Fundamentals of
FINANCIAL ACCOUNTING

FUNDAMENTALS OF FINANCIAL ACCOUNTING
Published by McGraw-Hill/Irwin, a business unit of The McGraw-Hill Companies, Inc., 1221
Avenue of the Americas, New York, NY, 10020. Copyright © 2006 by The McGraw-Hill
Companies, Inc. All rights reserved. No part of this publication may be reproduced or distributed
in any form or by any means, or stored in a database or retrieval system, without the prior written
consent of The McGraw-Hill Companies, Inc., including, but not limited to, in any network or
other electronic storage or transmission, or broadcast for distance learning.

Some ancillaries, including electronic and print components, may not be available to customers
outside the United States.

This book is printed on acid-free paper.

1 2 3 4 5 6 7 8 9 0 WCK/WCK 0 9 8 7 6 5 4

ISBN 0-07-111636-2

www.mhhe.com

Fundamentals of FINANCIAL ACCOUNTING

Fred Phillips
University of Saskatchewan

Robert Libby
Cornell University

Patricia A. Libby
Ithaca College

McGraw-Hill
Irwin

Boston   Burr Ridge, IL   Dubuque, IA   Madison, WI   New York
San Francisco   St. Louis   Bangkok   Bogotá   Caracas   Kuala Lumpur
Lisbon   London   Madrid   Mexico City   Milan   Montreal   New Delhi
Santiago   Seoul   Singapore   Sydney   Taipei   Toronto

GETTING THE MOST FROM THIS BOOK

We're tired of people saying that accounting is deadly boring. So we wrote this textbook to show just how interesting it can be. Here are a few tips to help you get the most from this book and this course.

- **Read the book.** Seriously.
- **Get the point.** Even though you're going to read all the assigned chapters (right?), you'll want to know what's important and likely to be on your test. The learning objectives tell you. Find them in the first exhibit in each chapter.
- **Consult the coach.** Each coach in Coach's Corner will walk you through tough problems and give you advice on improving your game.
- **Keep on track.** The self-study quizzes gauge whether you've been thinking hard enough as you read. There's no point in blasting through the chapter just to finish. Cover the self-study quiz answers with your thumb and give the questions a try.
- **Practice, practice, practice.** We can't say it enough. You can't just read about accounting, you have to do it. So be sure to do all the questions that you've been assigned. If you're assigned the Group A problems, you can do the Group B problems for extra practice and use the coached problems when reviewing for tests and exams.
- **Get extra help.** The DVD and Online Learning Center are full of digital tools that will help you pull it all together.

One last tip. Enjoy yourself. Do the crossword puzzles in the book while you wait for class to start. Ask questions. Share the cartoons with friends who aren't even taking this course. Discover for yourself that accounting isn't boring.

Fred Phillips   Bob Libby   Pat Libby

ABOUT THE AUTHORS

Fred Phillips

Fred Phillips is a Professor and the George C. Baxter Chartered Accountants of Saskatchewan Scholar at the University of Saskatchewan, where he teaches introductory financial accounting. He also has taught introductory accounting at the University of Texas at Austin and the University of Manitoba. Fred has an undergraduate accounting degree, a professional accounting designation, and a PhD from the University of Texas at Austin. He previously worked as an audit manager at KPMG.

Fred's main interest is accounting education. He has won eight teaching awards, including two national case-writing competitions. He has published instructional cases and numerous articles in journals such as *Issues in Accounting Education, Journal of Accounting Research*, and *Organizational Behavior and Human Decision Processes*. Fred currently serves as an associate editor of *Issues in Accounting Education*, and he is a member of the Teaching & Curriculum and Two-Year College sections of the American Accounting Association. In his spare time, he likes to work out, play video games, and drink iced cappuccino.

Robert Libby

Robert Libby is the David A. Thomas Professor of Management at the Johnson Graduate School of Management at Cornell University, where he teaches the introductory financial accounting course. He previously taught at the University of Illinois, Pennsylvania State University, the University of Texas at Austin, the University of Chicago, and the University of Michigan. He received his BS from Pennsylvania State University and his MAS and PhD from the University of Illinois; he is also a CPA.

Bob is a widely published author specializing in behavioral accounting. He was selected as the AAA Outstanding Educator in 2000. One of his

prior texts, *Accounting and Human Information Processing* (Prentice Hall, 1981), was awarded the AICPA/AAA Notable Contributions to the Accounting Literature Award. He received this award again in 1996 for a paper. He has published numerous articles in the *Journals of Accounting Research; Accounting, Organizations, and Society;* and other accounting journals. He is Vice President-Publications of the American Accounting Association and is a member of the American Institute of CPAs and the editorial boards of *Accounting, Organizations, and Society; Journal of Accounting Literature;* and *Journal of Behavioral Decision Making.*

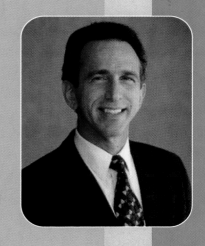

Patricia A. Libby

Patricia Libby is Associate Professor of Accounting and Coordinator of the MBA in Professional Accountancy Program at Ithaca College, where she teaches the undergraduate financial accounting course. She previously taught graduate and undergraduate financial accounting at Eastern Michigan University and the University of Texas at Austin. Before entering academe, she was an auditor with Price Waterhouse (now PricewaterhouseCoopers) and a financial administrator at the University of Chicago. She received her BS from Pennsylvania State

University, her MBA from DePaul University, and her PhD from the University of Michigan; she is also a CPA.

Pat conducts research on using cases in the introductory course and other parts of the accounting curriculum. She has published articles in *The Accounting Review, Issues in Accounting Education,* and *The Michigan CPA*. She has also conducted seminars nationwide on active learning strategies, including cooperative learning methods.

THE CLOSER YOU LOOK,

Phillips, Libby & Libby's

If you could peel away the exterior of a large company, what would you see? As our cover illustrates, at first glance it might seem just short of chaos—a hive of hectic activity that seems to defy comprehension. Look closer, however, and order begins to emerge: people at different levels of the organization are working with one another. Business activities occurring on the ground floor are analyzed and their financial effects are captured by accounting personnel on the second floor, who report these results to decision-makers on the top floor. Financial accounting is the thread that unites these various roles—on our cover and throughout the business world.

Like a complex picture whose details can be appreciated only through close inspection, the subtle messages conveyed by financial information become useful after examination with a trained and careful eye. Put another way, **the closer you look at financial accounting data, the more you understand.** *Fundamentals of Financial Accounting* gives students the ability to make sense of business activities, to prepare and interpret financial information in an accurate and relevant way, and it does so like no other book on the market.

Fundamentals of FINANCIAL ACCOUNTING

THE MORE YOU UNDERSTAND

How does *Fundamentals of Financial Accounting* differ from the competition? It all boils down to one quality:
Phillips/Libby/Libby is the most student-friendly financial book on the market. The following pages are filled with examples and highlights of Phillips' innovative student-centered approach. Four of the most compelling examples include:

Writing that students can read.
What does it mean to say that a book is "readable"? In the case of *FFA*, it simply means the most enjoyable accounting textbook your students have ever read. Through a mix of conversational wording, humor, and everyday examples, *FFA* achieves a relaxed style that maintains rigor while never sacrificing student engagement. Open *FFA* to almost any page at random, read a few paragraphs and see for yourself: *Fundamentals of Financial Accounting* offers **the most engaging read** of any financial text.

> I LOVE the authors' writing style. I think more and more of our students either don't read, or have difficulty reading, accounting textbooks. . . . I think [this book] will be more readable to our students and they may even enjoy reading it.
>
> — *Antoinette Clegg, Palm Beach Community College*

Focus companies.
In an approach pioneered by co-authors Robert Libby and Patricia Libby, each chapter of *Fundamentals of Financial Accounting* makes financial accounting come alive by using **a real world focus company** to teach fundamental accounting concepts. Your students learn why accounting is important and how businesses use accounting information to make decisions. All of the companies featured in *FFA* are **real companies whose products and services are popular with**

students, including Skechers (shoes), Activision (video games), and Oakley (sunglasses). (See page VIII for more on the focus companies.)

A CD-ROM made with students in mind.
Topic Tackler Plus takes advantage of the latest multimedia technology to provide **truly helpful audiovisual reinforcement** to your students. In particular, the Flash tutorials combine animation with audio narration to make reviewing each chapter's key concepts a snap. (See page XVI for more on Topic Tackler Plus.)

A framework you can USE.
The **USER** framework uses the cover illustration as a roadmap to each chapter, delineating how accounting works at all levels of a company. Students learn to **<u>U</u>nderstand** the business decisions that managers make on the ground floor, **<u>S</u>tudy** the accounting methods used on the second floor, **<u>E</u>valuate** the reported results from the viewpoint of financial statement users on the top floor, and **<u>R</u>econsider** how the accounting methods affect the evaluation of results, which indicate the quality of business decisions that managers have made (uniting the whole building). This framework ensures students will develop the ability to make sense of business activities, be able to prepare financial statements, and know how to interpret financial information in an accurate and relevant way.

By taking the most thorough student-oriented approach on the market, *Fundamentals of Financial Accounting* shows students that the more they look at financial accounting data, the more they'll understand of it. Read the following pages for further proof that *FFA* combines student-friendliness and academic rigor better than any other financial book on the market.

KEEP YOUR CLASS FOCUSED ON THE REAL WORLD

The best way to learn to prepare and use financial statements is to study accounting in real business contexts. This is the key idea behind *FFA's* focus company approach, which is introduced in the first chapter and which integrates each chapter's material around a focus company, its decisions, and its financial statements.

The one thing that consistently amazes me and makes me VERY happy is the choice of companies that the authors use to demonstrate chapter concepts. The use of Cedar Fair . . . an amusement park!!!! Everyone can relate to an amusement park and see that the needs of this business (for LT assets) are completely different from other businesses. Then there was Mattel, Supercuts, etc. The companies grab the interest of the reader and make them want to know more. As a "reader," I was drawn into the discussion because it interests me!!!

Cheryl Bartlett
Albuquerque TVI Community College

chapter **nine**

Reporting and Interpreting Long-Lived Tangible and Intangible Assets

If you're an average American, you gobble about three pounds of peanut butter per year, which equals 1,500 peanut butter sandwiches eaten before your high school graduation.[1] That makes you an expert at knowing how much peanut butter to spread on sandwiches. It also prepares you for learning how to report depreciation on long-lived assets. Really. Reporting depreciation is a lot like spreading peanut butter on sandwiches. The amount of peanut butter to spread on each sandwich is just like the amount of depreciation to spread over each accounting period. It depends on three factors: (1) the amount that you begin with in the jar (or the cost you begin with in the account), (2) the amount you want to leave in the jar (or account), and (3) the number of sandwiches (or accounting periods) that you'll be spreading it over. Just like peanut butter on a sandwich, there'll be a little depreciation if it's spread over many years or lots if it's spread over fewer years.

For the rest of this chapter, we're going to focus on the amusement park business at **CEDAR FAIR.** We're not leaving peanuts completely behind, because just as Mickey is Disney's mascot and Bugs Bunny gives character to Six Flags, Snoopy and the whole Charlie Brown gang from the PEANUTS® comic strip are featured at Cedar Fair. With seven amusement parks and six waterparks throughout the United States, Cedar Fair is one of the biggest and best amusement park businesses in the world.[2] As of December 31, 2003, its rides, hotels, and other long-lived assets accounted for over 96 percent of its total assets, so it's the perfect setting for you to learn how these assets are reported and the analyses you can conduct to determine how well they're managed.

[1]Retrieved May 3, 2004, from www.peanutbutter.com/funfacts.asp.

[2]"Cedar Fair, L.P.'s Flagship Park, Cedar Point, again Voted Best Amusement Park in the World," company press release, August 26, 2003.

One of Cedar Fair's rides reaches 120 mph

We consulted extensively with students in choosing *FFA's* focus companies, taking care that our companies' products and services are used by students and so will appeal to their curiosity. We further heighten student engagement by injecting our discussions with issues and questions that actually matter in the real world. *How can a slight improvement in gross profit percentage translate into over half a billion dollars of profit for Wal-Mart? What decisions does Cedar Fair make when investing in and reporting its roller coasters and other long-lived assets? How does Nautilus Group monitor and manage its fluctuating cash flows during the pre- and post-holiday seasons?* These are but a few of the companies and issues discussed over the course of this book.

INSIDE LOOKING OUT

SIDE KING IN

hapter focuses on how long-lived le and intangible assets and their ciation or amortization are reported in ial statements. We focus on Cedar which is currently the owner of the s biggest and fastest roller coaster.

in just four seconds.

A Warm Welcome in Every Chapter

Students often feel they lack the real-world experience needed to understand accounting, a subject they believe has little impact on their daily lives. *FFA's* chapter openers provide entertaining analogies that illustrate how accounting principles can inform even the most seemingly mundane things, from making peanut-butter sandwiches to catching a roommate stealing snacks. There's no better way to help students feel comfortable with accounting topics and to trigger an interest that invites them into the chapter. (To see how peanut-butter sandwiches relate to depreciation, take a look at Chapter 9.)

> I think the authors have written some difficult ideas in simple terms and that is good. I like the choice of theme parks as the underlying business because I believe this will interest students.
>
> *Gail Wright*
> *Bryant College*

> I hope students will enjoy learning about accounting for tangible and intangible assets in the context of our amusement parks. After reading this chapter students will truly understand the important business decisions that relate to tangible and intangible assets, and how the results of these decisions are reported to financial statement users.
>
> *Bruce A. Jackson*
> *Corporate Vice President and Chief Financial Officer*
> *Cedar Fair, L.P.*

AN *FFA* READER IS
NEVER ALONE

The cover of *Fundamentals of Financial Accounting* illustrates the maxim that underpins the book: the closer you look, the more you understand. More than that, it serves to introduce the characters and tools that accompany your students as they read the book. Many of the text's most innovative and student-friendly pedagogical features are marked with an element of the cover illustration—a visual shorthand that makes it a breeze to find additional help or insight while reading.

COACH'S CORNER
Loss in inventory value is typically combined into selling expenses or cost of goods sold for purposes of external reporting.

Coach's Corner.
Virtually every student has been inspired by a great coach at some point, and *FFA* features not one but two Coaches who appear throughout the text to offer tips, advice, and good ideas about how to learn. *FFA* is unique in that its in-text "coaches" appear in the end-of-chapter material as well, giving students additional encouragement as they work to reinforce the material they've learned.

COACH'S CORNER
If you want the DDB worksheet function in Microsoft Excel to match the formula presented here, set the "salvage" factor to 0.

I really like the Coach's Corner in the text and at the end-of-chapter materials. They are well written and will help the students focus on important points.

— *Margaret Houston, Wright State University*

YOU SHOULD KNOW

Declining-balance is a method that allocates the cost of an asset over its useful life based on a multiple of the straight-line rate (often two times).

You Should Know.
Look to the owl for wisdom, knowledge—and a quick recap of an important text point.

POINT OF INTEREST
Not every press release is trustworthy. A 23-year-old student was sentenced to 44 months in federal prison for sending out his own phony press release about Emulex Corporation, which allegedly defrauded investors of $241,814.

Points of Interest.
It always helps to take a little break now and then, and Points of Interest provide attention-grabbing topical diversions for students as they read. From the surprising origins of Nike to the bogus investment opportunity created by the SEC, Points of Interest illuminate the topic at hand with amusing and unusual facts that introduce a breath of fresh air into students' reading.

Ethical Issue.

We've seen all too plainly what can happen when accounting data are distorted or used inappropriately, and *FFA* makes sure your students start off with a solid grounding in ethics. Ethical Issues prompt your students to think about tough ethical decisions in each chapter and to practice making these decisions themselves in end-of-chapter cases.

Topic Tackler Plus.

For an animated tour of how transaction analysis and the rules of debits and credits apply to revenues and expenses, check out the tutorial on the DVD for use with this book.

FFA's Topic Tackler Plus is loaded with digital study tools that can make a real impact on how well your students perform in the course. All text content receiving expanded treatment on the Student CD is marked with this icon.

Fast Flashback.

FAST FLASHBACK
A merchandiser is a company that sells goods it has obtained from a supplier. A manufacturer is a company that sells goods it made itself.

Every student knows the frustration of learning a new concept or term only to forget it a few chapters later, requiring tedious backtracking through previously read material to find the original definition. *FFA's* Fast Flashbacks eliminate this hurdle: when a topic from a previous chapter is re-introduced, a Fast Flashback provides a brief, convenient refresher.

OUTSIDE LOOKING IN
This chapter focuses on how long-lived tangible and intangible assets and their depreciation or amortization are reported in financial statements. We focus on Cedar Fair, which is currently the owner of the world's biggest and fastest roller coaster.

Outside Looking In/ Inside Looking Out.

Different people use accounting information in different ways: those within the firm must choose when and how to report events, while those outside it rely on those reports to make their own decisions. Instances of this dual nature of accounting information are highlighted in the Outside Looking In/Inside Looking Out feature, using an analogy from students' own experiences to highlight the personal relevance of the chapter's topics.

A BOOK WITH ITS OWN

Fundamentals of Financial Accounting is loaded with so many innovative pedagogical features, you'd swear we shrinkwrapped a TA with the book. From quick review tools to head-scratching ethical dilemmas, *FFA's* pedagogy gives students every opportunity to reinforce and expand on what they're learning.

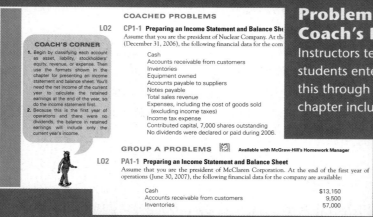

Problems With (and Without) the Coach's Help

Instructors tell us how important decision-making skills are for students entering the accounting profession, and *FFA* recognizes this through an innovative approach to problem-solving. Every chapter includes three problem sets: Coached Problems, Group A, and Group B problems. The Coached Problems go beyond the traditional check figures to advise students on the *process* of solving a problem rather than just its outcome. This feature will save students the inefficient and frustrating experience of having to work backwards from solutions to develop their own (possibly erroneous) problem-solving rules. When students can solve the coached problems, they'll be ready to tackle the Group A or Group B problems, which echo the content without the advice offered by the Coached Problems.

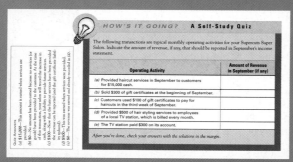

"How's It Going?"

Nothing helps like a quiz for mastering tricky subjects, so *FFA* provides plenty of these innovative review boxes throughout each chapter. **"How's It Going?"** boxes pose a review question about the recent material and provide the answer right there on the page, printed sideways so that students don't accidentally read it before answering the question.

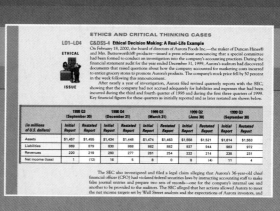

Ethics Cases

The last five years have seen controversies that brought the ethics of the accounting profession to the forefront of public debate. Young people entering the business world, whether as accountants or other business majors, simply must have a strong ethical grounding, so *FFA* includes **two ethics cases in every chapter.**

TEACHING ASSISTANT
INCLUDED

Transaction Analysis Revisited

Now that you've been introduced to debits, credits, journal entries, and T-accounts, you are ready to revisit the five-step DECIDE approach used earlier to analyze transactions. To include these new concepts in the accounting process, we need to add two more steps, as highlighted in Exhibit 2.8.

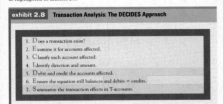

exhibit 2.8   Transaction Analysis: The DECIDES Approach

1. Does a transaction exist?
2. Examine it for accounts affected.
3. Classify each account affected.
4. Identify direction and amount.
5. Debit and credit the accounts affected.
6. Ensure the equation still balances and debits = credits.
7. Summarize the transaction effects in T-accounts.

In the remainder of this section, we will work with you to use this transaction analysis approach to record the monthly transactions that were presented earlier in this chapter for your Supercuts Super Salon. Because we have completed steps 1–4 of the transaction analysis for these events already, we will not show them below, but you should understand that these steps *would* be performed had we not analyzed them earlier. The analysis below focuses on the results of steps 5–7, which involve the new concepts of debits, credits, journal entries, and T-accounts.

A Good Accountant DECIDES

The DECIDES decision model provides students the structure they need to tackle challenging topics. This model helps students to decide on the accounting effects of transactions by thinking through the following steps:

1. **Does** a transaction exist? Go to step 2 only if your answer is "yes."
2. **Examine** it for the accounts affected. Put a name on what is given and received.
3. **Classify** each account as asset (A), liability (L), or stockholders' equity (SE).
4. **Identify** the direction and amount of the effects. By how much does each asset, liability, and stockholders' equity account increase or decrease?
5. **Ensure** the basic accounting equation still balances and that debits = credits.
6. **Summarize** the transaction effects in T-accounts.

The DECIDES model is introduced in Chapter 2, expanded in Chapter 3, and reinforced throughout the remaining chapters.

> DECIDE is an excellent learning tool which should help the students understand the process of transaction analysis.
>
> *Patsy Lee*
> *University of Texas at Arlington*

Do you know what managers worry about when making inventory decisions, how the results of their decisions are reported, and how you can use the reported results to evaluate the quality of their inventory decisions? If any of your answers are no, then you're doing exactly what you should be doing—reading this chapter. In it, we address these questions, which cover the specific learning objectives shown in Exhibit 8.1.

exhibit 8.1   Your Learning Objectives

Understand key inventory management decisions.
LO1   Describe inventory management goals.
Study inventory costing and reporting decisions.
LO2   Describe the different types of inventory.
LO3   Compute costs using four inventory costing methods.
LO4   Explain why inventory is reported at the lower of cost or market.
Evaluate inventory management practices.
LO5   Compute and interpret the inventory turnover ratio.
Reconsider how inventory reporting decisions affect analyses.
LO6   Explain how accounting methods affect evaluations of inventory management.

The USER Framework

The USER framework uses the cover illustration as a "roadmap" to each chapter, delineating how accounting functions work at all levels of the firm. Students learn to **Understand** the business decisions that managers make (ground floor), **Study** the accounting methods used (second floor), **Evaluate** the reported results from the viewpoint of financial statement users (top floor), and **Reconsider** how the accounting methods affect the evaluation of results, which indicate the quality of managers' decisions (the whole building).

THE FINEST END-OF-CHAPTER MATERIAL TO BE FOUND.

FINANCIAL REPORTING AND ANALYSIS CASES

C&DS5-1 Finding Financial Information

Refer to the financial statements of Landry's Restaurants in Appendix A at the end of this book, or download the annual report from the Cases section of the text's Web site at www.mhhe.com/phillips.

Required:

1. Calculate the debt-to-assets ratio for 2003 and 2002. Based on these calculations, has Landry's financing become more or less risky in 2003 than in 2002?
2. Calculate the asset turnover ratio for 2003 and 2002. (Total assets at December 31, 2001 were $690,171,196.) Based on these calculations, has Landry's used its assets more or less efficiently in 2003 than in 2002?
3. Calculate the net profit margin ratio for 2003 and 2002. Based on these calculations, has Landry's generated more or less profit per dollar of sales in 2003 than in 2002?

LO1–LO4

C&DS5-2 Comparing Financial Information

Refer to the financial statements of Dave & Buster's in Appendix B at the end of this book, or download the annual report from the Cases section of the text's Web site at www.mhhe.com/phillips. Note that Dave & Buster's ends its fiscal year on February 1, 2004, which doesn't perfectly match Landry's year ended December 31, 2003. In the questions that follow, assume Dave & Buster's financial statements for the year ended February 1, 2004, present the results for 2003. (This is a reasonable assumption given that Dave and Buster's fiscal year simply replaces January 2003 with January 2004.)

LO1–LO4

Annual Report Cases

There's no substitute for working on real-world data, so *FFA* comes complete with an annual report for Landry's Restaurants bundled free with every new copy. The end-of-chapter cases make extensive use of these data, showing students how to draw information from an annual report and providing them with a valuable perspective on how financial accounting information is used in decision making.

Team Cases

Every chapter also includes a team case that directs groups to search the Internet for companies to analyze, using the tools covered in that chapter. Students not only learn useful research skills but gain valuable practice solving accounting problems in group settings.

LO1–LO3 **C&DS1-3 Internet-Based Team Research: Examining an Annual Report**

As a team, select an industry to analyze. Reuters provides lists of industries and their makeup at www.investor.reuters.com/Industries.aspx. Each group member should acquire the annual report (or Form 10-K filed with the SEC) for one publicly traded company in the industry, with each member selecting a different company. (In addition to the company's own Web site, a great source is the SEC's Electronic Data Gathering, Analysis, and Retrieval (EDGAR) service. This free source is available by going to the "Filings & Forms" section of www.sec.gov and clicking on "Search for Company Filings" and then "Companies & Other Filers." Another great site that pulls information from EDGAR is edgarscan.pwcglobal.com.)

TEAM CASE

Required:

1. On an individual basis, each team member should write a short report that lists the following information:
   a. What type of business organization is it?
   b. What types of products or services does it sell?
   c. On what day of the year does its fiscal year end?
   d. For how many years does it present complete balance sheets? Income statements? Cash flow statements?
   e. Are its financial statements audited by independent CPAs? If so, by whom?
   f. Did its total assets increase or decrease over the last year?
   g. Did its net income increase or decrease over the last year?
2. Then, as a team, write a short report comparing and contrasting your companies using these attributes. Discuss any patterns across the companies that you as a team observe. Provide potential explanations for any differences discovered.

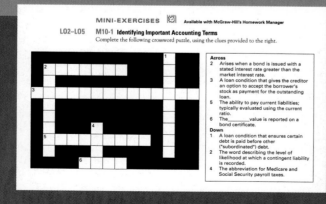

MINI-EXERCISES Available with McGraw-Hill's Homework Manager

LO2–LO5 **M10-1 Identifying Important Accounting Terms**

Complete the following crossword puzzle, using the clues provided to the right.

Across
2 Arises when a bond is issued with a stated interest rate greater than the market interest rate.
3 A loan condition that gives the creditor an option to accept the borrower's stock as payment for the outstanding loan.
5 The ability to pay current liabilities; typically evaluated using the current ratio.
6 The_____value is reported on a bond certificate.

Down
1 A loan condition that ensures certain debt is paid before other ("subordinated") debt.
2 The word describing the level of likelihood at which a contingent liability is recorded.
4 The abbreviation for Medicare and Social Security payroll taxes.

Crossword Puzzles

Yet another example of what makes *FFA* so much fun for students. Rather than memorize definitions through rote learning, students practice learning the language of business in a format that they'll want to complete even if it's not assigned. (If you don't believe us, try it for yourself. Point out the crossword puzzles to students, but don't assign them. We bet you'll find they do them anyway!)

The end-of-chapter material is traditionally where students go from reading to doing: answering review questions, solving problems, and wrestling with issues that help them to assimilate the material and apply it in a realistic context. While *FFA* doesn't see reading as a passive process — our pedagogy does more to maintain student interest and engagement than any competing book — the end-of-chapter material offers a wealth of opportunities for students to connect to the material, and for you to enliven your class with a variety of assignments and discussion questions.

Simplify with Spreadsheets

Why do the same calculations over and over again when you can enter them once, and then just copy and paste? Every chapter includes at least one spreadsheet problem that allows students to skip the tedium of repetitious number-crunching and focus instead on "what if" analyses and interpretations. And don't worry if your students haven't had formal training with spreadsheets: each problem includes relaxed, student-friendly advice on the steps needed to perform basic spreadsheet calculations.

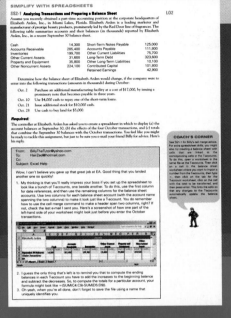

Multiple-Choice Questions

Students are likely to see these kinds of questions on tests and exams, so give them some practice with these quick checks of basic concepts.

Peachtree® Designated Exercises and Problems

Students entering the accounting profession can never have too much practice working on Peachtree, so *FFA*'s end-of-chapter material includes specially designated problems to be solved with the educational version of Peachtree Complete (see page XVIII). These problems are marked with an icon and make ideal homework assignments.

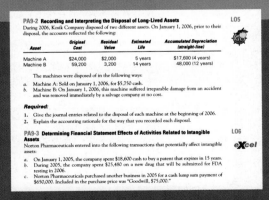

> The authors, as they have done throughout the book, have done a very good job on all of the end of chapter material.
>
> *Philip Fink*
> *University of Toledo*

FFA'S **STUDENT-CENTRIC** **APPROACH**

OnePass

It can be a challenge remembering all the different passwords and access codes for the many online assets available with *Fundamentals of Financial Accounting*. To make life easier for your students, McGraw-Hill is pleased to introduce OnePass. With McGraw-Hill's OnePass, just one code gets your students total access to McGraw-Hill's Homework Manager, Topic Tackler Plus, NetTutor, and the online version of the textbook. Moreover, the OnePass card fits in your students' wallets for safekeeping.

McGraw-Hill's Homework Manager

is a Web-based supplement that duplicates problem structures directly from the end-of-chapter material in your textbook, using algorithms to provide a limitless supply of online self-graded practice for students, or assignments and tests with unique versions of every problem. Say goodbye to cheating in your classroom; say hello to the power and flexibility you've been waiting for in creating assignments.

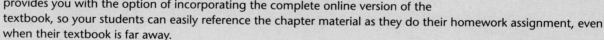

The enhanced version of McGraw-Hill's Homework Manager integrates all of *FFA's* online and multimedia assets to allow your students to brush up on a topic before doing their homework. You now have the option to give your students pre-populated hints and feedback. The test bank has been added to Homework Manager so you can create online quizzes and exams and have them autograded and recorded in the same gradebook as your homework assignments. Lastly, the enhanced version provides you with the option of incorporating the complete online version of the textbook, so your students can easily reference the chapter material as they do their homework assignment, even when their textbook is far away.

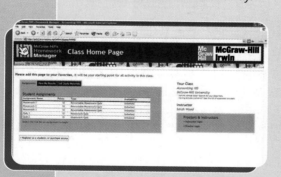

McGraw-Hill's Homework Manager is also a useful grading tool. All assignments can be delivered over the Web and are graded automatically, with the results stored in your private grade book. Detailed results let you see at a glance how each student does on an assignment or an individual problem—you can even see how many tries it took them to solve it.

Students receive full access to McGraw-Hill's Homework Manager when they purchase OnePass, or you can have Homework Manager pass codes shrinkwrapped with the textbook. Students can also purchase access to Homework Manager directly from their class homepage.

Topic Tackler Plus, the *FFA* student CD-ROM, is designed to accompany your students from the first day of class to the last, with text-specific study aids and helpful additional content that can make a real difference on overall student performance. It's one more reason why *Fundamentals of Financial Accounting* is the most student-friendly book of its kind.

DOESN'T STOP AT THE TEXTBOOK.

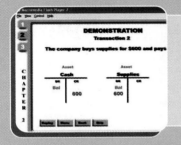

Animated Flash Tutorials

The toughest and most important topics of each chapter are reviewed in animated, audio-narrated tutorials powered by Flash technology. These tutorials take the main points of the textbook and put them in motion, with step-by-step instructions that can eliminate the need for holding midterm and end-of-term review sessions.

Video Segments

Combining original location footage, interviews, eye-catching graphics, and spoken narration, these vignettes explain how the concepts covered in each chapter make a difference in the world of business.

Animated Crossword Puzzles

These puzzles provide countless variations on the highly popular format for learning key terms.

Net Tutor

Many students work or have other commitments outside of class, making it difficult for them to get help with their questions during regular hours. NetTutor is a breakthrough program that connects your students with qualified tutors online, so they can get help at their convenience. Students can communicate with tutors through the Live Tutor Center, where students can view tutor-created spreadsheets, T-accounts, and instant responses to their questions, or through the Q&A Center, which allows students to submit questions anytime and receive answers within 48 hours.

With OnePass, students receive unlimited access to NetTutor for the length of the course.

THE BEST IN DIGITAL STUDY

Online Learning Center

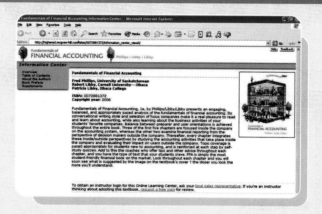

Fundamentals of Financial Accounting includes an Online Learning Center (OLC) that follows the book chapter by chapter. It doesn't require any building or maintenance on your part; it's ready to go the moment your students type in the address.

www.mhhe.com/phillips

As your students study, they can visit the OLC and work with a multitude of helpful tools:

- Tutorial
- Glossary
- Study Guide Sample Chapter
- Working Papers Sample Chapter
- Updates
- Mobile Resources link
- NetTutor link
- Chapter Objectives
- Chapter Overview
- Focus Company Links
- PowerPoint Presentations
- Excel Template Assignments

OnePass (see previous page) gives students total access to the Online Learning Center, including premium content such as the *FFA* online text.

A secured Instructor Resource Center stores your essential course materials to save you prep time before class. Everything you need to run a lively classroom and an efficient course is included:

- Link to OSCAR (MHHE Accounting Supersite)
- Instructors Manual
- Sample Syllabi
- Additional appendices or chapter material
- Transition Notes
- Ordering and Packaging info
- Updates
- PageOut link
- Mobile Resources link
- Solutions to Excel Template Assignments
- Solutions Manual
- PowerPoint Presentations
- Focus Company Links

Carol Yacht's General Ledger and Peachtree Complete 2004 CD-ROM

From one of the most trusted names in computer accounting education, Carol Yacht, comes a general ledger package that's a perfect fit for your course, no matter how you like to teach it.

The CD-ROM includes two full-featured accounting applications on one disk: **Carol Yacht's General Ledger**, a suite developed under Yacht's direction to provide the utmost in flexibility and power, and **Peachtree Complete**, the same software relied upon by thousands of firms throughout the world.

AND COURSE MANAGEMENT TOOLS

Students using Carol Yacht's General Ledger can move from financial statements to the specific journal entries with just a click of the mouse; **changing an entry updates the financial statement on the fly**, allowing students to see instantly how journal entries impact financial statements.

If you want your students to practice on the same software the professionals use, the educational version of Peachtree Complete 2004 is bundled on the CD with no disabled features to work around!

Carol Yacht's General Ledger and Peachtree CD-ROM can add incredible value to your FFA adoption. Contact your McGraw-Hill/Irwin representative for details.

PageOut
McGraw-Hill's Course Management System

PageOut is the easiest way to create a Web site for your financial accounting course.

There's no need for HTML coding, graphic design, or a thick how-to book. Just fill in a series of boxes with plain English and click on one of our professional designs. In no time, your course is online with a Web site that contains your syllabus!

Should you need assistance in preparing your Web site, we can help you. Our team of product specialists is ready to take your course materials and build a custom Web site to your specifications. You simply call a McGraw-Hill/Irwin PageOut specialist to start the process. Best of all, PageOut is free when you adopt *FFA*! To learn more, please visit **www.pageout.net**.

Third-Party Course Management Systems

For the ambitious instructor, we offer *FFA* content for complete online courses. To make this possible, we have joined forces with the most popular delivery platforms currently available. These platforms are designed for instructors who want complete control over course content and how it is presented to students. You can customize the *FFA* Online Learning Center content and author your own course materials. It's entirely up to you.

Products like WebCT, Blackboard, and eCollege all expand the reach of your course. Online discussion and message boards will now complement your office hours. Thanks to a sophisticated tracking system, you will know which students need more attention – even if they don't ask for help. That's because online testing scores are recorded and automatically placed in your grade book, and if a student is struggling with coursework, a special alert message lets you know.

Remember, *FFA's* content is flexible enough to use with any platform currently available. If your department or school is already using a platform, we can help. For information on McGraw-Hill/Irwin's course management supplements, including Instructor Advantage and Knowledge Gateway, contact your McGraw-Hill/Irwin representative.

SUPPLEMENTS FOR INSTRUCTORS

Instructor's Resource CD-ROM
0072948922

This is your all-in-one in-class re-source. Create stimulating custom presentations from your own materials or from the many text-specific materials provided in the CD's asset library:

- Instructor's Resource Manual
- Solutions Manual
- Computerized Test Bank (see right)
- Microsoft PowerPoint® Slides, a multimedia lecture slide package that illustrates chapter concepts and procedures. It allows revision of lecture slides and includes a viewer, allowing screens to be shown with or without the software.
- Excel Template Exercises
- Link to PageOut
- Video Clips

Instructor's Resource Manual
0072948884

This manual contains (for each chapter) a Lecture Outline, a chart linking all assignment materials to Learning Objectives, a list of relevant active learning activities, and additional visuals with transparency masters. An electronic version is available on the Web site and on the Instructor's Resource CD-ROM.

PowerPoint Slides

Available on the Instructor's CD-ROM and online. These offer a great visual complement to your lectures. A complete set of slides covers the key concepts presented in each chapter.

Solutions Manual
0072948876

Contains solutions for all in-text problems and exercises.

Solution Acetates 0072948914

Computerized Test Bank

This electronic test-generating engine is stocked with hundreds of true/false, multiple choice, and short answer questions; generating quizzes and tests is as easy as clicking a mouse.

Test Bank

0072948892

Contains thousands of questions in true/false, multiple choice, and short answer format written specifically for *FFA*. A Windows-compatible Computerized Test Bank is also available.

Check Figures

Available only online, these provide key answers for selected exercises and problems.

SUPPLEMENTS FOR STUDENTS

Online Learning Center
0072948930
See page XVIII for details on *FFA's* Online Learning Center.

Study Guide
0072948965
This helpful supplement augments each chapter and appendix with reviews of the learning objectives, outlines of the chapters, summaries of chapter materials, and additional problems with solutions.

Topic Tackler Plus
0072948973
See page XVI for details on Topic Tackler Plus.

Landry's Restaurants Inc. 2003 Annual Report
0072948906
Students use this report—containing the very same information distributed to Landry's stockholders and potential investors—to solve problems and exercises, in the process gaining an understanding of how real financial data are prepared and used.

Carol Yacht's General Ledger and Peachtree Complete CD-ROM
0072948981
See page XVIII for details on Carol Yacht's General Ledger and Peachtree Complete CD-ROM.

McGraw-Hill's Homework Manager
0073105511
See page XVI for details on McGraw-Hill's Homework Manager.

Working Papers
0072948949
Working Papers are provided to assist students in solving complex text assignments. The Working Papers are available both in print and as Excel spreadsheets.

Computerized Accounting Practice Sets
Gold Run Snowmobile, Inc. (0072957883)
Granite Bay Jet Ski, Inc. (0073080160)

When it comes to financial accounting, there's no such thing as too much practice. Our Computerized Practice Sets give students even more opportunities to work with realistic accounting information and make a great addition to your financial accounting course.

ACKNOWLEDGMENTS

We are deeply indebted to the following individuals who helped develop, critique, and shape the extensive ancillary package: Cheryl Bartlett, Albuquerque TVI Community College; Jon Booker, Tennessee Technological University; Charles Caldwell, Tennessee Technological University; Rita Kingery Cook, University of Delaware; Philip Fink, University of Toledo; Jeanne Franco, Paradise Valley Community College; Susan Galbreath, Tennessee Technological University; Mark Holtzman, Seton Hall University; Harry Hooper, Santa Fe Community College; Ken Johnson, Drury University; Barbara Schnathorst, The Write Solution; and Kimberly Temme, Maryville University.

We also received invaluable input and support from present and former colleagues and students, in particular Jocelyn Allard, Anders Bergstrom, Shari Boyd, Kara Chase, Shana M. Clor, Nicole Dewan, Erin Ferguson, Aaron Ferrara, Robin Harrington, Lee Harris, Blair Healy, Carrie Hordichuk, Lorraine Hurst, Nancy Kirzinger, Alan Koop, Deborah Loran, Diana Mark, Roger Martin, Jason Matshes, Jennifer Millard, Kimberley Olfert, Ryan Olson, David Pooler, Jessica Pothier, Emery Salahub, Bailey Schergevitch, and Marie Tait.

We thank the extraordinary efforts of a talented group of individuals at McGraw-Hill/Irwin, including Brent Gordon, our editorial director; Stewart Mattson, our publisher; Rich Kolasa, our marketing manager; Charlie Fisher, our project manager; Sesha Bolisetty, our production supervisor; Carol Loreth, our supplements producer; Jeremy Cheshareck, our photo research coordinator; and David Tietz, our photo researcher. We are especially grateful to Steve DeLancey, senior sponsoring editor, for his foresight and vision; Kimberly Hooker, senior developmental editor, for her unwavering support through all aspects of the project; Glenn Turner at Burrston House, developmental editor, for his sage advice; Tracey Douglas, our permissions researcher, for her persistence; Adam Rooke, our designer, for his endless patience; David Bartholomew at Cenveo, our artist, for his diligence and creativity; and Daniel Wiencek, senior copywriter, for all of his creative efforts.

We also want to recognize the valuable input of all those who helped guide our developmental decisions:

Reviewers

Cheryl Bartlett, *Albuquerque TVI Community College*

Bridgett Bell, *North Harris Community College*

Jon A. Booker, *Tennessee Tech University*

Robert Braun, *Southeastern Louisiana University*

Daniel Brickner, *Easter Michigan University*

Chiaho Chang, *Montclair State University*

Antoinette Clegg, *Palm Beach Community College*

Lola Dudley, *Eastern Illinois University*

Philip Fink, *University of Toledo*

Norman Godwin, *Auburn University*

Sharron Graves, *Steven F. Austin University*

James Harden, *University of North Carolina—Greensboro*

Jack Hatcher, *Purdue University*

Harry Hooper, *Sante Fe Community College*

Margaret Houston, *Wright State University*

Sung-soo Kim, *Rutgers University*

Rita Kingery Cook, *University of Delaware*

Phillip Landers, *Pennsylvania College of Technology*

Cathy Larson, *Middlesex Community College*

Patsy Lee, *University of Texas at Arlington*

Marina Nathan, *Houston Community College*

Emeka Ofobike, *University of Akron*

Khursheed Omer, *University of Houston—Downtown*

Meg Pollard, *American River College*

Roderick Posey, *University of Southern Mississippi*

Pamela Stuerke, *Case Western Reserve University*

Paul Swanson, *Bradley University*

Marilyn Vito, *Richard Stockton College*

Gail Wright, *Bryant College*

Faculty Focus Group Attendees

Vernon Allen, *Central Florida Community College*

Debbie Beard, *Southeastern Missouri State*

Daisy Beck, *Louisiana State University*

Bridgett Bell, *North Harris Community College*

Robert Braun, *Southeastern Louisiana University*

Antoinette Clegg, *Palm Beach Community College*

Lola Dudley, *Eastern Illinois University*

Wendell Edwards, *Texas A&M University*

Philip Empey, *Purdue University*

Diane Glowacki, *Tarrant County Community College*

Sharron Graves, *Steven F. Austin University*

James Harden, *University of North Carolina—Greeensboro*

Harry Hooper, *Sante Fe Community College*

Norma Jacobs, *Austin Community College*

Howard Keller, *Indiana University—Indianapolis*

Alice Ketchand, *Sam Houston State University*

Mehmet Kocakulah, *Pennsylvania College of Technology*

Cathy Larson, *Middlesex Community College*

Doug Larson, *Salem State College*

Larry Larson, *Triton College*

Patricia Lopez, *Valencia Community College*

Marcia Lucas, *Western Illinois University*

Khursheed Omer, *University of Houston—Downtown*

Roderick Posey, *University of Southern Mississippi*

Lawrence Roman, *Cuyahoga Community College*

Al Ruggiero, *Suffolk County Community College*

Sandy Scheuermann, *University of Louisiana/Lafayette*

Scott Steinkamp, *College of Lake County*

Paul Swanson, *Bradley University*

Amy Troutman, *University of Texas—Dallas*

Student Focus Group Attendees

Yekaterina Bardash, *College of New Jersey*

John Caramanna, *Camden County College*

Penelope Chambers, *Bucks County Community College*

Robert Derstine, *Villanova University*

Jonathan Hoffman, *Camden County College*

Gerald Miller, *College of New Jersey*

Rebecca Parker, *Bucks County Community College*

Richard Sarkisian, *Camden County College*

Megan Solek, *Bucks County Community College*

Matt Stout, *College of New Jersey*

Judith Toland, *Bucks County Community College*

Jennifer Tran, *Villanova University*

Dava Wiegand, *Villanova University*

brief contents

Fundamentals of
FINANCIAL ACCOUNTING

chapter one

Reporting and Interpreting the Financial Results of Business Activities

1

I t's never easy to break bad news to someone. Just how do you tell your best friend that you lost his car keys last night or that his girlfriend is planning to break up with him? You want to convince him that it won't happen again and that things will get better, but that's not going to be easy. It's also difficult to be in your friend's position on the receiving end of bad news, because it's tough to know for sure what happened and who's to blame.

The same thing is true in the business world. Just imagine the problem faced by the executives at **MATTEL,** the maker of Barbie® dolls and Hot Wheels® cars. They had to break the news to investors that their company had lost $431 million during a recent year. That's a $431 million problem. It's tough to convince investors that things aren't so bad when the company just lost more than a million dollars a day. Also imagine yourself on the other side of this news, as one of Mattel's investors. How could you decide whether to believe what the executives were telling you? Was the future really as bright as what they were claiming, or had the sparkle faded from Barbie's eyes? These are the kinds of questions that come up when reporting and interpreting the financial results of business activities.

INSIDE LOOKING OUT

OUTSIDE LOOKING IN

In every chapter, we introduce a key accounting decision that is made *inside* a real-world company, and, later in the chapter, we show how people *outside* the company are affected by it. This chapter features Mattel, the company that makes toys and games that everyone has enjoyed at one time in their lives. As you will see in this chapter, this industry isn't child's play—toys are one of the riskiest of all businesses to manage.

Toys and Games.

We make the kid in you.

Mattel is a leader in the toys and family games industry.

COACH'S CORNER

Throughout this course, I'll pass along some advice to you in my Coach's Corner like this. To make effective use of these points, read them after each paragraph that they appear beside. The You Should Know margin notes contain definitions that will be most useful when you review for a test. The Points of Interest are fun facts for you to enjoy.

YOU SHOULD KNOW

Financial statements are reports that summarize the financial results of business activities.

Financial statement users are people who base their decisions, in part, on information reported in a company's financial statements.

Wait a second. Did you just skip over the inside/outside feature story for Mattel? We suspect that you're used to seeing stories like it in textbooks for other courses and that you may even have developed a habit of skipping them in a rush to get to the "important" part of those courses. We urge you not to do so with the stories in this book because we frequently refer to them throughout the chapters, so skipping over them would be like arriving late to a movie. Plus, you'd miss one of the most interesting parts of accounting. The glimpse inside the company reveals some of the key decisions that accountants make and sets the stage for topics that will be discussed in greater detail in the chapter. The glance outside the company should help you to understand how business people use accounting information and why they consider it so important in their decision making.

In addition to seeing the inside/outside framework in the feature story, you also will see it throughout each chapter of this book. As you read the first part of this chapter, which begins with a look inside Mattel, focus on understanding how and where the financial results of Mattel's business activities are presented in accounting reports called the **financial statements.** In the second part of the chapter, after you have learned about what is reported in the financial statements, we describe how outsiders use Mattel's financial statements to make important business decisions such as determining whether to invest in or lend money to Mattel. In this part, your main goal should be to understand the information these **financial statement users,** as they are often called, use when making their decisions. At the end of the chapter, we'll return to Mattel's $431 million problem to let you test whether you understand how, on the inside, Mattel's managers will deal with this problem in the company's financial statements and how, on the outside, users will use this financial statement information in their decision making. Exhibit 1.1 presents a roadmap to the chapter. Think of the learning objectives (LO1–LO4) as our tips on what's going to be really important in the rest of the chapter.

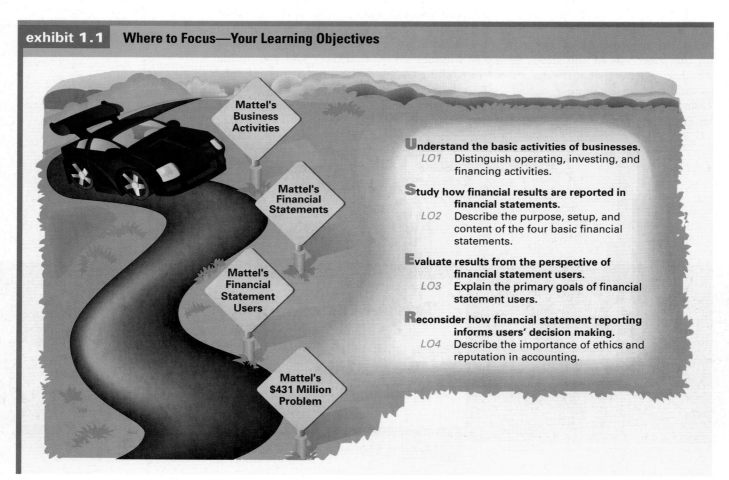

exhibit 1.1   Where to Focus—Your Learning Objectives

Mattel's Business Activities

Mattel's Financial Statements

Mattel's Financial Statement Users

Mattel's $431 Million Problem

Understand the basic activities of businesses.
LO1   Distinguish operating, investing, and financing activities.

Study how financial results are reported in financial statements.
LO2   Describe the purpose, setup, and content of the four basic financial statements.

Evaluate results from the perspective of financial statement users.
LO3   Explain the primary goals of financial statement users.

Reconsider how financial statement reporting informs users' decision making.
LO4   Describe the importance of ethics and reputation in accounting.

UNDERSTAND

THE BASIC ACTIVITIES OF BUSINESSES

The Development of Mattel's Business

Mattel's history provides an interesting look at how a business can change in form as it grows. Its history also provides a good context for introducing the three main types of business activities: **operating, investing,** and **financing.** You will find that one of the first steps to understanding accounting is to start thinking about business activities in terms of these three main categories. Operating activities are those day-to-day events that occur when running a business. Investing activities involve making significant investments in things like factory equipment. Financing activities are exchanges of money between a business and its lenders or owners. Look for the operating, investing, and financing activities in the following paragraph that describes how Mattel developed into an international toy monster.

  The toy company that claims to sell a couple of Barbie dolls every second started its business in a Southern California garage in 1945. Two friends, Harold "Matt" Matson and Elliot Handler, combined their names, money, and artistic skills to form a partnership that initially was in business to produce picture frames and dollhouse furniture. Matt left the business soon after it was started and was replaced by Elliot's wife Ruth. With the picture frame business struggling and opportunities growing in the dollhouse business, the Handlers decided they needed to get serious about toys. They changed their business from a **partnership** to a **corporation** in 1948, and borrowed money from a bank to expand their company. After a decade of satisfactory but not stellar performance, Mattel struck it big in 1959 with the introduction of Barbie. She was an instant success, selling over 350,000 dolls in the first year. The Handlers quickly realized that Mattel needed to expand the production facilities to try to keep up with growing worldwide toy demand. The money for financing the expansion this time didn't come from a bank loan. Instead, Elliot and Ruth decided Mattel should become a **public company,** which attracted hordes of investors who gave money to Mattel in exchange for a share of its ownership. This share of a company's ownership is indicated on stock certificates.

  Like most public companies, Mattel started out small but continually evolved from one type of business organization to another.[1] As the business grew, so did the variety of its activities. Were you able to slot the business activities into their operating, investing, and financing categories? Check whether you were on track by reading Exhibit 1.2.

YOU SHOULD KNOW

Operating activities include day-to-day events involved in running a business.
Investing activities involve buying or selling long-lived items such as land, buildings, and equipment.
Financing activities are related to exchanging money with lenders or owners.

YOU SHOULD KNOW

Partnerships are business organizations owned by two or more people. Each partner often is personally liable for debts that the partnership cannot pay.
Corporations operate as businesses separate from their owners. Owners of corporations (often called stockholders) are *not* personally responsible for debts of the corporation.
Public companies have their stock bought and sold on stock exchanges. (Private companies' stock is bought and sold privately.)

COACH'S CORNER

Researchers have found that people learn more from exhibits when they look at the pictures in them, then read the explanations in their captions, and then look again at the pictures.

---

exhibit 1.2 **Categorizing Mattel's Business Activities**

Operating Activities

Investing Activities

Financing Activities

Explanation: Based on the discussion of Mattel's activities in the text, you should have included making and selling picture frames, dollhouse furniture, and toys as operating activities. Investing activities would have included the purchase of production facilities during Mattel's expansion. Mattel's financing activities consisted of borrowing money from the bank and obtaining money from investors in exchange for a share of the ownership of the business.

---

[1]The only form of business organization not mentioned above is the sole proprietorship, which is like a partnership but with only one owner.

In reality, companies like Mattel become involved in hundreds of different types of operating, investing, and financing activities. Rather than bombard you with all possible examples in this course, we'll stick to the main business activities that affect about 99 percent of today's companies. Although we'll focus on how these activities affect the company in terms of dollars and cents, we don't want you to get the impression that this financial information is all that matters. In fact, to run a company successfully, business managers also need information about other aspects of their business, such as how much time Mattel's production line takes to roll out a Magic 8 Ball®. To ensure this other information is available, most modern businesses install sophisticated computer systems (also called accounting information systems) that monitor business activities in both financial and nonfinancial terms. This information then is reported in either the financial statements or other accounting reports.

POINT OF INTEREST
Mattel's Magic 8 Ball, in digital form, is online at www.mattelgames.com.

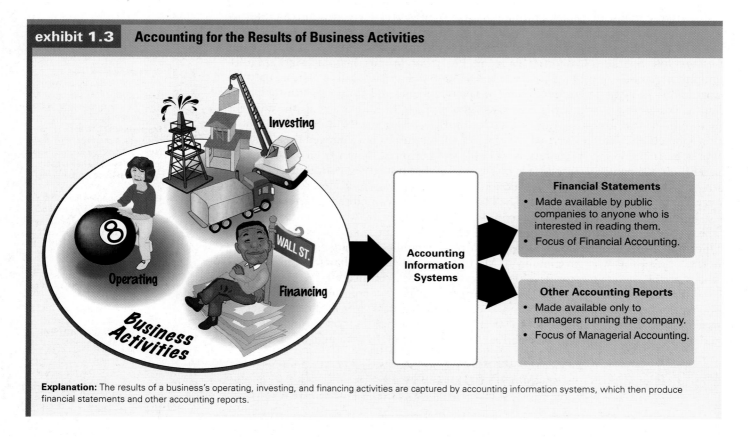

exhibit 1.3   **Accounting for the Results of Business Activities**

Explanation: The results of a business's operating, investing, and financing activities are captured by accounting information systems, which then produce financial statements and other accounting reports.

YOU SHOULD KNOW

Accounting is the process of capturing and reporting the results of a business's operating, investing, and financing activities.

Exhibit 1.3 shows how these different aspects of **accounting** fit together and what courses you'll take to learn more about them. Accounting Information Systems courses focus on how to design systems to capture and report the information that is needed in financial statements and other accounting reports. Financial Accounting courses (like this one) focus on preparing and using the financial statements that are made available by public companies to anyone who's interested in reading them. Managerial Accounting courses focus on other accounting reports that are not released to the general public, but instead are prepared and used by accountants and managers who run the business.

┌─ **STUDY** ────────────────
│ **HOW FINANCIAL RESULTS ARE REPORTED IN FINANCIAL STATEMENTS**

Financial Statements

The term "financial statements" typically refers to the following four accounting reports:

1. **Balance Sheet**
2. **Income Statement**
3. **Statement of Retained Earnings**
4. **Statement of Cash Flows**

One of the most confusing things for people first learning about accounting (or anything new, for that matter) is that different people use different terms to mean exactly the same thing. We will avoid doing this, but we can't stop others from doing it. So look to the coach for help with interpreting alternative names that people use in accounting.

Financial statements can be prepared at any time during the year, although they are most commonly prepared monthly, every three months (known as *quarterly reports*), and at the end of the year (known as *annual reports*). Companies are allowed to choose any date for the end of their accounting (or *fiscal*) year. Mattel chose a December 31 year-end because this is the start of its slow business period. Fewer toys are sold in January through May than in the first three weeks of December. The Green Bay Packers end their financial year on March 31, the month after the season wraps up with the Pro Bowl.

Each of the four statements has a specific and unique purpose, so we will begin by studying them one at a time. Later you will see how the four statements fit together, but for now just focus on learning what goes into each individual financial statement. Specifically, look for the answers to these questions:

a. **Purpose.** What is each statement attempting to explain?
b. **Setup.** How is the information on each statement organized?
c. **Content.** What kind of information is found on each statement?

Remember that this chapter is intended to provide an overview of financial statements, so focus on the "big picture." You will have the opportunity to learn details about specific financial statement items when we discuss them in depth in Chapters 2 through 5.

1. The Balance Sheet

a. **Purpose.** The balance sheet reports at a point in time what a business owns (**assets**), what it owes to outsiders (**liabilities**), and what is leftover for the owners of the company's stock (**stockholders' equity**). In effect, the balance sheet asks, Does a business have enough resources to pay its bills and still have something left for its owners? The business itself, not the individual stockholders who own the business, is viewed as owning the assets and owing the liabilities on its balance sheet. This is also the idea behind the **separate entity** assumption, which requires that a business's balance sheet include the assets, liabilities, and stockholders' equity of only that business and not those of the stockholders. In accounting language, assets are the resources owned by the business, and liabilities and stockholders' equity represent the claims that interested parties have over the assets. These claims exist because the interested parties have provided the financing for the business to buy the assets.

b. **Setup.** The balance sheet, like the other three basic financial statements, starts with a *heading* that answers three questions: (*i*) who—the name of the company, (*ii*) what—the name of the financial statement, and (*iii*) when—the date of the financial statement. The heading is followed by a *body* that lists dollar amounts for various aspects of the business. The body of every balance sheet contains three interrelated parts: assets, liabilities, and stockholders' equity. The relationship that unites these three parts of the balance sheet is often called the **basic accounting equation** and it is represented by the following:

The body of the balance sheet always shows that assets equal liabilities plus stockholders' equity. This basic accounting equation is true by definition because each asset on the balance sheet has been financed by either **creditors** or stockholders. Financing provided by creditors creates a liability. Financing provided by stockholders creates stockholders' equity.

c.   *Content.* Now that you know the purpose and setup for the balance sheet, you can probably predict its content. The balance sheet should have a heading that is followed by a body, which lists the business's assets, liabilities, and stockholders' equity at a particular point in time. You can learn lots about the balance sheet just by reading it from the top. As you read the following paragraphs, glance at Mattel's balance sheet in Exhibit 1.4, which we have adapted from the "investors" section of Mattel's Web site at www.mattel.com.

The heading indicates *who* (Mattel, Inc.), *what* (Balance Sheet), and *when* (At December 31, 2003). The balance sheet is like a snapshot indicating the financial position of a company at a particular point in time. The heading of Mattel's balance sheet includes a fourth line that states the unit of measure—in this case "in millions of U.S. dollars." Because Mattel is based in the United States, it reports in U.S. dollars. This is the **unit of measure** assumption. We see it in the currency used by companies in other countries: Nestlé (Swiss francs), Lego (Danish krone), and Adidas (euros). Like most big companies, our Mattel example in Exhibit 1.4 rounds to the nearest million (U.S. dollars), which involves dropping the last six digits.

Let's move on to the body of the balance sheet, focusing first on the Assets section. The five items listed there are common names that many companies use to describe the assets that they own and use in their business activities. If these **accounts,** as they are often called, don't adequately describe the company's assets, then the list would be expanded.

exhibit 1.4	Sample Balance Sheet and Explanation of Items

MATTEL, INC.
Balance Sheet
At December 31, 2003
(in millions of U.S. dollars)

Who: Name of the business
What: Title of the statement
When: Accounting period (at a point in time)
Other: Unit of measure

Assets		
Cash	$1,153	The amount of cash in the company's bank accounts
Accounts Receivable	544	Amounts owed to Mattel by customers for prior credit sales
Inventories	389	Toys being made and finished toys ready to be sold
Property, Plant, and Equipment	626	Land, factories, and production machinery
Other Assets	1,799	Trademarks, brand names, and other assets bought by Mattel
Total Assets	$4,511	Total must equal total liabilities and stockholders' equity below
Liabilities		
Accounts Payable	$1,468	Amounts still owed by Mattel for prior purchases on credit
Notes Payable	827	Amounts owed based on written debt contracts
Total Liabilities	2,295	
Stockholders' Equity		
Contributed Capital	1,509	Amounts invested in the business by stockholders
Retained Earnings	707	Past earnings minus past distributions to stockholders
Total Stockholders' Equity	2,216	
Total Liabilities and Stockholders' Equity	$4,511	Total must equal total assets above

Assets. The first three assets (*Cash, Accounts Receivable,* and *Inventories*) relate to Mattel's main operating activities. The amount shown for the *Cash* account indicates that Mattel has over $1.1 billion in its bank accounts (remember that the amounts in the exhibit are rounded to the nearest million dollars, so $1,153 is actually $1,153,000,000). The second asset account, *Accounts Receivable,* indicates the total amount of money that Mattel expects to collect from its customers for toys it has sold on credit. Think of this as an IOU that gives Mattel the right to collect cash from customers in the future. The third asset account, *Inventories,* reports the cost of all toys that Mattel has made or bought to be sold in the future.

Mattel's remaining asset accounts relate to its investing activities. The fourth asset account listed, *Property, Plant, and Equipment,* indicates that Mattel has invested a great deal of money in the land, factories, and production machinery that are used to make toys. The final asset shown, *Other Assets,* is a catchall that includes a variety of assets, including trademarks and brand names (like View-Master® and Matchbox®) that Mattel has bought from other companies.

COACH'S CORNER
Assets are listed on the balance sheet in order of how quickly they are used up or converted into cash. This is called order of liquidity.

Liabilities. Financing for Mattel to buy its assets has come from liabilities and stockholders' equity. Under the Liabilities category, Mattel's balance sheet in Exhibit 1.4 lists two items. *Accounts Payable* includes amounts owed to other companies for purchases of goods or services on credit. For example, when Mattel buys the material for Barbie's hair, which is the very same as that used to make Saran Wrap™,[2] it doesn't pay cash upfront. Instead, Mattel promises to pay within a short interest-free period of 60 days or less. The amount owed is included in accounts payable. If Mattel were to need a longer period of time to pay, the accounts payable could be converted to *Notes Payable*—the next liability listed on Mattel's balance sheet. Notes payable are like accounts payable except that they (*a*) are not interest-free, (*b*) will not be paid as soon as accounts payable, and (*c*) are documented using formal written debt contracts known as "notes." So if your friend buys a DVD for you with the understanding that you'll pay her back right away, you would have an account payable. If you arrange and sign for a car loan through your bank, you would have a note payable.

Stockholders' Equity. The Stockholders' Equity section of the balance sheet is called *stockholders'* equity to emphasize that Mattel is a corporation owned by stockholders. This section lists two accounts, both of which represent financing provided by stockholders. *Contributed Capital* reports the amount of cash injected into the business by stockholders who bought stock directly from the company. *Retained Earnings* represents the company's total earnings (and losses) less all **dividends** paid to the stockholders since the formation of the corporation. We'll discuss this account in more detail later in this chapter when we get to the statement of retained earnings.

YOU SHOULD KNOW

 Dividends are payments a company periodically makes to its stockholders as a return on their investment.

COACH'S CORNER
If you're thinking of leaving out the self-study quiz just to "get through" the chapter, don't. The best way to know whether you've been reading the chapter carefully enough is to see how well you do on the self-study quiz.

HOW'S IT GOING?   A Self-Study Quiz

1. Mattel's *assets* are listed in one section of the balance sheet and *liabilities* and *stockholders' equity* are in other sections. Notice that, according to the basic accounting equation, these sections must balance. In the following chapters, you will learn that this basic accounting equation is the main building block for the entire accounting process. Your task in this quiz is to show that Mattel's reported assets of $4,511 (million) is correct, by using the numbers for liabilities and stockholders' equity presented in Exhibit 1.4. Fill in the blanks in the basic accounting equation:

---

[2]"Impressive Tresses: Designing Barbie® Doll's Hair," retrieved June 2, 2004, from www.barbiecollectibles.com/about/design_200104.asp.

Assets	**=**	**Liabilities**	**+ Stockholders' Equity**
$4,511	=	☐	+ ☐

(amounts rounded to the nearest million)

2. Learning which items belong in each of the balance sheet categories is an important first step in understanding their meaning. Without referring to Exhibit 1.4, mark each balance sheet item in the following list with letters to show it as an Asset, Liability, or Stockholders' Equity account.

☐ Accounts Payable   ☐ Inventories
☐ Accounts Receivable   ☐ Property, Plant, and Equipment
☐ Cash   ☐ Notes Payable
☐ Contributed Capital   ☐ Retained Earnings

When working on these questions, cover up the solutions in the margin with your thumb. After you're done, check the answers in the margin.

2. The Income Statement

YOU SHOULD KNOW

Net income is equal to revenues minus expenses.
Revenues are increases in a company's resources, arising primarily from its operating activities.
Expenses are decreases in a company's resources, arising primarily from its operating activities.

a. **Purpose.** In the same way that your personal tax return shows how much you made during the year, the income statement reports whether a business made a profit (**net income**) from selling goods and providing services (**revenues**) after subtracting the costs of doing business (**expenses**). The income statement summarizes these financial results *over a particular time period,* such as one month, a quarter (three months), or an entire year.

b. **Setup.** Like the balance sheet, the income statement starts with a heading that shows *who, what,* and *when.* Following this is a body, which reports the various operating activities of the business along with related dollar amounts. These operating activities are classified as revenues or expenses. The amount by which revenues exceed expenses is reported as net income. (It's called a net loss if expenses are greater than revenues.) These three main parts of the income statement are connected through the following relationship:

Revenues − Expenses = Net Income

COACH'S CORNER

Unlike the heading of the balance sheet, which says it is prepared at a point in time, the headings of the three other basic financial statements—income statement, statement of retained earnings, and statement of cash flows—indicate that they cover a period of time that ends at the balance sheet date.

c. **Content.** As you can see from Exhibit 1.5, the heading of the income statement indicates that it covers a period of time ("For the Year Ended"). This means that the net income of $537 million shown in the body is the amount by which Mattel's revenues exceeded its expenses during the period from January 1 through December 31, 2003. The specific types of revenues and expenses reported in the body of the income statement depend on the nature of the business, as discussed below.

Revenues.   Mattel's (adapted) income statement in Exhibit 1.5 reports only one type of revenue (*Sales*), which implies they only sell goods. If you were to look instead at Blockbuster's income statement, you would see three types of revenues: movie rentals, merchandise sales, and the ever-mysterious "other revenues." The main rule of all reported revenues, whether they relate to Blockbuster's DVD rentals or Mattel's sales of Survivor™ games, is that revenues are reported when the product or service is given to a

---

exhibit 1.5   **Sample Income Statement and Explanation of Items**

MATTEL, INC. Income Statement For the Year Ended December 31, 2003 (in millions of U.S. dollars)		*Who:* Name of the business *What:* Title of the statement *When:* Accounting period (for the year) *Other:* Unit of measure
Revenues		
Sales Revenue	$4,960	Revenue earned from selling toys
Total Revenues	4,960	
Expenses		
Cost of Goods Sold Expense	2,531	Costs to produce the toys that were sold
Advertising and Promotion Expenses	636	Expenses to run ads and provide coupons
Other Selling and Administrative Expenses	991	Expenses to sell toys and manage the business
Interest Expense	62	Cost of using borrowed funds
Income Tax Expense	203	Cost of taxes charged on income earned
Total Expenses	4,423	Total of all expenses
Net Income	$ 537	Total of all revenues minus all expenses

---

customer *whether or not they are paid for in that period*. Some companies may collect cash at the time a sale is made, like when Blockbuster rents you a video, but others do not (such as when Mattel sells toys to Wal-Mart on credit). Either way, revenues include all sales (cash and credit) made during the period.

Expenses.   In addition to sales revenue, we see from Mattel's income statement in Exhibit 1.5 that its operating activities result in several types of expenses, which are the costs of running the business. The biggest expense is the $2.5 billion cost of making the toys that were sold in 2003 (called *Cost of Goods Sold Expense*). Another big expense for Mattel was the $636 million in *Advertising and Promotion Expenses*. It's pretty easy for Mattel to run up costs like this because it sells about 100 different lines of toys, and a single full-page ad for only one product in *Teen People* costs $75,500.[3] We could go on, but you probably already get the point: companies, like Mattel, incur many different kinds of expenses to generate revenues. All expenses are reported on the income statement.

Throughout this course, you will learn that some expenses involve immediate cash payments, while others involve payments at a later date. Expenses also can arise from selling or using assets that have been paid for in a prior period. We'll sort through all of this in Chapters 2–4, but for now you should note that expenses are reported in the period in which they are incurred to generate revenues *whether or not they are paid for in cash during that period*.

Net Income.   To understand how successful Mattel was in generating a profit from its business operations, we need to consider both the revenues and the expenses at the same time. *Net Income* does this by meshing revenues and expenses into a single number. This combined (or "net") number indicates whether the inflow of resources from making sales (revenues) was greater or less than the outflow of resources (expenses) to generate those sales. In Mattel's case in 2003, the net income (or "bottom line") was $537 million. Nice.

COACH'S CORNER

When expenses equal revenues, a company is said to "break even." When expenses exceed revenues, the business reports a "net loss." A company is "in the red" when it reports a net loss.

---

[3]Mediamark Research Inc. database, retrieved June 2, 2004, from www.mriplus.com.

HOW'S IT GOING?   A Self-Study Quiz

1. Learning which items belong in each of the income statement categories is an important first step in understanding their meaning. Without referring to Exhibit 1.5, mark each income statement item in the following list with a letter to indicate whether it is a <u>R</u>evenue or an <u>E</u>xpense.

   ☐ Cost of goods sold   ☐ Sales
   ☐ Advertising and promotion   ☐ Selling and administrative

2. During 2003, Mattel delivered toys for which customers paid or promised to pay amounts totaling $4,960 (million). During the same period, it collected $4,907 (million) in cash from its customers. Without referring to Exhibit 1.5, pick which of these two amounts will be shown on Mattel's income statement as *sales revenue* for 2003. Why did you pick this answer?

3. During 2003, Mattel *produced* toys with a total cost of production of $2,763 (million). During the same period, it *delivered* to customers toys that cost a total of $2,531 (million) to produce. Without referring to Exhibit 1.5, pick which of the two numbers will be shown on Mattel's income statement as *cost of goods sold expense* for 2003. Why did you pick this answer?

After you're done, check your answers with the solutions in the margin.

3. The Statement of Retained Earnings

a. **Purpose.** The statement of retained earnings shows the amount of earnings that have been retained in the business and the amount of the company's resources paid out to stockholders as dividends.

b. **Setup.** As shown in Exhibit 1.6 on page 13, Mattel's (adapted) statement of retained earnings has the customary heading and is followed by a body that reports the way that net income and dividends affected the company's financial position during the accounting period. The equation for the statement of retained earnings is:

Beginning Retained Earnings + Net Income − Dividends Declared = Ending Retained Earnings

Net income earned during the period increases the retained earnings balance. When a company **declares** dividends during the period, *Retained Earnings* decreases.

YOU SHOULD KNOW

A dividend is said to be **declared** when a company formally promises to pay out some of its resources to its owners.

c. **Content.** The statement begins with Mattel's beginning-of-year *Retained Earnings* balance of $341 million. This beginning balance indicates the total net income of the company that has not been distributed to stockholders, added up from when the corporation was formed in 1948 to the beginning of the current year. The current year's *Net Income* of $537 million (as we saw earlier on the income statement in Exhibit 1.5) is then added to the beginning retained earnings balance. The next line subtracts *Dividends* totaling $171 million that were declared in 2003 to be paid to stockholders. The last line reports the new end-of-year retained earnings balance, which for Mattel was $707 million at December 31, 2003.

Notice that the ending retained earnings balance in Exhibit 1.6 is the same as the amount reported for *Retained Earnings* on Mattel's balance sheet in Exhibit 1.4 on page 8.

exhibit 1.6	Sample Statement of Retained Earnings and Explanation of Items

MATTEL, INC. Statement of Retained Earnings For the Year Ended December 31, 2003 (in millions of U.S. dollars)		*Who:* Name of the business *What:* Title of the statement *When:* Accounting period (for the year) *Other:* Unit of measure
Retained Earnings, January 1, 2003	$341	Balance carried forward from previous year
Net Income for 2003	537	"Bottom line" from the income statement
Dividends Declared for 2003	(171)	Declared distributions to stockholders
Retained Earnings, December 31, 2003	$707	Balance at the end of this year

Thus, the statement of retained earnings shows how the income statement (and net income, in particular) links to the balance sheet (and retained earnings). We'll talk about this link in more detail later in this chapter.

4. The Statement of Cash Flows

a. **Purpose.** Most people are keenly interested in monitoring the balance in their own bank accounts, often asking questions such as: Why do I have only $23 left? Didn't my paycheck get deposited? Where did I spend all that money? These are precisely the kinds of questions that a statement of cash flows answers. The purpose of the statement of cash flows is to summarize how a business's operating, investing, and financing activities caused its cash balance to change over a particular period of time.

b. **Setup.** The statement of cash flows contains the now-familiar heading and a body. The body, unlike your personal bank statement, classifies cash increases (inflows) and decreases (outflows) into the three categories of business activities (operating, investing, and financing). As you can see from Mattel's (adapted) statement of cash flows in Exhibit 1.7 on page 14, cash inflows are shown as positive numbers and cash outflows appear as negative numbers (in parentheses). A subtotal (called *net cash flow*) is reported at the bottom of each of the three main categories, and these three subtotals are added together to yield a total *Net Change in Cash*. When this total change is added to the *Beginning-of-Year Cash* balance, an *End-of-Year Cash* balance pops out. This end-of-year cash balance is precisely the amount reported for the asset account *Cash* on the balance sheet.

c. **Content.** *Cash Flows from Operating Activities* are cash flows that are directly related to earning income. For example, when Wal-Mart, Toys "R" Us, and other customers pay Mattel for the toys delivered to them, the statement of cash flows lists the amounts collected as "cash collected from customers." From the first line of the operating activities section of the statement of cash flows in Exhibit 1.7 on page 14, you can see that Mattel received nearly $5 billion in cash from its customers during 2003. When Mattel pays salaries to its employees at its Design Center in El Segundo, California, or pays bills received from supply companies like Dow Chemical, the statement of cash flows includes the amounts as "cash paid to suppliers and employees," as shown in the second line of the operating activities section. Other cash outflows for operating activities are shown in a similar manner.

    Cash Flows from Investing Activities include cash flows related to the acquisition or sale of the company's long-term assets. Exhibit 1.7 reports only one cash outflow from investing activities, the purchase of additional manufacturing equipment to meet growing demand for Mattel's toys. The company also reported a cash inflow of $25 million, which it received from selling some equipment and other long-term assets.

COACH'S CORNER

Notice that dividends are reported in the statement of retained earnings *not* the income statement. Dividends are not an expense. They are a distribution of profits to stockholders.

COACH'S CORNER

Negative amounts are reported in parentheses in the financial statements.

exhibit 1.7	Sample Statement of Cash Flows and Explanation of Items

MATTEL, INC.
Statement of Cash Flows
For the Year Ended December 31, 2003
(in millions of U.S. dollars)

Who: Name of the business
What: Title of the statement
When: Accounting period (for the year)
Other: Unit of measure

Cash Flows from Operating Activities

Cash collected from customers	$4,907	
Cash paid to suppliers and employees	(2,763)	Cash flow from making and selling toys
Cash paid for other operating activities	(1,772)	
Net cash flow from operating activities	372	

Cash Flows from Investing Activities

Cash paid to purchase equipment and other assets	(206)	
Cash received from selling equipment and other assets	25	Cash flow from buying/selling long-term assets
Net cash flow from investing activities	(181)	

Cash Flows from Financing Activities

Cash paid on notes payable and other financing	(134)	
Cash paid for dividends	(171)	Cash flow from dealings with lenders/stockholders
Net cash flow from financing activities	(305)	
Net Change in Cash During the Year	(114)	Change in cash (372 − 181 − 305)
Cash at Beginning of Year	1,267	Last period's ending cash balance
Cash at End of Year	$1,153	This period's ending cash on the balance sheet

Cash Flows from Financing Activities are directly related to financing the company itself. These cash flows involve receipt or payment of money to lenders and stockholders. We see from Exhibit 1.7 that Mattel paid down $134 million of its notes payable and other financing, and it also paid out $171 million in dividends to stockholders in 2003.

HOW'S IT GOING?   A Self-Study Quiz

1. During 2003, Mattel delivered toys to customers who paid or promised to pay amounts totaling $4,960 (million). During the same period, Mattel collected $4,907 (million) in cash from its customers. Without referring to Exhibit 1.7, indicate which of the two amounts will be shown on Mattel's cash flow statement for 2003.

2. Learning which items belong in each cash flow statement category is an important first step in understanding their meaning. Without referring to Exhibit 1.7, use a letter to mark each item in the following list as a cash flow from Operating, Investing, or Financing activities. **Put parentheses around the letter if it is a cash *outflow* and use no parentheses if it's an *inflow.***

☐ Cash paid to suppliers and employees   ☐ Cash paid to purchase equipment
☐ Cash paid on note payable   ☐ Cash collected from customers
☐ Cash paid for dividends   ☐ Cash received from selling equipment

After you're done, check your answers with the solutions in the margin.

Quiz Answers

1. $4,907 (million) will be reported in the cash flow statement because this represents the actual cash collected from customers related to current and prior years' sales.

2. Column 1: (O), (F), (F)
   Column 2: (I), O, I

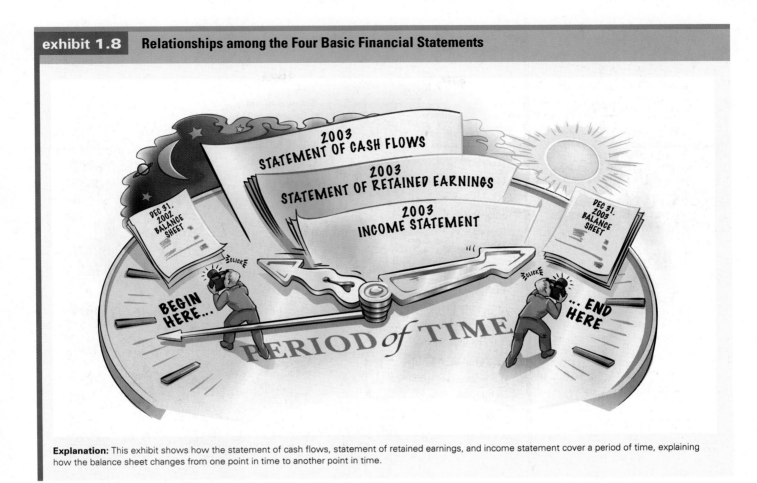

exhibit 1.8   **Relationships among the Four Basic Financial Statements**

Explanation: This exhibit shows how the statement of cash flows, statement of retained earnings, and income statement cover a period of time, explaining how the balance sheet changes from one point in time to another point in time.

Relationships among the Four Basic Financial Statements

The goal for this section is to show how the four statements fit together. Exhibit 1.8 presents one way to picture this, by reminding you that a balance sheet reports a snapshot of the company at a *point* in time whereas the other three statements cover a *period* of time. Think of the balance sheet on December 31, 2002, as the starting point for 2003 and the other three statements as explanations of what happened during the year (2003), ending on December 31, 2003, with a new balance sheet that presents an updated picture of the company.

In the real world, most companies do, in fact, present balance sheets at the two points in time shown in Exhibit 1.8. Rather than create two separate reports, though, they report these balance sheets using two columns of numbers on a single report. One column displays the balances at the end of the previous period (which is the starting point for the current period), and the other displays balances at the end of the current period. An example of this **comparative** balance sheet format is shown in Exhibit 1.9 on page 16. This comparative balance sheet acts as our starting point for showing how the financial statements connect together in the real world.

Think of actually splitting the balance sheet apart to form two points on a timeline, with one end on the far left side of the page and the other on the far right. Imagine that, for *Cash* and *Retained Earnings*, there are lines linking their beginning and ending balance sheet amounts. If you click on the cash link, the statement of cash flows would pop up, showing how the cash balance changed during the year. If you click on the retained earnings link, the statement of retained earnings would pop up, showing how the retained earnings balance changed during the year. If you were to click on the net income number within the statement of retained earnings, the income statement would pop up,

COACH'S CORNER

Learning how the four statements fit together is very important. Slow down and spend a little extra time on the next couple of pages.

YOU SHOULD KNOW

Comparative financial statements report numbers for two or more periods to make it easy for users to compare account balances from one period to the next.

exhibit 1.9   Comparative Balance Sheet

MATTEL, INC.
Balance Sheet
At December 31
(in millions of U.S. dollars)

Assets	2002	2003
Cash	$1,267	$1,153
Accounts Receivable	490	544
Inventories	339	389
Property, Plant, and Equipment	600	626
Other Assets	1,764	1,799
Total Assets	$4,460	$4,511
Liabilities		
Accounts Payable	$1,649	$1,468
Notes Payable	832	827
Total Liabilities	2,481	2,295
Stockholders' Equity		
Contributed Capital	1,638	1,509
Retained Earnings	341	707
Total Stockholders' Equity	1,979	2,216
Total Liabilities and Stockholders' Equity	$4,460	$4,511

explaining how the company's operations improved or harmed Mattel's financial position during the year. Exhibit 1.10 shows the end result of these clicks and pop-ups. An animated graphic on the DVD that comes with this textbook brings them to life.

Notes to the Financial Statements

In addition to the four reports that we've just described, the financial statements include one additional part that you should know about. This part is called the **notes** to the financial statements (or "footnotes") and it appears on the pages immediately after the four financial statements.

There are three types of financial statement notes:

1. **Accounting policies.** This type of note describes the accounting decisions that were made when preparing financial statements. For example, Mattel's accounting policy note for advertising and promotion describes how (and when) these costs are reported in Mattel's financial statements.
2. **Contents included.** This type of note presents additional detail about what's included in certain financial statement account balances. For example, Mattel's notes tell us that its "other assets" include the costs of trademarks and brand names.
3. **Additional information.** The third type of note provides additional financial disclosures about items not listed on the statements themselves. For example, Mattel rents warehouse space in California, Kentucky, New Jersey, Texas, and Wisconsin. The terms of these rental agreements (also known as leases) are disclosed in a note.

We've covered a lot of material to this point in the chapter. Exhibit 1.11 on page 18 summarizes the main points for each of the four basic financial statements. Notice that

exhibit 1.10 **Linking the Four Basic Statements**

MATTEL, INC.
Statement of Cash Flows
For the Year Ended December 31, 2003
(in millions of U.S. dollars)

Cash Flows from Operating Activities

Cash collected from customers	$4,907
Cash paid to suppliers and employees	(2,763)
Cash paid for other operating activities	(1,772)
Net cash flow from operating activities	372

Cash Flows from Investing Activities

Cash paid to purchase equipment and other assets	(206)
Cash received from selling equipment	25
Net cash flow from investing activities	(181)

Cash Flows from Financing Activities

Cash paid on notes payable and other financing	(134)
Cash paid for dividends	(171)
Net cash flow from financing activities	(305)
Net Change in Cash During the Year	(114)
Cash at Beginning of Year	1,267
Cash at End of Year	$1,153

MATTEL, INC.
Balance Sheet
At December 31
(in millions of U.S. dollars)

	2002	2003
Assets		
Cash	$1,267	$1,153
Accounts Receivable	490	544
Inventories	339	389
Property, Plant, and Equipment	600	626
Other Assets	1,764	1,799
Total Assets	$4,460	$4,511
Liabilities		
Accounts Payable	$1,649	$1,468
Notes Payable	832	827
Total Liabilities	2,481	2,295
Stockholders' Equity		
Contributed Capital	1,638	1,509
Retained Earnings	341	707
Total Stockholders' Equity	1,979	2,216
Total Liabilities and Stockholders' Equity	$4,460	$4,511

MATTEL, INC.
Statement of Retained Earnings
For the Year Ended December 31, 2003
(in millions of U.S. dollars)

Retained Earnings, January 1, 2003	$341
Net Income for 2003	537
Dividends Declared for 2003	(171)
Retained Earnings, December 31, 2003	$707

MATTEL, INC.
Income Statement
For the Year Ended December 31, 2003
(in millions of U.S. dollars)

Revenues

Sales Revenue	$4,960
Total Revenues	4,960

Expenses

Cost of Goods Sold Expense	2,531
Advertising and Promotion Expenses	636
Other Selling and Administrative Expenses	991
Interest Expense	62
Income Tax Expense	203
Total Expenses	4,423
Net Income	$ 537

| | exhibit 1.11 | Summary of Key Points |

Financial Statement	Purpose: To report . . .	Setup	Examples of Content
1. Balance sheet (also called the statement of financial position)	. . . what the business owns *at a particular point in time* and whether the financing for these items came from creditors or stockholders.	Assets = Liabilities + Stockholders' Equity	*Assets* include Mattel's cash in the bank, production equipment, and toys Mattel has made but not yet sold. *Liabilities* include amounts owed but not yet paid. *Stockholders' Equity* shows the amount owners have invested in the company.
2. Income statement (also called the statement of income, statement of operations, statement of profit and loss)	. . . what the business has earned from its operating activities *over a period of time.*	Revenues − Expenses = Net Income	*Revenues* include what Mattel earns from selling toys. *Expenses* include Mattel's costs of running its business.
3. Statement of retained earnings	. . . the accumulated earnings retained in the business *over a period of time.*	Beginning Retained Earnings + Net Income (this period) − Dividends Declared (this period) = Ending Retained Earnings	*Net Income* is the net amount earned by the business during the period. *Dividends* indicate how much is distributed to the business's stockholders during the period.
4. Statement of cash flows	. . . the cash received and paid out by the business *over a period of time.*	Operating Activities Cash Flow + Investing Activities Cash Flow + Financing Activities Cash Flow = Change in Cash Balance + Beginning Cash Balance = Ending Cash Balance	*Operating* cash flow includes cash received from customers and cash paid to suppliers during the period. *Investing* cash flow includes cash used to buy factory buildings during the period. *Financing* cash flow includes exchanges of cash with lenders and owners during the period.

the fourth column provides examples of items included in each financial statement. For more formal definitions of these financial statement items, see the You Should Know boxes presented earlier in the chapter.

Generally Accepted Accounting Principles (GAAP)

Just as the inventors of Monopoly® had to come up with rules for that game, someone has to determine the rules for financial reporting, and for ensuring that the accounting rules keep up with the ever-changing nature of business. As it turns out, the system of financial statement reporting in use today has a long history—all the way back to a publication in 1494 by an Italian monk and mathematician, Luca Pacioli. Despite this long history, few hard-and-fast accounting rules existed until 1933. Until that time, most companies decided for themselves how and what to report in their financial statements. Following the dramatic stock market decline of 1929, the U.S. Congress passed the Securities Act of 1933 and the Securities Exchange Act of 1934 into law. These acts created the **Securities and Exchange Commission** (SEC)—a government agency that was given many powers and responsibilities, including the power to establish accounting rules that must be followed by all public companies.

As shown in Exhibit 1.12, the SEC currently has given the primary responsibility for setting the underlying rules of accounting to the **Financial Accounting Standards Board** (FASB). Statements published by the FASB, as a group, are the main source of rules

YOU SHOULD KNOW

GAAP (generally accepted accounting principles) are the underlying rules for financial reporting and are established by the **Financial Accounting Standards Board** (FASB) under the authority granted by the **Securities and Exchange Commission** (SEC). The **Public Company Accounting Oversight Board** (PCAOB) establishes the rules used by **auditors,** who report on whether a public company's financial statements are, in fact, prepared following GAAP.

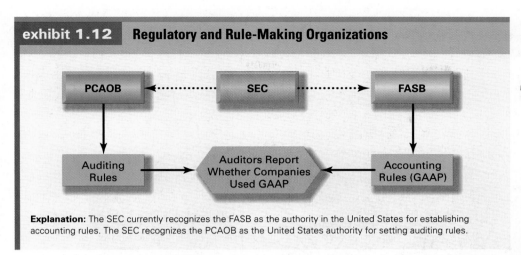

exhibit 1.12 | **Regulatory and Rule-Making Organizations**

Explanation: The SEC currently recognizes the FASB as the authority in the United States for establishing accounting rules. The SEC recognizes the PCAOB as the United States authority for setting auditing rules.

TOPIC TACKLER PLUS

For an animated tour of what financial statement users look at in a company's annual report, check out the animated walkthrough on the DVD for use with this book.

called **generally accepted accounting principles,** or GAAP for short (pronounced like the name of the clothing store). To ensure accountants follow GAAP when preparing their company's financial statements, the SEC requires that each public company hire independent **auditors** to scrutinize its financial records. Following rules approved by the **Public Company Accounting Oversight Board** (PCAOB), these auditors report whether, beyond reasonable doubt, the financial statements represent what they claim to represent and whether they comply with GAAP. In a sense, GAAP are to auditors and accountants what the criminal code is to lawyers and the public.

EVALUATE

RESULTS FROM THE PERSPECTIVE OF FINANCIAL STATEMENT USERS

Who Cares?

Now that you see what goes into financial statements, it's time to ask *who cares?* As Exhibit 1.13 shows, lots of people care. Financial statements are used by people inside the company and those external to it. In this course, we focus on decisions made by two important groups of external financial statement users: *investors* and *creditors*.

In general, investors and creditors use the four basic financial statements (and notes) to

1. **Understand the current state of the business.**
2. **Predict how the business is likely to do in the future.**

1. Using the Balance Sheet

Investors and creditors look at the balance sheet to see whether the company owns enough (assets) to pay all that it owes to creditors (liabilities) and still have enough left to distribute as dividends to stockholders and fund future operations (stockholders' equity). It's not good if assets are barely enough to cover liabilities, because if a company does not pay its creditors on time, it can be forced to sell its assets to pay its liabilities. When this happens, the law requires that creditors be paid before investors receive any money, as illustrated in Exhibit 1.14 on page 21.

Balance sheet

Assets

Liabilities

Stockholders' Equity

exhibit 1.13   Financial Statement Users

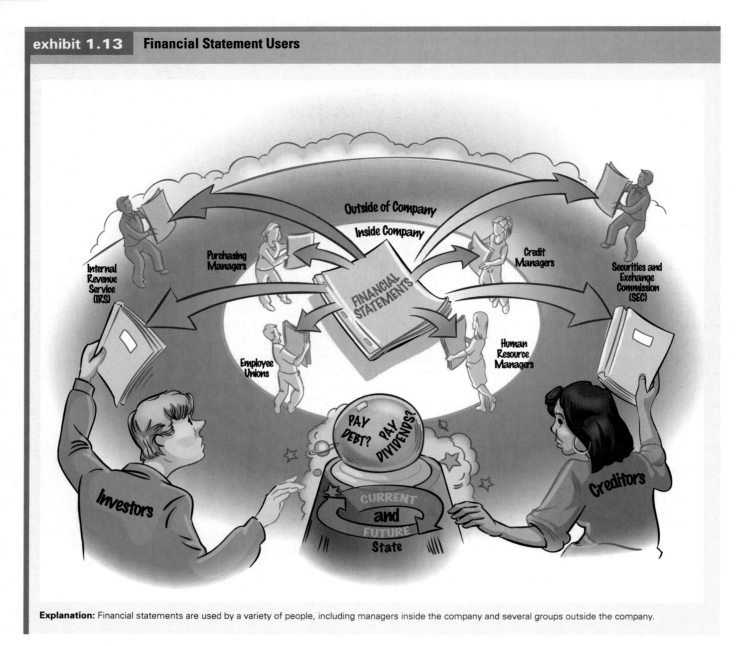

Explanation: Financial statements are used by a variety of people, including managers inside the company and several groups outside the company.

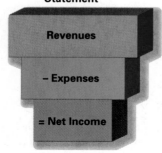

Income Statement

Revenues

– Expenses

= Net Income

Statement of Retained Earnings

Retained earnings, 1/1/06

\+ Net income (2006)

– Dividends declared (2006)

= Retained earnings, 12/31/06

2. Using the Income Statement

Investors and creditors are eager to analyze the income statement because it indicates whether a company made a profit during the current period. Also, by looking for a trend in a company's net income from year to year, users can get clues about the company's future earnings. Estimated future earnings are important to investors because they buy stock when they believe that future earnings will improve and lead to a higher stock price. These estimates also are important to creditors because future earnings provide the resources to repay loans.

3. Using the Statement of Retained Earnings

Creditors closely monitor the retained earnings statement because a company's policy on dividend payments to stockholders affects its ability to repay its debts. Every dollar from earnings that Mattel pays to stockholders as dividends is not available to use in paying

exhibit 1.14	**Creditor and Stockholder Claims**

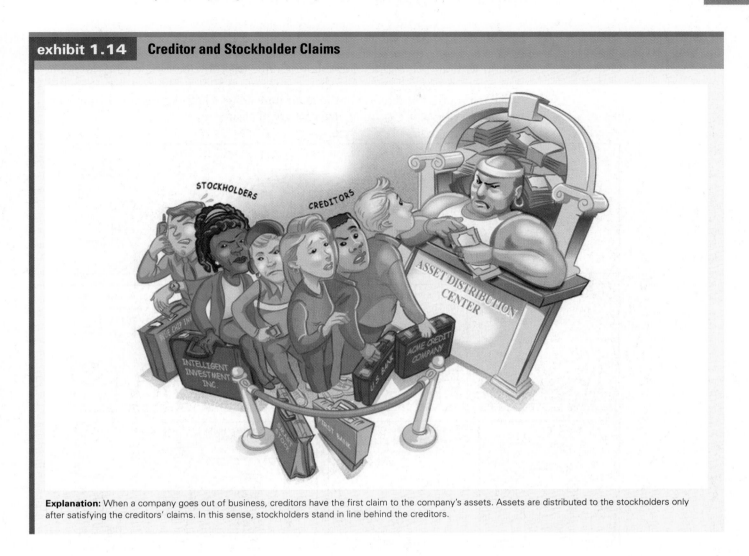

Explanation: When a company goes out of business, creditors have the first claim to the company's assets. Assets are distributed to the stockholders only after satisfying the creditors' claims. In this sense, stockholders stand in line behind the creditors.

back its debt to banks and other creditors. Investors, on the other hand, use the statement of retained earnings to evaluate whether the company favors paying out dividends or retaining its earnings to support future growth. Some investors, perhaps your grandparents, prefer steady dividends, whereas others are concerned that every dollar that Mattel pays as dividends is not available for investing in additional factories and the latest manufacturing equipment.

4. Using the Statement of Cash Flows

The statement of cash flows indicates to investors and creditors how the company obtained and spent its money during the accounting period. The Operating Activities section indicates the company's ability to generate cash from sales to meet its current cash needs, and the Investing and Financing Activities sections indicate whether any money left over from operations was used to expand the company, pay back the bank debt, or pay dividends to stockholders. By comparing Mattel's statement of cash flows from year to year, users can find that Mattel generates plenty of cash from operations but has reduced its dividends in recent years.

Using the Notes and Other Reports

All financial statement users need to understand the rules used in computing the numbers on the financial statements. A swim coach would never try to evaluate a swimmer's

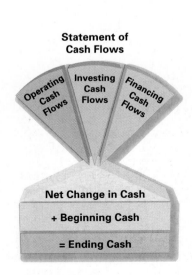

time in the 100 freestyle without first asking if the time was for a race in meters or in yards. Likewise, a financial statement user should never attempt to use accounting information without reading the notes that describe the rules used to prepare the financial statements. As the following cartoon suggests, information in the notes can dramatically influence your interpretation of the main statements. Consider them the equivalent of the Surgeon General's warning on a package of cigarettes.

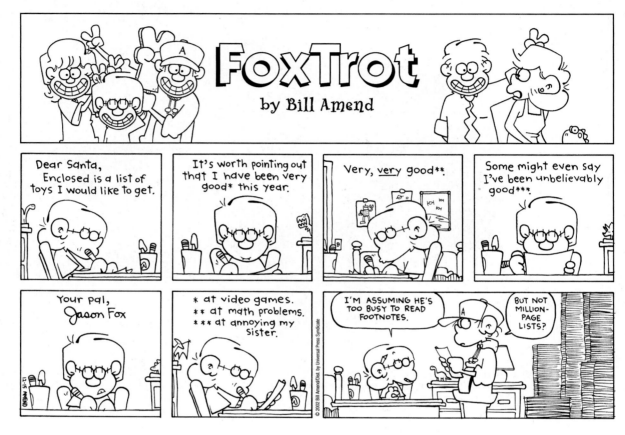

In addition to reading the notes to the financial statements, users also consider the information reported in the auditors' report. This report describes whether the financial statements present a fair picture of the company, and whether they are prepared using methods allowed by GAAP. The purpose of the auditors' report isn't to tell you if a company is about to go broke, but it is the best protection against having a company's accountants and executives unintentionally or intentionally prepare misleading financial reports.

RECONSIDER

HOW FINANCIAL STATEMENT REPORTING INFORMS USERS

The Glimpse Inside

ETHICAL

ISSUE

Do you remember Mattel's problem from the opening of this chapter? Its managers had to tell investors and creditors that the company lost $431 million (in 2000) without alarming them. They needed to be ethical and report the bad news about the loss honestly and, at the same time, convey to users good news that Mattel was still strong. By being honest with the bad news, Mattel's managers could begin to develop a reputation for honest reporting. This reputation could help in the long run because it would make users more likely to believe Mattel's managers when they have good news to report in the future.

© 1997 Randy Glasbergen.

"The bad news is, you do less work than anyone in this office. The good news is, you make the fewest mistakes."

Fortunately for Mattel, the $431 million loss in 2000 wasn't caused by poor toy sales. Instead, it was a result of a failed attempt to get into the software entertainment industry. Mattel had bought The Learning Company (TLC)—a business that produced kids' computer software under the Reader Rabbit® brand name. At the time of Mattel's purchase, TLC seemed to be doing well, having generated sales increases of 25 percent in each of the last three quarters leading up to the purchase. In the quarter after the purchase, however, Mattel ran into big losses from TLC. Mattel stuck with TLC for a year and a half, trying to make it profitable. But the longer Mattel tried, the more the losses mounted. Finally, Mattel admitted defeat and decided to get rid of TLC, confirming what some analysts had been calling one of the biggest acquisition failures of all time.

A Glance Outside

How did users take the news when Mattel announced the losses from TLC? Not well. Mattel's stock price fell about 30 percent. In addition to selling their Mattel stock, stockholders filed a lawsuit claiming that TLC's financial statements, which led Mattel to buy TLC, were fraudulently misstated. In an ironic turn of events, Mattel was named as a defendant in this lawsuit as TLC's former owner.[4] Mattel has since settled the lawsuit for $122 million.

What's Coming Up

In this chapter, you studied the basic financial statements that give external users an idea of how things are doing inside the company. The next chapter will take you deep inside a company to learn about the detailed steps involved in determining the amounts reported in each financial statement. To get ready for Chapter 2, use the materials in the following sections to review and practice what we covered in this chapter.

---

[4]U.S. District Court Class Action Complaint 99-CV-10619, retrieved June 2, 2004, from http://securities. stanford.edu/1009/MAT99/003.html.

POINT OF INTEREST
Mattel executives have learned the importance of honest financial reporting. Three decades earlier, six Mattel executives were charged with including fictitious sales in the company's financial statements. The fun and games ended with the Mattel execs paying over $30 million to settle lawsuits filed by angry investors and creditors. As the saying goes, today's good decisions come from experience, which itself comes from yesterday's bad decisions.

FOR YOUR REVIEW

DEMONSTRATION CASE

The introductory case presented here reviews the items reported on the income statement and balance sheet, using the financial statements of Krispy Kreme Donuts. The stores owned and franchised by Krispy Kreme Donuts can each make between 4,000 and 10,000 donuts per day. This capacity and the fanatical loyalty of its customers have made this expanding company a great success. Following is a list of the financial statement items and amounts adapted from a recent Krispy Kreme Donuts Inc. balance sheet and income statement. The numbers are presented in thousands of dollars for the year ended January 28.

eXcel

Accounts payable	$ 14,697
Accounts receivable	24,733
Cash	7,026
Contributed capital	85,060
General and administrative expenses	20,061
Income tax expense	9,058
Inventories	12,031
Net income	14,725
Notes payable	3,526
Operating expenses	250,690
Other assets	49,363
Other expenses	6,181
Other liabilities	26,474
Property and equipment	78,340
Retained earnings	41,736
Sales revenues	300,715
Total assets	171,493
Total expenses	285,990
Total liabilities	44,697
Total liabilities and stockholders' equity	171,493
Total revenues	300,715
Total stockholders' equity	126,796

Required:

1. Prepare a balance sheet and an income statement for the year, following the formats in Exhibits 1.4 and 1.5.
2. Describe the content of these two statements.
3. Name the other two statements that Krispy Kreme would include in its financial statements.
4. Did financing for Krispy Kreme's assets come primarily from liabilities or stockholders' equity?
5. Explain why Krispy Kreme would subject its statements to an independent audit.

Suggested Solution

1.

KRISPY KREME DONUTS INC.
Balance Sheet
At January 28
(in thousands of dollars)

Assets	
Cash	$ 7,026
Accounts receivable	24,733
Inventories	12,031
Property and equipment	78,340
Other assets	49,363
Total assets	**$171,493**
Liabilities	
Accounts payable	$ 14,697
Notes payable	3,526
Other liabilities	26,474
Total liabilities	44,697
Stockholders' Equity	
Contributed capital	85,060
Retained earnings	41,736
Total stockholders' equity	126,796
Total liabilities and stockholders' equity	**$171,493**

KRISPY KREME DONUTS INC. **Income Statement** **For the Year Ended January 28** **(in thousands of dollars)**	
Revenues	
Sales revenues	$300,715
Total revenues	300,715
Expenses	
Operating expenses	250,690
General and administrative expenses	20,061
Income tax expense	9,058
Other expenses	6,181
Total expenses	285,990
Net income	**$ 14,725**

2. The balance sheet reports the amount of assets, liabilities, and stockholders' equity of a business at a point in time. The income statement reports the most common measure of financial performance for a business: net income (revenues minus expenses during the accounting period).

3. Krispy Kreme would also present a statement of retained earnings and a statement of cash flows.

4. Financing for Krispy Kreme's assets is provided primarily from stockholders' equity ($126,796) rather than liabilities ($44,697).

5. Users will have greater confidence in the accuracy of financial statement information if they know that it has been audited, particularly because the people who audited the statements are required to meet professional standards of ethics and competence.

CHAPTER SUMMARY

Distinguish operating, investing, and financing activities. p. 5

LO1

-   *Operating activities* include day-to-day events involved in making and delivering goods and services.
-   *Investing activities* involve buying or selling longer-term assets such as land and buildings.
-   *Financing activities* are related to exchanging money with lenders or owners.

Describe the purpose, setup, and content of the four basic financial statements. p. 7

LO2

-   The *balance sheet* reports what the business owns (reported as assets) at a particular point in time and whether the financing for these assets came from creditors (reported as liabilities) or stockholders (reported as stockholders' equity).
-   The *income statement* reports the net amount that a business earned (net income) over a period of time by subtracting the costs of running the business (expenses) from the total amount earned (revenues).
-   The *statement of retained earnings* explains changes in the retained earnings account over a period of time by considering increases (from net income) and decreases (from dividends to stockholders).
-   The *statement of cash flows* explains changes in the cash account over a period of time by reporting inflows and outflows of cash from the business's operating, investing, and financing activities.

Explain the primary goals of financial statement users. p. 19

LO3

-   Although the particular interests of the various financial statement users differ somewhat, they ultimately are interested in using the financial statements to

1. Understand the current state of the business.
2. Predict how the business is likely to do in the future.

LO4   **Describe the importance of ethics and reputation in accounting. p. 22**

- Users have confidence in the accuracy of financial statement numbers when the people associated with their preparation and audit have reputations for ethical behavior and competence.

KEY TERMS TO KNOW

Accounting p. 6
Assets p. 7
Balance Sheet (Statement of Financial Position) p. 7
Basic Accounting Equation p. 7
Expenses p. 10
Financial Statements p. 4
Financial Statement Users p. 4

Financing Activities p. 5
Generally Accepted Accounting Principles (GAAP) p. 18
Income Statement (Statement of Income, Statement of Operations, or Statement of Profit and Loss) p. 10
Investing Activities p. 5
Liabilities p. 7

Net Income p. 10
Notes (Footnotes) p. 16
Operating Activities p. 5
Revenues p. 10
Statement of Cash Flows p. 13
Statement of Retained Earnings p. 12
Stockholders' Equity p. 7

FOR YOUR PRACTICE

QUESTIONS

1. Define *accounting*.
2. Briefly distinguish financial accounting from managerial accounting.
3. The accounting process generates financial reports for both internal and external users. Describe some of the specific groups of internal and external users.
4. Briefly distinguish investors from creditors.
5. Explain what the separate entity concept means when it says a business is treated as separate from its owners for accounting purposes.
6. Complete the following:

Name of Statement	Alternative Title
a. Income statement	*a.* _____
b. Balance sheet	*b.* _____

7. What information should be included in the heading of each of the four primary financial statements?
8. What are the purposes of (*a*) the balance sheet, (*b*) the income statement, (*c*) the statement of retained earnings, and (*d*) the statement of cash flows?
9. Explain why the income statement, statement of retained earnings, and statement of cash flows would be dated "For the Year Ended December 31, 2006," whereas the balance sheet would be dated "At December 31, 2006."
10. Briefly explain the importance of assets and liabilities to the decisions of investors and creditors.
11. Briefly define the following: *net income* and *net loss*.
12. Describe the basic accounting equation that underlies the balance sheet. Define the three major components reported on the balance sheet.
13. Describe the equation that underlies the income statement. Explain the three major items reported on the income statement.
14. Describe the equation that underlies the statement of retained earnings. Explain the four major items reported on the statement of retained earnings.

15. Describe the equation that underlies the statement of cash flows. Explain the three major types of activities reported on the statement.

16. Briefly describe the organizations that are responsible for developing accounting measurement rules (generally accepted accounting principles) in the United States.

MULTIPLE CHOICE

To practice more multiple choice questions, check out the DVD for use with this book.

1. Which of the following is *not* one of the four basic financial statements?

   a.   The balance sheet   *c.*   The income statement

   b.   The audit report   *d.*   The statement of cash flows

2. Which of the following is true regarding the income statement?

   a.   The income statement is sometimes called the statement of operations.

   b.   The income statement reports revenues, expenses, and liabilities.

   c.   The income statement only reports revenue for which cash was received at the point of sale.

   d.   The income statement reports the financial position of a business at a particular point in time.

3. Which of the following is false regarding the balance sheet?

   a.   The accounts shown on a balance sheet represent the basic accounting equation for a particular business.

   b.   The retained earnings balance shown on the balance sheet must agree to the ending retained earnings balance shown on the statement of retained earnings.

   c.   The balance sheet summarizes the net changes in specific account balances over a period of time.

   d.   The balance sheet reports the amount of assets, liabilities, and stockholders' equity of a business at a point in time.

4. Which of the following regarding retained earnings is false?

   a.   Retained earnings is increased by net income.

   b.   Retained earnings is a component of stockholders' equity on the balance sheet.

   c.   Retained earnings is an asset on the balance sheet.

   d.   Retained earnings represents earnings not distributed to stockholders in the form of dividends.

5. Which of the following is not one of the items required to be shown in the heading of a financial statement?

   a.   The financial statement preparer's name.

   b.   The title of the financial statement.

   c.   The financial reporting date or period.

   d.   The name of the business entity.

6. How many of the following statements regarding the statement of cash flows are true?

   •   The statement of cash flows separates cash inflows and outflows into three major categories: operating, investing, and financing.

   •   The ending cash balance shown on the statement of cash flows must agree with the amount shown on the balance sheet at the end of the same period.

   •   The total increase or decrease in cash shown on the statement of cash flows must agree to the "bottom line" (net income or net loss) reported on the income statement.

   a.   None

   b.   One

   c.   Two

   d.   Three

7. Which of the following is not a typical footnote included in an annual report?

   a.   A note describing the auditors' opinion of the management's past and future financial planning for the business.

   b.   A note providing more detail about a specific item shown in the financial statements.

   c.   A note describing the accounting rules applied in the financial statements.

   d.   A note describing financial disclosures about items not appearing in the financial statements.

8. Which of the following regarding GAAP is true?

   a.   GAAP is an abbreviation for goodie, another accounting problem.

   b.   Changes in GAAP do not affect the amount of income reported by a company.

   c.   GAAP is the abbreviation for generally accepted accounting principles.

   d.   Changes to GAAP must be approved by the Senate Finance Committee.

9. Which of the following is true?
   a.   FASB creates SEC.
   b.   GAAP creates FASB.
   c.   SEC creates CPA.
   d.   FASB creates GAAP.

10. Which of the following would *not* be a goal of external users reading a company's financial statements?
   a.   Understanding the current financial state of the company.
   b.   Assessing the company's contribution to social and environmental policies.
   c.   Predicting the company's future financial performance.
   d.   Evaluating the company's ability to generate cash from sales.

MINI-EXERCISES   **Available with McGraw-Hill's Homework Manager**

L01-L03   **M1-1 Identifying Important Accounting Terms and Abbreviations**

Complete the following crossword puzzle, using the clues provided to the right.

Across
1 The statement on which liabilities are reported.
3 The abbreviation for the principles that are used in external financial statement reporting.
5 Statement of cash _____.
7 Revenues minus expenses.
8 The organization that is currently responsible for establishing accounting rules in the United States.
9 The balance sheet category for resources owned by the business.

Down
2 Amounts owed by a business that will be paid, fulfilled, or otherwise satisfied in the future.
4 Declared by the board of directors for distribution to stockholders.
6 The government agency that was given the power to establish accounting rules for public companies.

L03   **M1-2 Identifying Definitions with Abbreviations**

The following is a list of important abbreviations used in the chapter. These abbreviations also are used widely in business. For each abbreviation, give the full designation. The first one is an example.

Abbreviation	Full Designation
1. CPA	Certified Public Accountant
2. GAAP	_____
3. FASB	_____
4. SEC	_____

L01-L03   **M1-3 Matching Definitions with Terms or Abbreviations**

Match each definition with its related term or abbreviation by entering the appropriate letter in the space provided.

Term or Abbreviation	Definition

____	1.	SEC
____	2.	Investing activities
____	3.	Private company
____	4.	Corporation
____	5.	Accounting
____	6.	Audit report
____	7.	Partnership
____	8.	FASB
____	9.	Financing activities
____	10.	Unit of measure
____	11.	GAAP
____	12.	Public company
____	13.	Operating activities

A. A system that collects and processes financial information about an organization and reports that information to decision makers.

B. Measurement of information about a business in the monetary unit (dollars or other national currency).

C. An unincorporated business owned by two or more persons.

D. A company that sells shares of its stock privately and does not release its financial statements to the public.

E. An incorporated business that issues shares of stock as evidence of ownership.

F. Purchases and disposals of long-term assets.

G. Transactions with lenders (borrowing and repaying cash) and stockholders (selling company stock and paying dividends).

H. Day-to-day activities related to a company's core business.

I. A report that describes the auditors' opinion of the fairness of the financial statement presentations and the evidence gathered to support that opinion.

J. Securities and Exchange Commission.

K. Financial Accounting Standards Board.

L. A company that has its stock bought and sold by investors on established stock exchanges.

M. Generally accepted accounting principles.

M1-4 Matching Items to Balance Sheet and Income Statement Categories

LO2

According to its annual report, "Procter & Gamble markets a broad range of laundry, cleaning, paper, beauty care, health care, food and beverage products in more than 140 countries around the world, with leading brands including Tide, Ariel, Crest, Crisco, Vicks and Max Factor." The following are items taken from its recent balance sheet and income statement. Mark each item in the following list with letters to indicate whether it would be reported as an Asset, Liability, or Stockholders' Equity account on the balance sheet or a Revenue or Expense account on the income statement.

P&G

____	1.	Accounts payable	____	7.	Interest expense
____	2.	Accounts receivable	____	8.	Inventories
____	3.	Cash	____	9.	Selling and administrative expenses
____	4.	Cost of goods sold expense	____	10.	Sales revenue
____	5.	Property, plant, and equipment	____	11.	Notes payable
____	6.	Income tax expense	____	12.	Retained earnings

M1-5 Matching Financial Statement Items to Balance Sheet and Income Statement Categories

LO2

Mark each item in the following list with letters to indicate whether it would be reported as an Asset, Liability, or Stockholders' Equity account on the balance sheet or a Revenue or Expense account on the income statement.

____	1.	Retained earnings	____	5.	Cost of goods sold expense
____	2.	Accounts receivable	____	6.	Inventories
____	3.	Sales revenue	____	7.	Advertising expense
____	4.	Property, plant, and equipment	____	8.	Accounts payable

LO2   **M1-6** **Matching Financial Statement Items to Balance Sheet and Income Statement Categories**

Tootsie Roll Industries manufactures and sells candy. Major products include Tootsie Roll, Tootsie Roll Pops, Tootsie Pop Drops, Tootsie Flavor Rolls, Charms, and Blow-Pop lollipops. The following items were listed on Tootsie Roll's recent income statement and balance sheet. Mark each item from the balance sheet as an <u>A</u>sset, <u>L</u>iability, or <u>S</u>tockholders' <u>E</u>quity and each item from the income statement as a <u>R</u>evenue or <u>E</u>xpense.

____	1.	Accounts payable	____ 7.	Cash
____	2.	Accounts receivable	____ 8.	Machinery
____	3.	Cost of goods sold expense	____ 9.	Promotion and advertising expenses
____	4.	Selling and administrative expenses	____ 10.	Sales revenue
____	5.	Income tax expense	____ 11.	Notes payable to banks
____	6.	Inventories	____ 12.	Retained earnings

LO2   **M1-7** **Matching Financial Statement Items to Balance Sheet and Income Statement Categories**

General Mills is a manufacturer of food products, such as Lucky Charms cereal, Pillsbury crescent rolls, and Jolly Green Giant vegetables. The following items were presented in the company's financial statements. Mark each item from the balance sheet as an <u>A</u>sset, <u>L</u>iability, or <u>S</u>tockholders' <u>E</u>quity and each item from the income statement as a <u>R</u>evenue or <u>E</u>xpense.

____	1.	Inventories	____ 7.	Cash
____	2.	Accounts payable	____ 8.	Retained earnings
____	3.	Contributed capital	____ 9.	Cost of goods sold expense
____	4.	Property, plant, and equipment	____ 10.	Selling and administration expenses
____	5.	Accounts receivable	____ 11.	Income tax expense
____	6.	Notes payable	____ 12.	Sales revenue

LO2   **M1-8** **Matching Financial Statement Items to Balance Sheet and Income Statement Categories**

Microsoft Corporation manufactures home entertainment devices like Xbox®, creates software like Word®, and operates networks like MSN Hotmail®. The following items were presented in the company's financial statements. Mark each item from the balance sheet as an <u>A</u>sset, <u>L</u>iability, or <u>S</u>tockholders' <u>E</u>quity and each item from the income statement as a <u>R</u>evenue or <u>E</u>xpense.

____	1.	Accounts payable	____ 7.	Contributed capital
____	2.	Inventories	____ 8.	Accounts receivable
____	3.	Cash	____ 9.	Sales revenue
____	4.	Retained earnings	____ 10.	Selling and administration expenses
____	5.	Property and equipment	____ 11.	Promotion expense
____	6.	Notes payable	____ 12.	Cost of goods sold expense

LO1, LO2   **M1-9** **Matching Financial Statement Items to the Four Basic Financial Statements**

Match each element with its financial statement by entering the appropriate letter in the space provided.

	Element		Financial Statement
____ 1.	Expenses	A.	Balance sheet
____ 2.	Cash flows from investing activities	B.	Income statement
____ 3.	Assets	C.	Statement of retained earnings
____ 4.	Dividends declared	D.	Statement of cash flows
____ 5.	Revenues		
____ 6.	Cash flows from operating activities		
____ 7.	Liabilities		
____ 8.	Cash flows from financing activities		

M1-10 Matching Financial Statement Items to the Four Basic Financial Statements

LO1, LO2

Oakley, Inc., manufactures sunglasses, goggles, shoes, watches, footwear, and clothing. Recently, the company reported the following items in its financial statements. Indicate whether these items appeared on the balance sheet (B/S), income statement (I/S), statement of retained earnings (SRE), or statement of cash flows (SCF).

_____ 1.   Total stockholders' equity

_____ 2.   Sales revenue

_____ 3.   Total assets

_____ 4.   Cash flows from operating activities

_____ 5.   Total liabilities

_____ 6.   Net income

_____ 7.   Cash flows from financing activities

_____ 8.   Dividends declared

M1-11 Reporting Amounts on the Income Statement

LO2

During a recent year, General Mills delivered boxes of cereal for which customers paid or promised to pay amounts totaling $10,506,000,000. During the same period, it collected $6,375,410,000 in cash from its customers. Indicate which of these two amounts will be shown on General Mills' income statement as *sales revenue*.

M1-12 Reporting Amounts on the Income Statement

LO2

During a recent year, Microsoft delivered software for which customers paid or promised to pay amounts totaling $32,200,000,000. During the same period, it collected $25,375,600,000 in cash from its customers. Indicate which of these two amounts will be shown on Microsoft's income statement as *sales revenue*.

M1-13 Reporting Amounts on the Income Statement

LO2

During a recent year, General Mills *produced* breakfast cereal with a total cost of production of $3,005,560,000. During the same period, it *delivered* to customers cereal that cost a total of $6,100,500,000 to produce. Indicate which of the two numbers will be shown on General Mills' income statement as *cost of goods sold expense*.

M1-14 Reporting Amounts on the Income Statement

LO2

During a recent year, Microsoft *produced* software with a total cost of production of $4,325,500,000. During the same period, it *delivered* to customers software that cost a total of $5,680,500,000 to produce. Indicate which of the two numbers will be shown on Microsoft's income statement as *cost of goods sold expense*.

M1-15 Reporting Amounts on the Statement of Cash Flows

LO1

During a recent year, General Mills delivered breakfast cereal to customers who paid or promised to pay amounts totaling $10,506,000,000. During the same period, General Mills collected $6,375,410,000 in cash from its customers. Indicate which of the two amounts will be shown on General Mills' cash flow statement.

M1-16 Reporting Amounts on the Statement of Cash Flows

LO1

During a recent year, Microsoft delivered software to customers who paid or promised to pay amounts totaling $32,200,000,000. During the same period, Microsoft collected $25,375,600,000 in cash from its customers. Indicate which of the two amounts will be shown on Microsoft's cash flow statement.

M1-17 Reporting Amounts on the Statement of Cash Flows

LO1

Learning which items belong in each cash flow statement category is an important first step in understanding their meaning. Use a letter to mark each item in the following list as a cash flow from Operating, Investing, or Financing activities. **Put parentheses around the letter if it is a cash *outflow* and use no parentheses if it's an *inflow*.**

____ 1.   Cash paid for dividends   ____ 4.   Cash paid to suppliers and employees

____ 2.   Cash collected from customers   ____ 5.   Cash paid to purchase equipment

____ 3.   Cash received from notes payable   ____ 6.   Cash received from issuing stock

LO1

M1-18 Reporting Amounts on the Statement of Cash Flows

Learning which items belong in each category of the statement of cash flows is an important first step in understanding their meaning. Use a letter to mark each item in the following list as a cash flow from Operating, Investing, or Financing activities. **Put parentheses around the letter if it is a cash *outflow* and use no parentheses if it's an *inflow*.**

_____ 1. Cash paid to purchase equipment   _____ 4. Cash paid for dividends

_____ 2. Cash collected from customers   _____ 5. Cash paid to suppliers and employees

_____ 3. Cash received from selling equipment   _____ 6. Cash received from issuing stock

EXERCISES   Available with McGraw-Hill's Homework Manager

LO2

E1-1 Reporting Amounts on the Four Basic Financial Statements

Using the figures listed in the table below and the equations underlying each of the four basic financial statements, show (*a*) that the balance sheet is in balance, (*b*) that net income is properly calculated, (*c*) what caused changes in the retained earnings account, and (*d*) what caused changes in the cash account.

Assets	$18,200	Beginning Retained Earnings	$3,500
Liabilities	13,750	Ending Retained Earnings	4,300
Stockholders' Equity	4,450	Cash Flows from Operating Activities	1,600
Revenue	10,500	Cash Flows from Investing Activities	(1,000)
Expenses	9,200	Cash Flows from Financing Activities	(900)
Net Income	1,300	Beginning Cash	1,000
Dividends	500	Ending Cash	700

LO2

E1-2 Reporting Amounts on the Four Basic Financial Statements

Using the figures listed in the table below and the equations underlying each of the four basic financial statements, show (*a*) that the balance sheet is in balance, (*b*) that net income is properly calculated, (*c*) what caused changes in the retained earnings account, and (*d*) what caused changes in the cash account.

Assets	$79,500	Beginning Retained Earnings	$20,500
Liabilities	18,500	Ending Retained Earnings	28,750
Stockholders' Equity	61,000	Cash Flows from Operating Activities	15,700
Revenue	32,100	Cash Flows from Investing Activities	(7,200)
Expenses	18,950	Cash Flows from Financing Activities	(5,300)
Net Income	13,150	Beginning Cash	3,200
Dividends	4,900	Ending Cash	6,400

LO2, LO3

E1-3 Preparing a Balance Sheet

Dave & Buster's Inc. is a restaurant/entertainment company. Founded in 1982, D&B provides high-quality food and beverage items, combined with an extensive array of interactive entertainment attractions such as pocket billiards, shuffleboard, state-of the-art simulators, and virtual reality and traditional carnival-style amusements and games of skill. A recent November 3 balance sheet contained the following items (in thousands).

Cash	$ 5,841
Contributed capital	114,969
Accounts payable	42,948
Inventories	26,249
Notes payable	94,550

Property and equipment	255,252
Other assets	15,974
Retained earnings	50,849
Total assets	303,316
Total liabilities and stockholders' equity	?

Required:

1. Prepare the balance sheet as of November 3, solving for the missing amount.
2. What is Dave & Buster's biggest asset?
3. As of November 3, did most of the financing for assets come from creditors or stockholders?

E1-4 Completing a Balance Sheet and Inferring Net Income

LO2, LO3

Terry Lloyd and Joan Lopez organized Read More Store as a corporation; each contributed $50,000 cash to start the business and received 4,000 shares of stock. The store completed its first year of operations on December 31, 2006. On that date, the following financial items for the year were determined: December 31, 2006, cash on hand and in the bank, $48,900; December 31, 2006, amounts due from customers from sales of books, $26,000; property and equipment, $48,000; December 31, 2006, amounts owed to publishers for books purchased, $8,000; one-year note payable to a local bank for $2,120. No dividends were declared or paid to the stockholders during the year.

Required:

1. Complete the following balance sheet as of the end of 2006.

Assets		Liabilities	
Cash	$ _____	Accounts payable	$ _____
Accounts receivable	_____	Note payable	_____
Property and equipment	_____	Total liabilities	$ _____
		Stockholders' Equity	
		Contributed capital	_____
		Retained earnings	12,780
		Total stockholders' equity	_____
Total assets	$ _____	**Total liabilities and stockholders' equity**	$ _____

2. Using the retained earnings equation and an opening balance of $0, compute the amount of net income for the year.
3. As of December 31, 2006, did most of the financing for assets come from creditors or stockholders?

E1-5 Analyzing Revenues and Expenses and Preparing an Income Statement

LO2

Assume that you are the owner of The Collegiate Shop, which specializes in selling college T-shirts and caps. At the end of January 2006, you find (for January only) this information:

a. Sales, per the cash register tapes, of $120,000, plus one sale on credit (a special situation) of $1,000.
b. With the help of a friend, you determined that all of the goods sold during January had cost $40,000 to purchase.
c. During the month, according to the checkbook, you paid $38,000 for selling, administration, interest, and other expenses; however, you have not yet paid the $600 monthly advertising expense for January.

Required:

On the basis of the data given (and ignoring income taxes), what was the amount of income for January? Show computations.

LO2, LO3

E1-6   Preparing an Income Statement and Inferring Missing Values

Wal-Mart Stores, Inc., is the largest retail chain in the United States, operating more than 2,000 stores. Its recent quarterly income statement contained the following items (in thousands):

Cost of goods sold expense	$16,200,873
Interest expense	184,190
Net income	?
Sales revenue	20,417,717
Selling and administrative expenses	3,340,263
Income tax expense	339,422
Total expenses	?

Required:

1. Solve for the missing amounts and prepare an income statement for the quarter ended October 31.
2. What is Wal-Mart's biggest expense?

LO2

E1-7   Analyzing Revenues and Expenses and Completing an Income Statement

Home Realty, Incorporated, has been operating for three years and is owned by three investors. J. Doe owns 60 percent of the total outstanding stock of 9,000 shares and is the managing executive in charge. On December 31, 2007, the following financial items for the entire year were determined: sales revenue earned and collected in cash, $150,000, plus $16,000 not yet collected; selling expenses paid, $97,000; interest expense paid, $5,775 (not including December interest of $525 yet to be paid); promotion and advertising expenses paid, $9,025; and income tax expense paid, $18,500. There were no other unpaid expenses at December 31. Also during the year, the company declared and paid the owners dividends amounting to $12,000. Complete the following income statement:

_____		
_____		
_____		
Revenues		
Sales revenue		$ _____
Expenses		
Selling expenses	$ _____	
Interest expense	_____	
Promotion and advertising expenses	_____	
Income tax expense	_____	
Total expenses		_____
Net income		$ 35,175

LO2

E1-8   Inferring Values Using the Income Statement and Balance Sheet Equations

Review the chapter explanations of the income statement and the balance sheet equations. Apply these equations in each of the following independent cases to compute the two missing amounts for each case. Assume that it is the end of 2007, the first full year of operations for the company.

Independent Cases	Total Revenues	Total Expenses	Net Income (Loss)	Total Assets	Total Liabilities	Stockholders' Equity
A	$100,000	$82,000	$_____	$150,000	$70,000	$_____
B	_____	80,000	12,000	112,000	_____	60,000
C	80,000	86,000	_____	104,000	26,000	_____
D	50,000	_____	13,000	_____	22,000	77,000
E	_____	81,000	(6,000)	_____	73,000	28,000

E1-9 Preparing an Income Statement and Balance Sheet

LO2, LO3

Five individuals organized Clay Corporation on January 1, 2006. At the end of January 2006, the following monthly financial data are available:

Total revenues	$130,000
Other expenses (excluding income taxes)	80,000
Income tax expense (all paid as of January 31)	15,000
Cash balance, January 31, 2006	30,000
Accounts receivable from customers (all considered collectible)	15,000
Inventory (by inventory count at cost)	42,000
Accounts payable to suppliers for merchandise purchased from them (will be paid during February 2006)	26,000
Contributed capital (2,600 shares)	26,000

No dividends were declared or paid during January.

Required:

1. Complete the following balance sheet and income statement for the month of January.

CLAY CORPORATION
Income Statement
For the Month of January 2006

Total revenues	$ _____
Other expenses (excluding income tax)	_____
Income tax expense	_____
Net income	$ _____

CLAY CORPORATION
Balance Sheet
At January 31, 2006

Assets

Cash	$ _____
Accounts receivable	_____
Inventory	_____
Total assets	$ _____

Liabilities

Accounts payable	$ _____
Total liabilities	_____

Stockholders' Equity

Contributed capital	_____
Retained earnings	_____
Total stockholders' equity	_____
Total liabilities and stockholders' equity	$ _____

2. Discuss whether Clay Corporation will be able to pay its liabilities.

LO3 **E1-10 Analyzing and Interpreting an Income Statement**

Three individuals organized Pest Away Corporation on January 1, 2006, to provide insect extermination services. At the end of 2006, the following income statement was prepared:

PEST AWAY CORPORATION Income Statement For the Year Ended December 31, 2006		
Revenues		
Sales revenue (cash)	$192,000	
Sales revenue (credit)	24,000	
Total revenues		$216,000
Expenses		
Cost of goods sold expense	$ 76,000	
Selling expense	33,000	
Advertising expense	14,000	
Interest expense	8,000	
Income tax expense	21,000	
Other expenses	25,000	
Total expenses		177,000
Net income		$ 39,000

Required:

1. What was the amount of average monthly revenue?
2. What was the average amount of monthly selling expense?
3. Explain why cost of goods sold is reported as an expense.
4. Explain why interest is reported as an expense.
5. Can you determine how much cash the company had on December 31, 2006? Answer yes or no, and explain your reasoning.

LO1 **E1-11 Matching Cash Flow Statement Items to Business-Activity Categories**

Tech Data Corporation is a leading distributor of computer peripherals and network solutions, and recently was ranked by *Fortune* as the second most admired company in its industry category. The following items were taken from its recent cash flow statement. Mark each item in the following list with a letter to indicate whether it is a cash flow from Operating, Investing, or Financing activities. **Put parentheses around the letter if it is a cash *outflow* and use no parentheses if it's an *inflow*.**

_____ 1.   Cash paid to suppliers and employees

_____ 2.   Cash received from customers

_____ 3.   Cash received from borrowing long-term debt

_____ 4.   Cash received from issuing stock

_____ 5.   Cash paid to purchase equipment

LO1 **E1-12 Matching Cash Flow Statement Items to Business-Activity Categories**

The Coca-Cola Company is one of the world's leading manufacturers, marketers, and distributors of nonalcoholic beverage concentrates and syrups, which produce more than 300 beverage brands. Mark each item in the following list with a letter to indicate whether it is a cash flow from Operating, Investing, or Financing activities. **Put parentheses around the letter if it is a cash *outflow* and use no parentheses if it's an *inflow*.**

_____ 1.   Purchases of property, plant, and equipment

_____ 2.   Cash received from customers

_____ 3. Cash received from issuing stock
_____ 4. Cash paid to suppliers and employees
_____ 5. Cash paid on notes payable
_____ 6. Cash received from selling equipment

SIMPLIFY WITH SPREADSHEETS

SS1-1 Preparing an Income Statement and Balance Sheet

LO2

eXcel

Electronic Arts is the world's leading developer and publisher of interactive entertainment software for personal computers and advanced entertainment systems made by Sony, Nintendo, and Microsoft. Assume that the company is revising its methods for displaying its financial statements, and the controller in the accounting department has asked you to create electronic worksheets that they can use as their standard format for financial statement reporting. The controller has provided you with an alphabetical list of statement categories and account names (below), with corresponding balances as of September 30. She has asked you to use a spreadsheet program to create two worksheets that organize the accounts into a properly formatted balance sheet and income statement, and use formulas to compute amounts marked by a ? below.

Accounts Payable	$120,200	Other Liabilities	333,600
Accounts Receivable	139,300	Promotion Expense	55,500
Assets		Property and Equipment	307,100
Cash	920,800	Retained Earnings	660,600
Contributed Capital	731,200	Revenue	
Cost of Goods Sold Expense	198,900	Sales Revenue	450,500
Expenses		Selling Expense	98,100
Income Tax Expense	22,500	Stockholders' Equity	
Inventories	36,800	Total Assets	?
Liabilities		Total Expenses	?
Net Income	?	Total Liabilities	?
Notes Payable	1,400	Total Liabilities and	
Other Assets	443,000	Stockholders' Equity	?
Other Expenses	29,600	Total Stockholders' Equity	?

Not knowing quite where to start, you e-mailed your friend Billy for advice on using a spreadsheet. Billy is an extreme Type A personality, which explains his very detailed reply, as shown below.

Required:

Follow Billy's advice to create a balance sheet and income statement, with each statement saved on a separate worksheet in a file called *me*EA.xls where the *me* part of the filename uniquely identifies you.

From: BillyTheTutor@yahoo.com
To: HairZed@hotmail.com
Cc:
Subject: Excel Help

Hey pal. Long time, no chat. Here's the scoop on creating those worksheets, with a screenshot that shows how to go. If you need more help, let me know and I'll submit an application for your position there. ☺

1. Start-up Excel to open a new spreadsheet file. You'll need only two worksheets for this assignment, so delete the third worksheet by clicking on the *Sheet3* tab at the bottom of the worksheet and selecting Edit/Delete Sheet in the pull-down menu. While you're at it, rename *Sheet1* and *Sheet2* to *Balance Sheet* and *Income Statement* by double-clicking on the worksheet tabs and typing in the new names.

2. Plan the layout for your reports. Use the first column as a blank margin, the second column for account names and their headings, and the third column for the numbers corresponding to each account name or total. If you want to apply the same format to all worksheets, begin by right-clicking on the tab at the bottom of a worksheet and choosing Select All Sheets. Next, resize the first column by clicking

on the A at the top of that column, selecting Format/Column/Width . . . from the pull-down menu, and choosing a width of 2. Using this same procedure, resize columns B and C to 50 and 15, respectively.

3. Starting with cell B1, enter the company's name. Enter the report name and date in cells B2 and B3. To merge cells so these headings span more than one column, select the cells to be merged and then click on ▦. Continue with the body of the report in cell B5, entering any necessary amounts in column C.

4. To use formulas to compute subtotals and totals, the equals sign = is entered first into the cell and is followed immediately by the formula. So, to subtract cell C16 from C13, enter =C16-C13. To add a series of amounts, say C6 through C10, use a formula like =SUM(C6:C10), as shown in the screenshot below.

5. After you get all the data entered and totals calculated, be sure to save the file. To do this, just click on File/Save As . . . and enter the filename.

6. If you need to print the worksheets, it might be best to highlight what you want printed, then click File/Print . . . and choose Selection in the dialog box that pops up.

7. Go to it, you accounting guru!

Microsoft Excel - SS1-1.xls			
File Edit View Insert Format Tools Data Window Help Acrobat			
C11		fx =SUM(C6:C10)	
A	B		C
1	Electronic Arts, Inc.		
2	Balance Sheet		
3	As of September 30		
4			
5	ASSETS		
6	Cash		$ 920,800
7	Accounts Receivable		139,300
8	Inventories		36,800
9	Property and Equipment		307,100
10	Other Assets		443,000
11	Total Assets		$ 1,847,000
12			

Balance Sheet / Income Statement
Ready   NUM

COACHED PROBLEMS

CP1-1 Preparing an Income Statement and Balance Sheet

Assume that you are the president of Nuclear Company. At the end of the first year of operations (December 31, 2006), the following financial data for the company are available:

Cash	$ 25,000
Accounts receivable from customers	12,000
Inventories	90,000
Equipment owned	45,000
Accounts payable to suppliers	47,370
Notes payable	2,000
Total sales revenue	140,000
Expenses, including the cost of goods sold (excluding income taxes)	89,100
Income tax expense	15,270
Contributed capital, 7,000 shares outstanding	87,000
No dividends were declared or paid during 2006.	

Required (show computations):

1. Prepare an income statement for the year 2006.
2. Prepare a balance sheet at December 31, 2006.

GROUP A PROBLEMS Available with McGraw-Hill's Homework Manager

PA1-1 Preparing an Income Statement and Balance Sheet

Assume that you are the president of McClaren Corporation. At the end of the first year of operations (June 30, 2007), the following financial data for the company are available:

Cash	$13,150
Accounts receivable from customers	9,500
Inventories	57,000

Equipment owned	36,000
Accounts payable to suppliers	31,500
Notes payable	1,500
Total sales revenue	90,000
Expenses, including the cost of goods sold (excluding income taxes)	60,500
Income tax expense	8,850
Contributed capital, 5,000 shares outstanding	62,000

No dividends were declared or paid during 2007.

Required (show computations):

1.   Prepare an income statement for the year ended June 30, 2007.
2.   Prepare a balance sheet at June 30, 2007.

GROUP B PROBLEMS

PB1-1 **Preparing an Income Statement and Balance Sheet**   L02

Assume that you are the president of Riterong Corporation. At the end of the first year of operations (April 30, 2007), the following financial data for the company are available:

Cash	$ 39,150
Accounts receivable from customers	27,500
Inventories	135,000
Equipment owned	108,000
Accounts payable to suppliers	57,800
Notes payable	3,500
Total sales revenue	270,000
Expenses, including the cost of goods sold (excluding income taxes)	180,500
Income tax expense	27,150
Contributed capital, 5,000 shares outstanding	186,000

No dividends were declared or paid during 2007.

Required (show computations):

1.   Prepare an income statement for the year ended April 30, 2007.
2.   Prepare a balance sheet at April 30, 2007.

CASES & DISCUSSION STARTERS

FINANCIAL REPORTING AND ANALYSIS CASES

C&DS1-1 **Finding Financial Information**   L01-L03

Refer to the financial statements of Landry's Restaurants in Appendix A at the end of this book, or download the annual report from the *Cases* section of the text's Web site at www.mhhe.com/phillips.

Required:

1.   What is the amount of net income for 2003?
2.   What amount of revenue was earned in 2003?
3.   How much inventory does the company have at the end of 2003?
4.   How much does Landry's have in cash at the end of 2003?
5.   Landry's stock is traded on the New York Stock Exchange under the symbol LNY. What kind of company does this make Landry's?

C&DS1-2 **Comparing Financial Information**   L01-L03

Refer to the financial statements of Dave & Buster's in Appendix B at the end of this book, or download the annual report from the *Cases* section of the text's Web site at www.mhhe.com/

phillips. Note that Dave & Buster's ends its fiscal year on February 1, 2004, which doesn't perfectly match Landry's year ended December 31, 2003. In the questions that follow, assume Dave & Buster's financial statements for the year ended February 1, 2004, present the results for 2003. (This is a reasonable assumption given that Dave and Buster's fiscal year simply replaces January 2003 with January 2004.)

Required:

1. Was Dave & Buster's net income for 2003 greater or less than Landry's?
2. Was Dave & Buster's revenue for 2003 greater or less than Landry's?
3. Did Dave & Buster's have more or less inventories than Landry's at the end of 2003?
4. Did Dave & Buster's have more or less cash than Landry's at the end of 2003?
5. Is Dave & Buster's the same type of business organization as Landry's?
6. On an overall basis, was Dave & Buster's or Landry's more successful in 2003?

LO1-LO3

TEAM CASE

C&DS1-3 Internet-Based Team Research: Examining an Annual Report

As a team, select an industry to analyze. Reuters provides lists of industries and their makeup at www.investor.reuters.com/Industries.aspx. Each group member should acquire the annual report (or Form 10-K filed with the SEC) for one publicly traded company in the industry, with each member selecting a different company. (In addition to the company's own Web site, a great source is the SEC's Electronic Data Gathering, Analysis, and Retrieval (EDGAR) service. This free source is available by going to the "Filings & Forms" section of www.sec.gov and clicking on "Search for Company Filings" and then "Companies & Other Filers." Another great site that pulls information from EDGAR is edgarscan.pwcglobal.com.)

Required:

1. On an individual basis, each team member should write a short report that lists the following information:
    a. What type of business organization is it?
    b. What types of products or services does it sell?
    c. On what day of the year does its fiscal year end?
    d. For how many years does it present complete balance sheets? Income statements? Cash flow statements?
    e. Are its financial statements audited by independent CPAs? If so, by whom?
    f. Did its total assets increase or decrease over the last year?
    g. Did its net income increase or decrease over the last year?
2. Then, as a team, write a short report comparing and contrasting your companies using these attributes. Discuss any patterns across the companies that you as a team observe. Provide potential explanations for any differences discovered.

ETHICS AND CRITICAL THINKING CASES

LO2-LO4

ETHICAL

ISSUE

C&DS1-4 Ethical Decision Making: A Real-Life Example

In September 2002, John Rigas, his three sons, and another executive from Adelphia Communications were charged with defrauding investors and lenders of over a billion dollars. If convicted, each would face over 30 years in prison. To understand the charges, you need to first understand a bit about Adelphia's history. Adelphia started as a one-town cable company in 1952 and, at the time the fraud accusations were made public, had grown into the sixth-largest cable television provider in the country. With the company starting as a family-owned business, Adelphia's operations were always a central part of the personal lives of the Rigas family members. However, the extent to which their personal lives were mixed in with the business activities was never clear to stockholders—at least, not nearly as clear as when they were reported in an article in the August 12, 2002, issue of *Fortune*. Below the following questions we present a table from that article, which summarizes how the Rigas family allegedly used over $1.2 billion dollars of Adelphia's money—money that ultimately belonged to Adelphia's stockholders.

1. What is the accounting concept that the Rigas family is accused of violating?
2. Based on the information provided in the following table, can you determine which of the family's dealings are clearly inappropriate and which are clearly appropriate?

3. As a stockholder, how might you attempt to ensure that this kind of behavior does not occur or, at least, does not occur without you knowing about it?

4. Aside from Adelphia's stockholders, who else might be harmed by these actions committed by the Rigas family?

Family Assets, Sort Of
Some of the notable ways the Rigas family used Adelphia shareholder dollars.

On the Receiving End . . .	Who's Behind the Entity	How Much?
Dobaire Designs	Adelphia paid this company, owned by Doris Rigas (John's wife), for design services.	$371,000
Wending Creek Farms	Adelphia paid John Rigas's farm for lawn care and snowplowing.	$2 million
SongCatcher Films	Adelphia financed the production of a movie by Ellen Rigas (John's daughter).	$3 million
Eleni Interiors	The company made payments to a furniture store run by Doris Rigas and owned by John.	$12 million
The Golf Club at Wending Creek Farms	Adelphia began developing a ritzy golf club.	$13 million
Wending Creek 3656	The company bought timber rights that would eventually revert to a Rigas family partnership.	$26 million
Praxis Capital Ventures	Adelphia funded a venture capital firm run by Ellen Rigas's husband.	$65 million
Niagara Frontier Hockey LP	Adelphia underwrote the Rigases' purchase of the Buffalo Sabres hockey team.	$150 million
Highland 2000	Adelphia guaranteed loans to a Rigas family partnership, which used the funds to buy stock.	$1 billion
Total		**$1,271,371,000**

C&DS1-5   Ethical Decision Making: A Mini-Case

LO4
ETHICAL

ISSUE

You are one of three partners who own and operate Mary's Maid Service. The company has been operating for seven years. One of the other partners has always prepared the company's annual financial statements. Recently, you proposed that the statements be audited each year because it would benefit the partners and prevent possible disagreements about the division of profits. The partner who prepares the statements proposed that his Uncle Ray, who has a lot of financial experience, can do the job and at little cost. Your other partner remained silent.

Required:

1. What position would you take on the proposal? Justify your response.
2. What would you strongly recommend? Give the basis for your recommendation.

C&DS1-6   Critical Thinking: Developing a Balance Sheet and Income Statement

LO2, LO3

On September 30, Jill and Jack started arguing about who is better off. Jack said he was better off because he had the latest PlayStation console that he bought last year for $350. Jill, on the other hand, argued that she was better off because she had $1,000 and a '75 Mustang that she bought two years ago for $800. Jack countered that Jill still owed $250 on her car and that Jack's dad promised to buy him a Porsche if he gets a great score in his accounting class. Jill pointed out that she inherited a collection of trading cards that she figured she could sell for about $250. Jack said he had $6,000 in his bank account right now because he just received a $4,800 student loan. Jill knows that Jack still owes an installment of $800 on this term's tuition.

Jill and Jack met again in early November. They asked how each other was doing. Jill claimed that she'd become much more successful than Jack. She had a part-time job, where she earned $500 per month. Jack laughed at Jill because he had won $950 on a lottery ticket he bought in October, and that was merely for the "work" of standing in line for a minute. It was just what he needed because his apartment costs $450 each month. Jill, on the other hand, pays $120 for her share of the rent. Both Jill and Jack have other normal living costs that total $300 each month.

1. Prepare a report that compares what Jill and Jack each own and owe on September 30. Note any decisions you had to make when preparing your report. Which of the two is better off?

2. Prepare a report that compares what Jill and Jack each earned during October. Note any decisions you had to make when preparing your report. Which of the two is more successful?

chapter two

Reporting Investing and Financing Results on the Balance Sheet

2

Do you spend hours looking for e-mail messages that you got just a couple of weeks ago? Have you ever found the perfect Web site, only to later misplace your bookmark to it? Does your directory of file folders contain meaningless labels like "stuff"? If so, you probably could use an organizing system that neatly sorts every e-mail, bookmark, and file into categories. With such a system, you might be able to quickly find that funny joke about the magician and the parrot, or the stats assignment that is due tomorrow.

Businesses also need systems for organizing information. Just think what could happen if a system didn't exist to track the 5 million packages and $53 million in revenues handled by FedEx every day, or the 270 million phone calls and $51 million in daily operating expenses at AT&T. Clearly, big companies need well-organized systems for tracking their business activities and financial results. But it's not just the big guys who need accounting systems. Small businesses, like your local **SUPERCUTS** store, need them too. In this chapter, we'll focus on the decisions that business managers make when starting up a single Supercuts salon and how their accounting systems track the financial results of the salon's investing and financing activities. In later chapters, you'll see how things are basically the same, only bigger, at Regis Corporation—a public company that owns over 1,700 Supercuts stores and 7,900 other hair salons. With that many stores, Regis is the main player in the U.S. hair business, which all combined generates $53 billion of revenue and 365,000 tons of hair clippings every year.

INSIDE LOOKING OUT

OUTSIDE LOOKING IN

This chapter introduces the system of accounting, which gathers financial information and produces the balance sheet as well as the other financial statement reports. We focus on the investing and financing activities of Supercuts, one of over twenty lines of hair care salons owned by Regis Corporation.

The Beauty of Our Business
REGIS CORPORATION

SUPERCUTS®
mia & maxx HAIR STUDIO
SmartStyle®

Learn more about Regis at www.regiscorp.com

FAST FLASHBACK

The basic accounting equation is A = L + SE.

You may remember our promise in Chapter 1 that you'd have time to learn the details about specific financial statement accounts in Chapters 2 through 4. That time has come: We begin this chapter with a look at the balance sheet and its accounts. This is a good place to start because the balance sheet is based on the basic accounting equation, which also happens to be the framework on which accounting systems are built. After you spend a bit of time becoming reacquainted with the balance sheet, you'll be all set to learn about the system of accounting—a topic that you'll be hearing lots about in this chapter and in Chapters 3 and 4. Although the accounting system tracks the results of all types of business activities, we focus on investing and financing in this chapter. (We'll spend Chapters 3 and 4 looking at how accounting systems track the results of operating activities, which affect both balance sheet and income statement accounts.) This chapter closes with a look at concepts that relate to the balance sheet. The goals that you should be trying to achieve when reading Chapter 2 are presented in Exhibit 2.1 below.

exhibit 2.1	Your Learning Objectives

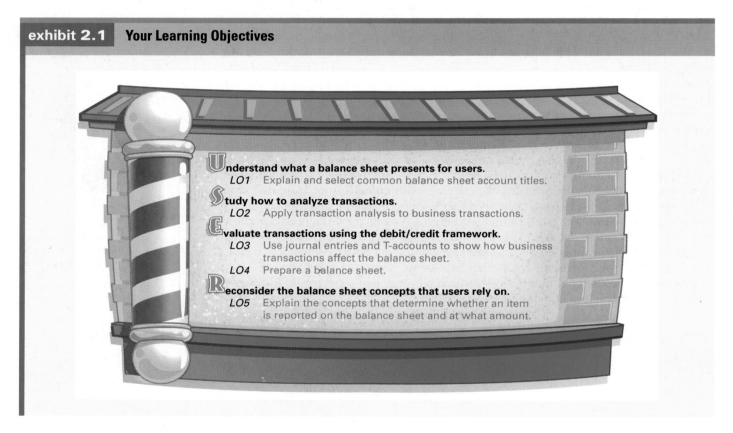

Understand what a balance sheet presents for users.
  LO1 Explain and select common balance sheet account titles.

Study how to analyze transactions.
  LO2 Apply transaction analysis to business transactions.

Evaluate transactions using the debit/credit framework.
  LO3 Use journal entries and T-accounts to show how business transactions affect the balance sheet.
  LO4 Prepare a balance sheet.

Reconsider the balance sheet concepts that users rely on.
  LO5 Explain the concepts that determine whether an item is reported on the balance sheet and at what amount.

UNDERSTAND

WHAT A BALANCE SHEET PRESENTS FOR USERS

Business Activities and Common Balance Sheet Accounts

To understand the items reported on the balance sheet of a Supercuts store, it's useful to first think about what's involved in getting a hair salon up and running. First, you will need to decide on a location. Because the idea behind Supercuts is to make hair care convenient for customers, you'll try to find space for your salon in a neighborhood shopping mall, anchored by either a major grocery chain or mass merchandiser. This will ensure your salon attracts what are known as "destination shoppers." These are customers who avoid spending time driving from the grocery store to the video store to a hair salon. They want to do it all at one place, and your mall location makes this possible.

Okay, now that you've selected a location, you'll need to start investing in some assets. First, you'll need to renovate your salon space so that it presents an open and airy environment, consistent with the standard Supercuts design. Typically, these renovations take four to six weeks to complete and cost about $42,000. You'll also need to spend an additional $18,000 to buy furniture and equipment for the salon. This might seem like a lot of money, but the next time you get your hair cut, just take a look around at all the different furnishings in a hair salon. You'll likely see a reception desk, lighting fixtures, styling chairs, shampoo stations, computer hardware (and software), mirrors, scissors, trimmers, razors, curlers, and dryers—and those fuzzy pink rollers.

But wait! You (and your parents) have got only $50,000 to contribute to starting up a company. To finance the cost of all those assets, you'll need to consider getting a loan from a bank. A $20,000 loan would give the company enough cash to pay for furniture and equipment and still leave some money to pay for operating supplies like shampoo and all that other hair gunk.

From the above description and what you remember from Chapter 1, try to think of the accounts that are likely to appear on the balance sheet of your Supercuts store. Really, cover up Exhibit 2.2 and take 10 seconds to picture what should be on the balance sheet of your business. When you're done, compare it to the balance sheet in Exhibit 2.2.

exhibit 2.2	**Sample Balance Sheet and Explanation of Items**

SUPERCUTS SUPER SALON
Balance Sheet
At August 31, 2005
(in U.S. dollars)

Who
What
When
Unit of measure

Assets

Current Assets		
Cash	$10,000	Cash in company's bank account
Supplies	630	Shampoo and other hair gunk to be used on customers
Total Current Assets	10,630	= 10,000 + 630
Furnishings & Equipment	60,000	Cost of store renovations, furniture, and equipment
Total Assets	$70,630	= 10,630 + 60,000

Liabilities

Current Liabilities		
Accounts Payable	$ 630	Amount owed to supplier for purchases of supplies on account
Total Current Liabilities	630	
Notes Payable	20,000	Amount owed to bank for loan (under a formal agreement)
Total Liabilities	20,630	= 630 + 20,000

Stockholders' Equity

Contributed Capital	50,000	Amount contributed by stockholders (you and your parents)
Retained Earnings	0	No operations yet, so no earnings to report as retained
Total Stockholders' Equity	50,000	= 50,000 + 0
Total Liabilities and Stockholders' Equity	$70,630	= 20,630 + 50,000

So, how did you do? The most important thing at this stage is that you knew to think about assets, liabilities, and stockholders' equity accounts. To extend your thinking a bit, Exhibit 2.2 separately classifies some assets and liabilities as "current." This is called a **classified balance sheet.** We haven't created new accounts to do this. We've simply cut the assets and liabilities into current and long-term sections when reporting them in the

YOU SHOULD KNOW

 A **classified balance sheet** is one that classifies assets and liabilities into current and other (long-term) categories.

balance sheet, as suggested in Exhibit 2.3. **Current assets** are the resources that your business will use up or turn into cash within the next 12 months. Your business will spend the *Cash* and use the *Supplies* that are reported at August 31, 2005, during the next 12 months, so they are classified as current. On the other hand, the *Furnishings & Equipment* will last five to ten years, so they are reported outside of the current asset category to indicate that they are **long-term assets.** Notice that assets are listed in order of how fast they will be used up or can be turned into cash. Note also that *all* assets share the key feature of having probable future economic benefits.

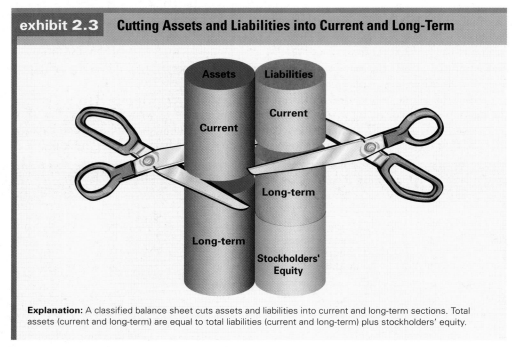

exhibit 2.3   **Cutting Assets and Liabilities into Current and Long-Term**

Explanation: A classified balance sheet cuts assets and liabilities into current and long-term sections. Total assets (current and long-term) are equal to total liabilities (current and long-term) plus stockholders' equity.

In the liabilities section of the balance sheet, back in Exhibit 2.2, you again see the "current" subheading. Go ahead, take a look. **Current liabilities** are debts and other obligations that are to be paid or fulfilled within the next 12 months. In our example, *Accounts Payable* is the only current liability. This line on the balance sheet shows the amounts still owed for things that were bought on credit and will be paid off within the next 12 months. Liabilities not included as current are considered **long-term liabilities.** In our example, *Notes Payable* represents amounts that your Supercuts store owes to the bank. More than likely, your company has signed an agreement (or "note") to repay these amounts several years from now. Notice that *all* liabilities (whether current or long-term) require a future sacrifice of resources—this is one of their key features.

The first account in the stockholders' equity section, *Contributed Capital*, includes the amount of financing contributed to the company by stockholders. The next account is *Retained Earnings*. In our Supercuts example, there is no amount reported for this account. This makes sense because your business isn't open to customers yet and so there can be no earnings to report as having been retained by the company.

Don't be surprised if you used account names that differ from what we used in Exhibit 2.2. It's okay to use different account names as long as they have the same meaning as ours and are properly classified as assets, liabilities, or stockholders' equity. In the real world of financial reporting, even commonly used accounts are given different labels by different companies. Depending on the company, you may see a liability for a bank loan called a "note payable," "loan payable," or simply "long-term debt." When choosing names, most companies will attempt to use names that already exist, if appropriate, or come up with one that describes the underlying business activity. Once an account name is selected, it is given a reference number (for the accounting system to recognize), and this exact name and number are used for all business activities affecting that account.

exhibit 2.4	**Excerpt from Chart of Accounts**

Account Number and Name	Description
ASSETS	
100 Cash	Includes cash in the bank and in the cash register
110 Accounts Receivable	Amounts owed to your business by customers for sales on credit
120 Interest Receivable	Interest owed to your business by others
130 Inventories	Goods on hand that are being held for resale
140 Supplies	Items on hand that will be used to make goods or provide services
150 Prepaid Expenses	Rent, insurance, and other expenses paid for future services
160 Notes Receivable	Amounts loaned to others under a formal agreement ("note")
170 Property & Equipment	Cost of land, buildings, and equipment
180 Intangible Assets	Trademarks, brand names, other rights that lack a physical presence
190 Other Assets	A variety of assets with smaller balances
LIABILITIES	
300 Accounts Payable	Amounts owed to suppliers for goods or services bought on credit
310 Wages Payable	Amounts owed to employees for salaries, wages, and bonuses
320 Accrued Liabilities	Amounts owed to others for advertising, utilities, interest, etc.
330 Unearned Revenues	Amounts (customer deposits) received in advance of providing goods or services to customers
340 Notes Payable	Amounts borrowed from lenders, involves signing a promissory note
350 Bonds Payable	Amounts borrowed from lenders, involves issuance of bonds
360 Other Liabilities	A variety of liabilities with smaller balances
STOCKHOLDERS' EQUITY	
500 Contributed Capital	Amount of cash received for stock issued
510 Retained Earnings	Amount of accumulated earnings not distributed as dividends

COACH'S CORNER

Read this chart of accounts but don't memorize it. Also, don't try to force this chart of accounts on all problems. When using account names in homework problems, follow a process similar to what companies do. Consider whether a common name already exists or is given in the problem. If there isn't one, make up a descriptive one. After you have chosen an account name, be sure to use it consistently throughout the problem.

A summary of account names and numbers, called the **chart of accounts,** is kept by each company and is used to ensure consistency in reporting its own financial results. A simple example from one company is given in Exhibit 2.4. The accounts in dark blue are used in this chapter and other accounts are used in Chapters 3 and later.

YOU SHOULD KNOW

The **chart of accounts** is a summary of all account names and corresponding account numbers used to record financial results in the accounting system.

STUDY

HOW TO ANALYZE TRANSACTIONS

Transaction Analysis

You may not have realized it, but in the previous section of this chapter you were already beginning to learn one of the key steps of accounting: analyzing business activities and determining their financial statement effects. Your instructor is likely to refer to this step as **transaction analysis.** Although a single phrase is used to describe this step, it actually has two parts: (1) analyzing business activities and (2) identifying transactions. The first part describes what you look at (business activities), and the second part describes what you look for (transactions). In other words, transaction analysis involves thinking about each business activity of your company with the goal of finding transactions that should be recorded in the accounting information system. To do this well, you first need to know what a transaction is.

An accounting **transaction** is an exchange or event that has a direct economic effect on the assets, liabilities, or stockholders' equity of a business. Transactions include three types of events:

1. ***Observable external events.*** These are exchanges involving assets, liabilities, and stockholders' equity that you can see between the company and someone else. When Starbucks sells you one of its exclusive Frappucino® coffee-blended beverages, it is exchanging an icy taste of heaven for your cash. This is an external transaction that needs to be recorded in Starbucks' accounting system.

2. ***Observable internal events.*** These events do not involve exchanges with anyone else but rather occur within the company itself. For example, when the Austrian company Red Bull combines sugar, water, taurine, and caffeine, something magical happens: These ingredients turn into Red Bull Energy Drink. This internal event is a transaction because some assets (supplies of sugar, etc.) are used up to create an inventory of Red Bull.

3. ***Unobservable events.*** As the name suggests, these are the trickiest transactions to identify because you can't really see them occur. An example of this type of transaction involves the interest cost that racks up on a bank loan as time passes. You don't *see* anything happen (other than the calendar page flipping over), but an event has occurred that has a direct economic effect on the business: It now has an obligation (liability) to pay the interest that the bank charges.

Although many business activities have direct economic effects on a company, some have only indirect effects, which are not recorded. For example, signing an agreement is not considered a transaction because it typically involves the exchange of only promises, not assets, liabilities, or stockholders' equity. If you were to sign an employment contract to hire a new stylist at your Supercuts store, no transaction occurs from an accounting point of view because no exchange of assets, liabilities, or stockholders' equity occurred when the contract was signed. The company merely agreed to pay the stylist, and she merely agreed to snip away at your customers' heads. This was only an exchange of promises. Sure, when she actually pulls out her scissors and leaves a mound of your professor's hair on the floor, your business will then be obligated to pay her for the services she has provided to your business, resulting in a transaction. However, until that time, there is only a promise of an exchange to occur at some time in the future. Of course, if you were to actually pay a cash bonus for her to sign the contract, like the $2.25 million the Los Angeles Dodgers reportedly paid to shortstop Irvin Joel Guzman when he was 16 years old, then it would involve an exchange that is considered a transaction.[1]

---

[1]"Dodgers Agree to Terms with 16-Year-Old," *Houston Chronicle*, March 7, 2001.

The Ideas behind Transaction Analysis

Two simple ideas are used when analyzing transactions:

1. **Duality of effects.** It's a fancy name, but the idea is simple. Every transaction has at least two effects on the basic accounting equation. To remember this, just think of expressions like "give and take" or "push and pull" or, if you're a closet scientist, Newton's Third Law of Motion. Just as every story has at least two sides, every transaction affects at least two accounts.

2. **A = L + SE.** You know this already, right? Well, just remember that assets *always* must equal liabilities plus stockholders' equity for every accounting transaction. If it doesn't, then you are missing something and you should go back to the first (duality of effects) idea.

Let's do a few examples to show how these ideas are used when analyzing transactions. Suppose that your Supercuts store paid cash to buy Tigi's Hard Head Hair Spray (supplies). This is a transaction because an exchange exists between your business and Tigi. Applying the duality of effects idea, look for the "give and take" in this transaction:

	Transaction	Supercuts Gives	Supercuts Takes
Duality of Effects	Purchased hair spray supplies for cash	Cash	Supplies

Now, let's check to see whether the basic accounting equation still holds:

	A	**=**	**L**	**+**	**SE**
Accounting Equation	⇓ Cash				
	⇑ Supplies	=	No change	+	No change

As you can see, the decrease in one asset (cash) is offset by the increase in another asset (supplies) and there are no changes in liabilities or stockholders' equity. Consequently, the accounting equation remains in balance, as it should.

In the above example, your Supercuts store paid cash to Tigi immediately upon receiving the supplies. When most companies buy goods or services from another company, they do so on credit with the promise to pay for it later. For the next example, let's assume that your store receives a case of Shine Junkie from Tigi and pays for this purchase at the end of the month. In this example, your Supercuts store has entered into *two* transactions: (1) the purchase of an asset on credit and (2) the eventual payment. In the first, your business "takes" supplies (an increase in an asset) and in return "gives" a promise to pay later called accounts payable (an increase in a liability).

	Transaction	Supercuts Gives	Supercuts Takes
Duality of Effects	(1) Purchased hair supplies on credit	Accounts payable (promise to pay)	Supplies

Notice that A = L + SE for this transaction, as shown below.

Accounting Equation	A	=	L	+	SE
	(1) ⇑ Supplies	=	⇑ Accounts Payable	+	No change

In the second transaction, your store gives up cash (a decrease in an asset) to fulfill its promise to pay Tigi and, as a result, takes back its promise (a decrease in the liability called accounts payable). Check the following table to see whether this analysis fits the duality of effects requirement described above.

Duality of Effects	Transaction	Supercuts Gives	Supercuts Takes
	(2) Paid the amount owed on account payable	Cash	Accounts payable (the promise has been fulfilled)

Now, let's make sure that the basic accounting equation is still in balance after we enter these effects:

Accounting Equation	A	=	L	+	SE
	(2) ⇓ Cash	=	⇓ Accounts Payable	+	No change

Note that the accounting equation remained in balance after each of the two transactions. In the first, the increase in an asset was accompanied by a corresponding increase in a liability and, in the second, the decrease in an asset was accompanied by a corresponding decrease in a liability. Although you haven't seen it yet in this chapter, you also will run into transactions where a stockholders' equity account changes and is accompanied by a corresponding change in either an asset or liability account.

We should warn you that when first learning transaction analysis, you might be tempted to rush to identifying what accounts are affected while accidentally skipping over the important task of determining whether a transaction even exists. Remember, for a transaction to exist, there must be some kind of exchange or event that has a direct economic effect on your company. If your store sent an order to Tigi for more slick-styling products and Tigi promised to send them next week, no transaction has taken place from an accounting point of view. Only two promises have been exchanged. As soon as the goods are shipped to your Supercuts store, however, your business has *exchanged* a promise to pay for goods that you actually received, so a transaction has taken place, and the financial statements of your Supercuts store will be affected.

DECIDE: A Systematic Approach to Transaction Analysis

Use these steps when analyzing transactions, to **DECIDE** on the accounting effects:

1. **D**oes a transaction exist? Go to step 2 only if your answer is yes.
2. **E**xamine it for the accounts affected. Put a name on what is given and received.
3. **C**lassify each account as asset (A), liability (L), or stockholders' equity (SE).
4. **ID**entify the direction and amount of the effects. By how much does each asset, liability, and stockholders' equity account increase or decrease?
5. **E**nsure the basic accounting equation still balances.

Because the best way to learn how to account for business activities is to work through examples, let's analyze some typical financing and investing transactions, using this DECIDE approach. Assume the following events took place in August.

(a) **You incorporate Supercuts Super Salon on August 1. The company issues stock to you and your parents in exchange for $50,000, which is deposited in the company's bank account.**

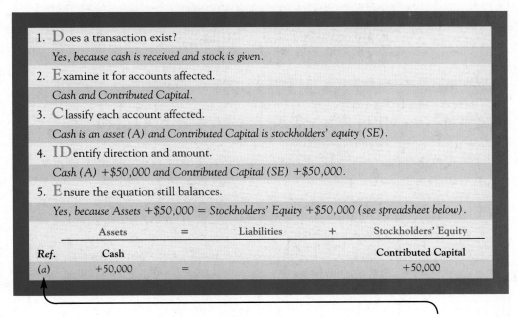

1. **D**oes a transaction exist?

   Yes, because cash is received and stock is given.

2. **E**xamine it for accounts affected.

   Cash and Contributed Capital.

3. **C**lassify each account affected.

   Cash is an asset (A) and Contributed Capital is stockholders' equity (SE).

4. **ID**entify direction and amount.

   Cash (A) +$50,000 and Contributed Capital (SE) +$50,000.

5. **E**nsure the equation still balances.

   Yes, because Assets +$50,000 = Stockholders' Equity +$50,000 (see spreadsheet below).

	Assets	=	Liabilities	+	Stockholders' Equity
Ref.	**Cash**				**Contributed Capital**
(a)	+50,000	=			+50,000

Notice that in the table above, we included a transaction reference (*a*) so that we can refer back to the original transaction description if needed. You too should use transaction letters (or numbers or dates) as references in your homework problems.

When first learning how to account for transactions, some people forget that they should examine them from the point of view of the company, not the company's owners. As you saw in Chapter 1, the separate entity concept states that personal transactions of the owners of a business are not to be mixed in with the results of the business itself. So if you thought transaction (*a*) involved an increase in an *asset* called "stock investment" (or something like that), you probably forgot to analyze the transaction from the company's point of view. For Supercuts Super Salon, the issuance of stock is a financing activity (not an investment), which was recorded as contributed capital in stockholders' equity.

(b) **A construction company renovates your store space at a cost of $42,000, which your company pays in cash.**

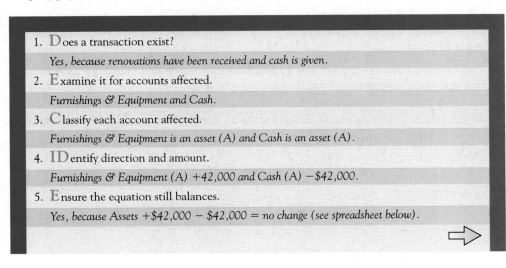

1. **D**oes a transaction exist?

   Yes, because renovations have been received and cash is given.

2. **E**xamine it for accounts affected.

   Furnishings & Equipment and Cash.

3. **C**lassify each account affected.

   Furnishings & Equipment is an asset (A) and Cash is an asset (A).

4. **ID**entify direction and amount.

   Furnishings & Equipment (A) +42,000 and Cash (A) −$42,000.

5. **E**nsure the equation still balances.

   Yes, because Assets +$42,000 − $42,000 = no change (see spreadsheet below).

	Assets		=	Liabilities	+	Stockholders' Equity
Ref.	Cash	Furnishings & Equipment				Contributed Capital
(a)	+50,000		=			+50,000
(b)	−42,000	+42,000	=		No change	

(c) Your company installs $10,000 of equipment in the salon, paying $8,000 in cash and promising to pay the remaining $2,000 at the end of the month.

1. **D**oes a transaction exist?

Yes, because equipment has been received, and cash and a promise to pay have been given.

2. **E**xamine it for accounts affected.

Furnishings & Equipment, Cash, and Accounts Payable.

3. **C**lassify each account affected.

Furnishings & Equipment is an asset (A), Cash is an asset (A), and Accounts Payable is a liability (L).

4. **ID**entify direction and amount.

Furnishings & Equipment (A) +10,000, Cash (A) −$8,000, and Accounts Payable (L) +$2,000.

5. **E**nsure the equation still balances.

Yes, because Assets +$2,000 = Liabilities +$2,000 (see spreadsheet below).

	Assets		=	Liabilities	+	Stockholders' Equity
Ref.	Cash	Furnishings & Equipment		Accounts Payable		Contributed Capital
(a)	+50,000		=			+50,000
(b)	−42,000	+42,000	=		No change	
(c)	−8,000	+10,000	=	+2,000		

If you ever run into a transaction that you have no idea how to analyze, simply break it down. Rather than trying to "solve" it all at once, begin by looking just for what is received. This **E**xamine step is crucial, and you may find that the reason you were having trouble is that there was more than one item received. After you find what is received, look just for what is given. Again, you may find that, as in event (c) here, more than one item is involved. After you **C**lassify and **ID**entify, **E**nsure the accounting equation remains in balance, because this may give you a clue about whether you've detected all the accounts affected.

(d) Your company borrows $20,000 from a bank, depositing those funds in its bank account and signing a formal agreement to repay the loan in two years.

1. **D**oes a transaction exist?

Yes, because cash has been received and a formal promise to pay ("note") has been given.

2. **E**xamine it for accounts affected.

Cash and Notes Payable.

3. **C**lassify each account affected.

Cash is an asset (A) and Notes Payable is a liability (L).

4. **ID**entify direction and amount.

Cash (A) +20,000 and Notes Payable (L) +$20,000.

5. **E**nsure the equation still balances.

Yes, because Assets +$20,000 = Liabilities +$20,000 (see spreadsheet below).

	Assets		=	Liabilities		+	Stockholders' Equity
Ref.	Cash	Furnishings & Equipment		Accounts Payable	Notes Payable		Contributed Capital
(a)	+50,000		=				+50,000
(b)	−42,000	+42,000	=		No change		
(c)	−8,000	+10,000	=	+2,000			
(d)	+20,000		=		+20,000		

(e) **Your company orders $800 of shampoo and other operating supplies from Tigi. None have been received yet.**

1. **D**oes a transaction exist?

No, because nothing has been received and only a promise has been given.

Okay, it's time for you to start taking over. As you read transactions (*f*)–(*h*) below, use the five-step **DECIDE** approach and fill in the highlighted blanks in the self-study quiz. The spreadsheet for you to summarize the effects of each transaction on the accounting equation is provided at the end of the self-study quiz.

HOW'S IT GOING? A Self-Study Quiz

(f) **Your company buys $8,000 of furniture, paying the full amount in cash.**

1. **D**oes a transaction exist?

Yes, because cash is given and furniture is received.

2. **E**xamine it for accounts affected.

Cash and Furnishings & Equipment.

3. **C**lassify each account affected.

Cash is an asset (A) and Furnishings & Equipment is [( )   ]

4. **ID**entify direction and amount.

Cash (A) −$8,000 and Furnishings & Equipment [( ) $]

5. **E**nsure the equation still balances.

Yes, because Assets +$8,000 − $8,000 = no change. [(see spreadsheet)]

(g) **Your company pays the $2,000 owed to the equipment supplier in (c).**

1. **D**oes a transaction exist?

Yes, because [   ]

2. **E**xamine it for accounts affected.

Cash and Accounts Payable.

3. **C**lassify each account affected.

Cash is an asset (A) and Accounts Payable is a liability (L).

4. **ID**entify direction and amount.

Cash (A) −$2,000 and Accounts Payable (L) −$2,000.

5. **E**nsure the equation still balances.

Yes, because [*(see spreadsheet)*] .

Note that (g) doesn't increase the *Furnishings & Equipment* asset again because the equipment was recorded in (c) at its full cost ($10,000) rather than at the amount of cash given when the equipment was received. This is an important concept (called the cost principle) that we will return to at the end of the chapter.

(h) **Your company receives $630 of the supplies ordered in (e) and promises to pay for them next month.**

1. **D**oes a transaction exist?

Yes, because supplies are received and a promise to pay is given.

2. **E**xamine it for accounts affected.

Supplies and Accounts Payable.

3. **C**lassify each account affected.

Supplies is an asset (A) and Accounts Payable is a liability (L).

4. **ID**entify direction and amount.

Supplies (A) [+$]   *Accounts Payable (L)* [+$]

5. **E**nsure the equation still balances.

Yes, because assets and liabilities increase by the same amount. [*(see spreadsheet)*]

	Assets			=	Liabilities		+	Stockholders' Equity
Ref.	Cash	Supplies	Furnishings & Equipment		Accounts Payable	Notes Payable		Contributed Capital
(a)	+50,000			=				+50,000
(b)	−42,000		+42,000	=		No change		
(c)	−8,000		+10,000	=	+2,000			
(d)	+20,000			=		+20,000		
(f)	−8,000		[ ]	=		No change		
(g)	[ ]			=	[ ]			
(h)		[ ]		=	[ ]			
Total	10,000	630	60,000		630	20,000		50,000

After you have finished, check your answers with the solutions presented in the margin.

COACH'S CORNER

The self-study quiz that you just finished involved a company's first month of operations. As a result, the net changes during the month lead directly to the ending balances, which would be reported on a balance sheet. Notice that the totals in the self-study quiz correspond to the amounts shown in Exhibit 2.2 on page 47.

EVALUATE

TRANSACTIONS USING THE DEBIT/CREDIT FRAMEWORK

It's possible to use a spreadsheet for entering the effects of transactions directly into the various accounts. By adding the increases, subtracting the decreases, and including the balances at the beginning of the month for each account, we could compute the ending balance in each account to then be reported on the balance sheet. Although this method would work, you can just imagine how impractical it would be in a company like Regis Corporation, which has transactions with about 12 million customers and 51,000 employees every month. Rather than create a spreadsheet as big as three football fields, a more sophisticated system is used to record and summarize transactions.

Fortunately, your experience as a student has made you familiar with a system of learning similar to the system used in accounting. Day after day, you go to class, take notes, go to class, take notes, rinse, repeat. The reason you take notes is to create a record of what happened each class, kind of like an academic diary or journal. Then, when preparing for exams, you probably copy these notes to summary sheets to study from. These summary sheets make it easier to understand all those things you noted earlier in the month.

The system of accounting also uses this combination of note-taking and summarizing. First, a daily record of events (transactions) is noted in a journal. These journal entries are copied ("posted") to summary sheets that show, for each balance sheet account, the effects of the month's transactions. These summary sheets (which, as a group, are called a ledger) then become the basis for preparing financial statements. Exhibit 2.5 illustrates this process. Notice how the transaction on August 1 to issue stock, which increased the company's cash and contributed capital (as noted in the journal), is summarized in the *Cash* and *Contributed Capital* accounts (in the ledger).

exhibit 2.5 Recording and Summarizing Processes

Typically, when people are first shown an accounting **journal** and **ledger,** they have a tough time telling them apart. Take a quick look at Exhibit 2.5 again. Does it seem like the journal and ledger pages look a lot alike? Both include dates, amounts, and lots of columns, so do they really differ from one another? Actually, yes. We will highlight their differences in the following sections by using simplified formats that strip away many of the lines (and some of the columns) that can make a journal and ledger look alike. These simplified formats should make it easier for you to distinguish the two types of accounting records and to focus on the main benefits of a journal (to take note of daily transactions) and a ledger (to summarize—for each account—the effects of those transactions). We'll

YOU SHOULD KNOW

A **journal** is a record of each day's transactions. A **ledger** is a collection of records that summarize the effects of transactions entered in the journal.

start with the simplified version of a ledger account, which is called a **T-account.** One more glance at the ledger page in Exhibit 2.5 should reveal how a T-account gets its name. (Can you see the "T" in the ledger account for *Cash?*)

T-Accounts: Separating Increases and Decreases in the Basic Accounting Equation

Each item on the balance sheet has its own T-account, which separately summarizes the increases and decreases that occur during the accounting period. Because assets appear on the left-hand side of the basic accounting equation (A = L + SE), each asset T-account includes increases on the left side of the T (decreases go on the right of the T). For liabilities and stockholders' equity, which appear on the right-hand side of the accounting equation, increases are included on the right side of the T (and decreases go on the left).

Assets		=	Liabilities		+	Stockholders' Equity	
+ Increases	Decreases −		− Decreases	Increases +		− Decreases	Increases +

Take a moment to see how the increase symbol + appears on the left side of the T for accounts on the left side of the accounting equation and on the right side of the T for accounts on the right side of the equation. This same balancing logic applies to decreases, which are on the side of the T closest to the equals sign.

Now, just as boating enthusiasts use special terms like "port" and "starboard" to refer to different sides of a boat, accountants also use special terms to refer to different sides of an account.[2] The term **debit** refers to the left side and **credit** refers to the right, as Exhibit 2.6 shows. These terms (and their abbreviations *dr* and *cr*) are based on Latin words that had real meaning back in the day, but today they just mean "left" and "right."

---

exhibit 2.6   **The Difference between Debits and Credits**

---

[2]Thanks to Rita Cook for sharing this analogy.

To make this as easy for you as possible, we've combined these ideas in Exhibit 2.7, which we call the transaction analysis model. As you work on more transaction analysis exercises later in this chapter, you should refer to this model as often as you need to, until you can create it on your own without help.

You should note the following from the transaction analysis model in Exhibit 2.7:

There's a great animated explanation of the transaction analysis model and the rules of debits and credits on the DVD for use with this book.

- Asset accounts increase on the left (debit) side. Because they increase on the left, they almost always have debit balances at the end of a month. It would be highly unusual for an asset account, such as inventory, to have a negative (credit) balance.

- Liabilities and stockholders' equity accounts increase on the right (credit) side, and normally have credit balances. It's highly unusual for a liability or stockholders' equity account, such as retained earnings, to have a negative (debit) balance.

- In every transaction, the total dollar value of all debits equals the total dollar value of all credits. Later, we will add this equality check (Debits = Credits) to our DECIDE transaction analysis approach.

COACH'S CORNER

Here's another way to picture how debits and credits affect accounts:

	dr	cr
Assets	⇑	⇓
Liabilities	⇓	⇑
Stockholders' **E**quity	⇓	⇑

---

exhibit 2.7   **Transaction Analysis Model**

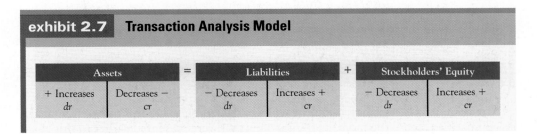

Assets		=	Liabilities		+	Stockholders' Equity	
+ Increases dr	Decreases − cr		− Decreases dr	Increases + cr		− Decreases dr	Increases + cr

---

Okay, now that you've seen how the T-account works as a simplified version of a ledger account, let's move on to the simplified format for noting each day's transactions in a journal.

Journal Entries

A debit-and-credit format is used when transactions are initially entered into the journal. The formal format for these **journal entries,** as they are called, was shown in Exhibit 2.5. For purposes of this course, we will use the following simplified format:

YOU SHOULD KNOW

Journal entries note the effects of each day's transactions on financial statement accounts.

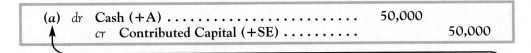

(a)   dr   **Cash (+A)** 50,000
        cr   **Contributed Capital (+SE)** 50,000

Notice the following about the simplified journal entry format shown above:

- The source of the transaction is referenced using a number or letter, like the (a) given in our original description of the transaction.

- Debits are written first (at the top) and credits are written below the debits. The account names and amounts to be credited are indented to the right. We recommend you also distinguish debits from credits by using dr and cr before the name of each account that is to be debited or credited.

- Total debits equal total credits ($50,000 = $50,000).

While you are learning to perform transaction analysis, use the symbols A, L, and SE after each account name, like we did. By identifying accounts as assets (A), liabilities (L), or stockholders' equity (SE), you will become more familiar with the various types of accounts and you'll make it easier for others to interpret your journal entries. In the next few chapters, we include the direction of the effect before the symbol. For example, if the asset account *Cash* is to be increased (debited), we will show it as dr Cash (+A).

Transaction Analysis Revisited

Now that you've been introduced to debits, credits, journal entries, and T-accounts, you are ready to revisit the five-step DECIDE approach used earlier to analyze transactions. To include these new concepts in the accounting process, we need to add two more steps, as highlighted in Exhibit 2.8.

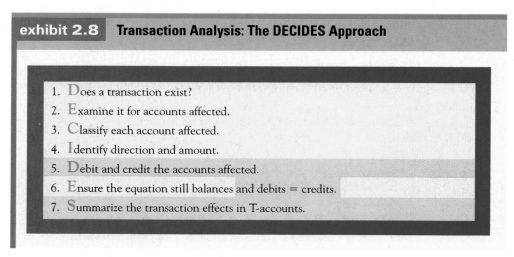

exhibit 2.8 | Transaction Analysis: The DECIDES Approach

1. Does a transaction exist?
2. Examine it for accounts affected.
3. Classify each account affected.
4. Identify direction and amount.
5. Debit and credit the accounts affected.
6. Ensure the equation still balances and debits = credits.
7. Summarize the transaction effects in T-accounts.

In the remainder of this section, we will work with you to use this transaction analysis approach to record the monthly transactions that were presented earlier in this chapter for your Supercuts Super Salon. Because we have completed steps 1–4 of the transaction analysis for these events already, we will not show them below, but you should understand that these steps *would* be performed had we not analyzed them earlier. The analysis below focuses on the results of steps 5–7, which involve the new concepts of debits, credits, journal entries, and T-accounts.

(*a*) **You incorporate Supercuts Super Salon on August 1. The company issues stock to you and your parents in exchange for $50,000, which is deposited in the company's bank account.**

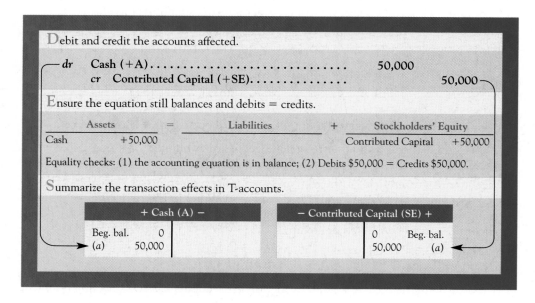

Debit and credit the accounts affected.

dr	Cash (+A)	50,000	
cr	Contributed Capital (+SE)		50,000

Ensure the equation still balances and debits = credits.

Assets		=	Liabilities	+	Stockholders' Equity	
Cash	+50,000				Contributed Capital	+50,000

Equality checks: (1) the accounting equation is in balance; (2) Debits $50,000 = Credits $50,000.

Summarize the transaction effects in T-accounts.

+ Cash (A) −			− Contributed Capital (SE) +	
Beg. bal.	0		0	Beg. bal.
(*a*)	50,000		50,000	(*a*)

Your homework exercises will likely ask you to create a list of journal entries for *all* transactions before posting any of them to T-accounts. We show the journal entries and T-account postings together here, to show you how the posting to T-accounts simply involves copying the debit or credit amount from each line of the journal entry to the debit or credit side of the corresponding T-accounts.

(b) **A construction company renovates your store space at a cost of $42,000, which your company pays in cash.**

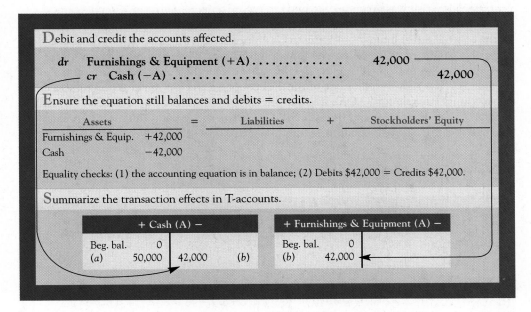

Notice above that the *Cash* T-account includes the postings for transactions (a) and (b). This accumulation of cash effects will continue until all of the month's transactions involving cash are included, at which time we will compute a total balance in the account by adding all the amounts in the debit column (increases) and subtracting all the amounts in the credit column (decreases). The excess of debits over credits will become the ending balance in this asset account, and it will carry over to become the beginning balance in the following month. But we've got a bunch more transactions in the month to **journalize** and post before we start totaling the T-accounts.

(c) **Your company installs $10,000 of equipment in the salon, paying $8,000 in cash and promising to pay the remaining $2,000 at the end of the month.**

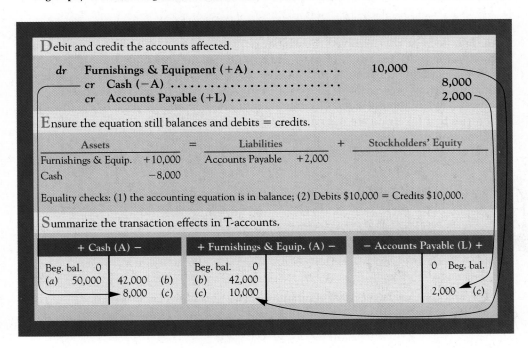

Let's briefly go over transaction (*c*), which affects three accounts: *Furnishings & Equipment*, *Cash*, and *Accounts Payable*. Because equipment was received, we need to record an increase in the asset account *Furnishings & Equipment*. The debit/credit rules indicate that asset increases are recorded on the left (debit) side of the T-account, so the journal entry includes a debit to Furnishings & Equipment for the $10,000 equipment cost. Because cash was given up, we need to record a decrease in the asset account *Cash*. The debit/credit rules indicate that asset decreases are recorded on the right (credit) side, so the journal entry includes a credit to Cash for the $8,000 given up. Because the company also gave a promise to pay the remaining $2,000, we need to record an increase in the liability *Accounts Payable*. The debit/credit rules indicate that liability increases are recorded on the right (credit) side of the T-account, so the journal entry includes a credit to Accounts Payable for $2,000. The net increase in assets of $2,000 ($10,000 − 8,000) is equal to the increase in liabilities of $2,000 (so the accounting equation is in balance), and the debit of $10,000 equals total credits of $10,000 ($8,000 + 2,000).

(d) **Your company borrows $20,000 from a bank, depositing those funds in its bank account and signing a formal agreement to repay the loan in two years.**

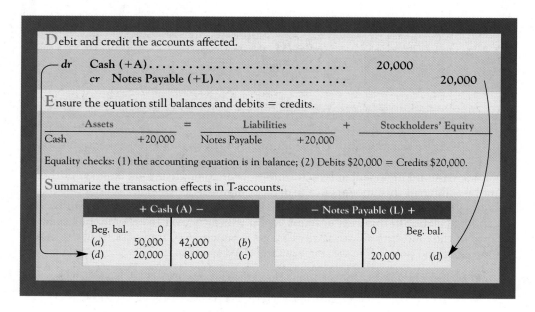

Let's move on to event (*e*), which involved ordering (but yet not receiving) supplies from Tigi. Because this involved the exchange of only promises, it was not considered a transaction. For this reason, no journal entry is needed for event (*e*).

Are you getting the hang of it? The best way to know for sure is to try accounting for some transactions on your own. In the following self-study quiz, we will provide you with space to complete journal entries for three transactions. Complete each of the three journal entries first (as if you are recording transactions for a real company on a daily basis), and then summarize the effects in the corresponding T-accounts (as if you are posting the journal entries at the end of the month). The T-accounts are in Exhibit 2.9 on page 64.

HOW'S IT GOING?   **A Self-Study Quiz**

For events (*f*), (*g*), and (*h*) below, complete the journal entries and then post their effects to the T-accounts in Exhibit 2.9. Then check your answers with the solution at the end of the illustration.

(f) **Your company buys $8,000 of furniture, paying the full amount in cash.**

Debit and credit the accounts affected.

dr [_____]([____]) . . . . [____]
cr   Cash (−A)   8,000

Ensure the equation still balances and debits = credits.

Assets	=	Liabilities	+	Stockholders' Equity
Furnishings & Equip. +8,000				
Cash −8,000				

Equality checks: (1) the accounting equation is in balance; (2) Debits $8,000 = Credits $8,000.

Summarize the transaction effects in T-accounts.

T-accounts are presented together in Exhibit 2.9.

(g) Your company pays the $2,000 owed to the equipment supplier in (c).

Debit and credit the accounts affected.

dr   Accounts Payable (−L)   2,000
cr [_____]([____]) . . . .   [____]

Ensure the equation still balances and debits = credits.

Assets	=	Liabilities	+	Stockholders' Equity
Cash −2,000		Accounts Payable −2,000		

Equality checks: (1) Does the accounting equation balance? [____] (2) Debits $2,000 = Credits $2,000.

Summarize the transaction effects in T-accounts.

T-accounts are presented together in Exhibit 2.9.

(h) Your company receives $630 of the supplies ordered in (e) and promises to pay for them next month.

Debit and credit the accounts affected.

dr [_____]([____]) . . . . [____]
cr [_____]([____]) . . . .   [____]

Ensure the equation still balances and debits = credits.

Assets	=	Liabilities	+	Stockholders' Equity
Supplies +630		Accounts Payable +630		

Equality checks: (1) the accounting equation is in balance; (2) Debits $[____] = Credits $[____].

Summarize the transaction effects in T-accounts.

T-accounts are presented together in Exhibit 2.9.

To compute the balance in T-accounts, draw a single line through each T-account below the amounts that you wish to total. Then calculate the ending balance by converting each T-account into equation form, as shown here for Cash and Accounts Payable:

	Cash		Accounts Payable	
Beginning balance	$ 0		$ 0	
Add: + side	+ 70,000	(50,000 + 20,000)	+ 2,630	(2,000 + 630)
Minus: − side	− 60,000	(42,000 + 8,000 + 8,000 + 2,000)	− 2,000	
Ending balance	$10,000		$ 630	

exhibit 2.9	T-Accounts Summarizing Transactions (a)–(h)

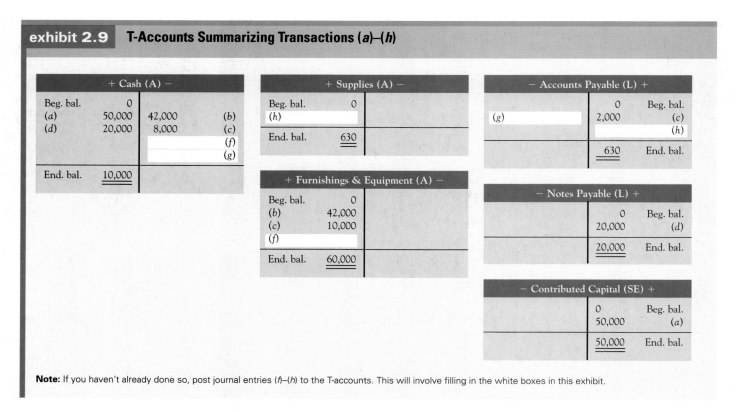

+ Cash (A) –			
Beg. bal.	0		
(a)	50,000	42,000	(b)
(d)	20,000	8,000	(c)
			(f)
			(g)
End. bal.	10,000		

+ Supplies (A) –		
Beg. bal.	0	
(h)		
End. bal.	630	

+ Furnishings & Equipment (A) –		
Beg. bal.	0	
(b)	42,000	
(c)	10,000	
(f)		
End. bal.	60,000	

– Accounts Payable (L) +		
	0	Beg. bal.
(g)	2,000	(c)
		(h)
	630	End. bal.

– Notes Payable (L) +		
	0	Beg. bal.
	20,000	(d)
	20,000	End. bal.

– Contributed Capital (SE) +		
	0	Beg. bal.
	50,000	(a)
	50,000	End. bal.

Note: If you haven't already done so, post journal entries (f)–(h) to the T-accounts. This will involve filling in the white boxes in this exhibit.

Notice in Exhibit 2.9, the ending balances are positive so they are shown on the + side with a double underline.

Preparing a Balance Sheet

It's possible to prepare a balance sheet at any point in time using the ending balances in the T-accounts. For example, to prepare a balance sheet for your Supercuts Super Salon after recording transactions (a)–(h) above, just take the ending balances from each T-account in Exhibit 2.9 and group them as assets, liabilities, and stockholders' equity in balance sheet format. If you do this, you should end up with a balance sheet that looks like the one we presented back in Exhibit 2.2. We realize that the odds of you flipping all the way back to page 47 right now are slim, so we'll take this opportunity to show you a slightly different balance sheet format used by some companies. Exhibit 2.10 shows an alternative balance sheet layout called the account format. Accountants can use either this format or the one shown in Exhibit 2.2, just as long as it balances (that is, total assets must equal the total of liabilities and stockholders' equity).

Occasionally, you may find that your balance sheet is out of balance. This only happens when you've made a mistake. Don't give up and hit Ctrl-Alt-Delete because there are some shortcuts for finding the error. They all involve looking at the amount of the difference between total assets and total liabilities plus stockholders' equity.

1. If the difference is *the same as* one of your account balances, you probably forgot to include the account in the balance sheet.
2. If the difference is *twice* the amount of *an account balance*, you may have reported the account in the wrong category of A, L, or SE.
3. If the difference is *two times* the amount of *a particular transaction*, you may have posted a debit as a credit or a credit as a debit in your T-accounts.
4. If the difference is *evenly divisible by 9*, you may have reversed the order of two digits in a number or left a zero off the end of a number.
5. If the difference is *evenly divisible by 3*, you may have hit the key above or below the one you intended to hit (like a 9 instead of a 6) on your calculator or numeric keypad.

exhibit 2.10	Balance Sheet in Account Format

SUPERCUTS SUPER SALON
Balance Sheet
At August 31, 2005
(in U.S. dollars)

Assets		Liabilities	
Current Assets		Current Liabilities	
Cash	$10,000	Accounts Payable	$ 630
Supplies	630	Total Current Liabilities	630
Total Current Assets	10,630	Notes Payable	20,000
		Total Liabilities	20,630
		Stockholders' Equity	
		Contributed Capital	50,000
Furnishings & Equipment	60,000	Retained Earnings	0
		Total Stockholders' Equity	50,000
Total Assets	$70,630	Total Liabilities and Stockholders' Equity	$70,630

Now that you've seen how a balance sheet is created from the ending balances in ledger/T-accounts, which summarize journal entries that record each day's transactions, it's time to take a step back and think about what the balance sheet means for financial statement users.

┌ *RECONSIDER* ─────────────
│ THE BALANCE SHEET CONCEPTS THAT USERS RELY ON

The Effects of a Transaction Focus

Some people mistakenly believe that the balance sheet reports what a business is actually worth. To them, this isn't a crazy idea because the balance sheet lists the company's assets and liabilities, so the net difference between the two must be the company's worth. In fact, "net worth" is a term that many accountants and analysts use when referring to stockholders' equity. So then, why is it wrong to think that the balance sheet reports what a business is actually worth?

The answer comes from knowing that accounting is based on recording and reporting *transactions*, as you have seen over and over in this chapter. This focus on transactions does two things to the balance sheet: (1) it affects what is (and is not) recorded, and (2) it affects the amounts assigned to recorded items.

1. **What is (and is not) recorded?** Because accounting is based on transactions, an item will only be recorded if it comes from an identifiable transaction. The asset *Furnishings & Equipment* on your Supercuts Super Salon balance sheet comes from having bought furniture and equipment. Other events that do *not* involve identifiable transactions are not entered into the accounting system and, therefore, do not make it to the balance sheet. For example, Regis Corporation will not report one of its most valuable assets (the name "Regis Salons") on its balance sheet because it wasn't acquired in an identifiable transaction. This doesn't mean that the name isn't valuable in attracting customers or isn't relevant when estimating the value of Regis Corporation's business. It *is* valuable and relevant. Rather, all it means is that it wasn't possible for Regis Corporation to point to a particular transaction and say, "there's where

POINT OF INTEREST
Regis Salons account for 26 percent of the sales of Regis Corporation. Supercuts makes up only 12 percent of all sales.

our name got its value." And, without an identifiable transaction, there is no recognition in the balance sheet (or in the other financial statements).

2. ***Amounts assigned to recorded items.*** Assets and liabilities are initially recorded at their original cost to the company. This **cost principle,** as it is called, is one of the main principles of accounting. While these amounts are accurate at the time a transaction is entered into, there is no guarantee that these amounts will continue to represent the value of an asset or liability at a later time. It is possible that some assets and liabilities will change in value as time passes. However, the cost principle does not allow increases in asset values (and decreases in liability values) to be recorded unless additional transactions have caused the change in value. So, although real estate values in Chattanooga and the 250,000-square-foot distribution center that Regis Corporation built there may have increased in value since 2001, this extra value would not be reported in the balance sheet of Regis Corporation because measurement (the dollar amount used to report transactions) is based on the original cost to the company.

Does this mean that an asset continues to be reported at its original, transaction-based cost if its value falls over time? No, because there is yet another accounting concept that comes into play—a concept called conservatism. **Conservatism** requires that special care be taken to avoid reporting assets at too high an amount or reporting liabilities at too low an amount. Essentially, conservatism requires that, when there is doubt about the amount at which assets and liabilities should be reported, the least optimistic measurement should be used.

What happens if someone doesn't follow the conservatism concept? Just ask the former president and chief financial officer for Rent-Way who was found guilty of ordering his employees to violate the conservatism concept. Or ask the former chief accounting officer who concocted 10 different schemes that led Rent-Way to overstate assets and understate liabilities by nearly $100 million. The last we heard, they were both in jail serving 16 months.

What's Coming Up

As you can see, you need to know quite a bit about the "how to" of accounting to be able to prepare financial statements. We will take a closer look at using the financial statements in decision making in Chapter 5, but first you need to learn how the accounting system handles transactions related to the operating activities of a business and how it produces an income statement. That's the focus for Chapters 3 and 4. Before hitting those chapters, though, you should review and practice what we covered in this chapter.

FOR YOUR REVIEW

DEMONSTRATION CASE

eXcel

On April 1, 2006, three ambitious college students started Goodbye Grass Corporation (GGC). A summary of GGC's transactions completed through April 30, 2006 follows:

a. Issued shares of stock to the three investors in exchange for cash totaling $9,000.
b. Acquired rakes and other hand tools (equipment) for $600, paying the hardware store $200 cash and signing a note for the balance, payable in three months.
c. Ordered three lawn mowers and two edgers costing $4,000 from XYZ Lawn Supply, Inc.
d. Purchased four acres of land for the future site of a storage garage. Paid cash, $5,000.
e. Received the mowers and edgers that had been ordered, and signed a note to pay XYZ Lawn Supply in full in 60 days.
f. Sold for $1,250 one acre of land to the city for a park. Accepted a six-month note from the city for payment.
g. One of the owners borrowed $3,000 from a local bank for personal use.

Required:

1. Analyze each transaction using the DECIDES approach outlined in the chapter. Show journal entries and equality checks for each transaction listed above.

2. Set up T-accounts for Cash, Notes Receivable (from the city), Equipment (hand tools and mowing equipment), Land, Notes Payable (to hardware store and equipment supply company), and Contributed Capital. Indicate the beginning balances of $0 in each T-account. Post all journal entries to the appropriate T-accounts. Identify each amount with its letter in the preceding list.

3. Use the amounts in the T-accounts, developed in requirement 2, to prepare a classified balance sheet for Goodbye Grass Corporation at April 30, 2006. Show the balances for all assets, liabilities, and stockholders' equity accounts.

4. As of April 30, 2006, has financing for GGC's assets come primarily from liabilities or stockholders' equity?

Check your answers with the solution in the following section.

Suggested Solution

1. Transaction analysis and journal entries:

(a) *dr* Cash (+A)................................   9,000
      cr Contributed Capital (+SE)   9,000

Assets		=	Liabilities	+	Stockholders' Equity	
Cash	+9,000				Contributed Capital	+9,000

Equality checks: (1) the accounting equation is in balance; (2) Debits $9,000 = Credits $9,000.

(b) *dr* Equipment (+A).............................   600
      cr Cash (−A)   200
      cr Notes Payable (+L)   400

Assets		=	Liabilities		+	Stockholders' Equity
Equipment	+600		Notes Payable	+400		
Cash	−200					

Equality checks: (1) the accounting equation is in balance; (2) Debits $600 = Credits $600.

(c) This is not an accounting transaction. No exchange has taken place. No accounts are affected.

(d) *dr* Land (+A)..................................   5,000
      cr Cash (−A)   5,000

Assets		=	Liabilities	+	Stockholders' Equity
Land	+5,000				
Cash	−5,000				

Equality checks: (1) the accounting equation is in balance; (2) Debits $5,000 = Credits $5,000.

(e) *dr* Equipment (+A).............................   4,000
      cr Notes Payable (+L)   4,000

Assets		=	Liabilities		+	Stockholders' Equity
Equipment	+4,000		Notes Payable	+4,000		

Equality checks: (1) the accounting equation is in balance; (2) Debits $4,000 = Credits $4,000.

(f) *dr* Notes Receivable (+A)   1,250
      cr Land (−A)   1,250

Assets		=	Liabilities	+	Stockholders' Equity
Notes Receivable	+1,250				
Land	−1,250				

Equality checks: (1) the accounting equation is in balance; (2) Debits $1,250 = Credits $1,250.

(*g*) This is not a transaction of the company. The separate entity assumption states that transactions of the owners are separate from transactions of the business.

2.   Posting journal entries to T-accounts:

+ Cash (A) −				
(dr)		(cr)		
Beg. bal.	0			
(*a*)	9,000	(*b*)	200	
		(*d*)	5,000	
End. bal. 3,800				

+ Equipment (A) −		(cr)
(dr)		
Beg. bal.	0	
(*b*)	600	
(*e*)	4,000	
End. bal. 4,600		

− Notes Payable (L) +		
(dr)	(cr)	
	Beg. bal.	0
	(*b*)	400
	(*e*)	4,000
	End. bal. 4,400	

+ Notes Receivable (A) −		(cr)
(dr)		
Beg. bal.	0	
(*f*)	1,250	
End. bal. 1,250		

+ Land (A) −		
(dr)	(cr)	
Beg. bal.	0	
(*d*)	5,000	(*f*) 1,250
End. bal. 3,750		

− Contributed Capital (SE) +		
(dr)	(cr)	
	Beg. bal.	0
	(*a*)	9,000
	End. bal. 9,000	

3.   Preparing a balance sheet from the T-accounts:

GOODBYE GRASS CORPORATION
Balance Sheet
At April 30, 2006

Assets		Liabilities	
Current Assets		*Current Liabilities*	
Cash	$ 3,800	Notes Payable	$ 4,400
Notes Receivable	1,250		
Total Current Assets	5,050	**Stockholders' Equity**	
Equipment	4,600	Contributed Capital	9,000
Land	3,750	**Total Liabilities and**	
Total Assets	**$13,400**	**Stockholders' Equity**	**$13,400**

4.   The primary source of financing for GGC's assets (totaling $13,400) has come from stockholders' equity ($9,000) rather than liabilities ($4,400).

CHAPTER SUMMARY

LO1   **Explain and select common balance sheet account titles. p. 46**

- A *classified balance sheet* separately classifies assets as current if they will be used up or converted into cash within one year. Liabilities are classified as current if they will be paid, settled, or fulfilled within one year.

- Typical balance sheet account titles include the following:

  Assets: Cash, Accounts Receivable, Inventories, Supplies, Property and Equipment.

  Liabilities: Accounts Payable, Notes Payable, Bonds Payable.

  Stockholders' Equity: Contributed Capital, Retained Earnings.

Apply transaction analysis to business transactions. p. 49   **LO2**

- Transactions include observable external events, observable internal events, and unobservable events.

- Transaction analysis is based on the duality of effects and the basic accounting equation. *Duality of effects* means that every transaction affects at least two accounts.

- Transaction analysis follows a systematic approach of determining whether a transaction exists; examining the transaction for the accounts affected; classifying the accounts as assets, liabilities, or stockholders' equity; identifying the direction and amount of the effects; and evaluating whether the accounting equation remains in balance.

Use journal entries and T-accounts to show how business transactions affect the balance sheet. p. 58   **LO3**

- Debit means left and credit means right.

- Debits increase assets and decrease liabilities and stockholders' equity.

- Credits decrease assets and increase liabilities and stockholders' equity.

- Journal entries express, in debit-equals-credit form, the effects of a transaction on various asset, liability, and stockholders' equity accounts. Journal entries are used to enter financial information into the accounting system, which is later summarized by account in the ledger (T-accounts).

- T-accounts are a simplified version of the ledger, which summarizes transaction effects for each account. T-accounts show increases on the left (debit) side for assets, which are on the left side of the accounting equation.
  T-accounts show increases on the right (credit) side for liabilities and stockholders' equity, which are on the right side of the accounting equation.

Prepare a balance sheet. p. 64   **LO4**

- Classified balance sheets are structured with

  Assets categorized as "current assets" (those to be used up or turned into cash within the year), followed by all other (noncurrent) assets, such as property and equipment, and intangible assets.

  Liabilities categorized as "current liabilities" (those that will be paid with current assets), followed by all other (long-term) liabilities.

  Stockholders' equity accounts are listed as Contributed Capital first followed by Retained Earnings.

Explain the concepts that determine whether an item is reported on the balance sheet and at what amount. p. 65   **LO5**

- Because accounting is transaction-based, the balance sheet does not necessarily represent the current value of a business.

- Some assets are not recorded because they do not arise from transactions.

- The amounts recorded for assets and liabilities may not represent current values because under the cost principle they generally are recorded at cost, using the exchange amounts established at the time of the initial transaction.

- The concept of conservatism states that when uncertainty exists about the value of an asset or liability, care should be taken to not overstate the reported value of assets or understate the reported value of liabilities.

KEY TERMS TO KNOW

Classified Balance Sheet p. 47

Conservatism p. 66

Contributed Capital p. 48

Current Assets p. 48

Current Liabilities p. 48

Debits and Credits p. 58

Journal p. 57

Journal Entry p. 59

Ledger p. 57

Long-Term Assets p. 48

Long-Term Liabilities p. 48

Retained Earnings p. 48

Stockholders' Equity, (Owners' Equity or Shareholders' Equity) pp. 47, 48

T-account p. 58

Transaction p. 50

Transaction Analysis p. 50

FOR YOUR PRACTICE

QUESTIONS

1. Define the following:
   - *a.* Asset
   - *b.* Current asset
   - *c.* Liability
   - *d.* Current liability
   - *e.* Contributed capital
   - *f.* Retained earnings

2. Define a business transaction in the broad sense, and give an example of observable external, observable internal, and unobservable events.

3. For accounting purposes, what is an account? Explain why accounts are used in an accounting system.

4. What is the basic accounting equation?

5. Explain what *debit* and *credit* mean.

6. Briefly explain what is meant by *transaction analysis*. What are the two principles underlying transaction analysis? What are the steps of the DECIDES approach to transaction analysis?

7. What two different accounting equalities must be maintained in transaction analysis?

8. What is a *journal entry*? What is the typical format of a journal entry?

9. What is a *T-account*? What is its purpose?

10. What is the key feature that all assets possess? What is the key feature of all liabilities?

11. Explain what the following accounting terms mean:
   - *a.* Cost principle
   - *b.* Conservatism

MULTIPLE CHOICE

To practice more multiple choice questions, check out the DVD for use with this book.

1. Which of the following is not an asset?
   - *a.* Cash
   - *b.* Land
   - *c.* Equipment
   - *d.* Contributed Capital

2. How many of the following statements describe transactions that would be recorded in the accounting system?
   - An exchange of one asset for another asset.
   - An exchange of a promise for an asset.
   - An exchange of a promise for another promise.
   - *a.* None
   - *b.* One
   - *c.* Two
   - *d.* Three

3. Total assets on a balance sheet prepared on any date must agree with which of the following?
   - *a.* The sum of total liabilities and net income as shown on the income statement.
   - *b.* The sum of total liabilities and contributed capital.
   - *c.* The sum of total liabilities and retained earnings.
   - *d.* The sum of total liabilities and contributed capital and retained earnings.

4. The "duality of effects" can best be described as follows:
   - *a.* When one records a transaction in the accounting system, at least two effects on the basic accounting equation will result.
   - *b.* When an exchange takes place between two parties, both parties must record the transaction.
   - *c.* When a transaction is recorded, both the balance sheet and the income statement must be impacted.
   - *d.* When a transaction is recorded, one account will always increase and one account will always decrease.

5. The T-account is used to summarize which of the following?
   - *a.* Increases and decreases to a single account in the accounting system.
   - *b.* Debits and credits to a single account in the accounting system.
   - *c.* Changes in specific account balances over a time period.
   - *d.* All of the above describe how T-accounts are used by accountants.

6. Which of the following describes how assets are listed on the balance sheet?

   a. In alphabetical order.

   b. In order of magnitude, lowest value to highest value.

   c. From most current to least current.

   d. From least current to most current.

7. A company was recently formed with $5,000 cash contributed to the company by stockholders. The company then borrowed $2,000 from a bank, and bought $1,000 of inventory on account. The company also purchased $5,000 of equipment by paying $2,000 in cash and issuing a note for the remainder. What is the amount of total assets to be reported on the balance sheet?

   a. $11,000   c. $9,000

   b. $10,000   d. None of the above

8. How many of the following are true regarding *debits* and *credits*?

   • In any given transaction, the total dollar amount of the debits and the total dollar amount of the credits must be equal.

   • Debits decrease certain accounts and credits decrease certain accounts.

   • Liabilities and Stockholders' Equity accounts usually end in credit balances, while assets usually end in debit balances.

   a. None   c. Two

   b. One   d. Three

9. How many of the following statements are true regarding the Balance Sheet?

   • One cannot determine the true "current value" of a company by reviewing just its balance sheet.

   • Certain assets, which are not acquired through identifiable transactions, are not reported on a company's balance sheet.

   • A balance sheet shows only the ending balances, in a summarized format, of all "balance sheet accounts" in the accounting system as of a particular date.

   a. None   c. Two

   b. One   d. Three

10. If a publicly traded company is trying to maximize its perceived value to decision makers external to the corporation, the company is most likely to *understate* which of the following on its balance sheet?

   a. Assets   c. Retained earnings

   b. Liabilities   d. Contributed capital

MINI-EXERCISES   Available with McGraw-Hill's Homework Manager

M2-1 Identifying Important Accounting Terms   LO2–LO5

Complete the following crossword puzzle, using the clues provided to the right.

Across
1. A simplified version of a ledger account.
6. The place in which each day's transactions are initially entered.
8. The requirement to use least optimistic numbers when uncertain about the value of an asset or liability.
9. Has the effect of decreasing assets.
10. The (right or left) side of the T-account on which decreases in stockholders' equity are recorded.

Down
2. The name for a balance sheet that separately reports certain assets and liabilities as current.
3. An exchange or event that has a direct economic effect on the business.
4. The accounting principle that describes the amount at which transactions should be recorded.
5. The portion that will be used up or will come due within the next 12 months.
7. Has the effect of decreasing liabilities.

LO3   **M2-2 Identifying Increase and Decrease Effects on Balance Sheet Accounts**

Complete the following table by entering either the word *increases* or *decreases* in each column.

	Debit	Credit
Assets	_____	_____
Liabilities	_____	_____
Stockholders' Equity	_____	_____

LO3   **M2-3 Identifying Debit and Credit Effects on Balance Sheet Accounts**

Complete the following table by entering either the word *debit* or *credit* in each column.

	Increase	Decrease
Assets	_____	_____
Liabilities	_____	_____
Stockholders' Equity	_____	_____

LO2, LO3, LO5   **M2-4 Matching Terms with Definitions**

Match each term with its related definition by entering the appropriate letter in the space provided. There should be only one definition per term (that is, there are more definitions than terms).

Term	Definition
_____ 1. Journal entry	A. An exchange of more than promises between a business and other parties.
_____ 2. A = L + SE; Debits = Credits	B. Four periodic financial statements.
_____ 3. Transaction	C. The two equalities in accounting that aid in providing accuracy.
_____ 4. Liabilities	D. The results of transaction analysis in debit equals credit format.
_____ 5. Assets	
_____ 6. Income statement, balance sheet, statement of retained earnings, and statement of cash flows	E. The account that is debited when money is borrowed from a bank.
	F. Probable future economic benefits owned by a business.
	G. Cumulative earnings of a company that are not distributed to the owners.
	H. Every transaction has at least two effects.
	I. Debts or obligations to be paid with assets or fulfilled with services.
	J. Assigning dollar amounts to transactions.

LO1, LO4   **M2-5 Classifying Accounts on a Balance Sheet**

The following are a few of the accounts of Gomez-Sanchez Company:

COACH'S CORNER

For help, see the Chart of Accounts in Exhibit 2.4 on page 49.

_____ 1.	Accounts Payable	_____ 9.	Leasehold Improvements
_____ 2.	Accounts Receivable	_____ 10.	Notes Payable (due in three years)
_____ 3.	Buildings	_____ 11.	Notes Receivable (due in six months)
_____ 4.	Cash	_____ 12.	Prepaid Rent
_____ 5.	Contributed Capital	_____ 13.	Retained Earnings
_____ 6.	Land	_____ 14.	Supplies
_____ 7.	Merchandise Inventory	_____ 15.	Utilities Payable
_____ 8.	Income Taxes Payable	_____ 16.	Wages Payable

In the space provided, classify each as it would be reported on a balance sheet. Use the following code:

CA = current asset   CL = current liability   SE = stockholders' equity

NCA = noncurrent asset   NCL = noncurrent liability

M2-6 Identifying Accounts on a Classified Balance Sheet and Their Normal Debit or Credit Balances

LO1, LO4

According to a recent report of Hasbro, Inc., the company is "a worldwide leader in children's and family games and toys." Hasbro produces products under several brands including Tonka, Milton Bradley, Playskool, and Parker Brothers. The following are several of the accounts from a recent balance sheet:

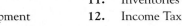

1.	Accounts Receivable	7.	Retained Earnings
2.	Short-Term Loan	8.	Accounts Payable
3.	Contributed Capital	9.	Cash
4.	Long-Term Debt	10.	Accrued Liabilities Payable
5.	Intangibles	11.	Inventories
6.	Property, Plant, and Equipment	12.	Income Taxes Payable

Required:

Indicate how each account normally should be categorized on a classified balance sheet. Use CA for current asset, NCA for noncurrent asset, CL for current liability, NCL for noncurrent liability, and SE for stockholders' equity. Also indicate whether the account normally has a debit or credit balance.

M2-7 Identifying Accounts on a Classified Balance Sheet and Their Normal Debit or Credit Balances

LO1, LO4

Blockbuster, Inc., is the world's leading provider of rentable DVDs, videogames, and videocassettes. Blockbuster estimates that 64 percent of the U.S. population lives within a 10-minute drive of a Blockbuster store. The following are several of the accounts included in a recent balance sheet:

1.	Accounts Receivable	8.	Retained Earnings
2.	Movie Rental Supplies	9.	Accounts Payable
3.	Contributed Capital	10.	Cash
4.	Long-Term Debt	11.	Accrued Liabilities Payable
5.	Prepaid Rent	12.	Long-Term Liabilities
6.	Intangibles	13.	Merchandise Inventories
7.	Property and Equipment	14.	Income Taxes Payable

Required:

Indicate how each account normally should be categorized on a classified balance sheet. Use CA for current asset, NCA for noncurrent asset, CL for current liability, NCL for noncurrent liability, and SE for stockholders' equity. Also indicate whether the account normally has a debit or credit balance.

M2-8 Identifying Events as Accounting Transactions

LO2

Do the following events result in a recordable transaction for The Toro Company? Answer yes or no for each.

_____ 1. Toro purchased robotic manufacturing equipment that it paid for by signing a note payable.

_____ 2. Six investors in Toro sold their stock to another investor.

_____ 3. The company lent $150,000 to a member of the board of directors.

_____ 4. The Toro Company ordered supplies from Office Max to be delivered next week.

_____ 5. The president of The Toro Company purchased additional stock in another company.

_____ 6. The company borrowed $1,000,000 from a local bank.

M2-9 Identifying Events as Accounting Transactions

LO2

Half Price Books is the country's largest family-owned new and used bookstore chain with 80 locations in 12 states. More than 1,800 employees currently generate annual revenues exceeding $125 million, placing Half Price Books in the top 200 of the nation's Top 500 Women-Owned

Businesses. Do the following events result in a recordable transaction for Half Price Books? Answer yes or no for each.

_____ 1. Half Price Books bought an old laundromat in Dallas.

_____ 2. The privately held company issued stock to family members and corporate officers.

_____ 3. The company signed an agreement to rent store space in Columbia Plaza near Cleveland.

_____ 4. The company paid for renovations to prepare its Seattle store for operations.

_____ 5. The vice president of the company spoke at a literacy luncheon in Indiana, which contributed to building the company's reputation as a responsible company.

LO2   **M2-10** **Determining Financial Statement Effects of Several Transactions**

For each of the following transactions of Nardozzi Inc. for the month of January 2006, indicate the accounts, amounts, and direction of the effects on the accounting equation. A sample is provided.

_a._ (*Sample*) Borrowed $1,000 from a local bank on a note due in six months.

_b._ Issued $3,000 stock to investors.

_c._ Purchased $500 in equipment, paying $100 cash and promising the rest on a note due in one year.

_d._ Paid $100 cash for supplies.

_e._ Lent $200 to an employee who signed a note promising to repay the company in 60 days.

	Assets	=	Liabilities	+	Stockholders' Equity
a. Sample: Cash	+1,000	Notes Payable	+1,000		

LO3   **M2-11** **Preparing Journal Entries**

For each of the transactions in M2-10 (including the sample), write the journal entry using the format shown in this chapter.

LO3   **M2-12** **Posting to T-Accounts**

For each of the transactions in M2-10 (including the sample), post the effects to the appropriate T-accounts and determine ending account balances.

+ Cash (A) −	+ Notes Receivable (A) −	+ Equipment (A) −

+ Supplies (A) −	− Notes Payable (L) +	− Contributed Capital (SE) +

LO4   **M2-13** **Reporting a Classified Balance Sheet**

Given the transactions in M2-10 (including the sample), prepare a classified balance sheet for Nardozzi Inc. as of January 31, 2006.

EXERCISES   Available with McGraw-Hill's Homework Manager

LO1, LO2, LO5   **E2-1** **Matching Terms with Definitions**

Match each term with its related definition by entering the appropriate letter in the space provided. There should be only one definition per term (that is, there are more definitions than terms).

Term

_____ 1. Transaction

_____ 2. Separate entity concept

_____ 3. Balance sheet

_____ 4. Liabilities

_____ 5. Assets = Liabilities + Stockholders' Equity

_____ 6. Current assets

_____ 7. Notes payable

_____ 8. Duality of effects

_____ 9. Retained earnings

_____ 10. Debit

Definition

A. Economic resources to be used or turned into cash within one year.

B. Reports assets, liabilities, and stockholders' equity.

C. Decrease assets; increase liabilities and stockholders' equity.

D. Increase assets; decrease liabilities and stockholders' equity.

E. An exchange of more than promises between a business and other parties.

F. The assumption that businesses will operate into the foreseeable future.

G. Accounts for a business separate from its owners.

H. The principle that assets should be recorded at their original cost to the company.

I. A standardized format used to accumulate data about each item reported on financial statements.

J. The basic accounting equation.

K. The two equalities in accounting that aid in providing accuracy.

L. The account that is credited when money is borrowed from a bank.

M. Cumulative earnings of a company that are not distributed to the owners.

N. Every transaction has at least two effects.

O. Probable debts or obligations to be paid with assets or services.

E2-2 Identifying Account Titles

LO2, LO5

The following are independent situations.

a. A company orders and receives 10 personal computers for office use for which it signs a note promising to pay $25,000 within three months.

b. A company purchases for $21,000 cash a new delivery truck that has a list, or sticker, price of $24,000.

c. A women's clothing retailer orders 30 new display stands for $300 each for future delivery.

d. A new company is formed and sells 100 shares of stock for $12 per share to investors.

e. A company purchases a piece of land for $50,000 cash. An appraiser for the buyer valued the land at $52,500.

f. The owner of a local company buys a $10,000 car for personal use. Answer from the company's point of view.

g. A company borrows $1,000 from a local bank and signs a six-month note for the loan.

h. A company pays $1,500 owed on its note payable (ignore interest).

Required:

1. Indicate titles of the appropriate accounts, if any, affected in each of the preceding events. Consider what the company gives and takes.

2. At what amount would you record the delivery truck in *b?* The piece of land in *e?* What measurement principle are you applying?

3. What reasoning did you apply in *c?* For *f,* what accounting concept did you apply?

E2-3 Classifying Accounts and Their Usual Balances

LO1, LO4

As described in a recent annual report, Digital Diversions, Inc. (DDI) designs, develops, and distributes videogames for computers and advanced game systems such as Paystation, Y-Box, Tamecube, and Gamegirl. DDI has been operating for only one full year.

Required:

For each of the following accounts from DDI's recent balance sheet, complete the following table. Indicate whether the account is classified as a current asset (CA), noncurrent asset (NCA), current liability (CL), noncurrent liability (NCL), or stockholders' equity (SE), and whether the account usually has a debit (*dr*) or credit (*cr*) balance.

Account	Balance Sheet Classification	Debit or Credit Balance
1. Land	_____	_____
2. Retained Earnings	_____	_____
3. Notes Payable (due in three years)	_____	_____

(continues)

COACH'S CORNER

If an account has a balance, it almost always will be on the side that increases the account.

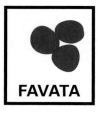

FAVATA

Account	Balance Sheet Classification	Debit or Credit Balance
4. Accounts Receivable		
5. Leasehold Improvements		
6. Contributed Capital		
7. Machinery and Equipment		
8. Accounts Payable		
9. Cash		
10. Taxes Payable		

LO2   **E2-4 Determining Financial Statement Effects of Several Transactions**

The following events occurred for Favata Company:

a. Received $20,000 cash by organizers and issued stock to them.
b. Borrowed $6,000 cash from a bank.
c. Purchased land for $12,000; paid $1,000 in cash and signed a note for the balance.
d. Loaned $300 to an employee who signed a note.
e. Purchased $8,000 of equipment, paying $1,000 in cash and signing a note for the rest.

Required:

For each of the events *a* through *e*, perform transaction analysis and indicate the account, amount, and direction of the effect (+ for increase and − for decrease) on the accounting equation. Check that the accounting equation remains in balance after each transaction. Use the following headings:

Event	Assets	=	Liabilities	+	Stockholders' Equity

LO2   **E2-5 Determining Financial Statement Effects of Several Transactions**

Nike, Inc., with headquarters in Beaverton, Oregon, is one of the world's leading manufacturers of athletic shoes and sports apparel. The following activities occurred during a recent year. The amounts are presented in millions of dollars.

a. Purchased $216.3 in property, plant, and equipment; paid by signing a $5 long-term note and fulfilling the rest with cash.
b. Issued $21.1 in additional stock for cash.
c. Several Nike investors sold their own stock to other investors on the stock exchange for $21 per share of stock.

Required:

1. For each of these events, perform transaction analysis and indicate the account, amount (in millions), and direction of the effect on the accounting equation. Check that the accounting equation remains in balance after each transaction. Use the following headings:

Event	Assets	=	Liabilities	+	Stockholders' Equity

2. Explain your response to transaction *c*.

LO3   **E2-6 Recording Investing and Financing Activities**

Refer to E2-4.

Required:

For each of the events in E2-4, prepare journal entries, checking that debits equal credits.

LO3   **E2-7 Recording Investing and Financing Activities**

Refer to E2-5.

Required:

1. For each of the events in E2-5, prepare journal entries, checking that debits equal credits.
2. Explain your response to event *c*.

E2-8 Analyzing the Effects of Transactions in T-Accounts

LO2, LO3, LO5

Mulkeen Service Company, Inc., was organized by Conor Mulkeen and five other investors. The following activities occurred during the year:

a.   Received $60,000 cash from the investors; each was issued 1,000 shares of capital stock.
b.   Purchased equipment for use in the business at a cost of $12,000; one-fourth was paid in cash and the company signed a note for the balance (due in six months).
c.   Signed an agreement with a cleaning service to pay it $120 per week for cleaning the corporate offices, beginning next week.
d.   Lent $2,000 to one of the investors who signed a note due in six months.
e.   Conor Mulkeen borrowed $10,000 for personal use from a local bank, signing a one-year note.

Required:

1.   Create T-accounts for the following accounts: Cash, Notes Receivable, Equipment, Notes Payable, and Contributed Capital. Beginning balances are zero. For each of the above transactions, record its effects in the appropriate T-accounts. Include good referencing and totals for each T-account.
2.   Using the balances in the T-accounts, fill in the following amounts for the accounting equation:
     Assets $_____ = Liabilities $_____ + Stockholders' Equity $_____
3.   Explain your response to events c and e.

E2-9 Inferring Investing and Financing Transactions and Preparing a Balance Sheet

LO2, LO4, LO5

During its first week of operations, January 1–7, 2006, Faith's Fine Furniture Corporation completed six transactions with the dollar effects indicated in the following schedule:

	Dollar Effect of Each of the Six Transactions						
Accounts	1	2	3	4	5	6	Ending Balance
Cash	$12,000	$50,000	$(4,000)	$4,000	$(7,000)		
Equipment					7,000		
Land			12,000			$3,000	
Long-term Debt		50,000	8,000	4,000		3,000	
Contributed Capital	12,000						

Required:

1.   Write a brief explanation of transactions 1 through 6. Explain any assumptions that you made.
2.   Compute the ending balance in each account and prepare a classified balance sheet for Faith's Fine Furniture Company on January 7, 2006.
3.   As of January 7, 2006, has most of the financing for Faith's investment in assets come from liabilities or stockholders' equity?

E2-10 Inferring Investing and Financing Transactions and Preparing a Balance Sheet

LO2, LO4, LO5

During its first month of operations, March 2006, Faye's Fashions, Inc., completed four transactions with the dollar effects indicated in the following schedule:

	Dollar Effect of Each of the Four Transactions				
Accounts	1	2	3	4	Ending Balance
Cash	$50,000	$(4,000)	$5,000	$(4,000)	
Computer Equipment				4,000	
Delivery Truck		25,000			
Short-term Bank Loan			5,000		
Long-term Notes Payable		21,000			
Contributed Capital	50,000				

Required:

1. Write a brief explanation of transactions 1 through 4. Explain any assumptions that you made.
2. Compute the ending balance in each account and prepare a classified balance sheet for Faye's Fashions, Inc., at the end of March 2006.
3. As of March 31, 2006, has most of the financing for Faye's investment in assets come from liabilities or stockholders' equity?

LO1, LO3   **E2-11 Recording Journal Entries**

Assume Down.com was organized on May 1, 2006 to compete with Despair.com—a company that sells de-motivational posters and office products. The following events occurred during the first month of Down.com's operations.

a. Received $60,000 cash from the investors who organized Down.com Corporation.
b. Borrowed $20,000 cash and signed a note due in two years.
c. Ordered lighting fixtures costing $16,000.
d. Purchased $10,000 in equipment, paying $1,000 in cash and signing a six-month note for the balance.
e. Received and paid for the lighting fixtures ordered in c.

Required:

Prepare journal entries for each transaction. (Remember that debits go on top and credits go on the bottom, indented.) Be sure to use good referencing and categorize each account as an asset (A), liability (L), or stockholders' equity (SE). If a transaction does not require a journal entry, explain the reason.

LO2–LO4   **E2-12 Analyzing the Effects of Transactions Using T-Accounts, Preparing and Interpreting a Balance Sheet**

Lee Delivery Company, Inc. (LDC), was organized in 2005. The following transactions occurred during the year:

a. Received $40,000 cash from organizers in exchange for stock in the new company.
b. Purchased land for $12,000, signing a two-year note (ignore interest).
c. Bought two used delivery trucks at the start of the year at a cost of $10,000 each; paid $2,000 cash and signed a note due in three years for the rest (ignore interest).
d. Sold one-fourth of the land for $3,000 to Birkins Moving, which signed a six-month note.
e. Paid $2,000 cash to a truck repair shop for a new motor for one of the trucks. (*Hint:* Increase the account you used to record the purchase of the trucks since the productive life of the truck has been improved.)
f. Traded the other truck and $6,000 cash for a new one.
g. Stockholder Jonah Lee paid $22,000 cash for land for his personal use.

Required:

1. Set up appropriate T-accounts with beginning balances of $0 for Cash, Notes Receivable, Land, Equipment, Notes Payable, and Contributed Capital. Using the T-accounts, record the effects of these transactions.
2. Prepare a classified balance sheet for LDC at the end of 2005.
3. Using the balance sheet, indicate whether LDC's assets at the end of the year were financed primarily by liabilities or stockholders' equity.

LO2, LO3   **E2-13 Explaining the Effects of Transactions on Balance Sheet Accounts Using T-Accounts**

Heavey and Lovas Furniture Repair Service, a company with two stockholders, began operations on June 1, 2005. The following T-accounts indicate the activities for the month of June.

Cash (A)				Notes Receivable (A)				Building (A)		
(a)	17,000	(b)	10,000	(c)	1,500			(b)	50,000	
		(c)	1,500							

Notes Payable (L)		Contributed Capital (SE)	
(b)	40,000	*(a)*	17,000

Required:

Explain events *a* through *c* that resulted in the entries in the T-accounts. That is, for each account what transactions made it increase and/or decrease?

SIMPLIFY WITH SPREADSHEETS

SS2-1 Analyzing Transactions and Preparing a Balance Sheet

LO2

Assume you recently obtained a part-time accounting position at the corporate headquarters of Elizabeth Arden, Inc., in Miami Lakes, Florida. Elizabeth Arden is a leading marketer and manufacturer of prestige beauty products, prominently led by the Red Door line of fragrances. The following table summarizes accounts and their balances (in thousands) reported by Elizabeth Arden, Inc., in a recent September 30 balance sheet.

Cash	14,300	Short-Term Notes Payable	125,000
Accounts Receivable	285,400	Accounts Payable	111,800
Inventories	199,700	Other Current Liabilities	75,700
Other Current Assets	31,600	Long-Term Debt	323,600
Property and Equipment	35,800	Other Long-Term Liabilities	10,100
Other Noncurrent Assets	224,100	Contributed Capital	101,800
		Retained Earnings	42,900

Determine how the balance sheet of Elizabeth Arden would change, if the company were to enter into the following transactions (amounts in thousands) during October:

Oct. 2 Purchase an additional manufacturing facility at a cost of $17,000, by issuing a promissory note that becomes payable in three years.

Oct. 10 Use $4,000 cash to repay one of the short-term loans.

Oct. 21 Issue additional stock for $10,000 cash.

Oct. 28 Use cash to buy land for $5,000.

Required:

The controller at Elizabeth Arden has asked you to create a spreadsheet in which to display (*a*) the account balances at September 30, (*b*) the effects of the four October transactions, and (*c*) totals that combine the September 30 balances with the October transactions. You feel like you might be ready to tackle this assignment, but just to be sure you e-mail your friend Billy for advice. Here's his reply.

From: BillyTheTutor@yahoo.com
To: HairZed@hotmail.com
Cc:
Subject: Excel Help

Wow, I can't believe you gave up that great job at EA. Good thing that you landed another one so quickly!

1. My thinking is that you'll really impress your boss if you set up the spreadsheet to look like a bunch of T-accounts, one beside another. To do this, use the first column for date references, and then use the remaining columns for the balance sheet accounts. Use two columns for each balance sheet account (with the account name spanning the two columns) to make it look just like a T-account. You do remember how to use the cell merge command to make a header span two columns, right? If not, check the last e-mail I sent you. Here's a screenshot of how one part of the left-hand side of your worksheet might look just before you enter the October transactions.

COACH'S CORNER

See SS1-1 for Billy's cell merge advice. For extra spreadsheet skills, you might also try creating a balance sheet with cells that are linked to the corresponding cells in the T-accounts. To do this, open a worksheet in the same file as the T-accounts. Then click on a cell in the balance sheet worksheet where you want to import a number from the T-accounts, then type =, then click on the tab for the T-account worksheet, click on the cell with the total to be transferred, and then press enter. This links the cells so that any changes to the T-accounts automatically update the balance sheet.

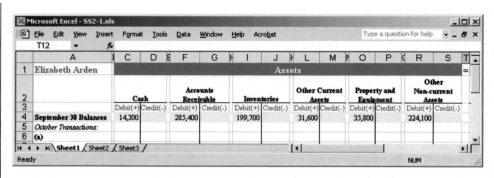

2. I guess the only thing that's left is to remind you that to compute the ending balances in each T-account you have to add the increases to the beginning balance and subtract the decreases. So, to compute the totals for a particular account, your formula might look like =(SUM(C4:C9)-SUM(D5:D9)).

3. Oh yeah, when you're all done, don't forget to save the file using a name that uniquely identifies you.

COACHED PROBLEMS

L01, L02

CP2-1 Determining Financial Statement Effects of Various Transactions

Lester's Home Healthcare Services (LHHS) was organized on January 1, 2005, by four friends. Each organizer invested $10,000 in the company and, in turn, was issued 8,000 shares of stock. To date, they are the only stockholders. During the first month (January 2005), the company had the following six events:

COACH'S CORNER

b. Five different accounts are affected.
c. Has this transaction caused LHHS to give or receive anything?
f. Remember to think about what LHHS has given up and what it has received.

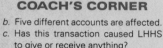

a. Collected a total of $40,000 from the organizers and, in turn, issued the shares of stock.
b. Purchased a building for $65,000, equipment for $16,000, and three acres of land for $12,000; paid $13,000 in cash and signed a note for the balance, which is due to be paid in 15 years.
c. One stockholder reported to the company that 500 shares of his Lester's stock had been sold and transferred to another stockholder for $5,000 cash.
d. Purchased supplies for $3,000 cash.
e. Sold one acre of land for $4,000 cash to another company.
f. Lent one of the shareholders $5,000 for moving costs, receiving a signed six-month note from the shareholder.

Required:

1. Was Lester's Home Healthcare Services organized as a partnership or corporation? Explain the basis for your answer.

2. During the first month, the records of the company were inadequate. You were asked to prepare the summary of the preceding transactions. To develop a quick assessment of their economic effects on Lester's Home Healthcare Services, you have decided to complete the spreadsheet that follows and to use plus (+) for increases and minus (−) for decreases for each account. The first transaction is used as an example.

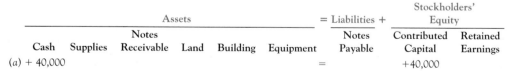

		Assets				= Liabilities +	Stockholders' Equity	
Cash	Supplies	Notes Receivable	Land	Building	Equipment	Notes Payable	Contributed Capital	Retained Earnings
(a) + 40,000						=	+40,000	

3. Did you include the transaction between the two stockholders—event c—in the spreadsheet? Why?

4. Based only on the completed spreadsheet, provide the following amounts (show computations):
   a. Total assets at the end of the month.
   b. Total liabilities at the end of the month.
   c. Total stockholders' equity at the end of the month.

d. Cash balance at the end of the month.

e. Total current assets at the end of the month.

5. As of January 31, 2005, has the financing for LHHS's investment in assets primarily come from liabilities or stockholders' equity?

CP2-2 Recording Transactions (in a Journal and T-Accounts), Preparing and Interpreting the Balance Sheet

LO1-LO5

Patrie Plastics Company (PPC) has been operating for three years. The December 31, 2005, account balances are:

Cash	$ 35,000	Other assets	$ 5,000
Accounts receivable	5,000	Accounts payable	37,000
Inventory	40,000	Notes payable (due 2008)	80,000
Notes receivable	2,000	Contributed capital	150,000
Equipment	80,000	Retained earnings	50,000
Factory building	150,000		

COACH'S CORNER

You won't need different accounts to record the transactions described below, so have a quick look at the ones listed before you start to answer this question.

f. Three different accounts are affected.

g. Does PPC owe anything to its new president for the year ended December 31, 2006?

h. What does PPC give up and take back?

During the year 2006, the company had the following summarized activities:

a. Purchased equipment that cost $30,000; paid $10,000 cash and signed a two-year note for the balance.

b. Issued an additional 2,000 shares of stock for $20,000 cash.

c. Lent $12,000 to a supplier who signed a six-month note.

d. Borrowed $20,000 cash from a local bank, payable June 30, 2008.

e. Purchased an "other asset" for $6,000 cash.

f. Built an addition to the factory for $42,000; paid $15,000 in cash and signed a three-year note for the balance.

g. Hired a new president on the last day of the year. The contract was for $85,000 for each full year worked.

h. Returned $2,000 of defective equipment to the manufacturer, receiving a cash refund.

Required:

1. Prepare journal entries to record transactions *a–h*.

2. Create T-accounts for each of the accounts on the balance sheet and enter the balances at the end of 2005 as beginning balances on January 1, 2006.

3. Enter the effects of the transactions in T-accounts (including referencing) and determine the December 31, 2006, balances.

4. Explain your response to event *g*.

5. Prepare a classified balance sheet at December 31, 2006.

6. As of December 31, 2006, has the financing for PPC's investment in assets primarily come from liabilities or stockholders' equity?

GROUP A PROBLEMS Available with McGraw-Hill's Homework Manager

PA2-1 Determining Financial Statement Effects of Various Transactions

LO1, LO2, LO5

Mallard Incorporated (MI) is a small manufacturing company that makes model trains to sell to toy stores. It has a small service department that repairs customers' trains for a fee. The company has been in business for five years. At the end of the most recent year, 2005, the accounting records reflected total assets of $500,000 and total liabilities of $200,000. During the current year, 2006, the following summarized events occurred:

a. Issued additional shares of stock for $100,000 cash.

b. Borrowed $120,000 cash from the bank and signed a 10-year note.

c. Built an addition on the factory for $200,000 and paid cash to the contractor.

d. Purchased equipment for the new addition for $30,000, paying $3,000 in cash and signing a note due in six months for the balance.

e. Returned a $3,000 piece of equipment, from *d*, because it proved to be defective; received a reduction of the note payable.

f. Purchased a delivery truck (equipment) for $10,000; paid $5,000 cash and signed a nine-month note for the remainder.
g. At the end of 2006, lent $2,000 cash to the company president, Jennifer Mallard, who signed a note due in one year.
h. A stockholder sold $5,000 of his capital stock in Mallard Incorporated to his neighbor.

Required:

1. Complete the spreadsheet that follows, using plus (+) for increases and minus (−) for decreases for each account. The first transaction is used as an example.

	Assets			=	Liabilities	+	Stockholders' Equity	
Cash	Notes Receivable	Equipment	Building		Notes Payable		Contributed Capital	Retained Earnings
(a) + 100,000				=			+100,000	

2. Did you include event *h* in the spreadsheet? Why or why not?
3. Based on beginning balances plus the completed spreadsheet, provide the following amounts (show computations):
    a. Total assets at the end of the year.
    b. Total liabilities at the end of the year.
    c. Total stockholders' equity at the end of the year.
4. As of December 31, 2006, has the financing for MI's investment in assets primarily come from liabilities or stockholders' equity?

LO1-LO5   **PA2-2** **Recording Transactions (in a Journal and T-Accounts), Preparing and Interpreting the Balance Sheet**

Ethan Allen Interiors Inc. is a leading manufacturer and retailer of home furnishings in 315 retail stores in the United States and abroad. The following is adapted from a recent Ethan Allen balance sheet as of June 30. Dollars are in thousands.

Cash	$ 75,688	Other assets	$ 6,665
Accounts receivable	32,845	Accounts payable	80,993
Inventories	174,147	Wages and other expenses payable	48,028
Prepaid expenses and		Long-term debt	9,321
other current assets	36,076	Other long-term liabilities	39,224
Property, plant, and equipment	293,626	Contributed capital	116,719
Intangibles	69,708	Retained earnings	394,470

Assume that the following events occurred in the quarter ended September 30:

a. Paid $3,400 cash for an additional "other asset."
b. Issued additional shares of stock for $1,020 in cash.
c. Purchased property, plant, and equipment; paid $1,830 in cash and will pay the remaining $9,400 in two years.
d. Sold, at cost, other assets for $310 cash.
e. Conducted negotiations to purchase a sawmill, which is expected to cost $34,000.

Required:

1. Prepare journal entries to record transactions *a–e*.
2. Create T-accounts for each of the accounts on the balance sheet and enter the balances at the end of June as beginning balances for the July 1–September 30 quarter.
3. Enter the effects of the transactions in T-accounts (including referencing) and determine the September 30 balances.
4. Explain your response to event *e*.
5. Prepare a classified balance sheet at September 30.
6. As of September 30, has the financing for Ethan Allen's investment in assets primarily come from liabilities or stockholders' equity?

GROUP B PROBLEMS

PB2-1   Determining Financial Statement Effects of Various Transactions

LO1, LO2, LO5

Swish Watch Corporation manufactures, sells, and services expensive, ugly watches. The company has been in business for three years. At the end of the most recent year, 2006, the accounting records reported total assets of $2,255,000 and total liabilities of $1,780,000. During the current year, 2007, the following summarized events occurred:

a.   Issued additional shares of stock for $109,000 cash.
b.   Borrowed $186,000 cash from the bank and signed a 10-year note.
c.   A stockholder sold $5,000 of his capital stock in Swish Watch Corporation to another investor.
d.   Built an addition on the factory for $200,000 and paid cash to the construction company.
e.   Purchased equipment for the new addition for $44,000, paying $12,000 in cash and signing a six-month note for the balance.
f.   Returned a $4,000 piece of equipment, from e, because it proved to be defective; received a cash refund.
g.   At the end of 2006, lent $2,000 cash to the company president, Thor Gunnarson, who signed a note with terms requiring repayment of the loan in one year.

Required:

1.   Complete the spreadsheet that follows, using plus (+) for increases and minus (−) for decreases for each account. The first transaction is used as an example.

	Assets			=	Liabilities	+	Stockholders' Equity	
Cash	Notes Receivable	Equipment	Building		Notes Payable		Contributed Capital	Retained Earnings
(a) + 109,000				=			+109,000	

2.   Did you include event c in the spreadsheet? Why?

3.   Based on beginning balances plus the completed spreadsheet, provide the following amounts (show computations):
   a.   Total assets at the end of the year.
   b.   Total liabilities at the end of the year.
   c.   Total stockholders' equity at the end of the year.

4.   As of December 31, 2007, has the financing for Swish Watch Corporation's investment in assets primarily come from liabilities or stockholders' equity?

PB2-2   Recording Transactions (in a Journal and T-Accounts), Preparing and Interpreting the Balance Sheet

LO1-LO5

Starbucks is a coffee company—a big coffee company. During a 10-year period, the number of Starbucks locations grew from 165 to over 5,800 stores—an average increase of 43 percent every year. The following is adapted from a recent Starbucks annual report. Starbucks' year-end is September 30 and dollars are reported in thousands.

Cash	$ 174,500	Accounts payable	$462,600
Accounts receivable	97,500	Short-term bank loans	74,900
Inventories	263,200	Long-term debt	5,100
Other current assets	312,100	Other long-term liabilities	23,500
Property, plant, and equipment	1,265,800	Contributed capital	930,300
Other long-term assets	179,500	Retained earnings	796,200

Assume that the following events occurred in the following quarter, which ended December 31:

a.   Paid $10,400 cash for additional other long-term assets.
b.   Issued additional shares of stock for $5,300 in cash.
c.   Purchased property, plant, and equipment; paid $11,800 in cash and signed additional long-term loans for $8,900.
d.   Sold, at cost, other long-term assets for $3,000 cash.
e.   Conducted negotiations to purchase a coffee farm, which is expected to cost $7,400.

Required:

1. Prepare journal entries to record transactions *a–e*.
2. Create T-accounts for each of the accounts on the balance sheet and enter the balances at the end of September as beginning balances for the October 1–December 31 quarter.
3. Enter the effects of the transactions in T-accounts (including referencing) and determine the December 31 balances.
4. Explain your response to event *e*.
5. Prepare a classified balance sheet at December 31.
6. As of December 31, has the financing for the investment in assets made by Starbucks primarily come from liabilities or stockholders' equity?

CASES & DISCUSSION STARTERS

FINANCIAL REPORTING AND ANALYSIS CASES

LO1, LO5

C&DS2-1 Finding Financial Information

Refer to the financial statements of Landry's Restaurants in Appendix A at the end of this book, or download the annual report from the *Cases* section of the text's Web site at www.mhhe.com/phillips.

Required:

1. What is the company's fiscal year-end? Where did you find the exact date?
2. Use the company's balance sheet to determine the amounts in the accounting equation (A = L + SE).
3. On the balance sheet, the company reports inventories of $47,772,298. Does this amount represent the expected selling price? Why or why not?
4. What is the amount of the company's current liabilities?
5. Has financing for the company's investment in assets primarily come from liabilities or stockholders' equity?

LO1, LO5

C&DS2-2 Comparing Financial Information

Refer to the financial statements of Dave & Buster's in Appendix B at the end of this book, or download the annual report from the *Cases* section of the text's Web site at www.mhhe.com/phillips.

Required:

1. Use the company's balance sheet to determine the amounts in the accounting equation (A = L + SE). Is Dave & Buster's or Landry's larger in terms of total assets?
2. Does Dave & Buster's have more or less inventories to sell than Landry's?
3. Does Dave & Buster's have more or less current liabilities than Landry's?
4. Has financing for the Dave & Buster's investment in assets primarily come from liabilities or stockholders' equity? Thinking back to Chapter 1, what does this imply about the risk assumed by Dave & Buster's investors, relative to those investing in Landry's Restaurants?

LO1, LO5

C&DS2-3 Internet-Based Team Research: Examining the Balance Sheet

As a team, select an industry to analyze. Using your Web browser, each team member should acquire the annual report or 10-K for one publicly traded company in the industry, with each member selecting a different company. (See C&DS1-3 in Chapter 1 for a description of possible resources for these tasks.)

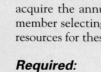

**TEAM
CASE**

Required:

1. On an individual basis, each team member should write a short report that lists the following information.
   a.   The date of the balance sheet.
   b.   The major noncurrent asset accounts and any significant changes in them.
   c.   The major noncurrent liability accounts and any significant changes in them.

  d. Any significant changes in total stockholders' equity.

  e. Whether financing for the investment in assets primarily comes from liabilities or stockholders' equity.

2. Then, as a team, write a short report comparing and contrasting your companies using the above dimensions. Discuss any similarities across the companies that you as a team observe, and provide potential explanations for any differences discovered.

ETHICS AND CRITICAL THINKING CASES

C&DS2-4 Ethical Decision Making: A Real-Life Example

LO1, LO2, LO5

ETHICAL

ISSUE

Charles Ponzi started the Security Exchange Company on December 26, 1919. He thought he had discovered a way to purchase American stamps in a foreign country at significantly lower amounts than they were worth in the U.S. He claimed his idea was so successful that anyone who gave money to his company would be repaid their original loan plus 50 percent interest within 90 days. Friends and family quickly offered their money to Ponzi and they were handsomely rewarded, being repaid their original loan and the 50 percent interest within just 45 days. Thanks to an article in the *New York Times,* word spread quickly about Ponzi's business, attracting thousands of people seeking a similar payback. He might have had a successful business had his idea actually worked. The problem, however, was that it didn't. The 50 percent interest paid to early investors did not come from the profits of a successful underlying business idea (which didn't even exist) but instead was obtained fraudulently from funds contributed by later lenders. Eventually, the Ponzi scheme collapsed on August 10, 1920, after an auditor examined his accounting records.

1. Assume that on December 27, 1919, Ponzi's first three lenders provided his company with $5,000 each. Use the basic accounting equation to show the effects of these transactions on December 27, 1919.

2. If the first two lenders are repaid their original loan amounts plus the 50 percent interest promised to them, how much cash is left in Ponzi's business to repay the third lender? Given what you discovered, how was it possible for Ponzi's company to remain in "business" for over eight months?

3. Who was harmed by Ponzi's scheme?

Epilogue: After taking in nearly $15 million from 40,000 people, Ponzi's company failed with just $1.5 million in total assets. Ponzi spent four years in prison before jumping bail, to become involved in fraudulently selling swampland in Florida. We're not kidding.

C&DS2-5 Ethical Decision Making: A Mini-Case

LO1, LO5

ETHICAL

ISSUE

You work as an accountant for a small land development company that desperately needs additional financing to continue in business. The president of your company is meeting with the manager of a local bank at the end of the month to try to obtain this financing. The president has approached you with two ideas to improve the company's reported financial position. First, he claims that because a big part of the company's value comes from its knowledgeable and dedicated employees, you should report their "Intellectual Abilities" as an asset on the balance sheet. Second, he claims that although the local economy is doing poorly and almost no one is buying land or new houses, he is optimistic that eventually things will turn around. For this reason, he asks you to continue reporting the company's land on the balance sheet at its cost, rather than the much lower amount that real estate appraisers say it's really worth.

1. Thinking back to Chapter 1, why do you think the president is so concerned with the amount of assets reported on the balance sheet?

2. What accounting concept introduced in Chapter 2 relates to the president's first suggestion to report "Intellectual Abilities" as an asset?

3. What accounting concept introduced in Chapter 2 relates to the president's second suggestion to continue reporting land at its cost?

4. Who might be hurt by the president's suggestions, if you were to do as he asks? What should you do?

C&DS2-6 Critical Thinking: Evaluating the Reliability of a Balance Sheet

LO1, LO4, LO5

Betsey Jordan asked a local bank for a $50,000 loan to expand her small company. The bank asked Betsey to submit a financial statement of the business to supplement the loan application. Betsey prepared the following balance sheet.

Balance Sheet June 30, 2007	
Assets	
Cash	$ 9,000
Inventory	30,000
Equipment	46,000
Personal residence (monthly payments, $2,800)	300,000
Remaining assets	20,000
Total assets	**$405,000**
Liabilities	
Short-term debt to suppliers	$ 62,000
Long-term debt on equipment	38,000
Total debt	**100,000**
Stockholder's equity	**305,000**
Total liabilities and stockholder's equity	**$405,000**

Required:

The balance sheet has several flaws. However, there is at least one major deficiency. Identify it and explain its significance.

www.mhhe.com/phillips

chapter three

Reporting Operating Results on the Income Statement

3

Aside from music, what do Toni Braxton, the San Jose Symphony, and TLC have in common? Here's a hint. They're in the same club as Enron, Kmart, United Airlines, and WorldCom (now called MCI). That's right, they all have experienced bankruptcy. It may be difficult to believe that these big names could be involved in bankruptcy proceedings, with TLC having enjoyed six top-10 singles in the United States prior to the group's bankruptcy filing and with Kmart celebrating its 100-year anniversary only three years before its bankruptcy filing. But it's true. Despite generating millions and millions of dollars in sales, these celebrities and huge corporations lived beyond their means—a problem that eventually led them to bankruptcy.

Toni Braxton's bankruptcy is an interesting tale that involves love, the law, and an income statement. Well, actually, it doesn't involve an income statement—that was part of the problem. Without an income statement to compare her revenues to her expenses, Toni had no way of seeing that she was headed for financial trouble. As it turns out, her personal revenues were "only" $400,000 a year—hardly enough to cover all the expenses that come from living a lavish celebrity lifestyle. She spent over $10,000 to attend a weekend runway show in New York, $15,000 to buy her Vera Wang wedding dress, and $1,200 to get hair extensions. If only she had known that these and other costs totaled more than her personal revenues—perhaps she could have had her hair done at **SUPER-CUTS,** where the average customer pays a mere $12.[1]

---

[1]Information for this chapter opener has been obtained from www.bankruptcydata.com/Research/15_Largest.htm; A. M. Dickerson, "Bankruptcy Reform: Does the End Justify the Means?" *American Bankruptcy Law Journal*, April 2001, p. 243; "A Star is Broke," *Entertainment Weekly*, February 20, 1998; www.chl.ca/JamMusicArtistsB/braxton_toni.html; Regis Corporation's 2003 Form 10-K; and http://people.aol.com/people/news/now/0,10958,123191,00.html.

INSIDE LOOKING OUT

OUTSIDE LOOKING IN

This chapter continues our discussion of the accounting system, with an emphasis on how the financial results of operating activities are tracked inside the company, and how they are reported to outsiders using the income statement. We also continue to focus on Supercuts and its parent, Regis Corporation.

The Beauty of Our Business
REGIS CORPORATION

SUPERCUTS

mia & maxx HAIR STUDIO

REGIS

Regis Corporation has never experienced an annual same-store sales decrease in over 80 years of business.

T he first goal of this chapter is to help you to see how an income statement indicates whether a business generated a profit or loss from the day-to-day business activities that occurred during the accounting period. Then we'll discuss various operating activities and show how the DECIDES transaction analysis approach from Chapter 2 can be used to analyze and record income statement transactions. Finally, at the close of the chapter, we will help you learn about the key accounting concepts that underlie income statement reporting. The most important things to get out of this chapter are summarized in Exhibit 3.1.

exhibit 3.1	**Your Learning Objectives**

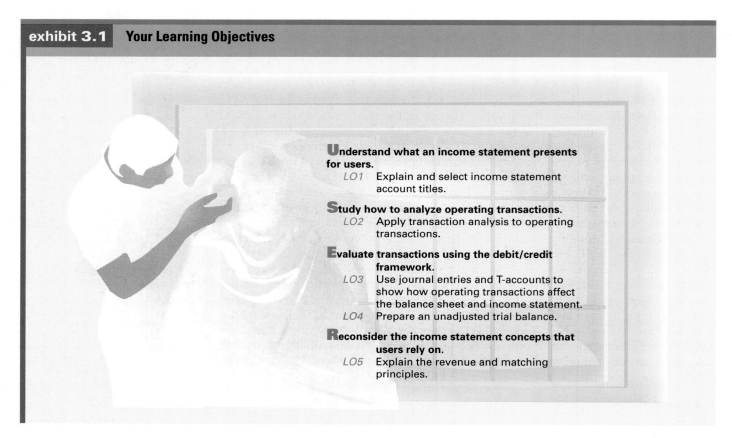

Understand what an income statement presents for users.
LO1   Explain and select income statement account titles.

Study how to analyze operating transactions.
LO2   Apply transaction analysis to operating transactions.

Evaluate transactions using the debit/credit framework.
LO3   Use journal entries and T-accounts to show how operating transactions affect the balance sheet and income statement.
LO4   Prepare an unadjusted trial balance.

Reconsider the income statement concepts that users rely on.
LO5   Explain the revenue and matching principles.

┌ *UNDERSTAND*
WHAT AN INCOME STATEMENT PRESENTS FOR USERS

Revenues and Expenses

Just as it was useful in Chapter 2 to understand the balance sheet by thinking about the investing and financing activities needed to start up your Supercuts Super Salon, you will better understand the income statement if you spend a few minutes considering a salon's operating activities. Think back to the last time you got your hair cut. How does your salon generate revenues and what expenses does it incur? For hair salons and most other businesses, **revenues** represent the amounts charged to customers. Specifically, revenues represent the increases in a company's resources that result from providing goods or services to customers. So if your salon gives 1,560 haircuts in a month and charges customers $10 per cut, revenues would total $15,600. The amount of revenues earned during the period is reported in the top part of the body of the income statement.

    The costs of operating the business are reported as **expenses** in the body of the income statement just underneath revenues. In general, expenses include any costs incurred to generate revenues in the period covered by the income statement. For hair salons, the big expenses relate to manager salaries and stylist wages, rent, advertising,

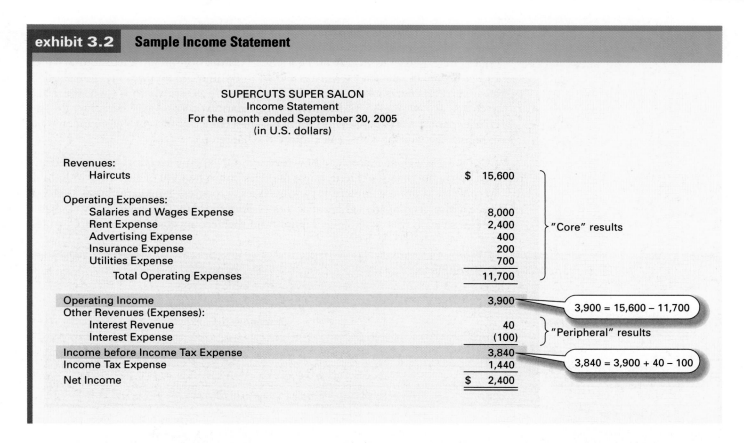

exhibit 3.2 | **Sample Income Statement**

SUPERCUTS SUPER SALON
Income Statement
For the month ended September 30, 2005
(in U.S. dollars)

Revenues:	
Haircuts	$ 15,600
Operating Expenses:	
Salaries and Wages Expense	8,000
Rent Expense	2,400
Advertising Expense	400
Insurance Expense	200
Utilities Expense	700
Total Operating Expenses	11,700
Operating Income	3,900
Other Revenues (Expenses):	
Interest Revenue	40
Interest Expense	(100)
Income before Income Tax Expense	3,840
Income Tax Expense	1,440
Net Income	$ 2,400

"Core" results

3,900 = 15,600 – 11,700

"Peripheral" results

3,840 = 3,900 + 40 – 100

insurance, and various utilities (telephone, fax, Internet, power, water). Our friends in the business tell us that a small salon that gives 1,560 haircuts in a month would typically incur operating expenses of $8,000 for salaries and wages, $2,400 for rent, $400 for advertising, $200 for insurance, and $700 for utilities. Big hair companies have similar expenses—for Regis Corporation, each expense is about 8,000 times bigger.

In addition to these typical or "core" operating activities, businesses often have other "peripheral" (normal but not central) transactions that result in revenues or expenses. For example, in addition to its core business of cutting hair, your Supercuts Super Salon might earn interest revenue from investing its cash in a certificate of deposit at the bank. Alternatively, it might have to pay interest expense on a bank loan. It might even generate a **gain** or **loss** from selling land that it owned. These items are not considered a central part of business operations because they have more to do with investing and financing than with how the business is run. To put it simply, hair salons are in business to generate a profit from selling haircuts, not from selling land or earning interest on their investments. Nonetheless, these peripheral transactions do affect net income, so these effects are included in the income statement, as shown in Exhibit 3.2.

We've highlighted two new things in Exhibit 3.2 that you need to know about:

1. **The results of core transactions are separated from peripheral transactions.** Notice that the income statement introduces a subtotal called *Operating income*, which combines revenues and expenses from only core operating transactions. This little subtotal actually is quite a useful addition to the income statement. By excluding peripheral transactions, which are less likely to recur in the future, operating income can act as a starting point for forecasting how much profit will be generated in future accounting periods. That is, if hair keeps growing at ½ inch per month, as scientists say it will, the $3,900 of operating income shown in Exhibit 3.2 is likely to be earned in later months, too. Of course, operating income isn't the final story on whether the business made a profit overall. To get to that "bottom line" net income number, we have to consider the results of peripheral transactions and income taxes charged on the company's profit.

COACH'S CORNER

There is no rule about the order for reporting the various types of operating expenses. In many cases, operating expenses are listed from the largest to smallest amount.

YOU SHOULD KNOW

A **gain** occurs when, as part of a peripheral transaction, a business sells something for an amount greater than what it's recorded at in the accounting records. A **loss** occurs when the business sells it for less than the amount recorded in the accounting records. Just like revenues, gains increase net income. Just like expenses, losses reduce net income.

2. **Income tax expense is reported separately.** Income tax is calculated on all the revenues and expenses of the company. For this reason, the company combines its revenues and expenses from core and peripheral transactions in another subtotal called *Income before income tax expense*, as shown in Exhibit 3.2 on page 91. *Income before income tax expense* is used to determine *Income tax expense*, which is then subtracted to arrive at *Net income*. (Although tax calculations can be very complex, for this course income tax expense will simply be a percentage of income before income tax expense. We will show this calculation in Chapter 4.)

Exhibit 3.2 is a great example of how revenue and expense accounts are arranged and reported on the income statement, but it includes only a handful of accounts. In Exhibit 3.3, we provide a more complete list of revenues, expenses, gains, and losses that you might see within a company's chart of accounts. As we said in Chapter 2, every company is different, so even this example will differ from the accounts used by other companies.

exhibit 3.3   Excerpt from Chart of Accounts

Account Number and Name	Description
Revenues	
600 Sales Revenues	Sales of products in the ordinary course of business
610 Service Revenues	Sales of services in the ordinary course of business
620 Rental Revenues	Amounts earned by renting out company property
630 Interest Revenues	Amounts earned on savings accounts and certificates of deposit
640 Dividend Revenues	Dividends earned from investing in other companies
650 Other Revenues	Miscellaneous sources of revenues
Expenses	
700 Cost of Goods Sold	Cost of products sold in the ordinary course of business
710 Repairs & Maintenance	Cost of routine maintenance and upkeep of buildings/equipment
720 Advertising Expense	Cost of advertising services obtained during the period
721 Depreciation Expense	Cost of plant and equipment used up during the period
722 Insurance Expense	Cost of insurance coverage for the current period
723 Salaries & Wages Expense	Cost of employees' salaries and wages for the period
724 Rent Expense	Cost of rent for the period
725 Supplies Expense	Cost of supplies used up during the period
726 Transportation Expense	Cost of freight to transport goods out to customers
727 Utilities Expense	Cost of power, light, heat, internet, and telephone for the period
728 Amortization Expense	Cost of intangible assets used up or expired during the period
730 Interest Expense	Interest charged on outstanding debts owed
740 Income Tax Expense	Taxes charged on reported earnings
Gains	
800 Gains on Asset Sales	Gains on asset sales (not central part of the business)
810 Gains on Sale of Investments	Gains from selling investments in other companies
Losses	
900 Losses on Asset Sales	Losses on asset sales (not central part of the business)
910 Losses on Sale of Investments	Losses from selling investments in other companies

Exhibit 3.3 isn't intended to be all-inclusive. It's just supposed to give you ideas about possible account names for companies that aren't in the hair business.

Before you move on to the next section, we need to make sure you aren't confusing the terms "expenses" and "expenditures," which are used interchangeably in everyday life. In accounting, these terms have precise and different meanings. **Expenditures** are any outflows of cash for any purpose—whether to pay down a bank loan, buy land, or pay an employee. Expenses, on the other hand, are defined as the costs incurred to generate revenue. Expenses can be incurred by spending cash, using up another asset, or incurring a liability—they don't always involve an immediate outflow of cash.

YOU SHOULD KNOW

Expenditures are any outflows of cash for any purpose.

STUDY

HOW TO ANALYZE OPERATING TRANSACTIONS

Cash-Based Measurements

Like most people, you probably look at the balance in your bank account to gauge your financial performance. If the overall balance increased this month, you'll likely take that as a sign that you've done a good job of managing your finances. If it has gone down, that's a clue that you need to tame yourself a little next month. The reason that the change in your bank balance tends to give a decent measure of financial performance is that your cash flows (in and out) occur close in time to the activities that cause those cash flows. For example, if you participate in a psychology experiment, you'll probably get paid on the spot, so the cash inflow is a good measure of how much your participation improved your financial situation. Similarly, if you pay cash for snacks, your declining cash balance will provide a timely measure of how much your snacking is costing you. As shown in Exhibit 3.4, when there is little delay between the underlying activities and the reporting of their effects on your bank balance, this **cash basis** of accounting is good enough.

YOU SHOULD KNOW

Cash basis accounting records revenues when cash is received and expenses when cash is paid.

exhibit 3.4	**Cash Basis Sometimes Provides a Decent Measure of Performance**

Explanation: The results of receiving cash from participating in an experiment and spending cash on junk food (the underlying activities) soon show up as changes in your bank account balance, which sometimes makes your bank balance a decent measure of financial performance.

POINT OF INTEREST
College students double their average credit-card debt and triple the number of credit cards in their wallets from the time they arrive on campus until graduation. *Source: Pittsburgh-Tribune Review,* January 6, 2002.

Generally speaking, the cash basis of accounting doesn't measure financial performance very well when transactions are conducted using credit rather than cash. The problem is that credit often introduces a significant delay between the time an activity occurs and the time it impacts the bank account balance. You probably realize that if you get a paycheck from your regular job only once a month, the results of your hard work don't show up until the end of the month. Similarly, if you go swipe-crazy with your credit card at the mall, these transactions won't affect your bank balance in the current month. This joyride only hits your cash balance the following month (or months) when you have to pay for what you bought. As shown in Exhibit 3.5, this delay in reporting the effects of the underlying activity makes the fluctuating bank balance a less useful measure of financial performance.

---

exhibit 3.5   Cash Basis Sometimes Provides a Poor Measure of Performance

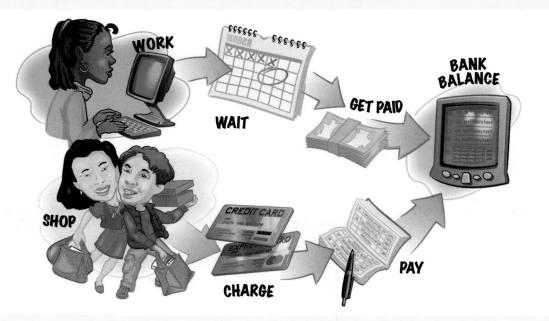

Explanation: The results of working and shopping (the underlying activities) eventually show up as changes in your bank account balance, but only after a significant delay. The delays between the underlying activities and their effects on the bank balance can cause your bank balance to be a poor measure of your financial performance.

Because most businesses use credit for their transactions, the cash basis of accounting is not likely to correspond to the business activities that actually occurred during a given period of time. For this reason, generally accepted accounting principles do not allow cash basis accounting to be used for external reporting of income. Instead, generally accepted accounting principles require the **accrual basis** of accounting. The "rule of accrual" is that the financial effects of business activities are measured and reported when the activities actually occur, not when the cash related to them is received or paid. That is, *revenues are reported when they are* **earned** *and expenses are reported when they are* **incurred.**

Accrual-Based Measurement of Revenues

Do you know what it means to recognize revenues when they are *earned?* Quite simply, it means a company reports revenue *when it performs the acts promised to the customer.* These promised acts might involve providing services (like a haircut) or transferring to the customer ownership of goods (such as a tube of hair gel). Although the company expects to receive cash in exchange for providing goods and services, the timing of that cash receipt

YOU SHOULD KNOW

Accrual basis accounting records revenues when they are earned and expenses when they are incurred, regardless of the timing of cash receipts or payments. Revenues are **earned** when goods or services are provided to customers at a determined price and with reasonable assurance of collection. Expenses are **incurred** when the economic benefits of an item are used up in the current period, resulting in a decrease in the company's resources.

does not dictate when revenues are reported. Instead, the key factor in determining when to report revenue is whether the company has done what it promised. This means that cash can be received (1) in the *same* period as the promised acts are performed, (2) in a period *before* the promised acts are performed, or (3) in a period *after* the promised acts are performed, as shown on the timeline in Exhibit 3.6. Let's see how to handle each of these cases.

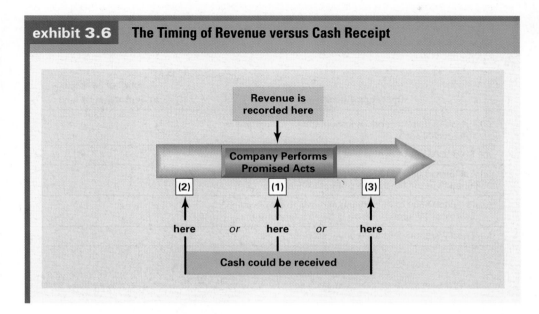

exhibit 3.6 **The Timing of Revenue versus Cash Receipt**

1. ***Cash is received in the*** **same** ***period as the promised acts are performed.*** This is a common occurrence for Supercuts stores because customers pay within a few minutes of getting a haircut. In these cases, when cash is received in the same period as the promised acts are performed, the company reports an increase in its cash and a corresponding increase in revenues. Notice that this transaction affects both the balance sheet (*cash*) and the income statement (*revenues*).

2. ***Cash is received in a period*** **before** ***the promised acts are performed.*** This situation occurs, for example, when your Supercuts Super Salon receives cash for gift certificates that can be used to pay for *future* haircuts. You know that your Supercuts Super Salon has to record the cash received, but it hasn't done anything yet to earn the revenue—so how does it account for this other part of the transaction? When cash is received before promised acts are performed, the company receiving the cash will report an increase in cash and an increase in a liability, which represents the obligation to perform the acts in the future. The liability for these advances from customers is called **unearned revenue.** There is no impact on the income statement at this time because the company has merely exchanged a promise for the customer's cash. When the company provides the promised goods or services to the customer, revenue will be reported on the income statement and the liability reduced.

3. ***Cash is to be received in a period*** **after** ***the promised acts are performed.*** This situation typically arises when a company sells to a customer on account. In these cases, the company will record revenue when the promised act has been performed and at that time also will record an asset called accounts receivable. When the company later collects cash from the customer, it will report an increase in cash and a corresponding reduction in accounts receivable. Again, notice that the income statement is affected in the period in which the promised acts are performed, not necessarily when cash is received.

It's worthwhile making sure you understand what sparks the recording of revenues because, later in this chapter, you'll see that this also triggers the recording of expenses.

COACH'S CORNER
When cash is received in the *same* period that the company performs the promised acts, revenues determined using accrual accounting do not differ from cash basis revenues.

YOU SHOULD KNOW

Unearned revenue is a liability representing a company's obligation to provide goods or services to customers in the future.

FAST FLASHBACK
An account receivable is like an IOU that gives the company the right to collect cash from a customer in the future.

To ensure that you've got a handle on this, spend a couple of minutes on the Self-Study Quiz.

HOW'S IT GOING?   A Self-Study Quiz

The following transactions are typical monthly operating activities for your Supercuts Super Salon. Indicate the amount of revenue, if any, that should be reported in September's income statement.

Operating Activity	Amount of Revenue in September (if any)
(a) Provided haircut services in September to customers for $15,000 cash.	
(b) Sold $300 of gift certificates at the beginning of September.	
(c) Customers used $100 of gift certificates to pay for haircuts in the third week of September.	
(d) Provided $500 of hair styling services to employees of a local TV station, which is billed every month.	
(e) The TV station paid $300 on its account.	

After you're done, check your answers with the solutions in the margin.

Quiz Answers

(a) $15,000—This amount is earned when services are provided.

(b) $0—No amount has been earned because no services (or goods) have been provided to the customer. At the time of this transaction, your salon will record the increase in cash, along with a liability to provide future services.

(c) $100—Now that the haircut services have been provided the revenue can be reported (and the gift certificate liability reduced).

(d) $500—This was earned when services were provided.

(e) $0—The revenue was earned and already recorded in *(d)*.

Accrual-Based Measurement of Expenses

Companies encounter a variety of **costs** when running a business. Initially, when costs are first incurred, accountants must decide whether to report them as assets or expenses. As Exhibit 3.7 indicates, this decision depends on whether the costs lead to something with a probable future economic benefit extending beyond the end of the current accounting period. Costs that do *not* benefit future periods are immediately reported as expenses on the income statement as they are incurred. For example, the cost of electrical services to power the hair dryers at your Supercuts Super Salon this month doesn't benefit future months (follow the top line in Exhibit 3.7), so it is reported as an expense on the income statement (called *Utilities Expense*).

In contrast, costs that have probable future economic benefits are **capitalized** initially as assets and later are transferred from assets (on the balance sheet) to expenses (on the income statement) when the assets' future benefits are used up with the passage of time or through physical use. When your Supercuts store pays for three months of rent in advance, the benefits from this cost extend over three months (see the downward-sloping line in Exhibit 3.7), so this cost is initially reported as an asset (*Prepaid Rent*). Later, as each month passes, your store will report *Rent Expense* equal to the amount of the prepaid rent benefit used up during that month (see the upward-sloping line in Exhibit 3.7).

When a company pays cash or uses credit to obtain something that doesn't benefit future periods, the transaction affects the balance sheet (reduced cash or increased liabilities) and the income statement (increased expenses). In other instances where costs involve items that benefit future periods, such as those jars of Barbicide that you see in hair salons, the downward-sloping line in Exhibit 3.7 indicates that these costs initially affect only the balance sheet (e.g., the asset *Supplies* increases at the same time cash is paid or credit is used). Eventually, when some of the asset's economic benefits are used up, these costs will move from the asset account (*Supplies*) on the balance sheet to an expense account (*Supplies Expense*) on the income statement (the upward-sloping line). The point to take away from this discussion is that expenses are the decreases in a company's resources when the

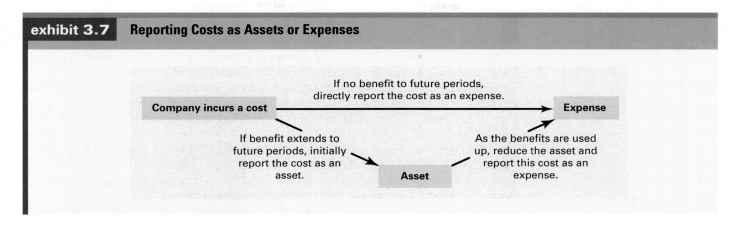

| exhibit 3.7 | **Reporting Costs as Assets or Expenses** |

company either (*a*) incurs a cost that does not benefit future periods or (*b*) uses up the economic benefits of an existing asset.

It's time for you to practice determining which costs should be reported as expenses on an income statement prepared according to accrual basis accounting. As you work through the Self-Study Quiz below, feel free to glance at Exhibit 3.7 for help.

HOW'S IT GOING? A Self-Study Quiz

This self-study quiz continues our look at the typical monthly operating activities for your Supercuts Super Salon, focusing this time on costs incurred by your salon. Indicate the amount of expense, if any, that should be reported in September's income statement.

Operating Activity	Amount of Expense in September (if any)
(f) Paid stylists $8,000 for wages related to services they provided in September.	
(g) Paid September, October, and November rent in advance, at a total cost of $7,200.	
(h) Paid $2,400 for an insurance policy that covers the period from September 1 until August 31 of next year.	
(i) Received a bill for $400 for running a newspaper ad in September. The bill will be paid in October.	
(j) Paid utility bills totaling $700 for services received and billed in September.	

After you're done, check your answers with the solutions in the margin.

Quiz Answers

(*f*) $8,000

(*g*) $2,400—The $7,200 provides mall space for three months, so only 1/3 of this cost is used up this month (1/3 × $7,200 = $2,400).

(*h*) $200—The $2,400 provides insurance coverage for a whole year, so only 1/12 of that has been used up this month ($2,400 × 1/12 = $200).

(*i*) $400—The newspaper ad ran in the current month.

(*j*) $700—The utilities services were received in the current month.

EVALUATE

TRANSACTIONS USING THE DEBIT/CREDIT FRAMEWORK

As you have seen, businesses can be involved in a variety of operating activities, many of which affect the income statement. Chapter 2 did not discuss how to account for these income statement effects because it focused on investing and financing activities, and their effects on assets, liabilities, and contributed capital. Now that you have seen how operating activities can result in revenues and expenses, you need to know how the debit/credit framework works with revenues and expenses. We present these effects by adding a little jet fuel to the transaction analysis model from Chapter 2.

For an animated tour of how transaction analysis and the rules of debits and credits apply to revenues and expenses, check out the tutorial on the DVD for use with this book.

Including Revenues and Expenses in the Transaction Analysis Model

Let's start with the basic ingredients from Chapter 2. That is, assets equals liabilities plus stockholders' equity, or A = L + SE. For now, we're going to focus on the stockholders' equity category. As you already know from Chapters 1 and 2, stockholders' equity represents the stockholders' investment in the company, which comes either from (1) *capital contributed* to the company by the stockholders (in exchange for stock) or (2) *earnings* that are *retained* in the company (rather than being distributed to stockholders as dividends).

What's new in this chapter is that we've introduced revenue and expense accounts. (We've also introduced gains and losses, but rather than make things overly complicated, we'll just focus on revenues and expenses for now. As you will see later, gains are accounted for just like revenues and losses are accounted for just like expenses.) You can think of the revenue and expense accounts as subcategories within the retained earnings account. The effects of revenue and expense transactions *eventually* flow into retained earnings, as suggested in Exhibit 3.8, but they aren't initially recorded there. Instead, each type of revenue and expense is accumulated in a separate account, making it easier to identify the amount to report for each of these line-items on the income statement.

Because revenue and expense accounts are subcategories of retained earnings, they are affected by debits and credits in the same way as all stockholders' equity accounts. You already know that increases in stockholders' equity are recorded on the right side. You also know that revenues increase net income, which increases the stockholders' equity account called retained earnings. So putting these ideas together should lead to the conclusion that **revenues are recorded on the right (credit).** Here's the logic again: increases in stockholders' equity are on the right, revenues increase stockholders' equity, so revenues are recorded on the right. *Decreases* in stockholders' equity are recorded on the left side, so since expenses decrease net income and retained earnings, **expenses are recorded on the left (debit).** Exhibit 3.8 summarizes these effects. The coach gives you another way of picturing how debits and credits affect the accounts.

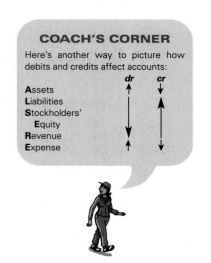

COACH'S CORNER

Here's another way to picture how debits and credits affect accounts:

	dr	*cr*
Assets		
Liabilities		
Stockholders' Equity		
Revenue		
Expense		

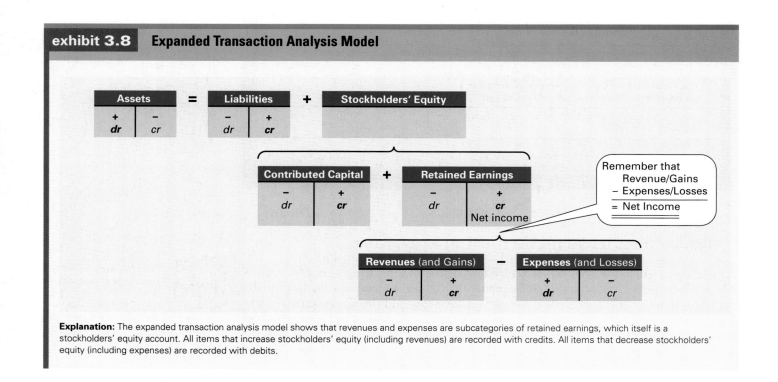

exhibit 3.8 Expanded Transaction Analysis Model

Explanation: The expanded transaction analysis model shows that revenues and expenses are subcategories of retained earnings, which itself is a stockholders' equity account. All items that increase stockholders' equity (including revenues) are recorded with credits. All items that decrease stockholders' equity (including expenses) are recorded with debits.

Using the DECIDES Approach with Revenues and Expenses

Okay, revenues are recorded with credits (on the right) and expenses are recorded with debits (on the left). Looks like you're ready to practice analyzing some transactions using the DECIDES approach from Chapter 2. To avoid adding too many new things all at once, we'll analyze the same transactions that appeared in the self-study quizzes earlier in this chapter. Don't skip this part because although you might understand *what* you're trying to do, the step of actually getting the accounting system to do what you want (using journal entries) requires practice, practice, and more practice.

To get a glimpse of the revenue accounting process at Sprint Corporation, check out the video on the DVD for use with this book.

Revenues

(a) Provided haircut services in September to customers for $15,000 cash.

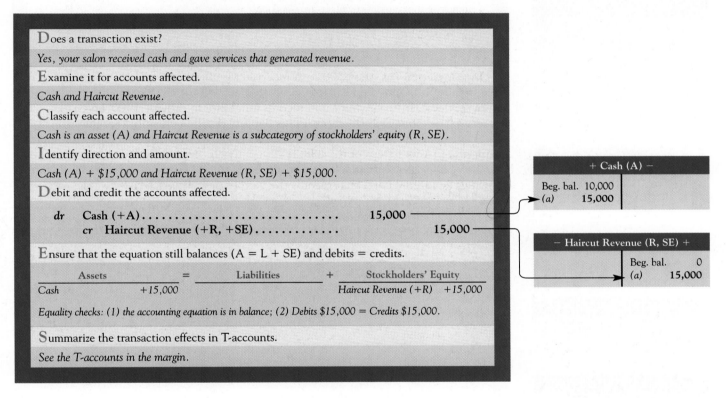

Does a transaction exist?
Yes, your salon received cash and gave services that generated revenue.
Examine it for accounts affected.
Cash and Haircut Revenue.
Classify each account affected.
Cash is an asset (A) and Haircut Revenue is a subcategory of stockholders' equity (R, SE).
Identify direction and amount.
Cash (A) + $15,000 and Haircut Revenue (R, SE) + $15,000.
Debit and credit the accounts affected.

	dr	Cash (+A)	15,000	
	cr	Haircut Revenue (+R, +SE)		15,000

Ensure that the equation still balances (A = L + SE) and debits = credits.

Assets	=	Liabilities	+	Stockholders' Equity
Cash	+15,000			Haircut Revenue (+R) +15,000

Equality checks: (1) the accounting equation is in balance; (2) Debits $15,000 = Credits $15,000.

Summarize the transaction effects in T-accounts.

See the T-accounts in the margin.

+ Cash (A) −	
Beg. bal. 10,000	
(a) 15,000	

− Haircut Revenue (R, SE) +	
	Beg. bal. 0
	(a) 15,000

The arrows above show how the journal entry is posted to the Cash and Haircut Revenue accounts. You've probably noticed that the Cash account has a beginning balance of $10,000. This is simply the balance from August 31 (in Chapter 2) that carries over to September 1 (in this chapter). The Haircut Revenue account has a balance of zero at the beginning of September because this is the first month of store operations.

(b) Sold $300 of gift certificates at the beginning of September.

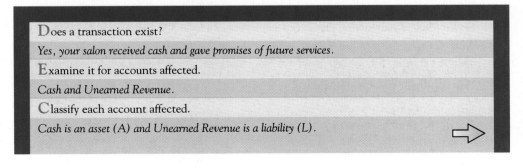

Does a transaction exist?
Yes, your salon received cash and gave promises of future services.
Examine it for accounts affected.
Cash and Unearned Revenue.
Classify each account affected.
Cash is an asset (A) and Unearned Revenue is a liability (L).

+ Cash (A) –	
Beg. bal. 10,000	
(a) 15,000	
(b) 300	

– Unearned Revenue (L) +	
	Beg. bal. 0
	(b) 300

Identify direction and amount.

Cash (+A) $300 and Unearned Revenue (+L) $300.

Debit and credit the accounts affected.

dr	**Cash (+A)**......................	300	
	cr Unearned Revenue (+L)		300

Ensure that the equation still balances (A = L + SE) and debits = credits.

Assets	=	Liabilities	+	Stockholders' Equity
Cash	+300	Unearned Revenue	+300	

Equality checks: (1) the accounting equation is in balance; (2) Debits $300 = Credits $300.

Summarize the transaction effects in T-accounts.

See the T-accounts in the margin.

In transaction *(b)*, the $300 cash received for gift certificates isn't recorded as revenue because it hasn't been earned yet (customers will use the gift certificates to pay for future services). Instead, your salon records a liability to provide $300 worth of services (or return the money) in the future. This liability is called unearned revenue.

As you may have noticed, a journal entry basically sums up the analyses completed during the first four steps of the DECIDES approach. Because we've already done these four steps as part of earlier self-study quizzes, in the remaining examples we'll start by showing the journal entry that records the various operating activities.

(c) Customers used $100 of gift certificates to pay for haircuts in the third week of September.

– Unearned Revenue (L) +	
	Beg. bal. 0
(c) 100	(b) 300

– Haircut Revenue (R, SE) +	
	Beg. bal. 0
	(a) 15,000
	(c) 100

Debit and credit the accounts affected.

dr	**Unearned Revenue (−L)**	100	
	cr Haircut Revenue (+R, +SE).............		100

Ensure that the equation still balances (A = L + SE) and debits = credits.

Assets	=	Liabilities	+	Stockholders' Equity
		Unearned Revenue	−100	Haircut Revenue (+R) +100

Equality checks: (1) the accounting equation is in balance; (2) Debits $100 = Credits $100.

Summarize the transaction effects in T-accounts.

See the T-accounts in the margin.

In transaction *(c)*, your Supercuts Super Salon provided services worth $100, which need to be recorded as revenue. In return for these services, your salon took back $100 of gift certificates, which reduces its liability for honoring them in the future. To account for this, journal entry *(c)* reduces the liability Unearned Revenue and increases Haircut Revenue.

(d) Provided $500 of hair styling services to employees of a local TV station, which is billed every month.

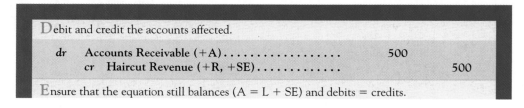

Debit and credit the accounts affected.

dr	**Accounts Receivable (+A)**...................	500	
	cr Haircut Revenue (+R, +SE).............		500

Ensure that the equation still balances (A = L + SE) and debits = credits.

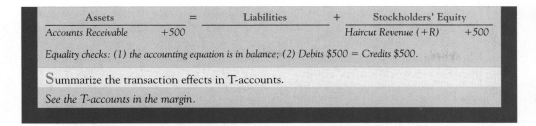

Assets	=	Liabilities	+	Stockholders' Equity	
Accounts Receivable	+500			*Haircut Revenue (+R)*	+500

Equality checks: (1) the accounting equation is in balance; (2) Debits $500 = Credits $500.

Summarize the transaction effects in T-accounts.

See the T-accounts in the margin.

+ Accounts Receivable (A) −	
Beg. bal. 0	
(d) 500	

− Haircut Revenue (R, SE) +	
	Beg. bal. 0
	(a) 15,000
	(c) 100
	(d) 500

Transaction (d) shows yet another instance where revenues are recorded based on whether services have been provided, not whether cash has been received. Because services have been provided, your salon has earned revenue and now has the right to collect $500 from the TV station. The right to collect money is an asset called Accounts Receivable.

(e) The TV station paid $300 on its account.

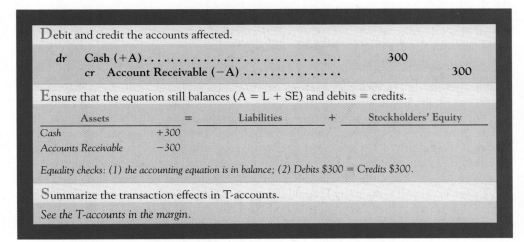

Debit and credit the accounts affected.

dr	Cash (+A)...............................	300	
	cr Account Receivable (−A)		300

Ensure that the equation still balances (A = L + SE) and debits = credits.

Assets	=	Liabilities	+	Stockholders' Equity
Cash	+300			
Accounts Receivable	−300			

Equality checks: (1) the accounting equation is in balance; (2) Debits $300 = Credits $300.

Summarize the transaction effects in T-accounts.

See the T-accounts in the margin.

+ Cash (A) −	
Beg. bal. 10,000	
(a) 15,000	
(b) 300	
(e) 300	

+ Accounts Receivable (A) −	
Beg. bal. 0	
(d) 500	(e) 300

Expenses

Okay, now it's time to switch to transactions involving expenses. Remember that expenses are decreases in a company's resources that arise when the company either incurs a cost that does not benefit future periods or uses up the economic benefits of an existing asset.

(f) Paid stylists $8,000 for wages related to services they provided in September.

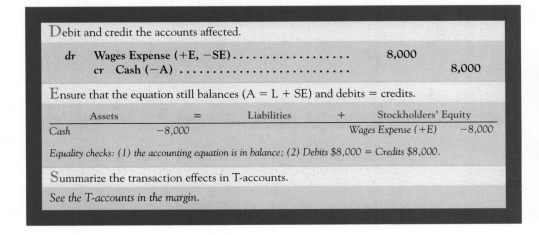

Debit and credit the accounts affected.

dr	Wages Expense (+E, −SE).................	8,000	
	cr Cash (−A)		8,000

Ensure that the equation still balances (A = L + SE) and debits = credits.

Assets	=	Liabilities	+	Stockholders' Equity	
Cash	−8,000			*Wages Expense (+E)*	−8,000

Equality checks: (1) the accounting equation is in balance; (2) Debits $8,000 = Credits $8,000.

Summarize the transaction effects in T-accounts.

See the T-accounts in the margin.

+ Wages Expense (E, SE) −	
Beg. bal. 0	
(f) 8,000	

+ Cash (A) −	
Beg. bal. 10,000	
(a) 15,000	(f) 8,000
(b) 300	
(e) 300	

The cost incurred in transaction (*f*) does not create a future benefit for your Supercuts Super Salon because it relates to work done earlier in the month, so it is recorded as an expense of the current month. The increase in wages expense is shown as a *negative* change in stockholders' equity (see the "Ensure" step) because increases in expenses cause decreases in stockholders' equity.

(g) Paid September, October, and November rent in advance, at a total cost of $7,200.

+ Prepaid Rent (A) –	
Beg. bal. 0	
(g) 7,200	

+ Cash (A) –			
Beg. bal. 10,000			
(a) 15,000	(f)		8,000
(b) 300	(g)		7,200
(e) 300			

Debit and credit the accounts affected.

dr	**Prepaid Rent (+A)**........................	7,200	
	cr **Cash (−A)**		7,200

Ensure that the equation still balances (A = L + SE) and debits = credits.

Assets		=	Liabilities	+	Stockholders' Equity
Cash	−7,200				
Prepaid Rent	+7,200				

Equality checks: (1) the accounting equation is in balance; (2) Debits $7,200 = Credits $7,200.

Summarize the transaction effects in T-accounts.

See the T-accounts in the margin.

Notice that *not* every operating transaction immediately affects the income statement. Transaction (*g*) involves paying for the right to use the rented mall space for three months following the payment. At the time the payment is made, this cost provides a future economic benefit to your Supercuts Super Salon (mall space for three months), so it is reported as an asset called Prepaid Rent. Each month, after the rented space has been used, your salon will reduce the Prepaid Rent asset and show the amount used up as rent expense. The adjustment needed to report September's rent expense of $2,400 will be covered in Chapter 4.

(h) Paid $2,400 for an insurance policy that covers the period from September 1 until August 31 of next year.

+ Prepaid Insurance (A) –	
Beg. bal. 0	
(h) 2,400	

+ Cash (A) –			
Beg. bal. 10,000			
(a) 15,000	(f)		8,000
(b) 300	(g)		7,200
(e) 300	(h)		2,400

Debit and credit the accounts affected.

dr	**Prepaid Insurance (+A)**....................	2,400	
	cr **Cash (−A)**		2,400

Ensure that the equation still balances (A = L + SE) and debits = credits.

Assets		=	Liabilities	+	Stockholders' Equity
Cash	−2,400				
Prepaid Insurance	+2,400				

Equality checks: (1) the accounting equation is in balance; (2) Debits $2,400 = Credits $2,400.

Summarize the transaction effects in T-accounts.

See the T-accounts in the margin.

Transaction (*h*) provides another example of a prepayment that is initially recorded as an asset. The adjustment to record September's insurance expense of $200 will be covered in Chapter 4.

(i) Received a bill for $400 for running a newspaper ad in September. The bill will be paid in October.

Debit and credit the accounts affected.

> dr Advertising Expense (+E, −SE)............ 400
>   cr Accounts Payable (+L) 400

Ensure that the equation still balances (A = L + SE) and debits = credits.

Assets	=	Liabilities	+	Stockholders' Equity
		Accounts Payable +400		Advertising Expense (+E) −400

Equality checks: (1) the accounting equation is in balance; (2) Debits $400 = Credits $400.

Summarize the transaction effects in T-accounts.

See the T-accounts in the margin.

+ Advertising Expense (E, SE) −		
Beg. bal.	0	
(i)	400	

− Accounts Payable (L) +		
		Beg. bal. 630
		(i) 400

HOW'S IT GOING?   A Self-Study Quiz

For transaction *(j)*, complete the journal entry and then check your answer against the solution in the margin. If you need some help, take a look back at transaction *(f)*.

(j) Paid utility bills totaling $700 for services received and billed in September.

Debit and credit the accounts affected.

> dr [ ] .... [ ]
>   cr [ ] .... [ ]

Ensure that the equation still balances (A = L + SE) and debits = credits.

Assets	=	Liabilities	+	Stockholders' Equity
Cash −700				Utilities Expense (+E) −700

Equality checks: (1) the accounting equation is in balance; (2) Debits $700 = Credits $700.

Summarize the transaction effects in T-accounts.

See the T-accounts in the margin.

+ Utilities Expense (E, SE) −		
Beg. bal.	0	
(j)	700	

+ Cash (A) −			
Beg. bal. 10,000			
(a)	15,000	*(f)*	8,000
(b)	300	*(g)*	7,200
(e)	300	*(h)*	2,400
		(j)	700

Calculating Account Balances

Now that the effects of the journal entries have been entered into the T-accounts, it's time to calculate the ending account balances. In Exhibit 3.9 on page 104, we have included all the T-accounts for your Supercuts Super Salon (from this chapter as well as Chapter 2). You've heard it before, but we'll just remind you that the ending balance in each account is determined by adding the amounts on the + side and subtracting the amounts on the − side.

Unadjusted Trial Balance

After posting journal entries to the various accounts, it's usually a good idea to check that the total recorded debits equal the total recorded credits. Unlike computerized accounting systems that prevent you from letting the accounting records get out of balance, it's

exhibit 3.9   Supercuts Super Salon T-Accounts (beginning balances are taken from Exhibit 2.9)

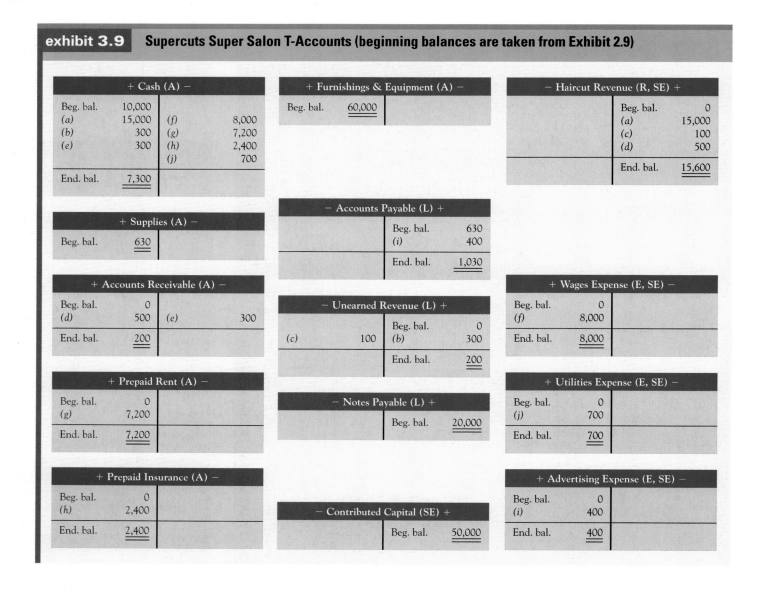

+ Cash (A) −

Beg. bal.	10,000		
(a)	15,000	(f)	8,000
(b)	300	(g)	7,200
(e)	300	(h)	2,400
		(j)	700
End. bal.	7,300		

+ Supplies (A) −

Beg. bal.	630

+ Accounts Receivable (A) −

Beg. bal.	0		
(d)	500	(e)	300
End. bal.	200		

+ Prepaid Rent (A) −

Beg. bal.	0	
(g)	7,200	
End. bal.	7,200	

+ Prepaid Insurance (A) −

Beg. bal.	0	
(h)	2,400	
End. bal.	2,400	

+ Furnishings & Equipment (A) −

Beg. bal.	60,000	

− Accounts Payable (L) +

	Beg. bal.	630
	(i)	400
	End. bal.	1,030

− Unearned Revenue (L) +

		Beg. bal.	0
(c)	100	(b)	300
		End. bal.	200

− Notes Payable (L) +

	Beg. bal.	20,000

− Contributed Capital (SE) +

	Beg. bal.	50,000

− Haircut Revenue (R, SE) +

	Beg. bal.	0
	(a)	15,000
	(c)	100
	(d)	500
	End. bal.	15,600

+ Wages Expense (E, SE) −

Beg. bal.	0	
(f)	8,000	
End. bal.	8,000	

+ Utilities Expense (E, SE) −

Beg. bal.	0	
(j)	700	
End. bal.	700	

+ Advertising Expense (E, SE) −

Beg. bal.	0	
(i)	400	
End. bal.	400	

YOU SHOULD KNOW

A **trial balance** is a list of all accounts and their balances, which is used to check on the equality of recorded debits and credits.

easy to make mistakes when you're doing it by hand. Typical mistakes involve (a) posting a debit as a credit, (b) posting only part of a journal entry, (c) recording the wrong amount, or (d) miscalculating the ending balance.

The best way to ensure your accounts are "in balance" is to prepare a **trial balance.** The trial balance isn't part of the financial statements. It's actually an internal report used to determine whether total debits equal total credits. Exhibit 3.10 shows a trial balance, which lists all of the account names in one column (usually in financial statement order) and their ending balances (from Exhibit 3.9) in the appropriate debit or credit column.

If your trial balance indicates that total debits don't equal total credits, you will experience a sickening feeling in your stomach because this means you've made an error somewhere in preparing or posting the journal entries. Don't panic or start randomly changing numbers. The first thing to do when you find yourself in a hole is stop digging. Calmly go back to your journal entries and T-account postings and find what you did wrong (using the hints on page 64).

If you haven't already scanned the trial balance in Exhibit 3.10, take a moment to do it now. Notice that the title says *unadjusted* trial balance. It is called this because several adjustments will have to be made at the end of the accounting period to update the accounts. For example, some of the benefits of prepaid rent and prepaid insurance were

exhibit 3.10   Sample Unadjusted Trial Balance

SUPERCUTS SUPER SALON
Unadjusted Trial Balance
As of September 30

Account Name	Debits	Credits
Cash	$ 7,300	
Supplies	630	
Accounts Receivable	200	
Prepaid Rent	7,200	
Prepaid Insurance	2,400	
Furnishings & Equipment	60,000	
Accounts Payable		$ 1,030
Unearned Revenue		200
Notes Payable		20,000
Contributed Capital		50,000
Haircut Revenue		15,600
Wages Expense	8,000	
Utilities Expense	700	
Advertising Expense	400	
Totals	$86,830	$86,830

COACH'S CORNER

Even if total debits equal total credits, it's still possible that you've made an error. For example, if you accidentally debit an asset rather than an expense, total debits would still equal total credits. So if they don't balance, you know you've made an error. If they do balance, it's still possible that a mistake has been made (and you just don't know it).

used up in September, but this wasn't recorded yet. If you're really sharp, you'll also have noticed that income taxes haven't been calculated and recorded yet. Although it's possible to prepare preliminary financial statements using the numbers on the unadjusted trial balance, most companies don't. Typically, they wait until after the final adjustments are made. These adjustments will ensure the revenues and expenses are up-to-date and complete so that the (adjusted) net income number will provide a good indication about whether the company was profitable during the period. Don't worry about how to make the end-of-period adjustments yet. We'll spend all of Chapter 4 on that. For now, just realize that the accounts still have to be adjusted before we can prepare financial statements that follow generally accepted accounting principles.

Summarizing How to Account for Revenues and Expenses

To this point of the chapter, you've analyzed some transactions—10 actually—that involve operating activities. While this is a good introduction, it doesn't quite prepare you for the variety of operating activities that most companies engage in. What you really need is a general summary of everything you've learned about revenues, expenses, and journal entries, and then lots of practice applying it to a broad range of activities.

In the following sections, we summarize the basic structure of journal entries that are used to account for a variety of operating transactions. The exhibits in these sections can save time and make things clear for you, but only if you read them and understand them. So take the time now to read each exhibit and think about how the specific transactions that you saw earlier in this chapter fit with the summaries.

Accounting for Revenues: A Summary

Remember that revenues are recorded when the business fulfills its promise to provide goods or services to customers, which is not necessarily the same time that cash is received. Because of this, we look at three cases, where cash is received (1) at the *same* time as the promised acts are performed, (2) *before* the promised acts are performed, and (3) *after* the promised acts are performed. Start by reading the explanation in Exhibit 3.11 on page 106 and then read the middle, left, and right panels (in that order).

exhibit 3.11   A Summary of How Revenues Are Recorded

Accrual Basis Journal Entries for Revenues

(2) If cash is received **before** the company delivers goods/services, a liability (*Unearned Revenue*) is created because the company still owes goods/services. Later, when revenue is earned, this liability is reduced and *Revenue* is recorded.

(1) If cash is received in the **same** period that the company delivers goods/services, only one journal entry is needed to record both *Cash* received and the type of *Revenue* earned.

(3) If cash is not received until **after** the company delivers goods/services, an asset account (*Accounts Receivable*) is created when the *Revenue* is recorded. Later, this asset is reduced when the customers pay *Cash* to the company for the amount the company is owed.

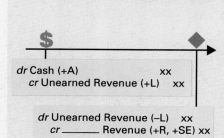

cash received BEFORE revenue is earned

dr Cash (+A)   xx
  cr Unearned Revenue (+L)   xx

dr Unearned Revenue (−L)   xx
  cr _____ Revenue (+R, +SE) xx

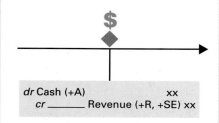

cash at the SAME time as revenue

dr Cash (+A)   xx
  cr _____ Revenue (+R, +SE) xx

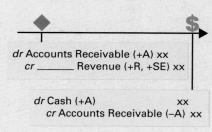

cash received AFTER revenue is earned

dr Accounts Receivable (+A) xx
  cr _____ Revenue (+R, +SE) xx

dr Cash (+A)   xx
  cr Accounts Receivable (−A) xx

Explanation: In the three different situations above, the red diamond (◆) indicates the point in time at which the company performs the promised act of delivering to the customer goods/services. The green dollar sign ($) indicates the point in time at which the company receives cash from the customer for the promised act.

COACH'S CORNER

Journal entries in the left panel of Exhibit 3.11 correspond to transactions *(b)* and *(c)* earlier in this chapter. The middle panel corresponds to transaction *(a)*. The right panel corresponds to transactions *(d)* and *(e)*.

Did you notice how the panels in Exhibit 3.11 correspond to the revenue transactions for Supercuts Super Salon analyzed earlier in this chapter? If you didn't, see the coach for some hints. In Exhibit 3.11, we use a generic label "_____ Revenue" with the expectation that you will fill in the blank with whatever type of revenue you are recording. That is, when accounting for revenue from cutting hair, you should use an account name like Haircut Revenue. If it's revenue generated from sales of inflatable sumo costumes, you could call it Sales Revenue.

Accounting for Expenses: A Summary

Under accrual accounting, expenses are recorded when incurred (by acquiring items that do not have future economic benefits or by using up the economic benefits of assets that were acquired in previous periods). Expenses are not necessarily incurred at the same time that cash is paid. Because of this, we look at three cases, where cash is paid (1) at the *same* time the expense is incurred, (2) *before* the expense is incurred, and (3) *after* the expense is incurred. Start by reading the explanation at the bottom of Exhibit 3.12 and then read the middle, left, and right panels (in that order). Go ahead and read the exhibit before continuing on below.

COACH'S CORNER

The first journal entry in the left panel of Exhibit 3.12 corresponds to transactions *(g)* and *(h)* earlier in this chapter. The middle panel corresponds to transactions *(f)* and *(j)*. The first journal entry in the right panel corresponds to transaction *(i)*.

Did you notice which panels in Exhibit 3.12 correspond to the expense transactions for Supercuts Super Salon analyzed earlier in this chapter? If you didn't, see the coach for some help. In Exhibit 3.12, we use a generic label "_____ Expense" with the expectation that you will fill in the blank with whatever type of expense you are recording. Similarly, we use the generic asset name "Prepaid Expense" with the expectation that you will use more specific asset names such as prepaid rent or supplies.

You've now seen how the operating activities of a business are analyzed to determine revenues, expenses, and net income for the period. In the final section of this chapter, we'll take a closer look at the accounting concepts that make this all possible.

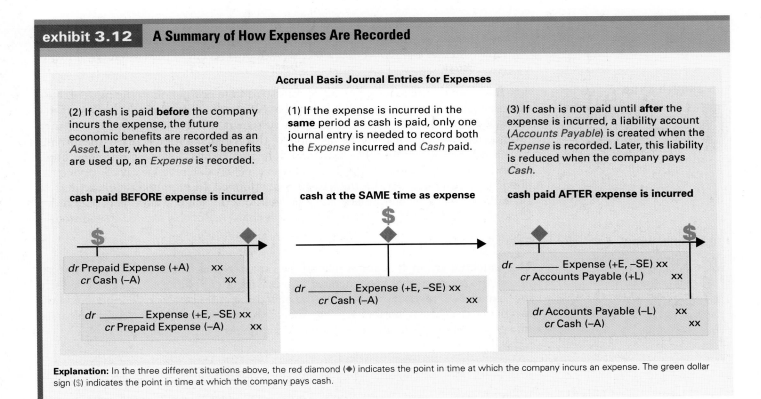

exhibit 3.12 **A Summary of How Expenses Are Recorded**

Accrual Basis Journal Entries for Expenses

(2) If cash is paid **before** the company incurs the expense, the future economic benefits are recorded as an *Asset*. Later, when the asset's benefits are used up, an *Expense* is recorded.

(1) If the expense is incurred in the **same** period as cash is paid, only one journal entry is needed to record both the *Expense* incurred and *Cash* paid.

(3) If cash is not paid until **after** the expense is incurred, a liability account (*Accounts Payable*) is created when the *Expense* is recorded. Later, this liability is reduced when the company pays *Cash*.

cash paid BEFORE expense is incurred

dr Prepaid Expense (+A)   xx
  cr Cash (–A)   xx

dr _____ Expense (+E, –SE) xx
  cr Prepaid Expense (–A)   xx

cash at the SAME time as expense

dr _____ Expense (+E, –SE) xx
  cr Cash (–A)   xx

cash paid AFTER expense is incurred

dr _____ Expense (+E, –SE) xx
  cr Accounts Payable (+L)   xx

dr Accounts Payable (–L)   xx
  cr Cash (–A)   xx

Explanation: In the three different situations above, the red diamond (◆) indicates the point in time at which the company incurs an expense. The green dollar sign ($) indicates the point in time at which the company pays cash.

RECONSIDER

THE INCOME STATEMENT CONCEPTS THAT USERS RELY ON

Some people mistakenly think that net income, as reported on the income statement, is money that can be paid out to stockholders. As you've learned in this chapter, net income is not the same thing as cash. Revenues and expenses are not recorded based on the timing of cash receipts and payments. Instead, they are reported according to two key concepts: the *revenue principle* and the *matching principle*.

The Revenue Principle

The **revenue principle** defines when it is appropriate to record revenues in the accounting system. Earlier in this chapter, you learned to record revenues by focusing on whether the acts promised to customers (haircuts) had been performed. You may not have realized it, but there actually were three more conditions that were met, allowing revenue to be reported.[2] The four conditions of the revenue principle are:

1. *Delivery has occurred or services have been rendered.* The company must perform all or substantially all of the acts promised to the customer (by providing goods or services).
2. *There is persuasive evidence of an arrangement for customer payment.* In exchange for the company's performance, the customer must provide cash or a promise to pay cash.
3. *The price is fixed or determinable.* The company must be able to put a reliable number on the amount of revenue related to performing the promised acts.

YOU SHOULD KNOW

The **revenue principle** is a concept that requires that revenues be recorded when they are earned, rather than when cash is received for them.

---

[2]For a thorough discussion of these conditions, see Thomas Phillips, Michael Leuhlfing, and Cynthia Daily, "The Right Way to Recognize Revenue," *Journal of Accountancy*, June 2001, pp. 39–46.

4. *Collection is reasonably assured.* For cash sales, collection is never in question since cash is received when promised acts are performed. For credit sales, the company will judge whether cash collection is likely based on a review of the customer's ability to pay.

To ensure that revenue reporting is consistent from one period to the next, all businesses adopt a **revenue recognition policy** that defines the time at which they report revenues from providing goods or services to customers. Most companies describe their revenue recognition policy in the first note to their financial statements. Typically, revenue is reported when the above four conditions are first met. Like your Supercuts Super Salon, Regis Corporation has the policy of recording its salon revenues when services are provided to customers. At this time, Regis has performed the promised act of cutting hair (Condition 1) and a determinable price (Condition 3) is paid by customers (Condition 2), so the probability of collecting cash is (more than) reasonably assured (Condition 4).

The Matching Principle

The **matching principle** requires that all relevant expenses be recorded in the same period as the revenues that are generated from having incurred the expenses. By "matching" expenses to revenues recorded in the period, expenses can then be subtracted from revenues to produce a "bottom line" net income number that provides a reasonable measure of the company's financial performance for the period.

Unethical Violations of the Revenue Principle and the Matching Principle

ETHICAL

ISSUE

What happens to corporate executives who violate the revenue and matching principles? Well, if their violations result in fraudulent financial statements, they'll likely go to jail. Exhibit 3.13 shows a few recent cases where this has happened.

Imagine what it must be like to be the guy in Exhibit 3.13 who is starting a 12-year prison sentence at the age of 71. It's probably just as bad as having to face 25 years in jail when you're only 23. That's what Barry Minkow got in the 1980s when the company he was managing defrauded investors by recording revenue and accounts receivable that didn't even exist. He's served his time and now is actually helping government regulators, investigators, and prosecutors unravel the kinds of fraud that he once committed.

exhibit 3.13   **Unethical Behavior and Its Consequences**

The CEO	The Fraud	Conviction/Plea	The Outcome
Martin Grass, 49 Rite Aid Corp.	Booked rebates from drug companies before they were earned.	Pleaded guilty, June 2003.	Sentenced to eight years.
Donald Ferrarini, 71 Underwriters Financial Group	Reported nonexistent revenues; made a losing company look like a profit maker.	Convicted, February 1999.	Sentenced to 12 years, one month.
Chan Desaigoudar, 61 California Micro Devices	Led staff to record sales for products not shipped—or not even manufactured.	Convicted, July 1998.	Sentenced to three years.
Paul Safronchik, 35 Home Theater Products Intl.	Invented customers and sales to show profits when, in reality, the company lost money.	Pleaded guilty, December 1996.	Sentenced to three years, one month.

What's Coming Up

In this chapter, we discussed how accountants analyze a company's operating activities, as the starting point for determining net income for the period. The next step will be to fully adjust the financial statements so that they are complete and up to date at the end of the accounting period. This adjustment process is the main topic for Chapter 4.

FOR YOUR REVIEW

DEMONSTRATION CASE

This case is a continuation of the Goodbye Grass Corporation case introduced in Chapter 2. The company was established and property and equipment were purchased. The balance sheet at April 30, 2006, based on only the investing and financing activities (from Chapter 2) is as follows:

GOODBYE GRASS CORPORATION			
Balance Sheet			
At April 30, 2006			
Assets		**Liabilities**	
Current Assets:		*Current Liabilities:*	
Cash	$ 3,800	Notes Payable	$ 4,400
Notes Receivable	1,250		
Total Current Assets	5,050	**Stockholders' Equity**	
Equipment	4,600	Contributed Capital	9,000
Land	3,750	**Total Liabilities and**	
Total Assets	**$13,400**	**Stockholders' Equity**	**$13,400**

The following activities also occurred during April 2006:

a.   Purchased and used gasoline for mowers and edgers, paying $90 in cash at a local gas station.

b.   In early April, received $1,600 cash from the city in advance for lawn maintenance service for April through July ($400 each month). The entire amount is to be recorded as Unearned Revenue.

c.   In early April, purchased $300 of insurance covering six months, April through September. The entire payment is to be recorded as Prepaid Insurance.

d.   Mowed lawns for residential customers who are billed every two weeks. A total of $5,200 of service was billed in April.

e.   Residential customers paid $3,500 on their accounts.

f.   Paid wages every two weeks. Total cash paid in April was $3,900.

g.   Received a bill for $320 from the local gas station for additional gasoline purchased on account and used in April.

h.   Paid $40 interest on notes owed to XYZ Lawn Supply and the hardware store.

i.   Paid $100 on accounts payable.

Required:

1.   a.   On a separate worksheet, set up T-accounts for Cash, Accounts Receivable, Notes Receivable, Prepaid Insurance, Equipment, Land, Accounts Payable, Unearned Revenue, Notes Payable, Contributed Capital, Retained Earnings, Mowing Revenue, Wages Expense, Fuel Expense, and Interest Expense. For the accounts shown on the balance sheet above, enter the balance as the opening balance in the corresponding T-accounts. For the remaining T-accounts, enter a beginning balance of $0.

b.   Analyze each transaction with the goal of preparing a separate worksheet that shows journal entries and indicates their effects on the basic accounting equation (Assets =

Liabilities + Stockholders' Equity). Include the equality checks: (1) the accounting equation is in balance, and (2) Debits = Credits.

c.   Enter the effects of each transaction in the appropriate T-accounts. Identify each amount with its letter in the list of activities above.

d.   Compute balances in each of the T-accounts.

2.   Use the amounts in the T-accounts to prepare an unadjusted trial balance for Goodbye Grass Corporation at April 30, 2006.

After completing the above requirements, check your answers with the following suggested solution.

Suggested Solution

1.   *Transaction analysis, journal entries, and T-accounts:*

(a)   dr   Fuel Expense (+E, −SE).   90
       cr   Cash (−A)   90

Assets		=	Liabilities	+	Stockholders' Equity	
Cash	− 90				Fuel Expense (+E)	− 90

Equality checks: (1) the accounting equation is in balance; (2) Debits $90 = Credits $90.

(b)   dr   Cash (+A).   1,600
       cr   Unearned Revenue (+L)   1,600

Assets		=	Liabilities		+	Stockholders' Equity
Cash	+ 1,600		Unearned Revenue	+ 1,600		

Equality checks: (1) the accounting equation is in balance; (2) Debits $1,600 = Credits $1,600.

(c)   dr   Prepaid Insurance (+A)   300
       cr   Cash (−A)   300

Assets		=	Liabilities	+	Stockholders' Equity
Cash	− 300				
Prepaid Insurance	+ 300				

Equality checks: (1) the accounting equation is in balance; (2) Debits $300 = Credits $300.

(d)   dr   Accounts Receivable (+A)   5,200
       cr   Mowing Revenue (+R, +SE)   5,200

Assets		=	Liabilities	+	Stockholders' Equity	
Accounts Receivable	+ 5,200				Mowing Revenue (+R)	+ 5,200

Equality checks: (1) the accounting equation is in balance; (2) Debits $5,200 = Credits $5,200.

(e)   dr   Cash (+A).   3,500
       cr   Accounts Receivable (−A)   3,500

Assets		=	Liabilities	+	Stockholders' Equity
Cash	+ 3,500				
Accounts Receivable	− 3,500				

Equality checks: (1) the accounting equation is in balance; (2) Debits $3,500 = Credits $3,500.

(f)   dr   Wages Expense (+E, −SE).   3,900
       cr   Cash (−A)   3,900

Assets	=	Liabilities	+	Stockholders' Equity
Cash − 3,900				Wages Expense (+E) − 3,900

Equality checks: (1) the accounting equation is in balance; (2) Debits $3,900 = Credits $3,900.

(g) dr Fuel Expense (+E, −SE)........................ 320
    cr Accounts Payable (+L) 320

Assets	=	Liabilities	+	Stockholders' Equity
		Accounts Payable + 320		Fuel Expense (+E) − 320

Equality checks: (1) the accounting equation is in balance; (2) Debits $320 = Credits $320.

(h) dr Interest Expense (+E, −SE).................... 40
    cr Cash (−A) 40

Assets	=	Liabilities	+	Stockholders' Equity
Cash − 40				Interest Expense (+E) − 40

Equality checks: (1) the accounting equation is in balance; (2) Debits $40 = Credits $40.

(i) dr Accounts Payable (−L)........................ 100
    cr Cash (−A) 100

Assets	=	Liabilities	+	Stockholders' Equity
Cash − 100		Accounts Payable − 100		

Equality checks: (1) the accounting equation is in balance; (2) Debits $100 = Credits $100.

T-accounts:

+ Cash (A) −			
Bal. fwd. 3,800			
(b) 1,600	90	(a)	
(e) 3,500	300	(c)	
	3,900	(f)	
	40	(h)	
	100	(i)	
End. bal. 4,470			

+ Accounts Receivable (A) −			
Beg. bal. 0			
(d) 5,200	3,500	(e)	
End. bal. 1,700			

+ Notes Receivable (A) −	
Bal. fwd. 1,250	
End. bal. 1,250	

+ Prepaid Insurance (A) −	
Beg. bal. 0	
(c) 300	
End. bal. 300	

+ Equipment (A) −	
Bal. fwd. 4,600	
End. bal. 4,600	

+ Land (A) −	
Bal. fwd. 3,750	
End. bal. 3,750	

− Accounts Payable (L) +			
		0	Beg. bal.
(i) 100		320	(g)
		220	End. bal.

− Unearned Revenue (L) +		
	0	Beg. bal.
	1,600	(b)
	1,600	End. bal.

− Notes Payable (L) +		
	4,400	Bal. fwd.
	4,400	End. bal.

− Contributed Capital (SE) +		
	9,000	Bal. fwd.
	9,000	End. bal.

− Retained Earnings (SE) +		
	0	Beg. bal.
	0	End. bal.

− Mowing Revenue (R) +		
	0	Beg. bal.
	5,200	(d)
	5,200	End. bal.

+ Wages Expense (E) −		
Beg. bal. 0		
(f) 3,900		
End. bal. 3,900		

+ Fuel Expense (E) −		
Beg. bal. 0		
(a) 90		
(g) 320		
End. bal. 410		

+ Interest Expense (E) −		
Beg. bal. 0		
(h) 40		
End. bal. 40		

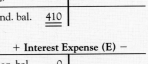

COACH'S CORNER

Balances carried forward from the previous month (Chapter 2) are indicated by the abbreviation Bal. fwd.

2. *Unadjusted trial balance:*

GOODBYE GRASS CORPORATION		
Unadjusted Trial Balance		
As of April 30, 2006		
Account Name	**Debits**	**Credits**
Cash	$ 4,470	
Accounts Receivable	1,700	
Notes Receivable	1,250	
Prepaid Insurance	300	
Equipment	4,600	
Land	3,750	
Accounts Payable		$ 220
Unearned Revenue		1,600
Notes Payable		4,400
Contributed Capital		9,000
Retained Earnings		0
Mowing Revenue		5,200
Wages Expense	3,900	
Fuel Expense	410	
Interest Expense	40	
Totals	**$20,420**	**$20,420**

CHAPTER SUMMARY

LO1 Explain and select income statement account titles. p. 90

- The income statement reports net income, which is calculated by combining

    Revenues—increases in assets or settlements of liabilities from ongoing operations.

    Expenses—decreases in assets or increases in liabilities from ongoing operations.

    Gains—increases in assets or settlements of liabilities from peripheral activities.

    Losses—decreases in assets or increases in liabilities from peripheral activities.

- See Exhibit 3.3 on page 92 for a list of common account titles.

LO2 Apply transaction analysis to operating transactions. p. 93

- Revenues are recognized when earned, which is usually when the company performs the acts promised to customers. The timing of cash receipt does not dictate when revenues are recognized.

- Expenses are recognized when incurred, which happens when the economic benefits of an item are used up in the current period, resulting in a decrease in the company's resources. The timing of cash payment does not dictate when expenses are recognized.

LO3 Use journal entries and T-accounts to show how operating transactions affect the balance sheet and income statement. p. 97

- The expanded transaction analysis model includes revenues and expenses as subcategories of retained earnings:

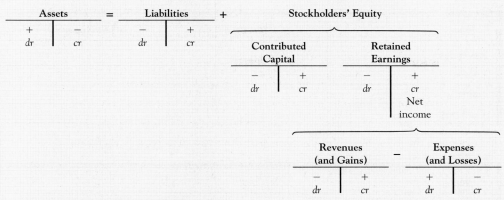

- In journal entry format, increases in revenues are recorded with credits and increases in expenses are recorded with debits.

Prepare an unadjusted trial balance. p. 103   **LO4**

- The unadjusted trial balance is a list of all accounts and their unadjusted balances, and is used to check on the equality of recorded debits and credits.

Explain the revenue and matching principles. p. 107   **LO5**

- The two key concepts underlying the income statement are

  Revenue principle—recognize revenues when (1) delivery has occurred, (2) there is persuasive evidence of an arrangement for customer payment, (3) the price is fixed or determinable, and (4) collection is reasonably assured.

  Matching principle—recognize expenses when they are incurred in generating revenue.

KEY TERMS TO KNOW

Accrual Basis
  Accounting p. 94
Capitalized p. 96
Cash Basis
  Accounting p. 93
Costs p. 96

Expenditures p. 93
Expenses p. 90
Gains p. 91
Losses p. 91
Matching Principle p. 108

Revenues p. 90
Revenue Principle p. 107
Revenue Recognition
  Policy p. 108

FOR YOUR PRACTICE

QUESTIONS

1. Indicate the income statement equation and define each element.
2. Explain the difference between
   a. Revenues and gains.
   b. Expenses and losses.
3. Define *accrual accounting* and contrast it with cash basis accounting.
4. What four conditions must normally be met for revenue to be recognized under accrual basis accounting?
5. Explain the matching principle.
6. Explain why stockholders' equity is increased by revenues and decreased by expenses.
7. Explain why revenues are recorded as credits and expenses as debits.
8. Complete the following table by entering either *debit* or *credit* in each cell:

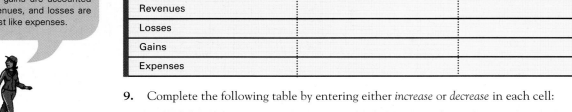

Item	Increase	Decrease
Revenues		
Losses		
Gains		
Expenses		

9. Complete the following table by entering either *increase* or *decrease* in each cell:

Item	Debit	Credit
Revenues		
Losses		
Gains		
Expenses		

MULTIPLE CHOICE

To practice more multiple choice questions, check out the DVD for use with this book.

1. Which of the following items is not a specific account in a company's chart of accounts?
   a. Gain on sale of investments.   c. Revenue.
   b. Net income.   d. Unearned revenue.

2. Which of the following is not one of the four conditions that normally must be met for revenue to be recognized according to the revenue principle for accrual basis accounting?
   a. The price is fixed or determinable.
   b. Services have been performed.
   c. Cash already has been collected.
   d. Evidence of an arrangement for customer payment exists.

3. The matching principle controls
   a. Where on the income statement expenses should be presented.
   b. How costs are allocated between Cost of Goods Sold (sometimes called Cost of Sales) and general and administrative expenses.
   c. The ordering of current assets and current liabilities on the balance sheet.
   d. When costs are recognized as expenses on the income statement.

4. Which of the following would not be considered a recurring item on the income statement?
   a. Administrative expenses.   c. Selling expenses.
   b. Sales revenues.   d. Loss on disposal of a business division.

5. If a company decides to record an expenditure as an asset rather than as an expense, how will this decision affect net income in the current period?
   a. Net income will be higher.
   b. Net income will be lower.
   c. Net income will not be affected by this decision.
   d. It's a mystery; nobody really knows.

6. When should a company report the cost of an insurance policy as an expense?
   a. When the company first signs the policy.
   b. When the company pays for the policy.
   c. When the company receives the benefits from the policy, over its period of coverage.
   d. When the company receives payments from the insurance company for its insurance claims.

7. When expenses exceed revenues in a given period (and there are no gains or losses),
   a. Stockholders' equity will not be impacted.
   b. Stockholders' equity will be increased.
   c. Stockholders' equity will be decreased.
   d. One cannot determine the impact on stockholders' equity without additional information.

8. Which account is *least* likely to be debited when revenue is recorded?
   a. Accounts payable   c. Cash
   b. Accounts receivable   d. Unearned revenue

9. Guessco reported the following amounts on its income statement: total revenues, $31,500; interest expense, $300; net income, $1,600; income tax expense, $900; and operating income, $2,800. What was the amount of Guessco's operating expenses?
   a. $1,200
   b. $28,700
   c. $29,000
   d. $29,900
10. Which of the following is the entry to be recorded by a law firm when it receives a retainer from a new client that will be earned when services are provided in the future?
   a. *Debit* to Accounts Receivable; *credit* to Legal Services Revenue.
   b. *Debit* to Unearned Revenue; *credit* to Legal Services Revenue.
   c. *Debit* to Cash; *credit* to Unearned Revenue.
   d. *Debit* to Unearned Revenue; *credit* to Cash.

MINI-EXERCISES Available with McGraw-Hill's Homework Manager

M3-1 Identifying Important Accounting Terms
LO1, LO2, LO5

Complete the following crossword puzzle, using the clues provided in the box on the right.

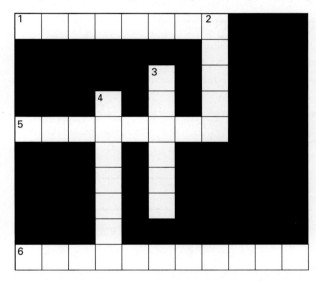

Across
1 The principle that requires expenses to be recorded when incurred to earn revenue.
5 Costs that result when a company sacrifices resources to generate revenue.
6 An outflow of cash for any purpose.

Down
2 Arise from peripheral transactions; have the effect of increasing net income.
3 Arise from peripheral transactions; have the effect of decreasing net income.
4 The principle that determines when sales should be reported.

M3-2 Reporting Cash Basis versus Accrual Basis Income
LO1, LO2

Mostert Music Company had the following transactions in March:

a. Sold instruments to customers for $10,000; received $6,000 in cash and the rest on account. The cost of the instruments was $7,000.
b. Purchased $4,000 of new instruments inventory; paid $1,000 in cash and owed the rest on account.
c. Paid $600 in wages for the month.
d. Received a $200 bill for utilities that will be paid in April.
e. Received $1,000 from customers as deposits on orders of new instruments to be sold to the customers in April.

Complete the following statements:

Cash Basis Income Statement		Accrual Basis Income Statement	
Revenues:		Revenues:	
Cash sales	$	Sales to customers	$
Customer deposits			
Expenses:		Expenses:	
Inventory purchases		Cost of sales	
Wages paid		Wages expense	
		Utilities expense	
Cash income	$_____	Net income	$_____

FAST FLASHBACK

Cash basis accounting records revenues when cash is received and expenses when cash is paid. **Accrual basis** accounting records revenues when they are earned and expenses when they are incurred, regardless of the timing of cash receipts or payments.

LO2 M3-3 Identifying Revenues

The following transactions are July 2007 activities of Bob's Bowling, Inc., which operates several bowling centers. If revenue is to be recognized in July, indicate the amount. If revenue is not to be recognized in July, explain why.

Activity	Amount or Explanation
a. Bob's collected $10,000 from customers for games played in July.	
b. Bob's billed a customer for $200 for a party held at the center on the last day of July. The bill is to be paid in August.	
c. Bob's received $1,000 from credit sales made to customers last month (in June).	
d. The men's and women's bowling leagues gave Bob's advance payments totaling $1,500 for the fall season that starts in September.	

LO2 M3-4 Identifying Expenses

The following transactions are July 2007 activities of Bob's Bowling, Inc., which operates several bowling centers. If an expense is to be recognized in July, indicate the amount. If an expense is not to be recognized in July, explain why.

Activity	Amount or Explanation
e. Bob's paid $1,000 to plumbers for repairing a broken pipe in the restrooms.	
f. Bob's paid $2,000 for the June electricity bill and received the July bill for $2,200, which will be paid in August.	
g. Bob's paid $4,000 to employees for work in July.	

LO3 M3-5 Recording Revenues

For each of the transactions in M3-3, write the journal entry using the format shown in the chapter.

LO3 M3-6 Recording Expenses

For each of the transactions in M3-4, write the journal entry using the format shown in the chapter.

LO2 M3-7 Determining the Financial Statement Effects of Operating Activities Involving Revenues

The following transactions are July 2007 activities of Bob's Bowling, Inc., which operates several bowling centers. For each of the following transactions, complete the spreadsheet, indicating the amount and effect (+ for increase and − for decrease) of each transaction. Write NE if there is no effect. The first transaction is provided as an example. (*Hint:* Remember that revenues and expenses affect the balance sheet because they are subcategories of retained earnings.)

Transaction	Balance Sheet			Income Statement		
	Assets	Liabilities	Stockholders' Equity	Revenues	Expenses	Net Income
a. Bob's collected $10,000 from customers for games played in July.	+10,000	NE	+10,000	+10,000	NE	+10,000
b. Bob's billed a customer for $200 for a party held at the center on the last day of July. The bill is to be paid in August.						

c. Bob's received $1,000 from credit sales made to customers last month (in June).	
d. The men's and women's bowling leagues gave Bob's advance payments totaling $1,500 for the fall season that starts in September.	

M3-8 Determining the Financial Statement Effects of Operating Activities Involving Expenses

LO2

The following transactions are July 2007 activities of Bob's Bowling, Inc., which operates several bowling centers. For each of the following transactions, complete the spreadsheet, indicating the amount and effect (+ for increase and − for decrease) of each transaction. Write NE if there is no effect. The first transaction is provided as an example.

	Balance Sheet			Income Statement		
Transaction	**Assets**	**Liabilities**	**Stockholders' Equity**	**Revenues**	**Expenses**	**Net Income**
e. Bob's paid $1,000 to plumbers for repairing a broken pipe in the restrooms.	−1,000	NE	−1,000	NE	+1,000	−1,000
f. Bob's paid $2,000 for the June electricity bill and received the July bill for $2,200, which will be paid in August.						
g. Bob's paid $4,000 to employees for work in July.						

M3-9 Preparing an Income Statement

LO4

Given the transactions in M3-7 and M3-8 (including the examples), prepare an income statement for Bob's Bowling, Inc., for the month of July 2007.

EXERCISES   Available with McGraw-Hill's Homework Manager

E3-1 Matching Definitions with Terms

LO1, LO5

Match each definition with its related term by entering the appropriate letter in the space provided.

Term	Definition
____ 1. Expenses	A. Record expenses when incurred in earning revenue.
____ 2. Matching principle	B. A liability account used to record the obligation to provide future services or return cash that has been received before revenues have been earned.
____ 3. Revenue principle	
____ 4. Cash basis accounting	
____ 5. Unearned revenue	C. Costs that result when a company sacrifices resources to generate revenues.
____ 6. Accrual basis accounting	
____ 7. Prepaid expenses	D. Record revenues when certain criteria are met (delivery of goods or services has occurred, there is persuasive evidence of an arrangement, the price is fixed or determinable, and collection is reasonably assured).
	E. Record revenues when received and expenses when paid.
	F. An asset account used to record the benefits obtained when cash is paid before expenses are incurred.
	G. Record revenues when earned and expenses when incurred.

LO1, LO2   **E3-2 Identifying Revenues**

Revenues are normally recognized when the delivery of goods or services has occurred, there is persuasive evidence of an arrangement, the price is fixed or determinable, and collection is reasonably assured. The amount recorded is the sales price. The following transactions occurred in September:

a. A customer orders and receives 10 personal computers from Gateway.com. The customer promises to pay $25,000 within three months. Answer from Gateway's standpoint.

b. For $21,000 cash, Sam Shell Dodge sells a truck with a list, or "sticker," price of $24,000.

c. Dillard's Department Store orders 1,000 men's shirts from Arrow Shirt Company for $18 each for future delivery. The terms require payment in full within 30 days of delivery. Answer from Arrow's standpoint.

d. Arrow Shirt Company completes production of the shirts described in *c* and delivers the order. Answer from Arrow's standpoint.

e. Arrow receives payment from Dillard's for the order described in *c*. Answer from Arrow's standpoint.

f. A customer purchases a ticket from American Airlines in September for $500 cash to travel in December. Answer from American Airlines' standpoint.

Required:

For each of the transactions, if revenue is to be recognized in September, indicate the amount. If revenue is not to be recognized in September, explain why.

LO1, LO2   **E3-3 Identifying Revenues**

Revenues are normally recognized when the delivery of goods or services has occurred, there is persuasive evidence of an arrangement, the price is fixed or determinable, and collection is reasonably assured. The amount recorded is the sales price. The following transactions occurred in September:

a. General Motors issues $26 million in new common stock.

b. Cal State University receives $20,000,000 cash for 80,000 five-game season football tickets. None of the games have been played.

c. Cal State plays the first football game referred to in *b*.

d. Hall Construction Company signs a contract with a customer for the construction of a new $500,000 warehouse. At the signing, Hall receives a check for $50,000 as a deposit to be applied against amounts earned during the first phase of construction. Answer from Hall's standpoint.

e. A popular snowboarding magazine company receives a total of $1,800 today from subscribers. The subscriptions begin in the next fiscal year. Answer from the magazine company's standpoint.

f. Sears sells a $100 minifridge to a customer who charges the sale on his store credit card. Answer from the standpoint of Sears.

Required:

For each of the transactions, if revenue is to be recognized in September, indicate the amount. If revenue is not to be recognized in September, explain why.

LO1, LO2   **E3-4 Identifying Expenses**

Expenses are decreases in a company's resources that occur when the company either (1) incurs a cost that does not benefit future periods, or (2) uses up the economic benefits of existing assets. Assume the following transactions occurred in January:

a. Gateway pays its computer service technicians $90,000 in salary for the two weeks ended January 7. Answer from Gateway's standpoint.

b. At the beginning of January, Turner Construction Company pays $4,500 in worker's compensation insurance for the first three months of the year.

c. The McGraw-Hill Companies—publisher of this textbook and *BusinessWeek*—uses $1,000 worth of electricity and natural gas in January for which it has not yet been billed.

d. Pooler Company receives and pays in January a $1,500 invoice from a consulting firm for services received in January.

e. The campus bookstore receives 500 accounting texts at a cost of $50 each. The terms indicate that payment is due within 30 days of delivery.

f. Schergevitch Incorporated has its delivery van repaired in January for $280 and charges the amount on account.

Required:

For each of the transactions, if an expense is to be recognized in January, indicate the amount. If an expense is not to be recognized in January, indicate why.

E3-5 Identifying Expenses

LO1, LO2

Expenses are decreases in a company's resources that occur when the company either (1) incurs a cost that does not benefit future periods, or (2) uses up the economic benefits of existing assets. The following transactions occurred in January:

a. Sam Shell Dodge pays its salespersons $3,500 in commissions related to December automobile sales. Answer from Sam Shell Dodge's standpoint.
b. On January 31, Sam Shell Dodge determines that it will pay its salespersons $4,200 in commissions related to January sales. The payment will be made in early February. Answer from Sam Shell Dodge's standpoint.
c. A new grill is purchased and installed at a McDonald's restaurant at the end of the day on January 31. A $12,000 cash payment is made on that day.
d. The University of Florida orders 60,000 season football tickets from its printer and pays $6,000 in advance for the custom printing. The first game will be played in September. Answer from the university's standpoint.
e. A Houston Community College employee works eight hours, at $15 per hour, on January 31; however, payday is not until February 3. Answer from the college's point of view.
f. Wang Company paid $3,600 for a fire insurance policy on January 1. The policy covers 12 months beginning on January 1. Answer from Wang's point of view.
g. Ziegler Company, a farm equipment company, receives its phone bill at the end of January for $230 for January calls. The bill has not been paid to date.

Required:

For each of the transactions, if an expense is to be recognized in January, indicate the amount. If an expense is not to be recognized in January, indicate why.

E3-6 Determining Financial Statement Effects of Various Transactions

LO2

The following transactions occurred during a recent year:

a. Issued stock to owners for cash (example).
b. Borrowed cash from local bank.
c. Purchased equipment on credit.
d. Earned revenue, collected cash.
e. Incurred expenses, on credit.
f. Earned revenue, on credit.
g. Paid cash on account.
h. Incurred expenses, paid cash.
i. Earned revenue, collected half in cash, balance on credit.
j. Collected cash from customers on account.
k. Incurred expenses, paid half in cash, balance on credit.
l. Paid income tax expense for the period.

Required:

For each of the transactions, complete the table below, indicating the effect (+ for increase and − for decrease) of each transaction. Write NE if there is no effect. The first transaction is provided as an example. For a hint, see M3-7.

	Balance Sheet			Income Statement		
Transaction	Assets	Liabilities	Stockholders' Equity	Revenues	Expenses	Net Income
(a) (example)	+	NE	+	NE	NE	NE

LO2   **E3-7 Determining Financial Statement Effects of Various Transactions**

Wolverine World Wide, Inc., manufactures military, work, sport, and casual footwear and leather accessories under a variety of brand names, such as Caterpillar, Hush Puppies, Wolverine, and Steve Madden. The following transactions occurred during a recent year. Dollars are in thousands.

a.   Issued common stock to investors for $49,000 cash (example).
b.   Purchased $300,000 of additional supplies on account.
c.   Borrowed $58,000 on long-term notes.
d.   Purchased $18,600 in additional property, plant, and equipment.
e.   Incurred $87,000 in selling expenses, paying two-thirds in cash and owing the rest on account.
f.   Incurred $4,700 in interest expense.

Required:

For each of the transactions, complete the table below, indicating the effect (+ for increase and − for decrease) and amount of each transaction. Write NE if there is no effect. The first transaction is provided as an example. For a hint, see M3-7.

	Balance Sheet			Income Statement		
Transaction	**Assets**	**Liabilities**	**Stockholders' Equity**	**Revenues**	**Expenses**	**Net Income**
(a) (example)	+49,000	NE	+49,000	NE	NE	NE

LO2, LO3   **E3-8 Recording Journal Entries**

Sysco, formed in 1969, is America's largest marketer and distributor of food service products, serving nearly 250,000 restaurants, hotels, schools, hospitals, and other institutions. The following transactions are typical of those that occurred in a recent year. (All amounts are rounded to the nearest thousand.)

a.   Borrowed $80,000 from a bank, signing a short-term note payable.
b.   Provided $10,000 in service to customers, with $9,500 on account and the rest received in cash.
c.   Purchased plant and equipment for $130,000 in cash.
d.   Purchased $8,000 of inventory on account.
e.   Paid employee wages of $1,000.
f.   Received $410 on account from a customer.
g.   Purchased and used fuel of $400,000 in delivery vehicles during the year (paid for in cash).
h.   Paid $8,200 cash on accounts payable.
i.   Incurred $20,000 in utility expenses during the year, of which $15,000 was paid in cash and the rest owed on account.

Required:

For each of the transactions, prepare journal entries. Determine whether the accounting equation remains in balance and debits equal credits after each entry.

LO2, LO3   **E3-9 Recording Journal Entries**

Greek Peak Incorporated is a ski resort in upstate New York. The company sells lift tickets, ski lessons, and ski equipment. It operates several restaurants and rents townhouses to vacationing skiers. The following hypothetical December transactions are typical of those that occur at the resort.

a.   Borrowed $500,000 from the bank on December 1, signing a note payable, due in six months.
b.   Purchased a new snowplow for $20,000 cash on December 31.
c.   Purchased ski supplies for $10,000 on account to sell in the ski shop.
d.   Incurred $22,000 in routine maintenance expenses for the chairlifts; paid cash.
e.   Sold $72,000 of partial season passes (beginning in the new year) and received cash.
f.   Daily lift passes were sold this month for a total of $76,000 cash.
g.   Received a $320 deposit on a townhouse to be rented for five days in January.
h.   Paid half the charges incurred on account in c.
i.   Paid $18,000 in wages to employees for the month of December.

Required:

Prepare journal entries for each transaction. Be sure to categorize each account as an asset (A), liability (L), stockholders' equity (SE), revenue (R), or expense (E), and check that debits equal credits for each journal entry.

E3-10 Recording Journal Entries

L02, L03

Rowland & Sons Air Transport Service, Inc., has been in operation for three years. The following transactions occurred in February:

Feb. 1	Paid $200 for rent of hangar space in February.
Feb. 2	Purchased fuel supplies costing $450 on account for the next flight to Dallas.
Feb. 4	Received customer payment of $800 to ship several items to Philadelphia next month.
Feb. 7	Flew cargo from Denver to Dallas; the customer paid $900 for the air transport.
Feb. 10	Paid pilot $1,200 in wages for flying in January.
Feb. 14	Paid $60 for an advertisement run in the local paper on February 14.
Feb. 18	Flew cargo for two customers from Dallas to Albuquerque for $1,700; one customer paid $500 cash and the other asked to be billed.
Feb. 25	Purchased on account $1,350 in spare parts for the planes.

Required:

Prepare journal entries for each transaction. Be sure to categorize each account as an asset (A), liability (L), stockholders' equity (SE), revenue (R), or expense (E).

E3-11 Recording Journal Entries and Posting to T-Accounts

L02, L03, L05

Hurst's Piano Rebuilding Company has been operating for one year (2007). At the start of 2008, its income statement accounts had zero balances and its balance sheet account balances were as follows:

Cash	$ 6,000	Accounts payable	$ 8,000
Accounts receivable	25,000	Unearned revenue (deposits)	3,200
Supplies	1,200	Notes payable	40,000
Equipment	8,000	Contributed capital	8,000
Land	6,000	Retained earnings	9,000
Building	22,000		

Required:

1. Create T-accounts for the balance sheet accounts and for these additional accounts: Piano Rebuilding Revenue, Rent Revenue, Wages Expense, and Utilities Expense. Enter the beginning balances.

2. Prepare journal entries for the following January 2008 transactions, using the letter of each transaction as a reference:
    a. Received a $500 deposit from a customer who wanted her piano rebuilt.
    b. Rented a part of the building to a bicycle repair shop for $300 rent received in January.
    c. Delivered five rebuilt pianos to customers who paid $14,500 in cash.
    d. Delivered two rebuilt pianos to customers for $7,000 charged on account.
    e. Received $6,000 from customers as payment on their accounts.
    f. Received an electric and gas utility bill for $350 for January services to be paid in February.
    g. Ordered $800 in supplies.
    h. Paid $1,700 on account in January.
    i. Paid $10,000 in wages to employees in January for work done this month.
    j. Received and paid cash for the supplies in g.

3. Post the journal entries to the T-accounts. Show the unadjusted ending balances in the T-accounts.

LO4   **E3-12 Preparing an Unadjusted Trial Balance**

Refer to E3-11.

Required:

Use the balances in the completed T-accounts in E3-11 to prepare an unadjusted trial balance at the end of January 2008.

LO2, LO3, LO4   **E3-13 Inferring Operating Transactions and Preparing an Unadjusted Trial Balance**

ElectroGolf Corporation operates indoor golf simulators that allow individual customers and golf club members to experience courses like Pebble Beach and Augusta without leaving their own neighborhood. Its stores are located in rented space in malls and shopping centers. During its first month of business ended April 30, 2008, ElectroGolf Corporation completed eight transactions with the dollar effects indicated in the following schedule:

| Accounts | Dollar Effect of Each of the Eight Transactions | | | | | | | | Ending Balance |
	a	b	c	d	e	f	g	h	
Cash	$100,000	$(30,000)	$ (200)	$ 9,000	$(2,000)	$(1,000)		$2,000	
Accounts receivable				1,000					
Supplies			1,000						
Prepaid expenses					2,000				
Equipment		30,000							
Accounts payable			800				$1,200		
Unearned revenue								2,000	
Contributed capital	100,000								
Sales revenue				10,000					
Wages expense						1,000			
Utilities expense							1,200		

Required:

1. Write a brief explanation of transactions *a* through *h*. Include any assumptions that you made.
2. Compute the ending balance in each account and prepare an unadjusted trial balance for ElectroGolf Corporation on April 30, 2008.

LO1, LO2, LO3   **E3-14 Inferring Transactions and Computing Effects Using T-Accounts**

A recent annual report of Dow Jones & Company, the world leader in business and financial news and information (and publisher of *The Wall Street Journal*), included the following accounts. Dollars are in millions.

+ Accounts Receivable (A) –		+ Prepaid Expenses (A) –		– Unearned Revenue (L) +	
1/1	313	1/1	25		240	1/1
	2,573	?		43	?	?	328
12/31	295	12/31	26		253	12/31

Required:

1. For each T-account, describe the typical transactions that cause it to increase and decrease.
2. Express each T-account in equation format and then solve for the missing amounts (in millions). For example, the Accounts Receivable T-account can be expressed as: $313 + 2{,}573 - ? = 295$. By rearranging the equation, you can solve for $313 + 2{,}573 - 295 = ?$.

E3-15 Finding Financial Information as an Investor

You are evaluating your current portfolio of investments to determine those that are not performing to your expectations. You have all of the companies' most recent annual reports.

LO1, LO2

Required:

For each of the following, indicate where you would locate the information in an annual report.

1. The total cost incurred for repairs and maintenance during the year.
2. Accounts receivable.
3. Description of a company's revenue recognition policy.
4. The cost of wages incurred during the year.

SIMPLIFY WITH SPREADSHEETS

SS3-1 Analyzing Transactions and Preparing an Unadjusted Trial Balance

LO2, LO3, LO4

Assume you recently started up a new company that rents machines for making frozen drinks like smoothies, frozen juices, tea slush, and iced cappuccinos. For $100, your business will deliver a machine, provide supplies (straws, paper cups), set up the machine, and pick up the machine the next morning. Drink mix and other supplies are sold by other businesses in your city. Being a one-person operation, you are responsible for everything from purchasing to marketing to operations to accounting.

You've decided that you'll just write notes about what happens during the month and then do the accounting at the end of the month. You figure this will be more efficient. Plus, by waiting until the end of the month to do the accounting, you'll be less likely to make a mistake because by that time you'll be way past the accounting cycle chapters. Your notes said the following about your first month of operations:

Oct. 2	Incorporated Slusher Gusher Inc. and contributed $10,000 for stock in the company.
Oct. 12	Paid cash to buy three frozen drink machines on eBay at a total cost of $1,500. What a deal!
Oct. 13	Paid cash to buy $70 of supplies. Wal-Mart was packed.
Oct. 16	Received $500 cash for this past week's rentals. I'm rich!
Oct. 17	Determined that $45 of supplies had been used up. Hmm, looks like I'll need some more.
Oct. 20	Bought $100 of supplies on account. I can't believe the party store gave me credit like that.
Oct. 23	Feeling tired after a busy week (6 rentals this time). Received $400 cash and expect to receive $200 more sometime this week.
Oct. 25	Received $100 cash from one of the customers who hadn't paid up yet. Called the other customer to remind him I'm waiting.
Oct. 26	Ran an ad in the local paper today for $25 cash. Maybe that'll drum up some business.
Oct. 27	Received $150 cash for a two-machine All Saints Day party to be held on November 1. It's a good thing I got this money because no other bookings are in sight for the rest of the month.

Required:

Create a spreadsheet in which to record the effects of the October transactions and calculate end-of-month totals. Using the spreadsheet, prepare a trial balance that checks whether debits = credits. Because you're dealing with your own business this time, you want to be extra sure that you do this just right, so you e-mail your friend Billy for advice. Here's his reply:

From:	BillyTheTutor@yahoo.com
To:	HairZed@hotmail.com
Cc:	
Subject:	Excel Help

Wow, you're a CEO already? I always thought you were a mover and a shaker! So you want my advice on how to set up your spreadsheet? My advice is *read the last e-mail I sent*. The main thing that's new here is you'll need to include some columns for revenue and expenses under the stockholders' equity heading. Here's a screenshot of how the right-hand side of your worksheet might look just before you enter the October transactions. Notice that because stockholders' equity is decreased by expenses, the debit side is used to record expenses.

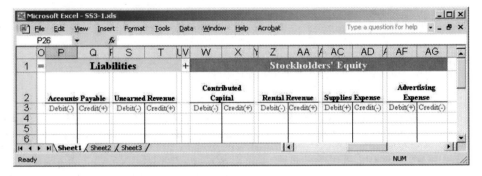

To prepare the trial balance, create three columns. In the first, copy and paste the account names (one per row). In the second column, link in each debit balance by entering = in a cell and then clicking on the debit total from the T-account. Repeat this with all the accounts. Then do the same with the credit balances. At the bottom of the trial balance, use the SUM function to compute totals.

Don't forget to save the file using a name that uniquely identifies you (as my true hero).

COACHED PROBLEMS

LO1, LO2, LO3

CP3-1   Recording Nonquantitative Journal Entries

The following list includes a series of accounts for B-ball Corporation, which has been operating for three years. These accounts are listed alphabetically and numbered for identification. Following the accounts is a series of transactions. For each transaction, indicate the account(s) that should be debited and credited by entering the appropriate account number(s) to the right of each transaction. If no journal entry is needed, write *none* after the transaction. The first transaction is used as an example.

Account No.	Account Title	Account No.	Account Title
1	Accounts payable	8	Income taxes payable
2	Accounts receivable	9	Note payable
3	Cash	10	Prepaid insurance
4	Contributed capital	11	Service revenue
5	Equipment	12	Supplies expense
6	Rent expense	13	Supplies
7	Income tax expense	14	Wages expense
		15	Wages payable

	Transactions	Debit	Credit
a.	Example: Purchased equipment for use in the business; paid one-third cash and signed a note payable for the balance.	5	3, 9
b.	Issued stock to new investors.		
c.	Paid cash for rent this period.		
d.	Collected cash for services performed this period.		
e.	Collected cash on accounts receivable for services performed last period.		
f.	Performed services this period on credit.		

COACH'S CORNER

h. Remember what the matching principle says.

k. You can think of this as two transactions: (1) incur expense and liability, and (2) pay part of the liability.

g. Paid cash on accounts payable for expenses incurred last period. _____ _____

h. Employees worked this period but won't be paid until next period. _____ _____

i. Purchased supplies to be used later; paid cash. _____ _____

j. Used some of the supplies for operations. _____ _____

k. Paid three-fourths of the income tax expense for the year; the balance will be paid next year. _____ _____

l. On the last day of the current period, paid cash for an insurance policy covering the next two years. _____ _____

CP3-2 Recording Journal Entries

LO2, LO3

Ryan Olson organized a new company, CollegeCaps, Inc. The company operates a small store in an area mall and specializes in baseball-type caps with logos printed on them. Ryan believes that his target market is college and high school students. You have been hired to record the transactions occurring in the first two weeks of operations.

a. May 1: Issued 1,000 shares of stock to investors for $30 per share.
b. May 1: Borrowed $50,000 from the bank to provide additional funding to begin operations; the note is due in two years.
c. May 1: Paid $2,400 for a one-year fire insurance policy (recorded as prepaid insurance).
d. May 3: Purchased furniture and fixtures for the store for $15,000 on account. The amount is due within 30 days.
e. May 4: Purchased a supply of Texas Tech, UNLV, and Washington State University baseball caps for the store for $1,800 cash.
f. May 5: Placed advertisements in local college newspapers for a total of $250 cash.
g. May 9: Sold caps for $400 cash. The caps had originally been bought by CollegeCaps for $150, as part of the May 4 transaction.
h. May 14: Made full payment for the furniture and fixtures purchased on account on May 3.

COACH'S CORNER

c. For convenience, simply record the full amount of the payment as an asset (called prepaid insurance). At the end of the month, this account will be adjusted to its proper balance. We will study this adjustment process in Chapter 4, so just leave it as prepaid insurance for now.

g. Notice that this is actually two transactions: (1) sale of caps to customers for cash, and (2) reduction of cap inventory, creating an expense.

Required:

For each of the transactions, prepare journal entries. Be sure to categorize each account as an asset (A), liability (L), stockholders' equity (SE), revenue (R), or expense (E).

CP3-3 Analyzing the Effects of Transactions Using T-Accounts and Preparing an Unadjusted Trial Balance

LO1, LO2, LO3, LO4

e**X**cel

Barbara Jone, a connoisseur of fine chocolate, opened Barb's Sweets in Stillwater on February 1, 2006. The shop specializes in a selection of gourmet chocolate candies. You have been hired as manager. Your duties include maintaining the store's financial records. The following transactions occurred in February 2006, the first month of operations.

a. Received four shareholders' contributions totaling $16,000 cash to form the corporation; issued stock.
b. Paid three months' rent for the store at $800 per month (recorded as prepaid rent).
c. Purchased supplies for $300 cash.
d. Purchased and received candy for $5,000, on account, due in 60 days.
e. Negotiated a two-year loan at the bank, depositing $10,000 in the company's bank account.
f. Used all of the money from e to purchase a computer for $2,500 and the balance for furniture and fixtures for the store.
g. Placed a grand opening advertisement in the local paper for $425 cash.
h. Made sales on Valentine's Day totaling $1,800; $1,525 was in cash and the rest on accounts receivable. The cost of the candy sold was $1,000.
i. Made a $500 payment on accounts payable.
j. Incurred and paid employee wages of $420.
k. Collected accounts receivable of $50 from customers.
l. Made a repair to one of the display cases for $120 cash.

COACH'S CORNER

b. For convenience, simply record the full amount of the payment as an asset (called prepaid rent). At the end of the month, this account will be adjusted to its proper balance. We will study this adjustment process in Chapter 4, so just leave it as prepaid rent for now.

h. Notice that this is actually two transactions: (1) sales to customers for cash and on account, and (2) reduction of candy inventory, creating a cost of goods sold expense.

l. Most repairs involve costs that do *not* provide extra future economic benefits. Repairs merely maintain an asset's existing benefits.

1. When preparing the T-accounts, you might find it useful to group them by type: assets, liabilities, stockholders' equity, revenues, and expenses.

Required:

1. Set up appropriate T-accounts for Cash, Accounts Receivable, Supplies, Candy Inventory, Prepaid Rent, Equipment, Furniture and Fixtures, Accounts Payable, Notes Payable, Contributed Capital, Sales Revenue, Cost of Goods Sold (Expense), Advertising Expense, Wages Expense, and Repair Expense. All accounts begin with zero balances.

2. Record in the T-accounts the effects of each transaction for Barb's Sweets in February, referencing each transaction in the accounts with the transaction letter. Show the unadjusted ending balances in the T-accounts.

3. Prepare an unadjusted trial balance at the end of February.

4. Refer to the revenues and expenses shown on the unadjusted trial balance. Based on this information, write a short memo to Barbara offering your opinion on the results of operations during the first month of business.

GROUP A PROBLEMS   Available with McGraw-Hill's Homework Manager

LO1, LO2, LO3

PA3-1 Recording Nonquantitative Journal Entries

The following is a series of accounts for Dewan & Allard, Incorporated, which has been operating for two years. The accounts are listed alphabetically and numbered for identification. Following the accounts is a series of transactions. For each transaction, indicate the account(s) that should be debited and credited by entering the appropriate account number(s) to the right of each transaction. If no journal entry is needed, write *none* after the transaction. The first transaction is given as an example.

Account No.	Account Title	Account No.	Account Title
1	Accounts payable	9	Land
2	Accounts receivable	10	Note payable
3	Advertising expense	11	Prepaid insurance
4	Buildings	12	Service revenue
5	Cash	13	Supplies expense
6	Contributed capital	14	Supplies
7	Income tax expense	15	Wages expense
8	Income taxes payable	16	Wages payable

	Transactions	Debit	Credit
a.	Example: Issued stock to new investors.	5	6
b.	Performed services for customers this period on credit.		
c.	Purchased on credit but did not use supplies this period.		
d.	Prepaid a fire insurance policy this period to cover the next 12 months.		
e.	Purchased a building this period by making a 20 percent cash downpayment and signing a note payable for the balance.		
f.	Collected cash this year for services that had been provided and recorded in the prior year.		
g.	Paid cash this period for wages that had been earned and recorded last period.		
h.	Paid cash for supplies that had been purchased on accounts payable in the prior period.		
i.	Paid cash for advertising expense incurred in the current period.		
j.	Incurred advertising expenses on credit to be paid next period, but recorded this period.		
k.	Collected cash for services rendered this period.		
l.	Used supplies on hand to clean the offices.		
m.	Recorded income taxes for this period to be paid at the beginning of the next period.		
n.	This period a shareholder sold some shares of her stock to another person for an amount above the original issuance price.		

LO2, LO3

PA3-2 Recording Journal Entries

Diana Mark is the president of ServicePro, Inc., a company that provides temporary employees for not-for-profit companies. ServicePro has been operating for five years; its revenues are increasing with each passing year. You have been hired to help Diana in analyzing the following transactions for the first two weeks of April:

April 2	Purchased office supplies for $500 on account.
April 5	Billed the local United Way office $1,950 for temporary services provided.
April 8	Paid $250 for supplies purchased and recorded on account last period.
April 8	Placed an advertisement in the local paper for $400 cash.
April 9	Purchased a new computer for the office costing $2,300 cash.
April 10	Paid employee wages of $1,200. Of this amount, $200 had been earned by employees in the prior period and already recorded in the Wages Payable account.
April 11	Received $1,000 on account from the local United Way office billed on April 5.
April 12	Purchased land as the site of a future office for $10,000. Paid $2,000 down and signed a note payable for the balance.
April 13	Issued 2,000 additional shares of stock for $40 per share in anticipation of building a new office.
April 14	Billed Family & Children's Service $2,000 for services rendered this month.
April 15	Received the April telephone bill for $245 to be paid next month.

Required:

For each of the transactions, prepare journal entries. Be sure to categorize each account as an asset (A), liability (L), stockholders' equity (SE), revenue (R), or expense (E).

PA3-3 Analyzing the Effects of Transactions Using T-Accounts and Preparing an Unadjusted Trial Balance

LO1, LO2, LO3, LO4

Spicewood Stables, Inc., was established in Dripping Springs, Texas, on April 1, 2007. The company provides stables, care for animals, and grounds for riding and showing horses. You have been hired as the new Assistant Controller. The following transactions for April 2007 are provided for your review.

a. Received contributions from five investors of $200,000 in cash ($40,000 each).
b. Built a barn for $142,000. The company paid half the amount in cash on April 1, 2007 and signed a three-year note payable for the balance.
c. Provided $15,260 in animal care services for customers, all on credit.
d. Rented stables to customers who cared for their own animals; received cash of $13,200.
e. Received from a customer $1,500 to board her horse in May, June, and July (record as unearned revenue).
f. Purchased hay and feed supplies on account for $3,210.
g. Paid $840 in cash for water utilities incurred in the month.
h. Paid $1,700 on accounts payable for previous purchases.
i. Received $1,000 from customers on accounts receivable.
j. Paid $4,000 in wages to employees who worked during the month.
k. At the end of the month, prepaid a two-year insurance policy for $3,600.
l. Received an electric utility bill for $1,200 for usage in April; the bill will be paid next month.

Required:

1. Set up appropriate T-accounts. All accounts begin with zero balances.
2. Record in the T-accounts the effects of each transaction for Spicewood Stables in April, referencing each transaction in the accounts with the transaction letter. Show the unadjusted ending balances in the T-accounts.
3. Prepare an unadjusted trial balance as of April 30, 2007.
4. Refer to the revenues and expenses shown on the unadjusted trial balance. Based on this information, write a short memo to the five owners offering your opinion on the results of operations during the first month of business.

GROUP B PROBLEMS

LO1, LO2, LO3

PB3-1 Recording Nonquantitative Journal Entries

Abercrombie & Fitch Co. is a specialty retailer of casual apparel. The company's brand was established in 1892. It became a public company in 1996 and then was spun off from The Limited in 1998. The following is a series of accounts for Abercrombie. The accounts are listed alphabetically and numbered for identification. Following the accounts is a series of transactions. For each transaction, indicate the account(s) that should be debited and credited by entering the appropriate account number(s) to the right of each transaction. If no journal entry is needed, write *none* after the transaction. The first transaction is given as an example.

Account No.	Account Title	Account No.	Account Title
1	Accounts payable	8	Rent expense
2	Accounts receivable	9	Supplies expense
3	Cash	10	Supplies
4	Contributed capital	11	Unearned revenue
5	Equipment	12	Wages expense
6	Interest revenue	13	Wages payable
7	Prepaid rent		

	Transactions	Debit	Credit
a.	Example: Incurred wages expense; paid cash.	12	3
b.	Collected cash on account.		
c.	Used up supplies (cash register tapes, etc.) this period.		
d.	Sold gift certificates to customers; none redeemed this period.		
e.	Purchased equipment, paying part in cash and charging the balance on account.		
f.	Paid cash to suppliers on account.		
g.	Issued additional stock for cash.		
h.	Paid rent to landlords for next month's use of mall space.		
i.	Earned and received cash for interest on investments.		

LO2, LO3

PB3-2 Recording Journal Entries

Robin Harrington established Time Definite Delivery on January 1. The following transactions occurred during the company's most recent quarter.

a. Issued stock for $80,000.
b. Provided delivery service to customers, receiving $72,000 in accounts receivable and $16,000 in cash.
c. Purchased equipment costing $82,000 and signed a long-term note for the full amount.
d. Incurred repair costs of $3,000 on account.
e. Collected $65,000 from customers on account.
f. Borrowed $90,000 by signing a long-term note.
g. Prepaid $74,400 cash to rent equipment and aircraft next quarter.
h. Paid employees $38,000 for work done during the quarter.
i. Purchased (with cash) and used $49,000 in fuel for delivery equipment.
j. Paid $2,000 on accounts payable.
k. Ordered, but haven't yet received, $700 in supplies.

Required:

For each of the transactions, prepare journal entries. Be sure to categorize each account as an asset (A), liability (L), stockholders' equity (SE), revenue (R), or expense (E).

LO1, LO2, LO3, LO4

PB3-3 Analyzing the Effects of Transactions Using T-Accounts and Preparing an Unadjusted Trial Balance

Jessica Pothier opened FunFlatables on June 1, 2006. The company rents out moon walks and inflatable slides for parties and corporate events. The company also has obtained the use of an abandoned ice rink located in a local shopping mall, where its rental products are displayed and available for casual hourly rental by mall patrons. The following transactions occurred during the first month of operations.

a. Jessica contributed $50,000 cash to the company in exchange for its stock.
b. Purchased inflatable rides and inflation equipment, paying $20,000 cash.
c. Received $5,000 cash from casual hourly rentals at the mall.
d. Rented rides and equipment to customers for $10,000. Received cash of $2,000 and the rest is due from customers.
e. Received $2,500 from a large corporate customer as a deposit on a party booking for July 4.
f. Began to prepare for the July 4th party by purchasing various party supplies on account for $600.
g. Paid $6,000 in cash for renting the mall space this month.
h. Prepaid next month's mall space rental charge of $6,000.
i. Received $1,000 from customers on accounts receivable.
j. Paid $4,000 in wages to employees for work done during the month.
k. Paid $1,000 for running a television ad this month.

Required:

1. Set up appropriate T-accounts. All accounts begin with zero balances.
2. Record in the T-accounts the effects of each transaction for FunFlatables in June, referencing each transaction in the accounts with the transaction letter. Show the unadjusted ending balances in the T-accounts.
3. Prepare an unadjusted trial balance for the end of June 2006.
4. Jessica has become alarmed at how quickly the company's cash balance has fallen. Refer to the revenues and expenses shown on the unadjusted trial balance and write a short memo to Jessica offering your opinion on the results of operations during the first month of business.

CASES & DISCUSSION STARTERS

FINANCIAL REPORTING AND ANALYSIS CASES

C&DS3-1 Finding Financial Information   LO1

Refer to the financial statements of Landry's Restaurants in Appendix A at the end of this book, or download the annual report from the *Cases* section of the text's Web site at www.mhhe.com/phillips.

Required:

1. Have Landry's total revenues increased or decreased in the most recent year? By how much? Calculate this change as a percentage of the previous year's total revenues by dividing the amount of the change by the previous year's revenues and multiplying by 100%.
2. State the amount of the largest expense on the most recent income statement and describe the transaction represented by the expense. Did this expense increase or decrease from the previous year and by what percentage?
3. Did Landry's report any nonoperating items in its most recent income statement? What percentage of revenues did these items represent? What percentage of net income did these items represent?

C&DS3-2 Comparing Financial Information   LO1

Refer to the financial statements of Dave & Buster's in Appendix B at the end of this book, or download the annual report from the *Cases* section of the text's Web site at www.mhhe.com/phillips.

Required:

1. Has Dave & Buster's total revenues increased or decreased in the most recent year? By how much? Calculate this change as a percentage of the previous year's total revenues. Is the trend in Dave & Buster's revenues more or less favorable than Landry's?

2. State the amount of the largest expense on the most recent income statement and describe the transaction represented by the expense. Did this expense increase or decrease and by what percentage, as compared to the previous year? Is the trend in Dave & Buster's largest expense more or less favorable than the trend for Landry's largest expense?

3. Did Dave & Buster's report any nonoperating items in its most recent income statement? What percentage of revenues did these items represent? What percentage of net income did these items represent? Do nonoperating items have a greater influence on the net income of Dave & Buster's or Landry's?

LO1, LO5

TEAM CASE

C&DS3-3 Internet-Based Team Research: Examining the Income Statement

As a team, select an industry to analyze. Using your Web browser, each team member should acquire the annual report or 10-K for one publicly traded company in the industry, with each member selecting a different company. (See C&DS1-3 in Chapter 1 for a description of possible resources for these tasks.)

Required:

1. On an individual basis, each team member should write a short report that lists the following information:
   a. The major revenue and expense accounts on the most recent income statement.
   b. Description of how the company has followed the conditions of the revenue principle.
   c. The percentage of revenues that go to covering expenses, and that are in excess of expenses (in other words, the percentage that remains as net income).

2. Then, as a team, write a short report comparing and contrasting your companies using these attributes. Discuss any patterns across the companies that you as a team observe. Provide potential explanations for any differences discovered.

ETHICS AND CRITICAL THINKING CASES

LO1, LO2, LO3, LO5

ETHICAL

ISSUE

C&DS3-4 Ethical Decision Making: A Real-Life Example

Read the following excerpt from a September 2, 2002, article in *Fortune* magazine and answer the questions that appear below.

> Forget about fraud. Companies don't need to lie, cheat, and steal to fool investors. Clever managers have always had, and continue to have, access to perfectly legal tricks to help make their balance sheets and income statements look better than they really are—tricks that *even today* won't jeopardize their ability to swear to the SEC that their books are on the up and up. . . . One of the most controversial of all number games—the one that got WorldCom in trouble—is to capitalize expenses. That can have a tremendous impact on the bottom line.

1. In this chapter, you learned that when a company incurs a cost, its accountants have to decide whether to record the cost as an asset or expense. This builds on Chapter 2, where you learned that it was appropriate to capitalize costs as assets, provided that they possess certain characteristics. What are those characteristics?

2. The author of the article argues that even with clear rules like those referenced in question 1 above, accounting still allows managers to use "tricks" like *capitalizing expenses*. What do you suppose the author means by the expression *capitalizing expenses*?

3. Suppose that, in the current year, a company inappropriately records a cost as an asset when it should be recorded as an expense. What is the effect of this accounting decision on the current year's net income? What is the effect of this accounting decision on the following year's net income?

4. Later in the article (not shown) the author says that the videogame industry is one where companies frequently capitalize software development costs as assets. These costs include wages paid to programmers, fees paid to graphic designers, and amounts paid to game testers. Evaluate whether software development costs are likely to possess the main characteristics possessed by all assets. Can you think of a situation where software development costs might not possess these main characteristics?

5. Do you think it is always easy and straightforward to determine whether costs should be capitalized or expensed? Do you think it is always easy and straightforward to determine whether a manager is acting ethically or unethically? Give examples to illustrate your views.

C&DS3-5 Ethical Decision Making: A Mini-Case

LO1, LO2, LO5

ETHICAL

ISSUE

Mike Lynch is the manager of an upstate New York regional office for an insurance company. As the regional manager, his pay package includes a base salary, commissions, and a bonus when the region sells new policies in excess of its quota. Mike has been under enormous pressure lately, stemming largely from two factors. First, he is experiencing a mounting personal debt due to a family member's illness. Second, compounding his worries, the region's sales of new insurance policies have dipped below the normal quota for the first time in years.

You have been working for Mike for two years, and like everyone else in the office, you consider yourself lucky to work for such a supportive boss. You also feel great sympathy for his personal problems over the last few months. In your position as accountant for the regional office, you are only too aware of the drop in new policy sales and the impact this will have on the manager's bonus. While you are working on the year-end financial statements, Mike stops by your office.

Mike asks you to change the manner in which you have accounted for a new property insurance policy for a large local business. A check for the premium, substantial in amount, came in the mail on December 31, the last day of the reporting year. The premium covers a period beginning on January 5. You deposited the check and correctly debited cash and credited an *unearned revenue* account. Mike says, "Hey, we have the money this year, so why not count the revenue this year? I never did understand why you accountants are so picky about these things anyway. I'd like you to change the way you've recorded the transaction. I want you to credit a *revenue* account. And anyway, I've done favors for you in the past, and I am asking for such a small thing in return." With that, he leaves your office.

Required:

How should you handle this situation? What are the ethical implications of Mike's request? Who are the parties who would be helped or harmed if you went along with the request? If you fail to comply with his request, how will you explain your position to him?

C&DS3-6 Critical Thinking: Analyzing Changes in Accounts and Preparing a Trial Balance

LO1, LO2, LO4

Hordichuk Painting Service Company was organized on January 20, 2008, by three individuals, each receiving 5,000 shares of stock from the new company. The following is a schedule of the cumulative account balances immediately after each of the first 10 transactions ending on January 31, 2008.

Accounts	Cumulative Balances								
	a	b	c	d	e	f	g	h	i
Cash	$75,000	$70,000	$85,000	$71,000	$61,000	$61,000	$46,000	$44,000	$60,000
Accounts receivable			12,000	12,000	12,000	26,000	26,000	26,000	10,000
Supplies					5,000	5,000	4,000	4,000	4,000
Office fixtures		20,000	20,000	20,000	20,000	20,000	20,000	20,000	20,000
Land				18,000	18,000	18,000	18,000	18,000	18,000
Accounts payable					3,000	3,000	3,000	1,000	1,000
Notes payable		15,000	15,000	19,000	19,000	19,000	19,000	19,000	19,000
Contributed capital	75,000	75,000	75,000	75,000	75,000	75,000	75,000	75,000	75,000
Paint revenue			27,000	27,000	27,000	41,000	41,000	41,000	41,000
Supplies expense							1,000	1,000	1,000
Wages expense					8,000	8,000	23,000	23,000	23,000

Required:

1. Analyze the changes in this schedule for each transaction; then explain the transaction. Transactions *a* and *b* are examples:

    a.   Cash increased $75,000, and Contributed Capital (stockholders' equity) increased $75,000. Therefore, transaction *a* was an issuance of the capital stock of the corporation for $75,000 cash.

    b.   Cash decreased $5,000, office fixtures (an asset) increased $20,000, and notes payable (a liability) increased $15,000. Therefore, transaction *b* was a purchase of office fixtures that cost $20,000. Payment was made as follows: cash, $5,000; notes payable, $15,000.

2. Based only on the preceding schedule after transaction *i*, prepare an unadjusted trial balance.

chapter four

Adjustments, Financial Statements, and the Quality of Financial Reporting

4

If you've ever used an online course management system, like Blackboard or WebCT, you'll know how great it is to be able to check your course standing at any given time. Even if you haven't used a system like this, just imagine what it would be like to be able to find out your course grade whenever you want. The key for making this kind of system work effectively is ensuring that it uses grade information that is up to date and complete. To be up to date, it needs to be adjusted for any test-score changes that your instructor has approved. To be complete, it needs to include the results of all assignments and tests that you've had graded. With up-to-date and complete information like this, you can know exactly where you stand in the course and you can make better-informed decisions about where to devote your limited study time during the upcoming week.

The same needs exist in business. For investors and creditors to decide where to devote their limited resources, they need financial reports that contain up-to-date and complete information. To ensure this kind of information is available, accountants adjust their company's accounting records before financial statements are prepared and released to users. These adjustments are used to update amounts already recorded in the accounting records and to include events that have occurred but haven't yet been recorded as transactions. For **SUPERCUTS** and Regis Corporation, this includes updating the supplies account for shampoo used during the month and including the interest that mounted on debt owed by the company. These kinds of adjustments are needed to ensure the financial statements include the financial results of *all* the company's activities for the period. They're also a key part of generally accepted accounting principles.

INSIDE LOOKING OUT

OUTSIDE LOOKING IN

This chapter continues our discussion of the accounting system, focusing specifically on the adjustments that are needed under accrual basis accounting. We continue to focus on Supercuts and its parent, Regis Corporation.

The Beauty of Our Business
REGIS CORPORATION

SUPERCUTS

mia & maxx HAIR STUDIO

STYLE AMERICA Family Hair Salon

Regis Corporation is nearly eight times larger than its nearest competitor.

FAST FLASHBACK

Accrual basis accounting requires that revenues and expenses be recorded *based on the activities of the accounting period*, regardless of whether cash has been received or paid during that period.

n the next section of this chapter, we'll help you to understand why adjustments are a necessary part of accrual basis accounting. Once you understand the purpose of adjustments, you'll be in a better position to learn about the process involved in figuring out what adjustments are needed and how they are recorded using journal entries, which is the focus for the second part of this chapter. In the third section, we consider how adjustments can affect external financial statement users. The final section reconsiders the complete process involved in preparing financial statements.

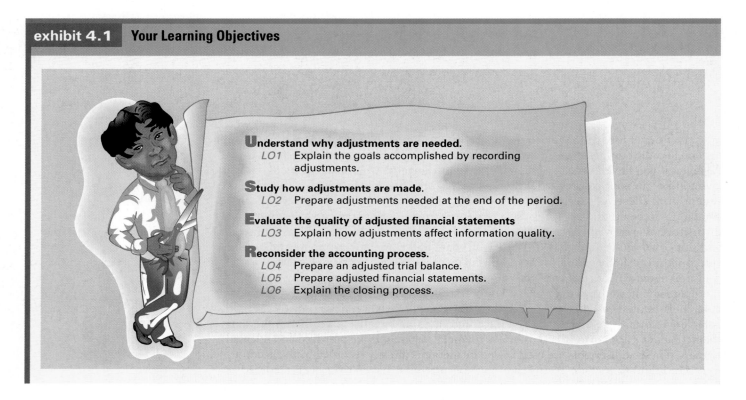

exhibit 4.1 **Your Learning Objectives**

Understand why adjustments are needed.
  LO1 Explain the goals accomplished by recording adjustments.

Study how adjustments are made.
  LO2 Prepare adjustments needed at the end of the period.

Evaluate the quality of adjusted financial statements
  LO3 Explain how adjustments affect information quality.

Reconsider the accounting process.
  LO4 Prepare an adjusted trial balance.
  LO5 Prepare adjusted financial statements.
  LO6 Explain the closing process.

UNDERSTAND

WHY ADJUSTMENTS ARE NEEDED

COACH'S CORNER

Deferral adjustments involve (1) updating amounts previously recorded ("deferred") as assets or liabilities, and (2) adjusting their related expenses or revenues. The accounts in a *deferral adjustment* always go in opposite directions. That is, a decrease in an asset goes with an increase in an expense, and a decrease in a liability goes with an increase in revenue.

Accounting systems are designed to record most recurring daily transactions, particularly any involving cash. This focus on cash is okay, but it does create a small problem. The problem is that cash is not always received in the period the company earns revenue and cash is not always paid in the period the company incurs expenses. The solution for this timing difference is to record journal entries at the end of every accounting period to adjust the amounts reported as revenues and expenses. After making these adjustments, the accounting system will include *all* of the revenues and expenses of the period, which ensures the income statement provides a meaningful measure of business success. These adjustments also ensure the related accounts on the balance sheet are (1) up to date and (2) complete. Two types of adjustments are recorded to accomplish these goals:

1. Deferral Adjustments

Deferral adjustments are used for updating accounts involving previously recorded transactions. If cash is exchanged before the related revenue or expense is recorded, deferral adjustments may be needed at the end of the accounting period to bring the accounting records *up to date*. In particular, deferral adjustments are needed in either of the following situations:

a. Some or all of an asset's future benefits have expired or been used up in the current period (but these expenses haven't been recorded as of the end of the period).

b. The company provides goods or services in the current period to satisfy an existing liability (but these revenues haven't been recorded as of the end of the period).

Many of the accounts that are affected by deferral adjustments are summarized in the middle column in Exhibit 4.2. The lines in the exhibit indicate that deferral adjustments affect assets and their related expenses, or liabilities and their related revenues.

2. Accrual Adjustments

Accrual adjustments are used for including transactions **not** *previously recorded.* If cash is not exchanged until after the related revenue is earned or expense is incurred, an accrual adjustment may be needed to make the accounting records *complete* at the end of the period. In particular, accrual adjustments are needed in either of the following situations:

a. Assets and revenues are generated in the current period but haven't been recorded as of the end of the period (perhaps because cash hasn't been received yet).

b. Liabilities and expenses are incurred in the current period but haven't been recorded as of the end of the period (perhaps because cash hasn't been paid yet).

Many of the accounts that are affected by accrual adjustments are summarized in the right-hand column of Exhibit 4.2. Notice that accrual adjustments create corresponding adjustments to assets and revenues, or liabilities and their related expenses.

If you didn't already read the explanation in Exhibit 4.2, read it now. Notice that every adjustment involves a pair of balance sheet and income statement accounts. The best way to determine what specific adjustments are needed is to scan the unadjusted trial balance, while thinking about each different transaction the company enters into and considering whether the pair of accounts affected by these transactions are up to date and complete as of the financial statement date. Has the company earned revenues or incurred expenses in this period but not yet recorded them? If so, the accounting records need to be adjusted before financial statements are prepared.

> **COACH'S CORNER**
>
> Accrual adjustments involve the inclusion ("accrual") of new amounts in balance sheet and income statement accounts. Accounts in an *accrual adjustment* always go in the same direction. That is, an increase in an asset goes with an increase in revenue, and an increase in a liability goes with an increase in an expense.

> **COACH'S CORNER**
>
> Don't try to memorize Exhibit 4.2. Instead, use it to understand how balance sheet and income statement accounts are related. Also, you'll find it useful as a reference when doing homework.

exhibit 4.2 Types of Adjustments

	Deferral Adjustments	Accrual Adjustments
a. What we want to accomplish:	Report **up-to-date** information.	Report **complete** information.
b. How do we accomplish it?	Update what's already recorded.	Include what's not yet recorded.
c. What accounts do they affect?	**Assets** — **Expenses** **Balance Sheet** — **Income Statement** Inventories — Cost of Goods Sold Supplies — Supplies Expense Prepaid Rent — Rent Expense **Liabilities** — **Revenues** Unearned Ticket Revenue — Ticket Sales Revenue Subscriptions Paid in Advance — Subscriptions Revenue	**Assets** — **Revenues** **Balance Sheet** — **Income Statement** Interest Receivable — Interest Revenue Rent Receivable — Rent Revenue **Liabilities** — **Expenses** Income Taxes Payable — Income Tax Expense Wages Payable — Wages Expense Interest Payable — Interest Expense

Explanation: *Deferral adjustments* are used to ensure that the information reported in financial statements is updated to the financial statement date. Each deferral adjustment affects an asset and expense account, or liability and revenue account. *Accrual adjustments* are used to ensure that the information reported in financial statements is complete. Unlike deferral adjustments, each accrual adjustment affects an asset and revenue account, or a liability and expense account.

STUDY

HOW ADJUSTMENTS ARE MADE

To make each necessary adjustment, apply the following steps:

1. Obtain the current unadjusted balances in the pair of accounts to be adjusted.
2. Calculate the amount of the adjustment needed.
3. Prepare a journal entry to make the adjustment (called an **adjusting journal entry**).

Step 1 is easy. Look in the accounting records (T-accounts or unadjusted trial balance) for the balances in the pair of balance sheet and income statement accounts that you will be adjusting. Sometimes it's enough to know the unadjusted balance in either the balance sheet or income statement account, but where possible, you should always try to identify the balances in both of the related accounts.

Step 2 is more challenging. To calculate the adjustment needed, you will use information gathered in Step 1 along with facts about the transactions that affect each pair of accounts to be adjusted. When calculating the amount of revenues or expenses that relate to the current period, it's useful to draw pictures or timelines, as we do in later examples.

Step 3 involves converting the calculations from Step 2 into journal-entry format. This step is made easier by using T-accounts to picture what you're trying to accomplish.

Examples of Deferral Adjustments

Let's begin by looking at common examples of deferral adjustments, which again are adjustments used to make the accounting records up to date—in this case, at the end of September.

Supplies—Supplies Expense

(a) **In August 2005, your salon received its first shipment of hair supplies, which was recorded in Chapter 2 with the following journal entry:**

dr	Supplies (+A).	630	
	cr Accounts Payable (+L).		630

Supplies were used during September, but their use wasn't recorded because it simply wasn't efficient to record a journal entry each day that the supplies were used. Instead, it's easier to make an end-of-period adjustment, determined as follows.

Step 1: The unadjusted trial balance at September 30 (in Exhibit 3.10 on page 105) shows that the unadjusted balances are $630 for *Supplies* and $0 for *Supplies Expense*.

Step 2: At the end of September 2005, by counting the bottles of shampoo and tubes of gel on hand, your salon manager determined that $400 of supplies were left. If only $400 of supplies are left from the $630 on hand at the start of the month, the $230 difference must be the cost of supplies used this month. The matching principle says this cost should be expensed in September.

Step 3: The *Supplies* T-account shown at the top of the next page (on the left) currently has an unadjusted balance of $630, but as we just calculated in Step 2 the desired adjusted balance is $400. To go from $630 to $400, we need an adjustment to decrease (credit) this asset by $230.

The *Supplies Expense* T-account (on the right) currently has an unadjusted balance of $0, but the balance should be the cost of supplies used up so far this year, which means the desired adjusted balance is $230. To go from $0 to $230, we need an adjustment to increase (debit) the expense by $230.

TOPIC TACKLER PLUS

For an animated explanation of adjustments, check out the tutorial on the DVD for use with this book.

COACH'S CORNER

Adjustment *(a)* focuses on the journal entry needed to record supplies used up. The accounts payable portion of the original journal entry does not require adjustment. That account will be reduced when the supplier is paid in cash.

+ Supplies (A) −				+ Supplies Expense (E) −		
Unadjusted bal.	630			Unadjusted bal.	0	
		230	Adjustment	Adjustment	230	
Desired adj. bal.	400			Desired adj. bal.	230	

Taken together, this analysis indicates our adjusting journal entry should debit *Supplies Expense* and credit *Supplies* by $230, shown as follows:

dr	**Supplies Expense (+E, −SE)**.		230	
cr	**Supplies (−A)**.			230

When posted to the accounts, the above adjusting journal entry will reduce the asset *Supplies* and increase *Supplies Expense*, as shown in the T-accounts above. The effects of this adjusting journal entry on the accounting equation are shown below and the financial statement effects are pictured in Exhibit 4.3.

FAST FLASHBACK
A journal entry is "posted" when its effects are entered into the accounts affected by it.

Assets		=	Liabilities	+	Stockholders' Equity	
Supplies	−230				Supplies Expense (+E)	−230

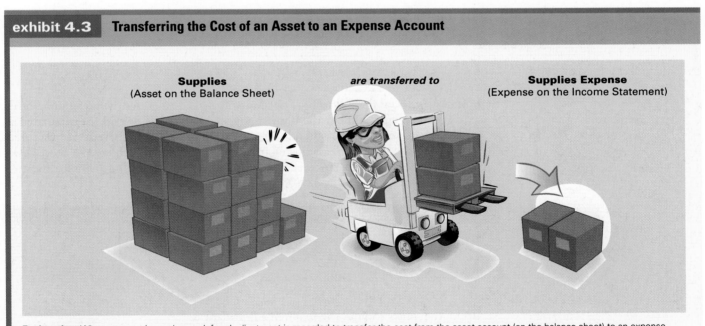

exhibit 4.3   **Transferring the Cost of an Asset to an Expense Account**

Supplies
(Asset on the Balance Sheet)

are transferred to

Supplies Expense
(Expense on the Income Statement)

Explanation: When an asset is used up, a deferral adjustment is recorded to transfer the cost from the asset account (on the balance sheet) to an expense account (on the income statement). In the above illustration, the cost of supplies used this month is removed from the asset account *Supplies* (on the balance sheet) and added to *Supplies Expense* (on the income statement).

Prepaid Rent—Rent Expense; Prepaid Insurance—Insurance Expense

Back in Chapter 3, your Supercuts Super Salon had prepaid its rent and insurance. Now that some of the benefits of these prepayments have been used up as of the end of September, the salon needs to adjust the accounts related to these prepaid expenses. We will show how to make the adjustment for prepaid rent in part (*b*) and then give you some practice with a Self-Study Quiz to adjust prepaid insurance in (*c*).

(b) **In September 2005, your salon paid $7,200 rent for September, October, and November. This $7,200 prepayment was recorded in Chapter 3 as an asset (***Prepaid Rent***).**

Step 1: The account balances (obtained from the unadjusted trial balance) are $7,200 for *Prepaid Rent* and $0 for *Rent Expense*.

Step 2: The timeline in Exhibit 4.4 shows that the September prepayment of $7,200 represented three equal pieces of $2,400. The benefits of the first piece (pictured in red) have now expired, so only two of the three months (²⁄₃) remain prepaid at September 30. Thus, the $7,200 that was prepaid on September 1 needs to be adjusted on September 30 to $4,800 (= ²⁄₃ × $7,200), which is the cost of the two remaining months of prepaid rent (pictured in blue).

---

exhibit 4.4   **Using a Timeline to Calculate Adjustments**

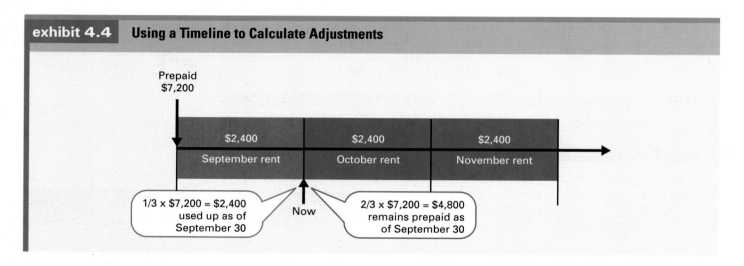

Step 3: As shown in the following T-accounts, *Prepaid Rent* currently has an unadjusted balance of $7,200 but the desired adjusted balance is $4,800 (as calculated in Step 2), so we require an adjustment to decrease (credit) the asset by $2,400. *Rent Expense* has an unadjusted balance of $0 but (as calculated in Step 2) the desired adjusted balance is $2,400, so we require an adjustment to increase (debit) the expense by $2,400.

+ Prepaid Rent (A) −		
Unadjusted bal. 7,200		
	2,400	**Adjustment**
Desired adj. bal. 4,800		

+ Rent Expense (E) −		
Unadjusted bal. 0		
Adjustment 2,400		
Desired adj. bal. 2,400		

In journal entry format, the required adjustment is

dr	**Rent Expense (+E, −SE)**	2,400	
	cr **Prepaid Rent (−A)**		2,400

Assets		=	Liabilities	+	Stockholders' Equity	
Prepaid Rent	−2,400				Rent Expense (+E)	−2,400

For *(c)* in the self-study quiz that follows, fill in the missing information and complete the adjusting journal entry.

HOW'S IT GOING? A Self-Study Quiz

(c) Your salon prepaid $2,400 for an insurance policy that covers the period from September 1 until August 31 of next year. The full amount was recorded as *Prepaid Insurance*. No *Insurance Expense* has been reported.

Step 1: The unadjusted balances are $ _____ for *Prepaid Insurance* and $ _____ for *Insurance Expense*.

Step 2: The benefits from the $2,400 payment relate to 12 months (September 1 through August 31). As of September 30, one month of these benefits (1/12) has been used up and 11/12 of them remain. To reflect this, the balance in *Prepaid Insurance* should be adjusted to $2,200 (= 11/12 × $2,400). *Insurance Expense* should be adjusted to $ _____ (= 1/12 × $2,400).

Step 3:

+ Prepaid Insurance (A) −		+ Insurance Expense (E) −	
Unadjusted bal. 2,400		Unadjusted bal. 0	
	Adjustment	Adjustment	
Desired adj. bal. 2,200		Desired adj. bal. 200	

September 30 adjusting journal entry:

dr Insurance Expense (+E, −SE) . . . . `_____`

    cr Prepaid Insurance (−A). . . . . `_____`

Assets	=	Liabilities	+	Stockholders' Equity	
Prepaid Insurance −200				Insurance Expense (+E) −200	

When you're done, check your answers with the solution in the margin.

Notice that for events *(a)*, *(b)*, and *(c)*, the deferral adjustments have two effects: (1) they reduce the **carrying value** of assets on the balance sheet, and (2) they transfer the amount of the reductions to related expense accounts. This happens whether we're recording the use of supplies, prepaid expenses, or even long-term assets like property and equipment. When accounting for the use of property and equipment, there is one slight difference in how the carrying value is reduced, as we'll explain next.

Property and Equipment (Accumulated Depreciation)—Depreciation Expense

The matching principle implies that when buildings and equipment are used to generate revenues in the current period, part of their cost should be transferred to an expense account in that period. This process is referred to as **depreciation,** so an account named *Depreciation Expense* is used to report the cost of these assets used up during the period. The use of an expense account to record the part of the assets used up is not new to you. What is new, however, is that rather than take the amount of depreciation directly out of the asset accounts, a **contra-account** is created to keep track of all the depreciation that is recorded against the property and equipment. As shown in Exhibit 4.5, this contra-account, named *Accumulated Depreciation*, is reported in the assets section of the balance sheet and is *subtracted* from the *Property and Equipment* account.

By recording depreciation in *Accumulated Depreciation* separate from *Property and Equipment*, it's possible to report both the original cost of the property and equipment and the amount that has already been depreciated. This gives users a rough idea of how

YOU SHOULD KNOW

Carrying value simply means the amount an asset or liability is reported at ("carried at") in the financial statements. It is also known as "net book value" or simply "book value."

YOU SHOULD KNOW

Depreciation is the process of allocating the cost of property and equipment to the accounting periods in which they are used.
A **contra-account** is an account that is an offset to, or reduction of, another account.

exhibit 4.5   Recording Depreciation Expense and Accumulated Depreciation

Before Depreciation Is Recorded

Road Runner Corporation
Partial Balance Sheet
As of January 1, 2006

Property & equipment $80,000

After Depreciation Is Recorded

Road Runner Corporation
Partial Balance Sheet
As of December 31, 2006

Property & equipment	$80,000
Less: Accumulated depreciation	(20,000)
Property & equip., net	60,000

Road Runner Corporation
Partial Income Statement
Year Ended December 31, 2006

Sales Revenue	$300,000
Expenses:	
Depreciation	20,000

Explanation: In the example shown here, a truck is bought on January 1 for $80,000, representing future benefits equal to $20,000 for each of its four years of usefulness. At the end of the year, $20,000 of the truck's cost is used up and is reported on the income statement as depreciation expense. On the balance sheet, total depreciation is accumulated in a contra-asset account, which reduces the truck's carrying value from $80,000 to $60,000.

COACH'S CORNER

Unlike depreciation expense, which relates only to the current period's depreciation, accumulated depreciation is a running total of depreciation. Each year's depreciation is added to the total from previous years. In this way, accumulated depreciation does actually *accumulate* all the depreciation that has been recorded since the underlying asset was originally acquired.

much of the asset's original cost (and original usefulness) has been used up as of the balance sheet date and how much remains to be depreciated (and used) in the future.

Before showing how depreciation is recorded for your Supercuts Super Salon, we need to ensure you don't misunderstand what it is. Some people mistakenly think that depreciation reflects an asset's decline in market value. People often say that a new car "depreciates" when it is driven off the lot because it has become a "used" car. From an accounting standpoint, a car is not depreciated until it actually is used to generate revenues. And that's because depreciation is used in accounting to *match* part of an asset's original cost to the revenues generated in the periods the asset is used. In accounting, depreciation is never intended to show a reduction in market value. In some cases, depreciation might appear to mirror a decline in market value but that's just a fluke.

One of the challenges in accounting for depreciation is figuring out how much to record. Unlike prepaid rent or prepaid insurance, there's no written agreement that states the number of periods for which buildings or equipment will be used, so it's tough to know exactly how much depreciation to report. For now, we'll tell you the amount to use. In Chapter 9, you'll learn the methods commonly used for estimating depreciation.

(d) In Chapter 2, your salon had bought furnishings and equipment costing $60,000. Your salon manager figures that depreciation for this month should be $1,000.

Step 1: The unadjusted account balances are $0 for *Accumulated Depreciation* and $0 for *Depreciation Expense*.

Step 2: Only one month of depreciation ($1,000) needs to be recorded for September.

Step 3: We don't need T-accounts to figure out what's needed. To go from the unadjusted balances of $0 to the desired adjusted balances of $1,000, we increase the expense and contra-account balances as follows:

dr	**Depreciation Expense (+E, −SE)**	1,000	
	cr **Accumulated Depreciation (+xA, −A)**		1,000

Assets	=	Liabilities	+	Stockholders' Equity	
Accumulated Depn. (+xA)	−1,000			Depreciation Expense (+E)	−1,000

Note that a contra-account always is recorded in a way that opposes the account that it offsets. For example, in *(d)*, the increase in *Accumulated Depreciation* was recorded with a credit because this account reduces the carrying value of an underlying asset, *Furnishings and Equipment*, which was recorded as a debit.

Unearned Revenues—Sales or Service Revenues

Just as deferral adjustments are used to record expenses incurred when assets are used up, they also can be used to record the revenues earned when a company fulfills its obligation to provide goods or services to customers—an example we look at in adjustment *(e)*.

(e) On the last day of September, one of the stylists discovered $75 in gift certificates at her station that customers had given her as payment for haircuts done that day. She had forgotten to report these sales.

Step 1: The unadjusted trial balance in Exhibit 3.10 includes $15,600 of *Haircut Revenue* and $200 of *Unearned Revenue* recorded earlier in September (in Chapter 3). The unearned revenue balance of $200 represents the $300 of gift certificates that were sold in early September less the $100 of gift certificates that were redeemed and recorded in the third week of September.

Step 2: Because the recently discovered gift certificates of $75 relate to haircuts provided on the last day of September, these revenues have been earned and should be recorded in September, to bring total revenue to $15,675. Also, by taking in $75 of additional gift certificates, the salon's liability for honoring gift certificates in the future should be reduced by $75 (from $200 to $125).

Step 3: The analysis in Step 2 indicates that an adjustment is needed to record a $75 increase in haircut revenue and a $75 decrease in unearned revenue. Let's double-check to see if this will bring the T-accounts to the desired balances:

− Unearned Revenue (L) +		
	Unadjusted bal.	200
Adjustment	75	
	Desired adj. bal.	125

− Haircut Revenue (R) +		
	Unadjusted bal.	15,600
	Adjustment	75
	Desired adj. bal.	15,675

That'll do the trick. Here's the adjusting journal entry to make it happen (along with a check to see that the accounting equation remains in balance).

dr	**Unearned Revenue (−L)**	75	
	cr **Haircut Revenue (+R, +SE)**		75

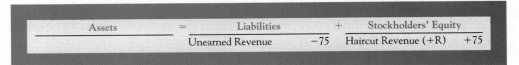

Assets	=	Liabilities	+	Stockholders' Equity	
		Unearned Revenue	−75	Haircut Revenue (+R)	+75

Examples of Accrual Adjustments

Let's now look at common examples of accrual adjustments, which are adjustments that make the accounting records complete by including transactions that have not been previously recorded—in this case, by the end of September.

Interest Receivable—Interest Revenue

(f) On September 1, your salon moved some cash into a certificate of deposit (CD) at the bank. A CD is a special type of bank account that pays a higher interest rate than a regular savings account but it only pays this interest after a specified period of time. The CD that your salon acquired will pay $120 interest on November 30.

Step 1: No amounts have been recorded for interest earned.

Step 2: The timeline shown in Exhibit 4.6 indicates that the $120 interest that will be received on November 30 actually is *earned* over the three previous months. The revenue principle says that interest earned in September should be recorded in September.

exhibit 4.6   Using a Timeline to Calculate Adjustments

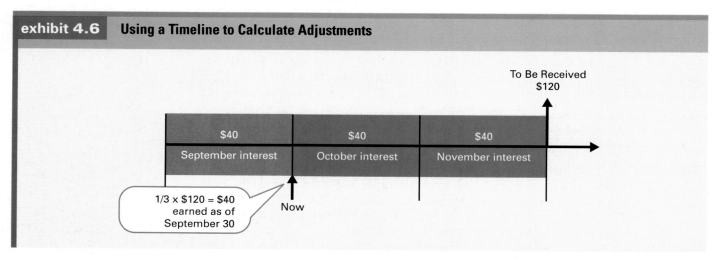

Step 3: The adjusting journal entry to record the interest earned and receivable as of September 30 is

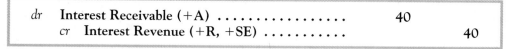

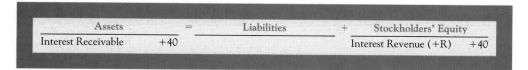

Interest Payable—Interest Expense

(g) Your salon has not paid or recorded the $100 interest that it owes this month on its note payable to the bank. (The note payable was issued in Chapter 2.)

Step 1: No amounts have been recorded for interest incurred.

Step 2: Because interest is incurred in September, a liability and expense need to be recorded, increasing the balances from $0 to $100.

Step 3: The adjusting journal entry needed to record the interest incurred and owed as of September 30 is

dr	Interest Expense (+E, −SE)	100	
cr	Interest Payable (+L)		100

Assets	=	Liabilities	+	Stockholders' Equity	
		Interest Payable	+100	Interest Expense (+E)	−100

Accrual adjustments also may be required for salaries, utilities, and property taxes that are incurred and owed during the current period (but not yet recorded). The adjusting journal entry required for each of these items would be identical to the one shown in (g), except that the word "interest" would be replaced with the particular type of cost incurred and the appropriate amounts would be used. For purposes of your Supercuts Super Salon example, we'll assume that the only remaining expense to record is the accrual of income taxes that are incurred this month but won't be paid until a later accounting period.

Income Taxes Payable—Income Tax Expense

Just like you, a corporation is responsible for income tax when it generates income in the current period. It is calculated by multiplying (1) the company's (adjusted) income before income taxes by (2) the company's tax rate. Let's calculate the first part (adjusted income before income taxes) by starting with the unadjusted revenue and expense numbers for your Supercuts Super Salon, which were included in the unadjusted trial balance (in Exhibit 3.10). Then we'll update these numbers for the adjustments made in this chapter.

	Revenues (and Gains)	Expenses (and Losses)	
Unadjusted totals	$15,600	$ 9,100	← Calculated from Exhibit 3.10
Adjustments:			
(a)		230	
(b)		2,400	
(c)		200	
(d)		1,000	
(e)	75		
(f)	40		
(g)		100	
Adjusted totals	$15,715 −	$13,030	= $2,685 ← Adjusted income before income tax

COACH'S CORNER

Always calculate income tax expense *after* adjusting all other revenue and expense accounts. This way, you'll have the adjusted *Income before income taxes* number available for calculating the amount of income taxes.

(h) **Your Supercuts Super Salon pays income tax at an average rate equal to 40 percent of the salon's income before taxes. No income tax has been recorded for September.**

Step 1: No amounts have been recorded for income taxes.

Step 2: Because income was earned in September, the matching principle requires that we record an expense in September. Because these taxes haven't been paid yet, a liability also is recorded. The amount of tax is $1,074, which is calculated as $2,685 (income before income tax) × 40% (tax rate).

Step 3: Nothing has been recorded for income taxes, so the adjusting journal entry needed to record income taxes incurred and owed as of September 30 is

dr	Income Tax Expense (+E, −SE)	1,074	
cr	Income Taxes Payable (+L)		1,074

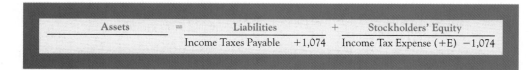

Assets	=	Liabilities	+	Stockholders' Equity
		Income Taxes Payable +1,074		Income Tax Expense (+E) −1,074

Dividends Payable—Dividends Declared

Now that your Supercuts Super Salon has generated a profit, it's time stockholders got a return for having invested in the business. This comes in the form of a dividend that will be paid to stockholders in cash. This decision to pay a dividend is made by a board of directors, which is a group of people who represent and act on behalf of the stockholders. The declaration of a dividend isn't taken lightly. According to law, an obligation is created the moment a dividend is declared.

(i) Your Supercuts Super Salon declared a dividend on September 30. The dividend (totaling $500) will be paid in cash to stockholders in early October.

Step 1: No amounts have been recorded for the dividend declared on September 30.

Step 2: An adjustment is needed to record a liability for the legal obligation to pay the dividend. The adjustment also must record the dividend as a reduction in stockholders' equity. Because it is declared only after the company generates profits and it is declared on behalf of the stockholders, **a dividend is *not* considered an expense of the business,** so it is recorded in its own special account (which is not included in the income statement but instead appears on the statement of retained earnings).

Step 3: The adjusting journal entry needed to record the dividend declared on September 30 is

dr	**Dividends Declared (+D, −SE)**.	500	
	cr **Dividends Payable (+L)**		500

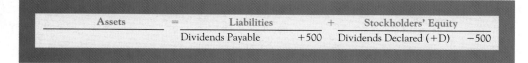

Assets	=	Liabilities	+	Stockholders' Equity
		Dividends Payable +500		Dividends Declared (+D) −500

One Final Note

There's one last thing to understand before leaving this section. Notice that none of the adjusting journal entries affected the *Cash* account. **Adjusting journal entries never involve cash.**

EVALUATE

THE QUALITY OF ADJUSTED FINANCIAL STATEMENTS

Adjustments for Good, Not Evil

ETHICAL

ISSUE

No doubt you've read articles or heard stories about accounting fraud and how managers have encouraged their accountants to use adjusting journal entries to defer expenses or accrue revenues that didn't exist. There's something about this topic that fascinates people, so it's always in the news. The problem with all this hype is that it gives the impression that *all* managers and accountants report assets and revenues that don't exist or they fail to report liabilities and expenses that do exist. And while you hear lots about the damage done by a few high-profile cases of fraud each year, you don't hear about all the other instances where deferral and accrual adjustments have helped financial statement users to better judge how well a company is performing.

So are adjustments good or evil? Many accounting research studies have looked into the question of whether accrual and deferral adjustments make financial statements more or less informative. They've found that while some managers may have used adjustments for evil, overall, adjustments significantly improve the quality of financial statements. By ensuring that revenues are recognized when they are earned and expenses are recorded when incurred to generate those revenues, these adjustments help financial statement users to better evaluate past decisions and predict future financial results.[1]

POINT OF INTEREST
If a company bases its adjustments on honest but optimistic estimates that lead to a higher net income, most people will refer to the company as "aggressive" and its earnings as "lower quality."

RECONSIDER
THE ACCOUNTING PROCESS

You're now through the hardest part of the accounting process. Exhibit 4.7 shows the complete process from start to finish. The steps in purple are done **every day** during the accounting period. The blue boxes show what is done at the end of **each period,** and the gold boxes show what is done at the end of **each year.** At this point in the chapter, we're ready to post our adjusting journal entries to the accounts, so let's get on with it.

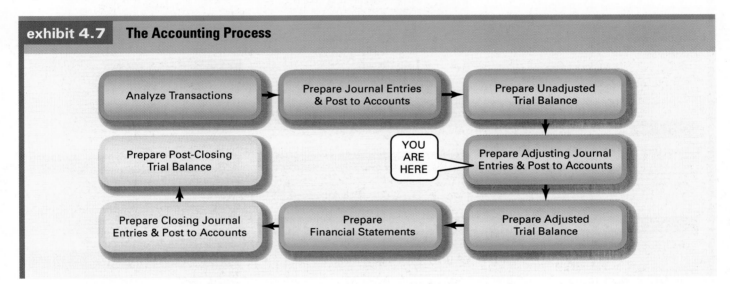

exhibit 4.7 **The Accounting Process**

To make life easier for you, we've posted all but one of this chapter's adjusting journal entries (AJEs) to the T-accounts (summarized in Exhibit 4.8). Just so you don't forget how it's done, we've left AJE (a) for you to post to Exhibit 4.8 on page 148. AJE (a) was

dr	**Supplies Expense (+E, −SE)**	230	
	cr **Supplies (−A)**		230

After you post this adjusting journal entry to the T-accounts, we'll check to see that the accounts are still in balance and then we'll prepare the financial statements.

Preparing the Adjusted Trial Balance

Just like the *unadjusted* trial balance in Chapter 3, an **adjusted trial balance** is prepared to check that the accounts are still in balance. The only difference is that it is prepared after the adjustments have been posted. Exhibit 4.9 on page 149 presents an adjusted trial balance, which involves simply copying and adding up the ending balances from the T-accounts shown in Exhibit 4.8.

YOU SHOULD KNOW

An **adjusted trial balance** is a list of all accounts and their adjusted balances to check on the equality of recorded debits and credits.

---

[1]P. Healy and J. Whalen, "A Review of the Earnings Management Literature and Its Implications for Standard Setting," *Accounting Horizons* 13, no. 4 (December 1999).

exhibit 4.8   Supercuts Super Salon T-Accounts (unadjusted balances come from Exhibit 3.9)

+ Cash (A) –

Unadj. bal.	7,300		

+ Supplies (A) –

Unadj. bal.	630		
		AJE (a)	
Adj. bal.	400		

+ Accounts Receivable (A) –

Unadj. bal.	200		

+ Interest Receivable (A) –

Unadj. bal.	0		
AJE (f)	40		
Adj. bal.	40		

+ Prepaid Rent (A) –

Unadj. bal.	7,200		
		AJE (b)	2,400
Adj. bal.	4,800		

+ Prepaid Insurance (A) –

Unadj. bal.	2,400		
		AJE (c)	200
Adj. bal.	2,200		

+ Furnishings & Equipment (A) –

Unadj. bal.	60,000		

– Accumulated Depreciation (xA) +

		Unadj. bal.	0
		AJE (d)	1,000
		Adj. bal.	1,000

– Accounts Payable (L) +

		Unadj. bal.	1,030

– Unearned Revenue (L) +

		Unadj. bal.	200
AJE (e)	75		
		Adj. bal.	125

– Interest Payable (L) +

		Unadj. bal.	0
		AJE (g)	100
		Adj. bal.	100

– Income Taxes Payable (L) +

		Unadj. bal.	0
		AJE (h)	1,074
		Adj. bal.	1,074

– Dividends Payable (L) +

		Unadj. bal.	0
		AJE (i)	500
		Adj. bal.	500

– Notes Payable (L) +

		Unadj. bal.	20,000

– Contributed Capital (SE) +

		Unadj. bal.	50,000

+ Dividends Declared (D, SE) –

Unadj. bal.	0		
AJE (i)	500		
Adj. bal.	500		

– Haircut Revenue (R, SE) +

		Unadj. bal.	15,600
		AJE (e)	75
		Adj. bal.	15,675

– Interest Revenue (R, SE) +

		Unadj. bal.	0
		AJE (f)	40
		Adj. bal.	40

+ Wages Expense (E, SE) –

Unadj. bal.	8,000		

+ Utilities Expense (E, SE) –

Unadj. bal.	700		

+ Advertising Expense (E, SE) –

Unadj. bal.	400		

+ Supplies Expense (E, SE) –

Unadj. bal.	0		
AJE (a)			
Adj. bal.	230		

+ Rent Expense (E, SE) –

Unadj. bal.	0		
AJE (b)	2,400		
Adj. bal.	2,400		

+ Insurance Expense (E, SE) –

Unadj. bal.	0		
AJE (c)	200		
Adj. bal.	200		

+ Depreciation Expense (E, SE) –

Unadj. bal.	0		
AJE (d)	1,000		
Adj. bal.	1,000		

+ Interest Expense (E, SE) –

Unadj. bal.	0		
AJE (g)	100		
Adj. bal.	100		

+ Income Tax Expense (E, SE) –

Unadj. bal.	0		
AJE (h)	1,074		
Adj. bal.	1,074		

exhibit 4.9   Sample Adjusted Trial Balance

SUPERCUTS SUPER SALON
Adjusted Trial Balance
As of September 30

Account Name	Debits	Credits
Cash	$ 7,300	
Supplies	400	
Accounts Receivable	200	
Interest Receivable	40	
Prepaid Rent	4,800	
Prepaid Insurance	2,200	
Furnishings & Equipment	60,000	
Accumulated Depreciation		1,000
Accounts Payable		1,030
Unearned Revenue		125
Interest Payable		100
Income Taxes Payable		1,074
Dividends Payable		500
Notes Payable		20,000
Contributed Capital		50,000
Retained Earnings		0
Dividends Declared	500	
Haircut Revenue		15,675
Interest Revenue		40
Wages Expense	8,000	
Utilities Expense	700	
Advertising Expense	400	
Supplies Expense	230	
Rent Expense	2,400	
Insurance Expense	200	
Depreciation Expense	1,000	
Interest Expense	100	
Income Tax Expense	1,074	
Totals	$89,544	$89,544

Now that we know the accounts are in balance, financial statements can be prepared. Typically, the income statement is prepared first because the net income number from it flows into the statement of retained earnings, and then the retained earnings number from the statement of retained earnings flows into the balance sheet. As you will see in later chapters of this book, the statement of cash flows and notes to the financial statements are prepared last because they include information obtained from the income statement, statement of retained earnings, and balance sheet (plus other sources).

Preparing the Income Statement and Statement of Retained Earnings

To prepare the income statement, just copy (from the adjusted trial balance) the names and amounts for any revenues, expenses, gains, and losses, as shown in Exhibit 4.10 on page 150.[2] Make sure your income statement includes the subtotals discussed in Chapter 3 (and shown in Exhibit 4.10). Also, it's common for companies to squish together similar accounts into a single amount, as we do in Exhibit 4.10 by combining five expense accounts into a single line-item called "General and Administrative Expenses."

Exhibit 4.10 shows that preparation of the statement of retained earnings also involves copying account balances. Notice, however, that the amount coming from the adjusted trial balance is the beginning-of-year balance for *Retained Earnings*. This account balance doesn't yet include revenues, expenses, and dividends declared for the current

FAST FLASHBACK

For a quick look at how the four financial statements fit together, see Exhibit 1.10 on page 17.

COACH'S CORNER

Accounts are combined ("aggregated") to avoid cluttering up the financial statements with too much detail.

[2]Thanks to Philip Fink for suggesting this format.

exhibit 4.10   **Preparing the Income Statement and Statement of Retained Earnings**

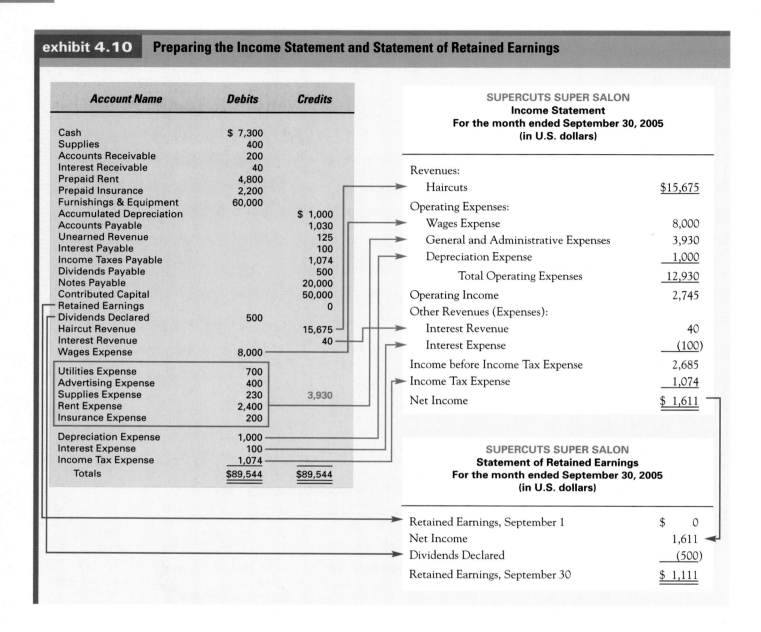

year because they've been recorded in their own separate accounts. Eventually we will transfer ("close") those accounts into *Retained Earnings*, but that's only done at the end of the year. For now, the retained earnings account on the adjusted trial balance provides the opening amount on the statement of retained earnings. You can get the net income number for the statement of retained earnings from the income statement and the dividends declared number from the adjusted trial balance.

Preparing the Balance Sheet

To prepare the balance sheet, copy the balance sheet account names and amounts from the adjusted trial balance, combining any similar accounts into a single amount, as shown in Exhibit 4.11. When preparing the balance sheet, watch out for two things. First, remember that *Accumulated Depreciation* is subtracted from *Furnishings & Equipment*. Second, get the retained earnings balance from the statement of retained earnings, not from the adjusted trial balance. (The retained earnings account on the adjusted trial balance still only contains this period's opening balance.)

exhibit 4.11 **Preparing the Balance Sheet**

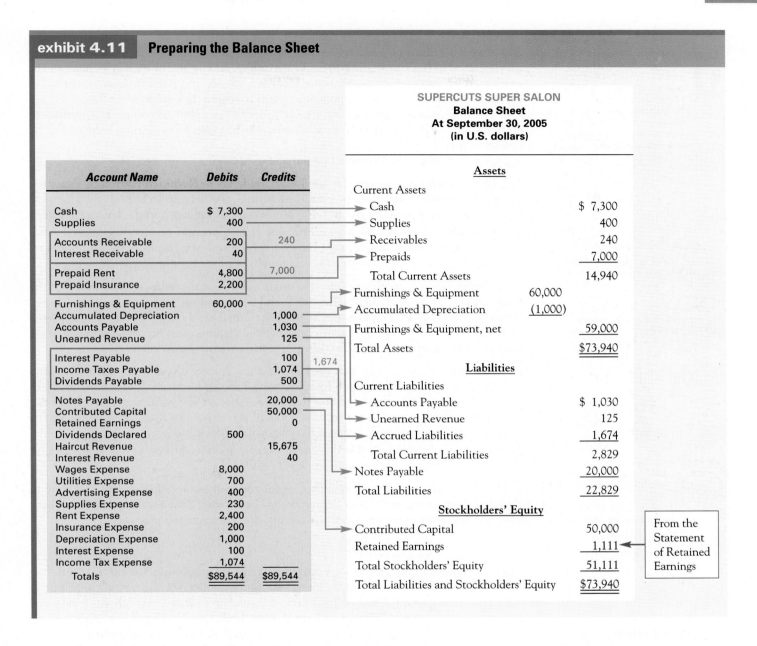

Account Name	Debits	Credits
Cash	$ 7,300	
Supplies	400	
Accounts Receivable	200	240
Interest Receivable	40	
Prepaid Rent	4,800	7,000
Prepaid Insurance	2,200	
Furnishings & Equipment	60,000	
Accumulated Depreciation		1,000
Accounts Payable		1,030
Unearned Revenue		125
Interest Payable		100
Income Taxes Payable		1,074
Dividends Payable		500
Notes Payable		20,000
Contributed Capital		50,000
Retained Earnings		0
Dividends Declared	500	
Haircut Revenue		15,675
Interest Revenue		40
Wages Expense	8,000	
Utilities Expense	700	
Advertising Expense	400	
Supplies Expense	230	
Rent Expense	2,400	
Insurance Expense	200	
Depreciation Expense	1,000	
Interest Expense	100	
Income Tax Expense	1,074	
Totals	$89,544	$89,544

1,674

SUPERCUTS SUPER SALON
Balance Sheet
At September 30, 2005
(in U.S. dollars)

Assets

Current Assets		
Cash		$ 7,300
Supplies		400
Receivables		240
Prepaids		7,000
Total Current Assets		14,940
Furnishings & Equipment	60,000	
Accumulated Depreciation	(1,000)	
Furnishings & Equipment, net		59,000
Total Assets		$73,940

Liabilities

Current Liabilities	
Accounts Payable	$ 1,030
Unearned Revenue	125
Accrued Liabilities	1,674
Total Current Liabilities	2,829
Notes Payable	20,000
Total Liabilities	22,829

Stockholders' Equity

Contributed Capital		50,000
Retained Earnings		1,111
Total Stockholders' Equity		51,111
Total Liabilities and Stockholders' Equity		$73,940

From the Statement of Retained Earnings

Preparing the Statement of Cash Flows and Notes to the Financial Statements

If you didn't look so tired, we'd spend another hour here talking about how the statement of cash flows (SCF) and notes to the financial statements are prepared. But it looks like you'll be ready for a break soon, so we'll leave the SCF for Chapter 12 and we'll slide information about financial statement notes into each of the remaining chapters.

The last two topics that we cover in this chapter relate to cleaning up the accounting records at the end of each year, to get them ready to begin tracking the results in the following year. Take a quick glance at Exhibit 4.7 on page 147 to see where we are in the accounting process. We're now entering the gold-colored boxes—the final steps.

Closing the Income Statement and Dividend Accounts

In Chapter 3, you learned to think of revenue and expense (and gain and loss) accounts as subcategories of *Retained Earnings*, which are used to track earnings-related transactions of the current year. Earlier in this chapter, you saw that a dividends declared account is similarly used to track dividends declared during the current year. All revenue, expense, gain, loss, and dividends declared accounts are known as **temporary accounts** because they are used to track only the current year's results. At the end of each year, after all the year's transactions and adjustments are recorded, closing journal entries are recorded to move the balances from the temporary accounts to where they belong—in *Retained Earnings*. The retained earnings account, like all other balance sheet accounts, is a **permanent account** because its ending balance from one year becomes its beginning balance for the following year.

Closing journal entries serve two purposes:

1. ***They transfer net income (or loss) and dividends to Retained Earnings.*** After the closing journal entries are prepared and posted, the balance in the *Retained Earnings* account will agree with the statement of retained earnings and the balance sheet.

2. ***To establish zero balances in all income statement and dividend accounts.*** After the closing journal entries are prepared and posted, the balances in the temporary accounts are reset to zero to start accumulating next year's results.

Closing journal entries follow the usual debits-equal-credits format used for the transaction journal entries (in Chapters 2 and 3) and adjusting journal entries (shown earlier in this chapter). Because they're the last thing done during the year, they're posted immediately to the accounts. (Some computerized systems even prepare and post closing journal entries automatically.) Two closing journal entries are needed:[3]

1. Debit each revenue and each gain account for the amount of its credit balance and credit each expense and each loss account for the amount of its debit balance. If total revenues and gains are greater than total expenses and losses for the year, the difference will be equal to net income and will be credited to *Retained Earnings*. (If the company has a net loss, *Retained Earnings* will be debited.)

2. Credit the dividends declared account for the amount of its debit balance and debit *Retained Earnings* for the same amount.

Exhibit 4.12 shows the closing process for your Supercuts Super Salon (if it were to close its books on the last day of September). The top part shows the closing journal entries, and the bottom part shows the accounts after these entries are posted.

Post-Closing Trial Balance

After the closing journal entries are posted, all temporary accounts should have zero balances. These accounts will be ready for recording transactions in the new accounting period. The ending balance in *Retained Earnings* is now up to date (it matches the year-end amount on the statement of retained earnings and balance sheet) and is carried forward as the beginning balance for the next period. As the last step of the accounting process, you should prepare a ***post-closing trial balance*** (as shown in Exhibit 4.13 on page 154). In this context, *post* means "after," so a post-closing trial balance is an "after-closing" trial balance that is prepared as a final check that total debits still equal total credits and that all temporary accounts have been closed.

What's Coming Up

This chapter discussed the final steps of the internal accounting process. This end to the internal part of the accounting process, however, is just the beginning of the process of communicating accounting information to external financial statement users. In the next chapter, we take a closer look at the process by which financial information is made available to external users. In that chapter, you'll also learn more about what they do when analyzing and interpreting information in the financial statements.

---

[3]Some companies use a four-step process, by closing (1) revenue and (2) expense accounts to a special summary account, called Income Summary, (3) which then is closed to Retained Earnings, (4) along with dividends declared.

exhibit 4.12 Preparing and Posting the Closing Journal Entries

Preparing the Closing Journal Entries (CJEs)

1. Close revenue and expense accounts:

dr	Haircut Revenue (−R)	15,675	
dr	Interest Revenue (−R)	40	
cr	Wages Expense (−E)		8,000
cr	Utilities Expense (−E)		700
cr	Advertising Expense (−E)		400
cr	Supplies Expense (−E)		230
cr	Rent Expense (−E)		2,400
cr	Insurance Expense (−E)		200
cr	Depreciation Expense (−E)		1,000
cr	Interest Expense (−E)		100
cr	Income Tax Expense (−E)		1,074
cr	Retained Earnings (+SE)		1,611

2. Close the dividends declared account:

dr	Retained Earnings (−SE)	500	
cr	Dividends Declared (−D)		500

COACH'S CORNER

If you've prepared the first closing journal entry correctly, the credit to *Retained Earnings* should equal the year's net income. (A net loss for the year, where expenses exceed revenues, would result in a debit to Retained Earnings).

Posting the Closing Journal Entries (CJEs)

− Haircut Revenue (R, SE) +

		Adj. bal.	15,675
CJE (1)	15,675		
		Closed bal.	0

+ Supplies Expense (E, SE) −

Adj. bal.	230		
		CJE (1)	230
Closed bal.	0		

+ Income Tax Expense (E, SE) −

Adj. bal.	1,074		
		CJE (1)	1,074
Closed bal.	0		

− Interest Revenue (R, SE) +

		Adj. bal.	40
CJE (1)	40		
		Closed bal.	0

+ Rent Expense (E, SE) −

Adj. bal.	2,400		
		CJE (1)	2,400
Closed bal.	0		

+ Wages Expense (E, SE) −

Adj. bal.	8,000		
		CJE (1)	8,000
Closed bal.	0		

+ Insurance Expense (E, SE) −

Adj. bal.	200		
		CJE (1)	200
Closed bal.	0		

− Retained Earnings (SE) +

		Adj. bal.	0
CJE (2)	500	CJE (1)	1,611
		Closed bal.	1,111

+ Utilities Expense (E, SE) −

Adj. bal.	700		
		CJE (1)	700
Closed bal.	0		

+ Depreciation Expense (E, SE) −

Adj. bal.	1,000		
		CJE (1)	1,000
Closed bal.	0		

+ Advertising Expense (E, SE) −

Adj. bal.	400		
		CJE (1)	400
Closed bal.	0		

+ Interest Expense (E, SE) −

Adj. bal.	100		
		CJE (1)	100
Closed bal.	0		

+ Dividends Declared (D, SE) −

Adj. bal.	500		
		CJE (2)	500
Closed bal.	0		

exhibit 4.13   Sample Post-Closing Trial Balance

SUPERCUTS SUPER SALON
Post-Closing Trial Balance
As of September 30

Account Name	Debits	Credits
Cash	$ 7,300	
Supplies	400	
Accounts Receivable	200	
Interest Receivable	40	
Prepaid Rent	4,800	
Prepaid Insurance	2,200	
Furnishings & Equipment	60,000	
Accumulated Depreciation		$ 1,000
Accounts Payable		1,030
Unearned Revenue		125
Interest Payable		100
Income Taxes Payable		1,074
Dividends Payable		500
Notes Payable		20,000
Contributed Capital		50,000
Retained Earnings		1,111
Dividends Declared	0	
Haircut Revenue		0
Interest Revenue		0
Wages Expense	0	
Utilities Expense	0	
Advertising Expense	0	
Supplies Expense	0	
Rent Expense	0	
Insurance Expense	0	
Depreciation Expense	0	
Interest Expense	0	
Income Tax Expense	0	
Totals	$74,940	$74,940

COACH'S CORNER

Total debits on the post-closing trial balance don't equal the total assets on the balance sheet because accumulated depreciation (a credit balance on the trial balance) is subtracted from assets on the balance sheet.

FOR YOUR REVIEW

DEMONSTRATION CASE

We take our final look at the accounting activities of Goodbye Grass Corporation by illustrating the activities at the end of the accounting cycle: the adjustment process, financial statement preparation, and the closing process. No adjustments had been made to the accounts yet to reflect *all* revenues earned and expenses incurred in April. Your starting point will be the following unadjusted trial balance as of April 30, 2006:

GOODBYE GRASS CORPORATION
Unadjusted Trial Balance
As of April 30, 2006

Account Name	Debits	Credits
Cash	$ 4,470	
Accounts Receivable	1,700	
Interest Receivable	0	
Notes Receivable	1,250	
Prepaid Insurance	300	

Equipment	4,600		
Accumulated Depreciation		$	0
Land	3,750		
Accounts Payable			220
Unearned Revenue			1,600
Wages Payable			0
Income Taxes Payable			0
Notes Payable			4,400
Contributed Capital			9,000
Retained Earnings			0
Mowing Revenue			5,200
Interest Revenue			0
Wages Expense	3,900		
Fuel Expense	410		
Insurance Expense	0		
Depreciation Expense	0		
Interest Expense	40		
Income Tax Expense	0		
Totals	$20,420		$20,420

In reviewing the trial balance, three deferred accounts (Prepaid Insurance, Equipment, and Unearned Revenue) may need to be adjusted and additional accruals may be necessary related to wages, income taxes, and interest earned on Notes Receivable. The following information is determined at the end of the accounting cycle:

Deferral Adjustments

a. One-fourth of the $1,600 cash received from the city at the beginning of April for future mowing service has been earned in April. The $1,600 in Unearned Revenue represents four months of service (April through July).
b. Insurance purchased at the beginning of April for $300 provides coverage for six months (April through September). The insurance coverage for April has now been used.
c. Mowers, edgers, rakes, and hand tools (equipment) have been used in April to generate revenues. The company estimates $300 in depreciation each year.

Accrual Adjustments

d. Interest earned and receivable on Goodbye Grass Corporation's outstanding note receivable from the city is $25 for the month of April.
e. Wages have been paid through April 28. Employees worked the last two days of April and will be paid in May. Wages amount to $200 per day.
f. The estimated income tax rate for Goodbye Grass Corporation is 35 percent.

Required:

1. Using the process outlined in this chapter, determine the adjusting journal entries required at the end of April.
2. Set up T-accounts for each account affected by the adjusting journal entries in 1. Enter the amounts from the unadjusted trial balance as beginning balances, post the adjusting journal entries from 1 into the accounts, and calculate April 30 balances.
3. Prepare an adjusted trial balance to ensure debit and credit balances are equal, remembering to include all accounts in the trial balance (and not just the ones affected by the adjusting journal entries).
4. Prepare an income statement, statement of retained earnings, and balance sheet from the amounts in the adjusted trial balance. Don't worry about combining ("aggregating") similar accounts.
5. Prepare the closing journal entries that would be required if Goodbye Grass Corporation's fiscal year ended April 30, 2006.

After completing requirements 1–5, check your answers with the following solution.

Suggested Solution

1. **Adjusting journal entries required:**
   a. *Unearned Revenue—Mowing Revenue*
      Step 1: The unadjusted balances are $1,600 for Unearned Revenue and $5,200 for Mowing Revenue.
      Step 2: One-fourth of the $1,600 has been earned in April ($400 = ¼ × $1,600) bringing total mowing revenues for the month to $5,600 (= $5,200 + $400). Three-fourths of the $1,600 remain unearned at the end of April ($1,200 = ¾ × $1,600).
      Step 3: The T-accounts below show that to reach the desired balances, we need an adjustment that decreases Unearned Revenue by $400 and increases Mowing Revenue by $400.

− Unearned Revenue (L) +			− Mowing Revenue (R) +	
	Unadjusted bal. 1,600			Unadjusted bal. 5,200
Adjustment 400				Adjustment 400
	Desired adj. bal. 1,200			Desired adj. bal. 5,600

The adjusting journal entry needed to accomplish this is

dr Unearned Revenue (−L)	400	
cr Mowing Revenue (+R, +SE)		400

Assets	=	Liabilities	+	Stockholders' Equity	
		Unearned Revenue	−400	Mowing Revenue (+R)	+400

   b. *Prepaid Insurance—Insurance Expense*
      Step 1: The unadjusted balances are $300 for Prepaid Insurance and $0 for Insurance Expense.
      Step 2: One-sixth of the $300 has expired in April resulting in an insurance expense for the month of $50 (= ⅙ × $300). Five of the six months of insurance coverage remain unused at the end of April ($250 = ⅚ × $300).
      Step 3: The T-accounts below show that to reach the desired balances, we need an adjustment that decreases Prepaid Insurance by $50 and increases Insurance Expense by $50.

+ Prepaid Insurance (A) −			+ Insurance Expense (E) −	
Unadjusted bal. 300			Unadjusted bal. 0	
	50 Adjustment		Adjustment 50	
Desired adj. bal. 250			Desired adj. bal. 50	

The adjusting journal entry needed to accomplish this is

dr Insurance Expense (+E, −SE)	50	
cr Prepaid Insurance (−A)........................		50

Assets	=	Liabilities	+	Stockholders' Equity	
Prepaid Insurance	−50			Insurance Expense (+E)	−50

   c. *Equipment (Accumulated Depreciation)—Depreciation Expense*
      Step 1: The unadjusted balances are $0 for Accumulated Depreciation and $0 for Depreciation Expense.
      Step 2: Yearly depreciation of $300 equals just $25 for one month (= $300 × 1/12).
      Step 3: To go from the unadjusted balances of $0 to the desired adjusted balances of $25, we increase the expense and contra-account balances as follows.

− Accumulated Depreciation (xA) +		+ Depreciation Expense (E) −	
	Unadjusted bal. 0	Unadjusted bal. 0	
	Adjustment 25	Adjustment 25	
	Desired adj. bal. 25	Desired adj. bal. 25	

The adjusting journal entry needed to accomplish this is

dr	Depreciation Expense (+E, −SE)	25
	cr Accumulated Depreciation (+xA, −A)	25

Assets	=	Liabilities	+	Stockholders' Equity	
Accumulated				Depreciation	
Depreciation (+xA) −25				Expense (+E) −25	

d. *Interest Receivable—Interest Revenue*

   Step 1: The unadjusted balances are $0 for Interest Receivable and $0 for Interest Revenue.

   Step 2: Interest earned and receivable was $25 for the month of April.

   Step 3: The following adjusting journal entry is needed to increase Interest Receivable and Interest Revenue from $0 to $25:

dr	Interest Receivable (+A)	25
	cr Interest Revenue (+R, +SE).....................	25

Assets	=	Liabilities	+	Stockholders' Equity	
Interest Receivable +25				Interest Revenue (+R) +25	

e. *Wages Payable—Wages Expense*

   Step 1: The unadjusted balances are $0 for Wages Payable and $3,900 for Wages Expense.

   Step 2: Because the final two days of work done in April are unpaid, we need to record a liability for $400 (= 2 × $200). Total wages expense for the month should include the $3,900 paid for work from April 1–28 plus the $400 not yet paid for work on April 29 and 30.

   Step 3: The T-accounts below show that to reach the desired balances, we need an adjustment increasing Wages Payable by $400 and Wages Expense by $400.

− Wages Payable (L) +		+ Wages Expense (E) −	
Unadjusted bal.	0	Unadjusted bal. 3,900	
Adjustment	**400**	**Adjustment** **400**	
Desired adj. bal.	400	Desired adj. bal. 4,300	

The adjusting journal entry needed to accomplish this is

dr	Wages Expense (+E, −SE)	400
	cr Wages Payable (+L)............................	400

Assets	=	Liabilities	+	Stockholders' Equity	
		Wages Payable +400		Wages Expense (+E) −400	

f. *Income Taxes Payable—Income Tax Expense*

   Step 1: The unadjusted balances are $0 for Income Taxes Payable and $0 for Income Tax Expense.

   Step 2: Information given for Goodbye Grass Corporation indicates that income taxes are calculated as 35 percent of adjusted income before tax for the month, which is calculated as follows:

	Revenues and Gains	Expenses and Losses	
Unadjusted totals	$5,200	$4,350	← Calculated from unadjusted trial balance
Adjustments: (a)	400		
(b)		50	
(c)		25	
(d)	25		
(e)		400	
Adjusted totals	$5,625	$4,825	

	Revenues and Gains	**Expenses and Losses**	
Adjusted totals	$5,625	− $4,825	= $800 Adjusted income before income tax
			× 35% Tax rate
			$280 Income tax

Step 3: The following adjusting journal entry will increase Income Taxes Payable and Income Tax Expense from $0 to $280.

> dr   Income Tax Expense (+E, −SE)   280
>   cr   Income Taxes Payable (+L)......................   280
>
> | Assets | = | Liabilities | + | Stockholders' Equity |
> |---|---|---|---|---|
> | | | Income Taxes Payable   +280 | | Income Tax Expense (+E)   −280 |

2.   T-accounts:

+ Prepaid Insurance (A) −				− Wages Payable (L) +				+ Insurance Expense (E) −	
Bal. fwd.	300				0	Beg. bal.	Beg. bal.	0	
		50	(b)		400	(e)	(b)	50	
End. bal.	250				400	End. bal.	End. bal.	50	

+ Interest Receivable (A) −			− Income Taxes Payable (L) +			+ Depreciation Expense (E) −	
Beg. bal.	0			0	Beg. bal.	Beg. bal.	0
(d)	25			280	(f)	(c)	25
End. bal.	25			280	End. bal.	End. bal.	25

− Accumulated Depreciation (xA) +			− Mowing Revenue (R) +			+ Wages Expense (E) −	
	0	Beg. bal.		5,200	Bal. fwd.	Bal. fwd.	3,900
	25	(c)		400	(a)	(e)	400
	25	End. bal.		5,600	End. bal.	End. bal.	4,300

− Unearned Revenue (L) +			− Interest Revenue (R) +			+ Income Tax Expense (E) −	
	1,600	Bal fwd.		0	Beg. bal.	Beg. bal.	0
(a)	400			25	(d)	(f)	280
	1,200	End. bal.		25	End. bal.	End. bal.	280

3.   Adjusted trial balance:

GOODBYE GRASS CORPORATION
Adjusted Trial Balance
As of April 30, 2006

Account Name	Debits	Credits
Cash	$4,470	
Accounts Receivable	1,700	
Interest Receivable	25	
Notes Receivable	1,250	
Prepaid Insurance	250	
Equipment	4,600	
Accumulated Depreciation		$ 25
Land	3,750	
Accounts Payable		220
Unearned Revenue		1,200
Wages Payable		400
Income Taxes Payable		280

Notes Payable		4,400
Contributed Capital		9,000
Retained Earnings		0
Mowing Revenue		5,600
Interest Revenue		25
Wages Expense	4,300	
Fuel Expense	410	
Insurance Expense	50	
Depreciation Expense	25	
Interest Expense	40	
Income Tax Expense	280	
Totals	$21,150	$21,150

4. Income statement, statement of retained earnings, and balance sheet:

GOODBYE GRASS CORPORATION
Income Statement
For the Month Ended April 30, 2006

Operating Revenues:	
Mowing Revenue	$5,600
	5,600
Operating Expenses:	
Wages Expense	4,300
Fuel Expense	410
Insurance Expense	50
Depreciation Expense	25
	4,785
Operating Income	815
Other Items:	
Interest Revenue	25
Interest Expense	(40)
Income before Income Taxes	800
Income Tax Expense	280
Net Income	**$ 520**

GOODBYE GRASS CORPORATION
Statement of Retained Earnings
For the Month Ended April 30, 2006

Balance, April 1, 2006	$	0
Net Income		520
Dividends Declared		0
Balance, April 30, 2006	$	520

GOODBYE GRASS CORPORATION
Balance Sheet
April 30, 2006

Assets			**Liabilities**		
Current Assets:			Current Liabilities:		
Cash	$	4,470	Accounts Payable	$	220
Accounts Receivable		1,700	Unearned Revenues		1,200
Interest Receivable		25	Wages Payable		400
Notes Receivable		1,250	Income Tax Payable		280
Prepaid Insurance		250	Notes Payable		4,400
Total Current Assets		7,695	Total Current Liabilities		6,500
Land		3,750	**Stockholders' Equity**		
Equipment		4,600			
Less: Accumulated Depreciation		(25)	Contributed Capital		9,000
			Retained Earnings		520
Total Assets		**$16,020**	**Total Liabilities and Stockholders' Equity**		**$16,020**

5. **Closing journal entry:**

If Goodbye Grass Corporation had adopted an April 30 year-end, the company would require a journal entry to close its revenue and expense accounts into retained earnings. Because the company has not declared a dividend, there is no dividends declared account to close into retained earnings. The closing journal entry needed to close revenues and expenses into retained earnings is

dr	Mowing Revenue (−R)	5,600	
dr	Interest Revenue (−R)	25	
	cr Wages Expense (−E)		4,300
	cr Fuel Expense (−E)		410
	cr Insurance Expense (−E)		50
	cr Depreciation Expense (−E)		25
	cr Interest Expense (−E)		40
	cr Income Tax Expense (−E)		280
	cr Retained Earnings (+SE)		520

CHAPTER SUMMARY

LO1   Explain the goals accomplished by recording adjustments. p. 136

Adjustments are recorded for two primary reasons:

- Make the financial statements *up to date* by updating previously recorded ("deferred") assets and liabilities, along with their corresponding expense and revenue accounts.

- Make the financial statements *complete* by including ("accruing") assets and liabilities not previously recorded, along with their corresponding revenue and expense accounts.

LO2   Prepare adjustments needed at the end of the period. p. 138

- The three-step process for preparing adjustments includes
  1. Identify the unadjusted balances in the pair of balance sheet and income statement accounts to be adjusted.
  2. Calculate the amount of the adjustment needed, using a timeline where appropriate.
  3. Prepare an adjusting journal entry to make the adjustment.
- Adjusting journal entries never affect the Cash account.

LO3   Explain how adjustments affect information quality. p. 146

Research shows that, overall, adjustments significantly improve the quality of financial statements, allowing financial statement users to better evaluate past decisions and predict future financial results.

LO4   Prepare an adjusted trial balance. p. 147

An adjusted trial balance is a list of all accounts with their adjusted debit or credit balances indicated in the appropriate column to provide a check on the equality of the debits and credits.

LO5   Prepare adjusted financial statements. p. 149

Adjusted account balances are used in preparing the following financial statements:

- Income Statement: Revenues − Expenses = Net Income.
- Statement of Retained Earnings: Beginning Retained Earnings + Net Income − Dividends Declared = Ending Retained Earnings.
- Balance Sheet: Assets = Liabilities + Stockholders' Equity.

The statement of cash flows and notes to the financial statements are important components of adjusted financial statements, but they will be studied in later chapters.

Explain the closing process. p. 151

LO6

- Closing journal entries are required to *(a)* transfer net income (or loss) and dividends declared into retained earnings, and *(b)* prepare all temporary accounts (revenues, gains, expenses, losses, dividends) for the following year by establishing zero balances in these accounts.

- Two closing journal entries are needed:

    1. Debit each revenue and gain account, credit each expense and loss account, and record the difference (equal to net income) in retained earnings.

    2. Credit the dividends declared account for the amount of its balance and debit retained earnings for the same amount.

KEY TERMS TO KNOW

Accrual Adjustments p. 137
Adjusted Trial Balance p. 147
Adjusting Journal Entries p. 138
Carrying Value (Net Book Value, Book Value) p. 141

Closing Journal Entries p. 152
Contra-Account p. 141
Deferral Adjustments p. 136
Depreciation p. 141

Permanent Accounts p. 152
Post-Closing Trial Balance p. 152
Temporary Accounts p. 152

FOR YOUR PRACTICE

QUESTIONS

1. Briefly explain the purpose of adjustments. List the two types of adjustments, and give an example of an adjustment affecting revenues and expenses for each type.
2. Explain the effect of adjusting journal entries on cash.
3. What is a contra-asset? Give an example of one.
4. What is an adjusted trial balance? What is its purpose?
5. What is the equation for each of the following statements: *(a)* income statement, *(b)* balance sheet, and *(c)* statement of retained earnings?
6. Explain how the financial statements in question 5 relate to each other.
7. What is the purpose of closing journal entries?
8. How do permanent accounts differ from temporary accounts?
9. Why are the income statement accounts closed but the balance sheet accounts are not?
10. What is a post-closing trial balance? Is it a useful part of the accounting cycle? Explain.

MULTIPLE CHOICE

1. Which of the following accounts would not appear in a closing journal entry?
    a. Interest revenue
    b. Accumulated depreciation
    c. Retained earnings
    d. Salary expense
2. Which account is least likely to appear in an adjusting journal entry?
    a. Cash
    b. Interest receivable
    c. Income tax expense
    d. Salaries payable

To practice more multiple choice questions, check out the DVD for use with this book.

3. When a concert promotions company collects cash for ticket sales two months in advance of the show date, which of the following accounts is recorded?

   a.   Accrued liability

   b.   Accounts receivable

   c.   Prepaid expense

   d.   Unearned revenue

4. On December 31, an adjustment is made to reduce unearned revenue and report (earned) revenue. How many accounts will be included in this adjusting journal entry?

   a.   None   *c.*   Two

   b.   One   *d.*   Three

5. An adjusting journal entry to recognize accrued salaries payable would cause which of the following?

   a.   A decrease in assets and stockholders' equity.

   b.   A decrease in assets and liabilities.

   c.   An increase in expenses, liabilities, and stockholders' equity.

   d.   An increase in expenses and liabilities and a decrease in stockholders' equity.

6. An adjusted trial balance

   a.   Shows the ending balances in a "debit" and "credit" format before posting the adjusting journal entries.

   b.   Is prepared after closing entries have been posted.

   c.   Is a tool used by financial analysts to review the performance of publicly traded companies.

   d.   Shows the ending balances resulting from the adjusting journal entries in a "debit" and "credit" format.

7. Company A owns a building. Which of the following statements regarding depreciation is false from an accounting perspective?

   a.   As the value of the building decreases over time, it "depreciates."

   b.   Depreciation is an estimated expense to be recorded each period during the building's life.

   c.   As depreciation is recorded, stockholders' equity is reduced.

   d.   As depreciation is recorded, total assets are reduced.

8. Which of the following trial balances are used as a source for preparing the income statement?

   a.   Unadjusted trial balance

   b.   Pre-adjusted trial balance

   c.   Adjusted trial balance

   d.   Post-closing trial balance

9. Assume the balance in Prepaid Insurance is $2,500 but it should be $1,500. The adjusting journal entry should include which of the following?

   a.   Debit to Prepaid Insurance for $1,000.

   b.   Credit to Insurance Expense for $1,000.

   c.   Debit to Insurance Expense for $1,000.

   d.   Debit to Insurance Expense for $1,500.

10. Assume a company receives a bill for $10,000 for advertising done during the current year. If this bill is not yet recorded at the end of the year, what will the adjusting journal entry include?

   a.   Debit to Advertising Expense of $10,000.

   b.   Credit to Advertising Expense of $10,000.

   c.   Debit to Accrued Liabilities of $10,000.

   d.   Need more information to determine.

Mutiple-Choice Solutions to Questions
1.*b*   2.*a*   3.*d*   4.*c*   5.*d*   6.*d*   7.*a*   8.*c*   9.*c*   10.*a*

MINI-EXERCISES   Available with McGraw-Hill's Homework Manager

LO2, LO4, LO6   **M4-1   Identifying Important Accounting Terms**

Complete the crossword puzzle on the next page, using the clues provided in the box on the right.

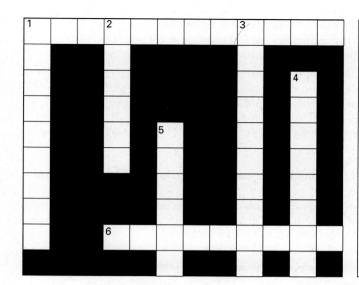

Across
1 A check on the equality of all debit and credit account balances.
6 The type of account that is never closed.

Down
1 The type of account that is closed at the end of the accounting year.
2 The verb that means to *include* an additional amount in the financial statements.
3 Needed to bring an account to its desired balance.
4 One name for the value that an asset or liability is reported at in the financial statements.
5 A type of account that is an offset to another account.

M4-2 Preparing an Adjusted Trial Balance   LO4

DeVita Company has the following adjusted accounts and balances at year-end (June 30, 2006):

Accounts payable	$ 200	Contributed capital	$300	Land	$ 200
Accounts receivable	350	Cost of goods sold	820	Long-term debt	1,300
Accrued liabilities	150	Depreciation expense	110	Prepaid expenses	40
Accumulated		Income taxes expense	110	Salaries expense	660
depreciation	250	Income taxes payable	30	Sales revenue	2,400
Buildings and		Interest expense	80	Rent expense	400
equipment	1,400	Interest revenue	50	Retained earnings	120
Cash	120	Inventories	610	Unearned revenue	100

Required:

Prepare an adjusted trial balance for DeVita Company at June 30, 2006.

M4-3 Matching Transactions with Type of Adjustment   LO1, LO2

Match each transaction with the type of adjustment that will be required, by entering the appropriate letter in the space provided.

	Transaction	Type of Adjustment
____ 1.	Revenue has been collected in advance and will be earned later.	A. Accrual adjustment
____ 2.	Office supplies on hand will be used next accounting period.	
____ 3.	Rent has not yet been collected, but is already earned.	B. Deferral adjustment
____ 4.	An expense has been incurred, but not yet paid or recorded.	
____ 5.	An expense has not yet been incurred, but has been paid in advance.	

M4-4 Matching Transactions with Type of Adjustment   LO1, LO2

Match each transaction with the type of adjustment that will be required, by entering the appropriate letter in the space provided.

	Transaction	Type of Adjustment
____ 1.	At year-end, wages payable of $3,600 had not been recorded or paid.	A. Accrual adjustment
____ 2.	Supplies for office use were purchased during the year for $500, and $100 of the office supplies remained on hand (unused) at year-end.	
____ 3.	Interest of $250 on a note receivable was earned at year-end, although collection of the interest is not due until the following year.	B. Deferral adjustment
____ 4.	At year-end, service revenue of $2,000 was collected in cash but was only partly earned.	

LO2   **M4-5 Recording Adjusting Journal Entries (Deferral Accounts)**

For each of the following transactions for SkyZaa Company, give the adjusting journal entry required at the end of the month on December 31, 2006:

a.   Collected $900 rent for the period December 1, 2006, to February 28, 2007, which was credited to Unearned Rent Revenue on December 1, 2006.

b.   Paid $2,400 for a two-year insurance premium on December 1, 2006; debited Prepaid Insurance for that amount.

c.   Used a machine purchased on December 1, 2006. The company estimates *annual* depreciation of $3,600.

LO2, LO5   **M4-6 Determining Financial Statement Effects of Adjusting Journal Entries (Deferral Accounts)**

For each of the transactions in M4-5, indicate the amounts and direction of effects of the adjusting journal entry on the elements of the balance sheet and income statement. Using the following format, indicate + for increase, − for decrease, and NE for no effect.

	Balance Sheet			Income Statement		
Transaction	Assets	Liabilities	Stockholders' Equity	Revenues	Expenses	Net Income
a						
b						
c						

LO2   **M4-7 Recording Adjusting Journal Entries (Accrual Accounts)**

For each of the following transactions for SkyZaa Company, give the adjusting journal entry required at the end of the month on December 31, 2006:

a.   Received a $220 utility bill for electricity usage in December to be paid in January 2007.

b.   Owed wages to 10 employees who worked three days at $120 each per day at the end of December. The company will pay employees at the end of the first week of January 2007.

c.   On December 1, 2006, loaned money to an executive who agreed to repay the loan in one year along with one full year of interest equal to $360.

LO2, LO5   **M4-8 Determining Financial Statement Effects of Adjusting Journal Entries (Accrual Accounts)**

For each of the transactions in M4-7, indicate the amounts and direction of effects of the adjusting journal entry on the elements of the balance sheet and income statement. Using the following format, indicate + for increase, − for decrease, and NE for no effect.

	Balance Sheet			Income Statement		
Transaction	Assets	Liabilities	Stockholders' Equity	Revenues	Expenses	Net Income
a						
b						
c						

LO5   **M4-9 Reporting an Income Statement**

SkyZaa Company has the following adjusted trial balance at December 31, 2006. No dividends were declared.

	Debit	Credit
Cash	$ 1,500	
Accounts receivable	2,000	
Interest receivable	30	
Prepaid insurance	2,300	
Notes receivable	3,000	
Equipment	12,000	
Accumulated depreciation		$ 300
Accounts payable		1,600
Accrued expenses payable		3,820
Income taxes payable		2,900
Unearned rent revenue		600
Contributed capital		2,400
Retained earnings		1,000
Sales revenue		42,000
Interest revenue		30
Rent revenue		300
Wages expense	21,600	
Depreciation expense	300	
Utilities expense	220	
Insurance expense	100	
Rent expense	9,000	
Income tax expense	2,900	
Total	$54,950	$54,950

Prepare an income statement for 2006. SkyZaa's core operations relate to computer technology services. How much net income did SkyZaa Company generate during 2006?

M4-10 Reporting a Statement of Retained Earnings   **LO5**

Refer to M4-9. Prepare a statement of retained earnings for 2006.

M4-11 Reporting a Balance Sheet   **LO5**

Refer to M4-7, M4-9, and M4-10. Prepare a classified balance sheet at December 31, 2006. Are SkyZaa Company's assets financed primarily by debt or equity?

M4-12 Recording Closing Journal Entries   **LO6**

Refer to the adjusted trial balance in M4-9. Prepare closing journal entries on December 31, 2006.

M4-13 Preparing and Posting Adjusting Journal Entries   **LO2**

At December 31, the unadjusted trial balance of H&R Tacks reports Supplies Inventory of $8,400 and Supplies Expense of $0. On December 31, supplies costing $1,300 are on hand. Prepare the adjusting journal entry on December 31. In separate T-accounts for each account, enter the unadjusted balances, post the adjusting journal entry, and report the adjusted balance.

M4-14 Preparing and Posting Adjusting Journal Entries   **LO2**

At December 31, the unadjusted trial balance of H&R Tacks reports Equipment of $28,000 and zero balances in Accumulated Depreciation and Depreciation Expense. Depreciation for the period is estimated to be $5,400. Prepare the adjusting journal entry on December 31. In separate T-accounts for each account, enter the unadjusted balances, post the adjusting journal entry, and report the adjusted balance.

M4-15 Preparing and Posting Adjusting Journal Entries   **LO2**

At December 31, the unadjusted trial balance of H&R Tacks reports Prepaid Insurance of $4,800 and Insurance Expense of $0. The insurance was purchased on July 1 and provides coverage for 12 months. Prepare the adjusting journal entry on December 31. In separate T-accounts for each account, enter the unadjusted balances, post the adjusting journal entry, and report the adjusted balance.

M4-16 Preparing and Posting Adjusting Journal Entries   **LO2**

At December 31, the unadjusted trial balance of H&R Tacks reports Unearned Revenue of $3,000 and Sales and Service Revenues of $31,800. One-half of the unearned revenues have been earned as of December 31. Prepare the adjusting journal entry on December 31. In separate T-accounts for each account, enter the unadjusted balances, post the adjusting journal entry, and report the adjusted balance.

LO2   M4-17 Preparing and Posting Adjusting Journal Entries

At December 31, the unadjusted trial balance of H&R Tacks reports Wages Payable of $0 and Wages Expense of $17,000. Employees have been paid for work done up to December 27, but the $900 they have earned for December 28–31 has not yet been paid or recorded. Prepare the adjusting journal entry on December 31. In separate T-accounts for each account, enter the unadjusted balances, post the adjusting journal entry, and report the adjusted balance.

LO2   M4-18 Preparing and Posting Adjusting Journal Entries

At December 31, the unadjusted trial balance of H&R Tacks reports Interest Payable of $0 and Interest Expense of $0. Interest incurred and owed in December totals $200. Prepare the adjusting journal entry on December 31. In separate T-accounts for each account, enter the unadjusted balances, post the adjusting journal entry, and report the adjusted balance.

LO2   M4-19 Preparing and Posting Adjusting Journal Entries

At December 31, the unadjusted trial balance of H&R Tacks reports Dividends Declared of $0 and Dividends Payable of $0. A $500 dividend was declared on December 27, with payment in cash to occur three weeks later. Prepare the adjusting journal entry on December 31. In separate T-accounts for each account, enter the unadjusted balances, post the adjusting journal entry, and report the adjusted balance.

LO4   M4-20 Preparing an Adjusted Trial Balance

The unadjusted trial balance for H&R Tacks reported the following account balances: Cash $3,000; Accounts Receivable $500; Supplies Inventory $8,400; Prepaid Insurance $4,800; Equipment $28,000; Accounts Payable $1,200; Unearned Revenue $3,000; Notes Payable $5,000; Contributed Capital $15,000; Retained Earnings $5,700; Sales and Service Revenue $31,800; and Wages Expense $17,000. Prepare an adjusted trial balance as of December 31 that includes the adjustments required in M4-13 through M4-19.

LO2, LO4–LO6   M4-21 Organizing the Steps in the Accounting Process

The following eight steps are included in the accounting process. In one column write the numbers 1 through 8. Beside each number, indicate the steps in their proper order: (a) prepare financial statements, (b) analyze transactions, (c) prepare a post-closing trial balance, (d) prepare an adjusted trial balance, (e) prepare journal entries and post to accounts, (f) prepare closing journal entries and post to accounts, (g) prepare adjusting journal entries and post to accounts, and (h) prepare an unadjusted trial balance.

EXERCISES   Available with McGraw-Hill's Homework Manager

LO4   E4-1 Preparing an Adjusted Trial Balance from Adjusted Account Balances

Goodison Consultants, Inc., provides marketing research for clients in the retail industry. The company had the following unadjusted balances at September 30, 2007:

Cash	Accumulated Depreciation	Accrued Liabilities
173,000	18,100	25,650

Wages and Benefits Expense	General and Administrative Expense	Supplies
1,590,000	320,050	12,200

Accounts Receivable	Prepaid Expenses	Interest Expense
225,400	10,200	17,200

Income Taxes Payable	Consulting Fees Earned	Retained Earnings
2,030	2,564,200	?

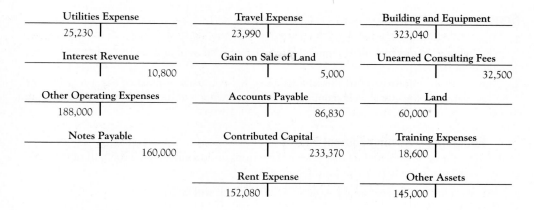

Utilities Expense		Travel Expense		Building and Equipment	
25,230		23,990		323,040	

Interest Revenue		Gain on Sale of Land		Unearned Consulting Fees	
	10,800		5,000		32,500

Other Operating Expenses		Accounts Payable		Land	
188,000			86,830	60,000	

Notes Payable		Contributed Capital		Training Expenses	
	160,000		233,370	18,600	

Rent Expense		Other Assets	
152,080		145,000	

Required:

Prepare an adjusted trial balance for Goodison Consultants, Inc., at September 30, 2007. Solve for the "?" in retained earnings.

E4-2 Identifying Adjustments by Scanning a Trial Balance   L01

Coach, Inc.—the maker of handbags and other women's and men's accessories—was previously owned by Sara Lee Corporation until April 2001, when Coach was spun off as a separate company. Assume the following adjusted balances were reported in Coach's trial balance and were used to prepare its June 28, 2003, year-end financial statements.

COACH INCORPORATED Adjusted Trial Balance At June 28, 2003 (millions of dollars)		
	Debit	**Credit**
Cash	$ 229,176	
Accounts receivable	35,470	
Inventories	143,807	
Prepaid expenses	18,821	
Property and equipment	291,838	
Accumulated depreciation		$ 173,291
Other assets	71,831	
Accounts payable		26,637
Accrued liabilities		108,273
Income taxes payable		26,471
Notes payable		3,615
Other liabilities		25,727
Contributed capital		216,314
Retained earnings		63,987
Sales revenue		953,226
Cost of sales	275,797	
Selling, general, and administrative expenses	433,667	
Other expenses	7,608	
Interest revenue		1,754
Interest expense	695	
Income tax expense	90,585	
	$1,599,295	$1,599,295

Required:

1. Based on the information in the trial balance, list two pairs of balance sheet and income statement accounts that likely required *deferral adjustments* as of June 28 (no computations are necessary).
2. Based on the information in the trial balance, list two pairs of balance sheet and income statement accounts that likely required *accrual adjustments* as of June 28 (no computations are necessary).

LO1, LO2

E4-3   Recording Adjusting Journal Entries

Cell Yell Company completed its first year of operations on December 31, 2006. All of the 2006 entries have been recorded, except for the following:

a.   At year-end, employees earned wages of $6,000, which will be paid on the next payroll date, January 6, 2007.
b.   At year-end, the company had earned interest revenue of $3,000. It will be collected March 1, 2007.

Required:

1. What is the annual reporting period for this company?
2. Identify whether each required adjustment is a deferral or an accrual. Using the process illustrated in the chapter, give the required adjusting journal entry for transactions *a* and *b*.
3. Why are these adjustments needed?

LO1, LO2

E4-4   Recording Adjusting Journal Entries and Reporting Balances in Financial Statements

Fes Company is making adjusting journal entries for the year ended December 31, 2007. In developing information for the adjusting journal entries, you learned the following:

a.   A two-year insurance premium of $7,200 was paid on January 1, 2007, for coverage beginning on that date. As of December 31, 2007, the unadjusted balances were $7,200 for Prepaid Insurance and $0 for Insurance Expense.
b.   At December 31, 2007, you obtained the following data relating to shipping supplies.

Unadjusted balance in Shipping Supplies on December 31, 2007	$15,000
Unadjusted balance in Shipping Supplies Expense on December 31, 2007	72,000
Shipping supplies on hand, counted on December 31, 2007	11,000

Required:

1. Of the $7,200 paid for insurance, what amount should be reported on the 2007 income statement as Insurance Expense? What amount should be reported on the December 31, 2007, balance sheet as Prepaid Insurance?
2. What amount should be reported on the 2007 income statement as Shipping Supplies Expense? What amount should be reported on the December 31, 2007, balance sheet as Shipping Supplies?
3. Using the process illustrated in the chapter, prepare an adjusting journal entry for insurance at December 31, 2007.
4. Using the process illustrated in the chapter, prepare an adjusting journal entry for shipping supplies at December 31, 2007.

LO2, LO5

E4-5   Determining Financial Statement Effects of Adjusting Journal Entries

Refer to E4-3 and E4-4.

Required:

For each of the transactions in E4-3 and E4-4, indicate the amount and direction of effects of each adjusting journal entry on the elements of the balance sheet and income statement. Using the following format, indicate + for increase, − for decrease, and NE for no effect.

	Balance Sheet			**Income Statement**		
Transaction	**Assets**	**Liabilities**	**Stockholders' Equity**	**Revenues**	**Expenses**	**Net Income**
E4-3 *a*						
E4-3 *b*						
E4-4 *a*						
E4-4 *b*						

E4-6 Recording Seven Typical Adjusting Journal Entries

LO1, LO2

Bauer's Board Store is completing the accounting process for its first year ended December 31, 2006. The transactions during 2006 have been journalized and posted. The following data are available to determine adjusting journal entries:

a. The unadjusted balance in Office Supplies at December 31, 2006, was $850. A year-end count showed $300 of supplies on hand.

b. Wages earned by employees during December 2006, unpaid and unrecorded at December 31, 2006, amounted to $2,700. The last paychecks were issued December 28; the next payments will be made on January 6, 2007.

c. A portion of the store's basement is rented for $1,100 per month to N. Myers. On November 1, 2006, the store collected six months' rent in the amount of $6,600 in advance from Myers. It was credited in full to Unearned Rent Revenue when collected.

d. The remaining basement space is rented to Kim's Specialty Shop for $520 per month, payable monthly. On December 31, 2006, the rent for November and December 2006 had not been collected or recorded. Collection is expected January 10, 2007.

e. The store purchased delivery equipment at the beginning of the year. The estimated depreciation for 2006 is $3,000, although none has been recorded yet.

f. On December 31, 2006, the unadjusted balance in Prepaid Insurance was $3,600. This was the amount paid in the middle of the year for a two-year insurance policy with coverage beginning on July 1, 2006. The unadjusted balance in Insurance Expense was $800, which was the cost of insurance from January 1 to June 30, 2006.

g. Bauer's operates a repair shop, doing some work for Myers. At the end of December 31, 2006, Myers had not paid for work completed amounting to $750. This amount has not yet been recorded as Repair Shop Revenue. Collection is expected during January 2007.

Required:

1. For each of the items listed above, identify whether an accrual adjustment, a deferral adjustment, or no adjustment is required.

2. Using the process illustrated in the chapter, prepare for each situation the adjusting journal entry that should be recorded for Bauer's at December 31, 2006.

E4-7 Determining Financial Statement Effects of Seven Typical Adjusting Journal Entries

LO2, LO5

Refer to E4-6.

Required:

For each of the transactions in E4-6, indicate the amount and direction of effects of the adjusting journal entry on the elements of the balance sheet and income statement. Using the following format, indicate + for increase, − for decrease, and NE for no effect.

	Balance Sheet			**Income Statement**		
Transaction	**Assets**	**Liabilities**	**Stockholders' Equity**	**Revenues**	**Expenses**	**Net Income**
a						
b						
c						
etc.						

LO2, LO6

E4-8 Recording Transactions Including Adjusting and Closing Journal Entries

The following accounts are used by Mouse Potato, Inc., a computer game maker.

Codes	Accounts	Codes	Accounts
A	Cash	K	Contributed capital
B	Office supplies	L	Retained earnings
C	Accounts receivable	M	Dividends declared
D	Office equipment	N	Service revenue
E	Accumulated depreciation	O	Interest revenue
F	Note payable	P	Wage expense
G	Wages payable	Q	Depreciation expense
H	Interest payable	R	Interest expense
I	Dividends payable	S	Supplies expense
J	Unearned service revenue	T	None of the above

Required:

For each of the following independent situations, give the journal entry by entering the appropriate code(s) and amount(s). We've done the first one for you as an example.

	Debit		Credit	
Independent Situations	**Code**	**Amount**	**Code**	**Amount**
a. Accrued wages, unrecorded and unpaid at year-end, $400 (example).	P	400	G	400
b. Service revenue collected in advance, $800.				
c. Dividends declared during year but not yet paid, $900.				
d. Depreciation expense for year, $1,000.				
e. Service revenue earned but not yet collected at year-end, $600.				
f. Balance in office supplies account, $400; supplies on hand at year-end, $150.				
g. At year-end, interest on note payable not yet recorded or paid, $220.				
h. Balance at year-end in Service Revenue account, $62,000. Give the journal entry to close this one account at year-end.				
i. Balance at year-end in Interest Expense account, $420. Give the journal entry to close this one account at year-end.				

LO1, LO2

E4-9 Inferring Transactions from Accrual Accounts

Deere & Company was incorporated in 1868 and today is the world's leading producer of agricultural equipment. Oddly enough the company also provides credit, managed health care plans, and insurance products for businesses and the general public. The following information is taken from a recent annual report (in millions of dollars):

Income Tax Payable			Dividends Payable			Interest Payable		
	Beg. bal.	87		Beg. bal.	53		Beg. bal.	65
84	(a)	?	(b) ?		211	544	(c)	?
	End. bal.	227		End. bal.	53		End. bal.	79

Required:

1. For each accrued liability account, describe the typical transactions that cause it to increase and decrease.

2. Express each T-account in equation format and then solve for the missing amounts for a, b, and c (in millions). For example, the Interest Payable T-account can be expressed as: $65 + ? - 544 = 79$. By rearranging the equation, you can solve for $? = 79 + 544 - 65$.

E4-10 Analyzing the Effects of Adjusting Journal Entries on the Income Statement and Balance Sheet

LO2, LO5

On December 31, 2006, Alan and Company prepared an income statement and balance sheet but the boneheads failed to take into account four adjusting journal entries. The income statement, prepared on this incorrect basis, reported income before income taxes of $30,000. The balance sheet (before the effect of income taxes) reflected total assets, $90,000; total liabilities, $40,000; and stockholders' equity, $50,000. The data for the four adjusting journal entries follow:

a. Depreciation of $8,000 for the year on equipment was not recorded.
b. Wages amounting to $17,000 for the last three days of December 2006 were not paid and not recorded (the next payroll will be on January 10, 2007).
c. Rent revenue of $4,800 was collected on December 1, 2006, for office space for the three-month period December 1, 2006, to February 28, 2007. The $4,800 was credited in full to Unearned Rent Revenue when collected.
d. Income taxes were not recorded. The income tax rate for the company is 30 percent.

Required:

Complete the following table to show the effects of the four adjusting journal entries (indicate deductions with parentheses):

Items	Net Income	Total Assets	Total Liabilities	Stockholders' Equity
Amounts reported	$30,000	$90,000	$40,000	$50,000
Effect of depreciation				
Effect of wages				
Effect of rent revenue				
Adjusted balances	6,600	82,000	55,400	26,600
Effect of income taxes				
Correct amounts				

E4-11 Preparing Adjusting Journal Entries and Indicating Their Effects on the Income Statement and Balance Sheet

LO2, LO5

On December 31, 2005, the bookkeeper for Tait Company prepared the following income statement and balance sheet summarized here, but neglected to consider three adjusting journal entries.

	As Prepared	Effects of Adjusting Journal Entries	Adjusted Amounts
Income Statement			
Revenues	$98,000		
Expenses	(72,000)		
Income tax expense			
Net income	$26,000		
Balance Sheet			
Assets			
Cash	$20,000		
Accounts receivable	22,000		
Rent receivable			
Equipment	50,000		
Accumulated depreciation	(10,000)		
	$82,000		
Liabilities			
Accounts payable	$10,000		
Income taxes payable			
Stockholders' Equity			
Contributed capital	40,000		
Retained earnings	32,000		
	$82,000		

Data on the three adjusting journal entries follow.

a.   Depreciation of $5,000 on the equipment for 2005 was not recorded.
b.   Rent revenue of $2,000 earned during December 2005 was neither collected nor recorded.
c.   Income tax expense of $6,900 for 2005 was neither paid nor recorded.

Required:

1.   Prepare the three adjusting journal entries that were omitted. Use the account titles shown in the income statement and balance sheet above.
2.   Complete the two columns to the right in the above table to show the correct amounts on the income statement and balance sheet.

LO2, LO5   **E4-12 Reporting an Adjusted Income Statement**

Dyer, Inc., completed its first year of operations on December 31, 2006. Because this is the end of the annual accounting period, the company bookkeeper prepared the following tentative income statement:

Income Statement, 2006		
Rental revenue		$114,000
Expenses:		
Salaries and wages expense	$28,500	
Maintenance expense	12,000	
Rent expense	9,000	
Utilities expense	4,000	
Gas and oil expense	3,000	
Other expenses	1,000	
Total expenses		57,500
Income		$ 56,500

You are an independent CPA hired by the company to audit the company's accounting systems and financial statements. In your audit, you developed additional data as follows:

a.   Wages for the last three days of December amounting to $310 were not recorded or paid.
b.   The $400 telephone bill for December 2006 has not been recorded or paid.
c.   Depreciation on rental autos, amounting to $23,000 for 2006, was not recorded.
d.   Interest of $500 was not recorded on the note payable by Dyer, Inc.
e.   The Unearned Rental Revenue account includes $4,000 revenue to be earned in January 2007.
f.   Maintenance expense excludes $600, which is the cost of maintenance supplies used during 2006.
g.   The income tax expense for 2006 is $7,000, but it won't actually be paid until 2007.

Required:

1.   What adjusting journal entry for each item a through g should be recorded at December 31, 2006? If none is required, explain why.
2.   Prepare an adjusted income statement for 2006.

LO2, LO5   **E4-13 Adjusting Unearned Subscriptions**

You are the regional sales manager for Abruzzo News Company. Abruzzo is making adjusting journal entries for the year ended March 31, 2007. On September 1, 2006, $18,000 cash was received from customers in your region for three-year magazine subscriptions beginning on that date. The magazines are published and mailed to customers every month. These were the only subscription sales in your region during the year.

Required:

1.   What amount should be reported on the 2007 income statement for subscriptions revenue?

2. What amount should be reported on the March 31, 2007, balance sheet for unearned subscriptions revenue?

3. Give the adjusting journal entry at March 31, 2007, assuming that the subscriptions received on September 1, 2006, were recorded for the full amount in Unearned Subscriptions Revenue.

E4-14 Recording Four Adjusting Journal Entries and Preparing an Adjusted Trial Balance   LO2, LO4

Seneca Company prepared the following unadjusted trial balance at the end of its second year of operations ending December 31, 2005. To simplify this exercise, the amounts given are in thousands of dollars.

Account Titles	Debit	Credit
Cash	38	
Accounts receivable	9	
Prepaid insurance	6	
Machinery	80	
Accumulated depreciation		
Accounts payable		9
Wages payable		
Income taxes payable		
Contributed capital		76
Retained earnings		4
Sales revenue		80
Cost of goods sold expense	26	
Wages expense	10	
Totals	169	169

Other data not yet recorded at December 31, 2005:

a. Insurance expired during 2005, $5.
b. Depreciation expense for 2005, $4.
c. Wages payable, $7.
d. Income tax expense, $9.

Required:

1. Prepare the adjusting journal entries for 2005.
2. Using T-accounts, determine the adjusted balances in each account and prepare an adjusted trial balance as of December 31, 2005.

E4-15 Reporting an Income Statement, Statement of Retained Earnings,   LO5
and Balance Sheet

Refer to E4-14.

Required:

Using the adjusted balances in E4-14, prepare an income statement, statement of retained earnings, and balance sheet for 2005.

E4-16 Recording Closing Entries   LO6

Refer to E4-14.

Required:

Using the adjusted balances in E4-14, give the closing journal entry for 2005. What is the purpose of "closing the books" at the end of the accounting period?

SIMPLIFY WITH SPREADSHEETS

LO4, LO5   **SS4-1** **Aggregating Accounts on an Adjusted Trial Balance to Prepare an Income Statement, Statement of Retained Earnings, and Balance Sheet**

Assume you recently were hired for a job in Evansville, Indiana, at the head office of Escalade, Inc.—the company that makes Goalrilla™ and Goaliath® basketball systems, and is the exclusive supplier of Ping Pong® and Stiga® equipment for table tennis. Your first assignment is to review the company's lengthy adjusted trial balance to determine the accounts that can be combined ("aggregated") into single line-items that will be reported on the financial statements. By querying the accounting system, you were able to obtain the following alphabetical list of accounts and their adjusted balances as of December 31.

Accounts payable	$ 2,792	Inventory of finished goods	$10,263	Prepaid insurance	$ 108
Accounts receivable	34,141	Inventory of goods being made	4,536	Prepaid rent	434
Accrued interest payable	42	Inventory of supplies		Rent expense	7,350
Accrued wages payable	5,856	and materials	5,750	Retained earnings	27,571
Accrued warranties payable	1,324	Long-term bank loan	14,000	Salaries expense	3,582
Accumulated depreciation	26,198	Long-term contract payable	1,837	Sales commissions expense	3,349
Cash	3,370	Long-term note payable	2,700	Sales of basketball systems	98,998
Contributed capital	7,165	Manufacturing equipment	12,962	Sales of other products	28,710
Cost of goods sold	111,164	Notes payable (current)	11,390	Sales of ping pong tables	27,747
Depreciation expense	862	Notes receivable	400	Shipping expenses	1,448
Factory buildings	7,070	Office building	2,301	Transport equipment	7,560
Income tax expense	5,804	Office equipment	2,363	Unearned revenue	8,144
Income tax payable	1,189	Office supplies expense	69	Utilities expense	2,111
Insurance expense	2,368	Other accrued liabilities	1,638	Wages expense	3,024
Interest expense	950	Other long-term assets	28,310	Warranties expense	1,226
Interest receivable	415	Packaging expenses	1,010	Warehouse buildings	3,001

Required:

With the above account names and balances, prepare an adjusted trial balance using a spreadsheet. Also prepare an income statement, statement of retained earnings, and balance sheet that import their numbers from the adjusted trial balance or from the other statements where appropriate. If similar accounts can be aggregated into a single line-item for each financial statement, use a formula to compute the aggregated amount. To be sure that you understand how to import numbers from other parts of a spreadsheet, you e-mail your friend Billy for advice. Here's his reply.

From: BillyTheTutor@yahoo.com
To: HairZed@hotmail.com
Cc:
Subject: Excel Help

Hey pal. You're bouncing from job to job like one of those ping-pong balls that your company sells. Okay, to import a number from another spreadsheet, you first click on the cell where you want the number to appear. For example, if you want to enter the Cash balance in the balance sheet, click on the cell in the balance sheet where the cash number is supposed to appear. Enter the equals sign (=) and then click on the tab that takes you to the worksheet containing the adjusted trial balance. In that worksheet, click on the cell that contains the amount you want to import into the balance sheet and then press enter. This will create a link from the adjusted trial balance cell to the balance sheet cell. At the end of this message, I've pasted a screen shot showing the formula I would enter on the balance sheet to import the total of three related inventory accounts from the adjusted trial balance. Don't forget to save the file using a name that indicates who you are.

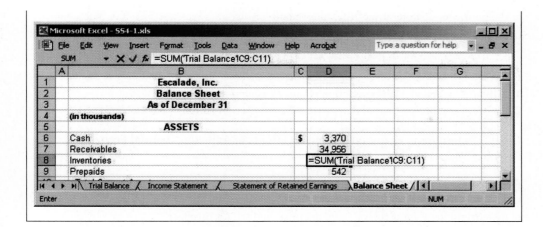

COACHED PROBLEMS

CP4-1 Preparing an Adjusted Trial Balance, Closing Journal Entry, and Post-Closing Trial Balance

LO4, LO6

Dell Computer Corporation, which originally was named PC's Limited, is the world's largest computer systems company selling directly to customers. The following is a list of accounts and amounts reported for the year ended January 31, 2003. The accounts have normal debit or credit balances and the dollars are rounded to the nearest million.

COACH'S CORNER

Notice that the income statement accounts for the year ended January 31, 2003, haven't yet been closed into retained earnings.

Accounts payable	$ 5,989	Long-term debt	$ 506
Accounts receivable	2,586	Other assets	7,027
Accrued liabilities	2,944	Other liabilities	1,158
Accumulated depreciation	749	Property, plant, and equipment	1,662
Cash	4,638	Research and development	
Contributed capital	1,479	expense	455
Cost of goods sold	29,055	Retained earnings	1,272
Income tax expense	905	Sales revenue	35,404
Interest revenue	183	Selling, general, and	
Inventories	306	administrative expenses	3,050

Required:

1. Prepare an adjusted trial balance at January 31, 2003. Is the Retained Earnings balance of $1,272 the amount that would be reported on the balance sheet as of January 31, 2003?
2. Prepare the closing entry required at January 31, 2003.
3. Prepare a post-closing trial balance at January 31, 2003.

CP4-2 Recording Adjusting Journal Entries

LO1, LO2

McCall Company's annual accounting year ends on December 31. It is now December 31, 2006, and all of the 2006 entries have been made except for the following:

COACH'S CORNER

a. $4,800 for six months equals $800 per month. This means $3,200 is earned during the four months from September 1–December 31, and $1,600 remains unearned at December 31.

c. $4,200 for 12 months equals $350 per month.

h. Adjusted income based on *a* through *g* is $30,000.

a. On September 1, 2006, McCall collected six months' rent of $4,800 on storage space. At that date, McCall debited Cash and credited Unearned Rent Revenue for $4,800.

b. The company earned service revenue of $3,000 on a special job that was completed December 29, 2006. Collection will be made during January 2007. No entry has been recorded.

c. On November 1, 2006, McCall paid a one-year premium for property insurance, $4,200, for coverage starting on that date. Cash was credited and Prepaid Insurance was debited for this amount.

d. At December 31, 2006, wages earned by employees totaled $1,100. The employees will be paid on the next payroll date, January 15, 2007.

e. Depreciation of $1,000 must be recognized on a service truck purchased this year.

f. On December 27, 2006, the company received a tax bill of $400 from the city for 2006 property taxes on land. The tax bill is payable during January 2007.

g. The company owes interest of $400 on a bank loan taken out on October 1, 2006. The interest will be paid when the loan is repaid on September 30, 2007.

eXcel

h. The income before any of the adjustments or income taxes was $27,400. The company's federal income tax rate is 30 percent. Compute adjusted income based on *a.* through *g.* to determine and record income tax expense.

Required:

1. Indicate whether each transaction relates to a deferral or accrual.
2. Give the adjusting journal entry required for each transaction at December 31, 2006.

LO2, LO5

CP4-3 Determining Financial Statement Effects of Adjusting Journal Entries
Refer to CP4-2.

Required:

Using the following headings, indicate the effect of each adjusting journal entry and the amount of the effect. Use + for increase, − for decrease, and NE for no effect.

	Balance Sheet			Income Statement		
Transaction	**Assets**	**Liabilities**	**Stockholders' Equity**	**Revenues**	**Expenses**	**Net Income**
a						
b						
c						
etc.						

LO2, LO5

CP4-4 Analyzing a Student's Business and Preparing an Adjusted Income Statement
During the summer between her junior and senior years, Susan Irwin needed to earn enough money for the coming academic year. Unable to obtain a job with a reasonable salary, she decided to try the lawn care business for three months. After a survey of the market potential, Susan bought a used pickup truck on June 1 for $1,500. On each door she painted "Susan's Lawn Service, Phone 555-4487." She also spent $900 for mowers, trimmers, and tools. To acquire these items, she borrowed $2,500 cash by signing a note payable promising to pay the $2,500 plus interest of $75 at the end of the three months (ending August 31).

At the end of the summer, Susan realized that she had done a lot of work, and her bank account looked good. This fact made her think about how much profit the business had earned.

A review of the check stubs showed the following: Bank deposits of collections from customers totaled $12,600. The following checks had been written: gas, oil, and lubrication, $920; pickup repairs, $210; mower repair, $75; miscellaneous supplies used, $80; helpers, $4,500; payroll taxes, $175; payment for assistance in preparing payroll tax forms, $25; insurance, $125; telephone, $110; and $2,575 to pay off the note including interest (on August 31). A notebook kept in the pickup, plus some unpaid bills, reflected that customers still owed her $800 for lawn services provided and that she owed $200 for gas and oil (credit card charges). She estimated that the depreciation on the truck and the other equipment amounted to $500 for three months.

Required:

1. Prepare an accrual basis income statement for Susan's Lawn Service covering the quarter from June 1–August 31, 2006. Assume the business is not subject to income tax.
2. Assuming Susan's Lawn Service remains in business, do you see a need for one or more additional financial reports for this company for 2006 and thereafter? Explain.

LO1, LO2, LO4–LO6

CP4-5 Comprehensive Review Problem: From Recording Transactions (including Adjusting Journal Entries) to Preparing Financial Statements and Closing Journal Entries (Chapters 2, 3, and 4)
Brothers Harry and Herman Hausyerday began operations of their machine shop (H & H Tool, Inc.) on January 1, 2004. The annual reporting period ends December 31. The trial balance on January 1, 2006, follows (the amounts are rounded to thousands of dollars to simplify):

Account No.	Account Titles	Debit	Credit
01	Cash	3	
02	Accounts receivable	5	
03	Supplies	12	
04	Land		
05	Equipment	60	
06	Accumulated depreciation (on equipment)		6
07	Other assets	4	
11	Accounts payable		5
12	Notes payable		
13	Wages payable		
14	Interest payable		
15	Income taxes payable		
16	Dividends payable		
21	Contributed capital		65
31	Retained earnings		8
32	Dividends declared		
35	Service revenue		
40	Depreciation expense		
41	Income tax expense		
42	Interest expense		
43	Supplies and other operating expenses		
	Totals	84	84

COACH'S CORNER

e. When credit is used for operating costs, accounts payable typically is used rather than accrued liabilities. The account accrued liabilities typically is used only for accrual adjustments made at the end of the period.

k. When a dividend is declared, the company establishes a liability and records the dividend itself in a temporary account.

l. Payment of the dividend in cash reduces the dividend liability.

m. What was the unadjusted balance in the supplies account at the end of the year?

Transactions during 2006 (summarized in thousands of dollars) follow:

a. Borrowed $10 cash on a short-term note payable dated March 1, 2006.
b. Purchased land for future building site, paid cash, $9.
c. Earned revenues for 2006, $160, including $40 on credit and $120 collected in cash.
d. Issued additional shares of stock for $3.
e. Recognized operating expenses for 2006, $85, including $15 on credit and $70 paid in cash.
f. Collected accounts receivable, $24.
g. Purchased other assets, $10 cash.
h. Paid accounts payable, $13.
i. Purchased supplies on account for future use, $18.
j. Signed a $25 service contract to start February 1, 2007.
k. Declared a dividend, $17.
l. Paid the $17 dividend in cash.

Data for adjusting journal entries:

m. Supplies counted on December 31, 2006, $14.
n. Depreciation for the year on the equipment, $6.
o. Accrued interest on notes payable of $1.
p. Wages earned since the December 24 payroll not yet paid, $12.
q. Income tax for the year was $8. It will be paid in 2007.

Required:

1. Set up T-accounts for the accounts on the trial balance and enter beginning balances.
2. Record journal entries for transactions *a* through *l* and post them to the T-accounts.
3. Prepare an unadjusted trial balance.
4. Record and post the adjusting journal entries *m* through *q*.
5. Prepare an adjusted trial balance.
6. Prepare an income statement, statement of retained earnings, and balance sheet.
7. Prepare and post the closing journal entries.
8. Prepare a post-closing trial balance.
9. How much net income did H & H Tool, Inc. generate during 2006? Is the company financed primarily by debt or equity?

GROUP A PROBLEMS   Available with McGraw-Hill's Homework Manager

PA4-1 Preparing a Trial Balance, Closing Journal Entry, and Post-Closing Trial Balance

Starbucks Corporation purchases and roasts high-quality whole bean coffees and sells them along with fresh-brewed coffees, its exclusive line of Frappucino® blended beverages, Italian-style espresso beverages, and premium teas, all in a variety of pompously named sizes. In addition to sales through its company-operated retail stores, Starbucks also sells coffee and tea products through other channels of distribution. The following is a simplified list of accounts and amounts reported in recent financial statements. The accounts have normal debit or credit balances and the dollars are rounded to the nearest million. Assume the year ended on September 30, 2006.

Accounts payable	$ 56	Interest revenue	$ 9
Accounts receivable	48	Inventories	181
Accrued liabilities	131	Long-term debt	40
Accumulated depreciation	321	Other current assets	72
Cash	66	Other long-lived assets	106
Contributed capital	647	Other operating expenses	51
Cost of goods sold	741	Prepaid expenses	19
Depreciation expense	98	Property, plant, and equipment	1,081
General and administrative		Retained earnings	212
expenses	90	Service revenues	1,680
Income tax expense	62	Short-term bank debt	64
Interest expense	1	Store operating expenses	544

Required:

1. Prepare an adjusted trial balance at September 30, 2006. Is the Retained Earnings balance of $212 the amount that would be reported on the balance sheet as of September 30, 2006?
2. Prepare the closing entry required at September 30, 2006.
3. Prepare a post-closing trial balance at September 30, 2006.

PA4-2 Recording Adjusting Journal Entries

Big Towing Company is at the end of its accounting year, December 31, 2006. The following data that must be considered were developed from the company's records and related documents:

a.   On July 1, 2006, a three-year insurance premium on equipment in the amount of $1,200 was paid and debited in full to Prepaid Insurance on that date. Coverage began on July 1.

b.   At the end of 2006, the unadjusted balance in the office supplies account was $1,000. A physical count of supplies on December 31, 2006, indicated supplies costing $300 were still on hand.

c.   On December 31, 2006, YY's Garage completed repairs on one of the company's trucks at a cost of $800. The amount is not yet recorded. It will be paid during January 2007.

d.   In December, the 2006 property tax bill for $1,600 was received from the city. The taxes, which have not been recorded, will be paid on February 15, 2007.

e.   On December 31, 2006, the company completed a contract for an out-of-state company for $8,000 payable by the customer within 30 days. No cash has been collected, and no journal entry has been made for this transaction.

f.   On July 1, 2006, the company purchased a new hauling van. Depreciation for July–December 2006, estimated to total $2,750, has not been recorded.

g.   The company owes interest of $500 on a bank loan taken out on October 1, 2006. The interest will be paid when the loan is repaid on September 30, 2007.

h.   The income before any of the adjustments or income taxes was $30,000. The company's federal income tax rate is 30 percent. Compute adjusted income based on all of the preceding information, and then determine and record income tax expense.

Required:

1. Indicate whether each transaction relates to a deferral or accrual.
2. Give the adjusting journal entry required for each transaction at December 31, 2006.

PA4-3 Determining Financial Statement Effects of Adjusting Journal Entries

Refer to PA4-2.

LO2, LO5

e**X**cel

Required:

Using the following headings, indicate the effect of each adjusting journal entry and the amount of each. Use + for increase, − for decrease, and NE for no effect.

	Balance Sheet			Income Statement		
Transaction	**Assets**	**Liabilities**	**Stockholders' Equity**	**Revenues**	**Expenses**	**Net Income**
a						
b						
c						
etc.						

PA4-4 Analyzing a Student's Business and Preparing an Adjusted Income Statement

LO2, LO5

Upon graduation from high school, John Abel immediately accepted a job as an electrician's assistant for a large local electrical repair company. After three years of hard work, John received an electrician's license and decided to start his own business. He had saved $12,000, which he invested in the business. First, he transferred this amount from his savings account to a business bank account for Abel Electric Repair Company, Incorporated. His lawyer had advised him to start as a corporation. He then purchased a used panel truck for $9,000 cash and secondhand tools for $1,500; rented space in a small building; inserted an ad in the local paper; and opened the doors on October 1, 2007. Immediately, John was very busy; after one month, he employed an assistant.

Although John knew practically nothing about the financial side of the business, he realized that a number of reports were required and that costs and collections had to be controlled carefully. At the end of the year, prompted in part by concern about his income tax situation (previously he had to report only salary), John recognized the need for financial statements. His wife Jane developed some financial statements for the business. On December 31, 2007, with the help of a friend, she gathered the following data for the three months just ended. Bank account deposits of collections for electric repair services totaled $32,000. The following checks had been written: electrician's assistant, $8,500; payroll taxes, $175; supplies purchased and used on jobs, $9,500; oil, gas, and maintenance on truck, $1,200; insurance, $700; rent, $500; utilities and telephone, $825; and miscellaneous expenses (including advertising), $600. Also, uncollected bills to customers for electric repair services amounted to $3,000. The $200 rent for December had not been paid. John estimated that the depreciation on the truck and tools during the three months was $1,200. Income taxes for the three-month period were $3,480.

Required:

1. John knows that you're good with numbers, so he has asked you to prepare a quarterly income statement for Abel Electric Repair for the three months October through December 31, 2007. Do it.

2. Do you think that John may have a need for one or more additional financial reports for 2007 and thereafter? Explain.

PA4-5 Comprehensive Review Problem: From Recording Transactions (including Adjusting Journal Entries) to Preparing Financial Statements and Closing Journal Entries (Chapters 2, 3, and 4)

LO1, LO2, LO4–LO6

Drs. Glenn Feltham and Gary Entwistle began operations of their physical therapy clinic called Northland Physical Therapy on January 1, 2005. The annual reporting period ends December 31. The trial balance on January 1, 2006, was as follows (the amounts are rounded to thousands of dollars to simplify):

Account No.	Account Titles	Debit	Credit
01	Cash	7	
02	Accounts receivable	3	
03	Supplies	3	
04	Equipment	6	
05	Accumulated depreciation (equipment)		1
06	Other assets	6	
11	Accounts payable		5
12	Notes payable		
13	Wages payable		
14	Interest payable		
15	Income taxes payable		
16	Unearned revenue		
17	Dividends payable		
21	Contributed capital		15
31	Retained earnings		4
32	Dividends declared		
35	Service revenue		
40	Depreciation expense		
41	Income tax expense		
42	Interest expense		
43	Supplies and other operating expenses		
	Totals	25	25

Transactions during 2006 (summarized in thousands of dollars) follow:

a. Borrowed $22 cash on July 1, 2006, signing a short-term note payable.
b. Purchased equipment for $20 cash on July 1, 2006.
c. Issued additional shares of stock for $5.
d. Earned revenues for 2006, $55, including $8 on credit and $47 received in cash.
e. Recognized operating expenses for 2006, $30, including $5 on credit and $25 in cash.
f. Purchased other assets, $3 cash.
g. Collected accounts receivable, $9.
h. Paid accounts payable, $7.
i. Purchased on account supplies for future use, $8.
j. Received a $3 deposit from a hospital for a contract to start January 5, 2007.
k. Declared a dividend, $4.
l. Paid the $4 dividend in cash.

Data for adjusting journal entries:

m. Supplies of $4 were counted on December 31, 2006.
n. Depreciation for 2006, $5.
o. Accrued interest on notes payable of $1.
p. Wages earned since the December 27 payroll not yet paid, $2.
q. Income tax for 2006 was $4, and will be paid in 2007.

Required:

1. Set up T-accounts for the accounts on the trial balance and enter beginning balances.
2. Record journal entries for transactions a through l and post them to the T-accounts.
3. Prepare an unadjusted trial balance.
4. Record and post the adjusting journal entries m through q.
5. Prepare an adjusted trial balance.
6. Prepare an income statement, statement of retained earnings, and balance sheet.
7. Prepare and post the closing journal entries.
8. Prepare a post-closing trial balance.
9. How much net income did the physical therapy clinic generate during 2006? Is the business financed primarily by debt or equity?

GROUP B PROBLEMS

PB4-1 Preparing a Trial Balance, Closing Journal Entry, and Post-Closing Trial Balance

LO4, LO6

Pacific Sunwear of California, Inc. operates three chains of retail stores under the names "Pacific Sunwear" (also known as "PacSun"), "Pacific Sunwear (PacSun) Outlet," and "d.e.m.o." The following is a simplified list of accounts and amounts reported in the company's financial statements for the year ended February 1, 2003.

Accounts payable	$ 28,456	Income taxes payable	$ 8,000
Accounts receivable	2,916	Interest expense	594
Accrued liabilities	34,522	Inventories	123,433
Accumulated depreciation	97,131	Long-term liabilities	24,024
Cash	36,438	Net sales	846,393
Contributed capital	93,503	Other current assets	4,975
Cost of goods sold	530,257	Other long-lived assets	15,597
Depreciation expense	32,453	Prepaid expenses	14,871
Selling, general, and		Property, plant, and equipment	298,644
administrative expenses	202,445	Retained earnings	159,211
Income tax expense	30,967	Short-term loans	2,350

Required:

a. Prepare an adjusted trial balance at February 1, 2003. Is the Retained Earnings balance of $159,211 the amount that would be reported on the balance sheet as of February 1, 2003?
b. Prepare the closing entry required at February 1, 2003.
c. Prepare a post-closing trial balance at February 1, 2003.

PB4-2 Recording Adjusting Journal Entries

LO1, LO2

Brandon Company's annual accounting year ends on June 30. It is June 30, 2006, and all of the 2006 entries except the following adjusting journal entries have been made:

a. On March 30, 2006, Brandon paid a six-month premium for property insurance, $3,200, for coverage starting on that date. Cash was credited and Prepaid Insurance was debited for this amount.
b. At June 30, 2006, wages of $900 were earned by employees but not yet paid. The employees will be paid on the next payroll date, July 15, 2006.
c. On June 1, 2006, Brandon collected two months' maintenance revenue of $450. At that date, Brandon debited Cash and credited Unearned Maintenance Revenue for $450.
d. Depreciation of $1,500 must be recognized on a service truck purchased on July 1, 2005.
e. Cash of $4,200 was collected on May 1, 2006, for services to be rendered evenly over the next year beginning on May 1. Unearned Service Revenue was credited when the cash was received.
f. The company owes interest of $600 on a bank loan taken out on February 1, 2006. The interest will be paid when the loan is repaid on January 31, 2007.
g. The company earned service revenue of $2,000 on a special job that was completed June 29, 2006. Collection will be made during July 2006; no entry has been recorded.
h. The income before any of the adjustments or income taxes was $31,675. The company's federal income tax rate is 30 percent. Compute adjusted income based on all of the preceding information, and then determine and record income tax expense.

Required:

1. Indicate whether each transaction relates to a deferral or accrual.
2. Give the adjusting journal entry required for each transaction at June 30, 2006.

PB4-3 Determining Financial Statement Effects of Adjusting Journal Entries

LO2, LO5

Refer to PB4-2.

Required:

Using the following headings, indicate the effect of each adjusting journal entry and the amount of the effect. Use + for increase, − for decrease, and NE for no effect.

	Balance Sheet			Income Statement		
Transaction	**Assets**	**Liabilities**	**Stockholders' Equity**	**Revenues**	**Expenses**	**Net Income**
a						
b						
c						
etc.						

LO2, LO5   **PB4-4 Analyzing a Student's Business and Preparing an Adjusted Income Statement**

Before she could start college in the spring, Kelly Gordon needed to make some money. She was a pro at using presentation software and had a good handle of other cutting edge graphics software, so she thought the best way to make some money would be to develop some fun applications that her high-school teachers could use in their classes. Based on the advice from a friend of her family, she created a corporation called Gordon's Flash. On July 1, 2007, Kelly began her business by investing $1,000 of her own money in the company and by having her mother invest an additional $3,000 in it. She immediately used some of this money to buy some computer hardware and software, at a total cost of $3,000. She then rented space in a small building; sent a flyer to her former teachers; and got to work creating a website and some sample applications. In no time, several of her teachers contacted her and agreed to purchase her services.

After a couple of months of working like mad, Kelly's business teacher asked her how things were going. She told him that she had enough work to keep busy every single minute of her life, but her company's bank account didn't seem to be reflecting that. Her teacher suggested that she prepare an income statement to get a better idea of whether her business was profitable. With his help, she gathered the following data for the three months ended September 30, 2007. The company's bank account showed deposits totaling $3,000 that Kelly had collected for preparing computer-based presentations. The following checks had been written: assistant's pay, $1,800; payroll taxes, $60; computer supplies purchased and used on jobs, $200; insurance, $165; rent, $400; utilities, telephone, and cable modem, $325; and miscellaneous expenses (including advertising), $300. Also, uncollected bills to customers for software programming services amounted to $1,400. The $200 rent for September had not been paid. Kelly estimated that depreciation on the computer hardware and software during the three months was $450. Income taxes for the three-month period were $500.

Required:

1. Prepare a quarterly income statement for Gordon's Flash for the three months July through September 2007.

2. Do you think that Kelly may have a need for one or more additional financial reports for 2007 and thereafter? Explain.

LO1, LO2, LO4–LO6   **PB4-5 Comprehensive Review Problem: From Recording Transactions (including Adjusting Journal Entries) to Preparing Financial Statements and Closing Journal Entries (Chapters 2, 3, and 4)**

Alison and Chuck Renny began operations of their furniture repair shop (Lazy Sofa Furniture, Inc.) on January 1, 2004. The annual reporting period ends December 31. The trial balance on January 1, 2005, was as follows (the amounts are rounded to thousands of dollars to simplify):

Account No.	Account Titles	Debit	Credit
01	Cash	5	
02	Accounts receivable	4	
03	Supplies	2	
04	Small tools	6	
05	Equipment		
06	Accumulated depreciation (equipment)		
07	Other assets	9	
11	Accounts payable		7

12	Notes payable		
13	Wages payable		
14	Interest payable		
15	Income taxes payable		
16	Unearned revenue		
17	Dividends payable		
21	Contributed capital		15
31	Retained earnings		4
32	Dividends declared		
35	Service revenue		
40	Depreciation expense		
41	Income tax expense		
42	Interest expense		
43	Supplies and other operating expenses		
	Totals	26	26

Transactions during 2005 (summarized in thousands of dollars) follow:

a. Borrowed $20 cash on July 1, 2005, signing a short-term note payable.
b. Purchased equipment for $18 cash on July 1, 2005.
c. Issued additional shares of stock for $5.
d. Earned revenues for 2005, $65, including $9 on credit and $56 received in cash.
e. Recognized operating expenses for 2005, $35, including $7 on credit and $28 in cash.
f. Purchased additional small tools, $3 cash.
g. Collected accounts receivable, $8.
h. Paid accounts payable, $11.
i. Purchased on account supplies for future use, $10.
j. Received a $3 deposit on work to start January 15, 2006.
k. Declared a dividend, $10.
l. Paid the $10 dividend in cash.

Data for adjusting journal entries:

m. Supplies of $4 were counted on December 31, 2005.
n. Depreciation for 2005, $2.
o. Accrued interest on notes payable of $1.
p. Wages earned since the December 24 payroll not yet paid, $3.
q. Income tax for 2005 was $4, and will be paid in 2006.

Required:

1. Set up T-accounts for the accounts on the trial balance and enter beginning balances.
2. Record journal entries for transactions a through l and post them to the T-accounts.
3. Prepare an unadjusted trial balance.
4. Record and post the adjusting journal entries m through q.
5. Prepare an adjusted trial balance.
6. Prepare an income statement, statement of retained earnings, and balance sheet.
7. Prepare and post the closing journal entries.
8. Prepare a post-closing trial balance.
9. How much net income did Lazy Sofa Furniture, Inc., generate during 2005? Is the company financed primarily by debt or equity?

FINANCIAL REPORTING AND ANALYSIS CASES

C&DS4-1 Finding Financial Information

LO1, LO5

Refer to the financial statements of Landry's Restaurants in Appendix A at the end of this book, or download the annual report from the *Cases* section of the text's Web site at www.mhhe.com/phillips.

RESTAURANTS, INC.

Required:

1. The company's Prepaid Expenses are included in the balance sheet line-item called Other Current Assets. Refer to the notes to the financial statements to determine the amount of Prepaid Expenses as of December 31, 2003.

2. Refer to the notes to the financial statements to determine what is included in the balance sheet line-item called Accrued Liabilities. For two of these specific liabilities, explain why Landry's would make an adjustment.

3. How much did Landry's owe for salaries, wages, and other payroll costs at its year-end? Was this an increase or decrease from the previous year?

4. In which line of the income statement does Landry's include the expense for renting restaurant buildings?

LO1, LO5

C&DS4-2 Comparing Financial Information

Refer to the financial statements of Dave & Buster's in Appendix B at the end of this book, or download the annual report from the *Cases* section of the text's Web site at www.mhhe.com/phillips.

Required:

1. Does Dave & Buster's report more or less for Prepaid Expenses than Landry's?

2. Refer to the notes to the financial statements to determine what is included in the balance sheet line-item called Accrued Liabilities. For two of the accrued liabilities, explain why Dave & Buster's would have made an accrual adjustment.

3. How much did Dave & Buster's owe for salaries, wages, and other payroll costs at its year-end? Are these accrued payroll liabilities more or less than Landry's accrued payroll liabilities? Provide one reason that would explain the difference between the two companies' accrued payroll liabilities.

4. In which line of the income statement does Dave & Buster's include the expense for renting restaurant buildings? Can you determine from the income statement whether Dave & Buster's or Landry's incurs the largest rent expense?

LO1, LO5

C&DS4-3 Internet-Based Team Research: Examining Deferrals and Accruals

As a team, select an industry to analyze. Using your Web browser, each team member should acquire the annual report or 10-K for one publicly traded company in the industry, with each member selecting a different company. (See C&DS1-3 in Chapter 1 for a description of possible resources for these tasks.)

TEAM CASE

Required:

1. On an individual basis, each team member should write a short report listing the following:
   a. The company's total assets and total liabilities at the end of each year.
   b. The company's prepaid expenses and accrued liabilities at the end of each year.
   c. The percentage of prepaid expenses to total assets and the percentage of accrued liabilities to total liabilities.
   d. Describe and explain the types of accrued liabilities reported in the notes to the financial statements.

2. Discuss any patterns that you as a team observe. Then, as a team, write a short report comparing and contrasting your companies according to the preceding attributes. Provide potential explanations for any differences discovered.

ETHICS AND CRITICAL THINKING CASES

LO1, LO3, LO5

ETHICAL

C&DS4-4 Ethical Decision Making: A Real-Life Example

On December 12, 2002, the SEC filed a lawsuit against four executives of Safety-Kleen Corp., one of the country's leading providers of industrial waste collection and disposal services. The primary issue was that the executives had directed others in the company to record improper adjustments in 1999 and 2000, which had the effect of overstating net income during those periods. The following table was included in the SEC's court documents to demonstrate the (combined) effect of proper and improper adjustments on net income. (All amounts are in millions.)

ISSUE

	Year (Quarter)				
	1999(Q1)	*1999(Q2)*	*1999(Q3)*	*1999(Q4)*	*2000(Q1)*
Net income before adjustments	$ 90.9	$ 76.7	$ 47.9	$ 57.3	$ 47.0
Effect of adjustments	36.6	30.9	75.5	53.1	69.8
Net income after adjustments	$127.5	$107.6	$123.4	$110.4	$116.8

The following excerpts from the SEC's complaint describe two of the allegedly improper adjustments:

Improper Capitalization of Operating Expenses

26. As part of the fraudulent accounting scheme, (three top executives) improperly recorded several adjusting entries to capitalize certain operating expenses. These adjustments caused the company to materially overstate both its assets and its earnings. For example, at the end of the third quarter of fiscal 1999, they improperly capitalized approximately $4.6 million of payroll expenses relating to certain marketing and start-up activities.

Improper Treatment of Accruals

33. During the fourth quarter of fiscal 1999, Humphreys (the CFO) created additional fictitious income by directing (other accounting executives) to eliminate a $7.6 million accrual that had been established to provide for management bonuses that had been earned in fiscal 1999, but were to be paid the following quarter. Humphreys' action suggested that no bonuses were going to be paid for that year. In fact, the bonuses for 1999 were paid as scheduled.

Required:

1. Discuss whether large adjustments, such as those included by Safety-Kleen in 1999 and 2000, necessarily indicate improper accounting procedures.

2. What does the SEC's document mean in paragraph 26 when it says three top executives "improperly recorded several adjusting entries to *capitalize* certain operating expenses." For a distinction between capitalize and expense, refer to Exhibit 3.7 (in Chapter 3). Drawing on concepts presented in Chapters 2 and 3, explain why it is improper to capitalize payroll expenses relating to marketing activities.

3. Assume the $7.6 million in bonuses referred to in paragraph 33 were recorded in the third quarter of 1999. What journal entry would have been used to record this accrual? Assume this accrual was eliminated in the fourth quarter of 1999. What adjusting journal entry would have been recorded to eliminate (remove) the previous accrual? What journal entry would have been used to record the $7.6 million in bonuses paid in the first quarter of 2000 (assuming the accrual had been removed in the fourth quarter of 1999)? What accounting concept is violated by recording an expense for management bonuses when they are paid rather than when they are earned by managers?

C&DS4-5 Ethical Decision Making: A Mini-Case

LO1, LO3, LO5

Assume you work as an assistant accountant in the head office of a national bricks-and-mortar video rental store. With the increasing popularity of online movie rental operations, your company has struggled to meet its earnings targets for the year. It's important for the company to meet its earnings targets this year because the company is renegotiating a bank loan next month, and the terms of that loan are likely to depend on the company's reported financial success. Also, the company plans to issue more stock to the public in the upcoming year, to obtain funds for establishing its own presence in the online movie rental business. The chief financial officer (CFO) has approached you with a solution to the earnings dilemma. She proposes that the depreciation period for the stock of reusable DVDs be extended from 3 months to 15 months. She explains that by lengthening the depreciation period, a smaller amount of depreciation expense

ETHICAL

ISSUE

will be recorded in the current year, resulting in a higher net income. She claims that generally accepted accounting principles require estimates like this, so it wouldn't involve doing anything wrong.

Required:

Discuss the CFO's proposed solution. In your discussion, consider the following questions. Will the change in depreciation affect net income in the current year in the way that the CFO described? How will it affect net income in the following year? Is the CFO correct when she claims that the change in estimated depreciation is allowed by GAAP? Who relies on the video company's financial statements when making decisions? Why might their decisions be affected by the CFO's proposed solution? Is it possible that their decisions would not be affected? What should you do?

LO1, LO2, LO5   **C&DS4-6** **Critical Thinking: Adjusting an Income Statement and Balance Sheet for Deferrals and Accruals**

Masterful Moving Corporation has been in operation since January 1, 2006. It is now December 31, 2006, the end of the annual accounting period. The company has not done well financially during the first year, although revenue has been fairly good. Three stockholders manage the company, but they have not given much attention to recordkeeping. In view of a serious cash shortage, they have applied to your bank for a $20,000 loan. As a loan officer, you requested a complete set of financial statements. The following 2006 annual financial statements were prepared by the company's office staff.

MASTERFUL MOVING CORPORATION		
Income Statement **For the Period Ended December 31, 2006**	**Balance Sheet** **At December 31, 2006**	
Transportation revenue $85,000	**Assets**	
Expenses:		
Salaries expense 17,000	Cash	$ 2,000
Supplies expense 12,000	Receivables	3,000
Other expenses 18,000	Supplies	6,000
Total expenses 47,000	Equipment	40,000
	Prepaid insurance	4,000
Net income $38,000	Remaining assets	27,000
	Total assets	$82,000
	Liabilities	
	Accounts payable	$ 9,000
	Stockholders' Equity	
	Contributed capital	35,000
	Retained earnings	38,000
	Total liabilities and stockholders' equity	$82,000

After briefly reviewing the statements and "looking into the situation," you requested that the statements be redone (with some expert help) to "incorporate depreciation, accruals, supply counts, income taxes, and so on." As a result of a review of the records and supporting documents, the following additional information was developed:

a.   The supplies of $6,000 shown on the balance sheet has not been adjusted for supplies used during 2006. A count of the supplies on hand on December 31, 2006, showed $1,800.

b.   The insurance premium paid in 2006 was for years 2006 and 2007. The total insurance premium was debited in full to Prepaid Insurance when paid in 2006 and no adjustment has been made.

c.   The equipment cost $40,000 when purchased January 1, 2006. It had an estimated annual depreciation of $8,000. No depreciation has been recorded for 2006.

d.   Unpaid (and unrecorded) salaries at December 31, 2006, amounted to $2,200.

e. At December 31, 2006, transportation revenue collected in advance amounted to $7,000. This amount was credited in full to Transportation Revenue when the cash was collected earlier during 2006.

f. Income taxes for the year are calculated as 25 percent of income before tax.

Required:

1. Prepare the adjusting journal entries required on December 31, 2006, based on the preceding additional information. You may need to create new accounts not yet included in the income statement or balance sheet.

2. Redo the preceding statements after taking into account the adjusting journal entries. One way to organize your response follows:

Items	Amounts Reported	Changes Plus	Minus	Corrected Amounts
(List here each item from the two statements)				

3. The effects of recording the adjusting journal entries were to
   a. *Increase* or *decrease* (select one) Net income by $_____.
   b. *Increase* or *decrease* (select one) Total assets by $_____.

4. Write a letter to the company explaining the results of the adjustments and your preliminary analysis.

chapter five

Understanding Financial Statements and the Financial Reporting Environment

5

A friend asks you to look at how his favorite basketball team did last season and to advise him on who's likely to win this season. While it's tempting to just look in the newspaper to see who won last year or to recommend the tallest team for this year, you know you'll have to drill down deeper than that. There's no guarantee that last year's champ will do well this year, because not all the players will be returning and who knows how good the new recruits will be. Also, the tallest team isn't always the best. Some teams make more out of their talents than others. Plus, you need to know what's happening with other teams in the league to do a good job of interpreting what it all means for the future.

You'll face the same issues when predicting how your friend's favorite company will do this year. If you're evaluating **ACTIVISION**—a leading maker of videogames for Sony, Nintendo, and Microsoft—you might be tempted to just look at how many different games it produces, but you really should analyze its published financial reports. Start by looking at the sales levels and then drill down further, considering such things as the income generated from those sales and the investment in assets needed to generate those sales. To predict future results, you'll need to consider whether the Tony Hawk and Spiderman games are likely to continue as top-10 sellers. These two "returning players" make up about 30 percent of Activision's game sales. You'll also consider new games that will hit the market in upcoming periods, as well as key changes in the industry, such as game titles that are being introduced by competitors like Electronic Arts and Take-Two Interactive Software. After gathering all this information, you'll have to somehow pull it together to figure out what it implies about the company's past and future financial performance. In this chapter, we'll guide you through this with a simple framework for financial statement analysis. Game on.

INSIDE LOOKING OUT

OUTSIDE LOOKING IN

This chapter focuses on how financial statement users analyze financial statements to get information to use in their decision making. We focus on Activision, Inc., one of the most popular videogame makers in the world.

Activision has a licensing agreement with Tony Hawk that doesn't expire until 2015.

POINT OF INTEREST
Of all Americans age six and older, 50 percent play video and computer games. Of these, 39 percent are women. *Source: Top Ten Industry Facts,* www.theesa.com.

Your parents would never have imagined that you could make money from videogames, but there's a whole industry doing just that. For example, game testers can earn a $28,000 salary, tournament competitors in the Cyberathlete Professional League vie for $100,000 in prize money, and some game developers turned $250 and a good game idea into a $28 million enterprise.[1] It's clear that videogames can be as much about making money as having fun. This chapter will help you to understand how to use accounting information when making investment decisions. You'll study how to analyze financial statements to evaluate how well a company is being run, and you'll find out about other sources of information that you can use to judge a company's success. Finally, you'll see how all of this fits within the financial reporting environment and what you need to remember to make informed investment decisions. This isn't just a role in a sim game—these are also your learning objectives, as summarized in Exhibit 5.1.

exhibit 5.1   Your Learning Objectives

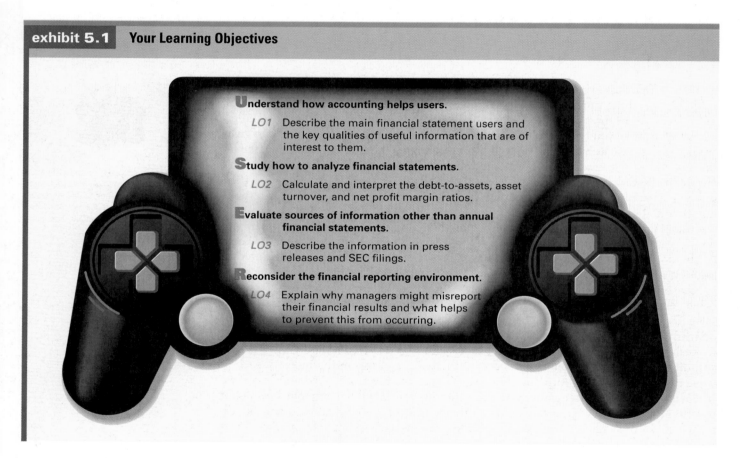

Understand how accounting helps users.

LO1   Describe the main financial statement users and the key qualities of useful information that are of interest to them.

Study how to analyze financial statements.

LO2   Calculate and interpret the debt-to-assets, asset turnover, and net profit margin ratios.

Evaluate sources of information other than annual financial statements.

LO3   Describe the information in press releases and SEC filings.

Reconsider the financial reporting environment.

LO4   Explain why managers might misreport their financial results and what helps to prevent this from occurring.

UNDERSTAND
HOW ACCOUNTING HELPS USERS

Who Are the Main Users and What Do They Need?

Chapter 1 provided a quick look at the many people who use financial statements to make decisions. A more detailed analysis of four main user groups is presented in Exhibit 5.2. As you can see, each group needs accounting information for different purposes.

---

[1]"Game Boy," *Fortune,* July 8, 2002, p. 122, and retrieved March 12, 2004, from www.thecpl.com.

exhibit 5.2	**Users and Uses of Accounting Information**	

Accounting information is used by . . .	to . . .	This is called . . .
Managers	Run the business	Management
Directors	Oversee the business	Governance
Creditors	Administer business contracts	Contracting
Investors	Value the business	Valuation

Managers

Managers at all levels within a company use accounting information to run the business. To make good decisions at Activision, managers need to know detailed information such as sales by game (e.g., Tony Hawk) and game platform (Sony, Nintendo, Microsoft, PC), profits by genre (e.g., action, role-playing, etc.), and costs by game developer (e.g., Gray Matter Studios). When accounting information is used in this way, to make business decisions, it is being used to fulfill a *management* function.

Directors

"Directors" is the short title often used to describe members of the board of directors. As the stockholders' own elected representatives, directors ensure that managers make decisions that benefit stockholders. Just as air traffic controllers use radar to keep flights on course, directors use accounting information to oversee management of the business, hopefully avoiding financial turbulence. When accounting information is used in this way, to oversee the business, it is being used in a *governance* role.

Creditors

Creditors use accounting information in several ways. Suppliers, for example, use it to decide whether to enter into contracts with another company. Bankers often use it to limit a company's activities, by requiring the company to satisfy certain financial targets such as minimum levels of assets or stockholders' equity. These **loan covenants,** as they are called, help to ensure the company will have money to repay the loan to the bank when it comes due. When accounting information is used in these ways, to administer contracts, it is being used in a *contracting* role.

Investors

Investors (and their advisers) look to accounting information to help evaluate the financial strength of a business and ultimately to estimate its value. In early 2004, when this text was written, investment advisers had mixed opinions about Activision's stock. Many recommended buying it, but some advised investors to "hold," which basically means investors should hit the pause button—the price is not attractive enough to recommend buying the company's stock nor is it bad enough to recommend selling the stock. When accounting information is used to assess stock prices, it is being used in a *valuation* role.

What Do Users Get?

Because managers and directors work for the company that they run or oversee, they can gain access to all the information they need directly from the company's accounting system. In contrast to these internal users, creditors and investors are external to the company and usually must rely on the accounting information reported in the financial statements. For this reason, *the primary objective of external financial reporting is to provide economic information that is useful to creditors and investors.*

Stockholders

↓ elect

Directors

↓ oversee

Managers

YOU SHOULD KNOW

Loan covenants are terms of a loan agreement which, if broken, entitle the lender to demand immediate repayment or renegotiation of the loan.

POINT OF INTEREST

For more information about analysts and their recommendations, see the SEC's report called "Analyzing Analyst Recommendations" in the investor alerts at www.sec.gov.

Okay, so what exactly makes information "useful"? To be useful, financial statement information must possess four main characteristics: (1) **reliability,** (2) **relevance,** (3) **consistency,** and (4) **comparability.** At this point in the course, we're not going to get into a detailed discussion of these characteristics—you'll get that in Chapter 13. For now, we just want you to be aware of these characteristics so you can begin to understand why accounting is done the way it is. Let's briefly look at each of the four characteristics and help you to see how they relate back to some of the topics in Chapters 1–4.

Reliability

Is the information accurate? The two equality checks that you have used throughout the recording of every transaction (A = L + SE and Debits = Credits) help to prevent errors from occurring, leading to more accurate information, which enhances its reliability.

Relevance

Does the information help in making decisions? The adjustments made under accrual basis accounting help to ensure the financial statements are complete and up to date, thereby enhancing their relevance.

Consistency

Does the company handle similar events in the same way from one period to the next? The chart of accounts ensures that transactions in the current month are recorded in the same accounts as similar transactions in previous months, thereby enhancing consistency. From a broader perspective, companies are required to use the rules of GAAP consistently from period to period. Consistent rules result in consistent information.

Comparability

Do different companies handle similar events in the same way? The rules of GAAP must be followed by all companies that prepare financial statements for external reporting, which enhances the comparability of different companies' financial statements.

These four characteristics underlie many other aspects of accounting, but this is enough for now. As you learn additional accounting rules in Chapters 6–13, think about how those rules ensure that financial statements are reliable, relevant, consistent, and comparable.

The Role of Auditors and Analysts

After the financial statements are prepared, they are checked and analyzed by two important groups of professionals: auditors and analysts. Have you heard of the auditor and analyst firms that work with the four companies shown in Exhibit 5.3?

As we saw in Chapter 1, the SEC requires publicly traded companies to have their financial statements audited by certified public accountants. Many privately owned companies also have their financial statements audited, often at the request of lenders or private investors who want to be sure the financial statements possess the four characteristics described earlier. The auditors, who are experts in financial reporting,

exhibit 5.3	Companies, Auditors, and Analysts	
Focus Company	**Auditors**	**Analysts**
Chap. 5—Activision	PricewaterhouseCoopers	Bear Stearns
Chap. 6—Wal-Mart	Ernst & Young	Goldman Sachs
Chap. 10—General Mills	KPMG	J. P. Morgan
Chap. 11—Ross Stores	Deloitte & Touche	Merrill Lynch

issue a one-page report that states whether the company's financial statements appear to have been prepared using GAAP. We say "appear to" because auditors can't check every single business transaction to ensure it was accurately reported, so they can't be 100 percent sure the financial statements *exactly* follow GAAP. But they do check enough to be "reasonably" sure the financial statements are "fair"—which is what their audit report says. If the audit report is **unqualified,** the company can point to it as further evidence that the financial statements are useful and that creditors and investors can trust what is reported. For an example of an unqualified audit report, see the one on page 7 of the annual report for Landry's Restaurants in Appendix A at the back of this book.

Stock analysts produce multipage reports that evaluate an individual company's past performance, make predictions about its future earnings, and conclude with a recommendation about whether investors should buy, hold, or sell stock in the company. To make these evaluations, **earnings forecasts,** and stock recommendations, analysts rely heavily on insights they gain from following developments occurring in the company, its industry, and the economy, and by analyzing the company's financial statements. Credit analysts also evaluate a company's past performance, but rather than make stock recommendations, their goal is to assess the risk that the company will be unable to pay its liabilities. In the next section of this chapter, we present a simple business and financial analysis model that stock and credit analysts use in their analyses.

YOU SHOULD KNOW

Being unqualified for a job is a bad thing. Getting an **unqualified audit report** is a good thing. Auditors "qualify" their reports when (1) financial statements do not follow GAAP, or (2) they are not able to complete tests needed to determine if the financial statements follow GAAP.

YOU SHOULD KNOW

An **earnings forecast** is a prediction of the amount of earnings expected for future accounting periods.

STUDY

HOW TO ANALYZE FINANCIAL STATEMENTS

A Model of Activision's Business

Before evaluating or predicting Activision's financial performance, it is useful to first get an idea of what's involved in running the videogame company. If you're not a fan of videogames, think about movie studios or book companies—they're very similar except that videogames generate more sales than the movie box office. Simply put, there are four parts to the business:

1. *Obtain financing* from lenders and investors, which is used to invest in assets.
2. *Invest in assets,* which are used to generate revenues.
3. *Generate revenues,* which produce net income.
4. *Produce net income,* which is needed to satisfy lenders and investors.

Based on this description of Activision's business, a skeleton of a business model can be developed, as shown in Exhibit 5.4.

POINT OF INTEREST
In 2002, the videogame business became bigger than the movie box office, generating approximately $10.3 billion in sales (compared to $9 billion for box office receipts).
Source: Fortune, November 25, 2002, p. 195.

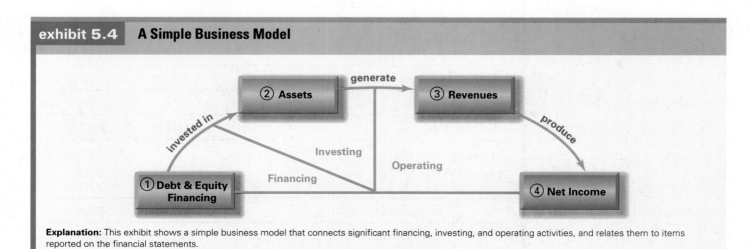

exhibit 5.4   A Simple Business Model

Explanation: This exhibit shows a simple business model that connects significant financing, investing, and operating activities, and relates them to items reported on the financial statements.

Now it's time to pack some muscle on the skeleton business model in Exhibit 5.4, with numbers from the financial statements. Information about Activision's debt and equity financing (in box 1 of Exhibit 5.4) is indicated by the liabilities and stockholders' equity sections of the balance sheet in Exhibit 5.5. There we see that the company relies very little on debt (total liabilities = $107 million) and instead looks to investors for most of its financing (total stockholders' equity = $598 million). By minimizing its reliance on debt financing, Activision can avoid the interest costs that lenders charge. Also, because stockholders' equity doesn't have to be repaid (like liabilities do), this is considered a less risky financing strategy.

Activision's balance sheet also helps us to understand the company's investment in assets (box 2 of Exhibit 5.4). As of March 31, 2003, Activision held lots of cash and short-term investments (nearly $407 million). For most companies, it's rare for cash and

exhibit 5.5	**Comparative Balance Sheet (modified)**

ACTIVISION, INC.
Balance Sheet
(in thousands of US dollars)

	March 31, 2003	March 31, 2002
Assets		
Current Assets:		
Cash and Short-Term Investments	$406,954	$279,007
Accounts Receivable	15,822	76,733
Inventories	19,577	20,736
Other Current Assets	84,552	80,397
Total Current Assets	526,905	456,873
Software Development and Intellectual Property Licenses	72,224	14,153
Property and Equipment, Net	22,265	17,832
Long-Term Investments and Other Assets	15,403	32,037
Goodwill	68,019	35,992
Total Assets	$704,816	$556,887
Liabilities and Stockholders' Equity		
Current Liabilities:		
Accounts Payable	$ 45,749	$ 64,578
Accrued Liabilities	58,656	59,096
Total Current Liabilities	104,405	123,674
Long-Term Debt	2,671	3,122
Total Liabilities	107,076	126,796
Stockholders' Equity:		
Contributed Capital	467,176	365,707
Retained Earnings	130,564	64,384
Total Stockholders' Equity	597,740	430,091
Total Liabilities and Stockholders' Equity	$704,816	$556,887

short-term investments to make up more than half of the total assets. Rather than have cash just sitting in the bank earning a tiny bit of interest, most companies would use these funds to buy additional property and equipment, which would help them make and sell more products and generate greater profits. Activision doesn't need a lot of property and equipment, however, because most of its games are physically manufactured by Sony, Nintendo, and Microsoft. Plus, the key isn't to produce more of the same games. Instead, to be successful, what Activision has to do is produce new and exciting games. Activision can do this by developing new games itself or acquiring smaller companies that have developed new games. It appears that Activision is able to do both. With all of its cash and short-term investments, Activision can buy game developers on a moment's notice. In addition, by looking at the balance sheet in Exhibit 5.5, we see that Activision also has spent $72 million on "software development and intellectual property licenses" as of March 31, 2003. This long-term asset suggests that Activision is in the process of developing games that'll likely be hitting the market at the same time you read this book.

For information on revenues and net income (boxes 3 and 4 in the business model in Exhibit 5.4 on page 193), we look at the income statement in Exhibit 5.6. There we see that revenues for the year ended March 31, 2003 were $864 million, which produced net income of $66 million.

POINT OF INTEREST
Activision uses a tough five-step review process to evaluate games under development. This process is used to ensure that any games passing through all five stages are likely to produce significant future economic benefits.
Source: 2003 Activision 10-K.

exhibit 5.6   Income Statement (modified)

ACTIVISION, INC.
Income Statement
(in thousands of US dollars)

	Year ended March 31,		
	2003	**2002**	**2001**
Net Revenues	$864,116	$786,434	$620,183
Costs and Expenses:			
Cost of Sales	565,173	534,731	414,609
Product Development	56,971	40,960	41,396
Sales and Marketing	100,646	86,161	85,378
General and Administrative	46,479	44,008	38,993
Total Operating Expenses	769,269	705,860	580,376
Operating Income	94,847	80,574	39,807
Interest Revenue (Expense), Net	8,560	2,546	(7,263)
Income before Income Tax Expense	103,407	83,120	32,544
Income Tax Expense	37,227	30,882	12,037
Net Income	$ 66,180	$ 52,238	$ 20,507

Analyzing Financial Statement Levels

If you're like most people, you probably find it hard to know whether $66 million in net income or $864 million in revenues are decent levels for these items. To interpret amounts like these, it's useful to have points of comparison, or "benchmarks." Two commonly used benchmarks are

1. **Prior periods.** By comparing Activision's current period results to its own results in prior periods, we can gain a sense of how the company's performance is changing over time. The trend is your friend. In Wall Street language, this comparison of the same company over a *series* of prior *time* periods is called **time-series analysis.**

YOU SHOULD KNOW
A **time-series analysis** compares a company's results for one period to its own results over a series of time periods.

| **exhibit 5.7** | **Chart of Activision's Time-Series Analysis** |

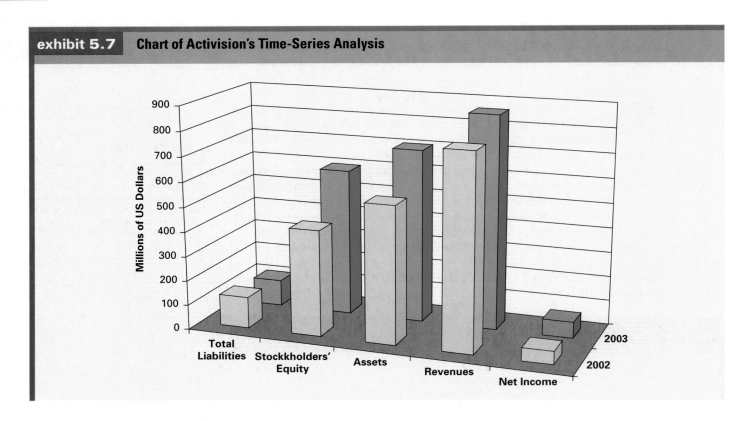

Cross-sectional analysis compares the results of one company with those of others in the same section of the industry.

COACH'S CORNER

To make charts using Excel, click on the Chart Wizard icon that looks like this 📊.

COACH'S CORNER

Average ratios for each industry can be obtained from a variety of sources such as the investing part of moneycentral.msn.com and the *Annual Statement Studies* published by the Risk Management Association.

2. ***Competitors.*** Although an analysis focused on one company is useful, it doesn't show what's happening in the industry. It's possible that Activision is improving (good), but still hasn't caught up to others in the same industry (not so good). Or it could be that Activision's performance is declining (bad), but it hasn't yet experienced the financial problems others face (not so bad). To get this industrywide perspective, most analysts will compare competitors within a particular industry. The name for comparing *across* companies that compete in the same *section* of an industry is **cross-sectional analysis.**

In Exhibit 5.7, we present a time-series chart that compares Activision to itself on each of the dimensions of our business model (which was pictured in Exhibit 5.4 on page 193). From this chart, we can see that Activision's financial profile changed between 2002 and 2003. In comparison to Activision's 2002 year-end balance, less debt was outstanding at the end of 2003. This reduction in liabilities was accompanied by an increase in stockholders' equity, suggesting that Activision's financing strategy shifted away from debt toward equity. We also see from Exhibit 5.7 that Activision grew significantly, with total assets, revenues, and net income in 2003 overshadowing that in 2002.

In Exhibit 5.8, we present a cross-sectional chart that compares Activision to two of its main competitors—Take-Two Interactive Software and Electronic Arts—based on financial statement data for the 2003 fiscal year.

From Exhibit 5.8, we learn that Activision is similar to Take-Two in many ways, as indicated by their almost identical bar heights across the various financial measures. We also see the towering bars of Electronic Arts, which suggest that this company dominates play in the industry. In fact, Electronic Arts is bigger than both Activision and Take-Two *combined* in every category. Given these mammoth differences in size, should we simply conclude that Electronic Arts is the winner and give them our pocketful of investment tokens? In a word, no. All that this means is that Electronic Arts is a bigger company. It says nothing about whether it's best at using the resources provided to it. This kind of conclusion usually requires some fraction action, which business professionals refer to more formally as financial statement ratio analyses.

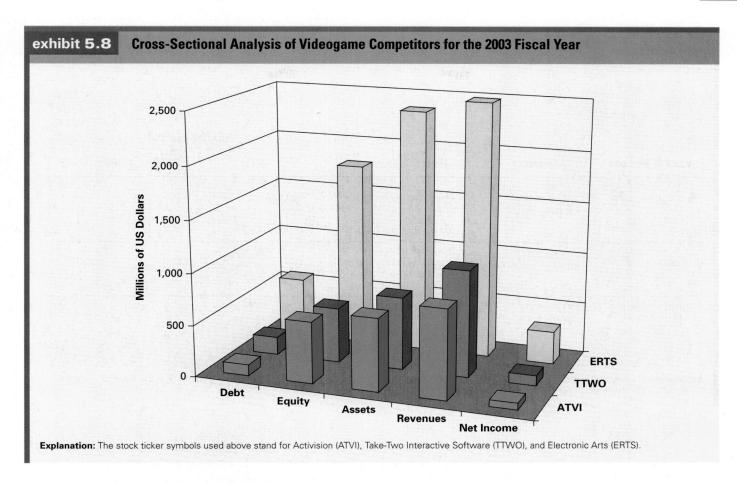

exhibit 5.8 **Cross-Sectional Analysis of Videogame Competitors for the 2003 Fiscal Year**

Explanation: The stock ticker symbols used above stand for Activision (ATVI), Take-Two Interactive Software (TTWO), and Electronic Arts (ERTS).

Analyzing Financial Statement Ratios

The goal of ratio analysis is to get to the heart of how well each company performed given the resources it had available. Huge companies with vast sources of financing should be expected to invest in more assets, which generate greater revenues, which produce larger profits. The real question is, given the financing available, how well did the company perform? To answer this question, we add three ratios to our business model in Exhibit 5.4 to create the version in Exhibit 5.9.

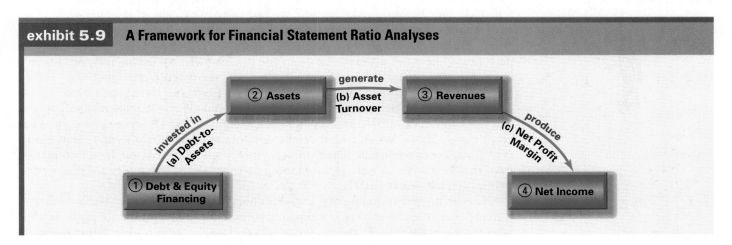

exhibit 5.9 **A Framework for Financial Statement Ratio Analyses**

Rather than examine the levels of financial statement accounts at each stage of the business model, ratio analyses focus on *relationships* between stages. Although it is possible

exhibit 5.10	Summary of Financial Statement Ratio Analyses

Name of Measure	Formula	What It Tells You	2003 FISCAL YEAR ATVI	2003 FISCAL YEAR ERTS	2003 FISCAL YEAR TTWO	SELF-STUDY QUIZ 2002 ATVI
a. Debt-to-assets ratio	$\dfrac{\text{Total Liabilities}}{\text{Total Assets}}$	• The percentage of assets financed by debt • A higher ratio means greater financing risk ☺	$=\dfrac{107{,}076}{704{,}816}$ $= 0.152$ or 15.2%	24.4%	24.6%	
b. Asset turnover ratio	$\dfrac{\text{Sales Revenue}}{\text{Average Total Assets}}$	• How well assets are used to generate sales • A higher ratio means greater efficiency ☺	$=\dfrac{864{,}116}{(704{,}816 + 556{,}887)/2}$ $= 1.37$	1.22	1.72	
c. Net profit margin ratio	$\dfrac{\text{Net Income}}{\text{Sales Revenue}}$	• The ability to generate sales while controlling expenses • A higher ratio means better performance ☺	$=\dfrac{66{,}180}{864{,}116}$ $= 0.077$ or 7.7%	12.8%	9.5%	

Explanation: This table uses financial statement data to calculate the ratios pictured in Exhibit 5.9. The stock ticker symbols used above stand for Activision (ATVI), Take-Two Interactive Software (TTWO), and Electronic Arts (ERTS).

COACH'S CORNER

To understand why ratio calculations differ, think about whether the pieces of data for each ratio came from the same basic financial statement.

to consider relationships that cut across the stages, say between *Assets* (box 2) and *Net Income* (box 4), this chapter focuses on only the links between neighboring stages. Also, because this chapter is your first look at financial statement ratio analyses, we discuss only one ratio per link—ratios that use totals in the financial statements. In later chapters, we will analyze links that cut across the stages and we will introduce additional ratios that replace totals with data from specific accounts (e.g., inventories, cost of goods sold).

The formula for each ratio named in Exhibit 5.9 on page 197 and an example of its calculation (using numbers reported in Activision's 2003 year-end financial statements) are presented in Exhibit 5.10. We also have presented the corresponding ratios for Electronic Arts and Take-Two Interactive Software for their 2003 fiscal year-ends for comparison and, for practice, a final column that you can complete as part of an upcoming self-study quiz. Before you do the quiz, we first need to explain why some ratios are reported as percentages but others aren't, and why averages are used in some ratios but not others. By looking at Exhibits 5.9 and 5.10, can you detect why ratio *b* isn't shown as a percentage like ratios *a* and *c*? Also, can you discover why we use an average in ratio *b* but not in ratios *a* and *c*? If you want help, see what the coach has to say.

Did you discover that ratio *b* takes information from both the balance sheet and income statement, whereas *a* and *c* use information from only one statement? This explains why asset turnover, ratio *b*, isn't reported as a percentage like the debt-to-assets and net profit margin ratios. When a ratio combines information from two separate statements, it typically is not reported as a percentage. Only those ratios that combine information from the same statement are reported using percentages. A percentage is calculated by multiplying the ratio by 100%, as in $0.152 \times 100\% = 15.2\%$.

The key to understanding why averages are included in some ratios but not others is to remember that the income statement reports the results of an entire *period* of time whereas the balance sheet reports the results at a single *point* in time. Some ratios are calculated by combining information from both the income statement and balance sheet. The asset turnover ratio, for example, takes sales revenues from the income statement for the top part of the ratio and total assets from the balance sheet for the bottom. To allow the bottom part of the ratio to represent the same time period as the top, we need to calculate the average of the beginning *and* ending balance sheet amounts to include in the bottom part of the ratio, as shown in Exhibit 5.11.

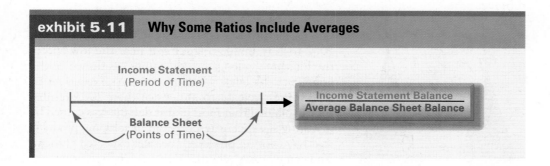

exhibit 5.11   Why Some Ratios Include Averages

Income Statement
(Period of Time)

$$\frac{\text{Income Statement Balance}}{\text{Average Balance Sheet Balance}}$$

Balance Sheet
(Points of Time)

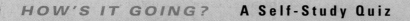

HOW'S IT GOING?   A Self-Study Quiz

Compute the ratios for the final column in Exhibit 5.10 using financial statement information in Exhibits 5.5 and 5.6, as well as the following information obtained from Activision's March 31, 2001, balance sheet. As of March 31, 2001, Activision reported (in thousands of U.S. dollars) assets totaling $359,957. When you're done, check your answers with the solutions in the margin.

Interpreting the Ratios

Most newcomers to ratio analyses want to be told rules of thumb that indicate "good" or "bad" levels for each ratio. The truth is ratios vary so much from industry to industry that rules of thumb aren't that useful. It's more informative to compare over time or across competitors, as we do here.

***a.* Debt-to-Assets Ratio.**   This ratio indicates the proportion of total assets that are financed by debt. It's important to know how much debt is used to finance assets because debt has to be repaid whether or not a company is doing well financially. If assets are financed primarily by debt, rather than equity, then this ratio will be high, which would suggest the company has adopted a risky financing strategy. Ultimately, a company would be forced into bankruptcy if it took on more debt than it ever could repay.

Exhibit 5.10 and the graphic to the right indicate that all three companies have debt-to-assets ratios less than 25 percent, with Activision having the lowest percentage of debt financing at 15.2 percent. Activision's ratio is down slightly from 22.8 percent in 2002 and down significantly from 2001, when it stood at 49.6 percent. This continued reduction in debt levels is consistent with a shift in Activision's financing strategy toward greater reliance on investors for funding the company's growth.

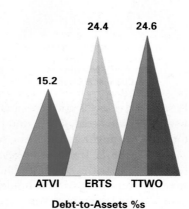

Debt-to-Assets %s
(2003 Fiscal Year)

b. Asset Turnover Ratio.   The asset turnover ratio represents sales revenue per dollar invested in the assets of the business. So the higher this ratio is, the more efficiently the business is utilizing its assets. An efficiently run business produces lots of sales for each dollar invested in assets. On the other hand, an inefficiently run business will tend to have assets sitting around idle and not generating sales, which results in a lower asset turnover ratio.

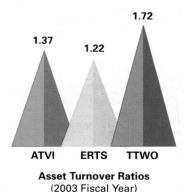

Asset Turnover Ratios
(2003 Fiscal Year)

Exhibit 5.10 on page 198 indicates that Activision's asset turnover ratio fell significantly from 1.72 in 2002 to 1.37 in 2003, landing it near the low end of the big three videogame companies (as shown in the graphic to the left). When Activision's executives issued a press release to announce their 2003 results, they explained that most of this decline was caused by investing significant resources in developing products that have not yet produced the sales expected of them. The game bosses reported that this decline prompted them to revise their product development strategy to focus on making fewer games that will be higher in quality, which should translate in the future into higher sales for each dollar invested.

c. Net Profit Margin Ratio.   This ratio measures the amount of net income ("profit") generated from each dollar of sales. This is a key ratio because it indicates how well executives manage the tricky balancing act between generating more sales and controlling expenses. What's so tricky about increasing sales and reducing expenses? Well, videogame makers have found that consumers won't spend more than $50 for a new game, so they can't jack the price to increase total sales revenues. Instead, they try to increase sales levels by making and selling cool new games. The problem is that new games require lots of advertising and promotion, which increases the company's expenses. The trick is to find the right balance between generating new game sales and controlling the expenses needed to generate those new sales. A company generating tons of sales will go bankrupt if its expenses are out of control, and a company that tightly controls its expenses will fail if it doesn't generate enough sales. Net profit margin takes this tradeoff into account, and indicates the company's ability to generate sales while controlling expenses.

Net Profit Margin %s
(2003 Fiscal Year)

Exhibit 5.10 (and the graphic to the left) indicates that Activision's profit margin, at 7.7 percent, is slightly below Take-Two and well below Electronic Arts. Activision and Take-Two have incurred significant expenses in what, so far, have been somewhat unsuccessful attempts to market several new lines of games. In contrast, Electronic Arts has focused its efforts (and expenses) on game titles that sell like crazy, with *SimCity 4* paving the way.

Until 2003, almost every analyst ranked the top three videogame makers as (1) Electronic Arts, (2) Activision, and (3) Take-Two Interactive Software.

Based on the levels and ratio analyses that we've just conducted in this chapter, who do you think wins gold, silver, and bronze in 2003? While there's no single correct answer for this, you might consider the summary of financial statement ratios in Exhibit 5.12.

Exhibit 5.12 (ratio *a*) suggests that Take-Two was financed with the largest proportion of debt. As the coach explains, this also implies the company was financed with the smallest proportion of stockholders' equity. We also know, from ratios *b* and *c*, that Take-Two had the largest asset turnover and earned a higher net profit margin than Activision. Taken together, these three ratios imply that Take-Two was more efficient than Activision at using its stockholders' investments to generate revenues and earn profits in 2003.

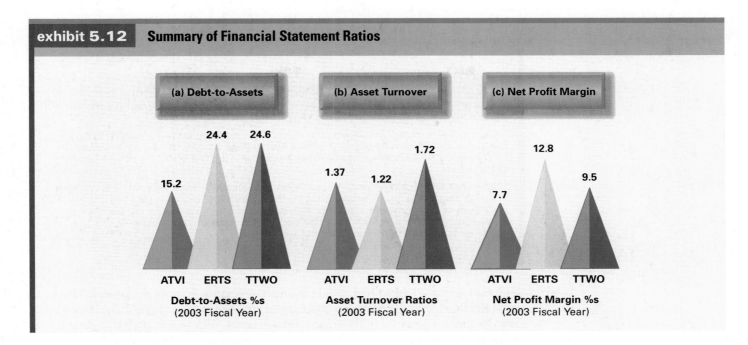

exhibit 5.12 Summary of Financial Statement Ratios

(a) Debt-to-Assets

	ATVI	ERTS	TTWO
	15.2	24.4	24.6

Debt-to-Assets %s
(2003 Fiscal Year)

(b) Asset Turnover

	ATVI	ERTS	TTWO
	1.37	1.22	1.72

Asset Turnover Ratios
(2003 Fiscal Year)

(c) Net Profit Margin

	ATVI	ERTS	TTWO
	7.7	12.8	9.5

Net Profit Margin %s
(2003 Fiscal Year)

Although Take-Two is not as big as Electronic Arts, it does appear to do a lot with what's available to it. Most analysts still considered Electronic Arts the industry leader in 2003, primarily because it had the largest amount of assets, revenues, and net income (as indicated by our analysis of "levels" shown in Exhibit 5.8). However, many analysts believed Take-Two had earned its name in 2003 by taking over the number-two spot in the industry, leaving Activision to activate a vision for getting back in the game.

TOPIC TACKLER PLUS

For a review of financial statement analyses, check out the animated tutorial on the DVD for use with this book.

EVALUATE

SOURCES OF INFORMATION OTHER THAN ANNUAL FINANCIAL STATEMENTS

Although our discussion in this chapter has focused on annual financial statements, we don't want you to get the impression that this is the only source of information about a company's financial performance. No, there are lots of other places you can go to learn more—some of them useful and others not so useful. In this section, you'll learn about which sources are likely to provide information that sheds light on the company's results and which are dark alleys.

Press Releases

To provide timely information for all external users, Activision and almost all other public companies announce quarterly and annual earnings through a press release that is sent to news agencies. This press release isn't issued until three or four weeks after the accounting period ends because it takes time to identify and compute all of the necessary adjusting journal entries that you learned about in Chapter 4. The press release typically includes key figures, management's discussion of the results, and attachments containing a condensed income statement and balance sheet. The information in a press release is fairly reliable because it's not released until the numbers in it have been checked by management (and by auditors in the case of *annual* earnings releases). Exhibit 5.13 shows an excerpt from a typical quarterly press release for Activision. Notice that it took four weeks from the end of the company's quarter to prepare, check, and release this information.

You should realize that management often is motivated to emphasize positive aspects of their financial performance in the press release. A common tactic for emphasizing the positive is to make up "what-if" or **pro forma** numbers that suggest how the company's

POINT OF INTEREST
Not every press release is trustworthy. A 23-year-old student was sentenced to 44 months in federal prison for sending out his own phony press release about Emulex Corporation, which allegedly defrauded investors of $241,814.

YOU SHOULD KNOW

Pro forma numbers show what a company's results would have been had certain events not occurred.

exhibit 5.13	Earnings Press Release for Activision, Inc.

ACTIVISION REPORTS RECORD THIRD QUARTER AND NINE MONTH FISCAL 2004 RESULTS

Santa Monica, CA—January 28, 2004—Activision, Inc. (Nasdaq: ATVI) today announced results for the third fiscal quarter and nine months ended December 31, 2003.

Net revenues were $508.5 million or 34% higher, as compared to net revenues of $378.7 million reported for the fiscal year 2003 third quarter. Net income for the third quarter rose to $77.0 million, a 74% increase, compared with net income of $44.3 million for the previous third quarter.

Robert A. Kotick, Chairman and CEO of Activision, commented, "We have one of the strongest balance sheets in our industry and ended the quarter with $552 million in cash and short-term investments, low inventories, and $796 million in shareholders' equity. Our planned product slate combined with the growing installed base of console hardware should enable us to continue to expand the scale and scope of our business."

results would have looked had certain events not occurred during the period. These pro forma numbers typically present a company in a more favorable light than the full set of GAAP numbers reported in the financial statements, with recent studies finding this to be the case about 85 percent of the time.[2] Activision doesn't follow this iffy practice of using pro forma to emphasize the positive, so to provide an example of pro forma reporting, Exhibit 5.14 takes one from Take-Two. Although you aren't expected to know what all the excluded items are, you probably can understand from this example why some analysts refer to pro forma earnings numbers as "earnings before bad stuff."

exhibit 5.14	Earnings Press Release for Take-Two Interactive Software

Excluding operating impairment charges on Internet assets, loss on Internet investments, gain on sale of a subsidiary, extraordinary loss on the early extinguishment of debt and cumulative effect of change in accounting principle, pro forma net income was $14.3 million.

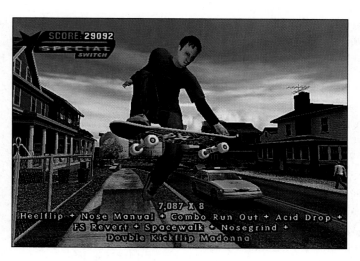

Many companies, including Activision, follow their press releases with a conference call broadcast on the Internet that allows analysts to grill the company's senior executives with questions about the financial results. By listening to these calls, you can learn a lot about a company's business strategy, its expectations for the future, and the key factors that analysts consider when they evaluate a company. You can check out this useful source of information by visiting each company's own Web site or the archive of conference calls at biz.yahoo.com/cc.

Annual and Quarterly Reports

Companies issue a formal quarterly or annual report several weeks after the press release. They aren't issued at the same time as the press release because it takes some time to gather and report all the detailed information that goes into the financial statement notes.

[2]Barbara Lougee and Carol Marquardt, "Earnings Informativeness and Strategic Disclosure: An Empirical Examination of 'Pro Forma' Earnings," *The Accounting Review*, July 2004.

The annual reports of many publicly traded companies are a thing of beauty. The first half of the report usually begins with a friendly letter to investors from the company's top executives. This is followed by glossy pictures of the company's products and glowing commentaries about the company's brilliant positioning to take over its industry. Having developed the right mood with these jazzy marketing tactics in the first half of the report, the annual report then presents the real core: the financial section. This section contains

For an animated tour of what's in a company's annual report, click on the annual report walkthrough (Chapter 1) that is on the DVD for use with this book.

1. *Summarized financial data*—key figures covering a period of 5 or 10 years.
2. *Management's discussion and analysis (MD&A)*—an honest and detailed analysis of the company's financial condition and operating results.
3. *Financial statements*—the four basic statements that provide the data for the financial analyses you just learned about in this chapter.
4. *Notes*—further information about the financial statements. As you will learn in later chapters, this part is crucial to understanding the financial statement data.
5. *Auditor's report*—the auditor's conclusion about whether GAAP was followed. The warning alarms should go off if this report is qualified.
6. *Recent stock price data*—brief summary of highs and lows during the year.
7. *Unaudited quarterly data*—condensed summary of each quarter's results.
8. *Directors and officers*—a list of who's overseeing and running the company.

COACH'S CORNER
The MD&A is a must-read for any serious financial statement user.

Now that you've got a handle on what's in an annual report, it'll be easy for you to understand what's in a quarterly report because it's merely a supercondensed version of an annual report. Quarterly reports normally begin with a short letter to stockholders. This is followed by a condensed income statement for the quarter, which often shows less detail than the annual income statement, a condensed balance sheet dated at the end of the quarter, and a condensed statement of cash flows. These condensed financial statements are not audited, so they are labeled as unaudited. Quarterly reports often omit the statement of retained earnings and many notes to the financial statements which are redundant with those in the company's annual report. Obviously, with all these limitations, the quarterly reports aren't quite as informative as the annual reports, but they have the benefit of being released on a timelier basis (every three months rather than every year).

Securities and Exchange Commission (SEC) Filings

Public companies are required to electronically file certain reports with the SEC, including an annual report on Form 10-K, quarterly reports on Form 10-Q, and current event reports on Form 8-K. When referring to these filings, most people simply say their number (for example, the "10-K"). In general, the 10-K and 10-Q present much of the same information as the glossy annual and quarterly reports, but with fewer images and less hype. In addition, the SEC filings include some really useful additional management discussion and required schedules. For example, in Part I of Activision's 2003 10-K, management describes 25 significant business risks that the company faces and outlines the business strategies for addressing those risks. Schedule II of the same 10-K provides detailed information about discounts given to customers. The 8-K is used to report significant business events that occur between financial statement dates, such as the acquisition of another company, a change in year-end, or a change in auditor.

POINT OF INTEREST
To provide timelier reporting, the SEC will require (by December 15, 2005) most large public companies to meet the following filing deadlines: 10-K within 60 days of year-end, 10-Q within 35 days of quarter-end, and 8-K within four days of the reported event.

These filings are available to the public as soon as they are received by the SEC's Electronic Data Gathering and Retrieval Service (EDGAR). As a result, most users can get all the details about a company's financial results in the SEC filings several weeks before they see them in the company's glossy reports. To find a company's SEC filings, click on "Search for Company Filings" at www.sec.gov or go to edgarscan.pwcglobal.com.

Investor Information Web Sites

In addition to companies' own Web sites, Hoovers.com, TheStreet.com, Fool.com, and Yahoo!Finance are four of the thousands of investor information Web sites that contain information about public companies. Some sections of investor information Web sites

POINT OF INTEREST

Lucent Technologies lost 30 percent of its stock value in 2001 when someone on an online stock messaging board falsely reported that the company was going to file for bankruptcy protection.
Source: www.forbes.com/2001/04/05/0405topnews.

provide useful information for evaluating and predicting a company's financial performance, whereas others do not. For example, at Yahoo!Finance, you can obtain valuable financial information about a company and its industry sector, including financial ratios similar to those you've read about earlier in this chapter. However, at messages.yahoo.com, you also can chat it up with someone using the alias plum_cray_z.

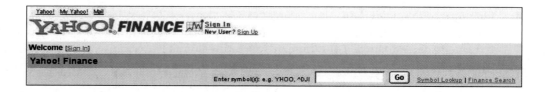

The obvious problem with many of these sites is that it's difficult to sort out what's good versus bad information. Another problem, particularly in the case of financial ratios, is that you're rarely told whether the underlying information is audited or unaudited. As a consequence, it's tough to know whether the analyses are as reliable as they might seem. An additional problem is that many Web sites do not show the formulas used to calculate ratios. That can be a big deal because *ratios with similar sounding names might be calculated differently*. For example, a few Web sites use long-term debt, rather than total liabilities, to calculate the debt-to-assets ratio. This could cause the ratio to be reported as 6 percent when it's actually 22 percent using the ratio shown in this chapter. As with most things in life, be sure you understand and trust it before using it.

RECONSIDER
THE FINANCIAL REPORTING ENVIRONMENT

ETHICAL

ISSUE

In Chapter 4, you learned that it was possible for management to dilute the quality of financial reporting by misrepresenting their company's actual financial results. Over the last few years, companies including Enron, WorldCom (now MCI), Global Crossing, and Xerox have discovered that their top managers led financial statement users astray by misreporting their financial results. In one famous case, managers at Bausch & Lomb shipped as much as two years' worth of contact lenses to opticians who hadn't even ordered them and recorded it all as sales revenue at artificially high prices.[3] In an even more blatant case, managers at Miniscribe—a computer disk drive manufacturer—boxed up spare parts and bricks, shipped them to customers, and then counted them as regular sales.[4] There's no question about whether this is ethical. Can you imagine what would lead someone to do this? In this section, we'll dig into some possible reasons, see how it could occur given the financial reporting process outlined in this chapter, and describe what you can do as a financial statement user to protect yourself from relying on faulty financial figures.

Why Would Management Misrepresent the Financial Results?

Financial misreporting is both unethical and illegal, so there must be some strong incentives driving some managers to act so despicably. These incentives fit into two categories: (1) creating business opportunities and (2) satisfying personal greed.

1. *Creating Business Opportunities*

Management is under constant pressure to produce pleasing financial results for at least three business reasons:

---

[3]"Blind Ambition: How the Pursuit of Results Got Out of Hand at Bausch & Lomb," *BusinessWeek*, October 23, 1995.

[4]"Miniscribe Report Describes Massive Fraud," *Washington Post*, September 9, 1989.

a. Satisfy loan covenants. As you learned earlier in this chapter, lenders rely on financial statements to determine whether a company has violated its loan covenants by failing to meet certain financial targets. If managers overstate their company's financial condition, they can avoid violating loan covenants which otherwise could require the company to pay a higher interest rate, repay its loan balance on demand, and offer extra collateral to secure the loan.

b. Increase equity financing. The amount of money obtained from issuing stock depends, in part, on the price of the stock when it is issued. An issuance of 100,000 shares will yield double the money if the stock price is $20 per share rather than $10 per share. Managers can lead investors to pay more than a company is really worth, if they overstate the company's reported financial performance.

c. Attract business partners. By making the business appear more stable than it actually is, management can mislead suppliers and other companies into wanting to pursue a business relationship with the company.

2. Satisfying Personal Greed

By producing pleasing financial results, members of top management can benefit personally in three ways:

a. Enhance job security. The financial statements are a report card on both the company and the company's management. If top management reports strong financial results, they'll likely get to keep their high-paying jobs.

b. Increase personal wealth. Members of top management often own shares in the company's stock, so their personal shareholdings will be worth more (and their personal wealth will increase) if their company reports financial results that send its stock price skyward.

c. Obtain bigger paycheck. Managers often receive cash bonuses based on the strength of their company's reported financial performance. Better reported results mean larger bonuses.

Exhibit 5.15 summarizes the above reasons.

exhibit 5.15	**Possible Incentives for Misreporting Financial Results**
Creating Business Opportunities	*Satisfying Personal Greed*
a. Satisfy loan covenants b. Increase equity financing c. Attract business partners	a. Enhance job security b. Increase personal wealth c. Obtain bigger paycheck

Why Would Management *Not* Misrepresent the Financial Results?

Now that we've shown several reasons why a manager might behave dishonestly, we should point out many good reasons for managers to report honestly. First, there's the personal satisfaction and pride that comes from doing the right thing. The **full disclosure principle** of accounting makes it clear that the right thing is to reliably report all information that is relevant to financial statement users. A second reason is that managers can develop reputations for honest reporting, which leads investors to place more trust in them and their financial reports. For most people, these reasons are more than enough to encourage them to report honestly. However, for the few other morally bankrupt people, there's a third reason to report honestly: the Sarbanes-Oxley Act and its new corporate fraud laws have introduced prison terms of 20-plus years and fines of up to $5,000,000 for managers who knowingly report fraudulent financial results. These criminals also have to repay any bonuses they received or profits from stock sales obtained as a result of their fraud. The law makes sure that they can't get out of repaying these fines by simply declaring bankruptcy.[5] It seems likely that Jamie Olis, a 38-year-old midlevel executive at Dynegy Inc., wished he had been more honest as he quietly wept with his wife and six-month-old daughter after being sentenced to over 24 years in federal prison, without opportunity for parole.

How Could Misreporting Occur?

Exhibit 5.16 summarizes the financial reporting process, which was outlined earlier in this chapter. As the figure suggests, management can get away with misreporting only if the company's directors, auditors, analysts, investors, and creditors are tricked into going along with the misreported results. Although it's difficult to imagine that management could dupe all of these groups, it has happened in the past. As a financial statement user, you'll have to be on your toes to make sure you don't become the next victim.

exhibit 5.16	**The Financial Reporting Process**

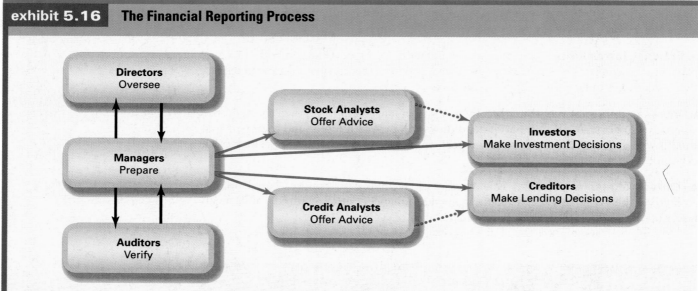

Explanation: The financial reporting process begins with management preparing financial statements, with oversight from directors. Auditors will then verify the financial statements (if annual) and issue an audit report. The audited financial statements are then distributed to analysts, investors, and creditors as indicated by the solid lines. Dotted lines indicate that analyst reports, which are based in part on a company's financial statements, are provided to investors and creditors.

POINT OF INTEREST
To educate investors about the risk of relying on false information, the SEC has created a false investment opportunity that promises huge returns to investors. To see this site, go to www.mcwhortle.com.

Some investment advisers have claimed that management is able to mislead investors and the other user groups in Exhibit 5.16 only if these users are lax in evaluating a company and its reported results. If you want to avoid becoming the next "point of interest" in a future edition of this book, you should ensure you understand a company's business and its financial statements before investing in it. This sounds a lot like some advice the SEC recently offered to financial statement users on how to avoid becoming a victim of financial reporting fraud. Excerpts of the SEC's advice appear in Exhibit 5.17.

Whereas it might be a while before you can use the SEC's advice in your daily life, we can offer some advice that will help you right now, right here in this course. As you read the remaining chapters in this book, keep your eyes open for places where accounting numbers are based on estimates or where management can choose from alternative accounting rules. Historically, these are two places where management has made accounting decisions that deceived all but the wisest of financial statement users.

---

[5]Sections 903, 1106, 304 and 803 of the Sarbanes-Oxley Act of 2002, retrieved March 25, 2004, from www.law.uc.edu/CCL/SOact/toc.html.

exhibit 5.17	How to Avoid Becoming a Victim of Financial Reporting Fraud

Investor Alert: Stock Market Fraud "Survivor" Checklist
- *Independently verify claims.* Don't rely solely on claims by companies or promoters about new product developments, lucrative contracts, or the company's financial health.
- *Research the company.* Always ask for, and carefully read, the company's current financial statements.
- *Be skeptical.* When you see an offer on the Internet, consider it a scam until you can prove it's legitimate through your own independent research.
- *Consider the source.* Remember that people touting a stock may be company insiders or paid promoters who stand to profit at your expense.

Source: Retrieved July 21, 2004, from SEC Web site, www.sec.gov/investor/pubs/fraudsurvivor.htm.

FOR YOUR REVIEW

DEMONSTRATION CASE

Earlier in this chapter, we said the videogame production and sales business was similar to the book production and sales business. In this demonstration case, we'll take a look at just how similar they are in terms of financial results. While we're tempted to analyze the financial statements of the company that published this textbook, it wouldn't provide a clean comparison because McGraw-Hill doesn't just publish books—it also runs Standard & Poor's (a financial services company). So, instead, we'll analyze the financial statements of one of our publisher's main competitors, John Wiley & Sons—a company that operates only in the book business. Shortened versions of that company's financial statements are shown below:

JOHN WILEY & SONS, INC. Income Statement (modified) (U.S. dollars in thousands) For the Years Ended April 30		
	2003	**2002**
Sales Revenue	$853,971	$734,396
Cost of Sales	288,925	243,196
Operating and Administrative Expenses	432,700	373,463
Other Expenses	12,085	29,974
Operating Income	120,261	87,763
Interest Expense	7,702	6,645
Income before Taxes	112,559	81,118
Income Tax Expense	25,284	23,802
Net Income	$ 87,275	$ 57,316

JOHN WILEY & SONS, INC. Balance Sheet (modified) (U.S. dollars in thousands) April 30		
Assets		
	2003	**2002**
Current Assets	$283,844	$275,259
Other Assets	672,128	620,886
Total Assets	$955,972	$896,145

Liabilities and Shareholders' Equity

Current Liabilities	$323,265	$320,393
Other Liabilities	288,703	299,102
Total Liabilities	611,968	619,495
Shareholders' Equity	344,004	276,650
Total Liabilities and Shareholders' Equity	$955,972	$896,145

Required:

1. Compute Wiley's debt-to-assets ratio at the end of the 2003 and 2002 fiscal years. How has Wiley changed its financing strategy from 2002 to 2003? Is this likely to be considered a riskier or safer strategy? How similar is the proportion of debt financing used by the book publisher to that used by the videogame companies analyzed in Exhibit 5.10?

2. Compute Wiley's asset turnover ratio for 2003 and 2002. (In thousands, Wiley's total assets at April 30, 2001, were $588,032.) Between 2002 and 2003, was there a change in Wiley's efficiency in using its assets to generate revenues? Does the book publisher generate more or less sales from each dollar invested in assets than the videogame companies analyzed in Exhibit 5.10?

3. Compute Wiley's net profit margin ratio for the 2003 and 2002 fiscal years. How has this aspect of Wiley's financial performance changed? Does the book publisher make more or less profit from each dollar of sales than the videogame companies analyzed in Exhibit 5.10?

4. In the aftermath of the 2001 Enron financial scandal, one of the biggest auditing firms in the world (Arthur Andersen) shut down. On April 15, 2002, John Wiley & Sons announced that KPMG would replace Arthur Andersen as the company's auditor. How would Wiley report this news to the SEC?

After completing requirements 1–4, check your answers with the following solution.

Suggested Solution

1. **Debt-to-Assets Ratio = Total Liabilities ÷ Total Assets**

	2003	*2002*
$\dfrac{\text{Total Liabilities}}{\text{Total Assets}}$	$\dfrac{\$611,968}{\$955,972} = 0.640$ or 64.0%	$\dfrac{\$619,495}{\$896,145} = 0.691$ or 69.1%

Wiley has moved toward a safer financing strategy in 2003, by relying less on debt (down from 69.1 percent in 2002 to 64.0 percent in 2003). Despite this change, Wiley still relies much more on debt than the videogame companies in Exhibit 5.10, which financed less than 25 percent of their total assets using debt.

2. **Asset Turnover Ratio = Sales Revenue ÷ Average Total Assets**

	2003	*2002*
$\dfrac{\text{Sales Revenue}}{\text{Average Total Assets}}$	$\dfrac{\$853,971}{(\$955,972 + 896,145)/2} = 0.92$	$\dfrac{\$734,396}{(\$896,145 + 588,032)/2} = 0.99$

Wiley generated fewer sales per dollar invested in assets in 2003 (0.92) than in 2002 (0.99). In comparison to the videogame companies in Exhibit 5.10, it appears Wiley's assets are not generating sales with nearly the same efficiency. The videogame company that was least efficient at using assets to generate sales (with an asset turnover ratio of 1.22) was still better than Wiley.

3. **Net Profit Margin Ratio = Net Income ÷ Sales Revenue**

	2003	*2002*
$\dfrac{\text{Net Income}}{\text{Sales Revenue}}$	$\dfrac{\$87,275}{\$853,971} = 0.102$ or 10.2%	$\dfrac{\$57,316}{\$734,396} = 0.078$ or 7.8%

Wiley has improved its net profit margin from 7.8 percent in 2002 to 10.2 percent in 2003. This means that, in 2003, Wiley made about 10.2 cents of profit for each dollar of sales. These ratios are in the same range as those for the videogame companies.

4. **Form 8-K** is used to report significant events such as this change in auditor.

CHAPTER SUMMARY

Describe the main financial statement users and the key qualities of useful information that are of interest to them. p. 190   LO1

- The four main financial statement users are

    Managers, who use accounting information to run the business.

    Directors, who use accounting information to oversee the business.

    Creditors, who use accounting information to administer business contracts.

    Investors, who use accounting information to value the business.

- The key qualities of useful information are (1) reliability, (2) relevance, (3) consistency, and (4) comparability.

Calculate and interpret the debt-to-assets, asset turnover, and net profit margin ratios. p. 193   LO2

- The debt-to-assets ratio is calculated by dividing total liabilities by total assets. It indicates the percentage of assets financed by debt, with a higher ratio indicating a riskier financing strategy.

- The asset turnover ratio is calculated by dividing sales revenue for the period by average total assets held during the period. Average total assets usually is calculated by adding the beginning and ending total assets together and dividing by 2. The asset turnover ratio indicates how well assets are used to generate sales, with a higher ratio indicating greater efficiency.

- The net profit margin ratio is calculated by dividing net income by sales revenue. It indicates the ability to generate sales while controlling expenses, with a higher ratio indicating better performance.

Describe the information in press releases and SEC filings. p. 201   LO3

- Press releases typically include key figures (sales revenues, net income), management's discussion of the results, and attachments containing a condensed income statement and balance sheet.

- Form 10-K is the SEC's version of the annual report, which includes the annual financial statements, auditor's report, management's discussion and analysis, stock price data, and other financial schedules.

- Form 10-Q is the SEC's version of the quarterly report, which includes the quarterly financial statements and management's discussion and analysis.

- Form 8-K is the SEC's form that companies use to report significant current events, such as changes in auditors, press releases issued, and acquisitions of other companies.

Explain why managers might misreport their financial results and what helps to prevent this from occurring. p. 204   LO4

- Managers can be motivated to misreport financial results to create business opportunities (by satisfying loan covenants, increasing equity financing, and attracting business partners) and to satisfy personal greed (enhancing job security, increasing personal wealth, and obtaining a bigger paycheck).

- Managers are deterred from misrepresenting their financial results because doing so is unethical and illegal, and it can result in significant financial and legal penalties. Also, honest managers can develop a reputation for honest reporting, which leads investors to place more trust in them and their financial reports.

FINANCIAL STATEMENT ANALYSIS TIPS

To determine the percentage of assets financed by debt—as a sign of the company's financing risk—calculate the debt-to-assets ratio:

$$\text{Debt-to-Assets Ratio} = \frac{\text{Total Liabilities}}{\text{Total Assets}}$$

To determine how well assets are used to generate sales, calculate the asset turnover ratio:

$$\text{Asset Turnover Ratio} = \frac{\text{Sales Revenue}}{\text{Average Total Assets}}$$

To determine a company's ability to generate sales while controlling expenses, calculate the net profit margin ratio:

$$\text{Net Profit Margin Ratio} = \frac{\text{Net Income}}{\text{Sales Revenue}}$$

KEY TERMS TO KNOW

Asset Turnover Ratio p. 210
Comparable p. 192
Consistent p. 192
Cross-Sectional
  Analysis p. 196
Debt-to-Assets Ratio p. 210

Earnings Forecast p. 193
Full Disclosure
  Principle p. 205
Loan Covenants p. 191
Net Profit Margin
  Ratio p. 210

Pro Forma p. 201
Relevant p. 192
Reliable p. 192
Time-Series Analysis p. 195
Unqualified Audit
  Report p. 193

FOR YOUR PRACTICE

QUESTIONS

1. Describe one decision that each of the four main financial statement user groups makes with financial statement information.
2. What are the four characteristics of *useful* information? Briefly describe each.
3. What roles do auditors and analysts play in the financial reporting process?
4. Explain the simple business model that starts with obtaining financing and then proceeds through other investing and operating decisions.
5. What two benchmarks are commonly used to interpret and evaluate amounts reported for specific financial statement items?
6. Why are some ratios expressed as percentages whereas others are not?
7. Why do some ratios use just the ending balance sheet amounts whereas others use averages of the beginning and ending balances?
8. What are the key business activities that the debt-to-assets, asset turnover, and net profit margin ratios assess?
9. What are two potential problems with relying on investor information Web sites for financial statement ratio analyses?
10. Why would managers misrepresent the financial results of their companies? What are the incentives for doing this? What are the reasons for not misrepresenting financial results?
11. Some people say that a company's earnings are like a student's grades. In what ways do you agree with this? In what ways do you disagree with this?

MULTIPLE CHOICE

1. If total assets increase but total liabilities remain the same, what is the impact on the debt-to-assets ratio?
   a. Increases.
   b. Decreases.
   c. Remains the same.
   d. Cannot be determined without additional information.

2. Costco and Sam's Club are two companies that offer low prices for items packaged in bulk. This strategy increases total sales volume, but generates less profit for each dollar of sales. Which of the following ratios is improved by this strategy?
   a. Net profit margin.
   b. Asset turnover.
   c. Debt-to-assets.
   d. All of the above.

3. Which of the following would increase the net profit margin ratio in the current period?
   a. Increase the amount of research and development in the last month of the year.
   b. Decrease the amount of sales in the last month of the year.
   c. Postpone routine maintenance checks that were to be done this year.
   d. All of the above.

4. The asset turnover ratio is directly affected by which of the following categories of business decisions?
   a. Operating and investing decisions.
   b. Operating and financing decisions.
   c. Investing and financing decisions.
   d. Operating, investing, and financing decisions.

5. Which of the following reports is filed annually with the SEC?
   a. Form 10-Q   c. Form 8-K
   b. Form 10-K   d. Press release

6. Which of the following describes a cross-sectional analysis of your academic performance?
   a. Counting the number of A's on your transcript.
   b. Comparing the number of A's you received this year to the number you received last year.
   c. Comparing the number of A's you received this year to the number your friend received.
   d. Counting the total number of A's given out to your class as a whole.

7. Which of the following is not a normal function of a financial analyst?
   a. Make predictions about a company's future earnings.
   b. Examine the records underlying the financial statements to verify the use of GAAP.
   c. Make buy, hold, and sell recommendations on a company's stock.
   d. Evaluate a company's past performance.

8. Which of the following is always included in an annual report but never in a quarterly report?
   a. Balance sheet.
   b. Income statement.
   c. Management's discussion and analysis.
   d. Auditor's report.

9. Which of the following transactions will increase the debt-to-assets ratio?
   a. The company issues stock to investors.
   b. The company uses cash to buy land.
   c. The company issues a note payable to buy machinery.
   d. None of the above.

10. What type of audit report does a company hope to include with its annual report?
    a. Conservative report   c. Comparable report
    b. Qualified report   d. Unqualified report

Solutions to Multiple-Choice Questions

1. b 2. b 3. c 4. a 5. b 6. c 7. b 8. d 9. c 10. d

MINI-EXERCISES Available with McGraw-Hill's Homework Manager

M5-1 Identifying Important Accounting Terms

LO1, LO2

Complete the following crossword puzzle, using the clues provided in the box on the right. Omit hyphens.

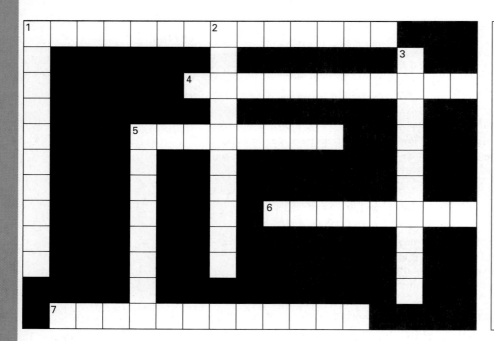

Across
1 A type of analysis that compares across companies.
4 The type of audit report that says the financial statements follow GAAP.
5 A characteristic of information that means it is accurate, unbiased, and verifiable.
6 The name given to the type of report that shows financial results after excluding certain events.
7 The name of the ratio that indicates the percentage of assets that are financed by debt.

Down
1 A characteristic of information that allows it to be compared across companies.
2 A characteristic of information that allows it to be compared over time.
3 A type of analysis that compares across time periods.
5 A characteristic of information that means it can affect a decision.

LO1

M5-2 Matching Players in the Financial Reporting Process with Their Definitions

Match each player with the related definition by entering the appropriate letter in the space provided.

Players	Definitions
___ 1. Directors	A. Advisers who analyze financial and other economic information to form forecasts and stock recommendations.
___ 2. Independent auditors	
___ 3. External users	B. Investors and creditors (among others).
___ 4. Financial analysts	C. People who are elected by stockholders to oversee a company's management.
	D. CPAs who examine financial statements and attest to their fairness.

LO3

M5-3 Identifying the Sequence of Financial Reports and Disclosures

Indicate the order in which the following reports and disclosures are normally issued by public companies in any given year.

No.	Title
___	Annual report
___	Form 10-K
___	Press release announcing annual earnings

LO2

M5-4 Determining the Effects of Transactions on the Balance Sheet and Income Statement

Complete the following table, indicating the sign and amount of the effect (+ for increase, − for decrease, and NE for no effect) of each transaction. Consider each item independently.

a. Recorded services provided on account for $100.
b. Recorded advertising expense of $10 incurred but not paid for.

	Balance Sheet			Income Statement		
Transaction	Assets	Liabilities	Stockholders' Equity	Revenues	Expenses	Net Income
a						
b						

M5-5 Determining the Effects of Transactions on Debt-to-Assets, Asset Turnover, and Net Profit Margin

LO2

Using the transactions in M5-4, complete the following table by indicating the sign of the effect (+ for increase, − for decrease, NE for no effect, and CD for cannot determine) of each transaction. Consider each item independently.

Transaction	Debt-to-Assets	Asset Turnover	Net Profit Margin
a			
b			

M5-6 Determining the Effects of Transactions on the Balance Sheet and Income Statement

LO2

Complete the following table, indicating the sign and amount of the effect (+ for increase, − for decrease, and NE for no effect) of each transaction. Consider each item independently.

a. Equipment costing $4,000 was purchased by issuing a note payable.
b. Issued 10,000 shares of stock for $90,000 cash.
c. Recorded depreciation of $1,000 on the equipment.

	Balance Sheet			Income Statement		
Transaction	Assets	Liabilities	Stockholders' Equity	Revenues	Expenses	Net Income
a						
b						
c						

M5-7 Determining the Effects of Transactions on Debt-to-Assets, Asset Turnover, and Net Profit Margin

LO2

Using the transactions in M5-6, complete the following table by indicating the sign of the effect (+ for increase, − for decrease, NE for no effect, and CD for cannot determine) of each transaction. Consider each item independently.

Transaction	Debt-to-Assets	Asset Turnover	Net Profit Margin
a			
b			
c			

M5-8 Computing and Interpreting the Net Profit Margin Ratio

LO2

Gilmore Golf Corporation recently reported the following December 31 amounts in its financial statements (in thousands):

	Current Year	Prior Year
Operating income	$ 170	$140
Net income	85	70
Total assets	1,000	900
Total stockholders' equity	800	750
Sales revenue	900	700

Compute the net profit margin ratio for the current and prior years. What do these analyses indicate?

LO2

M5-9 Computing and Interpreting the Debt-to-Assets Ratio
Using the data in M5-8, compute the debt-to-assets ratio for the current and prior years. What do these analyses indicate?

LO2

M5-10 Computing and Interpreting the Asset Turnover Ratio
Using the data in M5-8, compute the asset turnover ratio for the current year. Assuming the asset turnover ratio in the prior year was 85.2 percent (0.852), what does your analysis indicate?

EXERCISES   Available with McGraw-Hill's Homework Manager

LO1, LO3

E5-1 Matching Components of the Financial Reporting Process with Their Definitions
Match each component with the related definition by entering the appropriate letter in the space provided.

Components	Definitions
_____ 1. SEC	A. Adviser who analyzes financial and other economic information to form forecasts and stock recommendations.
_____ 2. Independent auditor	
_____ 3. Investor	B. Financial institution or supplier that lends money to the company.
_____ 4. CEO and CFO	
_____ 5. Creditor	C. Chief executive officer and chief financial officer who have primary responsibility for the information presented in financial statements.
_____ 6. Financial analyst	
_____ 7. Investor information Web site	D. Independent CPA who examines financial statements and attests to their fairness.
	E. Securities and Exchange Commission, which regulates financial disclosure requirements.
	F. Gathers, combines, and transmits financial and related information from various sources.
	G. Individual who purchases stock in companies for personal ownership or for pension funds or mutual funds.

LO3

E5-2 Matching Definitions with Information Releases Made by Public Companies
Following are the titles of various information releases. Match each definition with the related release by entering the appropriate letter in the space provided.

Information Release	Definitions
___ 1. Annual report	A. A company-prepared news announcement that is normally distributed to major news agencies.
___ 2. Form 8-K	
___ 3. Press release	B. Annual report filed by public companies with the SEC that contains detailed financial information.
___ 4. Form 10-Q	
___ 5. Quarterly report	C. Quarterly report filed by public companies with the SEC that contains unaudited financial information.
___ 6. Form 10-K	
	D. Comprehensive report containing the four basic financial statements and related notes, statements by management and auditors, and other descriptions of the company's activities.
	E. Brief unaudited report for the quarter, normally containing condensed income statement and balance sheet (unaudited).
	F. Report of special events (e.g., auditor changes, mergers and acquisitions) filed by public companies with the SEC.

LO3

E5-3 Finding Financial Information: Matching Information Items to Financial Reports
Following are information items included in various financial reports. Match each information item with the report(s) where it would most likely be found by entering the appropriate letter(s) in the space provided.

Information Item		Report	
____ 1.	Summarized financial data for 5- or 10-year period.	A.	Annual report
____ 2.	Initial announcement of quarterly earnings.	B.	Form 8-K
____ 3.	Initial announcement of a change in auditors.	C.	Press release
____ 4.	Complete quarterly income statement, balance sheet, and cash flow statement.	D.	Form 10-Q
		E.	Quarterly report
____ 5.	The four basic financial statements for the year.	F.	Form 10-K
____ 6.	Summarized income statement information for the quarter.	G.	None of the above
____ 7.	Detailed discussion of the company's business risks and strategies.		
____ 8.	Detailed notes to financial statements.		
____ 9.	Recent stock price data.		
____ 10.	Initial announcement of hiring of new vice president for sales.		

E5-4 Understanding the Financial Reporting Process   LO3

During the first half of 2004, Papa John's International filed reports with the SEC and issued various reports to the public. Two of the reports were filed/issued on the same day. Match each date in the table below with the related report by entering the appropriate letter in the space provided.

Date Filed/Issued		Report	
____ 1.	February 24, 2004	A.	Annual report
____ 2.	February 24, 2004	B.	Form 8-K announcing press release
____ 3.	March 10, 2004	C.	Annual earnings press release
____ 4.	June 1, 2004	D.	Form 10-K

E5-5 Matching Events with Concepts   LO1

Following are the concepts of accounting covered in Chapters 2 through 5. Match each event with its related concept by entering the appropriate letter in the space provided. Use one letter for each blank.

Concepts		Events	
____ 1.	Users of financial statements	A.	Counted unsold items of inventory at the end of the period and valued them in U.S. dollars.
____ 2.	Objective of financial statements	B.	Reported the amount of depreciation expense because it likely will affect important decisions of statement users.
____ 3.	Relevance	C.	Maintained a list of all parties who requested a copy of the financial statements.
____ 4.	Reliability	D.	Engaged an outside independent CPA to audit the financial statements.
____ 5.	Consistency	E.	Established an accounting policy that sales revenue shall be recognized only when ownership to the goods sold passes to the customer.
____ 6.	Comparability		
____ 7.	Separate entity	F.	Prepared and distributed financial statements that provide useful economic information.
____ 8.	Unit of measure	G.	Established a policy not to include in the financial statements the personal financial affairs of the owners of the business.
____ 9.	Cost principle		
____ 10.	Revenue principle	H.	Changed the company's year-end to correspond with that used by others in the industry.
____ 11.	Matching principle	I.	Valued an asset, such as land, at less than its purchase cost because its value had declined permanently.
____ 12.	Full disclosure principle	J.	Disclosed all relevant financial information about the business in the financial statements (including the notes to the financial statements).
____ 13.	Conservatism		
		K.	Established a policy to report the company's recurring business activities in the same way from year to year.
		L.	Adjusted the rent accounts to show the cost of rent relating to the current period.
		M.	Acquired a vehicle for use in the business, reporting it at the agreed-upon purchase price rather than its higher sticker price.

LO1–LO3

E5-6 Understanding the Characteristics of Useful Financial Information and the Financial Reporting Process

The second page of this chapter mentioned someone who created a $28 million enterprise from $250 and a new game idea. The new idea was a game called Pong and the enterprise was Atari Incorporated. Over the years, Atari has been owned by a variety of companies, including Time-Warner, Hasbro, and most recently Infogrames (a public company in France). Infogrames made the following announcement in 2003:

> On March 28, 2003, the Company announced that it has changed its fiscal year-end from June 30 to March 31. As a result of this change, the Company's fiscal year 2003 was a nine-month period. The Company believes that the March 31 year-end is consistent with more of its peers in the video game industry, allowing for more meaningful analysis and comparisons within the sector.

Required:

1. To which of the four characteristics of useful information is the company referring? (*Hint*: Rather than look for key words in the announcement, read it for meaning.)
2. On what SEC form would the change in year-end be reported?
3. Since the 2003 fiscal period includes only nine months, will the debt-to-assets, asset turnover, and net profit margin ratios be meaningful in 2003? Explain your reasoning.

LO1–LO3

E5-7 Understanding the Characteristics of Useful Financial Information and the Financial Reporting Process

THQ, Inc., is among the five biggest videogame makers in the world, and is one of Activision's main competitors. On February 13, 2003, THQ made the following announcement:

> On February 13, 2003, we announced a fiscal year end change from December 31 of each year to March 31 of each year, effective March 31, 2003. We believe that the change in fiscal year will better reflect our natural business year and allow us to provide financial guidance after the holiday selling season.

Required:

1. Does the reason given for the change in year-end indicate that this change will make THQ's financial statements more useful to users? Can you think of a reason that the change in year-end ultimately will result in more useful information for users?
2. On what SEC form would the change in year-end be reported?
3. Since the March 31, 2003 fiscal period includes only three months, will the debt-to-assets, asset turnover, and net profit margin ratios be meaningful in this period? Explain your reasoning.

LO2

E5-8 Computing and Interpreting the Net Profit Margin Ratio

Boise Cascade Corporation manufactures all kinds of lumber and paper products, and sells office supplies through its Office Max division. On January 22, the company issued a press release that reported the following amounts (in thousands) for the year just ended on December 31:

	Current Year	Prior Year
Sales revenue	$8,245	$7,412
Operating income	148	118
Net income	8	11

Required:

Compute the net profit margin ratio for the current and prior years. What do these analyses indicate?

E5-9 Understanding the Financial Reporting Process

LO3

1. The information in E5-8 indicated that the Boise Cascade press release was issued on January 22, yet the company's year-end was three weeks earlier on December 31. Why did the company wait so long to issue the press release? Why weren't the financial results announced on January 1?

2. The press release stated that the 10-K would be filed sometime in March. Why would the company wait so long to file the 10-K? Why wouldn't they file it at the same time the press release was issued?

3. Is the company's glossy annual report likely to be issued before or after the 10-K?

E5-10 Analyzing and Interpreting Asset Turnover and Net Profit Margin

LO1, LO2

Papa John's is one of the fastest-growing pizza delivery and carryout restaurant chains in the country. Presented here are selected income statement and balance sheet amounts (in millions).

	Current Year	Prior Year
Total revenues	$917	$946
Net income	34	47
Average total assets	357	377

Required:

1. Compute the asset turnover and net profit margin ratios for the current and prior years.

2. Would security analysts more likely increase or decrease their estimates of stock value on the basis of these changes? Explain by interpreting what the changes in these two ratios mean.

E5-11 Analyzing and Interpreting Asset Turnover and Net Profit Margin

LO1, LO2

RadioShack Corporation has populated the world with its stores, from Greece to Chile to Canada, and in the United States, an estimated 94 percent of all Americans live or work within five minutes of one of its stores—not bad for a company that originally started business as American Hide & Leather Company. Presented here are selected amounts (in millions) reported in RadioShack's income statement and balance sheet.

	2003	2002	2001
Net sales	$4,649	$4,577	$4,776
Net income	299	263	167
Total assets	2,244	2,228	2,245
Total liabilities	1,474	1,500	1,467

Required:

1. Compute the asset turnover and net profit margin ratios for 2003 and 2002.

2. Would investment analysts be more likely to increase or decrease their estimates of stock value on the basis of these changes? Explain what the changes in these two ratios mean.

3. Compute the debt-to-assets ratio for 2003 and 2002.

4. Would credit analysts be more likely to increase or decrease their estimates of RadioShack's ability to repay lenders on the basis of this change? Explain by interpreting what the change in this ratio means.

E5-12 Determining the Effects of Transactions on the Balance Sheet and Income Statement

LO2

Rowe Furniture Corporation is a Virginia-based manufacturer of furniture. Listed here are selected aggregate transactions from the first quarter of a recent year (in millions). Complete the following table, indicating the sign (+ for increase, − for decrease, and NE for no effect) and amount of the effect of each transaction. Consider each item independently.

a. Recorded collections of cash from customers of $32.
b. Repaid $10 on a note payable to a bank.

	Balance Sheet			Income Statement		
Transaction	Assets	Liabilities	Stockholders' Equity	Revenues	Expenses	Net Income
a						
b						

LO2

E5-13 Determining the Effects of Transactions on Debt-to-Assets, Asset Turnover, and Net Profit Margin

Using the transactions in E5-12, complete the following table by indicating the sign of the effect (+ for increase, − for decrease, NE for no effect, and CD for cannot determine) of each transaction. Consider each item independently.

Transaction	Debt-to-Assets	Asset Turnover	Net Profit Margin
a			
b			

SIMPLIFY WITH SPREADSHEETS

LO2

SS5-1 Computing, Charting, and Interpreting Time-Series and Cross-Sectional Analyses

Assume that *Candy Industry Magazine* has contracted you to write an article discussing the financial status of Hershey Foods Corporation over the last few years. The editor suggests that your article should also compare Hershey's recent financial performance to competitors like Tootsie Roll Industries and gum-maker Wm. Wrigley Jr. You gather the following information from the three companies' 10-Ks (all have December 31 year-ends).

(in millions of U.S. dollars)	Hershey Foods Corporation			Tootsie Roll Industries	Wm. Wrigley Jr. Company
	2001	2002	2003	2003	2003
Total Liabilities	$2,100	$2,109	$2,302	$128	$ 700
Total Assets	$3,247	$3,481	$3,583	$665	$2,520
Sales Revenues	$4,137	$4,120	$4,172	$393	$3,069
Net Income	$ 207	$ 403	$ 458	$ 65	$ 446

Required:

Enter the above information into a spreadsheet and perform the following analyses:

1. *Time-series analysis:* Demonstrate the changes in Hershey's size over the last three years by charting its total liabilities, total assets, sales revenues, and net income.
2. *Cross-sectional analysis:* Demonstrate the size of Hershey relative to Tootsie Roll and Wm. Wrigley Jr. by charting the three companies' total liabilities, total assets, sales revenues, and net income for 2003.
3. *Ratio analysis:* Compare the performance of Hershey relative to Tootsie Roll and Wm. Wrigley Jr. by computing the debt-to-assets and net profit margin ratios for 2003.

Although you're confident you can use a spreadsheet to complete the ratio analyses, you realize you'll need Billy's help with the charting to be done in the time-series and cross-sectional analyses. Here's his reply.

> From: BillyTheTutor@yahoo.com
> To: HairZed@hotmail.com
> Cc:
> Subject: Excel Help

I can imagine that the readers of Candy Industry Magazine are on a constant sugar rush, so that's a great idea to present the time-series and cross-sectional analyses in easily digested charts. Using the charting function in Excel isn't too difficult. The first thing to do is enter the data into a spreadsheet exactly as it appears in the table. Next, display the chart toolbar by clicking on View/Toolbar/Chart.

To produce the time-series chart, click on the cell containing Hershey's 2003 total liabilities and drag to the cell containing Hershey's 2001 net income. With these cells selected, click on the 3D column chart icon to chart the data. You can change the layout by clicking on the chart and then Chart/Source Data in the pull-down menu. Click on the Data Range tab to indicate whether the data are presented as columns or rows in your spreadsheet (select Columns). To add labels, click on the Series tab, select each series one at a time, and enter a name for each (Series 1 should be named 2003). Before you close the box, click on the icon beside the "Category (X) axis labels:" which will take you back to your spreadsheet. Once there, select the financial statement category names by clicking on the name "total liabilities" and dragging to "net income." After selecting these cells, hit enter on the keyboard. If you followed these directions exactly, you should have a decent looking time-series chart. Play around with the appearance by selecting 3-D View . . . from the Chart pull-down menu. Follow these same basic steps to produce the cross-sectional chart.

COACH'S CORNER

CP5-1*d*. Remember that declared dividends are considered distributions of retained earnings, rather than expenses of the current period.

COACHED PROBLEMS

CP5-1 Determining the Effects of Transactions on the Balance Sheet and Income Statement

LO2

Yahoo! Inc. is a leading provider of Internet products and services. (Like you needed to be told that.) Listed here are selected aggregate transactions from 2003 (in millions). Complete the following table, indicating the sign (+ for increase, − for decrease, and NE for no effect) and amount of the effect of each transaction. Consider each item independently.

a. Recorded marketing revenues on account of $663.
b. Borrowed $750 cash by issuing a note payable.
c. Incurred research and development expense of $121, which was paid in cash.
d. Declared, but haven't yet paid, a dividend of $5.

	Balance Sheet			Income Statement		
Transaction	**Assets**	**Liabilities**	**Stockholders' Equity**	**Revenues**	**Expenses**	**Net Income**
a						
b						
c						
d						

CP5-2 Determining the Effects of Transactions on Debt-to-Assets, Asset Turnover, and Net Profit Margin

LO2

Using the transactions in CP5-1, complete the following table by indicating the sign of the effect (+ for increase, − for decrease, NE for no effect, and CD for cannot determine) of each transaction. Consider each item independently.

LO2

Transaction	Debt-to-Assets	Asset Turnover	Net Profit Margin
a			
b			
c			
d			

CP5-3 Relating Debt-to-Assets Ratio to Vertical Analysis

The debt-to-assets ratio divides total liabilities by total assets to determine the percentage of assets financed by debt. This same type of analysis can be conducted to determine what percentage of assets are financed by each individual type of liability, such as accounts payable and notes payable. Also, you can determine how significant each individual type of asset is by dividing the amount shown for each asset by the total assets. This kind of analysis, which compares each individual line item to a total on that statement, often is called a vertical, or common size, analysis. Below, we present a condensed balance sheet for Activision and a partially completed vertical analysis.

	ACTIVISION, INC.				
(in millions of U.S. dollars)	**Balance Sheet (summarized)** **March 31, 2003**				
Cash and short-term investments	$407	58%	Accounts payable	$ 46	7%
Accounts receivable	16	2	Accrued liabilities	58	(d)
Inventories	20	3	Long-term debt	3	0
Other current assets	85	(a)	Total Liabilities	107	(e)
Software development	72	(b)	Contributed capital	467	66
Property and equipment	22	(c)	Retained earnings	131	19
Other assets	83	12	Total Stockholders' Equity	598	85
Total Assets	$705	100%	Total Liabilities & Stockholders' Equity	$705	100%

Required:

1. Complete the vertical analysis by computing each line-item (a)–(e) as a percentage of total assets.
2. What percentages of Activision's assets relate to software development versus property and equipment? What reasons can you think of that would explain this relative emphasis?
3. Does the (rounded) percentage that you calculated in 1 (e) correspond to the debt-to-assets ratio reported in Exhibit 5.10?

LO2

CP5-4 Relating Net Profit Margin Ratio to Vertical Analysis

The net profit margin ratio divides net income by total revenues to determine the percentage of profits produced from sales. This same type of analysis can be conducted to determine what percentage of total revenues each individual expense represents. This kind of analysis, which compares each individual line item to a total on that statement, often is called a vertical, or common size, analysis. Below, we present a condensed income statement for Activision along with a partially completed vertical analysis.

	ACTIVISION, INC.				
(in millions of U.S. dollars)	**Income Statement (summarized)** **For the Year Ended March 31**				
	2003			**2002**	
Net revenues	$864		100%	$786	100%
Cost of sales	565	(a)		535	68
Product development	57		7	41	5

Sales and marketing	101	(b)		86	11
General and administrative	46	(c)		44	5
Operating income	95	11		80	11
Interest revenue	8	1		3	—
Income before income taxes	103	12		83	11
Income tax expense	37	4		31	4
Net income	$ 66	(d)	%	$ 52	7%

Required:

1. Complete the vertical analysis by computing each line-item (a)–(d) as a percentage of net revenues.

2. Does Activision's 2003 cost of sales, as a percentage of revenues, represent better or worse performance as compared to 2002?

3. Does the (rounded) percentage that you calculated in 1(d) correspond to the net profit margin reported in Exhibit 5.10?

GROUP A PROBLEMS   Available with McGraw-Hill's Homework Manager

PA5-1 Determining the Effects of Transactions on the Balance Sheet and Income Statement

LO2

Papa John's International began in the back of a tavern in Jefferson, Indiana, and has since become the third-largest pizza company in America. Listed here are transactions that occur each year (in millions). Complete the following table, indicating the sign (+ for increase, − for decrease, and NE for no effect) and amount of the effect of each transaction. Consider each item independently.

a. Recorded royalty revenues on account of $10.
b. Paid cash to purchase property and equipment costing $4.
c. Purchased additional property and equipment costing $3, by issuing a note payable.
d. Repaid bank loan payable of $10.

	Balance Sheet			Income Statement		
Transaction	**Assets**	**Liabilities**	**Stockholders' Equity**	**Revenues**	**Expenses**	**Net Income**
a						
b						
c						
d						

PA5-2 Determining the Effects of Transactions on Debt-to-Assets, Asset Turnover, and Net Profit Margin

LO2

Using the transactions in PA5-1, complete the following table by indicating the sign of the effect (+ for increase, − for decrease, NE for no effect, and CD for cannot determine) of each transaction. Consider each item independently.

Transaction	**Debt-to-Assets**	**Asset Turnover**	**Net Profit Margin**
a			
b			
c			
d			

LO2

PA5-3 Relating Debt-to-Assets Ratio to Vertical Analysis

The debt-to-total assets ratio divides total liabilities by total assets to determine the percentage of assets financed by debt. This same type of analysis can be conducted to determine what percentage of assets are financed by each individual type of liability, such as accounts payable and notes payable. Also, you can determine how significant each individual type of asset is by dividing the amount shown for each asset by the total assets. This kind of analysis, which compares each individual line-item to a total on that statement, often is called a vertical analysis. Below, we present a condensed balance sheet for Kellwood Company and a partially completed vertical analysis.

KELLWOOD COMPANY					
Balance Sheet (summarized)					
(in millions of U.S. dollars)			**January 31, 2004**		
Cash and short-term investments	$ 179	14%	Current liabilities	$ 305	24%
			Long-term liabilities	343	26
Accounts receivable	321	25	Total Liabilities	648	(b)
Inventories	316	24			
Other current assets	66	(a)	Contributed capital	144	(c)
Property and equipment	97	8	Retained earnings	500	39
Other assets	313	24	Total Stockholders' Equity	644	(d)
Total Assets	$1,292	100%	Total Liabilities & Stockholders' Equity	$1,292	100%

Required:

1. Complete the vertical analysis by computing each line item (*a*)–(*d*) as a percentage of total assets.

2. What percentages of Kellwood's assets relate to inventories versus property and equipment? What does this tell you about the relative significance of these two assets to Kellwood's business?

3. What percentage of Kellwood's assets is financed by total stockholders' equity? By total liabilities?

LO2, LO3

PA5-4 Relating Net Profit Margin Ratio to Vertical Analysis and Identifying SEC Filing

The net profit margin ratio divides net income by total revenues to determine the percentage of profits produced from sales. This same type of analysis can be conducted to determine what percentage of total revenues each individual expense represents. This kind of analysis, which compares each individual line-item to a total on that statement, often is called a vertical analysis. Below, we present a condensed income statement for Kellwood Company along with a partially completed vertical analysis.

KELLWOOD COMPANY					
Income Statement (summarized)					
(in millions of U.S. dollars)	**For the Year Ended**				
	January 31, 2004			**February 1, 2003**	
Sales revenues	$2,346		100%	$2,167		100%
Cost of products sold	1,845		79	1,734	(d)	
Selling, general, and administrative expenses	358	(a)		324		15
Other operating expenses	10		0	18		1
Interest expense	25	(b)		28		1
Income before income taxes	108		5	63	(e)	
Income tax expense	37		2	21		1
Net income	$ 71	(c)	%	$ 42	(f)	%

Required:

1. Complete the vertical analysis by computing each line-item (*a*)–(*f*) as a percentage of sales revenues.
2. Does Kellwood's cost of products sold for the year ended January 31, 2004, as a percentage of revenues, represent better or worse performance as compared to that for the year ended February 1, 2003?
3. Do the percentages that you calculated in 1(*c*) and (*f*) indicate whether Kellwood's net profit margin has changed over the two years?
4. On January 8, 2004, Kellwood issued an exciting press release announcing that Russell Simmons—the founder of Def Jam Records and legendary "Godfather of Hip Hop"—had agreed to sell Phat Fashions to Kellwood for nearly $140 million. In addition to the press release, what other report would Kellwood be required to file?

GROUP B PROBLEMS

PB5-1 Determining the Effects of Transactions on the Balance Sheet and Income Statement   LO2

Regal Entertainment Group is the largest movie company in the world, taking in over 20 percent of the box office receipts in the United States. Listed here are transactions that occur each quarter (in millions). Complete the following table, indicating the sign (+ for increase, − for decrease, and NE for no effect) and amount of the effect of each transaction. Consider each item independently.

a. Recorded cash admissions revenues of $440.
b. Paid cash to purchase property and equipment costing $27.
c. Declared and paid cash dividend totaling $41.
d. Recorded depreciation on property and equipment totaling $75.

	Balance Sheet			Income Statement		
Transaction	**Assets**	**Liabilities**	**Stockholders' Equity**	**Revenues**	**Expenses**	**Net Income**
a						
b						
c						
d						

PB5-2 Determining the Effects of Transactions on Debt-to-Assets, Asset Turnover, and Net Profit Margin   LO2

Using the transactions in PB5-1, complete the following table by indicating the sign of the effect (+ for increase, − for decrease, NE for no effect, and CD for cannot determine) of each transaction. Consider each item independently.

Transaction	**Debt-to-Assets**	**Asset Turnover**	**Net Profit Margin**
a			
b			
c			
d			

PB5-3 Relating Debt-to-Assets Ratio to Vertical Analysis   LO2

The debt-to-assets ratio divides total liabilities by total assets to determine the percentage of assets financed by debt. This same type of analysis can be conducted to determine what percentage of assets are financed by each individual type of liability, such as accounts payable and notes payable. Also, you can determine how significant each individual type of asset is by dividing the amount shown for each asset by the total assets. This kind of analysis, which compares each individual line item to a total on that statement, often is called a vertical analysis. Below, we present a condensed balance sheet for Southwest Airlines and a partially completed vertical analysis.

SOUTHWEST AIRLINES Balance Sheet (summarized)							
(in millions of U.S. dollars)			December 31, 2003				
Cash	$1,865		19%	Current liabilities	$1,723		18%
Accounts receivable	132		2	Long-term liabilities	3,103	(b)	
Inventory of parts				Total Liabilities	4,826		49
and supplies	93		1	Contributed capital	1,047		11
Other current assets	223		2	Retained earnings	4,005		40
Property and				Total Stockholders'			
equipment	7,443	(a)		Equity	5,052	(c)	
Other assets	122		1	Total Liabilities &			
Total Assets	$9,878		100%	Stockholders'			
				Equity	$9,878		100%

Required:

1. Complete the vertical analysis by computing each line-item (a)–(c) as a percentage of total assets.
2. What percentages of Southwest's assets relate to inventory of parts and supplies versus property and equipment? What does this tell you about the relative significance of these two assets to Southwest's business?
3. What percentage of Southwest's assets is financed by total stockholders' equity? By total liabilities?

LO2, LO3   **PB5-4** **Relating Net Profit Margin Ratio to Vertical Analysis and Identifying SEC Filing**
The net profit margin ratio divides net income by total revenues to determine the percentage of profits produced from sales. This same type of analysis can be conducted to determine what percentage of total revenues each individual expense represents. This kind of analysis, which compares each individual line-item to a total on that statement, often is called a vertical analysis. Below, we present a condensed income statement for Southwest Airlines along with a partially completed vertical analysis.

SOUTHWEST AIRLINES Income Statement (summarized)						
(in millions of U.S. dollars)	For the Year Ended December 31					
	2003			**2002**		
Sales revenues	$5,937		100%	$5,522		100%
Salaries, wages, and benefits	2,224		38	1,993	(d)	
Fuel, oil, repairs, and						
maintenance	1,260	(a)		1,152		21
Other operating expenses	1,970	(b)		1,960		35
Other expenses (revenues						
and gains)	(225)		(4)	24		1
Income before income taxes	708		12	393	(e)	
Income tax expense	266		5	152		3
Net income	$ 422	(c)	%	$ 241	(f)	%

Required:

1. Complete the vertical analysis by computing each line-item (a)–(f) as a percentage of sales revenues.

2.   Does the percentage that you calculated in 1(a) suggest that Southwest tried to increase its profit by cutting repairs and maintenance costs in 2003 compared to 2002?

3.   According to Southwest's Web site at www.southwest.com/swatakeoff/plane_talk.html#wright, if the company had averaged 2.3 fewer passengers on each of its flights over the 15 months following 9/11, the company would have reported a loss rather than a profit. Do the percentages that you calculated in 1(c) and (f) indicate whether Southwest's net profit margin is continuing to improve, or is it declining?

CASES & DISCUSSION STARTERS

FINANCIAL REPORTING AND ANALYSIS CASES

C&DS5-1 Finding Financial Information

Refer to the financial statements of Landry's Restaurants in Appendix A at the end of this book, or download the annual report from the *Cases* section of the text's Web site at www.mhhe.com/phillips.

LO1–LO4

Required:

1.   Calculate the debt-to-assets ratio for 2003 and 2002. Based on these calculations, has Landry's financing become more or less risky in 2003 than in 2002?

2.   Calculate the asset turnover ratio for 2003 and 2002. (Total assets at December 31, 2001 were $690,171,196.) Based on these calculations, has Landry's used its assets more or less efficiently in 2003 than in 2002?

3.   Calculate the net profit margin ratio for 2003 and 2002. Based on these calculations, has Landry's generated more or less profit per dollar of sales in 2003 than in 2002?

C&DS5-2 Comparing Financial Information

Refer to the financial statements of Dave & Buster's in Appendix B at the end of this book, or download the annual report from the *Cases* section of the text's Web site at www.mhhe.com/phillips. Note that Dave & Buster's ends its fiscal year on February 1, 2004, which doesn't perfectly match Landry's year ended December 31, 2003. In the questions that follow, assume Dave & Buster's financial statements for the year ended February 1, 2004, present the results for 2003. (This is a reasonable assumption given that Dave and Buster's fiscal year simply replaces January 2003 with January 2004.)

LO1–LO4

Required:

1.   Calculate the debt-to-assets ratio at February 1, 2004. Based on this calculation, was Dave & Buster's financing more or less risky than Landry's in 2003?

2.   Calculate the asset turnover ratio for the year ended February 1, 2004. Based on this calculation, did Dave & Buster's use its assets more or less efficiently than Landry's in 2003?

3.   Calculate the net profit margin ratio for the year ended February 1, 2004. Based on this calculation, did Dave & Buster's generate more or less profit per dollar of sales than Landry's in 2003?

C&DS5-3 Internet-Based Team Research: Examining an Annual Report

As a team, select an industry to analyze. Using your Web browser, each team member should acquire the annual report or 10-K for one publicly traded company in the industry, with each member selecting a different company. (See C&DS1-3 in Chapter 1 for a description of possible resources for these tasks.)

LO2, LO3

TEAM CASE

Required:

1.   On an individual basis, each team member should write a short report that incorporates the following:
   a.   Calculate the debt-to-assets ratio at the end of the current and prior year, and explain any change between the two years.

b. Calculate the asset turnover ratio at the end of the current and prior year, and explain any change between the two years. (To calculate average assets for the prior year, you will need the total assets number for the beginning of the prior year. If this isn't reported in the summarized financial data section in the current annual report, you will need to get it from the prior annual report or 10-K.)

c. Calculate the net profit margin ratio at the end of the current and prior year, and explain any change between the two years.

2. Then, as a team, write a short report comparing and contrasting your companies using these attributes. Discuss any patterns across the companies that you as a team observe. Provide potential explanations for any differences discovered.

ETHICS AND CRITICAL THINKING CASES

L01–L04   **C&DS5-4** **Ethical Decision Making: A Real-Life Example**

ETHICAL

ISSUE

On February 18, 2000, the board of directors of Aurora Foods Inc.—the maker of Duncan Hines® and Mrs. Butterworth's® products—issued a press release announcing that a special committee had been formed to conduct an investigation into the company's accounting practices. During the financial statement audit for the year ended December 31, 1999, Aurora's auditors had discovered documents that raised questions about how the company accounted for marketing costs incurred to entice grocery stores to promote Aurora's products. The company's stock price fell by 50 percent in the week following this announcement.

After nearly a year of investigation, Aurora filed revised quarterly reports with the SEC, showing that the company had not accrued adequately for liabilities and expenses that had been incurred during the third and fourth quarter of 1998 and during the first three quarters of 1999. Key financial figures for these quarters as initially reported and as later restated are shown below.

(in millions of U.S. dollars)	1998 Q3 (September 30)		1998 Q4 (December 31)		1999 Q1 (March 31)		1999 Q2 (June 30)		1999 Q3 (September 30)	
	Initial Report	Restated Report	Initial Report	Restated Report	Initial Report	Restated Report	Initial Report	Restated Report	Initial Report	Restated Report
Assets	$1,457	$1,455	$1,434	$1,448	$1,474	$1,463	$1,558	$1,521	$1,614	$1,553
Liabilities	869	879	830	868	862	882	937	944	983	972
Revenues	220	219	280	277	261	254	222	214	238	231
Net income (loss)	1	(12)	16	5	8	0	8	(4)	11	4

The SEC also investigated and filed a legal claim alleging that Aurora's 36-year-old chief financial officer (CFO) had violated federal securities laws by instructing accounting staff to make false journal entries and prepare two sets of records—one for the company's internal use and another to be provided to the auditors. The SEC alleged that her actions allowed Aurora to meet the net income targets set by Wall Street analysts and the expectations of Aurora investors, and to obtain loans from Chase Manhattan Bank and other lenders. The CFO pled guilty to the charges, was sentenced to 57 months in prison, was barred for life from ever serving as an executive of a public company, and had to return to the company the stock and bonuses that had been awarded to her on the basis of Aurora's false and substantially inflated financial results.

Epilogue: On December 8, 2003, Aurora Foods filed for bankruptcy protection after violating several of its lenders' loan covenants. On March 19, 2004, Aurora emerged from bankruptcy and has since merged with Pinnacle Foods, the maker of Vlasic pickles and Swanson TV dinners.

Required:

1. Using the initially reported numbers, calculate the debt-to-assets ratio (reported as a percentage) at the end of each quarter.

2. Using the restated numbers, calculate the debt-to-assets ratio (reported as a percentage) at the end of each quarter.

3. On an overall basis, did the initially reported numbers suggest more or less financing risk than the restated numbers? Of the financial statement users mentioned earlier in this chapter in Exhibit 5.2, which would be most influenced by this impact on the debt-to-assets ratio?

4. Using the initially reported numbers, calculate the asset turnover ratio for the last quarter of 1998 and the first three quarters of 1999. (Note that the asset turnover ratio will be substantially less than the examples shown earlier in this chapter because they use only three months of revenues. Do not attempt to convert them to annual amounts.)

5. Using the restated numbers, calculate the asset turnover ratio for the last quarter of 1998 and the first three quarters of 1999.

6. On an overall basis, did the initially reported numbers or the restated numbers present Aurora in a better light? Of the financial statement users mentioned earlier in this chapter in Exhibit 5.2, which would be most influenced by this impact on the asset turnover ratio?

7. Using the initially reported numbers, calculate the net profit margin ratio (reported as a percentage) at the end of each quarter.

8. Using the restated numbers, calculate the net profit margin ratio (reported as a percentage) at the end of each quarter.

9. On an overall basis, did the initially reported numbers or the restated numbers present Aurora in a better light? Of the financial statement users mentioned earlier in this chapter in Exhibit 5.2, which would be most influenced by this impact on the net profit margin ratio?

10. What important role(s) did Aurora's auditors play in this case?

11. Based on specific information in the case, identify the incentives or goals that might have led the CFO to misreport Aurora's financial results. Looking back at the consequences of her dishonest actions, did she fulfill those goals?

C&DS5-5 Ethical Decision Making: A Mini-Case

Assume you've been hired to replace an accounting clerk for a small public company. After your second month on the job, the chief financial officer (CFO) approached you directly with a "special project." The company had just finished installing a new production line earlier in the year, and the CFO wanted you to go through all of the company's expense accounts with the goal of finding any costs that might be related to the machinery's installation or to "tinkering with it" to get the line working just right. He said that the previous accounting clerk, who you had replaced, didn't understand that these costs should have been recorded as part of the production line (an asset) rather than as expenses of the period. The CFO indicated that there was some urgency, as the company had to finalize its quarterly financial statements so that they could be filed with the SEC. Also, the company was close to violating its loan covenants and that it needed a few extra dollars of profit this quarter to ensure the bank didn't demand immediate repayment of the loan. As you thought about this situation, you tried to remember what Chapter 2 in your accounting textbook said regarding the key characteristics of assets.

ETHICAL

ISSUE

Required:

1. Which of the three ratios discussed in this chapter (debt-to-assets, asset turnover, and net profit margin) are affected by the decision to record costs as an asset rather than an expense? Indicate whether each ratio will be higher or lower if costs are recorded as an asset rather than an expense.

2. Is there anything in the case that makes you uncomfortable with the work that you've been asked to do?

3. What should you do?

C&DS5-6 Critical Thinking: Analyzing Income Statement–Based Executive Bonuses

Callaway Golf believes in tying executives' compensation to the company's performance as measured by accounting numbers. Suppose, in a recent year, Callaway had agreed to pay its executive officers bonuses of up to 70 percent of base salary provided that *asset turnover* and *net profit margin* met or exceeded target amounts. Callaway's income statements for the relevant years are presented here.

(in thousands)	Year Ended December 31,	
	2002	**2001**
Net sales	$792,064	$816,163
Cost of goods sold	393,068	411,585
Gross profit	398,996	404,578
Selling expenses	200,153	188,306
General and administrative expenses	56,580	71,058
Research and development costs	32,182	32,697
Income from operations	110,081	112,517
Other revenue (expense)		
Interest and other revenue, net	1,590	5,597
Other unrealized losses	—	(19,922)
Income before income taxes	111,671	98,192
Provision for income taxes	42,225	39,817
Net income	$ 69,446	$ 58,375

Callaway executives receive bonuses if *asset turnover* meets (or exceeds) 0.8 or *net profit margin* meets (or exceeds) 5.0 percent. Their bonuses are even larger if asset turnover meets (or exceeds) 1.6 and net profit margin meets (or exceeds) 7.0 percent. Average total assets were $663,724 (thousand) in 2002.

Required:

1. Use the preceding information to determine whether Callaway executives received any bonuses for 2002. Did they approach the maximum possible bonuses?
2. Explain why the bonus arrangement might be based on both *asset turnover* and *net profit margin* ratios, rather than just one of these two ratios.
3. Callaway was able to improve its net profit margin from 2001 to 2002, when its net sales had decreased. Based on the comparative income statements, briefly describe what led to this achievement.

chapter six

Internal Control and Financial Reporting for Merchandising Operations

6

During a long night of studying, there's nothing like a revitalizing snack to perk you up, right? Imagine your disappointment if you went to snack a stack of Pringles™ chips but discovered the container was empty. How could this have happened? Did you forget that you already ate them, or did that sneaky roommate of yours pilfer them? Oh well, there's always the yogurt you've got in the fridge. Oh wait, it's moldy. Looks like you'll have to go to the ATM so you can buy more goodies at a nearby convenience store. But what if you found that someone had emptied almost all of your bank account last month? What an unpleasant surprise that would be! All of these problems could have been avoided had you exercised tighter control over your day-to-day activities.

Good controls also are needed by every business, ranging from small 7-Eleven stores to massive **WAL-MART** Supercenters. At a very basic level, these businesses face many of the same potential problems as you did in our opening example. They need to ensure they have inventory on hand to meet their customers' needs, but they don't want too much inventory hanging around because it can become spoiled, stale, damaged, obsolete, or stolen before it is sold to customers. To combat these potential problems, most businesses use special accounting systems to track and control inventory purchases and sales. These companies also implement strict controls to monitor their cash levels because, like many inventory items, cash is easy to carry and ready to use—two features that make it attractive to thieves. We'll discuss some common controls in this chapter, which will help you to gain a better understanding of how business operations are managed. It also should give you some useful ideas on how to ensure that your own snacks and cash don't unknowingly disappear.

INSIDE LOOKING OUT

OUTSIDE LOOKING IN

This chapter focuses on how merchandisers track and report operating activities related to cash, product purchases, and sales. We focus on Wal-Mart, the biggest merchandising company in the world.

WAL★MART®
ALWAYS LOW PRICES.
Always.

Low Prices

WAL★MART
SUPERCENTER

Wal-Mart Stores, Inc. is the world's largest retailer.

T he company was only founded in 1962, but by 1979, Wal-Mart rang up a billion dollars in sales. By 1993, it sold that much in a week. By 2001, it took only a day to reach that level of sales.[1] With its trucks transporting 50 million pallets of goods and its greeters welcoming over 100 million customers every week,[2] Wal-Mart needs state-of-the-art accounting systems to track its inventory purchases and sales and to ensure the cash related to these activities is properly recorded in its accounts. In this chapter, you will learn about unique aspects of operating a merchandising company like Wal-Mart and systems that control operating activities. You'll also learn what to look for in a merchandiser's financial statements and how this differs from analyzing the financial statements of other types of companies. Exhibit 6.1 provides the specifics about where you should focus in this chapter.

exhibit 6.1   Your Learning Objectives

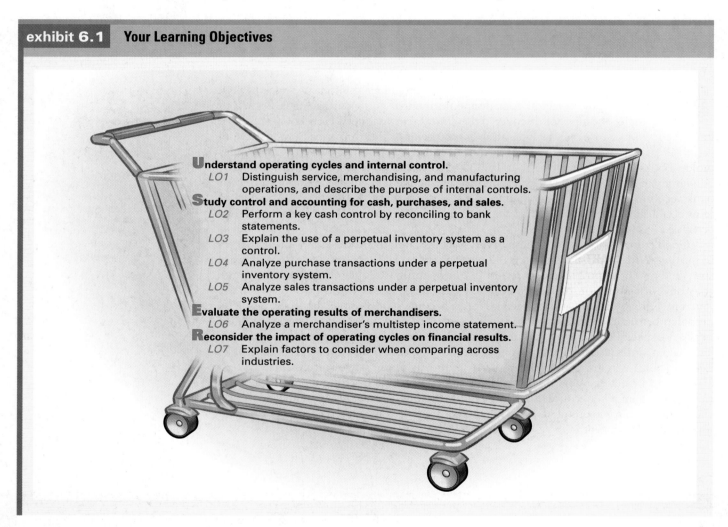

Understand operating cycles and internal control.
- LO1   Distinguish service, merchandising, and manufacturing operations, and describe the purpose of internal controls.

Study control and accounting for cash, purchases, and sales.
- LO2   Perform a key cash control by reconciling to bank statements.
- LO3   Explain the use of a perpetual inventory system as a control.
- LO4   Analyze purchase transactions under a perpetual inventory system.
- LO5   Analyze sales transactions under a perpetual inventory system.

Evaluate the operating results of merchandisers.
- LO6   Analyze a merchandiser's multistep income statement.

Reconsider the impact of operating cycles on financial results.
- LO7   Explain factors to consider when comparing across industries.

┌ UNDERSTAND ─────────
└ OPERATING CYCLES AND INTERNAL CONTROL

Service, Merchandising, and Manufacturing Operating Activities

Based on their operating activities, businesses can be classified into three types: (1) **service companies**, (2) **merchandising companies**, and (3) **manufacturing companies**.

YOU SHOULD KNOW

A **service company** sells services rather than physical goods. A **merchandising company** sells goods that have been obtained from a supplier. A **manufacturing company** sells goods that it has made itself.

---

[1]"The 2002 Fortune 500," *Fortune.com*, March 31, 2002.
[2]"Lord of the Things," *Business 2.0 Magazine*, March 1, 2002.

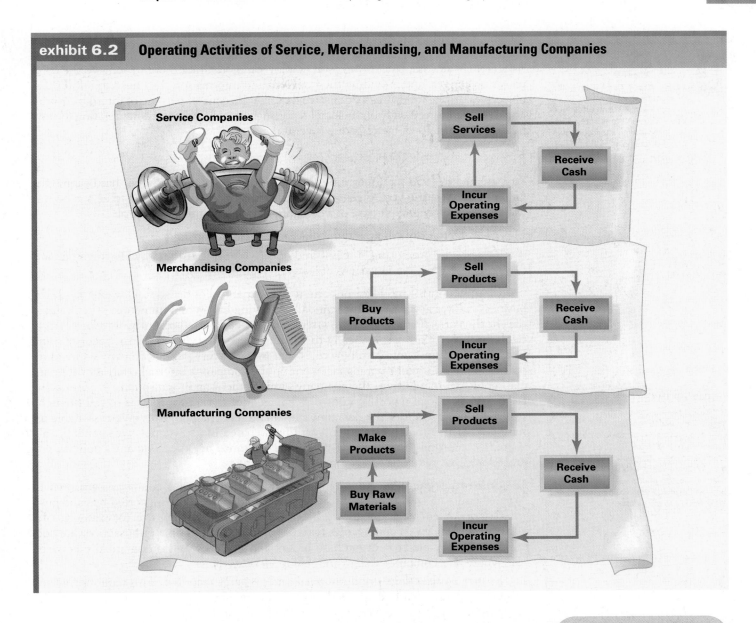

exhibit 6.2 **Operating Activities of Service, Merchandising, and Manufacturing Companies**

Exhibit 6.2 shows the primary differences among these types of business operations. As the name suggests, service companies sell services, ranging from fitness training to Internet access to hairstyling, which you already learned about through the operations of Regis Corporation in Chapters 2–4. In contrast, merchandising companies sell physical products, which are purchased from a supplier. When talking about merchandising companies, most businesspeople refer to two specific subcategories: *retail* merchandising companies that sell directly to consumers, as Wal-Mart does, and *wholesale* merchandising companies, like LA Shades, that sell to retailers rather than end consumers. The discussion in this chapter applies equally to retail and wholesale merchandisers. Manufacturing companies, like Mattel in Chapter 1, also sell physical products, but rather than acquire these in a ready-to-sell format, manufacturing companies make their own products from raw goods that they buy from suppliers.

Despite the differences in operating activities shown in Exhibit 6.2, all types of companies share one thing in common: to be successful, they have to be in control of their operations. In other words, they must be able to achieve what they want and avoid problems and surprises along the way. To achieve this state of control, companies include as part of their operating activities a variety of procedures and policies that are referred to as

COACH'S CORNER

In addition to showing the various types of operating cycles, Exhibit 6.2 also reinforces two additional concepts. First, the arrows indicate that operating activities involve both inflows and outflows of cash. Second, by lining up sales of services/products with operating expenses, it suggests that operating performance should be measured using accrual basis accounting, where expenses are matched to sales revenues.

internal controls. Internal control is a big idea that includes much more than just accounting. For example, it includes setting strategic objectives for the company, identifying risks facing the company, hiring good employees, motivating them to achieve the company's objectives, and providing the resources and information they need to fulfill those objectives. In the following sections, we describe the general purpose of internal controls and then focus specifically on financial reporting controls and procedures relating to cash, purchases, and sales of merchandise inventory.

Internal Control: To Protect and to Serve

First created in 1955 for a magazine contest, "To Protect and to Serve" has become the familiar motto of the Los Angeles Police Department.[3] It also happens to be a good way to describe the general purpose of a company's system of internal control:

- **To protect** against theft and fraudulent financial reporting.
- **To serve** by promoting efficient and effective operations and by alerting company officials to possible violations of laws and regulations.

Internal control has been important to companies for decades. However, with the business failures and accounting scandals involving Enron and numerous other companies in the early 2000s, a lot more attention has been placed recently on controls, particularly those relating specifically to financial reporting. In 2003, the Securities and Exchange Commission issued new rules that require every public company's annual report to include a report from management on the company's internal control over financial reporting. In addition, the company's independent auditor also must report on the company's financial reporting controls. The goal of these new rules is to tell financial statement users whether the company's financial reporting controls give reasonable assurance that its financial statements will be prepared in accordance with generally accepted accounting principles. Of greatest importance are the company's policies and procedures that meet the following control objectives:

1. **Ensure adequate records are maintained.** This requires company personnel to make sure all transactions of the business are identified and supported by valid business documents. This has always been the case at Wal-Mart where, for example, sales revenues are based on cash register receipts. Similarly, purchase transactions are documented by electronic purchase orders and invoices sent automatically between Wal-Mart's computer system and its suppliers' systems.

2. **Ensure transactions are authorized and properly recorded.** This requires that top management clearly define responsibilities and appropriate behaviors for each employee, starting at the very top of the company. According to Rob Walton, chairman of Wal-Mart's board of directors, "setting the right ethical tone at the top is the first step towards good corporate governance at Wal-Mart."[4] From there on down through the company, each employee is made aware of what they can and cannot do. And, just to be sure, a team of employees (called internal auditors) checks to ensure everyone follows the company's code of conduct.

3. **Prevent or detect unauthorized activities involving the company's assets.** To effectively protect (or "safeguard") assets, a variety of controls can be used. Some are rather obvious steps like physically locking up sensitive assets (such as Wal-Mart's inventory of videogames) and electronically securing access to other assets (such as requiring a password to open a Wal-Mart cash register). Other controls are designed into the accounting system itself. For example, a control commonly called **segregation of duties** involves assigning responsibilities so that one employee can't make a mistake or commit a dishonest act without someone else knowing it. That's why you

[3]"The LAPD Motto Was Developed from a Contest," retrieved January 4, 2004 from www.lapdonline.org/general_information/did_you_know/did_you_know_main.htm.

[4]"A Letter from the Chairman of the Board," 2003 Annual Report, Wal-Mart Stores, Inc.

wait for a Wal-Mart manager to approve price changes at the checkout. Without this control, cashiers could ring up a sale, collect cash from the customer, and later reduce the amount of the sale and pocket the excess cash without anyone knowing. Segregation of duties is most effective when responsibilities for related activities are assigned to two or more people and when responsibilities for record keeping are assigned to people who do not also handle the assets that they are accounting for.

To meet these three objectives, a company's top management will implement a vast number of specific controls. We can't possibly cover them all, so our goal in the next section is to *introduce* you to a few examples, specifically focusing on cash, purchases, and sales of merchandise inventory. You'll study the topic of internal control in much greater detail in advanced courses in accounting and management.

STUDY

CONTROL AND ACCOUNTING FOR CASH, PURCHASES, AND SALES

Cash Control and Reporting

Every type of company—service, merchandising, and manufacturing—keeps tight control over its **cash.** You probably use some of the same controls as many companies, without even knowing it. Go ahead, fill in the following checklist, and we'll tell you how you're doing.

Do you ...	Yes	No
... keep a limited supply of cash on hand?	☐	☐
... prevent others from writing checks against your bank account?	☐	☐
... regularly account for differences between the balance in your checkbook and the balance on your bank statement?	☐	☐

If you're like most people, you probably answered yes to the first two questions, and no to the third. Unfortunately, this is one instance where two out of three *is* bad. The process of accounting for differences between your cash records and your bank's records is called "reconciling," and it is one of the most important of all cash controls. By preparing a **bank reconciliation,** you can identify differences that exist between your records and those kept by someone independent of you, which essentially means it's a way to double-check the accuracy of what you've recorded. Businesses consider bank reconciliations so important that they prepare a new one every month. You should, too. In the remainder of this section, we'll show you how.

Need for Reconciliation

A bank reconciliation involves comparing your own cash records to the cash balance reported in your bank's statement of account to see whether the records are in agreement. Your records can differ from your bank's records for two basic reasons: (1) you've recorded some items in your records that the bank doesn't know about at the time it prepares your statement of account, or (2) the bank recorded some items in its records that you don't know about until you read your bank statement. Examples of these differences are summarized in Exhibit 6.3 and are discussed below.

1. Bank errors.   Bank errors happen in real life just like they do in Monopoly®. If you discover a bank error, you'll need to ask the bank to correct its records, but you needn't change yours.

exhibit 6.3	Possible Differences between What You and Your Bank Know

Your bank may not know about . . .	*You may not know about . . .*

1. Errors made by the bank
2. Time lags
   a. Deposits that you made recently
   b. Checks that you wrote recently
	3. Interest the bank has put into your account
	4. Service charges taken out of your account
	5. Customer checks you deposited but that bounced
	6. Errors made by you

2. Time lags.   Time lags are very common. A time lag occurs, for example, when you make a deposit after the bank's normal business hours. *You* know you've made the deposit, but your bank doesn't know until it processes the deposit the next day. Time lags involving deposits are called *deposits in transit*. Another common time lag is an *outstanding check*. This occurs when you write and mail a check, say to your cable company, but your bank doesn't find out about it until the cable company deposits the check in its own bank, which then notifies your bank. As you will see later, deposits in transit and outstanding checks are a significant part of a bank reconciliation but they do not require any further action on your part.

3. Interest deposited.   You may know that your bank pays interest to you, but you probably don't know exactly how much interest you'll get because it varies depending on the average balance in your account during that month. When you read your bank statement, you'll learn how much interest you need to add to your records.

4. Service charges.   These are amounts the bank charges you for processing your transactions. Rather than send a bill to you and wait for you to pay it, the bank just takes the amount directly out of your account. You'll need to reduce your records for these charges.

5. Bounced checks.   These are checks that you have previously deposited in your bank account but are later rejected by your bank because the check writer did **not** have **sufficient funds** to cover the check. Because the bank increased your account when you first deposited the check, the bank will decrease your account when it discovers it was not a valid deposit. You will need to reduce the cash balance in your records for these bounced checks, and you'll have to try once again to collect the amount still owed to you by the check writer.

6. Your errors.   These are mistakes that you've made or amounts that you haven't yet recorded in your checkbook, such as those ATM slips that you didn't get around to recording before they went through the wash. You'll now have to adjust your records for these items.

The Bank Statement

Before we get into the nitty gritty of how you can prepare a bank reconciliation, let's have a quick look at what a typical bank statement reports. Exhibit 6.4 presents a typical bank statement for Wonderful Merchandise and Things (WMT).

Reconciling the Accounting Records and Bank Statement

Usually, the ending cash balance as shown on the bank statement does not agree with the ending cash balance shown by the related *Cash* account on the books of the company. For example, the *Cash* account of WMT at the end of June might contain the information shown in the T-account.

exhibit 6.4   Example of a Bank Statement

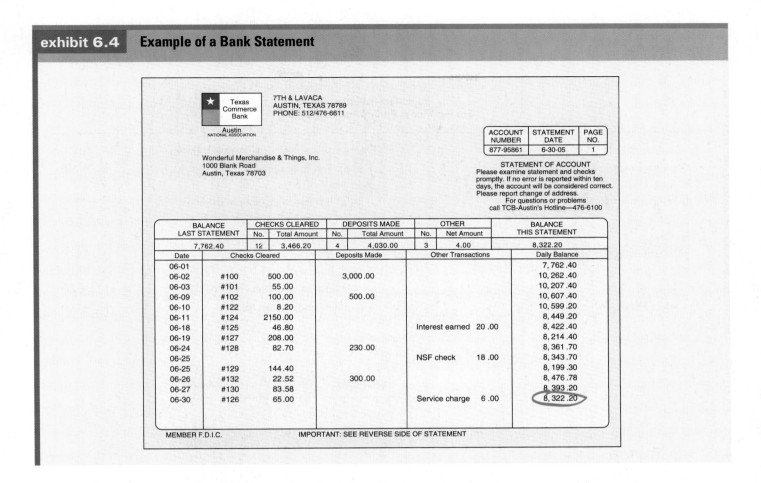

+ Cash (A) –			
June 1 balance	6,971.40		
June deposits	5,830.00	June checks written	3,743.40
Ending balance	9,058.00		

The $8,322.20 ending cash balance shown on the bank statement (Exhibit 6.4) differs from WMT's ending cash balance of $9,058.00. To determine the appropriate cash balance, these balances need to be reconciled. Exhibit 6.5 shows the bank reconciliation prepared by WMT for the month of June. The completed reconciliation finds that the up-to-date cash balance is $9,045.00, an amount that differs from both the bank's statement and WMT's accounting records. This balance is the amount that WMT will report on its balance sheet after adjusting its *Cash* balance with the adjusting journal entries presented below—after we describe the steps WMT uses to prepare the bank reconciliation.

WMT followed these steps in preparing the bank reconciliation in Exhibit 6.5:

1. Identify the deposits in transit. A comparison of WMT's recorded deposits with those listed on the bank statement revealed that WMT made a deposit of $1,800 on June 30 that was not listed on the bank statement. More than likely, the bank won't process this deposit until July 1. Because this amount was in WMT's books on June 30, it is entered on the reconciliation as an addition to update the bank's records.

2. Identify the outstanding checks. A comparison of the checks listed on the bank statement with the company's record of written checks showed the following were still outstanding (had not been processed by the bank) at the end of June:

exhibit 6.5	Bank Reconciliation Illustrated

WONDERFUL MERCHANDISE AND THINGS, INC.
Bank Reconciliation
For the Month Ending June 30, 2005

Bank Statement		Company's Books	
Ending cash balance per bank statement	$ 8,322.20	Ending cash balance per books	$9,058.00
Additions		Additions	
(1) Deposit in transit	1,800.00	(3a) Interest received from the bank	20.00
	10,122.20		9,078.00
Deductions		Deductions	
(2) Outstanding checks	1,077.20	(3b) NSF check of R. Smith	18.00
		(3c) Bank service charges	6.00
		(4) Error in recording check no. 126	9.00
Up-to-date ending cash balance	$ 9,045.00	Up-to-date ending cash balance	$9,045.00

Check No.	Amount
103	$ 145.00
123	815.00
131	117.20
Total	$1,077.20

This total was entered on the reconciliation (in Exhibit 6.5) as a deduction from the bank account because the bank will eventually deduct these checks when they clear the bank. (They've already been deducted from the company's cash records.)

3. Record other transactions on the bank statement.

a.   *Interest received* from the bank, $20—entered on the bank reconciliation as an addition to the book balance because it's included in the bank balance but not yet in the company's books.

b.   *NSF check* of R. Smith, $18—entered on the bank reconciliation as a deduction from the book balance because it was deducted from the bank statement balance but not yet deducted from the company's cash records.

c.   *Service charges,* $6—entered on the bank reconciliation as a deduction from the book balance because it has been deducted from the bank balance but not yet removed from the *Cash* account in the company's books.

COACH'S CORNER

This example involves the company's error in recording the amount of the check. In other cases, the bank errs if it processes the check at the wrong amount. In all instances, the amount written on the check is the correct amount at which the transaction should be recorded.

4. Determine the impact of errors.
After performing the three steps listed above, WMT found that the reconciliation was out of balance by $9. Upon checking the journal entries made during the month, WMT found that check no. 126 was recorded in the company's accounts as $56 when, in fact, the check had been filled out for $65 (in payment of an account payable). As Exhibit 6.4 shows on page 237, the bank correctly processed the check (on June 30) as $65. To correct its own error, WMT must deduct $9 (= $65 − $56) from the company's books side of the bank reconciliation.

Now that we know the up-to-date cash balance is $9,045.00, we need to prepare and record adjusting journal entries that will bring the *Cash* account to that balance. Remember that the entries on the *Bank Statement* side of the bank reconciliation do not need to be adjusted by WMT because they will work out automatically when the bank processes them next month. Only the items on the *Company's Books* side of the bank reconciliation need to be adjusted in the company's records, using the following entries:

Interest Received:

| (*a*) | *dr* | Cash (+A) . . . . | 20 | |
| | *cr* | Interest Revenue (+R, +SE) . . . . | | 20 |

To record interest received from the bank.

NSF Check:

| (*b*) | *dr* | Accounts Receivable (+A) . . . . | 18 | |
| | *cr* | Cash (−A) . . . . | | 18 |

To record amount rejected by bank and still owed by customer.

Service Charges:

| (*c*) | *dr* | Other Expenses (+E, −SE) . . . . | 6 | |
| | *cr* | Cash (−A) . . . . | | 6 |

To record service charge deducted by bank.

> **COACH'S CORNER**
> Because service charges are so small in relation to other expenses, they typically are considered an "other expense."

Company Error:

| (*d*) | *dr* | Accounts Payable (−L) . . . . | 9 | |
| | *cr* | Cash (−A) . . . . | | 9 |

To correct error made in recording a check paid to a creditor.

Assets		=	Liabilities		+	Stockholders' Equity	
Cash (+20 −18 −6 −9)	−13		Accounts Payable	−9		Interest Revenue	+20
Accounts Receivable	+18					Other Expenses (+E)	−6

HOW'S IT GOING?   A Self-Study Quiz

Indicate which of the following items discovered when preparing a company's bank reconciliation will require an adjustment to the *Cash* balance on the company's books.

1. Outstanding checks.

2. Deposits in transit.

3. Bank service charges.

4. NSF checks that were deposited.

After you have finished, check your answers with the solutions presented in the margin.

In addition to preparing a monthly bank reconciliation, other common cash controls include reconciling cash receipts to bank deposit slips and matching purchase orders to supplier invoices before authorizing payments to suppliers. Speaking of suppliers, let's now take a look at how merchandising companies control and account for purchases of inventory from suppliers.

Inventory Controls and Tracking Systems

Merchandising companies spend a great deal of time and money tracking their inventory transactions because, after all, inventory management is vital in their business. A strong accounting system plays three roles in the inventory management process. First, it must provide up-to-date information on inventory quantities and costs, so that managers can make informed decisions. Second, it has to provide accurate information for preparing financial statements. Inventory is reported as an asset on the balance sheet until it is sold, at which time it is removed from the balance sheet and reported on the income statement as an expense called cost of goods sold. The third role for an inventory system is to provide information that controls inventory and helps protect it from theft. Companies use one of two types of inventory accounting systems: *perpetual* or *periodic*.

Perpetual Inventory System

In a **perpetual inventory system,** the inventory records are updated every time an item is bought, sold, or returned. You may not realize it, but the bar-code readers at Wal-Mart's checkouts serve two purposes: (1) they calculate and record the sales revenue for each product you're buying, and (2) they remove the product and its cost from Wal-Mart's inventory records. Similar scanners are used back in the "employees only" part of the store where products are unloaded from the trucks or returned to suppliers. As a result of this continuous or "perpetual" updating on a transaction-by-transaction basis, the *Inventory* and *Cost of Goods Sold* accounts always contain updated balances.

Periodic Inventory System

A **periodic inventory system** differs from a perpetual system in several ways, most of which we describe in detail later in this chapter. For now, however, the most important difference for you to understand is that, rather than update the inventory records immediately after each purchase and sale (as is done in a perpetual system), a periodic system updates the inventory records only *at the end of the accounting period.* Consequently, an accurate record of inventory on hand and inventory sold is not available during the period. To determine these amounts, the inventory has to be physically counted. This is what's going on at stores that you see closed "for inventory." This inventory count is then used to compute the correct balances for *Inventory* and *Cost of Goods Sold* and adjust them at the end of the period.

Inventory Control

Perpetual inventory systems provide more timely information than periodic systems, allowing companies to keep just the right quantity of products on the shelves for the right amount of time. One study has found that Wal-Mart's perpetual inventory system has created tremendous efficiencies, accounting for over half of the productivity gains in general merchandise sales in the U.S. economy during 1995–99.[5] This unbelievable performance

---

[5]"Retail: The Wal-Mart Effect," *The McKinsey Quarterly*, no. 1 (2002).

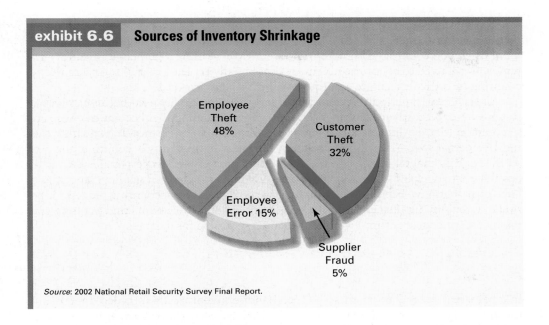

exhibit 6.6 | **Sources of Inventory Shrinkage**

Employee Theft 48%

Customer Theft 32%

Employee Error 15%

Supplier Fraud 5%

Source: 2002 National Retail Security Survey Final Report.

is likely to continue into the future, as the company adopts new microchip technologies that use radio waves to transmit data automatically from every inventory item that enters, moves within, exits, and later re-enters its stores. With this technology, it might even be possible for Wal-Mart to identify shoppers who bought their clothing at one of its stores.

Another benefit of a perpetual inventory system is that it allows managers to estimate "shrinkage," which is the politically correct term for loss of inventory from theft, fraud, and error. When it comes to shrinkage, who do you think managers should fear most? Results from a survey of 118 retail companies, shown in Exhibit 6.6, indicates that most companies believed their own employees were their biggest source of inventory losses.

You might wonder how companies can estimate how much of their inventory has gone missing, because isn't it, by definition, *missing*? Here's how they do it and how you can use a similar process to figure out if your roommate is swiping your stuff. It relies on knowing the kinds of transactions that are recorded in the inventory account.

1. *Determine what's on hand at the beginning of the period.*

2. *Monitor every piece of inventory entering and exiting your stock during the period.*

   a. *Add purchases.*

   b. *Subtract goods sold.*

   By perpetually tracking every movement, your inventory records should match exactly the amount of inventory on hand—unless items have been wrongfully removed.

3. *Count the inventory to determine what's actually there.* If your records say you have more on hand than what you counted, it's likely that the difference is the amount of inventory that has been removed without your permission ("shrinkage"). In plain English, you've been robbed.

October 1

October 31

+

−

October 31

=

Shrinkage =

POINT OF INTEREST
Prior to 2002, Nordstrom department stores relied on a periodic system, using loose-leaf binders to track inventory levels.
Source: BusinessWeek, July 30, 2001, p. 9.

COACH'S CORNER

Inventory includes only merchandise purchased for sale. Other purchases, such as supplies for internal use, are recorded in different accounts.

Notice that you can't do this kind of detective work with a periodic inventory system because it doesn't provide an up-to-date record of the inventory that *should* be on hand when you count it. Also note that, even if you're using a perpetual inventory system, you still need to count the inventory occasionally (at least yearly) to ensure the accounting records are accurate and that any shrinkage is detected.

Until recently, periodic inventory systems were commonly used because perpetual systems were too costly to implement. But now this technology has become so cheap and so common that it's difficult for a merchandiser to survive in business today without using a perpetual system. To ensure you learn the latest in inventory accounting, the next section of this chapter focuses on the accounting process used in perpetual systems. It's possible that you could encounter a periodic system, particularly in smaller companies or large ones that have been slow to switch, so we do discuss the accounting process for periodic systems in Supplement A at the end of this chapter. You should find out from your instructor (or course outline) whether you are responsible for it.

Purchases, Purchase Returns and Allowances, and Purchase Discounts

Purchases

In a perpetual system, all purchases of merchandise inventory are recorded directly into the *Inventory* account. As you learned in earlier chapters, most companies use credit rather than cash to purchase goods, so *Accounts Payable* usually is the other account used in the journal entry to record these purchases. For example, if Wal-Mart purchased some super soaker water blasters on account for $5,000, the journal entry and accounting equation effects would be as follows:

dr	**Inventory (+A)**	5,000
	cr **Accounts Payable (+L)**................	5,000

Assets		=	Liabilities		+	Stockholders' Equity
Inventory	+5,000		Accounts Payable	+5,000		

Transportation Cost

The inventory that Wal-Mart purchases doesn't just magically appear in its stockroom. It has to be shipped from the supplier's location to Wal-Mart's premises. Often, the supplier will pay the cost of transportation and recover it by charging more for the inventory. In this situation, transportation cost is built into the purchaser's cost of the inventory so there are no additional costs to record. In other cases, however, an outside trucking company might be hired to transport inventory from the supplier to Wal-Mart. To illustrate, assume Wal-Mart pays $300 cash to a trucker who delivers goods to Wal-Mart. In this situation, the additional cost of transporting the goods to Wal-Mart (called freight-in) would be added to the *Inventory* account, using the following journal entry:

COACH'S CORNER

A general principle is that a purchaser should include in its *Inventory* account any costs needed to get its inventory into a condition and location ready for sale. Any costs incurred after the inventory is ready for sale (such as freight-out to deliver goods to customers) are considered selling, general, and administrative expenses.

dr	**Inventory (+A)**	300
	cr **Cash (−A)**	300

Assets		=	Liabilities	+	Stockholders' Equity
Cash	−300				
Inventory	+300				

Purchase Returns and Allowances

When goods purchased from a supplier do not meet specifications or arrive in damaged condition, the buyer can either return them for a full refund or keep them and ask for a cost reduction (called an "allowance"). These **purchase returns and allowances** are accounted for by reducing the cost of the inventory and recording the cash refund or the reduction in the liability owed to the supplier. For example, assume that Wal-Mart returned to its supplier some crushed water blasters—or what the inventory clerks referred to as hurt squirt—and received a $400 reduction in the balance it owed. This transaction would be recorded as follows:

YOU SHOULD KNOW

Purchase returns and allowances are a reduction in the cost of inventory purchases associated with unsatisfactory goods.

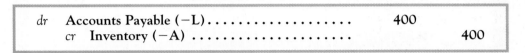

dr	**Accounts Payable (−L)**	400	
cr	**Inventory (−A)**		400

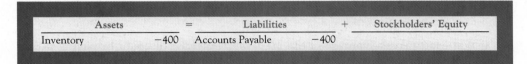

Assets		=	Liabilities		+	Stockholders' Equity
Inventory	−400		Accounts Payable	−400		

Purchase Discounts

When merchandise is bought on credit, terms such as 2/10, n/30 are sometimes specified. The 2/10 part means that if the purchaser pays within 10 days of the date of purchase, a 2 percent **purchase discount** is given off the purchaser's cost. Although 2 percent might seem small, if taken consistently on all purchases made throughout the year, it can add up to substantial savings. The n/30 part implies that if payment is not made within the 10-day discount period, the full amount is due 30 days after the purchase. If a purchaser fails to pay by the end of this credit period, interest will be charged, further credit can be denied, and nice people from a collection agency may contact the purchaser to collect the amount owed. Exhibit 6.7 illustrates a 2/10, n/30 purchase occurring on November 1.

YOU SHOULD KNOW

A **purchase discount** is a cash discount received for prompt payment of a purchase on account.

When a purchase discount is offered, the purchaser accounts for it in two stages. Initially, the purchase is accounted for at its full cost because at the time a company purchases goods, it's not clear whether it will take advantage of the purchase discount. Later, *if payment is made within the discount period*, the purchaser will reduce the *Inventory* account for the purchase discount because this discount, in effect, reduces the cost of the inventory. Let's work through an example of this. You do the first part—the initial purchase of the inventory—and then we'll show the journal entry for recording the purchase discount, assuming the purchaser pays within the discount period.

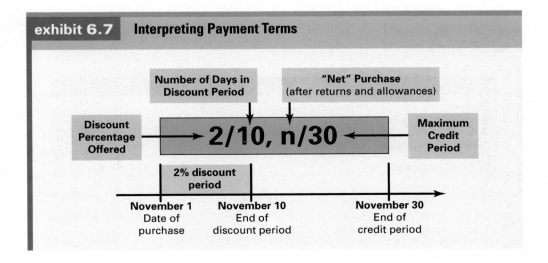

exhibit 6.7 **Interpreting Payment Terms**

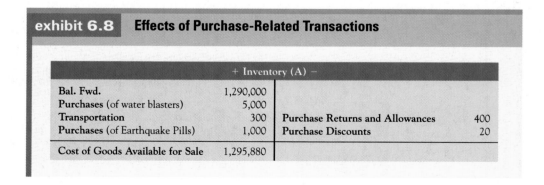

HOW'S IT GOING?   **A Self-Study Quiz**

Assume Wal-Mart receives a crate of Earthquake Pills that it bought from Acme Supply Company. The invoice shows a price of $1,000 and terms of 2/10, n/30. Prepare the journal entry and show the accounting equation effects for this purchase transaction.

dr [   ] .... [   ]

cr [   ] .... [   ]

Assets	=	Liabilities	+	Stockholders' Equity

After you have finished, check your answers with the solutions presented in the margin.

Quiz Answers

dr Inventory (+A) 1,000
  cr Accounts Payable (+L) 1,000

Assets	=	Liabilities	+	Stockholders' Equity
Inventory +1,000		Accounts Payable +1,000		

If Wal-Mart takes advantage of the 2/10, n/30 purchase discount by paying within the 10-day discount period, it would record the following journal entry:

dr	**Accounts Payable (−L)**	1,000	
cr	**Cash (−A)**		980
cr	**Inventory (−A)**		20

Assets		=	Liabilities		+	Stockholders' Equity
Cash	−980		Accounts Payable	−1,000		
Inventory	−20					

COACH'S CORNER

The 2 percent discount is calculated using the initial purchase cost ($20 = 2% × $1,000). Because the discount actually reduces the purchaser's inventory cost, the purchaser records it as a reduction of the *Inventory* account.

If Wal-Mart decided to *not* take advantage of the purchase discount, it would pay the full $1,000 owed, recording a debit to *Accounts Payable* and a credit to *Cash* for $1,000.[6]

Summary of Purchase-Related Transactions

You've now seen several types of purchase-related transactions. Before you learn how to account for sales of this merchandise, make sure you understand how these purchase-related transactions affect *Inventory*, as summarized in the T-account in Exhibit 6.8.

exhibit 6.8	Effects of Purchase-Related Transactions

	+ Inventory (A) −		
Bal. Fwd.	1,290,000		
Purchases (of water blasters)	5,000		
Transportation	300	Purchase Returns and Allowances	400
Purchases (of Earthquake Pills)	1,000	Purchase Discounts	20
Cost of Goods Available for Sale	1,295,880		

---

[6]An alternative approach to accounting for purchase discounts (called the net method) exists, but we leave that topic for discussion in intermediate accounting textbooks.

Sales, Sales Returns and Allowances, Sales Discounts, and Credit Card Discounts

Sales

For all merchandisers, inventory is considered "sold" when ownership of the goods transfers to the customer. For a retail merchandiser like Wal-Mart, this transfer occurs when a customer takes the goods to the checkout and agrees to pay for them, using cash or a credit card. For a wholesale merchandiser, this transfer of ownership occurs at a time stated in a written sales agreement between the seller and the customer. Most sales agreements use one of two possible times: (i) when the goods leave the *shipping* department at the seller's premises, or (ii) when the goods reach their *destination* at the customer's premises.[7] For the examples in this textbook, we assume that ownership transfers when the goods leave the seller's premises.

In a perpetual system, two journal entries are made when inventory is sold:

1. Record the increase in *Sales Revenue* and a corresponding increase in either *Cash* (if it is a cash sale) or *Accounts Receivable* (if the sale is made on credit).
2. Record a reduction in *Inventory* and a corresponding increase in *Cost of Goods Sold*.

For example, assume Wal-Mart sells you a Schwinn mountain bike for $225 cash when the cost of the bike to Wal-Mart was $175. The two journal entries and their effects on the accounting equation are as follows:

dr **Cash (+A)**	225	
cr **Sales Revenue (+R, +SE)**		225

dr **Cost of Goods Sold (+E, −SE)**	175	
cr **Inventory (−A)**		175

Assets		=	Liabilities	+	Stockholders' Equity	
Cash	+225				Sales Revenue (+R)	+225
Inventory	−175				Cost of Goods Sold (+E)	−175

> **COACH'S CORNER**
>
> Notice that profit on sale is not directly recorded in any account. Rather, the pair of journal entries that record the sale and cost of goods sold combine to result in a profit. This important subtotal, called "gross profit," is discussed later in this chapter.

Sales Returns and Allowances

Sales returns and allowances are the same thing as purchase returns and allowances except that instead of looking at them from the purchaser's perspective, we're now seeing them from the seller's side. For example, suppose that after you bought the Schwinn mountain bike from Wal-Mart, the idea of performing an "involuntary dismount" on a street curb caused you to change your mind and return the bike to Wal-Mart. Assuming that the bike is still like new, you can expect Wal-Mart to roll back $225 to you, take back the bike, and pretend as if the sale had never been made in the first place.

To allow its accounting records to reflect this, Wal-Mart will record two journal entries that are basically the opposite of what this stellar seller recorded above when the bike was initially sold. We say "basically" because there is one catch: Wal-Mart will not directly reduce its *Sales Revenue* account. Instead, Wal-Mart will track the amount of sales returns and allowances in a contra-revenue account, which is deducted from total sales revenue. By using a contra-revenue account, rather than directly reducing the *Sales* account, Wal-Mart can quickly determine the amount of goods that customers return,

> **YOU SHOULD KNOW**
>
> **Sales returns and allowances** are reductions given to customers after goods have been sold and found unsatisfactory.

> **COACH'S CORNER**
>
> Just as a contra-asset account (like *Accumulated Depreciation*) reduces the total in an asset account (*Plant and Equipment*), a contra-revenue account (like *Sales Returns and Allowances*) is subtracted from the total in a revenue account (*Sales Revenues*).

---

[7] These two possible arrangements often are referred to as *FOB (free on board) shipping point* and *FOB destination*, but in most instances these are not the correct labels (FOB refers only to shipments by sea or inland waterway). The International Chamber of Commerce website (www.iccwbo.org/index_incoterms.asp) precisely defines FOB and other trade terms.

which can provide clues about whether Wal-Mart's customers are happy with the quality and price of its products.[8] This is an example where accounting information functions as an internal control that serves to promote efficient and effective operations. Here are the journal entries and their effects:

dr	Sales Returns and Allowances (+xR, −SE)	225	
	cr Cash (−A)		225

dr	Inventory (+A)	175	
	cr Cost of Goods Sold (−E, +SE)		175

Assets		=	Liabilities	+	Stockholders' Equity	
Cash	−225				Sales Returns and Allow. (+xR)	−225
Inventory	+175				Cost of Goods Sold (−E)	+175

Sales Discounts

You already know that buyers are sometimes given purchase discounts to encourage them to pay promptly for purchases they've made on account. From the seller's point of view, these discounts are called **sales discounts.** Just like purchase discounts, sales discounts involve two parts: (1) the initial sale, and (2) the discount given for prompt payment.

Let's split up and use this as another chance for you to practice the part that you've already seen—recording the initial sale using a perpetual inventory system. We'll then show you the journal entry needed when the discount is taken.

HOW'S IT GOING?   A Self-Study Quiz

Assume that Wal-Mart's warehouse store (called Sam's Club) sells neon printer paper to your college bookstore on account for $1,000, with payment terms of 2/10, n/30. The paper had cost Wal-Mart $670. Prepare the journal entries Wal-Mart will record in its perpetual inventory system and show their effects on the accounting equation.

dr	[_____]	. . . .	[_____]
cr	[_____]	. . . .	[_____]
dr	[_____]	. . . .	[_____]
cr	[_____]	. . . .	[_____]

Assets	=	Liabilities	+	Stockholders' Equity

After you have finished, check your answers with the solutions presented in the margin.

Quiz Answers

dr Accounts Receivable (+A). 1,000
    cr Sales Revenue (+R, +SE). . .   1,000
dr Cost of Goods Sold (+E, −SE). .   670
    cr Inventory (−A).   670

Assets	=	Liabilities	+	Stockholders' Equity	
Accts. Rec. +1,000				Sales Revenue (+R)	+1,000
Inventory −670				Cost of Goods Sold (+E)	−670

---

[8]We have assumed that the return occurs in the same period as the sale. When significant returns are likely to occur after the period of sale, the seller records an estimate of those expected returns, using methods described in Chapter 7.

If Wal-Mart receives the customer's payment within the 10-day discount period, it would record the following journal entry:

dr	Cash (+A)	980	
dr	Sales Discounts (+xR, −SE)...............	20	
	cr Accounts Receivable (−A)		1,000

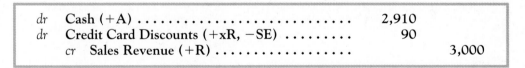

Assets		=	Liabilities	+	Stockholders' Equity	
Cash	+980				Sales Discounts (+xR)	−20
Accts. Receiv.	−1,000					

If the customer pays the full amount to Wal-Mart *after* the discount period, Wal-Mart would record a debit to *Cash* and a credit to *Accounts Receivable* for $1,000. What if a customer doesn't pay? We discuss that important issue in detail in Chapter 7.

Before leaving the topic of sales discounts, we need to clear up a common misconception. Sales discounts differ from the "discount" that you get as a consumer buying clearance items at a reduced selling price. The sales discounts discussed in this section are given in business-to-business (B2B) transactions for prompt payment. As a consumer, you're not likely to be offered this kind of discount. Boo hoo.

Credit Card Discounts

Most retail merchandise companies allow their customers to pay for goods using credit cards like Visa, MasterCard, American Express, and Discover Card. This practice helps to increase sales, speed up cash collections (because Wal-Mart is able to deposit credit card receipts directly into its bank account as if it's actually cash), and reduce losses from customers writing bad checks. But these benefits come at a cost: the credit card company charges a fee for the service it provides. When Wal-Mart deposits its credit card receipts in the bank, it might receive credit for only 97 percent of the sales price. The credit card company is charging a 3 percent fee (called a **credit card discount**) for its service. If we assume Wal-Mart made a credit card sale of $3,000 under these terms, the $90 credit card discount ($3,000 × 3%) would be recorded using the journal entry shown below.

dr	Cash (+A)	2,910	
dr	Credit Card Discounts (+xR, −SE)	90	
	cr Sales Revenue (+R)		3,000

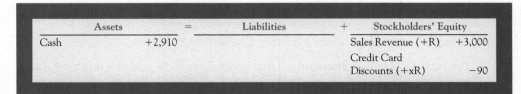

Assets		=	Liabilities	+	Stockholders' Equity	
Cash	+2,910				Sales Revenue (+R)	+3,000
					Credit Card Discounts (+xR)	−90

In addition to recording the credit card sale (above), Wal-Mart's perpetual inventory system would record a reduction in *Inventory* and increase in *Cost of Goods Sold* at the time of sale. If the cost of the products sold was $1,750, the corresponding journal entry would be

dr	Cost of Goods Sold (+E, −SE)	1,750	
	cr Inventory (−A)		1,750

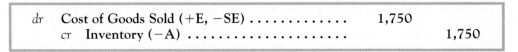

	Assets	=	Liabilities	+	Stockholders' Equity	
Inventory	−1,750				Cost of Goods Sold (+E)	−1,750

Summary of Sales-Related Transactions

For a review of how purchases and sales are accounted for in perpetual inventory systems, check out the animated tutorial on the DVD for use with this book.

The various sales-related transactions introduced in this section were recorded using contra-revenue accounts.[9] Their effects on sales reporting are summarized in Exhibit 6.9.

As we discussed, contra-revenue accounts are used as an internal control to allow managers to separately monitor and control how credit cards, sales discounts, and sales returns affect the company's revenues. For example, if customers are frequently returning a product for being defective, it would show up as an increase in the *Sales Returns and Allowances* account. Upon seeing the increase, Wal-Mart's managers could decide to discontinue selling the product or find a new supplier for it. This kind of detailed information is a key part of a merchandiser's business strategy, so to avoid revealing these secrets to competitors, most companies allow only *internal* financial statement users to see the balances in these contra-revenue accounts. For external reporting purposes, contra-revenue accounts are subtracted from total *Sales Revenue*, as shown in Exhibit 6.9, but this calculation is made "behind the scenes." Rather than show all of these accounts, externally reported income statements usually just begin with *Net Sales*. Despite this secrecy, external financial statement users can still conduct useful financial statement analyses, as we'll see in the next section.

exhibit 6.9   Effects of Sales-Related Transactions

Sales Revenue		$4,225
Less:	Sales Returns and Allowances	225
	Sales Discounts	20
	Credit Card Discounts	90
Net Sales		$3,890

Explanation: The various contra-revenue accounts are subtracted from *Sales Revenue* to compute *Net Sales*. For reasons discussed in the text, most companies only report *Net Sales* in their externally reported income statements. The detailed breakdown shown above is available only to internal financial statement users.

EVALUATE

THE OPERATING RESULTS OF MERCHANDISERS

Drilling Down in a Multistep Income Statement

One of the basic facts of merchandising is that goods have to be sold at a profit for a merchandiser to survive. Sure, cash has to be controlled, but the fact remains that there won't be much cash to control unless goods are sold at a profit. That's the only way companies like Wal-Mart can generate enough money to cover their operating expenses. To make it easy for financial statement users to see how much is earned from product sales, without being clouded by other operating costs, merchandise companies often present their income statement using a multistep format. A multistep income statement is similar to what you've seen in earlier chapters, with expenses being subtracted from revenues to arrive at net income. The key difference for financial statement users is that a multi-

---

[9]Some companies use an alternative form of reporting that classifies credit card discounts as expenses (rather than contra-revenues) on the income statement.

exhibit 6.10   Sample Multistep Income Statement

See the video on the DVD for use with this book for a brief explanation of how the income statement format differs between merchandise and service companies.

WAL-MART STORES, INC.
Income Statements
Fiscal Years Ended January 31

(amounts in millions)	2003	2002	2001
Net Sales	$244,520	$217,800	$191,330
Cost of Goods Sold	191,840	171,560	150,260
Gross Profit	52,680	46,240	41,070
Selling, General, and Administrative Expenses	39,040	34,300	29,760
Operating Income	13,640	11,940	11,310
Interest and Other Expenses	1,120	1,370	1,320
Income before Income Taxes	12,520	10,570	9,990
Income Tax Expenses	4,480	3,900	3,690
Net Income	$ 8,040	$ 6,670	$ 6,300

step format separates *Cost of Goods Sold* from other expenses. As shown in Exhibit 6.10, this extra step produces a subtotal called **Gross Profit,** which is the amount the company earned from selling goods, over and above the cost of the goods. If you buy something for $70 and sell it for $100, you'll have a gross profit of $30.

Notice in Exhibit 6.10 that after the gross profit line, the multistep income statement presents other items in a similar format to what you saw for a service company in Chapter 3 (Exhibit 3.2). The category called Selling, General, and Administrative Expenses includes a variety of operating expenses including wages, utilities, advertising, and rent. These expenses are subtracted from Gross Profit to yield Operating Income, which is a measure of the company's income from regular operating activities, before considering the effects of interest, income taxes, and any nonrecurring items.

Gross Profit Percentage

Let's focus again on the gross profit line on the income statement in Exhibit 6.10. Although the dollar amount of gross profit can be impressive—yes, Wal-Mart really did generate over $52 billion of gross profit in 2003—this number is difficult to interpret by itself. In Exhibit 6.10, we see that Wal-Mart's gross profit increased from 2001 to 2002 to 2003. The problem is that Wal-Mart also increased its sales over these three years, so we don't know whether the increase in gross profit dollars arises because Wal-Mart increased its sales volume or whether it is generating more profit per sale. To determine the amount of gross profit included in each dollar of sales, analysts typically evaluate **gross profit percentage,** which is calculated as follows:

YOU SHOULD KNOW

Gross Profit (also called Gross Margin or simply "margin") is net sales minus cost of goods sold. It is a subtotal, not an account.

YOU SHOULD KNOW

Gross profit percentage indicates how much above cost a company sells its products.

$$\frac{\text{Gross Profit}}{\text{Percentage}} = \frac{\text{Gross Profit}}{\text{Net Sales}} \times 100\% = \frac{(\text{Net Sales} - \text{Cost of Goods Sold})}{\text{Net Sales}} \times 100\%$$

The gross profit percentage measures how much above cost a company sells its products. As discussed below, this ratio is used to (1) analyze changes in the company's operations over time, (2) compare one company to another, and (3) determine whether a company is earning enough on each sale to cover its operating expenses. A higher gross profit percentage means that, all else being equal, a company will have more resources to cover operating expenses, leading to greater net income.

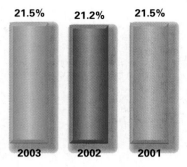

21.5%   **21.2%**   **21.5%**

2003   **2002**   **2001**

Gross Profit Percentage

COACH'S CORNER

A product is considered "high-margin" if the gross profit percentage from it is greater than the average gross profit percentage from other products.

As we can see in the graphic to the left, Wal-Mart's gross profit percentage dipped ever so slightly in 2002, and recovered in 2003. Each dollar of sales in 2003 and 2001 included 21.5 cents of gross profit whereas in 2002, each dollar of sales included 21.2 cents. So not only did Wal-Mart sell more in 2003 than in 2002, it also generated more profit per sale. How was this possible? To find out, we read the Management's Discussion and Analysis section of Wal-Mart's annual report. The word from the company's top people was that customers bought more "high-margin" products in 2003. You might wonder whether it's even worth talking about changes of less than half a percentage point, but just remember that a small change in the gross profit percentage can lead to a big change in net income. In Wal-Mart's case, because the company has such a huge volume of sales, the increase in gross profit of just three-tenths of a percentage point in 2003 translates into about three-quarters of a billion dollars. Yes, that's billion with a "b."

RECONSIDER

THE IMPACT OF OPERATING CYCLES ON FINANCIAL RESULTS

The gross profit percentage is particularly useful when analyzing merchandising and manufacturing companies because it shows how much profit is included in the selling price of an average product. Although it's less obvious to think of service companies, like hotels, movie theaters, and restaurants, as selling a product, some service-oriented companies report gross profit. For service companies, gross profit represents the amount of profit earned over and above the cost of each customer transaction, without considering general and administrative costs like advertising and corporate salaries.

Comparing Operating Results across Companies and Industries

Exhibit 6.11 shows that gross profit percentages can vary greatly between service, merchandising, and manufacturing companies, as well as within these broad categories. For example, pharmaceutical companies recently reported an average gross profit percentage of 51.2 percent compared to the 22.0 percent reported by automakers. Of course, these across-industry differences are expected because drug companies need a higher gross profit percentage than carmakers because they have more research and development expenses to cover.

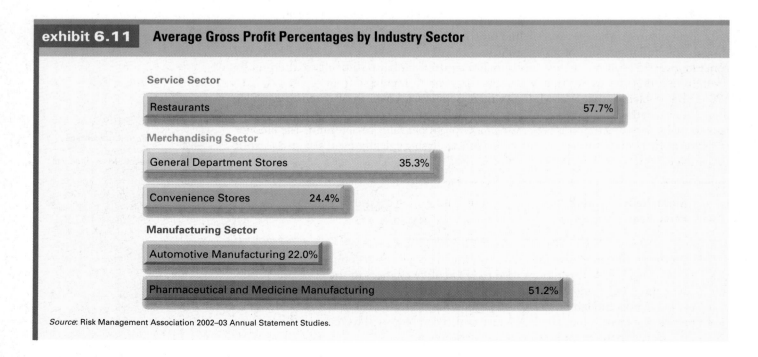

exhibit 6.11   **Average Gross Profit Percentages by Industry Sector**

Service Sector

Restaurants — 57.7%

Merchandising Sector

General Department Stores — 35.3%

Convenience Stores — 24.4%

Manufacturing Sector

Automotive Manufacturing 22.0%

Pharmaceutical and Medicine Manufacturing — 51.2%

Source: Risk Management Association 2002–03 Annual Statement Studies.

Even within a single industry sector, however, gross profit percentages are likely to vary from company to company depending on its business strategy and the nature of its products. Saks' high-end department stores enjoy a 36 percent gross profit percentage, whereas Wal-Mart's 21.5 percent is characteristic of its business strategy, which is true to its slogan of selling at "Low Prices, Always." The industry average of 35.3 percent shown in Exhibit 6.11 suggests that Wal-Mart's competitors charge an extra 13.8 cents on every dollar of sales. Fortunately for Wal-Mart, its low-price strategy attracts herds of customers who buy lots of merchandise. This enhanced sales volume counteracts the lower gross profit percentage, which allowed Wal-Mart to gross a hefty $52 billion in 2003.

Be on the Alert

Because gross profit percentages vary so much depending on the nature of a company's products, strategy, and operating cycle, they are more useful in comparing one company to itself over time than in comparing across companies. Even when comparing across years, though, you shouldn't jump to the conclusion that a change in gross profit percentage in one year will continue in the following years. To truly know whether changes represent onetime blips or a sustained effect, you must understand the sources of the change. For example, an increase in the gross profit percentage resulting from selling more high-margin winter clothing during a hard winter is likely to be a one-hit wonder, whereas an increase that comes from selling an entirely new line of products is likely to continue in future periods.

What's Coming Up

Throughout our discussions in this chapter, we quietly assumed that all sales ultimately are collected as cash. Unfortunately, this isn't always the case in the real world—companies aren't always successful in collecting every account receivable that is created by sales on account. In Chapter 7, you'll learn how companies account for the situation where they sell on account to customers, some of whom won't end up paying all that they owe. But before we start looking down the road to the collection of credit sales, you first need to review and practice the material covered in this chapter.

FOR YOUR REVIEW

DEMONSTRATION CASE A

Kat Bardash, a student at a small state college, has just received her first checking account statement for the month ended September 30. This was her first chance to attempt a bank reconciliation. The bank's statement of account showed the following:

Bank balance, September 1	$1,150
Deposits during September	650
Checks cleared during September	900
Bank service charge	25
Interest earned	5
Bank balance, September 30	880

Kat was surprised that her bank had not yet reported the deposit of $50 she made on September 29 and was pleased that her rent check of $200 had not cleared her account. Her September 30 checkbook balance was $750.

Required:

1. Complete Kat's bank reconciliation. What adjustments, if any, does she need to make in her checkbook?
2. Why is it important for individuals and businesses to do a bank reconciliation each month?

Suggested Solution

1. Kat's bank reconciliation:

Bank Statement		Kat's Books	
September 30 cash balance	$880	September 30 cash balance	$750
Additions		Additions	
Deposit in transit	50	Interest earned	5
Deductions		Deductions	
Outstanding check	(200)	Bank service charge	(25)
Up-to-date cash balance	$730	Up-to-date cash balance	$730

Kat should increase her checkbook balance by $5 for the cash given by the bank for interest and reduce her checkbook balance by $25 for the cash given to the bank for service charges.

2. Bank statements, whether personal or business, should be reconciled each month to help ensure that a correct balance is reflected in the depositor's books. Failure to reconcile a bank statement increases the chance that an error will not be discovered and may result in bad checks being written. Businesses reconcile their bank statements for an additional reason: The up-to-date balance that is calculated during reconciliation is reported on the balance sheet.

DEMONSTRATION CASE B

Assume Oakley Incorporated—the maker of stylish sunglasses, goggles, and many other leading products—made merchandise costing $137,200 and sold it on credit to Sunglass Hut for $405,000 with terms 2/10, n/30. Some of the merchandise differed from what Sunglass Hut had ordered, so Oakley agreed to give an allowance of $5,000. Sunglass Hut satisfied the remaining balance (of $400,000) by paying within the discount period.

Required:

1. Assuming that both companies use perpetual inventory systems, prepare the journal entries that both Oakley and Sunglass Hut would use to record the following transactions:
    a. Sale from Oakley to Sunglass Hut.
    b. Allowance granted by Oakley.
    c. Payment made by Sunglass Hut to Oakley.
2. Compute Oakley's net sales, assuming that sales returns and allowances and sales discounts are treated as contra-revenues.
3. Compute Oakley's gross profit and gross profit percentage on the sale. Compare this ratio to the 72.0 percent gross profit percentage recently reported by the Luxottica Group—the Italian company that makes Killer Loop® and Ray-Ban® sunglasses, which are sold through its Sunglass Hut stores. What does it imply about the two companies?

Suggested Solution

1. Journal entries:
    a. **Sale from Oakley to Sunglass Hut**

Oakley				Sunglass Hut			
dr	Accounts Receivable (+A)	405,000		dr	Inventory (+A)	405,000	
	cr Sales Revenue (+R, +SE)		405,000		cr Accounts Payable (+L).		405,000
dr	Cost of Goods Sold (+E, −SE)	137,200					
	cr Inventory (−A).		137,200					

b. Allowance granted by Oakley

Oakley			Sunglass Hut		
dr Sales Returns and Allowances (+xR, −SE)	5,000		dr Accounts Payable (−L)	5,000	
cr Accounts Receivable (−A). . . .		5,000	cr Inventory (−A).		5,000

c. Payment made by Sunglass Hut to Oakley

Oakley			Sunglass Hut		
dr Cash (+A)	392,000		dr Accounts Payable (−L)	400,000	
dr Sales Discounts (+xR, −SE)	8,000		cr Cash (−A).		392,000
cr Accounts Receivable (−A). . . .		400,000	cr Inventory (−A).		8,000
($8,000 = $400,000 × 2%)					

2. Sales returns and allowances and sales discounts should be subtracted from sales revenue to compute net sales:

COACH'S CORNER

Transaction *b* depicts an allowance but no return of goods. Had goods been returned, Oakley also would increase its inventory and decrease its cost of goods sold.

Sales Revenue		$405,000
Less: Sales Returns and Allowances		5,000
Sales Discounts [0.02 × (405,000 − 5,000)]		8,000
Net Sales		$392,000

3. Gross profit and gross profit percentage are calculated as follows:

	In Dollars	Percent of Net Sales
Net Sales (calculated in 2)	$392,000	100.0%
Less: Cost of Goods Sold	137,200	35.0
Gross Profit	$254,800	65.0%

The 65% gross profit percentage indicates that Oakley generates 7 cents less gross profit on each dollar of sales than Luxottica (7.0 = 72.0 − 65.0). This difference implies that Luxottica is including a higher markup in its selling prices.

CHAPTER SUMMARY

Distinguish service, merchandising, and manufacturing operations, and describe the purpose of internal controls. p. 232

LO1

- Service companies sell services rather than physical goods; consequently, their income statements show costs of services rather than cost of goods sold.

- Merchandise companies sell goods that have been obtained from a supplier. Retail merchandise companies sell direct to consumers whereas wholesale merchandise companies sell to retail companies.

- Manufacturing companies sell goods that they have made themselves.

- Internal controls are used to protect (against theft and fraudulent financial reporting) and to serve (by promoting efficient and effective operations and by alerting company officials to possible violations of laws and regulations).

Perform a key cash control by reconciling to bank statements. p. 235

LO2

- The bank reconciliation requires determining two categories of items: (1) those that have been recorded in the company's books but not in the bank's statement of account, and (2) those that have been reported in the bank's statement of account but not in the company's books. The second category of items provides the data needed to adjust the Cash records to the balance reported on the balance sheet.

LO3   **Explain the use of a perpetual inventory system as a control. p. 240**

- Perpetual inventory systems protect against undetectable theft because they provide an up-to-date record of inventory that should be on hand at any given time, which can be compared to a count of the physical quantity that actually is on hand.

- Perpetual inventory systems serve to promote efficient and effective operations because they are updated every time inventory is purchased, sold, or returned.

LO4   **Analyze purchase transactions under a perpetual inventory system. p. 242**

- In a perpetual inventory system, the *Inventory* account is increased every time inventory is purchased. The account should include any costs, such as transportation-in, that are needed to get the inventory into a condition and location ready for sale.

- In a perpetual inventory system, the purchaser's *Inventory* account is decreased whenever the purchaser returns goods to the supplier or is given a discount for prompt payment.

LO5   **Analyze sales transactions under a perpetual inventory system. p. 245**

- In a perpetual inventory system, two entries are made every time inventory is sold: one entry records the sale (and corresponding debit to cash or accounts receivable) and the other entry records the cost of the goods sold (and corresponding credit to inventory).

- By recording *sales discounts, credit card discounts,* and *sales returns and allowances* as contra-revenues, net sales are reduced.

LO6   **Analyze a merchandiser's multistep income statement. p. 248**

- One of the key items in a merchandiser's multistep income statement is Gross Profit, which is a subtotal calculated by subtracting *Cost of Goods Sold* from *Net Sales*. The gross profit percentage can be calculated by dividing Gross Profit by Net Sales. This measure indicates the amount of gross profit that is included in each dollar of sales.

LO7   **Explain factors to consider when comparing across industries. p. 250**

- As with other measures of operating performance, the gross profit percentage varies between companies depending on the nature of the operating cycle (e.g., service, merchandising, manufacturing), business strategy, and product mix.

FINANCIAL STATEMENT ANALYSIS TIP

To determine the amount of gross profit included in every dollar of sales, calculate the gross profit percentage:

$$\text{Gross Profit Percentage} = \frac{\text{Gross Profit}}{\text{Net Sales}} \times 100\% = \frac{(\text{Net Sales} - \text{Cost of Goods Sold})}{\text{Net Sales}} \times 100\%$$

KEY TERMS TO KNOW

Bank Reconciliation p. 235

Cash p. 235

Credit Card Discount p. 247

Gross Profit (or Gross Margin) p. 249

Gross Profit Percentage p. 249

Internal Control p. 234

Manufacturing Company p. 232

Merchandising Company p. 232

NSF (Not Sufficient Funds) Check p. 236

Periodic Inventory System p. 240

Perpetual Inventory System p. 240

Purchase Discounts p. 243

Purchase Returns and Allowances p. 243

Sales Discounts p. 246

Sales Returns and Allowances p. 245

Segregation of Duties p. 234

Service Company p. 232

SUPPLEMENT A: PERIODIC INVENTORY SYSTEMS

As described in the body of this chapter, a *periodic* inventory system updates the inventory records only *at the end of the accounting period.* Unlike the perpetual inventory system, a periodic system does not track the cost of goods sold during the accounting period. Instead, this information is determined by following a four-step process:

1. ***Determine beginning inventory.*** You get this simply by looking in the T-account or balance sheet for last period's ending inventory balance.

2. ***Track this period's purchases.*** The cost of all transactions related to inventory is recorded in separate accounts called *Purchases*, *Purchase Discounts*, and *Purchase Returns and Allowances*.

3. ***Determine ending inventory.*** The number of units of inventory on hand at the end of the period is determined through an inventory count. These quantities are then multiplied by the cost of each unit to determine the cost of ending inventory.

4. ***Calculate the cost of goods sold.*** This step combines data from the first three steps to "force out" the cost of goods sold. You start with the cost of beginning inventory and add the cost of every piece of inventory that you bought during the period (net of any purchase discounts or purchase returns and allowances). The result is the cost of all of the goods that *could* have been sold during the period. If you sold everything, this would be the cost of goods sold. But you know that some of the goods weren't sold because you counted a bunch of items during the inventory count. So the cost of what you did sell is equal to the difference between what you could have sold and what you didn't sell. In other words, the **cost of goods sold equation** is:

YOU SHOULD KNOW

The **cost of goods sold equation** is:
Beginning Inventory
+ Purchases
− Purchase Discounts
− Purchase Returns and
 Allowances

Cost of Goods Available for Sale
− Ending Inventory (counted)

Cost of Goods Sold

> Cost of Goods Sold = Beginning Inventory + Net Purchases − Ending Inventory

where Net Purchases = Purchases − Purchase Discounts − Purchase Returns and Allowances.

Comparison of the Accounting Processes Used in Periodic and Perpetual Systems

The typical journal entries recorded in a periodic inventory system are presented below and contrasted with the entries that would be recorded in a perpetual inventory system. The effects of these journal entries on the accounting equation then are summarized. Note that the total effects are identical, and only the timing and nature of recording differs.

Assume, for this illustration only, that Wal-Mart stocks and sells only one item, the Iowna Clone Phone, and that only the following events occurred in 2006:

Jan. 1   Beginning inventory: 800 units, at unit cost of $50.

Apr. 14   Purchased: 1,100 additional units on account, at unit cost of $50.

Nov. 30   Sold: 1,300 units on account, at unit sales price of $83.

Dec. 31   Counted: 600 units, at unit cost of $50.

Periodic Records	Perpetual Records

Periodic Records

A. Record purchases
April 14, 2006:

```
dr  Purchases (+A) (1,100 units at $50)..........    55,000
     cr  Accounts Payable (+L).................            55,000
```

B. Record sales (but not cost of goods sold)
November 30, 2006:

```
dr  Accounts Receivable (+A).................   107,900
     cr  Sales Revenue (+R, +SE)
         (1,300 units at $83).......................        107,900

No cost of goods sold entry
```

C. Record end-of-period adjustments
At the end of the period, compute cost of goods sold using the four-step process and adjust the inventory accounts.

1. Beginning inventory (last period's ending)	$40,000
2. Add net purchases	55,000
Cost of goods available for sale	95,000
3. Deduct ending inventory (physical count—600 units at $50)	30,000
4. Cost of goods sold	$65,000

December 31, 2006:
Transfer beginning inventory and net purchases to cost of goods sold: (act *as if* all goods were sold)

```
dr  Cost of Goods Sold (+E, −SE)..............   95,000
     cr  Inventory (−A) (beginning)..............        40,000
     cr  Purchases (−A).......................        55,000
```

Adjust the cost of goods sold by subtracting the amount of ending inventory still on hand: (recognize that not all goods were sold)

```
dr  Inventory (+A) (ending) ...................   30,000
     cr  Cost of Goods Sold (−E, +SE)............        30,000
```

Assets		=	Liabilities	+	Stockholders' Equity	
Purchases	+55,000		Accounts Payable +55,000			
Accts. Rec.	+107,900				Sales Revenue	+107,900
Inventory	−40,000				Cost of Goods Sold (+E)	−95,000
Purchases	−55,000					
Inventory	+30,000				Cost of Goods Sold (+E)	+30,000
Totals	+97,900		+55,000			+42,900

Perpetual Records

A. Record purchases
April 14, 2006:

```
dr  Inventory (+A) (1,100 units at $50) ..........    55,000
     cr  Accounts Payable (+L).................            55,000
```

B. Record sales and cost of goods sold
November 30, 2006:

```
dr  Accounts Receivable (+A).................   107,900
     cr  Sales Revenue (+R, +SE)
         (1,300 units at $83).......................        107,900
dr  Cost of Goods Sold (+E, −SE)..............    65,000
     cr  Inventory (−A) (1,300 units at $50) .......        65,000
```

C. Record end-of-period adjustments
At the end of the accounting period, the balance in the *Cost of Goods Sold* account is reported on the income statement. It is not necessary to compute cost of goods sold because the *Cost of Goods Sold* account is up to date. Also, the *Inventory* account shows the ending inventory amount reported on the balance sheet. A physical inventory count is still necessary to assess the accuracy of the perpetual records and identify theft and other forms of shrinkage. Any shrinkage would be recorded by reducing the *Inventory* account and increasing an expense account (such as *Inventory Shrinkage* or *Cost of Goods Sold*). This illustration assumes no shrinkage is detected.

```
No entry
```

Assets		=	Liabilities	+	Stockholders' Equity	
Inventory	+55,000		Accounts Payable +55,000			
Accts. Rec.	+107,900				Sales Revenue	+107,900
Inventory	−65,000				Cost of Goods Sold (+E)	−65,000
Totals	+97,900		+55,000			+42,900

QUESTIONS

1. What is the distinction between service and merchandising companies? What is the distinction between merchandising and manufacturing companies? What is the distinction between retail and wholesale merchandising companies?

2. Summarize the primary purposes of an internal control system.

3. What are the three internal control objectives for financial reporting?

4. Why should responsibilities for certain duties, like cash handling and cash recording, be separated? What types of responsibilities should be separated?

5. Define *cash* and indicate the types of items that should be reported as cash.

6. What are the purposes of a bank reconciliation? What balances are reconciled?

7. What is the main distinction between perpetual and periodic inventory systems? Which type of system provides better internal control over inventory? Explain why.

8. Describe how transportation costs to obtain inventory (freight-in) are accounted for by a merchandising company using a perpetual inventory system. Explain the reasoning behind this accounting treatment.

9. What is the distinction between *purchase returns and allowances* and *purchase discounts?*

10. What is a purchase discount? Use 1/10, n/30 in your explanation.

11. Describe in words the journal entries that are made in a perpetual inventory system when inventory is sold on credit.

12. Explain the difference between sales revenue and net sales.

13. How are purchase discounts and sales discounts similar? How are they different?

14. What is a credit card discount? How does it affect amounts reported on the income statement?

15. What is gross profit? How is the gross profit percentage computed? Illustrate its calculation and interpretation assuming net sales revenue is $100,000 and cost of goods sold is $60,000.

MULTIPLE CHOICE

To practice more multiple choice questions, check out the DVD for use with this book.

1. Mountain Gear, Inc. buys bikes, tents, and climbing supplies from Rugged Rock Corporation for sale to consumers. What type of company is Mountain Gear, Inc.?

    a. Service

    b. Retail merchandiser

    c. Wholesale merchandiser

    d. Manufacturer

2. Which of the following does not enhance internal control?

    a. Ensuring transactions are authorized and properly recorded.

    b. Ensuring adequate records are maintained.

    c. Hiring good employees.

    d. None of the above—all enhance internal control.

3. Upon review of your bank statement, you discover that you recently deposited a check from a customer that was rejected by your bank as NSF. Which of the following describes the actions to be taken when preparing your bank reconciliation?

	Balance per Bank	Balance per Books
a.	Decrease	No change
b.	Increase	Decrease
c.	No change	Decrease
d.	Decrease	Increase

4. Upon review of the most recent bank statement, you discover that a check was made out to your supplier for $76 but was recorded in your *Cash* and *Accounts payable* accounts as $67. Which of the following describes the actions to be taken when preparing your bank reconciliation?

	Balance per Bank	Balance per Books
a.	Decrease	No change
b.	Increase	Decrease
c.	No change	Decrease
d.	Decrease	Increase

5. Which of the following is false regarding a perpetual inventory system?

   a. Physical counts are never needed since records are maintained on a transaction-by-transaction basis.

   b. The balance in the inventory account is updated with each inventory purchase and sale transaction.

   c. Cost of goods sold is increased as sales are recorded.

   d. The account *Purchases* is not used as inventory is acquired.

6. Purchase discounts with terms 2/10, n/30 mean

   a. 10 percent discount for payment within 30 days.

   b. 2 percent discount for payment within 10 days or the full amount (less returns) is due within 30 days.

   c. Two-tenths of a percent discount for payment within 30 days.

   d. None of the above.

7. Which of the following describes how payments to suppliers, made within the purchase discount period, are recorded in a perpetual inventory system (using the method shown in the chapter)?

   a. Reduce cash, reduce accounts payable.

   b. Reduce cash, reduce accounts payable, reduce inventory.

   c. Reduce cash, reduce accounts payable, increase purchase discounts.

   d. Reduce cash, reduce accounts payable, decrease purchase discounts.

8. Which of the following is not a component of net sales?

   a. Sales returns and allowances.

   b. Sales discounts.

   c. Cost of goods sold.

   d. Credit card discounts.

9. What is the best description of a *credit card discount*?

   a. The discount offered by a seller to a consumer for using a national credit card like Visa.

   b. The fee charged by a seller to a consumer for the right to use a credit card, calculated as a percentage of total revenue for the sale.

   c. The discount offered by a seller to a customer for early payment of an account receivable.

   d. The percentage fee charged by a credit card company to a seller.

10. Earlier this year, your company negotiated larger purchase discounts when paying for its merchandise inventory, which it has consistently taken throughout the year. What effect will this factor have on the company's gross profit percentage this year, in comparison to last year?

   a. The ratio will not change.

   b. The ratio will increase.

   c. The ratio will decrease.

   d. Either *b* or *c*.

Solutions to Multiple-Choice Questions
1. *b* 2. *d* 3. *c* 4. *c* 5. *a* 6. *b* 7. *b* 8. *c* 9. *d* 10. *b*

MINI-EXERCISES Available with McGraw-Hill's Homework Manager

L01–L06 **M6-1 Identifying Important Accounting Terms**

Complete the following crossword puzzle, using the clues provided to the right. Omit hyphens.

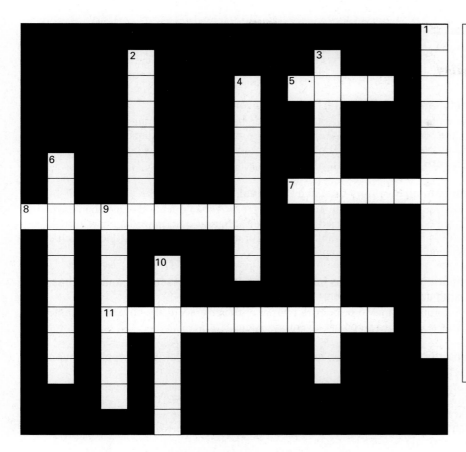

Across
5 Money or any instrument that banks will accept for deposit.
7 The one-word term used to mean gross profit.
8 An inventory system that updates inventory records every time inventory is bought, sold, or returned.
11 The name for a category of checks that have been written but not yet processed by the bank.

Down
1 A type of company that sells goods that have been purchased from a supplier.
2 A type of company that sells services rather than physical goods.
3 A type of company that sells goods that it has made itself.
4 The two-word name of the first line item reported in most income statements prepared for external reporting.
6 An alternative (hyphenated) name that purchasers use for transportation costs incurred to acquire inventory.
9 An inventory system that updates inventory records only at the end of the accounting period.
10 Sales _____ and allowances.

M6-2 Identifying Internal Controls over Financial Reporting   LO1

Fox Erasing has a system of internal control with the following procedures. Match the procedure to the corresponding financial reporting control objective.

Procedure		Financial Reporting Control Objective
____ 1.	Only the treasurer may sign checks.	A. Ensure adequate records are maintained.
____ 2.	The treasurer is not allowed to make bank deposits.	B. Ensure transactions are authorized and properly recorded.
____ 3.	The company's checks are prenumbered.	C. Prevent or detect unauthorized activities involving the company's assets.

M6-3 Organizing Items on the Bank Reconciliation   LO2

Indicate whether the following items would be added (+) or subtracted (−) from the company's books or the bank statement side of a bank reconciliation.

Reconciling Item	Bank Statement	Company's Books
a. Outstanding checks of $12,000		
b. Bank service charge of $15		
c. Deposit in transit of $2,300		
d. Interest earned of $5		

M6-4 Preparing Journal Entries after a Bank Reconciliation   LO2

Using the information in M6-3, prepare any journal entries needed to adjust the company's books.

LO3   **M6-5** **Choosing between a Perpetual and Periodic Inventory System**

Nordstrom, Inc., started in business in 1901. It only took 100 years, but eventually the company changed from a periodic inventory system to a perpetual inventory system (in 2002). Write a brief report describing how this change is likely to improve the company's inventory control.

LO3   **M6-6** **Calculating Shrinkage in a Perpetual Inventory System**

Koonce's Campus Store has $25,000 of inventory on hand at the beginning of the month. During the month, the company buys $4,000 of merchandise and sells merchandise that had cost $15,000. At the end of the month, $13,000 of inventory is on hand. How much "shrinkage" occurred during the month?

LO4   **M6-7** **Determining Inventory Cost in a Perpetual System**

Assume Anderson's General Store in Toledo bought, on credit, a truckload of merchandise costing $23,000. If the company was charged $650 in transportation cost, immediately returned goods costing $1,200, and then took advantage of a 2/10, n/30 purchase discount, how much should Anderson's report as the cost of inventory?

LO4   **M6-8** **Preparing Journal Entries for Purchases, Purchase Discounts, and Purchase Returns Using a Perpetual System**

Using the information in M6-6, prepare journal entries to record the inventory transactions, assuming Anderson's uses a perpetual inventory system.

LO3-LO5   **M6-9** **Recording Journal Entries for Purchases and Sales Using a Perpetual Inventory System**

Inventory at the beginning of the year cost $13,400. During the year, the company purchased (on account) inventory costing $54,000 and inventory, which had cost $60,000, was sold on account for $75,000. At the end of the year, inventory was counted and its cost was determined to be $7,400. Prepare journal entries to record these transactions, assuming a perpetual inventory system is used.

LO5   **M6-10** **Reporting Net Sales and Gross Profit with Sales Discounts**

Merchandise costing $1,500 is sold for $2,000 on terms 2/10, n/30. If the buyer pays within the discount period, what amount will be reported on the income statement as net sales and as gross profit?

LO5   **M6-11** **Recording Journal Entries for Sales and Sales Discounts**

Using the information in M6-10, prepare the journal entries needed at the time of sale and collection, assuming the company uses a perpetual inventory system.

LO5   **M6-12** **Journal Entries to Record Sales Discounts**

Inventory that cost $500 is sold for $700, with terms of 2/10, n/30. Give the journal entries to record (a) the sale of merchandise and (b) collection of the accounts receivable assuming that it occurs during the discount period. (Use the method shown in the chapter for recording sales discounts.)

LO5   **M6-13** **Reporting Net Sales with Sales Discounts, Credit Card Discounts, and Sales Returns**

Total sales for the period include the following:

Sales paid by credit card (discount 3%)	$8,000
Sales made on account (terms 2/15, n/60)	$9,500

Sales returns relating to sales on account were $500. All returns were made by customers before they paid their account balances. One-half of the sales on account (net of returns) was paid within the discount period. The company records all discounts and returns as contra-revenues. What amount will be reported on the income statement as net sales?

LO6   **M6-14** **Preparing a Multistep Income Statement**

Sheehan Publishing Inc. reported the following amounts in its adjusted trial balance prepared as of its December 31, 2006 fiscal year-end: Administrative expenses, $2,300; Cost of goods sold, $12,300; Gain on sale of equipment, $500; General expenses, $6,700; Income tax expense, $2,400,

Interest expense, $1,300; Sales revenue, $36,000; Sales discounts $2,400; Sales returns and allowances, $920; and Delivery (freight-out) expense $2,500. Prepare a multistep income statement for distribution to external financial statement users, using the format shown in Exhibit 6.10.

M6-15 Computing and Interpreting the Gross Profit Percentage

LO6, LO7

Ziehart Pharmaceuticals reported net sales of $178,000 and cost of goods sold of $58,000. Candy Electronics Corp. reported net sales of $36,000 and cost of goods sold of $26,200. Calculate the gross profit percentage for both companies. From these calculations, can you determine which company is more successful? Explain.

EXERCISES   Available with McGraw-Hill's Homework Manager

E6-1 Identifying Internal Control Procedure and Financial Reporting Control Objective

LO1

At most movie theaters, one employee sells tickets and another employee collects them. One night, when you're at the movies, your friend comments that this is a waste of the theater's money.

Required:

1. Identify the name of the control procedure and control objective to which this situation relates.
2. Explain to your friend what could happen if the same person did both jobs.

E6-2 Identifying Financial Reporting Control Objectives

LO1

Your student club recently volunteered to go door-to-door collecting cash donations on behalf of a local charity. The charity's accountant went absolutely berserk when you happened to say you bothered to write receipts only for donors who asked for one.

Required:

Identify the control objective or objectives that you violated, and explain why the accountant reacted so strongly. What controls might be appropriate to use in the future?

E6-3 Preparing a Bank Reconciliation and Journal Entries, and Reporting Cash

LO2

Jones Company's June 30, 2006, bank statement and the June ledger account for cash are summarized here:

Bank Statement

	Checks	Deposits	Other	Balance
Balance, June 1, 2006				$ 7,200
Deposits during June		$17,000		24,200
Checks cleared during June	$18,100			6,100
Bank service charges			$50	6,050
Balance, June 30, 2006				6,050

	+ Cash (A) −			
June 1 Balance	6,800	June	Checks written	18,400
June Deposits	19,000			

Required:

1. Prepare a bank reconciliation. A comparison of the checks written with the checks that have cleared the bank shows outstanding checks of $700. Some of the checks that cleared in June were written prior to June. No deposits in transit were noted in May, but a deposit is in transit at the end of June.
2. Give any journal entries that should be made as a result of the bank reconciliation.
3. What is the balance in the *Cash* account after the reconciliation entries?
4. In addition to the balance in its bank account, Jones Company also has $300 cash on hand. This amount is recorded in a separate T-account called *Cash on Hand*. What is the total amount of cash that should be reported on the balance sheet at June 30?

LO2

E6-4 Preparing a Bank Reconciliation and Journal Entries, and Reporting Cash

The September 30, 2006, bank statement for Cadieux Company and the September ledger account for cash are summarized here:

Bank Statement

	Checks	Deposits	Other	Balance
Balance, September 1, 2006				$ 6,300
Deposits recorded during September		$27,000		33,300
Checks cleared during September	$28,500			4,800
NSF checks—Betty Brown			$150	4,650
Bank service charges			50	4,600
Balance, September 30, 2006				4,600

+ Cash (A) −				
Sept. 1	Balance	6,300	June	Checks written	28,600
Sept.	Deposits	28,000			

No outstanding checks and no deposits in transit were noted in August. However, there are deposits in transit and checks outstanding at the end of September.

Required:

1. Prepare a bank reconciliation.
2. Give any journal entries that should be made as the result of the bank reconciliation.
3. What should the balance in the *Cash* account be after recording the journal entries in requirement 2?
4. If the company also has $400 of cash on hand (recorded in a separate account), what total amount of cash should the company report on the September 30 balance sheet?

LO3

E6-5 Inferring Shrinkage Using a Perpetual Inventory System

Calculate the amount of shrinkage for each of the following independent cases:

Cases	Beginning Inventory	Purchases	Cost of Goods Sold	Ending Inventory (as counted)	Shrinkage
A	$100	$700	$300	$420	$?
B	200	800	850	150	?
C	150	500	200	440	?
D	260	600	650	200	?

LO3

E6-6 Inferring Shrinkage Using a Perpetual Inventory System

JCPenney Company, Inc., is a major retailer with department stores in all 50 states. The main part of the company's business consists of providing merchandise and services to consumers through department stores. In a recent annual report, JCPenney reported cost of goods sold of $10,969 million, ending inventory for the current year of $3,058 million, and ending inventory for the previous year of $2,969 million.

Required:

If you knew that the cost of inventory purchases was $11,060 million, could you estimate the cost of shrinkage during the year? If so, prepare the estimate and if not, explain why.

LO4

E6-7 Recording the Cost of Purchases for a Merchandiser

Apparel.com purchased 80 new shirts and recorded a total cost of $3,015 determined as follows:

Invoice cost	$2,600
Transportation cost (freight-in)	165
Estimated cost of shipping to customers	250
	$3,015

Required:

Calculate the correct inventory cost and give the journal entry or entries to record the above purchase information in the correct amount, assuming a perpetual inventory system. Show computations.

E6-8 Reporting Purchases and Purchase Discounts Using a Perpetual Inventory System   LO4

During the months of January and February, Axe Corporation purchased goods from three suppliers. The sequence of events was as follows:

Jan.	6	Purchased goods for $1,000 from Green with terms 2/10, n/30.
	6	Purchased goods from Munoz for $800 with terms 2/10, n/30.
	14	Paid Green in full.
Feb.	2	Paid Munoz in full.
	28	Purchased goods for $500 from Reynolds with terms 2/10, n/45.

Required:

Assume that Axe uses a perpetual inventory system, the company had no inventory on hand at the beginning of January, and no sales were made during January and February. Calculate the cost of inventory as of February 28.

E6-9 Recording Journal Entries for Purchases and Purchase Discounts Using a   LO4
Perpetual Inventory System

Using the information in E6-8, prepare journal entries to record the transactions, assuming Axe uses a perpetual inventory system.

E6-10 Reporting Purchases, Purchase Discounts, and Purchase Returns Using a   LO4
Perpetual Inventory System

During the month of June, Ace Incorporated purchased goods from two suppliers. The sequence of events was as follows:

June	3	Purchased goods for $2,200 from Zip Inc. with terms 2/10, n/30.
	5	Returned goods costing $1,200 to Zip Inc. for full credit.
	6	Purchased goods from Nadda Corp. for $2,000 with terms 2/10, n/30.
	11	Paid the balance owed to Zip.
	22	Paid Nadda in full.

Required:

Assume that Ace uses a perpetual inventory system, and that the company had no inventory on hand at the beginning of the month. Calculate the cost of inventory as of June 30.

E6-11 Recording Journal Entries for Purchases, Purchase Discounts, and Purchase   LO4
Returns Using a Perpetual Inventory System

Using the information in E6-10, prepare journal entries to record the transactions, assuming Ace uses a perpetual inventory system.

E6-12 Reporting Net Sales with Credit Sales and Sales Discounts   LO5

During the months of January and February, Zax Corporation sold goods to three customers. The sequence of events was as follows:

Jan.	6	Sold goods for $1,000 to Blue Inc. with terms 2/10, n/30. The goods cost Zax $700.
	6	Sold goods to VeraCorp for $800 with terms 2/10, n/30. The goods cost Zax $600.
	14	Collected cash due from Blue Inc.
Feb.	2	Collected cash due from VeraCorp.
	28	Sold goods for $500 to Wrapp with terms 2/10, n/45. The goods cost Zax $300.

Required:

Assuming that sales discounts are reported as contra-revenue, compute net sales for the two months ended February 28.

LO5

E6-13 Recording Journal Entries for Net Sales with Credit Sales and Sales Discounts

Using the information in E6-12, prepare journal entries to record the transactions, assuming Zax uses a perpetual inventory system.

LO5

E6-14 Reporting Net Sales with Credit Sales, Sales Discounts, and Credit Card Sales

The following transactions were selected from the records of Evergreen Company:

July	12	Sold merchandise to Wally Butler, who charged the $1,000 purchase on his Visa credit card. Visa charges Evergreen a 2 percent credit card fee. The goods cost Evergreen Company $600.
	15	Sold merchandise to Claudio's Chair Company at a selling price of $5,000 on terms 3/10, n/30. The goods cost Evergreen Company $3,500.
	20	Sold merchandise to Otto's Ottomans at a selling price of $3,000 on terms 3/10, n/30. The goods cost Evergreen Company $1,900.
	23	Collected payment from Claudio's Chair Company from July 15 sale.
Aug.	25	Collected payment from Otto's Ottomans from July 20 sale.

Required:

Assuming that sales discounts are reported as contra-revenue, compute net sales for the two months ended August 31.

LO5

E6-15 Recording Journal Entries for Net Sales with Credit Sales, Sales Discounts, and Credit Card Sales

Using the information in E6-14, prepare journal entries to record the transactions, assuming Evergreen Company uses a perpetual inventory system.

LO5

E6-16 Reporting Net Sales with Credit Sales, Sales Discounts, Sales Returns, and Credit Card Sales

The following transactions were selected from among those completed by Bear's Retail Store in 2006:

Nov.	20	Sold two items of merchandise to Cheryl Jahn, who charged the $400 sales price on her Visa credit card. Visa charges Bear's a 2 percent credit card fee. The goods cost Bear's $300.
	25	Sold 20 items of merchandise to Vasko Athletics at a selling price of $4,000 (total); terms 3/10, n/30. The goods cost Bear's $2,500.
	28	Sold 10 identical items of merchandise to Nancy's Gym at a selling price of $6,000 (total); terms 3/10, n/30. The goods cost Bear's $4,000.
	29	Nancy's Gym returned one of the items purchased on the 28th. The item was defective, and credit was given to the customer.
Dec.	6	Nancy's Gym paid the account balance in full.
	30	Vasko Athletics paid in full for the invoice of November 25, 2006.

COACH'S CORNER

For E6-17, note that defective items are not returned to inventory. Assume they remain as an expense.

Required:

Assuming that sales returns, sales discounts, and credit card discounts are reported as contra-revenues, compute net sales for the two months ended December 31, 2006.

LO5

E6-17 Recording Journal Entries for Net Sales with Credit Sales, Sales Discounts, Sales Returns, and Credit Card Sales

Using the information in E6-16, prepare journal entries to record the transactions, assuming Bear's Retail Store uses a perpetual inventory system.

E6-18 Determining the Effects of Credit Sales, Sales Discounts, Credit Card Sales, and Sales Returns and Allowances on Income Statement Categories

LO5

Rockland Shoe Company records sales returns and allowances, sales discounts, and credit card discounts as contra-revenues. Complete the following table, indicating the amount and direction of effect (+ for increase, − for decrease, and NE for no effect) of each transaction on Rockland.

July	12	Rockland sold merchandise to Kristina Zee at its factory store. Kristina charged the $300 purchase on her American Express card. American Express charges Rockland a 1 percent credit card fee.
July	15	Sold merchandise to Shoe Express at a selling price of $5,000, with terms 3/10, n/30.
July	20	Collected cash due from Shoe Express.
July	21	Sold merchandise to Fleet Foot Co. at a selling price of $2,000, with terms 2/10, n/30.
July	23	Fleet Foot Co. returned $1,000 of shoes, and promised to pay for the remaining goods in August.

Transaction	Sales Revenue	Sales Returns and Allowances	Sales Discounts	Credit Card Discounts	Net Sales
July 12					
July 15					
July 20					
July 21					
July 23					

E6-19 Recording Sales and Purchases with Discounts

LO4, LO5

Cycle Wholesaling sells merchandise on credit terms of 2/10, n/30. A sale invoiced at $800 (cost of goods sold of $500) was made to Sarah's Cycles on February 1, 2006. On March 4, 2006, Cycle Wholesaling purchased bicycles and accessories from a supplier on credit, invoiced at $8,000 with terms 1/15, n/30. Assume Cycle Wholesaling uses a perpetual inventory system.

Required:

Sales Transactions

1. Give the journal entry Cycle Wholesaling would make to record the sale to Sarah's Cycles.
2. Give the journal entry to record the collection of the account, assuming it was collected in full on February 9, 2006.
3. Give the journal entry, assuming, instead, that the account was collected in full on March 2, 2006.

Purchase Transactions

4. Give the journal entry to record the purchase on credit.
5. Give the journal entry to record the payment of Cycle Wholesaling's account, assuming it was paid in full on March 12, 2006.
6. Give the journal entry, assuming, instead, that the account was paid in full on March 28, 2006.

E6-20 Inferring Missing Amounts Based on Income Statement Relationships

LO6

Supply the missing dollar amounts for the 2006 income statement of Williamson Company for each of the following independent cases:

	Case A	Case B	Case C
Sales revenue	$8,000	$6,000	$?
Sales returns and allowances	150	?	275
Net sales revenue	?	?	5,920
Cost of goods sold	5,750	4,050	5,400
Gross profit	?	1,450	?

LO6   E6-21 Inferring Missing Amounts Based on Income Statement Relationships

Supply the missing dollar amounts for the 2006 income statement of Lewis Retailers for each of the following independent cases:

Cases	Sales Revenue	Beginning Inventory	Purchases	Cost of Goods Sold	Cost of Ending Inventory	Gross Profit
A	$ 650	$100	$700	$300	?	$?
B	900	200	800	?	150	?
C	?	150	?	200	300	400
D	800	?	600	650	250	?
E	1,000	50	900	?	?	500

LO6   E6-22 Analyzing Gross Profit Percentage on the Basis of a Multistep Income Statement

The following summarized data were provided by the records of Mystery Incorporated for the year ended December 31, 2006:

Sales of merchandise for cash	$220,000
Sales of merchandise on credit	32,000
Cost of goods sold	147,000
Selling expense	40,200
Administrative expense	19,000
Sales returns and allowances	7,000
Income tax expense	11,600

Required:

1. Based on these data, prepare a multistep income statement (showing both gross profit and operating income).
2. What was the amount of gross profit? What was the gross profit percentage? Explain what these two amounts mean.

LO6, LO7   E6-23 Analyzing Gross Profit Percentage on the Basis of an Income Statement

Wolverine World Wide Inc. prides itself as being the "world's leading marketer of U.S. branded non-athletic footwear." The following data were taken from its recent annual report (in thousands):

Sales of merchandise	$413,957
Income taxes	10,047
Cash dividends paid	2,347
Selling and administrative expense	85,993
Cost of products sold	290,469
Interest expense	3,678
Other revenues	297

Required:

1. Based on these data, prepare a multistep income statement.
2. How much was the gross profit? What was the gross profit percentage (rounded to the nearest tenth of a percent)? Explain what these two amounts mean.
3. Compare Wolverine's gross profit percentage to Wal-Mart's average gross profit percentage of 21.5 percent. From this information, can you determine which company is more successful? Why or why not?

LO4, LO5   E6-24 (Supplement) Recording Purchases and Sales Using Perpetual and Periodic Inventory Systems

Kangaroo Jim Company reported beginning inventory of 100 units at a unit cost of $25. It had the following purchase and sales transactions during 2006:

Jan. 14   Sold 25 units at unit sales price of $45 on account.

Apr. 9   Purchased 15 additional units at unit cost of $25 on account.

Sep. 2   Sold 50 units at sales price of $50 on account.

Dec. 31   Counted inventory and determined 40 units were still on hand.

Required:

Record each transaction, assuming that Kangaroo Jim Company uses (*a*) a perpetual inventory system and (*b*) a periodic inventory system.

SIMPLIFY WITH SPREADSHEETS

SS6-1 Preparing Multistep Income Statements and Calculating Gross Profit Percentage

LO5–LO7

Assume that you have been hired by Big Sky Corporation as a summer student. The company is in the process of preparing their annual financial statements. To help in the process, you are asked to prepare an income statement for internal reporting purposes and an income statement for external reporting purposes. Your boss has also requested that you determine the company's gross profit percentage based on the statements that you are to prepare. The following adjusted trial balance was created from the general ledger accounts on May 31, 2007.

Account Titles	Debit	Credit
Cash	$ 57,000	
Accounts receivable	67,000	
Inventory	103,000	
Property and equipment	252,000	
Accumulated depreciation		$103,000
Liabilities		75,000
Contributed capital		120,000
Retained earnings, June 1, 2006		145,900
Sales revenue		369,000
Sales returns and allowances	9,000	
Sales discounts	13,000	
Credit card discounts	1,500	
Cost of goods sold	248,000	
Selling expense	19,000	
Administrative expense	23,000	
General expenses	5,000	
Income tax expense	15,400	
Totals	$812,900	$812,900

Your boss wants you to create the spreadsheet in a way that automatically recalculates net sales and any other related amounts whenever changes are made to the contra-revenue accounts. To do this, you know that you'll have to use formulas throughout the worksheets and even import or link cells from one worksheet to another. Once again, your friend Billy is willing to help.

From: BillyTheTutor@yahoo.com
To: HairZed@hotmail.com
Cc:
Subject: Excel Help

Sounds like you are going to get some great experience this summer. Okay, to import a number from another spreadsheet, you first click on the cell where you want the number to appear. For example, if you want to enter the Net sales balance in the external income statement, click on the cell in the external income statement where the net sales number is supposed to appear. Enter the equals sign (=) and then click on the tab that takes you to the worksheet containing the internal income statement.

In that worksheet, click on the cell that contains the amount you want to import into the external income statement and then press enter. This will create a link from the internal income statement cell to the external income statement cell. Here's a screen shot showing the formula that will appear after you import the number.

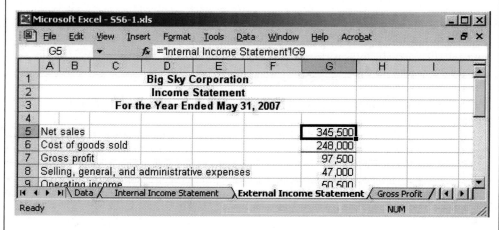

Don't forget to save the file using a name that indicates who you are.

Required:

Enter the trial balance information into a spreadsheet and complete the following:

1. Prepare a multistep income statement that would be used for internal reporting purposes. Classify sales returns and allowances, sales discounts, and credit card discounts as contra-revenue accounts.

2. Prepare a multistep income statement that would be used for external reporting purposes, beginning with the amount for *net sales*.

3. Compute the gross profit percentage.

COACHED PROBLEMS

LO2

CP6-1 Preparing a Bank Reconciliation and Journal Entries, and Reporting Cash

The bookkeeper at Hopkins Company has not reconciled the bank statement with the *Cash* account, saying, "I don't have time." You have been asked to prepare a bank reconciliation and review the procedures with the bookkeeper.

The April 30, 2006, bank statement and the April T-account for cash showed the following (summarized):

Bank Statement

	Checks	Deposits	Other	Balance
Balance, April 1, 2006				$25,850
Deposits during April		$37,050		62,900
Interest earned			$20	62,920
Checks cleared during April	$44,200			18,720
NSF checks—A. B. Wright			140	18,580
Bank service charges			50	18,530
Balance, April 30, 2006				18,530

	+ Cash (A) −			
Apr. 1 Balance	23,250	Apr.	Checks written	43,800
Apr. Deposits	42,000			

Hopkins Company's bank reconciliation at the end of March 2006 showed outstanding checks of $2,200. No deposits were in transit at the end of March, but a deposit was in transit at the end of April.

Required:

1. Prepare a bank reconciliation for April.
2. Prepare any journal entries required as a result of the bank reconciliation. Why are they necessary?
3. After the reconciliation journal entries are posted, what balance will be reflected in the *Cash* account in the ledger?
4. If the company also has $100 on hand, which is recorded in a different account called *Cash on Hand*, what total amount of cash should be reported on the balance sheet at the end of April?

CP6-2 Identifying Outstanding Checks and Deposits in Transit and Preparing a Bank Reconciliation and Journal Entries

LO2

The August 2006 bank statement for Martha Company and the cash T-account for August 2006 follow:

Bank Statement

Date	Checks	Deposits	Other	Balance
Aug.1				$17,470
2	$300			17,170
3		$12,000		29,170
4	400			28,770
5	250			28,520
9	890			27,630
10	310			27,320
15		4,000		31,320
21	400			30,920
24	21,000			9,920
25		7,000		16,920
30	800			16,120
30			Interest earned $20	16,140
31			Service charge 10	16,130

COACH'S CORNER

Put a check mark beside each item that appears on both the bank statement and what's already recorded in the accounting records (either in the T-account this month or the outstanding items from last month). Any item in the accounting records without check marks should appear on the bank statement side of the bank reconciliation. Any items in the bank statement without check marks should appear on the company's books side of the bank reconciliation.

	+ Cash (A) −		
Aug. 1 Balance	16,520	Checks written	
Deposits		Aug. 2	310
Aug. 2	12,000	4	890
12	4,000	15	290
24	7,000	17	550
31	5,000	18	800
		18	400
		23	21,000

Outstanding checks at the end of July were for $250, $400, and $300. No deposits were in transit at the end of July.

Required:

1. Identify and list the deposits in transit at the end of August.
2. Identify and list the outstanding checks at the end of August.
3. Prepare a bank reconciliation for August.
4. Give any journal entries that the company should make as a result of the bank reconciliation. Why are they necessary?
5. After the reconciliation journal entries are posted, what balance will be reflected in the *Cash* account in the ledger?
6. If the company also has $100 on hand, which is recorded in a different account called *Cash on Hand*, what total amount of cash should be reported on the August 31, 2006, balance sheet?

LO5, LO6

CP6-3 Preparing a Multistep Income Statement with Sales Discounts and Sales Returns and Allowances and Computing the Gross Profit Percentage

Psymon Company, Inc., sells heavy construction equipment. The annual fiscal period ends on December 31. The following adjusted trial balance was created from the general ledger accounts on December 31, 2006:

COACH'S CORNER

Remember that contra-revenue accounts are rarely reported in financial statements used for external reporting.

Account Titles	Debit	Credit
Cash	$ 42,000	
Accounts receivable	18,000	
Inventory	65,000	
Property and equipment	50,000	
Accumulated depreciation		$ 21,000
Liabilities		30,000
Contributed capital		90,000
Retained earnings, January 1, 2006		11,600
Sales revenue		182,000
Sales returns and allowances	7,000	
Sales discounts	8,000	
Cost of goods sold	98,000	
Selling expense	17,000	
Administrative expense	18,000	
General expenses	2,000	
Income tax expense	9,600	
Totals	$334,600	$334,600

Required:

1. Prepare a multistep income statement that would be used for internal reporting purposes. Treat sales discounts as a contra-revenue.

2. Prepare a multistep income statement that would be used for external reporting purposes, beginning with the amount for *net sales*.

3. Compute the gross profit percentage and explain its meaning.

LO4, LO5

CP6-4 Recording Sales and Purchases with Discounts and Returns

Campus Stop, Incorporated, is a student co-op. Campus Stop uses a perpetual inventory system. The following transactions (summarized) have been selected from 2007:

COACH'S CORNER

Inventory includes only merchandise purchased for sale. Other purchases, such as supplies for internal use, are recorded in separate accounts.

a.	Sold merchandise for cash (cost of merchandise $137,500).	$275,000
b.	Received merchandise returned by customers as unsatisfactory, for cash refund (original cost of merchandise $800).	1,600
	Purchased items from suppliers on credit:	
c.	Purchased merchandise from Super Supply Company with terms 3/10, n/30.	5,000
d.	Purchased merchandise from other suppliers with terms 3/10, n/30.	120,000
e.	Purchased equipment for use in store; paid cash.	2,200
f.	Purchased office supplies for future use in the store; paid cash.	700
g.	Freight on merchandise purchased; paid cash.	400
	Paid accounts payable in full during the period as follows:	
h.	Paid Super Supply Company after the discount period.	5,000
i.	Paid other suppliers within the 3 percent discount period.	116,400

Required:

Prepare journal entries for each of the preceding transactions.

CP6-5 Reporting Sales and Purchase Transactions between Wholesale and Retail Merchandisers, with Sales/Purchase Allowances and Sales/Purchase Discounts Using Perpetual Inventory Systems

The transactions listed below are typical of those involving Ghostmaker Garments and First Fashions. Ghostmaker is a wholesale merchandiser and First Fashions is a retail merchandiser. Assume the following transactions between the two companies occurred in the order listed during the year ended December 31, 2007. Assume all sales of merchandise from Ghostmaker to First Fashions are made with terms 2/10, n/30, and that the two companies use perpetual inventory systems.

Transactions during 2007:

a. Ghostmaker sold merchandise to First Fashions at a selling price of $230,000. The merchandise had cost Ghostmaker $175,000.
b. Two days later, First Fashions complained to Ghostmaker that some of the merchandise differed from what First Fashions had ordered. Ghostmaker agreed to give an allowance of $5,000 to First Fashions.
c. Just three days later, First Fashions paid Ghostmaker, which settled all amounts owed.

Required:

1. For each of the events *a* through *c*, indicate the amount and direction of the effect (+ for increase, − for decrease, and NE for no effect) on Ghostmaker Garments in terms of the following items.

Sales Revenues	Sales Returns and Allowances	Sales Discounts	Net Sales	Cost of Goods Sold	Gross Profit

2. Which of the above items are likely to be reported on Ghostmaker's external financial statements, and which items will be combined "behind the scenes."
3. Indicate the effect (direction and amount) of each transaction on the balance in First Fashions' inventory account.

CP6-6 Journalizing Sales and Purchase Transactions between Wholesale and Retail Merchandisers, with Sales/Purchase Allowances and Sales/Purchase Discounts Using Perpetual Inventory Systems

Use the information presented in CP6-5 to complete the following requirements.

Required:

1. Prepare the journal entries that Ghostmaker Garments would record, and show any computations.
2. Prepare the journal entries that First Fashions would record, and show any computations.

CP6-7 (Supplement) Journalizing Sales and Purchase Transactions between Wholesale and Retail Merchandisers, with Sales/Purchase Allowances and Sales/Purchase Discounts Using Periodic Inventory Systems

Use the information presented in CP6-5 and transaction *a* (only) to complete the following requirements, except assume that both companies use periodic inventory systems.

Required:

1. Prepare the journal entry (or entries) that Ghostmaker Garments would record for transaction *a* only.
2. Prepare the journal entry (or entries) that First Fashions would record for transaction *a* only.
3. Assume that, during the year, First Fashions sold merchandise on credit for $160,000. Prepare the journal entry (or entries) that First Fashions would record.
4. Assume that, at the end of the year, First Fashions counted the inventory on hand that had been purchased from Ghostmaker Garments and determined that its cost was $80,000. Prepare any journal entries that First Fashions would record, and show any computations.

LO4–LO6

COACH'S CORNER

1a. Gross profit is a subtotal which is affected when a company records sales and cost of goods sold.
1b. When an allowance is granted and no inventory is returned, the seller records only one journal entry.

LO4, LO5

COACH'S CORNER

When using a perpetual inventory system, the seller always makes two journal entries when goods are sold.

COACH'S CORNER

When using a periodic inventory system, the seller only makes one journal entry when goods are sold.

LO2

PA6-1 Preparing a Bank Reconciliation and Journal Entries, and Reporting Cash

The bookkeeper at Martin Company has asked you to prepare a bank reconciliation as of May 31, 2007. The May 31, 2007, bank statement and the May T-account for cash showed the following (summarized):

Bank Statement

	Checks	Deposits	Other	Balance
Balance, May 1, 2007				$11,500
Deposits during May		$18,000		29,500
Interest earned			$120	29,620
Checks cleared during May	$22,100			7,520
NSF checks—B. A. Dugry				
(customer)			280	7,240
Bank service charges			60	7,180
Balance, May 31, 2007				7,180

		+ Cash (A) −			
May 1	Balance	8,800	May	Checks written	23,400
May	Deposits	22,000			

Martin Company's bank reconciliation at the end of April 2006 showed outstanding checks of $2,700. No deposits were in transit at the end of April, but a deposit was in transit at the end of May.

Required:

1. Prepare a bank reconciliation for May.
2. Prepare any journal entries required as a result of the bank reconciliation. Why are they necessary?
3. After the reconciliation journal entries are posted, what balance will be reflected in the *Cash* account in the ledger?
4. If the company also has $50 on hand, which is recorded in a different account called *Cash on Hand*, what total amount of cash should be reported on the balance sheet at the end of May?

LO2

PA6-2 Identifying Outstanding Checks and Deposits in Transit and Preparing a Bank Reconciliation and Journal Entries

The December 2006 bank statement for Stewart Company and the cash T-account for December 2006 follow:

Bank Statement

Date	Checks	Deposits	Other		Balance
Dec. 1					$48,000
2	$400; 300	$17,000			64,300
4	7,000; 90				57,210
6	120; 180; 1,600				55,310
11	500; 1,200; 70	28,000			81,540
13	480; 700; 1,900				78,460
17	12,000; 8,000				58,460
23	60; 23,500	36,000			70,900
26	900; 2,650				67,350
28	2,200; 5,200				59,950
30	17,000; 1,890	19,000	NSF*	$300	59,760
31	1,650; 1,350		Interest earned	50	
			Service charge	150	56,660

*NSF check from J. Left, a customer.

```
                         + Cash (A) −
Dec. 1   Balance      64,100 │ Checks written during December:
Deposits                     │    60      5,000    2,650
Dec.     11    28,000        │ 17,000     5,200    1,650
         23    36,000        │   700      1,890    2,200
         30    19,000        │  3,300     1,600    7,000
         31    13,000        │  1,350      120      300
                             │   180       90       480
                             │ 12,000    23,500    8,000
                             │    70       500     1,900
                             │   900      1,200
```

The November 2006 bank reconciliation showed the following: up-to-date cash balance at November 30, $64,100; deposits in transit on November 30, $17,000; and outstanding checks on November 30, $400 + $500 = $900.

Required:

1. Identify and list the deposits in transit at the end of December.
2. Identify and list the outstanding checks at the end of December.
3. Prepare a bank reconciliation for December.
4. Give any journal entries that the company should make as a result of the bank reconciliation. Why are they necessary?
5. After the reconciliation journal entries are posted, what balance will be reflected in the *Cash* account in the ledger?
6. If the company also has $300 on hand, which is recorded in a different account called *Cash on Hand*, what total amount of cash should be reported on the December 31, 2006, balance sheet?

PA6-3 Preparing a Multistep Income Statement with Sales Discounts and Sales Returns and Allowances and Computing the Gross Profit Percentage

LO5, LO6

Big Tommy Corporation is a local grocery store organized seven years ago as a corporation. The store is in an excellent location, and sales have increased each year. At the end of 2006, the bookkeeper prepared the following statement (assume that all amounts are correct, but note the incorrect terminology and format):

BIG TOMMY CORPORATION Profit and Loss December 31, 2006		
	Debit	**Credit**
Sales		$420,000
Cost of goods sold	$279,000	
Sales returns and allowances	10,000	
Sales discounts	6,000	
Selling expense	58,000	
Administrative expense	16,000	
General expenses	1,000	
Income tax expense	15,000	
Net profit	35,000	
Totals	$420,000	$420,000

Required:

1. Prepare a multistep income statement that would be used for internal reporting purposes. Treat sales discounts as a contra-revenue.
2. Prepare a multistep income statement that would be used for external reporting purposes, beginning with the amount for *net sales*.
3. Compute the gross profit percentage and explain its meaning.

LO4, LO5

PA6-4 Recording Sales and Purchases with Discounts and Returns

Hair World Inc. is a wholesaler of hair supplies. Hair World uses a perpetual inventory system. The following transactions (summarized) have been selected from 2007:

a.	Sold merchandise for cash (cost of merchandise $30,600).	$51,200
b.	Received merchandise returned by customers as unsatisfactory, for cash refund (original cost of merchandise $360).	600

Purchased items from suppliers on credit:

c.	Purchased merchandise from Cari's Comb Company with terms 3/10, n/30.	1,000
d.	Purchased merchandise from other suppliers with terms 3/10, n/30.	24,000
e.	Purchased equipment for use in store; paid cash.	400
f.	Purchased office supplies for future use in the store; paid cash.	140
g.	Freight on merchandise purchased; paid cash.	100

Paid accounts payable in full during the period as follows:

h.	Paid Cari's Comb Company after the discount period.	1,000
i.	Paid other suppliers within the 3 percent discount period.	23,280

Required:

Prepare journal entries for each of the preceding transactions.

LO4–LO6

eXcel

PA6-5 Reporting Sales and Purchase Transactions between Wholesale and Retail Merchandisers, with Sales/Purchase Allowances and Sales/Purchase Discounts Using Perpetual Inventory Systems

The transactions listed below are typical of those involving New Books Inc. and Readers' Corner. New Books is a wholesale merchandiser and Readers' Corner is a retail merchandiser. Assume the following transactions between the two companies occurred in the order listed during the year ended August 31, 2007. Assume all sales of merchandise from New Books to Readers' Corner are made with terms 2/10, n/30, and that the two companies use perpetual inventory systems.

Transactions during the year ended August 31, 2007:

a. New Books sold merchandise to Readers' Corner at a selling price of $550,000. The merchandise had cost New Books $415,000.
b. Two days later, Readers' Corner complained to New Books that some of the merchandise differed from what Readers' Corner had ordered. New Books agreed to give an allowance of $10,000 to Readers' Corner.
c. Just three days later, Readers' Corner paid New Books, which settled all amounts owed.

Required:

1. For each of the events *a* through *c*, indicate the amount and direction of the effect (+ for increase, − for decrease, and NE for no effect) on New Books in terms of the following items.

Sales Revenues	Sales Returns and Allowances	Sales Discounts	Net Sales	Cost of Goods Sold	Gross Profit

2. Which of the above items are likely to be reported on New Books' external financial statements, and which items will be combined "behind the scenes."
3. Indicate the effect (direction and amount) of each transaction on the balance in Readers' Corner's inventory account.

LO4, LO5

PA6-6 Journalizing Sales and Purchase Transactions between Wholesale and Retail Merchandisers, with Sales/Purchase Allowances and Sales/Purchase Discounts Using Perpetual Inventory Systems

Use the information presented in PA6-5 to complete the following requirements.

Required:

1. Prepare the journal entries that New Books would record, and show any computations.
2. Prepare the journal entries that Readers' Corner would record, and show any computations.

PA6-7 (Supplement) Journalizing Sales and Purchase Transactions between Wholesale and Retail Merchandisers, with Sales/Purchase Allowances and Sales/Purchase Discounts Using Periodic Inventory Systems

Use the information presented in PA6-5 and transaction *a* (only) to complete the following requirements, except assume that both companies use periodic inventory systems.

Required:

1. Prepare the journal entries that New Books would record for transaction *a* only.
2. Prepare the journal entries that Readers' Corner would record for transaction *a* only.
3. Assume that, during the year, Readers' Corner sold merchandise on credit for $250,000. Prepare the journal entries that Readers' Corner would record.
4. Assume that, at the end of the year, Readers' Corner counted the inventory it had purchased from New Books and determined that its cost was $135,000. Prepare any journal entries that Readers' Corner would record, and show any computations.

GROUP B PROBLEMS

PB6-1 Preparing a Bank Reconciliation and Journal Entries, and Reporting Cash   LO2

The bookkeeper at Tony Company has asked you to prepare a bank reconciliation as of February 28, 2006. The February 28, 2006, bank statement and the February T-account for cash showed the following (summarized):

Bank Statement

	Checks	Deposits	Other	Balance
Balance, February 1, 2006				$52,600
Deposits during February		$30,650		83,250
Interest earned			$150	83,400
Checks cleared during February	$49,200			34,200
NSF checks—S. H. Schaffer			320	33,880
Bank service charges			40	33,840
Balance, February 28, 2006				33,840

+ Cash (A) −					
Feb. 1	Balance	49,400	Feb.	Checks written	50,400
Feb.	Deposits	38,450			

Tony Company's bank reconciliation at the end of January 2006, showed outstanding checks of $3,200. No deposits were in transit at the end of January, but a deposit was in transit at the end of February.

Required:

1. Prepare a bank reconciliation for February.
2. Prepare any journal entries required as a result of the bank reconciliation. Why are they necessary?
3. After the reconciliation journal entries are posted, what balance will be reflected in the *Cash* account in the ledger?
4. If the company also has $50 on hand, which is recorded in a different account called *Cash on Hand*, what total amount of cash should be reported on the balance sheet at the end of February?

PB6-2 Identifying Outstanding Checks and Deposits in Transit and Preparing a Bank   LO2
Reconciliation and Journal Entries

The September 2007 bank statement for Terrick Company and the cash T-account for September 2007 follow:

Bank Statement

Date	Checks	Deposits	Other		Balance
Sept.1					$75,900
2	$620; 550	$25,000			99,730
4	2,000; 200				97,530
6	1,500; 870; 21,000				74,160
11	300; 1,500; 600	14,000			85,760
13	650; 600; 6,550				77,960
17	10,000; 9,000				58,960
23	90; 500	27,000			85,370
26	700; 3,220				81,450
28	8,000; 8,200				65,250
29	730; 3,200	17,000	NSF*	$500	77,820
30	400; 4,400		Interest earned	60	
			Service charge	40	73,040

*NSF check from B. Frank, a customer.

	+ Cash (A) −			
Sept. 1 Balance	98,780	Checks written during September:		
Deposits		730	8,000	3,220
Sept. 11	14,000	21,000	200	550
23	27,000	600	3,680	4,400
29	17,000	700	650	9,000
30	21,000	6,550	3,200	600
		560	500	840
		2,000	8,200	10,000
		90	300	400
		870	1,500	

The August 2007 bank reconciliation showed the following: up-to-date cash balance at August 30, $98,780; deposits in transit on August 31, $25,000; and outstanding checks on August 31, $620 + $1,500 = $2,120.

Required:

1. Identify and list the deposits in transit at the end of September.
2. Identify and list the outstanding checks at the end of September.
3. Prepare a bank reconciliation for September.
4. Give any journal entries that the company should make as a result of the bank reconciliation. Why are they necessary?
5. After the reconciliation journal entries are posted, what balance will be reflected in the *Cash* account in the ledger?
6. If the company also has $200 on hand, which is recorded in a different account called *Cash on Hand*, what total amount of cash should be reported on the September 30, 2007, balance sheet?

LO5, LO6   **PB6-3 Preparing a Multistep Income Statement with Sales Discounts and Sales Returns and Allowances and Computing the Gross Profit Percentage**

Emily's Greenhouse Corporation is a local greenhouse organized 10 years ago as a corporation. The greenhouse is in an excellent location, and sales have increased each year. At the end of 2007, the bookkeeper prepared the following statement (assume that all amounts are correct, but note the incorrect terminology and format):

EMILY'S GREENHOUSE CORPORATION		
Profit and Loss		
December 31, 2007		
	Debit	**Credit**
Sales		$504,000
Cost of goods sold	$311,000	
Sales returns and allowances	11,000	

Sales discounts	8,000	
Selling expense	61,000	
Administrative expense	13,000	
General expenses	3,000	
Income tax expense	18,000	
Net profit	79,000	
Totals	$504,000	$504,000

Required:

1. Prepare a multistep income statement that would be used for internal reporting purposes. Treat sales discounts as a contra-revenue.

2. Prepare a multistep income statement that would be used for external reporting purposes, beginning with the amount for *net sales*.

3. Compute the gross profit percentage and explain its meaning.

PB6-4 Recording Sales and Purchases with Discounts and Returns

LO4, LO5

Larry's Hardware, Incorporated, is a locally owned and operated hardware store. Larry's Hardware uses a perpetual inventory system.

The following transactions (summarized) have been selected from 2007:

a.	Sold merchandise for cash (cost of merchandise $325,000).	$500,000
b.	Received merchandise returned by customers as unsatisfactory, for cash refund (original cost of merchandise $1,900).	3,000

Purchased items from suppliers on credit:

c.	Purchased merchandise from Do It Yourself Company with terms 3/10, n/30.	27,000
d.	Purchased merchandise from other suppliers with terms 3/10, n/30.	237,000
e.	Purchased equipment for use in store; paid cash.	5,000
f.	Purchased office supplies for future use in the store; paid cash.	400
g.	Freight on merchandise purchased; paid cash.	350

Paid accounts payable in full during the period as follows:

h.	Paid Do It Yourself Company after the discount period.	27,000
i.	Paid other suppliers within the 3 percent discount period.	229,890

Required:

Prepare journal entries for each of the preceding transactions.

PB6-5 Reporting Sales and Purchase Transactions between Wholesale and Retail Merchandisers, with Sales/Purchase Allowances and Sales/Purchase Discounts Using Perpetual Inventory Systems

LO4–LO6

The transactions listed below are typical of those involving Southern Sporting Goods and Sports R Us. Southern Sporting Goods is a wholesale merchandiser and Sports R Us is a retail merchandiser. Assume the following transactions between the two companies occurred in the order listed during the year ended December 31, 2007. Assume all sales of merchandise from Southern Sporting Goods to Sports R Us are made with terms 2/10, n/30, and that the two companies use perpetual inventory systems.

Transactions during 2007:

a. Southern Sporting Goods sold merchandise to Sports R Us at a selling price of $125,000. The merchandise had cost Southern Sporting Goods $94,000.

b. Two days later, Sports R Us complained to Southern Sporting Goods that some of the merchandise differed from what Sports R Us had ordered. Southern Sporting Goods agreed to give an allowance of $3,000 to Sports R Us.

c. Just three days later Sports R Us paid Southern Sporting Goods, which settled all amounts owed.

Required:

1. For each of the events *a* through *c*, indicate the amount and direction of the effect (+ for increase, − for decrease, and NE for no effect) on Southern Sporting Goods in terms of the following items.

Sales Revenues	Sales Returns and Allowances	Sales Discounts	Net Sales	Cost of Goods Sold	Gross Profit

2. Which of the above items are likely to be reported on Southern Sporting Goods' external financial statements, and which items will be combined "behind the scenes."
3. Indicate the effect (direction and amount) of each transaction on the balance in Sports R Us' inventory account.

LO4, LO5   **PB6-6 Journalizing Sales and Purchase Transactions between Wholesale and Retail Merchandisers, with Sales/Purchase Allowances and Sales/Purchase Discounts Using Perpetual Inventory Systems**

Use the information presented in PB6-5 to complete the following requirements.

Required:

1. Prepare the journal entries that Southern Sporting Goods would record, and show any computations.
2. Prepare the journal entries that Sports R Us would record, and show any computations.

PB6-7 (Supplement) Journalizing Sales and Purchase Transactions between Wholesale and Retail Merchandisers, with Sales/Purchase Allowances and Sales/Purchase Discounts Using Periodic Inventory Systems

Use the information presented in PB6-5 and transaction *a* (only) to complete the following requirements, except assume that both companies use periodic inventory systems.

Required:

1. Prepare the journal entries that Southern Sporting Goods would record for transaction *a* only.
2. Prepare the journal entries that Sports R Us would record for transaction *a* only.
3. Assume that, during the year, Sports R Us sold merchandise on credit for $97,000. Prepare the journal entries that Sports R Us would record.
4. Assume that, at the end of the year, Sports R Us counted the inventory it had purchased from Southern Sporting Goods and determined that its cost was $43,000. Prepare any journal entries that Sports R Us would record, and show any computations.

CASES & DISCUSSION STARTERS

FINANCIAL REPORTING AND ANALYSIS CASES

LO2, LO3, LO6   **C&DS6-1 Finding Financial Information**

Refer to the financial statements of Landry's Restaurants in Appendix A at the end of this book, or download the annual report from the *Cases* section of the text's Web site at www.mhhe.com/phillips.

Required:

1. How much cash (including cash equivalents) does the company report at the end of the current year?
2. Assuming that *cost of revenues* is the same thing as cost of goods sold, compute the company's gross profit percentage for the most recent two years. Has it risen or fallen? Explain the meaning of the change.
3. Assume that Landry's experienced no shrinkage in the most current year. Using the balance sheet and income statement, estimate the amount of purchases in the most recent year.

C&DS6-2 Comparing Financial Information

LO2, LO3, LO6

Refer to the financial statements of Dave & Buster's in Appendix B at the end of this book, or download the annual report from the *Cases* section of the text's Web site at www.mhhe.com/phillips. Note that Dave & Buster's ends its fiscal year on February 1, 2004, which doesn't perfectly match Landry's year ended December 31, 2003. In the questions that follow, assume Dave & Buster's financial statements for the year ended February 1, 2004, present the results for 2003. (This is a reasonable assumption given that Dave & Buster's fiscal year simply replaces January 2003 with January 2004.)

1. Does Dave & Buster's report more or less cash (including cash equivalents) than Landry's at the end of the year?

2. Assuming that *cost of revenues* is the same thing as cost of goods sold, compute the company's gross profit percentage for the most recent two years. Is it greater or less than Landry's? Explain the meaning of the comparison.

3. Assume that Dave & Buster's experienced no shrinkage in the most recent year. Using the balance sheet and income statement, estimate the amount of purchases in the most recent year. How much greater (or less) were Dave & Buster's purchases than Landry's for the most recent year?

C&DS6-3 Internet-Based Team Research: Examining an Annual Report

LO1, LO6, LO7

As a team, select an industry to analyze. Using your Web browser, each team member should acquire the annual report or 10-K for one publicly traded company in the industry, with each member selecting a different company. (See C&DS1-3 in Chapter 1 for a description of possible resources for these tasks.)

TEAM CASE

Required:

1. On an individual basis, each team member should write a short report that incorporates the following:
   a. Describe the company's business in sufficient detail to be able to classify it as a service, merchandising, or manufacturing company. What products or services does the company provide?
   b. Calculate the gross profit percentage at the end of the current and prior year, and explain any change between the two years.

2. Then, as a team, write a short report comparing and contrasting your companies using these attributes. Discuss any patterns across the companies that you as a team observe. Provide potential explanations for any differences discovered.

ETHICS AND CRITICAL THINKING CASES

C&DS6-4 Ethical Decision Making: A Real-Life Example

LO1, LO3

ETHICAL

When some people think about inventory theft, they imagine a shoplifter running out of a store with goods stuffed inside a jacket or bag. But that's not what the managers thought at the Famous Footwear store on Chicago's Madison Street. No, they suspected their own employees were the main cause of their unusually high shrinkage. One scam involved dishonest cashiers who would let their friends take a pair of Skechers without paying for them. To make it look like the shoes had been bought, cashiers would ring up a sale, but instead of charging $50 for shoes, they would charge only $2 for a bottle of shoe polish. That's when the company's managers decided to put its accounting system to work. In just two years, the company cut its Madison Street inventory losses in half. Here's how a newspaper described the store's improvements:

ISSUE

> **Retailers Crack Down on Employee Theft**
> *SouthCoast Today,* September 10, 2000, Chicago
> By Calmetta Coleman, *Wall Street Journal* Staff Writer
>
> . . . Famous Footwear installed a chainwide register-monitoring system to sniff out suspicious transactions, such as unusually large numbers of refunds or voids, or repeated sales of cheap goods. *(continues)*

... [B]efore an employee can issue a cash refund, a second worker must be present to see the customer and inspect the merchandise.

... [T]he chain has set up a toll-free hotline for employees to use to report suspicions about co-workers.

These improvements in inventory control came as welcome news for investors and creditors of Brown Shoe Company, the company that owns Famous Footwear. Despite these improvements at the Chicago store, Brown Shoe has been forced to shut down operations in other cities.

Required:

1. Explain how the register-monitoring system would allow Famous Footwear to cut down on employee theft.
2. What is the name of the control and the financial reporting control objective that is addressed by Famous Footwear's new cash refund procedure?
3. If Famous Footwear used a periodic inventory system, rather than a perpetual inventory system, how would the company detect shrinkage?
4. Think of and describe at least four different parties that are harmed by the type of inventory theft described in this case.

LO5, LO6

ETHICAL

ISSUE

C&DS6-5 Ethical Decision Making: A Mini-Case

Assume you work as an accountant in the merchandising division of a large public company that makes and sells athletic clothing. To encourage the merchandising division to earn as much profit on each individual sale as possible, the division manager's pay is based, in part, on the division's gross profit percentage. To encourage control over the division's operating expenses, the manager's pay also is based on the division's net income.

You are currently preparing the division's financial statements. The division had a good year, with sales of $100,000, cost of goods sold of $50,000, sales returns and allowances of $5,000, sales discounts of $2,000, credit card discounts of $3,000, and other selling expenses of $30,000. (Assume the division does not report income taxes.) The division manager stresses that "*it would be in your personal interest*" to classify sales returns and allowances, credit card discounts, and sales discounts as selling expenses rather than as contra-revenues on the division's income statement. He justifies this "friendly advice" by saying that he's not asking you to fake the numbers—he just believes that those items are more accurately reported as expenses. Plus, he claims, being a division of a larger company, you don't have to follow GAAP.

Required:

1. Prepare an income statement for the division using the classifications shown in this chapter. Using this income statement, calculate the division's gross profit percentage.
2. Prepare an income statement for the division using the classifications advised by the manager. Using this income statement, calculate the division's gross profit percentage.
3. What reason (other than reporting "more accurately") do you think is motivating the manager's advice to you?
4. Do you agree with the manager's statement that "he's not asking you to fake the numbers"?
5. Do you agree with the manager's statement about not having to follow GAAP?
6. How should you respond to the division manager's "friendly advice"?

LO1, LO2

C&DS6-6 Critical Thinking: Analyzing

Cripple Creek Company has one trusted employee who, as the owner said, "handles all of the bookkeeping and paperwork for the company." This employee is responsible for counting, verifying, and recording cash receipts and payments, making the weekly bank deposit, preparing checks for major expenditures (signed by the owner), making small expenditures from the cash register for daily expenses, and collecting accounts receivable. The owners asked the local bank for a $20,000 loan. The bank asked that an audit be performed covering the year just ended. The independent auditor (a local CPA), in a private conference with the owner, presented some evidence of the following activities of the trusted employee during the past year:

a. Cash sales sometimes were not entered in the cash register, and the trusted employee pocketed approximately $50 per month.

b. Cash taken from the cash register (and pocketed by the trusted employee) was replaced with expense memos with fictitious signatures (approximately $12 per day).

c. $300 collected on an account receivable from a valued out-of-town customer was pocketed by the trusted employee and was covered by making a $300 entry as a debit to *Sales Returns* and a credit to *Accounts Receivable*.

d. $800 collected on an account receivable from a local customer was pocketed by the trusted employee and was covered by making an $800 entry as a debit to *Sales Discounts* and a credit to *Accounts Receivable*.

Required:

1. What was the approximate amount stolen during the past year?
2. What would be your recommendations to the owner?

chapter seven

Reporting and Interpreting Receivables, Bad Debt Expense, and Interest Revenue

INSIDE LOOKING OUT

OUTSIDE LOOKING IN

This chapter focuses on how to account for receivables and the cost of bad debts. We focus on Skechers USA, a designer and marketer of footwear for men, women, and children.

One of the most challenging parts of your academic and professional careers will involve managing things that you can't completely control. For example, think about a group project that you have to complete this term. You might believe that, in theory, the work should take only six days from start to finish. But you know from experience that someone in your group is likely to be late with the assigned work or not complete his or her task at all. The problem is you don't know for sure which particular group member will be late, nor do you know how late that person will be—these matters are largely beyond your control. To allow for the possibility that someone will be late, you might set a shorter time period (say four days) for group members to finish their work. By subtracting this two-day allowance, you'll have a realistic basis for planning and successfully completing the group project.

This situation is similar to a problem faced by many companies, including **SKECHERS,** a shoe company that sells to Foot Locker and about 3,000 other companies. When Skechers sells to a company on account, it's not clear whether that customer will actually pay on time and, more important, it's not clear whether the customer will even pay at all. Skechers' managers know from experience that some customers won't end up paying what they owe. The problem is that, at the time a sale is made, it's not possible to identify who these "bad" customers are. In the rest of this chapter you'll learn about a method of accounting for these uncertainties that is similar to the allowance approach described above for your group project. This method allows Skechers' managers to report in a timely manner how much money their company is likely to collect from customers, which gives financial statement users a realistic basis for making decisions.

Skechers sells more than 1,500 styles, in over 100 countries and territories.

T he most important topics in this chapter are summarized in Exhibit 7.1 as learning objectives. You'll learn about key tradeoffs managers consider when they decide whether to allow sales on account, how the business decision to extend credit affects accounting methods, the analyses that financial statement users rely on to evaluate **accounts receivable** management practices, and how these analyses can be affected by decisions made when accounting for accounts receivable.

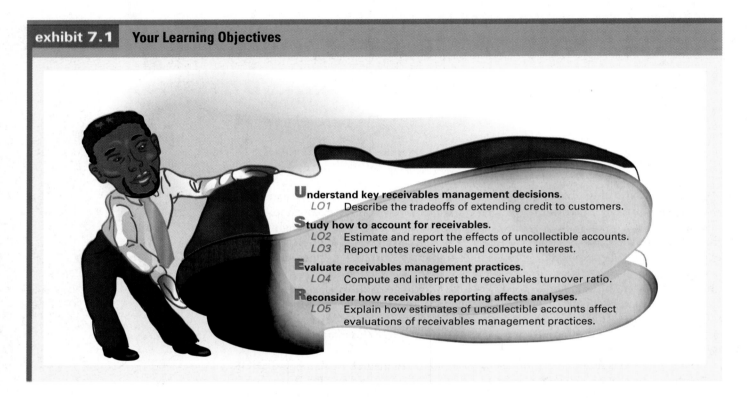

exhibit 7.1   **Your Learning Objectives**

Understand key receivables management decisions.
    LO1   Describe the tradeoffs of extending credit to customers.

Study how to account for receivables.
    LO2   Estimate and report the effects of uncollectible accounts.
    LO3   Report notes receivable and compute interest.

Evaluate receivables management practices.
    LO4   Compute and interpret the receivables turnover ratio.

Reconsider how receivables reporting affects analyses.
    LO5   Explain how estimates of uncollectible accounts affect evaluations of receivables management practices.

UNDERSTAND

KEY RECEIVABLES MANAGEMENT DECISIONS

The Pros and Cons of Extending Credit to Customers

Although Skechers operates a few stores at which it sells directly to consumers, over 75 percent of its sales are made to other companies (called retailers), who in turn sell to consumers.[1] A key issue for Skechers' managers is to decide whether to extend credit to these retail companies. If Skechers decides not to allow sales on account, these companies are likely to buy instead from Timberland, Kenneth Cole, Reebok, or Nike. To be in the running to get business from these retailers, Skechers will need to consider extending credit to them. When making this decision, Skechers' managers realize that by extending credit the company will incur the following additional costs:

1. ***Increased employee costs.*** Skechers will need employees to (*a*) evaluate whether each customer is creditworthy, (*b*) track how much each customer owes, and (*c*) follow up to ensure they collect the receivable from each customer.

2. ***Bad debt costs.*** Inevitably, some customers dispute what they owe and pay only a portion of the total amount that they've been charged. In extreme circumstances (such as a retailer's bankruptcy), Skechers may never collect the amount that is

---

[1]Skechers U.S.A., Inc., 2003 Form 10-K.

receivable from the customer. These "bad debts," as they are called, can be a significant additional cost of extending credit.

3. **Delayed receipt of cash.** Even if Skechers were to collect in full from customers, it will likely have to wait 30–60 days before receiving the cash. During this period of time, it's possible Skechers would have to take out a short-term bank loan to obtain cash for other business activities. The interest on such a loan would be another cost of extending credit to customers.

Most managers find that the sales revenue (or, more accurately, the gross profit) to be gained from selling on account is greater than the additional costs listed above. They attempt to control these costs by using accounting records, which we discuss in the next section, to carefully screen and monitor customers.

In cases where a customer is having difficulty paying its balance, Skechers could establish a formal repayment schedule for the customer, which essentially converts the account receivable into a "note receivable." A **note receivable** is a formal contract stating (1) specified payments to be received at definite future dates and (2) a specified rate of interest, which is charged on the outstanding balance. By converting from an account receivable to a note receivable, Skechers establishes in writing its legal right to collect the original amount owed plus any additional interest charged by Skechers. In our examples below, we show how interest is charged and recorded on unpaid notes receivable. (We'll save you the trouble of learning how to record interest on unpaid accounts receivable by simply telling you it's basically the same as for notes receivable.)

FAST FLASHBACK

Gross profit is the amount by which the selling price exceeds the cost of goods sold.

YOU SHOULD KNOW

A **note receivable** is a promise that requires another party to pay the business according to a written agreement.

STUDY

HOW TO ACCOUNT FOR RECEIVABLES

In this section, we describe how to account for Accounts Receivable and Notes Receivable. Exhibit 7.2 shows how Skechers reports these two accounts in its financial statements for the year ended December 31, 2003.

As you can see in the balance sheet excerpt in Exhibit 7.2, Skechers reported over $98 million in *Trade Accounts Receivable* and over $4.5 million in *Notes Receivable* at December 31, 2003. Notice that both of these items are classified as *current* assets, indicating that they are expected to be collected in cash sometime in 2004.

POINT OF INTEREST

Before cash was invented, business transactions involved trading assets or services. The term "trade" is still used today by some companies to describe receivables that arise in the ordinary course of business.

exhibit 7.2 | **Balance Sheet Disclosure of Receivables**

SKECHERS U.S.A., INC.
(Partial) Balance Sheet
December 31, 2003 and 2002
(in thousands)

Current Assets	2003	2002
Cash and Cash Equivalents	$113,479	$124,830
Trade Accounts Receivable, Less Allowances of $7,861 in 2003 and $8,498 in 2002	98,751	97,419
Notes Receivable	4,533	7,761
Inventories	137,917	147,984
Prepaid Expenses and Other Current Assets	17,987	15,482
Total Current Assets	**372,667**	**393,476**

The Allowance Method of Accounting for Accounts Receivable and Bad Debts

Notice in Exhibit 7.2 that trade accounts receivable were reported "less allowances." In this section, we explain what these allowances are and where they come from.

When Skechers extends credit to retail stores, like Foot Locker or Kohl's Department Stores, it knows that some of these customers are not likely to pay their debts. It's just like that friend of yours who *says* he'll pay you later, but for one reason or another, never gets around to it. Following the conservatism principle, accounting rules require that Skechers report accounts receivable at the amount it actually expects to collect rather than the total that it would collect if everyone paid. At the same time, the matching principle requires that all expenses, including the cost of bad debts, be recorded in the accounting period in which the related credit sales are made. These two principles point to the same solution: reduce both accounts receivable and net income by the amount of credit sales included this period in receivables and net income but which is unlikely to ever be converted into cash.

The only problem with this solution is that, just as it takes you a while to find out which friends you can't trust, some time will pass before Skechers discovers which particular credit sales and customer balances aren't going to be paid. More than likely, it will be discovered in an accounting period following the sale, rather than in the same period as the sale. Skechers resolves the problem and satisfies the conservatism and matching principles by using the **allowance method** to report uncollectible amounts. The allowance method uses a two-step process, which we walk through with you below:

1. **Record an estimated bad debt expense in the period in which the sale took place** by making an adjusting journal entry at the end of that period.
2. **Remove ("write off") specific customer balances in the period that they are determined to be uncollectible.**

1. Record Estimated Bad Debt Expense

Bad debt expense (also called doubtful accounts expense or uncollectible accounts expense) is an estimate of this period's credit sales that the company won't collect from customers. By reading the company's annual report, we learned that Skechers estimated bad debt expense for the year ended December 31, 2003, to be $7,318 (all numbers in thousands of dollars). The following adjusting journal entry would have been used to record this estimate at the end of the accounting period:[2]

dr	**Bad Debt Expense (+E, −SE)**	7,318
cr	**Allowance for Doubtful Accounts (+xA, −A)**	7,318

Assets	=	Liabilities	+	Stockholders' Equity
Allowance for Doubtful Accounts (+xA) −7,318				Bad Debt Expense (+E) −7,318

The credit in the journal entry could not be recorded to *Accounts Receivable* because, at the time the journal entry is prepared, there is no way to know which customers' accounts receivable are bad. So the credit is made, instead, to a contra-asset account called **Allowance for doubtful accounts** (also called allowance for bad debts, allowance for uncollectible accounts, reserve for bad debts, or simply allowance). As a contra-asset, the

---

[2]In this estimate, Skechers also includes estimated future sales returns and allowances. For ease of understanding, we refer to only the estimated bad debts. Skechers records estimated future sales returns and allowances in the same manner as estimated bad debts.

exhibit 7.3	Interpreting Gross and Net Receivables		
		2003	**Explanation**
Recorded in accounting records as . . .			
Gross accounts receivable		$106,612	Total amount owed to Skechers
Less: Allowance for doubtful accounts		(7,861)	Amount unlikely to be collected
Net accounts receivable		98,751	Amount likely to be collected
Reported on the balance sheet as . . .			
Trade accounts receivable, less allowance of $7,861 in 2003		98,751	Amount likely to be collected

balance in *Allowance for Doubtful Accounts* is subtracted from the balance of the asset *Accounts Receivable*, thereby reducing the reported accounts receivable without directly reducing a particular customer balance in that account. To make it clear which account we're talking about, we'll refer to the total amount receivable as Gross Accounts Receivable and we'll use the name Net Accounts Receivable to refer to the amount receivable after subtracting the allowance for doubtful accounts. The top part of Exhibit 7.3 shows this relationship using the amounts reported by Skechers at December 31, 2003. The bottom part shows how most companies report these amounts in the balance sheet.

2. Remove (Write Off) Specific Customer Balances

When it becomes clear that a particular customer will not pay its balance, Skechers will record a journal entry to remove the account receivable from its accounting records. With the receivable removed, there's no longer a need to include an allowance for it, so the corresponding amount also is removed from the allowance for doubtful accounts. This act of removing the uncollectible account and its corresponding allowance is called a **write-off.** Skechers reported in its annual report that, in 2003, it gave up all hopes of collecting customer accounts totaling $7,955. The journal entry to summarize Skechers' write-offs of these previously allowed for doubtful accounts is:

dr Allowance for Doubtful Accounts (−xA, +A) ..	7,955	
cr Accounts Receivable (−A)		7,955

Assets		=	Liabilities	+	Stockholders' Equity
Accounts Receivable	−7,955				
Allowance for Doubtful Accounts (−xA)	+7,955				

Notice in the above journal entry that the write-off did not affect income statement accounts. The estimated bad debt expense relating to these uncollectible accounts was already recorded with an adjusting journal entry in the period the sale was recorded, so there is no additional expense when the account is written off. Also, notice that the journal entry does not change the amount reported as Net accounts receivable because the decrease in Gross accounts receivable is offset by the decrease in the Allowance for doubtful accounts.

Recovery of an Uncollectible Account   In the same way that someone you've written off as a friend might do something to win you back, a customer might pay an account balance that was previously written off. Collection of a previously written off account is called a recovery and it is accounted for in two parts. First, put the receivable back on the books by recording a journal entry opposite to what was recorded to write off the account in the first place. Second, record the collection of the account. To illustrate, let's assume that Skechers collects $50 on an account that had been previously written off. This recovery would be recorded using the following journal entries:

(1)	dr	Accounts Receivable (+A)	50
	cr	Allowance for Doubtful Accounts (+xA, −A)		50
(2)	dr	Cash (+A)	50
	cr	Accounts Receivable (−A)		50

Assets	=	Liabilities	+	Stockholders' Equity
Cash +50				
Accounts Receivable +50 − 50 = no change				
Allowance for Doubtful Accounts (+xA) −50				

Summary of the Allowance Method   To make it easy for you to review the two main steps of the allowance method, here's a quick summary:

Step	Timing	Journal Entry	Financial Statement Effects		

1. Record adjustment for estimated bad debts	End of the period in which sales are made	dr Bad Debt Expense (+E, −SE)
		    cr Allowance for Doubtful
		    Accounts (+xA, −A)
			Balance Sheet
			Gross accounts receivable *none*
			    Less: Allowance ↑
			Net accounts receivable ↓
				Income Statement
				Revenues *none*
				Expenses
				    Bad Debt Expense ↑
				Net Income ↓	

2. Identify and write off actual bad debts	As accounts are determined uncollectible	dr Allowance for Doubtful
		    Accounts (−xA, +A)
		    cr Accounts Receivable (−A)
			Balance Sheet
			Gross accounts receivable ↓
			    Less: Allowance ↓
			Net accounts receivable *none*
				Income Statement
				Revenues *none*
				Expenses
				    Bad Debt Expense *none*
				Net Income *none*	

Estimating Bad Debts

In our earlier example, we simply gave you the amount of the estimated bad debt expense to be recorded. In the real world, the amount of bad debt expense is estimated based on either (1) total credit sales for the period or (2) an aging of accounts receivable. Both methods are acceptable under GAAP and are widely used in practice.[3]

Percentage of Credit Sales Method   Many companies come up with bad debt estimates using the **percentage of credit sales method,** which bases bad debt expense on the historical percentage of credit sales that result in bad debts. Because of its focus on income statement accounts (sales and bad debt expense), this method is also known as the income statement method. The estimated bad debt expense is estimated by multiplying the current year's credit sales by the average percentage of credit sales that in prior years

---

[3]To avoid having too many different numbers running around, we make assumptions in our examples that lead both methods to produce the same estimated bad debt expense. Although it's rare for both methods to lead to *exactly* the same numbers in the real world, they generally lead to similar estimates.

resulted in bad debts. For example, if Skechers has credit sales in the current year of $1,463,600, and it had experienced bad debt losses of ½ of 1 percent of credit sales in prior years, Skechers could estimate the current year's bad debt expense as:

Credit sales this year	$1,463,600
× Bad debt loss rate (0.5%)	× .005
Bad debt expense this year	$ 7,318

This amount would be recorded using the following journal entry, which you saw earlier in this chapter.

dr	**Bad Debt Expense (+E, −SE)**	**7,318**
cr	**Allowance for Doubtful Accounts**	
	(+xA, −A)	**7,318**

The effects of this journal entry on the account balances are shown in the T-accounts below:

− Allowance for Doubtful Accounts (xA) +				+ Bad debt expense (E) −		
		8,498	Beginning balance			
Write-offs	7,955	7,318	% of sales adjustment	*% of sales adjustment*	7,318	
		7,861	Ending balance	Ending balance	7,318	

Aging of Accounts Receivable Method   As an alternative to the percentage of credit sales method, many companies use the **aging of accounts receivable method.** This method relies on the fact that, as accounts receivable become older and more overdue, it is less likely that they will prove to be collectible. For example, a receivable that was due in 30 days but remains unpaid after 120 days is less likely to be collected, on average, than a similar receivable that has been unpaid for just 45 days. Based on prior experience, the company can estimate the proportion of receivables of different ages that will not be collected. Because of its focus on balance sheet accounts (accounts receivable and allowance for doubtful accounts), this method is also known as the balance sheet method.

To see how this method works, assume that Skechers prepared the aged listing of accounts receivable shown in Exhibit 7.4 on page 290. This listing separates the total amount owed by each customer into aging categories that represent how many days have passed since uncollected amounts were first recorded in the customer's account. The total receivable for each aging category on this listing is multiplied by *estimated* bad debt loss rates for each category to estimate the amount of allowance needed to cover bad debts in each category. The total of the estimated uncollectible amounts across all the aging categories represents the balance that *should be* in the Allowance for Doubtful Accounts at the end of the period. In our example in Exhibit 7.4, this estimated uncollectible balance is $7,861 (= $557 + 1,099 + 2,530 + 3,675).

The aging method records the estimated bad debt expense by debiting and crediting the same accounts as the percentage of credit sales method, but the method for computing the amount of the journal entry differs. When we used the percentage of credit sales method earlier, we simply calculated the amount to be recorded as *Bad Debt Expense* on the income statement and added that same amount to the *Allowance for Doubtful Accounts*. **The aging method requires two steps: (1) compute the *final ending balance* that we expect to have in the** *Allowance for Doubtful Accounts* **after we make the adjusting entry for bad debt expense, and (2) calculate the amount of the adjustment needed to reach that balance.** As shown below, the difference between the unadjusted

| exhibit 7.4 | Aged Listing of Accounts Receivable | | | | | |

| Customer | Total | NUMBER OF DAYS UNPAID | | | |
		0–30	31–60	61–90	Over 90
Adam's Sports Stores	$ 648	$ 405	$ 198	$ 45	—
Backyard Shoe Company	2,345	—	—	—	$ 2,345
...	...	...	...	...	...
Zero Fear Inc.	10,566	7,444	2,331	550	241
Total Receivable	**$106,612**	**$55,681**	**$27,472**	**$12,650**	**$10,809**
× Estimated bad debt rates		1%	4%	20%	34%
= **Estimated uncollectible**	**$ 7,861**	**$ 557**	**$ 1,099**	**$ 2,530**	**$ 3,675**

balance and the estimated uncollectible balance is recorded as the adjusting entry for bad debt expense for the period:

− Allowance for Doubtful Accounts (xA) +			
Write-offs	7,955	Beginning balance	8,498
		Unadjusted balance	543
		Bad debt expense adjustment	?
		Final ending balance	7,861

Step 2. Calculate Amount of Adjustment
(= $7,861 − 543 = $7,318)

Step 1. Compute Estimated Uncollectible
(see Exhibit 7.4 calculation)

The adjustment of $7,318 would be recorded using the following journal entry, which would affect the account balances in the manner shown in the T-accounts below:

dr	Bad Debt Expense (+E, −SE)	7,318	
	cr Allowance for Doubtful Accounts		
	(+xA, −A).		7,318

− Allowance for Doubtful Accounts (xA) +			
		8,498	Beginning balance
Write-offs	7,955	7,318	Aging adjustment
		7,861	Ending balance

+ Bad Debt Expense (E) −		
Aging adjustment	7,318	
Ending balance	7,318	

Actual Write-Offs Compared with Estimates

The amount of uncollectible accounts actually written off seldom equals the estimated amount previously recorded. This situation is resolved when the adjusting entry is made at the end of the next accounting period: A higher or lower amount is recorded to make up for the previous period's error in estimate. *When estimates are found to be incorrect, financial statement values for prior annual accounting periods are not corrected.*

HOW'S IT GOING? A Self-Study Quiz

1. Assuming that Skechers estimated that 0.5 percent of credit sales would prove uncollectible for the year, what adjusting journal entry would be needed to record bad debts at the end of a year in which credit sales were $700,000 (in thousands of U.S. dollars)?

2. In an earlier year, Skechers reported beginning and ending balances in the Allowance for Doubtful Accounts of $7,113 and $8,498, respectively. It also reported that write-offs of bad accounts amounted to $3,578 (all numbers in thousands). Assuming that no previously written-off accounts had been collected (there were no recoveries), what amount did Skechers record as bad debt expense for the period? Use the Allowance for Doubtful Accounts T-account to solve for the missing value.

− Allowance for Doubtful Accounts (xA) +

After you're done, check your answers with the solution in the margin.

Quiz Answers

1. Bad debt expense (+E, −SE) 3,500
   Allowance for doubtful accounts (+xA, −A) 3,500

2. − Allowance for Doubtful Accounts (xA) +

Write-offs	3,578	Beg. bal.	7,113
		Bad debt expense (*solve*)	**4,963**
		End. bal.	8,498

Beginning + Bad debt expense − Write-offs = Ending
7,113 + x − 3,578 = 8,498; x = 4,963

Reporting Accounts Receivable and Bad Debts

For many large companies, bad debt expense typically isn't reported separately in the income statement. Instead, it usually is combined with other selling expenses in an appropriately named line-item like "Selling expenses." Similarly, accounts receivable write-offs are not reported separately in the financial statements. Although they are not reported separately, these numbers are potentially informative because changes in the level of bad debt expense from one period to another, for example, suggest whether the company is extending credit to riskier customers. Fortunately, if you're analyzing a public company and the amount of bad debt expense and accounts receivable write-offs are significant ("material"), the SEC requires public companies to report these amounts on a schedule included in the 10-K annual report. Exhibit 7.5 presents a condensed version of this schedule from Skechers' 2003 filing.

FAST FLASHBACK

10-K is the abbreviated name of a form that public companies file with the Securities and Exchange Commission, containing the annual report and other important information.

exhibit 7.5	Accounts Receivable Valuation Schedule (Form 10-K)

SKECHERS U.S.A., INC.
Valuation and Qualifying Amounts
(dollars in thousands)

		Additions	Deductions	
Description	Balance at Beginning of Period	Charged to Bad Debt Expense	Write-Offs	Balance at End of Period
Allowance for doubtful accounts:				
Year ended				
December 31, 2003	$8,498	$7,318	$7,955	$7,861
December 31, 2002	7,113	4,963	3,578	8,498
December 31, 2001	5,152	5,507	3,546	7,113

See the animated tutorial reviewing the allowance method on the DVD for use with this book.

Exhibit 7.5 shows that the amount charged to bad debt expense during 2003 ($7,318) was greater than in the two prior years ($4,963 and $5,507). This increase could indicate a decline in the company's ability to collect from customers, consistent with the jump in total write-offs recorded in 2003 (up to $7,955 from $3,578).

Other Methods of Accounting for Accounts Receivable and Bad Debts

In the previous section, you learned how to use the allowance method to account for bad debts arising from sales to customers on credit. This method requires that either the percentage of credit sales method or aging of accounts receivable method be used to estimate future bad debts so that they can be recorded in the period sales are made. You should be aware that some small companies use an alternative method called the direct write-off method. This alternative method violates the conservatism concept and the matching principle, so it is not considered a generally accepted accounting method. The Internal Revenue Service (IRS) however does use this method for tax purposes. Because of this potential use, we demonstrate it in Supplement A at the end of this chapter. Check with your instructor (or your course outline) to see whether you are responsible for this supplement.

Accounting for Notes Receivable

Receivables don't only come from sales. Skechers, for example, reports *notes* receivable of approximately $4.5 million at December 31, 2003. This type of receivable represents amounts that are owed to Skechers under formal written contracts (called "notes").

Most notes receivable arise when a company lends money to another business or individual, such as when Skechers lends money to its executives and key employees for various reasons (such as financing their relocation to a different city). Because notes receivable provide a stronger legal claim than accounts receivable, notes may also be used for big-dollar sales transactions, such as when your car dealer sells a car to you on credit. Regardless of the reason for the note, each note typically outlines the amount owed (called the *principal*), the date by which it is to be repaid to the company (called the *maturity date*), and the interest rate charged while the note remains unpaid. Let's begin by looking at how interest is calculated.

To calculate interest, three variables must be considered: (1) the principal, which is simply the amount of cash that is owed, (2) the interest rate, which always is given in annual terms, and (3) the time period covered in the interest calculation. Because interest rates are stated in terms of a full year, the "time" variable is used when interest is calculated for a period shorter than a year. It indicates how many months out of 12 the interest period covers. The following **interest formula** shows that, to calculate interest, the three variables are multiplied together:

> Interest = Principal × Interest Rate × Time

To illustrate, assume that on November 1, 2004, Skechers loans $100,000 cash to an inventor who is developing a new line of extra-springy shoes that will be used by adults as a self-contained exercise device and by kids as a self-propelled bouncing toy. The loan agreement says that Skechers will be paid 12 percent interest on the note. The interest is split into two installments, payable on April 30, 2005, and October 31, 2005. Skechers is to receive the $100,000 principal when the final interest payment is made on the maturity date of October 31, 2005. Here's a timeline that shows what the promissory note says.

POINT OF INTEREST

The former CEO of Tyco International—Dennis Kozlowski—is accused of loaning over $100 million to employees who used the money to buy outrageous items, such as a $6,000 shower curtain. It has been alleged that these loans were written off later without collecting a penny.
Source: BusinessWeek, December 23, 2002, p. 64.

YOU SHOULD KNOW

The **interest formula** is:
 I = P × R × T
where I = interest calculated, P = principal, R = annual interest rate, and T = time period covered in the interest calculation (number of months out of 12).

COACH'S CORNER

If interest is calculated for a full year, the time variable is 12 months out of 12. Because 12/12 equals 1, this is a case in which the time variable has no effect on the interest calculation.

Establishing a Note Receivable

To record the $100,000 note receivable established by loaning cash to the inventor on November 1, 2004, Skechers would use the following journal entry:

dr	Note Receivable (+A).....................	100,000	
	cr Cash (−A)		100,000

Assets		=	Liabilities	+	Stockholders' Equity
Note Receivable	+100,000				
Cash	−100,000				

Recording Interest Earned

Under accrual basis accounting, interest revenue is recorded when it is earned rather than when the interest payment is actually received in cash. Skechers earned *two* months of interest revenue in the year ended December 31, 2004, because its note receivable was outstanding for all of November and December 2004. As you learned in Chapter 4, when interest is earned in the current period, but not received until a later period, an adjusting journal entry is used at the end of the current period to accrue the interest earned. The amount of interest to be recorded for the two months of 2004 is computed as follows:

Interest	=	Principal	×	Interest Rate	×	Time
$2,000	=	$100,000	×	12%	×	$2/12$

The adjusting journal entry to record the $2,000 of interest revenue that is receivable on December 31, 2004, is

dr	Interest Receivable (+A)	2,000	
	cr Interest Revenue (+R, +SE)		2,000

Assets		=	Liabilities	+	Stockholders' Equity	
Interest Receivable	+2,000				Interest Revenue (+R)	+2,000

Recording Interest Received

On April 30, 2005, Skechers receives the first interest payment of $6,000, which was calculated as $100,000 × 12% × 6/12. This receipt of cash includes the $2,000 of interest that was receivable at December 31, 2004, plus $4,000 of interest that has been earned during the first four months of 2005 (from January 1 to April 30, 2005). To record the collection of this interest, Skechers would make the following journal entry:

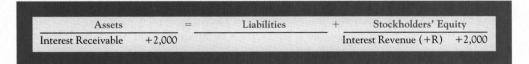

dr	Cash (+A)	6,000	
	cr Interest Receivable (−A)		2,000
	cr Interest Revenue (+R, +SE)		4,000

	Assets	=	Liabilities	+	Stockholders' Equity	
Cash	+6,000					
Interest Receivable	−2,000				Interest Revenue (+R)	+4,000

Recording Receipt of Interest and Principal at Maturity

Let's assume Skechers does not make any more entries for the note until it comes due on October 31, 2005. On that date, Skechers will receive the second interest payment of $6,000 plus the principal of $100,000. Let's record this in two parts. First, the receipt of $6,000 cash for interest would be recorded using the following journal entry:

dr	**Cash (+A)**	6,000	
	cr **Interest Revenue (+R, +SE)**		6,000

	Assets	=	Liabilities	+	Stockholders' Equity	
Cash	+6,000				Interest Revenue (+R)	+6,000

A second journal entry is needed to record the collection of the $100,000 principal owed on the note receivable. For our example, this journal entry would be

dr	**Cash (+A)**	100,000	
	cr **Note Receivable (−A)**		100,000

	Assets	=	Liabilities	+	Stockholders' Equity
Cash	+100,000				
Note Receivable	−100,000				

Accounting for Uncollectible Notes

Just as a customer might fail to pay its accounts receivable balance, some companies also might fail to pay the principal (and interest) that they owe on a note receivable. When the collectibility of notes receivable is in doubt, a company should record an allowance for doubtful accounts against the notes receivable, just as it records an allowance for doubtful accounts against accounts receivable.

⌐EVALUATE
RECEIVABLES MANAGEMENT PRACTICES

Receivables Turnover Analysis

Managers, directors, investors, and creditors evaluate the effectiveness of a company's credit-granting and collection activities by conducting a receivables turnover analysis. The idea behind a receivables turnover analysis is shown in Exhibit 7.6. As a company sells goods or services on credit, its receivables balance goes up, and as it collects from customers, the receivables balance goes down. This process of selling and collecting is called **receivables turnover** and it is repeated over and over during each accounting period, for each customer.

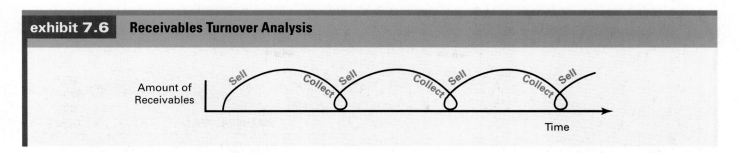

| exhibit 7.6 | **Receivables Turnover Analysis** |

To assess how many times, on average, this process of selling and collecting is repeated over and over during the period, financial statement users calculate the receivables turnover ratio:

$$\text{Receivables Turnover Ratio} = \frac{\text{Net Credit Sales Revenue}}{\text{Average Net Trade Receivables}} = \frac{\text{Net Credit Sales Revenue}}{\dfrac{(\text{Beginning Receivables} + \text{Ending Receivables})}{2}}$$

COACH'S CORNER

The average receivables balance outstanding over the entire year is used in the bottom of the ratio to correspond with the top part of the ratio, which also represents the year's results. Ideally, the ratio would use net *credit* sales, but it is not reported separately, so analysts typically use net sales instead.

The higher the ratio, the faster the collection of receivables. And the faster the collection of receivables, the more cash your company will have available. That's a good thing. A lower ratio is a warning sign, suggesting that the company is offering a longer time for customers to pay. As you learned earlier in this chapter, the longer an account goes without being collected, the bigger the risk that it will never be collected. Analysts watch for changes in the receivables turnover ratio, because a sudden decline may mean that a company is recording sales that customers are likely to return later or is allowing them a longer-than-normal period of time to pay their accounts to entice them to buy as much as possible—a practice known in business as "stuffing the channel."

Rather than evaluate the number of times accounts receivable turn over during a year, some people find it easier to think in terms of the amount of time (in days) it takes to collect accounts receivable. It's easy to convert a year's receivables turnover ratio into the average days to collect: simply calculate 365 ÷ receivables turnover ratio and you'll have the average **days to collect**:

$$\text{Days to Collect} = \frac{365}{\text{Receivables Turnover Ratio}}$$

This measure doesn't say anything different about the company's ability to collect receivables—it's just a little easier to interpret. In terms of Exhibit 7.6, the receivables turnover ratio counts the number of loops in a given period of time, whereas the days to collect tells you the average number of days between loops.

Be on the Alert

Receivables turnover ratios and the number of days to collect can vary across industries, as Exhibit 7.7 suggests, with The Boeing Company having a turnover ratio of 10.6 times, which means a jet-fast collection period of about 34 days. Verizon Communications—the phone company that has popularized the cell yell—is much more sluggish, as indicated by its receivables turnover ratio of 6.0 times. This is about 60 days to collect. Skechers turned over its receivables 9.8 times during 2003, which is once every 37 days. With this big a range in ratios between industries, you should compare a company's turnover only with its figures from prior periods or with figures for other companies in the

YOU SHOULD KNOW

 Days to collect is a measure of the average number of days from the time a sale is made on account to the time it is collected. Calculate it by dividing 365 by the year-long receivables turnover ratio. Other names for days to collect are the number of days' sales in receivables or the average days' sales uncollected.

exhibit 7.7   Summary of Receivables Ratio Analyses

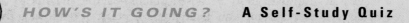

Name of Measure	Formula	What It Tells You	2003 FISCAL YEAR Boeing	2003 FISCAL YEAR Verizon Communications	2003 FISCAL YEAR Skechers	SELF-STUDY QUIZ 2002 Skechers
a. Receivables turnover ratio	Net Sales Revenue / Average Net Trade Receivables	• The number of times receivables turn over • A higher ratio means faster turnover ☺	10.6 times	6.0 times	$= \dfrac{960{,}385}{(98{,}751 + 97{,}419)/2}$ = 9.8 times	
b. Days to collect	365 / Receivables Turnover	• Average number of days from sale on account to collection • A higher number means a longer time to collect ☹	34.4 days	60.8 days	$= \dfrac{365}{9.8}$ = 37.2 days	

same industry. For practice at computing and comparing to prior periods, try the following Self-Study Quiz, which asks you to calculate Skechers' receivables turnover ratio and days to collect in 2002.

HOW'S IT GOING?   A Self-Study Quiz

Compute the ratios for the final column in Exhibit 7.7 using financial statement information in Exhibit 7.2, as well as the following information. Skechers reported net sales revenues of $960,385 in 2003 and $943,582 in 2002, and net trade receivables of $120,285 at December 31, 2001 (in thousands of U.S. dollars). Did Skechers' receivables turnover improve or decline in 2003, as compared to 2002?

After you're done, check your answers with the solutions in the margin.

Quiz Answers
a. 943,582/(97,419 + 120,285) / 2 = 8.7 times
b. 365 ÷ 8.7 = 42.0 days
Skechers' receivables turnover improved significantly in 2003.

Factoring Receivables

To generate the cash needed to pay for a company's business activities, managers must ensure that receivables are collected on a timely basis. You might wonder what managers can do to speed up sluggish receivables collections. One obvious tactic is to start hounding customers for payment. This brute force approach has at least two drawbacks: (1) it is time-consuming and costly, and (2) it can annoy customers and cause them to take their business elsewhere. An alternative approach is to sell outstanding accounts receivable to another company (called a factor). The way this **factoring** arrangement works is that your company receives cash for the receivables it sells to the factor (minus a factoring fee) and the factor then has the right to collect the outstanding amounts owed by your customers. In the same way that you can get cash immediately at a local Checks Cashed store for any check, factoring is a fast and easy way for your company to get cash for its receivables. However, this does come at a cost: The factoring fee can be as much as 3 percent of the receivables sold. If Skechers sold $100,000 of receivables to a factor under such an arrangement, Skechers would receive only $97,000 cash and would give up the potential to collect the full $100,000, resulting in an expense of $3,000 that is

YOU SHOULD KNOW

Factoring is an arrangement where receivables are sold to another company (called a factor) for immediate cash (minus a factoring fee).

reported on Skechers' income statement. For a company that regularly sells its receivables, the cost of factoring is included with selling expenses. If a company factors infrequently, the fee is considered a peripheral "other" expense.

⌐ RECONSIDER
HOW RECEIVABLES REPORTING AFFECTS ANALYSES

The Impact of Estimation

As we have noted throughout this chapter, the Allowance for Doubtful Accounts and Bad Debt Expense accounts are based on estimates of future events. Although these estimates might be accurate forecasts of what will happen in the future, they can be a source of misstatement. In some cases, managers have been unintentionally biased by their natural managerial optimism, estimating greater collections on account than what actually turned out to be true. In other cases, they have acted dishonestly to understate Bad Debt Expense to boost net income and overstate Net accounts receivable to make the balance sheet appear stronger. Either way, overly optimistic estimates can mislead financial statement users.

Financial statement users also can be misguided by overly pessimistic bad debt estimates. Some managers have made unethical accounting decisions by overestimating bad debts in years of strong sales and high gross profits to build up a cushion (or "cookie jar reserve") in the Allowance for Doubtful Accounts. The extra bad debt expense recorded in those years is more than offset by extra sales and gross profits, so financial statement users do not react adversely to the increase in bad debt expense. The extra cushion in the Allowance for Doubtful Accounts allows managers to reduce the amount of bad debt expense that is added to it in a later year while still ensuring an adequate ending balance in the Allowance for Doubtful Accounts. The result is that the net income in the current year is understated (the good year does not appear quite so good) and the net income in the later year is overstated (the bad year does not appear quite so bad). This dishonest behavior is known as **income smoothing**. The following example shows how this could mislead users.

Assume that we have a crystal ball that accurately tells us what should be recorded in the Allowance for Doubtful Accounts and on the income statement in three years:

ETHICAL

ISSUE

YOU SHOULD KNOW

Income smoothing is the dishonest practice of manipulating accounting estimates to keep net income levels stable or "smooth" over a series of periods.

Accurate Allowance for Doubtful Accounts	Year 1	Year 2	Year 3
Allowance for doubtful accounts, beginning	$8	$8	$8
Add: Bad debts estimated for current year	4	4	4
Less: Write-offs in current year	(4)	(4)	(4)
Allowance for doubtful accounts, ending	$8	$8	$8

Accurate Income Statements	Year 1	Year 2	Year 3
Sales revenues	$130	$135	$130
Total expenses (excluding bad debt expense)	(115)	(117)	(115)
Bad debt expense	(4)	(4)	(4)
Net income	$ 11	$ 14	$ 11

Now let's see how overly pessimistic forecasts about future collections affect the financial statements. Assume that at the end of year 2, managers can see that year 3 is going to be less successful than year 2. Instead of accurately recording $4 of bad debt expense at the end of year 2, managers estimate it to be $6. In year 3, they make up for the overestimate in the previous year by recording a smaller bad debt expense, which also reduces the Allowance for Doubtful Accounts to a more appropriate balance. The Allowance for Doubtful Accounts and income statements under this scenario are

Allowance for Doubtful Accounts (pessimistic in year 2)	Year 1	Year 2	Year 3
Allowance for doubtful accounts, beginning	$8	$ 8	$10
Add: Bad debts estimated for current year	4	6	2
Less: Write-offs in current year	(4)	(4)	(4)
Allowance for doubtful accounts, ending	$8	$10	$ 8

Income Statements (pessimistic in year 2)	Year 1	Year 2	Year 3
Sales revenues	$130	$135	$130
Total expenses (excluding bad debt expense)	(115)	(117)	(115)
Bad debt expense	(4)	(6)	(2)
Net income	$ 11	$ 12	$ 13

As a financial statement user, you are likely to form different impressions about the company based on the net income reported in the income statements. The effects of the bad debt estimates on net income are shown in Exhibit 7.8. Had bad debt expense been forecasted accurately, the company would have reported that its earnings kicked up in year 2 but then took a step backward in year 3. This would leave you with lots of uncertainty about what is likely to happen in year 4. In contrast, because bad debt expense was overestimated in year 2 and readjusted in year 3, the income statements report that the company's net income increased from year to year. Based on the smooth net income trend, many people would predict that the company is a shoo-in for continuing to increase its earnings again in year 4.

The SEC and financial statement auditors recently have devoted extra attention to detecting bad debt estimates that are overly optimistic or overly pessimistic. These efforts are likely to catch unscrupulous managers who blatantly misreport these estimates. So, as a financial statement user, you shouldn't have to worry that you're being duped. However, when evaluating a company's results or comparing two companies, you will want to be aware of the degree of optimism or pessimism in their bad debt estimates. Here are some steps that you can take when evaluating them:

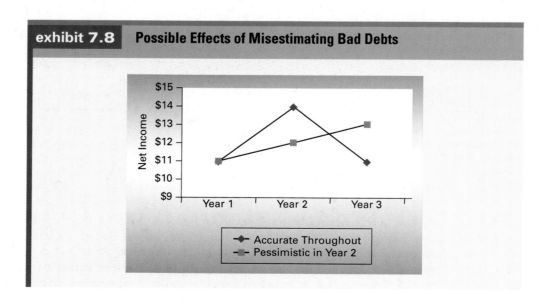

exhibit 7.8   **Possible Effects of Misestimating Bad Debts**

1. ***Assess the consistency of estimates.*** In normal circumstances, the allowance for doubtful accounts should be a fairly consistent percentage of gross accounts receivable. Also, the bad debt expense should be a consistent percentage of net sales. If you notice any unexplained fluctuations, it might be cause for concern.

2. ***Don't rely on just one number.*** In our example, by focusing on net income, users would have overlooked other clues that bad debts were misestimated. An overly optimistic estimate about the collectibility of accounts receivable has the effect of decreasing bad debt expense, which increases net income, but it has the opposite effect on the receivables turnover ratio—if a company records too little bad debt expense in the current period, its receivables turnover will appear to have slowed. On the other hand, if the company records too much bad debt expense in the current period, its receivables turnover will appear to have picked up but its net income will have dropped. This is one of the good features about double-entry accounting and financial statement reporting: It's difficult to misstate them in a way that doesn't raise *some* questions or "red flags."

3. ***Understand how management develops estimates.*** In addition to evaluating the estimates themselves, assess the process used to generate the estimates. You wouldn't go on a blind date without knowing how your friend picked "the one for you," so don't just accept the estimated bad debt expense and allowance for doubtful accounts numbers without knowing how they're estimated. Companies describe their methods in the Summary of Significant Accounting Policies note to their financial statements and may explain them in even greater detail in the annual report section called Management's Discussion and Analysis. We'll close this chapter with Exhibit 7.9, which shows what Skechers says about its approach for managing and estimating bad debts.

COACH'S CORNER

Calculate the allowance as a percentage of gross accounts receivable as follows:

$$\frac{\text{Allowance}}{\text{Gross accounts receivable}} \times 100\%$$

exhibit 7.9	**Excerpt of Skechers' Receivables Policy**

We insure selected customer account balances both greater than $200,000 and accepted by the insurance company should our customer not pay. We also provide a reserve against our receivables for estimated losses that may result from our customers' inability to pay, and disputed and returned items. We determine the amount of the reserve by analyzing known uncollectible accounts, aged receivables, economic conditions in the customers' country or industry, historical losses and our customers' credit-worthiness. Amounts later determined and specifically identified to be uncollectible are charged or written off against this reserve. To minimize the likelihood of uncollectibility, customers' credit-worthiness is reviewed periodically based on external credit reporting services and our experience with the account and adjusted accordingly. Should a customer's account become past due, we generally place a hold on the account and discontinue further shipments to that customer, minimizing further risk of loss.

Source: Skechers U.S.A., Inc. 2003 Form 10-K.

COACH'S CORNER

Notice how Skechers controls the risk of bad debt losses by insuring its receivables and by placing a hold on overdue accounts. Some of the best places for learning about these business strategies are the notes to the financial statements and the financial section of the company's annual report.

What's Coming Up

We'll continue our journey down the assets side of the balance sheet in Chapter 8 by focusing on inventory and the related income statement account called *Cost of Goods Sold*. Just as you saw in this chapter for receivables, inventory reporting also involves choosing among alternative accounting methods and considering estimates of future value when reporting current balances. So be sure you get a good handle on how to account for receivables in the following review and practice problems—it only makes things easier as you progress through the next chapters.

FOR YOUR REVIEW

DEMONSTRATION CASE

Shooby Dooby Shoe (SDS) sold $950,000 in merchandise on credit during 2006. Also during 2006, SDS determined that it would not be able to collect a $500 account balance that was owed by a deceased customer (Captain Cutler).

Required:

1. Prepare a journal entry to write off the account receivable from Captain Cutler, and show its effects on the accounting equation.

2. Assume that SDS uses the percentage of credit sales method for estimating bad debt expense and that it estimates that 1 percent of credit sales will result in bad debts. Prepare a journal entry to record bad debt expense for 2006, and show its effects on the accounting equation.

3. Assume instead that SDS uses the aging of accounts receivable method and that it estimates that $11,000 of its year-end accounts receivable is uncollectible. As of December 31, 2006, the Allowance for Doubtful Accounts had an unadjusted credit balance of $3,000. Prepare a journal entry to record bad debt expense for 2006, and show its effects on the accounting equation.

4. Assume that SDS reported net accounts receivable of $160,000 at December 31, 2006, and $150,000 at December 31, 2005. Calculate the receivables turnover ratio for 2006.

5. If the receivables turnover ratio was 6.4 in 2005, what was the number of days to collect in 2005? Given your calculations in 4, conclude whether SDS collections are faster or slower in 2006 than in 2005.

6. Assume that, on October 1, 2006, SDS signed a $5,000 note receivable from an employee. The note states an annual interest rate of 8 percent, with the first payment to be made on March 31, 2007. Prepare journal entries to record the issuance of the note on October 1 and any interest revenue earned in 2006.

Take 10 minutes to attempt the requirements, and then check your answers with the following solution.

Suggested Solution

1. The journal entry to write-off this account is

dr	Allowance for Doubtful Accounts (−xA, +A)	500	
	cr Accounts Receivable (−A)		500

Assets		=	Liabilities	+	Stockholders' Equity
Accounts Receivable	−500				
Allowance for Doubtful Accounts (−xA)	+500				

2. The percentage of credit sales method directly estimates the amount of bad debt expense to record.

dr	Bad Debt Expense (+E, −SE) (0.01 × $950,000)	9,500	
	cr Allowance for Doubtful Accounts (+xA, −A)		9,500

Assets		=	Liabilities	+	Stockholders' Equity	
Allowance for Doubtful Accounts (+xA)	−9,500				Bad Debt Expense (+E)	−9,500

3. Under the aging of accounts receivable method, we determine the estimated balance for the allowance for doubtful accounts and then subtract its unadjusted balance to determine the amount of the adjustment.

dr	Bad Debt Expense (+E, −SE)			8,000	
	cr Allowance for Doubtful Accounts (+xA, −A)				
	($11,000 − $3,000)				8,000

Assets	=	Liabilities	+	Stockholders' Equity	
Allowance for Doubtful				Bad Debt	
Accounts (+xA) −8,000				Expense (+E) −8,000	

4. Receivables turnover ratio is calculated as Net sales ÷ Average accounts receivable. The average accounts receivable in 2006 was $155,000 (= ($160,000 + 150,000)/2), so the receivables turnover ratio for 2006 was 6.13 (= $950,000 ÷ 155,000).

5. Days to collect is calculated as 365 ÷ receivables turnover ratio. The 6.4 turnover in 2005 equates to 57 days (and the 6.13 turnover in 2006 equates to 60 days). Collections are slower in 2006 than in 2005.

6. The entry to record the issuance of the note on October 1, 2006 is

dr	Note Receivable (+A)			5,000	
	cr Cash (−A)				5,000

Assets	=	Liabilities	+	Stockholders' Equity
Note Receivable +5,000				
Cash −5,000				

Interest revenue is earned when the note is outstanding during the accounting period, not when the interest payment is received. During 2006, the loan has been outstanding for October, November, and December, which equals 3 months (out of 12). The adjusting journal entry to accrue this is

dr	Interest Receivable (+A) (5,000 × 8% × 3/12)			100	
	cr Interest Revenue (+R, +SE).....................				100

Assets	=	Liabilities	+	Stockholders' Equity
Interest Receivable +100				Interest Revenue +100

CHAPTER SUMMARY

Describe the tradeoffs of extending credit to customers. p. 284   **LO1**

- By extending credit to customers, a company is likely to attract a greater number of customers willing to buy from it.

- The additional costs of extending credit include increased employee costs, bad debt costs, and delayed receipt of cash.

Estimate and report the effects of uncollectible accounts. p. 286   **LO2**

- When bad debts are material, the company must use the allowance method to account for uncollectibles. This method involves the following steps:

  1. Estimate and record uncollectibles with an end-of-period adjusting journal entry to bad debt expense and the allowance for doubtful accounts.

  2. Identify and write off specific customer balances in the period that they are determined to be uncollectible.

- The adjusting entry reduces net income as well as net accounts receivable. The write-off affects neither.

Report notes receivable and compute interest. p. 292   **LO3**

- A note receivable specifies the amount loaned, when it is to be repaid, and the interest rate associated with the note receivable. As time passes and interest is earned on the note, accountants must record an adjusting journal entry that accrues the interest revenue that is receivable on the note.

LO4   **Compute and interpret the receivables turnover ratio. p. 294**

- The receivables turnover ratio measures the effectiveness of credit-granting and collection activities. It reflects how many times average trade receivables were recorded and collected during the period.

- Analysts and creditors watch this ratio because a sudden decline in it may mean that a company is extending payment deadlines in an attempt to prop up lagging sales or even is recording sales that later will be returned by customers.

LO5   **Explain how estimates of uncollectible accounts affect evaluations of receivables management practices. p. 294**

- Receivables are reported net of *estimated* uncollectible accounts. If these estimates are overly optimistic, net receivables will be too high and bad debt expense will be too low (which causes net income to be too high). To guard against overly optimistic or overly pessimistic estimates, analysts should: assess the consistency of the estimates, rely on more than one single estimate or number, and consider the process management uses to develop the estimates.

FINANCIAL STATEMENT ANALYSIS TIPS

To determine the average number of times that accounts receivable are recorded and collected during the period, calculate the receivables turnover ratio:

$$\text{Receivables Turnover Ratio} = \frac{\text{Net Credit Sales Revenue}}{\text{Average Net Trade Receivables}} = \frac{\text{Net Credit Sales Revenue}}{\dfrac{(\text{Beginning Receivables} + \text{Ending Receivables})}{2}}$$

Calculate the following to express the annual receivables turnover ratio in terms of number of days to collect:

$$\text{Days to Collect} = \frac{365}{\text{Receivables Turnover Ratio}}$$

KEY TERMS TO KNOW

Accounts Receivable p. 284
Aging of Accounts
   Receivable Method p. 289
Allowance for Doubtful
   Accounts p. 286
Allowance Method p. 286

Bad Debt Expense p. 286
Days to Collect p. 295
Factoring p. 296
Income Smoothing p. 297
Interest Formula p. 292

Percentage of Credit Sales
   Method p. 288
Receivables Turnover
   Ratio p. 294
Notes Receivable p. 285
Write-Off p. 287

SUPPLEMENT A: DIRECT WRITE-OFF METHOD

As described in the body of this chapter, an alternative method exists to account for uncollectible accounts. This alternative approach, called the direct write-off method, is okay for tax purposes but it is not acceptable under generally accepted accounting principles. Consequently, it isn't used very often for external financial reporting.

The reason the direct write-off method isn't considered a GAAP method is that it ignores the conservatism concept and the matching principle. It breaks the conservatism concept by reporting accounts receivable at the total amount owed by customers (an overly optimistic point of view) rather than what is estimated to actually be collectible (a more realistic viewpoint). Under the direct write-off method, an allowance for doubtful accounts is not used. The direct write-off method breaks the matching principle by recording bad debt expense in the period that customer accounts are determined to be bad rather than matching the expense to the revenues reported in the period when the credit sales are actually made. The journal entry used by the direct write-off method to record $1,000 of bad debt expense is

dr	Bad Debt Expense (+E, −SE)	1,000	
	cr Accounts Receivable (−A)		1,000

It's easy to see why this method is defective if you imagine a case where a company provides services to customers on account for $1,000 in year 1, but then discovers in year 2 that none of the amounts will be collected. Under the direct write-off method, the company would report sales of $1,000 and no bad debt expense in year 1, but in year 2 would then report no sales and bad debt expense of $1,000. By failing to match expenses to revenues, the direct write-off method doesn't provide useful information for evaluating the company's financial performance.

FOR YOUR PRACTICE

QUESTIONS

1. What's the difference between accounts receivable and notes receivable?
2. Which basic accounting principles does the allowance method of accounting for bad debts satisfy?
3. Using the allowance method, is bad debt expense recognized in the period in which (a) sales related to the uncollectible account were made or (b) the seller learns that the customer is unable to pay?
4. What is the effect of the write-off of bad debts (using the allowance method) on (a) net income and (b) net accounts receivable?
5. What are the three components of the interest formula? Explain how this formula adjusts for interest periods that are less than a full year.
6. Are interest revenues recognized in the period in which (a) a note receivable has remained unpaid or (b) the company receives a cash payment for the interest?
7. Does an increase in the receivables turnover ratio generally indicate faster or slower collection of receivables? Explain.
8. What two approaches can managers take to speed up sluggish collections of receivables? List one advantage and disadvantage for each approach.
9. Define income smoothing and explain how it can potentially mislead financial statement users.
10. (Supplement A) Describe how (and when) the direct write-off method accounts for uncollectible accounts. What are the disadvantages of this method?

MULTIPLE CHOICE

1. When a company using the allowance method writes off a specific customer's account receivable from the accounting system, how many of the following are true?
   - Total stockholders' equity remains the same.
   - Total assets remain the same.
   - Total expenses remain the same.

   a. None
   b. One
   c. Two
   d. Three

2. When using the allowance method, as bad debt expense is recorded,
   a. Total assets remain the same and stockholders' equity remains the same.
   b. Total assets decrease and stockholders' equity decreases.
   c. Total assets increase and stockholders' equity decreases.
   d. Total liabilities increase and stockholders' equity decreases.

3. You have determined that Carefree Company estimates bad debt expense using the aging of accounts receivable method. Assuming Carefree has no write-offs or recoveries, its estimate of uncollectible receivables resulting from the aging analysis equals
    a. Bad debt expense for the current period.
    b. The ending balance in the allowance for doubtful accounts for the period.
    c. The change in the allowance for doubtful accounts for the period.
    d. Both *a* and *c*.

4. Which of the following best describes the proper presentation of accounts receivable in the financial statements?
    a. Gross accounts receivable plus the allowance for doubtful accounts in the asset section of the balance sheet.
    b. Gross accounts receivable in the asset section of the balance sheet and the allowance for doubtful accounts in the expense section of the income statement.
    c. Gross accounts receivable less bad debt expense in the asset section of the balance sheet.
    d. Gross accounts receivable less the allowance for doubtful accounts in the asset section of the balance sheet.

5. If the allowance for doubtful accounts opened with a $10,000 balance, ended with an adjusted balance of $20,000, and included write-offs of $5,000 (with no recoveries) during the period, what was the amount of bad debt expense?
    a. $5,000
    b. $10,000
    c. $15,000
    d. Cannot determine without knowing whether percentage of credit sales or aging of accounts receivable method was used.

6. When an accounts receivable is "recovered,"
    a. Total assets increase.
    b. Total assets decrease.
    c. Stockholders' equity increases.
    d. None of the above.

7. If a 10 percent note receivable for $10,000 is created on January 1, 2006, and it has a maturity date of December 31, 2010,
    a. No interest revenue will be recorded in 2006.
    b. The note receivable will be classified as a current asset.
    c. Interest revenue of $1,000 will be recorded in 2006.
    d. None of the above.

8. If the receivables turnover ratio decreased during the year,
    a. The days to collect also decreased.
    b. Receivables collections slowed down.
    c. Sales revenues increased at a faster rate than receivables increased.
    d. None of the above.

9. All else equal, if Skechers incurs a 3 percent fee to factor $10,000 of its accounts receivable, its net income will
    a. Increase by $10,000.
    b. Increase by $9,700.
    c. Increase by $300.
    d. Decrease by $300.

10. Which of the following steps can financial statement users take to evaluate the degree of optimism in management's bad debt estimates?
    a. Assess the consistency of estimates.
    b. Don't rely on just one number like net income.
    c. Understand how management develops its estimates.
    d. All of the above.

MINI-EXERCISES   **Available with McGraw-Hill's Homework Manager**

L01–L05   **M7-1** **Identifying Important Accounting Terms**

Complete the following crossword puzzle, using the clues provided in the box on the right. Omit hyphens.

Across

2 A listing that categorizes receivables by the number of days unpaid.

4 The term to describe the act of removing an uncollectible account and its corresponding allowance from the accounting records.

8 An arrangement where receivables are sold to another company.

9 The type of receivable documented by formal written contracts.

10 The term still used today to refer to accounts receivable arising in the ordinary course of business.

Down

1 The allowance for doubtful accounts is a _____ account.

2 The name of the method that reduces accounts receivable for an estimate of uncollectible accounts.

3 The dishonest practice of manipulating accounting estimates to keep net income levels stable over a series of periods.

5 The term for the collection of a previously written off account.

6 Multiplied by the interest rate and time period to calculate interest.

7 The term used to describe the complete process of making credit sales and later collecting those receivables.

M7-2 Evaluating the Decision to Extend Credit   LO1

On December 22, 2003, Bally Total Fitness issued a press release announcing that it had sold a significant portion of its accounts receivable. The CEO justified the decision by stating "we focused on simplifying the business." Explain how Bally's decision will simplify its business.

M7-3 Reporting Accounts Receivable and Recording Write-Offs Using the Allowance   LO2
Method

At the end of 2005, Bully's Full Fitness has adjusted balances of $600,000 in gross accounts receivable and $44,000 in allowance for doubtful accounts. On January 2, 2006, the company learns that certain customer accounts are not collectible, so management authorizes a write-off of these accounts totaling $8,000.

a. Show how the company would have reported its receivable accounts on December 31, 2005. As of that date, what amount did Bully's Full Fitness expect to collect?

b. Prepare the journal entry to write off the accounts on January 2, 2006.

c. Assuming no other transactions occurred between December 31, 2005, and January 3, 2006, show how Bully's Full Fitness would have reported its receivable accounts on January 3, 2006. As of that date, what amount did Bully's Full Fitness expect to collect? Has this changed from December 31, 2005? Explain why or why not.

M7-4 Recording Recoveries Using the Allowance Method   LO2

Let's go a bit further with the example from M7-3. Assume that on February 2, 2006, Bully's Full Fitness received a payment of $500 from one of the customers whose balance had been written off. Prepare the journal entries to record this transaction.

M7-5 Recording Write-Offs and Bad Debt Expense Using the Allowance Method   LO2

Prepare journal entries for each transaction listed.

a. During the period, customer balances are written off in the amount of $17,000.

b. At the end of the period, bad debt expense is estimated to be $14,000.

LO2   **M7-6 Determining Financial Statement Effects of Write-Offs and Bad Debt Expense Using the Allowance Method**

Using the following categories, indicate the effects of the following transactions. Use + for increase and − for decrease and indicate the accounts affected and the amounts.

a.   During the period, customer balances are written off in the amount of $8,000.
b.   At the end of the period, bad debt expense is estimated to be $10,000.

Assets	=	Liabilities	+	Stockholders' Equity

LO3   **M7-7 Using the Interest Formula to Compute Interest**

Complete the following table by computing the missing amounts (?) for the following independent cases.

Principal Amount on Note Receivable	Annual Interest Rate	Time Period	Interest Earned
a. $100,000	10%	6 months	?
b. ?	10%	12 months	$4,000
c. $ 50,000	?	9 months	$3,000

LO3   **M7-8 Recording Note Receivable Transactions**

Scotia Corporation hired a new corporate controller and agreed to provide her a $20,000 relocation loan on a six-month, 7 percent note. Prepare journal entries to record the following transactions for Scotia Corporation. Rather than use letters to reference each transaction, use the date of the transaction.

a.   The company loans the money on January 1, 2006.
b.   The new employee pays Scotia the full principal and interest on its maturity date.

LO3   **M7-9 Recording Note Receivable Transactions**

RecRoom Equipment Company received an $8,000, six-month, 10 percent note to settle an unpaid balance owed by a customer. Prepare journal entries to record the following transactions for RecRoom. Rather than use letters to reference each transaction, use the date of the transaction.

a.   The note is accepted by RecRoom on November 1, 2006, causing the company to increase its notes receivable and decrease its accounts receivable.
b.   RecRoom adjusts its records for interest earned to December 31, 2006.
c.   RecRoom receives the principal and interest on the note's maturity date.

LO4   **M7-10 Determining the Effects of Credit Policy Changes on Receivables Turnover Ratio and Days to Collect**

Indicate the most likely effect of the following changes in credit policy on the receivables turnover ratio and days to collect (+ for increase, − for decrease, and NE for no effect).

a.   Granted credit with shorter payment deadlines.
b.   Increased effectiveness of collection methods.
c.   Granted credit to less creditworthy customers.

LO4   **M7-11 Evaluating the Effect of Factoring on the Receivables Turnover Ratio and Computing the Cost of Factoring**

After noting that its receivables turnover ratio had declined, Imperative Company decided to sell $500,000 of receivables to a factoring company. The factor charges a factoring fee of 3 percent of the receivables sold. All else equal, how will this affect Imperative's receivables turnover ratio in the future? How much cash does Imperative receive on the sale? Calculate the factoring fee and describe how it is reported by Imperative Company.

M7-12 (Supplement) Recording Write-Offs and Reporting Accounts Receivable Using the Direct Write-Off Method

Complete all the requirements of M7-3, except assume that Bully's Full Fitness uses the direct write-off method. Note that this means Bully's does not have an allowance for doubtful accounts balance.

EXERCISES   Available with McGraw-Hill's Homework Manager

E7-1 Recording Bad Debt Expense Estimates and Write-Offs Using the Percentage of Credit Sales Method   LO2

During 2006, Kimberly Productions, Inc., recorded credit sales of $650,000. Based on prior experience, the company estimates a 1.5 percent bad debt rate on credit sales.

Required:

Prepare journal entries for each transaction.

a. The appropriate bad debt expense adjustment was recorded for the year 2006.
b. On December 31, 2006, an account receivable for $1,000 from March 2006 was determined to be uncollectible and was written off.

E7-2 Determining Financial Statement Effects of Bad Debt Expense Estimates and Write-Offs   LO2

Using the following categories, indicate the effects of the transactions listed in E7-1. Use + for increase and − for decrease and indicate the accounts affected and the amounts.

Assets	=	Liabilities	+	Stockholders' Equity

E7-3 Recording Write-Offs, Recoveries, and Bad Debt Expense Estimates Using the Percentage of Credit Sales Method   LO2

During 2006, Gonzales Electronics, Incorporated, recorded credit sales of $720,000. Based on prior experience, it estimates a 0.5 percent bad debt rate on credit sales.

Required:

Prepare journal entries for each transaction.

a. On August 31, 2006, a customer balance for $300 from a prior year was determined to be uncollectible and was written off.
b. On December 15, 2006, the customer balance for $300 written off on August 31, 2006 was collected in full.
c. On December 31, 2006, the appropriate bad debt expense adjustment was recorded for the year 2006.

E7-4 Determining Financial Statement Effects of Write-Offs, Recoveries, and Bad Debt Expense Estimates   LO2

Using the following categories, indicate the effects of the transactions listed in E7-3. Use + for increase and − for decrease and indicate the accounts affected and the amounts.

Assets	=	Liabilities	+	Stockholders' Equity

E7-5 Recording and Determining the Effects of Write-Offs, Recoveries, and Bad Debt Expense Estimates on the Balance Sheet and Income Statement   LO2

Copy Catchers Corporation operates a plagiarism detection service for universities and community colleges. While most of its customers reliably pay amounts owed, the company has historically experienced a 2 percent rate of bad debts on credit sales. The company estimates bad debts with the percentage of credit sales method.

Required:

1. Prepare journal entries for each transaction below.
   a. On March 31, 2007, ten customers were billed for detection services totaling $50,000.
   b. On October 31, 2007, a customer balance for $1,600 from a prior year was determined to be uncollectible and was written off.
   c. On December 15, 2007, a customer paid an old balance of $600, which had been written off in a prior year.
   d. On December 31, 2007, the appropriate bad debt expense adjustment was recorded for the year 2007.
2. Complete the following table, indicating the amount and effect (+ for increase, − for decrease, and NE for no effect) of each transaction.

Transaction	Net Receivables	Net Sales	Income from Operations
a			
b			
c			
d			

LO2

E7-6 Computing Bad Debt Expense Using Aging of Accounts Receivable Method

Brown Cow Dairy uses the aging approach to estimate bad debt expense. The balance of each account receivable is aged on the basis of three time periods as follows: (1) 1–30 days old, $12,000, (2) 31–90 days old, $5,000, and (3) more than 90 days old, $3,000. Experience has shown that for each age group, the average loss rate on the amount of the receivable due to uncollectibility is (1) 2 percent, (2) 10 percent, and (3) 30 percent, respectively. At December 31, 2006 (end of the current year), the Allowance for Doubtful Accounts balance was $300 (credit) before the end-of-period adjusting entry is made.

Required:

1. What amount should be recorded as Bad Debt Expense for the current year?
2. If the unadjusted balance in the Allowance for Doubtful Accounts was a $600 debit balance, what would be the amount of bad debt expense in 2006?

LO2

E7-7 Recording and Reporting Allowance for Doubtful Accounts Using Aging of Accounts Receivable Method

Arias Company uses the aging approach to estimate bad debt expense. The balance of each account receivable is aged on the basis of three time periods as follows: (1) 1–30 days old, $65,000, (2) 31–90 days old, $10,000, and (3) more than 90 days old, $4,000. Experience has shown that for each age group, the average loss rate on the amount of the receivable due to uncollectibility is (1) 1 percent, (2) 15 percent, and (3) 40 percent, respectively. At December 31, 2007 (end of the current year), the Allowance for Doubtful Accounts balance was $100 (credit) before the end-of-period adjusting entry is made.

Required:

1. Prepare the appropriate bad debt expense adjusting entry for the year 2007.
2. Show how the various accounts related to accounts receivable should be shown on the December 31, 2007, balance sheet.

LO2

E7-8 Recording, Reporting, and Evaluating a Bad Debt Estimate

During the year ended December 31, 2007, Kelly's Camera Shop had sales revenue of $170,000, of which $85,000 was on credit. At the start of 2007, Accounts Receivable showed a $10,000 debit balance, and the Allowance for Doubtful Accounts showed an $800 credit balance. Collections of accounts receivable during 2007 amounted to $68,000.

Data during 2007 follows:

a. On December 10, 2007, a customer balance of $1,500 from a prior year was determined to be uncollectible, so it was written off.
b. On December 31, 2007, a decision was made to continue the accounting policy of basing estimated bad debt losses on 2 percent of credit sales for the year.

Required:

1. Give the required journal entries for the two events in December 2007.
2. Show how the amounts related to Accounts Receivable and Bad Debt Expense would be reported on the income statement and balance sheet for 2007.
3. On the basis of the data available, does the 2 percent rate appear to be reasonable? Explain.

LO3

E7-9 Recording Note Receivable Transactions, Including Accrual Adjustment for Interest

The following transactions took place for Big Whiskers Grooming Service.

2006	July 1	Loaned $10,000 to the president of the company and received back a one-year, 10 percent note.
	Dec. 31	Accrued interest on the note.
2007	July 1	Received principal and interest on the note. (No interest has been accrued since December 31.)

Required:

Prepare the journal entries that Big Whiskers would record for the above transactions.

E7-10 Recording Note Receivable Transactions, Including Accrual Adjustment for Interest

LO3

To attract retailers to its shopping center, the Marketplace Mall will lend money to tenants under formal contracts, provided that they use it to renovate their store space. On November 1, 2005, the company loaned $10,000 to a new tenant on a one-year note with a stated annual interest rate of 6 percent. Interest is to be received by Marketplace Mall on April 30, 2006, and at maturity on October 31, 2006.

Required:

Prepare journal entries that Marketplace Mall would record related to this note on the following dates: (a) November 1, 2005; (b) December 31, 2005 (Marketplace Mall's fiscal year-end); (c) April 30, 2006; and (d) October 31, 2006.

E7-11 Using Financial Statement Disclosures to Infer Write-Offs and Bad Debt Expense and to Calculate the Receivables Turnover Ratio

LO2, LO4

Microsoft develops, produces, and markets a wide range of computer software including the Windows operating system. On a recent balance sheet, Microsoft reported the following information about net sales revenue and accounts receivable.

	Current Year	**Prior Year**
Accounts receivable, net of allowances of $76 and $57	$ 338	$ 270
Net revenues	3,753	2,759

According to its Form 10-K, Microsoft recorded bad debt expense of $47 and did not recover any previously written-off accounts during the current year.

Required:

1. What amount of bad debts was written off during the current year?
2. Assuming that Microsoft uses the percentage of sales method to estimate bad debt expense, solve for the percentage the company used in estimating bad debt expense for the current year.
3. What was Microsoft's receivables turnover ratio in the current year?

E7-12 Using Financial Statement Disclosures to Infer Bad Debt Expense

LO2

A recent annual report for Sears contained the following information at the end of its fiscal year:

	Year 1	**Year 2**
Accounts receivable	$7,022,075,000	$7,336,308,000
Allowance for doubtful accounts	(86,605,000)	(96,989,000)
	$6,935,470,000	$7,239,319,000

A footnote to the financial statements disclosed that accounts receivable write-offs amounted to $55,000,000 during year 1 and $69,000,000 during year 2. Assume that Sears did not record any recoveries.

Required:

Determine the bad debt expense for year 2 based on the above facts.

LO2, LO4

SEARS

E7-13 Determining the Effects of Uncollectible Accounts on the Receivables Turnover Ratio

Refer to the information about Sears given in E7-12.

Required:

Complete the following table indicating the direction of the effect (+ for increase, − for decrease, and NE for no effect) of each transaction during year 2:

Transaction	Net Credit Sales	Average Net Accounts Receivable	Receivables Turnover Ratio
a. Write-off of $69,000,000 in uncollectible accounts.			
b. Recording bad debt expense.			

LO4

E7-14 Analyzing and Interpreting Receivables Turnover Ratio and Days to Collect

A recent annual report for Federal Express contained the following data (in thousands):

	Current Year	Previous Year
Accounts receivable	$1,034,608	$805,495
Less: Allowance for doubtful accounts	36,800	38,225
Net accounts receivable	$ 997,808	$767,270
Net sales (assume all on credit)	$7,015,069	

Required:

1. Determine the accounts receivable turnover ratio and days to collect for the current year.
2. Explain the meaning of each number.

LO2, LO4

E7-15 Determining the Effects of Bad Debts on Receivables Turnover Ratio

During 2006, Jesse Enterprises Corporation recorded credit sales of $650,000. Based on prior experience, the company estimates a 1 percent bad debt rate on credit sales. At the beginning of the year, the balance in Net trade accounts receivable was $50,000. At the end of the year, but *before* the bad debt expense adjustment was recorded and *before* any bad debts had been written off, the balance in Net trade accounts receivable was $55,500.

Required:

1. Assume that on December 31, 2006, the appropriate bad debt expense adjustment was recorded for the year 2006 and accounts receivable totaling $6,000 for the year were determined to be uncollectible and written off. What was the receivables turnover ratio for 2006?
2. Assume instead that on December 31, 2006, the appropriate bad debt expense adjustment was recorded for the year 2006 and $7,000 of accounts receivable was determined to be uncollectible and written off. What was the receivables turnover ratio for 2006?
3. Explain why the answers to requirements 1 and 2 differ or do not differ.

E7-16 (Supplement) Recording Write-Offs and Reporting Accounts Receivable Using the Direct Write-Off Method

Trevorson Electronics is a small company privately owned by Jon Trevorson, an electrician who installs wiring in new homes. Because the company's financial statements are prepared only for tax purposes, Jon uses the direct write-off method. During 2005, its first year of operations, Trevorson Electronics sold $30,000 of services on account. The company collected $26,000 of these receivables during the year, and Jon believed that the remaining $4,000 was fully collectible. In 2006, Jon discovered that none of the $4,000 would be collected, so he wrote off the entire amount. To make matters worse, Jon sold only $5,000 of services during the year.

Required:

1. Prepare journal entries to record the transactions in 2005 and 2006.
2. Using only the information provided (ignore other operating expenses), prepare comparative income statements for 2005 and 2006. Was 2005 really as profitable as indicated by its income statement? Was 2006 quite as bad as indicated by its income statement? What should Jon do if he wants better information for assessing his company's ability to generate profit?

SIMPLIFY WITH SPREADSHEETS

SS7-1 Using an Aging Schedule to Estimate Bad Debts and Improve Collections from Customers

LO2

Assume you were recently hired by Caffe D'Amore, the company that formulated the world's first flavored instant cappuccino and now manufactures several lines of coffee flavored cappuccino mixes. The company recently has experienced tremendous growth in its sales to retailers, given that there are now an estimated 8 million weekly drinkers of iced cappuccino nationwide. Given its tremendous sales growth, Caffe D'Amore's receivables also have grown. Your job is to evaluate and improve collections of the company's receivables.

By analyzing collections of accounts receivable over the past five years, you were able to estimate bad debt loss rates for balances of varying ages. To estimate this year's uncollectible accounts, you jotted down the historical loss rates on the last page of a recent aged listing of outstanding customer balances (see below).

		Number of Days Unpaid				
Customer	**Total**	**1–30**	**31–60**	**61–90**	**91–120**	**Over 120**
Subtotal from previous page	$280,000	$150,000	$60,000	$40,000	$20,000	$10,000
Jumpy Jim's Coffee	1,000					1,000
Pasadena Coffee Company	24,500	14,500	8,000	2,000		
Phillips Blender House	17,000	12,000	4,000		1,000	
Pugsly's Trading Post	26,600	19,600	7,000			
Q-Coffee	12,400	8,400	3,000	1,000		
Special Sips	10,000	6,000	4,000			
Uneasy Isaac's	3,500	500				3,000
Total accounts receivable	375,000	211,000	86,000	43,000	21,000	14,000
Bad debt loss rates		1%	5%	8%	12%	20%

Required:

1. With a spreadsheet, use the above information to calculate the total estimated uncollectible accounts.
2. Prepare the year-end adjusting journal entry to adjust the allowance for doubtful accounts to the balance you calculated above. Assume the allowance account has an unadjusted credit balance of $10,000.
3. Of the customer account balances shown above on the last page of the aged listing, which should be your highest priority for contacting and pursuing collection?
4. Assume Jumpy Jim's Coffee account is determined to be uncollectible. Prepare the journal entry to write off the entire account balance.

COACHED PROBLEMS

CP7-1 Recording Accounts Receivable Transactions Using the Allowance Method

LO2

The Gillette Company is well known for its shaving products, as well as its Duracell batteries and Oral-B toothbrushes. Assume the company recently reported the following amounts in its unadjusted trial balance as of December 31, 2005 (all amounts in millions):

	Debits	*Credits*
Accounts receivable	$973	
Allowance for doubtful accounts		$ 13
Sales		9,200

Required:

1. Assume Gillette uses 1/2 of 1 percent of sales to estimate its bad debt expense for the year. If you also assume that no bad debt expense has been recorded for 2005, what adjusting journal entry would be required at December 31, 2005, for bad debt expense?

2. Assume Gillette uses the aging of accounts receivable method and estimates that $53 of accounts receivable will be uncollectible. Prepare the adjusting journal entry required at December 31, 2005, for recording bad debt expense.

3. Repeat requirement 2, except this time assume the unadjusted balance in Gillette's allowance for doubtful accounts at December 31, 2005, was a debit balance of $10.

4. If one of Gillette's main customers declared bankruptcy in 2006, what journal entry would be used to write off its $8 balance?

LO2   **CP7-2** **Interpreting Disclosure of Allowance for Doubtful Accounts**

Saucony, Inc., designs, develops, and markets performance-oriented athletic footwear, athletic apparel, and casual leather footwear. It recently disclosed the following information concerning the allowance for doubtful accounts on its Form 10-K annual report submitted to the Securities and Exchange Commission.

SCHEDULE II Valuation and Qualifying Accounts (dollars in thousands)				
Allowance for Doubtful Accounts	**Balance at Beginning of Year**	**Additions Charged to Bad Debt Expense**	**Deductions from Allowance**	**Balance at End of Year**
2004	$2,406	$4,453	$5,751	$1,108
2003	2,457	?	4,803	2,406
2002	2,047	5,767	?	2,457

Required:

1. Create a T-account for the allowance for doubtful accounts and enter into it the 2004 amounts from the above schedule. Then write the T-account in equation format to prove that the above items account for the changes in the account.

2. Record summary journal entries for 2004 related to (*a*) estimating bad debt expense and (*b*) writing off specific balances.

3. Supply the missing dollar amounts noted by ? for 2003 and 2002.

4. If Saucony had written off an additional $200 of accounts receivable during 2004, how would net receivables been affected? How would net income have been affected? Explain why.

LO3   **CP7-3** **Recording Notes Receivable Transactions**

Jung & Newbicalm Advertising (JNA) recently hired a new creative director, Howard Rachell, for its Madison Avenue office in New York. To persuade Howard to move from San Francisco, JNA agreed to advance him $100,000 on April 30, 2006, on a one-year, 10 percent note, with interest payments required on October 31, 2006, and April 30, 2007. JNA issues quarterly financial statements on March 31, June 30, September 30, and December 31.

Required:

1. Prepare the journal entry that JNA will make to record the promissory note created on April 30, 2006.

2. Prepare the journal entries that JNA will make to record the interest accruals at each quarter end and interest payments at each payment date.

3. Prepare the journal entry that JNA will make to record the principal payment at the maturity date.

CP7-4 Recording and Reporting Accounts Receivable and Notes Receivable Transactions

LO2, LO3

Sports USA, Inc., distributes athletic gear to sporting goods stores throughout the country. Most of its sales are made on account, but some particularly large items (such as sport court systems) are sold in exchange for notes receivable. Sports USA reported the following balances in its December 31, 2005, unadjusted trial balance:

	Debit	Credit
Accounts receivable	$1,110,000	
Allowance for doubtful accounts		$ 5,000
Bad debt expense	0	
Interest receivable	0	
Interest revenue		0
Notes receivable	25,200	
Sales made on account		5,600,000
Sales in exchange for notes		25,200

Notes receivable consists of principal owed by a customer on a two-year, 5 percent note accepted on November 1, 2005. The note requires the customer to make annual interest payments on October 31, 2006, and 2007. Sports USA has no concerns about the collectibility of this note. Sports USA does estimate, however, that 1 percent of its sales made on account will be uncollectible.

Required:

1. Prepare the December 31, 2005, adjusting journal entries related to accounts receivable and notes receivable.

2. Show how the adjusted balances for the above balance sheet accounts will be reported on Sports USA's classified balance sheet as of December 31, 2005.

CP7-5 Analyzing Allowance for Doubtful Accounts, Receivables Turnover Ratio, and Days to Collect

LO4

Mattel and Hasbro are two of the largest and most successful toymakers in the world, in terms of the products they sell and their receivables management practices. To evaluate their ability to collect on credit sales, consider the following information reported in their 2003 and 2002 annual reports (amounts in millions).

	Mattel			Hasbro		
Fiscal Year Ended:	**2003**	**2002**	**2001**	**2003**	**2002**	**2001**
Net sales	$4,960	$4,885	$4,688	$3,139	$2,816	$2,856
Gross accounts receivable	572	514	722	647	606	621
Allowance for doubtful accounts	28	23	56	39	51	49
Net accounts receivable	544	491	666	608	555	572

Required:

1. Calculate the receivables turnover ratios and days to collect for Mattel and Hasbro for 2003 and 2002. (Round to one decimal place.) Which of the companies is quicker to convert its receivables into cash?

2. Comment on the trend in each company's allowance for doubtful accounts over the three years. Is each company growing more or less optimistic about its ability to collect its accounts receivable? Consider the dollar amount of the allowance for doubtful accounts as well as its percentage of gross accounts receivable.

3. In its annual report filed with the SEC, Mattel's management discusses and analyzes its financial results. As part of this discussion, Mattel admits that it sold $456 million of receivables in 2003 and $437 in 2002 to a group of banks. Given this additional information, recalculate what the receivables turnover ratio and days to collect would have been in 2003 if Mattel had not factored its receivables. Does this help to explain the apparent differences determined in requirement 1 above?

GROUP A PROBLEMS   Available with McGraw-Hill's Homework Manager

LO2

PA7-1 Recording Accounts Receivable Transactions Using the Allowance Method

Kraft Foods Inc. is the second-largest food and beverage company in the world. Assume the company recently reported the following amounts in its unadjusted trial balance as of December 31, 2005 (all amounts in millions):

	Debits	Credits
Accounts receivable	$3,483	
Allowance for doubtful accounts		$ 114
Sales		31,010

Required:

1. Assume Kraft uses ½ of 1 percent of sales to estimate its bad debt expense for the year. If you also assume that no bad debt expense has been recorded for 2005, what adjusting journal entry would be required at December 31, 2005, for bad debt expense?

2. Assume Kraft uses the aging of accounts receivable method and estimates that $253 of accounts receivable will be uncollectible. Prepare the adjusting journal entry required at December 31, 2005, for recording bad debt expense.

3. Repeat requirement 2, except this time assume the unadjusted balance in Kraft's allowance for doubtful accounts at December 31, 2005, was a debit balance of $10.

4. If one of Kraft's main customers declared bankruptcy in 2006, what journal entry would be used to write off its $10 balance?

LO2

PA7-2 Interpreting Disclosure of Allowance for Doubtful Accounts

Rocky Mountain Chocolate Factory (RMCF) is one of several national companies that manufacture and sell chocolates which, according to the Department of Commerce, are consumed by the average American at a rate of 12 pounds per year. The majority of RMCF's sales are made on credit to other companies that operate Rocky Mountain stores through the United States. In addition to these accounts receivable, RMCF also has long-term notes receivable arising from the sale of 28 of its stores to other companies during 2001 and 2002. In Schedule II of its recent annual report filed with the SEC, RMCF reported the following changes in its allowance for doubtful accounts, which relates to both its accounts receivable and its notes receivable:

Balance at Beginning of Period	Charged to Costs and Expenses	Amounts Written Off	Balance at End of Period
$298,959	$1,754,524	$1,938,920	$114,563

Required:

1. Create a T-account for the allowance for doubtful accounts and enter into it the amounts from the above schedule. Then write the T-account in equation format to prove that the above items account for the changes in the account.

2. Record summary journal entries related to (a) estimating bad debt expense and (b) writing off specific balances during the year. (*Note:* Use the generic account name "receivables" to refer to the combined accounts receivable and notes receivable.)

3. If RMCF had written off an additional $20,000 of accounts receivable during the period, how would net accounts and notes receivable been affected? How would net income have been affected? Explain why.

PA7-3 Recording Notes Receivable Transactions

C&S Marketing (CSM) recently hired a new marketing director, Jeff Otos, for its downtown Minneapolis office. As part of the arrangement, CSM agreed on February 28, 2006, to advance Jeff $50,000 on a one-year, 8 percent note, with interest payments required on August 31, 2006, and February 28, 2007. CSM issues quarterly financial statements on March 31, June 30, September 30, and December 31.

Required:

1. Prepare the journal entry that CSM will make to record the execution of the note.
2. Prepare the journal entries that CSM will make to record the interest accruals at each quarter end and interest payments at each payment date.
3. Prepare the journal entry that CSM will make to record the principal payment at the maturity date.

PA7-4 Recording and Reporting Accounts Receivable and Notes Receivable Transactions

Merle Adventures, Inc., is a distributor of kayaks, kayaking equipment, and kayaking accessories. The company ships mainly to retail stores in the northeastern United States. Most of its sales are made on account, but some particularly large orders are sold in exchange for notes receivable. Merle Adventures reported the following balances in its December 31, 2005, unadjusted trial balance:

	Debit	Credit
Accounts receivable	$2,500,000	
Allowance for doubtful accounts		$ 10,000
Bad debt expense	0	
Interest receivable	0	
Interest revenue		0
Notes receivable	120,000	
Sales on account		10,225,000
Sales in exchange for notes		120,000

Notes receivable consists of principal owed by a customer on a two-year, 6 percent note accepted on November 1, 2005. The note requires the customer to make annual interest payments on October 31, 2006, and 2007. Merle Adventures has no concerns about the collectibility of this note. Merle Adventures does estimate, however, that 1 percent of its sales made on account will be uncollectible.

Required:

1. Prepare the December 31, 2005, adjusting journal entries related to accounts receivable and notes receivable.
2. Show how the adjusted balances for the above balance sheet accounts will be reported on Merle Adventures' classified balance sheet as of December 31, 2005.

PA7-5 Analyzing Allowance for Doubtful Accounts, Receivables Turnover Ratio, and Days to Collect

Coca-Cola and PepsiCo are two of the largest and most successful beverage companies in the world in terms of the products that they sell and in terms of their receivables management practices. To evaluate their ability to collect on credit sales, consider the following information reported in their 2003 and 2002 annual reports (amounts in millions).

	Coca-Cola			PepsiCo		
Fiscal Year Ended:	2003	2002	2001	2003	2002	2001
Net sales	$21,044	$19,564	$17,545	$26,971	$25,112	$23,512
Gross accounts receivable	2,152	2,152	1,941	2,935	2,647	2,263
Allowance for doubtful accounts	61	55	59	105	116	121
Net accounts receivable	2,091	2,097	1,882	2,830	2,531	2,142

Required:

1. Calculate the receivables turnover ratios and days to collect for Coca-Cola and PepsiCo for 2003 and 2002. (Round to one decimal place.) Which of the companies is quicker to convert its receivables into cash?

2. Comment on the trend in each company's allowance for doubtful accounts over the three years. Is each company growing more or less optimistic about its ability to collect its accounts receivable? Consider the dollar amount of the allowance for doubtful accounts as well as the percentage of gross accounts receivable that the allowance represents.

GROUP B PROBLEMS

L02   PB7-1 Recording Accounts Receivable Transactions Using the Allowance Method

Intel Corporation is a well-known supplier of computer chips, boards, systems, and software building blocks. Assume the company recently reported the following amounts in its unadjusted trial balance as December 31, 2005 (all amounts in millions):

	Debits	*Credits*
Accounts receivable	$3,015	
Allowance for doubtful accounts		$ 55
Sales		30,141

Required:

1. Assume Intel uses ½ of 1 percent of sales to estimate its bad debt expense for the year. If you also assume that no bad debt expense has been recorded for 2005, what adjusting journal entry would be required at December 31, 2005, for bad debt expense?

2. Assume Intel uses the aging of accounts receivable method and estimates that $175 of accounts receivable will be uncollectible. Prepare the adjusting journal entry required at December 31, 2005, for recording bad debt expense.

3. Repeat requirement 2, except this time assume the unadjusted balance in Intel's allowance for doubtful accounts at December 31, 2005, was a debit balance of $25.

4. If one of Intel's main customers declared bankruptcy in 2006, what journal entry would be used to write off its $15 balance?

L02   PB7-2 Interpreting Disclosure of Allowance for Doubtful Accounts

Xerox Corporation is the company that made the photocopier popular, although it now describes itself as a technology and services enterprise that helps businesses deploy document management strategies and improve productivity. Wow, how impressive is that? It recently disclosed the following information concerning the allowance for doubtful accounts on its Form 10-K annual report submitted to the Securities and Exchange Commission.

SCHEDULE II **Valuation and Qualifying Accounts** **(dollars in millions)**				
Allowance for Doubtful Accounts	**Balance at Beginning of Year**	**Additions Charged to Bad Debt Expense**	**Deductions from Allowance**	**Balance at End of Year**
2003	$282	$ 72	$136	$218
2002	306	?	208	282
2001	289	184	?	306

Required:

1. Create a T-account for the allowance for doubtful accounts and enter into it the 2003 amounts from the above schedule. Then, write the T-account in equation format to prove that the above items account for the changes in the account.

2. Record summary journal entries for 2003 related to (a) estimating bad debt expense and (b) writing off specific balances.

3. Supply the missing dollar amounts noted by ? for 2002 and 2001.

4. If Xerox had written off an additional $20 of accounts receivable during 2003, how would net accounts receivable been affected? How would net income have been affected? Explain why.

PB7-3 Recording Notes Receivable Transactions

LO3

Stinson Company recently agreed to loan its CEO $100,000 for the purchase of a new house. The loan was executed on May 31, 2006, and is a one-year, 7 percent note, with interest payments required on November 30, 2006, and May 31, 2007. Stinson Co. issues quarterly financial statements on March 31, June 30, September 30, and December 31.

Required:

1. Prepare the journal entry that Stinson Co. will make to record the execution of the note.

2. Prepare the journal entries that Stinson Co. will make to record the interest accruals at each quarter end and interest payments at each payment date.

3. Prepare the journal entry that Stinson Co. will make to record the principal payment at the maturity date.

PB7-4 Recording and Reporting Accounts Receivable and Notes Receivable Transactions

LO2, LO3

Tractors-R-Us is a supplier of garden tractors. Most of its sales are made on account, but some particularly large orders are sold in exchange for notes receivable. Tractors-R-Us reported the following balances in its December 31, 2005, unadjusted trial balance:

	Debit	Credit
Accounts receivable	$1,650,000	
Allowance for doubtful accounts		$ 15,000
Bad debt expense	0	
Interest receivable	0	
Interest revenue		0
Notes receivable	105,000	
Sales on account		8,250,000
Sales in exchange for notes		105,000

Notes receivable consists of principal owed by a customer on a two-year, 5 percent note accepted on July 1, 2005. The note requires the customer to make annual interest payments on June 30, 2006, and 2007. Tractors-R-Us has no concerns about the collectibility of this note. Tractors-R-Us does estimate, however, that 1 percent of its sales made on account will be uncollectible.

Required:

1. Prepare the December 31, 2005, adjusting journal entries related to accounts receivable and notes receivable.

2. Show how the adjusted balances for the above balance sheet accounts will be reported on Tractors-R-Us' classified balance sheet as of December 31, 2005.

PB7-5 Analyzing Allowance for Doubtful Accounts, Receivables Turnover Ratio, and Days to Collect

LO4

Wal-Mart and Target are two of the largest and most successful retail chains in the world. To evaluate their ability to collect on credit sales, consider the following information reported in their 2004 and 2003 annual reports (amounts in millions).

	Wal-Mart			Target		
Fiscal Year Ended:	2004	2003	2002	2004	2003	2002
Net sales	$256,329	$229,616	$204,011	$46,781	$42,722	$39,114
Gross accounts receivable	1,355	1,721	2,189	6,195	5,964	4,092
Allowance for doubtful accounts	101	152	189	419	399	261
Net accounts receivable	1,254	1,569	2,000	5,776	5,565	3,831

Required:

1. Calculate the receivables turnover ratios and days to collect for Wal-Mart and Target for 2004 and 2003. (Round to one decimal place.) Which of the companies is quicker to convert its receivables into cash?

2. Comment on the trend in each company's allowance for doubtful accounts over the three years. Is each company growing more or less optimistic about its ability to collect its accounts receivable? Consider the dollar amount of the allowance for doubtful accounts as well as the percentage of gross accounts receivable that the allowance represents.

CASES & DISCUSSION STARTERS

FINANCIAL REPORTING AND ANALYSIS CASES

LO2, LO4

C&DS7-1 Finding Financial Information

Refer to the financial statements of Landry's Restaurants in Appendix A at the end of this book, or download the annual report from the *Cases* section of the text's Web site at www.mhhe.com/phillips.

1. Does the company report an allowance for doubtful accounts on the balance sheet or in the notes? Explain why it does or does not. (*Hint:* Consider the nature of its receivables.)

2. Compute the company's receivables turnover ratio and days to collect for the most recent year. Are these comparable to the examples shown in Exhibit 7.7? Explain any unusual differences.

LO2, LO4

C&DS7-2 Comparing Financial Information

Refer to the financial statements of Dave & Buster's in Appendix B at the end of this book, or download the annual report from the *Cases* section of the text's Web site at www.mhhe.com/phillips.

1. Does the company report accounts receivable or an allowance for doubtful accounts in its financial statements? Explain why it does or does not. (*Hint:* Consider the nature of its business operations.)

2. Based on your observations for requirement 1, describe the usefulness of the receivables turnover ratio and days to collect analyses for companies that are only involved in operating restaurants. Can you think of any other businesses for which this description might apply?

LO1, LO2, LO4

C&DS7-3 Internet-Based Team Research: Examining an Annual Report

As a team, select an industry to analyze. Using your Web browser, each team member should acquire the annual report or 10-K for one publicly traded company in the industry, with each member selecting a different company. (See C&DS1-3 in Chapter 1 for a description of possible resources for these tasks.)

Required:

TEAM CASE

1. On an individual basis, each team member should write a short report that incorporates the following:

a. Calculate the receivables turnover ratio for the current and prior year, and explain any change between the two years. (To obtain the beginning accounts receivable number for the prior year, you will need the prior year's annual report.)

b. Look in the 10-K for the Schedule II analysis of "Valuation and Qualifying Accounts," which provides additional disclosures concerning the allowance for doubtful accounts. From this schedule, determine the level of bad debt expense, as a percentage of sales, for the current and prior year.

2. Then, as a team, write a short report comparing and contrasting your companies using these attributes. Discuss any patterns across the companies that you as a team observe. Provide potential explanations for any differences discovered.

ETHICS AND CRITICAL THINKING CASES

C&DS7-4 Ethical Decision Making: A Real-Life Example

LO2, LO3, LO5

ETHICAL

ISSUE

As an auditor for a large international accounting firm, you have been assigned the job of evaluating whether your client's allowance for doubtful accounts balance is a fair estimate of its uncollectible accounts. You've obtained an aged listing of the company's customer account balances for each month of the year to see if any particular customer accounts appear uncollectible. As you scan the listings, you notice something odd. An account receivable from a customer named CT&T first appeared early in the year. This customer's account balance continued to grow and age with each passing month because the customer wasn't paying the balance it owed to your client. CT&T owed $30 million to your client by the middle of the year and $100 million just one month before your client's year-end. Then in the final month of the year, CT&T's balance disappeared. Upon looking more closely at the aged listings, you notice a similar pattern for a customer called Telemedia. Its balance had grown to $2 million before disappearing in the final month of the year. You ask the accounts receivable manager, Walter Pavlo, what happened. He said the two customers "obtained some financing . . . I guess out of nowhere" and then paid off their accounts receivable balances. As strange as this seemed, you decided that these customer accounts no longer existed, so they weren't your concern.

To estimate what your client's allowance for doubtful accounts balance should be, you combine the year-end aged listing of accounts receivable balances with an analysis of your client's historical bad debt loss rates. You calculated an estimate that was significantly higher than what your client had recorded in the allowance for doubtful accounts. Walter had left for the day, so you asked his assistant why the recorded amount wasn't higher. The staff member replied, "The $35 million owed to us by Hi-Rim, which is included in the over 120 days category, doesn't require an allowance because Hi-Rim will pay it off as soon as Walter advances funds to Hi-Rim as part of the promissory note that we're arranging with Hi-Rim."

Required:

1. Discuss whether it makes sense to exclude a particular customer account from an aged listing of accounts receivable when using historical bad debt loss rates to estimate uncollectible accounts.

2. Given what you learned about Hi-Rim, what do you think may have happened with the accounts receivable from CT&T and Telemedia? Should you investigate this matter further? Explain why or why not.

Epilogue: Your client, it turns out, is MCI (formerly WorldCom) and the events described above are based on a June 10, 2002, issue of *Fortune* magazine that describes how, in the mid-1990s, Walter Pavlo contributed to WorldCom's $11 billion fraud by hiding hundreds of millions of dollars in uncollectible receivables.

C&DS7-5 Ethical Decision Making: A Mini-Case

LO2, LO5

ETHICAL

ISSUE

Having just graduated with a business degree, you're excited to begin working as a junior accountant at Clear Optics, Inc. The company supplies lenses, frames, and sunglasses to opticians and retailers throughout the country. Clear Optics is currently in the process of finalizing its third quarter (Q3) operating results. All Q3 adjusting entries have been made, except for bad debt expense. The preliminary income statement for Q3 is shown below, along with reported results for Q2 and Q1.

	CLEAR OPTICS, INC.		
	Quarterly Income Statements		
	(amounts in thousands of U.S. dollars)		
	Q3 (preliminary)	Q2 (as reported)	Q1 (as reported)
Net sales	$135,800	$135,460	$130,100
Cost of goods sold	58,400	58,250	55,990
Gross profit	77,400	77,210	74,110
Selling, general, and administrative expenses	56,560	53,975	53,690
Bad debt expense	—	6,050	4,200
Income before income taxes	20,840	17,185	16,220
Income tax expense	5,620	5,155	5,020
Net income	$ 15,220	$ 12,030	$ 11,200

The corporate controller has asked you to examine the allowance for doubtful accounts and use the aged listing of accounts receivable to determine the adjustment needed to record estimated bad debts for the quarter. The controller states that, "Although our customers are somewhat slower in paying this quarter, we can't afford to increase the allowance for doubtful accounts. If anything, we need to decrease it—an adjusted balance of about $8,000 is what I'd like to see. Play around with our estimated bad debt loss rates until you get it to work."

You were somewhat confused by what the controller had told you, but you chalked it up to your lack of experience and decided to analyze the allowance for doubtful accounts. You summarized the transactions recorded in the allowance for doubtful accounts using the T-account below:

Allowance for Doubtful Accounts			
		7,900	**January 1 bal. fwd.**
Q1 Write-offs	4,110	4,200	Q1 Bad debts estimate
		7,990	**March 31 adjusted**
Q2 Write-offs	4,120	6,050	Q2 Bad debts estimate
		9,920	**June 30 adjusted**
Q3 Write-offs	4,030	—	
		5,890	**September 30 unadjusted**

Required:

1. What bad debts estimate for Q3 will produce the $8,000 balance that the controller would like to see?

2. Prepare the adjusting journal entry that would be required to record this estimate.

3. If the entry in requirement 2 is made, what does it do to the Q3 income and the trend in earnings? (Assume that income tax expense does not change.)

4. Reconsider the statement the controller made to you. Is his suggestion a logical way to use the aging method to estimate bad debts?

5. What would be the Q3 net income if the bad debt expense estimate was the average of bad debt expense in Q2 and Q1? What would this do to the trend in net income across the three quarters? (Assume that income tax expense does not change.)

6. Is there any evidence of unethical behavior in this case? Explain your answer.

LO1, LO4   **C&DS7-6 Critical Thinking: Analyzing**

Problem Solved Company has been operating for five years as a software consulting firm. During this period, it has experienced rapid growth in sales revenue and in accounts receivable. To solve its growing receivables problem, the company hired you as its first corporate controller. You have put into place more stringent credit-granting and collection procedures that you expect will reduce receivables by approximately one-third by year-end. You have gathered the following data related to the changes (in thousands):

	Beginning of Year	End of Year (projected)
Accounts receivable	$1,000,608	$ 660,495
Less: Allowance for doubtful accounts	36,800	10,225
Net accounts receivable	$ 963,808	$ 650,270

	Prior Year	Current Year (projected)
Net sales (assume all on credit)	$7,515,444	$7,015,069

Required:

1. Compute the accounts receivable turnover ratio based on three different assumptions:
    a. The stringent credit policies reduce the balance in Net accounts receivable and decrease Net sales as projected in the tables above.
    b. The stringent credit policies reduce the balance in Net accounts receivable as projected in the tables above but do not decrease Net sales from the prior year.
    c. The stringent credit policies are not implemented, resulting in no change from the beginning of the year accounts receivable balance and no change in Net sales from the prior year.

2. On the basis of your findings in requirement 1, write a brief memo explaining the potential benefits and drawbacks of more stringent credit policies and how they are likely to affect the accounts receivable turnover ratio.

chapter eight

Reporting and Interpreting Inventories and Cost of Goods Sold

8

It's just past the middle of the term, so it's time to ask yourself how you're doing. Suppose you've taken three tests and scored 30 percent on the first, 60 percent on the second, and 90 percent on the third. Does this mean you're doing great, terrible, or average? It could be any of these three interpretations, depending on whether you focus on the first test, the last test, or the average of all three. Wouldn't this be a lot easier to figure out if there were rules describing how to interpret your test scores?

The same issue exists when companies report the cost of their inventories. Inflation can cause these costs to increase over time, while technological innovation can cause them to decrease. Either way, inventory is likely to be made up of some items acquired at lower unit costs and others at higher costs. Suppose **OAKLEY,** the sunglass maker for Annika Sorenstam, produces three pairs of its Straight Jacket sunglasses, at costs of $30, $60, and $90 each. Do these numbers suggest that their cost is low, moderate, or high? As with your test scores, it could mean any of the three, depending on how you look at it. Fortunately, in accounting, certain rules are used when determining the cost of inventory on hand and the cost of inventory sold. The tricky part is that these rules allow accountants to use one of several possible methods when determining the costs of inventories and goods sold, with each method leading to a different number. This flexibility of choice can be a good thing because it allows managers to use the method that best fits their business environment. This flexibility also makes it essential, however, that you know which methods are being used and how they work. That's what we'll be reflecting on in this chapter.

INSIDE
LOOKING
OUT

OUTSIDE
LOOKING IN

This chapter focuses on how the costs of inventories and goods sold are reported in financial statements. We focus on Oakley Inc., a company that sells goggles, sunglasses, watches, and other apparel.

Oakley produces about three million frames a year, and estimates that another million are made by counterfeiters.

D o you know what managers worry about when making inventory decisions, how the results of their decisions are reported, and how you can use the reported results to evaluate the quality of their inventory decisions? If any of your answers are no, then you're doing exactly what you should be doing—reading this chapter. In it, we address these questions, which cover the specific learning objectives shown in Exhibit 8.1.

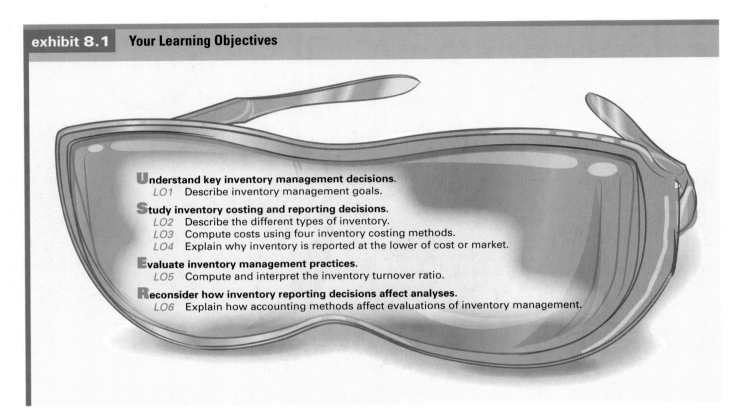

exhibit 8.1 **Your Learning Objectives**

Understand key inventory management decisions.
  LO1 Describe inventory management goals.

Study inventory costing and reporting decisions.
  LO2 Describe the different types of inventory.
  LO3 Compute costs using four inventory costing methods.
  LO4 Explain why inventory is reported at the lower of cost or market.

Evaluate inventory management practices.
  LO5 Compute and interpret the inventory turnover ratio.

Reconsider how inventory reporting decisions affect analyses.
  LO6 Explain how accounting methods affect evaluations of inventory management.

UNDERSTAND
KEY INVENTORY MANAGEMENT DECISIONS

The Business of Inventory Management

You may not make or sell inventory, but you buy it all the time. The things that concern you as a consumer are the same issues that concern managers who make inventory decisions. The primary goals of inventory managers are to (1) ensure sufficient quantities of inventory are available to meet customers' needs and (2) ensure inventory quality meets customers' expectations and company standards. At the same time, they try to (3) minimize the costs of acquiring and carrying inventory (including costs related to purchasing, production, storage, spoilage, theft, obsolescence, and financing). Purchasing or producing too few units of a hot-selling item causes stock-outs that mean lost sales revenue and decreases in customer satisfaction. Conversely, purchasing too many units of a slow-selling item increases storage costs as well as interest costs on short-term borrowings that finance the purchases. It may even lead to losses if the merchandise becomes outdated and cannot be sold at regular prices.

Oakley's managers will agree that inventory cost, quantity, and quality are important factors when managing their inventories, but they'll claim there's a fourth factor that drives their inventory decisions: product innovation. Oakley believes so strongly in product innovation that it once described itself as "a technology company, in business to seek out problems with existing consumer products and solve them in ways that redefine product

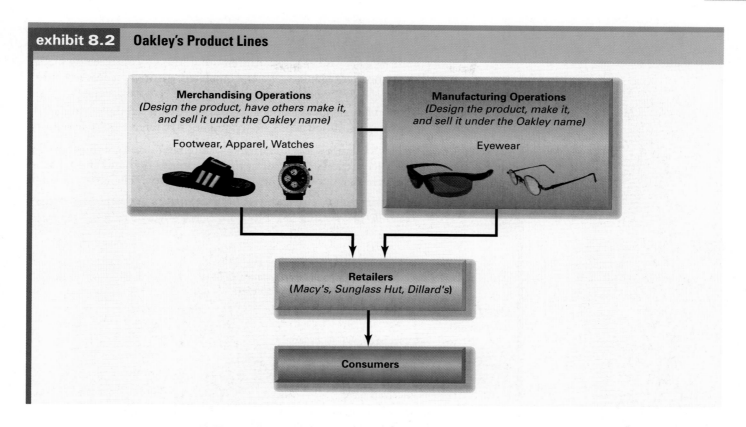

exhibit 8.2 **Oakley's Product Lines**

Merchandising Operations
(Design the product, have others make it, and sell it under the Oakley name)

Footwear, Apparel, Watches

Manufacturing Operations
(Design the product, make it, and sell it under the Oakley name)

Eyewear

Retailers
(Macy's, Sunglass Hut, Dillard's)

Consumers

categories."[1] Wow, with all the different products that Oakley sells (shown in Exhibit 8.2), the company may have solved more problems than you've been assigned so far in this course.

STUDY

INVENTORY COSTING AND REPORTING DECISIONS

Items Included in Inventory

Inventory includes goods that are (1) held for sale in the normal course of business or (2) used to produce goods for sale. Inventory is reported on the balance sheet as a current asset because it is used or converted into cash within a company's operating cycle, which is normally less than one year. Goods in inventory are initially recorded at cost, which is the amount given up to acquire the asset and bring it into a condition and location ready for sale. The general name "inventory" can include several specific types of inventory, which usually differ between merchandisers and manufacturers. Since Oakley is both a merchandiser and a manufacturer, let's briefly describe how its various types of inventory differ:

- **Merchandisers** hold *merchandise inventory*, which usually is acquired in a finished condition and is ready for sale without further processing.
- **Manufacturers** often hold three types of inventory, with each representing a different stage in the manufacturing process:
  1. *Raw materials inventory* includes materials that eventually are processed further to produce finished goods. Oakley owns lots of different raw materials, including a stock of Titanium that gives the same lightweight strength to sunglasses that it gives to jet engines. Items are included in raw materials inventory until they

---

[1]Oakley Incorporated 2002 Form 10-K.

enter the production process, at which time they become part of work in process inventory.

2. *Work in process inventory* includes goods that are in the process of being manufactured, but are not yet complete. When completed, work in process inventory becomes finished goods inventory.

3. *Finished goods inventory* includes manufactured goods that are complete and ready for sale. At this stage, finished goods are treated just like merchandise inventory.

Excerpts from Oakley's balance sheet and financial statement notes are shown in Exhibit 8.3. The balance sheet reports the total of the inventories on hand and refers to Note 3, which provides details about the various types of inventory included in the total.

exhibit 8.3	Inventory Reporting Sample

OAKLEY, INC.
Consolidated Balance Sheets
(in thousands)

December 31,	2003	2002	2001
Assets			
Current Assets			
Cash and Cash Equivalents	$ 49,211	$ 22,248	$ 5,612
Accounts Receivable, net	77,989	68,116	74,775
Inventories (Note 3)	98,691	87,007	77,270
Prepaid Income Taxes and Other Expenses	21,395	21,965	29,034
Total Current Assets	247,286	199,336	186,691

OAKLEY, INC.
Notes to the Consolidated Financial Statements
(in thousands)

Note 3—Inventories
Inventories at December 31 consist

of the following:	2003	2002	2001
Raw Materials	$21,310	$22,188	$23,137
Finished Goods	77,381	64,819	54,133
	$98,691	$87,007	$77,270

Notice that Note 3 includes only two categories of inventories: raw materials and finished goods. As with many companies that have both merchandising and manufacturing operations, Oakley combines *merchandise inventory* with manufactured *finished goods inventory* because both categories relate to goods that are ready to sell. You'll also notice that Oakley did not report any *work in process inventory*. Although it's possible that Oakley did not have any semicompleted goods in production at year-end, the more likely explanation is that Oakley had an insignificant amount of them, so their costs are included with either raw materials or finished goods inventories. This illustrates an accounting concept called **materiality,** which states that relatively small amounts not likely to influence decisions may be recorded and reported in the most cost-beneficial way. Based on this concept, Oakley separately reports only those amounts that are large enough to influence a user's decision.

Cost of Goods Sold

As highlighted in the income statement excerpt below in Exhibit 8.4, the cost of goods sold (CGS) expense is directly related to sales revenue. Sales revenue for an accounting period is the number of units sold multiplied by the sales price. The calculation for cost of goods sold uses the same number of units used to calculate sales revenue, except it is multiplied by the unit *cost* of the items sold. The difference between these two line-items is a subtotal called gross profit.

exhibit 8.4	Sample Income Statement

OAKLEY, INC.
Consolidated Income Statements
(in thousands)

For the Years Ended December 31,	2003	2002	2001
Net Sales	$521,549	$489,552	$429,267
Cost of Goods Sold	226,846	211,962	174,332
Gross Profit	294,703	277,590	254,935

Now let's examine the relationship between cost of goods sold on the income statement and inventory on the balance sheet. Oakley starts each accounting period with a stock of inventory called *beginning inventory* (BI). During the accounting period, new *purchases* (P) are added to inventory. As shown in Exhibit 8.5, the sum of these two amounts is the **goods available for sale** during that period. What remains unsold at the end of the period is reported as *ending inventory* (EI) on the balance sheet. The portion of goods available for sale that is sold becomes *cost of goods sold* on the income statement. The ending inventory for one accounting period then becomes the beginning inventory for

YOU SHOULD KNOW

Goods available for sale
refers to the sum of beginning inventory and purchases for the period.

exhibit 8.5	Cost of Goods Sold for Merchandise Inventory

Beginning Inventory $40,000

Purchases $55,000

Goods Available for Sale $95,000

Still here

Sold

Ending Inventory $35,000

Cost of Goods Sold $60,000

(Balance Sheet)

(Income Statement)

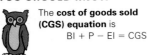
the next period. The relationships between these various inventory amounts are brought together in the **cost of goods sold (CGS) equation.**

To illustrate, assume that Oakley began the period with $40,000 of Detonator™ watches in beginning inventory, purchased additional merchandise during the period for $55,000, and had $35,000 left in inventory at the end of the period. These amounts can be combined as follows to compute cost of goods sold of $60,000:

Beginning inventory	$40,000
+ Purchases of merchandise during the year	+ 55,000
= Goods available for sale	= 95,000
− Ending inventory	− 35,000
= Cost of goods sold	= $60,000

These same relationships can be represented in the merchandise inventory T-account as follows:

+ Merchandise Inventory (A) −			
Beginning inventory	40,000		
Purchases of inventory	55,000	Cost of goods sold	60,000
Ending inventory	35,000		

If three of these four values are known, either the cost of goods sold equation or the inventory T-account can be used to solve for the fourth value. You get a chance to practice this in the following Self-Study Quiz.

HOW'S IT GOING? A Self-Study Quiz

Assume the following facts for Oakley's Overdrive™ golf shoe product line for the year 2007:

Beginning inventory 500 units at unit cost of $75.

Purchases of inventory 1,200 units at unit cost of $75.

Sales of 1,100 units at a sales price of $100 (cost per unit $75).

1. Using the cost of goods sold equation or the T-account, compute the dollar amount of Overdrive golf shoes in inventory at the end of the period.

			+ Merchandise Inventory (A) −	
Beginning inventory	$ ☐		BI ☐	
+ Purchases of merchandise during the year	☐		P ☐	☐ CGS
− Ending inventory	☐			
= Cost of goods sold	$ ☐		EI ☐	

2. Prepare the first three lines of the income statement (showing computation of gross profit) for the Overdrive golf shoe line for the year 2007.

After you have finished, check your answers with the solutions in the margin.

Quiz Answers

1. BI = 500 × $75 = $37,500
   P = 1,200 × $75 = $90,000
   CGS = 1,100 × $75 = $82,500

   BI + P − EI = CGS
   37,500 + 90,000 − EI = 82,500
   37,500 + 90,000 − 82,500 = EI
   45,000 = EI

2. Net sales $110,000
   Cost of goods sold   82,500
   Gross profit $ 27,500

Inventory Costing Methods

In the Overdrive golf shoes example presented in the Self-Study Quiz, the cost of all units of the shoes was the same—$75. If inventory costs normally stayed constant like this, we'd be done right now. But just as you don't always get 90 percent on every test, the cost of goods doesn't stay constant forever. In recent years, the costs of many manufactured items such as automobiles have risen moderately. In some industries, such as computers and electronics, costs of production have dropped dramatically.

When inventory costs change, how inventory items are treated (as sold or remaining in inventory) can turn profits into losses and cause companies to pay or save hundreds of millions of dollars in taxes. A simple example will illustrate these dramatic effects.

Assume that one of Oakley's *Icon* stores experienced the following:

Jan.	1	Beginning inventory: Two units of Wisdom™ snow goggles at $70 each.
March	12	Purchased four units of Wisdom snow goggles at $80 each.
June	9	Purchased one unit of Wisdom snow goggles at $100.
Nov.	5	Sold four units for $120 each.

Note that cost of the goggles *rose* rapidly between January and June. On November 5, four units are sold for $120 each, so revenues of $480 are recorded. What amount is recorded as cost of goods sold? The answer depends on which goggles we assume were sold. Four generally accepted inventory costing methods are available for determining this:

1. *Specific identification.*
2. *First-in, first-out (FIFO).*
3. *Last-in, first-out (LIFO).*
4. *Weighted average.*

The four inventory costing methods are alternative ways to split the total dollar amount of goods available for sale between (1) ending inventory and (2) cost of goods sold. The first method specifically identifies which items remain in inventory and which are sold. The remaining three methods *assume* inventory costs flow in a certain way from *Inventory* on the balance sheet to *Cost of Goods Sold* on the income statement.

Specific Identification Method

When the **specific identification method** is used, the cost of each item sold is individually identified and recorded as cost of goods sold. This method requires keeping track of the purchase cost of each item. This is done by either (1) coding the purchase cost on each unit before placing it in stock or (2) keeping a separate record of the unit and identifying it with a serial number. In the snow goggles example, any four of the items could have been sold. If we assume that one of the $70 items, two of the $80 items, and the one $100 item have been sold, the cost of those items ($70 + $80 + $80 + $100) would become cost of goods sold ($330). The cost of the remaining items ($70 + $80 + $80) would be included in ending inventory ($230).

The specific identification method is impractical when large quantities of similar items are stocked. On the other hand, when dealing with expensive and unique items such as houses or fine jewelry, this method is appropriate. A drawback of this method is that it can allow for the unethical manipulation of financial results when the units are identical because it's possible to alter the cost of goods sold and ending inventory accounts by picking and choosing from among the different unit costs.

To prevent accounting manipulations that can occur using the specific identification method, inventory often is accounted for using one of three cost flow assumptions. Under these cost flow assumptions, *inventory costs are not based on the actual physical flow of goods* on and off the shelves. Rather, they are based on an assumed flow of costs from the balance sheet to the income statement. This is why they are called cost flow *assumptions.* A useful tool for imagining inventory cost flow assumptions is a bin, or container, as shown on page 330. Try picturing the following inventory costing methods as flows of inventory costs in and out of the bin. We will apply the methods *as if* all purchases during the period take place before any sales and cost of goods sold are recorded.[2]

---

[2]You might think it's odd that we said in Chapter 6 that most modern companies use perpetual inventory systems and then, in this chapter, we illustrate the cost flow assumptions using a periodic system. We actually have several good reasons for doing this, which we explain in Supplement A at the end of this chapter. For those who would like to learn how certain cost flow assumptions are applied in perpetual inventory systems, see Supplement A. For purposes of examples shown in the chapter and for problem materials at the end of this chapter, we assume no shrinkage (a topic discussed in Chapter 6).

YOU SHOULD KNOW

Specific identification is the inventory costing method that identifies the cost of the specific item that was sold.

ETHICAL

ISSUE

COACH'S CORNER

Although the actual physical flow of goods can differ from the cost flow assumption used, it's useful to picture in your mind how the costs flow from the balance sheet to the income statement.

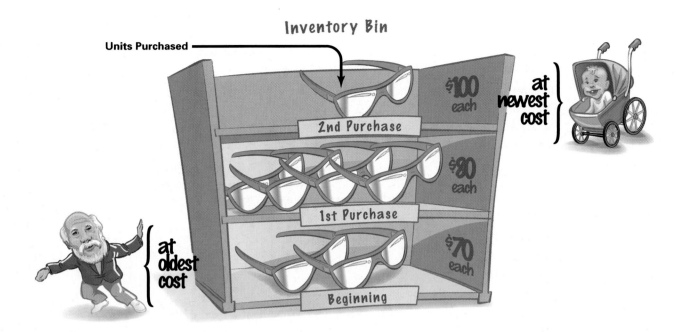

Inventory Bin

Units Purchased

2nd Purchase $100 each   at newest cost

1st Purchase $80 each

Beginning $70 each

at oldest cost

First-In, First-Out (FIFO) Method

No, it's not the name of a dog. The **first-in, first-out method,** usually called **FIFO,** is a method for computing inventory costs. It assumes that the costs for the oldest goods (the first ones in) are used first to calculate cost of goods sold and the newer costs are left to calculate ending inventory. It's as if costs flow in and out of an inventory bin that works like a gumball machine (as shown in Exhibit 8.6),[3] corresponding to the following two-step process.

Step 1: Each purchase is treated as if it were deposited in the bin from the top in sequence. In our example, the costs for the oldest units (two units in beginning inventory at $70) are first in followed by the next oldest (four units at $80), and finally the most recent purchase (one unit at $100). In total, these costs result in goods available for sale that cost $560.

Step 2: The cost of each unit sold is then removed from the bottom in sequence, as if the bottom of the bin swung open and the *first* costs *in* are the *first* costs *out*. In our example, four units are sold, so the cost of goods sold is calculated as the cost of the first two units in at $70 and two more units from the next layer at $80 each. These costs totaling $300 are reported as the cost of goods sold (CGS).

The costs of any remaining units (two units at $80 and one at $100 = $260) are reported as ending inventory. FIFO allocates the *oldest* unit costs *to cost of goods sold* and the *newest* unit costs *to ending inventory*.

Last-In, First-Out (LIFO) Method

The **last-in, first-out method,** usually called **LIFO,** assumes that the costs for the newest goods (the last ones in) are used first and the oldest costs are left in ending inventory. Picture this kind of cost flow as picking paving stones from the top of a stack at a home improvements store. Go ahead, flip ahead to Exhibit 8.7, take a look, and then come right back here.

Step 1: As in FIFO, each purchase is treated as if it were deposited from the top (two units at $70 followed by four units at $80, and one unit at $100) resulting in the goods available for sale of $560.

---

[3]Thanks to Cathy Larson for suggesting this analogy.

exhibit 8.6	**Inventory Cost Flows Using FIFO (First-in, first-out)**

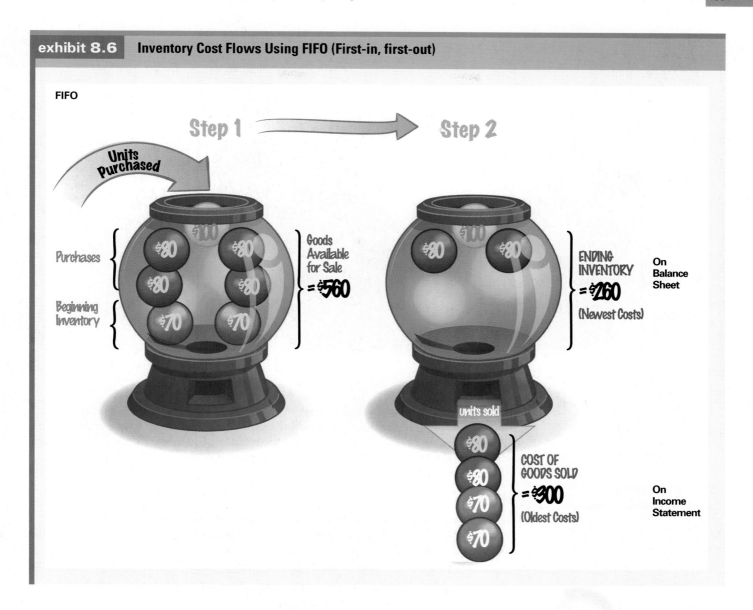

Step 2: Unlike FIFO, where costs are removed from the bottom of the bin, in LIFO each item sold is treated as if its cost were removed in sequence from the top of a stack (beginning with the most recent purchases). In our example, this would mean we assume the four units sold consist of one unit at $100 followed by three units at $80. The total cost of these four *last-in* goods ($340) is *first out* when reported as cost of goods sold (CGS).

The costs of the remaining units (one at $80 and two at $70) are reported as ending inventory. LIFO allocates the *newest* unit costs *to cost of goods sold* and the *oldest* unit costs *to ending inventory.*

Notice that the cost flows assumed for LIFO are the exact opposite of FIFO.

POINT OF INTEREST

You won't see many Canadian companies use LIFO—their government doesn't allow it in income tax calculations. In the United States, the LIFO Conformity Rule requires that if LIFO is used on the income tax return, it also must be used to calculate inventory and cost of goods sold for the financial statements.

	Cost of Goods Sold *(on the income statement)*	Inventory *(on the balance sheet)*
FIFO	First-in (oldest) unit costs	Newest unit costs
LIFO	Last-in (newest) unit costs	Oldest unit costs

exhibit 8.7   Inventory Cost Flows Using LIFO (Last-in, first-out)

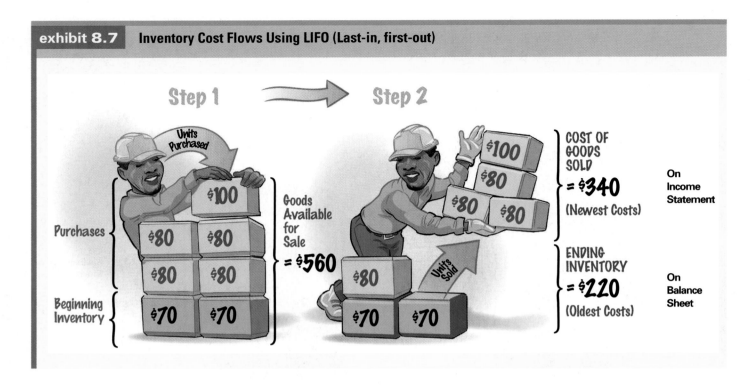

Also notice that the name of the costing method describes the unit costs that are *first out* of inventory. The name doesn't mention the unit costs that are still here in ending inventory. When calculating the cost of ending inventory, you might find it useful to think of the costs that are still here. For LIFO, the first-in costs are still here, so think LIFO = FISH (first-in, still here).

Weighted Average Cost Method

The **weighted average cost method** requires calculating the weighted average unit cost of goods available for sale. This weighted average unit cost is then used to assign a dollar amount to cost of goods sold and to ending inventory. The weighted average unit cost of goods available for sale is computed as shown in Steps 1*a* and 1*b*.

Step 1a. Determine the number of units and cost of goods available for sale. Using our example, these would be calculated as follows:

Number of Units	×	Unit Cost	=	Total Cost
2	×	$ 70	=	$140
4	×	$ 80	=	320
1	×	$100	=	100
7		Available for Sale		$560

Step 1b. Calculate the weighted average cost per unit, as follows:

$$\text{Weighted Average Cost} = \frac{\text{\$ Cost of Goods Available for Sale}}{\text{\# Number of Units Available for Sale}}$$

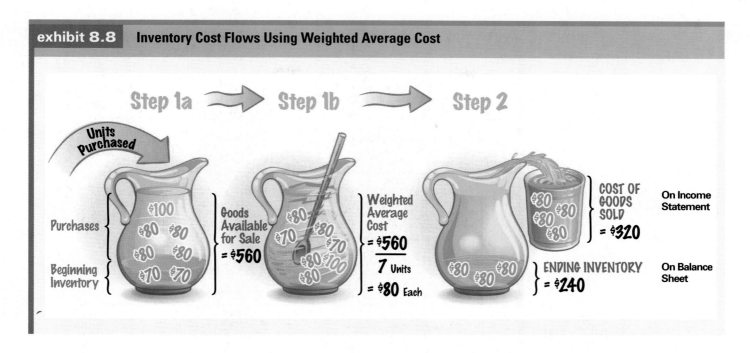

exhibit 8.8   **Inventory Cost Flows Using Weighted Average Cost**

This step has the effect of mixing all the unit costs together like Kool-Aid in a jug, as shown in Exhibit 8.8. For our example, this would be calculated as follows:

$$\text{Weighted Average Cost} = \frac{\$560}{7 \text{ Units}} = \$80 \text{ per unit}$$

Step 2. Assign the same weighted average unit cost to cost of goods sold and ending inventory. In our example, this would be calculated as follows

$$\text{Cost of Goods Sold} = 4 \text{ units} \times \$80 = \$320$$

$$\text{Ending Inventory} = 3 \text{ units} \times \$80 = \$240$$

Financial Statement Effects of Inventory Costing Methods

Exhibit 8.9 summarizes the financial statement effects of the FIFO, LIFO, and weighted average methods in our example. Remember that the methods differ only in how they allocate the cost of goods available for sale to cost of goods sold versus ending inventory. If a cost goes into ending inventory, it doesn't go into cost of goods sold. For that reason, the method that gives the highest dollar amount to ending inventory also gives the lowest to cost of goods sold. When costs are rising, as they are in our example, FIFO leads to a higher inventory value (making the balance sheet *appear* stronger) and a lower cost of goods sold (resulting in a higher gross profit, making the company *look* more profitable). The effects are opposite when costs are falling, with FIFO giving the lowest ending inventory amount as well as the highest cost of goods sold—a double whammy. Remember that these are not "real" economic effects because the same number of units is either sold or still on hand in ending inventory—*all that differs are the costs assigned to them.* Also remember that managers can choose any of the four inventory costing methods.

Given these effects, you might wonder why a company would ever use a method that produces a lower inventory amount and a higher cost of goods sold. The answer is suggested

Inventory costing methods are reviewed in a video and are demonstrated in an animated tutorial—both of which are available on the DVD for use with this book.

exhibit 8.9	Financial Statement Effects of Inventory Costing Methods		

	FIFO	LIFO	Weighted Average
Cost of Goods Sold Calculation			
Beginning inventory	$140	$140	$140
Add: Purchases	420	420	420
Goods available for sale	560	560	560
Subtract: Ending inventory (to balance sheet)	260	220	240
Cost of goods sold (to income statement)	$300	$340	$320
Effect on the Income Statement			
Sales	$480	$480	$480
Cost of goods sold	300	340	320
Gross profit	180	140	160
Other expenses	80	80	80
Income before income taxes	100	60	80
Income tax expense (25%)	25	15	20
Net income	75	45	60
Effect on the Balance Sheet			
Inventory	$260	$220	$240

in Exhibit 8.9, in the line called *Income tax expense*. When faced with increasing costs per unit, as in our example, a company that uses FIFO will have a higher income tax expense. This income tax effect is a real cost, in the sense that the company will actually have to pay more income taxes in the current year, thereby reducing the company's cash. Given a choice between FIFO and LIFO, most stockholders would want managers to use the method that results in the lowest income taxes because this saves the company money. Managers, on the other hand, might prefer the method that produces the highest net income, particularly if they are paid a bonus based on reported profits. Clearly, a manager who selects an accounting method that is not optimal for the company solely to increase his or her own pay is engaging in questionable ethical behavior.

ETHICAL

ISSUE

A common question people ask is can a manager choose LIFO one period, FIFO the next, and then back to LIFO, depending on whether unit costs are rising or declining during the period? Because this would make it difficult to compare financial results across periods, accounting rules (and tax rules) prevent it. A change in method is allowed only if it will improve the accuracy with which financial results and financial position are measured, and that's likely to happen only once during a company's life. Companies can, however, use different inventory methods for different product lines included in inventory, as long as the methods are used consistently over time.

POINT OF INTEREST

SIFCO Industries, a metal works company, uses FIFO, LIFO, and specific identification for its different product lines.

Additional Inventory Cost Flow Computations

Now that you've seen how these cost flow assumptions work and that they actually make a difference in the reported results, you could probably use some practice with a more complex example. In the following problem, we will show you how to calculate the cost of ending inventory using the FIFO cost flow assumption and then "force out" the cost of goods sold using the CGS equation. Pay close attention to this example because you'll be using the same numbers in LIFO computations in the Self-Study Quiz that follows it.

Assume Oakley started buying and selling a new line of products during the year and had the following transactions, which resulted in a total cost of goods available for sale of $5,350. Based on a year-end inventory count, Oakley determined that 200 units were still on hand. The cost of ending inventory is calculated using the first-in, first-out (FIFO) cost flow assumption, and the remainder of the cost of goods available for sale is the cost of goods sold (as indicated by the CGS equation).

Date	Description	Units	Unit Cost	Total Cost
January 1	Beginning Inventory	0	$ 0	$ 0
March 13	Purchase	50	10	500
April 27	Purchase	100	11	1,100
June 15	Purchase	150	12	1,800
August 11	Purchase	150	13	1,950
	Goods Available for Sale	450		$5,350

Still here   or   *Sold*

FIFO Ending Inventory	Units	Unit Cost	Total Cost
Last units in (August 11)	150	$13	$1,950
Next units in (June 15)	50	12	600
Total	200		$2,550

FIFO Cost of Goods Sold	Total Cost
Goods Available for Sale	$5,350
− Ending Inventory	2,550
Cost of Goods Sold	$2,800

In the above example, we used the CGS equation to force out the cost of goods sold. This approach will always produce the correct cost of goods sold if the cost of goods available for sale and cost of ending inventory are calculated correctly. There's always the risk, however, that you made a mistake when calculating them. To double-check your calculations, you can calculate the cost of goods sold directly by applying the FIFO cost flow assumption to the 250 units sold, as shown below. Notice that we assume that only 100 units from the June 15 purchase are sold, which complements our earlier assumption that 50 units from this purchase are still sitting in ending inventory.

FIFO Cost of Goods Sold	Units	Unit Cost	Total Cost
First units in (March 13)	50	$10	$ 500
Next units in (April 27)	100	11	1,100
Next units in (June 15)	100	12	1,200
Total	250		$2,800

COACH'S CORNER

Under FIFO, newest costs are assigned to ending inventory (last-in, still here). Because the number of units in ending inventory (200) is greater than the 150 units bought on August 11, we go to the next most recent purchases for unit costs. That is, we assume that 50 of the 150 units bought on June 15 remain in ending inventory.

COACH'S CORNER

This direct calculation of cost of goods sold is a great way to prove that the number forced out of the CGS equation is correct.

HOW'S IT GOING? A Self-Study Quiz

Using the information provided above, compute (1) the LIFO cost of ending inventory and (2) the LIFO cost of goods sold (using the CGS equation).

LIFO **Ending Inventory**	Units	Unit Cost	Total Cost	LIFO **Cost of Goods Sold**	Total Cost
First units in				Goods Available for Sale	
Next units in				− Ending Inventory	
Next units in				Cost of Goods Sold	
Total					

After you have finished, check your answers with the solutions in the margin.

Reporting Inventory at the Lower of Cost or Market

You've spent a bunch of time learning how to calculate inventory costs using different methods. And it's been time well spent because most of the time inventories are reported at cost, just like the cost principle says. However, you're not quite done yet because you need to know what happens when inventory value falls below its recorded cost. The value of inventory can fall below its recorded cost for two reasons: (1) it's easily replaced by identical goods at a lower cost, or (2) it's become outdated or damaged. The first case typically involves high-tech goods like cell phones or Oakley's Plutonite® lenses, which become cheaper to make when companies become more efficient at making them. The second case commonly occurs with fad or seasonal goods, like Oakley's board shorts, when their value drops at the end of the season. In either instance, when the value of inventory falls below its recorded cost, the amount recorded for *Inventory* is written down to its lower market value. This rule is known as reporting inventories at the **lower of cost or market (LCM)**, which ensures inventory assets are not reported at more than they're worth. Let's look at how the inventory write-down is determined and recorded.

Assume Oakley's ending inventory includes two items where their replacement costs have recently fallen as a result of significant improvements in production technology. Each item's replacement cost is used as an estimate of market value, which is then compared to the recorded cost per unit. The lower of these two amounts is called the lower of cost or market, and it is multiplied by the number of units on hand to calculate the amount that this inventory should be reported at after all adjustments have been made.

Item	Quantity	Cost per Item	Replacement Cost (Market) per Item	LCM per Item	Total Lower of Cost or Market
Plutonite lenses	1,000	$165	$150	$150	1,000 × $150 = $150,000
Unobtainium inlays	400	20	25	20	400 × $ 20 = 8,000

Because the market value of the 1,000 Plutonite lenses ($150) is *lower* than the recorded cost ($165), the amount recorded for ending inventory needs to be written down by $15 per unit ($165 − 150), using the following journal entry:

Loss in Inventory Value (+E, −SE) [1,000 × ($165 − 150)]	15,000	
Inventory (−A)		15,000

Assets	=	Liabilities	+	Stockholders' Equity
Inventory −15,000				Loss in Inventory Value (+E) −15,000

exhibit 8.10	**Sample Inventory Accounting Policy Note**

OAKLEY, INC.
Notes to the Consolidated Financial Statements

Note 1—Significant Accounting Policies
Inventories—Inventories are stated at the lower of cost to purchase and/or manufacture the inventory or the current estimated market value of the inventory. The Company regularly reviews its inventory quantities on hand and records a provision for excess and obsolete inventory based primarily on the Company's estimated forecast of product demand and production requirements.

Because the replacement cost of the inlays ($25) is still higher than the original cost ($20), no write-down is necessary. The inlays remain on the books at their cost of $20 per unit ($8,000 in total). They are not *increased* in value to the higher replacement cost because GAAP requires that they be reported at the *lower* of cost or market.

Most companies explain the use of the LCM rule for inventory in Note 1 in their financial statement footnotes. Oakley's is shown in Exhibit 8.10.

The failure to estimate the market value of inventory appropriately is one of the most common types of financial statement errors. To learn more about how these and other inventory errors can affect the financial statements, see Supplement B at the end of this chapter.

EVALUATE
INVENTORY MANAGEMENT PRACTICES

Interpreting Changes in Inventory Levels

If you see a company's inventory balance increase from $100,000 in one period to $130,000 in the next, is it good news or bad news? It could be good news, if it occurs because management is building up stock in anticipation of increasing sales in the near future. On the other hand, it could be bad news if the buildup is a result of having bought or made a bunch of crusty old inventory that nobody wants. If you work inside the company, it's easy to determine whether the reason for a change in inventory levels is good or bad news: you just talk to the sales managers. But if you're a typical financial statement user on the outside, how can you tell? The method used by most analysts is called an **inventory turnover** analysis. Does this sound familiar? Yes, it's similar to the receivables turnover analysis that you studied in Chapter 7, except that this time we're dealing with inventory and cost of goods sold.

Inventory Turnover Analysis

The idea behind an inventory turnover analysis is shown in Exhibit 8.11. As a company buys goods, its inventory balance goes up, and as it sells goods, the inventory balance goes down. This process of buying and selling is called inventory turnover, and it is repeated over and over during each accounting period, for each line of products.

Analysts assess how many times average inventory has been bought (or made) and sold during the period by calculating the inventory turnover ratio:

YOU SHOULD KNOW

Inventory turnover is the process of buying and selling inventory.

COACH'S CORNER

Notice that the top number in this ratio is Cost of Goods Sold (not sales revenue). This makes the top part of the ratio comparable to the bottom part, which also is based on costs. Also, you should realize that beginning inventory for the current year is the same as ending inventory for the prior year.

$$\text{Inventory Turnover Ratio} = \frac{\text{Cost of Goods Sold}}{\text{Average Inventory}} = \frac{\text{Cost of Goods Sold}}{\dfrac{(\text{Beginning Inventory} + \text{Ending Inventory})}{2}}$$

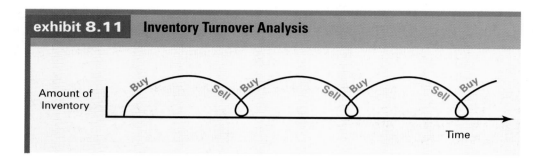

exhibit 8.11   **Inventory Turnover Analysis**

A higher ratio indicates that inventory moves more quickly from purchase (or production) to the ultimate customer, reducing storage and obsolescence costs. Because less money is tied up in inventory, the excess can be invested to earn interest income or reduce borrowing, which reduces interest expense. More efficient purchasing and production techniques as well as high product demand cause this ratio to be high. Analysts and creditors compare the inventory turnover ratio from period to period because a sudden decline may mean that a company is facing an unexpected drop in demand for its products or is becoming sloppy in its inventory management.

Some people find it easier to think in terms of the amount of time it takes to sell inventory, rather than the number of times inventory is turned over during a particular year. It's easy to convert the inventory turnover ratio into the average days to sell. Simply calculate 365 ÷ inventory turnover ratio and you'll have the average **days to sell**:

YOU SHOULD KNOW

Days to sell is a measure of the average number of days from the time inventory is bought to the time it is sold. It is calculated by dividing the year-long inventory turnover ratio into 365. Other names for days to sell are days in inventory and days' sales in inventory.

$$\text{Days to Sell} = \frac{365}{\text{Inventory Turnover Ratio}}$$

This measure doesn't say anything different about the company's ability to buy and sell inventory—it's just a little easier to interpret. In terms of Exhibit 8.11, the inventory turnover ratio counts the number of loops in a given period of time, whereas the days to sell tells you the average number of days between loops.

Be on the Alert

Inventory turnover ratios and the number of days to sell vary by type of company. For merchandisers, inventory turnover refers to the time between buying and selling goods. For manufacturers, it refers to the time required to produce and deliver inventory to customers. Turnover also varies by industry, as shown in Exhibit 8.12, with McDonald's having a turnover ratio of 35.8, which means it takes about 10 days to sell its entire food inventory (including the stuff in its freezers). The motorcycles at Harley-Davidson hog more time, as indicated by its inventory turnover ratio of 13.9, which equates to about 26 days to produce and sell. Oakley's inventory turned over only 2.4 times during the year, which is just once every 152 days. With differences this big, you should compare a company's inventory turnover only with its figures from prior periods or with figures for other companies in the same industry. For practice at calculating and comparing to prior years, calculate Oakley's 2002 turnover and days to sell in the following Self-Study Quiz.

HOW'S IT GOING?   A Self-Study Quiz

Compute the ratios for the final column in Exhibit 8.12 using financial statement information in Exhibits 8.3 and 8.4. Did Oakley's inventory turnover improve or decline in 2003, as compared to 2002? When you're done, check your answers with the solutions in the margin.

Quiz Answers

a. $\dfrac{211,962}{(87,007+77,270)\,/\,2} = 2.6$ times

b. $365 \div 2.6 = 140$ days

Oakley's inventory turnover declined in 2003, resulting in goods being on hand an average of 12 more days.

exhibit 8.12   Summary of Inventory Ratio Analyses

Name of Measure	Formula	What It Tells You	McDonald's	Harley-Davidson	Oakley	SELF-STUDY QUIZ 2002 Oakley
				2003 FISCAL YEAR		
a. Inventory turnover	$\dfrac{\text{Cost of Goods Sold}}{\text{Average Inventory}}$	• The number of times inventory turns over • A higher ratio means faster turnover ☺	35.8 times	13.9 times	$= \dfrac{226{,}846}{(98{,}691 + 87{,}007)/2}$ $= 2.4$ times	
b. Days to collect	$\dfrac{365}{\text{Inventory Turnover}}$	• Average number of days from purchase to sale • A higher number means a longer time in stock ☹	10.2 days	26.3 days	$= \dfrac{365}{2.4}$ $= 152.1$ days	

⌐RECONSIDER──────────
HOW INVENTORY REPORTING DECISIONS AFFECT ANALYSES

The Impact of Inventory Costing Methods

As you saw earlier in Exhibit 8.9, the use of different inventory cost flow assumptions can lead to different amounts being reported for inventory and cost of goods sold, *even when the underlying business transactions are identical.* Because inventory and cost of goods sold numbers are the main inputs into the inventory turnover ratio and average days to sell calculations, these two measures of turnover will be affected by the cost flow assumption used. This is a bit of a problem for you, as a financial statement user, because as shown in the graphic to the right, not all companies use the same cost flow assumption.

As you might expect, the accounting rule makers who develop GAAP knew that by allowing companies to choose alternative cost flow assumptions, they would run the risk that financial statements wouldn't be comparable across companies. To get around this, the accounting rules require that any companies that choose to use LIFO must report in the financial statement notes what their inventory balance would have been had they used FIFO. This isn't a big burden on accountants because most companies that report using LIFO actually keep track of the costs of inventory and goods sold during the year using FIFO and then simply adjust the balance to LIFO at the end of the year, using what is called a LIFO reserve. Exhibit 8.13 shows an example of how this adjustment is presented in the notes to the financial statements of Deere & Company, the manufacturer of John Deere farm, lawn, and construction equipment. Until John Deere made its LIFO adjustment at the end of 2003, its inventory was reported in its books at a FIFO cost of $2,316 million. After the adjustment to LIFO, John Deere reported only $1,366 million of inventories on its balance sheet.

Notice how huge the difference between FIFO and LIFO can be for an old business like John Deere, which was incorporated in 1868. The cost of inventory using the FIFO assumption ($2,316 in 2003) was almost 70 percent bigger than the cost calculated with the LIFO assumption ($1,366 in 2003). These kinds of differences can have similarly large effects when inventory numbers are used in analyses such as the inventory turnover ratio. The lesson here for now is that, when analyzing a company's inventory or cost of

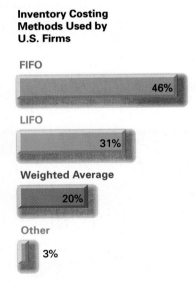

Inventory Costing Methods Used by U.S. Firms

FIFO   46%

LIFO   31%

Weighted Average   20%

Other   3%

exhibit 8.13	**LIFO Inventory Reporting**

DEERE & COMPANY
Notes to the Consolidated Financial Statements

Note 13—Inventories

Most inventories owned by Deere & Company and its United States equipment subsidiaries are valued at cost, on the "last-in, first-out" (LIFO) basis. If all inventories had been valued on a FIFO basis, estimated inventories at October 31 in millions of dollars would have been as follows:

	2003	**2002**
Total FIFO value	$2,316	$2,320
Adjustment to LIFO basis	950	948
Inventories	$1,366	$1,372

Explanation: This exhibit shows how companies using the LIFO method also report, in their financial statement notes, what their inventories would be if FIFO were used. In this example, costs have increased over the years, so the FIFO amounts ($2,316 and $2,320) are substantially larger than the LIFO amounts ($1,366 and $1,372).

goods sold numbers, you should compare that company only to its own results in prior periods or to another company that uses the same cost flow assumption.[4]

What's Coming Up

This chapter completes our look at current assets. Chapter 9 will focus on long-lived assets, which are the assets that allow companies to produce and sell inventory and provide services. You'll see yet again that different accounting methods are allowed—this time when accounting for long-lived assets. So before you move on to learn about new accounting methods, make sure you review and practice the material covered in this chapter.

---

[4]LIFO cost of goods sold numbers can be converted to FIFO equivalents using information in the financial statement notes, but we'll leave that calculation for intermediate accounting textbooks.

FOR YOUR REVIEW

DEMONSTRATION CASE

Ebert Electronics distributes a number of consumer electronics goods. One product, DVD recorders, has been selected for purposes of this case. Assume that the following summarized transactions were completed during the year ended December 31, 2006, in the order given (assume that all transactions are cash):

	Units	*Unit Cost*
a. Beginning inventory (January 1)	11	$200
b. New inventory purchases (March 15)	5	209
c. New inventory purchases (July 21)	9	220
d. Sales (selling price, $420)	12	

Required:

1. Compute the following amounts, assuming the application of the FIFO, LIFO, and weighted average inventory costing methods:

| | Ending Inventory | | Cost of Goods Sold | |
| | Units | Dollars | Units | Dollars |

FIFO
LIFO
Weighted average

2. Assuming that inventory cost was expected to follow current trends and that Ebert wants to minimize its income taxes, which method would you suggest that Ebert select to account for these inventory items? Explain your answer.

3. Assuming that other operating expenses were $500 and the income tax rate is 25 percent, prepare the income statement for the period using the method selected in requirement 2.

4. Compute and interpret the inventory turnover ratio for the current period using the selected method.

Suggested Solution

1.

	Ending Inventory		Cost of Goods Sold	
	Units	**Dollars**	**Units**	**Dollars**
FIFO	13	$2,816	12	$2,409
LIFO	13	2,618	12	2,607
Weighted average	13	2,717	12	2,508

Computations

Description	Units	Unit Cost	Total Cost
Beginning Inventory	11	$200	$2,200
Purchase	5	209	1,045
Purchase	9	220	1,980
Goods Available for Sale	25		$5,225

Still here   or   Sold

FIFO Ending Inventory	Units	Unit Cost	Total Cost
Last units in (July 21)	9	$220	$1,980
Next units in (March 15)	4	209	836
Total	13		$2,816

FIFO Cost of Goods Sold	Total Cost
Goods Available for Sale	$5,225
− Ending Inventory	2,816
Cost of Goods Sold	$2,409

Direct CGS Calculations

FIFO:
11 units × $200 =	$2,200
1 unit × $209 =	209
12 units	$2,409

LIFO Ending Inventory	Units	Unit Cost	Total Cost
First units in (January 1)	11	$200	$2,200
Next units in (March 15)	2	209	418
Total	13		$2,618

LIFO Cost of Goods Sold	Total Cost
Goods Available for Sale	$5,225
− Ending Inventory	2,618
Cost of Goods Sold	$2,607

LIFO:
9 units × $220 =	$1,980
3 units × $209 =	627
12 units	$2,607

Weighted Average Computations

$$\text{Average Cost} = \frac{\$5,225}{25 \text{ Units}} = \$209 \text{ per unit}$$

Ending Inventory = 13 units × $209 = $2,717
Cost of Goods Sold = 12 units × $209 = $2,508

2. LIFO should be selected. Because costs are rising, LIFO produces higher cost of goods sold, lower income before income taxes, and lower income taxes.

3.

EBERT ELECTRONICS **Statement of Income** **Year Ended December 31, 2006**	
Sales (12 × $420)	$5,040
Cost of goods sold	2,607
Gross profit	2,433
Other expenses	500
Income before income taxes	1,933
Income tax expense (25%)	483
Net income	$1,450

4. Inventory turnover ratio = Cost of Goods Sold ÷ Average Inventory

= $2,607 ÷ [($2,200 + $2,618) ÷ 2 = $2,409]

= 1.08

The inventory turnover ratio reflects how many times average inventory was bought and sold during the period. Based on our calculations, Ebert Electronics bought and sold its average inventory a little more than just once during the year, meaning its days to sell was 338 days (365 ÷ 1.08). This seems pitiful when you think Best Buy turns over its inventory of electronics, on average, in just 46 days.

CHAPTER SUMMARY

LO1 **Describe inventory management goals. p. 324**

- Make or buy a sufficient *quantity*, of *quality* and *innovative* products, at the lowest possible *cost*.
- Minimize the costs of obtaining and carrying inventory (purchasing, production, storage, spoilage, theft, obsolescence, and financing) while avoiding stock-outs that mean lost sales revenue and decreases in customer satisfaction.

LO2 **Describe the different types of inventory. p. 325**

- Inventory is initially recorded at cost, which includes all amounts given up to acquire the asset and bring it into a condition and location ready for sale.
- When *raw materials* enter the production process, they become *work in process* inventory, which is further transformed into *finished goods* that are ultimately sold to customers. *Merchandise inventory* is bought in a ready to sell format.

LO3 **Compute costs using four inventory costing methods. p. 328**

- Any of four generally accepted methods can be used to allocate the cost of inventory available for sale between goods that are sold and goods that remain on hand at the end of the accounting period.
- Specific identification assigns costs to ending inventory and cost of goods sold by tracking and identifying each specific item of inventory.
- Under FIFO, the costs first in are assigned to cost of goods sold, and the costs last in (most recent) are assigned to the inventory that is still on hand in ending inventory.
- Under LIFO, the costs last in are assigned to cost of goods sold, and the costs first in (oldest) are assigned to the inventory that is still on hand in ending inventory.
- Under weighted average cost, the weighted average cost per unit of inventory is assigned equally to goods sold and those still on hand in ending inventory.

LO4 **Explain why inventory is reported at the lower of cost or market. p. 336**

- The accounting concept of conservatism requires that, when the value of an asset like inventory is uncertain, it should be reported at the lowest value expected to be recovered.

Compute and interpret the inventory turnover ratio. p. 337   **LO5**

- The inventory turnover ratio measures the efficiency of inventory management. It reflects how many times average inventory was produced and sold during the period. The inventory turnover ratio is calculated by dividing Cost of Goods Sold by Average Inventory. It can be divided into 365 to determine the average number of days to sell inventory.

Explain how accounting methods affect evaluations of inventory management. p. 339   **LO6**

- To help financial statement users compare the inventory levels and ratios of companies that use different inventory cost flow assumptions, accounting rules require any LIFO companies to also report FIFO numbers in their financial statement notes. Most companies use a LIFO reserve to show how FIFO numbers are converted into LIFO numbers.

FINANCIAL STATEMENT ANALYSIS TIPS

To determine how frequently inventory turns over during the period, calculate the inventory turnover ratio:

$$\text{Inventory Turnover Ratio} = \frac{\text{Cost of Goods Sold}}{\text{Average Inventory}} = \frac{\text{Cost of Goods Sold}}{\dfrac{(\text{Beginning Inventory} + \text{Ending Inventory})}{2}}$$

Calculate the following to express the annual inventory turnover ratio in terms of number of days to sell:

$$\text{Days to Sell} = \frac{365}{\text{Inventory Turnover Ratio}}$$

KEY TERMS TO KNOW

Cost of Goods Sold
  Equation p. 328
Days to Sell p. 338
First-In, First-Out
  (FIFO) p. 330

Goods Available for
  Sale p. 327
Inventory p. 325
Inventory Turnover p. 337
Last-In, First-Out
  (LIFO) p. 330

Lower of Cost or Market
  (LCM) p. 336
Materiality p. 326
Specific Identification p. 329
Weighted Average
  Cost Method p. 332

SUPPLEMENT A: APPLYING FIFO AND LIFO IN A PERPETUAL INVENTORY SYSTEM

There were several good reasons for showing, in the body of this chapter, how cost flow assumptions are applied in a periodic inventory system, even though most modern companies use perpetual inventory systems. First, only the LIFO and weighted average calculations differ between periodic and perpetual inventory systems. FIFO calculations don't differ between periodic and perpetual systems. Second, most LIFO companies actually use FIFO during the period and then adjust to LIFO at the end of the period. By waiting to the end of the period to calculate this LIFO adjustment, it's *as if* all purchases during the period *were* recorded before the cost of goods sold is calculated and recorded. In other words, it's *as if* these companies use a periodic inventory system to determine their LIFO inventory numbers, even though they actually track the number of units bought and sold on a perpetual basis. Third, the periodic inventory system is much easier to visualize, so for pedagogical reasons, it's an appropriate way to be introduced to cost flow assumptions.

Despite these reasons, it can be useful to know how to apply cost flow assumptions in a perpetual inventory system. In this supplement, we show how to use the LIFO cost flow assumption to calculate the cost of goods sold and cost of ending inventory on a perpetual basis.[5] In a perpetual

---

[5]Use of the weighted average cost flow assumption in perpetual inventory systems is discussed in intermediate financial accounting textbooks.

inventory system, LIFO numbers are calculated using the cost of goods last in *as of the date of sale*. This differs from a periodic system, where the cost of goods sold is calculated as if all sales occurred at the end of the period.

Assume that one of Oakley's *Icon* stores experienced the following:

Jan.	1	Beginning inventory: Two units of Wisdom snow goggles at $70 each.
March	12	Purchased four units of Wisdom snow goggles at $80 each.
April	27	Sold four units of Wisdom snow goggles for $120 each.
June	9	Purchased one unit of Wisdom snow goggles at $100.

Note that this example is identical to the one presented in the body of this chapter, except for one important difference. The example in the chapter assumes that four units are sold on November 5 after all purchases have been made. In the current example, the units are sold (and recorded) on April 27 *before* the June 9 purchase is made and recorded. This small difference changes the LIFO cost of goods sold and ending inventory calculations because at the time of the sale, the goggles last in were acquired on March 12 at $80 each, which excludes the unit purchased on June 9 at $100. Because this purchase occurs after the cost of goods sold is recorded in the perpetual system, it is included in the cost of inventory still on hand at the end of the period. These perpetual LIFO cost flows are illustrated in Exhibit 8A.1.

| **exhibit 8A.1** | **Inventory Cost Flows Using LIFO in a Perpetual System** |

Notice that, in this example of rising costs, the perpetual LIFO cost of goods sold of $320 shown in Exhibit 8A.1 is lower than the periodic LIFO cost of goods sold of $340 calculated in the body of the chapter. Because perpetual LIFO cost of goods sold is lower, income before income taxes is higher, which means that income tax expense is higher under perpetual LIFO than under periodic LIFO. The potential tax savings that can be gained from using periodic LIFO is yet another reason that explains why many LIFO companies calculate and adjust their cost of goods sold and ending inventory at the end of the accounting period *as if* they were using a periodic LIFO inventory system.

SUPPLEMENT B: THE EFFECTS OF ERRORS IN ENDING INVENTORY

POINT OF INTEREST
Greeting card maker Gibson Greetings overstated its net income one year by 20 percent because one of its divisions had overstated its ending inventory for the year.

As mentioned in the body of the chapter, the failure to apply the LCM rule correctly to ending inventory is considered an error. Other errors can occur when inappropriate quantities or unit costs are used in calculating inventory cost. Regardless of the reason, errors in inventory can significantly affect both the balance sheet and the income statement. As the cost of goods sold equation indicates, a direct relationship exists between ending inventory and cost of goods sold because items not in the ending inventory are assumed to have been sold. Thus, any errors in ending inventory will affect the balance sheet (current assets) and the income statement (cost of goods sold, gross profit, and net income). The effects of inventory errors are felt in more than one year because the ending inventory for one year becomes the beginning inventory for the next year.

To determine the effects of inventory errors on the financial statements in both the current year and the following year, use the cost of goods sold equation. For example, let's assume that ending inventory was overstated by $10,000 due to an error that was not discovered until the following year. This would have the following effects in the current year:

Current Year	
Beginning inventory	Accurate
+ Purchases of merchandise during the year	Accurate
− Ending inventory	Overstated $10,000
= Cost of goods sold	Understated $10,000

Because cost of goods sold was understated, gross profit and income before income taxes would be overstated by $10,000 in the current year. (Net income would be overstated as well, although the effects would be offset somewhat by overstated income tax expense.)

The current year's ending inventory becomes next year's beginning inventory, so the error above would have the following effects next year (assuming that ending inventory is calculated correctly that year):

Next Year	
Beginning inventory	Overstated $10,000
+ Purchases of merchandise during the year	Accurate
− Ending inventory	Accurate
= Cost of goods sold	Overstated $10,000

Because cost of goods sold is overstated, gross profit and income before income taxes would be understated by the same amount in the next year. (Net income would be understated as well, although the effects would be offset somewhat by understated income tax expense.)

Ignoring income taxes, the effects of these errors on net income in each of the two years is shown in Exhibit 8B.1. Notice that the cost of goods sold is overstated in the first year and

exhibit 8B.1   Two-Year Income Effects of Inventory Error

	CURRENT YEAR		NEXT YEAR	
	With an Error	**Without an Error**	**With an Error**	**Without an Error**
Sales	$120,000	$120,000	$110,000	$110,000
Beginning inventory	$ 50,000	$ 50,000	$ 45,000	$ 35,000
Purchases	75,000	75,000	70,000	70,000
Cost of goods available for sale	125,000	125,000	115,000	105,000
Ending inventory	45,000	35,000	20,000	20,000
Cost of goods sold	80,000	90,000	95,000	85,000
Gross profit	40,000	30,000	15,000	25,000
Operating expenses	10,000	10,000	10,000	10,000
Net income	$ 30,000	$ 20,000	$ 5,000	$ 15,000

Net income overstated by $10,000 ⟶ cancels out ⟵ Net income understated by $10,000

understated in the second year. Over the two years, these errors offset one another. Inventory errors will "self-correct" like this only if ending inventory is accurately calculated at the end of the following year and adjusted to that correct balance.

FOR YOUR PRACTICE

QUESTIONS

1. What are four goals of inventory management?
2. Describe the specific types of inventory reported by merchandisers and manufacturers.
3. Explain how the concept of materiality is applied to inventory reporting.
4. Define *goods available for sale*. How does it differ from cost of goods sold?
5. Define *beginning inventory* and *ending inventory*.
6. The chapter discussed four inventory costing methods. List the four methods and briefly explain each.
7. Explain how income can be manipulated when the specific identification inventory costing method is used for identical units of inventory.
8. Contrast the effects of LIFO versus FIFO on ending inventory when (*a*) costs are rising and (*b*) costs are falling.
9. Contrast the income statement effect of LIFO versus FIFO (on cost of goods sold and gross profit) when (*a*) costs are rising and (*b*) costs are falling.
10. Explain briefly the application of the LCM concept to ending inventory. Describe its effect on the balance sheet and income statement when market is lower than cost.
11. (Supplement A) Distinguish perpetual inventory systems from periodic inventory systems by describing when and how cost of goods sold is calculated.
12. (Supplement B) Explain why an error in ending inventory in one period affects the following period.

MULTIPLE CHOICE

To practice more multiple choice questions, check out the DVD for use with this book.

1. How many of the following statements are true regarding *Cost of Goods Sold*?
   - Cost of goods sold represents the cost that a company incurred to purchase or produce inventory in the current period.
   - Cost of goods sold is an expense on the income statement.
   - Cost of goods sold is affected by the inventory method selected by a company (FIFO, LIFO, etc.).
   a. None
   b. One
   c. Two
   d. Three

2. The inventory costing method selected by a company can affect
   a. The balance sheet.
   b. The income statement.
   c. The statement of retained earnings.
   d. All of the above.

3. Which of the following is not a name for a specific type of inventory?
   a. Finished goods.
   b. Merchandise inventory.
   c. Raw materials.
   d. Goods available for sale.

4. Each period, the cost of goods available for sale is allocated between
   a. Assets and liabilities.
   b. Assets and expenses.
   c. Assets and revenues.
   d. Expenses and liabilities.

5. A New York bridal dress designer that makes high-end custom wedding dresses and needs to know the exact cost of each dress most likely uses which inventory costing method?
   a. FIFO
   b. LIFO
   c. Weighted average
   d. Specific identification

6. If costs are rising, which of the following will be true?
   a. The cost of goods sold will be greater if LIFO is used rather than weighted average.
   b. The cost of ending inventory will be greater if FIFO is used rather than LIFO.
   c. The gross profit will be greater if FIFO is used rather than LIFO.
   d. All of the above are true.

7. Which inventory method provides a better matching of current costs with sales revenue on the income statement but also results in older values being reported for inventory on the balance sheet?
   a. FIFO
   b. Weighted average
   c. LIFO
   d. Specific identification

8. How many of the following regarding the *lower of cost or market* rule for inventory are true?
   • The lower of cost or market rule is an example of the historical cost principle.
   • When the replacement cost of inventory drops below the cost shown in the financial records, net income is reduced.
   • When the replacement cost of inventory drops below the cost shown in the financial records, total assets are reduced.
   a. None
   b. One
   c. Two
   d. Three

9. An increasing inventory turnover ratio
   a. Indicates a longer time span between the ordering and receiving of inventory.
   b. Indicates a shorter time span between the ordering and receiving of inventory.
   c. Indicates a shorter time span between the purchase and sale of inventory.
   d. Indicates a longer time span between the purchase and sale of inventory.

10. Which of the following is true regarding companies that report their inventories on a LIFO basis?
    a. They will always have a higher income tax expense.
    b. They also must report the cost of ending inventory on a FIFO basis.
    c. Both of the above.
    d. None of the above.

MINI-EXERCISES Available with McGraw-Hill's Homework Manager

M8-1 Identifying Important Accounting Terms LO2–LO5

Complete the following crossword puzzle, using the clues provided in the box on the right. Omit hyphens and spaces.

Across
4 The concept behind the lower of cost or market rule.
5 A name used to describe the process of buying and selling inventory.
7 The type of manufactured inventory that is similar to merchandise inventory.

Down
1 An inventory costing method that assigns newest costs to ending inventory.
2 The concept behind the requirement to report only the amounts that are likely to influence decisions.
3 The days to sell will _____ (increase or decrease) if the inventory turnover ratio decreases.
6 An inventory costing method that assigns oldest costs to ending inventory.

LO2   **M8-2 Matching Inventory Items to Type of Business**

Match the type of inventory with the type of business by placing checkmarks in the applicable columns:

	Type of Business	
Type of Inventory	*Merchandising*	*Manufacturing*
Merchandise		
Finished goods		
Work in process		
Raw materials		

LO3   **M8-3 Inferring Purchases Using the Cost of Goods Sold Equation**

Dillard's, Inc., operates 328 department stores located in 29 states primarily in the Southwest, Southeast, and Midwest. The company uses the LIFO method to determine the cost of 97 percent of inventories and the specific identification method for the remaining 3 percent. In its annual report for the year ended January 31, 2004, the company reported cost of goods sold of $5,170 million, ending inventory for the current year of $1,632 million, and ending inventory for the previous year of $1,594 million. Is it possible to develop a reasonable estimate of the merchandise purchases for the year? If so, prepare the estimate. If not, explain why.

LO3   **M8-4 Matching Financial Statement Effects to Inventory Costing Methods**

Complete the following table by indicating which inventory costing method (FIFO or LIFO) would lead to the effects noted in the rows, for each of the circumstances described in the columns.

	1. Rising Costs	*2. Declining Costs*
a. Highest net income		
b. Highest ending inventory		

LO3   **M8-5 Matching Inventory Costing Method Choices to Company Circumstances**

Indicate whether a company interested in minimizing its income taxes should choose the FIFO or LIFO inventory costing method under each of the following circumstances.

a.   Rising costs   _____

b.   Declining costs   _____

LO3   **M8-6 Calculating Cost of Goods Sold and Ending Inventory under Periodic FIFO, LIFO, and Weighted Average**

In its first month of operations, Reading for Dummies opened a new bookstore and bought merchandise in the following order: (1) 200 units at $6 on January 1, (2) 300 units at $7 on January 8, and (3) 500 units at $8 on January 29. Assuming 600 units are on hand at the end of the month, calculate the cost of goods sold and ending inventory on January 31 under the (*a*) FIFO, (*b*) LIFO, and (*c*) weighted average cost flow assumptions. Assume a periodic inventory system is used.

LO4   **M8-7 Reporting Inventory under Lower of Cost or Market**

The Jewel Fool had the following inventory items on hand at the end of the year.

	Quantity	*Cost per Item*	*Replacement Cost per Item*
Necklaces	50	$75	$70
Bracelets	25	60	50

Determine the lower of cost or market per unit and the total amount that should be reported on the balance sheet for each item of inventory.

M8-8 Determining the Effects of Inventory Management Changes on the Inventory Turnover Ratio   LO5

Indicate the most likely effect of the following changes in inventory management on the inventory turnover ratio (+ for increase, − for decrease, and NE for no effect).

_____ *a.* Inventory delivered by suppliers daily (small amounts) instead of weekly (larger amounts).

_____ *b.* Shorten production process from 10 days to 8 days.

_____ *c.* Extend payments for inventory purchases from 15 days to 30 days.

M8-9 Calculating the Inventory Turnover Ratio and Days to Sell   LO5

Using the data in M8-3, calculate the inventory turnover ratio and days to sell for Dillard's. In a recent year, Macy's reported an inventory turnover ratio of 2.55. Which company's inventory turnover is faster?

M8-10 Reporting FIFO Ending Inventory in the Financial Statement Notes   LO6

Koss Corporation is a public company with 108 employees involved exclusively in making and selling stereo headphones. Koss reported ending inventory at June 30, 2003, of $7,333,772 under the LIFO costing method. In Note 1 to its financial statements, Koss reported that its FIFO inventory cost was $1,009,586 higher than LIFO at June 30, 2003. Using Exhibit 8.13 as a guide, show how Koss would report this in its financial statement notes.

M8-11 (Supplement A) Calculating Cost of Goods Sold and Ending Inventory under Perpetual FIFO and LIFO

Repeat M8-6 (parts *a* and *b* only), except assume Reading for Dummies uses a perpetual inventory system and it sold 400 units between January 9 and January 28.

M8-12 (Supplement B) Determining the Financial Statement Effects of Inventory Errors

Assume the 2005 ending inventory of Shea's Shrimp Shack was understated by $10,000. Explain how this error would affect the amounts reported for cost of goods sold and gross profit for 2005 and 2006.

M8-13 (Supplement B) Determining the Financial Statement Effects of Inventory Errors

Repeat M8-12, except assume the 2005 ending inventory was *over*stated by $100,000.

EXERCISES   Available with McGraw-Hill's Homework Manager

E8-1 Inferring Missing Amounts Based on Income Statement Relationships   LO3

Supply the missing dollar amounts for the 2006 income statement of Lewis Retailers for each of the following independent cases:

Cases	Sales Revenue	Beginning Inventory	Purchases	Total Available	Ending Inventory	Cost of Goods Sold	Gross Profit	Operating Expenses	Operating Income or (Loss)
A	$ 650	$100	$700	$?	$500	$?	$?	$200	$?
B	900	200	800	?	?	?	?	150	0
C	?	150	?	?	300	200	400	100	?
D	800	?	600	?	250	?	?	250	$100
E	1,000	?	900	$1,100	?	?	500	?	(50)

E8-2 Inferring Merchandise Purchases   LO3

The Gap, Inc., is a specialty retailer that operates stores selling clothes under the trade names Gap, GapKids, BabyGap, and Banana Republic. Assume that you are employed as a stock analyst and your boss has just completed a review of the new Gap annual report. She provided you with her notes, but they are missing some information that you need. Her notes show that the ending inventory for Gap in the current year was $243,482,000 and in the previous year was $193,268,000. Net sales for the current year were $1,586,596,000. Gross profit was $540,360,000 and net income was $97,628,000. For your analysis, you determine that you need to know the amount of purchases for the year and cost of goods sold.

Required:

Do you need to ask your boss for her copy of the annual report, or can you develop the information from her notes? Explain and show calculations.

LO3   **E8-3 Calculating Cost of Ending Inventory and Cost of Goods Sold under Periodic FIFO, LIFO, and Weighted Average**

Assume Oahu Kiki's uses a periodic inventory system, which shows the following for the month of January, when it sold 120 units.

	Date	Units	Unit Cost	Total Cost
Beginning Inventory	January 1	60	$ 8	$ 480
Purchase	January 15	190	9	1,710
Purchase	January 24	100	11	1,100
Total				$3,290

Required:

1. Calculate the cost of ending inventory using the (a) FIFO, (b) LIFO, and (c) weighted average cost methods.
2. Given your answer to requirement 1, use the cost of goods sold equation to force out the cost of goods sold under (a) FIFO, (b) LIFO, and (c) weighted average cost methods.
3. Double-check your answer to requirement 2 by directly calculating the cost of the 120 units sold under the (a) FIFO, (b) LIFO, and (c) weighted average cost methods.

LO3   **E8-4 Analyzing and Interpreting the Financial Statement Effects of FIFO, LIFO, and Weighted Average**

Lunar Company uses a periodic inventory system. At the end of the annual accounting period, December 31, 2005, the accounting records provided the following information:

Transactions	Units	Unit Cost
a. Inventory, December 31, 2004	3,000	$12
For the year 2005:		
b. Purchase, April 11	9,000	10
c. Purchase, June 1	8,000	13
d. Sale, May 1 (sold for $40 per unit)	5,000	
e. Sale, July 3 (sold for $40 per unit)	6,000	
f. Operating expenses (excluding income tax expense), $195,000		

Required:

1. Compute the cost of goods sold under (a) FIFO, (b) LIFO, and (c) weighted average.
2. Prepare an income statement that shows 2005 amounts for the FIFO method in one column, the LIFO method in another column, and the weighted average method in a final column. Include the following line-items in the income statement: sales, cost of goods sold, gross profit, operating expenses, and operating income.
3. Compare the operating income and the ending inventory amounts that would be reported under the three methods. Explain the similarities and differences.
4. Which inventory costing method may be preferred by Lunar for income tax purposes? Explain.

LO3   **E8-5 Analyzing and Interpreting the Financial Statement Effects of FIFO, LIFO, and Weighted Average**

Scoresby Inc. uses a periodic inventory system. At the end of the annual accounting period, December 31, 2006, the accounting records provided the following information:

Transactions	Units	Unit Cost
a. Inventory, December 31, 2005	6,000	$ 8
For the year 2006:		
b. Purchase, March 5	19,000	9
c. Purchase, September 19	10,000	11
d. Sale, April 15 (sold for $29 per unit)	8,000	
e. Sale, October 31 (sold for $31 per unit)	16,000	
f. Operating expenses (excluding income tax expense), $500,000		

Required:

1. Compute the cost of goods sold under (*a*) FIFO, (*b*) LIFO, and (*c*) weighted average.

2. Prepare an income statement that shows 2006 amounts for the FIFO method in one column, the LIFO method in another column, and the weighted average method in a final column. Include the following line-items in the income statement: sales, cost of goods sold, gross profit, operating expenses, and operating income.

3. Compare the operating income and the ending inventory amounts that would be reported under the two methods. Explain the similarities and differences.

4. Which inventory costing method may be preferred by Scoresby for income tax purposes? Explain.

E8-6 Evaluating the Effects of Inventory Methods on Operating Income, Income Taxes, and Net Income

LO3

Courtney Company uses a periodic inventory system. Data for 2005: beginning merchandise inventory (December 31, 2004), 2,000 units at $35; purchases, 8,000 units at $38; operating expenses (excluding income taxes), $142,000; ending inventory per physical count at December 31, 2005, 1,800 units; sales price per unit, $70; and average income tax rate, 30 percent.

Required:

1. Prepare income statements under the FIFO, LIFO, and weighted average costing methods. Use a format similar to the following:

		Inventory Costing Method		
Income Statement	**Units**	**FIFO**	**LIFO**	**Weighted Average**
Sales revenue	_____	$_____	$_____	$_____
Cost of goods sold				
Beginning inventory	_____	_____	_____	_____
Purchases	_____	_____	_____	_____
Goods available for sale	_____	_____	_____	_____
Ending inventory	_____	_____	_____	_____
Cost of goods sold	_____	_____	_____	_____
Gross profit		_____	_____	_____
Operating expenses		_____	_____	_____
Operating income		_____	_____	_____
Income tax expense		_____	_____	_____
Net income		_____	_____	_____

2. Between FIFO and LIFO, which method is preferable in terms of (*a*) maximizing operating income or (*b*) minimizing income taxes? Explain.

3. What would be your answer to requirement 2 if costs were falling? Explain.

E8-7 Evaluating the Effects of Inventory Methods on Operating Income, Income Taxes, and Net Income

LO3

Following is partial information for the income statement of Timber Company under three different inventory costing methods, assuming the use of a periodic inventory system:

	FIFO	LIFO	Weighted Average
Sales ($50 per unit)			
Cost of goods sold			
Beginning inventory (330 units)	$11,220	$11,220	$11,220
Purchases (475 units)	17,100	17,100	17,100
Goods available for sale			
Ending inventory (510 units)			
Cost of goods sold			
Expenses	1,600	1,600	1,600
Income before income taxes			

Required:

1. Compute cost of goods sold under the FIFO, LIFO, and weighted average inventory costing methods.
2. Prepare an income statement (up to income before income taxes) that compares each method.
3. Rank the three methods in order of (a) highest income before income taxes and (b) lowest income taxes.

LO3   **E8-8**   **Choosing LIFO versus FIFO When Costs Are Rising and Falling**

Use the following information to complete this exercise: sales, 500 units for $12,500; beginning inventory, 300 units; purchases, 400 units; ending inventory, 200 units; and operating expenses, $4,000. Begin by setting up the following table and then complete the requirements that follow.

		Costs Rising		Costs Falling	
		Situation A FIFO	Situation B LIFO	Situation C FIFO	Situation D LIFO
Sales revenue		$12,500	$12,500	$12,500	$12,500
Beginning inventory	3,600				
Purchases	5,200				
Goods available for sale	8,800				
Ending inventory	2,600				
Cost of goods sold		6,200			
Gross profit		6,300			
Operating expenses		4,000	4,000	4,000	4,000
Operating income		2,300			
Income tax expense (30%)		690			
Net income		$ 1,610			

Required:

1. Complete the table for each situation. In Situations A and B (costs rising), assume the following: beginning inventory, 300 units at $12 = $3,600; purchases, 400 units at $13 = $5,200. In Situations C and D (costs falling), assume the opposite; that is, beginning inventory, 300 units at $13 = $3,900; purchases, 400 units at $12 = $4,800. Use periodic inventory procedures.
2. Describe the relative effects on operating income as demonstrated by requirement 1 when costs are rising and when costs are falling.
3. Describe the relative effects on income taxes for each situation.
4. Would you recommend FIFO or LIFO? Explain.

LO4   **E8-9**   **Reporting Inventory at Lower of Cost or Market**

Peterson Furniture Designs is preparing the annual financial statements dated December 31, 2005. Ending inventory information about the five major items stocked for regular sale follows:

	Ending Inventory, 2005		
Item	**Quantity on Hand**	**Unit Cost When Acquired (FIFO)**	**Replacement Cost (Market) at Year-End**
Alligator Armoires	50	$15	$13
Bear Bureaus	75	40	40
Cougar Beds	10	50	52
Dingo Cribs	30	30	30
Elephant Dressers	400	8	6

COACH'S CORNER

To apply the LCM rule, set up a table similar to the one shown in the chapter, with columns for Item, Quantity, Cost per Item, Market per Item, LCM per Item, and Total LCM.

Required:

Compute the amount that should be reported for the 2005 ending inventory using the LCM rule applied to each item.

LO4

E8-10 Reporting Inventory at Lower of Cost or Market

Sandals Company was formed on January 1, 2006 and is preparing the annual financial statements dated December 31, 2006. Ending inventory information about the four major items stocked for regular sale follows:

	Ending Inventory, 2006		
Product Line	**Quantity on Hand**	**Unit Cost When Acquired (FIFO)**	**Replacement Cost (Market) at Year-End**
Air Flow	20	$12	$13
Blister Buster	75	40	38
Coolonite	35	55	52
Dudesly	10	30	35

COACH'S CORNER

1. See my advice for E8-9.

2. Calculate the write-down by determining the total cost of ending inventory and comparing it to the LCM calculated in requirement 1.

Required:

1. Compute the amount that should be reported for the 2006 ending inventory using the LCM rule applied to each item.
2. How will the write down of inventory to lower of cost or market affect the amount of cost of goods sold (or selling expenses) reported for the year ended December 31, 2006?

E8-11 Preparing the Journal Entry to Record Lower of Cost or Market (LCM) Adjustments

LO4

Tropical Sportswear International Corporation makes and sells several clothing brands including Savane®, Farah®, and Authentic Chino Casuals®. In its annual report filed with the SEC for the year ended September 27, 2003, the company reported that it wrote down excess and slow-moving inventory by approximately $12.3 million because its cost exceeded its market value. Show the journal entry that the company would have made to record this adjustment, as well as its effects on the accounting equation.

E8-12 Analyzing and Interpreting the Inventory Turnover Ratio

LO5

Polaris Industries Inc. is the biggest snowmobile manufacturer in the world. It reported the following amounts in its financial statements (in millions):

	2003	*2002*	*2001*
Net sales revenue	$1,606	$1,521	$1,488
Cost of sales	1,246	1,189	1,181
Average inventory	169	154	148

Required:

1. Determine the inventory turnover ratio and average days to sell inventory for 2003, 2002, and 2001.
2. Comment on any trends, and compare the effectiveness of inventory managers at Polaris to inventory managers at its main competitor, Arctic Cat, where inventory turns over 6.7 times per year (54 days to sell). Both companies use the same inventory costing method (FIFO).

LO3, LO5   ### E8-13   Analyzing and Interpreting the Effects of the LIFO/FIFO Choice on Inventory Turnover Ratio

Simple Plan Enterprises uses a periodic inventory system. Its records at the end of January 2006 showed the following:

Inventory, December 31, 2005, using FIFO → 19 Units @ \$14 = \$266

Inventory, December 31, 2005, using LIFO → 19 Units @ \$10 = \$190

Transactions	Units	Unit Cost	Total Cost
Purchase, January 9, 2006	25	15	\$375
Purchase, January 20, 2006	50	16	800
Sale, January 11, 2006 (at \$38 per unit)	40		
Sale, January 27, 2006 (at \$39 per unit)	28		

Required:

Compute the inventory turnover ratio under the FIFO and LIFO inventory costing methods (show computations).

LO6   ### E8-14   Analyzing Notes to Adjust Inventory from LIFO to FIFO and Calculating the Effects on the Inventory Turnover Ratio and Days to Sell

The Ford Motor Company uses the LIFO method to determine the cost of most of its inventories, which were reported at a recent year-end as follows:

	Inventory (in \$ millions)	
	Current Year	**Previous Year**
Finished products	\$3,413.8	\$3,226.7
Raw material and work in process	2,983.9	2,981.6
Additional materials	419.1	429.9
Total	\$6,816.8	\$6,638.2

If FIFO were used by the company, inventories would have been \$1,235 million higher than reported at the current year-end and \$1,246 million higher than reported last year.

Required:

1. What would be the amount of Ford's LIFO reserve at the end of the current year?
2. Determine the amount that would have been reported for ending inventory in the current year if Ford had used only FIFO.
3. The cost of goods sold reported by Ford for the current year was \$74,315 million. If Ford had used FIFO, its cost of goods sold would have been \$74,326 for the current year. Calculate the inventory turnover ratio and days to sell under LIFO and FIFO, and comment on the significance of the inventory costing methods to these analyses of Ford's inventory.

E8-15   (Supplement A) Calculating Cost of Ending Inventory and Cost of Goods Sold under Perpetual FIFO and LIFO

Refer to the information in E8-3. Assume Oahu Kiki uses a perpetual inventory system and that its 120 units were sold between January 16 and 23. Calculate the cost of ending inventory and cost of goods sold using the FIFO and LIFO methods.

E8-16 (Supplement A) Calculating Cost of Ending Inventory and Cost of Goods Sold under Perpetual FIFO and LIFO

Refer to the information in E8-4. Assume Lunar uses a perpetual inventory system. Calculate the cost of ending inventory and cost of goods sold using the FIFO and LIFO methods.

E8-17 (Supplement B) Analyzing and Interpreting the Impact of an Inventory Error

Dallas Corporation prepared the following two income statements:

	First Quarter 2005		Second Quarter 2005	
Sales revenue		$15,000		$18,000
Cost of goods sold				
Beginning inventory	$ 3,000		$ 4,000	
Purchases	7,000		12,000	
Goods available for sale	10,000		16,000	
Ending inventory	4,000		9,000	
Cost of goods sold		6,000		7,000
Gross profit		9,000		11,000
Operating expenses		5,000		6,000
Operating income		$ 4,000		$ 5,000

During the third quarter, the company's internal auditors discovered that the ending inventory for the first quarter should have been $4,400. The ending inventory for the second quarter was correct.

Required:

1. What effect would the error have on the total operating income for the two quarters combined? Explain.
2. What effect would the error have on the operating income for each of the two quarters? Explain.
3. Prepare corrected income statements for each quarter.

SIMPLIFY WITH SPREADSHEETS

SS8-1 Calculating and Recording the Effects of Lower of Cost or Market (LCM) on Ending Inventory

LO4

Assume you recently obtained a job in the Miami head office of Perfumania, the largest specialty retailer of discounted fragrances in the United States. Your job is to estimate the amount of write-down required to value inventory at the lower of cost or market. The cost of inventory is calculated using the weighted average cost method and, at approximately $70 million, it represents the company's biggest and most important asset. Assume the corporate controller asked you to prepare a spreadsheet that can be used to determine the amount of LCM write-down for the current year. The controller provides the following hypothetical numbers for you to use in the spreadsheet.

Product Line	Quantity on Hand	Weighted Average Unit Cost	Replacement Cost (Market) at Year-End
Alfred Sung Shi	80	$22	$20
Animale	75	15	16
Azzaro	50	10	10
Mambo	30	16	17
OP Juice	400	8	7

You realize that you'll need to multiply the quantity of each item by the lower of cost or market per unit, but you can't figure out how to get the spreadsheet to choose the *lower* number. You e-mailed your friend Billy for help, and here's his reply.

From: BillyTheTutor@yahoo.com
To: HairZed@hotmail.com
Cc:
Subject: Excel Help

So you don't have a sniff about how to pick the lower of cost or market? You can do this several different ways, but the easiest is to use the MIN command. Set up your spreadsheet similar to the table you sent me, and then add two new columns. In the first new column, enter the command "=MIN(costcell, marketcell)" where costcell is the cell containing the cost per unit and marketcell is the cell containing the market value per unit. Next, in the second new column, multiply the quantity by the LCM per unit. Here's a screenshot of what this will probably look like in your spreadsheet.

Microsoft Excel - ss8-1problem.xls

File   Edit   View   Insert   Format   Tools   Data   Window   Help   Acrobat

G5   =MIN(E5,F5)

Perfumania LCM Spreadsheet

Product	Quantity	Cost	Market	LCM	Total LCM
Alfred Sung Shi	80	$22	$20	$20	
Animale	75	15	16		
Azzaro	50	10	10		
Mambo	30	16	17		
OP Juice	400	8	7		
TOTAL					

Be sure to enter a formula to sum down the Total LCM column for all the products so that this grand total can be subtracted from the cost presently recorded in the inventory accounting records to determine the write-down.

Required:

1. Prepare a spreadsheet that calculates total LCM for inventory, applied on an item-by-item basis.

2. Prepare a journal entry to record the write-down needed for the five products in this problem.

COACHED PROBLEMS

LO3

CP8-1 Analyzing the Effects of Four Alternative Inventory Methods in a Periodic Inventory System

Scrappers Supplies uses a periodic inventory system. At the end of the annual accounting period, December 31, 2007, the inventory records showed the following:

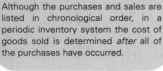

Transactions	Units	Unit Cost
Beginning inventory, January 1, 2007	400	$30
Transactions during 2007:		
a. Purchase, March 2	600	32
b. Sale, April 1 ($46 each)	(700)	
c. Purchase, June 30	500	36
d. Sale, August 1 ($46 each)	(100)	

Required:

1. Compute the cost of goods available for sale, cost of ending inventory, and cost of goods sold at December 31, 2007, under each of the following inventory costing methods:

    a.   Last-in, first-out.
    b.   Weighted average cost.
    c.   First-in, first-out.
    d.   Specific identification, assuming that the April 1, 2007, sale was selected one-fifth from the beginning inventory and four-fifths from the purchase of March 2, 2007. Assume that the sale of August 1, 2007, was selected from the purchase of June 30, 2007.

2.   Of the four methods, which will result in the highest gross profit? Which will result in the lowest income taxes?

CP8-2 Evaluating the Income Statement and Income Tax Effects of Lower of Cost or Market

LO4

Smart Company prepared its annual financial statements dated December 31, 2005. The company used the FIFO inventory costing method, but it failed to apply LCM to the ending inventory. The preliminary 2005 income statement follows:

Sales revenue		$280,000
Cost of goods sold		
Beginning inventory	$ 30,000	
Purchases	182,000	
Goods available for sale	212,000	
Ending inventory (FIFO cost)	44,000	
Cost of goods sold		168,000
Gross profit		112,000
Operating expenses		61,000
Operating income		51,000
Income tax expense (30%)		15,300
Net income		$ 35,700

COACH'S CORNER

Inventory write-downs do not affect the cost of goods available for sale. Instead, the effect of the write-down is to reduce ending inventory, which increases cost of goods sold and then affects other amounts reported lower in the income statement.

Assume that you have been asked to restate the 2005 financial statements to incorporate LCM. You have developed the following data relating to the 2005 ending inventory:

Item	Quantity	Acquisition Cost Per Unit	Acquisition Cost Total	Current Replacement Unit Cost (Market)
A	3,000	$3	$ 9,000	$4
B	1,500	4	6,000	2
C	7,000	2	14,000	4
D	3,000	5	15,000	3
			$44,000	

Required:

1.   Restate the income statement to reflect LCM valuation of the 2005 ending inventory. Apply LCM on an item-by-item basis and show computations.

2.   Compare and explain the LCM effect on each amount that was changed in requirement 1.

3.   What is the conceptual basis for applying LCM to merchandise inventories?

CP8-3 Calculating and Interpreting the Inventory Turnover Ratio and Days to Sell

LO5

Circuit City is a leading national retailer of brand-name consumer electronics, personal computers, and entertainment software. The company reported the following amounts in its financial statements (in millions), after excluding results of the CarMax auto superstore that Circuit City owned until October 1, 2002.

	2003	*2002*
Net sales revenue	$9,953	$9,518
Cost of sales	7,603	7,180
Beginning inventory	1,234	1,411
Ending inventory	1,410	1,234

LO3

Required:

1. Determine the inventory turnover ratio and average days to sell inventory for 2003 and 2002.
2. Comment on any changes in these measures, and compare the effectiveness of inventory managers at Circuit City to inventory managers at Best Buy, where inventory turns over 7.9 times per year (46 days to sell).
3. Circuit City uses the weighted average cost method to determine the cost of goods sold and ending inventory. In contrast, Best Buy uses the FIFO method. If the cost of electronics merchandise is falling, which of these two costing methods will produce the higher cost of goods sold? Will this method produce a higher or lower ending inventory cost than the other method? Taken together, which method will suggest a faster inventory turnover?

CP8-4 (Supplement A) Analyzing the Effects of the LIFO Inventory Method in a Perpetual Inventory System

Using the information in CP8-1, calculate the cost of goods sold and ending inventory for Scrappers Supplies assuming it uses the LIFO cost method in combination with a perpetual inventory system. Compare these amounts to the periodic LIFO calculations in requirement 1a of CP8-1. Does the use of a perpetual inventory system result in a higher or lower cost of goods sold when costs are rising?

CP8-5 (Supplement B) Analyzing and Interpreting the Effects of Inventory Errors

Partial income statements for Murphy & Murphy (M & M) reported the following summarized amounts:

	2003	2004	2005	2006
Sales revenue	$50,000	$49,000	$71,000	$58,000
Cost of goods sold	32,500	35,000	43,000	37,000
Gross profit	$17,500	$14,000	$28,000	$21,000

After these amounts were reported, M & M's accountant determined that the inventory on December 31, 2004, was understated by $3,000. The inventory balance on December 31, 2005, was accurately stated.

Required:

1. Restate the income statements to reflect the correct amounts, after fixing the inventory error.
2. Compute the gross profit percentage for each year (*a*) before the correction and (*b*) after the correction. Do the results lend confidence to your corrected amounts? Explain.

GROUP A PROBLEMS   Available with McGraw-Hill's Homework Manager

PA8-1 Analyzing the Effects of Four Alternative Inventory Methods in a Periodic Inventory System

Gladstone Company uses a periodic inventory system. At the end of the annual accounting period, December 31, 2005, the accounting records for the most popular item in inventory showed the following:

Transactions	Units	Unit Cost
Beginning inventory, January 1, 2005	1,800	$2.50
Transactions during 2005:		
a. Purchase, January 30	2,500	3.10
b. Sale, March 14 ($5 each)	(1,450)	
c. Purchase, May 1	1,200	4.00
d. Sale, August 31 ($5 each)	(1,900)	

Required:

1. Compute the amount of goods available for sale, ending inventory, and cost of goods sold at December 31, 2005, under each of the following inventory costing methods:
   a.   Last-in, first-out.
   b.   Weighted average cost.

   c.   First-in, first-out.

   d.   Specific identification, assuming that the March 14, 2005, sale was selected two-fifths from the beginning inventory and three-fifths from the purchase of January 30, 2005. Assume that the sale of August 31, 2005, was selected from the remainder of the beginning inventory, with the balance from the purchase of May 1, 2005.

2. Of the four methods, which will result in the highest gross profit? Which will result in the lowest income taxes?

PA8-2 Evaluating the Income Statement and Income Tax Effects of Lower of Cost or Market

LO4

Springer Anderson Gymnastics prepared its annual financial statements dated December 31, 2006. The company used the FIFO inventory costing method, but it failed to apply LCM to the ending inventory. The preliminary 2006 income statement follows:

Sales revenue		$140,000
Cost of goods sold		
Beginning inventory	$ 15,000	
Purchases	91,000	
Goods available for sale	106,000	
Ending inventory (FIFO cost)	22,000	
Cost of goods sold		84,000
Gross profit		56,000
Operating expenses		31,000
Operating income		25,000
Income tax expense (30%)		7,500
Net income		$ 17,500

    Assume that you have been asked to restate the 2006 financial statements to incorporate LCM. You have developed the following data relating to the 2006 ending inventory:

Item	Quantity	Acquisition Cost Per Unit	Acquisition Cost Total	Current Replacement Unit Cost (Market)
A	1,500	$3	$ 4,500	$4
B	750	4	3,000	2
C	3,500	2	7,000	4
D	1,500	5	7,500	3
			$22,000	

Required:

1. Restate the income statement to reflect LCM valuation of the 2006 ending inventory. Apply LCM on an item-by-item basis and show computations.

2. Compare and explain the LCM effect on each amount that was changed in requirement 1.

3. What is the conceptual basis for applying LCM to merchandise inventories?

PA8-3 Calculating and Interpreting the Inventory Turnover Ratio and Days to Sell

LO5

Harmon International Industries is a world leading producer of loudspeakers and other electronics products, which are sold under brand names like JBL, Infinity, and Harmon/Kardon. The company reported the following amounts in its financial statements (in millions):

	2003	2002
Net sales revenue	$2,229	$1,826
Cost of sales	1,577	1,326
Beginning inventory	330	318
Ending inventory	350	330

Required:

1. Determine the inventory turnover ratio and average days to sell inventory for 2003 and 2002.

2. Comment on any changes in these measures, and compare the effectiveness of inventory managers at Harmon to inventory managers at Boston Acoustics, where inventory turns over 3.7 times per year (99 days to sell). Both companies use the same inventory costing method (FIFO).

PA8-4 (Supplement A) Analyzing the Effects of the LIFO Inventory Method in a Perpetual Inventory System

Using the information in PA8-1, calculate the cost of goods sold and ending inventory for Gladstone Company assuming it uses the LIFO cost method in combination with a perpetual inventory system. Compare these amounts to the periodic LIFO calculations in requirement 1a of PA8-1. Does the use of a perpetual inventory system result in a higher or lower cost of goods sold when costs are rising?

PA8-5 (Supplement B) Analyzing and Interpreting the Effects of Inventory Errors

The income statement for Sherwood Company summarized for a four-year period shows the following:

	2003	2004	2005	2006
Sales revenue	$2,000,000	$2,400,000	$2,500,000	$3,000,000
Cost of goods sold	1,400,000	1,660,000	1,770,000	2,100,000
Gross profit	$ 600,000	$ 740,000	$ 730,000	$ 900,000

An audit revealed that in determining these amounts, the ending inventory for 2004 was overstated by $20,000. The inventory balance on December 31, 2005, was accurately stated. The company uses a periodic inventory system.

Required:

1. Restate the income statements to reflect the correct amounts, after fixing the inventory error.

2. Compute the gross profit percentage for each year (*a*) before the correction and (*b*) after the correction. Do the results lend confidence to your corrected amounts? Explain.

GROUP B PROBLEMS

PB8-1 Analyzing the Effects of Four Alternative Inventory Methods in a Periodic Inventory System

L03

Mojo Industries uses a periodic inventory system. At the end of the annual accounting period, January 31, 2007, the inventory records showed the following for an item that sold at $18 per unit:

Transactions	Units	Total Cost
Inventory, January 1, 2007	500	$2,500
Sale, January 10	(400)	
Purchase, January 12	600	3,600
Sale, January 17	(300)	
Purchase, January 26	160	1,280

Required:

1. Compute the amount of goods available for sale, ending inventory, and cost of goods sold at January 31, 2007, under each of the following inventory costing methods:
   a. Weighted average cost.
   b. First-in, first-out.
   c. Last-in, first-out.
   d. Specific identification, assuming that the January 10 sale was from the beginning inventory and the January 17 sale was from the January 12 purchase.

2. Of the four methods, which will result in the highest gross profit? Which will result in the lowest income taxes?

PB8-2 Evaluating the Income Statement and Income Tax Effects of Lower of Cost or Market

LO4

Mondetta Clothing prepared its annual financial statements dated December 31, 2007. The company used the FIFO inventory costing method, but it failed to apply LCM to the ending inventory. The preliminary 2007 income statement follows:

Sales revenue		$420,000
Cost of goods sold		
Beginning inventory	$ 45,000	
Purchases	273,000	
Goods available for sale	318,000	
Ending inventory (FIFO cost)	66,000	
Cost of goods sold		252,000
Gross profit		168,000
Operating expenses		93,000
Operating income		75,000
Income tax expense (30%)		22,500
Net income		$ 52,500

Assume that you have been asked to restate the 2007 financial statements to incorporate LCM. You have developed the following data relating to the 2007 ending inventory:

		Acquisition Cost		Current Replacement Unit Cost
Item	Quantity	Per Unit	Total	(Market)
A	3,000	$4.50	$13,500	$6.00
B	1,500	6.00	9,000	4.00
C	7,000	3.00	21,000	6.00
D	3,000	7.50	22,500	4.50
			$66,000	

Required:

1. Restate the income statement to reflect LCM valuation of the 2007 ending inventory. Apply LCM on an item-by-item basis and show computations.
2. Compare and explain the LCM effect on each amount that was changed in requirement 1.
3. What is the conceptual basis for applying LCM to merchandise inventories?

PB8-3 Calculating and Interpreting the Inventory Turnover Ratio and Days to Sell

LO5

Amazon.com reported the following amounts in its financial statements (in millions):

	2003	2002
Net sales revenue	$5,264	$3,933
Cost of sales	4,007	2,940
Beginning inventory	202	144
Ending inventory	294	202

Required:

1. Determine the inventory turnover ratio and average days to sell inventory for 2003 and 2002.
2. Comment on any changes in these measures and compare the inventory turnover at Amazon.com to inventory turnover at Borders, where inventory turned over 2.2 times during 2003 (166 days to sell). Based on your own experience, what's the key difference between Amazon.com and Borders that leads one company's results to be the picture of über-efficiency and the other to seem like a library?

3. On January 1, 2002, Amazon.com changed its inventory costing method from specific identification to FIFO. In its notes to the financial statements, the company explained that this change makes its record keeping process more efficient and comparable to others in the industry, while having a minor impact on the financial results. The change caused an increase of $0.8 million in the 2002 ending inventory, and it did not affect the reported cost of sales. Verify that the change in inventory costing method had a minor impact on financial results by subtracting the $0.8 million from 2002 ending inventory and recalculating the inventory turnover ratio. Is Amazon.com trying to fool us? Did the change have a minor impact?

PB8-4 (Supplement A) Analyzing the Effects of the LIFO Inventory Method in a Perpetual Inventory System

Using the information in PB8-1, calculate the cost of goods sold and ending inventory for Mojo Industries assuming it uses the LIFO cost method in combination with a perpetual inventory system. Compare these amounts to the periodic LIFO calculations in requirement 1a of PB8-1. Does the use of a perpetual inventory system result in a higher or lower cost of goods sold when costs are rising?

PB8-5 (Supplement B) Analyzing and Interpreting the Effects of Inventory Errors

"Oops" was the song being sung by the accountants at Spears & Cantrell when they announced inventory had been overstated by $30 (million) at the end of the second quarter. The error wasn't discovered and corrected in the company's periodic inventory system until after the end of the third quarter. The following table shows the amounts (in millions) that were originally reported by the company.

	Q1	Q2	Q3
Sales revenue	$3,000	$3,600	$3,750
Cost of goods sold	2,100	2,490	2,655
Gross profit	$ 900	$1,110	$1,095

Required:

1. Restate the income statements to reflect the correct amounts, after fixing the inventory error.
2. Compute the gross profit percentage for each quarter (*a*) before the correction and (*b*) after the correction. Do the results lend confidence to your corrected amounts? Explain.

CASES & DISCUSSION STARTERS

FINANCIAL REPORTING AND ANALYSIS CASES

LO2–LO5   ### C&DS8-1 Finding Financial Information

Refer to the financial statements of Landry's Restaurants in Appendix A at the end of this book, or download the annual report from the *Cases* section of the text's Web site at www.mhhe.com/phillips.

1. How much inventory does the company hold at the end of the most recent year? Does this represent an increase or decrease in comparison to the prior year?
2. What method(s) does the company use to determine the cost of its inventory? Describe where you found this information.
3. Compute the company's inventory turnover ratio and days to sell for the most recent year. Are these comparable to McDonald's numbers shown in Exhibit 8.12? What does this analysis suggest to you?

LO2–LO6   ### C&DS8-2 Comparing Financial Information

Refer to the financial statements of Dave & Buster's in Appendix B at the end of this book, or download the annual report from the *Cases* section of the text's Web site at www.mhhe.com/phillips.

1. Does Dave & Buster's hold more or less inventory than Landry's at the end of the most recent year?

2. What method does Dave & Buster's use to determine the cost of its inventory? Comment on how this affects comparisons you might make between Dave & Buster's and Landry's inventory turnover ratios.

3. Compute Dave & Buster's inventory turnover ratio for the most recent year and compare it to Landry's. What does this analysis suggest to you?

C&DS8-3 Internet-Based Team Research: Examining an Annual Report

LO1–LO6

As a team, select an industry to analyze. Using your Web browser, each team member should acquire the annual report or 10-K for one publicly traded company in the industry, with each member selecting a different company. (See C&DS1-3 in Chapter 1 for a description of possible resources for these tasks.)

TEAM CASE

Required:

1. On an individual basis, each team member should write a short report that incorporates the following:
   a. Describe the types of inventory held by the company. Does the company indicate its inventory management goals anywhere in its annual report?
   b. Describe the inventory costing method that is used. Why do you think the company chose this method rather than the other acceptable methods? Do you think its inventory costs are rising or falling?
   c. Calculate the inventory turnover ratio for the current and prior year, and explain any change between the two years. (To obtain the beginning inventory number for the prior year, you will need the prior year's annual report.)
   d. Search the 10-K for information about the company's approach for applying the LCM rule to inventory. Did the company report the amount of inventory written down during the year?

2. Then, as a team, write a short report comparing and contrasting your companies using these attributes. Discuss any patterns across the companies that you as a team observe. Provide potential explanations for any differences discovered.

ETHICS AND CRITICAL THINKING CASES

C&DS8-4 Ethical Decision Making: A Real-Life Example

LO3, LO4

ETHICAL

ISSUE

Assume you are on a jury hearing a trial involving a large national drugstore company. Your immediate task is to identify suspicious events in the following evidence that suggest financial fraud may have occurred.

In just seven years, the company grew from 15 to 310 stores, reporting sales of more than $3 billion. Some retail experts believed the company was going to be the next Wal-Mart. The apparent secret to the company's success was its ability to attract customers to its stores by selling items below cost. Then the company would make it easy for customers to buy other items, particularly pharmaceuticals, which earned a high gross profit. This strategy appeared to be working, so the company's top executives built up massive pharmaceutical inventories at its stores, causing total inventory to increase from $11 million to $36 million to $153 million in the last three years. The company hadn't installed a perpetual inventory system, so inventory had to be physically counted at each store to determine the cost of goods sold. To help its auditors verify the accuracy of these inventory counts, top management agreed to close selected stores on the day inventory was counted. All they asked was that they be given advance notice of which stores' inventory counts the auditors were planning to attend, so that the temporary closures could be conveyed to employees and customers at those stores. The external auditors selected four stores to test each year and informed the company several weeks in advance. To further assist the auditors with counting the inventory, top management reduced the inventory levels at the selected stores by shipping some of their goods to other stores that the auditors weren't attending.

After the inventory was counted and its cost was calculated, the company applied the LCM test. On a store-by-store basis, top management compared the unit cost and market value of inventory items and then prepared journal entries to write down the inventory. Some of the journal entries were large in amount and involved debiting an account called "cookies" and crediting the inventory account. Management reported that the cookies account was used to accumulate the required write-downs for all the company's stores. Just before the financial statements were finalized, the cookies account was emptied by allocating it back to each of the stores. In one instance, $9,999,999.99 was allocated from cookies to a store's account called "accrued inventory."

Required:

Prepare a list that summarizes the pieces of evidence that indicate that fraud might have occurred and, for each item on the list, explain why it contributes to your suspicion.

Epilogue: This case is based on a fraud involving Phar Mor, as described by David Cottrell and Steven Glover in the July 1997 issue of the *CPA Journal.* Phar Mor's management was collectively fined over $1 million and two top managers received prison sentences ranging from 33 months to five years. The company's auditors paid over $300 million in civil judgments for failing to uncover the fraud.

LO3

ETHICAL

ISSUE

C&DS8-5 Ethical Decision Making: A Mini-Case

David Exler is the CEO of AquaGear Enterprises, a seven-year-old manufacturer of boats. After many long months of debate with the company's board of directors, David obtained the board's approval to expand into water ski sales. David firmly believed that AquaGear could generate significant profits in this market, despite recent increases in the cost of skis. A board meeting will be held later this month for David to present the financial results for the first quarter of ski sales. As AquaGear's corporate controller, you reported to David that the results weren't great. Although sales were better than expected at $330,000 (3,000 units at $110 per unit), the cost of goods sold was $295,000. This left a gross profit of $35,000. David knew this amount wouldn't please the board. Desperate to save the ski division, David asks you to "take another look at the cost calculations to see if there's any way to reduce the cost of goods sold. I know you accountants have different methods for figuring things out, so maybe you can do your magic now when I need it most." You dig out your summary of inventory purchases for the quarter to recheck your calculations, using the LIFO method that has always been used for the company's inventory of boats.

	Date	Units	Unit Cost	Total Cost
Beginning inventory of water skis	January 1	0	—	—
Purchases	January 15	1,500	$ 60	$ 90,000
Purchases	February 18	2,000	90	180,000
Purchases	March 29	2,500	100	250,000

Required:

1. Calculate cost of goods sold using the LIFO method. Does this confirm the statement you made to David about the gross profit earned on water ski sales in the first quarter?
2. Without doing any calculations, is it likely that any alternative inventory costing method will produce a lower cost of goods sold?
3. Calculate cost of goods sold using the FIFO method. Would use of this method solve David's current dilemma?
4. Is it acceptable within GAAP to report the water skis using one inventory costing method and the boats using a different method?
5. Do you see any problems with using the FIFO numbers for purposes of David's meeting with the board?

LO3

ETHICAL

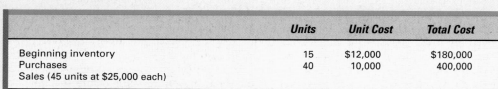

ISSUE

C&DS8-6 Critical Thinking: Income Manipulation under the LIFO Inventory Method

Mandalay Industries sells electronic test equipment. During the year 2005, the inventory records reflected the following:

	Units	Unit Cost	Total Cost
Beginning inventory	15	$12,000	$180,000
Purchases	40	10,000	400,000
Sales (45 units at $25,000 each)			

Inventory is valued at cost using the LIFO inventory method. On December 28, 2005, the unit cost of the test equipment declined to $8,000. The cost is expected to fall again during the first quarter of next year but then increase later in the year.

Required:

1. Complete the following income statement summary assuming LIFO is applied with a periodic inventory system (show computations):

Sales revenue	$ _____
Cost of goods sold	_____
Gross profit	_____
Operating expenses	300,000
Operating income	$ _____
Ending inventory	$ _____

2. Although costs are likely to fall again early next year, Mandalay's management is considering buying 20 additional units on December 31, 2005, at $8,000 each. Redo the income statement (and ending inventory), assuming that this purchase is made on December 31, 2005.

3. How much did operating income change because of the decision to purchase additional units on December 31, 2005? Is there any evidence of deliberate income manipulation? Explain.

chapter nine

Reporting and Interpreting Long-Lived Tangible and Intangible Assets

9

If you're an average American, you gobble about three pounds of peanut butter per year, which equals 1,500 peanut butter sandwiches eaten before your high school graduation.[1] That makes you an expert at knowing how much peanut butter to spread on sandwiches. It also prepares you for learning how to report depreciation on long-lived assets. Really. Reporting depreciation is a lot like spreading peanut butter on sandwiches. The amount of peanut butter to spread on each sandwich is just like the amount of depreciation to spread over each accounting period. It depends on three factors: (1) the amount that you begin with in the jar (or the cost you begin with in the account), (2) the amount you want to leave in the jar (or account), and (3) the number of sandwiches (or accounting periods) that you'll be spreading it over. Just like peanut butter on a sandwich, there'll be a little depreciation if it's spread over many years or lots if it's spread over fewer years.

For the rest of this chapter, we're going to focus on the amusement park business at **CEDAR FAIR.** We're not leaving peanuts completely behind, because just as Mickey is Disney's mascot and Bugs Bunny gives character to Six Flags, Snoopy and the whole Charlie Brown gang from the PEANUTS® comic strip are featured at Cedar Fair. With seven amusement parks and six waterparks throughout the United States, Cedar Fair is one of the biggest and best amusement park businesses in the world.[2] As of December 31, 2003, its rides, hotels, and other long-lived assets accounted for over 96 percent of its total assets, so it's the perfect setting for you to learn how these assets are reported and the analyses you can conduct to determine how well they're managed.

---

[1]Retrieved May 3, 2004, from www.peanutbutter.com/funfacts.asp.

[2]"Cedar Fair, L.P.'s Flagship Park, Cedar Point, again Voted Best Amusement Park in the World," company press release, August 26, 2003.

One of Cedar Fair's rides reaches 120 mph within just four seconds.

The main topics of this chapter are summarized in Exhibit 9.1. When you begin the next section, focus on understanding what long-lived assets are and why they're important to many business decisions. In the second section, you'll study the accounting methods and procedures used inside the business to track these assets from the time they are first acquired, to when they are used, to when they are discarded. In the last parts of the chapter, you'll see how analysts outside the organization evaluate how effectively these assets have been used, and then you'll pull it all together by considering how different accounting methods and procedures for these long-lived assets can affect analyses of reported financial results.

exhibit 9.1   Your Learning Objectives

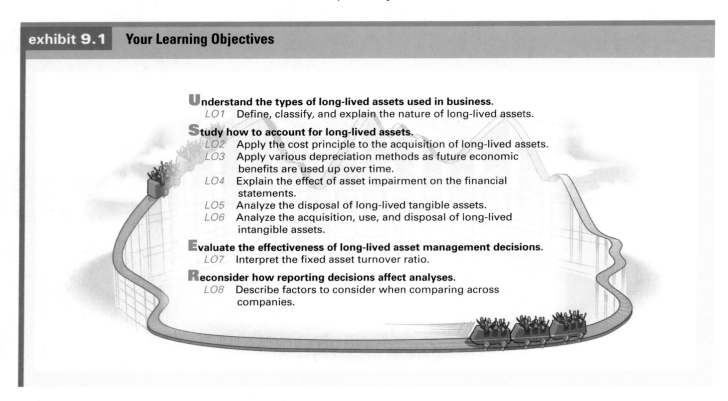

Understand the types of long-lived assets used in business.
   LO1   Define, classify, and explain the nature of long-lived assets.

Study how to account for long-lived assets.
   LO2   Apply the cost principle to the acquisition of long-lived assets.
   LO3   Apply various depreciation methods as future economic benefits are used up over time.
   LO4   Explain the effect of asset impairment on the financial statements.
   LO5   Analyze the disposal of long-lived tangible assets.
   LO6   Analyze the acquisition, use, and disposal of long-lived intangible assets.

Evaluate the effectiveness of long-lived asset management decisions.
   LO7   Interpret the fixed asset turnover ratio.

Reconsider how reporting decisions affect analyses.
   LO8   Describe factors to consider when comparing across companies.

UNDERSTAND
THE TYPES OF LONG-LIVED ASSETS USED IN BUSINESS

Defining and Classifying Long-Lived Assets

Long-lived assets are any assets that will not be used up within the next year. For most companies, these assets are the heart of their businesses. Without them, Mattel wouldn't have the robotics that make toys, Supercuts wouldn't have the salons for providing hair-care services, Wal-Mart wouldn't have the stores for selling its products, and Oakley wouldn't have the legal rights for protecting its sunglasses from counterfeiting and piracy. So when you hear the label "long-lived assets," don't just think of rusty old equipment, because this class of assets is much broader than that. Long-lived assets include the following:

1. ***Tangible assets.*** These are long-lived assets that have physical substance, which simply means that you can see, touch, or kick them. The most prominent examples of tangible assets are land, buildings, factories, machinery, and office equipment, which are typically grouped into a single line-item on the balance sheet called property, plant, and equipment. This category includes the four-lane causeway that Cedar Fair built to cross Sandusky Bay in Ohio and the 50 roller coasters that race through its parks.

2. **Intangible assets.** These long-lived assets have special rights, but no physical substance. Most intangible assets are evidenced only by legal documents. Unlike the various tangible assets like the store buildings and cash registers that you see in your daily life, you probably have less familiarity with intangible assets. For this reason, we'll spend a bunch of time later in this chapter describing the various types of intangibles. For now you can think of this category as including things like brand names, trademarks, and licensing rights that allow Cedar Fair to use PEANUTS® characters in its Knott's Berry Farm and throughout its other parks.

Exhibit 9.2 indicates just how important these two categories of assets are to Cedar Fair, by showing the assets section of its balance sheet at December 31, 2003 and 2002.

exhibit 9.2	Cedar Fair's Assets		
December 31,		**2003**	**2002**
(in thousands)			
Assets			
Current Assets			
Cash		$ 2,194	$ 2,171
Receivables		6,560	6,623
Inventories		14,905	13,895
Prepaids		6,118	6,548
Total Current Assets		29,777	29,237
Property and Equipment			
Land		150,144	149,380
Land Improvements		131,765	127,919
Buildings		257,102	254,512
Rides and Equipment		553,927	522,234
Construction in Progress		10,832	21,811
		1,103,770	1,075,856
Less Accumulated Depreciation		(326,731)	(294,354)
		777,039	781,502
Intangibles and Other Assets, Net of Accumulated Amortization		12,525	11,518
		$ 819,341	$ 822,257

COACH'S CORNER

Land improvements differ from **land** because they will deteriorate over time, whereas land is assumed to last forever. Land improvements include, for example, the pavement and trees that are added to the land.

Construction in progress includes the costs of constructing new property and equipment. These costs are moved from this account into the applicable property and equipment account(s) when the construction is completed.

Accumulated depreciation is reported here as a total for the entire tangible assets category. Alternatively, it can be reported separately for each type of tangible asset.

STUDY

HOW TO ACCOUNT FOR LONG-LIVED ASSETS

In this section, you will study the accounting decisions that relate to long-lived assets. We'll start with *tangible* long-lived assets and consider key accounting decisions related to their (1) acquisition, (2) use, and (3) disposal. Accounting for *intangible assets* will be the focus of the last part of this section.

Acquisition of Tangible Assets

The general rule for tangible assets, under the cost principle, is that all reasonable and necessary costs of acquiring and preparing an asset for use should be recorded as a cost of

ETHICAL

ISSUE

the asset. The act of recording costs as assets (rather than as expenses) is what accountants and analysts call **capitalizing** the costs.

For tangible assets, it's not always obvious whether a cost is reasonable and necessary for acquiring or preparing them for use, so the decision to capitalize versus expense a cost is one that can involve lots of judgment. It's also one that has been exploited in recent years. An $11 billion accounting fraud was committed at WorldCom (now called MCI) in the early 2000s, in part by capitalizing costs that were a lot like rent and should have been expensed. This accounting decision led WorldCom to report huge increases in assets (rather than expenses) in the periods in which the costs were incurred. The result was a balance sheet that appeared stronger (larger assets) and an income statement that appeared more profitable (lower expenses) than if these costs had been expensed. One of the cases at the end of this chapter (C&DS9-4) shows what happened in more detail. For now, as you read the next couple of pages, focus on learning what kinds of costs should be capitalized and what kinds should be expensed.

Costs Incurred at the Time of Acquiring Tangible Assets

To help you understand the types of costs that should be capitalized when a tangible asset is acquired, we list several costs below that are considered necessary for acquiring and preparing tangible assets for use. Notice that the costs to be capitalized are not just the amounts paid to purchase or construct the assets themselves. For example, the land account at Cedar Fair would include legal fees incurred to purchase the arm of land that you can see crossing Sandusky Bay in the picture below. Fees to hire land surveyors and commissions paid to real estate brokers to purchase other pieces of land also would be capitalized in the land account. Take a moment right now to read the other similar types of costs that are capitalized when acquiring buildings and equipment.

Land

Purchase cost
Legal fees
Survey fees
Broker's commissions

Equipment

Purchase/construction cost
Sales taxes
Transportation costs
Installation costs

Buildings

Purchase/construction cost
Legal fees
Appraisal fees
Architect fees

In some instances, land, buildings, and equipment will be purchased as a group, as they were when Cedar Fair bought Six Flags Worlds of Adventure amusement park on April 8, 2004, for $145 million. When this kind of "basket purchase" occurs, the total cost is broken up and allocated to each asset in proportion to the market value of the assets as a whole. For example, if Cedar Fair were to pay $10 million for a hotel and the land surrounding it, based on an appraisal that estimates the land contributes 40 percent of the property's value and the building makes up the remaining 60 percent, Cedar Fair would record 40 percent of the total cost as land ($4 million) and the other 60 percent as buildings ($6 million). This allocation of the total purchase price among individual assets is necessary because the cost of each different type of asset will be spread over different periods of time.

To illustrate how the costs of tangible assets are recorded, let's consider the Top Thrill Dragster that Cedar Fair purchased in 2002 from Intamin, a Swiss roller-coaster manufacturing company. At the time this book was being written, the Top Thrill Dragster was the biggest and fastest roller coaster in the world. Some of its specs are presented in the following graphic.

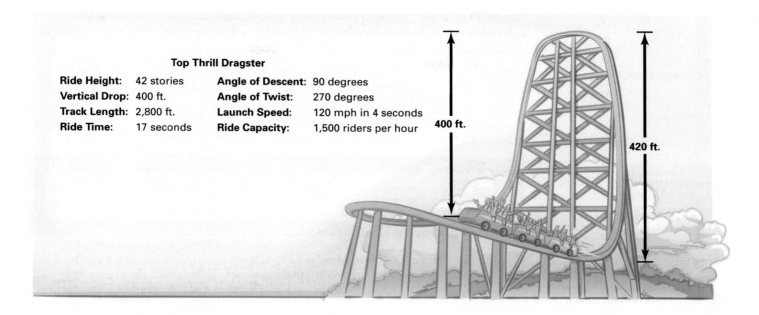

Top Thrill Dragster

Ride Height:	42 stories	**Angle of Descent:**	90 degrees
Vertical Drop:	400 ft.	**Angle of Twist:**	270 degrees
Track Length:	2,800 ft.	**Launch Speed:**	120 mph in 4 seconds
Ride Time:	17 seconds	**Ride Capacity:**	1,500 riders per hour

400 ft.

420 ft.

We'll assume that the list price for the roller coaster (including sales taxes) was $26 million, but Cedar Fair received a discount of $1 million from this. This means that the net purchase price of the roller coaster to Cedar Fair was actually $25 million. In addition, we'll assume Cedar Fair paid $125,000 to have the roller coaster delivered and $625,000 to have it assembled and prepared for use. Cedar Fair would calculate the costs to be capitalized (as *Rides and Equipment*) as follows:

Invoice price	$26,000,000
Less: Discount	1,000,000
Net cash invoice price	25,000,000
Add: Transportation costs paid by Cedar Fair	125,000
Installation costs paid by Cedar Fair	625,000
Total cost of the roller coaster	$25,750,000

The journal entry required to record this asset depends on whether the purchase is paid for in cash or financed using credit.

Cash Purchase. Assuming that Cedar Fair paid cash for the roller coaster and related transportation and installation costs, the transaction is recorded as follows:

dr	Rides and Equipment (+A)	25,750,000	
cr	Cash (−A)		25,750,000

Assets		=	Liabilities	+	Stockholders' Equity
Cash	−25,750,000				
Rides and Equipment	+25,750,000				

You might find it hard to believe that Cedar Fair would pay cash for assets that cost over $25 million, but this really isn't unusual. Companies often use cash that has been generated from operations or that has been borrowed recently. It's also possible for the seller to extend credit to the buyer, a situation that we examine next.

Credit Purchase. If we were to assume that Cedar Fair signed a note payable for the new roller coaster and paid cash for the transportation and installation costs, Cedar Fair would record the following journal entry:

dr	Rides and Equipment (+A)	25,750,000	
	cr Cash (−A)		750,000
	cr Note Payable (+L)		25,000,000

Assets		=	Liabilities	+	Stockholders' Equity
Cash	−750,000		Note Payable +25,000,000		
Rides and Equipment	+25,750,000				

YOU SHOULD KNOW

A **capital lease** is a long-term agreement between two companies that is accounted for like a credit purchase.
Capitalized interest represents interest expenditures included in the cost of a self-constructed asset.

Another form of financing often used to acquire fixed assets is called a **capital lease**. It is accounted for just like the credit purchase shown above, with the company recording both a long-lived tangible asset and a long-term liability (called a capital lease obligation).

Self-Constructed Tangible Assets. In some cases, a company may construct a tangible asset for its own use instead of buying it from a manufacturer. When a company does this, the cost of the asset should include all the necessary costs associated with construction, such as labor, materials, and, in most situations, a portion of the interest incurred during the construction period, called **capitalized interest.** The amount of interest to be capitalized is a complex computation discussed in other accounting courses.

In a recent year, the New Bakery Company of Ohio opened a new computer-integrated baking plant priced at $21 million. The plant can make 3,420 buns per minute, which are enough buns for 1.2 billion Wendy's sandwiches a year. Assume that the company paid $800,000 for sales taxes on the plant; $70,000 for transportation costs; and $50,000 for installation and preparation of the assets before use.

Source: American Way, February 1, 2003, p. 53.

1. Compute the acquisition cost to be recorded as property, plant, and equipment (PPE).

2. Under the following assumptions, indicate the effects of the acquisition on the accounting equation. Use + for increase and − for decrease, and indicate the accounts and amounts.

	Assets	=	Liabilities	+	Stockholders' Equity
a. Paid all in cash.					
b. Paid 30 percent in cash and the rest by signing a note payable.					

After you're done, check your answers with the solutions in the margin.

Quiz Answers

1. $21,000,000 + 800,000 + 70,000 + 50,000 = $21,920,000

2.

Assets	=	Liabilities	+	Stockholders' Equity
a. PPE +21,920,000				
Cash −21,920,000				
b. PPE +21,920,000		Note Payable +15,344,000		
Cash −6,576,000				

Use of Tangible Assets

Maintenance Costs Incurred during Time of Use

Most tangible assets require substantial expenditures over the course of their lives to maintain or enhance their ability to operate. Maintenance is a big deal in the roller coaster industry where it's important to have safe rides. Despite the tremendous stress created by frequent use and wicked-fast speeds, surprisingly few accidents occur, with a recent estimate reporting the odds of a serious amusement park injury at 1 in 23 million. You're 38 times more likely to get hit by lightening.[3] This level of safety comes from spending lots of money on two types of maintenance during a ride's period of use:

1. Ordinary repairs and maintenance. Ordinary repairs and maintenance are expenditures for routine maintenance and upkeep of long-lived assets. Just like an oil change for your car, these expenditures are recurring in nature, involve relatively small amounts at each occurrence, and do not directly lengthen the useful life of the asset. Because these expenditures occur frequently and maintain the productive capacity of the asset for a short period of time, they are recorded as *expenses* in the current period.

In the case of Cedar Fair, examples of ordinary repairs and maintenance include greasing the tracks on the Steel Venom roller coaster at Valleyfair in Minnesota, replacing the lights on the eight-story tall Ferris wheel at Michigan's Adventure, and tightening the seams on a water slide at Knott's Soak City in California.

2. Extraordinary repairs, replacements, and additions. These expenditures occur infrequently, involve large amounts, and increase an asset's economic usefulness in the future through increased efficiency, increased capacity, or longer life. Examples include additions, major overhauls, complete reconditioning, and major replacements and improvements, such as the complete replacement of the passenger train on a roller coaster. Because these costs increase the usefulness of tangible assets beyond their original condition, they are added to the appropriate *asset* accounts.

Exhibit 9.3 presents a brief excerpt from the Management's Discussion and Analysis (MD&A) section of Cedar Fair's 2003 annual report, which describes the policies used to account for expenditures made when buildings, rides, and equipment are being used. After reading how Cedar Fair explains its accounting policy, take a minute to try the self-study quiz that follows it.

YOU SHOULD KNOW

Ordinary repairs and maintenance are expenditures for routine operating upkeep of long-lived assets, and are recorded as expenses.

YOU SHOULD KNOW

Extraordinary repairs are expenditures that increase a tangible asset's economic usefulness in the future, and are recorded as increases in asset accounts, not as expenses. In contrast to ordinary repairs, extraordinary repairs are done less frequently and yield longer-lasting benefits.

---

exhibit 9.3	**Cedar Fair's Policy on Expenditures Made during Use of Tangible Assets**

Key Accounting Policies

Expenditures made to maintain (tangible) assets in their original operating condition are expensed as incurred, and improvements and upgrades are capitalized.

---

[3] "Newtonian Nightmare Rack-and-Pinion Inversions and Pneumatic Accelerators. This Is Fun?" *Forbes*, July 23, 2001, p. 112.

HOW'S IT GOING?   A Self-Study Quiz

As you know from living in an apartment, dorm, or house, buildings require continuous maintenance and repair. For each of the following expenditures, indicate whether it should be expensed in the current period or capitalized as part of the cost of the building.

	Expense or Capitalize?
1. Replacing electrical wiring throughout the building.	
2. Repairing the hinge on the front door of the building.	
3. Yearly cleaning of the building's air conditioning filters.	
4. Repairing major structural damage from a rare flood.	

After you're done, check your answers with the solutions in the margin.

Quiz Answers
1. Capitalize—extends life.
2. Expense
3. Expense
4. Capitalize—extends life.

Depreciation Expense

YOU SHOULD KNOW

Depreciation is the allocation of the cost of long-lived tangible assets over their productive lives using a systematic and rational method.

COACH'S CORNER

Because depreciation involves allocating the *cost* of tangible assets, rather than determining their current values, the amounts reported on a balance sheet for long-lived tangible assets are likely to differ from their current market values.

YOU SHOULD KNOW

Book (or carrying) value is the acquisition cost of an asset less accumulated depreciation.

In addition to repairs and maintenance, another expense is reported every period that a tangible asset is used. This expense, called **depreciation,** does not involve new costs arising from using the asset. Instead, depreciation expense is the *allocation of existing costs* that have been recorded as a long-lived tangible asset. The idea is that the cost of a long-lived tangible asset is essentially a prepaid cost representing future benefits. These benefits are used up when the asset is used, so a portion of its cost is allocated to the period of its use and is reported as an expense. You should recognize that this corresponds to the *matching principle*, which requires expenses to be reported in the same period as the revenues they generate. For Cedar Fair, revenues are earned when its rides are open to customers, so depreciation expense also is recorded at that time to show the allocated cost of the tangible assets that are used to generate those revenues.

In Chapter 4, you learned the adjusting journal entry that is needed at the end of each period to reflect the use of property and equipment for the period:

dr **Depreciation Expense (+E, −SE)**	**xxxxx**	
cr **Accumulated Depreciation (+xA, −A)** . . .		**xxxxx**

The amount of depreciation recorded during each period is reported on the income statement as *Depreciation Expense.* The amount of depreciation expense accumulated since the acquisition date is reported on the balance sheet as a contra-account, *Accumulated Depreciation,* and deducted from the related asset's cost. The net amounts on the balance sheet are called *book values* or *carrying values.* The **book (or carrying) value** of a long-lived asset is its acquisition cost less the accumulated depreciation from acquisition date to the balance sheet date. If you're not crystal clear on how these things are reported, take a quick look at Exhibit 9.2 on page 369. You should see that, at the end of 2003, Cedar Fair's total cost of property and equipment (in thousands) was $1,103,770, accumulated depreciation was $326,731, and the book (or carrying) value was $777,039 ($1,103,770 − 326,731). Depreciation expense (of $44,693) is included in Cedar Fair's 2003 income statement. Although some companies report depreciation expense as a separate type of operating expense, many (including Cedar Fair) combine it with other operating expenses for external reporting purposes.

To calculate depreciation expense, you need three amounts:

1. **Asset cost.** This includes all the costs capitalized for the asset. You saw earlier in this chapter that this cost can include purchase cost, sales tax, legal fees, and other related costs.

2. *Residual value.* **Residual value** is an estimate of the amount that the company will get when it disposes of the asset. Cedar Fair will recover some of the initial cost of its roller coasters when it disposes of them by either selling them "as is" to local amusement companies or by dismantling them and selling their parts to other roller coaster or scrap metal companies.

3. *Useful life.* **Useful life** is an estimate of the asset's useful economic life *to the company* (rather than its economic life to all potential users). Economic life may be expressed in terms of years or units of asset capacity, such as the number of units it can produce or the number of miles it will travel. **Land is the only tangible asset that's assumed to have an unlimited (indefinite) useful life. Because of this, land is not depreciated.**

The basic idea of depreciation is to allocate the amount of the asset that will be used up (asset cost minus residual value) over the periods it will be used to generate revenue (useful life). Just as you might plan to leave some peanut butter in the jar for your roommate when you're done making your sandwich, you plan to leave a little of the asset's cost in the accounts when you're done depreciating it. You do this because, when you dispose of the asset, you're likely to get back some of what you initially paid for it. So, ultimately, the "true" net cost of the asset is what you paid minus what you get back (asset cost minus residual value). This amount is often called the **depreciable cost.** The total depreciation expense that accumulates over an asset's useful life should not exceed depreciable cost, which also means that an asset's end-of-life book value should equal its estimated residual value.

If every company used the same techniques for calculating depreciation, we'd stop right here. However, because companies own different assets and use them differently, accountants have not been able to agree on a single best method of depreciation. As a result, managers are allowed to choose from several different acceptable depreciation methods, basing their decision on how they believe their assets will generate revenues over time. These alternative depreciation methods produce different depreciation numbers, so you need to understand how the alternative methods work to understand how to interpret differences in depreciation.

Alternative Depreciation Methods

We will discuss the three most common depreciation methods:

- Straight-line
- Units-of-production
- Declining-balance

To show how each method works, let's assume that Cedar Fair acquired a new go-cart ride on January 1, 2006. The relevant information is shown in Exhibit 9.4.

exhibit 9.4	**Information Used to Show Depreciation Computations under Alternative Methods**

CEDAR FAIR—Acquisition of a New Go-Cart Ride

Cost, purchased on January 1, 2006	$62,500		
Estimated residual value	$2,500		
Estimated useful life	3 years	**OR**	100,000 miles
Actual miles driven in: 2006			30,000 miles
2007			50,000 miles
2008			20,000 miles

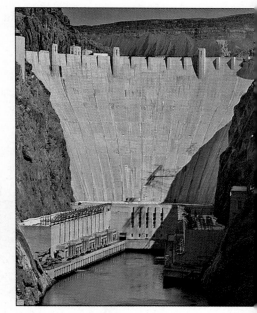

Water structures and facilities, such as the Hoover Dam shown above, are depreciated over periods extending to 100 years.

Source: U.S. Department of the Interior, Bureau of Reclamation, 2002 Annual Report.

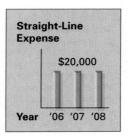

Straight-Line Method.   Under the **straight-line** method, an equal portion of an asset's depreciable cost is allocated to each accounting period over its estimated useful life. The formula to estimate annual depreciation expense is

$$(\text{Cost} - \text{Residual Value}) \times \frac{1}{\text{Useful Life}} = \text{Depreciation Expense}$$

$$(\$62,500 - \$2,500) \times \frac{1}{3 \text{ years}} = \$20,000 \text{ per year}$$

Straight-Line Formula:

In the straight-line formula, "Cost minus Residual Value" is the total amount to be depreciated (the *depreciable cost*). "1 ÷ Useful Life" is the *straight-line rate*. Using the information in Exhibit 9.4, the depreciation expense for Cedar Fair's new ride would be $20,000 per year. A depreciation schedule for the entire useful life of the ride follows:

Amount for the Adjusting Journal Entry

Cost less Accumulated Depreciation

Year	Yearly Computation	INCOME STATEMENT Depreciation Expense	BALANCE SHEET Cost	Accumulated Depreciation	Book Value
At acquisition			$62,500	$ 0	$62,500
2006	($62,500 − $2,500) × 1/3	$20,000	62,500	20,000	42,500
2007	($62,500 − $2,500) × 1/3	20,000	62,500	40,000	22,500
2008	($62,500 − $2,500) × 1/3	20,000	62,500	60,000	2,500
	Total	$60,000			

Notice that, as the name "straight-line" suggests,

1.   Depreciation expense is a *constant* amount each year.
2.   Accumulated depreciation increases by an *equal* amount each year.
3.   Book value decreases by the same *equal* amount each year.

Notice also that the straight-line method relies on estimates of an asset's useful life and its residual value at the end of that life. These are difficult things to estimate with precision, so accountants are encouraged to update depreciation calculations regularly for new estimates of useful lives and residual values, as discussed in Supplement A at the end of the chapter.

Units-of-Production Method.   Like the straight-line method, the **units-of-production** method allocates each asset's depreciable cost over its useful life—only there's one key difference. Whereas straight-line defines useful life by number of years, units-of-production defines it by production. Specifically, the units-of-production method relates depreciable cost to the total number of estimated units of output. This output could be in terms of miles, products, or machine hours operated. The formula to estimate depreciation expense under the units-of-production method is as follows:

Depreciation Rate per unit = $.60 per mile

Units-of-Production Formula:

$$\frac{(\text{Cost} - \text{Residual Value})}{\text{Estimated Total Production}} \times \text{Actual Production} = \text{Depreciation Expense}$$

$$\frac{(\$62,500 - \$2,500)}{100,000 \text{ miles}} \times \frac{30,000 \text{ miles}}{\text{in 2006}} = \$18,000 \text{ in 2006}$$

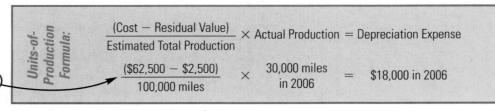

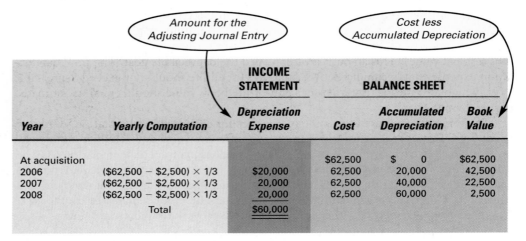

Dividing the depreciable cost by the estimated total production yields the depreciation rate per unit of production, which is then multiplied by the actual production for the period to determine depreciation expense. In our illustration, for every mile that the ride travels, Cedar Fair would record depreciation expense of $0.60. The depreciation schedule for the ride under the units-of-production method would appear as follows:

| | | INCOME STATEMENT | BALANCE SHEET | | |
| | | Depreciation | | Accumulated | Book |
Year	Yearly Computation	Expense	Cost	Depreciation	Value
At acquisition			$62,500	$ 0	$62,500
2006	$.60 rate × 30,000 miles	$18,000	62,500	18,000	44,500
2007	$.60 rate × 50,000 miles	30,000	62,500	48,000	14,500
2008	$.60 rate × 20,000 miles	12,000	62,500	60,000	2,500
	Total	$60,000			

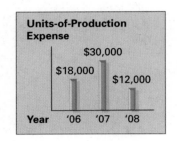

Units-of-Production Expense

$18,000 $30,000 $12,000

Year   '06   '07   '08

Notice that, from period to period, depreciation expense, accumulated depreciation, and book value vary directly with the units produced. Notice also that the units-of-production method is based on an estimate of an asset's total future productive capacity or output. This is another example of the degree of wiggle room in accounting.

Declining-Balance Method.   Under the **declining-balance method**, depreciation expense amounts are higher in the early years of an asset's life and lower in the later years. This is why it is sometimes called an *accelerated depreciation* method. Although accelerated methods aren't often used for financial reporting purposes in the United States, they are commonly used in financial reporting in other countries like Japan and Canada and in tax reporting in the United States (a point we discuss in greater detail below).

Declining-balance depreciation is based on applying a depreciation rate to the book value of the asset at the beginning of the accounting period. The rate is often double (two times) the straight-line rate and, therefore, is termed the *double-declining-balance rate*. For example, if the straight-line rate is 20 percent (1 ÷ 5 years) for a five-year estimated useful life, then the double-declining-balance rate is 40 percent (2 × the straight-line rate). Other typical acceleration rates are 1.5 times and 1.75 times. Double-declining is the rate adopted most frequently by companies that choose an accelerated method, so we will use it in our illustration.

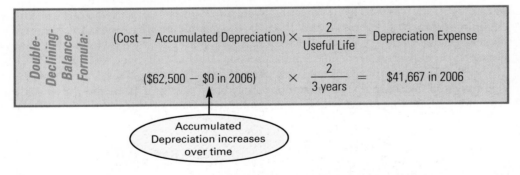

Double-Declining-Balance Formula:

$$(\text{Cost} - \text{Accumulated Depreciation}) \times \frac{2}{\text{Useful Life}} = \text{Depreciation Expense}$$

$$(\$62,500 - \$0 \text{ in } 2006) \times \frac{2}{3 \text{ years}} = \$41,667 \text{ in } 2006$$

Accumulated Depreciation increases over time

COACH'S CORNER

If you want the DDB worksheet function in Microsoft Excel to match the formula presented here, set the "salvage" factor to 0.

Notice in our example that we use the beginning of year accumulated depreciation balance. Also note that *residual value is not included in the formula for computing depreciation expense*, so you have to take extra care to ensure an asset's book value is not being depreciated below its residual value. If the normal depreciation calculated for the year reduces book value below residual value, a lower amount of depreciation must be recorded, so that book value equals residual value. Let's show you what we mean by computing depreciation for each of the three years of our example:

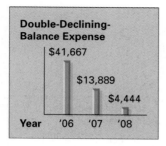

Double-Declining-Balance Expense

$41,667
$13,889
$4,444

Year   '06   '07   '08

Year	Yearly Computation	INCOME STATEMENT Depreciation Expense	BALANCE SHEET Cost	Accumulated Depreciation	Book Value
At acquisition			$62,500	$ 0	$62,500
2006	($62,500 − $0) × 2/3	$41,667	62,500	41,667	20,833
2007	($62,500 − $41,667) × 2/3	13,889	62,500	55,556	6,944
2008	($62,500 − $55,556) × 2/3	~~4,629~~	62,500	~~60,185~~	~~2,315~~
		4,444	62,500	60,000	2,500
	Total	$60,000			

Computed amount is too large

If the calculated depreciation expense for 2008 ($4,629) were recorded, the asset's book value would fall below its residual value. This isn't allowed, so in the final year of the asset's life, just enough depreciation is recorded ($4,444) to make the book value of the asset equal to its residual value of $2,500.

Summary.   The following table summarizes the three depreciation methods and computations. The graph shows the differences in depreciation expense patterns over the asset's useful life for each method.

Depreciation Expense Summary

Year   '06   '07   '08

Method	Computation
Straight-line	(Cost − Residual Value) × 1/Useful Life
Units-of-production	[(Cost − Residual Value)/Estimated Total Production] × Actual Production
Double-declining-balance	(Cost − Accumulated Depreciation) × 2/Useful Life

Managers are allowed to choose any rational and systematic depreciation methods, provided that they describe them in their financial statement notes (in keeping with the full disclosure principle discussed in Chapter 5). Also, because not every tangible asset is identical, different depreciation methods can be used for different classes of assets, provided the methods are used consistently over time so that financial statement users can easily compare across time periods. So what methods do companies use? In a recent survey, straight-line was used by 84 percent of companies, units-of-production by 5 percent, declining-balance by 3 percent, and others by 9 percent.[4] Straight-line is the preferred choice because it's the easiest to use and understand, plus it does a good job of matching depreciation expense to revenues when assets are used evenly over their useful lives. Units-of-production typically is used only when asset use fluctuates significantly from period to period. Declining-balance methods apply best to assets that are most productive when they are new and quickly lose their usefulness as they get older.

TOPIC TACKLER PLUS

See the animated tutorial reviewing these depreciation methods on the DVD for use with this book.

HOW'S IT GOING?   A Self-Study Quiz

Assume that Cedar Fair has acquired new computer equipment at a cost of $240,000. The equipment has an estimated life of six years, an estimated operating life of 50,000 hours, and an estimated residual value of $30,000. Determine depreciation expense for the first full year under each of the following methods:

---

[4]AICPA 2003 *Accounting Trends & Techniques.*

1. Straight-line method.

2. Double-declining-balance method.

3. Units-of-production method (assume the equipment ran for 8,000 hours in the first year).

After you're done, check your answers with the solutions in the margin.

Tax Depreciation.   Before we leave the topic of depreciation methods, we should note that most public companies use one method of depreciation for reporting to stockholders and a different method for determining income taxes. Essentially, these companies keep two sets of accounting records. When some people first learn that companies maintain two sets of books, they question the ethics or legality of the practice. In reality, *it is both legal and ethical to maintain separate records for tax and financial reporting purposes.*

The reason that it's legal to maintain two sets of books is simple: The objectives of GAAP and the Internal Revenue Code differ.

Financial Reporting (GAAP)	Tax Reporting (Internal Revenue Code)
The objective of financial reporting is to provide economic information about a business that is useful in projecting future cash flows of the business. Financial reporting rules follow generally accepted accounting principles.	The objective of the Internal Revenue Code is to raise sufficient revenues to pay for the expenditures of the federal government. Many of the Code's provisions are designed to encourage certain behaviors that are thought to benefit society (e.g., contributions to charities are made tax deductible to encourage people to support worthy programs).

While it is easy to understand why two sets of accounting records are permitted, perhaps the more interesting question is why managers would be willing to pay the extra cost of maintaining two sets of books. In some cases, differences in the accounting rules permitted under the Internal Revenue Code and GAAP leave the manager no choice but to maintain separate records. In other cases, the explanation is an economic one, called the *least and the latest rule*. All taxpayers want to pay the least tax that is legally permitted, and at the latest possible date. If you had the choice of paying $10,000 to the federal government at the end of this year or at the end of next year, you would choose the end of next year. By doing so, you could invest the money for an extra year and earn a significant return on the investment.

Similarly, by maintaining two sets of books, corporations can defer (delay) paying millions and sometimes billions of dollars in taxes. The following companies report deferring significant tax obligations in a recent year. Much of these deferrals were due to differences in the depreciation methods used for tax and financial reporting purposes.

Company	Deferred Tax Liabilities	Percentage Due to Applying Different Depreciation Methods
AT&T Corp.	$5,755 million	86%
Southwest Airlines	1,537 million	94
Revlon, Inc.	29 million	90

Most corporations use the IRS-approved Modified Accelerated Cost Recovery System (MACRS) to calculate depreciation expense for their tax returns. MACRS is similar to the declining-balance method, and is applied over relatively short asset lives set by the IRS to yield high tax deductions for depreciation expense in the early years. *MACRS is not acceptable for financial reporting purposes.*

Asset Impairment Losses

Because the goal of depreciation is to allocate costs, rather than value assets, it's possible that the carrying value of long-lived tangible assets could exceed the value of their future benefits—particularly if the assets become impaired. *Impairment* occurs when events or changed circumstances cause the estimated future cash flows (future benefits) of these assets to fall below their book value. If the estimated future cash flows are less than the asset's book value, the asset's book value should be written down, with the amount of the write-down reported as an impairment loss. Impairment losses typically are included with other expenses reported below "operating income" in the bottom part of the income statement.

Cedar Fair recorded a write-down in 2002 after a rare engineering phenomenon called "vortex shedding" reportedly caused a steel support tower in one of its VertiGo slingshot rides to snap during the off-season. Even though only one of the rides was affected, Cedar Fair dismantled and removed its two VertiGo rides.[5] To see how this bizarre event would be accounted for, let's assume that the book value of Cedar Fair's VertiGo rides was $8 million. We'll also assume that the future cash flows from the rides were only $4.8 million, because let's face it, few people are willing to go on a ride that came apart, even if it is fixable. If the fair value of the rides is estimated to be $4.8 million, which represents what other amusement park companies and scrap dealers were expected to pay for the rides' parts and 265-foot steel towers, the impairment loss is calculated as $8 million minus $4.8 million. To record this impairment loss, a write-down of $3.2 million is needed as shown in the following journal entry:

dr	**Loss Due to Impairment of Assets**	
	(+E, −SE)	3,200,000
cr	Rides and Equipment (−A)	3,200,000

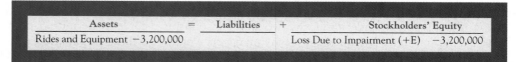

Assets	=	Liabilities	+	Stockholders' Equity
Rides and Equipment −3,200,000				Loss Due to Impairment (+E) −3,200,000

When Cedar Fair reported this loss on the income statement, it caused a huge reduction in net income. Because the loss was so large and unusual in nature, it was reported as a separate line-item called "non-recurring loss." Cedar Fair also described the impairment loss and asset write-down in the financial statement notes, as shown in Exhibit 9.5.

exhibit 9.5	**Financial Statement Note Describing Write-Down of VertiGo Rides**

Impairment of Long-Lived Assets During the first quarter of 2002, we removed certain fixed assets from service at our parks, and recorded a provision of $3.2 million for the estimated portion of the net book value of these assets that may not be recoverable.

---

[5]"Insurer Refuses Damage Payment to Sandusky, Ohio-Based Amusement Park Company," *Knight Ridder/Tribune Business News*, February 11, 2003.

Disposal of Tangible Assets

In some cases, a business may *voluntarily* decide not to hold a long-term asset for its entire life. For example, your local gym might decide to replace its treadmills with elliptical trainers, or a company may drop a product from its line and no longer need the equipment that was used to produce its product. To get rid of used assets, companies do just what you do. They trade them in on a new asset, sell them on eBay, or "retire" them to a junkyard. Sometimes, assets are damaged or destroyed in storms, fires, or accidents, creating what are politely called *involuntary disposals*.

Disposals of long-term assets seldom occur on the last day of the accounting period. Therefore, depreciation must be recorded to the date of disposal. The disposal of a depreciable asset usually requires journal entries to

1. *Update the depreciation expense and accumulated depreciation accounts.*
2. *Record the disposal.* The cost of the asset and any accumulated depreciation at the date of disposal must be removed from the accounts. The difference between any resources received on disposal of an asset and its book value at the date of disposal is treated as a gain or loss on the disposal of the asset, which is reported on the income statement. It's not really operating revenue (or an operating expense) because it arises from peripheral or incidental activities, so it's usually shown below "operating income" in the bottom half of the income statement.

Assume that in the middle of year 17, Cedar Fair sold one of its hotels for $5 million cash. The original cost of the hotel of $20 million was depreciated using the straight-line method over 20 years with no residual value ($1 million depreciation expense per year). The last accounting for depreciation was at the end of year 16, so depreciation expense must be recorded for the first half of year 17. Journal entry (1) to update depreciation expense for the first half of year 17 is

dr	**Depreciation Expense (+E, −SE)**	500,000	
	cr **Accumulated Depreciation**		
	(+xA, −A)		500,000

The gain or loss on disposal is calculated as follows:

Cash received		$5,000,000
Original cost of hotel	$20,000,000	
Less: Accumulated depreciation ($1,000,000 × 16.5 years)	16,500,000	
Book value at date of sale		3,500,000
Gain on sale of hotel		$1,500,000

Journal entry (2) to record the sale of the hotel and the resulting gain is

dr	**Cash (+A)**	5,000,000	
dr	**Accumulated Depreciation**		
	(−xA, +A)	16,500,000	
	cr **Buildings (−A)**		20,000,000
	cr **Gain on Sale of Hotel Building**		
	(+R, +SE)		1,500,000

COACH'S CORNER

Although gains on disposal work the same as revenues (recorded with a credit and cause an increase in net income), they are not reported with sales revenues because they arise from peripheral or incidental activities rather than normal operations. Instead, they are reported below "operating income" in the bottom half of the income statement.

The accounting equation effects of the two entries (to update depreciation and record the gain on asset sale) are

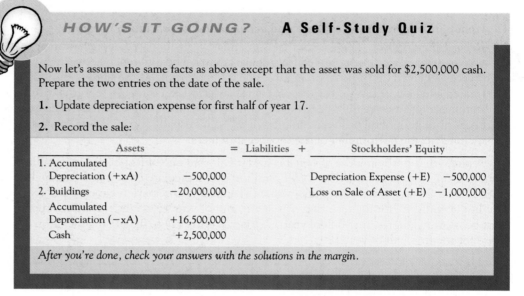

Assets	= Liabilities +	Stockholders' Equity	
1. Accumulated			
Depreciation (+xA)	−500,000	Depreciation Expense (+E)	−500,000
2. Buildings	−20,000,000	Gain on Sale of Asset (+R)	+1,500,000
Accumulated			
Depreciation (−xA)	+16,500,000		
Cash	+5,000,000		

Quiz Answers

1. dr Depreciation expense (+E) 500,000
   cr Accumulated depreciation (+xA, −A) 500,000
2. dr Cash (+A) 2,500,000
   dr Accumulated depreciation (−xA, +A) 16,500,000
   dr Loss on sale of hotel (+E, −SE) 1,000,000
   cr Buildings (−A) 20,000,000

HOW'S IT GOING?   A Self-Study Quiz

Now let's assume the same facts as above except that the asset was sold for $2,500,000 cash. Prepare the two entries on the date of the sale.

1. Update depreciation expense for first half of year 17.

2. Record the sale:

Assets	= Liabilities +	Stockholders' Equity	
1. Accumulated			
Depreciation (+xA)	−500,000	Depreciation Expense (+E)	−500,000
2. Buildings	−20,000,000	Loss on Sale of Asset (+E)	−1,000,000
Accumulated			
Depreciation (−xA)	+16,500,000		
Cash	+2,500,000		

After you're done, check your answers with the solutions in the margin.

It's time now to move on to accounting for intangibles, which are long-lived assets that lack physical substance and, instead, are evidenced by legal documents.

Types of Intangible Assets

Trademarks. A **trademark** is a special name, image, or slogan identified with a product or a company. The symbol ® signifies a trademark registered with the U.S. Patent and Trademark Office and ™ indicates unregistered trademarks.

Copyrights. A **copyright** gives the owner the exclusive right to publish, use, and sell a literary, musical, artistic, or dramatic work for a period not exceeding 70 years after the author's death. The book you are reading is copyrighted, which makes it illegal, for example, for an instructor to copy several chapters from this book and hand them out in class without first obtaining permission from the copyright owner.

Patents. A **patent** is an exclusive right granted by the federal government for a period of 20 years, typically to whoever invents a new product or discovers a new process. The patent enables the owner to be the only one who can use, manufacture, or sell the patented item. This protection is intended to encourage people to be inventive because it prevents others from simply copying innovations until after the inventor has had time to earn some money from the new product or process. One of the first roller-coaster patents was granted in 1884 for what was then called a "gravity pleasure road."

Licensing Rights. **Licensing rights** are limited permissions to use something according to specific terms and conditions. Your university or college likely has obtained the licensing right to make computer programs available for use on your campus network. A licensing right also is what allows Cedar Fair to showcase Snoopy at its parks, in the same way that MetLife flies him on their two blimps that travel 120,000 miles a year.

YOU SHOULD KNOW

A **trademark** is a special name, image, or slogan identified with a product or company.
A **copyright** is a form of protection provided to the original authors of literary, musical, artistic, dramatic, and other works of authorship.
A **patent** is a right to exclude others from making, using, selling, or importing an invention.

YOU SHOULD KNOW

A **licensing right** is the limited permission to use property according to specific terms and conditions set out in a contract.

Technology. The **technology** category of intangible assets includes a company's Web site and any computer programs written by its employees. The number of companies that reported technology intangible assets jumped by 82 percent between 2001 and 2002.

Franchises. A **franchise** is a contractual right to sell certain products or services, use certain trademarks, or perform activities in a geographical region. Krispy Kreme, for example, granted the Icon Doughnut Development Co. the franchise rights to operate stores using the Krispy Kreme name, store format, recipes, and ingredients in the Pacific Northwest. Krispy Kreme typically grants these rights in exchange for an up-front fee ranging from $20,000 to $40,000 per store plus ongoing fees of 4.5–5.5 percent of store sales.[6]

Goodwill. Goodwill tops the charts as the most frequently reported intangible asset. It encompasses lots of good stuff like a favorable location, an established customer base, a great reputation, and successful business operations. Although many companies have probably built up their own goodwill, GAAP doesn't allow it to be reported as an intangible asset on the balance sheet unless it has been purchased from another company. To understand the reasons behind this, keep reading. We explain them in the next section.

Acquisition, Use, and Disposal of Intangible Assets

Aside from being invisible, one of the biggest things distinguishing intangibles from long-lived tangible assets is that *almost all intangible assets are recorded as assets only if they have been purchased*. The costs of almost all *self-constructed or internally developed intangibles are reported as* **research and development** *expenses*. (We say "almost all" because there is one exception relating to internally developed computer software, but we'll leave details about that topic for an intermediate accounting book.) The primary reason that self-developed intangibles are not reported as assets is that it's easy for Joe Schmo to claim that he's developed a valuable (but invisible) intangible asset. But to believe what Joe is saying, you really need to see some evidence that it's worth what Joe says it's worth. In other words, an intangible asset is not reported as an asset until there's proof that it exists. And that only happens when someone gives up their hard-earned cash to buy it. At that time, the *purchaser* can record the intangible asset *at its acquisition cost*.

Some people describe goodwill as the value paid for unidentifiable net assets. Huh? Did you read that right—"the value paid for unidentifiable net assets"? How can you put a value on something you can't identify? Actually, it is possible. When one company buys another business, the purchase price often is greater than the value of all of the **net assets** of the business. Why would a company pay more for a business as a whole than it would pay if it bought the assets individually? The answer is to obtain its goodwill. You could easily buy equipment to produce and sell a bunch of generic chocolate-wafer cookies, but this strategy likely wouldn't be as successful as acquiring the goodwill associated with the Oreo business.

For accounting purposes, goodwill (also called "cost in excess of net assets acquired") is defined as the difference between the purchase price of a company as a whole and the fair market value of its net assets:

Purchase price
− Fair market value of identifiable assets, net of liabilities
= Goodwill to be reported

Both parties to the sale estimate an acceptable amount for the goodwill of the business and add it to the appraised fair value of the business's net assets. Then the sales price of the business is negotiated. In conformity with the *cost principle*, the resulting goodwill is recorded as an intangible asset only when it is actually purchased at a measurable cost.

---

[6]Krispy Kreme 2003 Annual Report, and May 1, 2001 press release, "Krispy Kreme Continues Expansion through New Area Developer Agreements and New Store Openings."

Okay, that's enough on the acquisition of intangible assets. Let's talk about what happens to the cost of intangible assets after they have been purchased. The accounting rules here depend on whether the intangible asset has a limited or unlimited life.

- *Limited life.* The cost of an intangible asset with a limited life, such as a patent or copyright, is allocated on a straight-line basis over each period of its useful life in a process called **amortization**, which is similar to depreciation. Most companies do not estimate a residual value for their intangible assets because, unlike tangible assets that can be sold as scrap, intangibles have no value at the end of their useful lives. Amortization expense is included on the income statement each period and the intangible assets are reported on the balance sheet at cost net of accumulated amortization.

Let's assume a company purchases the patent for a jet-propelled surfboard for $800,000 and intends to use it for 20 years. The adjusting entry each year to record $40,000 in patent amortization expense ($800,000 ÷ 20 years) is as follows:

dr	Patent Amortization Expense (+E)......	40,000
cr	Accumulated Amortization (+xA, −A).................	40,000

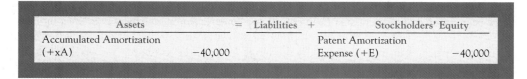

Assets	= Liabilities +	Stockholders' Equity
Accumulated Amortization (+xA) −40,000		Patent Amortization Expense (+E) −40,000

- *Unlimited life.* Intangibles with unlimited (or indefinite) lives, such as goodwill and trademarks, are not amortized.

Just like long-lived tangible assets, each intangible is tested for possible impairment and the asset's book value is written down (decreased) to its fair value if impaired. Similarly, disposals of intangible assets result in gains (or losses) if the amounts received on disposal are greater than (less than) their book values.

The accounting rules for long-lived tangible and intangible assets are summarized and compared in Exhibit 9.6.

exhibit 9.6   Accounting Rules for Long-Lived Tangible and Intangible Assets

Stage	Subject	Tangible Assets	Intangible Assets
Acquire	**Purchased asset**	Capitalize all related costs	Capitalize all related costs
	Self-constructed asset	Capitalize all related costs	Expense all related costs (unless software products)
Use	**Repairs/maintenance** Ordinary	Expense related costs	Not applicable
	Extraordinary	Capitalize related costs	Not applicable
	Depreciation/amortization Limited life	One of several methods: • Straight-line • Units-of-production • Declining-balance	Typically use only the straight-line method
	Unlimited life	Do not depreciate (e.g., land)	Do not amortize (e.g., goodwill)
	Impairment test	Write down if necessary	Write down if necessary
Dispose	**Report gain (loss) when . . .**	Receive more (less) on disposal than book value	Receive more (less) on disposal than book value

EVALUATE

THE EFFECTIVENESS OF LONG-LIVED ASSET MANAGEMENT DECISIONS

What's an Optimal Level of Investment?

One of the major challenges business managers face is forecasting the right amount to invest in tangible and intangible assets. If they underestimate the amount needed to produce goods or provide services for customers, they will miss an opportunity to earn revenue. On the other hand, if they overestimate the amount needed, their companies will incur excessive costs that will reduce profitability.

If you've ever played RollerCoaster Tycoon®, you know the amusement park business provides an outstanding example of the difficulties involved in these long-lived asset decisions. If an amusement park builds more rides than it needs to satisfy park-goers, the rides will run with empty seats. The company will still incur all of the costs to run the rides, but it will generate only a fraction of the possible revenue. Unlike merchandise companies, an amusement park cannot build up an "inventory" of unused seats to be sold in the future. On the other hand, an amusement park also can run into trouble if it doesn't have enough rides to satisfy park-goers. Just think how you felt the last time you had to wait an hour or more in line. To keep its customers on rides rather than in lines, Cedar Fair is always adding new rides. This is one of the reasons its main park is voted no. 1 in the amusement industry for best ride capacity, year after year.[7]

In addition to accurately forecasting the right *number* of rides, a business like Cedar Fair also has to pick the right *type* of ride. This is a key feature that distinguishes Cedar Fair from competitors like Disney, Six Flags, and Universal Studios. Cedar Fair prides itself on having the tallest and fastest roller coasters in the world. Cedar Fair's business strategy is to continually introduce the latest ride technologies into its parks, which enables it to compete head on with the other big-name companies that instead emphasize other aspects of their parks.

POINT OF INTEREST
The $10 million Power Tower ride blasts you up and down its 24-story tall towers, at speeds of up to 60 mph! This ride handles 12 people at a time on each of its four steel towers. That can translate into over 1.4 million riders a season.

POINT OF INTEREST
For a break from roller-coaster action, Cedar Fair's Oceans of Fun waterpark features a 1,000-gallon bucket that fills and empties every five minutes, gushing water on anyone and everyone below.

Evaluating the Use of Long-Lived Tangible Assets

Just as managers carefully plan what to invest in long-lived tangible and intangible assets, financial analysts closely evaluate how well management uses these assets to generate revenues. The fixed asset turnover ratio provides a good measure of this.

---

[7]See footnote 2.

$$\text{Fixed Asset} \atop \text{Turnover Ratio} = \frac{\text{Net Sales Revenue}}{\text{Average Net Fixed Assets}} = \frac{\text{Net Sales Revenue}}{\left(\begin{matrix}\text{Beginning Net} \\ \text{Fixed Assets}\end{matrix} + \begin{matrix}\text{Ending Net} \\ \text{Fixed Assets}\end{matrix}\right) \Big/ 2}$$

The fixed asset turnover ratio measures the sales dollars generated by each dollar invested in fixed assets. Just as mpg (miles per gallon) provides a measure of a car's fuel efficiency, the fixed asset turnover ratio provides a measure of fixed asset operating efficiency. Generally speaking, a high or increasing turnover ratio suggests better use of fixed assets whereas a low or declining ratio usually means the opposite.

Be on the Alert

A low or declining ratio doesn't *always* mean bad news. A declining ratio, for example, could be caused by a company acquiring additional assets during the current period in anticipation of higher sales in future periods. Higher future sales are always a good thing. Similarly, a high or increasing fixed asset turnover ratio doesn't *always* mean good news. It could be caused by renting rather than buying fixed assets. For example, Kimberly-Clark—the Kleenex and Huggies company—admits in its annual report that it "acquires the use of automobiles, fork lifts, office equipment, warehouses and some manufacturing equipment" through short-term rental agreements, whereby "no asset . . . is recorded on the Corporation's balance sheet." This arrangement is called an **operating lease.** Under an operating lease, a company can obtain the use of fixed assets without buying them. This allows a company to generate revenues by using fixed assets that are not reported in the fixed asset accounts, which has the effect of increasing the fixed asset turnover ratio.[8]

YOU SHOULD KNOW

An **operating lease** is an arrangement where a company rents fixed assets from other companies, but does not record them on its balance sheet.

Note that fixed asset turnover ratios can vary between industries. A company like Yahoo!, for example, needs fewer fixed assets to generate revenues, so it is likely to have a high turnover ratio in comparison to companies like Cedar Fair and Six Flags, which need to invest lots of money in fixed assets to attract customers. In Exhibit 9.7, we've shown the fixed asset turnover ratios for these three companies in 2003. The details of the Cedar Fair calculations are shown, which divide the total net revenues of $509,976 (million) in 2003 by the average of the net fixed asset numbers reported in Cedar Fair's balance sheet in Exhibit 9.2. The Self-Study Quiz that follows gives you a chance to see whether you understand how to calculate this ratio.

exhibit 9.7   **Summary of Fixed Asset Turnover Ratio Analyses**

| Name of Measure | Formula | What It Tells You | 2003 FISCAL YEAR | | | SELF-STUDY QUIZ 2002 |
			Yahoo!	Six Flags	Cedar Fair	Cedar Fair
Fixed Asset Turnover Ratio	Net Sales Revenue / Average Net Fixed Assets	• The efficiency with which fixed assets generate revenue • A higher ratio means greater efficiency ☺	3.96 times	0.45 times	$= \dfrac{509,976}{(777,039 + 781,502)/2}$ $= 0.65$ times	

---

[8]Operating and capital leases (mentioned earlier) are discussed in detail in intermediate accounting.

RECONSIDER

HOW REPORTING DECISIONS AFFECT ANALYSES

The Impact of Depreciation Differences

As you've seen in the last section, differences in the nature of business operations affect financial analyses and the conclusions that you draw from them. The same is true for differences in depreciation, whether they arise from using different depreciation methods, different estimated useful lives, or different estimated residual values. In this section, we present a simple example to show how different depreciation methods can affect analyses throughout the life of a long-lived asset. Don't let the simplicity of this example fool you. The differences in this example are identical to what often happens in the real world.

Assume that Cedar Fair and Six Flags each acquire a new roller coaster at the beginning of the year for $15.5 million, and estimate that the roller coasters will have residual values of $1.5 million at the end of their seven-year useful lives. Everything about the roller coasters is identical, except we'll assume Cedar Fair uses the straight-line depreciation method and Six Flags uses the double-declining-balance method. Exhibit 9.8 shows the yearly depreciation to be reported by the two companies. Notice that early in the asset life, prior to year 4, the straight-line depreciation expense reported by Cedar Fair is less than the declining-balance depreciation expense reported by Six Flags. This means that even if the two companies draw exactly the same number of customers, which lead to exactly the same total revenues, the reported net income will differ just because the two companies use different (but equally acceptable) methods of depreciation. This example shows why, as a user of financial statements, you need to understand what accounting methods are used by companies that you may be comparing.

COACH'S CORNER

For tips and practice involving the calculations in Exhibit 9.8, try SS9-1 at the end of this chapter.

exhibit 9.8	Straight-Line and Double-Declining-Balance Depreciation Schedules

CEDAR FAIR (STRAIGHT-LINE)				SIX FLAGS (DOUBLE-DECLINING-BALANCE)		
Depreciation Expense	Accumulated Depreciation	Book Value	Year	Depreciation Expense	Accumulated Depreciation	Book Value
$2,000,000	$ 2,000,000	$13,500,000	1	$4,429,000	$ 4,429,000	$11,071,000
2,000,000	4,000,000	11,500,000	2	3,163,000	7,592,000	7,908,000
2,000,000	6,000,000	9,500,000	3	2,259,000	9,851,000	5,649,000
2,000,000	8,000,000	7,500,000	4	1,614,000	11,465,000	4,035,000
2,000,000	10,000,000	5,500,000	5	1,153,000	12,618,000	2,882,000
2,000,000	12,000,000	3,500,000	6	823,000	13,441,000	2,059,000
2,000,000	14,000,000	1,500,000	7	559,000	14,000,000	1,500,000

exhibit 9.9   Calculations of Gain/Loss on Disposal

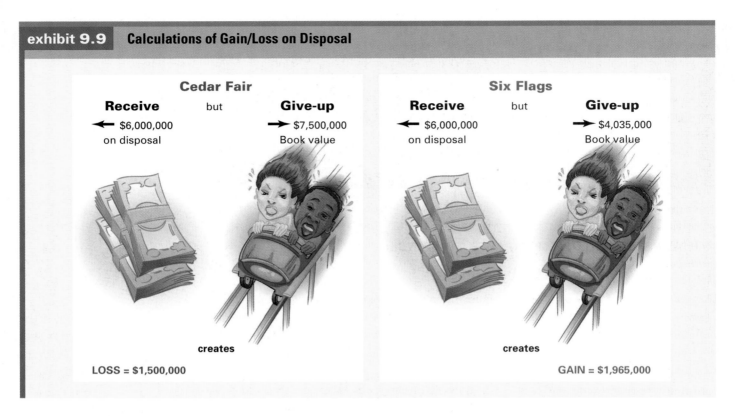

The differences don't stop at depreciation expense, however. Let's take the example one step further and assume that the two companies sell the roller coasters at the end of year 4 for $6,000,000. Since we've assumed the disposal occurs on the last day of the year, a full year of depreciation will be recorded prior to the disposal. Thus, at the time of disposal, Cedar Fair's asset will have a book value of $7,500,000 whereas Six Flags will have a book value of $4,035,000, as shown in the highlighted line in Exhibit 9.8 on the previous page. To account for the disposal at the end of year 4, the companies will record what they receive, remove what they give up (the book value of the asset), and recognize a gain or loss for the difference between what is received and given up. Exhibit 9.9 shows these calculations for the two companies.

Based on the information in Exhibit 9.9, which company appears better managed? Someone who doesn't understand accounting is likely to say Six Flags is better managed because it reports a gain on disposal whereas Cedar Fair reports a loss. You know that this can't be right because both companies have experienced exactly the same business events. They bought the same asset at the same cost ($15.5 million) and sold it for the same amount of money ($6 million). The only difference between them is that Cedar Fair reported less depreciation over the years leading up to the disposal, so its roller coaster has a larger book value at the time of disposal. Six Flags reported more depreciation in years 1–4, so it has a smaller book value at the time of disposal. As a financial statement user, you should realize that any disposal gain or loss reported on the income statement tells you as much (and, in many cases, more) about the method previously used to depreciate assets than about the apparent "wisdom" or management ability to negotiate the sale of long-lived assets.

Although our example used different depreciation methods, the same effects can exist between two companies that use the same depreciation methods but estimate different useful lives or different residual values for their long-lived assets. How big can these differences get? Well, even within the same industry, sizable differences can exist. The financial statement notes of various companies in the airline industry, for example, reveal the following differences in estimated useful lives of their airplanes and other flight equipment:

COACH'S CORNER

Useful lives vary for several reasons, including differences in (a) the type of equipment used by each company, (b) the frequency of repairs and maintenance, (c) the frequency and duration of use, and (d) the degree of conservatism in management's estimates.

Company	Estimated Life (in years)
US Airways	Up to 30
Southwest	Up to 25
Alaska Airlines	Up to 20
Singapore Airlines	Up to 15

Some analysts try to sidestep possible differences in depreciation calculations by focusing on financial measures that exclude the effects of depreciation. One popular measure is called **EBITDA** (pronounced something like *'e bit, duh*). This might seem like a goofy name, but it's actually the first letters of "earnings before interest, taxes, depreciation, and amortization." Analysts calculate EBITDA by starting with net income and adding back depreciation and amortization expense (as well as nonoperating expenses like interest and taxes). The idea is that this measure allows analysts to conduct financial analyses without having to think about possible differences in depreciation and amortization.

YOU SHOULD KNOW

EBITDA is an abbreviation for "earnings before interest, taxes, depreciation, and amortization," which is a measure of operating performance that some managers and analysts use in place of net income.

What's Coming Up

This chapter concludes our look at the assets side of the balance sheet. In Chapter 10, we will study the liabilities that are needed to help finance asset purchases. For now, though, spend some time reviewing and practicing the material covered in this chapter.

FOR YOUR REVIEW

DEMONSTRATION CASE

Diversified Industries started as a house construction company. In recent years, it has expanded into heavy construction, ready-mix concrete, sand and gravel, construction supplies, and earth-moving services. The company completed the following transactions during 2006. Amounts have been simplified.

2006

Jan. 1   The management decided to buy a 10-year old building for $175,000 and the land on which it was situated for $130,000. It paid $100,000 in cash and signed a note payable for the rest.

Jan. 3   Paid $38,000 in cash for renovations to the building prior to its use.

July 10   Paid $1,200 cash for ordinary repairs on the building.

Dec. 31   Considered the following information to determine year-end adjustments:

a. The building will be depreciated on a straight-line basis over an estimated useful life of 30 years. The estimated residual value is $33,000.

b. Diversified purchased another company several years ago at $100,000 more than the fair values of the net assets acquired. The goodwill has an unlimited life.

c. At the beginning of the year, the company owned equipment with a cost of $650,000 and accumulated depreciation of $150,000. The equipment is being depreciated using the double-declining-balance method, with a useful life of 20 years and no residual value.

d. At year-end, the company tested its long-lived assets for possible impairment of their value. Included in its equipment was a piece of old excavation equipment with a cost of $156,000 and book value of $120,000 (after making the adjustment for c). Due to its smaller size and lack of safety features, the old equipment has limited use. The future cash flows and fair value are expected to be $35,000. Goodwill was found not to be impaired.

December 31, 2006, is the end of the annual accounting period.

Required:

1. Indicate the accounts affected and the amount and direction (+ for increase and − for decrease) of the effect of each of the preceding events on the financial statement categories at the end of the year. Use the following headings:

Date	Assets	=	Liabilities	+	Stockholders' Equity

2. Prepare the journal entries to record each event that occurred during the year and the adjusting journal entries required at December 31.

3. Show the December 31, 2006, balance sheet classification and amount for each of the following items:
   - Fixed assets—land, building, and equipment.
   - Intangible asset—goodwill.

4. Assuming that the company had sales of $1,000,000 for the year and a book value of $500,000 for fixed assets at the beginning of the year, compute the fixed asset turnover ratio. Explain its meaning.

Suggested Solution

1. **Effects of events** (with computations in notes below the table):

Date	Assets		=	Liabilities		+	Stockholders' Equity	
Jan. 1	Cash	−100,000		Note Payable	+205,000			
	Land	+130,000						
	Building	+175,000						
Jan. 3	Cash	−38,000						
(1)	Building	+38,000						
July 10	Cash	−1,200					Repairs Expense (+E)	−1,200
(2)								
Dec. 31 *a*	Accumulated Depreciation (+xA)	−6,000					Depreciation Expense (+E)	−6,000
(3)								
Dec. 31 *b*	No entry							
(4)								
Dec. 31 *c*	Accumulated Depreciation (+xA)	−50,000					Depreciation Expense (+E)	−50,000
(5)								
Dec. 31 *d*	Equipment	−85,000					Loss Due to Asset Impairment (+E)	−85,000
(6)								

(1) Capitalize the $38,000 expenditure because it is necessary to prepare the asset for use.

(2) This is an ordinary repair and should be expensed.

(3)

Cost of building		**Straight-line depreciation**
Initial payment	$175,000	($213,000 cost − $33,000 residual value) ×
Renovations prior to use	38,000	1/30 years = *$6,000* annual depreciation
Acquisition cost	$213,000	

(4) Goodwill has indefinite life and is therefore not amortized. Goodwill is tested for impairment but, as described later in the case, was found not to be impaired.

(5) **Double-declining-balance depreciation**

($650,000 cost − $150,000 accumulated depreciation) × 2/20 years = $50,000 annual depreciation

(6) **Asset impairment test**

The book value of old equipment ($120,000) exceeds expected future cash flows ($35,000). The asset has become impaired, so it needs to be written down to its fair value.

Impairment Loss:

Book value	$120,000
Less: Fair value	− 35,000
Loss due to impairment	$ 85,000

2. **Journal entries for events during the year:**

January 1, 2006
dr	Land (+A)	130,000	
dr	Building (+A)	175,000	
	cr Cash (−A)		100,000
	cr Note Payable (+L)		205,000

January 3, 2006
dr	Building (+A)	38,000	
	cr Cash (−A)		38,000

July 10, 2006
dr	Repairs Expense (+E, −SE)	1,200	
	cr Cash (−A)		1,200

Adjusting journal entries at December 31, 2006:

a.
dr	Depreciation Expense (+E, −SE)	6,000	
	cr Accumulated Depreciation (+xA, −A)		6,000

b. No adjusting journal entry required because goodwill is assumed to have an unlimited (or indefinite) life.

c.
dr	Depreciation Expense (+E, −SE)	50,000	
	cr Accumulated Depreciation (+xA, −A)		50,000

d.
dr	Loss Due to Asset Impairment (+E, −SE)	85,000	
	cr Equipment (−A)		85,000

3. **Partial balance sheet, December 31, 2006:**

Assets		
Fixed assets		
Land		$130,000
Building	$213,000	
Less: Accumulated depreciation	6,000	207,000
Equipment ($650,000 − 85,000)	565,000	
Less: Accumulated depreciation		
($150,000 + 50,000)	200,000	365,000
Total fixed assets		702,000
Intangible asset		
Goodwill		100,000

4. **Fixed asset turnover ratio:**

$$\frac{\text{Sales}}{\text{(Beginning Net Fixed Asset Balance + Ending Net Fixed Asset Balance)} \div 2} = \frac{\$1,000,000}{(\$500,000 + \$702,000) \div 2} = 1.66$$

This construction company is capital intensive. The fixed asset turnover ratio measures the company's efficiency at using its investment in property, plant, and equipment to generate sales.

CHAPTER SUMMARY

LO1   **Define, classify, and explain the nature of long-lived assets. p. 368**

- Long-lived assets are those that a business retains for long periods of time for use in the course of normal operations rather than for sale. They may be divided into tangible assets (land, buildings, equipment) and intangible assets (including goodwill, patents, and franchises).

LO2   **Apply the cost principle to the acquisition of long-lived assets. p. 369**

- Acquisition cost of property, plant, and equipment is the cash-equivalent purchase price plus all reasonable and necessary expenditures made to acquire and prepare the asset for its intended use. These assets may be acquired using cash or debt, or through self-construction.

  Expenditures made after the asset is in use are either expensed or capitalized as a cost of the asset:

  a. Expenditures are *expensed* if they recur frequently, involve relatively small amounts, and do not directly lengthen the asset's useful life. These are considered ordinary repairs and maintenance expense.

  b. Expenditures are *capitalized as a cost of the asset* if they provide benefits for one or more accounting periods beyond the current period. This category includes extraordinary repairs, replacements, and additions.

LO3   **Apply various depreciation methods as future economic benefits are used up over time. p. 374**

- In conformity with the matching principle, the cost of long-lived tangible assets (less any estimated residual value) is allocated to depreciation expense over each period benefited by the assets.
- Because of depreciation, the book value of an asset declines over time and net income is reduced by the amount of the expense.
- Common depreciation methods include straight-line (a constant amount over time), units-of-production (a variable amount over time), and double-declining-balance (a decreasing amount over time).

LO4   **Explain the effect of asset impairment on the financial statements. p. 380**

- When events or changes in circumstances reduce the estimated future cash flows of a long-lived asset below its book value, the book value of the asset should be written down, with the amount of the write-down reported as an impairment loss.

LO5   **Analyze the disposal of long-lived tangible assets. p. 381**

When assets are disposed of through sale or abandonment,
- Record additional depreciation arising since the last adjustment was made.
- Remove the cost of the old asset and its related accumulated depreciation.
- Recognize the cash proceeds (if any).
- Recognize any gains or losses when the asset's book value is not equal to the cash received.

Analyze the acquisition, use, and disposal of long-lived intangible assets. p. 383   LO6

- Intangible assets are recorded at cost, but only when purchased. The costs of most internally developed intangible assets are expensed as research and development when incurred.

- Intangibles are reported at book value (cost less accumulated amortization) on the balance sheet.

- Amortization is calculated for intangibles with limited useful lives, using the straight-line method.

- Intangibles with unlimited useful lives, including goodwill, are not amortized, but are reviewed for impairment.

Interpret the fixed asset turnover ratio. p. 385   LO7

- The fixed asset turnover ratio measures the company's efficiency at using its investment in property, plant, and equipment to generate sales. Higher turnover ratios imply greater efficiency.

Describe factors to consider when comparing across companies. p. 387   LO8

- Companies in different industries require different levels of investment in long-lived assets. Beyond that, you should consider whether differences exist in depreciation methods, estimated useful lives, and estimated residual values, which can affect the book value of long-lived assets as well as ratios calculated using these book values and any gains or losses reported at the time of asset disposal.

FINANCIAL STATEMENT ANALYSIS TIP

To determine the amount of sales generated by each dollar invested in property, plant, and equipment, calculate the fixed asset turnover ratio:

$$\text{Fixed Asset Turnover Ratio} = \frac{\text{Net Sales Revenue}}{\text{Average Net Fixed Assets}} = \frac{\text{Net Sales Revenue}}{\left(\dfrac{\text{Beginning Net Fixed Assets} + \text{Ending Net Fixed Assets}}{2}\right)}$$

KEY TERMS TO KNOW

Amortization p. 384

Book (or Carrying) Value p. 374

Capital Lease p. 372

Capitalize p. 370

Capitalized Interest p. 372

Copyright p. 382

Declining-Balance Depreciation p. 377

Depreciable Cost p. 375

Depreciation p. 374

EBITDA p. 389

Estimated Useful Life p. 375

Extraordinary Repairs p. 373

Franchise p. 383

Goodwill (Cost in Excess of Net Assets Acquired) p. 383

Impairment p. 380

Intangible Assets p. 369

Licensing Right p. 382

Long-Lived Assets p. 368

Net Assets p. 383

Operating Lease p. 386

Ordinary Repairs and Maintenance p. 373

Patent p. 382

Research and Development p. 383

Residual (or Salvage) Value p. 375

Straight-Line Depreciation p. 376

Tangible Assets p. 368

Technology p. 383

Trademark p. 382

Units-of-Production Depreciation p. 376

SUPPLEMENT A: CHANGE IN DEPRECIATION ESTIMATES

Depreciation is based on two estimates, useful life and residual value. These estimates are made at the time a depreciable asset is acquired. As you gain experience with the asset, one or both of these initial estimates may need to be revised. In addition, extraordinary repairs and additions may be added to the original acquisition cost at some time during the asset's use. When it is clear that either estimate should be revised to a significant degree or that the asset's cost has changed, the undepreciated asset balance (less any residual value at that date) should be allocated over the remaining estimated life from the current year into the future. This is called a prospective *change in estimate*.

To compute the new depreciation expense due to a change in estimate for any of the depreciation methods described here, substitute the book value for the original acquisition cost, the new residual value for the original residual value, and the estimated remaining life for the original useful life. As an illustration, the formula using the straight-line method follows.

Original Straight-Line Formula Modified for a Change in Estimate:

$$(\text{Cost} - \text{Residual Value}) \times \frac{1}{\text{Useful Life}} = \text{Depreciation Expense}$$

$$(\text{Book Value} - \text{New Residual Value}) \times \frac{1}{\text{Remaining Life}} = \text{Depreciation Expense}$$

Assume Cedar Fair purchased the largest and fastest roller coaster in the universe for $60,000,000 with an estimated useful life of 20 years and estimated residual value of $3,000,000. Shortly after the start of year 5, Cedar Fair changed the initial estimated life to 25 years and lowered the estimated residual value to $2,400,000. At the end of year 5, the computation of the new amount for depreciation expense is as follows:

Original depreciation expense: ($60,000,000 − $3,000,000) × 1/20 = $ 2,850,000 per year
                                                     × 4 years

Accumulated depreciation at the end of year 4 $11,400,000

Book value at the end of year 4:

Acquisition cost	$60,000,000
Less: Accumulated depreciation	11,400,000
Book value	$48,600,000

Depreciation in years 5 through 25 based on changes in estimates:

(Book value − New residual value) × 1/remaining years = New depreciation expense

($48,600,000 − $2,400,000) × 1/21 (25 − 4 years) = $2,200,000 per year

---

Companies may also change depreciation methods (for example, from declining-balance to straight-line), although such a change requires significantly more disclosure, as described in intermediate accounting textbooks. Under GAAP, changes in accounting estimates and depreciation methods should be made only when a new estimate or accounting method "better measures" the periodic income of the business.

Margin box (left):

Straight-Line Depreciation Expense with a Change in Estimate

$2,850,000

$2,200,000

Years   1–4   5–25

Margin box (bottom left):

Quiz Answer

$50,000 (book value after five years)

÷ 2 years (remaining life)

= $25,000 Depreciation expense per year.

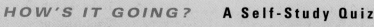

HOW'S IT GOING?   **A Self-Study Quiz**

Assume that Cedar Fair owned a bumper-car ride that originally cost $100,000. When purchased, the ride had an estimated useful life of 10 years with no residual value. After operating the ride for five years, Cedar Fair determined that the ride had only two more years of remaining life. Based on this change in estimate, what amount of depreciation should be recorded over the remaining life of the asset? Cedar Fair uses the straight-line method.

After you're done, check your answer with the solution in the margin.

QUESTIONS

1. Define *long-lived assets*. What are the two categories of long-lived assets? Describe each.
2. Under the cost principle, what amounts should be recorded as a cost of a long-lived asset?
3. What is it called when costs are recorded as assets rather than expenses?
4. Distinguish between ordinary repairs and extraordinary repairs. How is each accounted for?
5. Describe the relationship between the matching principle and accounting for long-lived assets.
6. In computing depreciation, three values must be known or estimated. Identify and describe each.
7. What type of depreciation expense pattern is used under each of the following methods and when is its use appropriate?
   a. The straight-line method.
   b. The units-of-production method.
   c. The double-declining-balance method.
8. What is an *asset impairment*? How is it accounted for?
9. What is book value? When equipment is sold for more than book value, how is the transaction recorded? How is it recorded when the selling price is less than book value?
10. Distinguish between depreciation and amortization.
11. Define *goodwill*. When is it appropriate to record goodwill as an intangible asset?
12. How is the fixed asset turnover ratio computed? Explain its meaning.
13. (Supplement) Over what period should an addition to an existing long-lived asset be depreciated? Explain.

MULTIPLE CHOICE

1. Which of the following should be capitalized when a piece of production equipment is acquired for a factory?
   a. Sales taxes.
   b. Transportation costs.
   c. Installation costs.
   d. All of the above.
2. When recording depreciation, which of the following statements are true?
   a. Total assets increase and stockholders' equity increases.
   b. Total assets decrease and total liabilities increase.
   c. Total assets decrease and stockholders' equity increases.
   d. None of the above are true.
3. Under what depreciation method(s) is an asset's book value used to calculate depreciation each year?
   a. Straight-line method.
   b. Units-of-production method.
   c. Declining-balance method.
   d. All of the above.
4. A company wishes to report the highest earnings possible according to GAAP. Therefore, when calculating depreciation for financial reporting purposes,
   a. It will follow the MACRS depreciation rates prescribed by the IRS.
   b. It will select the shortest lives possible for its assets according to GAAP.
   c. It will select the longest lives possible for its assets according to GAAP.
   d. It will estimate lower residual values for its assets.

To practice more multiple choice questions, check out the DVD for use with this book.

5. Barber, Inc., followed the practice of depreciating its building on a straight-line basis. A building was purchased on January 1, 2005, and it had an estimated useful life of 20 years and a residual value of $20,000. The company's depreciation expense for 2005 was $20,000 on the building. What was the original cost of the building?

   a. $360,000

   b. $380,000

   c. $400,000

   d. $420,000

6. ACME, Inc., uses straight-line depreciation for all of its depreciable assets. ACME sold a used piece of machinery on December 31, 2005, that it purchased on January 1, 2004, for $10,000. The asset had a five-year life, zero residual value and accumulated depreciation as of December 31, 2004, of $2,000. If the sales price of the used machine was $7,500, the resulting gain or loss on disposal was which of the following amounts?

   a.   Loss of $3,500.

   b.   Gain of $3,500.

   c.   Loss of $1,500.

   d.   Gain of $1,500.

7. What assets should be amortized using the straight-line method?

   a.   Land.

   b.   Intangible assets with limited lives.

   c.   Intangible assets with unlimited lives.

   d.   All of the above.

8. How many of the following statements regarding goodwill are true?

   • Goodwill is not reported unless purchased in an exchange.

   • Goodwill must be reviewed annually for possible impairment.

   • Impairment of goodwill results in a decrease in net income.

   a.   None

   b.   One

   c.   Two

   d.   Three

9. The Simon Company and the Allen Company each bought a new delivery truck on January 1, 2004. Both companies paid exactly the same cost, $30,000 for their respective vehicle. As of December 31, 2005, the book value of Simon's truck was less than the Allen Company's book value for the same vehicle. Which of the following are acceptable explanations for the difference in book value?

   a.   Both companies elected straight-line depreciation, but the Simon Company used a longer estimated life.

   b.   The Simon Company estimated a lower residual value, but both estimated the same useful life and both elected straight-line depreciation.

   c.   Because GAAP specifies rigid guidelines regarding the calculation of depreciation, this situation is not possible.

   d.   None of the above explain the difference in book value.

10. (Supplement) Thornton Industries purchased a machine for $45,000 and is depreciating it with the straight-line method over a life of 10 years, using a residual value of $3,000. At the beginning of the sixth year, a major overhaul was made costing $5,000, the estimated useful life was extended to 13 years, and no change was made to the estimated residual value. Depreciation expense for year 6 is

   a. $1,885

   b. $2,000

   c. $3,250

   d. $3,625

Solutions to Multiple-Choice Questions

1. d   2. d   3. c   4. c   5. d   6. d   7. b   8. d   9. b   10. c

MINI-EXERCISES   Available with McGraw-Hill's Homework Manager

M9-1 Identifying Important Accounting Terms

Complete the following crossword puzzle, using the clues provided in the box on the right.   LO1–LO6

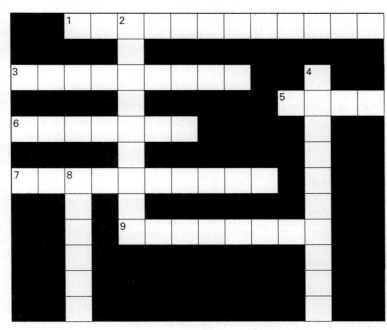

Across
1. Depreciation is to tangible assets what _____ is to intangibles.
3. A special name, image, or slogan identified with a product or company.
5. Recorded when an asset is sold for an amount greater than its book value.
6. _____ value is an alternative name for residual value.
7. Occurs when events cause the estimated future cash flows from an asset to fall below its book value.
9. The premium a company pays to obtain the favorable reputation and other intangible strengths associated with another company.

Down
2. The type of lease when a company rents a tangible asset but does not report it on its balance sheet.
4. To record a cost as an asset rather than an expense.
8. A right to exclude others from making, using, selling, or importing an invention.

M9-2 Classifying Long-Lived Assets and Related Cost Allocation Concepts   LO1, LO3, LO6

For each of the following long-lived assets, indicate its nature and related cost allocation concept. Use the abbreviations shown on the right:

Asset	Nature	Cost Allocation
1. Operating license	_____	_____
2. Property	_____	_____
3. New engine for old machine	_____	_____
4. Delivery vans	_____	_____
5. Production plant	_____	_____
6. Warehouse	_____	_____
7. Copyright	_____	_____
8. Trademark	_____	_____
9. Computers	_____	_____

Nature

L	Land
B	Building
E	Equipment
I	Intangible

Cost Allocation Concept

D	Depreciation
A	Amortization
NO	No cost allocation

M9-3 Identifying Capital and Revenue Expenditures   LO2, LO6

For each of the following items, enter the correct letter to the left to show whether the expenditure should be capitalized (C) or expensed (E).

Transactions

_____ 1. Paid $400 for ordinary repairs.
_____ 2. Paid $6,000 for extraordinary repairs.
_____ 3. Paid cash, $20,000, for addition to old building.
_____ 4. Paid for routine maintenance, $200, on credit.
_____ 5. Purchased a machine, $7,000; gave long-term note.
_____ 6. Purchased a patent, $4,300 cash.
_____ 7. Paid $10,000 for monthly salaries.

LO3   M9-4 Computing Book Value (Straight-Line Depreciation)

Calculate the book value of a three-year-old machine that cost $21,500, has an estimated residual value of $1,500, and has an estimated useful life of four years. The company uses straight-line depreciation.

LO3   M9-5 Computing Book Value (Units-of-Production Depreciation)

Calculate the book value of a three-year-old machine that cost $21,500, has an estimated residual value of $1,500, and has an estimated useful life of 20,000 machine hours. The company uses units-of-production depreciation and ran the machine 3,000 hours in year 1, 8,000 hours in year 2, and 7,000 hours in year 3.

LO3   M9-6 Computing Book Value (Double-Declining-Balance Depreciation)

Calculate the book value of a three-year-old machine that cost $21,500, has an estimated residual value of $1,500, and has an estimated useful life of four years. The company uses double-declining-balance depreciation. Round to the nearest dollar.

LO4   M9-7 Identifying Asset Impairment

For each of the following scenarios, indicate whether an asset has been impaired (Y for yes and N for no) and, if so, how much loss should be recorded.

	Book Value	Estimated Future Cash Flows	Fair Value	Is Asset Impaired?	If Yes, Amount of Loss?
a. Machine	$ 16,000	$ 9,000	$ 9,000		
b. Copyright	40,000	39,000	39,000		
c. Factory building	50,000	30,000	30,000		
d. Building	230,000	210,000	210,000		

LO5   M9-8 Recording the Disposal of a Long-Lived Asset

Prepare journal entries to record these transactions: (a) Morrell Corporation disposed of two computers at the end of their useful lives. The computers had cost $3,800 and their accumulated depreciation was $3,800. No residual value was received. (b) Assume the same information as (a), except that accumulated depreciation, updated to the date of disposal, was $3,600.

LO5   M9-9 Recording the Disposal of a Long-Lived Asset (Straight-Line Depreciation)

As part of a major renovation at the beginning of the year, Mullins' Pharmacy, Inc., sold shelving units (store fixtures) that were 10 years old for $1,400 cash. The shelves originally cost $6,200 and had been depreciated on a straight-line basis over an estimated useful life of 12 years with an estimated residual value of $200. Assuming that depreciation has been recorded to the date of sale, prepare the journal entry to record the sale of the shelving units.

LO6   M9-10 Capitalizing versus Expensing Intangible Asset Costs

Most highly visible companies spend significant amounts of money to protect their intellectual property, ensuring that no one uses this property without direct permission. For example, to include logos throughout this book, we had to obtain written permission from each company—a process that stretched over nearly a year and often resulted in requests being denied. Discuss whether companies should capitalize or expense the money paid to employees who evaluate requests for use of their logos and who search for instances where the companies' intellectual property has been used without permission. Draw an analogy to similar costs incurred for employees responsible for the use and upkeep of tangible assets.

LO6   M9-11 Computing Goodwill and Patents

Elizabeth Pie Company has been in business for 30 years and has developed a large group of loyal restaurant customers. Bonanza Foods made an offer to buy Elizabeth Pie Company for $5,000,000. The market value of Elizabeth Pie's recorded assets, net of liabilities, on the date of the offer is $4,600,000. Elizabeth Pie also holds a patent for a pie crust fluting machine that the company invented (the patent with a market value of $200,000 was never recorded by Elizabeth Pie because it was developed internally). How much has Bonanza Foods included for intangibles in its offer of

$5,000,000? Assuming Elizabeth Pie accepts this offer, which company will report goodwill on its balance sheet?

M9-12 Computing and Evaluating the Fixed Asset Turnover Ratio   LO7
The following information was reported by Amuse Yourself Parks (AYP) for 2005:

Net fixed assets (beginning of year)	$4,450,000
Net fixed assets (end of year)	4,250,000
Net sales for the year	3,250,000
Net income for the year	1,700,000

Compute the company's fixed asset turnover ratio for the year. What can you say about AYP's fixed asset turnover ratio when compared to Cedar Fair's 2003 ratio in Exhibit 9.7?

EXERCISES   Available with McGraw-Hill's Homework Manager

E9-1 Preparing a Classified Balance Sheet   LO1
The following is a list of account titles and amounts (in millions) reported by Hasbro, Inc., a leading manufacturer of games, toys, and interactive entertainment software for children and families:

Buildings and improvements	$197	Machinery and equipment	$ 346
Prepaid expenses and other current assets	319	Accumulated depreciation	227
Allowance for doubtful accounts	64	Inventories	335
Other noncurrent assets	131	Other intangibles, net	838
Cash and cash equivalents	178	Land and improvements	15
Goodwill	704	Accounts receivable	1,022

Required:
Prepare the asset section of a classified balance sheet for Hasbro, Inc.

E9-2 Computing and Recording a Basket Purchase and Straight-Line Depreciation   LO2, LO3
Sweet Company bought a building and the land on which it is located for $178,000 cash. The land is estimated to represent 60 percent of the purchase price. The company also paid renovation costs on the building of $23,200.

Required:
1. Give the journal entry to record the purchase of the property, including all expenditures. Assume that all transactions were for cash and that all purchases occurred at the start of the year.
2. Compute straight-line depreciation on the building at the end of one year, assuming an estimated 12-year useful life and a $14,000 estimated residual value.
3. What should be the book value of the land and building at the end of year 2?

E9-3 Determining Financial Statement Effects of an Asset Acquisition and   LO2, LO3
Straight-Line Depreciation
Conover Company ordered a machine on January 1, 2005, at a purchase price of $20,000. On date of delivery, January 2, 2005, the company paid $8,000 on the machine and signed a note payable for the balance. On January 3, 2005, it paid $250 for freight on the machine. On January 5, Conover paid installation costs relating to the machine amounting to $1,200. On December 31, 2005 (the end of the accounting period), Conover recorded depreciation on the machine using the straight-line method with an estimated useful life of 10 years and an estimated residual value of $3,450.

Required:
1. Indicate the effects (accounts, amounts, and + or −) of each transaction (on January 1, 2, 3, and 5) on the accounting equation. Use the following schedule:

Date	Assets	=	Liabilities	+	Stockholders' Equity

2. Compute the acquisition cost of the machine.

3. Compute the depreciation expense to be reported for 2005.
4. What should be the book value of the machine at the end of 2006?

LO2, LO3

E9-4 Recording Straight-Line Depreciation and Repairs

Wiater Company operates a small manufacturing facility. At the beginning of 2006, an asset account for the company showed the following balances:

Manufacturing equipment	$80,000
Accumulated depreciation through 2005	55,000

During 2006, the following expenditures were incurred for repairs and maintenance:

Routine maintenance and repairs on the equipment	$ 850
Major overhaul of the equipment that improved efficiency	10,500

The equipment is being depreciated on a straight-line basis over an estimated life of 15 years with a $5,000 estimated residual value. The annual accounting period ends on December 31.

Required:

1. Give the adjusting journal entry that would have been made at the end of 2005 for depreciation on the manufacturing equipment.
2. Starting at the beginning of 2006, what is the remaining estimated life?
3. Give the journal entries to record the two expenditures for repairs and maintenance during 2006.

LO2, LO3

E9-5 Determining Financial Statement Effects of Straight-Line Depreciation and Repairs

Refer to the information in E9-4.

Required:

Indicate the effects (accounts, amounts, and + or −) of the following two items on the accounting equation, using the headings shown below.

1. The adjustment for depreciation at the end of 2005.
2. The two expenditures for repairs and maintenance during 2006.

Item	Assets	=	Liabilities	+	Stockholders' Equity

LO3

E9-6 Computing Depreciation under Alternative Methods

Dorn Corporation bought a machine at the beginning of the year at a cost of $6,400. The estimated useful life was four years, and the residual value was $800. Assume that the estimated productive life of the machine is 80,000 units. Expected annual production was: year 1, 28,000 units; year 2, 22,000 units; year 3, 18,000 units; and year 4, 12,000 units.

Required:

Complete a depreciation schedule for each of the alternative methods.

a. Straight-line.
b. Units-of-production.
c. Double-declining-balance.

			Income Statement		Balance Sheet	
	Year	Computation	Depreciation Expense	Cost	Accumulated Depreciation	Book Value
At acquisition						
	1					
	2					
	3					
	4					

E9-7 Interpreting Management's Choice of Different Depreciation Methods for Tax and Financial Reporting   LO3

The annual report for Federal Express Corporation includes the following information:

> For financial reporting purposes, depreciation and amortization of property and equipment is provided on a straight-line basis over the asset's service life. For income tax purposes, depreciation is generally computed using accelerated methods.

Required:

Explain why Federal Express uses different methods of depreciation for financial reporting and tax purposes.

E9-8 Inferring Asset Age and Recording Impairment on a Long-Lived Asset (Straight-Line Depreciation)   LO3, LO4

On January 1, 2006, the records of Pastuf Corporation showed the following regarding production equipment:

Equipment (estimated residual value, $2,000)	$12,000
Accumulated depreciation (straight-line, one year)	2,000

On December 31, 2006, management determined that the equipment was impaired because its future cash flows and fair value were only $6,800.

Required:

1. Based on the data given, compute the estimated useful life of the truck.
2. Give all journal entries with respect to the equipment on December 31, 2006. Show computations.

E9-9 Demonstrating the Effect of Book Value on Recording an Asset Disposal   LO5

Federal Express is the world's leading express-distribution company. In addition to the world's largest fleet of all-cargo aircraft, the company has more than 53,700 ground vehicles that pick up and deliver packages. Assume that Federal Express sold a small delivery truck for $5,000. FedEx had originally purchased the truck for $18,000, and had recorded depreciation for three years.

Required:

1. Give the journal entry for the disposal of the truck, assuming that
   a. The accumulated depreciation was $13,000.
   b. The accumulated depreciation was $12,400.
   c. The accumulated depreciation was $13,400.
2. Based on the three preceding situations, explain how the amount of depreciation recorded up to the time of disposal affects the amount of gain or loss on disposal.

E9-10 Determining Financial Statement Effects of the Disposal of an Asset   LO5

Refer to the information in E9-9.

Required:

1. Using the following structure, indicate the effects (accounts, amounts, and + or −) for the disposal of the truck assuming that
   a. The accumulated depreciation was $13,000.
   b. The accumulated depreciation was $12,400.
   c. The accumulated depreciation was $13,400.

Assumption	Assets	=	Liabilities	+	Stockholders' Equity

2. Based on the three preceding situations, explain how the amount of depreciation recorded up to the time of disposal affects the amount of gain or loss on disposal.

LO6

E9-11 Computing and Reporting the Acquisition and Amortization of Three Different Intangible Assets

Kreiser Company had three intangible assets at the end of 2005 (end of the accounting year):

a. A patent purchased from J. Miller on January 1, 2005, for a cash cost of $5,640. Miller had registered the patent with the U.S. Patent Office five years ago.
b. An internally developed trademark was registered with the federal government for $10,000. Management decided the trademark has an indefinite life.
c. Computer software and Web development technology was purchased on January 1, 2004, for $60,000. The technology is expected to have a four-year useful life to the company.

Required:

1. Compute the acquisition cost of each intangible asset.
2. Compute the amortization of each intangible for the year ended December 31, 2005.
3. Show how these assets and any related expenses should be reported on the balance sheet and income statement for 2005.

LO4, LO6

E9-12 Recording the Purchase, Amortization, and Impairment of a Patent

Nutek, Inc., holds a patent for the Full Service™ handi-plate, which the company's 2003 10-K describes as "a patented plastic buffet plate that allows the user to hold both a plate and cup in one hand" and that "has a multitude of uses including social gatherings such as backyard barbecues, buffets, picnics, tailgate and parties of any kind." (No, we're not making this up.) Recently, Nutek also purchased a patent for $1,000,000 for "a specialty line of patented switch plate covers and outlet plate covers specifically designed to light up automatically when the power fails." Assume the switch plate patent was purchased January 1, 2003, and it is being amortized over a period of 10 years.

Required:

1. Give the journal entries to record the purchase and amortization of the switch plate patent in 2003.
2. After several months of unsuccessful attempts to manufacture the switch plate covers, Nutek determined the patent was significantly impaired and its book value on January 1, 2004, was written off. Give the journal entry to record the asset impairment.

LO7

E9-13 Computing and Interpreting the Fixed Asset Turnover Ratio from a Financial Analyst's Perspective

The following data were included in a recent Apple Computer annual report (in millions):

	2002	2001	2000	1999	1998	1997	1996	1995
Net sales	$5,742	$5,363	$7,983	$6,134	$5,941	$7,081	$9,833	$11,062
Net property, plant, and equipment	669	564	419	318	348	486	598	711

Required:

1. Compute Apple's fixed asset turnover ratio for 1996, 1998, 2000, and 2002 (the even years).
2. If you were a financial analyst, what would you say about the results of your analyses?

LO3, LO7

E9-14 Computing Depreciation and Book Value for Two Years Using Alternative Depreciation Methods and Interpreting the Impact on the Fixed Asset Turnover Ratio

Torge Company bought a machine for $65,000 cash. The estimated useful life was five years, and the estimated residual value was $5,000. Assume that the estimated useful life in productive units is 150,000. Units actually produced were 40,000 in year 1 and 45,000 in year 2.

Required:

1. Determine the appropriate amounts to complete the following schedule. Show computations.

Method of Depreciation	Depreciation Expense for		Book Value at the End of	
	Year 1	Year 2	Year 1	Year 2
Straight-line Units-of-production Double-declining-balance				

2.   Which method would result in the lowest net income for year 1? For year 2?
3.   Which method would result in the lowest fixed asset turnover ratio for year 1? Why?

E9-15 Evaluating the Impact of Capitalized Interest on Fixed Asset Turnover

LO2, LO7

You are a financial analyst charged with evaluating the asset efficiency of companies in the hotel industry. The financial statements for Hilton Hotels include the following note:

Summary of Significant Accounting Policies

Property, Equipment and Depreciation
Property and equipment are stated at cost. Interest incurred during construction of facilities is capitalized and amortized over the life of the asset.

Required:

1.   Assume that Hilton followed this policy for a major construction project this year. Would Hilton's policy increase, decrease, or not affect the fixed asset turnover ratio in the current year?
2.   Normally, if you saw a decrease in the fixed asset turnover ratio, what would you think about Hilton's effectiveness in utilizing fixed assets?
3.   If the fixed asset turnover ratio decreases due to interest capitalization, does this change indicate a real decrease in efficiency? Why or why not?

E9-16 Finding Financial Information as a Potential Investor

LO1–LO6

You are considering investing the cash gifts you received for graduation in various stocks. You have received several annual reports of major companies.

Required:

For each of the following, indicate where you would locate the information in an annual report:

1.   The detail on major classifications of long-lived assets.
2.   The accounting method(s) used for financial reporting purposes.
3.   The amount of assets written off as impaired during the year.
4.   Net amount of property, plant, and equipment.
5.   Policies on amortizing intangibles.
6.   Depreciation expense.
7.   Any significant gains or losses on disposals of fixed assets.
8.   Prior year's accumulated depreciation.

COACH'S CORNER
The information might be available in more than one location of the annual report.

E9-17 (Supplement) Recording a Change in Estimate

Refer to E9-4.

Required:

Give the adjusting entry that should be made at the end of 2006 for depreciation of the manufacturing equipment, assuming no change in the original estimated total life or residual value. Show computations.

E9-18 (Supplement) Determining Financial Statement Effects of a Change in Estimate

Refer to E9-4.

Required:

Using the following format, indicate the effects (accounts, amounts, and + or −) of the 2006 adjustment for depreciation of the manufacturing equipment, assuming no change in the estimated life or residual value. Show computations.

Date	Assets	=	Liabilities	+	Stockholders' Equity

SIMPLIFY WITH SPREADSHEETS

LO3

SS9-1 Preparing Depreciation Schedules for Straight-Line and Double-Declining-Balance

To make some extra money, you've started preparing templates of business forms and schedules for others to download from the Internet (for a small fee). After relevant information is entered into each template, it automatically performs calculations using formulas you have entered into the template. For the depreciation template, you decide to produce two worksheets—one that calculates depreciation and book value under the straight-line method and another that calculates these amounts using the double-declining-balance method. The templates perform straightforward calculations of depreciation and book value, when given the cost of an asset, its estimated useful life, and its estimated residual value. These particular templates won't handle disposals or changes in estimates—you plan to create a deluxe version for those functions. To illustrate that your templates actually work, you enter the information used to produce the depreciation schedules shown in Exhibit 9.8, with Cedar Fair and Six Flags as examples.

Although you're confident you can use appropriate formulas in the spreadsheet to create a template for the straight-line method, you're a little uncertain about how to make the double-declining-balance method work. As usual, you e-mail your friend Billy for advice. Here's what he said:

From: BillyTheTutor@yahoo.com
To: HairZed@hotmail.com
Cc:
Subject: Excel Help

I wish I'd thought of charging money for showing how to do ordinary accounting activities. You'd have made me rich by now. ☺ Here's how to set up your worksheets. Begin by creating an "input values" section. This section will allow someone to enter the asset cost, residual value, and estimated life in an area removed from the actual depreciation schedule. You don't want someone accidentally entering amounts over formulas that you've entered into the schedule.

The cells from the input values section will be referenced by other cells in the depreciation schedule. You will want to enter formulas in the cells for the first year row, and then copy and paste them to rows for the other years. When doing this, you will need to use what is called an "absolute reference," which means that the cell reference does not change when one row is copied and pasted to a different row. Unlike an ordinary cell reference that has a format of A1, an absolute reference has the format of A1, which prevents the spreadsheet from changing either the column (A) or row (1) when copying the cell to other cells. You may find this useful when preparing both the straight-line and double-declining-balance schedules.

To create the depreciation schedules, use five columns labeled: (1) year, (2) beginning of year accumulated depreciation, (3) depreciation, (4) end of year accumulated depreciation, and (5) end of year book value.

The double-declining-balance template will be the trickiest to create because you need to be concerned that the book value is not depreciated below the residual value in the last year of the asset's life. To force the template to automatically watch for this, you will need to use the IF function. Here's a screenshot of a template I created, using the IF function to properly calculate depreciation for all years of the asset's life. Notice the formula shown in the formula bar at the top.

COACH'S CORNER

To switch between displaying cell formulas and their values, press CTRL and ~ (tilde) at the same time.

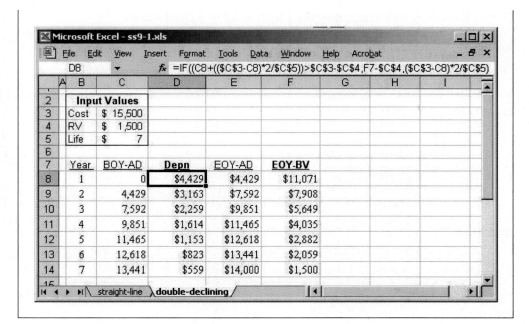

Required:

Create the spreadsheet templates to calculate depreciation and book value using the straight-line and double-declining-balance methods. Demonstrate that the template works by reproducing the schedules in Exhibit 9.8.

COACHED PROBLEMS

CP9-1 Computing Acquisition Cost and Recording Depreciation under Three Alternative Methods

At the beginning of the year, Montgomery Company bought three used machines from Hosey, Inc. The machines immediately were overhauled, installed, and started operating. Because the machines were different, each was recorded separately in the accounts.

	Machine A	Machine B	Machine C
Amount paid for asset	$7,600	$25,600	$6,800
Installation costs	300	500	200
Renovation costs prior to use	2,000	400	600
Repairs after production began	400	350	325

COACH'S CORNER

Remember that the formula for double-declining-balance uses accumulated depreciation (not residual value).

By the end of the first year, each machine had been operating 8,000 hours.

Required:

1. Compute the cost of each machine. Explain the rationale for capitalizing or expensing the various costs.
2. Give the journal entry to record depreciation expense at the end of year 1, assuming the following:

Machine	Life	Residual Value	Depreciation Method
		Estimates	
A	5 years	$1,500	Straight-line
B	40,000 hours	900	Units-of-production
C	4 years	2,000	Double-declining-balance

LO5

CP9-2   Recording and Interpreting the Disposal of Long-Lived Assets

During 2005, Jensen Company disposed of two different assets. On January 1, 2005, prior to their disposal, the accounts reflected the following:

Asset	Original Cost	Residual Value	Estimated Life	Accumulated Depreciation (straight-line)
Machine A	$20,000	$3,000	8 years	$12,750 (6 years)
Machine B	76,200	4,200	15 years	57,600 (12 years)

The machines were disposed of in the following ways:

a.   Machine A: Sold on January 2, 2005, for $8,200 cash.
b.   Machine B: On January 2, 2005, this machine suffered irreparable damage from an accident and was removed immediately by a salvage company at no cost.

Required:

1.   Give the journal entries related to the disposal of each machine at the beginning of 2005.
2.   Explain the accounting rationale for the way that you recorded each disposal.

LO6

CP9-3   Determining Financial Statement Effects of Activities Related to Intangible Assets

During the 2004 annual accounting period, Chu Corporation completed the following transactions:

a.   On January 1, 2004, purchased a license for $7,200 cash (estimated useful life, three years).
b.   On July 1, 2004, purchased another business for cash. The $120,000 purchase price included $115,000 for tangible assets of the business and $24,000 for its liabilities, which were assumed by Chu. The remainder was goodwill with an indefinite life.
c.   Expenditures during 2004 for research and development totaled $8,700.

Required:

1.   For each of these transactions, indicate the accounts, amounts and effects (+ for increase and − for decrease) on the accounting equation. Use the following structure:

Date	Assets	=	Liabilities	+	Stockholders' Equity

2.   For each of the intangible assets, compute amortization for the year ended December 31, 2004.

CP9-4   (Supplement) Analyzing and Recording Entries Related to a Change in Estimated Life and Residual Value

Reader's Digest is a global publisher of magazines, books, and music and video collections, and is one of the world's leading direct-mail marketers. Many direct-mail marketers use high-speed Didde press equipment to print their advertisements. These presses can cost more than $1 million. Assume that Reader's Digest owns a Didde press acquired at an original cost of $400,000. It is being depreciated on a straight-line basis over a 20-year estimated useful life and has a $50,000 estimated residual value. At the end of 2005, the press had been depreciated for a full eight years. In January 2006, a decision was made, on the basis of improved maintenance procedures, that a total estimated useful life of 25 years and a residual value of $73,000 would be more realistic. The accounting period ends December 31.

Required:

1.   Compute (a) the amount of depreciation expense recorded in 2005, and (b) the book value of the printing press at the end of 2005.
2.   Compute the amount of depreciation that should be recorded in 2006. Show computations.
3.   Give the adjusting entry for depreciation at December 31, 2006.

GROUP A PROBLEMS Available with McGraw-Hill's Homework Manager

PA9-1 Computing Acquisition Cost and Recording Depreciation under Three Alternative Methods

LO2, LO3

At the beginning of the year, Morgan Inc. bought three used machines from Abruzzo Corporation. The machines immediately were overhauled, installed, and started operating. Because the machines were different, each was recorded separately in the accounts.

	Machine A	Machine B	Machine C
Cost of the asset	$10,800	$32,500	$21,700
Installation costs	800	1,100	1,100
Renovation costs prior to use	600	1,400	1,600
Repairs after production began	200	300	300

By the end of the first year, each machine had been operating 7,000 hours.

Required:

1. Compute the cost of each machine. Explain the rationale for capitalizing or expensing the various costs.
2. Give the journal entry to record depreciation expense at the end of year 1, assuming the following:

	Estimates		
Machine	Life	Residual Value	Depreciation Method
A	4 years	$1,000	Straight-line
B	33,000 hours	2,000	Units-of-production
C	5 years	1,400	Double-declining-balance

PA9-2 Recording and Interpreting the Disposal of Long-Lived Assets

LO5

During 2006, Kosik Company disposed of two different assets. On January 1, 2006, prior to their disposal, the accounts reflected the following:

Asset	Original Cost	Residual Value	Estimated Life	Accumulated Depreciation (straight-line)
Machine A	$24,000	$2,000	5 years	$17,600 (4 years)
Machine B	59,200	3,200	14 years	48,000 (12 years)

The machines were disposed of in the following ways:

a. Machine A: Sold on January 1, 2006, for $5,750 cash.
b. Machine B: On January 1, 2006, this machine suffered irreparable damage from an accident and was removed immediately by a salvage company at no cost.

Required:

1. Give the journal entries related to the disposal of each machine at the beginning of 2006.
2. Explain the accounting rationale for the way that you recorded each disposal.

PA9-3 Determining Financial Statement Effects of Activities Related to Intangible Assets

LO6

Norton Pharmaceuticals entered into the following transactions that potentially affect intangible assets:

a. On January 1, 2005, the company spent $18,600 cash to buy a patent that expires in 15 years.
b. During 2005, the company spent $25,480 on a new drug that will be submitted for FDA testing in 2006.
c. Norton Pharmaceuticals purchased another business in 2005 for a cash lump sum payment of $650,000. Included in the purchase price was "Goodwill, $75,000."

Required:

1. For each of these transactions, indicate the accounts, amounts and effects (+ for increase and − for decrease) on the accounting equation. Use the following structure:

Item	Assets	=	Liabilities	+	Stockholders' Equity

2. For each of the intangible assets, compute amortization for the year ended December 31, 2005.

GROUP B PROBLEMS

LO2, LO3

PB9-1 Computing Acquisition Cost and Recording Depreciation under Three Alternative Methods

At the beginning of the year, Walters Company bought three used machines from American Chopper, Inc. The machines immediately were overhauled, installed, and started operating. Because the machines were different, each was recorded separately in the accounts.

	Machine A	*Machine B*	*Machine C*
Amount paid for asset	$19,600	$10,100	$9,800
Installation costs	300	500	200
Renovation costs prior to use	100	300	600
Repairs after production began	220	900	480

By the end of the first year, each machine had been operating 4,000 hours.

Required:

1. Compute the cost of each machine. Explain the rationale for capitalizing or expensing the various costs.
2. Give the journal entry to record depreciation expense at the end of year 1, assuming the following:

	Estimates		
Machine	*Life*	*Residual Value*	*Depreciation Method*
A	7 years	$1,100	Straight-line
B	40,000 hours	900	Units-of-production
C	4 years	2,000	Double-declining-balance

LO5

PB9-2 Recording and Interpreting the Disposal of Long-Lived Assets

During 2006, Rayon Corporation disposed of two different assets. On January 1, 2006, prior to their disposal, the accounts reflected the following:

Asset	*Original Cost*	*Residual Value*	*Estimated Life*	*Accumulated Depreciation (straight-line)*
Machine A	$60,000	$11,000	7 years	$28,000 (4 years)
Machine B	14,200	1,925	5 years	7,365 (3 years)

The machines were disposed of in the following ways:

a. Machine A: Sold on January 2, 2006, for $33,500 cash.
b. Machine B: On January 2, 2006, this machine suffered irreparable damage from an accident and was removed immediately by a salvage company at no cost.

Required:

1. Give the journal entries related to the disposal of each machine at the beginning of 2006.
2. Explain the accounting rationale for the way that you recorded each disposal.

LO6

PB9-3 Determining Financial Statement Effects of Activities Related to Intangible Assets

Fearn Company entered into the following transactions that potentially affect intangible assets:

a. Soon after Fearn Company started business, in January 2003, it purchased another business for a cash lump sum payment of $400,000. Included in the purchase price was "Goodwill, $60,000." The account balance hasn't changed in three years.

b. The company purchased a patent at a cash cost of $54,600 on January 1, 2005. The patent has an estimated useful life of 13 years.

c. In 2005, Fearn hired a director of brand development to create a marketable identity for the company's products. The director devoted the entire year to this work, at a cost to the company of $125,000.

Required:

1. For each of these transactions, indicate the accounts, amounts and effects (+ for increase and − for decrease) on the accounting equation in 2005. Use the following structure:

Item	Assets	=	Liabilities	+	Stockholders' Equity

2. For each of the intangible assets, compute amortization for the year ended December 31, 2005.

CASES & DISCUSSION STARTERS

FINANCIAL REPORTING AND ANALYSIS CASES

C&DS9-1 Finding Financial Information

LO2, LO3, LO6, LO7

Refer to the financial statements of Landry's Restaurants in Appendix A at the end of this book, or download the annual report from the *Cases* section of the text's Web site at www.mhhe.com/phillips.

Required:

1. What method of depreciation does the company use?
2. What is the amount of accumulated depreciation at the end of the current year? What percentage is this of the total cost of property and equipment?
3. For depreciation purposes, what is the estimated useful life of furniture, fixtures and equipment?
4. What amount of depreciation and amortization expense was reported for the current year? What percentage of total revenues is it?
5. What amount did the company report for intangible assets in the current year?
6. What is the fixed asset turnover ratio for the current year?
7. For each of the preceding questions, where did you locate the information?

C&DS9-2 Comparing Financial Information

LO2, LO3, LO6, LO7

Refer to the financial statements of Dave & Buster's in Appendix B at the end of this book, or download the annual report from the *Cases* section of the text's Web site at www.mhhe.com/phillips. In the questions that follow, assume Dave & Buster's financial statements for the year ended February 1, 2004, present the results for the 2003 calendar year.

Required:

1. What methods of depreciation does the company use? Why do you think Dave & Buster's would use a different method for some of its equipment assets than what Landry's uses? How would this affect depreciation expense in early years of these assets' lives?
2. What is the amount of accumulated depreciation at the end of the current year? What percentage is this of the total cost of property and equipment? Is this a larger (or smaller) percentage of the total cost of property and equipment than Landry's? What does it suggest to you about the length of time the assets have been depreciated?
3. Dave & Buster's estimated useful life of furniture, fixtures and equipment differs from that estimated by Landry's. How will this affect the fixed asset turnover ratios of the two companies?
4. What amount of depreciation and amortization expense was reported for the current year? What percentage of total revenues is it? Compare this percentage to that of Landry's and describe what this implies about the two companies' operations.

5.   What amount did the company report for intangible assets in the current year? What does the write-off of goodwill in 2002 suggest to you about the success of the Dave & Buster's business?

6.   What is the fixed asset turnover ratio for the current year? Compare this ratio to that of Landry's and describe what it implies about the operations of the two companies.

LO1, LO3, LO6, LO7

TEAM CASE

C&DS9-3   Internet-Based Team Research: Examining an Annual Report

As a team, select an industry to analyze. Using your Web browser, each team member should acquire the annual report or 10-K for one publicly traded company in the industry, with each member selecting a different company. (See C&DS1-3 in Chapter 1 for a description of possible resources for these tasks.)

Required:

1.   On an individual basis, each team member should write a short report that incorporates the following:
     a.   Describe the depreciation methods used.
     b.   Compute the percentage of fixed asset cost that has been depreciated. What does this imply about the length of time the assets have been depreciated?
     c.   Compute the fixed asset turnover ratios for the current and prior years. What does this tell you about the efficiency of the company's asset use?
     d.   Describe the kinds of intangible assets, if any, that the company reports on the balance sheet.

2.   Then, as a team, write a short report comparing and contrasting your companies using these attributes. Discuss any patterns across the companies that you as a team observe. Provide potential explanations for any differences discovered.

ETHICS AND CRITICAL THINKING CASES

LO2, LO7

ETHICAL ISSUE

C&DS9-4   Ethical Decision Making: A Real-Life Example

Assume you work as a staff member in a large accounting department for a multinational public company. Your job requires you to review documents relating to the company's equipment purchases. Upon verifying that purchases are properly approved, you prepare journal entries to record the equipment purchases in the accounting system. Typically, you handle equipment purchases costing $100,000 or less.

This morning, you were contacted by the executive assistant to the chief financial officer (CFO). She says that the CFO has asked to see you immediately in his office. Although your boss's boss has attended a few meetings where the CFO was present, you have never met the CFO during your three years with the company. Needless to say, you are anxious about the meeting.

Upon entering the CFO's office, you are warmly greeted with a smile and friendly handshake. The CFO compliments you on the great work that you've been doing for the company. You soon feel a little more comfortable, particularly when the CFO mentions that he has a special project for you. He states that he and the CEO have negotiated significant new arrangements with the company's equipment suppliers, which require the company to make advance payments for equipment to be purchased in the future. The CFO says that, for various reasons that he didn't want to discuss, he will be processing the payments through the operating division of the company rather than the equipment accounting group. Given that the payments will be made through the operating division, they will initially be classified as operating expenses of the company. He indicates that clearly these advance payments for property and equipment should be recorded as assets, so he will be contacting you at the end of every quarter to make an adjusting journal entry to capitalize the amounts inappropriately classified as operating expenses. He advises you that a new account, called "prepaid equipment," has been established for this purpose. He quickly wraps up the meeting by telling you that it is important that you not talk about the special project with anyone. You assume he doesn't want others to become jealous of your new important responsibility.

A few weeks later, at the end of the first quarter, you receive a voicemail from the CFO stating "The adjustment that we discussed is $771,000,000 for this quarter." Before deleting the message, you replay it to make sure you heard it right. Your company generates over $8 billion in revenues and incurs $6 billion in operating expenses every quarter, but you've never made a journal entry for that much money. So, just to be sure there's not a mistake, you send an e-mail to the CFO confirming the amount. He phones you back immediately to abruptly inform you, "There's no mistake. That's the number." Feeling embarrassed that you may have annoyed the CFO, you quietly make the adjusting journal entry.

For each of the remaining three quarters in that year and for the first quarter in the following year, you continue to make these end-of-quarter adjustments. The "magic number" as the CFO liked to call it was $560,000,000 for Q2, $742,745,000 for Q3, $941,000,000 for Q4, and $818,204,000 for Q1 of the following year. During this time, you've had several meetings and lunches with the CFO where he provides you the magic number, sometimes supported with nothing more than a Post-it note with the number written on it. He frequently compliments you on your good work, and promises that you'll soon be in line for a big promotion.

Despite the CFO's compliments and promises, you are growing increasingly uncomfortable with the journal entries that you've been making. Typically, whenever an ordinary equipment purchase involves an advance payment, the purchase is completed a few weeks later. At that time, the amount of the advance is removed from an "equipment deposit" account and transferred to the appropriate equipment account. This hasn't been the case with the CFO's special project. Instead, the "prepaid equipment" account has continued to grow, now standing at over $3.8 billion. There's been no discussion about how or when this balance will be reduced, and no depreciation has been recorded for it.

Just as you begin to reflect on the effect the adjustments have had on your company's fixed assets, operating expenses, and operating income, you receive a call from the vice-president for internal audit. She needs to talk with you this afternoon about "a peculiar trend in the company's fixed asset turnover ratio and some suspicious journal entries that you've been making."

Required:

1. Complete the following table to determine what the company's accounting records would have looked like had you not made the journal entries as part of the CFO's special project. Comment on how the decision to capitalize amounts, which were initially recorded as operating expenses, has affected the level of operating income in each quarter.

(amounts in millions of U.S. dollars)	Q1 Year 1 (March 31) With the Entries	Q1 Year 1 (March 31) Without the Entries	Q2 Year 1 (June 30) With the Entries	Q2 Year 1 (June 30) Without the Entries	Q3 Year 1 (September 30) With the Entries	Q3 Year 1 (September 30) Without the Entries	Q4 Year 1 (December 31) With the Entries	Q4 Year 1 (December 31) Without the Entries	Q1 Year 2 (March 31) With the Entries	Q1 Year 2 (March 31) Without the Entries
Property and equipment, net	$38,614	$	$35,982	$	$38,151	$	$38,809	$	$39,155	$
Sales revenues	8,825	8,825	8,910	8,910	8,966	8,966	8,478	8,478	8,120	8,120
Operating expenses	7,628		8,526		7,786		7,725		7,277	
Operating income	1,197		384		1,180		753		843	

2. Using the publicly reported numbers (which include the special journal entries that you recorded), compute the fixed asset turnover ratio for the periods ended Q2–Q4 of year 1 and Q1 of year 2. What does the trend in this ratio suggest to you? Is this consistent with the changes in operating income reported by the company?

3. Before your meeting with the vice-president for internal audit, you think about the above computations and the variety of peculiar circumstances surrounding the "special project" for the CFO. What in particular might have raised your suspicion about the real nature of your work?

4. Your meeting with internal audit was short and unpleasant. The vice-president indicated that she had discussed her findings with the CFO before meeting with you. The CFO claimed that he too had noticed the peculiar trend in the fixed assets turnover ratio, but that he hadn't had a chance to investigate it further. He urged internal audit to get to the bottom of things, suggesting that perhaps someone might be making unapproved journal entries. Internal audit had identified you as the source of the journal entries and had been unable to find any documents that approved or substantiated the entries. She ended the meeting by advising you to find a good lawyer. Given your current circumstances, describe how you would have acted earlier had you been able to foresee where it might lead you.

5. In the real case on which this one is based, the internal auditors agonized over the question of whether they had actually uncovered a fraud or whether they were jumping to the wrong

conclusion. The *Wall Street Journal* mentioned this on October 30, 2002, by stating, "it was clear . . . that their findings would be devastating for the company. They worried about whether their revelations would result in layoffs. Plus, they feared that they would somehow end up being blamed for the mess." Beyond the personal consequences mentioned in this quote, describe other potential ways in which the findings of the internal auditors would likely be devastating for the publicly traded company and those associated with it.

Epilogue: This case is based on a fraud committed at WorldCom (now called MCI). The case draws its numbers, the nature of the unsupported journal entries, and the CFO's role in carrying out the fraud from a report issued by WorldCom's bankruptcy examiner. Year 1 in this case was actually 2001 and year 2 was 2002. This case excludes other fraudulent activities that contributed to WorldCom's $11 billion fraud. At the time this textbook went to press, the CFO and four other employees in WorldCom's accounting group had pleaded guilty to securities fraud and a variety of other charges, and they were awaiting sentencing. The CEO has been charged with planning and executing the biggest fraud in the history of American business.

LO3, LO5   ### C&DS9-5 Ethical Decision Making: A Mini-Case

Assume you are one of three members of the accounting staff working for a small, private company. At the beginning of this year, the company expanded into a new industry by acquiring equipment that will be used to make several new lines of products. The owner and general manager of the company has indicated that, as one of the conditions for providing financing for the new equipment, the company's bank will receive a copy of the company's annual financial statements. Another condition of the loan is that the company's total assets cannot fall below $250,000. Violation of this condition gives the bank the option to demand immediate repayment of the loan. Before making the adjustment for this year's depreciation, the company's total assets are reported at $255,000. The owner has asked you to take a look at the facts regarding the new equipment and "work with the numbers to make sure everything stays onside with the bank."

A depreciation method has yet not been adopted for the new equipment. Equipment used in other parts of the company is depreciated using the double-declining-balance method. The cost of the new equipment was $35,000 and the manager estimates it will be worth "at least $7,000" at the end of its four-year useful life. Because the products made with the new equipment are only beginning to catch on with consumers, the company used the equipment to produce just 4,000 units this year. It is expected that, over all four years of its useful life, the new equipment will make a total of 28,000 units.

Required:

1. Calculate the depreciation that would be reported this year under each of the three methods shown in this chapter. Which of the methods would meet the owner's objective?

2. Evaluate whether it is ethical to recommend that the company use the method identified in requirement 1. What two parties are most directly affected by this recommendation? How would each party be benefited or harmed by the recommendation? Does the recommendation violate any laws or applicable rules? Are there any other factors that you would consider before making a recommendation?

LO3, LO5, LO8   ### C&DS9-6 Critical Thinking: Analyzing the Effects of Depreciation Policies on Income

As an aspiring financial analyst, you have applied to a major Wall Street firm for a summer job. To screen potential applicants, the firm provides you a short case study and asks you to evaluate the financial success of two hypothetical companies that started operations on January 1, 2004. Both companies operate in the same industry, use very similar assets, and have very similar customer bases. Among the additional information provided about the companies are the following comparative income statements.

	Fast Corporation		Slow Corporation	
	2005	**2004**	**2005**	**2004**
Net sales	$60,000	$60,000	$60,000	$60,000
Cost of goods sold	20,000	20,000	20,000	20,000
Gross profit	40,000	40,000	40,000	40,000
Selling, general, and administrative expenses	19,000	19,000	19,000	19,000
Depreciation expense	3,555	10,667	5,000	5,000
Operating income	17,445	10,333	16,000	16,000
Other gains (losses)	2,222	—	(1,000)	—
Income before income taxes	$19,667	$10,333	$15,000	$16,000

Required:

Prepare an analysis of the two companies with the goal of determining which company is better managed. If you could request two additional pieces of information from these companies' financial statements, describe specifically what they would be and explain how they would help you to make a decision.

chapter ten

Reporting and Interpreting Liabilities

10

They've turned in the reports, and they're just waiting to hear their letter grade. They're expecting an A and would be devastated if it's a B. Sounds like some high-achieving students, right? It could be. But it's actually the Jolly Green Giant, Lucky the Leprechaun, Poppin' Fresh, and their corporate bosses at **GENERAL MILLS.** That's right. This magically delicious company and all its characters receive a letter grade just like you and your friends. Their grading process differs a bit from yours, because their grade is assigned by credit rating agencies like Standard & Poor's, Fitch, and Moody's, indicating the company's ability to pay its liabilities on a timely basis. Another difference is that their grades can range from AAA to D. The AAA rating is given to companies in rock-solid financial condition, and the D goes to those likely to pay less than half of what they owe. In general, anything above BB is considered a good to high-quality credit rating, which is what General Mills typically earns.

In this chapter, you will learn about the accounting procedures and financial ratios used to report and interpret liabilities, and how they influence credit ratings. Although we focus on *corporate* reporting and analyses, this chapter also can help you to understand the kind of information others use to evaluate your own personal credit rating.

INSIDE LOOKING OUT

OUTSIDE LOOKING IN

This chapter focuses on reporting and interpreting the liabilities of General Mills, a leader in cereals, frozen foods, and snacks.

GENERAL MILLS

The Trix Rabbit and Lucky the Leprechaun were joined by Poppin' Fresh and the Jolly Green Giant in 2001 when General Mills acquired the Pillsbury Company.

FAST FLASHBACK

Liabilities are debts or probable obligations that result from past transactions and will be paid with assets or services.

As you might suspect, liabilities are a key ingredient in credit ratings. So that's where we'll start: helping you to understand what liabilities are and how they're accounted for. As Exhibit 10.1 shows, you'll use this knowledge later in the chapter when learning about the financial analyses and other information used to evaluate whether a company is likely to meet its financial obligations.

exhibit 10.1   Your Learning Objectives

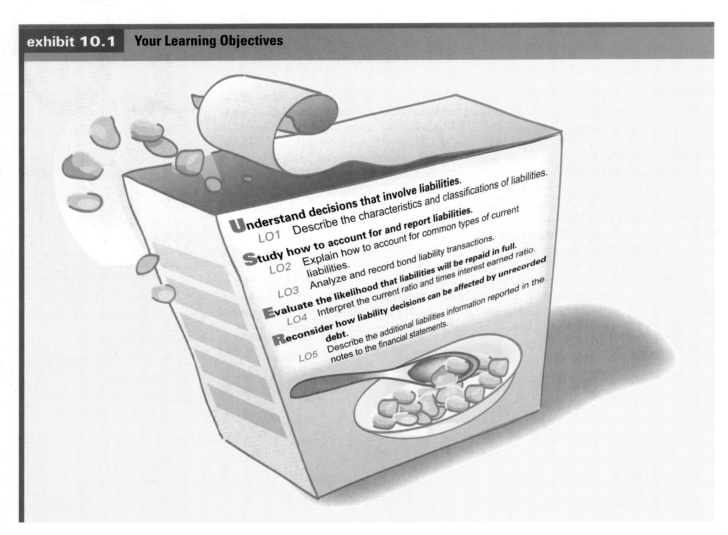

Understand decisions that involve liabilities.
LO1   Describe the characteristics and classifications of liabilities.

Study how to account for and report liabilities.
LO2   Explain how to account for common types of current liabilities.
LO3   Analyze and record bond liability transactions.

Evaluate the likelihood that liabilities will be repaid in full.
LO4   Interpret the current ratio and times interest earned ratio.

Reconsider how liability decisions can be affected by unrecorded debt.
LO5   Describe the additional liabilities information reported in the notes to the financial statements.

UNDERSTAND

DECISIONS THAT INVOLVE LIABILITIES

When a friend asks to borrow something and promises to pay you back later, you get to experience what it's like to be a credit manager for a company. Before lending something to a friend or extending credit to another company, two questions should quickly come to mind:

1. How much does the person or company owe to others? For what?
2. Can you expect the person or company to repay each of its debts? When?

Some of your friends might be offended if you came right out and asked these questions. Fortunately, if you're a credit manager, you can often find answers to these questions in a company's financial statements. Let's assume we are credit managers at Seneca Foods, a canned veggies supplier to Big G (that's the Wall Street nickname for General

exhibit 10.2	General Mills' Liabilities (in millions)		

Liabilities

	2003	2002
Current Liabilities		
Accounts Payable	$ 1,303	$ 1,217
Other Current Liabilities	800	682
Notes Payable	1,236	3,600
Current Portion of Long-Term Debt	105	248
Total Current Liabilities	3,444	5,747
Long-Term Debt	7,516	5,591
Other Liabilities	2,792	1,473
Total Liabilities	13,752	12,811

Mills). Let's see if we can answer these questions by looking at the liabilities section of the General Mills balance sheet at the end of its 2003 fiscal year, which is shown in Exhibit 10.2.

Starting with the first question, does General Mills owe anything to others? You bet! The liabilities section of the balance sheet, shown in Exhibit 10.2, indicates that General Mills owes over $13.7 billion at the end of 2003. If you knew nothing else about General Mills, you might feel uneasy about its creditworthiness because the company owes so much to others. Let's see if this feeling changes as we now move to the second question.

Classification of Liabilities

When can you expect General Mills to repay its debts? The balance sheet responds to this question by classifying some liabilities as current. **Current liabilities** are short-term obligations that will be paid with current assets within the current operating cycle of the business or within one year of the balance sheet date, whichever is longer. Because most companies have an operating cycle that is shorter than a year, the definition of current liabilities can be simplified as liabilities that are due within one year. This means that only $3.4 billion of the $13.7 billion of total liabilities shown in Exhibit 10.2 will be paid within one year. This should make you feel a little more comfortable, particularly if you require General Mills to pay your company in one year or less. The remaining $10.3 billion of liabilities are due more than a year from the balance sheet date. Although these longer-term obligations rarely get a separate subheading of their own, people often refer to them as noncurrent or long-term liabilities.

YOU SHOULD KNOW

Current liabilities are short-term obligations that will be paid with current assets within the current operating cycle or one year, whichever is longer. An operating cycle is the time it takes to make sales to customers, collect from them, and pay suppliers.

STUDY

HOW TO ACCOUNT FOR AND REPORT LIABILITIES

A company must record a liability when a transaction or event obligates the company to give up assets or services in the future. In this section, we will discuss various types of obligations that are reported as liabilities. But before we do that, let's make sure you clearly understand what the liability numbers on the balance sheet represent.

Measurement of Liabilities

The dollar amount reported for liabilities is the result of three things:

1. **The initial amount of the liability.** A liability is initially recorded at its cash equivalent, which is the amount of cash that a creditor would accept to settle the liability immediately after the transaction or event occurred.

2. **Additional amounts owed to the creditor.** Liabilities are increased whenever additional obligations arise, including interest charges that arise as time passes.

3. **Payments or services provided to the creditor.** Liabilities are reduced whenever the company makes payments or provides services to the creditor.

Notice that a liability is first recorded at a cash-equivalent amount, which excludes any interest charge. This makes sense because if you borrowed $10 from a friend and paid it back a split-second later, you wouldn't have to pay any interest. Interest arises only as time passes, so it is recorded as a liability only after time has passed.

Current Liabilities

Accounts Payable

Most companies purchase goods and services from other companies on credit. Typically, these transactions involve three stages: (1) order the goods/services, (2) receive the goods/services, and (3) pay for the goods/services. Accountants record liabilities at the stage that "obligates the company to give up assets or services." When do *you* think Big G becomes obligated to pay for the grain it buys to make Wheaties® or Cheerios®?

If the grain order is never filled, General Mills wouldn't be expected to pay for it. So the receipt of goods/services is the point at which a liability is created and recorded. Like Big G, most companies call this liability "accounts payable." According to Exhibit 10.2, General Mills owes about $1.3 billion in accounts payable at the end of 2003. The great thing about using accounts payable to buy goods/services is that suppliers don't charge interest on unpaid balances unless they are overdue.

Accrued Liabilities

Often, a business incurs an expense in one accounting period and makes a cash payment in a later period. To account for these situations, an adjusting entry typically is made at the end of the first of these periods to record a liability. Chapter 4 called this an accrual adjustment, so it seems appropriate that the liability account is called **accrued liabilities.** Companies record accrued liabilities for various expenses, including electricity, salaries, taxes, and interest.

The liabilities section of the balance sheet for General Mills doesn't separately report an account called accrued liabilities. While it's tempting to assume they're included in the $800 million of *Other current liabilities* shown in Exhibit 10.2 on page 417, to be sure we need to read the financial statement notes. That's where you often find what lurks within mysteriously named items like *Other current liabilities*. Sure enough, if you were to page through the notes, you'd make an important discovery in footnote 5, which we've cut and pasted into Exhibit 10.3. This exhibit shows that the $800 million of *Other current liabilities* includes accrued liabilities for payroll, taxes, and interest.

Accrued Payroll.   At the end of each accounting period, employees usually will have earned salaries that have not yet been paid. General Mills includes these unpaid salaries in its $243 million of accrued payroll. In addition to unpaid salaries, companies must report the cost of employment benefits promised to and earned by employees but not yet paid. These benefits include retirement programs, vacation time, and health insurance.

Payroll Taxes.   In addition to paying employees and providing vacation time, all businesses must account for a variety of payroll taxes including federal, state, and local income taxes, Social Security taxes, and federal and state unemployment taxes. If you've ever been an employee, you probably already know that the government requires your employer to deduct payroll taxes from your gross pay. Payroll taxes don't just hit the employees. Employers also are required to pay taxes (based on what employees are paid).

FAST FLASHBACK

The initial amount of a loan, which is called the "principal," does not include interest charges.

For an overview of the various types of liabilities, check out the video on the DVD for use with this book.

YOU SHOULD KNOW

Accrued liabilities report the liability for expenses that have been incurred but not paid at the end of the accounting period.

exhibit 10.3	**General Mills' Other Current Liabilities (in millions)**

	2003
Other Current Liabilities:	
Accrued Payroll	$243
Accrued Taxes	129
Accrued Interest	178
Miscellaneous	250
Total Other Current Liabilities	$800

Let's look at the two largest of these taxes. Accounting for other payroll taxes is similar to what we describe for these two bad boys.

- **Employee income taxes.** The government requires employers to withhold income taxes for each employee, essentially making employers collection agencies for the government. The amount of income tax withheld is recorded by the employer as a current liability on the day it is deducted from employees' pay. It remains as a current liability until the company forwards that amount to the government.

- **FICA taxes.** FICA taxes are amounts that the Federal Insurance Contributions Act requires employees and employers to pay for Medicare and Social Security. In 2004 (when this book was being written), employers were required to withhold 1.45 percent from each employee's earnings for Medicare and 6.2 percent (on earnings up to $87,900) for Social Security and forward it to the government. Employers also were required to pay an additional *employer* amount for FICA taxes equal to what was withheld from employees' pay.

A company's compensation expense (also called salaries and wages expense) includes all amounts earned by its employees, along with any compensation-related amounts paid to others. To illustrate, let's assume General Mills accumulated the following information in its payroll records for the first two weeks of June 2006:

Salaries and wages earned by employees	$1,800,000	
Less: Income taxes withheld from employees	275,000	} Owed to government
Less: FICA taxes withheld from employees	105,000	
Net pay to employees	$1,420,000	→ Paid to employees

The journal entries to record the payroll follow:

dr Compensation Expense (+E, −SE)	1,800,000	
cr Liability for Income Taxes Withheld (+L)		275,000
cr FICA Payable (+L)		105,000
cr Cash (−A)		1,420,000
dr Compensation Expense (+E, −SE)	105,000	
cr FICA Payable (+L)		105,000

COACH'S CORNER

Two journal entries are used, to make it easy to see that compensation expense and FICA payable include both employee FICA taxes (in the top journal entry) and employer FICA taxes (in the bottom).

Assets	=	Liabilities	+	Stockholders' Equity
Cash −1,420,000		FICA Payable +210,000		Compensation
		Liability for Income		Expense (+E) −1,905,000
		Taxes Withheld +275,000		

Accrued Taxes.   Corporations pay taxes not only on payroll but also on income they earn, just like you. The corporate tax return, which the IRS calls a Form 1120, is similar to the company's income statement, except that it calculates *taxable* income by subtracting tax-allowed expenses from revenues. This taxable income is then multiplied by a tax rate, which for most large corporations is about 35 percent. In 2003, for example, General Mills reported taxable income of $1,316 million, which when multiplied by 35 percent equaled its $460 million of income tax expense for the year. Corporate income taxes are due two and a half months after year-end, although most corporations are required to pay in installments during the year. This was the case with General Mills in 2003 because, of the $460 million in total income taxes for the year, only $129 million remained unpaid at the date of the balance sheet, as shown in Exhibit 10.3 on page 419.

Notes Payable

In Chapter 7, we described how a company accounts for promissory notes as *Notes Receivable* when it lends money to someone. In this section, you'll see how a company accounts for promissory notes as *Notes Payable* when they're used to borrow money.

For purposes of illustration, assume that on November 1, 2006, General Mills negotiates with Citigroup to borrow $100,000 cash on a *one-year* note. Citigroup charges 6 percent interest, which is the normal rate at the time. Interest payments are to be made in two cash installments, on April 30 and October 31. The principal is to be repaid on the note's October 31, 2007, maturity date. These transactions can be summarized graphically as follows:

COACH'S CORNER

Each interest payment of $3,000 is calculated as:

$$\$100{,}000 \times 6\% \times 6/12.$$

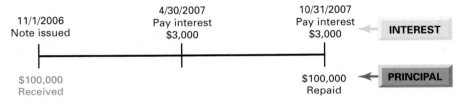

	4/30/2007	10/31/2007	
11/1/2006	Pay interest	Pay interest	**INTEREST**
Note issued	$3,000	$3,000	

| $100,000 | | $100,000 | **PRINCIPAL** |
| Received | | Repaid | |

During the first year of this note, journal entries are needed for three things:

1. *The initial recording of the note payable.*
2. *Additional amounts owed.*
3. *Payments made to the lender.*

1. Record the issuance of the note and receipt of cash.   When General Mills receives $100,000 cash from Citigroup on November 1, 2006, it has an obligation to repay that amount, which is recorded using the following journal entry:

dr **Cash (+A)**	100,000	
cr **Notes Payable (+L)**		100,000

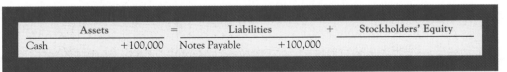

Assets		=	Liabilities		+	Stockholders' Equity
Cash	+100,000		Notes Payable	+100,000		

2. Record any interest owed by the end of the accounting period.   Interest is kind of like "rent" for using someone else's money over a period of time. Although interest becomes payable as each day passes, it is not paid nearly that often. Typically, interest is paid monthly or, in some cases, only once or twice per year. Rather than record the unpaid interest on each passing day, most companies record it at the end of the accounting period. These interest obligations often are reported in an account called interest payable or accrued interest, which is the name Big G used in Exhibit 10.3 on page 419.

If General Mills were to prepare financial statements as of December 31, 2006, it would update its accounting records for any interest expense that has been incurred but not yet paid at that time. (See the graphic in the margin.) As you may recall from Chapter 7, interest is calculated using the formula:

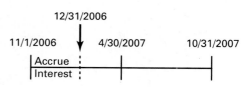

| Interest = Principal Owed × Interest Rate × Time |

As of December 31, the note has been outstanding for only two months, so the unpaid interest is $1,000 = $100,000 × 6% × 2/12. Notice in these calculations that the "principal owed" is the amount owed at the beginning of the interest period, which is equal to the amount of the liability recorded in the *Notes Payable* account on November 1. "Time" is the fraction of the year for which interest is being accrued (2 months out of 12). Rather than prepare the journal entry for you, we'll give you a Self-Study Quiz that lets you practice what you learned back in Chapter 4 about accruing a liability for unpaid interest.

 FAST FLASHBACK

Interest rates are usually expressed in annual terms.

HOW'S IT GOING? A Self-Study Quiz

Prepare the journal entry that General Mills would record on December 31 to accrue two months of interest on its promissory note. Show the effects on the accounting equation.

dr [   ] [   ]

cr [   ] [   ]

Assets	=	Liabilities	+	Stockholders' Equity

After you're done, check your answers with the solution in the margin.

Quiz Answers

dr Interest expense (+E, −SE) 1,000
  cr Interest payable (+L)......... 1,000

Assets	=	Liabilities	+	Stockholders' Equity
		Interest payable +1,000		Interest expense (+E) −1,000

3. Record payments made to the lender. General Mills makes its first interest payment on April 30, 2007, which is six months after the note was signed. This payment totals $3,000 (= $100,000 × 6% × 6/12). The interest payment includes two months of interest expense accrued above for 2006 ($1,000) plus four additional months of interest expense incurred from January 1 to April 30, 2007 ($2,000 = $100,000 × 6% × 4/12). The journal entry to record the payment follows:

dr **Interest Payable (−L)** 1,000
dr **Interest Expense (+E, −SE)** 2,000
  cr **Cash (−A)** 3,000

Assets		=	Liabilities		+	Stockholders' Equity	
Cash	−3,000		Interest Payable	−1,000		Interest Expense (+E)	−2,000

What happens after April 30, 2007? Well, assuming General Mills hasn't made any other entries for the note until it matures on October 31, 2007, the following journal entries will be needed. First, to account for the payment of interest for the six months from April 30 to October 31 ($3,000 = $100,000 × 6% × 6/12), Big G will record:

dr	**Interest Expense (+E, −SE)**	3,000	
	cr **Cash (−A)**		3,000

Second, to account for the principal payment, General Mills will make the following entry:

dr	**Notes Payable (−L)**	100,000	
	cr **Cash (−A)**		100,000

The combined effect of these two entries on the accounting equation is

Assets		=	Liabilities		+	Stockholders' Equity	
Cash	−103,000		Notes Payable	−100,000		Interest Expense (+E)	−3,000

After these entries are recorded, General Mills is done accounting for the note payable. And so are we. Let's move on to the final line-item that General Mills reports in the current liabilities section of the balance sheet.

Current Portion of Long-Term Debt

Remember when you were in grade 9 and it seemed like it would be forever before you'd graduate from high school? At that time, graduation was something that would happen in the long term. Later, however, when you made it to your senior year, high-school graduation had become a current event—something that was less than a year away. We remind you of this to help you understand what happens with long-term debt.

If a company borrows money with the promise to repay it in two years, the amount of the loan is classified as long-term debt. Only the accrued interest on the loan is reported as a current liability in that year's balance sheet. After a year passes, however, the loan becomes a current liability, just as your graduation became a current event. When that happens, the loan needs to be reported in the current liabilities section of the balance sheet. Accountants don't actually create a different account for this—they just take the amount of principal to be repaid in the upcoming year out of the total long-term debt and report it as a current liability called *Current Portion of Long-Term Debt*. Exhibit 10.2 on page 417 showed how General Mills did this in 2003 for $105 million of its long-term debt.

Quiz Answers

	As of December 31	
	2007	2006
Current Liabilities		
Current portion of long-term debt	$2,000	$ 1,000
Long-term debt	7,000	9,000
Total Liabilities	$9,000	$10,000

HOW'S IT GOING?   **A Self-Study Quiz**

Assume that on December 1, 2006, your company borrowed $10,000, a portion of which is to be repaid each year on November 30. Specifically, your company will make the following principal payments: 2007, $1,000; 2008, $2,000; 2009, $3,000; and 2010, $4,000. Show how this loan will be reported in the December 31, 2007 and 2006 balance sheets, assuming that principal payments will be made when required.

	As of December 31	
	2007	*2006*
Current Liabilities:		
Current Portion of Long-Term Debt	$	$
Long-Term Debt		
Total Liabilities	$9,000	$10,000

After you're done, check your answers with the solution in the margin.

Additional Current Liabilities

Because of the nature of Big G's business, it does not report certain current liabilities that are common to other companies. In this section, we will look at two of them.

Sales Tax Payable.   In all but five states, retail companies are required to charge a sales tax. (Big G isn't a retail company, so it doesn't charge sales tax.) Retailers collect sales tax from consumers at the time of sale and forward it to the state government. Just like payroll taxes, the tax collected by the company is reported as a current liability until it is forwarded to the government. It is not an expense because the retailer simply collects and passes on the sales tax. So if you bought a new plasma screen TV at Best Buy in Albuquerque, New Mexico, for $6,000 cash plus sales tax, the company would record the sale and 5 percent sales tax using the following journal entry:

dr	Cash (+A) 6,300	
	cr Sales Tax Payable (+L) ($6,000 × 5%) . . .	300
	cr Sales Revenue (+R, +SE)	6,000

Assets		=	Liabilities		+	Stockholders' Equity	
Cash	+6,300		Sales Tax Payable	+300		Sales Revenue (+R)	+6,000

When Best Buy pays the sales tax to the state government, *Sales Tax Payable* would be debited and *Cash* would be credited for the amount remitted.

Unearned Revenue.   Back in Chapter 4, you learned that some companies receive cash before they provide goods or services to customers. InterActiveCorp—the owner of Expedia, Match.com, and Ticketmaster—provides great examples of this. Expedia receives cash from customers on hotel and air bookings before the stay or flight occurs. Expedia accounts for this in two stages: (1) when the cash is received, Expedia records a liability for making the future booking, and (2) when the booking is made, Expedia removes the liability and records the revenue that has been earned.

   This two-step process applies to all instances where cash is received before revenue is earned. As an example, let's look at the journal entries for the subscription fee that InterActiveCorp collects before letting you loose with other subscribers in its Match.com chat rooms. Assume that on October 1, InterActiveCorp receives cash for a three-month subscription paid in advance at a rate of $10 per month (or $30 in total). The company will account for this in two stages:

1. *Record cash received and liability created* (on October 1):

dr	Cash (+A) 30	
	cr Unearned Revenue (+L).	30

Assets		=	Liabilities		+	Stockholders' Equity
Cash	+30		Unearned Revenue	+30		

2. *Reduce the liability as it is fulfilled and revenue is earned* (on October 31):

dr	Unearned Revenue (−L). 10	
	cr Subscription Revenue (+R, +SE).	10

Assets	=	Liabilities	+	Stockholders' Equity	
		Unearned Revenue −10		Subscription Revenue (+R) +10	

As each month passes, InterActiveCorp will make an adjusting journal entry to show that it has continued to fulfill its obligation and earn its subscription revenues. Don't let the tiny amounts in our examples fool you. Unearned revenues can be huge. For InterActiveCorp, they total over $500 million. That's more than the company's accounts payable.

Long-Term Liabilities

Long-term liabilities include all obligations that are not classified as current liabilities. These obligations may be created by borrowing money, or they may result from other activities. In this section, we focus on long-term liabilities that are created by borrowing.

Exhibit 10.4 illustrates how companies can borrow through (1) a private placement or (2) publicly issued debt certificates. Notice how the order of steps differs between the two methods of borrowing. In a private placement, the borrower identifies a potential lender, such as a bank, and negotiates terms for a loan with that lender. This is just like the notes payable that you studied in the previous section, except that this time it extends more than one year. Publicly issued debt certificates, on the other hand, are used when a company needs more money than any single lender can provide. Because several hundred (or thousand) lenders might be involved in this financing, the company can't possibly negotiate different loan terms with each potential lender. Instead, the company begins by setting standard terms that will apply to each lender. These loan terms are detailed in a

YOU SHOULD KNOW

The "lenders" involved in a bond issuance include companies and individuals who are interested in giving up money now in exchange for a series of fixed future payments of interest. This often appeals to retirees or their companies' pension funds.

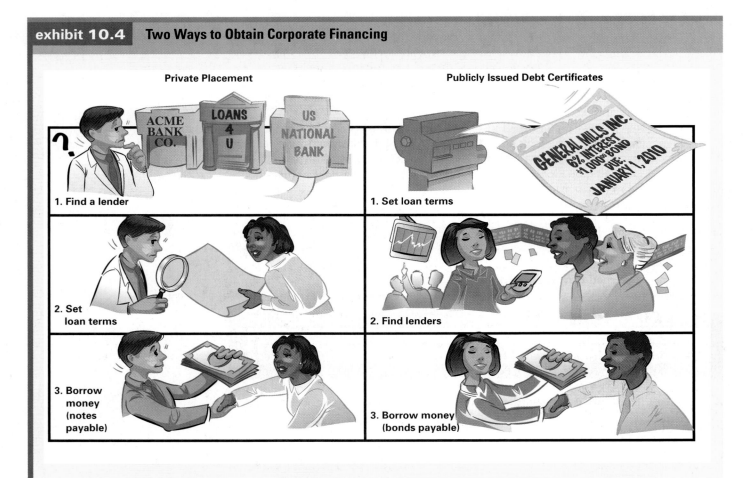

exhibit 10.4   **Two Ways to Obtain Corporate Financing**

Private Placement

1. Find a lender
2. Set loan terms
3. Borrow money (notes payable)

Publicly Issued Debt Certificates

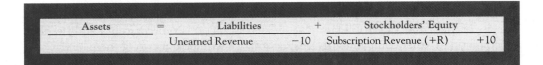

1. Set loan terms
2. Find lenders
3. Borrow money (bonds payable)

document called a bond certificate, which is issued on a bond market similar to the stock market. Interested lenders "buy" bonds by providing money to the company in exchange for the company's promise to repay the lender according to the terms stated on the bond certificate. When the company receives the cash generated from selling these bonds, a liability is created called *bonds payable*.

Bonds Payable

On the surface, a bond is a lot like your typical bank loan or long-term promissory note. It states the interest payments, a maturity date, and the amount that is to be paid at maturity (this "face value," as it is called, is often $1,000 per bond). These three facts are all that is needed to understand what the borrower will be required to pay to the lender from the day the bond is issued to the day it matures.

FAST FLASHBACK

Maturity date is the date by which a loan is to be repaid in full.

Let's look at an example. Assume that on January 1, 2006, General Mills receives $100,000 for bonds issued with a January 1, 2010, maturity date. The bonds pay $100,000 at maturity and also state an interest rate of 6 percent, which is paid each year on January 1.[1] These bond payments can be summarized graphically as follows:

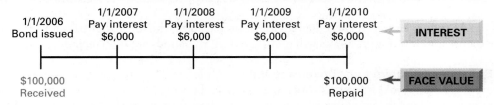

This looks a lot like the notes payable graphic shown on page 420, doesn't it? When lenders pay face value for the bonds, the accounting also is very similar.

COACH'S CORNER

Each interest payment of $6,000 is calculated as:
$$\$100,000 \times 6\% \times 12/12.$$

Accounting for Bonds Issued at Face Value.   When accounting for bonds, accountants are concerned with recording (1) the initial bond issuance, (2) additional amounts owed to the lender for interest, (3) payments to the lender, and (4) removal of the bond liability when it is paid off. In this section, we discuss the first three points using the bond described above as an example. The fourth point is discussed later in the chapter.

1. **Record the issuance of the bond and receipt of cash.**   The journal entry that the borrower, General Mills, uses to record the bond issuance on January 1, 2006, is

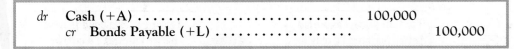

dr	Cash (+A)	100,000	
cr	Bonds Payable (+L)		100,000

	Assets	=	Liabilities	+	Stockholders' Equity
Cash	+100,000		Bonds Payable +100,000		

2. **Record any interest owed by the end of the accounting period.**   Interest expense on these bonds is calculated the same way as it was for notes payable, as explained earlier in this chapter. If we assume General Mills hasn't made any entries for the bonds since January 1, it will record a liability for interest expense for the 12 months ended December 31, 2006. The amount of interest is $6,000 (= $100,000 × 6% × 12/12), and it is recorded with the following journal entry:

dr	Interest Expense (+E, −SE)	6,000	
cr	Interest Payable (+L)		6,000

---

[1]For some bonds, interest is calculated and paid twice a year (semiannually). To keep things manageable, we consider only annual interest payments.

Assets	=	Liabilities		+	Stockholders' Equity	
		Interest Payable	+6,000		Interest Expense (+E)	−6,000

3. ***Record payments made to the lender.*** When General Mills pays the interest on January 1, 2007, the journal entry to record this payment would be

dr **Interest Payable (−L)**	6,000	
cr **Cash (−A)**		6,000

	Assets		=	Liabilities		+	Stockholders' Equity
Cash		−6,000		Interest Payable	−6,000		

As shown earlier in this chapter (for notes payable), the journal entries for interest expense and interest payments will continue until the bonds are fully repaid.

Bonds Issued below or above Face Value. If lenders always paid **face value** to acquire a bond, you'd have this topic aced already. However, sometimes the amount of money that lenders are willing to pay up-front differs from what the borrower repays at maturity. Before getting into the mechanics of accounting for this, it's useful to understand why this might occur.

The key to understanding this is to remember that the borrower sets the terms of a bond before identifying its lenders. If the borrower sets a **stated interest rate** (6 percent) that pays less than what lenders expect (say 8 percent), lenders won't be attracted to the bond. It's just like asking you to give up $1,000 for a stereo that doesn't have all the features you want. You aren't going to buy it unless (*a*) the necessary features are added, or (*b*) you're given a discount off the initial price. In the case of a bond, it's not practical to change its features because they're actually stated on the face of the bond. Instead, what happens is lenders are required to pay less money up-front to acquire the bond—they get a discount!

The opposite happens if bonds have features that make them attractive to lenders. Just as you might have to pay a premium to get tickets to popular concerts or sporting events, lenders have to give more money to acquire a bond that has popular features, such as an interest rate (6 percent) that is higher than what similar bonds in the market pay (say 4 percent). Lenders will be willing to pay a premium provided that they don't have to pay so much that they earn less than what they expect to earn from other similarly attractive bonds.

Before we discuss how to account for bonds issued at amounts other than face value, let's summarize some important terms. First, let's start with the things you can see on a bond certificate. The value stated on the bond is called the face value. For clarity, we will always use this term when referring to it, but you probably should be aware that other people use alternative terms (such as par value). The interest rate stated on the bond is called the stated interest rate. Again, we will always use this term, but alternatives exist (such as coupon rate or contract rate).

Now, instead of talking about what's written on the face of the bond, let's turn to the terms that describe its true substance. The amount that the borrower actually receives when a bond is issued is called the **issue price.** The exact amount of the issue price is determined by the lenders who decide how much they're willing to give up to acquire the bond. Theoretically, this amount is based on a mathematical calculation called a **present value,** which is discussed in Appendix C at the end of this book. Bond dealers and news reports typically quote the bond issue price as a percentage of the face value of the bond (although they don't include the percentage symbol). So a $1,000 bond issued at a price of 95 means the bond issued for 95 percent of $1,000, or $950. The interest rate that lenders in the bond market demand from the bond (and use in their present value calculations to determine the bond issue price) is called the **market interest rate.** Some people also refer to this as the yield, discount rate, or effective-interest rate. Okay, now you're ready to pull together all these terms by considering how they relate to premiums and discounts, as shown here.

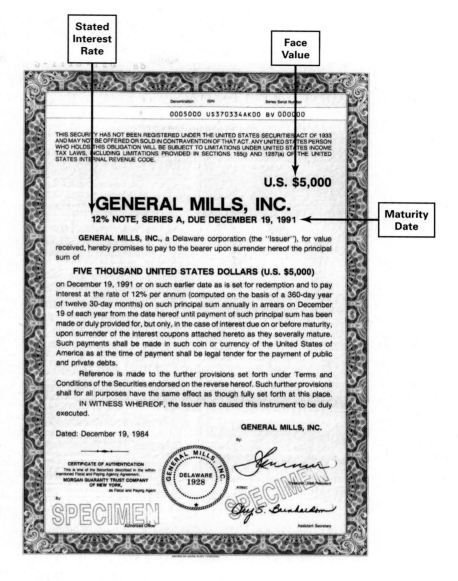

It's natural to feel a little overwhelmed by all of these new terms. Accountants use a little phrase when dealing with complex stuff like this that might help you here. The phrase is "substance over form," and what it means is that accountants try to account for

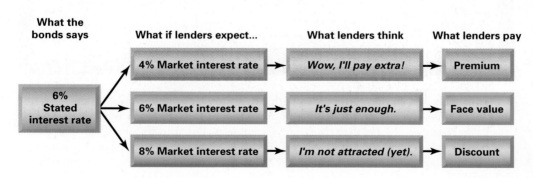

YOU SHOULD KNOW

The **issue price** is the amount of money that a lender pays (and the company receives) when a bond is issued.

Present value is based on a mathematical calculation that determines the amount that one or more payments made in the future are worth today.

The **market interest rate** is the rate of interest that lenders demand from a bond.

YOU SHOULD KNOW

A bond is issued at a **premium** when the issue price is greater than the face value. A bond is issued at a **discount** when the issue price is less than the face value.

the "true" substance of a transaction rather than what it suggests on the surface. In a way, you've already been exposed to this when you learned that expenses are accounted for using accrual not cash basis accounting. The same idea applies to bonds. Face value and stated interest rate reflect only the form of the bond. They merely describe the cash that the borrower repays to the lender. They do not reflect the substance of the bond or its cost of borrowing, which instead is reflected in the bond's actual *issue price* (the starting point for the bond liabilities) and *market interest rate* (used to compute interest expense). These ideas are summarized in Exhibit 10.5.

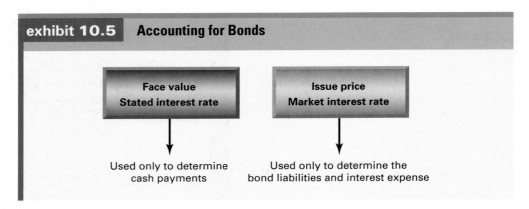

exhibit 10.5   Accounting for Bonds

Accounting for Bonds Issued at a Discount.   When a company issues a bond at a discount, the repayment terms of the bond don't change. Borrowers still pay according to the terms stated on the face of the bond. They just receive less money up-front from lenders. Let's look at the case where a $100,000, four-year General Mills bond pays a stated interest rate of 6 percent but lenders expect to earn the market interest rate of 8 percent. To get the 8 percent that they expect, the lenders are willing to pay an issue price of only $93,376. That is, they've determined (by using present value calculations shown in Appendix C) that if they pay $93,376 and receive back $6,000 interest every year plus $100,000 at maturity, in effect they will earn 8 percent on the amount they've lent. The journal entry to record the issuance of the $100,000 bond, on January 1, 2006, at $93,376 (quoted as 93.376) is

dr	Cash (+A)	93,376	
dr	Discount on Bonds Payable (+xL, −L)	6,624	
	cr Bonds Payable (+L)		100,000

Assets		=	Liabilities		+	Stockholders' Equity
Cash	+93,376		Bonds Payable	+100,000		
			Discount on Bonds			
			Payable (+xL)	−6,624		

Although the discount is recorded with a debit to *Discount on Bonds Payable*, it is not an asset. Rather, it is a contra-liability account, which means it is deducted from the *Bonds Payable* account on the balance sheet. An example is shown in Exhibit 10.6. The *Bonds Payable* account reports the amount that General Mills will owe on the bond at maturity, whereas the line called *Bonds Payable, Net of Discount* (often called the "carrying value") reports the liability based on what General Mills owed when the bond was issued.

In our example, General Mills received only $93,376 when the bond was issued, but must pay back $100,000 when the bond matures. Big G will pay back the extra cash as a way of adjusting the interest that lenders will earn. Remember that the terms of the bond

exhibit 10.6	Sample Balance Sheet Reporting of Bond Discount

GENERAL MILLS, INC.
Balance Sheet (excerpt)
January 1, 2006

Long-Term Liabilities	
Bonds Payable	$100,000
Less: Discount on Bonds Payable	6,624
Bonds Payable, Net of Discount	93,376

were already set when the bond was issued, so the only way to adjust the lenders' interest was to discount the issue price for the bond. By paying less than face value for the bond, in effect lenders will earn the market interest rate they expect. From the perspective of General Mills, **the effect of a discount is to provide the borrower less money than what is repaid at maturity, which increases the total cost of borrowing.** In effect, General Mills incurs interest equal to 8 percent on the amount actually borrowed ($93,376), rather than the 6 percent stated on the face of the bond.

To comply with the matching concept, this extra cost of borrowing must be matched to the periods in which the bond liability is owed. This is done each accounting period by taking an amount out of *Discount on Bonds Payable* and adding it to *Interest Expense* of that period. This process (called "amortizing" the discount) causes the *Discount on Bonds Payable* account to slowly decline to zero over the life of the bond, which causes the carrying value of the bond to increase until it reaches face value when the bond matures. This is shown in Exhibit 10.7.

exhibit 10.7	Amortization of Bond Discount

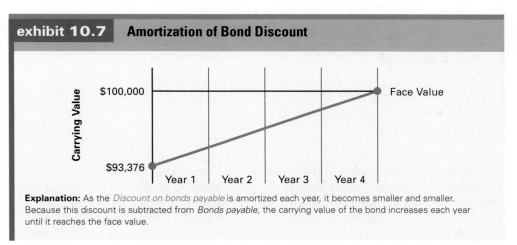

Explanation: As the *Discount on bonds payable* is amortized each year, it becomes smaller and smaller. Because this discount is subtracted from *Bonds payable,* the carrying value of the bond increases each year until it reaches the face value.

Two different amortization methods can be used to compute and record the amount to be taken out of *Discount on Bonds Payable* and added to *Interest Expense:* (1) straight-line, and (2) effective-interest. Generally accepted accounting principles require that the effective-interest method be used, unless the straight-line method results in numbers that are not significantly ("materially") different. Some people believe that straight-line is the easier method to understand, so we present it first in Supplement A at the end of this chapter. Effective-interest (a conceptually superior method) is detailed in Supplement B. An approach that blends the simplicity of the straight-line method with the conceptual strengths of the effective-interest method is presented in Supplement C. If you've been assigned any of these supplements, don't jump to them yet. We'll tell you later when it's best to read them.

Accounting for Bonds Issued at a Premium.   When a bond issues at a premium, *the borrower receives the face value of the bond plus the amount of the premium.* This means that, on the day of issue, the company owes more than just the face value of the bond. Let's look at the case where the market interest rate is 4 percent yet the General Mills bond states an interest rate of 6 percent. In this situation, lenders are willing to pay an issue price of $107,260 (which they've determined using present value calculations shown in Appendix C). The journal entry to record the issuance of the bond on January 1, 2006, for $107,260 is

dr	Cash (+A)	107,260	
	cr Bonds Payable (+L)		100,000
	cr Premium on Bonds Payable (+L)		7,260

Assets		=	Liabilities		+	Stockholders' Equity
Cash	+107,260		Bonds Payable	+100,000		
			Premium on Bonds Payable	+7,260		

The carrying value of the bond is the total of the two accounts, *Bonds Payable* and *Premium on Bonds Payable*, as shown in Exhibit 10.8.

exhibit 10.8	**Sample Balance Sheet Reporting of Bond Premium**

GENERAL MILLS, INC.
Balance Sheet (excerpt)
January 1, 2006

Long-Term Liabilities	
Bonds Payable	$100,000
Add: Premium on Bonds Payable	7,260
Bonds Payable, Including Premium	107,260

General Mills received $107,260 when the bond was issued but only repays $100,000 when the bond matures. **The effect of the premium is to provide the borrower more money than what is repaid at maturity, which reduces the total cost of borrowing.** As with a discount, the premium of $7,260 is allocated to each interest period. This amortization process reduces both *Premium on Bonds Payable* and *Interest Expense* in each period, causing the *Premium on Bonds Payable* account to decline to zero over the life of the bond. This also causes the carrying value of the bond to decrease until it reaches face value when the bond matures, as shown in Exhibit 10.9. Procedures that accomplish this are explained in chapter Supplements A, B, and C. At this point, read any of the chapter supplements that you have been assigned, then come back here and continue with the remainder of this section. The supplements begin on page 440.

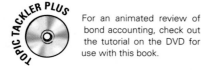

For an animated review of bond accounting, check out the tutorial on the DVD for use with this book.

Early Retirement of Debt.   Most bonds are retired (paid off) at maturity. There are some instances, however, where a company may decide to retire bonds before their maturity date. A company with lots of cash can retire debt early to reduce future interest expense, which increases net income in the future. Even companies that don't have extra cash might retire bonds early, particularly if interest rates have fallen since the original

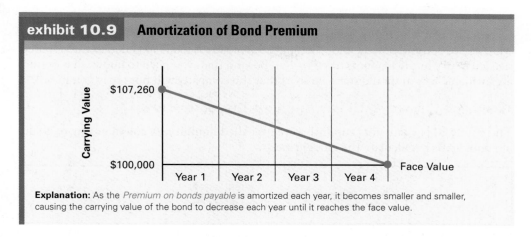

exhibit 10.9   **Amortization of Bond Premium**

Explanation: As the *Premium on bonds payable* is amortized each year, it becomes smaller and smaller, causing the carrying value of the bond to decrease each year until it reaches the face value.

bonds were issued. By issuing new bonds at the lower interest rate and using the money received from this new bond issuance to retire the old bonds before their maturity date, companies can reduce their future interest expense (which increases future earnings).

When bonds are retired before maturity, the company's accountants do three things: (1) remove the bond balances from the accounting records, (2) record the cash paid, and (3) record a loss (if the company has to pay more cash than the carrying value of the bond liability) or a gain (if the cash paid to retire the bonds is less than their carrying value).

To illustrate, assume that in 1997, General Mills issued $1 million of bonds at face value. Nine years later, in 2006, the headlines of *The Wall Street Journal* report that the bonds are being retired at 103. Here's the journal entry to record the debt retirement with a cash payment of $1,030,000 ($1 million × 103%):

dr	Bonds Payable (−L)	1,000,000	
dr	Loss on Bonds Retired (+E, −SE)..........	30,000	
	cr Cash (−A)		1,030,000

Assets		=	Liabilities		+	Stockholders' Equity	
Cash	−1,030,000		Bonds Payable	−1,000,000		Loss on Bonds Retired (+E)	−30,000

There are two things to note about the example above. First, the loss on bond retirement would be reported on the income statement with other gains and losses, somewhere between "operating income" and "income before income taxes." Second, the journal entry in our example doesn't remove a bond discount or bond premium account because we have assumed the bonds were issued at face value. Retirement of bonds issued below or above face value will be covered in intermediate accounting courses.

Now that you know how liabilities are accounted for on the inside of a company, let's consider them again from the outside. How do users judge whether liabilities are likely to be repaid in full?

EVALUATE

THE LIKELIHOOD THAT LIABILITIES WILL BE REPAID IN FULL

When evaluating the ability of another person or company to pay you, a great place to start is with credit reports issued by credit rating agencies. However, credit raters don't report on everyone (particularly smaller companies). Even if they did, their reports might be too general and not address your specific concerns. So you really need to understand how to analyze a set of financial statements yourself in the same way a credit rater would. Essentially, you're going to assess whether the company has the assets available to pay what you're currently owed, and whether the company is likely to generate the resources needed to pay future amounts owed to you. Beyond that, you need to know what options are available to you should there be signs that the company will not repay you in full.

Analyzing the Ability to Pay Amounts Currently Owed

The ability to pay amounts currently owed is called **liquidity.** A common way to evaluate liquidity is to calculate the **current ratio:**

$$\text{Current Ratio} = \frac{\text{Current Assets}}{\text{Current Liabilities}}$$

The current ratio measures whether the company has enough current assets to pay what it currently owes. Generally speaking, a high ratio suggests good liquidity. An old rule of thumb was that companies should have a current ratio between 1 and 2. Today, many successful companies use sophisticated management techniques to minimize the funds invested in current assets and, as a result, have current ratios below 1.

General Mills is a company that minimizes what it holds in current assets. As shown in Exhibit 10.10, its total current assets are less than its total current liabilities, which makes its ratio less than one ($3,179 ÷ 3,444 = 0.92). For many companies, a ratio less than one can be a significant concern. It's not a big deal for General Mills, however, because the company has arranged a **line of credit** with banks that provides cash on an as-needed basis. Rather than hold extra cash to enhance its liquidity, General Mills can use its line of credit to borrow only when money is actually needed, avoiding significant interest expense.

exhibit 10.10 **General Mills' Current Assets and Current Liabilities (in millions)**

Assets	2003	2002
Current Assets		
Cash	$ 703	$ 975
Receivables, Less Allowance for Doubtful Accounts	980	1,010
Inventories	1,082	1,055
Prepaid Expenses and Other Current Assets	414	397
Total Current Assets	3,179	3,437

Liabilities		
Current Liabilities		
Accounts Payable	$1,303	$1,217
Other Current Liabilities	800	682
Notes Payable	1,236	3,600
Current Portion of Long-Term Debt	105	248
Total Current Liabilities	3,444	5,747

| exhibit 10.11 | Summary of Current Ratio Analyses |

				2003		**SELF-STUDY QUIZ 2002**
Name of Measure	**Formula**	**What It Tells You**	**Kellogg's**	**Kraft Foods**	**General Mills**	**General Mills**
Current ratio	$\dfrac{\text{Current Assets}}{\text{Current Liabilities}}$	• Whether current assets are sufficient to pay current liabilities • A higher ratio means greater ability to pay ☺	0.66	0.91	$=\dfrac{3,179}{3,444}$ $= 0.92$	

To better understand a company's current ratio, it's useful to compare it to other companies in the same industry. The 2003 current ratios for Kellogg's, Kraft Foods, and General Mills are presented in Exhibit 10.11. We've also included a column for you to practice calculating the current ratio yourself, as described in the Self-Study Quiz that follows. As you can see in Exhibit 10.11, all three companies carry minimal levels of current assets relative to their current liabilities. They've been successfully managing their liquidity in this way for years.

HOW'S IT GOING?   A Self-Study Quiz

Using financial statement information in Exhibit 10.10, compute the current ratio for General Mills in 2002 to complete the final column in Exhibit 10.11. Did the current ratio increase or decrease in 2003, as compared to 2002?

When you're done, check your answers with the solutions in the margin.

Quiz Answers

$3,437 \div 5,747 = 0.60$

The current ratio increased a great deal in 2003 (because Big G paid down its current notes payable, as you can see in Exhibit 10.10).

Be on the Alert

The current ratio may be a misleading measure of liquidity if significant funds are tied up in assets that cannot be easily converted into cash. A company with a high current ratio might still have liquidity problems if the majority of its current assets are made up of slow-moving inventory. The current ratio also can be misleading because managers can manipulate it by entering into certain transactions just before the end of an accounting period. In most cases, for example, the current ratio can be improved by paying creditors just prior to the date of the financial statements. To watch out for this, it's useful to evaluate the current ratio at the end of each quarter and over several years.

Analyzing the Ability to Generate Resources to Pay Future Amounts Owed

By studying how (and when) accountants report interest owed on debt, you now know that liabilities do not include *all* of the future interest payments that will be made on existing liabilities. Liabilities include only the unpaid interest for periods ending before the balance sheet date. This means that the current ratio and any other ratios based on recorded liabilities don't tell you much about whether the company will be able to make

YOU SHOULD KNOW

Some analysts calculate a "quick ratio," which divides total cash, receivables, and short-term investments by current liabilities. A quick ratio greater than one means a company could cash in those assets, if needed, to instantly pay off its current liabilities.

future interest payments. One way to judge a company's future ability to pay interest is to analyze whether, in the past, it has generated enough income to cover its interest expense. Barring huge changes, the past can be a fair predictor of the future. The measure that most analysts use for this is the **times interest earned ratio:**

YOU SHOULD KNOW

The **times interest earned ratio** divides net income before interest and taxes by interest expense to determine the extent to which earnings before taxes and financing costs are sufficient to cover interest incurred for debt.

$$\text{Times Interest Earned Ratio} = \frac{\text{Net Income} + \text{Interest Expense} + \text{Income Tax Expense}}{\text{Interest Expense}}$$

Notice that the times interest earned ratio adds interest and income tax expenses back into net income. The reason for this is fairly simple. We want to know whether the company generates enough income **before the costs of financing and taxes** to cover its interest expense. The way to achieve this is to add these expenses back into net income.

The times interest earned ratio shows the amount of resources generated for each dollar of interest expense. In general, a high ratio is viewed more favorably than a low ratio. A high ratio indicates an extra margin of protection in the event that future profitability declines.

Using information in Big G's 2003 income statement (see the simplified version to the right), we have calculated and reported its times interest earned ratio in Exhibit 10.12. We've also included the ratios for Kellogg's and Kraft Foods. Notice that the ratios for all three companies show that they are generating income to cover interest expense comfortably. No doubt this is part of the reason that credit raters have given all three companies a favorable credit rating of BBB or higher.

Every now and then you'll likely see a negative times interest earned ratio. **A negative ratio basically says that the company does _not_ generate enough income to cover its interest expense.** This is a big problem. Most companies can survive for only a couple of years with negative times interest earned ratios before they have to declare bankruptcy.

GENERAL MILLS Income Statement For the Year 2003 (in millions)	
Net Sales	$10,506
Expenses:	
Cost of Sales	6,109
Selling, General, and Administrative	2,472
Interest, Net	547
Other Items, Net	1
Total Expenses	9,129
Income before Income Taxes	1,377
Income Taxes	460
Net Income	$ 917

exhibit 10.12   Summary of Times Interest Earned Ratio Analyses

Name of Measure	Formula	What It Tells You	2003		
			Kellogg's	Kraft Foods	General Mills
Times Interest Earned Ratio	$\dfrac{\text{(Net Income} + \text{Interest Expense} + \text{Income Tax Expense)}}{\text{Interest Expense}}$	• Whether sufficient resources are generated to cover interest costs • A higher ratio means greater coverage ☺	3.93	7.21	$\dfrac{917 + 547 + 460}{547}$ = 3.52

Be on the Alert

The method of accounting for certain interest costs can make the times interest earned ratio potentially misleading. As you learned in Chapter 9, companies are allowed to capitalize interest that is incurred to self-construct property, plant, and equipment. If this occurs, the company's reported interest expense will be less than its actual interest costs, causing the times interest earned ratio to suggest greater interest coverage than what is actually the case. So don't jump to conclusions after calculating the times interest earned ratio. Read the financial statement notes to see whether any interest has been capitalized because it might be distorting the ratio.

Understanding Common Features of Debt

Salty, sweet, crunchy, and chewy are adjectives that describe snacks that Big G sells (at a rate of four products every second from vending machines in the United States).[2] These adjectives are useful because they describe differences among the products, which help us to choose the products we want. In the same way, various adjectives are used to describe key terms in a debt agreement (e.g., secured, callable, convertible), which help creditors and borrowers choose the loan terms they want. We explain some of the more important ones below.

To reduce the risk of a loan, some lenders require borrowers to offer specific assets as "security" to creditors. This simply means that if the borrower does not satisfy its liability, the creditor may take ownership of the assets used as security. A liability supported by this type of agreement is called a secured debt. Most car loans and house loans require you to offer your car or house as security for the loan. Some creditors are willing to loan money without security (called unsecured debt), but they typically demand a higher interest rate in return for taking on this extra risk. Another tactic that reduces risk is to allow lenders to demand immediate repayment of the loan if certain ratios, calculated using the borrower's financial statements, get out of whack. "Escape hatches" like these, which are common in many lending agreements, are called *loan covenants*. Borrowers report significant loan covenants in their financial statement notes. Exhibit 10.13 lists these and other common loan terms along with explanations of them.

FAST FLASHBACK

Loan covenants are loan terms that lenders use to monitor and, in some cases, restrict management decisions made by the borrower.

exhibit 10.13	**Explanations of Important Loan Terms**

Loan Terms	What They Mean	Effects
Security	Security guarantees that the borrower's assets will be given to the creditor if the borrower doesn't pay.	Reduces risk to creditors, making them willing to accept a lower interest rate.
Loan Covenants	Allows the creditor to force immediate repayment of the loan if the borrower violates these terms.	Reduces risk to creditors, making them willing to accept a lower interest rate.
Seniority	Debt designated as "senior" is paid first in the event of bankruptcy, followed by "subordinated" debt.	Reduces risk to senior creditors, making them willing to accept a lower interest rate.
Convertibility	Gives the creditor an option to accept the borrower's stock as payment for the outstanding loan.	Gives greater control to creditors, reducing their risk and making them willing to accept a lower interest rate.
Callability	Gives the borrower control over the decision to fully repay the lender before the loan's maturity date.	Gives greater control to borrowers, increasing creditors' risk and causing them to demand a higher interest rate.

[2]General Mills, Inc., *2001 Annual Report*.

RECONSIDER

HOW LIABILITY DECISIONS CAN BE AFFECTED BY UNRECORDED DEBT

Hide and seek was a fun game to play as a kid. But when the executives at Enron used it as their guide to financial reporting, the fun ended. Investors, creditors, auditors, and practically everyone else in the business world has been affected by the Enron scandal that erupted in 2001. What exactly did Enron executives do wrong? Well, a lot of things. To understand precisely what they did, you'll need to take advanced courses in financial accounting. At a very simple level, however, one of their biggest offenses was to "hide" debt owed by the company. In essence, the company didn't report all of its true liabilities.

Unrecorded Liabilities

As a result of Enron, everyone in the business world has become much more sensitive to financial commitments that aren't reported on the balance sheet. As you will learn in this section, fraud isn't the only reason a company has unrecorded liabilities. In some cases, the accounting rules themselves actually require that certain liabilities *not* be reported on the balance sheet. We'll briefly introduce two topics where accounting rules can lead to unrecorded liabilities: leases and contingent liabilities. Both of these topics are covered in greater detail in intermediate accounting textbooks.

As you learned in Chapter 9, companies can use a lease to obtain the use of equipment and other property. In that chapter, we focused primarily on the *asset* obtained through the lease. Let's think now about the liabilities associated with leases. If a lease meets certain criteria, it is considered a *capital lease* and a long-term liability is recorded for the present value of all future lease payments. That's basically the same way you account for a long-term note or bond payable. If the lease doesn't meet those criteria, it is considered an *operating lease* and only the amounts past due are recorded as current liabilities on the balance sheet. If the company has kept up with all required payments, no liability is reported on the balance sheet for an operating lease. Thus, the classification of a lease as capital or operating can have a huge impact on total liabilities reported on the balance sheet. For example, even by conservative estimates, General Mills would have reported $370 million more liabilities had its operating leases been considered capital leases. The really interesting part of this is that it's sometimes a very fine line that distinguishes a capital lease from an operating lease, as you will learn in later accounting courses.

A **contingent liability** is a potential liability that arises as a result of past transactions or events, but the company is unable to determine whether it actually will be liable (or for what amount) until a future event occurs or fails to occur. The most common example of this is a lawsuit. Until it becomes clear that the company is liable and at what amount, the contingent liability is only reported in the company's notes to the financial statements. As you might expect, the actual accounting rules don't use loosey-goosey language like "until it becomes clear." Instead, they refer to the likelihood that the company will be found liable and whether it's possible to estimate the amount of liability. Exhibit 10.14 tells you all you need to know for now about accounting for contingent liabilities.

In closing, we'll remind you that these unrecorded liabilities aren't illegal or unethical. In fact, good accounting requires that they remain unrecorded, at least until there's a reliable basis for recording them. Some companies are so up-front about potentially significant unrecorded liabilities that they even direct you to them by including a line-item in the balance sheet (following the liabilities section) called "commitments and contingencies," which often references an explanatory note to the financial statements. Because these potential liabilities haven't been recorded in the accounting records, the line-item consists only of the name, without corresponding dollar amounts. It may look odd at first, but just think of it as a friendly reminder to consider potentially significant (but currently unrecorded) liabilities. The balance sheets of Landry's Restaurants and Dave and Buster's provide two good examples of this (in Appendixes A and B at the end of the book).

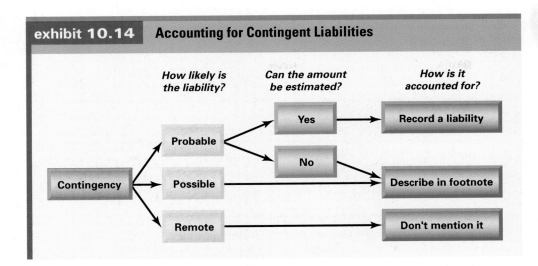

exhibit 10.14 | **Accounting for Contingent Liabilities**

What's Coming Up

This completes our in-depth coverage of liabilities. In Chapter 11, you will focus on the other section of the balance sheet related to a company's financing: stockholders' equity. You're likely to invest money in stock someday in the future, so it's important you learn about the various types of stock transactions and how they are reported. But before you move on to that, be sure to review and practice the material presented in this chapter.

FOR YOUR REVIEW

DEMONSTRATION CASE A (NOTES PAYABLE AND ACCRUED INTEREST)

On September 30, 2003, Nike received $50 million for promissory notes that it issued with a maturity date of October 1, 2013. The notes pay interest on April 1 and October 1 at the annual rate of 4.7 percent, which was comparable to other interest rates in the market at that time. Nike's second quarter ends on November 30. At the end of the first quarter, Nike had $5.0 billion in current assets and $2.0 billion in current liabilities.

Required:

1. Describe which sections of Nike's balance sheet are affected by the issuance of notes.
2. Give the journal entry on September 30, 2003, to record the issuance of the notes payable.
3. Give the journal entry on November 30, 2003, to record interest expense.
4. Give the journal entry on April 1, 2004, to record the first interest payment.
5. Compute Nike's current ratio at the end of its first quarter.
6. Assume that, as of November 30, 2003, Nike had not yet used the cash from the issuance of notes on September 30, 2003. What is the effect, if any, of the note issuance on the company's current ratio at the end of the second quarter?

Suggested Solution

1. The issuance of notes increases Nike's cash (a current asset) and its notes payable (a long-term liability) by $50 million.
2. September 30, 2003 (issuance date):

dr	Cash (+A)	50,000,000	
	cr Notes Payable (+L)		50,000,000

3. November 30, 2003 (accrual of interest expense for 2 months):

> dr   Interest Expense (+E, −SE)
> ($50,000,000 × 4.7% × 2/12) 391,667
>   cr   Interest Payable (+L)...........................   391,667

4. April 1, 2004 (first interest payment date):

> dr   Interest Expense (+E, −SE)
> ($50,000,000 × 4.7% × 4/12) 783,333
> dr   Interest Payable (−L) 391,667
>   cr   Cash (−A) ($50,000,000 × 4.7% × 6/12)   1,175,000

5. First quarter current ratio = Current assets ÷ Current liabilities
    = 5,000,000,000 ÷ 2,000,000,000 = 2.50

6. Second quarter current ratio = Current assets ÷ Current liabilities
    = (5,000,000,000 + 50,000,000) ÷ (2,000,000,000 + 391,667)
    = 2.52

The issuance of the notes increases the current ratio, because the cash from the notes increased current assets by a sizable amount, but the only increase in current liabilities was a relatively small amount of interest payable. The $50 million in notes payable increased long-term liabilities.

DEMONSTRATION CASE B (BONDS PAYABLE)

To raise funds to build a new plant, Reed Company issued bonds with the following terms:

Face value of the bonds: $100,000.

Dates: Issued February 1, 2006; due in 10 years on January 31, 2016.

Interest rate: 6 percent per year, payable on January 31 each year.

The bonds were issued on February 1, 2006, at 106. The annual accounting period for Reed Company ends on December 31.

Required:

1. How much cash did Reed Company receive from the sale of the bonds payable? Show computations.
2. What was the amount of premium on the bonds payable? Over how many months should it be amortized?
3. Give the journal entry on February 1, 2006, to record the sale and issuance of the bonds payable.

Suggested Solution

1. Sale price of the bonds: $100,000 × 106% = $106,000.
2. Premium on the bonds payable: $106,000 − $100,000 = $6,000.
    Months amortized: From date of issue, February 1, 2006, to maturity date, January 31, 2016
    = 10 years × 12 months per year = 120 months.
3. February 1, 2006 (issuance date):

> dr   Cash (+A)....................................... 106,000
>   cr   Premium on Bonds Payable (+L)   6,000
>   cr   Bonds Payable (+L)............................   100,000

CHAPTER SUMMARY

Describe the characteristics and classifications of liabilities. p. 416 **LO1**

- Liabilities are any probable future sacrifices of economic benefits that arise from past transactions. Examples include accounts payable, accrued liabilities, notes payable, and bonds payable.
- Liabilities are classified as current if due to be paid with current assets within the current operating cycle of the business or within one year of the balance sheet date (whichever is longer). All other liabilities are considered long term.

Explain how to account for common types of current liabilities. p. 418 **LO2**

- Liabilities are initially reported at their cash equivalent value, which is the amount of cash that a creditor would accept to settle the liability immediately after the transaction or event occurred.
- Liabilities are increased whenever additional obligations arise (including interest) and are reduced whenever the company makes payments or provides services to the creditor.

Analyze and record bond liability transactions. p. 425 **LO3**

- For most public issuances of debt (bonds), the amount borrowed by the company does not equal the amount repaid at maturity. The effect of a bond discount is to provide the borrower less money than the value stated on the face of the bond, which increases the cost of borrowing above the interest rate stated on the bond. The effect of a bond premium is to provide the borrower more money than repaid at maturity, which decreases the cost of borrowing below the stated interest rate.
- Interest expense reports the true cost of borrowing, which equals the periodic interest payments plus (or minus) the amount of the bond discount (or premium) amortized in that interest period.

Interpret the current ratio and times interest earned ratio. p. 432 **LO4**

- The current ratio measures liquidity, which is the company's ability to pay its current liabilities using its current assets.
- The times interest earned ratio measures a company's ability to meet its interest obligations with resources generated from its profit-making activities.

Describe the additional liabilities information reported in the notes to the financial statements. p. 436 **LO5**

- The notes to the financial statements describe significant financial commitments, such as leases, and contingencies.
- A contingent liability is a potential liability that has arisen as a result of a past transaction or event. Its ultimate outcome will not be known until a future event occurs or fails to occur.

FINANCIAL STATEMENT ANALYSIS TIPS

To determine how well a company is able to use its current assets to pay its current liabilities, calculate the current ratio:

$$\text{Current Ratio} = \frac{\text{Current Assets}}{\text{Current Liabilities}}$$

Calculate the following to determine the amount of income generated by the company (before interest and taxes) for each dollar of interest expense:

$$\text{Times Interest Earned Ratio} = \frac{\text{Net Income} + \text{Interest Expense} + \text{Income Tax Expense}}{\text{Interest Expense}}$$

KEY TERMS TO KNOW

Accrued Liabilities p. 418

Capital Lease p. 439

Contingent Liability p. 436

Current Liabilities p. 416

Current Ratio p. 432

Discount p. 427

Effective-Interest Method
(Supplement B) p. 441

Face Value p. 426

Issue Price p. 427

Line of Credit p. 432

Liquidity p. 432

Market Interest Rate p. 427

Operating Lease p. 439

Premium p. 427

Present Value p. 427

Stated Interest Rate p. 426

Straight-Line Method
(Supplement A) p. 440

Times Interest Earned
Ratio p. 434

SUPPLEMENT A: STRAIGHT-LINE AMORTIZATION OF BOND DISCOUNT AND PREMIUM

Straight-Line Amortization of Bond Discount

Earlier in the chapter, we described how, when a bond is issued at a discount, lenders provide the borrower less money than what is repaid at maturity, which increases the cost of borrowing above the interest rate stated on the bond. For example, if a $100,000 bond is issued for $93,376, the discount of $6,624 ($100,000 − 93,376) is an additional cost of borrowing, over and above the 6 percent annual interest stated on the face of the bond. To comply with the matching concept, this extra cost of borrowing must be matched to the periods in which the bond liability is owed. This is done each accounting period by taking an amount out of *Discount on Bonds Payable* and adding it to *Interest Expense* of that period.

The **straight-line method of amortization** spreads this additional cost equally over the life of the bond. In our example, the bond matures in four years. Thus, the amount amortized in each period would be $6,624 ÷ 4 = $1,656. We add this amount to the promised interest payment ($6,000) to compute interest expense for the period ($7,656). The journal entry to record interest on the bond on December 31, using the straight-line method of amortization, is

YOU SHOULD KNOW

The **straight-line method of amortization** allocates the amount of bond discount (or premium) evenly over each period of a bond's life to adjust interest expense for differences between its stated interest rate and market interest rate.

dr	Interest Expense (+E, −SE) ($6,000 + 1,656)	7,656	
	cr Interest Payable (+L) ($100,000 × 6% × 12/12).		6,000
	cr Discount on Bonds Payable (−xL, +L)		1,656

Assets	=	Liabilities		+	Stockholders' Equity
		Interest Payable	+6,000		Interest Expense (+E) −7,656
		Discount on Bonds Payable (−xL)	+1,656		

COACH'S CORNER

As the name suggests, the straight-line method results in an equal amount of discount amortization in each period.

When the interest payment is actually made, which in our example occurs on January 1, *Interest Payable* will be debited and *Cash* will be credited.

As shown graphically in the chapter, this process continues until the bond matures, at which point the *Discount on Bonds Payable* account will be fully amortized to zero. While you probably believe us on this, it's often useful to actually see how it happens. In Exhibit 10A.1, we summarize the changes that occur *during* each accounting period and how they affect the bond liability accounts on the balance sheet at the *end* of each period. You can see in Exhibit 10A.1 how the bond discount (column E) decreases each period after recording the amount of amortization (column B).

Straight-Line Amortization of Bond Premium

As with a discount, whenever a premium exists ($7,260 in our earlier example), it must be spread over each interest period. Using the straight-line method, the amortization of premium each year is $7,260 ÷ 4 periods = $1,815. This amount is subtracted from the interest that will be paid ($6,000) to calculate the amount of interest expense to report each period ($4,185). Notice that by amortizing the premium in this way, the company reports less interest expense than what will actually be paid as interest each period, which is consistent with our earlier comment that a premium has the effect of reducing the cost of borrowing below the stated interest rate that appears on the bond certificate.

exhibit 10A.1 Bond Discount Amortization Schedule

	CHANGES DURING THE PERIOD				ENDING BOND LIABILITY BALANCES		
Period Ended	**(A) Interest Payable**	**(B) Amortization of Discount**	**(C) (= A + B) Interest Expense**		**(D) Bonds Payable**	**(E) Discount on Bonds Payable**	**(F) (= D − E) Bonds Payable, Net of Discount**
01/01/06	—	—	—		100,000	6,624	93,376
12/31/06	6,000	1,656	7,656		100,000	4,968	95,032
12/31/07	6,000	1,656	7,656		100,000	3,312	96,688
12/31/08	6,000	1,656	7,656		100,000	1,656	98,344
12/31/09	6,000	1,656	7,656		100,000	0	100,000

Recorded each period with the following entry:

Reported at the end of each period on the balance sheet:

dr Interest Expense (+E, −SE) . . . . (C)
  cr Interest Payable (+L) . . . .   (A)
  cr Discount on Bonds Payable
     (−xL, +L). . . . . (B)

Liabilities:
Bonds payable $(D)
Less: Discount on bonds payable   (E)
Bonds payable, net of discount   (F)

For this bond premium example, the journal entry to record interest on December 31 is:

dr Interest Expense (+E, −SE) 4,185
dr Premium on Bonds Payable (−L) 1,815
  cr Interest Payable (+L)   6,000

Assets	=	Liabilities		+	Stockholders' Equity	
		Premium on Bonds Payable	−1,815		Interest Expense (+E)	−4,185
		Interest Payable	+6,000			

COACH'S CORNER

Don't forget to read the rest of the chapter if you haven't already done so. It picks up on page 430.

When the $6,000 interest payment is made on January 1, *Interest Payable* will be debited and *Cash* will be credited. Notice that the $6,000 interest payment each period is made up of $4,185 interest expense and $1,815 premium amortization. In other words, the payment includes interest expense for the current period plus a return of part of the premium that lenders paid when they first bought the bonds.

In Exhibit 10A.2 on page 442, we present a bond amortization schedule that summarizes the changes that occur *during* each interest period and how they affect the bond liability accounts on the balance sheet at the *end* of each period. Notice that the *Premium on Bonds Payable* (column E) decreases each period after recording the amount of amortization (column B), ultimately reaching zero at the end of the bond's four-year life.

SUPPLEMENT B: EFFECTIVE-INTEREST AMORTIZATION OF BOND DISCOUNT AND PREMIUM

The **effective-interest method** is considered a conceptually superior method of accounting for bonds because it correctly calculates interest expense by multiplying the true cost of borrowing times the amount of money actually owed to lenders. The true cost of borrowing is the market interest rate that lenders used to determine the bond issue price. The actual amount owed to lenders is the carrying value of the bond, which equals the cash received when the bond was issued plus any interest costs that haven't been paid.

To clearly understand the effective-interest method, it helps to see how a bond's issue price depends on the market interest rate. As we mentioned in the chapter, lenders decide how much

YOU SHOULD KNOW

The **effective-interest method of amortization** reduces the bond discount (or premium) for the amount by which the borrower's interest payments are less (more) than the true cost of borrowing. The true cost of borrowing is calculated by multiplying the carrying value of the bond times the market interest rate that lenders used to determine the bond issue price.

exhibit 10A.2 Bond Premium Amortization Schedule

	CHANGES DURING THE PERIOD				ENDING BOND LIABILITY BALANCES		
Period Ended	(A) Interest Payable	(B) Amortization of Premium	(C) (= A − B) Interest Expense		(D) Bonds Payable	(E) Premium on Bonds Payable	(F) (= D + E) Bonds Payable, Including Premium
01/01/06	—	—	—		100,000	7,260	107,260
12/31/06	6,000	1,815	4,185		100,000	5,445	105,445
12/31/07	6,000	1,815	4,185		100,000	3,630	103,630
12/31/08	6,000	1,815	4,185		100,000	1,815	101,815
12/31/09	6,000	1,815	4,185		100,000	0	100,000

Recorded each period with the following entry:

dr	Interest Expense (+E, −SE)	(C)	
dr	Premium on Bonds Payable (−L)		(B)
cr	Interest Payable (+L)		(B)

Reported at the end of each period on the balance sheet:

Liabilities:
Bonds payable	$(D)
Add: Premium on bonds payable	(E)
Bonds payable, including premium	(F)

to pay for a bond by using a mathematical calculation called a present value. You can read instructions about how to calculate present values in Appendix C at the end of this book, but for now just focus on understanding what a present value is. Present value is the idea that something is worth more if you get it today than if you get it some time in the future. For example, if someone offered to pay you $100,000 today or $100,000 five years from now, you'd be better off taking it today. You could invest the money and earn interest for five years, making it worth way more than $100,000 five years from now. So if you won the lottery and got to choose between receiving $100,000 in five years or some smaller amount today (hey, it could happen), you can figure out how much to accept today by calculating the present value of $100,000. The only pieces of information you need for this calculation are (1) the amounts to be received in the future, (2) the number of months between now and then, and (3) the interest rate you expect to earn during that time.

In the bond context, lenders get some of this information from the face of the bond and then they determine how much to pay for the bond by calculating the present value of the amounts paid periodically (as interest) and at maturity (as face value), using the interest rate that they want to earn. We have summarized this calculation in Exhibit 10B.1 for General Mills' 6 percent, four-year bond described in the chapter. We show three different scenarios, with each one yielding different market interest rates that would be earned by lenders. The first column calculates the amount of money that lenders would be willing to give up if they needed to earn 4 percent on the amount they pay for the bond. The second column calculates the amount lenders would pay if they wanted a bond returning an interest rate of 6 percent. The third column calculates the amount that lenders would be willing to pay if they wanted to earn 8 percent on the amount they pay for the bond. (For detailed calculations underlying the amounts in Exhibit 10B.1, see Appendix C at the end of the book.)

Notice that when the bond pays interest at a rate that exactly matches the rate expected by lenders in the market (6 percent), they are willing to pay face value for it. If the 6 percent paid on the bond is more than lenders expect, they pay a premium for the bond (as shown in the first column). If the 6 percent interest promised is less than the market interest rate, lenders pay less than face value for the bond, resulting in a discount as suggested in the third column. Let's now look at what happens to a bond discount and premium under the effective-interest amortization method.

Effective-Interest Amortization of a Bond Discount

When a company issues a bond at a discount, it receives less money up-front than it repays at maturity. This creates a true cost of borrowing that is greater than the interest rate stated on the face of the bond. In other words, the true interest expense is greater than the interest paid.

exhibit 10B.1	**Computing the Present Value of Bond Payments**

	MARKET INTEREST RATES		
	4%	6%	8%
Present value of $100,000 (face value) paid four years from now	$ 85,480	$ 79,210	$73,503
Present value of $6,000 (interest) paid once a year for four years	21,780	20,790	19,873
Amount to pay	**$107,260**	**$100,000**	**$93,376**

Under the effective-interest method, this unpaid interest is added to the true bond liability each period—a process known as amortizing the bond discount.

Let's continue the bond discount example presented earlier in the chapter. We had already recorded the issuance of bonds that stated a face value of $100,000 along with an annual interest rate of 6 percent paid on January 1 each year. The bonds were issued for $93,376, which implied a discount of $6,624 and a market interest rate of 8 percent.

Although the actual interest payment isn't made until January 1, the company has to record interest expense at the end of each year on December 31. Interest expense for the year is calculated by multiplying the amount actually borrowed by the market interest rate for the year ($93,376 × 8% × 12/12 = $7,470). The promised interest payment was indicated on the face of the bond as the face value times the stated interest rate for a full year ($100,000 × 6% × 12/12 = $6,000). The difference between the interest expense and the promised interest payment is the amount of discount that is amortized ($7,470 − 6,000 = $1,470). This is recorded with the following entry on December 31:

dr	Interest Expense (+E, −SE)	7,470	
cr	Discount on Bonds Payable (−xL, +L)		1,470
cr	Interest Payable (+L)		6,000

Assets	=	Liabilities	+	Stockholders' Equity
		Discount on Bonds Payable (−xL) +1,470		Interest Expense (+E) −7,470
		Interest Payable +6,000		

When the $6,000 interest payment is made on January 1, *Interest Payable* will be debited and *Cash* will be credited.

The T-account presented in the margin shows how the above journal entry reduces the balance of the *Discount on Bonds Payable* account. A reduction of this contra-liability account increases the carrying value of the long-term liability, as you can see by moving from left to right in Exhibit 10B.2.

Let's now consider the interest expense for 2007. As in 2006, the 2007 interest expense is calculated using the market interest rate. However, the amount of bonds payable actually owed at the end of 2006 increased, as shown in Exhibit 10B.2. Thus, interest expense also will increase, calculated as the unpaid balance on December 31, 2006 of $94,846 (see Exhibit 10B.2) times the market interest rate for the full year ($94,846 × 8% × 12/12 = $7,587 rounded). The difference between the 2007 interest expense ($7,587) and the promised cash payment ($6,000) is the amount of discount that is amortized ($1,587 = $7,587 − 6,000) in 2007. That is, because the true interest expense ($7,587) is greater than the promised payment ($6,000), the bond liability is increased (by reducing the contra-liability). This is recorded with the following entry on December 31:

Discount on Bonds Payable (xL)			
1/1/06	6,624		
		1,470	12/31/06
12/31/06	5,154		

exhibit 10B.2   Sample Balance Sheet Reporting of Bond Discount

GENERAL MILLS, INC.
Balance Sheet (excerpt)

Long-Term Liabilities	January 1, 2006	December 31, 2006
Bonds Payable	$100,000	$100,000
Less: Discount on Bonds Payable	6,624	5,154
Bonds Payable, Net of Discount	93,376	94,846

dr	Interest Expense (+E, −SE)	7,587	
	cr Discount on Bonds Payable (−xL, +L)		1,587
	cr Interest Payable (+L)		6,000

Assets	=	Liabilities		+	Stockholders' Equity	
		Discount on Bonds (−xL)	+1,587		Interest Expense (+E)	−7,587
		Interest Payable	+6,000			

Again, when the $6,000 interest payment is made on January 1, *Interest Payable* will be debited and *Cash* will be credited.

Some companies use a bond amortization schedule to summarize the detailed computations required under the effective-interest amortization method. A typical schedule is presented in Exhibit 10B.3. The following paragraph describes how to read the schedule.

The amortization schedule begins, in the first row, with the balance in *Bonds Payable* (column D, $100,000) and *Discount on Bonds Payable* (column E; $6,624) on the date of the bond issuance. The carrying value reported on the balance sheet as *Bonds Payable, Net of Discount* (column F, $93,376) is computed by subtracting the $6,624 discount from the $100,000 face value. This carrying value is then multiplied by the market interest rate for the full year ($93,376 × 8% × 12/12) to calculate interest expense for the first year (column A, $7,470). The interest to be paid (column B, $6,000) is computed by multiplying the face value of the bond by its stated interest rate for twelve months ($100,000 × 6% × 12/12). The amount of discount amortization (column C, $1,470) is computed by subtracting the promised interest payment of $6,000 (column B) from the interest expense of $7,470 (column A). The amount of discount amortization ($1,470) is subtracted from the previous balance in the *Discount on Bonds Payable* (column E; $6,624) to arrive at a new balance ($5,154), which is subtracted from the face value (column D, $100,000) to compute a new carrying value for the bonds (column D, $94,846). This new carrying value at the end of the first year (12/31/06) becomes the starting point for calculating interest expense in the following year. Take a moment right now to ensure you can calculate the amounts in Exhibit 10B.3 for the period ended 12/31/07. If you need help getting started, see the coach.

Effective-Interest Amortization of Bond Premium

The effective-interest method is applied in the same way for a premium as it was for a discount. Interest expense is computed by multiplying the current unpaid balance times the market interest rate for the length of the interest period. The amount of the bond premium to amortize is then calculated as the difference between interest expense and the cash interest payment promised on the bond. Let's use our earlier example of a bond premium to illustrate. The

exhibit 10B.3 Bond Discount Amortization Schedule

	CHANGES DURING THE PERIOD				ENDING BOND LIABILITY BALANCES		
Period Ended	(A) Interest Expense	(B) Interest Payable	(C) (= A + B) Amortization of Discount		(D) Bonds Payable	(E) Discount on Bonds Payable	(F) (= D − E) Bonds Payable, Net of Discount
01/01/06	—	—	—		100,000	6,624	93,376
12/31/06	7,470	6,000	1,470		100,000	5,154	94,846
12/31/07	7,587	6,000	1,587		100,000	3,567	96,433
12/31/08	7,715	6,000	1,715		100,000	1,852	98,148
12/31/09	7,852	6,000	1,852		100,000	0	100,000

Recorded each period with the following entry:

> dr Interest Expense (+E, −SE) . . . .   (A)
>   cr Interest Payable (+L) . . . .   (B)
>   cr Discount on Bonds Payable
>   (−xL, +L) . . . .   (C)

Reported at the end of each period on the balance sheet:

> **Liabilities:**
> Bonds payable $(D)
> Less: Discount on bonds payable   (E)
> Bonds payable, net of discount   (F)

example involved 6 percent bonds with a face value of $100,000 issued when the market interest rate was 4 percent. The issue price of the bonds was $107,260, and the bond premium was $7,260.

The interest expense at the end of the year is calculated by multiplying the amount actually owed times the market interest rate for the full year ($107,260 × 4% × 12/12 = $4,290). The promised interest payment is calculated by multiplying the face value by the stated interest rate for the full year ($100,000 × 6% × 12/12 = $6,000). The difference between the interest expense and the promised interest payment is the amount of premium that is amortized ($6,000 − $4,290 = $1,710), as shown in the following journal entry.

> dr Interest Expense (+E, −SE)   4,290
> dr Premium on Bonds Payable (−L)   1,710
>   cr Interest Payable (+L)   6,000

Assets	=	Liabilities	+	Stockholders' Equity	
		Premium on Bonds Payable −1,710		Interest Expense (+E)	−4,290
		Interest Payable +6,000			

COACH'S CORNER

Notice that, in each interest period, the borrower promises to pay more than its true cost of borrowing. The extra amount included in each payment goes to reducing the total bond liability (by reducing the premium).

When the $6,000 interest payment is made on January 1, *Interest Payable* will be debited and *Cash* will be credited. Notice in the journal entry above that the promised interest payment ($6,000) is greater than the true interest expense ($4,290), so the bond premium decreases. This illustrates the basic difference between effective-interest amortization of a bond premium versus a bond discount. Amortization of a premium reduces the carrying value of the liability whereas the amortization of a discount increases it. An amortization schedule for our premium example is provided in Exhibit 10B.4. We completed the first two annual interest periods and left the last two for you to complete as part of the Self-Study Quiz that follows.

COACH'S CORNER

Don't forget to read the rest of the chapter if you haven't already done so. It picks up on page 430.

exhibit 10B.4	**Bond Premium Amortization Schedule**

	CHANGES DURING THE PERIOD				ENDING BOND LIABILITY BALANCES		
Period Ended	(A) Interest Expense	(B) Interest Payable	(C) (= B − A) Amortization of Premium		(D) Bonds Payable	(E) Premium on Bonds Payable	(F) (= D + E) Bonds Payable, Including Premium
01/01/06	—	—	—		100,000	7,260	107,260
12/31/06	4,290	6,000	1,710		100,000	5,550	105,550
12/31/07	4,222	6,000	1,778		100,000	3,772	103,772
12/31/08	☐	☐	☐		☐	☐	☐
12/31/09	☐	☐	☐		☐	☐	☐

Recorded each period with the following entry:

dr	Interest Expense (+E, −SE)	(A)	
dr	Premium on Bonds Payable (−L)	(C)	
	cr Interest Payable (+L)		(B)

Reported at the end of each period on the balance sheet:

Liabilities:
Bonds payable	$(D)
Add: Premium on bonds payable	(E)
Bonds payable, including premium	(F)

HOW'S IT GOING?   **A Self-Study Quiz**

Complete the bond premium amortization schedule in Exhibit 10B.4 for the periods ended 12/31/08 and 12/31/09.

When you're done, check your answers with the solutions in the margin.

SUPPLEMENT C: A SIMPLIFIED APPROACH TO BOND ACCOUNTING USING EFFECTIVE-INTEREST AMORTIZATION

The approach shown in this supplement presents a simplified explanation of how bond liabilities and interest expense are accounted for. You should be aware that this approach involves taking a shortcut. While the shortcut will help you to focus on the line-items that ultimately are reported on the financial statements, it requires that we ignore a few accounts that are typically used in "real world" accounting systems. Be sure to check with your instructor (or course outline) to see whether you are expected to read this supplement.

If you're like most people, you probably have to really concentrate hard when reading about how a *reduction* in a contra-liability account causes an *increase* in the carrying value of a bond. You may even whisper this thought quietly to yourself a few times before it starts making sense. In this section, we present a shortcut when accounting for bonds that will allow you to avoid thinking in "double-negatives" like this. Hopefully it will also help you to stop whispering to yourself when you read. ☺

The shortcut involves simplifying only one aspect of what you studied earlier in this chapter. Rather than record a discount or premium in a separate account, we will record it with the bonds payable in an account that we will call *Bonds Payable, Net*. This name is used to remind you that we are focusing on what is ultimately reported in the financial statements rather than what is actually used "behind the scenes." This shortcut greatly simplifies how we account for (1) the initial bond issuance, (2) additional amounts owed to lenders for interest, (3) payments to the lenders, and (4) removal of the bond liability when it is retired.

Accounting for Bonds Issued Below Face Value

1. Record the issuance of the bond and the receipt of cash. Let's illustrate with the example from the chapter in which General Mills issued bonds on January 1, 2006 for $93,376 cash. The following journal entry would be used:

dr	Cash (+A)..	93,376	
	cr Bonds Payable, Net (+L).......................		93,376

Assets	=	Liabilities	+	Stockholders' Equity
Cash +93,376		Bonds Payable, Net +93,376		

Rather than record the *Bonds Payable* at face value ($100,000), with an offsetting *Discount on Bonds Payable* account (of $6,624), we have combined them together in an account called *Bonds Payable, Net* (resulting in $93,376).

With this simplified approach, we still describe bonds as being issued at a discount or premium because the recorded liability is either less or greater than the face value. What has changed, though, is that we no longer need a separate discount or premium account to adjust from the face value to the true liability. Instead, the true liability is reported directly in *Bonds Payable, Net*.

2. Record any interest owed by the end of the accounting period. One of the advantages of this simplified approach is that we no longer choose between the straight-line or effective-interest method of amortization because there is no discount or premium account to amortize. An additional advantage is that interest expense is calculated directly, using an interest formula similar to what you learned earlier:

$$\text{Interest} = \text{Amount Owed} \times \text{Interest Rate} \times \text{Time}$$

The amount owed is the cash that was received when the bond was issued plus any unpaid interest cost. With the simplified approach, the amount owed is the balance in the *Bonds Payable, Net* account at the beginning of the interest period. The rate of interest is the market interest rate that was actually used to determine the present value of the bond when it was issued.

Let's illustrate by recording interest owed for the first annual interest period ended December 31, 2006. The amount owed at the beginning of this period is the $93,376 reported in the *Bonds Payable, Net* account on January 1, 2006. From this, we calculate the interest expense as

$93,376 (amount owed) × 8% (market interest rate) × 12/12 (time) = $7,470 (interest expense).

This interest expense differs from what General Mills actually promised to pay. From the face of the bond we can calculate the amount of interest to be paid for this period as:

$100,000 (face value) × 6% (stated interest rate) × 12/12 (time) = $6,000 (interest payment).

Notice that General Mills is going to pay only $6,000 when its true interest expense is $7,470. Because the company pays less than the cost of interest, its *Bonds Payable, Net* liability will increase by the amount of interest expense that won't be paid this interest period ($1,470). This would be recorded on December 31, 2006, with the following adjusting journal entry:

dr	Interest Expense (+E, −SE)........................	7,470	
	cr Interest Payable (+L)............................		6,000
	cr Bonds Payable, Net (+L)........................		1,470

Assets	=	Liabilities		+	Stockholders' Equity	
		Interest Payable	+6,000		Interest Expense (+E)	−7,470
		Bonds Payable, Net	+1,470			

3. Record payments made to the lender. When interest is paid on January 1, 2007, General Mills would record

dr	Interest Payable (−L)	6,000	
	cr Cash (−A)		6,000

Assets		=	Liabilities		+	Stockholders' Equity
Cash	−6,000		Interest Payable	−6,000		

Let's look at the entries that will be made at the end of the next year.

Record any interest owed by the end of the accounting period. Interest expense is calculated by multiplying the amount owed at the beginning of the interest period times the market interest rate for the year. The amount owed at the beginning of 2007 is shown in the T-account in the margin. After the $1,470 was added to the *Bonds Payable, Net* account on December 31, 2006, the amount owed increased to $94,846. From this, we can calculate the interest expense for 2007 as:

$94,846 (amount owed) × 8% (market interest rate) × 12/12 (time) = $7,587.

Bonds Payable, Net (L)	
	93,376 1/1/06
	1,470 12/31/06
	94,846 1/1/07

The amount of interest payable is based on what General Mills actually promised to pay ($6,000). Notice that General Mills is going to pay only $6,000 when its true interest expense is $7,587. Because the company pays less than the cost of interest, its *Bonds Payable, Net* liability increases by the amount of interest expense that General Mills isn't going to pay in this interest period ($1,587). This would be recorded on December 31, 2007, with the following adjusting journal entry:

COACH'S CORNER

The interest expense for 2007 is greater than that for 2006 because the balance in *Bonds Payable, Net* was greater in 2007 than 2006.

dr	Interest Expense (+E, −SE)	7,587	
	cr Interest Payable (+L)		6,000
	cr Bonds Payable, Net (+L)		1,587

Assets	=	Liabilities		+	Stockholders' Equity	
		Interest Payable	+6,000		Interest Expense (+E)	−7,587
		Bonds Payable, Net	+1,587			

Record payments made to the lender. As before, when Big G pays interest on January 1, 2008, the following journal entry is required:

dr	Interest Payable (−L)	6,000	
	cr Cash (−A)		6,000

Assets		=	Liabilities		+	Stockholders' Equity
Cash	−6,000		Interest Payable	−6,000		

exhibit 10C.1 Bond Amortization Schedule

Period Ended	BEGINNING OF PERIOD (A) Bonds Payable, Net		CHANGES DURING THE PERIOD (B) Interest Expense	(C) Interest Payable	(D) = (B) − (C) Interest Added to Bonds Payable	END OF PERIOD (E) = (A) + (D) Bonds Payable, Net	
12/31/06	93,376	Used to calculate	7,470	6,000	1,470	94,846	Reported on
12/31/07	94,846	interest expense	7,587	6,000	1,587	96,433	the balance
12/31/08	96,433	for each interest	7,715	6,000	1,715	98,148	sheet at the
12/31/09	98,148	period.	7,852	6,000	1,852	100,000	end of each
							period.

Recorded during each period with the following entry:

dr	Interest Expense (+E, −SE). . . .	(B)
cr	Interest Payable (+L).	(C)
cr	Bonds Payable, Net (+L). . .	(D)

These journal entries for interest expense and interest payments will continue as long as the bonds remain outstanding, although the amounts will change as the *Bonds Payable, Net* balance changes.

In Exhibit 10C.1, we present a bond amortization schedule that summarizes the balance in *Bonds Payable, Net* at the beginning of each interest period (column A), the changes that occur during each interest period (columns B, C, and D), and the *Bonds Payable, Net* balance at the *end* of each period (column E). Notice in column E that as the bonds approach maturity (January 1, 2010), the *Bonds Payable, Net* account approaches the face value of the bonds.

The amortization schedule begins, in the first row, with the balance in *Bonds Payable, Net* immediately after the bond issuance. Interest expense (column B) is calculated by multiplying the amount owed at the beginning of the interest period (column A) times the market interest rate times the length of period. Interest payable (column C) is calculated as the face value times the stated interest rate times the length of period. Unpaid interest (column D) is the difference between the interest expense (column B) and the interest payment that will be made (column C). The ending balance in *Bonds Payable, Net* (column E) is the beginning balance (column A) plus the unpaid interest (column D). The ending balance for one year (column E) then becomes the beginning balance for the next year (column A), which is the starting point for calculating interest expense in that year.

Accounting for Bonds Issued above Face Value

The calculations and journal entries used to record interest expense and interest payments when a bond issues at a premium are similar to those shown in the previous section for a bond issued at a discount. The only difference is that because a premium reduces the cost of borrowing, interest expense is less than the promised cash payment for each interest period. The extra amount included in each payment goes to paying down *Bonds Payable, Net*. To illustrate, we extend the bond premium example introduced earlier in the chapter, which involved a four-year bond (with a face value of $100,000 and stated interest rate of 6%) that was issued at a price of $107,260. This price implies a market interest rate of 4%, so the interest expense for the first year is $4,290 ($107,260 × 4% × 12/12). The stated interest payment for the year is $6,000 ($100,000 × 6% × 12/12), which is greater than the interest expense of $4,290. The extra $1,710 included in the payment represents a repayment of the bond liability, which is recorded with the following journal entry:

dr	Interest Expense (+E, −SE).	4,290	
dr	Bonds Payable, Net (−L)	1,710	
	cr Interest Payable (+L).		6,000

Assets	=	Liabilities	+	Stockholders' Equity
		Interest Payable +6,000		Interest Expense (+E) −4,290
		Bonds Payable, Net −1,710		

When the $6,000 interest payment is made on January 1, *Interest Payable* will be debited and *Cash* will be credited. And, as we saw before, these entries to record interest expense and payments will continue each period until the bond matures or is retired early.

FOR YOUR PRACTICE

QUESTIONS

1. Define *liability*. What's the difference between a current liability and a long-term liability?
2. What three factors influence the dollar amount reported for liabilities?
3. Define *accrued liability*. Give an example of a typical accrued liability.
4. Why is *unearned revenue* considered a liability?
5. Why are *payroll taxes* and *sales taxes* considered liabilities?
6. If a company has a long-term loan that has only two years remaining until it matures, how is it reported on the balance sheet (*a*) this year, and (*b*) next year?
7. What are the reasons that some bonds are issued at a discount and others are issued at a premium?
8. Why are publicly issued debt certificates more likely to involve a discount or premium than a private placement of debt?
9. What is the difference between the stated interest rate and the market interest rate on a bond?
10. Will the stated interest rate be higher than the market interest rate or will the market interest rate be higher than the stated interest rate when a bond is issued at (*a*) face value, (*b*) a discount, and (*c*) a premium?
11. What is the carrying value of a bond payable?
12. What is the current ratio? How is it related to the classification of liabilities?
13. What is the difference between a secured and an unsecured loan? Which type carries more risk for the lender?
14. What amounts are reported as liabilities for *capital* versus *operating* leases?
15. What is a contingent liability? How is a contingent liability reported?
16. (Supplement A) How is interest expense calculated using the straight-line method of amortization for a bond issued at (*a*) a discount and (*b*) a premium?
17. (Supplement B) How is interest expense calculated using the effective-interest method of amortization for a bond issued at (*a*) a discount and (*b*) a premium?
18. (Supplement C) How is interest expense calculated using the simplified approach to the effective-interest method for a bond issued at (*a*) a discount and (*b*) a premium?

MULTIPLE CHOICE

To practice more multiple choice questions, check out the DVD for use with this book.

1. Which of the following best describes *accrued liabilities*?
   a. Long-term liabilities.
   b. Current amounts owed to suppliers of inventory.
   c. Expenses incurred, but not paid at the end of the accounting period.
   d. Revenues that have been collected, but not earned.

2. As of February 29, 2004, American Greetings Corporation had 9,800 full-time and 21,000 part-time employees. Assume that in the last pay period of the year, the company paid $8,000,000 to employees after deducting $2,000,000 for employee income taxes, $612,000 for FICA taxes, and $700,000 for other payroll taxes. No payments have been made to the government relating to these taxes. Which of the following statements is true regarding this pay period?

   a. FICA taxes payable is $612,000.
   b. FICA taxes payable is $1,224,000.
   c. Compensation expense is $8,000,000.
   d. None of the above is true.

3. Assume that Warnaco Group Inc., the makers of Fruit of the Loom® underwear, borrowed $100,000 from the bank to be repaid over the next five years, with principal payments beginning next month. Which of the following best describes the presentation of this debt in the balance sheet as of today (the date of borrowing)?

   a. $100,000 in the long-term liability section.
   b. $100,000 *plus* the interest to be paid over the five-year period in the long-term liability section.
   c. A portion of the $100,000 in the current liability section, and the remainder of the principal in the long-term liability section.
   d. A portion of the $100,000 plus interest in the current liability section, and the remainder of the principal plus interest in the long-term liability section.

4. Assume that Speedo International received $400,000 for long-term promissory notes that issued on November 1. The notes pay interest on April 30 and October 31 at the annual rate of 6 percent, which was comparable to other interest rates in the market at that time. Which of the following journal entries would be required at December 31?

   a. dr Interest Expense   4,000
          cr   Interest Payable   4,000
   b. dr Interest Expense   4,000
          cr   Cash   4,000
   c. dr Interest Expense   4,000
      dr Interest Payable   8,000
          cr   Cash   12,000
   d. dr Interest Expense   8,000
      dr Interest Payable   4,000
          cr   Cash   12,000

5. Which of the following does not impact the calculation of the cash interest payments to be made to bondholders?

   a. Face value of the bond.
   b. Stated interest rate.
   c. Market interest rate.
   d. The length of time between payments.

6. Which of the following is false when a bond is issued at a premium?

   a. The bond will issue for an amount above its face value.
   b. Interest expense will exceed the cash interest payments.
   c. The market interest rate is lower than the stated interest rate.
   d. All of the above are true when a bond is issued at a premium.

7. When the company that borrows money by issuing a bond has the right to terminate a relationship with a lender early and repay the amount borrowed ahead of schedule, we say that the loan is

   a. Convertible   c. Amortizable
   b. Secured   d. Callable

8. To determine if a bond will be issued at a premium, discount, or at face value, one must know which of the following pairs of information?

   a. The face value and the stated interest rate on the date the bonds were issued.
   b. The face value and the market interest rate on the date the bonds were issued.

c. The stated interest rate and the market interest rate on the date the bonds were issued.

d. You can't tell without having more information.

9. For the year ended December 31, 2003, Land O' Lakes, Inc., reported operating income of $109,382, net income of $83,538, interest expense of $82,948, and income tax expense of $18,103. What was this dairy company's times interest earned ratio for the year?

a. 0.76   c. 1.32

b. 1.01   d. 2.23

10. Big Hitter Corp. is facing a class-action lawsuit in the upcoming year. It is possible, but not probable, that the company will have to pay a settlement of approximately $2,000,000. How would this fact be reported, if at all, in the financial statements to be issued at the end of the current month?

a. Report $2,000,000 as a current liability.

b. Report $2,000,000 as a long-term liability.

c. Report the potential liability in the notes to the financial statements.

d. Reporting is not required in this case.

MINI-EXERCISES   Available with McGraw-Hill's Homework Manager

LO2–LO5   M10-1 Identifying Important Accounting Terms

Complete the following crossword puzzle, using the clues provided to the right.

Across

2 Arises when a bond is issued with a stated interest rate greater than the market interest rate.

3 A loan condition that gives the creditor an option to accept the borrower's stock as payment for the outstanding loan.

5 The ability to pay current liabilities; typically evaluated using the current ratio.

6 The_____value is reported on a bond certificate.

Down

1 A loan condition that ensures certain debt is paid before other ("subordinated") debt.

2 The word describing the level of likelihood at which a contingent liability is recorded.

4 The abbreviation for Medicare and Social Security payroll taxes.

LO2   M10-2 Recording Unearned Revenues

A local theater company sells 500 season ticket packages at a price of $300 per package. The first show in the five-show season starts this week. Prepare the journal entries to record (a) the sale of the season tickets before the first show and (b) the revenue earned after putting on the first show.

LO2   M10-3 Recording Sales and State Tax

Ahlers Clocks is a retailer of wall clocks, mantles, and grandfather clocks and is located in the Empire Mall in Sioux Falls, South Dakota. Assume that a customer bought a grandfather clock for $2,000 cash plus 4 percent sales tax. Prepare the journal entry Ahlers Clocks would use to record this transaction.

LO2   M10-4 Reporting Payroll Tax Liabilities

Lightning Electronics is a mid-sized manufacturer of lithium batteries. The company's payroll records for the November 1–14 pay period shows that employees earned wages totaling $90,000 but that employee income taxes totaling $14,000 and FICA taxes totaling $5,250 were withheld from this amount, leaving a net pay of $70,750, which was directly deposited into the employees' bank accounts. Prepare the journal entry or entries that Lightning would use to record the payroll. Include both employee and employer taxes.

M10-5 Reporting Current and Noncurrent Portions of Long-Term Debt
LO2

Assume that on December 1, 2005, your company borrowed $14,000, a portion of which is to be repaid each year on November 30. Specifically, your company will make the following principal payments: 2006, $2,000; 2007, $3,000; 2008, $4,000; and 2009, $5,000. Show how this loan will be reported in the December 31, 2006 and 2005 balance sheets, assuming that principal payments will be made when required.

M10-6 Recording a Note Payable
LO2

Farmer Corporation borrowed $100,000 on November 1, 2005. The note carried a 6 percent interest rate with the principal and interest payable on June 1, 2006. Prepare the journal entries to record (a) the note issued on November 1 and (b) the interest accrued on December 31, assuming no adjusting entries have been made.

M10-7 Reporting Interest and Long-Term Debt, Including Current Portion
LO2

Barton Chocolates used a promissory note to borrow $1,000,000 on July 1, 2005, at an annual interest rate of 6 percent. The note is to be repaid in yearly installments of $200,000, plus accrued interest, on every June 30th of every year until the note is paid in full (on June 30, 2010). Show how the results of this transaction would be reported in a classified balance sheet prepared as of December 31, 2005.

M10-8 Determining Bond Discount or Premium from Quoted Price
LO3

On May 14, 2004, Bondpickers.com quoted a bond price of 103.677 for Ford Motor Company's 6.375 percent bonds maturing on November 5, 2008. Were the bonds selling at a discount or premium? Does this mean the market interest rate was higher or lower than 6.375 percent?

M10-9 Computing and Reporting a Bond Liability at an Issuance Price of 98
LO3

Coopers Company plans to issue $500,000, 10-year, 4 percent bonds. Interest is payable annually on December 31. All of the bonds will be issued on January 1, 2005. Show how the bonds would be reported on the January 2, 2005, balance sheet if they are issued at 98.

M10-10 Computing and Reporting a Bond Liability at an Issuance Price of 103
LO3

Repeat M10-9 assuming the bonds are issued at 103.

M10-11 Recording Bonds Issued at Face Value
LO3

Schlitterbahn Waterslide Company issued 5,000, 10-year, 6 percent, $1,000 bonds on January 1, 2006, at face value. Interest is payable each January 1. Prepare journal entries to (a) record the issuance of these bonds on January 1, 2006, (b) accrue interest on December 31, 2006, and (c) record interest paid on January 1, 2007.

M10-12 Determining Financial Statement Effects of an Early Retirement of Debt
LO3

If the price of a bond increased after it was issued and the company decided to retire the debt early, would you expect the company to report a gain or loss on debt retirement? Describe the financial statement effects of a debt retirement under these circumstances.

M10-13 Computing the Current Ratio and the Times Interest Earned Ratio
LO4

The balance sheet for Shaver Corporation reported the following: total assets, $250,000; noncurrent assets, $150,000; current liabilities, $40,000; total stockholders' equity, $90,000; net income, $3,320; interest expense, $4,400; income before income taxes, $5,280. Compute Shaver's current ratio and times interest earned ratio. Based on these ratios, does it appear Shaver will be able to meet its obligations to pay current liabilities and future interest obligations as they become payable?

M10-14 Analyzing the Impact of Transactions on the Current Ratio
LO4

BSO, Inc., has a current ratio of 2.0. For each of the following transactions, determine whether the current ratio will increase, decrease, or remain the same.

a.   Paid accounts payable in the amount of $50,000.
b.   Recorded accrued salaries in the amount of $100,000.
c.   Borrowed $250,000 from a local bank, to be repaid in 90 days.
d.   Purchased $20,000 of new inventory on credit.

LO5   **M10-15 Reporting a Contingent Liability**
Buzz Coffee Shops is famous for its large servings of hot coffee. After a famous case involving McDonald's, the lawyer for Buzz warned management (during 2005) that it could be sued if someone were to spill hot coffee and be burned. "With the temperature of your coffee, I can guarantee it's just a matter of time before you're sued for $1,000,000." Unfortunately, in 2006, the prediction came true when a customer filed suit. The case went to trial in 2007, and the jury awarded the customer $400,000 in damages, which the company immediately appealed. During 2008, the customer and the company settled their dispute for $150,000. What is the proper reporting of this liability each year?

M10-16 (Supplement A) Recording Bond Issuance and Interest Payment (Straight-Line Amortization)
Simko Company issued $600,000, 10-year, 5 percent bonds on January 1, 2005. The bonds were issued for $580,000. Interest is payable annually on January 1. Using straight-line amortization, prepare journal entries to record (a) the bond issuance on January 1, 2005, (b) the accrual of interest on December 31, 2005, and (c) the payment of interest on January 1, 2006.

M10-17 (Supplement B) Recording Bond Issuance and Interest Payment (Effective-Interest Amortization)
Clem Company issued $800,000, 10-year, 5 percent bonds on January 1, 2005. The bonds sold for $741,000. Interest is payable annually on January 1. Using effective-interest amortization, prepare journal entries to record (a) the bond issuance on January 1, 2005, (b) the accrual of interest on December 31, 2005, and (c) the payment of interest on January 1, 2006. The market interest rate on the bonds is 6 percent.

M10-18 (Supplement C) Recording Interest Accrual and Interest Payment (Simplified Approach to Effective-Interest Amortization)
On December 31, 2005, the balance sheet of Buchheit Enterprises reported $95,000 in a liability called "Bonds payable, net." This liability related to a $100,000 bond with a stated interest rate of 5 percent that was issued when the market interest rate was 6 percent. Assuming that interest is paid each January 1, prepare separate journal entries to record (a) accrual of interest on December 31, 2006, and (b) payment of the interest on January 1, 2007, using the simplified approach shown in chapter supplement C.

EXERCISES   **Available with McGraw-Hill's Homework Manager**

LO2   **E10-1 Recording a Note Payable through Its Time to Maturity with Discussion of Management Strategy**
Many businesses borrow money during periods of increased business activity to finance inventory and accounts receivable. Target Corporation is one of America's largest general merchandise retailers. Each Christmas, Target builds up its inventory to meet the needs of Christmas shoppers. A large portion of Christmas sales are on credit. As a result, Target often collects cash from the sales several months after Christmas. Assume that on November 1, 2005, Target borrowed $4.5 million cash from Metropolitan Bank and signed a promissory note that matures in six months. The interest rate was 10 percent payable at maturity. The accounting period ends December 31.

Required:

1.   Give the journal entry to record the note on November 1.
2.   Give any adjusting entry required at the end of the annual accounting period.
3.   Give the journal entry to record payment of the note and interest on the maturity date, April 30, 2006.
4.   If Target needs extra cash during every Christmas season, should management borrow money on a long-term basis to avoid the necessity of negotiating a new short-term loan each year? Why or why not?

E10-2 Determining Financial Statement Effects of Transactions Involving Notes Payable

LO2

Use the information in E10-1 to complete the following requirements.

Required:

1. Indicate the accounts, amounts, and effects (+ for increase, − for decrease, and NE for no effect) of the (a) issuance of the note on November 1, (b) impact of the adjusting entry at the end of the accounting period, and (c) the payment of the note and interest on April 30, 2006, on the accounting equation. Use the following structure for your answer:

Date	Assets	Liabilities	Stockholders' Equity

2. If Target needs extra cash every Christmas season, should management borrow money on a long-term basis to avoid negotiating a new short-term loan each year? Explain your answer.

E10-3 Recording Payroll Costs with Discussion

LO2

McLoyd Company completed the salary and wage payroll for March 2006. The payroll provided the following details:

Salaries and wages earned	$230,000
Employee income taxes withheld	46,000
Union dues withheld	3,000
Insurance premiums withheld	1,200
FICA taxes withheld	16,445

Required:

1. Prepare the journal entry to record the payroll for March, including employee deductions (but excluding employer FICA taxes).
2. Prepare the journal entry to record the employer's FICA taxes.
3. Assume the amounts owed to governmental agencies and other organizations are paid on April 4, 2006. Prepare the journal entry to record this payment.
4. What was the total labor cost for the company? Explain.

E10-4 Determining the Impact of Current Liability Transactions, Including Analysis of the Current Ratio

LO2, LO4

Bryant Company sells a wide range of inventories, which are purchased on accounts payable. Occasionally, a short-term note payable is used to obtain cash for current use. The following transactions were selected from those occurring during 2006:

a. On January 10, 2006, purchased merchandise on credit for $18,000. The company uses a perpetual inventory system.
b. On March 1, 2006, borrowed $40,000 cash from City Bank and gave an interest-bearing note payable: face amount, $40,000, due at the end of six months, with an annual interest rate of 8 percent payable at maturity.

Required:

1. For each of the transactions, indicate the accounts, amounts, and effects (+ for increase, − for decrease, and NE for no effect) on the accounting equation. Use the following structure:

Date	Assets	=	Liabilities	+	Stockholders' Equity

2. What amount of cash is paid on the maturity date of the note?
3. Discuss the impact of each transaction on the current ratio. (Assume Bryant Company's current assets have always been greater than its current liabilities.)

E10-5 Determining and Recording the Financial Statement Effects of Unearned Subscription Revenue

LO2

Reader's Digest Association is a publisher of magazines, books, and music collections. The following note is from its annual report:

Revenues

Sales of subscriptions to magazines are recorded as unearned revenue at the time the order is received. Proportional shares of the subscription price are recognized as revenues when the subscription is fulfilled.

Assume that Reader's Digest collected $10 million in 2005 for magazines that will be delivered in future years. During 2006, the company delivered $8 million worth of magazines on those subscriptions.

Required:

1. Using the information given above, indicate the accounts, amounts, and effects (+ for increase, − for decrease, and NE for no effect) on the accounting equation. Use the following structure:

Date	Assets	=	Liabilities	+	Stockholders' Equity

2. Using the information given above, prepare the journal entries that would be recorded in each year.

LO3   **E10-6   Preparing Journal Entries to Record Issuance of a Bond, Accrual of Interest, and Payment of Interest**

On January 1, 2005, Applied Technologies Corporation (ATC) issued a $300,000 bond that matures in 10 years. The bond has a stated interest rate of 6 percent. When the bond was issued, the market rate was 6 percent. The bond pays interest once per year on January 1.

Required:

1. Determine the price at which the bond was issued and the amount that ATC received at issuance.
2. Prepare the journal entry to record the bond issuance.
3. Prepare the journal entry to accrue interest on December 31, 2005.
4. Prepare the journal entry to record the interest payment on January 1, 2006.

LO3   **E10-7   Preparing Journal Entries to Record Issuance of a Bond at Face Value, Accrual of Interest, Payment of Interest, and Early Retirement**

On January 1, 2005, Innovative Solutions, Inc., issued a $200,000 bond at face value. The bond has a stated interest rate of 6 percent. The bond matures in 10 years and pays interest once per year on January 1.

Required:

1. Prepare the journal entry to record the bond issuance.
2. Prepare the journal entry to accrue interest on December 31, 2005.
3. Prepare the journal entry to record the interest payment on January 1, 2006.
4. Assume the bond was retired immediately after the first interest payment on January 1, 2006, at a quoted price of 102. Prepare the journal entry to record the early retirement of the bond.

LO3, LO4   **E10-8   Describing the Effects of a Premium Bond Issue and Interest Payment on the Financial Statements, Current Ratio, and Times Interest Earned Ratio**

Grocery Corporation received $300,328 for $250,000, 11 percent bonds issued on January 1, 2006, at a market interest rate of 8 percent. The bonds stated that interest would be paid each January 1 and that they mature on January 1, 2016.

Required:

1. Describe how the bond issuance affects the financial statements, specifically identifying the account names and direction of effects (ignore amounts). Also, describe its impact on the current ratio and times interest earned ratios, if any.

2. Without doing calculations, describe how the financial statements are affected by the recording of interest on December 31, 2006. Also, describe the impact of the December 31 interest accrual and the January 1 interest payment on the current ratio and times interest earned ratio, if any.

E10-9 Calculating the Current Ratio and Times Interest Earned Ratio

LO4

According to its Web site, Kraft Foods Inc. sells enough Kool-Aid® mix to make 17 gallons of the nectar every second during the summer and over 560 million gallons each year. At a recent year-end, the company reported the following amounts (in millions) in its financial statements:

	Current Year	Prior Year
Total current assets	$8,124	$7,456
Total current liabilities	7,861	7,169
Interest and other debt expense	665	847
Income tax expense	1,866	1,869
Net income	3,476	3,394

Required:

1. Compute the current ratio and times interest earned ratio for the current and prior years.
2. Did Kraft appear to have increased or decreased its ability to pay current liabilities and future interest obligations as they become due?

E10-10 (Supplement A) Recording the Effects of a Premium Bond Issue and First Interest Payment (Straight-Line Amortization)

Refer to the information in E10-8 and assume Grocery Corporation uses the straight-line method to amortize the bond premium.

Required:

1. Prepare the journal entry to record the bond issuance.
2. Prepare the journal entry to record the interest accrual on December 31, 2006.

E10-11 (Supplement B) Recording the Effects of a Premium Bond Issue and First Interest Payment (Effective-Interest Amortization)

Refer to the information in E10-8 and assume Grocery Corporation uses the effective-interest method to amortize the bond premium.

Required:

1. Prepare the journal entry to record the bond issuance.
2. Prepare the journal entry to record the interest accrual on December 31, 2006.

E10-12 (Supplement C) Recording the Effects of a Premium Bond Issue and First Interest Payment (Simplified Approach to Effective-Interest Amortization)

Refer to the information in E10-8 and assume Grocery Corporation accounts for the bond using the shortcut approach shown in chapter supplement C.

Required:

1. Prepare the journal entry to record the bond issuance.
2. Prepare the journal entry to record the interest accrual on December 31, 2006.

E10-13 (Supplement A) Recording the Effects of a Discount Bond Issue and First Interest Payment and Preparing a Discount Amortization Schedule (Straight-Line Amortization)

On January 1, 2006, when the market interest rate was 9 percent, Seton Corporation sold a $200,000, 8 percent bond issue for $187,163. The bonds were dated January 1, 2006, pay interest each December 31, and mature 10 years from January 1, 2006. Seton amortizes the bond discount using the straight-line method.

Required:

1. Prepare the journal entry to record the bond issuance.
2. Prepare the journal entry to record the interest payment on December 31, 2006.
3. Prepare a bond discount amortization schedule for these bonds, using the format shown in Exhibit 10A.1.

E10-14 (Supplement B) Recording the Effects of a Discount Bond Issue and First Interest Payment and Preparing a Discount Amortization Schedule (Effective-Interest Amortization)

Refer to the information in E10-13 and assume Seton Corporation uses the effective-interest method to amortize the bond discount.

Required:

1. Prepare the journal entry to record the bond issuance.
2. Prepare the journal entry to record the interest payment on December 31, 2006.
3. Prepare a bond discount amortization schedule for these bonds, using the format shown in Exhibit 10B.3.

E10-15 (Supplement C) Recording the Effects of a Discount Bond Issue and First Interest Payment and Preparing a Discount Amortization Schedule (Simplified Approach to Effective-Interest Amortization)

Refer to the information in E10-13 and assume Seton Corporation accounts for the bond using the shortcut approach shown in chapter supplement C.

Required:

1. Prepare the journal entry to record the bond issuance.
2. Prepare the journal entry to record the interest payment on December 31, 2006.
3. Prepare a bond discount amortization schedule for these bonds, using the format shown in Exhibit 10C.1.

SIMPLIFY WITH SPREADSHEETS

SS10-1 (Supplement A) Preparing a Bond Amortization Schedule (Straight-Line Amortization)

Assume the authors of a popular introductory accounting text have hired you to create spreadsheets that will calculate bond discount amortization schedules like those shown in Exhibits 10A.1, 10B. 3, and 10C.1. As usual, you e-mail your friend Billy for some guidance. Much to your disappointment, you receive an auto-reply message from Billy indicating that he's gone skiing in New Zealand. After a bit of panicking, you realize you can refer to Billy's previous e-mail messages for spreadsheet advice that will help you complete this task. From his advice for Chapter 9, you decide to create a data input section for the stated interest rate, market interest rate, face value, issue price, and years to maturity. The spreadsheet file also will have a separate amortization schedule worksheet that contains only formulas, references to the cells in the data input section, and references to other cells in the amortization schedule. All amounts will be rounded to the nearest dollar (using the Round function in Excel), which means the discount amortization in the final year might be off a few dollars (unless you use the If function in Excel to eliminate any remaining discount in the final year of the bond's life, in the same way that Billy showed in Chapter 9 for declining-balance depreciation).

Required:

Prepare a worksheet that reproduces the straight-line bond discount amortization schedule shown in Exhibit 10A.1.

SS10-2 (Supplement B) Preparing a Bond Amortization Schedule (Effective-Interest Amortization)

Refer to the information in SS10-1 and prepare a worksheet that reproduces the effective-interest bond discount amortization schedule shown in Exhibit 10B.3.

SS10-3 (Supplement C) Preparing a Bond Amortization Schedule (Simplified Approach to Effective-Interest Amortization)

Refer to the information in SS10-1 and prepare a worksheet that reproduces the bond discount amortization schedule, shown in Exhibit 10C.1, for the simplified approach.

COACHED PROBLEMS

CP10-1 Recording and Reporting Current Liabilities with Evaluation of Effects on the Current Ratio

LO2, LO4

Curb Company completed the following transactions during 2005. The annual accounting period ends December 31, 2005.

Jan.	8	Purchased merchandise on account at a cost of $13,580. (Assume a perpetual inventory system.)
	17	Paid for the January 8 purchase.
Apr.	1	Received $40,000 from National Bank after signing a 12-month, 12 percent interest-bearing note payable.
June	3	Purchased merchandise on account at a cost of $17,820.
July	5	Paid for the June 3 purchase.
Aug.	1	Rented out a small office in a building owned by Curb Company and collected six months' rent in advance amounting to $5,100. (Use an account called unearned rent revenue.)
Dec.	20	Received a $100 deposit from a customer as a guarantee to return a large trailer "borrowed" for 30 days.
	31	Determined wages of $6,500 were earned but not yet paid on December 31 (ignore payroll taxes).

> **COACH'S CORNER**
>
> For the December 20 transaction, consider whether Curb Company has an obligation to return the money when the trailer is returned.

Required:

1. Prepare journal entries for each of the items listed above.
2. Prepare any adjusting entries required on December 31, 2005.
3. Show how all of the liabilities arising from these transactions are reported on the balance sheet at December 31, 2005.
4. For each transaction (including adjusting entries), state whether the current ratio is increased, decreased, or remains the same. (Assume Curb Company's current assets have always been greater than its current liabilities.)

CP10-2 Determining Financial Effects of Transactions Affecting Current Liabilities with Evaluation of Effects on the Current Ratio

LO2, LO4

Using data from CP10-1, complete the following requirements.

Required:

1. For each transaction (including adjusting entries) listed in CP10-1, indicate the accounts, amounts, and effects (+ for increase, − for decrease, and NE for no effect) on the accounting equation, using the following schedule:

Date	Assets	=	Liabilities	+	Stockholders' Equity

2. For each transaction (including adjusting entries), state whether the current ratio is increased, decreased, or there is no change. (Assume Curb Company's current assets have always been greater than its current liabilities.)

CP10-3 Recording and Reporting Current Liabilities

LO2

During 2006, Riverside Company completed the following two transactions. The annual accounting period ends December 31.

a. Paid and recorded wages of $130,000 during 2006; however, at the end of December 2006, three days' wages are unpaid and unrecorded because the weekly payroll will not be paid until January 6, 2007. Wages for the three days total $3,600.

b. Collected rent revenue of $2,400 on December 10, 2006, for office space that Riverside rented to another business. The rent collected was for 30 days from December 11, 2006, to January 10, 2007, and was credited in full to Rent Revenue.

Required:

1. Give the adjusting entry required on December 31, 2006, for unpaid wages from December 2006.
2. Give (a) the journal entry for the collection of rent on December 10, 2006, and (b) the adjusting journal entry on December 31, 2006.
3. Show how any liabilities related to these transactions should be reported on the company's balance sheet at December 31, 2006.
4. Explain why the accrual basis of accounting provides more relevant information to financial analysts than the cash basis.

LO3

CP10-4 Comparing Bonds Issued at Par, Discount, and Premium

Sikes Corporation, whose annual accounting period ends on December 31, issued the following bonds:

Date of bonds: January 1, 2005.

Maturity amount and date: $100,000 due in 10 years (December 31, 2014).

Interest: 10 percent per year payable each December 31.

Date sold: January 1, 2005.

Required:

1. Provide the following amounts to be reported on the January 1, 2005, financial statements immediately after the bonds are issued:

	Case A (issued at 100)	Case B (at 96)	Case C (at 102)
a. Bonds payable	$	$	$
b. Unamortized premium or discount			
c. Bonds payable, net			

2. Assume that you are an investment adviser and a retired person has written to you asking, "Why should I buy a bond at a premium when I can find one at a discount? Isn't that stupid? It's like paying list price for a car instead of negotiating a discount." Write a brief message in response to the question.

LO3

CP10-5 Comparing Carrying Value and Market Value and Recording Early Retirement of Debt

The name Hilton is well known for its hotels and notorious daughters. The Hilton annual report contained the following information concerning long-term debt:

> **Long-Term Debt**
>
> The estimated current market value of long-term debt is based on the quoted market price for the same or similar issues. The current carrying value for long-term debt is $1,132.5 (million) and the current market value is $1,173.5 (million).

Required:

1. Explain why there is a difference between the carrying value and the current market value of the long-term debt for Hilton.
2. Assume that Hilton retired all of its long-term debt early (a very unlikely event) by buying the bonds in the bond market. This required a cash payment equal to the current market value. Prepare the journal entry to record the transaction.

CP10-6 Determining Financial Statement Reporting of Contingent Liabilities

LO5

Brunswick Corporation is a multinational company that manufactures and sells marine and recreational products. A prior annual report contained the following information:

> ### Litigation
>
> A jury awarded $44.4 million in damages in a suit brought by Independent Boat Builders, Inc., a buying group of boat manufacturers and its 22 members. Under the antitrust laws, the damage award has been tripled, and the plaintiffs will be entitled to their attorney's fees and interest. The Company has filed an appeal contending the verdict was erroneous as a matter of law, both as to liability and damages.

COACH'S CORNER

Consider the different possible outcomes that could arise from the appeal.

Required:

What are the alternative ways in which Brunswick could account for this litigation?

CP10-7 (Supplement A) Recording Bond Issuance and Interest Payments (Straight-Line Amortization)

West Company issued bonds with the following details:

Maturity value: $600,000.

Interest: 9 percent per year payable each December 31.

Terms: Bonds dated January 1, 2005, due five years from that date.

The annual accounting period ends December 31. The bonds were issued at 104 on January 1, 2005, at an 8 percent market interest rate. Assume the company uses straight-line amortization.

COACH'S CORNER

Bonds pay face value at maturity.

Required:

1. Compute the issue (sale) price of the bonds (show computations).
2. Give the journal entry to record the issuance of the bonds.
3. Give the journal entries to record the payment of interest on December 31, 2005 and 2006.
4. How much interest expense would be reported on the income statements for 2005 and 2006? Show how the liability related to the bonds should be reported on the balance sheets at December 31, 2005 and 2006.

CP10-8 (Supplement B) Recording Bond Issuance and Interest Payments (Effective-Interest Amortization)

Complete the requirements of CP10-7, assuming West Company uses effective-interest amortization.

CP10-9 (Supplement C) Recording Bond Issuance and Interest Payments (Simplified Approach to Effective-Interest Amortization)

Complete the requirements of CP10-7, assuming West Company uses the simplified approach shown in chapter supplement C.

CP10-10 (Supplement A) Completing an Amortization Schedule (Straight-Line Amortization)

Asper Corporation issued bonds and received cash in full for the issue price. The bonds were dated and issued on January 1, 2004. The stated interest rate was payable at the end of each year. The bonds mature at the end of four years. The following schedule has been prepared (amounts in thousands):

COACH'S CORNER

The switch in amortization from $25 to $26 in 2007 is caused by rounding.

Date	Cash	Interest	Amortization	Balance
January 1, 2004				$6,101
End of year 2004	$450	$425	$25	?
End of year 2005	450	?	25	6,051
End of year 2006	450	?	25	6,026
End of year 2007	450	424	26	6,000

Required:

1. Complete the amortization schedule.
2. What was the maturity amount of the bonds?
3. How much cash was received at date of issuance (sale) of the bonds?
4. Was there a premium or a discount? If so, which and how much was it?
5. How much cash will be paid for interest each period and in total for the full life of the bond issue?
6. What is the stated interest rate?
7. What is the market interest rate?
8. What amount of interest expense should be reported on the income statement each year?
9. Show how the bonds should be reported on the balance sheet at the end of 2005 and 2006.

CP10-11 (Supplements B or C) Completing an Amortization Schedule (Effective-Interest Amortization or Simplified Approach)

Berkley Corporation issued bonds and received cash in full for the issue price. The bonds were dated and issued on January 1, 2004. The stated interest rate was payable at the end of each year. The bonds mature at the end of four years. The following schedule has been completed (amounts in thousands):

Date	Cash	Interest	Amortization	Balance
January 1, 2004				$6,101
End of year 2004	$450	$427	$23	6,078
End of year 2005	450	426	24	6,054
End of year 2006	450	?	?	?
End of year 2007	450	?	28	6,000

COACH'S CORNER

The stated interest rate can be calculated by comparing the cash payment to the face value of the bond (which is the balance paid at maturity).

Required:

1. Complete the amortization schedule.
2. What was the maturity amount of the bonds?
3. How much cash was received at date of issuance (sale) of the bonds?
4. Was there a premium or a discount? If so, which and how much was it?
5. How much cash will be paid for interest each period and in total for the full life of the bond issue?
6. What is the stated interest rate?
7. What is the market interest rate?
8. What amount of interest expense should be reported on the income statement each year?
9. Show how the bonds should be reported on the balance sheet at the end of 2004 and 2005.

GROUP A PROBLEMS Available with McGraw-Hill's Homework Manager

LO2, LO4

PA10-1 Recording and Reporting Current Liabilities with Evaluation of Effects on the Current Ratio

Rocko Hammer Company completed the following transactions during 2005. The annual accounting period ends December 31, 2005.

Apr.	30	Received $550,000 from Commerce Bank after signing a 12-month, 6 percent interest-bearing note payable.
June	6	Purchased merchandise on account at a cost of $75,820.
July	15	Paid for the June 6 purchase.
Aug.	31	Signed contract to provide security service to a small apartment complex and collected six months' fees in advance amounting to $12,000. (Use an account called unearned service revenue.)
Dec.	31	Determined salary and wages of $85,000 earned but not yet paid December 31 (ignore payroll taxes).

Required:

1. Prepare journal entries for each of these transactions.
2. Prepare all adjusting entries required on December 31, 2005.
3. Show how all of the liabilities arising from these transactions are reported on the balance sheet at December 31, 2005.
4. For each transaction, state whether the current ratio is increased, decreased, or remains the same. (Assume Rocko Hammer's current assets have always been greater than its current liabilities.)

PA10-2 Determining Financial Effects of Transactions Affecting Current Liabilities with Evaluation of Effects on the Current Ratio

LO2, LO4

Using data from PA10-1, complete the following requirements.

Required:

1. For each transaction (including adjusting entries) listed in PA10-1, indicate the accounts, amounts, and effects (+ for increase, − for decrease, and NE for no effect) on the accounting equation, using the following schedule:

Date	Assets	=	Liabilities	+	Stockholders' Equity

2. For each transaction, state whether the current ratio is increased, decreased, or there is no change. (Assume Rocko Hammer's current assets have always been greater than its current liabilities.)

PA10-3 Recording and Reporting Current Liabilities

LO2

During 2006, Lakeside Company completed the following two transactions. The annual accounting period ends December 31.

a. Paid and recorded wages of $80,000 during 2006; however, at the end of December 2006, three days' wages are unpaid and unrecorded because the weekly payroll will not be paid until January 6, 2007. Wages for the three days total $1,600.

b. Collected rent revenue of $3,600 on December 10, 2006, for office space that Lakeside rented to another business. The rent collected was for 30 days from December 11, 2006, to January 10, 2007, and was credited in full to Rent Revenue.

Required:

1. Give the adjusting entry required on December 31, 2006, for unpaid wages from December 2006.
2. Give (*a*) the journal entry for the collection of rent on December 10, 2006, and (*b*) the adjusting journal entry on December 31, 2006.
3. Show how any liabilities related to these transactions should be reported on the company's balance sheet at December 31, 2006.
4. Explain why the accrual basis of accounting provides more relevant information to financial analysts than the cash basis.

PA10-4 Comparing Bonds Issued at Par, Discount, and Premium

LO3

Allfer One Corporation, whose annual accounting period ends on December 31, issued the following bonds:

Date of bonds: January 1, 2006.

Maturity amount and date: $100,000 due in 10 years (December 31, 2015).

Interest: 10 percent per year payable each December 31.

Date sold: January 1, 2006.

Required:

1. Provide the following amounts to be reported on the January 1, 2006 financial statements immediately after the bonds were issued:

	Case A (issued at 100)	Case B (at 97)	Case C (at 101)
a. Bonds payable	$	$	$
b. Unamortized premium or discount			
c. Bonds payable, net			

2. Assume that you are an investment adviser and a retired person has written to you asking, "Why should I buy a bond at a premium when I can find one at a discount? Isn't that stupid? It's like paying list price for a car instead of negotiating a discount." Write a brief message in response to the question.

LO3

PA10-5 Comparing Carrying Value and Market Value and Recording Early Retirement of Debt

Quaker Oats is a well-known name at most breakfast tables. Before it was acquired by PepsiCo, Quaker Oats reported the following information about its long-term debt in its annual report:

Long-Term Debt

The fair value of long-term debt was $779.7 million at the end of the current fiscal year, which was based on market prices for the same or similar issues or on the current rates offered to the Company for similar debt of the same maturities. The carrying value of long-term debt as of the same date was $759.5 million.

Required:

1. Explain what is meant by "fair value." Explain why there is a difference between the carrying value and the fair value of the long-term debt for Quaker Oats.

2. Assume that Quaker Oats retired all of its long-term debt early (a very unlikely event) by buying the bonds in the bond market. This required a cash payment equal to the current market value. Prepare the journal entry to record the transaction.

LO5

PA10-6 Determining Financial Statement Reporting of Contingent Liabilities

Macromedia, Inc., is the maker of shockwave and flash technologies. Its 2002 annual report indicated that a lawsuit had been filed in 2000 against the company and five of its former officers for securities fraud in connection with allegedly making false or misleading statements about its financial results. The lawsuit was settled on January 9, 2002, as described in the following note:

Legal

The settlement amount was $48.0 million, of which approximately $19.5 million was paid by insurance. As a result, the Company recorded a $28.5 million charge as a component of other income (expense) in its consolidated statements of operations during fiscal year 2002.

Required:

Explain why Macromedia didn't record a contingent liability in 2000 when the lawsuit was filed.

GROUP B PROBLEMS

LO2, LO4

PB10-1 Recording and Reporting Current Liabilities with Evaluation of Effects on the Current Ratio

Little Rock Company completed the following transactions during 2005. The annual accounting period ends December 31, 2005.

Jan. 3 Purchased merchandise on account at a cost of $23,660. (Assume a perpetual inventory system.)

27 Paid for the January 3 purchase.

Apr. 1   Received $80,000 from Atlantic Bank after signing a 12-month, 8 percent interest-bearing note payable.

June 13   Purchased merchandise on account at a cost of $7,910.

July 25   Paid for the June 13 purchase.

Aug. 1   Rented out a small office in a building owned by Little Rock Company and collected eight months' rent in advance amounting to $8,000. (Use an account called unearned rent revenue.)

Dec. 31   Determined wages of $12,000 were earned but not yet paid on December 31 (ignore payroll taxes).

Required:

1. Prepare journal entries for each of the items listed above.
2. Prepare any adjusting entries required on December 31, 2005.
3. Show how all of the liabilities arising from these transactions are reported on the balance sheet at December 31, 2005.
4. For each transaction (including adjusting entries), state whether the current ratio is increased, decreased, or remains the same. (Assume Little Rock Company's current assets have always been greater than its current liabilities.)

PB10-2 Determining Financial Effects of Transactions Affecting Current Liabilities with Evaluation of Effects on the Current Ratio

LO2, LO4

Using data from PB10-1, complete the following requirements.

Required:

1. For each transaction (including adjusting entries) listed in PB10-1, indicate the accounts, amounts, and effects (+ for increase, − for decrease, and NE for no effect) on the accounting equation, using the following schedule:

Date	Assets	=	Liabilities	+	Stockholders' Equity

2. For each transaction (including adjusting entries), state whether the current ratio is increased, decreased, or there is no change. (Assume Little Rock Company's current assets have always been greater than its current liabilities.)

PB10-3 Recording and Reporting Current Liabilities

LO2

During 2006, Colorade Company completed the following two transactions. The annual accounting period ends December 31.

a. Paid and recorded wages of $240,000 during 2006; however, at the end of December 2006, two days' wages are unpaid and unrecorded because the weekly payroll will not be paid until January 5, 2007. Wages for the two days total $2,000.

b. Collected rent revenue of $1,500 on December 10, 2006, for office space that Colorade rented to another business. The rent collected was for 30 days from December 11, 2006, to January 10, 2007, and was credited in full to Rent Revenue.

Required:

1. Give the adjusting entry required on December 31, 2006, for unpaid wages from December 2006.
2. Give (a) the journal entry for the collection of rent on December 10, 2006, and (b) the adjusting journal entry on December 31, 2006.
3. Show how any liabilities related to these transactions should be reported on the company's balance sheet at December 31, 2006.
4. Explain why the accrual basis of accounting provides more relevant information to financial analysts than the cash basis.

PB10-4 Completing Schedule Comparing Bonds Issued at Par, Discount, and Premium

LO3

Quartz Corporation sold a $500,000, 7 percent bond issue on January 1, 2006. The bonds pay interest each December 31 and mature 10 years from January 1, 2006.

Required:

1. Provide the following amounts to be reported on the January 1, 2006, financial statements immediately after the bonds were issued:

	Case A (issued at 100)	Case B (at 98)	Case C (at 102)
a. Bonds payable	$	$	$
b. Unamortized premium or discount			
c. Bonds payable, net			

2. Assume that you are an investment adviser and a retired person has written to you asking, "Why should I buy a bond at a premium when I can find one at a discount? Isn't that stupid? It's like paying list price for a car instead of negotiating a discount." Write a brief message in response to the question.

LO3 **PB10-5 Understanding the Early Retirement of Debt**

AMC Entertainment, Inc., owns and operates 239 movie theaters worldwide, with 3,120 screens in 28 states. On August 12, 1992, the company sold 11 7/8 percent bonds in the amount of $52,720,000 and used the $52,720,000 cash proceeds to retire bonds with a coupon rate of 13.6 percent. At that time, the 13.6 percent bonds had a book value of $50,000,000.

Required:

1. Prepare the journal entries to record the issuance of the new bonds and the early retirement of the old bonds.
2. How should AMC report any gain or loss on this transaction?
3. Why might the company have issued new bonds to retire the old bonds?

CASES & DISCUSSION STARTERS

FINANCIAL REPORTING AND ANALYSIS CASES

LO4 **C&DS10-1 Finding Financial Information**

Refer to the financial statements of Landry's Restaurants in Appendix A at the end of this book, or download the annual report from the *Cases* section of the text's Web site at www.mhhe.com/phillips.

1. Calculate the company's current ratio at the most recent year end. Does this ratio cause you any concern about the company's ability to pay its current liabilities? As part of your answer, consider the financing that is available under the existing credit facilities (discussed in the third paragraph of Note 5).
2. Calculate the company's times interest earned ratio for the most recent year. Does this ratio cause you any concern about the company's ability to meet future interest obligations as they become payable?

LO4 **C&DS10-2 Comparing Financial Information**

Refer to the financial statements of Dave & Buster's in Appendix B at the end of this book, or download the annual report from the *Cases* section of the text's Web site at www.mhhe.com/phillips.

1. Calculate the company's current ratio at the most recent year end. Does this ratio cause you any concern about the company's ability to pay its current liabilities? As part of your answer, consider the financing that is available under the revolving credit facility (discussed in the second paragraph of Note 4). Based on your analyses of the current ratio and financing available on a line of credit (also called "letters of credit"), does Landry's or Dave & Buster's appear to be better able to pay its current liabilities?
2. Calculate the company's times interest earned ratio for the most recent year. Does it appear that Landry's or Dave & Buster's will be better able to meet future interest obligations as they become payable?

C&DS10-3 Internet-Based Team Research: Examining an Annual Report

As a team, select an industry to analyze. Using your Web browser, each team member should acquire the annual report or 10-K for one publicly traded company in the industry, with each member selecting a different company. (See C&DS1-3 in Chapter 1 for a description of possible resources for these tasks.)

Required:

1. On an individual basis, each team member should write a short report that incorporates the following:
   a. What are the most significant types of current liabilities owed by the company?
   b. Read the company's financial statement note regarding long-term debt and commitments and contingencies. Does the company have any significant amounts coming due in the next five years?
   c. Compute and analyze the current ratio and times interest earned ratio.
2. Then, as a team, write a short report comparing and contrasting your companies using these attributes. Discuss any patterns across the companies that you as a team observe. Provide potential explanations for any differences discovered.

ETHICS AND CRITICAL THINKING CASES

C&DS10-4 Ethical Decision Making: A Real-Life Example

Many retired people invest a significant portion of their money in bonds of corporations because of their relatively low level of risk. During the 1980s, significant inflation caused some interest rates to rise to as high as 15 percent. Retired people who bought bonds that paid only 6 percent continued to earn at the lower rate. During the 1990s, inflation subsided and interest rates declined. Many corporations took advantage of the callability feature of these bonds and retired the bonds early. Many of these early retirements of high interest rate bonds were replaced with low interest rate bonds.

Required:

In your judgment, is it ethical for corporations to continue paying low interest rates when rates increase but to call bonds when rates decrease? Why or why not?

C&DS10-5 Ethical Decision Making: A Mini-Case

Assume that you are a portfolio manager for a large insurance company. The majority of the money you manage is from retired school teachers who depend on the income you earn on their investments. You have invested a significant amount of money in the bonds of a large corporation and have just received a call from the company's president explaining that it is unable to meet its current interest obligations because of deteriorating business operations related to increased international competition. The president has a recovery plan that will take at least two years. During that time, the company will not be able to pay interest on the bonds and, she admits, if the plan does not work, bondholders will probably lose more than half of their money. As a creditor, you can force the company into immediate bankruptcy and probably get back at least 90 percent of the bondholders' money. You also know that your decision will cause at least 10,000 people to lose their jobs if the company ceases operations.

Required:

Given only these two options, what should you do? Consider who would be helped or harmed by the two options.

C&DS10-6 Critical Thinking: Evaluating Lease Alternatives

As the new vice president for consumer products at Acme Manufacturing, you are attending a meeting to discuss a serious problem associated with delivering merchandise to customers. Bob Smith, director of logistics, summarized the problem: "It's easy to understand, we just don't have enough delivery trucks given our recent growth." Barb Bader, from the accounting department responded: "Maybe it's easy to understand but it's impossible to do anything. Because of Wall Street's concern about the amount of debt on our balance sheet, we're under a freeze and cannot borrow money to acquire new assets. There's nothing we can do."

On the way back to your office after the meeting, your assistant offers a suggestion: "Why don't we just lease the trucks we need? That way we can get the assets we want without having to record a liability on the balance sheet."

Required:

How would you respond to this suggestion?

chapter eleven

Reporting and Interpreting Stockholders' Equity

11

Suppose you buy a DVD containing all the episodes of your favorite TV show from last season. Are you likely to watch one episode every few days, or will you save the DVD until you have free time for all of it? If you start into it now, you'll get some immediate enjoyment. But if you save it until you have an entire weekend free, it might be more fun, because then you'll be able to become totally engrossed in it. It's really a question of how you want to balance smaller immediate rewards with potentially greater long-term returns.

As an investor, you'll face a similar question. Do you want an immediate return on your stock (through dividends), or do you seek long-term returns (through higher stock prices)? Similarly, the directors at **ROSS STORES** have to decide whether the company should pay dividends to stockholders or reinvest those funds in the company. By paying dividends in the current period, the company provides an immediate return on stockholders' investments, but by reinvesting its funds, Ross can potentially create even greater long-run returns for stockholders. Again, it's a question of balancing immediate and long-term returns. This chapter focuses on issues like these, which involve stockholders' equity.

INSIDE LOOKING OUT

OUTSIDE LOOKING IN

This chapter focuses on reporting and interpreting the stockholders' equity of Ross Stores, a discount clothing company that prefers to call itself an "off-price" retailer.

Ross Stores, Inc. has over 560 stores in 25 states.

o make your shopping experience more efficient, stores like Ross assign names to their various departments. We've done the same thing for the main sections of this chapter. Take a moment to read Exhibit 11.1 to see what you'll be learning about. It'll make your reading more efficient.

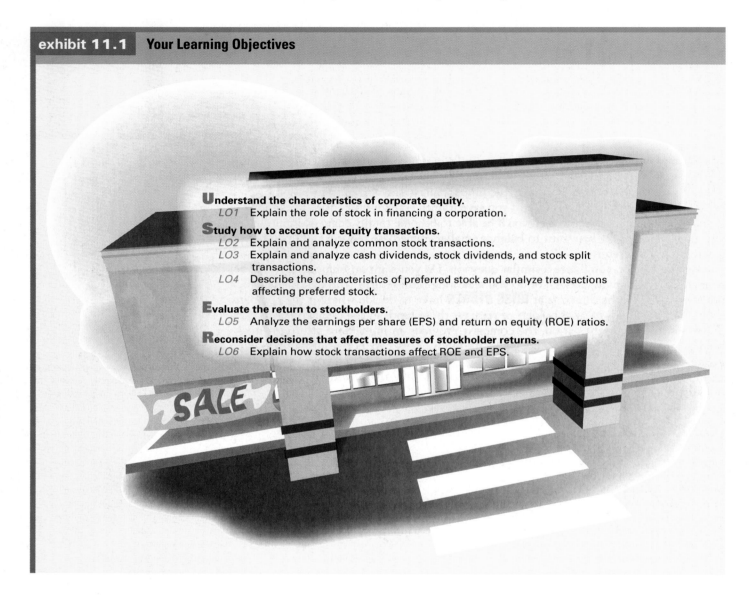

exhibit **11.1**	**Your Learning Objectives**

Understand the characteristics of corporate equity.
　　LO1　Explain the role of stock in financing a corporation.

Study how to account for equity transactions.
　　LO2　Explain and analyze common stock transactions.
　　LO3　Explain and analyze cash dividends, stock dividends, and stock split transactions.
　　LO4　Describe the characteristics of preferred stock and analyze transactions affecting preferred stock.

Evaluate the return to stockholders.
　　LO5　Analyze the earnings per share (EPS) and return on equity (ROE) ratios.

Reconsider decisions that affect measures of stockholder returns.
　　LO6　Explain how stock transactions affect ROE and EPS.

UNDERSTAND

THE CHARACTERISTICS OF CORPORATE EQUITY

Understanding Corporations

FAST FLASHBACK

A *corporation* is a business organized as a separate legal entity. An unincorporated business owned by one person is a sole proprietorship. An unincorporated business owned by more than one person is a partnership.

Some people think that every company's stock is publicly traded on a stock exchange. As you learned in Chapter 1, this isn't so. Many private corporations are able to obtain adequate financing from private owners (as equity) and banks (as debt). Another misconception is that the words *corporation* and *business* mean the same thing. This is understandable because corporations account for most business transactions. If you were to write the names of 50 familiar businesses on a piece of paper, probably all of them would be corporations, except perhaps for rare Cedar Fair, which actually is a partnership.

What makes the corporate form so popular? Corporations have one critical advantage over sole proprietorships and partnerships: They can raise large amounts of money because both large and small investors can easily participate in a corporation's ownership. This ease of participation is related to several factors.

- **Shares of stock can be purchased in small amounts.** According to finance. yahoo.com, as of May 18, 2004, you could have become one of Ross Stores' owners by buying a single share of the company's stock for just $25.

- **Ownership interests are transferable.** The shares of public companies are regularly bought and sold on established markets such as the New York Stock Exchange. So if you decide to sell your shares in Ross, or buy more, it's quick and easy to do. Ross is traded on the Nasdaq under the ticker symbol ROST.

- **Stockholders are not liable for the corporation's debts.** Creditors have no legal claim on the personal assets of stockholders like they do on the personal assets belonging to owners of sole proprietorships and partnerships. So if you owned stock in the old Montgomery Ward department store, which went bankrupt and was liquidated in 2000, you would lose what you paid to buy the stock, but you wouldn't have to pay the hundreds of millions that the company owed but couldn't pay.

About half of Americans own stock, either directly or indirectly through a mutual fund or pension program. Stock ownership offers them the opportunity to earn higher returns than the interest paid on bank accounts. Because stock ownership in corporations is so prevalent today, this chapter focuses on *corporate* equity. Chapter supplement A discusses accounting for equity in proprietorships, partnerships, and other business forms.

Exhibit 11.2 presents the stockholders' equity of Ross Stores at January 31, 2004. Unlike earlier chapters, where we used *Contributed Capital*, Ross uses *Common Stock* and *Additional Paid-In Capital*. This change in presentation is typical for most companies, for reasons that we discuss later in the chapter. Don't let this slight change concern you because these two accounts (Common Stock and Additional Paid-In Capital) together still represent the amount of money that stockholders have contributed by purchasing stock from the company. Also in Exhibit 11.2, you can see the amount that the company itself has contributed through its profit-making activities. That is, the *Retained Earnings* account reports the cumulative amount of net income earned less the cumulative amount of dividends declared since the corporation was first organized.

POINT OF INTEREST

Nasdaq used to stand for the National Association of Securities Dealers Automated Quotations. Today, it is the name of the company that operates the world's largest electronic, screen-based equity securities (stock) market.

exhibit 11.2	Excerpt from the Consolidated Balance Sheets of Ross Stores, Inc.

ROSS STORES, INC.
Partial Balance Sheets
(in thousands)

	January 31, 2004	February 1, 2003
Stockholders' Equity		
Common Stock, Par Value $0.01 Per Share		
Authorized 300,000,000 Shares		
Issued and Outstanding Shares 151,208,000 in 2004 and 154,982,000 in 2003	$ 1,512	$ 1,550
Additional Paid-In Capital	383,629	340,266
Retained Earnings	370,278	301,372
Total Stockholders' Equity	755,419	643,188

Ownership of a Corporation

The law recognizes a corporation as a separate legal entity. It may own assets, incur liabilities, expand and contract in size, sue others, be sued, and enter into contracts independently of its stockholder owners. A corporation exists separate and apart from its owners, which means it doesn't die when its owners die. Thomas Edison died in 1931, but his company continues in existence today.

To protect everyone's rights, the creation and oversight of corporations are tightly regulated by law. Corporations are created by submitting an application to a state government (not the federal government). On approval of the application, the state issues a charter, sometimes called the articles of incorporation.

Each state has different laws governing the organization of corporations created within its boundaries. Though the original Ross Stores company was incorporated in California in 1957, it elected to reincorporate in 1989 in the state of Delaware. More than half of the largest corporations in America are incorporated in Delaware. The reason is simple. Delaware has some of the most favorable laws for establishing corporations.

Benefits of Stock Ownership

When you invest in a corporation, you are known as a stockholder or shareholder. As a stockholder, you receive shares of stock that you later can sell. Owners of common stock receive a number of benefits:

- *Voting.* For each share you own, you get one vote on major issues such as who will serve on the board of directors and which accounting firm will be appointed as external auditors.
- *Dividends.* You receive a share of the profits when distributed as dividends.
- *Residual claim.* Should the company cease operations, creditors would be paid and you would share in any remaining assets.

As a stockholder, you have the ultimate authority in a corporation. You're the boss. As shown in Exhibit 11.3, the board of directors and, indirectly, all the employees are accountable to the stockholders. The organizational structure shown is typical of most corporations, but the specific structure depends on the nature of the company's business.

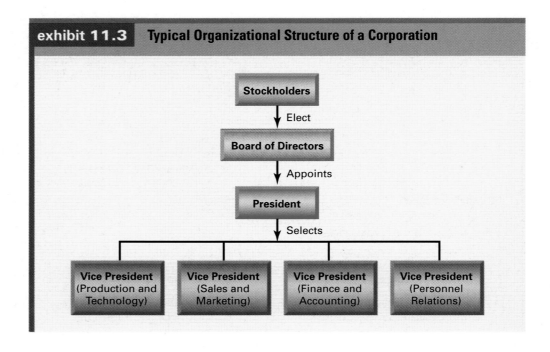

exhibit 11.3 **Typical Organizational Structure of a Corporation**

Authorized, Issued, and Outstanding Shares

Okay, so as a stockholder in Ross, you can be the company's ultimate authority—well, you and a whole bunch of other investors. To be the ultimate authority, you need to own a lot of shares. The financial statements report information concerning the maximum number of shares that can be sold and the number that have been sold to date. Let's look back at the share information reported by Ross as of January 31, 2004, shown in Exhibit 11.2 on page 473. For Ross, the maximum number of shares that can be sold, called the **authorized** number of shares, is 300,000,000. As of January 31, 2004, the company had distributed 151,208,000 shares of stock. These are called **issued shares.**

For a number of reasons, a company might want to buy back stock that has already been sold to the public. After buying back its stock, the company can hold onto it or cancel it. If the company holds onto its own shares of stock, these shares are called **treasury stock,** and they don't have voting, dividend, or other stockholder rights. Because a company can't own or invest in itself, treasury stock reduces the number of shares that are considered **outstanding** with investors. If the company cancels this stock later, it is removed from treasury stock, and from the number of shares considered issued. The relationship between authorized, issued, and outstanding stock is shown in Exhibit 11.4.

Notice in Exhibit 11.2 on page 473 that the number of issued shares was equal to the number outstanding in 2004 (at 151,208,000). This information implies that Ross held no shares as treasury stock at the balance sheet date.

YOU SHOULD KNOW

The **authorized** number of shares is the maximum number of shares of capital stock of a corporation that can be issued, as specified in the charter. **Issued shares** represent the total number of shares of stock that have been sold. **Treasury stock** consists of issued shares that have been bought back by the company. **Outstanding shares** consist of issued shares that are currently held by stockholders other than the corporation itself.

┌STUDY────────

HOW TO ACCOUNT FOR EQUITY TRANSACTIONS

Common Stock Transactions

All corporations are required to issue **common stock** when they are first incorporated. Common stock indicates which investors should be thought of as the ultimate owners of a corporation because common stockholders have the right to vote on important decisions of the corporation and to share in its profitability. This sharing of the company's profits is done through dividends, which are determined by the stockholders' representatives—the board of directors of the corporation. Corporations also have the option to

YOU SHOULD KNOW

Common stock is the basic voting stock issued by a corporation to stockholders.

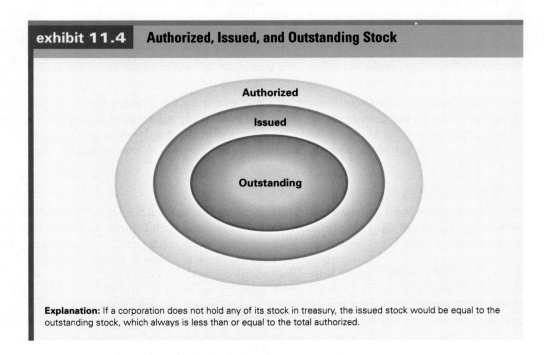

| exhibit 11.4 | Authorized, Issued, and Outstanding Stock |

Authorized

Issued

Outstanding

Explanation: If a corporation does not hold any of its stock in treasury, the issued stock would be equal to the outstanding stock, which always is less than or equal to the total authorized.

issue other types of stock, which we discuss later in this chapter, but for now let's focus on common stock.

Common stock normally has a **par value,** which is a nominal value per share established in the corporate charter. Par value is a token amount and has no relationship to the market value of a stock. Ross's balance sheet, in Exhibit 11.2, states that its common stock has a par value of $0.01, yet its market value (at the time of writing) is over $25 per share. For legal reasons, most states require stock to have a par value, but there are some that allow the issuance of **no-par value stock.** No-par value stock does not have a specified legal value per share.

Issuance of Stock

Two names are used for transactions involving the initial sale of a company's stock to the public. An *initial public offering,* or IPO, involves the very first sale of a company's stock to the public. This is what most people are referring to when they say a private company is "going public." After a company's stock has been traded on established markets, additional issuances of new stock by the company are called *seasoned new issues.* Whether stock is issued as part of an IPO or as a seasoned new issue, a company accounts for it in the same way. Note that a company does not account for the sale of stock from one stockholder to another because these transactions involve only the owners of the company and not the corporation itself. It's like an auto dealer who records the initial sale of a car to a customer, but doesn't later record another sale when the customer sells the car to someone else.

Most sales of stock to the public are cash transactions. To illustrate the accounting for an initial issuance of stock, assume that during the fiscal year ended January 29, 2005, Ross sold 100,000 shares of its $0.01 par value stock for $30 per share. The company would record the following journal entry:

dr **Cash (+A) (100,000 × $30)** 3,000,000		
cr **Common Stock (+SE)**		
(100,000 × $0.01).		1,000
cr **Additional Paid-In Capital (+SE)**		
($3,000,000 − 1,000)		2,999,000

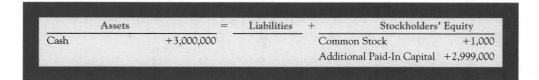

	Assets	=	Liabilities	+	Stockholders' Equity	
Cash	+3,000,000				Common Stock	+1,000
					Additional Paid-In Capital	+2,999,000

Notice that the common stock account is credited for the number of shares sold times the par value per share, and the additional paid-in capital account is credited for cash received in excess of this amount. If the corporate charter does not specify a par value for the stock, the total proceeds from the sale of stock will be entered in the common stock account.

Repurchase of Stock

A corporation may want to repurchase its stock from existing stockholders for a number of reasons: (1) to send a signal to investors that the company itself believes its own stock is worth purchasing, (2) to obtain shares that can be reissued as payment for purchases of other companies, and (3) to obtain shares to reissue to employees as part of employee stock plans that provide workers with shares of the company's stock as part of their pay. Because of Securities and Exchange Commission regulations concerning newly issued shares, it is generally less costly for companies to give employees repurchased shares than to issue new ones.

Most companies record the purchase of treasury stock based on the cost of the shares that were purchased. This approach is called the cost method. Assume that, on February

1, 2004, Ross bought 50,000 shares of its stock in the market when it was selling for $25 per share. Using the cost method, the company would record the following journal entry:

> dr   **Treasury Stock (+xSE, −SE) (50,000 × $25) . 1,250,000**
>   cr   **Cash (−A) . . . .**   **1,250,000**

	Assets	=	Liabilities	+	Stockholders' Equity	
Cash	−1,250,000				Treasury Stock (+xSE)	−1,250,000

Notice that *Treasury Stock* is not an asset. It is actually a contra-equity account, which means that it is subtracted from total stockholders' equity. This practice makes sense because treasury stock is stock that is not outstanding and therefore should not be included in total stockholders' equity. This treasury stock would be reported in the balance sheet as shown in Exhibit 11.5.

exhibit 11.5	**Reporting Treasury Stock on the Balance Sheet**

ROSS STORES, INC.
Partial Balance Sheets (modified)
(in thousands)

	February 1, 2004	January 31, 2004
Stockholders' Equity:		
Preferred Stock, 4,000,000 Authorized; None Issued	—	—
Common Stock, $0.01 Par Value, 300,000,000 Authorized; 151,208,000 Issued	1,512	1,512
Additional Paid-In Capital	383,629	383,629
Retained Earnings	370,278	370,278
	755,419	755,419
Less: Treasury Stock, at Cost (50,000 Shares)	1,250	—
Total Stockholders' Equity	754,169	755,419

HOW'S IT GOING? A Self-Study Quiz

1. Using the information in Exhibit 11.5, calculate the number of shares of common stock that was outstanding with investors as of February 1, 2004.

2. Work backward from the treasury stock information in Exhibit 11.5 to calculate the average cost per share of stock repurchased by the company.

3. Assume that Ross issued 10,000 shares of its common stock, par value $0.01, for $250,000 cash. Prepare the journal entry to record this transaction.

4. Assume that Ross repurchased 5,000 of its common shares in the stock market when it was selling for $20 per share. Record this transaction at its cost.

After you're done, check your answers with the solutions in the margin.

Quiz Answers

1. 151,208,000 − 50,000 = 151,158,000
2. $25 = $1,250,000 / 50,000 shares
3. *dr* Cash (+A)   250,000
    cr Common stock (+SE)   100
       (10,000 × $0.01)
    cr Additional paid-in capital (+SE)   249,900
4. *dr* Treasury stock (+xSE, −SE)   100,000
    cr Cash (−A) ($20 × 5,000)   100,000

Reissuance of Treasury Stock

When a company resells shares of its treasury stock, it does *not* report an accounting profit or loss on the transaction, even if it sells them for more or less than they cost. GAAP do not permit a corporation to report income or losses from investments in its own stock because transactions with the owners are not considered profit-making activities. Extending our previous example where Ross had repurchased its stock for $25 per share, assume now that it resold 5,000 shares of treasury stock for $26 per share. Ross would record the following journal entry:

COACH'S CORNER

Notice that the contra-account *Treasury Stock* is reduced only for the cost of each treasury share. Any amount received for treasury stock in excess of its cost is credited to *Additional Paid-In Capital*, as shown.

dr **Cash** (+A) (5,000 × $26)	130,000	
cr **Treasury Stock** (−xSE, +SE)		
(5,000 × $25)		125,000
cr **Additional Paid-In Capital** (+SE)		
(5,000 × ($26 − 25))		5,000

Assets	=	Liabilities	+	Stockholders' Equity	
Cash +130,000				Treasury Stock (−xSE)	+125,000
				Additional Paid-In Capital	+5,000

If treasury stock were reissued at a price *below* its repurchase price (say $23), the difference between the repurchase price ($25 per share) and the reissue price ($23 per share) is recorded as a reduction in *Additional Paid-In Capital*, as shown here:

dr **Cash** (+A) (5,000 × $23)	115,000	
dr **Additional Paid-In Capital** (−SE)		
[5,000 × ($25 − 23)].............	10,000	
cr **Treasury Stock** (−xSE, +SE)		
(5,000 × $25)		125,000

Assets	=	Liabilities	+	Stockholders' Equity	
Cash +115,000				Treasury Stock (−xSE)	+125,000
				Additional Paid-In Capital	−10,000

Statement of Stockholders' Equity

As you have seen, lots of different transactions affect the stockholders' equity accounts. To help users understand all the stockholders' equity transactions that occur during a period, companies often will replace the statement of retained earnings (shown earlier in this text) with a more complete statement of stockholders' equity. This statement summarizes the changes in not only *Retained Earnings* but also all other stockholders' equity accounts. Exhibit 11.6 shows what this statement would look like for Ross, given the following assumptions: (1) 50,000 shares of common stock were repurchased into treasury at $25 per share, (2) 5,000 shares of treasury stock were later issued at $26 per share, (3) 100,000 shares of $0.01 par value common stock were issued for $30 per share, (4) net income of $200 million was earned, and (5) dividends of $15 million were declared. Take two minutes right now to match these five transactions to the statement of stockholders' equity (in Exhibit 11.6) and to relate the first three line-items in the statement to the journal entries presented earlier in this section.

exhibit 11.6	Statement of Stockholders' Equity (amounts in thousands of dollars)				
	Common Stock	Additional Paid-In Capital	Retained Earnings	Treasury Stock	Total
Balance at January 31, 2004	$1,512	$383,629	$370,278	$ —	$755,419
Common Stock Purchased into Treasury				(1,250)	(1,250)
Treasury Stock Issued		5		125	130
Common Stock Issued	1	2,999			3,000
Net Income			200,000		200,000
Dividends Declared			(15,000)		(15,000)
Balance at January 29, 2005	$1,513	$386,633	$555,278	($1,125)	$942,299

Dividends on Common Stock

Investors buy common stock because they expect a return on their investment. This return can come in two forms: dividends and increases in stock price. Some investors prefer to buy stocks that pay little or no dividends (called a "growth" investment), because companies that reinvest the majority of their earnings tend to increase their future earnings potential, along with their stock price. Dell Corporation, for example, has never paid a dividend, yet if your parents had bought 100 Dell shares when they were first issued on June 22, 1988, for $850, the investment would be worth over $325,000 at the time this chapter was being written. Rather than wait for growth in stock value, other investors, such as retired people who need a steady income, prefer to receive their return in the form of dividends. These people often seek stocks that consistently pay dividends (called an "income" investment), such as Coca-Cola, which has paid cash dividends each year since 1893 and has increased its dividend 40 times in the last 40 years.[1]

A corporation does not have a legal obligation to pay dividends. It is a decision made by the board of directors, and it is made each time a dividend is to be paid. Once the board of directors formally declares a dividend, a liability is created. An actual press release announcing a dividend declaration for Ross contained the following information:

POINT OF INTEREST

According to the Motley Fool (www.fool.com), if you had purchased one share of Coca-Cola in its first year and used every dividend received to buy more Coke stock, you'd now receive an annual dividend of over $80,000.

Ross Stores Announces Quarterly Dividend

NEWARK, Calif., May 20, 2004—Ross Stores, Inc. (Nasdaq: ROST) announced today that the Company's Board of Directors declared a regular quarterly cash dividend of $.0425 per common share, payable on or about July 1, 2004 to stockholders of record as of June 14, 2004.

Notice that this announcement contains three important dates: (1) the declaration date (May 20), (2) the date of record (June 14), and (3) the date of payment (July 1).

1. **Declaration date—May 20, 2004.** The **declaration date** is the date on which the board of directors officially approves the dividend. As you learned in Chapter 4, as soon as the board makes the declaration, the company records a dividend liability. Assuming 1,000,000 shares are outstanding, the dividend of $42,500 ($0.0425 × 1,000,000) would be recorded as

YOU SHOULD KNOW

The **declaration date** is the date on which the board of directors officially approves a dividend.

---

[1]www2.standardandpoors.com/spf/xls/index/sp500_dividend_aristocrats.xls, retrieved October 31, 2003.

dr	**Dividends Declared (+D, −SE)**.	42,500	
	cr **Dividends Payable (+L)**		42,500

Assets	=	Liabilities	+	Stockholders' Equity
		Dividends Payable +42,500		Dividends Declared (+D) −42,500

2. **Date of record—June 14, 2004.** The **record date** follows the declaration. It is the date on which the corporation prepares the list of current stockholders based on its records. The dividend is payable only to those names listed on the record date. No journal entry is made on this date.

3. **Date of payment—July 1, 2004.** The **payment date** is the date on which the cash is disbursed to pay the dividend liability. It follows the date of record, as described in the dividend announcement. Continuing our example above, when the dividend is paid and the liability satisfied on July 1, the following journal entry is recorded:

dr	**Dividends Payable (−L)**	42,500	
	cr **Cash (−A)**		42,500

Assets	=	Liabilities	+	Stockholders' Equity
Cash −42,500		Dividends Payable −42,500		

Notice that the declaration of a cash dividend increases the temporary account *Dividends Declared*, which will reduce *Retained Earnings* when it is closed at the end of each fiscal year. Also notice that the payment of a cash dividend reduces *Cash* by the same amount. These two observations explain the two fundamental requirements for payment of a cash dividend:

1. *Sufficient retained earnings.* The corporation must have accumulated a sufficient amount of retained earnings to cover the amount of the dividend. State incorporation laws often limit cash dividends to the balance in the *Retained Earnings* account.

2. *Sufficient cash.* The corporation must have sufficient cash to pay the dividend and meet the operating needs of the business. The cash generated in the past by earnings represented in the *Retained Earnings* account may already have been spent before the dividend was declared. In the case of Ross, this money may have been used to acquire a designer shoe inventory, buy more clothing racks, or pay for the unfortunate lime green pants that were ordered last season. So the mere fact that the *Retained Earnings* account has a large credit balance does not mean that there is sufficient cash to pay a dividend. Remember, retained earnings is not cash.

HOW'S IT GOING?   **A Self-Study Quiz**

Answer the following questions concerning dividends:

1. On which dividend date is a liability created?

2. A cash outflow occurs on which dividend date?

3. What are the two fundamental requirements for the payment of a dividend?

After you're done, check your answers with the solutions in the margin.

Stock Dividends and Stock Splits

Stock Dividends

The term *dividend,* when used alone with no adjectives, implies a cash dividend. However, there are some dividends that are not paid with cash, but instead involve payment with additional shares of stock. These dividends, called **stock dividends,** are distributions of additional shares of a corporation's stock to its stockholders on a pro rata basis at no cost to the stockholder. The phrase "pro rata basis" means that each stockholder receives additional shares equal to the percentage of shares held. A stockholder with 10 percent of the outstanding shares would receive 10 percent of any additional shares issued as a stock dividend.

The value of a stock dividend is the subject of much debate. In reality, a stock dividend by itself has no economic value. All stockholders receive a pro rata distribution of shares, which means that each stockholder owns exactly the same proportion of the company as before. If you get change for a dollar, you do not have more wealth because you hold four quarters instead of only one dollar. Similarly, if you own 10 percent of a company, you are not wealthier simply because the company declares a stock dividend, fires up a laser printer, and gives you (and all other stockholders) more shares of stock.

So **why do corporations issue stock dividends?** Academics and financial executives offer two main reasons: (1) It reminds stockholders of their accumulating wealth in the company, and (2) It reduces the market price per share of stock. Let's look at both of these reasons in a little more depth, not only to help you become a smarter financial manager but also to explain how to account for stock dividends. As you will see below, the method of accounting depends on the reason that a stock dividend was issued.

1. Remind Stockholders.   As you read earlier in this chapter, some companies don't pay cash dividends to stockholders, either because they prefer to use it to fund operating and investing activities or they simply don't have the cash available to pay out. In either event, a stock dividend can be declared to remind stockholders that although they might not receive a cash dividend for the current year, the company is still thinking of them and is simply retaining their wealth in the corporation. When this is the primary reason behind a stock dividend, the stock dividend typically is small (less than 20–25 percent of the outstanding stock). The accounting for a "small stock dividend" like this involves recording a journal entry to indicate that new stock has been issued at the current market price and a dividend has been declared. For example, the following journal entry would be recorded if Ross had 1,000,000 shares of $0.01 par value common stock outstanding and issued a 5 percent stock dividend when the stock price was $20 per share:

dr	**Retained Earnings (−SE)**	
	($20 × 1,000,000 × 5% dividend) 1,000,000	
cr	**Common Stock (+SE)**	
	($0.01 × 1,000,000 × 5% dividend)	500
cr	**Additional Paid-In Capital (+SE)**	999,500

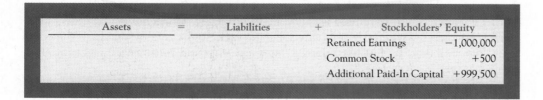

Assets	=	Liabilities	+	Stockholders' Equity	
				Retained Earnings	−1,000,000
				Common Stock	+500
				Additional Paid-In Capital	+999,500

Notice that this journal entry to record a stock dividend changes some of the stockholders' equity account balances, but it doesn't change total stockholders' equity.

2. Reduce Market Price.   Although a rising stock price generally is something that every investor and manager dreams of, the price can become so high that it is no longer attractive to new investors. Many investors prefer to buy stock in round lots, which are multiples of 100 shares. An investor with $10,000 might not buy a stock selling for $150, for instance, because she cannot afford to buy 100 shares. She might buy the stock if the price were less than $100 as the result of a stock dividend. So to reduce the market price per share of stock, a corporation can declare a stock dividend. The stock market reacts immediately when a stock dividend is issued, and the stock price falls proportionally. Theoretically, if the stock price was $60 before a stock dividend and the stock dividend causes the number of shares outstanding to double, the price would fall to $30. Thus, an investor would own 100 shares worth $6,000 before the stock dividend (100 × $60) and 200 shares worth $6,000 after the stock dividend (200 × $30).

Rather than issue a series of small stock dividends to gradually reduce the per-share stock price, most corporations will issue a big honkin' stock dividend of 100 percent or more. Because these "large stock dividends" have such a significant effect on stock price, they aren't accounted for at the current market price (like a "small stock dividend") but instead are recorded at par value. In the last decade, Ross has issued three 100 percent stock dividends, in March 1997, September 1999, and December 2003. If we assume that Ross issues yet another 100 percent stock dividend this year, consisting of 1,000,000 shares ($0.01 par value), the company would make the following journal entry:

dr	**Retained Earnings (−SE)**	
	($0.01 × 1,000,000)	**10,000**
cr	**Common Stock (+SE)**	**10,000**

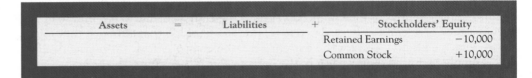

Assets	=	Liabilities	+	Stockholders' Equity	
				Retained Earnings	−10,000
				Common Stock	+10,000

As we noted earlier, the journal entry for a stock dividend moves an amount out of *Retained Earnings* and into other stockholders' equity accounts, but it doesn't change the total stockholders' equity.

Before we leave this section, we must caution you on a potential point of confusion. Most companies refer to the 100 percent stock dividend discussed in this section as a "stock split effected as a stock dividend." Although they *say* stock split, they actually mean a stock dividend as described above. A "true" stock split is different, both in terms of how it is done and how it is accounted for, as we discuss in the following section.

Stock Splits

Stock splits are not dividends. While they are similar to a stock dividend, they are quite different in terms of their impact on the stockholders' equity accounts. In a **stock split,** the total number of authorized shares is increased by a specified amount, such as 2-for-1. In this instance, each share held is called in and two new shares are issued in its place. Cash is not affected when the company splits its stock, so the total resources of the company do not change. It's just like taking a four-piece pizza and cutting each piece into two smaller pieces.

Typically, a stock split involves reducing the par value on each share of all authorized shares, so that the total par value of the shares is unchanged. For instance, if Ross executes a 2-for-1 stock split, it reduces the par value of its stock from $0.01 to $0.005 and doubles the number of shares outstanding. The decrease in par value per share offsets the increase in the number of shares, so that no journal entry is needed.

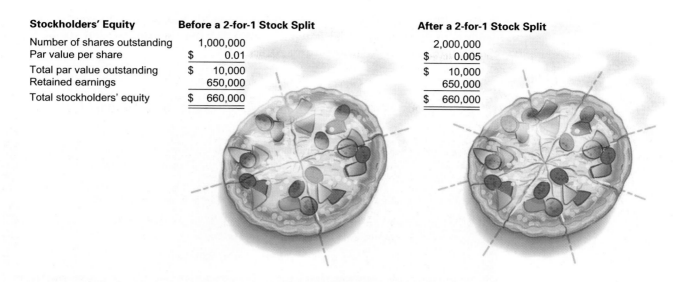

Stockholders' Equity	Before a 2-for-1 Stock Split	After a 2-for-1 Stock Split
Number of shares outstanding	1,000,000	2,000,000
Par value per share	$ 0.01	$ 0.005
Total par value outstanding	$ 10,000	$ 10,000
Retained earnings	650,000	650,000
Total stockholders' equity	$ 660,000	$ 660,000

Exhibit 11.7 reviews the similarities and differences between stock dividends and stock splits. Notice that the way these events are accounted for depends on the reasons for entering into them in the first place.

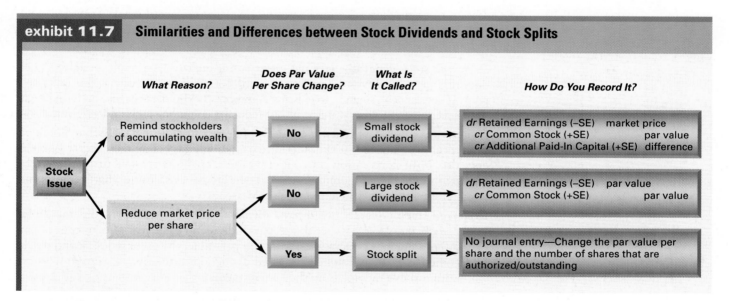

exhibit 11.7   **Similarities and Differences between Stock Dividends and Stock Splits**

If you're like most new financial managers, you probably wonder how a company chooses between a "large" 100 percent stock dividend and a 2-for-1 stock split when the goal of both is to reduce the per-share market price. The answer, it seems, is closely related to how stock dividends and splits are accounted for. As you can see in Exhibit 11.7, a stock dividend causes a reduction in *Retained Earnings*, whereas a "true" stock split doesn't. By itself, this accounting difference might not mean much, but remember that a company needs to have an adequate balance in retained earnings to declare cash dividends in the future. So if you're managing a company that expects some financial struggles in the future, you'll want to use a 2-for-1 stock split because this doesn't reduce retained earnings, which means it doesn't reduce your ability to declare cash dividends in the future. On the other hand, if your company is expecting financial success in the near future, you won't care that retained earnings is reduced by a stock dividend because future earnings will build up retained earnings enough to allow cash dividends to be declared. In fact, you'll probably *want* to use a stock dividend rather than a stock split just to show how confident you are that your company is expecting to do well in the near future. This reasoning suggests that **a third reason that companies declare stock dividends is to signal to financial statement users that the company expects strong financial performance in the near future.**

HOW'S IT GOING?   A Self-Study Quiz

Joey & Chandler's Penny Stores wanted to reduce the market price of its stock, so it issued 100,000 new shares of common stock (par value $10) in a 100 percent stock dividend when the market value was $30 per share.

1. Prepare the journal entry that J&C Penny would use to record this transaction.

2. What journal entry would be required if the transaction instead involved a 2-for-1 stock split? Theoretically, what would be the new stock price after the split?

After you're done, check your answers with the solutions in the margin.

Quiz Answers

1. *dr* Retained earnings (−SE)   1,000,000
   cr Common stock (+SE)   1,000,000

2. No journal entry is required in the case of a stock split. Theoretically, the new price would be one-half of what it was before the split ($30 × 1/2 = $15).

Preferred Stock

In addition to common stock, some corporations issue **preferred stock.** Preferred stock differs from common stock based on a number of rights granted to the stockholders. The most significant differences are:

■ *Preferred stock generally does not grant voting rights.* As a result, preferred stock does not appeal to investors who want some control over the operations of a company. It does appeal, though, to existing common stockholders because preferred stock allows a company to raise funds without reducing common stockholders' control.

■ *Preferred stock is less risky.* Generally, preferred stock is less risky than common stock because preferred stockholders are paid dividends before common stockholders. Also, if the corporation goes out of business, creditors are paid first, followed by preferred stockholders. Common stockholders are paid last, using whatever assets remain after having paid preferred stockholders.

■ *Preferred stock typically has a fixed dividend rate.* For example, "6 percent preferred stock, par value $10 per share" pays a dividend each year of 6 percent of par, or $0.60 per share. If preferred stock has no par value, the preferred dividend would be specified as $0.60 per share. The fixed dividend is attractive to certain investors who want a stable income from their investments.

To illustrate the accounting for an initial issuance of preferred stock, assume that during the fiscal year ended January 31, 2004, Ross issued 100,000 shares of $1 par value preferred stock for $5 per share. The company would record the following journal entry:

dr	Cash (+A) (100,000 × $5)	500,000	
	cr Preferred Stock (+SE) (100,000 × $1) . . .		100,000
	cr Additional Paid-In Capital (+SE)		400,000

Assets		=	Liabilities	+	Stockholders' Equity	
Cash	+500,000				Common Stock	+100,000
					Additional Paid-In Capital	+400,000

Dividends on Preferred Stock

Because investors who purchase preferred stock give up voting rights that are available to investors in common stock, preferred stock offers dividend preferences. The two most common dividend preferences are current and cumulative, both of which are explained below.

Current Dividend Preference.   This preference requires that the current preferred dividend be paid before any dividends are paid to holders of common stock. After the current dividend preference has been met and if no other preference exists, dividends can be paid to the common stockholders.

Let's look at an example, assuming that Ross's 100,000 shares of $1 par preferred stock had a 10 percent dividend rate. This means that preferred stockholders will be paid the first $10,000 of any dividends declared for the year ($10,000 = 100,000 shares outstanding × $1 par × 10% dividend rate). Any additional dividends would go entirely to common stockholders. If the declared dividends were less than this amount, no dividends would be paid to common stockholders and preferred stockholders would not get their full 10 percent dividend that year. The preferred stockholders would lose their rights to this unpaid portion, unless the preferred stock also has what is called a "cumulative dividend preference." Let's see what that means.

Cumulative Dividend Preference.   This preference states that if all or a part of the current dividend is not paid in full, the cumulative unpaid amount, known as **dividends in arrears,** must be paid before any future common dividends can be paid. To illustrate the cumulative dividend preference, let's assume that no dividends were declared by Ross in the year ended January 31, 2004, and that the Ross preferred stock carried a cumulative dividend preference. This means that, as of January 31, 2004, the dividends on Ross's preferred stock were $10,000 in arrears. Let's now assume that Ross declared total dividends of $400,000 during the year ended January 29, 2005. This dividend would be distributed to stockholders as follows:

Dividends Distributed to...

Dividends Declared	Preferred Stockholders	Common Stockholders

$400,000 declared for current year

$10,000 (in arrears)

$10,000 (100,000 × $1 × 10%) (current year)

$380,000 ($400,000 − 10,000 − 10,000)

(Remaining amount)

Because dividends are not an actual liability until the board of directors declares them, dividends in arrears are not reported on the balance sheet. Instead, they are disclosed in the notes to the statements. The following note from American Skiing—the company that operates ski, snowboard, and golf resorts throughout the United States, including Colorado's Steamboat and Vermont's Killington—is typical:

To view a video that summarizes the features of preferred stock, check out the DVD for use with this book.

As of July 27, 2003, cumulative dividends in arrears totaled approximately $10.1 million and $45.2 million for the Series C-1 Preferred Stock and Series C-2 Preferred Stock, respectively.

Okay, now that you know how dividends and other stockholders' equity transactions are accounted for inside a company, it's time to evaluate things from the outside. In the next section, you will learn to evaluate how well a company is using its capital to generate returns for the company and, ultimately, for its stockholders.

⌐ EVALUATE ─────────
THE RETURN TO STOCKHOLDERS

Earnings per Share (EPS)

The most famous of all ratios, earnings per share (EPS), reports how much profit is earned for each share of common stock outstanding. The calculation of EPS can involve many details and intricacies, but in its basic form, it is computed as

$$\text{Earnings per Share} = \frac{\text{Net Income}}{\text{Average Number of Common Shares Outstanding}}$$

Most companies calculate EPS at the end of each quarter and year and report it either on the income statement immediately below *Net income* or in the notes to the financial statements.[2]

You might be wondering why *earnings* per share is so popular when dividends and stock prices ultimately determine the return to stockholders. The reason is that current earnings can predict future dividends and stock prices. If a company generates increased earnings in the current year, it will be able to pay higher dividends in future years. In other words, current EPS influences expectations about future dividends, which investors factor into the stock price. That's why the stock price of Ross Stores changed by over 10 percent when the company announced a 7¢ change in EPS on March 4, 2004.

Another reason that EPS is so popular is that it allows you to easily compare over time. For example, for the year ended January 31, 2004, Ross earned net income of $228 million, compared to $201 million for the previous year. It's hard to know whether that's a good increase for stockholders, because it's possible that the number of shares increased at a faster rate than net income. By considering earnings on a per share basis, we adjust for the effect of additional stock issued, resulting in a clearer picture of what increases mean for each investor. In our example, the increase in net income translated into EPS growth from $1.29 to $1.50 for each investor. This 16 percent jump in EPS is right in line with the EPS growth goal of 15 percent that Ross set for itself in a recent annual report.

Be on the Alert

While EPS is an effective and widely used measure for comparing a company with itself over time, it is not appropriate for comparing across companies. As you have seen in earlier chapters, net income can be affected by differences in estimates of bad debts (Chapter 7), methods of inventory costing (Chapter 8), estimated useful lives of long-lived tangible assets (Chapter 9), and estimates of losses from contingent liabilities (Chapter 10). But even if companies use identical accounting methods, EPS will be misleading if the dollar amounts for the shares being compared differ significantly. Two companies reporting $2 EPS might appear comparable, but if shares in one company cost $10 while shares of the other cost $150, they are not. You spend a lot less for shares of stock in one company than you do for the other. Thus, when evaluating return to stockholders, it's important to consider not just the number of shares of stock but also how much they cost.

Fiscal Period

EPS bar chart showing values for fiscal periods 2001/02, 2002/03, and 2003/04, with EPS axis marked at $0.00, $0.50, $1.00, and $1.50.

---

[2]Although companies report their annual EPS numbers only at the end of their fiscal years, most analysts find it useful to update annual EPS as each quarter's results are reported. To do this, analysts will compute their own "trailing 12 months" EPS measure by summing the most recent four quarters of EPS. This way, they can get a timely measure of year-long EPS, without having to wait until the end of the fiscal year.

Return on Equity (ROE)

The return on equity (ROE) ratio takes into consideration the "cost" of stock, in terms of the dollars of stockholder investment and earnings reinvested in the company. ROE is computed as follows:

$$\text{Return on Equity} = \frac{\text{Net Income}}{\text{Average Stockholders' Equity}}$$

COACH'S CORNER

The bottom number in the return on equity ratio is calculated by summing the beginning and ending total stockholders' equity balances and dividing by 2.

Just as EPS is useful in understanding a company's stock price, so is ROE. In the long run, companies with higher ROE are likely to have higher stock prices than companies with lower ROE.

In its 2004 annual report, Ross Stores, Inc., said it would achieve 30 percent ROE in future years. For most companies in the retail apparel industry, this is a challenging goal; according to Yahoo! Finance, the average ROE in the industry is approximately 20 percent. For Ross, it's nothing spectacular, as the company's ROE over the last five years has ranged from about 31 to 34 percent. Exhibit 11.8 shows that Ross met its 30 percent ROE goal, placing it halfway between two of its biggest competitors: TJX Companies (owner of TJ Maxx) and Pacific Sunwear (owner of PacSun and d.e.m.o. stores). The Self-Study Quiz that follows gives you a chance to see whether you understand how to calculate this ratio, using the numbers for Ross in 2002–03.

HOW'S IT GOING? A Self-Study Quiz

Compute the ratio for the final column in Exhibit 11.8 using information in Exhibit 11.2 along with the following. In its financial statements for the year ended February 1, 2003, Ross reported net income of $201,178 and beginning total stockholders' equity of $544,455 (in thousands of U.S. dollars). Did the return on equity ratio improve or decline in 2003–04, as compared to 2002–03?

When you're done, check your answers with the solutions in the margin.

Quiz Answers

$$\frac{201,178}{(643,188 + 544,455) / 2} = .0339 \text{ or } 33.9\%$$

The 32.6% ratio in 2003–04 represented a slight decline from the 33.9% in 2002–03.

exhibit 11.8 Summary of Return on Equity (ROE) Ratio Analyses

Name of Measure	Formula	What It Tells You	2003–04 FISCAL YEAR			SELF-STUDY QUIZ 2002–03
			TJX Companies	Pacific Sunwear	Ross Stores	Ross Stores
Return on Equity Ratio	$\dfrac{\text{Net Income}}{\text{Average Stockholders' Equity}}$	• The amount earned for each dollar invested by stockholders • A higher ratio means stockholders are likely to enjoy greater returns ☺	44.4%	21.9%	$= \dfrac{228,102}{(755,419 + 643,188)/2}$ $= 0.326$, or 32.6%	

COACH'S CORNER

If a company has preferred stock outstanding, the ROE ratio can be adjusted to focus on the common stockholders' perspective. Simply deduct any preferred dividends from net income and exclude any preferred stock accounts from the calculation of average stockholders' equity.

Be on the Alert

Note that ROE is calculated from the company's point of view, using the dollar amount contributed to or reinvested in the company. This amount does not necessarily reflect what each individual investor pays to acquire the company's stock, nor does it represent the current value of all outstanding stock, which could be much more than what's reported on the balance sheet for stockholders' equity. Remember, these accounts are not updated for changes in stock value. Because of this, the ROE ratio does not equal the return that each individual stockholder will enjoy on his or her own investment in that company.

Equity versus Debt

Whenever a company needs a large amount of long-term financing, its executives will have to decide whether to obtain it through equity (issue stock) or debt (borrow money). Equity has certain advantages over debt, but it also has disadvantages. Exhibit 11.9 summarizes some of these pros and cons.

exhibit **11.9**	**Advantages and Disadvantages of Equity Financing (Relative to Debt)**

Advantages of Equity Financing

1. **Equity does not have to be repaid.**
   Debt must be repaid or refinanced.

2. **Dividends are optional.**
   Interest must be paid on debt.

Disadvantages of Equity Financing

1. **Change in stockholder control.**
   New stockholders get to vote and share in the earnings, diluting existing stockholders' control.

2. **Dividends are not tax deductible.**
   Interest on debt is tax deductible.

One additional issue is considered when choosing between equity and debt financing. If money can be invested in a project that generates a higher return than the rate of interest on a loan, debt financing will lead to a greater return on stockholders' equity. However, if the project happens to return less, then debt financing will lead to a lower return on equity. To illustrate, assume that Ozzy's Off-Price Offerings has stockholders' equity of $100,000 invested in a store and currently earns net income of $20,000 per year (before income taxes). Ozzy plans to open a new store, at the beginning of the following year, at a cost of $100,000. The new store is expected to earn an additional $20,000 per year (before tax). Ozzy has the choice of issuing new stock (for $100,000) or borrowing at a rate of 8 percent. Let's look at three cases: (1) Ozzy issues stock and income is as expected, (2) Ozzy borrows and income is as expected, and (3) Ozzy borrows but income is less than expected.

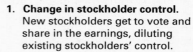

	Case 1: Stock	Case 2: Debt	Case 3: Debt
Income before interest and taxes	$40,000	$40,000	$25,000
Interest expense (8% × 100,000 × 12/12)	—	(8,000)	(8,000)
Income before taxes	40,000	32,000	17,000
Income taxes (35%)	(14,000)	(11,200)	(5,950)
Net income	$26,000	$20,800	$11,050
Average stockholders' equity	200,000	100,000	100,000
Return on equity (ROE)	13%	20.8%	11.05%
(= Net income / Average stockholders' equity)	$= \dfrac{26,000}{200,000}$	$= \dfrac{20,800}{100,000}$	$= \dfrac{11,050}{100,000}$

As you can see, the return on equity is increased by borrowing (Case 2) if the additional amount earned ($20,000) is greater than the cost of borrowing ($8,000), but the return on equity is decreased if the additional amount earned ($5,000) is less than the cost of borrowing ($8,000) (Case 3). This magnifying effect is known as financial leverage, which is an advantage when results are good but a disadvantage when results are bad.

RECONSIDER
DECISIONS THAT AFFECT MEASURES OF STOCKHOLDER RETURNS

In addition to evaluating the historical relationship between a company's earnings and stockholders' equity levels, investors also should keep their eyes open for events that might impact stockholders' equity in the future.

Retained Earnings Restrictions

Several types of business transactions may place restrictions on retained earnings to limit a company's ability to pay dividends in the future. The most typical example involves borrowing money from a bank. To reduce its risk, a bank might include a clause in its lending agreement that limits the amount of dividends a corporation can pay. If this loan covenant is violated, the bank can demand immediate repayment of the debt. Restrictions on retained earnings will be disclosed in the notes to the financial statements.

Stock Options and Diluted Earnings per Share

Most publicly traded companies grant stock options to their employees. The accounting rules for stock options are complex, so they're covered in detail in intermediate accounting courses. However, because stock options are so common, we should tell you in simple terms what they are and how they potentially affect financial statement users. Stock options are agreements that give employees the option to buy the company's stock at a fixed price in the future, say at $55 per share. If employees work hard to improve the company and increase its stock price to say $60, they can "exercise the option" to buy stock from the company for $55 per share. The result is a $5 per share benefit for employees, kind of like a bonus tied to the company's stock price.

For investors, employee stock option plans can be both good news and bad news. The good news is that they potentially motivate employees to improve the company's financial performance, which can increase the stock price, leading to an increase in investors' personal wealth. The bad news is that when stock options are exercised by employees, the company issues more common stock, which, all else equal, reduces or "dilutes" the existing stockholders' control of the company as well as their claims on the company's future earnings. For example, if a company has 40 shares outstanding and you own 4 of them, you'd be considered a 10 percent owner ($4 \div 40 = 10\%$). If the company then issued 10 additional shares to employees when they exercise their stock options, the total number of shares outstanding would increase to 50, causing your ownership percentage to fall to 8 percent ($4 \div 50 = 8\%$). In other words, you'd have less control of the company, and, when the company's earnings are distributed as dividends, you'd share them with more stockholders.

To advise financial statement users of these potential effects, accounting rules require companies to report two versions of the earnings per share (EPS) number. The first version, called basic EPS (shown earlier in this chapter), indicates what the current period's earnings are for each existing share of stock. The second version, called diluted EPS, shows what the current earnings would have been for each share of stock if the company had issued additional stock for unexercised stock options (and any other existing agreements that would require the company to issue additional stock).

Be on the Alert for Stock Repurchases

Before closing this chapter, we need to remind you to interpret changes in EPS and ROE in the light of your new knowledge about accounting for stock repurchases. As you know from the previous section in this chapter, stock repurchases cause a decrease in the

COACH'S CORNER
The bank imposes dividend restrictions because it doesn't want to lend money to a corporation and then have the corporation pay it out in dividends to stockholders.

POINT OF INTEREST
In 1998, for the first time in history, companies paid out more money for stock repurchases than for cash dividends.
Source: G. Grullon and R. Michaely, 2002 *Journal of Finance.*

number of outstanding shares as well as a decrease in total stockholders' equity. Because of these effects, stock repurchases lead to increases in EPS and ROE (other things being equal). Some people jump to the conclusion that increases in EPS and ROE mean the company has become more profitable in the current year. This is not necessarily true, because a company with the same $1 million of net income in two consecutive years can still report an increase in EPS and ROE if it repurchases its stock during the second year. So beware, changes in EPS and ROE can be caused by reductions in the bottom of the ratios (number of shares and average stockholders' equity) rather than improvements in the top (net income).

What's Coming Up

This completes our in-depth coverage of the balance sheet accounts. Chapter 12 returns to one of the four basic accounting reports introduced in Chapter 1: the statement of cash flows. Following that, Chapter 13 pulls everything together by demonstrating the analyses that can be conducted using a full set of financial statements and by reviewing the concepts that underlie financial accounting. But don't get ahead of yourself yet. Be sure to review and practice testing your understanding of what you've read in this chapter.

FOR YOUR REVIEW

DEMONSTRATION CASE A (STOCK ISSUANCE AND REPURCHASES)

This case focuses on selected transactions from the first year of operations of Zoogle Corporation, which became a public company on January 1, 2005, for the purpose of operating a lost-pet search business. The charter authorized the following stock:

> Common stock, no-par value, 20,000 shares.
>
> Preferred stock, 5 percent noncumulative, $100 par value, 5,000 shares.

The laws of the state specify that the legal capital for no-par stock is the full sale amount.

The following summarized transactions, selected from 2005, were completed on the dates indicated:

a.	Jan. 1	Issued a total of 8,000 shares of no-par value common stock for cash at $50 per share.
b.	Feb. 1	Sold 2,000 shares of preferred stock at $102 per share; cash collected in full.
c.	July 1	Purchased 400 shares of common stock that had been issued earlier. Zoogle Corporation paid the stockholder $54 per share for the stock, which is currently held in treasury.
d.	Aug. 1	Sold 30 shares of the common treasury stock at $56 per share.
e.	Dec. 31	The board decided not to declare any dividends for the current year.

Required:

1. Give the appropriate journal entries, and show calculations for each transaction.
2. Prepare the stockholders' equity section of the balance sheet for Zoogle Corporation at December 31, 2005. Assume retained earnings is $31,000.

Suggested Solution

1. **Journal entries:**
   a. Jan. 1, 2005

dr	Cash (+A) ($50 × 8,000 shares)	400,000	
cr	Common Stock (+SE)		400,000

b. Feb. 1, 2005

dr	Cash (+A) ($102 × 2,000 shares)	204,000	
	cr Preferred Stock (+SE)		
	($100 par × 2,000 shares)		200,000
	cr Additional Paid-In Capital (+SE)		4,000
	(($102 − 100) × 2,000 shares)		

c. July 1, 2005

dr	Treasury Stock (+xSE, −SE)	21,600	
	cr Cash (−A) ($54 × 400 shares)		21,600

d. Aug. 1, 2005

dr	Cash (+A) ($56 × 30 shares)	1,680	
	cr Treasury Stock (−xSE, +SE)		
	($54 × 30 shares)		1,620
	cr Additional Paid-In Capital (+SE)		
	($1,680 − 1,620)		60

e. Dec. 31, 2005   No journal entry is required.

2. **Stockholders' equity section of the balance sheet:**

ZOOGLE CORPORATION
Partial Balance Sheet
At December 31, 2005

Stockholders' Equity

Contributed capital

Preferred stock, 5% (par value $100; 5,000 authorized shares, 2,000 issued and outstanding shares)	$200,000	
Additional paid-in capital, preferred stock	4,000	
Common stock (no-par value; authorized 20,000 shares, issued 8,000 shares of which 370 shares are held as treasury stock)	400,000	
Additional paid-in capital, common stock	60	
Total contributed capital		$604,060
Retained earnings		31,000
Less: cost of common stock held in treasury (370 shares)		(19,980)
Total stockholders' equity		$615,080

DEMONSTRATION CASE B (CASH DIVIDENDS AND STOCK DIVIDENDS)

This case extends Demonstration Case A by focusing on dividend transactions occurring during Zoogle Corporation's second year. The following summarized transactions, selected from 2006, were completed on the dates indicated:

a. Nov. 1   To remind common stockholders of their accumulating wealth, the board declared and issued a 10 percent stock dividend on the outstanding common stock. The stock price was $49.80.

b. Dec. 1 The board declared a cash dividend on the preferred stock, payable on December 22, 2006 to stockholders of record as of December 15, 2006.

c. Dec. 31 The temporary dividends declared account was closed.

Required:

Give the appropriate journal entries, and show calculations for each transaction.

Suggested Solution

a. Nov. 1, 2006

dr	Retained Earnings (−SE)......................	379,974	
cr	Common Stock (+SE)		379,974
	[(8,000 common shares issued − 370 in treasury) × $49.80]		

b. Dec. 1, 2006

dr	Dividends Declared (+D, −SE)	10,000	
cr	Dividends Payable (+L)		10,000
	(2,000 preferred shares × $100 par × 5% dividend rate)		

Dec. 15, 2006 No journal entry is required.
Dec. 22, 2006

dr	Dividends Payable (−L)........................	10,000	
cr	Cash (−A)................................		10,000

c. Dec. 31, 2006

dr	Retained Earnings (−SE)......................	10,000	
cr	Dividends Declared (−D, +SE)		10,000

CHAPTER SUMMARY

LO1   **Explain the role of stock in financing a corporation. p. 472**

- The law recognizes corporations as separate legal entities. Owners invest in a corporation and receive capital stock that can be bought from and sold to other investors. Stock provides a number of rights, including the rights to vote, to receive dividends, and to share in residual assets at liquidation.

LO2   **Explain and analyze common stock transactions. p. 475**

- A number of key transactions involve common stock: (1) initial issuance of stock, (2) repurchase of stock into treasury, and (3) reissuance of treasury stock. Each is illustrated in this chapter.

LO3   **Explain and analyze cash dividends, stock dividends, and stock split transactions. p. 479**

- Cash dividends reduce stockholders' equity (retained earnings) and create a liability (dividends payable) when they are declared by the board of directors (on the date of declaration). The liability is reduced when the dividends are paid (on the date of payment).

- Stock dividends are pro rata distributions of a company's stock to existing owners. The transaction typically is accounted for by transferring an amount out of retained earnings and into common stock accounts.

- A stock split also involves the distribution of additional shares to owners but no additional amount is transferred into the common stock account. Instead, the par value of each share of stock is reduced.

Describe the characteristics of preferred stock and analyze transactions affecting preferred stock. p. 484

LO4

- Preferred stock provides investors certain advantages including current dividend preferences and a preference on asset distributions in the event the corporation is liquidated.
- If preferred stock carries cumulative dividend rights, any part of a current dividend that is not paid (called dividends in arrears) must be paid in full before any additional dividends can be paid.

Analyze the earnings per share (EPS) and return on equity (ROE) ratios. p. 486

LO5

- The earnings per share (EPS) ratio makes it easy to compare a company's earnings over time. Although EPS adjusts for differences in the number of shares outstanding, it does not take into account possible differences in the price of stock, making it a poor measure for comparing across companies.
- The return on equity ratio relates earnings to each dollar contributed to and retained by the company.

Explain how stock transactions affect ROE and EPS. p. 489

LO6

- Accounting rules require companies to report a "diluted EPS" number, which indicates how employee stock options (and other commitments to potentially issue additional shares of stock in the future) would have affected existing stockholders' claims to a company's earnings had additional shares been issued to fulfill these commitments.
- Stock repurchases reduce the number of and dollar amount reported for outstanding common stock, causing increases in EPS and ROE (assuming all else is equal).

FINANCIAL STATEMENT ANALYSIS TIPS

To determine the amount of income generated for each share of common stock, calculate the earnings per share (EPS) ratio:

$$\text{Earnings per Share} = \frac{\text{Net Income}}{\text{Average Number of Common Shares Outstanding}}$$

To determine the amount of income generated for each dollar contributed to and retained by a company, calculate the return on equity (ROE) ratio:

$$\text{Return on Equity} = \frac{\text{Net Income}}{\text{Average Stockholders' Equity}}$$

KEY TERMS TO KNOW

Authorized Number of
  Shares p. 475
Common Stock p. 475
Cumulative Dividend
  Preference p. 485
Current Dividend
  Preference p. 485

Declaration Date p. 479
Dividends in Arrears p. 485
Issued Shares p. 475
No-Par Value Stock p. 476
Outstanding Shares p. 475
Par Value p. 476

Payment Date p. 480
Preferred Stock p. 484
Record Date p. 480
Stock Dividend p. 481
Stock Split p. 482
Treasury Stock p. 475

SUPPLEMENT A: ACCOUNTING FOR EQUITY IN SOLE PROPRIETORSHIPS, PARTNERSHIPS, AND OTHER BUSINESS FORMS

Owner's Equity for a Sole Proprietorship

A sole proprietorship is an unincorporated business owned by one person. Only two owner's equity accounts are needed: (1) a capital account for the proprietor (H. Simpson, Capital) and (2) a drawing (or withdrawal) account for the proprietor (H. Simpson, Drawings).

The capital account of a sole proprietorship serves two purposes: to record investments by the owner and to accumulate periodic income or loss. The drawing account is used to record the owner's withdrawals of cash or other assets from the business, similar to recording dividends declared by corporations. The drawing account is closed to the capital account at the end of each accounting period. Thus, after the drawing account is closed, the capital account reflects the cumulative total of all investments by the owner and all earnings of the entity less all withdrawals from the entity by the owner.

In most respects, the accounting for a sole proprietorship is the same as for a corporation. Exhibit 11A.1 presents the recording of selected transactions of Homer's Dough Store and the owner's equity section of the balance sheet.

Because a sole proprietorship does not pay income taxes, its financial statements do not reflect income tax expense or income taxes payable. Instead, the net income of a sole proprietorship is taxed when it is included on the owner's personal income tax return. Likewise, the owner's salary

COACH'S CORNER

The capital account is like all the stockholders' equity accounts for a corporation combined into a single account. The drawing account is like the dividends declared account for a corporation.

COACH'S CORNER

Because a sole proprietorship does not issue stock, its equity is called owner's equity rather than stockholder's equity. We use OE to designate an owner's equity account.

---

exhibit 11A.1   Accounting for Owner's Equity for a Sole Proprietorship

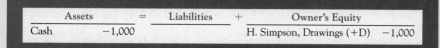

Selected Entries during 2006

January 1, 2006

H. Simpson started a retail store by investing $150,000 of personal savings. The journal entry follows:

dr	Cash (+A)	150,000	
	cr H. Simpson, Capital (+OE)		150,000

Assets		=	Liabilities	+	Owner's Equity	
Cash	+150,000				H. Simpson, Capital	+150,000

During 2006

Each month during the year, Homer withdrew $1,000 cash from the business for personal living costs. Accordingly, each month the following journal entry was made:

dr	H. Simpson, Drawings (+D, −OE)	1,000	
	cr Cash (−A)		1,000

Assets		=	Liabilities	+	Owner's Equity	
Cash	−1,000				H. Simpson, Drawings (+D)	−1,000

Note: At December 31, 2006, after the last withdrawal, the drawings account reflected a debit balance of $12,000.

is not recognized as an expense in a sole proprietorship because an employer/employee contractual relationship cannot exist with only one party involved. The owner's salary is therefore accounted for as a distribution of profits—a withdrawal—instead of salary expense, as it would be in a corporation.

Accounting for Partnership Equity

The Uniform Partnership Act, which most states have adopted, defines a partnership as "an association of two or more persons to carry on as co-owners of a business for profit." Small businesses and professionals such as accountants, doctors, and lawyers often use the partnership form of business.

A partnership is formed by two or more persons reaching mutual agreement about the terms of the relationship. The law does not require an application for a charter as in the case of a corporation. Instead, the agreement between the partners constitutes a partnership contract. This agreement should specify matters such as division of income, management responsibilities, transfer or sale of partnership interests, disposition of assets upon liquidation, and procedures to

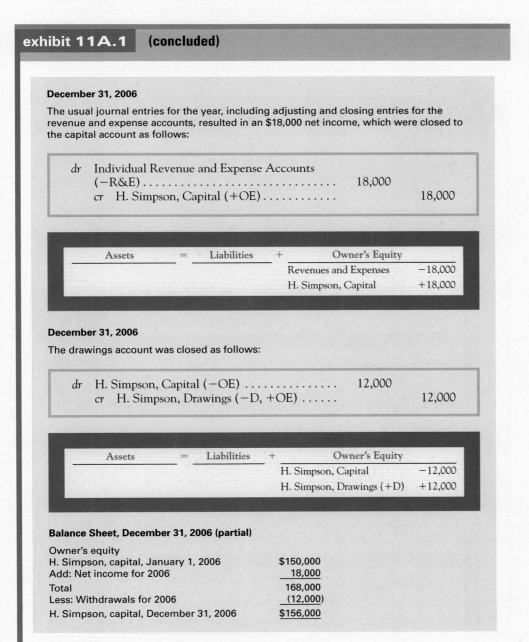

exhibit 11A.1   (concluded)

December 31, 2006

The usual journal entries for the year, including adjusting and closing entries for the revenue and expense accounts, resulted in an $18,000 net income, which were closed to the capital account as follows:

dr Individual Revenue and Expense Accounts (−R&E)	18,000
cr H. Simpson, Capital (+OE)	18,000

Assets	=	Liabilities	+	Owner's Equity	
				Revenues and Expenses	−18,000
				H. Simpson, Capital	+18,000

December 31, 2006

The drawings account was closed as follows:

dr H. Simpson, Capital (−OE)	12,000
cr H. Simpson, Drawings (−D, +OE)	12,000

Assets	=	Liabilities	+	Owner's Equity	
				H. Simpson, Capital	−12,000
				H. Simpson, Drawings (+D)	+12,000

Balance Sheet, December 31, 2006 (partial)

Owner's equity	
H. Simpson, capital, January 1, 2006	$150,000
Add: Net income for 2006	18,000
Total	168,000
Less: Withdrawals for 2006	(12,000)
H. Simpson, capital, December 31, 2006	$156,000

be followed in case of the death of a partner. If the partnership agreement does not specify these matters, the laws of the resident state are binding.

In comparison to a corporation, the primary advantages of a partnership are (1) ease of formation, (2) complete control by the partners, and (3) lack of income taxes on the business itself. The primary disadvantage is the unlimited liability of each partner for the partnership's debts. If the partnership does not have sufficient assets to satisfy outstanding debt, creditors of the partnership can seize each partner's personal assets. In some cases, this can even result in one partner being held responsible for another partner's share of the partnership's debt.

As with a sole proprietorship, accounting for a partnership follows the same underlying principles as any other form of business organization, except for those entries that directly affect owners' equity. Accounting for partners' equity follows the same pattern as for a sole proprietorship, except that separate capital and drawings accounts must be established for each partner. Investments by each partner are credited to that partner's capital account and withdrawals are debited to the respective drawings account. The net income of a partnership is divided among the partners in accordance with the partnership agreement and credited to each account. The respective drawings accounts are closed to the partner capital accounts. After the closing process, each partner's capital account reflects the cumulative total of all that partner's investments plus that partner's share of the partnership earnings less all that partner's withdrawals.

Exhibit 11A.2 presents selected journal entries and partial financial statements for AB Partnership to illustrate the accounting for the distribution of income and partners' equity.

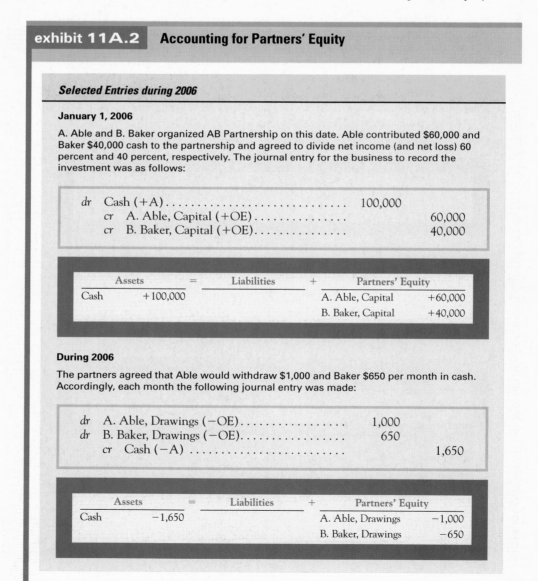

exhibit 11A.2   Accounting for Partners' Equity

Selected Entries during 2006

January 1, 2006

A. Able and B. Baker organized AB Partnership on this date. Able contributed $60,000 and Baker $40,000 cash to the partnership and agreed to divide net income (and net loss) 60 percent and 40 percent, respectively. The journal entry for the business to record the investment was as follows:

dr	Cash (+A)	100,000	
cr	A. Able, Capital (+OE)		60,000
cr	B. Baker, Capital (+OE)		40,000

Assets		=	Liabilities	+	Partners' Equity	
Cash	+100,000				A. Able, Capital	+60,000
					B. Baker, Capital	+40,000

During 2006

The partners agreed that Able would withdraw $1,000 and Baker $650 per month in cash. Accordingly, each month the following journal entry was made:

dr	A. Able, Drawings (−OE)	1,000	
dr	B. Baker, Drawings (−OE)	650	
cr	Cash (−A)		1,650

Assets		=	Liabilities	+	Partners' Equity	
Cash	−1,650				A. Able, Drawings	−1,000
					B. Baker, Drawings	−650

exhibit 11A.2 **(concluded)**

December 31, 2006

Assume that the normal closing entries for the revenue and expense accounts resulted in a net income of $30,000. The partnership agreement specified Able would receive 60 percent of earnings and Baker would get 40 percent. The closing entry was as follows:

dr Individual Revenue and Expense Accounts (−R&E)	30,000
cr A. Able, Capital (+OE) (60% × $30,000)	18,000
cr B. Baker, Capital (+OE) (40% × $30,000)	12,000

Assets	=	Liabilities	+	Partners' Equity	
				Revenues and Expenses	−30,000
				A. Able, Capital	+18,000
				B. Baker, Capital	+12,000

December 31, 2006

The journal entry required to close the drawings accounts follows:

dr A. Able, Capital (−OE)	12,000
dr B. Baker, Capital (−OE)	7,800
cr A. Able, Drawings (+OE)	12,000
cr B. Baker, Drawings (+OE)	7,800

Assets	=	Liabilities	+	Partners' Equity	
				A. Able, capital	−12,000
				B. Baker, capital	−7,800
				A. Able, drawings	+12,000
				B. Baker, drawings	+7,800

A separate statement of partners' capital, similar to the following, is customarily prepared to supplement the balance sheet:

AB PARTNERSHIP
Statement of Partners' Equity
For the Year Ended December 31, 2006

	A. Able	B. Baker	Total
Investment, January 1, 2006	$60,000	$40,000	$100,000
Add: Additional investments during the year	0	0	0
Net income for the year	18,000	12,000	30,000
Totals	78,000	52,000	130,000
Less: Drawings during the year	(12,000)	(7,800)	(19,800)
Partners' equity, December 31, 2006	$66,000	$44,200	$110,200

Other Business Forms

In addition to sole proprietorships, partnerships, and corporations, other forms of business have emerged. These new forms blend features of the "pure" organizational forms described earlier in this chapter to create hybrid business forms such as "S corporations," limited liability partnerships (LLPs), and limited liability companies (LLCs). The LLC in particular is an increasingly common form of business that combines legal characteristics of corporations (such as a separate legal identity and limited liability) with the tax treatment of partnerships (where tax is paid by the individual owners rather than by the business entity itself). Accounting for these hybrid entities generally follows the methods shown earlier in this chapter.

The financial statements of an LLC follow the same format as those for a partnership, which differs from a corporation in the following ways: (1) the financial statements include an additional section entitled Distribution of Net Income; (2) the owners' equity section of the balance sheet is detailed for each owner; (3) the income statement does not report income tax expense because these forms of business do not pay income tax (owners must report their share of the entity's profits on their individual tax returns); and (4) unless other contractual arrangements exist, amounts paid to the owners are not recorded as expenses but instead are treated as withdrawals of capital.

FOR YOUR PRACTICE

QUESTIONS

1. Identify the primary advantages of the corporate form of business.
2. Explain each of the following terms: (*a*) authorized common stock, (*b*) issued common stock, and (*c*) outstanding common stock.
3. What are the differences between common stock and preferred stock?
4. What is the distinction between par value and no-par value capital stock?
5. What are the usual characteristics of preferred stock?
6. What are the two basic sources of stockholders' equity? Explain each.
7. What is treasury stock? Why do corporations acquire treasury stock?
8. How is treasury stock reported on the balance sheet? How is the "gain or loss" on reissued treasury stock reported on the financial statements?
9. What are the two basic requirements to support the declaration of a cash dividend? What are the effects of a cash dividend on assets and stockholders' equity?
10. What is the difference between cumulative and noncumulative preferred stock?
11. What is a stock dividend? How does a stock dividend differ from a cash dividend?
12. What are the primary reasons for issuing a stock dividend?
13. Identify and explain the three important dates with respect to dividends.
14. Why is the EPS number so popular? What are its limitations?
15. What are the advantages and disadvantages of equity financing (relative to debt financing)?
16. How do stock repurchases affect the EPS and ROE ratios?

MULTIPLE CHOICE

To practice more multiple choice questions, check out the DVD for use with this book.

1. Which feature is not applicable to common stock ownership?
   a. Right to receive dividends before preferred stock shareholders.
   b. Right to vote on appointment of external auditor.
   c. Right to receive residual assets of the company should it cease operations.
   d. All of the above are applicable to common stock ownership.
2. Which statement regarding treasury stock is false?
   a. Treasury stock is considered to be issued but not outstanding.
   b. Treasury stock has no voting, dividend, or liquidation rights.
   c. Treasury stock reduces total stockholders' equity on the balance sheet.
   d. None of the above are false.

3. Which of the following statements about stock dividends is true?
   a. Stock dividends are reported on the income statement.
   b. Stock dividends are reported on the statement of stockholders' equity.
   c. Stock dividends increase total stockholders' equity.
   d. Stock dividends decrease total stockholders' equity.

4. Which of the following is ordered from the largest number of shares to the smallest number of shares?
   a. Shares authorized, shares issued, shares outstanding.
   b. Shares issued, shares outstanding, shares authorized.
   c. Shares outstanding, shares issued, shares authorized.
   d. Shares in treasury, shares outstanding, shares issued.

5. Which of the following statements about the relative advantages and disadvantages of equity and debt financing is false?
   a. An advantage of equity financing is that it does not have to be repaid.
   b. An advantage of equity financing is that dividends are optional.
   c. A disadvantage of equity financing is that new stockholders get to vote and share in the earnings of the company.
   d. A disadvantage of equity financing is that it always leads to a smaller return on stockholders' equity.

6. A journal entry is not recorded on what date?
   a. Date of declaration.
   b. Date of record.
   c. Date of payment.
   d. A journal entry is recorded on all of the above dates.

7. Which of the following transactions will increase the return on equity?
   a. Declare and issue a stock dividend.
   b. Split the stock 2-for-1.
   c. Repurchase the company's stock.
   d. None of the above.

8. Which statement regarding dividends is false?
   a. Dividends represent a sharing of corporate profits with owners.
   b. Both stock and cash dividends reduce retained earnings.
   c. Cash dividends paid to stockholders reduce net income.
   d. None of the above statements are false.

9. When treasury stock is purchased with cash, what is the impact on the balance sheet equation?
   a. No change—the reduction of the asset "Cash" is offset with the addition of the asset "Treasury Stock."
   b. Assets decrease and Stockholders' Equity increases.
   c. Assets increase and Stockholders' Equity decreases.
   d. Assets decrease and Stockholders' Equity decreases.

10. In what situation does an investor's personal wealth increase immediately?
    a. When receiving a cash dividend.
    b. When receiving a stock dividend.
    c. When a stock split is announced.
    d. An investor's wealth is increased instantly in all of the above situations.

MINI-EXERCISES **Available with McGraw-Hill's Homework Manager**

M11-1 Identifying Important Accounting Terms

LO2–LO4

Complete the following crossword puzzle, using the clues provided in the box on the right.

Across

2   The size of stock dividend typically used to remind stockholders of their accumulating wealth.

3   The category of shares that have at one time been sold by the company.

4   The type of stock that is recorded in a contra-equity account.

6   The name for the date on which stockholders are identified as the recipients of a dividend.

7   The name for the date on which a dividend is declared.

Down

1   The name for the date on which a dividend is paid.

3   The two-word term used to describe cumulative dividends that have not been paid.

5   The nominal value associated with each share of stock.

LO1 **M11-2 Evaluating Stockholders' Rights**

Name three rights of stockholders. Which of these is most important in your mind? Why?

LO1 **M11-3 Computing the Number of Unissued Shares**

The balance sheet for Crutcher Corporation reported 147,000 shares outstanding, 200,000 shares authorized, and 10,000 shares in treasury stock. Compute the maximum number of new shares that Crutcher could issue.

LO2 **M11-4 Recording the Sale of Common Stock**

To expand operations, Aragon Consulting issued 100,000 shares of previously unissued common stock with a par value of $1. The selling price for the stock was $75 per share. Record the sale of this stock. Would your answer be different if the par value was $2 per share? If so, record the sale of stock with a par value of $2.

LO2, LO4 **M11-5 Comparing Common Stock and Preferred Stock**

Your parents have just retired and have asked you for some financial advice. They have decided to invest $100,000 in a company very similar to Ross Stores. The company has issued both common and preferred stock. Which type of stock would you recommend? What factors would you consider in giving them advice?

LO2 **M11-6 Determining the Effects of Treasury Stock Transactions**

Trans Union Corporation purchased 20,000 shares of its own stock for $45 per share. The next year, the company sold 5,000 shares for $50 per share and the following year, it sold 10,000 shares for $37 per share. Determine the impact (increase, decrease, or no change) of each of these transactions on the following classifications:

1. Total assets.
2. Total liabilities.
3. Total stockholders' equity.
4. Net income.

LO3 **M11-7 Determining the Amount of a Dividend**

Jacobs Company has 300,000 shares of common stock authorized, 270,000 shares issued, and 50,000 shares of treasury stock. The company's board of directors declares a dividend of 50 cents per share. What is the total amount of the dividend that will be paid?

M11-8 Recording Dividends

LO3

On April 15, 2005, the board of directors for Auction.com declared a cash dividend of 20 cents per share payable to stockholders of record on May 20. The dividends will be paid on June 14. The company has 500,000 shares of stock outstanding. Prepare any necessary journal entries for each date.

M11-9 Determining the Impact of a Stock Dividend

LO3

Armstrong Tools, Inc., announced a 100 percent stock dividend. Determine the impact (increase, decrease, no change) of this dividend on the following:

1. Total assets.
2. Total liabilities.
3. Common stock.
4. Total stockholders' equity.
5. Market value per share of common stock.

M11-10 Determining the Impact of a Stock Split

LO3

Complete the requirements of M11-9 assuming that the company announced a 2-for-1 stock split.

M11-11 Recording a Stock Dividend

LO3

To reduce its stock price, Shriver Food Systems, Inc., declared and issued a 50 percent stock dividend. The company has 800,000 shares authorized and 200,000 shares outstanding. The par value of the stock is $5 per share and the market value is $100 per share. Prepare the journal entry to record this stock dividend.

M11-12 Determining the Amount of a Preferred Dividend

LO4

Colliers, Inc., has 200,000 shares of cumulative preferred stock outstanding. The preferred stock pays dividends in the amount of $2 per share but because of cash flow problems, the company did not pay any dividends last year. The board of directors plans to pay dividends in the amount of $1 million this year. What amount will go to preferred stockholders?

M11-13 Calculating and Interpreting Earnings Per Share (EPS) and Return on Equity (ROE)

LO5

Toonce's Driving School reported the following amount in its financial statements:

	2006	2005
Number of common shares	11,500	11,500
Net income	$ 23,000	$ 18,000
Cash dividends paid on common stock	$ 3,000	$ 3,000
Total stockholders' equity	$240,000	$220,000

Calculate 2006 EPS and ROE. Another driving school in the same city reported a higher net income ($45,000) in 2006, yet its EPS and ROE ratios were lower than those for Toonce's Driving School. Explain how this apparent inconsistency could occur.

M11-14 Determining the Impact of Transactions on Earnings Per Share (EPS) and Return on Equity (ROE)

LO6

Indicate the direction of effect (+ for increase, − for decrease, or NE for no effect) of each of the following transactions on EPS and ROE.

	EPS	ROE
a. Sold and issued 6,000 shares of common stock for cash.	————	————
b. Purchased 50 shares into treasury.	————	————
c. Declared and paid a cash dividend.	————	————
d. Declared and issued a stock dividend.	————	————
e. Sold inventory at an amount greater than cost.	————	————

M11-15 (Supplement) Comparing Stockholder's Equity to Owner's Equity

James Riggins contributed $20,000 to start his business. At the end of the year, the business had generated $30,000 in sales revenues, incurred $18,000 in operating expenses, and distributed $5,000 for James to use to pay some personal expenses. Prepare the section of the balance sheet showing (a) his stockholder's equity, assuming this is a corporation with no-par value stock, or (b) his owner's equity, assuming this is a sole proprietorship.

EXERCISES   Available with McGraw-Hill's Homework Manager

L01   E11-1 Computing Shares Outstanding

The 2003 annual report for Big Dog Sportswear disclosed that 30 million shares of common stock have been authorized. At the end of 2002, 9,698,284 shares had been issued and the number of shares in treasury stock was 1,455,152. During 2003, no additional common shares were issued, but additional shares were purchased for treasury stock and shares were sold from treasury stock. The net change was a decrease of 149,516 shares of treasury stock.

Required:

Determine the number of shares outstanding at the end of 2003.

L02, L03   E11-2 Reporting Stockholders' Equity and Determining Dividend Policy

Sampson Corporation was organized in 2005 to operate a financial consulting business. The charter authorized the following capital stock: common stock, par value $8 per share, 12,000 shares. During the first year, the following selected transactions were completed:

a. Sold and issued 6,000 shares of common stock for cash at $20 per share.
b. Sold and issued 2,000 shares of common stock for cash at $23 per share.

Required:

1. Give the journal entry required for each of these transactions.
2. Prepare the stockholders' equity section as it should be reported on the 2005 year-end balance sheet. At year-end, the accounts reflected a profit of $100.
3. Sampson has $30,000 in the company's bank account. Can the company declare cash dividends at this time? Explain.

L02, L04   E11-3 Preparing the Stockholders' Equity Section of the Balance Sheet

Skyhawk Corporation received its charter during January 2005. The charter authorized the following capital stock:

Preferred stock: 8 percent, par $10, authorized 20,000 shares.

Common stock: par $8, authorized 50,000 shares.

During 2005, the following transactions occurred in the order given:

a. Issued a total of 40,000 shares of the common stock to the four organizers at $11 per share.
b. Sold 5,000 shares of the preferred stock at $18 per share.
c. Sold 3,000 shares of the common stock at $14 per share and 1,000 shares of the preferred stock at $28.
d. Net income for the year was $48,000.

Required:

Prepare the stockholders' equity section of the balance sheet at December 31, 2005.

L02–L04   E11-4 Reporting a Statement of Stockholders' Equity

Shelby Corporation was organized in January 2005 by 10 stockholders to operate an air conditioning sales and service business. The charter issued by the state authorized the following capital stock:

Common stock, $1 par value, 200,000 shares.

Preferred stock, $10 par value, 6 percent, 50,000 shares.

During January and February 2005, the following stock transactions were completed:

a. Collected $40,000 cash from each of the 10 organizers and issued 2,000 shares of common stock to each of them.
b. Sold 15,000 shares of preferred stock at $25 per share; collected the cash and immediately issued the stock.

Net income for 2005 was $40,000; cash dividends declared and paid at year-end were $10,000.

Required:

Prepare a statement of stockholders' equity for the year ended December 31, 2005.

E11-5 Determining the Effects of the Issuance of Common and Preferred Stock   LO2, LO4

Kelly, Incorporated, was issued a charter on January 15, 2005, that authorized the following capital stock:

Common stock, $6 par, 100,000 shares.

Preferred stock, 7 percent, par value $10 per share, 5,000 shares.

During 2005, the following selected transactions were completed in the order given:

a. Sold and issued 20,000 shares of the $6 par common stock at $18 cash per share.
b. Sold and issued 3,000 shares of preferred stock at $22 cash per share.
c. At the end of 2005, the accounts showed net income of $38,000.

Required:

1. Prepare the stockholders' equity section of the balance sheet at December 31, 2005.
2. Assume that you are a common stockholder. If Kelly needed additional capital, would you prefer to have it issue additional common stock or additional preferred stock? Explain.

E11-6 Recording and Reporting Stockholders' Equity Transactions   LO2, LO4

Teacher Corporation obtained a charter at the start of 2005 that authorized 50,000 shares of no-par common stock and 20,000 shares of preferred stock, par value $10. During 2005, the following selected transactions occurred:

a. Collected $40 cash per share from four individuals and issued 4,000 shares of common stock to each.
b. Sold and issued 6,000 shares of common stock to an outside investor at $40 cash per share.
c. Sold and issued 8,000 shares of preferred stock at $20 cash per share.

Required:

1. Give the journal entries indicated for each of these transactions.
2. Prepare the stockholders' equity section of the balance sheet at December 31, 2005. At the end of 2005, the accounts reflected net income of $36,000.

E11-7 Finding Amounts Missing from the Stockholders' Equity Section   LO2, LO4

The stockholders' equity section on the December 31, 2006, balance sheet of Chemfast Corporation follows:

Stockholders' Equity	
Contributed capital	
Preferred stock (par $20; authorized 10,000 shares,	
? issued, of which 500 shares are held as treasury stock)	$104,000
Common stock (no-par; authorized 20,000 shares,	
issued and outstanding 8,000 shares)	600,000
Additional paid-in capital, preferred	14,300
Retained earnings	30,000
Cost of preferred treasury stock	9,500

Required:

Complete the following statements and show your computations.

1. The number of shares of preferred stock issued was _____.
2. The number of shares of preferred stock outstanding was _____.
3. The average sale price of the preferred stock when issued was $_____ per share.
4. The average issue price of the common stock was $_____.
5. The treasury stock transaction increased (decreased) stockholders' equity by _____.
6. How much did the treasury stock held cost per share? $_____.
7. Total stockholders' equity is $_____.

LO2, LO3

E11-8 Recording Treasury Stock Transactions and Analyzing Their Impact

During 2005, the following selected transactions affecting stockholders' equity occurred for Italy Corporation:

a.   Feb. 1   Purchased 200 shares of the company's own common stock at $22 cash per share.
b.   Jul. 15   Sold 100 of the shares purchased on February 1, 2005, for $24 cash per share.
c.   Sept. 1   Sold 60 more of the shares purchased on February 1, 2005, for $20 cash per share.

Required:

1. Give the indicated journal entries for each of the four transactions.
2. What impact does the purchase of treasury stock have on dividends paid?
3. What impact does the sale of treasury stock for an amount higher than the purchase price have on net income?

LO2, LO3

E11-9 Recording Stockholders' Equity Transactions

Halliburton is one of the world's largest providers of products and services to the oil and gas industries. The annual report for Halliburton reported the following transactions affecting stockholders' equity:

a.   Purchased $3.5 million in treasury stock.
b.   Declared and paid cash dividends in the amount of $254.2 million.
c.   Issued 100 percent common stock dividend involving 222.5 million additional shares with a total par value of $556.3 million.

Required:

Prepare journal entries to record each of these transactions.

LO3, LO4

E11-10 Computing Dividends on Preferred Stock and Analyzing Differences

The records of Hoffman Company reflected the following balances in the stockholders' equity accounts at December 31, 2006:

Common stock, par $12 per share, 40,000 shares outstanding.

Preferred stock, 8 percent, par $10 per share, 6,000 shares outstanding.

Retained earnings, $220,000.

On September 1, 2006, the board of directors was considering the distribution of a $62,000 cash dividend. No dividends were paid during 2004 and 2005.

Required:

1. Determine the total and per share amounts that would be paid to the common stockholders and to the preferred stockholders under two independent assumptions:
   a.   The preferred stock is noncumulative.
   b.   The preferred stock is cumulative.
2. Briefly explain why the dividends per share of common stock were less for the second assumption.
3. What factors would cause a more favorable dividend for the common stockholders?

E11-11 Recording the Payment of Dividends

LO3

A recent annual report for Sears disclosed that the company paid preferred dividends in the amount of $119.9 million. It declared and paid dividends on common stock in the amount of $2 per share. During the year, Sears had 1,000,000,000 shares of common authorized; 387,514,300 shares had been issued; 41,670,000 shares were in treasury stock. Assume that the dividend transaction occurred on July 15.

Required:

Prepare a journal entry to record the declaration and payment of dividends.

E11-12 Analyzing Stock Dividends

LO3

On December 31, 2005, the stockholders' equity section of the balance sheet of R & B Corporation reflected the following:

Common stock (par $10; authorized 60,000 shares, outstanding 25,000 shares)	$250,000
Additional paid-in capital	12,000
Retained earnings	75,000

On February 1, 2006, the board of directors declared a 12 percent stock dividend to be issued April 30, 2006. The market value of the stock on February 1, 2006, was $18 per share.

Required:

1. For comparative purposes, prepare the stockholders' equity section of the balance sheet (a) immediately before the stock dividend and (b) immediately after the stock dividend. (*Hint:* Use two columns for the amounts in this requirement.)
2. Explain the effects of this stock dividend on the assets, liabilities, and stockholders' equity.

E11-13 Recording Dividends

LO3

Black & Decker is a leading global manufacturer and marketer of power tools, hardware, and home improvement products. A press release on May 29, 2004, contained the following announcement:

> The Black & Decker Corporation announced today that its Board of Directors declared a quarterly cash dividend of $0.21 per share of the company's outstanding common stock payable June 25, 2004, to stockholders of record at the close of business on June 11, 2004.

At the time of the press release, Black & Decker had 150,000,000 shares authorized and 77,993,000 issued and outstanding. The par value for the company's stock is $.01 per share.

Required:

Prepare journal entries as appropriate for each of the three dates mentioned above.

E11-14 Comparing Stock Dividends and Splits

LO3

On July 1, 2004, Jones Corporation had the following capital structure:

Common stock (par $1, authorized shares)	$200,000
Common stock (par $1, unissued shares)	50,000
Additional paid-in capital	88,000
Retained earnings	172,000
Treasury stock	None

Required:

Complete the following table based on three independent cases involving stock transactions:

Case 1: The board of directors declared and issued a 20 percent stock dividend when the stock was selling at $4 per share.

Case 2: The board of directors declared and issued a 100 percent stock dividend when the stock was selling at $4 per share.

Case 3: The board of directors voted a 2-for-1 stock split. The market price prior to the split was $4 per share.

		Case 1	Case 2	Case 3
Items	**Before Stock Transactions**	**After 20% Stock Dividend**	**After 100% Stock Dividend**	**After Stock Split**
Number of shares outstanding				
Par per share	$ 1	$	$	$
Common stock account	$	$	$	$
Additional paid-in capital	88,000			
Retained earnings	172,000			
Total stockholders' equity	$	$	$	$

LO4

E11-15 Analyzing Dividends in Arrears

Mission Critical Software, Inc., was a leading provider of systems management software for Windows NT network and Internet infrastructure. Like many start-up companies, Mission Critical struggled with cash flows as it developed new business opportunities. A student found a financial statement for Mission Critical that stated that the increase in dividends in arrears on preferred stock this year was $264,000.

The student who read the note suggested that the Mission Critical preferred stock would be a good investment because of the large amount of dividend income that would be earned when the company started paying dividends again: "As the owner of the stock, I'll get dividends for the period I hold the stock plus some previous periods when I didn't even own the stock." Do you agree? Explain.

LO3, LO4

E11-16 Determining the Impact of Cash and Stock Dividends

Average Corporation has the following capital stock outstanding at the end of 2005:

Preferred stock, 6 percent, par $15, outstanding shares, 8,000.

Common stock, par $8, outstanding shares, 30,000.

On October 1, 2005, the board of directors declared dividends as follows:

Preferred stock: Full cash preference amount, payable December 20, 2005.

Common stock: 10 percent common stock dividend (i.e., one additional share for each 10 held), to be issued on December 20, 2005.

On December 20, 2005, the market prices were preferred stock, $40, and common stock, $32.

Required:

At each date indicated above, describe the overall effect of the cash and stock dividends on the assets, liabilities, and stockholders' equity of the company.

LO3, LO4

E11-17 Determining the Financial Statement Effects of Cash and Stock Dividends

Lynn Company has outstanding 60,000 shares of $10 par value common stock and 25,000 shares of $20 par value preferred stock (8 percent). On December 1, 2004, the board of directors voted an 8 percent cash dividend on the preferred stock and a 10 percent stock dividend on the common stock. At the date of declaration, the common stock was selling at $35 and the preferred at $20 per share. The dividends are to be paid, or issued, on February 15, 2005. The annual accounting period ends December 31.

Required:

Explain the comparative effects of the two dividends on the assets, liabilities, and stockholders' equity (a) through December 31, 2004, (b) on February 15, 2005, and (c) the overall effects from December 1, 2004, through February 15, 2005. A schedule using the following structure might be helpful:

	Comparative Effects Explained	
Item	**Cash Dividend on Preferred**	**Stock Dividend on Common**
(a) Through December 31, 2004:		
Effect on Assets		
Effect on Liabilities		
Effect on Stockholders' Equity		

E11-18 Preparing a Statement of Stockholders' Equity and Evaluating Dividend Policy   LO3, LO5

The following account balances were selected from the records of clothing retailer Blake Corporation at December 31, 2007, after all adjusting entries were completed:

Common stock (par $15; authorized 100,000 shares, issued 35,000 shares, of which 1,000 shares are held as treasury stock)	$525,000
Additional paid-in capital	180,000
Dividends declared and paid in 2007	18,000
Retained earnings, January 1, 2007	76,000
Treasury stock at cost (1,000 shares)	20,000

Net income for the year was $28,000.

Required:

1. Prepare the stockholders' equity section of the balance sheet at December 31, 2007.
2. Determine the number of shares of stock that received dividends.
3. Compute the ROE ratio, assuming total stockholders' equity was $629,000 on December 31, 2006. How does it compare to the ratios shown in Exhibit 11.8?

E11-19 Analyzing Stock Repurchases and Stock Dividends   LO3, LO6

Winnebago is a familiar name on vehicles traveling U.S. highways. The company manufactures and sells large motor homes for vacation travel. These motor homes can be quickly recognized because of the company's "flying W" trademark. A June 19, 2002, news article contained the following information:

Winnebago Industries, Inc., (NYSE: WGO) today announced that the board of directors has authorized the purchase of outstanding shares of the Company's common stock for an aggregate price of up to $15 million. This is the seventh stock repurchase program to be announced within the last five years.

Required:

1. Determine the impact of this stock buyback on the financial statements.
2. Why do you think the board decided to repurchase the stock?
3. What impact will this purchase have on Winnebago's future dividend obligations?

4. On January 14, 2004, the company's board of directors declared a 2-for-1 stock split effected in the form of a 100 percent stock dividend distributed on March 5, 2004. Why would Winnebago choose a stock dividend rather than an actual stock split?

5. What impact would this stock dividend have had on Winnebago's financial statements? What impact would it have had on the EPS and ROE ratios?

E11-20 (Supplement A) Comparing Stockholders' Equity Sections for Alternative Forms of Organization

Assume for each of the following independent cases that the annual accounting period ends on December 31, 2005, and that the total of all revenue accounts was $150,000 and the total of all expense accounts was $130,000.

Case A: Assume that the company is a *sole proprietorship* owned by Proprietor A. Prior to the closing entries, the capital account reflected a credit balance of $50,000 and the drawings account a balance of $8,000.

Case B: Assume that the company is a *partnership* owned by Partner A and Partner B. Prior to the closing entries, the owners' equity accounts reflected the following balances: A, Capital, $40,000; B, Capital, $38,000; A, Drawings, $5,000; and B, Drawings, $9,000. Profits and losses are divided equally.

Case C: Assume that the company is a *corporation*. Prior to the closing entries, the stockholders' equity accounts showed the following: Capital Stock, par $10, authorized 30,000 shares, outstanding 15,000 shares; Additional paid-in capital, $5,000; Retained Earnings, $65,000.

Required:

1. Give all the closing entries required at December 31, 2005, for each of the separate cases.
2. Show how the equity section of the balance sheet would appear at December 31, 2005, for each case.

SIMPLIFY WITH SPREADSHEETS

L01 **SS11-1 Charting Stock Price Movement around Important Announcement Dates**

Using a Web search engine like Google, find either an earnings or dividend announcement for two different companies. Using a source such as bigcharts.com, determine the closing stock price for each company for each day during the five business days before and after the announcement. Using a separate worksheet for each company, prepare a line chart of its stock price movement.

Required:

Examine the charts for each company. Does the stock price appear to change as a consequence of their announcements? Explain why or why not.

COACHED PROBLEMS

L02 **CP11-1 Preparing a Statement of Stockholders' Equity and Partial Balance Sheet after Selected Transactions**

Worldwide Company obtained a charter from the state in January 2005, which authorized 200,000 shares of common stock, $10 par value. The stockholders were 30 local citizens. During the first year, the company earned $38,200 and the following selected transactions occurred in the order given:

a. Sold 60,000 shares of the common stock at $12 per share.
b. Purchased 2,000 shares at $15 cash per share from one of the 30 stockholders who needed cash and wanted to sell the stock back to the company.
c. Resold 1,000 of the shares of the treasury stock purchased in transaction *b* two months later to another individual at $18 cash per share.

Required:

1. Prepare a statement of stockholders' equity for the year ended December 31, 2005.
2. Prepare the stockholders' equity section of the balance sheet at December 31, 2005.

COACH'S CORNER

See Exhibit 11.6 for an example of a statement of stockholders' equity.

CP11-2 Recording Dividends

Adobe Systems develops and markets computer software including Adobe Acrobat that enables users to access information across all print and electronic media. A recent news article contained the following information:

> September 16, 1999—Adobe Systems reported record revenue and operating profit for the third quarter of fiscal 1999. The Board of Directors announced a 100% stock dividend will occur on October 26, 1999, for stockholders of record on October 4, 1999. The Board also declared this quarter's cash dividend of $0.05 per share, payable on October 12, 1999, to stockholders of record as of September 28, 1999.

LO3

COACH'S CORNER

Because large stock dividends dramatically affect stock price, they are recorded using par value.

Required:

1. Prepare any journal entries that Adobe should make as the result of information in the preceding report. Assume that, on September 16, 1999, the company had one million shares outstanding, the par value was $0.50 per share, and the market value was $40 per share.
2. What two requirements would the board of directors have considered before making the dividend decision?

CP11-3 Finding Missing Amounts

At December 31, 2007, the records of Nortech Corporation provided the following selected and incomplete data:

Common stock (par $10; no changes during 2007).

Shares authorized, 200,000.

Shares issued, ___?___; issue price $17 per share.

Common stock account $1,250,000.

Shares held as treasury stock, 3,000 shares, cost $20 per share.

Net income for 2007, $118,000.

Dividends declared and paid during 2007, $73,200.

Retained earnings balance, January 1, 2007, $155,000.

LO2–LO5

COACH'S CORNER

To determine the number of shares issued, divide the balance in the common stock account by the par value per share.

Required:

1. Complete the following:
   Shares authorized _____.
   Shares issued _____.
   Shares outstanding _____.
2. The balance in the additional paid-in capital account would be $_____.
3. Earnings per share is $_____.
4. Dividends paid per share of common stock is $_____.
5. Treasury stock should be reported in the stockholders' equity section of the balance sheet in the amount of $_____.
6. Assume that the board of directors approved a 2-for-1 stock split. After the stock split, the par value per share will be $_____ and the number of outstanding shares will be _____. The treasury stock was acquired after the split was issued.
7. Disregard the stock split (assumed above). Assume instead that a 10 percent stock dividend was declared and issued after the treasury stock was acquired, when the market price of the common stock was $21. Give any journal entry that should be made.

CP11-4 Comparing Stock and Cash Dividends

Water Tower Company had the following stock outstanding and retained earnings at December 31, 2007:

LO2–LO4

eXcel

Common stock (par $8; outstanding, 30,000 shares)	$240,000
Preferred stock, 7% (par $10; outstanding, 6,000 shares)	60,000
Retained earnings	280,000

COACH'S CORNER

Preferred stockholders with cumulative dividends are paid dividends for any prior years (in arrears) *and* for the current year before common stockholders are paid.

The board of directors is considering the distribution of a cash dividend to the common and preferred stockholders. No dividends were declared during 2005 or 2006. Three independent cases are assumed:

Case A: The preferred stock is noncumulative; the total amount of dividends is $30,000.

Case B: The preferred stock is cumulative; the total amount of dividends is $12,600.

Case C: Same as Case B, except the amount is $66,000.

Required:

1. Compute the amount of dividends, in total and per share, that would be payable to each class of stockholders for each case. Show computations.

2. Assume that to remind stockholders of their accumulating wealth in the company, a 10 percent common stock dividend was issued when the market value per share was $24. Complete the following schedule.

	Amount of Dollar Increase (Decrease)	
Item	**Cash Dividend, Case C**	**Stock Dividend**
Assets	$	$
Liabilities	$	$
Stockholders' equity	$	$

LO5, LO6

CP11-5 Computing and Interpreting Return on Equity (ROE)

Two publicly traded rental companies reported the following in their 2003 financial statements (in thousands):

COACH'S CORNER

Remember that the bottom of the ROE ratio uses the *average* stockholders' equity.

	Aaron Rents, Inc.		Rent-A-Center, Inc.	
	2003	**2002**	**2003**	**2002**
Net income	$ 36,426	$ 27,440	$181,496	$172,173
Total stockholders' equity	320,186	280,545	794,830	842,400

Required:

1. Compute the 2003 ROE for each company. Which company appears to generate greater returns on stockholders' equity in 2003?

2. Rent-A-Center repurchased 2,544 (thousand) shares of common stock in June and July 2003 at $73 per share. Recalculate the company's ROE for 2003 assuming that this stock repurchase did not occur. Does this change your interpretation of the ROE ratios calculated in requirement 1?

GROUP A PROBLEMS   Available with McGraw-Hill's Homework Manager

LO2

PA11-1 Preparing a Statement of Stockholders' Equity and Partial Balance Sheet after Selected Transactions

Global Marine obtained a charter from the state in January 2005, which authorized 1,000,000 shares of common stock, $5 par value. During the first year, the company earned $429,000 and the following selected transactions occurred in the order given:

a. Sold 700,000 shares of the common stock at $54 per share. Collected the cash and issued the stock.

b. Purchased 25,000 shares at $50 cash per share to use as stock incentives for senior management.

Required:

1. Prepare a statement of stockholders' equity for the year ended December 31, 2005.

2. Prepare the stockholders' equity section of the balance sheet at December 31, 2005.

PA11-2 Recording Dividends

LO3

National Beverage Corp. produces soft drinks, bottled waters, and juices sold under the brand names Shasta®, Faygo®, and Everfresh®. A recent press release contained the following information:

> March 5, 2004—National Beverage Corp. today announced that its Board of Directors has declared a special "one-time" cash dividend of $1.00 per share on approximately 36.6 million outstanding shares (subsequent to the Company's payment of a 100% stock dividend on March 22, 2004). The dividend will be paid on or before April 30, 2004 to shareholders of record at the close of business on March 26, 2004.

Required:

1. Prepare any journal entries that National Beverage Corp. should make as the result of information in the preceding report. Assume that the company has 18.3 million shares outstanding on March 5, 2004, the par value is $0.01 per share, and the market value is $10 per share.
2. What two requirements would the board of directors have considered before making the dividend decisions?

PA11-3 Finding Missing Amounts

LO2–LO5

At December 31, 2005, the records of Kozmetsky Corporation provided the following selected and incomplete data:

Common stock (par $1; no changes during 2005).
Shares authorized, 5,000,000.
Shares issued, ___?___; issue price $80 per share.
Shares held as treasury stock, 100,000 shares, cost $60 per share.
Net income for 2005, $4,800,000.
Common stock account $1,500,000.
Dividends declared and paid during 2005, $2 per share.
Retained earnings balance, January 1, 2005, $82,900,000.

Required:

1. Complete the following:
   Shares issued _____.
   Shares outstanding _____.
2. The balance in the additional paid-in capital account would be $_____.
3. Earnings per share is $_____.
4. Total dividends paid on common stock during 2005 is $_____.
5. Treasury stock should be reported in the stockholders' equity section of the balance sheet in the amount of $_____.
6. Assume that the board of directors voted a 2-for-1 stock split. After the stock split, the par value per share will be $_____, and the number of outstanding shares will be _____. The treasury stock was acquired after the split was issued.
7. Disregard the stock split (assumed above). Assume instead that a 10 percent stock dividend was declared and issued after the treasury stock was acquired, when the market price of the common stock was $21. Explain how stockholders' equity will change.

PA11-4 Comparing Stock and Cash Dividends

LO2–LO4

Ritz Company had the following stock outstanding and retained earnings at December 31, 2006:

Common stock (par $1; outstanding, 500,000 shares)	$500,000
Preferred stock, 8% (par $10; outstanding, 21,000 shares)	210,000
Retained earnings	900,000

The board of directors is considering the distribution of a cash dividend to the common and preferred stockholders. No dividends were declared during 2004 or 2005. Three independent cases are assumed:

Case A: The preferred stock is noncumulative; the total amount of dividends is $25,000.
Case B: The preferred stock is cumulative; the total amount of dividends is $25,000.
Case C: Same as Case B, except the amount is $75,000.

Required:

1. Compute the amount of dividends, in total and per share, payable to each class of stockholders for each case. Show computations.
2. Assume that the company issued a 15 percent stock dividend on the outstanding common shares when the market value per share was $50. Complete the following comparative schedule, including explanation of the comparative differences.

	Amount of Dollar Increase (Decrease)	
Item	**Cash Dividend, Case C**	**Stock Dividend**
Assets	$	$
Liabilities	$	$
Stockholders' equity	$	$

LO5, LO6

eXcel

PA11-5 Computing and Interpreting Return on Equity (ROE)

Two magazine companies reported the following in their 2005 financial statements (in thousands):

	BusinessWorld		Fun and Games	
	2005	**2004**	**2005**	**2004**
Net income	$ 55,000	$ 54,302	$ 91,420	$172,173
Total stockholders' equity	587,186	512,814	894,302	934,098

Required:

1. Compute the 2005 ROE for each company. Which company appears to generate greater returns on stockholders' equity in 2005?
2. Fun and Games repurchased 32,804 (thousand) shares of common stock in 2005 at $4 per share. Recalculate the company's ROE for 2005 assuming that this stock repurchase did not occur. Does this change your interpretation of the ROE ratios calculated in requirement 1?

GROUP B PROBLEMS

LO2

PB11-1 Preparing a Statement of Stockholders' Equity and Partial Balance Sheet after Selected Transactions

Whyville Corporation obtained its charter from the state in January 2005, which authorized 500,000 shares of common stock, $1 par value. During the first year, the company earned $58,000 and the following selected transactions occurred in the order given:

a. Sold 200,000 shares of the common stock at $23 per share. Collected the cash and issued the stock.
b. Purchased 5,000 shares at $24 cash per share to use as stock incentives for senior management.

Required:

1. Prepare a statement of stockholders' equity for the year ended December 31, 2005.
2. Prepare the stockholders' equity section of the balance sheet at December 31, 2005.

LO3

PB11-2 Recording Dividends

Yougi Corp. is an animation studio operating in South Florida. A recent press release contained the following information:

April 1, 2004—Yougi Corp. today announced that its Board of Directors has declared a cash dividend of $0.50 per share on 605,000 outstanding preferred shares. The dividend will be paid on or before May 31, 2004, to preferred shareholders of record at the close of business on May 26, 2004. The Board of Directors also announced a 100% common stock dividend will occur on May 31, 2004, on its 1,900,000 outstanding $0.01 par common stock for stockholders of record on May 26, 2004.

Required:

1. Prepare any journal entries that Yougi Corp. should make as the result of information in the preceding report.
2. What two requirements would the board of directors have considered before making the dividend decision?

PB11-3 Finding Missing Amounts   LO2–LO5

At December 31, 2005, the records of Seacrest Enterprises provided the following selected and incomplete data:

Common stock (par $0.50; no changes during 2005).

Shares authorized, 10,000,000.

Shares issued, ___?___; issue price $10 per share.

Shares held as treasury stock, 50,000 shares, cost $11 per share.

Net income for 2005, $2,400,000.

Common stock account $750,000.

Dividends declared and paid during 2005, $1 per share.

Retained earnings balance, January 1, 2005, $36,400,000.

Required:

1. Complete the following:
   Shares issued _____.
   Shares outstanding _____.
2. The balance in the additional paid-in capital account would be $_____.
3. Earnings per share is $_____.
4. Total dividends paid on common stock during 2005 is $_____.
5. Treasury stock should be reported in the stockholders' equity section of the balance sheet in the amount of $_____.
6. Assume that the board of directors voted a 2-for-1 stock split. After the stock split, the par value per share will be $_____, and the number of outstanding shares will be _____. The treasury stock was acquired after the split was issued.
7. Disregard the stock split (assumed above). Assume instead that a 10 percent stock dividend was declared and issued after the treasury stock was acquired, when the market price of the common stock was $21. Explain how stockholders' equity will change.

PB11-4 Comparing Stock and Cash Dividends   LO2–LO4

Reuben Company had the following stock outstanding and retained earnings at December 31, 2006:

Common stock (par $1; outstanding, 490,000 shares)	$490,000
Preferred stock, 8% (par $10; outstanding, 19,000 shares)	190,000
Retained earnings	966,000

The board of directors is considering the distribution of a cash dividend to the common and preferred stockholders. No dividends were declared during 2004 or 2005. Three independent cases are assumed:

Case A: The preferred stock is noncumulative; the total amount of dividends is $24,000.

Case B: The preferred stock is cumulative; the total amount of dividends is $24,000.

Case C: Same as Case B, except the amount is $67,000.

Required:

1. Compute the amount of dividends, in total and per share, payable to each class of stockholders for each case. Show computations.

2. Assume that the company issued a 10 percent stock dividend on the outstanding common shares when the market value per share was $45. Complete the following comparative schedule, including explanation of the comparative differences.

	Amount of Dollar Increase (Decrease)	
Item	*Cash Dividend, Case C*	*Stock Dividend*
Assets	$	$
Liabilities	$	$
Stockholders' equity	$	$

LO5, LO6

PB11-5 Computing and Interpreting Return on Equity (ROE)

Two music companies reported the following in their 2005 financial statements (in thousands):

	Urban Youth		Sound Jonx	
	2005	*2004*	*2005*	*2004*
Net income	$ 27,500	$ 24,302	$ 41,500	$ 36,739
Total stockholders' equity	387,101	300,399	516,302	521,198

Required:

1. Compute the 2005 ROE for each company. Which company appears to generate greater returns on stockholders' equity in 2005?

2. Sound Jonx repurchased 5,000 (thousand) shares of common stock in 2005 at $13 per share. Recalculate the company's ROE for 2005 assuming that this stock repurchase did not occur. Does this change your interpretation of the ROE ratios calculated in requirement 1?

CASES & DISCUSSION STARTERS

FINANCIAL REPORTING AND ANALYSIS CASES

LO1–LO3, LO5

C&DS11-1 Finding Financial Information

Refer to the financial statements of Landry's Restaurants in Appendix A at the end of this book, or download the annual report from the *Cases* section of the text's Web site at www.mhhe.com/phillips.

COACH'S CORNER

The total stockholders' equity at the beginning of the prior year, which is needed for the calculation in requirement 5, is reported in the statement of stockholders' equity.

Required:

1. How many shares of common stock are authorized? How many shares are issued? How many shares are outstanding? What does this suggest to you about the number of shares held in treasury?

2. According to the statement of stockholders' equity, how much did the company declare in dividends during the current year? Using your answer to requirement 1, calculate approximately how much this was per share. Does this correspond to what is reported in Note 8 of the financial statements?

3. Note 8 to the financial statements indicates that Landry's purchased treasury stock for approximately $8.4 million. According to the statement of stockholders' equity, how much was it exactly? (You might find it odd that Landry's purchased treasury stock during the year but reported none at year-end. The explanation for this is that Landry's cancelled the treasury

stock during the year. This also is the reason that you see treasury stock being deducted directly from various stockholders' equity accounts on the statement of stockholders' equity. Cancellation of treasury stock is typically taught in intermediate accounting.)

4. How has Landry's basic earnings per share changed over the past three years? Based on this trend, what do you predict will happen in the following year? Does Landry's maintain a stock option plan? How can you tell?

5. Calculate the ROE ratio for Landry's in the current and prior year.

C&DS11-2 Comparing Financial Information

LO1–LO3, LO5

Refer to the financial statements of Dave & Buster's in Appendix B at the end of this book, or download the annual report from the *Cases* section of the text's Web site at www.mhhe.com/phillips.

Required:

1. Did Dave & Buster's have more or fewer authorized shares of common stock than Landry's?

2. From the statement of stockholders' equity, does it appear that Dave & Buster's declared dividends during the current year? Compared to Landry's, is Dave & Buster's policy on dividends better, worse, or just different?

3. Based on the balance sheet disclosures, how much did Dave & Buster's pay to repurchase its stock into treasury?

4. How has Dave & Buster's basic EPS changed over the past three years? Based on this trend, what do you predict will happen in the following year? Do you find it easier to predict EPS for Dave & Buster's or for Landry's? Does Dave & Buster's maintain a stock option plan? How can you tell?

5. Calculate the ROE ratio for Dave & Buster's in the current and prior year. (Total stockholders' equity at the beginning of the prior year is reported in the statement of stockholders' equity.) How does Dave & Buster's compare to Landry's on this ratio?

C&DS11-3 Internet-Based Team Research: Examining an Annual Report

LO3, LO5

As a team, select an industry to analyze. Using your Web browser, each team member should acquire the annual report or 10-K for one publicly traded company in the industry, with each member selecting a different company. (See C&DS1-3 in Chapter 1 for a description of possible resources for these tasks.)

**TEAM
CASE**

Required:

1. On an individual basis, each team member should write a short report that incorporates the following:
   a. Has the company declared cash or stock dividends during the past three years?
   b. What is the trend in the company's EPS over the past three years?
   c. Compute and analyze the return on equity ratio over the past two years.

2. Then, as a team, write a short report comparing and contrasting your companies using these attributes. Discuss any patterns across the companies that you as a team observe. Provide potential explanations for any differences discovered.

ETHICS AND CRITICAL THINKING CASES

C&DS11-4 Ethical Decision Making: A Real-Life Example

LO1, LO3

ETHICAL

ISSUE

Activision became a public company with an initial public offering of stock on June 9, 1983, at $12 per share. In June 2002, Activision issued 7.5 million additional shares to the public at approximately $33 per share in a seasoned new issue. In October 2002, when its stock was trading at about $22 per share, Activision executives announced that the company would spend up to $150 million to buy back stock from investors. On January 8, 2003, the *Wall Street Journal* reported that several analysts were criticizing Activision's executives because the company had sold the shares to the public at a high price ($33) and then were offering to buy them back at the going market price, which was considerably lower than the issue price in 2002.

Required:

1. Do you think it was inappropriate for Activision to offer to buy back the stock at a lower price in October 2002?

2. Would your answer to question 1 be different if Activision had not issued additional stock in June 2002?

3. The above *Wall Street Journal* article also reported that, in December 2002, Activision executives had purchased over 530,000 shares of stock in the company at the then-current price of $13.32 per share. If you were an investor, how would you feel about executives buying stock in their own company?

4. Would your answer to question 3 be different if you also learned that the executives had sold nearly 2.5 million shares of Activision stock earlier in the year, when the price was at least $26.08 per share?

LO3

ETHICAL

ISSUE

C&DS11-5 Ethical Decision Making: A Mini-Case

You are the president of a very successful Internet company that has had a remarkably profitable year. You have determined that the company has more than $10 million in cash generated by operating activities not needed in the business. You are thinking about paying it out to stockholders as a special dividend. You discuss the idea with your vice president, who reacts angrily to your suggestion:

> Our stock price has gone up by 200 percent in the last year alone. What more do we have to do for the owners? The people who really earned that money are the employees who have been working 12 hours a day, six or seven days a week to make the company successful. Most of them didn't even take vacations last year. I say we have to pay out bonuses and nothing extra for the stockholders.

As president, you know that you are hired by the board of directors, which is elected by the stockholders.

Required:

What is your responsibility to both groups? To which group would you give the $10 million? Why?

LO3

C&DS11-6 Critical Thinking: Making a Decision as an Investor

You have retired after a long and successful career as a business executive and now spend a good portion of your time managing your retirement portfolio. You are considering three basic investment alternatives. You can invest in (1) corporate bonds currently paying 7 percent interest, (2) conservative stocks that pay substantial dividends (typically 5 percent of the stock price every year), and (3) growth-oriented technology stocks that pay no dividends.

Required:

Analyze each of these alternatives and select one. Justify your selection.

www.mhhe.com/phillips

chapter twelve

Reporting and Interpreting the Statement of Cash Flows

12

If you're like most people, you probably feel like you gain weight in the fall and winter and then lose it in the spring and summer. To understand and control seasonal weight fluctuations, the President's Council on Physical Fitness recommends that you track your inflows and outflows of calories. By analyzing a summary of your total inflows and outflows over a period of time, you can better understand how to improve your weight situation. You might discover that it takes more than half an hour on the StairMaster to burn off the 500 calories that flow in when you down a Super Big Gulp of Coke.

The **NAUTILUS GROUP,** the maker of BowFlex and StairMaster fitness equipment, has *its* greatest gains in the spring. But we're not talking about pounds or calories anymore. Instead, we're focusing on the company's cash position. In 2003, for example, the first quarter alone generated an increase of nearly $30 million in cash. To control and report the causes of its seasonal fluctuations in cash position, Nautilus prepares a statement of cash flows that tracks inflows and outflows of cash related to its operating, investing, and financing activities. As you will see later in this chapter, it can also help you, as a financial statement user, to understand better the company's financial performance.

INSIDE
LOOKING
OUT

OUTSIDE
LOOKING IN

This chapter focuses on reporting and interpreting the statement of cash flows of the Nautilus Group, maker of BowFlex, StairMaster, and Schwinn fitness equipment.

The Nautilus Group sells fitness equipment to residential and commercial customers.

The king is here! No, we we're not talking about Elvis. The king, according to some analysts, is the cash that's reported on the statement of cash flows. These analysts aren't dismissing the accrual basis of accounting. They just believe it's crucial to consider the cash flows of a business too. As Exhibit 12.1 indicates, you'll begin this chapter by learning what the statement of cash flows reports. Then, to help you truly understand what the items on this statement represent, you'll study how to create this statement yourself. The third section of the chapter will arm you with what you need to know as an outsider using the cash flow statement. We'll pull it all together in the final section to show how you can use your knowledge about the statement of cash flows to evaluate the results reported in other financial statements.

exhibit 12.1 | **Your Learning Objectives**

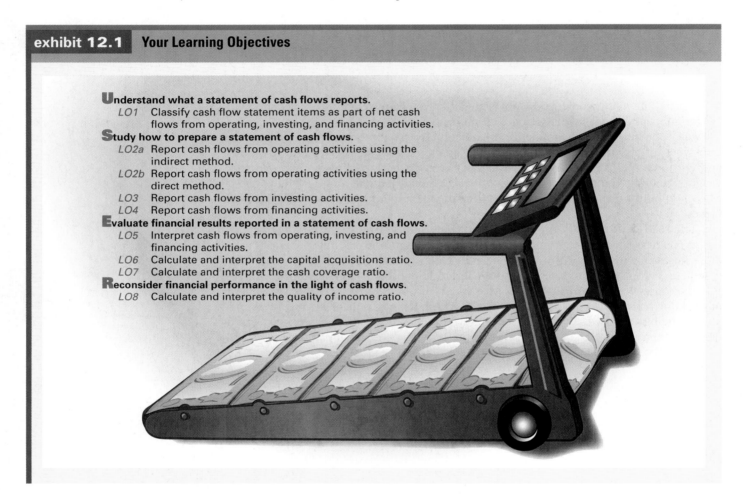

Understand what a statement of cash flows reports.
- *LO1* Classify cash flow statement items as part of net cash flows from operating, investing, and financing activities.

Study how to prepare a statement of cash flows.
- *LO2a* Report cash flows from operating activities using the indirect method.
- *LO2b* Report cash flows from operating activities using the direct method.
- *LO3* Report cash flows from investing activities.
- *LO4* Report cash flows from financing activities.

Evaluate financial results reported in a statement of cash flows.
- *LO5* Interpret cash flows from operating, investing, and financing activities.
- *LO6* Calculate and interpret the capital acquisitions ratio.
- *LO7* Calculate and interpret the cash coverage ratio.

Reconsider financial performance in the light of cash flows.
- *LO8* Calculate and interpret the quality of income ratio.

┌ UNDERSTAND
└ WHAT A STATEMENT OF CASH FLOWS REPORTS

The Need for a Statement of Cash Flows

Companies haven't always been required to report a statement of cash flows. So why are they now? One of the reasons is that, before the statement of cash flows was born, some companies ran out of cash even when they were reporting profits, catching many financial statement users by surprise. Now, with the statement of cash flows to report all the cash receipts and cash payments of a business, it's much easier to detect cases where this might occur. Another benefit is that it's very difficult for dishonest managers to manipulate both a statement of cash flows and an accrual-based income statement at the same time.

Clearly, net income is important, but seasonal fluctuations in sales, inventory purchases, and advertising expenditures can lead to odd combinations of income and cash flows. It's not unusual to have **high profits alongside net outflows of cash** in some quarters, and **losses combined with net cash inflows** in others. This occurs because, as we have seen in earlier chapters, the timing of revenues and expenses does not always line up with cash inflows and outflows. As a consequence, managers carefully monitor both cash flows and profits. For the same reasons, financial analysts consider the information in the statement of cash flows as well as the other financial statements.

The cash flow statement focuses attention on four things: (1) a company's ability to generate cash internally from its operating activities, (2) its management of current assets and current liabilities, (3) the amount spent on long-term assets, and (4) the amount received from external financing. It helps both managers and analysts answer important cash-related questions such as

The statement of cash flows is briefly introduced in a video on the DVD for use with this book.

- Will the company have enough cash to pay its short-term debts to suppliers and other creditors without additional borrowing?
- Is the company adequately managing its accounts receivable and inventory?
- Has the company purchased sufficient equipment and other long-term assets?
- Did the company generate enough cash flow internally to finance these purchases, or did it rely on external financing?
- Is the company changing the source of its external financing?

To understand how the statement of cash flows answers these questions, it's useful to first see how transactions are classified in the statement.

Classifications in the Statement of Cash Flows

Basically, the statement of cash flows explains how the amount of cash on the balance sheet at the end of the previous period became the amount of cash at the end of the current period. For purposes of this statement, the definition of cash includes cash and cash equivalents. **Cash equivalents** are short-term, highly liquid investments that are both

YOU SHOULD KNOW

A **cash equivalent** is a short-term, highly liquid investment with an original maturity of less than three months.

1. Readily convertible to known amounts of cash, and
2. So near to maturity that there is little risk their value will change.

For most companies, including Nautilus, cash and cash equivalents include cash on hand, cash deposited with banks, and highly liquid investments purchased within three months of maturity. In your personal life, cash equivalents could include checks you've received but not yet deposited into your bank account or certificates of deposit (CDs) that are about to mature.

Before we look at a sample statement, let's agree to two simplifications that'll allow you to read a little faster. First, rather than saying "cash and cash equivalents," let's just say "cash" with the understanding that it includes cash equivalents as well. Second, let's shorten statement of cash flows to SCF, which is what most accountants and analysts do in the real world. Okay, so let's look at the SCF. (See, you just saved two seconds.)

As you can see in Exhibit 12.2, the SCF reports cash inflows and outflows in three broad categories: (1) operating activities, (2) investing activities, and (3) financing activities. Looking only at the subtotals (which we've highlighted), you can see that operating activities generated a net cash inflow of about $16.4 million cash during the first three months of 2003. Investing activities resulted in an additional $14.0 million, whereas financing activities required the Nautilus Group to use up nearly $1.7 million cash. Together, these three cash flow categories show a net increase in cash of nearly $28.7 million (16.4 + 14.0 − 1.7). When this change is added to the beginning cash balance ($31.7 million), you arrive at the ending cash balance ($60.4 million), reported on the balance sheet. Let's begin to dissect the SCF a little further, by looking at what goes into each of the operating, investing, and financing activities.

FAST FLASHBACK

Operating activities include day-to-day events involved in running a business. *Investing activities* involve buying or selling long-lived items such as land, buildings, and equipment. *Financing activities* are related to exchanging money with lenders or owners.

exhibit 12.2	Sample Statement of Cash Flows—Indirect Method

THE NAUTILUS GROUP, INC.
Statement of Cash Flows*
Three Months Ended March 31, 2003

(unaudited—in thousands)

Cash Flows from Operating Activities:	
Net income	$ 13,689
Adjustments to reconcile net income to net cash provided by operating activities:	
Depreciation	2,764
Changes in assets and liabilities:	
Accounts receivable	8,614
Inventories	(3,022)
Prepaid expenses	(409)
Accounts payable	(11,970)
Accrued liabilities	6,766
Net cash provided by operating activities	16,432
Cash Flows from Investing Activities:	
Maturities of short-term investments	17,578
Purchases of equipment	(3,626)
Net cash provided by investing activities	13,952
Cash Flows from Financing Activities:	
Additional long-term debt borrowed	1,897
Proceeds from stock issuance	622
Cash dividends paid	(4,207)
Net cash used in financing activities	(1,688)
Net increase in cash and cash equivalents	28,696
Cash and cash equivalents at beginning of period	31,719
Cash and cash equivalents at end of period	$ 60,415

*Certain amounts have been adjusted to simplify the presentation.

Cash Flows from Operating Activities

Cash flows from operating activities (or simply called cash flows from operations) are the cash inflows and outflows that relate directly to revenues and expenses reported on the income statement. There are two alternative approaches for presenting the operating activities section of the statement:

1. The **direct method** reports the total cash inflow from each main operating activity that generates cash as well as the total cash outflow for each main operating activity that uses cash. Typical operating inflows and outflows of cash are listed below.

Inflows	Outflows
Cash provided by Customers Dividends and interest on investments	*Cash used for* Purchase of goods for resale and services (electricity, etc.) Salaries and wages Income taxes Interest on liabilities

The difference between these cash inflows and outflows is called *Net cash provided by (used for) operating activities*.

2. Although the FASB says it prefers the direct method, it is rarely used in the United States. Instead, nearly 99 percent of large U.S. companies, including the Nautilus Group, use the **indirect method**, which also is allowed by the FASB.[1] The indirect method starts with net income from the income statement and then adjusts it by removing items that do not involve cash but were included in net income. By eliminating these "noncash" items, we back into the *Net cash provided by (used for) operating activities*.

> Net income
> ± Adjustments for noncash items
> = Net cash provided by (used for) operating activities

For now, the most important thing to remember about the two methods is that they are simply different ways to arrive at the same number. The total amount of **cash flows from operating activities is always the same regardless of whether it is computed using the direct or indirect method.** Management's choice of method for presenting its operating cash flows does not affect the other sections of the SCF.

Cash Flows from Investing Activities

Cash flows from investing activities are cash inflows and outflows related to the purchase and disposal of long-lived assets. Typical cash flows from investing activities are listed below.

Inflows	Outflows
Cash provided by	*Cash used for*
Sale or disposal of property, plant, and equipment	Purchase of property, plant, and equipment
Sale or maturity of investments in securities	Purchase of investments in securities

The difference between these cash inflows and outflows is called *Net cash provided by (used for) investing activities*.

Cash Flows from Financing Activities

Cash flows from financing activities include exchanges of cash with stockholders and cash exchanges with lenders (for principal on loans). Common cash flows from financing activities are listed below.

Inflows	Outflows
Cash provided by	*Cash used for*
Borrowing from lenders through formal debt contracts	Repaying principal to lenders
Issuing stock to owners	Repurchasing stock from owners
	Paying dividends to owners

The difference between these cash inflows and outflows is called *Net cash provided by (used for) financing activities*.

To check that you understand these classifications, try the following Self-Study Quiz.

---

[1]AICPA 2003, *Accounting Trends & Techniques*.

HOW'S IT GOING?   **A Self-Study Quiz**

Brunswick Corporation—the billiards, bowling, boating, and "buffing" company—produces the Life Fitness line of gym equipment, which competes head on with the Nautilus Group. A listing of some of its cash flows follows. Indicate whether each item is disclosed in the operating activities (O), investing activities (I), or financing activities (F) section of the statement of cash flows.

☐ *a.* Stock issued to stockholders.   ☐ *d.* Purchase of plant and equipment.

☐ *b.* Collections from customers.   ☐ *e.* Acquisition of investment securities.

☐ *c.* Interest paid on debt.   ☐ *f.* Cash dividends paid.

After you're done, check your answers with the solutions in the margin.

STUDY

HOW TO PREPARE A STATEMENT OF CASH FLOWS

Relationships to the Balance Sheet and Income Statement

The cash flow statement is prepared by analyzing the income statement and changes in balance sheet accounts, and relating these changes to the three sections of the cash flow statement. To prepare the SCF, you need the following:

FAST FLASHBACK

A comparative balance sheet reports assets, liabilities, and stockholders' equity at the beginning and end of a period.

1. **Comparative balance sheets,** used in calculating the cash flows from all activities (operating, investing, and financing).
2. **A complete income statement,** used primarily in calculating cash flows from operating activities.
3. **Additional details** concerning selected accounts that increase and decrease as a result of investing and/or financing activities.

Our approach to preparing the cash flow statement focuses on the changes in the balance sheet accounts. It relies on a simple manipulation of the balance sheet equation:

First, assets can be split into cash and all the other assets (that we'll call noncash assets):

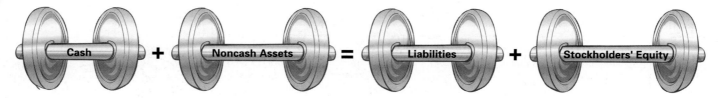

If we pick up the noncash assets and move them to the right side of the equation, we get:

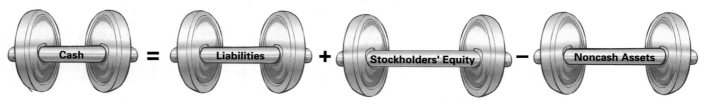

Given this relationship, the changes (Δ) in cash between the beginning and end of the period must equal the changes (Δ) in the amounts on the right side of the equation between the beginning and end of the period:

$$\Delta \text{ Cash} = \Delta \text{ Liabilities} + \Delta \text{ Stockholders' Equity} - \Delta \text{ Noncash Assets}$$

Thus, *any transaction that changes cash must be accompanied by a change in liabilities, stockholders' equity, or noncash assets.* Exhibit 12.3 illustrates this concept for selected cash transactions.

exhibit 12.3	Selected Cash Transactions and Their Effects on Other Balance Sheet Accounts

Category	Transaction	Cash Effect	Other Account Affected
Operating	Collect accounts receivable	+Cash	−Accounts Receivable (A)
	Pay accounts payable	−Cash	−Accounts Payable (L)
	Prepay rent	−Cash	+Prepaid Rent (A)
	Pay interest	−Cash	−Retained Earnings (SE)
	Sell goods/services for cash	+Cash	+Retained Earnings (SE)
Investing	Purchase equipment for cash	−Cash	+Equipment (A)
	Sell investment securities for cash	+Cash	−Investments (A)
Financing	Pay back debt to bank	−Cash	− Bank Loan Payable (L)
	Issue stock for cash	+Cash	+Contributed Capital (SE)

Reporting Cash Flows from Operating Activities

Because the operating section can be prepared in one of two formats, we will discuss them separately. Part A will describe the indirect method, and part B the direct method. Your instructor may choose to assign one, the other, or both. After you have completed the assigned part(s), you should move on to the discussion of Reporting Cash Flows from Investing Activities.

Remember that

1. Cash flow from operating activities is always the same regardless of whether it is computed using the direct or indirect method.

2. The investing and financing sections are always presented in the same manner, regardless of the format of the operating section.

Part A: Reporting Cash Flows from Operating Activities—Indirect Method

To prepare the operating section using the indirect method, we will follow the three steps shown in Exhibit 12.4 and explained in greater detail below. These steps draw extensively on the comparative balance sheet and the income statement for the Nautilus Group, which are shown together in Exhibit 12.5. To get a glimpse of what we're trying to accomplish, take a peek right now at Exhibit 12.6 on page 529. Really. That's what we should end up with when we complete the three steps in Exhibit 12.4.

Step 1. Mark an O beside the balance sheet accounts that relate to earning income (operating items). These accounts will include

■ ***Most current assets.*** Most current assets are used up or converted into cash through the company's regular operating activities. For example, when inventories are sold,

exhibit 12.4	**Steps to Determine Operating Cash Flows—Indirect Method**

Step 1:	Identify balance sheet accounts related to operating activities.
Step 2:	Create a schedule of operating activities (like the one shown in Exhibit 12.6), which begins by assuming net income is a cash inflow.
Step 3:	Remove the effects of accrual adjustments included in net income (Step 2), using changes in balance sheet accounts that relate to operations (Step 1).

they create accounts receivable, which are turned into cash when collected. When marking an O beside the current assets that relate to operating activities, exclude cash (because that's what we're trying to explain the change in) and exclude short-term investments (because this account relates to investing activities).

COACH'S CORNER

Dividends payable is an example of a current liability owed to owners. It relates to financing, not operating, activities.

- **Most current liabilities.** Most current liabilities arise from buying goods or services that are used in a company's operations. Any amounts owed to owners and loans owed to banks and other financial institutions, however, should not be marked with an O because they relate to financing activities.

- **Accumulated depreciation.** This contra-asset account increases each period by the amount of depreciation expense. Because depreciation expense affects net income, this account is related to operating activities.

- **Retained earnings.** This line-item includes activities related to both operating and financing. It increases each period by the amount of net income (which is the starting point for the operating section), and it decreases when dividends are paid (which is a financing activity). To show that the account relates to these two sections of the SCF, we mark it with O and F.

While you're at it, you might as well also mark whether the other balance sheet accounts relate to investing (I) or financing (F) activities. This will make it easier for you later when preparing the investing and financing sections of the SCF.

Step 2.   Create a schedule of operating activities, which begins with net income as reported on the income statement. Our Nautilus example (in Exhibit 12.6) begins with the $13,689 net income reported on the income statement in Exhibit 12.5. By starting with net income, it's like we assume all revenues resulted in cash inflows and all expenses resulted in cash outflows. There are lots of places where that isn't true, so the next step adjusts for this.

COACH'S CORNER

Use this table to remember how to adjust for changes in current assets and liabilities:

	Current Assets	Current Liabilities	
Increase	−	+	SCF Adjustment
Decrease	+	−	

To make it easy to "dial up" your memory, simplify this table even more:

	A	L
I	−	+
D	+	−

Step 3.   Adjust net income for the effects of items marked O that reflect differences in the timing of accrual basis net income and cash flows. The following adjustments are the ones most frequently encountered:

Income Statement Amounts or Balance Sheet Changes	*Impact on the SCF*
Net income	Starting point
Depreciation expense included in accumulated depreciation	Added
Decreases in current assets	Added
Increases in current liabilities	Added
Increases in current assets	Subtracted
Decreases in current liabilities	Subtracted

Step 3 is completed in two parts:

Step 3a.   Adjust net income for depreciation expense. Depreciation is subtracted on the income statement to determine net income, but depreciation does not affect cash. By

exhibit 12.5	The Nautilus Group: Comparative Balance Sheet and Current Income Statement

THE NAUTILUS GROUP, INC.
Balance Sheet*
(unaudited in thousands)

Related Cash Flow Section		March 31, 2003	December 31, 2002	*Change*
Δ in Cash	Assets			
	Current Assets:			
I	Cash and Cash Equivalents	$ 60,415	$ 31,719	+28,696
O	Short-Term Investments	—	17,578	−17,578
O	Accounts Receivable	41,485	50,099	−8,614
O	Inventories	66,820	63,798	+3,022
	Prepaid Expenses	11,319	10,910	+409
	Total Current Assets	180,039	174,104	
I	Equipment	118,994	115,368	+3,626
O	Less: Accumulated Depreciation	(15,583)	(12,819)	−2,764
	Total Assets	$283,450	$276,653	
	Liabilities and Stockholders' Equity			
	Current Liabilities:			
O	Accounts Payable	$ 29,318	$ 41,288	−11,970
O	Accrued Liabilities	30,559	23,793	+6,766
	Total Current Liabilities	59,877	65,081	
F	Long-Term Debt	11,046	9,149	+1,897
	Stockholders' Equity:			
F	Contributed Capital	677	55	+622
O, F[†]	Retained Earnings	211,850	202,368	+9,482
	Total Stockholders' Equity	212,527	202,423	
	Total Liabilities and Stockholders' Equity	$283,450	$276,653	

THE NAUTILUS GROUP, INC.
Statement of Operations*
(unaudited in thousands)

	Three Months Ended March 31, 2003
Net Sales	$129,449
Cost of Goods Sold	59,502
Gross Profit	69,947
Operating Expenses:	
Selling, General, and Administrative Expenses	45,692
Depreciation	2,764
Total Operating Expenses	48,456
Operating Income	21,491
Interest Expense	102
Net Income before Taxes	21,389
Income Tax Expense	7,700
Net Income	$ 13,689

*Certain balances have been adjusted to simplify the presentation.
[†]This line-item includes transactions related to both operating and financing activities.

adding depreciation expense to our starting point on the SCF, we remove the effect of having deducted it in the income statement. It's like depreciation expense digs a hole in the income statement and you need to fill the hole back in on the SCF by adding back the amount of depreciation expense. In the Nautilus case, we remove the effect of depreciation expense by adding back $2,764 to net income (see Exhibit 12.6).[2]

Step 3b. Adjust net income for changes in current assets and current liabilities. Each *change* in current assets (other than cash and short-term investments) and current liabilities (other than amounts owed to owners and financial institutions) causes a difference between net income and cash flow from operating activities. When converting net income to cash flow from operating activities, apply the following general rules:

■ *Add the change when a current asset decreases or current liability increases.*

■ *Subtract the change when a current asset increases or current liability decreases.*

Understanding what makes these current assets and current liabilities increase and decrease is the key to understanding the logic of these additions and subtractions.

+ Accounts Receivable (A) −	
Beg. bal.	
Sales revenue	Cash collected
End. bal.	

Change in Accounts Receivable. We will illustrate the logic behind Step 3b with the first operating item (O) listed on the Nautilus balance sheet in Exhibit 12.5, accounts receivable. The goal is to adjust the **sales** revenue included in net income to **cash** collected from customers. As shown in the equation below and in the T-account in the margin, sales revenues cause accounts receivable (A/R) to increase and cash collected from customers causes accounts receivable to decrease:

A/R (beginning) + Sales revenue − Cash collected = A/R (ending)

If we move A/R (beginning) to the right-hand side of the equation, we get

Sales revenue − Cash collected = A/R (ending) − A/R (beginning)

This equation says that the difference between the sales revenue included in net income and the cash collected from customers is equal to the change in accounts receivable. In other words, to adjust from accrual-basis net income to operating cash flows, we need to adjust for the change in accounts receivable. If we insert the numbers for Nautilus (from Exhibit 12.5) into the accounts receivable T-account and use bigger characters for bigger amounts, you can begin to understand why we *add* the change in accounts receivable when its balance decreases:

Accounts Receivable (A)			
Beginning balance	50,099	**Cash** collected from customers	138,063
Sales revenue (on account)	129,449		
Ending balance	41,485		

Change −$8,614

The **cash** collections were **bigger** than the sales included in net income, so the appropriate adjustment on the SCF is to **add** the amount by which cash collections are bigger than sales. (The opposite is true, as well. An increase in accounts receivable would have been subtracted.)

---

[2] Amortization expense for intangible assets (discussed in Chapter 9) is handled in exactly the same way as depreciation expense. Gains and losses on sales of equipment also are dealt with in a similar manner and are discussed in Chapter Supplement A. Other additions and subtractions for long-lived assets are discussed in more advanced accounting courses.

Take note that the adjustment on the SCF is not the total cash collections of $138,063. Because we started with net income, which already includes sales of $129,449, the amount of the adjustment is the difference between $138,063 and $129,449, which can be easily determined by computing the change in accounts receivable:

Beginning balance	$50,099
− Ending balance	41,485
= Change	$ 8,614

This actually provides a shortcut for determining the SCF adjustment: Simply adjust for the change in the balance sheet account. One way to remember whether the adjustment on the SCF should be an increase or decrease is to think about the accounts receivable T-account (shown below). If the change in the account is explained by a credit (a decrease), the SCF adjustment is reported just like a debit to cash (an increase).

Accounts Receivable (A)		
Beg. bal.	50,099	
		Decrease 8,614
End. bal.	41,485	

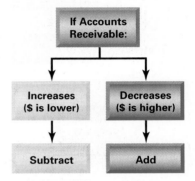

exhibit 12.6 | Nautilus Group: Schedule for Net Cash Flow from Operating Activities—Indirect Method

CONVERSION OF NET INCOME TO NET CASH FLOW FROM OPERATING ACTIVITIES

Items	Amount (in thousands)	Explanation
Net income, accrual basis	$13,689	From income statement.
Add (subtract) to convert to cash basis:		
Depreciation	+ 2,764	Add because depreciation expense does not affect cash but was subtracted when computing net income.
Accounts receivable decrease	+ 8,614	Add because the cash collected from customers is more than accrual basis revenues.
Inventory increase	− 3,022	Subtract because purchases are more than the cost of goods sold expense.
Prepaid expense increase	− 409	Subtract because cash prepayments for expenses are more than accrual basis expenses.
Accounts payable decrease	−11,970	Subtract because amounts purchased on account (borrowed from suppliers) are less than cash payments to suppliers.
Accrued liabilities increase	+ 6,766	Add because accrual basis expenses are more than the cash payments for expenses.
Net cash inflow (outflow)	$16,432	Subtotal for the SCF.

Change in Inventory. As shown in the T-account on the left below, purchases of goods increase the balance in inventory and recording the cost of goods sold decreases the balance in inventory. The income statement deducts the cost of goods sold when determining net income (our starting point for the indirect method SCF), yet we want the SCF to deduct the cash outflow for inventory purchases. Using the beginning and ending inventory numbers (from Exhibit 12.5) in the T-account on the right, we see that inventory increased $3,022 during the period. This means that the company bought more merchandise than it sold or, in other words, more was spent on inventory than was expensed as cost of goods sold. So to convert from COGS to the amount spent on inventory purchases, subtract the extra money spent on purchases, as shown in Exhibit 12.6.

The extra money spent on purchases is the amount by which inventory increased. (If inventory had decreased, that amount would be added on the SCF, as shown in the graphic in the margin.)

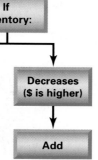

Inventories (A)	
Beg. bal.	
Purchases	Cost of goods sold
End. bal.	

Inventories (A)		
Beg. bal.	63,798	
Increase	3,022	
End. bal.	66,820	

Change in Prepaid Expenses. The income statement reflects expenses of the period, but cash flow from operating activities must reflect the cash payments. Cash prepayments increase the balance in prepaid expenses, and the balance decreases when prepaid expenses are used up and expensed on the income statement.

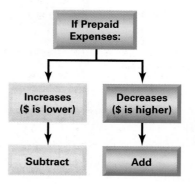

Prepaid Expenses (A)	
Beg. bal.	
Cash prepayments	Used up / expensed
End. bal.	

Prepaid Expenses (A)		
Beg. bal.	10,910	
Increase	409	
End. bal.	11,319	

The Nautilus balance sheet (Exhibit 12.5) indicates a $409 increase in prepaid expenses, which means that new cash prepayments were more than expenses. These extra cash prepayments must be *subtracted* on the SCF in Exhibit 12.6. (A decrease is added.)

Change in Accounts Payable. Cash flow from operations must reflect cash purchases, but not all purchases are made using cash. As shown in the T-account below, purchases on account increase accounts payable and cash paid to suppliers decreases accounts payable.

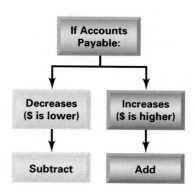

Accounts Payable (L)	
Cash payments	Beg. bal.
	Purchases on account
	End. bal.

Accounts Payable (L)		
		Beg. bal. 41,288
Decrease	11,970	
		End. bal. 29,318

Accounts payable *decreased* by $11,970 this period, which means that cash payments to suppliers were more than purchases on account. This decrease (the extra payments) must be *subtracted* in Exhibit 12.6. (An increase is added.)

Change in Accrued Liabilities. The income statement reflects all accrued and/or paid expenses, but the cash flow statement must reflect only those expenses paid in cash during the current period. When expenses like salaries and wages are accrued, the accrued liabilities account increases, and when they are paid off, it decreases.

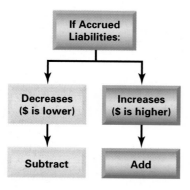

Accrued Liabilities (L)	
Pay off accruals	Beg. bal.
	Accrue expenses
	End. bal.

Accrued Liabilities (L)		
		Beg. bal. 23,793
		Increase 6,766
		End. bal. 30,559

Accrued liabilities for Nautilus (Exhibit 12.5) *increased* by $6,766, which indicates that more expenses were accrued than paid in cash. The increase in accrued liabilities (which represent noncash expenses deducted on the income statement) must be *added* back in Exhibit 12.6. (A decrease is subtracted.)

Summary. We can summarize the typical additions and subtractions that are required to reconcile net income with cash flow from operating activities as follows:

Item	ADDITIONS AND SUBTRACTIONS TO RECONCILE NET INCOME TO CASH FLOW FROM OPERATING ACTIVITIES	
	When Item Increases	**When Item Decreases**
Depreciation (and accumulated depreciation)	+	n/a
Accounts receivable	–	+
Inventory	–	+
Prepaid expenses	–	+
Accounts payable	+	–
Accrued expense liabilities	+	–

> **COACH'S CORNER**
> Notice in this table that, to reconcile net income to cash flows from operations, you
> • Add the change when the current asset decreases or current liability increases.
> • Subtract the change when the current asset increases or current liability decreases.

The additions and subtractions to reconcile Nautilus Group's net income to its cash flows from operating activities are summarized in Exhibit 12.6 and would be reported in the SCF in the format shown in Exhibit 12.2 on page 522.

TOPIC TACKLER PLUS

For a review of the indirect method, see the animated tutorial on the DVD for use with this book.

HOW'S IT GOING?   A Self-Study Quiz

Indicate which of the following items taken from Brunswick Corporation's cash flow statement would be added (+), subtracted (−), or not included (0) in the reconciliation of net income to cash flow from operations.

    [+]   *a.* Decrease in inventories.

    [+]   *b.* Increase in accounts payable.

    [+]   *c.* Depreciation expense.

    [−]   *d.* Increase in accounts receivable.

    [+]   *e.* Increase in accrued liabilities.

    [−]   *f.* Increase in prepaid expenses.

After you're done, check your answers with the solutions in the margin.

If your instructor has assigned only the indirect method, you should skip the next section and move on to the discussion of Reporting Cash Flows from Investing Activities (page 535).

Part B: Reporting Cash Flows from Operating Activities—Direct Method

The direct method presents a summary of all operating transactions that result in either a debit or a credit to cash. It is prepared by adjusting each individual revenue and expense on the income statement from the accrual basis to the cash basis. We will complete this process for all of the revenues and expenses reported in the Nautilus income statement in Exhibit 12.5, and accumulate them in a new schedule in Exhibit 12.7 on page 534. Notice that, with the direct method, we work directly with each revenue and expense listed on the income statement and ignore any totals or subtotals (like net income).

Converting Sales Revenues to Cash Inflows.   When sales are recorded, accounts receivable increases, and when cash is collected, accounts receivable decreases. Thus, if we see an overall increase in accounts receivable, it means sales were greater than cash collections. If accounts receivable decreases, then cash collected from customers was greater than the sales made that period. The following formula can be used to convert sales revenue (from the income statement) to cash collected from customers (for the SCF):

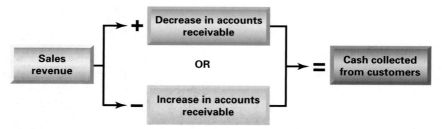

Using information from the Nautilus income statement and balance sheet presented in Exhibit 12.5, we can compute cash collected from customers as follows:

Accounts Receivable (A)	
Beg. bal. 50,099	
	Decrease 8,614
End. bal. 41,485	

Net sales	$129,449
+ Decrease in accounts receivable	8,614
Cash collected from customers	$138,063

Converting Cost of Goods Sold to Cash Paid to Suppliers.   Cost of goods sold represents the cost of merchandise sold during the accounting period. It may be more or less than the amount of cash paid to suppliers during the period. The balance sheet of Nautilus in Exhibit 12.5 shows that inventory increased during the quarter, which means the company bought more merchandise than it sold. If the company paid cash to suppliers for inventory, it would have paid more cash than what was reported as cost of goods sold. So, to compute cash paid to suppliers, the increase in inventory must be added to cost of goods sold.

In addition to the change in inventory, we have to consider the change in accounts payable because cash payments also are made to suppliers for inventory purchased on account. If the accounts payable balance decreases, it means cash payments to suppliers were greater than the inventory purchases that flowed through the inventory account. If accounts payable increases, it means cash payments weren't as great as that suggested by the change in inventory. In other words, to fully convert cost of goods sold to a cash basis, you must consider changes in both inventory and accounts payable in the following manner:

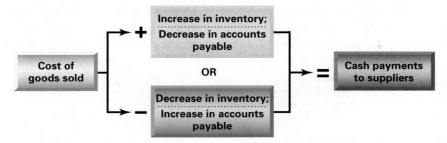

Using information from Exhibit 12.5, we can compute cash paid to suppliers as follows:

Cost of goods sold	$59,502
+ Increase in inventory	3,022
+ Decrease in accounts payable	11,970
Cash payments to suppliers	$74,494

Inventories (A)	
Beg. bal. 63,798	
Increase 3,022	
End. bal. 66,820	

Accounts Payable (L)	
	Beg. bal. 41,288
Decrease 11,970	
	End. bal. 29,318

Converting Operating Expenses to a Cash Outflow. The total amount of an expense on the income statement may differ from the cash outflow associated with that activity. Some amounts, like prepaid rent, are paid before they are recognized as expenses. When prepayments are made, the balance in the asset *Prepaid Expenses* increases. When expenses are recorded, *Prepaid Expenses* decreases. When we see Nautilus Group's prepaid expenses increase by $409 during the period, it means the company paid more cash than it recorded as operating expenses. Thus, to compute the cash paid for operating expenses, we must add the increase in prepaid expenses to the reported operating expenses.

Some other expenses, like accrued wages, are paid for after they are recorded. In this case, when expenses are recorded, the balance in the *Accrued Liabilities* account increases. When payments are made, *Accrued Liabilities* decreases. When Nautilus Group's accrued liabilities increase by $6,766, it means the company paid that much less cash than it recorded as operating expenses. This difference must be subtracted in computing cash paid for expenses.

Generally, other operating expenses can be converted from the accrual basis to the cash basis in the following manner:

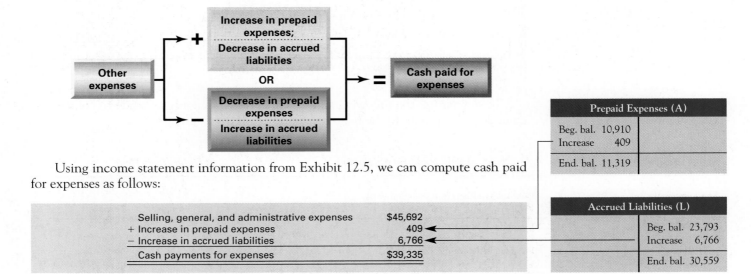

Using income statement information from Exhibit 12.5, we can compute cash paid for expenses as follows:

Selling, general, and administrative expenses	$45,692
+ Increase in prepaid expenses	409
− Increase in accrued liabilities	6,766
Cash payments for expenses	$39,335

Prepaid Expenses (A)	
Beg. bal. 10,910	
Increase 409	
End. bal. 11,319	

Accrued Liabilities (L)	
	Beg. bal. 23,793
	Increase 6,766
	End. bal. 30,559

You don't have to do anything to convert depreciation expense on the income statement to the cash basis for the SCF because depreciation doesn't involve cash. It is merely an allocation of previously incurred costs. Noncash expenses like depreciation (or revenues that don't affect cash) are omitted when the SCF is prepared using the direct method.

The next expense account listed on the income statement in Exhibit 12.5 is interest expense of $102. Because there is no balance in interest payable, interest must have been recorded as an expense when it was paid. Thus, interest expense equals interest paid.

Interest expense	$102
No change in interest payable	0
Cash payments for interest	$102

The same logic can be applied to income taxes. Nautilus presents income tax expense of $7,700. Because there is no balance in income taxes payable (or any other tax account) on the balance sheet in Exhibit 12.5, income tax paid is equal to income tax expense.

Income tax expense	$7,700
No change in taxes payable	0
Cash payments for income taxes	$7,700

Now that we've considered all the line-items shown in the income statement in Exhibit 12.5, it's time to gather all the operating cash inflows and outflows that we calculated above. This information is shown in Exhibit 12.7. If the Nautilus Group was to report its SCF using the direct method, the information in Exhibit 12.7 would replace the operating activities section shown in Exhibit 12.2 on page 522.

exhibit 12.7	**Nautilus Group: Schedule for Net Cash Flow from Operating Activities—Direct Method**

(in thousands)	
Cash Flows from Operating Activities:	
Cash collected from customers	$138,063
Cash payments to suppliers	(74,494)
Cash payments for operating expenses	(39,335)
Cash payments for interest	(102)
Cash payments for income taxes	(7,700)
Net cash inflow (outflow)	$ 16,432

To summarize, the following adjustments must commonly be made to convert income statement items to the related operating cash flow amounts:

Income Statement Account	+/− *Change in Balance Sheet Account(s)*	= *Operating Cash Flow*
Sales Revenue	+Decrease in Accounts Receivable (A) −Increase in Accounts Receivable (A)	= Collections from customers
Cost of Goods Sold	+Increase in Inventory (A) −Decrease in Inventory (A) −Increase in Accounts Payable (L) +Decrease in Accounts Payable (L)	= Payments to suppliers of inventory

Income Statement Account	+/− Change in Balance Sheet Account(s)	= Operating Cash Flow
Other Expenses	+Increase in Prepaid Expenses (A) −Decrease in Prepaid Expenses (A) −Increase in Accrued Expenses (L) +Decrease in Accrued Expenses (L)	= Payments to suppliers of services (e.g., rent, utilities, wages, interest)
Interest Expense	−Increase in Interest Payable (L) +Decrease in Interest Payable (L)	= Payments of interest
Income Tax Expense	+Increase in Prepaid Income Taxes (Deferred Taxes) (A) −Decrease in Prepaid Income Taxes (Deferred Taxes) (A) −Increase in Income Taxes Payable (Deferred Taxes) (L) +Decrease in Income Taxes Payable (Deferred Taxes) (L)	= Payments of income taxes

Again, note that the net cash inflow or outflow is the same regardless of whether the direct or indirect method of presentation is used (in this case, an inflow of $16,432). The two methods differ only in terms of the details reported on the statement.

HOW'S IT GOING? A Self-Study Quiz

Indicate which of the following items taken from a cash flow statement would be added (+), subtracted (−), or not included (0) when calculating cash flow from operations using the direct method.

[−]	*a.* Increase in inventories.
[0]	*b.* Payment of dividends to stockholders.
[+]	*c.* Cash collections from customers.
[0]	*d.* Purchase of plant and equipment for cash.
[−]	*e.* Payments of interest to lenders.
[−]	*f.* Payment of taxes to the government.

After you're done, check your answers with the solutions in the margin.

Quiz Answers
a. −, b. 0, c. +, d. 0, e. −, f. −

Reporting Cash Flows from Investing Activities

To prepare this section of the SCF, you must analyze accounts related to short-term investments and long-term asset accounts such as property, plant, and equipment.[3] The following relationships are the ones that you will encounter most frequently:

Related Balance Sheet Accounts	Investing Activity	Cash Flow Effect
Short-term investments	Purchase of investment securities for cash	Outflow
	Sale (maturity) of investment securities for cash	Inflow
Property, plant, and equipment	Purchase of property, plant, and equipment for cash	Outflow
	Sale of property, plant, and equipment for cash	Inflow

COACH'S CORNER

When analyzing investing activities, remember to include both of the following:
- Only purchases paid for with **cash** (or cash equivalents).
- The amount of **cash** received from the sale of these assets, regardless of whether the assets are sold at a gain or loss.

---

[3]Investing activities also include other long-term assets described in Chapter 9 (intangible assets) and Appendix D (long-term investments in other companies). Although not shown here, the cash flows for intangible assets are similar to those for property, plant, and equipment, and the cash flows for long-term investments are similar to those for short-term investments.

In the case of Nautilus, the balance sheet (Exhibit 12.5) shows two investing assets (noted with an I) that have changed during the period: Short-term investments and Equipment.

Short-Term Investments

To figure out the cause(s) for the changes in this account, accountants would examine the detailed accounting records for investments. Let's assume these records show that Nautilus sold its short-term investments and received $17,578 in cash, which is an investing cash inflow. The company did not purchase any additional investments during the period. We will include the cash from selling investments in a schedule of investing activities, shown in Exhibit 12.8. By itself, the sale of short-term investments explains the change in that account on the balance sheet.

Short-Term Investments (A)			
Beg. bal.	17,578		
		Sold	17,578
End. bal.	0		

Equipment

To figure out the cause(s) for the change in the equipment account, accountants would examine the detailed accounting records for equipment. For purposes of our example, we have assumed that Nautilus purchased equipment for $3,626 cash and did not sell any equipment during the quarter. The equipment purchase is a cash outflow, which we subtract in the schedule of investing activities in Exhibit 12.8. In our example, this purchase fully explains the increase in Equipment of $3,626.

Equipment (A)		
Beg. bal.	115,368	
Purchases	3,626	
End. bal.	118,994	

exhibit 12.8   **Nautilus Group: Schedule for Net Cash Flow from Investing Activities**

Items	Amount (in thousands)	Explanations
Maturities (sale) of short-term investments	$17,578	Receipt of cash from sale of short-term investments
Purchase of equipment	(3,626)	Payment of cash for equipment
Net cash inflow (outflow)	$13,952	Subtotal for the SCF

Reporting Cash Flows from Financing Activities

This section of the cash flow statement includes changes in current liabilities owed to owners (dividends payable) and financial institutions (bank loans payable, short-term notes payable, current portion of long-term debt), as well as changes in long-term liabilities and stockholders' equity accounts. The following relationships are the ones that you will encounter most often:

Related Balance Sheet Accounts	Financing Activity	Cash Flow Effect
Short-term debt (notes payable)	Borrowing cash from bank or other financial institutions	Inflow
	Repayment of loan principal	Outflow
Long-term debt	Issuance of bonds for cash	Inflow
	Repayment of bond principal	Outflow
Contributed capital	Issuance of stock for cash	Inflow
	Repurchase of stock with cash	Outflow
Retained earnings	Payment of cash dividends	Outflow

COACH'S CORNER

Remember that dividends received from investing in other companies, interest received, and interest paid all affect net income, so they are reported on the SCF as operating (not financing) activities.

To compute cash flows from financing activities, you should review changes in debt and stockholders' equity accounts. In the case of the Nautilus Group, when we look at changes in the balance sheet (Exhibit 12.5), we find that long-term debt, contributed capital, and retained earnings changed during the period (noted with an F).

Long-Term Debt

The change in long-term debt resulted from borrowing $1,897 during the period, as shown in the T-account below. We'll include this cash inflow in a schedule of financing activities, shown in Exhibit 12.9 on page 538.

Long-Term Debt (L)		
	Beg. bal.	9,149
	Borrowings	1,897
	End. bal.	11,046

Contributed Capital

The change in contributed capital resulted from the issuance of common stock to employees for $622 in cash, which is a cash inflow. This accounts for the $622 increase in contributed capital, and is listed in the schedule of financing activities in Exhibit 12.9.

Contributed Capital (SE)		
	Beg. bal.	55
	Issue new stock	622
	End. bal.	677

Retained Earnings

The change in retained earnings resulted from two things. First, the account increased by an amount equal to the Nautilus Group's net income of $13,689. Second, the company declared and paid cash dividends of $4,207. Together, these two amounts account for the $9,482 increase in retained earnings. The cash effects related to net income have been included in the operating activities section of the SCF, so the only change in retained earnings that is left to account for is the cash outflow for dividends paid. We include this in the schedule of financing activities in Exhibit 12.9.

Retained Earnings (SE)			
		Beg. bal.	202,368
Dividends	4,207	Net Income	13,689
		End. bal.	211,850

exhibit 12.9   Nautilus Group: Schedule for Net Cash Flow from Financing Activities

Items	Amount (in thousands)	Explanations
Additional borrowings of long-term debt	$1,897	Cash received when new loan obtained
Proceeds from stock issuance	622	Cash proceeds from issue of common stock
Cash dividends paid	(4,207)	Cash paid to stockholders as dividend
Net cash inflow (outflow)	($1,688)	Subtotal for the SCF

Summarizing Cash Flows from Operating, Investing, and Financing Activities

Now that you have determined the cash flows for the three main types of business activities, you can prepare the SCF. The Nautilus Group example in Exhibit 12.2 shows how the SCF combines the information from Exhibits 12.9, 12.8, and either 12.7 or 12.6 to produce an overall net increase (or decrease) in cash. This net change is added to the beginning cash balance to arrive at the ending cash balance, as summarized here:

COACH'S CORNER

For a complete example of a SCF, refer to Exhibit 12.2 on page 522.

Net cash provided by (used for) operating activities	$16,432
+ (−) Net cash provided by (used for) investing activities	13,952
+ (−) Net cash provided by (used for) financing activities	(1,688)
Net increase (decrease) in cash	28,696
Cash and cash equivalents at beginning of period	31,719
Cash and cash equivalents at end of period	$60,415

Additional SCF Information

In addition to their cash flows, all companies are required to report material investing and financing transactions that did not have cash flow effects (called "noncash investing and financing activities"). For example, the purchase of a $10,000 piece of equipment with a $10,000 note payable to the supplier does not cause either an inflow or an outflow of cash. As a result, these activities are not listed in the three main sections of the SCF. This important information is normally presented for users in a supplementary schedule to the SCF or in the financial statement notes. This supplementary information must also report (for companies using the indirect method) the amount of cash paid for interest and for income taxes.

COACH'S CORNER

When doing homework problems, assume that all changes in noncurrent account balances are caused by cash transactions (unless the problem specifically describes changes caused by noncash investing and financing activities).

⌐ EVALUATE ────────

FINANCIAL RESULTS REPORTED IN A STATEMENT OF CASH FLOWS

When evaluating the SCF, a good way to start is by looking at the totals of each of the three main sections. A healthy company will show positive cash flows from operations that are sufficiently large to pay for replacing current property, plant, and equipment and to pay dividends to stockholders. Any additional cash (called "free cash flow") can (1) be used to expand the business through additional investing activities, (2) be used for other financing activities, or (3) simply build up the company's cash balance. After considering where the company stands, in relation to this big picture, you're ready to look at the details within each of the sections.

Interpreting Cash Flows from Operating Activities

The operating activities section of the SCF indicates how well a company is able to generate cash internally through its operations and management of current assets and current liabilities. Most analysts believe that this is the most important section of the statement because, in the long run, operations are the only continuing source of cash. That is, investors will not invest in a company if they do not believe that cash generated from operations will be available to pay them dividends or expand the company. Similarly, creditors will not lend money if they do not believe that cash generated from operations will be sufficient to repay them. Many dot-com companies failed when investors stopped believing that internet companies would turn business ideas into cash flows from operations.

When evaluating the operating activities section of the SCF, consider the absolute amount of cash flow (is it positive or negative?), keeping in mind that operating cash flows have to be positive over the long run for a company to be successful. Also, look for trends from one period to another. Most companies have ups and downs in operating cash flows, particularly if they are just starting out or if they operate a seasonal business. The Nautilus Group, for example, experiences its strongest operating cash flows in the first quarter of the year because that's when it collects on all the December and January sales to people making New Year's fitness resolutions. As Exhibit 12.10 shows, the second quarter (April through June) is a completely different story for Nautilus, generating the weakest operating cash flows of the year. To evaluate these cash flow changes, consider explanations given by management (typically presented in the MD&A) in relation to the nature of the business and to what industry competitors are experiencing.

POINT OF INTEREST
The term "burn rate" was created to describe how quickly dot-coms would burn through cash received from creditors and stockholders before generating positive cash flows from operations.

FAST FLASHBACK
MD&A is the abbreviation for the section of annual and quarterly reports called Management's Discussion and Analysis.

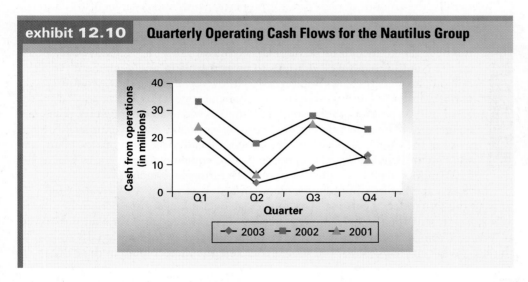

exhibit 12.10   **Quarterly Operating Cash Flows for the Nautilus Group**

Interpreting Cash Flows from Investing Activities

To maintain operating cash flows at their current levels, a company must replace existing equipment as it wears down. A good measure for determining whether the company is generating enough cash internally to purchase new long-term assets like equipment is the capital acquisitions ratio:

$$\text{Capital Acquisitions Ratio} = \frac{\text{Net Cash Flow from Operating Activities}}{\text{Cash Paid for Property, Plant, and Equipment}}$$

The capital acquisitions ratio reflects the extent to which purchases of property, plant, and equipment is financed from operating activities (without the need for outside debt or equity financing or the sale of other investments or long-term assets). A ratio greater than 1.0 indicates that, all else equal, outside financing was not needed to replace equipment in the current period. Generally speaking, the higher a company's capital acquisitions ratio, the less likely external financing will be needed to fund future expansion.

COACH'S CORNER
The amount of cash paid for property, plant, and equipment can be found within the investing activities section of the SCF. Although it is shown as a negative number on the SCF (because it is an outflow of cash), treat it as a positive number in the capital acquisitions ratio.

exhibit 12.11	**Summary of Capital Acquisitions Ratio Analyses**						

				2000–02			**SELF-STUDY QUIZ 1997–99**
Name of Measure	**Formula**	**What It Tells You**	**Brunswick**	**Cybex**	**Nautilus**		**Nautilus**
Capital Acquisitions Ratio	Net Cash from Operations / Cash Paid for PPE	• Whether operating cash flows are sufficient to pay for PPE purchases • A higher ratio means less need for external financing ☺	2.63	2.02	2.21		☐

Generally, the amount of cash paid for property, plant, and equipment (used in the bottom part of the ratio) is reported in the SCF's investing activities section in a line-item called something like "additions to property, plant, and equipment." Occasionally, it is necessary to include an additional amount with this line-item. In 2002, for example, Nautilus reported "additions to property, plant, and equipment" of $31.5 million plus an extra $24.1 million cash outflow representing the "Acquisition cost of StairMaster." Nautilus' notes to the financial statements indicated that, of the $24.1 million paid for StairMaster, $10.9 million was related to property, plant, and equipment. (The remainder was for accounts receivable and inventories.) For purposes of the capital acquisitions ratio, the total cash paid for property, plant, and equipment included the $31.5 million paid to equipment suppliers, as well as the $10.9 million paid for StairMaster's manufacturing equipment.

Because expenditures for property, plant, and equipment can vary greatly from year to year, the ratio often is calculated as an average over a longer time period. In Exhibit 12.11, we present the three-year average capital acquisitions ratio for Nautilus and its two biggest competitors (Brunswick Corporation and Cybex International). As part of the self-study quiz that follows, you should complete the final column in the exhibit.

HOW'S IT GOING?   A Self-Study Quiz

Compute the ratio for the final column in Exhibit 12.11 using the cash flow from operations and cash paid for property, plant, and equipment shown in the table below. How did the ratio change between 1997–99 and 2000–02? Suggest a possible reason for this change.

(in millions)	1997	1998	1999	Total
Cash flow from operating activities	$3.89	$15.9	$20.8	$40.6
Purchases of property, plant, and equipment	0.3	1.7	1.9	3.9
Equipment acquired as part of another company	0.0	0.0	12.3	12.3

When you're done, check your answers with the solutions in the margin.

Quiz Answers

$40.6 ÷ (3.9 + 12.3) = 2.51.

The ratio fell a little in 2000–02, in part because Nautilus significantly expanded its business during this period.

Be on the Alert

Because the needs for investment in plant and equipment differ dramatically across industries (for example, consider Nautilus versus Supercuts), a particular company's ratio should be compared only with its prior years' figures or with other companies in the same industry. Also, while a high ratio can indicate strong cash flows, it also might suggest a failure to update plant and equipment, which can limit a company's ability to compete in the future. The main point is that you have to interpret the ratio in relation to the company's activities and business strategy.

Interpreting Cash Flows from Financing Activities

The long-term growth of a company can be financed from internally generated funds (cash from operating activities), the issuance of stock (equity financing), and money borrowed on a long-term basis (debt financing). Debt financing is the riskiest source of financing because (1) interest *must* be paid on debt (dividends do not have to be paid) and (2) debt *must* be repaid (stock does not). To determine possible changes in the risk related to a company's financing strategy, look within the financing activities section. All else equal, a company that borrows additional money will be taking on greater risk than a company that pays down its debt.

In addition to considering changes in financing strategy, it also is useful to consider whether a company is generating sufficient cash flow to pay the interest it owes on debt. The times interest earned ratio (introduced in Chapter 10) is one way of assessing a company's ability to pay interest (by comparing net income before interest and taxes to the amount of interest expense). The problem with that ratio is that interest is paid with cash (not the net income used in that ratio). A more appropriate way to see whether a company has been able to pay its interest is to compare the cash flows generated from the company's operations to the cash paid for interest. The cash coverage ratio is used for this:

$$\text{Cash Coverage Ratio} = \frac{\text{Net Cash Flow from Operating Activities} + \text{Interest Paid} + \text{Income Taxes Paid}}{\text{Interest Paid}}$$

Interest and income taxes paid are added to net cash flow from operating activities because these outflows of cash were deducted in determining operating cash flows. By adding them back in, the cash coverage ratio can determine whether the company generates enough cash before the costs of financing and taxes to cover its interest payments.

RECONSIDER

FINANCIAL PERFORMANCE IN THE LIGHT OF CASH FLOWS

Using Net Operating Cash Flows to Evaluate Net Income

As you now know, both net operating cash flow and net income are important measures of a company's operating performance. Unlike net operating cash flow, which is based on actual cash inflows and outflows, net income *assumes* that all of the company's revenues eventually are realized as cash inflows and that its expenses are associated with outflows of cash. These assumptions are necessary if net income is to provide a timely measure of operating performance. A useful ratio for checking the extent to which these assumptions affect a particular company (and, more generally, for evaluating whether net income is in sync with cash flows from operations) is the quality of income ratio:

$$\text{Quality of Income Ratio} = \frac{\text{Net Cash Flow from Operating Activities}}{\text{Net Income}}$$

The quality of income ratio measures the portion of income that was generated in cash. All other things equal, a higher quality of income ratio indicates a higher likelihood that revenues are being realized in cash and that expenses are associated with cash out-flows. This ratio is most useful when compared to industry competitors or to prior time pe-riods. Any major deviations should be investigated. In some cases, a deviation may be nothing to worry about, but in others, it could be the first sign of big problems to come. Four potential causes of deviations to consider include

COACH'S CORNER

Think of increases in accounts receivable and inventory as a sign that cash is "tied up" in these assets. Decreases in these assets indicate that the amount previously invested in them has now been released into cash.

ETHICAL

ISSUE

1. *Seasonality.* As in the Nautilus case, seasonal variations in sales and inventory pro-duction can cause the ratio to fluctuate. Usually, this isn't a cause for alarm. ☺

2. *The corporate life cycle (growth in sales).* New companies often experience rapid sales growth. When sales are increasing, accounts receivable and inventory normally increase faster than accounts payable. This often reduces operating cash flows below net income, which, in turn, reduces the ratio. This isn't a big deal, provided that the start-up company can get cash from financing activities until operating activities be-gin to stabilize. ☺

3. *Changes in management of operating activities.* If a company's operating assets (like accounts receivable and inventories) are allowed to grow out of control, its operating cash flows and quality of income ratio will decrease. More efficient management will have the opposite effect. To investigate this potential cause more closely, use the ac-counts receivable and inventory turnover ratios covered in Chapters 7 and 8. ☺

4. *Changes in revenue and expense recognition.* Most cases of fraudulent financial re-porting involve aggressive revenue recognition (recording revenues earlier than usual) or delayed expense recognition (deferring expenses longer than usual). Both of these tactics cause net income to increase in the current period, making it seem as though the company has improved its performance. Neither of these tactics, though, affects cash flows from operating activities. As a result, if a manager changes revenue and expense recognition policies to boost net income, the quality of income ratio will drop, providing one of the first clues that the financial statements might contain errors or fraud. ☹

What's Coming Up

If you've been reading the chapters in the order presented, the next chapter will help you to pull together everything you've learned to this point in the course. If you've read this chapter just after completing the initial chapters that introduce the accounting cycle (Chapters 1–4), it's time to learn more about many of the decisions that are made when accounting for the variety of operating, investing, and financing transactions that a com-pany enters into. Either way, ensure you review and practice what was covered in this chapter before going on.

FOR YOUR REVIEW

DEMONSTRATION CASE A (INDIRECT METHOD)

During a recent quarter (ended March 31), Brunswick Corporation reported net income of $3,800 (all numbers in thousands). The balance in cash and cash equivalents on December 31 was $351,400, and at the end of the quarter on March 31 it was $280,000. The company also reported the following activities:

a. Borrowed $2,200 of short-term debt.
b. Accounts receivable increased by $40,300.
c. Paid $31,800 in cash for purchase of property, plant, and equipment.
d. Recorded depreciation of $35,600.
e. Salaries payable increased by $10,210.
f. Other accrued liabilities decreased by $35,000.
g. Prepaid expenses decreased by $14,500.
h. Inventories increased by $20,810.

i.   Accounts payable decreased by $10,200.
j.   Issued stock to employees for $400 in cash.

Required:

Based on this information, prepare the cash flow statement using the indirect method. Evaluate the cash flows reported in the statement.

Suggested Solution

BRUNSWICK CORPORATION Statement of Cash Flows For the Quarter Ended March 31 (in thousands)	
Cash Flows from Operating Activities	
Net Income	$ 3,800
Adjustments	
Depreciation	35,600
Change in accounts receivable	(40,300)
Change in inventories	(20,810)
Change in prepaid expenses	14,500
Change in accounts payable	(10,200)
Change in salaries payable	10,210
Change in other accrued liabilities	(35,000)
Net cash provided by (used for) operating activities	(42,200)
Cash Flows from Investing Activities	
Additions to property, plant, and equipment	(31,800)
Net cash provided by (used for) investing activities	(31,800)
Cash Flows from Financing Activities	
Proceeds from short-term debt borrowings	2,200
Proceeds from issuance of stock to employees	400
Net cash provided by (used for) financing activities	2,600
Increase (Decrease) in Cash and Cash Equivalents	(71,400)
Cash and cash equivalents, December 31	351,400
Cash and cash equivalents, March 31	$280,000

Despite reporting profits this quarter, the company has experienced a decline in cash flows from operations. This is caused primarily by build-ups of accounts receivable and inventories, with no corresponding reduction in spending for accounts payable and other accrued liabilities. This is potentially troublesome because it suggests the company may be encountering difficulties in selling its products and when collecting on past sales. In addition to the drain on cash for operating activities, the company also spent over $30 million for additional property, plant, and equipment. Financing activities had relatively little effect on cash flows during the period. The company entered this quarter with lots of cash (over $350 million) and, despite the shortfall in cash flow, still has lots remaining ($280 million) to finance future activities.

DEMONSTRATION CASE B (DIRECT METHOD)

During a recent quarter (ended March 29), Cybex International reported that its cash and cash equivalents had increased from $216 on December 31 to $469 on March 29 (all amounts in thousands). The company also indicated the following:

a.   Paid $13,229 to suppliers for inventory purchases.
b.   Borrowed $2,400 from one of the company's main stockholders.
c.   Paid $554 in cash for purchase of property, plant, and equipment.
d.   Reported sales on account of $20,608. The company reported accounts receivable of $13,628 at the beginning of the quarter and $12,386 at the end of the quarter.

e.   Paid operating expenses totaling $6,188.
f.   Cash payments for interest totaled $1,060.
g.   Made payments of $2,625 for principal owed on long-term debt.
h.   Paid $284 cash for other financing activities.
i.   Paid $57 cash for income taxes.

Required:

Based on this information, prepare the cash flow statement using the direct method. Evaluate the cash flows reported in the statement.

Suggested Solution

CYBEX INTERNATIONAL **Statement of Cash Flows** **For the Quarter Ended March 29** **(in thousands)**	
Operating Activities	
Cash collected from customers ($13,628 + 20,608 − 12,386)	$21,850
Cash paid to suppliers	(13,229)
Cash paid for operating expenses	(6,188)
Cash paid for interest	(1,060)
Cash paid for income taxes	(57)
Net cash flow from operating activities	1,316
Investing Activities	
Additions to property, plant, and equipment	(554)
Net cash flow from (used for) investing activities	(554)
Financing Activities	
Borrowed cash from related party (stockholder)	2,400
Repaid principal owed on long-term debt	(2,625)
Cash paid for other financing activities	(284)
Net cash flow from (used for) financing activities	(509)
Increase (Decrease) in Cash and Cash Equivalents	253
Cash and cash equivalents, December 31	216
Cash and cash equivalents, March 29	$ 469

Cybex reported a net inflow of $1,316 cash from operating activities during the quarter. These cash flows were more than enough to pay for the property, plant, and equipment purchased this quarter, as indicated by its capital acquisitions ratio of 2.38 (= $1,316 ÷ 554). Some of the extra cash from operations that was not used to purchase property, plant, and equipment (also called "free cash flow") could be used to pay down debt or to increase the company's cash balance. The financing activities section suggests that the company paid down a significant amount of long-term debt ($2,625), in part by borrowing funds from a related party ($2,400). Borrowing from a related party (particularly, a major stockholder) is unusual, which would prompt analysts to investigate further. The company's quarterly report explains that its lenders had demanded immediate repayment of their loans because the company had violated its debt covenants. A major stockholder loaned money to the company so that it could make this repayment.

CHAPTER SUMMARY

L01   Classify cash flow statement items as part of net cash flows from operating, investing, and financing activities. p. 520

- The statement has three main sections: cash flows from operating activities, which are related to earning income from normal operations; cash flows from investing activities, which are related to the acquisition and sale of productive assets; and cash flows from financing activities, which are related to external financing of the enterprise.

- The net cash inflow or outflow for the period is the same amount as the increase or decrease in cash and cash equivalents for the period on the balance sheet. Cash equivalents are highly liquid investments with original maturities of less than three months.

Report cash flows from operating activities using the indirect method. p. 525

LO2A

- The indirect method for reporting cash flows from operating activities reports a conversion of net income to net cash flow from operating activities. The conversion involves additions and subtractions for (1) noncurrent accruals, including expenses (such as depreciation expense) and revenues, which do not affect current assets or current liabilities, and (2) changes in each of the individual current assets (other than cash and short-term investments) and current liabilities (other than short-term debt to financial institutions and current portion of long-term debt, which relate to financing), which reflect differences in the timing of accrual basis net income and cash flows.

Report cash flows from operating activities using the direct method. p. 531

LO2B

- The direct method for reporting cash flows from operating activities accumulates all of the operating transactions that result in either a debit or a credit to cash into categories.
- The most common inflows are cash received from customers and dividends and interest on investments.
- The most common outflows are cash paid for purchase of services and goods for resale, salaries and wages, income taxes, and interest on liabilities.
- It is prepared by adjusting each item on the income statement from an accrual basis to a cash basis.

Report cash flows from investing activities. p. 535

LO3

- Investing activities reported on the cash flow statement include cash payments to acquire fixed assets and short- and long-term investments and cash proceeds from the sale of fixed assets and short- and long-term investments.

Report cash flows from financing activities. p. 536

LO4

- Cash inflows from financing activities include cash proceeds from issuance of short- and long-term debt and common stock.
- Cash outflows include cash principal payments on short- and long-term debt, cash paid for the repurchase of the company's stock, and cash dividend payments.
- Cash payments associated with interest are a cash flow from operating activities.

Interpret cash flows from operating, investing, and financing activities. p. 538

LO5

- A healthy company will generate positive cash flows from operations, some of which will be used to pay for purchases of property, plant, and equipment. Any additional cash (called "free cash flow") can be used to further expand the business, used to pay down some of the company's debt, or returned to stockholders.
- A company is in trouble if it is unable to generate positive cash flows from operations in the long run because eventually creditors will stop lending to the company and stockholders will stop investing in it.

Calculate and interpret the capital acquisitions ratio. p. 539

LO6

- The capital acquisitions ratio (Cash Flow from Operating Activities ÷ Cash Paid for Property, Plant, and Equipment) reflects the portion of purchases of property, plant, and equipment financed from operating activities without the need for outside debt or equity financing or the sale of other investments or fixed assets.
- A high ratio indicates less need for outside financing when replacing current equipment and expanding in the future.

Calculate and interpret the cash coverage ratio. p. 541

LO7

- The cash coverage ratio [(Cash Flow from Operating Activities + Interest Paid + Income Taxes Paid) ÷ Interest Paid] indicates the amount of cash generated by the company for each dollar of interest paid.

- A ratio greater than 1 suggests a company is likely to make its interest payments, with a higher ratio indicating a higher likelihood.

LO8   **Calculate and interpret the quality of income ratio. p. 541**

- Quality of income ratio (Cash Flow from Operating Activities ÷ Net Income) measures the portion of income that was generated in cash.
- All other things equal, a higher ratio also indicates a higher likelihood that revenues are being realized in cash and that expenses are associated with cash outflows.

FINANCIAL STATEMENT ANALYSIS TIPS

To determine a company's ability to finance purchases of property, plant, and equipment from operations, calculate the capital acquisitions ratio:

$$\text{Capital Acquisitions Ratio} = \frac{\text{Net Cash Flow from Operating Activities}}{\text{Cash Paid for Property, Plant, and Equipment}}$$

To determine whether a company has been able to pay the interest owed on debt, calculate the cash coverage ratio:

$$\text{Cash Coverage Ratio} = \frac{\text{Net Cash Flow from Operating Activities} + \text{Interest Paid} + \text{Income Taxes Paid}}{\text{Interest Paid}}$$

To determine the extent to which net income corresponds to actual operating cash flows, calculate the quality of income ratio:

$$\text{Quality of Income Ratio} = \frac{\text{Net Cash Flow from Operating Activities}}{\text{Net Income}}$$

KEY TERMS TO KNOW

Cash Equivalent p. 521
Cash Flows from Financing
    Activities p. 523

Cash Flows from Investing
    Activities p. 523
Cash Flows from Operating
    Activities (Cash Flows from
    Operations) p. 522

Direct Method p. 522
Indirect Method p. 523

SUPPLEMENT A: REPORTING SALES OF PROPERTY, PLANT, AND EQUIPMENT—INDIRECT METHOD

COACH'S CORNER

Cash received from the disposal of equipment is classified as an investing activity because the original purchase of equipment is considered an investing activity. Think of the disposal as "de-investing."

Whenever a company sells a piece of property, plant, and equipment (PPE), it records three things: (1) a decrease in the PPE account for the book value of the asset sold, (2) an increase in the cash account for the cash received on disposal, and (3) a gain if the cash received is more than the book value of the asset sold (or a loss if the cash received is less than the book value of the asset sold). The only part of this transaction that qualifies for the SCF is the cash received on disposal (classified as an investing activity).

Okay, that seems straightforward, so why do we have a separate chapter supplement for this kind of transaction? Well, there is one complicating factor. If the SCF is prepared using the indirect method, any gain or loss on disposal will have found its way into the SCF because it's included in or deducted from net income, which is the starting point for the operating activities section. So just as the SCF had to fill in the hole that depreciation created on the income statement, the SCF also has to fill in any holes created by losses reported on disposals of PPE. This means the operating activities section of an indirect method SCF will add back any losses deducted on the income statement. The flipside also is true. Any gains on disposal need to be taken out of net income in the operating activities section of the SCF. Let's look at one example.

Assume that Nautilus sold a piece of its manufacturing equipment for $80,000. The equipment originally cost $100,000 and had $22,000 of accumulated depreciation at the time of disposal. The journal entry to record the disposal was

dr	Cash (+A)	80,000	
dr	Accumulated Depreciation (−xA, +A)	22,000	
	cr Property, Plant, and Equipment (−A)		100,000
	cr Gain on Disposal (+R, +SE)		2,000

	Assets		=	Liabilities	+	Stockholders' Equity	
Cash		+80,000				Gain on disposal (+R)	+2,000
Accumulated Depreciation (−xA)		+22,000					
Property, Plant, and Equipment		−100,000					

The $80,000 inflow of cash is reported as an investing activity. Also, because the $2,000 gain was included in net income, we must remove (subtract) it in the operating activities section of the statement. Thus, the disposal would affect two parts of the SCF:

Cash provided by operating activities	
Net income	$21,998
Adjustments to reconcile net income to net cash from operations:	
Depreciation	3,767
Gain on disposal of property, plant, and equipment	(2,000)
. . .	. . .
Net cash provided by (used for) operating activities	. . .
Cash provided by (used for) investing activities	
Additions to property, plant, and equipment	(6,884)
Cash received from sale of property, plant, and equipment	80,000
. . .	. . .
Net cash provided by (used for) investing activities	. . .

SUPPLEMENT B: SPREADSHEET APPROACH— INDIRECT METHOD

As situations become more complex, the analytical approach that we used to prepare the statement of cash flows for the Nautilus Group becomes cumbersome and inefficient. In actual practice, many companies use a spreadsheet approach to prepare the statement of cash flows. The spreadsheet is based on the same logic that we used in the main body of the chapter. The spreadsheet's primary advantage is that it offers a more systematic way to keep track of information. You may find it useful even in simple situations.

Exhibit 12B.1 shows the Nautilus Group's spreadsheet, which we created as follows:

1. Make four columns to record dollar amounts. The first column is for the beginning balances for items reported on the balance sheet, the next two columns reflect debit and credit changes to those balances, and the final column contains the ending balances for the balance sheet accounts.

2. Enter each account name from the balance sheet in the far left of the top half of the spreadsheet.

3. As you analyze changes in each balance sheet account, enter the name of each item to be reported on the SCF in the far left of the bottom half of the spreadsheet.

exhibit 12B.1   Spreadsheet to Prepare Statement of Cash Flows, Indirect Method

THE NAUTILUS GROUP, INC.
Three Months Ended March 31, 2003
(in thousands)

	Beginning Balances, December 31, 2002	Analysis of Changes Debit		Analysis of Changes Credit		Ending Balances, March 31, 2003
Items from Balance Sheet						
Cash and Cash Equivalents (A)	31,719	(m)	28,696			60,415
Short-Term Investments (A)	17,578			(h)	17,578	—
Accounts Receivable (A)	50,099			(c)	8,614	41,485
Inventories (A)	63,798	(d)	3,022			66,820
Prepaid Expenses (A)	10,910	(e)	409			11,319
Equipment (A)	115,368	(i)	3,626			118,994
Accumulated Depreciation (xA)	12,819			(b)	2,764	15,583
Accounts Payable (L)	41,288	(f)	11,970			29,318
Accrued Liabilities (L)	23,793			(g)	6,766	30,559
Long-Term Debt (L)	9,149			(j)	1,897	11,046
Contributed Capital (SE)	55			(k)	622	677
Retained Earnings (SE)	202,368	(l)	4,207	(a)	13,689	211,850

	Cash Inflows		Cash Outflows		Subtotals
Statement of Cash Flows					
Cash Flows from Operating Activities:					
Net income	(a)	13,689			
Adjustments to reconcile net income to cash provided by operating activities					
Depreciation	(b)	2,764			
Changes in assets and liabilities:					
Accounts receivable	(c)	8,614			
Inventories			(d)	3,022	
Prepaid expenses			(e)	409	
Accounts payable			(f)	11,970	
Accrued liabilities	(g)	6,766			
					16,432
Cash Flows from Investing Activities:					
Maturities (sale) of short-term investments	(h)	17,578			
Purchases of equipment			(i)	3,626	
					13,952
Cash Flows from Financing Activities:					
Additional long-term debt borrowed	(j)	1,897			
Proceeds from stock issuance	(k)	622			
Cash dividends paid			(l)	4,207	
					(1,688)
Net increase in cash and cash equivalents			(m)	28,696	
		103,860		103,860	28,696

Changes in the various balance sheet accounts are analyzed in terms of debits and credits in the top half of the spreadsheet with the offsetting debits and credits being recorded in the bottom half of the spreadsheet in terms of their impact on cash flows. Each change in the noncash balance sheet accounts explains part of the change in the Cash account.

Let's go through each of the entries on the spreadsheet for Nautilus shown in Exhibit 12B.1, starting with the first one shown in the bottom half of the spreadsheet.

a.   Net income of $13,689 is shown as an inflow in the operating activities section of the SCF, with the corresponding credit going to *Retained Earnings* in the top half of the spreadsheet (to show that net income increased retained earnings).

b.   Depreciation expense of $2,764 is added back to net income because this type of expense does not cause a cash outflow when it is recorded. The corresponding credit explains the increase in the *Accumulated Depreciation* account during the period.

c.   The decrease in *Accounts Receivable* means that cash collections from customers were *bigger* than sales on account. Net income includes the sales number, so to adjust up to the actual cash collected, we add the extra amount. This shows up in our spreadsheet as an inflow in the spreadsheet (like a debit to cash) and a corresponding credit to accounts receivable.

d.   This entry reconciles the purchases of inventory with cost of goods sold. It is subtracted from net income because more inventory was purchased than was sold.

e.   This entry reconciles the prepayment of expenses with their expiration. It is subtracted from net income because cash payments for new prepayments are more than the amounts that expired.

f.   This entry reconciles cash paid to suppliers with purchases on account. It is subtracted because more was paid on account than was included as purchases on account.

g.   This entry reconciles the accrual of liabilities for operating expenses with payments for these expenses. It is added in the SCF because more expenses were accrued as liabilities than paid for in cash. The corresponding credit increases the accrued liabilities account.

h.   This entry records the receipt of cash on maturity of short-term investments.

i.   This entry records the purchases of new equipment for cash.

j.   This entry records cash provided by borrowing additional long-term debt.

k.   This entry records cash received from issuing stock.

l.   This entry records the payment of dividends in cash.

m.   This entry shows that the net increase from all liabilities, stockholders' equity, and noncash asset accounts, in effect, flows out of those accounts into cash.

The above entries complete the spreadsheet analysis because the beginning and ending balances of all accounts are reconciled and explained in terms of changes in cash. Check to see that Debits = Credits in your spreadsheet, because if they don't, you've missed something along the way. Notice that the bottom part of the spreadsheet can be used to prepare the formal statement of cash flows shown in Exhibit 12.2.

FOR YOUR PRACTICE

QUESTIONS

1.   Compare the purposes of the income statement, the balance sheet, and the statement of cash flows.

2.   What information does the statement of cash flows report that is not reported on the other required financial statements?

3.   What are cash equivalents? How are they reported on the statement of cash flows?

4.   What are the major categories of business activities reported on the statement of cash flows? Define each of these activities.

5.   What are the typical cash inflows from operating activities? What are the typical cash outflows from operating activities?

6.   Describe the types of items used to compute cash flows from operating activities under the two alternative methods of reporting.

7. Under the indirect method, depreciation expense is added to net income to report cash flows from operating activities. Does depreciation cause an inflow of cash?

8. Explain why cash outflows during the period for purchases and salaries are not specifically reported on a statement of cash flows prepared using the indirect method.

9. Explain why a $50,000 increase in inventory during the year must be included in computing cash flows from operating activities under both the direct and indirect methods.

10. What are the typical cash inflows from investing activities? What are the typical cash outflows from investing activities?

11. What are the typical cash inflows from financing activities? What are the typical cash outflows from financing activities?

12. What are noncash investing and financing activities? Give one example. How are noncash investing and financing activities reported on the statement of cash flows?

13. (Supplement A) How is the sale of equipment reported on the statement of cash flows using the indirect method?

MULTIPLE CHOICE

To practice more multiple choice questions, check out the DVD for use with this book.

1. Where is the change in cash shown in the statement of cash flows?
   a.   In the top part, before the operating activities section.
   b.   In one of the operating, investing, or financing activities sections.
   c.   In the bottom part, following the financing activities section.
   d.   None of the above.

2. In what order do the three sections of the statement of cash flows appear when reading from top to bottom?
   a.   Financing, investing, operating.
   b.   Investing, operating, financing.
   c.   Operating, financing, investing.
   d.   Operating, investing, financing.

3. Total cash inflow in the operating section of the statement of cash flows should include which of the following?
   a.   Cash received from customers at the point of sale.
   b.   Cash collections from customer accounts receivable.
   c.   Cash received in advance of revenue recognition (unearned revenue).
   d.   All of the above.

4. If the balance in prepaid expenses increased during the year, what action should be taken on the statement of cash flows when following the indirect method, *and why?*
   a.   The change in the account balance should be subtracted from net income, because the net increase in prepaid expenses did not impact net income but did reduce the cash balance.
   b.   The change in the account balance should be added to net income, because the net increase in prepaid expenses did not impact net income but did increase the cash balance.
   c.   The net change in prepaid expenses should be subtracted from net income, to reverse the income statement effect that had no impact on cash.
   d.   The net change in prepaid expenses should be added to net income, to reverse the income statement effect that had no impact on cash.

5. Which of the following would not appear in the investing section of the statement of cash flows?
   a.   Purchase of inventory.
   b.   Sale of short-term investments.
   c.   Purchase of land.
   d.   All of the above would appear in the investing section of the statement of cash flows.

6. Which of the following items would not appear in the financing section of the statement of cash flows?
   a.   The issuance of the company's own stock.
   b.   The receipt of dividends.
   c.   The repayment of debt.
   d.   The payment of dividends.

7. Which of the following is not added when computing cash flows from operations using the indirect method?
   a.   The net increase in accounts payable.
   b.   The net decrease in accounts receivable.

    c.   The net decrease in inventory.

    d.   All of the above should be added.

8. If a company engages in a material transaction that is noncash, which of the following is required?

    a.   The company must include an explanatory narrative or schedule along with the statement of cash flows.

    b.   No disclosure is necessary.

    c.   The company must include an explanatory narrative or schedule along with the balance sheet.

    d.   It must be reported in the investing and financing section of the statement of cash flows.

9. The *total* change in cash as shown near the bottom of the statement of cash flows for the year should agree to which of the following?

    a.   The difference in retained earnings when reviewing the comparative balance sheet.

    b.   Net income or net loss as found on the income statement.

    c.   The difference in cash when reviewing the comparative balance sheet.

    d.   None of the above.

10. Which of the following is a ratio used to assess the extent to which operating cash flows are sufficient to cover replacement of property, plant, and equipment?

    a.   Free cash flow.

    b.   Capital acquisitions ratio.

    c.   Cash coverage ratio.

    d.   Quality of income ratio.

Solutions to Multiple-Choice Questions

1.*c*   2.*d*   3.*d*   4.*a*   5.*a*   6.*b*   7.*d*   8.*a*   9.*c*   10.*b*

MINI-EXERCISES   Available with McGraw-Hill's Homework Manager

M12-1 Identifying Important Accounting Terms   LO1–LO5

Complete the following crossword puzzle, using the clues provided to the right.

Across

7 _____ cash flow is a measure of cash flows from operating activities that exceed amounts needed to pay dividends and replace property and equipment.

8 This category of business activities typically involves buying or selling long-lived assets.

9 These activities relate to transactions with owners and lenders.

Down

1 This SCF method converts each individual revenue and expense on the income statement to a cash basis.

2 These day-to-day activities relate to running the business.

3 If accounts receivable _____ (increase or decrease), the cash flows are less than what is included in sales on the income statement.

4 Dividends paid are classified as this type of activity.

5 Dividends received are classified as this type of activity.

6 This SCF method computes cash flow from operating activities by making adjustments to net income.

M12-2 Matching Items Reported to Cash Flow Statement Categories (Indirect Method)   LO1

The Buckle, Inc., operates over 300 stores in 38 states, selling brand name apparel like Lucky Jeans and Fossil belts and watches. Some of the items included in its 2004 statement of cash flows presented using the *indirect method* are listed here. Indicate whether each item is disclosed in the operating activities (O), investing activities (I), or financing activities (F) section of the statement or (NA) if the item does not appear on the statement.

_____ 1.   Proceeds from issuance of stock.

_____ 2.   Purchase of property and equipment.

_____ 3. Depreciation.

_____ 4. Accounts payable (decrease).

_____ 5. Inventories (decrease).

_____ 6. Purchase of investments.

LO2A   **M12-3 Determining the Effects of Account Changes on Cash Flows from Operating Activities (Indirect Method)**

Indicate whether each item would be added (+) or subtracted (−) in the computation of cash flow from operating activities using the indirect method.

_____ 1. Depreciation.

_____ 2. Inventories (increase).

_____ 3. Accounts payable (decrease).

_____ 4. Accounts receivable (decrease).

_____ 5. Accrued liabilities (increase).

LO1, LO2B   **M12-4 Matching Items Reported to Cash Flow Statement Categories (Direct Method)**

Nanupp Corporation reports the following items in its 2004 statement of cash flows presented using the *direct method*. Indicate whether each item is disclosed in the operating activities (O), investing activities (I), or financing activities (F) section of the statement or (NA) if the item does not appear on the statement.

_____ 1. Repayments of bank loan.

_____ 2. Dividends paid.

_____ 3. Proceeds from issuance of stock.

_____ 4. Interest paid.

_____ 5. Receipts from customers.

_____ 6. Payment for equipment purchase.

LO2A   **M12-5 Computing Cash Flows from Operating Activities (Indirect Method)**

For each of the following independent cases, compute cash flows from operating activities. Assume the list below includes all balance sheet accounts related to operating activities.

	Case A	Case B	Case C
Net income	$ 25,000	$ 36,000	$ 2,000
Depreciation expense	4,000	12,000	15,000
Accounts receivable increase (decrease)	10,000	(2,000)	20,000
Inventory increase (decrease)	(5,000)	5,000	(10,000)
Accounts payable increase (decrease)	(11,000)	7,000	12,000
Accrued liabilities increase (decrease)	6,000	(4,000)	(22,000)

LO2B   **M12-6 Computing Cash Flows from Operating Activities (Direct Method)**

For each of the following independent cases, compute cash flows from operating activities. Assume the list below includes all items relevant to operating activities.

	Case A	Case B	Case C
Sales revenue	$75,000	$55,000	$95,000
Cost of goods sold	35,000	32,000	65,000
Depreciation expense	10,000	2,000	10,000
Other operating expenses	5,000	13,000	8,000
Net income	25,000	8,000	12,000
Accounts receivable increase (decrease)	(1,000)	4,000	3,000
Inventory increase (decrease)	2,000	0	(4,000)
Accounts payable increase (decrease)	0	3,000	(2,000)
Accrued liabilities increase (decrease)	1,000	(1,000)	1,000

M12-7 Computing Cash Flows from Investing Activities

LO3

Based on the following information, compute cash flows from investing activities.

Cash collections from customers	$800
Purchase of used equipment	250
Depreciation expense	100
Sale of short-term investments	300

M12-8 Computing Cash Flows from Financing Activities

LO4

Based on the following information, compute cash flows from financing activities.

Purchase of short-term investments	$ 250
Dividends paid	800
Interest paid	400
Additional short-term borrowing from bank	1,000

M12-9 Reporting Noncash Investing and Financing Activities

LO3, LO4

Which of the following transactions would be considered noncash investing and financing activities?

____ 1. Purchase of equipment with short-term investments.

____ 2. Dividends paid in cash.

____ 3. Purchase of building with promissory note.

____ 4. Additional short-term borrowing from bank.

M12-10 Interpreting Cash Flows from Operating, Investing, and Financing Activities

LO5

Quantum Dots, Inc., is a nanotechnology company that manufactures "quantum dots," which are tiny pieces of silicon consisting of 100 or more molecules. Quantum dots can be used to illuminate very small objects, enabling scientists to see the blood vessels beneath a mouse's skin ripple with each heartbeat, at the rate of 100 times per second. Evaluate this research intensive company's cash flows, assuming the following was reported in its statement of cash flows.

COACH'S CORNER

See the demonstration cases for examples of evaluations of a statement of cash flows.

	Current Year	Previous Year
Cash Flows from Operating Activities		
Net cash provided by (used for) operating activities	$ (50,790)	$ (46,730)
Cash Flows from Investing Activities		
Purchases of research equipment	(250,770)	(480,145)
Proceeds from selling all short-term investments	35,000	—
Net cash provided by (used for) investing activities	(215,770)	(480,145)
Cash Flows from Financing Activities		
Additional long-term debt borrowed	100,000	200,000
Proceeds from stock issuance	140,000	200,000
Cash dividends paid	—	(10,000)
Net cash provided by (used for) financing activities	240,000	390,000
Net Increase (Decrease) in Cash	(26,560)	(136,875)
Cash at beginning of period	29,025	165,900
Cash at end of period	$ 2,465	$ 29,025

M12-11 Calculating and Interpreting the Capital Acquisitions Ratio

LO6

Airbow Kites Corporation reported the following information in its statement of cash flows:

	2004	*2003*	*2002*
Net cash flow from operating activities	$35,000	$32,000	$23,000
Interest paid	2,000	3,000	2,500
Income taxes paid	9,000	8,500	6,500
Purchases of property, plant, and equipment	31,818	22,857	20,325

Calculate the average capital acquisitions ratio for the period covering 2002–04 and the capital acquisitions ratio for *each* year during this period. What does this analysis tell you about the company's need for using external financing to replace property, plant, and equipment?

LO7 **M12-12** **Calculating and Interpreting the Cash Coverage Ratio**

Using the information in M12-11, calculate the cash coverage ratio for Airbow Kites for each of the three years. What do these ratios tell you about the company's ability to pay its interest costs?

LO8 **M12-13** **Calculating and Interpreting the Quality of Income Ratio**

Sea Leather Products, Inc., reported net income of $80,000, depreciation expense of $3,000, and cash flow from operations of $60,000. Compute the quality of income ratio. What does the ratio tell you about the company's accrual of revenues and/or deferral of expenses?

EXERCISES **Available with McGraw-Hill's Homework Manager**

LO1, LO2A **E12-1** **Matching Items Reported to Cash Flow Statement Categories (Indirect Method)**

Nike, Inc., is the best-known sports shoe, apparel, and equipment company in the world because of its association with sports stars such as LeBron James. Some of the items included in its recent statement of cash flows presented using the *indirect method* are listed here.

Indicate whether each item is disclosed in the operating activities (O), investing activities (I), or financing activities (F) section of the statement or (NA) if the item does not appear on the statement.

_____ 1. Depreciation.

_____ 2. Additions to property, plant, and equipment.

_____ 3. Increase (decrease) in notes payable. (The amount is owed to financial institutions.)

_____ 4. (Increase) decrease in other current assets.

_____ 5. Disposal of property, plant, and equipment.

_____ 6. Reductions in long-term debt including current portion.

_____ 7. Issuance of stock.

_____ 8. (Increase) decrease in inventory.

_____ 9. Net income.

_____ 10. Additions to long-term debt.

LO2A, LO2B **E12-2** **Comparing the Direct and Indirect Methods**

To compare statement of cash flows reporting under the direct and indirect methods, enter check marks to indicate which line-items are reported on the statement of cash flows with each method.

	Statement of Cash Flows Method	
Cash Flows (and Related Changes)	**Direct**	**Indirect**
1. Receipts from customers		
2. Accounts receivable increase or decrease		
3. Payments to suppliers		
4. Inventory increase or decrease		
5. Accounts payable increase or decrease		
6. Payments to employees		
7. Wages payable, increase or decrease		
8. Depreciation expense		
9. Net income		
10. Cash flows from operating activities		
11. Cash flows from investing activities		
12. Cash flows from financing activities		
13. Net increase or decrease in cash during the period		

LO2A **E12-3** **Reporting Cash Flows from Operating Activities (Indirect Method)**

The following information pertains to Day Company:

Sales		$80,000
Expenses:		
Cost of goods sold	$50,000	
Depreciation expense	6,000	
Salaries expense	12,000	68,000
Net income		$12,000
Accounts receivable increase	$ 5,000	
Merchandise inventory decrease	8,000	
Salaries payable increase	500	

Required:

Present the operating activities section of the statement of cash flows for Day Company using the indirect method.

E12-4 Reporting and Interpreting Cash Flows from Operating Activities from an Analyst's Perspective (Indirect Method)

LO2A, LO5

Kane Company completed its income statement and balance sheet for 2006 and provided the following information:

Service revenue		$50,000
Expenses:		
Salaries	$42,000	
Depreciation	7,300	
Utilities	7,000	
Other expenses	1,700	58,000
Net loss		($ 8,000)
Decrease in accounts receivable	$12,000	
Bought a small service machine	5,000	
Increase in salaries payable	9,000	
Decrease in other accrued liabilities	4,000	

Required:

1. Present the operating activities section of the statement of cash flows for Kane Company using the indirect method.

2. What were the major reasons that Kane was able to report a net loss but positive cash flow from operations?

3. Of the potential causes of differences between cash flow from operations and net income, which are the most important to financial analysts?

E12-5 Reporting and Interpreting Cash Flows from Operating Activities from an Analyst's Perspective (Indirect Method)

LO2A, LO5

Sizzler International, Inc., operates 465 family restaurants around the world. The company's annual report contained the following information (in thousands):

Operating Activities	
Net loss	$ (9,482)
Depreciation	33,305
Increase in receivables	170
Decrease in inventories	643
Increase in prepaid expenses	664
Decrease in accounts payable	2,282
Decrease in accrued liabilities	719
Increase in income taxes payable	1,861
Reduction of long-term debt	12,691
Additions to equipment	29,073

Required:

1. Based on this information, compute cash flow from operating activities using the indirect method.

2. What were the major reasons that Sizzler was able to report a net loss but positive cash flow from operations?

3. Of the potential causes of differences between cash flow from operations and net income, which are the most important to financial analysts?

LO2A

E12-6 Inferring Balance Sheet Changes from the Cash Flow Statement (Indirect Method)

Colgate-Palmolive was founded in 1806. Its statement of cash flows for the first quarter of 2004 reported the following information (in millions):

Operating Activities	
Net income	$338.5
Depreciation	79.9
Cash effect of changes in	
Accounts receivable	12.0
Inventories	(73.8)
Other current assets	8.0
Accounts payable	(26.6)
Other	33.3
Net cash provided by operations	$371.3

Required:

Based on the information reported in the operating activities section of the statement of cash flows for Colgate-Palmolive, determine whether the following accounts increased or decreased during the period: Accounts Receivable, Inventories, Other Current Assets, and Accounts Payable.

LO2A

E12-7 Inferring Balance Sheet Changes from the Cash Flow Statement (Indirect Method)

A prior statement of cash flows for Apple Computer contained the following information (in thousands):

Operating Activities	
Net income	$310,178
Depreciation	167,958
Changes in assets and liabilities	
Accounts receivable	(199,401)
Inventories	418,204
Other current assets	33,616
Accounts payable	139,095
Income taxes payable	50,045
Other current liabilities	39,991
Other adjustments	(222,691)
Net cash provided by operations	$736,995

Required:

For each of the asset and liability accounts listed in the operating activities section of the statement of cash flows, determine whether the account balances increased or decreased during the period.

LO2B, LO5

E12-8 Reporting and Interpreting Cash Flows from Operating Activities from an Analyst's Perspective (Direct Method)

Refer to the information for Kane Company in E12-4.

Required:

1. Present the operating activities section of the statement of cash flows for Kane Company using the direct method. Assume that other accrued liabilities relate to other expenses on the income statement.

2. What were the major reasons that Kane was able to report a net loss but positive cash flow from operations?

3. Of the potential causes of differences between cash flow from operations and net income, which are the most important to financial analysts?

E12-9 Reporting and Interpreting Cash Flows from Operating Activities from an Analyst's Perspective (Direct Method)

LO2B, LO5

Refer back to the information given for E12-5, plus the following summarized income statement for Sizzler International, Inc.:

Revenues	$136,500
Cost of sales	45,500
Gross margin	91,000
Salary expense	56,835
Depreciation	33,305
Other expenses	7,781
Net loss before income taxes	(6,921)
Income tax expense	2,561
Net loss	$ (9,482)

Required:

1. Based on this information, compute cash flow from operating activities using the direct method. Assume that prepaid expenses and accrued liabilities relate to other expenses.
2. What were the major reasons that Sizzler was able to report a net loss but positive cash flow from operations?
3. Of the potential causes of differences between cash flow from operations and net income, which are the most important to financial analysts?

E12-10 Analyzing Cash Flows from Operating Activities (Indirect Method) and Calculating and Interpreting the Quality of Income Ratio

LO2A, LO8

A recent annual report for PepsiCo contained the following information for the period (in millions):

Net income	$1,587.9
Depreciation	1,444.2
Increase in accounts receivable	161.0
Increase in inventory	89.5
Decrease in prepaid expense	3.3
Increase in accounts payable	143.2
Decrease in taxes payable	125.1
Decrease in other current liabilities	96.7
Cash dividends paid	461.6

Required:

1. Compute cash flows from operating activities for PepsiCo using the indirect method.
2. Compute the quality of income ratio.
3. What was the main reason that PepsiCo's quality of income ratio did not equal 1.0?

E12-11 Reporting Cash Flows from Investing and Financing Activities

LO3, LO4

Rowe Furniture Corporation is a Virginia-based manufacturer of furniture. In a recent quarter, it reported the following activities:

Net income	$ 4,135
Purchase of property, plant, and equipment	871
Borrowings under line of credit (bank)	1,417
Proceeds from issuance of stock	11
Cash received from customers	29,164
Payments to reduce long-term debt	46
Sale of short-term investments	134
Proceeds from sale of property and equipment	6,594
Dividends paid	277
Interest paid	90

Required:

Based on this information, present the cash flows from investing and financing activities sections of the cash flow statement.

LO3–LO5   **E12-12   Reporting and Interpreting Cash Flows from Investing and Financing Activities with Discussion of Management Strategy**

Gibraltar Steel Corporation is a Buffalo, New York–based manufacturer of steel products. In a prior year, it reported the following activities:

Net income	$ 5,213
Purchase of property, plant, and equipment	10,468
Payments of notes payable (bank)	8,598
Net proceeds of stock issuance	26,061
Depreciation	3,399
Long-term debt reduction	17,832
Proceeds from sale of short-term investments	131
Proceeds from sale of property, plant, and equipment	1,817
Proceeds from long-term debt borrowed	10,242
Decrease in accounts receivable	1,137
Proceeds from notes payable (bank)	3,848

Required:

1. Based on this information, present the cash flows from investing and financing activities sections of the cash flow statement.
2. Referring to your response to requirement 1, comment on what you think Gibraltar's management plan was for the use of the cash generated by the stock issuance.

LO6   **E12-13   Analyzing and Interpreting the Capital Acquisitions Ratio**

A recent annual report for Sportsnet Corporation contained the following data for the three most recent years (in thousands):

	2005	2004	2003
Cash flows from operating activities	$ 821	$1,460	$619
Cash flows from investing activities	(1,404)	(1,315)	(862)
Cash flows from financing activities	42,960	775	360

Assume that all investing activities involved acquisition of new plant and equipment.

Required:

1. Compute the capital acquisitions ratio for the three-year period in total.
2. What portion of Sportsnet's investing activities was financed from cash flows from operating activities? What portion was financed from external sources or preexisting cash balances during the three-year period?
3. What do you think is the likely explanation for the dramatic increase in cash flow from financing activities during the period?

LO6   **E12-14   Calculating and Interpreting the Capital Acquisitions Ratio**

AMC Theatres® is the world's second-largest theatre chain. The following information was extracted from its 2003 financial statements.

	2003	2002	2001
Net income (loss)	(20,302)	(11,468)	(105,886)
Net cash provided by operating activities	128,747	101,091	43,458
Purchase of property and equipment	(107,984)	(106,501)	(101,932)
Cash paid for interest	78,677	59,824	85,261
Cash paid (refunded) for income taxes	(9,757)	(3,579)	(6,583)

Required:

1. Calculate the average capital acquisitions ratio for the period covering 2001–03.
2. Interpret the results of your calculations in requirement 1. What do they suggest about the company's need for external financing to acquire property and equipment?

E12-15 Calculating and Interpreting the Cash Coverage Ratio   LO7

Refer to the information in E12-14.

Required:

1. Calculate the cash coverage ratio for each year.
2. Interpret the results of your calculations in requirement 1. What do they suggest about the company's ability to pay interest on its debt financing?

E12-16 Calculating and Interpreting the Quality of Income Ratio   LO8

Refer to the information in E12-14.

Required:

1. Calculate the quality of income ratio for each year.
2. Interpret the results of your calculations in requirement 1. Given what you know about the movie theatre business from your own personal observations, provide one reason that could explain the sizable difference between net income (loss) and net cash provided by operating activities.

E12-17 (Supplement A) Determining Cash Flows from the Sale of Property

The first in the theatre industry to introduce a customer loyalty program (like frequent flyer miles for movie watchers) was AMC Theatres. During 2003, the company sold property for $5,494,000 cash and recorded a gain on sale of $1,385,000. During 2002, the company sold property for $6,647,000 cash and recorded a gain on sale of $1,821,000.

Required:

For the property sold by AMC each year, show how these amounts would be reported on its comparative statements of cash flows, using the following format (which assumes the indirect method):

	2003	2002
Cash flows from operating activities		
Gain on sale of property		
Cash flows from investing activities		
Proceeds from disposition of property		

E12-18 (Supplement A) Determining Cash Flows from the Sale of Equipment

During the period, English Company sold some excess equipment at a loss. The following information was collected from the company's accounting records:

From the Income Statement	
Depreciation expense	$ 700
Loss on sale of equipment	3,000
From the Balance Sheet	
Beginning equipment	12,500
Ending equipment	8,000
Beginning accumulated depreciation	2,000
Ending accumulated depreciation	2,400

No new equipment was bought during the period.

Required:

For the equipment that was sold, determine its original cost, its accumulated depreciation, and the cash received from the sale.

E12-19 Preparing a Statement of Cash Flows, Indirect Method: Complete Spreadsheet (Supplement B)

To prepare a statement of cash flows for Mac's Relax Store, you examined the company's accounts, noting the following:

Purchased equipment, $20,000, and issued a promissory note in full payment.

Purchased a long-term investment for cash, $15,000.

Paid cash dividend, $12,000.

Sold equipment for $6,000 cash (cost, $21,000, accumulated depreciation, $15,000).

Issued shares of stock, 500 shares at $12 per share cash.

You also created the following spreadsheet to use when preparing the statement of cash flows.

	Beginning Balances, December 31, 2003	Analysis of Changes Debit	Analysis of Changes Credit	Ending Balances, December 31, 2004
Income Statement Items				
Sales			$140,000	
Cost of goods sold		$59,000		
Depreciation		3,000		
Wage expense		28,000		
Income tax expense		9,000		
Interest expense		5,000		
Other expenses		15,800		
Net income		20,200		
Balance Sheet Items				
Cash	$ 20,500			$ 19,200
Accounts receivable	22,000			22,000
Merchandise inventory	68,000			75,000
Investments, long-term	0			15,000
Equipment	114,500			113,500
Total debits	$225,000			$244,700
Accumulated depreciation	$ 32,000			$ 20,000
Accounts payable	17,000			14,000
Wages payable	2,500			1,500
Income taxes payable	3,000			4,500
Notes payable	54,000			74,000
Contributed capital	100,000			106,000
Retained earnings	16,500			24,700
Total credits	$225,000			$244,700

	Inflows	Outflows
Statement of Cash Flows		
Cash flows from operating activities		
Cash flows from investing activities		
Cash flows from financing activities		
Net increase (decrease) in cash		
Totals		

Required:

Complete the spreadsheet to prepare the statement of cash flows using the indirect method.

SIMPLIFY WITH SPREADSHEETS

SS12-1 Using a Spreadsheet that Calculates Cash Flows from Operating Activities (Indirect Method)

L02A

You've recently been hired by B2B Consultants to provide financial advisory services to small business managers. B2B's clients often need advice on how to improve their operating cash flows and, given your accounting background, you're frequently called upon to show them how operating cash flows would change if they were to speed up their sales of inventory and their collections of accounts receivable or delay their payment of accounts payable. Each time you're asked to show the effects of these business decisions on the cash flows from operating activities, you get the uneasy feeling that you might inadvertently miscalculate their effects. To deal with this once and for all, you e-mail your friend Billy and ask him to prepare a template that automatically calculates the net operating cash flows from a simple comparative balance sheet. You received his reply today.

From: BillyTheTutor@yahoo.com
To: HairZed@hotmail.com
Cc:
Subject: Excel Help

Hey pal. I like your idea of working smarter, not harder. Too bad it involved me doing the thinking. Anyhow, I've created a spreadsheet file that contains four worksheets. The first two tabs (labeled BS and IS) are the input sheets where you would enter the numbers from each client's comparative balance sheet and income statement. Your clients are small, so this template allows for only the usual accounts. Also, I've assumed that depreciation is the only reason for a change in accumulated depreciation. If your clients' business activities differ from these, you'll need to contact me for more complex templates. The third worksheet calculates the operating cash flows using the indirect method and the fourth does this calculation using the direct method. I'll attach the screenshots of each of the worksheets so you can create your own. To answer "what if" questions, all you'll need to do is change selected amounts in the balance sheet and income statement.

Microsoft Excel - ss12-1.xls

File Edit View Insert Format Tools Data Window Help Acrobat

	B	C	D	E
2	Small Business Client			
3	Balance Sheet			
4	As of December 31			
5	**ASSETS**	Current Year	Prior Year	Change
6	Cash	$ 8,000	$ 12,000	-4,000
7	Accounts receivable	16,900	8,500	+8,400
8	Inventories	37,600	25,900	+11,700
9	Total Current Assets	62,500	46,400	
10	Property, plant, and equipment	105,000	105,000	0
11	Less: accumulated depreciation	(20,000)	(10,000)	-10,000
12	*Total Assets*	$ 147,500	$ 141,400	
13	**LIABILITIES**			
14	Accounts payable	$ 31,400	$ 30,000	+1,400
15	Income taxes payable	3,000	4,000	-1,000
16	Interest payable	4,000	1,800	+2,200
17	Other accrued liabilities	11,000	14,000	-3,000
18	Total Current Liabilities	49,400	49,800	
19	Long-term debt	40,000	40,000	0
20	Total Liabilities	89,400	89,800	
21	**STOCKHOLDERS' EQUITY**			
22	Contributed Capital	10,000	10,000	0
23	Retained Earnings	48,100	41,600	+6,500
24	Total Stockholders' Equity	58,100	51,600	
25	*Total Liabilities and Stockholders' Equity*	$ 147,500	$ 141,400	

BS / IS / Indirect / Direct /

Microsoft Excel - ss12-1.xls

File Edit View Insert Format Tools Data Window Help Acrobat

	B	C
2	Small Business Client	
3	Income Statement	
4	For the Year Ended December 31	
5	Sales revenues	$ 102,000
6	Cost of goods sold	77,400
7	Depreciation expense	10,000
8	Other operating expenses	1,800
9	Operating income	12,800
10	Interest expense	2,800
11	Income before income taxes	10,000
12	Income tax expense	3,500
13	Net income	$ 6,500

BS \ IS / Indirect / [

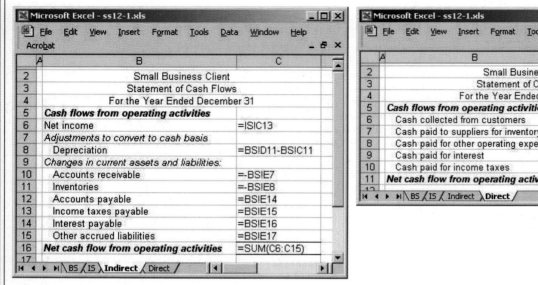

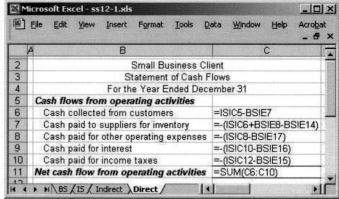

Required:

Copy the information from the worksheets for the balance sheet, income statement, and statement of cash flows (indirect method only) into a spreadsheet file. What was the net cash flow from operating activities?

LO2B   **SS12-2 Using a Spreadsheet that Calculates Cash Flows from Operating Activities (Direct Method)**

Refer to the information presented in SS12-1.

Required:

Copy the information from the worksheets for the balance sheet, income statement, and statement of cash flows (direct method only) into a spreadsheet file. What was the net cash flow from operating activities?

LO5   **SS12-3 Using a Spreadsheet to Answer "What If" Management Decisions (Indirect or Direct Method)**

Change the amounts for selected balance sheet accounts in the spreadsheets created for either SS12-1 or SS12-2 to calculate the cash flows from operating activities if, just before the current year-end, the company's management took the actions listed in the following requirements. Consider each question independently, unless indicated otherwise.

Required:

1. What if the company collected $10,000 of the accounts receivable?
2. What if the company had paid down its interest payable by an extra $2,000?
3. What if the company waited an additional month before paying $6,000 of its accounts payable?
4. What if the company had reported $5,000 more depreciation expense?
5. What if all four of the above events had taken place?

COACHED PROBLEMS

LO1   **CP12-1 Determining Cash Flow Statement Effects of Transactions**

Motorola, Inc., is best known for its cell phones and modems, which have become so small that they are being integrated into new high-tech sunglasses (scheduled for release in 2006). For each of the following first-quarter transactions, indicate whether operating (O), investing (I), or financing activities (F) are affected and whether the effect is a cash inflow (+) or outflow (−), or (NE) if the transaction has no effect on cash.

_____ 1. Recorded and paid income taxes to the federal government.

_____ 2. Issued shares of stock for cash.

_____ 3. Prepaid rent for the following period.

_____ 4. Recorded an adjusting entry for expiration of a prepaid expense.

_____ 5. Paid cash to purchase new equipment.

_____ 6. Issued long-term debt for cash.

_____ 7. Collected payments on account from customers.

_____ 8. Recorded and paid salaries to employees.

_____ 9. Purchased new equipment by signing a promissory note.

CP12-2 Computing Cash Flows from Operating Activities (Indirect Method)

LO2A

Beta Company's accountants just completed the 2004 income statement and balance sheet for the year and have provided the following information (in thousands):

Income Statement

Sales revenue	$20,600
Expenses:	
Cost of goods sold	9,000
Depreciation expense	2,000
Salaries expense	5,000
Rent expense	2,500
Insurance expense	800
Interest expense	600
Utilities expense	500
Net income	$ 200

Selected Balance Sheet Accounts

	2004	2003
Merchandise inventory	$ 82	$ 60
Accounts receivable	380	450
Accounts payable	240	210
Salaries payable	29	20
Utilities payable	20	60
Prepaid rent	2	7
Prepaid insurance	14	5

Required:

Prepare the cash flows from operating activities section of the 2004 statement of cash flows using the indirect method.

CP12-3 Computing Cash Flows from Operating Activities (Direct Method)

Refer to the information in CP12-2.

Required:

Prepare the cash flows from operating activities section of the 2004 statement of cash flows using the direct method.

LO2B

CP12-4 Preparing a Statement of Cash Flows (Indirect Method)

LO2A, LO3, LO4

eXcel

Hunter Company is developing its annual financial statements at December 31, 2004. The statements are complete except for the statement of cash flows. The completed comparative balance sheets and income statement are summarized:

	2004	2003
Balance sheet at December 31		
Cash	$ 44,000	$ 18,000
Accounts receivable	27,000	29,000
Merchandise inventory	30,000	36,000
Property and equipment	111,000	102,000
Less: Accumulated depreciation	(36,000)	(30,000)
	$176,000	$155,000
Accounts payable	$ 25,000	$ 22,000
Wages payable	800	1,000
Note payable, long-term	38,000	48,000
Contributed capital	80,000	60,000
Retained earnings	32,200	24,000
	$176,000	$155,000
Income statement for 2004		
Sales	$100,000	
Cost of goods sold	61,000	
Other expenses	27,000	
Net income	$ 12,000	

COACH'S CORNER

When evaluating the statement of cash flows in requirement 2, consider (*a*) are operating cash flows positive, (*b*) how much has the company spent on property and equipment, and (*c*) has the company had to take out new loans, issue more stock, or use up its cash, or has it been able to build up cash, pay down debt, or pay cash dividends? The demonstration cases provide good examples to follow.

Additional Data:

a. Bought equipment for cash, $9,000.
b. Paid $10,000 on the long-term note payable.
c. Issued new shares of stock for $20,000 cash.
d. Declared and paid a $3,800 cash dividend.
e. Other expenses included depreciation, $6,000; wages, $10,000; taxes, $3,000; other, $8,000.
f. Accounts payable includes only inventory purchases made on credit. Because there are no liability accounts relating to taxes or other expenses, assume that these expenses were fully paid in cash.

Required:

1. Prepare the statement of cash flows for the year ended December 31, 2004, using the indirect method.
2. Use the statement of cash flows to evaluate Hunter's cash flows.

GROUP A PROBLEMS   Available with McGraw-Hill's Homework Manager

LO1   **PA12-1 Determining Cash Flow Statement Effects of Transactions**

Stanley Furniture Company is a Virginia-based furniture manufacturer. For each of the following first-quarter transactions, indicate whether operating (O), investing (I), or financing activities (F) are affected and whether the effect is a cash inflow (+) or outflow (−), or (NE) if the transaction has no effect on cash.

____ 1. Paid cash to purchase new equipment.
____ 2. Declared and paid cash dividends to stockholders.
____ 3. Collected payments on account from customers.
____ 4. Recorded an adjusting entry to record accrued salaries expense.
____ 5. Recorded and paid interest on debt to creditors.
____ 6. Repaid principal on loan from bank.
____ 7. Prepaid rent for the following period.
____ 8. Bought used equipment for cash.
____ 9. Made payment to suppliers on account.

LO2A   **PA12-2 Computing Cash Flows from Operating Activities (Indirect Method)**

Gamma Company's accountants just completed the 2004 income statement and balance sheet for the year and have provided the following information (in thousands):

Income Statement

Sales revenue	$48,600
Expenses:	
Cost of goods sold	21,000
Depreciation expense	6,000
Salaries expense	9,000
Rent expense	4,500
Insurance expense	1,900
Interest expense	1,800
Utilities expense	1,400
Net income	$ 3,000

Selected Balance Sheet Accounts

	2004	2003
Merchandise inventory	$ 99	$ 77
Accounts receivable	280	290
Accounts payable	220	230
Salaries payable	44	35
Utilities payable	11	8
Prepaid rent	11	9
Prepaid insurance	13	14

Required:

Prepare the cash flows from operating activities section of the 2004 statement of cash flows using the indirect method.

PA12-3 Computing Cash Flows from Operating Activities (Direct Method)

Refer to the information in PA12-2.

L02B

Required:

Prepare the cash flows from operating activities section of the 2004 statement of cash flows using the direct method.

PA12-4 Preparing a Statement of Cash Flows (Indirect Method)

XS Supply Company is developing its annual financial statements at December 31, 2004. The statements are complete except for the statement of cash flows. The completed comparative balance sheets and income statement are summarized:

L02A, L03, L04

e**X**cel

	2004	2003
Balance sheet at December 31		
Cash	$ 34,000	$ 29,000
Accounts receivable	35,000	28,000
Merchandise inventory	41,000	38,000
Property and equipment	121,000	100,000
Less: Accumulated depreciation	(30,000)	(25,000)
	$201,000	$170,000
Accounts payable	$ 36,000	$ 27,000
Wages payable	1,200	1,400
Note payable, long-term	38,000	44,000
Contributed capital	88,600	72,600
Retained earnings	37,200	25,000
	$201,000	$170,000

Income statement for 2004

Sales	$120,000
Cost of goods sold	70,000
Other expenses	37,800
Net income	$ 12,200

Additional Data:

a. Bought equipment for cash, $21,000.
b. Paid $6,000 on the long-term note payable.
c. Issued new shares of stock for $16,000 cash.
d. No dividends were declared or paid.
e. Other expenses included depreciation, $5,000; wages, $20,000; taxes, $6,000; other, $6,800.
f. Accounts payable includes only inventory purchases made on credit. Because there are no liability accounts relating to taxes or other expenses, assume that these expenses were fully paid in cash.

Required:

1. Prepare the statement of cash flows for the year ended December 31, 2004, using the indirect method.
2. Evaluate the statement of cash flows.

GROUP B PROBLEMS

L01   **PB12-1 Determining Cash Flow Statement Effects of Transactions**

Fantatech Inc. designs, develops, and produces high-tech entertainment products, including VirtuaSports, that allow novice players to experience hazardous and difficult real-life sports in virtual reality. The company also produces a 4D theatre system that combines 3D visual effects with special effects such as vibrating chairs, simulated drops, and scented air blasts. For each of the following transactions listed in Fantatech's 2003 annual report, indicate whether operating (O), investing (I), or financing activities (F) are affected and whether the effect is a cash inflow (+) or outflow (−), or (NE) if the transaction has no effect on cash.

_____ 1. Recorded and paid interest to debt holders.
_____ 2. Issued shares of stock for cash.
_____ 3. Received deposits from customers for products to be delivered the following period.
_____ 4. Principal repayments on short-term loan.
_____ 5. Paid cash to purchase new equipment.
_____ 6. Received proceeds from short-term loan.
_____ 7. Collected payments on account from customers.
_____ 8. Recorded and paid salaries to employees.
_____ 9. Paid cash for building construction.

L02A   **PB12-2 Computing Cash Flows from Operating Activities (Indirect Method)**

Alpha Company's accountants just completed the 2004 income statement and balance sheet for the year and have provided the following information (in thousands):

Income Statement	
Sales revenue	$78,000
Expenses:	
Cost of goods sold	36,000
Depreciation expense	16,000
Salaries expense	10,000
Rent expense	2,500
Insurance expense	1,300
Interest expense	1,200
Utilities expense	1,000
Net income	$10,000

Selected Balance Sheet Accounts

	2004	2003
Merchandise inventory	$ 43	$ 49
Accounts receivable	180	150
Accounts payable	120	130
Salaries payable	45	30
Utilities payable	10	0
Prepaid rent	5	10
Prepaid insurance	7	9

Required:

Prepare the cash flows from operating activities section of the 2004 statement of cash flows using the indirect method.

PB12-3 Computing Cash Flows from Operating Activities (Direct Method)   LO2B

Refer to the information in PB12-2.

Required:

Prepare the cash flows from operating activities section of the 2004 statement of cash flows using the direct method.

PB12-4 Preparing a Statement of Cash Flows (Indirect Method)   LO2A, LO3, LO4

Audio City, Inc., is developing its annual financial statements at December 31, 2004. The statements are complete except for the statement of cash flows. The completed comparative balance sheets and income statement are summarized:

	2004	2003
Balance sheet at December 31		
Cash	$ 68,000	$ 65,000
Accounts receivable	15,000	20,000
Merchandise inventory	22,000	20,000
Property and equipment	210,000	150,000
Less: Accumulated depreciation	(60,000)	(45,000)
	$255,000	$210,000
Accounts payable	$ 8,000	$ 19,000
Wages payable	2,000	1,000
Note payable, long-term	60,000	75,000
Contributed capital	100,000	70,000
Retained earnings	85,000	45,000
	$255,000	$210,000
Income statement for 2004		
Sales	$190,000	
Cost of goods sold	90,000	
Other expenses	60,000	
Net income	$ 40,000	

Additional Data:

a. Bought equipment for cash, $60,000.
b. Paid $15,000 on the long-term note payable.
c. Issued new shares of stock for $30,000 cash.
d. No dividends were declared or paid.
e. Other expenses included depreciation, $15,000; wages, $20,000; taxes, $25,000.
f. Accounts payable includes only inventory purchases made on credit. Because a liability relating to taxes does not exist, assume that they were fully paid in cash.

Required:

1. Prepare the statement of cash flows for the year ended December 31, 2004, using the indirect method.
2. Evaluate the statement of cash flows.

CASES & DISCUSSION STARTERS

FINANCIAL REPORTING AND ANALYSIS CASES

LO1, LO5–LO7

C&DS12-1 Finding Financial Information

Refer to the financial statements of Landry's Restaurants in Appendix A at the end of this book, or download the annual report from the *Cases* section of the text's Web site at www.mhhe.com/phillips.

Required:

1. Which of the two basic reporting approaches for the cash flows from operating activities did Landry's use?
2. What amount of tax payments did Landry's make during the current year? Where did you find this information?
3. Including business acquisitions, what was the capital acquisitions ratio averaged across the three years shown in Landry's statement of cash flows? Ignoring business acquisitions, what was the capital acquisitions ratio averaged across the three years shown in Landry's statement of cash flows?
4. How much cash did Landry's pay for interest during the current year? Using this information, calculate and interpret the cash coverage ratio for the most recent year.
5. In the most recent year reported, Landry's generated $121,529,891 from operating activities and $148,093,497 from long-term debt (senior notes) borrowed. Where did Landry's spend this money? List the two largest cash outflows.

LO1, LO5–LO7

C&DS12-2 Comparing Financial Information

Refer to the financial statements of Dave & Buster's in Appendix B at the end of this book, or download the annual report from the *Cases* section of the text's Web site at www.mhhe.com/phillips. In the questions that follow, assume Dave & Buster's financial statements for the year ended February 1, 2004, present the results for 2003.

Required:

1. Which of the two basic reporting approaches for the cash flows from operating activities did Dave & Buster's use? Is this the same as what Landry's used?
2. What net amount of tax payments did Dave & Buster's make during the current year? Where did you find this information? Is this more or less than Landry's paid?
3. Including business acquisitions, what was the capital acquisitions ratio averaged across the three years shown in Dave & Buster's statement of cash flows? Ignoring business acquisitions, what was the capital acquisitions ratio averaged across the three years shown in Dave & Buster's statement of cash flows? Do net operating cash flows pay for a greater or lesser proportion of Dave & Buster's capital acquisitions than Landry's?
4. Ignoring capitalized interest, how much cash did Dave & Buster's pay for interest during the current year? Using this information, calculate and interpret the cash coverage ratio for Dave & Buster's for the most recent year. Compare this to Landry's and draw a conclusion about the companies' relative abilities to pay for interest.
5. In the most recent year reported, Dave & Buster's generated $45 million from operating activities and nearly $45 million from long-term debt borrowings. Where did Dave & Buster's spend this money? List the two largest cash outflows. Do these uses differ significantly from Landry's?

LO5–LO8

C&DS12-3 Internet-Based Team Research: Examining an Annual Report

As a team, select an industry to analyze. Using your Web browser, each team member should acquire the annual report or 10-K for one publicly traded company in the industry, with each member selecting a different company. (See C&DS1-3 in Chapter 1 for a description of possible resources for these tasks.)

Required:

1. On an individual basis, each team member should write a short report that incorporates the following:
   a. Has the company generated positive or negative operating cash flows during the past three years?
   b. Has the company been expanding over the period? If so, what appears to have been the source of financing for this expansion (operating cash flow, additional borrowing, issuance of stock)?
   c. Compute and analyze the capital acquisitions ratio averaged over the past three years.
   d. Compute and analyze the cash coverage ratio in each of the past three years.
   e. Compute and analyze the quality of income ratio in each of the past three years.

2. Then, as a team, write a short report comparing and contrasting your companies using these attributes. Discuss any patterns across the companies that you as a team observe. Provide potential explanations for any differences discovered.

TEAM CASE

ETHICS AND CRITICAL THINKING CASES

C&DS12-4 Ethical Decision Making: A Real-Life Example

In a February 19, 2004, press release, the Securities and Exchange Commission described a number of fraudulent transactions that Enron executives concocted in an effort to meet the company's financial targets. One particularly well-known scheme is called the "Nigerian barge" transaction, which took place in the fourth quarter of 1999. According to court documents, Enron arranged to sell three electricity-generating power barges moored off the coast of Nigeria. The "buyer" was the investment banking firm of Merrill Lynch. Although Enron reported this transaction as a sale in its income statement, it turns out this was no ordinary sale. Merrill Lynch didn't really want the barges and had only agreed to buy them because Enron guaranteed, in a secret side-deal, that it would arrange for the barges to be bought back from Merrill Lynch within six months of the initial transaction. In addition, Enron promised to pay Merrill Lynch a hefty fee for doing the deal. In an interview on National Public Radio on August 17, 2002, Michigan Senator Carl Levin declared, "(t)he case of the Nigerian barge transaction was, by any definition, a loan."

LO1, LO5

ETHICAL

ISSUE

Required:

1. Discuss whether the Nigerian barge transaction should have been considered a loan rather than a sale. As part of your discussion, consider the following questions. Doesn't the Merrill Lynch payment to Enron at the time of the initial transaction automatically make it a sale, not a loan? What aspects of the transaction are similar to a loan? Which aspects suggest that the four criteria for revenue recognition (summarized near the end of Chapter 3) are not fulfilled?

2. The income statement effect of recording the transaction as a sale rather than a loan is fairly clear: Enron was able to boost its revenues and net income. What is somewhat less obvious, but nearly as important, are the effects on the statement of cash flows. Describe how including the transaction with sales of other Merrill Lynch products, rather than as a loan, would change the statement of cash flows.

3. How would the difference in the statement of cash flows (described in your response to requirement 2) affect financial statement users?

C&DS12-5 Ethical Decision Making: A Mini-Case

Assume you serve on the board of a local golf and country club. In preparation for renegotiating the club's bank loans, the president indicates that the club needs to increase its operating cash flows before the end of the current year. With a wink and sly smile, the club's treasurer reassures the president and other board members that he knows a couple of ways to boost the club's operating cash flows. First, he says, the club can sell some of its accounts receivable to a collections company that is willing to pay the club $97,000 up front for the right to collect $100,000 of the overdue accounts. That will immediately boost operating cash flows. Second, he indicates that the club paid about $200,000 last month to relocate the 18th fairway and green closer to the clubhouse. The treasurer indicates that although these costs have been reported as expenses in the club's own monthly financial statements, he feels an argument can be made for reporting them as part of land

LO1, LO2A, LO2B, LO5

ETHICAL

ISSUE

and land improvements (a long-lived asset) in the year-end financial statements that would be provided to the bank. He explains that, by recording these payments as an addition to a long-lived asset, they will not be shown as a reduction in operating cash flows.

Required:

1. Does the sale of accounts receivable to generate immediate cash harm or mislead anyone? Would you consider it an ethical business activity?

2. If cash is spent on long-lived assets, such as land improvements, how is it typically classified in the statement of cash flows? If cash is spent on expenses, such as costs for regular upkeep of the grounds, how is it typically classified in the statement of cash flows?

3. What facts are relevant to deciding whether the costs of the 18th hole relocation should be reported as an asset or as an expense? Is it appropriate to make this decision based on the impact it could have on operating cash flows?

4. As a member of the board, how would you ensure that an ethical decision is made?

LO2A

C&DS12-6 Critical Thinking: Interpreting Adjustments Reported on the Statement of Cash Flows from a Management Perspective (Indirect Method)

QuickServe, a chain of convenience stores, was experiencing some serious cash flow difficulties because of rapid growth. The company did not generate sufficient cash from operating activities to finance its new stores, and creditors were not willing to lend money because the company had not produced any income for the previous three years. The new controller for QuickServe proposed a reduction in the estimated life of store equipment to increase depreciation expense; thus, "we can improve cash flows from operating activities because depreciation expense is added back on the statement of cash flows." Other executives were not sure that this was a good idea because the increase in depreciation would make it more difficult to have positive earnings: "Without income, the bank will never lend us money."

Required:

What action would you recommend for QuickServe? Why?

chapter thirteen

Measuring and Evaluating Financial Performance

13

Hey, you made it to Chapter 13 of the textbook. In accounting slang, "Chapter 11" and "Chapter 13" are labels used for different forms of bankruptcy protection that buy time for people rearranging their financial affairs, but that's not what Chapter 13 in this textbook is about. In fact, we focus on a company that's in just the opposite situation. In this chapter, you'll learn why analysts have judged **LANDRY'S RESTAURANTS** to be a strong, financially successful company.

Measuring and evaluating financial performance is like judging gymnastics or figure skating at the Olympics. You have to know three things: (1) the general categories to evaluate for each event, (2) the particular elements to consider within each category, and (3) how performance for each element is measured. You probably use a similar approach when judging your eating experience at one of Landry's restaurants, like Joe's Crab Shack. General categories, like enjoyment and value, can be broken down into particular elements like service, atmosphere, flavor, price, and serving size, which can be measured in terms of time, money, and pounds of crab. On the financial side, analysts consider general categories like profitability, liquidity, and solvency, which are broken down into particular elements like profit margin and asset turnover. For each of these elements, analysts measure performance using financial ratios, which themselves are based on information reported in the financial statements. By the time you finish reading this chapter, you'll understand why analysts are eating up Landry's financial results and, more generally, what you should look for when analyzing other companies' financial performance.

INSIDE LOOKING OUT

OUTSIDE LOOKING IN

This chapter reviews the measurement and analysis of financial performance, by focusing on Landry's Restaurants, the company that owns Joe's Crab Shack, Rainforest Cafè, and over a dozen other chains of seafood and steak houses.

Landry's estimates that Joe's Crab Shack serves over 12,000 gallons of gumbo and a quarter million pounds of shrimp every year.

n this chapter, we describe techniques commonly used to evaluate financial performance and then present a framework for organizing all the ratios you've learned throughout the previous chapters. Using the framework and ratios, we analyze the financial results of Landry's Restaurants. Later sections discuss how financial results relate to stock prices and then review key concepts that make financial accounting useful for evaluating a company and predicting its future. With a plateful of topics like this (summarized in Exhibit 13.1), you'd better get started.

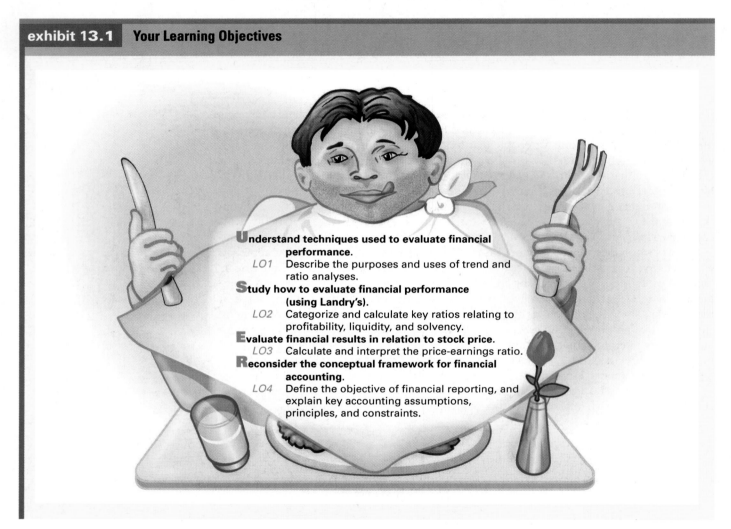

exhibit 13.1   Your Learning Objectives

Understand techniques used to evaluate financial performance.
LO1   Describe the purposes and uses of trend and ratio analyses.

Study how to evaluate financial performance (using Landry's).
LO2   Categorize and calculate key ratios relating to profitability, liquidity, and solvency.

Evaluate financial results in relation to stock price.
LO3   Calculate and interpret the price-earnings ratio.

Reconsider the conceptual framework for financial accounting.
LO4   Define the objective of financial reporting, and explain key accounting assumptions, principles, and constraints.

COACH'S CORNER

Year-over-year comparisons are also called "time series analyses" because they compare across a series of time periods. They also are called "horizontal analyses" because they involve comparing financial statement amounts horizontally.

UNDERSTAND

TECHNIQUES USED TO EVALUATE FINANCIAL PERFORMANCE

Before diving into an analysis of Landry's financial statements, we'll describe the two techniques that'll be used: (1) trend analysis and (2) ratio analysis. Trend analysis compares individual financial statement line-items over time, with the general goal of identifying significant sustained changes ("trends") that exist. These changes are typically described in terms of dollar amounts as well as year-over-year percentages. A year-over-year percentage simply expresses the change in the current year as a percentage of the prior year total, using the following calculation:

$$\text{Year-Over-Year Change (\%)} = \frac{\text{Change This Year}}{\text{Prior Year's Total}} \times 100\% = \frac{(\text{Current Year's Total} - \text{Prior Year's Total})}{\text{Prior Year's Total}} \times 100\%$$

For example, if sales for the current year are $240 million and they were $200 million in the prior year, the $40 million increase ($240 − 200) could be described as a year-over-year increase of 20 percent [20% = ($40 ÷ 200) × 100%].

The second technique that we will use is ratio analysis, which involves comparing an amount for one or more financial statement items to an amount for other items for the same year. Ratio analysis takes into account differences in the size of amounts being compared to allow you to evaluate how well a company has performed *given the existing level of other company resources*. For example, it's one thing to know that current assets total $1 million, but it's much more informative if you also know that current liabilities are $4 million and that current assets are only 25 percent (1/4) of the amount currently owed. A ratio this low suggests the company won't have sufficient resources to pay its creditors on time.

As shown throughout other chapters in this book, a company's ratios can be calculated for each year and then compared across years to identify additional trends not revealed in an analysis of individual financial statement line-items. Another possibility is to compare ratios from one company to those for close competitors and for the industry as a whole. In a competitive economy, companies strive to outperform one another, so this type of analysis provides clues as to which companies are likely to survive and thrive in the long run.

For the purposes of our analyses, we favor comparisons to similar competitors rather than to industrywide averages. The drawback of industry averages is that they encompass all sizes and types of restaurants ranging from massive fast-food chains like McDonald's to small, elegant restaurants. Rather than evaluate Landry's relative to all potential food outlets, we want to understand how it's doing in relation to its direct industry competitors. This means we'll compare Landry's ratios to those for Dave & Buster's (another big-name food and entertainment company for which we include an annual report in Appendix B), Darden Restaurants (owner of Red Lobster, Olive Garden, and Bahama Breeze), and Outback Steakhouse.

One final point before we present our analyses. The goal for the next section is to show you an example of trend and ratio analyses. Rather than present every possible trend and ratio covering every year and every competitor, we discuss the ones that do the best job of depicting Landry's performance and financial position. We don't show how every single number in the ratios were calculated because previous chapters already have shown how to calculate and interpret financial ratios. If you feel a need to refresh your memory, just flip back to the corresponding chapters for each of the ratios, which are summarized in Exhibit 13.5. The USER framework in each chapter makes it easy to find the ratio discussion (in the "Evaluate" section). For extra practice with these calculations, make sure you attempt SS13-1 at the end of this chapter, which asks you to calculate the ratios reported in this chapter. You can use these reported ratios as "check figures."

FAST FLASHBACK

Comparisons across companies operating in the same section of an industry are called cross-sectional analyses.

COACH'S CORNER

Industry averages are reported in the *Annual Statement Studies,* which are published by the Risk Management Association. You can obtain industry averages also from marketguide.com or edgarscan.pwcglobal.com, both of which were available for free at the time this book was written.

STUDY

HOW TO EVALUATE FINANCIAL PERFORMANCE (USING LANDRY'S)

The annual report of Landry's Restaurants appears in Appendix A at the end of the book. To save you the trouble of flipping back and forth, we've presented a summary of the balance sheets, income statements, and statements of cash flows from the three most recent years in Exhibits 13.2–13.4. Based on trends and ratios determined using these financial statements, we present a point-by-point analysis of Landry's results below.

For an animated tour of Landry's annual report, click on the annual report walkthrough on the DVD for use with this book.

Trend Analyses of Landry's Financial Statements

Landry's has grown significantly in recent years, with its balance sheets in Exhibit 13.2 showing a 35 percent increase in total assets from $690 million in 2001 to $933 million in 2002 [35% = ($933 − 690) ÷ $690 × 100%]. In 2003, total assets increased again, from $933 million in 2002 to $1.1 billion in 2003. Most of this growth appears in the *Property and Equipment* category. The financial highlights section of Landry's annual report explains the cause of this growth. The company added 95 new restaurants during 2002 and 2003, bringing the number of restaurants to 286 at December 31, 2003. The liabilities and stockholders' equity section of the balance sheets in Exhibit 13.2 suggest that the growth

exhibit 13.2 Summarized Balance Sheets

LANDRY'S RESTAURANTS, INC.
Balance Sheets
(in thousands)

	Year Ended December 31		
	2003	**2002**	**2001**
Assets			
Current Assets			
Cash	$ 35,211	$ 13,878	$ 31,081
Accounts Receivable	23,272	19,910	13,519
Inventories	47,772	40,879	33,563
Other Current Assets	14,349	18,002	15,958
Total Current Assets	120,604	92,669	94,121
Property and Equipment	965,575	830,930	587,829
Goodwill and Other Assets	16,606	9,416	8,221
Total Assets	$1,102,785	$933,015	$690,171
Liabilities and Stockholders' Equity			
Current Liabilities	$ 159,581	$148,354	$100,137
Long-Term Liabilities	338,654	217,586	196,364
Total Liabilities	498,235	365,940	296,501
Stockholders' Equity	604,550	567,075	393,670
Total Liabilities and Stockholders' Equity	$1,102,785	$933,015	$690,171

in these assets has been financed by both debt (total liabilities are up from $297 million in 2001 to $498 million in 2003) and equity (stockholders' equity is up from $394 million in 2001 to $605 million in 2003).

The income statements in Exhibit 13.3 show that this growth has significantly increased revenues, expenses, and net income in 2003 as compared to 2002 and 2001. The statements of cash flows in Exhibit 13.4 indicate that this growth also has produced increased cash flow from operating activities. The short story, based on these trend analyses, is that the company has been expanding its asset base, using financing provided by creditors and stockholders, who are being rewarded with increases in profits and operating cash flows.

Ratio Analyses Using Landry's Financial Statements

Our ratio analyses are split into three general categories of performance:

1. **Profitability**, which relates to performance in the *current period*. In particular, the focus is on the company's ability to generate income during the period.
2. **Liquidity**, which relates to the company's *short-term* survival. In particular, the focus is on the company's ability to use current assets to repay liabilities as they become due in the short-term.
3. **Solvency**, which relates to the company's *long-run* survival. In particular, the focus is on the company's ability to repay lenders when debt matures (and to make required interest payments prior to the date of maturity).

Exhibit 13.5 summarizes and groups the ratios from earlier chapters in terms of these three categories. The following analyses, focused on the restaurant industry, show how these ratios can be used to interpret and evaluate a company's financial performance.

YOU SHOULD KNOW

Profitability is the extent to which a company generates income. **Liquidity** is the extent to which a company is able to pay its currently maturing obligations. **Solvency** is the ability to survive long enough to repay lenders when debt matures.

exhibit 13.3	**Summarized Income Statements**

LANDRY'S RESTAURANTS, INC.
Income Statements
(in thousands)

	Year Ended December 31		
	2003	**2002**	**2001**
Revenues	$1,105,755	$894,795	$746,642
Cost of Revenues	321,783	257,945	219,684
Gross Profit	783,972	636,850	526,958
Operating and Other Expenses	717,018	571,676	478,540
Interest Expense	9,561	4,997	9,402
Income Tax Expense	11,492	18,655	12,096
Net Income	$ 45,901	$ 41,522	$ 26,920
Earnings per Share	$1.66	$1.60	$1.24

POINT OF INTEREST
Landry's net income in 2003 is bigger than the company's total revenues in 1993, the first year the company was publicly traded.

exhibit 13.4	**Summarized Statements of Cash Flows**

LANDRY'S RESTAURANTS, INC.
Statements of Cash Flows
(in thousands)

	Year Ended December 31		
	2003	**2002**	**2001**
Cash Flows from Operating Activities			
Net income	$ 45,901	$ 41,522	$ 26,920
Adjustments to reconcile to cash flows from operations	75,629	70,116	62,051
Net cash provided by operating activities	121,530	111,638	88,971
Cash Flows from Investing Activities			
Net cash paid for property and equipment	(162,895)	(113,806)	(72,713)
Cash paid for business acquisitions	(27,036)	(161,108)	(32,581)
Net cash used in investing activities	(189,931)	(274,914)	(105,294)
Cash Flows from Financing Activities			
Net cash from issuing (repurchasing) common stock	(6,591)	132,978	3,472
Amounts borrowed (paid) for other financing activities	96,325	13,095	17,772
Net cash provided by financing activities	89,734	146,073	21,244
Net increase in cash	21,333	(17,203)	4,921
Cash at beginning of year	13,878	31,081	26,160
Cash at end of year	$ 35,211	$ 13,878	$ 31,081
Supplemental Disclosure of Cash Flows			
Cash paid during the period for interest	$ 8,675	$ 5,567	$ 10,231
Cash paid during the period for income taxes	$ 5,699	$ 8,689	$ 0

exhibit 13.5   Ratios Used for Financial Analyses

Ratio	Basic Computation	Chapter/Page
Tests of Profitability		
a. Net profit margin	$\dfrac{\text{Net income}}{\text{Net sales revenue}}$	5 (p. 198)
b. Gross profit percentage	$\dfrac{\text{Net sales revenue} - \text{Cost of goods sold}}{\text{Net sales revenue}}$	6 (p. 249)
c. Asset turnover	$\dfrac{\text{Net sales revenue}}{\text{Average total assets}}$	5 (p. 198)
d. Fixed asset turnover	$\dfrac{\text{Net sales revenue}}{\text{Average net fixed assets}}$	9 (p. 386)
e. Return on equity	$\dfrac{\text{Net income}}{\text{Average stockholders' equity}}$	11 (p. 487)
f. Earnings per share	$\dfrac{\text{Net income}}{\text{Average number of shares of common stock outstanding}}$	11 (p. 486)
g. Quality of income	$\dfrac{\text{Net cash flows from operating activities}}{\text{Net income}}$	12 (p. 541)
Tests of Liquidity		
h. Receivables turnover	$\dfrac{\text{Net credit sales revenue}}{\text{Average net receivables}}$	7 (p. 295)
i. Inventory turnover	$\dfrac{\text{Cost of goods sold}}{\text{Average inventory}}$	8 (p. 337)
j. Current ratio	$\dfrac{\text{Current assets}}{\text{Current liabilities}}$	10 (p. 432)
Tests of Solvency		
k. Debt-to-assets	$\dfrac{\text{Total liabilities}}{\text{Total assets}}$	5 (p. 198)
l. Times interest earned	$\dfrac{\text{Net income} + \text{Interest expense} + \text{Income tax expense}}{\text{Interest expense}}$	10 (p. 434)
m. Cash coverage	$\dfrac{\text{Net cash flows from operating activities} + \text{Interest paid} + \text{Income taxes paid}}{\text{Interest paid}}$	12 (p. 541)
n. Capital acquisitions ratio	$\dfrac{\text{Net cash flows from operating activities}}{\text{Cash paid for property, plant, and equipment}}$	12 (p. 539)

COACH'S CORNER

Remember from the discussions in prior chapters that calculated ratios often differ from one industry to the next.

Profitability Ratios

The analyses in this section focus on how well the company did during the current period, in terms of its ability to generate profit.

a. **Net profit margin.** Net profit margin represents the percentage of sales revenues that ultimately make it into net income, after deducting expenses. Landry's net profit margins for each of the last three years are

Year Ended December 31		2003	2002	2001
Net profit margin $= \dfrac{\text{Net income}}{\text{Net sales revenue}}$		4.2%*	4.6%	3.6%

*4.2% = $45,901 ÷ 1,105,755 × 100%.

As you can see, Landry's net profit margin has fluctuated somewhat over the past three years. The 4.2 percent earned in 2003 indicates that, for each dollar of sales, Landry's generated 4.2¢ of net income. The decrease from 4.6 percent in 2002 to 4.2 percent in 2003 might seem small to you, but when considered in light of Landry's $1.1 billion in sales, this drop of 0.4 percent equates to $4.4 million of profit [$4.4 million = $1.1 billion × 0.4%]. To understand better the cause of this drop in net profit margin, we need to look at the gross profit percentage.

b. Gross profit percentage. The gross profit percentage indicates how much profit is made after deducting the cost of goods sold. Landry's gross profit percentage for the last three years are

Year Ended December 31		2003	2002	2001
Gross profit percentage =	$\dfrac{\text{Net sales } - \text{ Cost of goods sold}}{\text{Net sales}}$	70.9%*	71.3%	70.6%

*70.9% = ($1,105,755 − 321,783) ÷ 1,105,755 × 100%.

This analysis shows that, in 2003, after paying for the cost of the food, drinks, and t-shirts sold during the year, 70.9 percent of each sales dollar was leftover to cover other costs like employee wages, advertising, utilities, and other expenses. The 2003 gross profit percentage represents a decline of 0.4 percent (71.3 − 70.9%) from 2002, which is identical to the amount that net profit margin declined in 2003. According to Landry's MD&A, product costs increased in 2003 (without corresponding increases in selling prices). The result was a decline in both gross profit percentage and net profit margin.

c. Asset turnover. The asset turnover ratio indicates the amount of sales generated for each dollar invested in assets. The ratios for the three years are

Year Ended December 31		2003	2002	2001
Asset turnover =	$\dfrac{\text{Net sales revenue}}{\text{Average total assets}}$	1.09*	1.11	1.10

*1.09 = $1,105,755 ÷ [(1,102,785 + 933,015) / 2].

The asset turnover analysis suggests that Landry's wasn't as efficient at using assets to generate sales in 2003 as in prior years. To understand what caused this, it's useful to focus on key assets that are used to generate sales. For a restaurant company like Landry's, the key asset is restaurant property, which can be compared to sales using the fixed asset turnover ratio discussed next.

d. Fixed asset turnover. The fixed asset turnover ratio indicates how much the company generates in sales for each dollar invested in fixed assets like restaurant buildings and those stuffed seagulls hiding in the ceiling at Joe's Crab Shack. The ratios for three years are

Year Ended December 31		2003	2002	2001
Fixed asset turnover =	$\dfrac{\text{Net sales revenue}}{\text{Average net fixed assets}}$	1.23*	1.27	1.30

*1.23 = $1,105,755 ÷ [(965,575 + 830,930) / 2].

This analysis shows that Landry's has recently cranked out around $1.23–$1.30 of sales for each dollar of fixed assets. Is this good? Well, the declining trend isn't

FAST FLASHBACK
MD&A is the abbreviation for the section of annual and quarterly reports called "Management's Discussion and Analysis."

great, but it's understandable given that our trend analyses revealed that Landry's added 95 restaurants in just the past two years. It's likely that these restaurants will take some time to establish a strong customer base and begin generating sales at full capacity. Compared to its competitors, Landry's fixed asset turnover ratios are low. Landry's expects this, as it has adopted a strategy of owning about one-third of the buildings and waterfront properties in which its restaurants are located. Many of Landry's competitors rent, rather than own their properties, so they report higher levels of sales relative to their fixed assets. Dave & Buster's, for example, had a fixed asset turnover of 1.46 in 2003, because it owned only 4 of its 33 restaurant buildings. In a recent presentation to analysts, Landry's CEO justified his company's strategy by pointing out that Landry's has much lower rent costs than its competitors. "In case there are ever tough times, we own all this real estate. We can have a dip in business and never get strangled like a lot of other companies who pay 5–7 percent (of revenue) for rent."

e. *Return on equity (ROE).* The return on equity ratio compares the amount of net income to average stockholders' equity. Like the interest rate on your savings account, ROE reports the net amount earned this period as a percentage of each dollar contributed (by stockholders) and retained in the business. The ROE ratios for the three years are

Year Ended December 31	2003	2002	2001
Return on equity (ROE) = $\dfrac{\text{Net income}}{\text{Average stockholders' equity}}$	7.8%*	8.6%	7.1%

*7.8% = $45,901 ÷ [(604,550 + 567,075) / 2] × 100%.

In 2003, Landry's generated a return of 7.8 percent, which is down a little from 2002 because average stockholders' equity increased significantly in 2003 (as noted earlier in our trend analyses). This level of ROE is quite a bit below the returns generated by competitors Outback Steakhouse (17.0 percent in 2003) and Darden Restaurants (20.0 percent in 2003). Landry's lower ROE again reflects its strategy to buy property, which requires more financing and involves a higher level of stockholders' equity relative to net income.

f. *Earnings per share (EPS).* Earnings per share indicates the amount of earnings generated for each share of common stock. In Chapter 11, you saw that most companies report basic EPS and diluted EPS. For purposes of analyses in this course, focus on basic EPS. (Diluted EPS is studied in greater detail in intermediate accounting courses.)

Year Ended December 31	2003	2002	2001
Earnings per share (EPS) = $\dfrac{\text{Net income}}{\text{Average number of common shares}}$	$1.66*	$1.60	$1.24

*Reported on the income statement.

In contrast to ROE, which dropped in 2003, the EPS ratio increased in 2003. At first glance, this might seem inconsistent. However, by looking at the detailed breakdown of stockholders' equity in the company's actual balance sheet, you would find that the increase in stockholders' equity was the net result of a huge increase in retained earnings and a slight decrease in contributed capital. During 2003, Landry's bought back more shares than it issued, which combined with an increase in net income to bump EPS from $1.60 in 2002 to $1.66 in 2003.

g. *Quality of income.* The quality of income ratio relates operating cash flows (from the statement of cash flows) to net income, as follows:

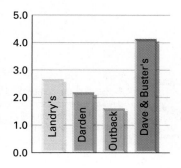

Year Ended December 31		2003	2002	2001
Quality of income = $\dfrac{\text{Net cash flows from operating activities}}{\text{Net income}}$		2.65*	2.69	3.31

*2.65 = $121,530 ÷ 45,901.

The ratio of 2.65 in 2003 shown above indicates that Landry's generated $2.65 of operating cash flow for every dollar of net income. This is substantially stronger than the 2003 ratios for competitors Darden (2.19) and Outback Steakhouse (1.58). The only potential concern with Landry's ratio is the declining trend over the years, but it's not unusual for a company to experience lower operating cash flows (relative to net income) when expanding quickly. Cash typically is used to buy additional food, beverage, and merchandise inventory and prepay insurance and other operating costs when opening new restaurants.

Let's pause to summarize what we've learned so far. In 2002 and 2003, Landry's greatly expanded the number of restaurants it owns and operates, causing both total assets and net sales to pass the $1 billion level. During this period of expansion, Landry's fixed asset turnover and return on equity ratios dipped slightly. Also during this period, product costs increased slightly, causing the company to experience a decline in both gross profit percentage and net profit margin. Fortunately, the company's expansion led to greater total sales volume, which despite the declining margin earned on each sale was still enough to increase overall net income (for the fourth year in a row).

To understand the issues that lenders and investors consider when evaluating a company, check out the video on the DVD for use with this book.

Liquidity Ratios

The analyses in this section focus on the company's ability to survive in the short-term, by generating cash that can be used to pay current liabilities as they come due.

h. *Receivables turnover.* Most restaurant companies have low levels of accounts receivable relative to sales revenues because the majority of their sales are collected immediately as cash. Although the formula calls for net credit sales in the top of the ratio, companies never separately report credit sales and cash sales. Consequently, financial statement users end up having to use total sales revenue in the formula, resulting in a receivables turnover ratio that is not terribly meaningful. This is particularly true in the case of restaurants, which make few sales on account. We present the ratio below simply to remind you how it's calculated.

Year Ended December 31		2003	2002	2001
Receivables turnover = $\dfrac{\text{Net credit sales revenue}}{\text{Average net receivables}}$		51.2*	53.5	61.8

*51.2 = $1,105,575 ÷ [(23,272 + 19,910) / 2].

i. *Inventory turnover.* As you probably know from personal experience, food can go bad quickly if it's left sitting out. The inventory turnover ratio (reported on the next page) indicates how frequently inventory is bought and sold during the year.

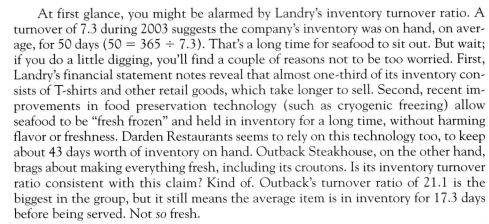

Year Ended December 31	2003	2002	2001
Inventory turnover = $\dfrac{\text{Cost of good sold}}{\text{Average inventory}}$	7.3*	6.9	6.4

*7.3 = $321,783 ÷ [(47,772 + 40,879) / 2].

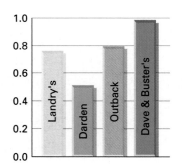

FAST FLASHBACK

To calculate the number of days to sell inventory, divide 365 by the annual inventory turnover ratio.

POINT OF INTEREST

To preserve their natural state (and flavor), oysters are frozen cryogenically at −109°F and are misted with water to form a glaze of ice that prevents freezer burn. *Source*: "Open up to the World of Oysters." *Food & Service News*, March 2001.

At first glance, you might be alarmed by Landry's inventory turnover ratio. A turnover of 7.3 during 2003 suggests the company's inventory was on hand, on average, for 50 days (50 = 365 ÷ 7.3). That's a long time for seafood to sit out. But wait; if you do a little digging, you'll find a couple of reasons not to be too worried. First, Landry's financial statement notes reveal that almost one-third of its inventory consists of T-shirts and other retail goods, which take longer to sell. Second, recent improvements in food preservation technology (such as cryogenic freezing) allow seafood to be "fresh frozen" and held in inventory for a long time, without harming flavor or freshness. Darden Restaurants seems to rely on this technology too, to keep about 43 days worth of inventory on hand. Outback Steakhouse, on the other hand, brags about making everything fresh, including its croutons. Is its inventory turnover ratio consistent with this claim? Kind of. Outback's turnover ratio of 21.1 is the biggest in the group, but it still means the average item is in inventory for 17.3 days before being served. Not *so* fresh.

j. **Current ratio.** The current ratio compares current assets to current liabilities, as follows:

Year Ended December 31	2003	2002	2001
Current ratio = $\dfrac{\text{Current assets}}{\text{Current liabilities}}$	0.76*	0.62	0.94

*0.76 = $120,604 ÷ 159,581.

Landry's current ratio indicates that the company's current assets are only 76 percent of its current liabilities. For many companies, this would be a big concern. It's not a problem for Landry's, for four reasons: (1) the company collects the majority of its revenues in cash as soon as its goods are sold, (2) the company sells its complete inventory of goods, on average, within 50 days of purchase, which is less than the 60 days of credit that suppliers typically offer, (3) over the years, the company has consistently generated significant positive cash flows from operations, and (4) like General Mills (discussed in Chapter 10), Landry's has arranged a line of credit with banks to cover times when the company is temporarily short on cash. Comparing across the restaurant industry, we find that Landry's current ratio is similar to Outback Steakhouse (at 0.79). Dave & Buster's is a little higher at 0.99 and Darden is a little lower at 0.51.

In summary, the liquidity ratios suggest that Landry's efficiently manages its short-term position. The company doesn't keep a lot of current assets on hand relative to its current liabilities. But then again, nobody really wants a restaurant to stockpile a bunch of food or let its cash sit idle in the bank.

Solvency Ratios

The analyses in this section focus on how well the company is positioned for long-term survival, in terms of its ability to repay debt when it matures, to pay interest until that time, and to finance the replacement and/or expansion of long-term assets.

k. **Debt-to-assets.** The debt-to-assets ratio indicates the proportion of total assets that are financed by creditors. Remember, creditors *have to be paid* regardless of how tough a year a company might have had, so the higher the ratio, the riskier the financing strategy. The ratio is calculated as

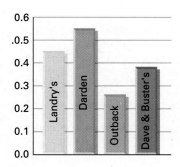

Year Ended December 31	2003	2002	2001
Debt-to-assets = $\dfrac{\text{Total liabilities}}{\text{Total assets}}$	0.45*	0.39	0.43

*0.45 = $498,235 ÷ 1,102,785.

Landry's ratio of 0.45 at the end of 2003 indicates that creditors have contributed 45 percent of the financing used by Landry's, which implies that stockholders' equity is the main source of financing at 55 percent. We can see from the ratios above that the proportion of debt financing is up from 2002, which suggests Landry's has increased its level of financing risk. Relative to its competitors, Landry's now has an average level of debt financing, as indicated by the chart in the margin. Outback Steakhouse has the lowest proportion of debt financing with a debt-to-assets ratio of 0.26, followed by Dave & Buster's at 0.38, and Darden at 0.55.

l. ***Times interest earned.*** The times interest earned ratio indicates how many times interest is covered by operating results. This ratio is calculated using accrual-based interest expense and net income (before interest and taxes), as follows:

Year Ended December 31	2003	2002	2001
Times interest earned = $\dfrac{\text{Net income + Interest expense + Income tax expense}}{\text{Interest expense}}$	7.0*	13.0	5.1

*7.0 = ($45,901 + 9,561 + 11,492) ÷ 9,561.

The message from the times interest earned ratio is that Landry's is generating more than enough profit from its business to cover its interest expense. Anything above 1.0 would indicate that net income (before the costs of financing and taxes) is sufficient to cover interest expense. A ratio of 7.0 is very comfortable.

m. ***Cash coverage ratio.*** Like the times interest earned ratio, the cash coverage ratio indicates how many times interest is covered by operating results. Rather than use accrual-based numbers, however, the cash coverage ratio compares the cash generated from the company's business operations (before interest and taxes) to its interest payments, as follows:

Year Ended December 31	2003	2002	2001
Cash coverage = $\dfrac{\text{Net cash flows from operations + Interest paid + Income taxes paid}}{\text{Interest paid}}$	15.7*	22.6	9.7

*15.7 = ($121,530 + 8,675 + 5,699) ÷ 8,675.

This analysis shows that if the cash generated from operations wasn't spent on other financing or investing activities, Landry's could cover its interest payments many times over, with a high of 22.6 times in 2002. Bankers and other long-term debtholders should sleep comfortably knowing that they will be paid interest on time.

n. ***Capital acquisitions ratio.*** The capital acquisitions ratio compares cash flows from operations to cash paid for property and equipment, as follows:

COACH'S CORNER

Instead of the debt-to-assets ratio, analysts might use a debt-to-equity ratio, which gives the same basic information as debt-to-assets. Debt-to-equity typically is calculated as total liabilities ÷ total stockholders' equity. As with debt-to-assets, the higher the debt-to-equity ratio, the more the company relies on debt (rather than equity) financing.

COACH'S CORNER

If the company reports a net loss, rather than net income, include the loss as a negative number in the formula. A negative ratio indicates that the operating results (before the costs of financing and taxes) are less than the interest costs.

FAST FLASHBACK

Information for the cash coverage ratio is obtained from the statement of cash flows.

Year Ended December 31		2003	2002	2001
Capital acquisitions ratio = $\dfrac{\text{Net cash flows from operations}}{\text{Cash paid for PPE}}$		0.64*	0.41	0.85

*0.64 = $121,530 ÷ (162,895 + 27,036).

The 0.41 capital acquisitions ratio in 2002 indicates that when Landry's acquired three different restaurant chains, its cash flow from operations was 41 percent of what it needed to buy property and equipment and other restaurant businesses. In 2003, when the company completed a series of relatively small acquisitions, its operating cash flows were 64 percent of what it needed to buy new property and equipment. These figures are typical of a company that is rapidly growing. In contrast, a company that grows one restaurant at a time is likely to have a much larger capital acquisitions ratio. And that's exactly what we find with Dave & Buster's, where its average ratio over the last three years was 1.37.

In summary, the solvency ratios depict a growing yet financially secure company. One story that emerges from these ratios is that growth in debt and stockholders' equity are providing the funds needed to buy up other businesses, allowing Landry's to use its operating cash flows to buy additional pieces of property and equipment, and to pay interest and principal owed on existing debt. Despite the company's rapid growth, its profile of long-term financing risk has changed only slightly.

Other Considerations

In the analyses just presented, we've compared Landry's with Dave & Buster's, Darden, and Outback Steakhouse. Where appropriate, we've discussed how differences in strategy (e.g., buying versus renting restaurant space) and business operations (e.g., selling food and merchandise versus food only) affect interpretations of the financial ratios. When comparing companies, you should consider two other matters: (1) are their accounting policies similar, and (2) are their results affected by nonrecurring or other special items? Let's look at item one below. The second item, nonrecurring and other special items, will be discussed in Supplement A at the end of this chapter.

Information about a company's accounting policies is presented in the notes to the financial statements. Exhibit 13.6 compares the policies used by the four restaurant companies when accounting for food inventory and depreciation—the areas with the greatest impact on the results of restaurant companies. As you can see, the four companies use similar, but not identical, policies. The inventory costing method varies, with Landry's and Darden using weighted average and Dave & Buster's and Outback using FIFO to calculate the costs of ending inventory and goods sold. Although these different methods

exhibit 13.6	**Comparison of Accounting Methods**			
	Landry's Restaurants	**Darden Restaurants**	**Outback Steakhouse**	**Dave & Buster's**
Food inventory	Weighted average cost	Weighted average cost	FIFO	FIFO
Depreciation	Straight-line Buildings: 5–40 yrs Equipment: 5–15 yrs	Straight-line Buildings: 7–40 yrs Equipment: 3–10 yrs	Straight-line Buildings: 5–32 yrs Equipment: 2–15 yrs	Straight-line Buildings: 5–40 yrs Equipment: 5–10 yrs

create somewhat different numbers, their overall impact on our ratios is likely to be minor because, at any point in time, inventory is a small part of the companies' total assets (less than 10 percent for each company).

The four companies calculate depreciation using the straight-line method with a similar range of estimated useful lives of buildings and equipment. Because buildings and equipment make up over two-thirds of each company's assets, these similarities go a long way toward making the financial results comparable across the companies. The conclusion from our analysis of Exhibit 13.6 is that although some differences exist among the companies' accounting policies, they are unlikely (in this case) to have a major impact on our comparisons.

Let's turn now from the main accounting measures of performance to the main market measure of performance: the price of the company's stock. Whether Nasdaq is streaking them across its quarter-acre MarketSite Tower in Times Square, or your computer is streaming them onto your desktop, or Kudlow & Cramer are screaming about them on CNBC, stock prices are everywhere. And if you pay attention to business news reports, you'll quickly see that stock prices depend a great deal on how well a company is doing.

EVALUATE

FINANCIAL RESULTS IN RELATION TO STOCK PRICE

The Relationship between Earnings and Stock Prices

Now that you know how to analyze a company's financial statements, does this mean that you're ready to tell people whether to buy stock in a company? No. The first thing to realize is that there's a difference between analyzing financial statements and predicting stock prices. When analyzing financial statements, you're trying to *evaluate* management's effectiveness. When predicting stock prices, you're trying to put a *value* on what the company is worth. To go from evaluation to valuation, you need additional tools and skills.

Sophisticated techniques to value a company are taught in advanced courses in corporate finance, but for this course, let's focus on a simple tool. The **price/earnings ratio** is the most basic way to determine the value investors place on a company's common stock. The P/E ratio, as most people call it, measures how many times more than current year's earnings investors are willing to pay for a company's stock. The P/E ratio is calculated as

$$\text{Price/Earnings Ratio} = \frac{\text{Stock Price (per share)}}{\text{Earnings per Share (annual)}}$$

Generally, a relatively high P/E ratio means investors expect the company to do better in the future and increase profits, so they have factored the future earnings into the current stock price. A relatively low P/E ratio typically means that they don't expect strong future performance. P/E ratios can vary significantly across industries, so you'll find them most meaningful when comparing a company over time with itself or with competitors in the same industry.

Be on the Alert

Some people think a high P/E ratio means a stock is priced too high or, conversely, the stock is cheap if the ratio is low. We caution against jumping to these conclusions. Often a low P/E ratio means a company is headed for trouble, or a high P/E ratio means the company has made an important discovery or acquisition that hasn't yet affected EPS. Landry's provides an excellent example of this. The company's P/E ratio jumped in the fall of 2000, from 8.8 to 16.6, when Landry's acquired Rainforest Café. Does this higher ratio mean that Landry's stock was overpriced at the end of December 2000? The answer appears to be no. Landry's EPS nearly tripled after December 2000. Like most ratios, the P/E ratio does not tell you the whole story by itself. Instead, it's most useful in alerting you to the need to learn more about how the company is changing.

RECONSIDER

THE CONCEPTUAL FRAMEWORK FOR FINANCIAL ACCOUNTING

The Objective of Financial Reporting

It shouldn't come as a surprise to you that financial statements are useful for evaluating performance and predicting the future. After all, the accounting rule makers at the FASB had these goals in mind when they developed the conceptual framework for financial accounting. This framework, shown in Exhibit 13.7, begins at the top of the pyramid with the primary objective of external financial reporting and is developed further in the other layers of the pyramid. The primary objective is to provide useful economic information about a business to help external parties, primarily investors and creditors, make sound financial decisions. The first box in the middle layer of Exhibit 13.7 lists and defines the financial statement elements that are expected to convey this useful information.

The second box in the middle layer of Exhibit 13.7 summarizes the primary characteristics that make information "useful," including its **relevance**, **reliability**, **comparability**, and **consistency**. Landry's financial statements provide relevant information because they give *feedback* on past results (how much property did the company acquire?), they

---

exhibit 13.7 | **Conceptual Framework for Financial Accounting and Reporting**

PRIMARY OBJECTIVE OF EXTERNAL FINANCIAL REPORTING
To provide useful economic information to external users (particularly investors and creditors) for decision making (assessing future cash flows) [Ch. 5]

ELEMENTS OF FINANCIAL STATEMENTS
Asset—economic resource with probable future benefits [Ch. 2]
Liability—probable future sacrifices of economic resources [Ch. 3]
Stockholders' Equity—financing provided by owners and operations (residual interest to owners) [Ch. 2]
Revenue—increase in assets or settlement of liabilities from ongoing operations [Ch. 3]
Expense—decrease in assets or increase in liabilities from ongoing operations [Ch. 3]
Gain—increase in assets or settlement of liabilities from peripheral activities [Ch. 3]
Loss—decrease in assets or increase in liabilities from peripheral activities [Ch. 3]

QUALITATIVE CHARACTERISTICS OF FINANCIAL INFORMATION
To be useful, information should possess:
Relevance—be capable of making a difference in decisions [Ch. 5]
 - feedback value (assess prior expectations)
 - predictive value (extrapolate into the future)
 - timeliness (available to help with decisions)
Reliability—can be relied upon [Ch. 5]
 - verifiability (can be verified independently)
 - representational faithfulness (represents reality)
 - neutrality (unbiased)
Information should also be **comparable** across companies and **consistent** over time [Ch. 5]

ASSUMPTIONS
Separate entity—activities of the business are separate from activities of the owners [Ch. 1]
Unit of measure—accounting measurements are in the national monetary unit [Ch. 1]
Time period—the long life of a company can be reported over a series of shorter time periods [Ch. 13]
Going concern (continuity)—entity will not go out of business in the near future [Ch. 13]

PRINCIPLES
Historical cost—cash equivalent price on the transaction date is used initially to measure elements [Ch. 2]
Revenue recognition—record revenue when earned, measurable, and realizable [Ch. 3]
Matching—record when expenses are incurred to generate revenues [Ch. 3]
Full disclosure—provide information sufficiently important to influence a decision [Ch. 5]

CONSTRAINTS
Conservatism—exercise care not to overstate assets and revenues or understate liabilities and expenses [Ch. 2]
Materiality—relatively small amounts not likely to influence decisions are to be recorded in the most cost-beneficial way [Ch. 8]
Industry practices—industry-specific measurements and reporting deviations may be acceptable [Ch. 13]
Cost-benefit—benefits to users should outweigh costs of providing information [Ch. 13]

are useful in *predicting* future results (the steady increase in EPS noted earlier suggests EPS will continue increasing in the future), and they are available on a *timely* basis (third quarter results were released the following month). Landry's results are reliable because they are capable of being checked or "*verified*" by someone else (in 2002 and 2003, this was done by Ernst & Young) and they *faithfully represent* what really happened during the period, with *neutrality* (without bias).

As the bottom layer of Exhibit 13.7 indicates, financial accounting is based on four main assumptions. We've already discussed the separate entity and unit of measure assumptions in earlier chapters, so we won't take up your time repeating them here. If you need a refresher, read the definition in the exhibit or flip back to the chapter where they were introduced (shown in brackets in Exhibit 13.7). The two assumptions that we haven't discussed yet are the time period and going-concern assumptions. The **time period assumption** is what allows Landry's accountants to divide the company's long life into a series of shorter periods so that measures of its performance and financial position can be obtained on a timely basis. Given the time period assumption, accountants can divide a company's indefinite life into monthly, quarterly, or annual periods for financial reporting purposes. This is the main reason that adjusting journal entries are needed (as discussed in Chapter 4). The **going-concern assumption** (also called the continuity assumption) states that a business is assumed capable of continuing its operations long enough to meet its obligations. If a company runs into severe financial difficulty (such as bankruptcy), this assumption may no longer be appropriate, leading to what is called a "going-concern problem." Some of the factors that contribute to going concern problems are listed in Exhibit 13.8.[1]

exhibit 13.8	**Factors Contributing to Going-Concern Problems**

Revealed by Financial Analyses	*Revealed by Other Analyses*
• Declining sales	• Overdependence on one customer
• Declining gross margin	• Insufficient product innovation/quality
• Significant one-time expenses	• Significant barriers to expansion
• Fluctuating net income	• Loss of key personnel without replacement
• Insufficient current assets	• Inability to negotiate favorable purchases
• Excessive reliance on debt financing	• Inadequate maintenance of long-lived assets
• Adverse financial commitments	• Loss of a key patent

The four main principles of accounting (summarized in the middle box in the bottom layer of Exhibit 13.7) have been introduced in earlier chapters. You also should be aware of the practical constraints listed in the bottom right of Exhibit 13.7, which may affect how things are reported in financial statements. In addition to issues like materiality and conservatism, which were discussed in earlier chapters, two additional constraints exist. A constraint related to **industry practices** is that companies in some industries have such special circumstances that they need to use accounting rules that differ from what other companies use. The **cost-benefit** constraint recognizes that it is costly for companies to gather all the financial information that could possibly be reported. Accounting rules should be implemented only to the extent that the benefits outweigh the costs of doing so.

Before closing the book on this topic (and possibly this course), take a moment to attempt the following Self-Study Quiz. It'll give you a good idea of whether you should do a detailed review of the concepts introduced in earlier chapters or whether you're ready to move on to review and practice the key aspects of this chapter.

---

[1]When there is substantial doubt about the company's ability to continue as a going concern, the auditor will draw attention to this issue in the auditor's report. When the going-concern (continuity) assumption is no longer appropriate for a company, all its assets and liabilities are measured at their liquidation values.

HOW'S IT GOING?   A Self-Study Quiz

Match each statement below to the characteristic, assumption, principle, or constraint to which it most closely relates.

1. I can use it, but only if I get it soon.   (a) Neutrality

2. Don't let your hopes or wishes influence what you say.   (b) Conservatism

3. Don't sweat it. It's not big enough to worry about.   (c) Going concern

4. We'll make an exception, but only because you're special.   (d) Timeliness

5. Tell me like it is, based on what really happened.   (e) Time period

6. I've told you everything you could possibly want to know.   (f) Cost-benefit

7. When in doubt, don't be overly optimistic.   (g) Materiality

8. I know it's a long time, but let's look at it in stages.   (h) Industry practices

9. You can reach a point where it's just not worth all the trouble.   (i) Full disclosure

10. At that rate, you may not survive past the end of the year.   (j) Representational faithfulness

Quiz Answers
1. (d) 2. (a) 3. (g) 4. (h) 5. (j) 6. (i) 7. (b)
8. (e) 9. (f) 10. (c)

FOR YOUR REVIEW

eXcel

DEMONSTRATION CASE

The following ratios for Dave & Buster's were presented as benchmarks for interpreting Landry's 2003 ratios:

Fixed asset turnover = 1.46

Current ratio = 0.99

Debt-to-assets = 0.38

Capital acquisitions ratio = 1.37 (three-year average)

Required:

With reference to the Dave & Buster's annual report in Appendix B, demonstrate how the ratios listed above for 2003 were calculated.

Suggested Solution

Fixed asset turnover = Net sales revenue ÷ Average net fixed assets
= \$362,822 ÷ [(247,161 + 249,451) / 2]
= 1.46

Current ratio = Current assets ÷ Current liabilities
= 35,357 ÷ 35,577
= 0.99

Debt-to-assets = Total liabilities ÷ Total assets
= (35,577 + 13,620 + 13,602 + 50,201) ÷ 295,889
= 0.38

Capital acquisitions = Cash from operations (three years) ÷ Cash paid for PPE (three years)

$$= (45{,}517 + 40{,}604 + 49{,}701) \div [(24{,}292 + 3{,}600) + 21{,}720 + 49{,}761]$$

$$= 1.37$$

CHAPTER SUMMARY

Describe the purposes and uses of trend and ratio analyses. p. 574   **LO1**

- Trend analyses compare financial statement items to comparable amounts in prior periods, with the goal of identifying sustained changes ("trends").

- Ratio analyses compare one or more financial statement items to an amount for other items for the same year. Ratios take into account differences in the size of amounts to allow for evaluations of performance given existing levels of other company resources.

- When comparing over time and across companies, watch out for possible differences in business strategy, operations, accounting policies, and nonrecurring events that can affect reported financial results.

Categorize and calculate key ratios relating to profitability, liquidity, and solvency. p. 576   **LO2**

- Profitability ratios focus on measuring the adequacy of income by comparing it to other items reported on the financial statements.

- Liquidity ratios measure a company's ability to meet its current maturing debt.

- Solvency ratios measure a company's ability to meet its long-term obligations.

- Exhibit 13.5 lists these ratios and shows how to compute them.

Calculate and interpret the price-earnings ratio. p. 585   **LO3**

- The price/earnings (P/E) ratio measures the relationship between the current market price of a stock and its earnings per share. Typically, the ratio will be high for companies that are expected to produce higher future earnings and low for companies that are expected to produce lower future earnings.

Define the objective of financial reporting, and explain key accounting assumptions, principles, and constraints. p. 586   **LO4**

- The primary objective of external financial reporting is to provide useful economic information about a business to help external parties, primarily investors and creditors, make sound financial decisions.

- Key accounting assumptions:

  a. Separate-entity assumption—transactions of the business are accounted for separately from transactions of the owner(s).

  b. Unit-of-measure assumption—financial information is reported in the national monetary unit.

  c. Time period assumption—the long life of a company can be reported over a series of shorter time periods.

  d. Going-concern (continuity) assumption—it is assumed that a business will continue to operate into the foreseeable future.

- Key accounting principles:

  a. Historical cost principle—financial statement elements should be recorded at the cash-equivalent cost on the date of the transaction.

  b. Revenue recognition principle —record revenue when earned, measurable, and realizable.

  c. Matching principle—record when expenses are incurred to generate revenues.

  d. Full disclosure principle—provide information sufficiently important to influence a decision.

- Key accounting constraints:
  - a. Conservatism—exercise care not to overstate assets and revenues or understate liabilities and expenses.
  - b. Materiality—relatively small amounts not likely to influence decisions are to be recorded in the most cost-beneficial way.
  - c. Industry practices—industry-specific measurements and reporting differences may be acceptable.
  - d. Cost-benefit—benefits to users should outweigh costs of providing information.

FINANCIAL STATEMENT ANALYSIS TIPS

All ratios are summarized in Exhibit 13.5 on page 578.

KEY TERMS TO KNOW

Cost-Benefit
   Constraint p. 587
Going-Concern (Continuity)
   Assumption p. 587

Industry Practices
   Constraint p. 587
Liquidity p. 576
Profitability p. 576

Solvency p. 576
Time Period
   Assumption p. 587

SUPPLEMENT A: NONRECURRING AND OTHER SPECIAL ITEMS

Nonrecurring Items

A company's income statement may include three different types of nonrecurring items: discontinued operations, extraordinary items, and cumulative effects of changes in accounting methods. Recently, R. J. Reynolds Tobacco Holdings, Inc., (RJR) reported all three types of nonrecurring items in a single comparative income statement, shown in Exhibit 13A.1. We discuss each of these below. (And, just in case you were wondering, no we aren't trying to quietly promote the tobacco industry. RJR is just one of the few real-world cases where all three types of nonrecurring items are reported in a single set of financial statements.)

Discontinued Operations

YOU SHOULD KNOW

Discontinued operations result from the disposal of a major component of the business and are reported net of income tax effects.

Discontinued operations result from abandoning or selling a major business component. The discontinued operations line-item on the income statement includes any gain or loss on disposal of the discontinued operation as well as any operating income generated during the current year prior to its disposal. Because gains or losses from discontinued operations appear below the income tax expense line on the income statement, any additional tax effects related to the gains or losses are included in their reported amounts.

RJR's net gain of $122 million in 2003 relates to the sale of an international business unit. Obviously, the sale of a particular business unit can happen only once, so these results are reported separately to inform users that they are not predictive of the company's future.

Extraordinary Items

YOU SHOULD KNOW

Extraordinary items are gains and losses that are both unusual in nature and infrequent in occurrence; they are reported net of tax on the income statement.

Extraordinary items are gains or losses that are considered both unusual in nature and infrequent in occurrence. Examples include losses suffered from natural disasters such as floods and hurricanes in parts of the world where such disasters are rare. Any items reported as extraordinary items must be explained in the notes to the financial statements. The extraordinary gain shown in Exhibit 13A.1 related to rather peculiar circumstances surrounding RJR's acquisition of the company that previously owned RJR (this kind of bizarre transaction is called a "reverse takeover"). Clearly, transactions like these are not likely to recur in the future, so they are reported immediately following discontinued operations. Because they appear below income tax expense, extraordinary items are reported net of any taxes directly related to them.

Cumulative Effects of Changes in Accounting Methods

The final nonrecurring item reflects the income statement effects of any adjustment made to balance sheet accounts because of a change to a different acceptable accounting method. These amounts are called **cumulative effects of changes in accounting methods** because balance sheet

exhibit 13A.1	**Reporting Nonrecurring Items on the Income Statement**

R.J. REYNOLDS TOBACCO HOLDINGS, INC.
Condensed Income Statements
December 31,
(in millions)

	2003	2002
Net Sales	$ 5,267	$6,211
Cost of Products Sold	3,218	3,732
Selling, General, and Administrative Expenses	1,327	1,463
Asset Impairment Expenses	4,563	237
Operating Income (loss)	(3,841)	779
Interest and Other Expenses, net	77	96
Income (loss) before Income Taxes	(3,918)	683
Income Tax Expense (benefit)	(229)	265
Net Income (loss) from Continuing Operations	(3,689)	418
Gain on Sale of Discontinued Operations, Net of Income Taxes	122	40
Extraordinary Item, Net of Income Taxes	121	—
Cumulative Effect of Accounting Change, Net of Income Taxes	—	(502)
Net Loss	$(3,446)	$ (44)

POINT OF INTEREST
Because financial losses related to the September 11, 2001, attacks were so widespread, the FASB concluded that no single line item could adequately capture them. As a result, the FASB ruled that the financial effects of these events should not be reported as extraordinary.

accounts contain the results of transactions that have accumulated over several periods. The goal is to determine what the balance sheet amount would be if the new accounting method had always been applied, net of any tax effects, and show the corresponding effect on net income.

While most changes in accounting methods involve implementing new FASB rules, it is possible that managers will determine that a change to an alternative accounting method is necessary because of changes in business activities. For example, managers might switch from FIFO to LIFO or from declining-balance to straight-line depreciation. Any time an accounting method is changed, note disclosure explaining the change is required. The change that RJR made and reported in 2002 (see Exhibit 13A.1) involved implementing a new accounting standard related to impairment of intangible assets. Again, because this particular change will happen only once, it isn't terribly relevant to predicting the company's future, so its effects are reported separately on the income statement.

Other Special Items

In some cases, you may see that companies include additional items on their income statement after the *Net Income* line. These items may be added to or subtracted from net income to arrive at something called *Comprehensive Income*. As you can learn in detail in intermediate courses in financial accounting, these items represent gains or losses relating to changes in the value of certain balance sheet accounts. While most gains and losses are included in the computation of net income, some (relating to changes in foreign currency exchange rates and the value of certain investments) are excluded from net income and included only when computing comprehensive income. The main reason for excluding these gains and losses from net income is that the changes in value that created them may very well disappear before they are ever realized (when the company gets rid of the assets or liabilities to which they relate). For this reason, most analysts will take a moment to consider the size of these special items in relation to net income but, if they are not large, will exclude them from the profitability ratios presented earlier in this chapter.[2]

YOU SHOULD KNOW

 Cumulative effects of changes in accounting methods are the amounts reflected on the income statement for adjustments made to balance sheet accounts when applying different accounting principles. They are reported net of income taxes.

---

[2]Rather than show the computation of comprehensive income on the face of the income statement, companies are allowed to show it instead either in a statement of stockholders' equity or in a separate statement of comprehensive income. In a recent survey, about 70 percent of companies chose to show its computation in a statement of stockholders' equity. (AICPA 2003 *Accounting Trends & Techniques*).

FOR YOUR PRACTICE

QUESTIONS

1. What is the general goal of trend analysis?
2. How is a year-over-year percentage calculated?
3. What is ratio analysis? Why is it useful?
4. What benchmarks are commonly used for interpreting ratios?
5. Into what three categories of performance are most financial ratios split? To what in particular do each of these categories relate?
6. What is one of the most basic ways to determine the value investors place on a company's stock?
7. Give two different interpretations of a high P/E ratio.
8. What is the primary objective of financial reporting?
9. Why is the time period assumption necessary?
10. What is the going-concern assumption? What is a "going-concern problem"? What factors can contribute to such a problem?
11. How do industry practices and cost-benefit constraints impact financial reporting?
12. (Supplement A) Name three types of nonrecurring items, and explain where and how they are reported on the income statement.

MULTIPLE CHOICE

To practice more multiple choice questions, check out the DVD for use with this book.

1. Which of the following ratios is *not* used to analyze profitability?
   a.   Quality of income ratio.
   b.   Gross profit percentage.
   c.   Current ratio.
   d.   Return on equity.
2. Which of the following would *not* change the receivables turnover ratio for a company?
   a.   Increases in the selling prices of your inventory.
   b.   A change in your credit policy.
   c.   Increases in the cost you incur to purchase inventory.
   d.   All of the above could change the receivables turnover ratio.
3. Which of the following ratios is used to analyze liquidity?
   a.   Earnings per share.
   b.   Debt-to-assets.
   c.   Current ratio.
   d.   Both *b* and *c*.
4. Analysts use ratios to
   a.   Compare different companies in the same industry.
   b.   Track a company's performance over time.
   c.   Compare a company's performance to industry averages.
   d.   All of the above describe ways that analysts use ratios.
5. Which of the following ratios incorporates cash flows from operations?
   a.   Inventory turnover.
   b.   Earnings per share.
   c.   Quality of income.
   d.   All of the above.
6. Given the following ratios for four companies, which company is least likely to experience problems paying its current liabilities promptly?

	Current Ratio	Receivable Turnover Ratio
a.	1.2	7.0
b.	1.2	6.0
c.	1.0	6.0
d.	0.5	7.0

7. A decrease in selling and administrative expenses would impact what ratio?
   a. Fixed asset turnover ratio.
   b. Times interest earned.
   c. Current ratio.
   d. None of the above.

8. A bank is least likely to use which of the following ratios when analyzing the likelihood that a borrower will pay all that it owes?
   a. Cash coverage ratio.
   b. Debt-to-assets ratio.
   c. Times interest earned ratio.
   d. Return on equity ratio.

9. Which of the following accounting concepts requires accountants to use adjusting journal entries?
   a. Cost benefit.
   b. Materiality.
   c. Industry practices.
   d. Time period assumption.

10. (Supplement A) Which of the following items is not reported net of related income taxes?
    a. Gain or loss from discontinued operations.
    b. Gain or loss from extraordinary items.
    c. Cumulative effect of accounting changes.
    d. All of the above are reported net of related income taxes.

MINI-EXERCISES **Available with McGraw-Hill's Homework Manager**

M13-1 Identifying Important Accounting Terms

LO2–LO4

Complete the following crossword puzzle, using the clues provided in the box on the right. Omit hyphens.

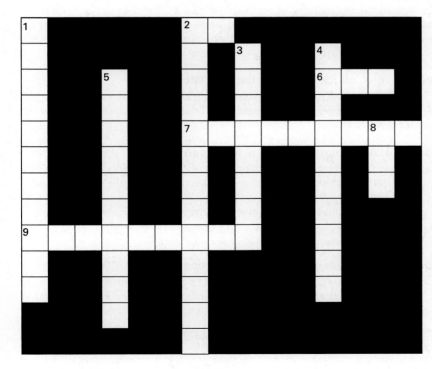

Across
2. The ratio that relates net income to the current market price of stock.
6. The ratio that relates net income to the average number of common shares outstanding.
7. The type of turnover ratio calculated using cost of goods sold.
9. The extent to which a company is able to pay its currently maturing obligations.

Down
1. The type of turnover ratio calculated using net credit sales.
2. The extent to which a company generates income.
3. The ability to survive long enough to repay lenders when debt matures.
4. A characteristic that means without bias.
5. Another name for the going-concern assumption.
8. The ratio that relates net income to the average stockholders' equity.

COACH'S CORNER

To calculate cost of goods sold in M13-2, work backwards from the gross profit percentage.

M13-2 Inferring Financial Information Using Gross Profit Percentage

LO2

Your campus computer store reported revenue of $1,680,000. The company's gross profit percentage was 60.0 percent. What amount of cost of goods sold did the company report?

LO2   **M13-3** **Inferring Financial Information Using Gross Profit Percentage and Year-over-Year Comparisons**

A consumer products company reported a 25 percent increase in sales from 2003 to 2004. Sales in 2003 were $20,000. In 2004, the company reported cost of goods sold in the amount of $15,000. What was the gross profit percentage in 2004?

LO2   **M13-4** **Computing the Return on Equity Ratio**

Compute the return on equity ratio for 2004 given the following data:

	2004	2003
Net income	$ 185,000	$ 160,000
Stockholders' equity	1,000,000	1,312,500
Total assets	2,400,000	2,600,000
Interest expense	40,000	30,000

LO2   **M13-5** **Analyzing the Inventory Turnover Ratio**

A manufacturer reported an inventory turnover ratio of 8.6 during 2003. During 2004, management introduced a new inventory control system that was expected to reduce average inventory levels by 25 percent without affecting sales volume. Given these circumstances, would you expect the inventory turnover ratio to increase or decrease during 2004? Explain.

LO2   **M13-6** **Inferring Financial Information Using the Current Ratio**

Scruggs Company reported total assets of $1,200,000 and noncurrent assets of $480,000. The company also reported a current ratio of 1.5. What amount of current liabilities did the company report?

LO2   **M13-7** **Analyzing the Impact of Accounting Alternatives**

Lexis Corporation operates in an industry where costs are rising. The company is considering changing its inventory method from FIFO to LIFO and wants to determine the impact that the change would have on selected accounting ratios in future years. In general, what impact would you expect on the following ratios: net profit margin, fixed asset turnover, and current ratio?

LO3   **M13-8** **Inferring Financial Information Using the P/E Ratio**

In 2003, Drago Company reported earnings per share of $8.50 when its stock was selling for $212.50. In 2004, its earnings increased by 20 percent. If all other relationships remain constant, what is the price of the stock? Explain.

M13-9 **(Supplement A) Analyzing the Impact of Nonrecurring Items**

Northern Drilling Corporation operates an oil exploration company in Alaska. In March 2004, one of the company's drilling platforms was destroyed by a tornado, resulting in an uninsured equipment loss of $4 million. How would this event, which is highly unusual for Alaska, affect the following ratios: net profit margin, fixed asset turnover, and current ratio?

EXERCISES 　 Available with McGraw-Hill's Homework Manager

LO1   **E13-1** **Preparing a Schedule Using Year-over-Year Percentages**

The average price of a gallon of gas in 2003 jumped $0.20 (15 percent) from $1.35 in 2002 (to $1.55 in 2003). Let's see whether these changes are reflected in the income statement of ChevronTexaco Inc. for the year ended December 31, 2003 (amounts in millions).

	2003	2002
Total revenues	$121,761	$98,913
Costs of crude oil and products	71,583	57,249
Other operating costs	37,408	37,508
Income before income tax expense	12,770	4,156
Income tax expense	5,344	3,024
Other items	196	—
Net income	$ 7,230	$ 1,132

Required:

Calculate the year-over-year changes in each line item. How did the change in gas prices compare to the changes in ChevronTexaco's total revenues and costs of crude oil and products?

E13-2 Computing Profitability Ratios

LO2

Use the information in E13-1 to complete the following requirements.

Required:

1. Compute the gross profit percentage for each year. Assuming that the change from 2002 to 2003 is the beginning of a sustained trend, is ChevronTexaco likely to earn more or less gross profit from each dollar of sales in 2004?

2. Compute the net profit margin for each year. Given your calculations here and in requirement 1, explain whether ChevronTexaco did a better or worse job of controlling expenses other than the costs of crude oil and products in 2003 relative to 2002.

3. ChevronTexaco reported average net fixed assets of $44.3 billion in 2003 and $43.5 billion in 2002. Compute the fixed asset turnover ratios for both years. Did the company better utilize its investment in fixed assets to generate revenues in 2003 or 2002?

4. ChevronTexaco reported average stockholders' equity of $33.9 billion in 2003 and $32.8 billion in 2002. Compute the return on equity ratios for both years. Did the company generate greater returns for stockholders in 2003 or 2002?

E13-3 Computing a Commonly Used Solvency Ratio

LO2

Use the information in E13-1 to complete the following requirement.

Required:

Interest expense in the amount of $474 million was included with "other operating costs" in 2003 ($565 million in 2002). Compute the times interest earned ratios for each year. In your opinion, does ChevronTexaco generate sufficient net income (before taxes and interest) to cover the cost of debt financing?

E13-4 Matching Each Ratio with Its Computational Formula

LO2

Match each ratio or percentage with its formula by entering the appropriate letter for each numbered item.

Ratios or Percentages	Formula
_____ 1. Net profit margin	A. Net income ÷ Net sales revenue.
_____ 2. Inventory turnover ratio	B. (Net sales revenue − Cost of goods sold) ÷ Net sales revenue.
_____ 3. Cash coverage ratio	
_____ 4. Fixed asset turnover	C. Current assets ÷ Current liabilities.
_____ 5. Capital acquisitions ratio	D. Cost of goods sold ÷ Average inventory.
_____ 6. Return on equity	E. Net credit sales revenue ÷ Average net receivables.
_____ 7. Current ratio	
_____ 8. Debt-to-assets ratio	F. Net cash flows from operating activities ÷ Net income.
_____ 9. Price/earnings ratio	
_____ 10. Receivables turnover ratio	G. Net income ÷ Average number of common shares outstanding.
_____ 11. Earnings per share	
_____ 12. Quality of income ratio	H. Total liabilities ÷ Total assets.
_____ 13. Gross profit percentage	I. (Net income + Interest expense + Income tax expense) ÷ Interest expense.
_____ 14. Times interest earned	
	J. Net cash flows from operating activities ÷ Cash paid for property, plant, and equipment.
	K. Current market price per share ÷ Earnings per share.
	L. Net income ÷ Average total stockholders' equity.
	M. Net cash flows from operating activities (before interest and taxes) ÷ Interest paid.
	N. Net sales revenue ÷ Average net fixed assets.

LO2   **E13-5 Computing Selected Liquidity Ratios**

DuckWing Stores reported sales for the year of $600,000, of which one-half was on credit. The average gross profit percentage was 40 percent on sales. Account balances follow:

	Beginning	Ending
Accounts receivable (net)	$40,000	$60,000
Inventory	70,000	30,000

Required:

1. Compute the turnover ratios for accounts receivable and inventory.
2. By dividing your ratios from requirement 1 into 365, calculate the average days to collect receivables and the average days to sell inventory.

LO2   **E13-6 Computing Liquidity Ratios**

Cintas Corporation is the largest uniform supplier in North America. More than five million people wear Cintas clothing each day. Selected information from the company's balance sheet follows. For 2003, the company reported sales revenue of $2,686,585,000 and cost of goods sold of $1,567,377,000.

Cintas	2003	2002
Balance Sheet (amounts in thousands)		
Cash	$ 32,239	$ 52,182
Accounts receivable, less allowance of $7,737 and $9,229	278,147	225,735
Inventories	228,410	164,906
Prepaid expenses	7,607	7,237
Other current assets	25,420	57,640
Accounts payable	53,909	60,393
Wages payable	25,252	29,004
Income taxes payable	69,545	73,163
Accrued liabilities	127,882	131,705
Long-term debt due within one year	28,251	18,369

Required:

Compute the current ratio, inventory turnover ratio, and accounts receivable turnover ratio (assuming that 60 percent of sales was on credit) for 2003.

LO2   **E13-7 Analyzing the Impact of Selected Transactions on the Current Ratio**

In its most recent annual report, Appalachian Beverages reported current assets of $54,000 and a current ratio of 1.8. Assume that the following transactions were completed: (1) purchased merchandise for $6,000 on account, and (2) purchased a delivery truck for $10,000, paying $1,000 cash and signing a two-year promissory note for the balance.

Required:

Compute the updated current ratio after each transaction.

LO2   **E13-8 Analyzing the Impact of Selected Transactions on the Current Ratio**

In its most recent annual report, Sunrise Enterprises reported current assets of $1,090,000 and current liabilities of $602,000.

Required:

Determine the impact of the following transactions on the current ratio for Sunrise: (1) sold long-term assets for cash, (2) accrued severance pay for terminated employees, (3) wrote down the carrying value of certain inventory items that were deemed to be obsolete, and (4) acquired new inventory by signing an 18-month promissory note (the supplier was not willing to provide normal credit terms).

E13-9 Analyzing the Impact of Selected Transactions on the Current Ratio

LO2

The Sports Authority, Inc., is the country's largest publicly traded full-line sporting goods retailer. Stores are operated under four brand names: Sports Authority, Gart Sports, Oshman's, and Sportmart. Assume one of the Sports Authority stores reported current assets of $88,000 and its current ratio was 1.75. Assume that the following transactions were completed: (1) paid $6,000 on accounts payable, (2) purchased a delivery truck for $10,000 cash, (3) wrote off a bad account receivable for $2,000, and (4) paid previously declared dividends in the amount of $25,000.

Required:

Compute the updated current ratio after each transaction.

E13-10 Analyzing the Impact of Selected Transactions on the Current Ratio

LO2

Current assets totaled $500,000, the current ratio was 2.0, and the company uses the perpetual inventory method. Assume that the following transactions were completed: (1) sold $12,000 in merchandise on short-term credit for $15,000, (2) declared but did not pay dividends of $50,000, (3) paid prepaid rent in the amount of $12,000, (4) paid previously declared dividends in the amount of $50,000, (5) collected an account receivable in the amount of $12,000, and (6) reclassified $40,000 of long-term debt as a current liability.

Required:

Compute the updated current ratio after each transaction.

E13-11 Computing the Accounts Receivable and Inventory Turnover Ratios

LO2

Procter & Gamble is a multinational corporation that manufactures and markets many products that are probably in your apartment or dorm room. Last year, sales for the company were $43,377 (all amounts in millions). The annual report did not report the amount of credit sales, so we will assume that all sales were on credit. The average gross margin rate was 49 percent on sales. Account balances follow:

	Beginning	*Ending*
Accounts receivable (net)	$3,038	$3,090
Inventory	3,640	3,456

Required:

1. Compute the turnover ratios for accounts receivable and inventory.
2. By dividing your ratios from requirement 1 into 365, calculate the average days to collect receivables and the average days to sell inventory.

E13-12 Inferring Financial Information from Profitability and Liquidity Ratios

LO2

Dollar General Corporation operates over 6,800 general merchandise stores that feature quality merchandise at low prices to meet the needs of middle-, low-, and fixed-income families in 29 southern, eastern, and midwestern states. For the year ended January 31, 2004, the company reported average inventories of $1,140 (in millions) and an inventory turnover of 4.25. Average total fixed assets were $990 (million), and the fixed asset turnover ratio was 6.94.

Required:

Rounded to one decimal place, calculate Dollar General's gross profit percentage for the year. What does this imply about the amount of gross profit made from each dollar of sales?

E13-13 Using Financial Information to Identify Mystery Companies

LO2

The following selected financial data pertain to four unidentified companies (balance sheet amounts reported in millions):

COACH'S CORNER

In E13-12, work backward from the fixed asset turnover and inventory turnover ratios to compute the amounts needed for the gross profit percentage.

	Companies			
	1	**2**	**3**	**4**
Balance Sheet Data				
Cash	$5.1	$8.8	$6.3	$10.4
Accounts receivable	13.1	41.5	13.8	4.9
Inventory	4.6	3.6	65.1	35.8
Property and equipment	53.1	23.0	8.8	35.7
Selected Ratios				
Gross profit percentage	N/A*	N/A	45.2	22.5
Net profit margin	0.3	16.0	3.9	1.5
Current ratio	0.7	2.2	1.9	1.4
Inventory turnover	N/A	N/A	1.4	15.5
Debt-to-equity	2.5	0.9	1.7	2.3

*N/A = Not applicable.

This financial information pertains to the following companies:

a.   Cable TV company.
b.   Grocery store.
c.   Accounting firm.
d.   Retail jewelry store.

Required:

Match each company with its financial information, and explain the basis for your answers.

L02   **E13-14**   **Analyzing the Impact of Alternative Inventory Methods on Selected Ratios**

Company A uses the FIFO method to cost inventory, and Company B uses the LIFO method. The two companies are exactly alike except for the difference in inventory costing methods. Costs of inventory items for both companies have been rising steadily in recent years, and each company has increased its inventory each year. Ignore income tax effects.

Required:

Identify which company will report the higher amount for each of the following ratios. If it is not possible to identify which will report the higher amount, explain why.

1.   Current ratio.
2.   Debt-to-assets ratio.
3.   Earnings per share.

SIMPLIFY WITH SPREADSHEETS

L02   **SS13-1**   **Using a Spreadsheet to Calculate Financial Statement Ratios**

Enter the financial statement information from Exhibits 13.2, 13.3, and 13.4 into three separate worksheets in one spreadsheet file. Using the cell referencing instructions given in SS6-1 for "importing" information from different worksheets, create a fourth worksheet that uses the formulas in Exhibit 13.5 to recalculate all the ratios for Landry's for 2002 and 2003. (For the EPS ratio, simply import the amount reported on the face of the income statement.)

COACHED PROBLEMS

L01   **CP13-1**   **Analyzing Comparative Financial Statements Using Year-over-Year Percentages**

The comparative financial statements prepared at December 31, 2004, for Golden Corporation showed the following summarized data:

			Increase (Decrease) 2004 over 2003	
	2004	**2003**	**Amount**	**Percentage**
Income Statement				
Sales revenue	$180,000*	$165,000		
Cost of goods sold	110,000	100,000		

Gross profit	70,000	65,000
Operating expenses	53,300	50,400
Interest expense	2,700	2,600
Income before income taxes	14,000	12,000
Income tax expense	4,000	3,000
Net income	$ 10,000	$ 9,000
Balance Sheet		
Cash	$ 4,000	$ 8,000
Accounts receivable (net)	14,000	18,000
Inventory	40,000	35,000
Property and equipment (net)	45,000	38,000
	$103,000	$ 99,000
Current liabilities (no interest)	$ 16,000	$ 19,000
Long-term liabilities (6% interest)	45,000	45,000
Common stock (par $5)	30,000	30,000
Retained earnings†	12,000	5,000
	$103,000	$ 99,000

*One-third of all sales are on account.

†During 2004, cash dividends amounting to $3,000 were declared and paid.

COACH'S CORNER

Calculate the increase (decrease) by subtracting 2003 from 2004. Calculate the percentage by dividing the amount of increase (decrease) by the 2003 balance.

Required:

1. Complete the two final columns shown beside each item in Golden Corporation's comparative financial statements.
2. Does anything significant jump out at you from the year-over-year analyses?

CP13-2 Analyzing Comparative Financial Statements Using Selected Ratios

Use the data given in CP13-1 for Golden Corporation.

LO2, LO3

e**X**cel

Required:

1. Compute the gross profit percentages in 2004 and 2003. Is the trend going in the right direction?
2. Compute the net profit margin ratios in 2004 and 2003. Is the trend going in the right direction?
3. Compute the earnings per share for 2004 and 2003. Does the trend look good or bad? Explain.
4. Stockholders' equity totaled $30,000 at the end of 2002. Compute the return on equity ratios for 2004 and 2003. Is the trend going in the right direction?
5. Net property and equipment totaled $35,000 at the end of 2002. Compute the fixed asset turnover ratios for 2004 and 2003. Is the trend going in the right direction?
6. Compute the debt-to-assets ratios for 2004 and 2003. Is debt providing financing for a larger or smaller proportion of the company's asset growth? Explain.
7. Compute the times interest earned ratios for 2004 and 2003. Do they look good or bad? Explain.
8. After Golden released its 2004 financial statements, the company's stock was trading at $30. After the release of its 2003 financial statements, the company's stock price was $21 per share. Compute the P/E ratios for both years. Does it appear that investors have become more (or less) optimistic about Golden's future success?

COACH'S CORNER

To calculate the number of shares outstanding, remember that the balance in the common stock account includes the par value per share times the number of shares. As discussed in Chapter 11, any amount received in excess of par value is recorded in a separate account (called additional paid-in capital).

CP13-3 Interpreting Profitability, Liquidity, Solvency, and P/E Ratios

Macy's is a national retail department store owned by Federated Department Stores (FDS). The company's total revenues in 2003 were $925 billion. Dillard's is a somewhat smaller national department store company with $161 billion of revenues for 2003. The following ratios for the two companies were obtained for a recent year from www.marketguide.com:

LO2, LO3

Ratio	FDS	Dillard's
Gross profit percentage	34.12 %	32.60 %
Net profit margin	8.07 %	0.49 %
Return on equity	12.85 %	1.73 %
EPS	$ 3.76	$ 0.11

(continues)

COACH'S CORNER

When evaluating the P/E ratio in requirement 4, remember that the top number in the ratio represents investors' expectations about future financial performance whereas the bottom number reports past financial performance.

Ratio	FDS	Dillard's
Receivables turnover ratio	5.19	6.83
Inventory turnover ratio	2.55	2.67
Current ratio	2.00	2.26
Debt-to-assets	0.40	0.47
P/E ratio	12.12	43.69

Required:

1. Which company appears more profitable? Describe the ratio(s) that you used to reach this decision.

2. Which company appears more liquid? Describe the ratio(s) that you used to reach this decision.

3. Which company appears more solvent? Describe the ratio(s) that you used to reach this decision.

4. Are the conclusions from your analyses in requirements 1–3 consistent with the value of the two companies suggested by the P/E ratios of the two companies? If not, offer one explanation for any apparent inconsistency.

LO2, LO3

CP13-4 Using Ratios to Compare Alternative Investment Opportunities

The 2004 financial statements for Armstrong and Blair companies are summarized here:

	Armstrong Company	Blair Company
Balance Sheet		
Cash	$ 35,000	$ 22,000
Accounts receivable (net)	40,000	30,000
Inventory	100,000	40,000
Property and equipment (net)	180,000	300,000
Other assets	45,000	408,000
Total assets	$400,000	$800,000
Current liabilities	$100,000	$ 50,000
Long-term debt	60,000	370,000
Total liabilities	160,000	420,000
Common stock (par $10)	150,000	200,000
Additional paid-in capital	30,000	110,000
Retained earnings	60,000	70,000
Total liabilities and stockholders' equity	$400,000	$800,000
Income Statement		
Sales revenue (1/3 on credit)	$450,000	$810,000
Cost of goods sold	(245,000)	(405,000)
Expenses (including interest and income tax)	(160,000)	(315,000)
Net income	$ 45,000	$ 90,000
Selected Data from 2003 Statements		
Accounts receivable (net)	$ 20,000	$ 38,000
Inventory	92,000	45,000
Property and equipment (net)	180,000	300,000
Long-term debt	60,000	70,000
Total stockholders' equity	231,000	440,000
Other Data		
Per share price at end of 2004	$ 18	$ 27
Average income tax rate	30%	30%
Dividends declared and paid in 2004	$ 36,000	$150,000

COACH'S CORNER

If you need to calculate the number of shares outstanding, remember that the balance in the common stock account includes the par value per share times the number of shares. As discussed in Chapter 11, any amount received in excess of par value is recorded in a separate account (called additional paid-in capital).

The companies are in the same line of business and are direct competitors in a large metropolitan area. Both have been in business approximately 10 years, and each has had steady growth. The management of each has a different viewpoint in many respects. Blair is more conservative, and as its president said, "We avoid what we consider to be undue risk." Neither company is publicly held. Blair Company has an annual audit by a CPA but Armstrong Company does not.

Required:

1. Complete a schedule similar to Exhibit 13.5 that reflects a ratio analysis of each company.
2. A client of yours has the opportunity to buy 10 percent of the shares in one or the other company at the per share prices at the end of 2004 and has decided to invest in one of the companies. Based on the data given, prepare a comparative written evaluation of the ratio analyses (and any other available information) and give your recommended choice with the supporting explanation.

CP13-5 Analyzing an Investment by Comparing Selected Ratios

LO2, LO3

You have the opportunity to invest $10,000 in one of two companies from a single industry. The only information you have follows. The word *high* refers to the top third of the industry; *average* is the middle third; *low* is the bottom third.

Ratio	Company A	Company B
Current	High	Average
Inventory turnover	Low	Average
Debt-to-assets	High	Average
Times interest earned	Low	Average
Price/earnings	Low	Average

COACH'S CORNER

When interpreting ratios, think about how they are related to one another. For example, the current ratio and the inventory turnover ratio both include the inventory balance. This means that the low inventory turnover ratio can help you to interpret the high current ratio.

Required:

Which company would you select? Write a brief explanation for your recommendation.

GROUP A PROBLEMS Available with McGraw-Hill's Homework Manager

PA13-1 Analyzing Financial Statements Using Ratios and Percentage Changes

LO1

The comparative financial statements prepared at December 31, 2004, for Taber Company showed the following summarized data:

	2004	2003	Increase (Decrease) 2004 over 2003 Amount	Percentage
Income Statement				
Sales revenue*	$110,000	$ 99,000		
Cost of goods sold	52,000	48,000		
Gross profit	58,000	51,000		
Operating expenses	36,000	33,000		
Interest expense	4,000	4,000		
Income before income taxes	18,000	14,000		
Income tax expense (30%)	5,400	4,200		
Net income	$ 12,600	$ 9,800		
Balance Sheet				
Cash	$ 49,500	$ 18,000		
Accounts receivable (net)	37,000	32,000		
Inventory	25,000	38,000		
Property and equipment (net)	95,000	105,000		
Total assets	$206,500	$193,000		
Accounts payable	$ 42,000	$ 35,000		
Income taxes payable	1,000	500		
Note payable, long-term	40,000	40,000		
Total liabilities	83,000	75,500		
Capital stock (par $10)	90,000	90,000		
Retained earnings†	33,500	27,500		
Total liabilities and stockholders' equity	$206,500	$193,000		

*One-half of all sales are on credit.

†During 2004, cash dividends amounting to $6,600 were declared and paid.

Required:

1. Complete the two final columns shown beside each item in Taber Company's comparative financial statements.
2. Does anything significant jump out at you from the year-over-year analyses?

LO2, LO3

PA13-2   Analyzing Comparative Financial Statements Using Selected Ratios

Use the data given in PA13-1 for Taber Company.

Required:

1. Compute the gross profit percentages in 2004 and 2003. Is the trend going in the right direction?
2. Compute the net profit margin ratios in 2004 and 2003. Is the trend going in the right direction?
3. Compute the earnings per share for 2004 and 2003. Does the trend look good or bad? Explain.
4. Stockholders' equity totaled $100,000 at the end of 2002. Compute the return on equity ratios for 2004 and 2003. Is the trend going in the right direction?
5. Net property and equipment totaled $110,000 at the end of 2002. Compute the fixed asset turnover ratios for 2004 and 2003. Is the trend going in the right direction?
6. Compute the debt-to-assets ratios for 2004 and 2003. Is debt providing financing for a larger or smaller proportion of the company's asset growth? Explain.
7. Compute the times interest earned ratios for 2004 and 2003. Do they look good or bad? Explain.
8. After Taber released its 2004 financial statements, the company's stock was trading at $18. After the release of its 2003 financial statements, the company's stock price was $15 per share. Compute the P/E ratios for both years. Does it appear that investors have become more (or less) optimistic about Taber's future success?

LO2, LO3

PA13-3   Interpreting Profitability, Liquidity, Solvency, and P/E Ratios

Coke and Pepsi are well-known international brands. Coca-Cola sells more than $13 billion worth of beverages each year while annual sales of Pepsi products exceed $22 billion. Compare the two companies as a potential investment based on the following ratios:

Ratio	Coca-Cola	PepsiCo	
Gross profit percentage	48.53 %	48.95 %	
Net profit margin	2.63 %	4.14 %	
Return on equity	66.19 %	23.27 %	
EPS	$ 3.40	$ 1.54	
Receivables turnover ratio	11.49	9.82	
Inventory turnover ratio	15.06	12.76	
Current ratio	1.47	1.40	
Debt-to-assets	0.94	0.72	
P/E ratio	16.35	18.70	

Required:

1. Which company appears more profitable? Describe the ratio(s) that you used to reach this decision.
2. Which company appears more liquid? Describe the ratio(s) that you used to reach this decision.
3. Which company appears more solvent? Describe the ratio(s) that you used to reach this decision.
4. Are the conclusions from your analyses in requirements 1–3 consistent with the value of the two companies suggested by the P/E ratios of the two companies? If not, offer one explanation for any apparent inconsistency.

LO2, LO3

PA13-4   Using Ratios to Compare Loan Requests from Two Companies

The 2004 financial statements for Rand and Tand companies are summarized here:

	Rand Company	*Tand Company*
Balance Sheet		
Cash	$ 25,000	$ 45,000
Accounts receivable (net)	55,000	5,000
Inventory	110,000	25,000
Property and equipment (net)	550,000	160,000
Other assets	140,000	57,000
Total assets	$880,000	$292,000
Current liabilities	$120,000	$ 15,000
Long-term debt	190,000	55,000
Capital stock (par $20)	480,000	210,000
Additional paid-in capital	50,000	4,000
Retained earnings	40,000	8,000
Total liabilities and stockholders' equity	$880,000	$292,000
Income Statement		
Sales revenue	$800,000	$280,000
Cost of goods sold	(480,000)	(150,000)
Expenses (including interest and income tax)	(240,000)	(95,000)
Net income	$ 80,000	$ 35,000
Selected Data from 2003 Statements		
Accounts receivable, net	$ 47,000	$ 11,000
Long-term debt	190,000	55,000
Property and equipment, net	550,000	160,000
Inventory	95,000	38,000
Total stockholders' equity	570,000	202,000
Other Data		
Per share price at end of 2004	$14.00	$11.00
Average income tax rate	30%	30%

These two companies are in the same line of business and in the same state but in different cities. One-half of Rand's sales are on credit, whereas one-quarter of Tand's sales are on credit. Each company has been in operation for about 10 years. Both companies received an unqualified audit opinion on the financial statements, which means the independent auditors found nothing wrong. Rand Company wants to borrow $75,000 cash, and Tand Company is asking for $30,000. The loans will be for a two-year period.

Required:

1. Complete a schedule that reflects a ratio analysis of each company. Compute the ratios discussed in the chapter.

2. Assume that you work in the loan department of a local bank. You have been asked to analyze the situation and recommend which loan is preferable. Based on the data given, your analysis prepared in requirement 1, and any other information, give your choice and the supported explanation.

PA13-5 Analyzing an Investment by Comparing Selected Ratios   LO2, LO3

You have the opportunity to invest $10,000 in one of two companies from a single industry. The only information you have is shown here. The word *high* refers to the top third of the industry; *average* is the middle third; *low* is the bottom third.

Ratio	*Company A*	*Company B*
Current	Low	High
Inventory turnover	High	Low
Debt-to-assets	Low	Average
Times interest earned	High	Average
Price/earnings	High	Average

Required:

Which company would you select? Write a brief explanation for your recommendation.

GROUP B PROBLEMS

LO1   **PB13-1** **Analyzing Financial Statements Using Ratios and Percentage Changes**

The comparative financial statements prepared at December 31, 2004, for Soon Company showed the following summarized data:

	2004	2003	Increase (Decrease) 2004 over 2003	
			Amount	Percentage
Income Statement				
Sales revenue*	$222,000	$185,000		
Cost of goods sold	127,650	111,000		
Gross profit	94,350	74,000		
Operating expenses	39,600	33,730		
Interest expense	4,000	3,270		
Income before income taxes	50,750	37,000		
Income tax expense (30%)	15,225	11,100		
Net income	$ 35,525	$ 25,900		
Balance Sheet				
Cash	$ 40,000	$ 38,000		
Accounts receivable (net)	18,500	16,000		
Inventory	25,000	22,000		
Property and equipment (net)	127,000	119,000		
Total assets	$210,500	$195,000		
Accounts payable	$ 27,000	$ 25,000		
Income taxes payable	3,000	2,800		
Note payable, long-term	75,500	92,200		
Total liabilities	105,500	120,000		
Capital stock (par $1)	25,000	25,000		
Retained earnings†	80,000	50,000		
Total liabilities and stockholders' equity	$210,500	$195,000		

*One-half of all sales are on credit.

†During 2004, cash dividends amounting to $5,525 were declared and paid.

Required:

1. Complete the two final columns shown beside each item in Soon Company's comparative financial statements.
2. Does anything significant jump out at you from the year-over-year analyses?

LO2, LO3   **PB13-2** **Analyzing Comparative Financial Statements Using Selected Ratios**

Use the data given in PB13-1 for Soon Company.

Required:

1. Compute the gross profit percentages in 2004 and 2003. Is the trend going in the right direction?
2. Compute the net profit margin ratios in 2004 and 2003. Is the trend going in the right direction?
3. Compute the earnings per share for 2004 and 2003. Does the trend look good or bad? Explain.
4. Stockholders' equity totaled $65,000 at the end of 2002. Compute the return on equity ratios for 2004 and 2003. Is the trend going in the right direction?
5. Net property and equipment totaled $115,000 at the end of 2002. Compute the fixed asset turnover ratios for 2004 and 2003. Is the trend going in the right direction?
6. Compute the debt-to-assets ratios for 2004 and 2003. Is debt providing financing for a larger or smaller proportion of the company's asset growth? Explain.
7. Compute the times interest earned ratios for 2004 and 2003. Do they look good or bad? Explain.

8. After Soon released its 2004 financial statements, the company's stock was trading at $17. After the release of its 2003 financial statements, the company's stock price was $12 per share. Compute the P/E ratios for both years. Does it appear that investors have become more (or less) optimistic about Soon's future success?

PB13-3 Interpreting Profitability, Liquidity, Solvency, and P/E Ratios

Mattel and Hasbro are the two biggest makers of games and toys in the world. Mattel sells nearly $5 billion of products each year while annual sales of Hasbro products exceed $3 billion. Compare the two companies as a potential investment based on the following ratios:

LO2, LO3

Ratio	Mattel	Hasbro
Gross profit percentage	48.30 %	58.67 %
Net profit margin	10.28 %	5.72 %
Return on equity	23.63 %	13.55 %
EPS	$1.23	$0.91
Receivables turnover ratio	7.17	6.39
Inventory turnover ratio	5.50	5.70
Current ratio	1.86	1.89
Debt-to-assets	0.24	0.33
P/E ratio	15.18	18.90

Required:

1. Which company appears more profitable? Describe the ratio(s) that you used to reach this decision.
2. Which company appears more liquid? Describe the ratio(s) that you used to reach this decision.
3. Which company appears more solvent? Describe the ratio(s) that you used to reach this decision.
4. Are the conclusions from your analyses in requirements 1–3 consistent with the value of the two companies suggested by the P/E ratios of the two companies? If not, offer one explanation for any apparent inconsistency.

PB13-4 Using Ratios to Compare Loan Requests from Two Companies

The 2004 financial statements for Thor and Gunnar Companies are summarized here:

LO2, LO3

	Thor Company	Gunnar Company
Balance Sheet		
Cash	$ 35,000	$ 54,000
Accounts receivable (net)	77,000	6,000
Inventory	154,000	30,000
Property and equipment (net)	770,000	192,000
Other assets	196,000	68,400
Total assets	$1,232,000	$350,400
Current liabilities	$ 168,000	$ 18,000
Long-term debt (12% interest rate)	266,000	66,000
Capital stock (par $20)	672,000	252,000
Additional paid-in capital	70,000	4,800
Retained earnings	56,000	9,600
Total liabilities and stockholders' equity	$1,232,000	$350,400
Income Statement		
Sales revenue	$1,120,000	$336,000
Cost of goods sold	(672,000)	(180,000)
Expenses (including interest and income tax)	(336,000)	(114,000)
Net income	$ 112,000	$ 42,000
Selected Data from 2003 Statements		
Accounts receivable, net	$ 65,800	$ 13,200
Inventory	133,000	45,600

(continues)

	Thor Company	*Gunnar Company*
Selected Data from 2003 Statements		
Property and equipment, net	770,000	192,000
Long-term debt (12% interest rate)	266,000	66,000
Total stockholders' equity	798,000	266,400
Other Data		
Per share price at end of 2004	$13.20	$19.60
Average income tax rate	30%	30%

These two companies are in the same line of business and in the same state but in different cities. One-half of Thor's sales are on credit, whereas one-quarter of Gunnar's sales are on credit. Each company has been in operation for about 10 years. Both companies received an unqualified audit opinion on the financial statements, which means the independent auditors found nothing wrong. Thor Company wants to borrow $105,000 cash, and Gunnar Company is asking for $36,000. The loans will be for a two-year period.

Required:

1. Complete a schedule that reflects a ratio analysis of each company. Compute the ratios discussed in the chapter.
2. Assume that you work in the loan department of a local bank. You have been asked to analyze the situation and recommend which loan is preferable. Based on the data given, your analysis prepared in requirement 1, and any other information, give your choice and the supported explanation.

LO2, LO3 **PB13-5 Analyzing an Investment by Comparing Selected Ratios**

You have the opportunity to invest $10,000 in one of two companies from a single industry. The only information you have is shown here. The word *high* refers to the top third of the industry; *average* is the middle third; *low* is the bottom third.

Ratio	*Company A*	*Company B*
EPS	High	High
Return on equity	High	Average
Debt-to-assets	High	Low
Current	Low	Average
Price/earnings	Low	High

Required:

Which company would you select? Write a brief explanation for your recommendation.

CASES & DISCUSSION STARTERS

FINANCIAL REPORTING AND ANALYSIS CASES

LO2, LO3 **C&DS13-1 Finding Financial Information**

Refer to the financial statements of Dave & Buster's in Appendix B at the end of this book, or download the annual report from the *Cases* section of the text's Web site at www.mhhe.com/phillips. From the list of ratios that were discussed in this chapter, select and compute the ratios that help you evaluate the company. Provide a written analysis that interprets your ratio computations. Assume that Dave & Buster's financial statements for the year ended February 1, 2004, present the results for 2003. (Disregard the cumulative effect of a change in accounting principle.)

LO2, LO3 **C&DS13-2 Comparing Financial Information**

Download the financial statements of Darden Restaurants for its May 30, 2004 and May 25, 2003 year-ends from the company's Web site or the sources listed in C&DS1-3. From the list of ratios that were discussed in this chapter, select, compute, and interpret the ratios that help you compare Darden to the 2003 and 2002 results for Landry's reported in the chapter. When comparing to Landry's, assume that Darden's financial statements for the year ended May 30, 2004, represent the results for 2003 and that the May 25, 2003, financial statements represent results for 2002.

C&DS13-3 Internet-Based Team Research: Examining an Annual Report

As a team, select an industry to analyze. Using your Web browser, each team member should acquire the annual report or 10-K for one publicly traded company in the industry, with each member selecting a different company. (See C&DS1-3 in Chapter 1 for a description of possible resources for these tasks.)

LO1–LO3

TEAM CASE

Required:

1. On an individual basis, each team member should write a short report that incorporates year-over-year percentage comparisons and as many of the ratios from the chapter as are applicable given the nature of the selected company.

2. Then, as a team, write a short report comparing and contrasting your companies using these attributes. Discuss any patterns across the companies that you as a team observe. Provide potential explanations for any differences discovered.

ETHICS AND CRITICAL THINKING CASES

C&DS13-4 Ethical Decision Making: A Real-Life Example

During its deliberations on the Sarbanes-Oxley Act, the U.S. Senate considered numerous reports evaluating the quality of work done by external auditors. One study by Weiss Ratings, Inc., focused on auditors' ability to predict bankruptcy. The study criticized auditors for failing to identify and report going-concern problems for audit clients that later went bankrupt. Based on a sample of 45 bankrupt companies, the Weiss study concluded that had auditors noted unusual levels for just two of seven typical financial ratios, they would have identified 89 percent of the sample companies that later went bankrupt. A follow-up to the Weiss study found that had the criteria in the Weiss study been applied to a larger sample of nonbankrupt companies, 46.9 percent of nonbankrupt companies would have been predicted to go bankrupt.* In other words, the Weiss criteria would have incorrectly predicted bankruptcy for nearly half of the companies in the follow-up study and would have led the auditors to report that these clients had substantial going-concern problems when, in fact, they did not. Discuss the negative consequences that arise when auditors fail to predict companies that go bankrupt. Who is harmed by these failures? Discuss the negative consequences that arise when auditors incorrectly predict bankruptcy. Who is harmed by these errors? In your opinion, which of the potential consequences is worse?

LO2, LO4

ETHICAL

ISSUE

*Michael D. Akers, Meredith A. Maher, and Don E. Giacomino, "Going-Concern Opinions: Broadening the Expectations Gap," *CPA Journal*, October 2003. Retrieved June 13, 2004 from www.nysscpa.org/cpajournal/2003/1003/features/f103803.htm.

C&DS13-5 Ethical Decision Making: A Mini-Case

Almost Short Company requested a sizable loan from First Federal Bank to acquire a large piece of land for future expansion. Almost Short reported current assets of $1,900,000 (including $430,000 in cash) and current liabilities of $1,075,000. First Federal denied the loan request for a number of reasons, including the fact that the current ratio was below 2:1. When Almost Short was informed of the loan denial, the controller of the company immediately paid $420,000 that was owed to several trade creditors. The controller then asked First Federal to reconsider the loan application. Based on these abbreviated facts, would you recommend that First Federal approve the loan request? Why? Are the controller's actions ethical?

LO2

ETHICAL

ISSUE

C&DS13-6 Critical Thinking: Analyzing the Impact of Alternative Depreciation Methods on Ratio Analysis

Speedy Company uses the double-declining-balance method to depreciate its property, plant, and equipment, and Turtle Company uses the straight-line method. The two companies are exactly alike except for the difference in depreciation methods.

LO2

Required:

1. Identify the financial ratios discussed in this chapter that are likely to be affected by the difference in depreciation methods.

2. Which company will report the higher amount for each ratio that you have identified? If you cannot be certain, explain why.

Landry's Restaurants, Inc. 2003 Annual Report

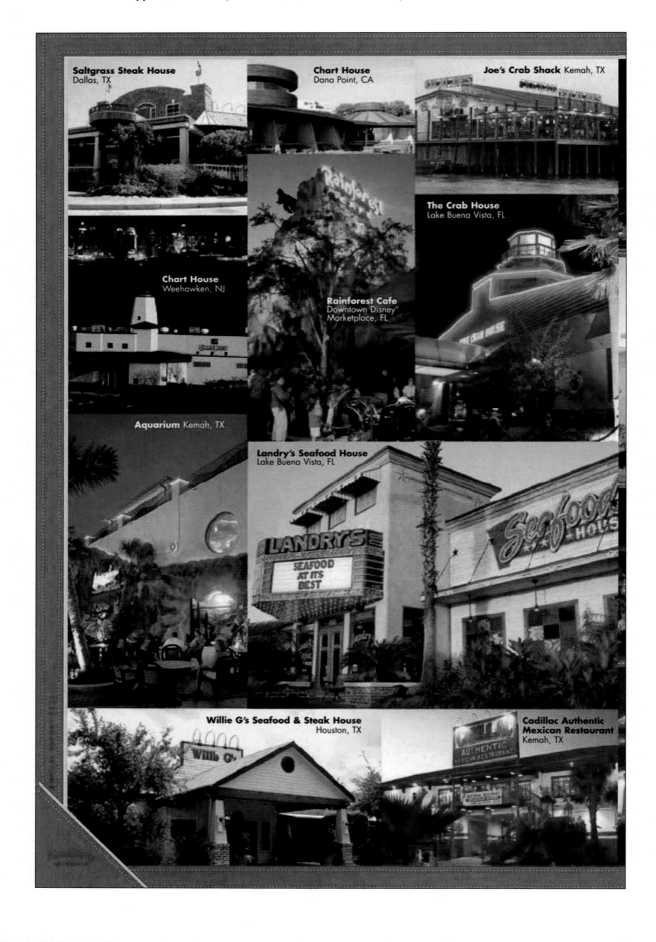

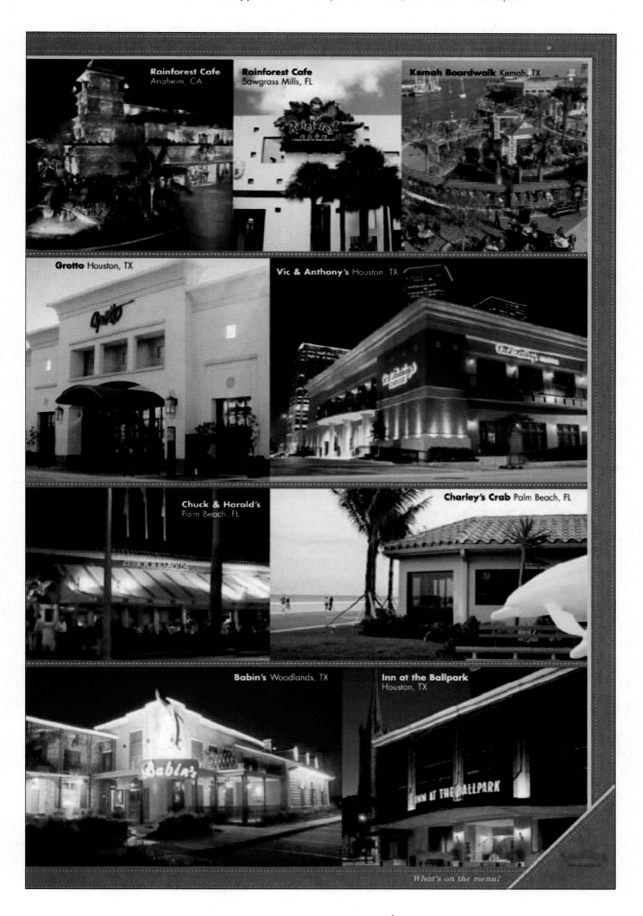

2003 HIGHLIGHTS

LANDRY'S AT A GLANCE

We celebrated our 10 year anniversary as a public company in 2003 and achieved milestones that once seemed insurmountable. While I had a deep-seated belief that we would be successful, I never imagined that within 10 short years, we would achieve the success that we have attained. A $10,000 investment in our Company in 1993 would have been worth approximately $42,867 at December 31, 2003. Our revenues topped over $1.1 billion in 2003, a far cry from the $34 million in revenues in 1993, and 2003 net income increased by a whopping 1100 percent from 1993.

The progress we have made in 2003 on the acquisitions completed in 2002 is extraordinary. Our development department completed major renovations and remodeling of nearly all of the Chart House and Muer restaurants, while our culinary team worked their magic in the kitchens re-engineering menus and training staff. Meanwhile, the Saltgrass team just kept doing what they do best, serving guests and pleasing customers.

Had we stopped there, 2003 would have been considered successful. However, because of the creative power and skills of the people who work here, we set the bar at new heights. We opened the Downtown Aquarium in Houston, Texas, a 6 acre entertainment complex featuring an aquarium, restaurants, amusement rides and the Shark Voyage – a train ride through a shark tank. We also opened a fire breathing Rainforest Cafe and River Adventure Ride in Galveston, Texas. In addition, our signature group of restaurants was launched, including a world-class steakhouse called Vic and Anthony's and an Italian masterpiece – Grotto's.

Our strong brands are the driving force behind our financial results. Joe's Crab Shack still continues to lead the way and contributed greatly to our success in 2003. Rainforest Cafe, our namesake concept - Landry's Seafood House, The Crab House, Saltgrass Steak House, Muer Restaurants and Chart House all chipped in to produce superior financial returns.

Landry's benefited from exceptional returns this past year because we successfully managed our business and increased customer satisfaction. For fiscal 2003, Landry's reported revenues of $1.1 billion, a 24 percent increase when compared with revenues of $894 million in 2002. Net income was $45.9 million for fiscal 2003 compared with net income of $41.5 million for fiscal 2002, an increase of 11 percent. As a result, our stock price at December 31, 2003 was $25.72, a 21 percent increase over the stock price at December 31, 2002.

We also kept a close guard over our balance sheet and managed our level of debt. We opportunistically fixed the rate on about half of our outstanding debt and renewed our existing line of credit. In addition to our revenues, total assets broke the billion dollar barrier in 2003. The resources at our disposal are tremendous.

We accomplished a lot last year, but I am confident that new challenges and much hard work lay ahead. Our management team is united and business is strong. We will continue to drive growth to deliver financial rewards to our shareholders. Nothing else will be acceptable.

Tilman J. Fertitta
Chairman of the Board, President
& Chief Executive Officer

FINANCIAL FEATURES

LANDRY'S AT A GLANCE

REVENUES
(in millions)

$1,105.8 — 03
$894.8 — 02
$746.6 — 01

UNITS
(#)

286* — 03
267 — 02
191 — 01

NET EARNINGS
(in millions)

$45.9 — 03
$41.5 — 02
$26.9 — 01

BOOK VALUES
(per share)

$21.86 — 03
$20.42 — 02
$17.90 — 01

Year Ended December 31	2003	2002	2001
Revenues	$ 1,105,755,057	$ 894,794,621	$ 746,642,287
Operating income	$ 68,416,764	$ 64,286,619	$ 48,361,365
Income before taxes	$ 57,392,832	$ 60,176,254	$ 39,015,299
Net earnings	$ 45,901,054	$ 41,521,616	$ 26,919,569
Net earnings per common share as reported (diluted)	$ 1.62	$ 1.54	$ 1.19

December 31	2003	2002	2001
Total assets	$ 1,102,785,506	$ 933,015,079	$ 690,171,196
Short-term debt	$ 1,963,189	$ 1,783,427	$ –
Long-term debt	$ 299,735,906	$ 189,403,599	$ 175,000,000
Stockholders' equity	$ 604,550,749	$ 567,075,437	$ 393,670,623

*We own several limited menu restaurants, specialty growth projects including the Kemah Boardwalk and hotel properties which have been excluded from the numerical unit count due to lack of materiality.

What's on the menu?

05

2003 MILESTONES

APPETIZING BITES

Strong leadership and diversified assets marked one more successful year for the Company

$1.1 BILLION

Revenues topped $1 billion in 2003, a 24% increase over fiscal 2002.

$45.9 MILLION

Net earnings for the year were $45.9 million, up 11% over fiscal 2002.

23%

Restaurant Level Profit rose 23% in 2003.

303 UNITS

Landry's ended fiscal 2003 with 303* units and 25,000 employees in 36 states and 8 international locations.

More facts

• The Company successfully integrated three major brands (Charley's Crab, Chart House and Saltgrass Steak House), achieving a turnaround to positive sales trends through renovations, employee rewards, management operational improvements and menu modifications.

• Landry's seafood brands including Joe's Crab Shack, Landry's Seafood House, Crab House, Charley's Crab and Chart House accounted for 70 percent of the Company's revenues in fiscal 2003.

• Non-seafood enterprises including Rainforest Cafe, Saltgrass Steak House and the Company's Kemah Boardwalk and specialty growth projects provided 30 percent of fiscal 2003 revenues.

• Landry's core management team, many of whom have grown with the Company, are the backbone of a stable, dedicated culture.

• In the past five years, Landry's stock performance has significantly outpaced its industry competition.

• Landry's diversified assets include $400 million in owned property, including 85 prime waterfront locations. The Company's high profile locations include units at Disney sites, the MGM Las Vegas, Mall of America, Fisherman's Wharf and Downtown Chicago.

*Unit count includes all company owned full service restaurants, several limited menu restaurants, specialty growth projects, hotels and retail shops.

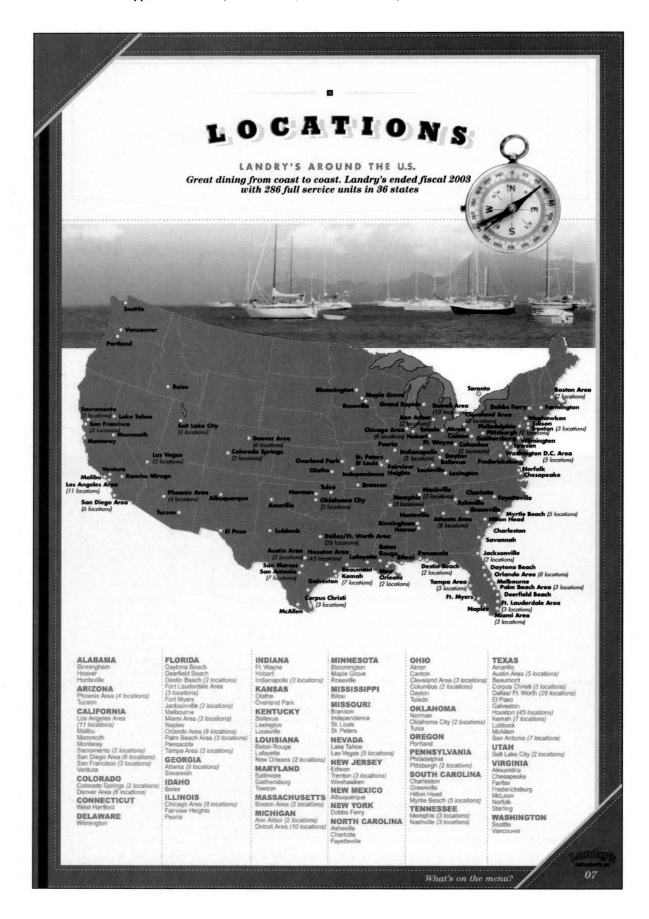

LOCATIONS

LANDRY'S AROUND THE U.S.

*Great dining from coast to coast. Landry's ended fiscal 2003
with 286 full service units in 36 states*

ALABAMA
Birmingham
Hoover
Huntsville

ARIZONA
Phoenix Area (4 locations)
Tucson

CALIFORNIA
Los Angeles Area
(11 locations)
Malibu
Mammoth
Monterey
Sacramento (2 locations)
San Diego Area (6 locations)
San Francisco (3 locations)
Ventura

COLORADO
Colorado Springs (2 locations)
Denver Area (6 locations)

CONNECTICUT
West Hartford

DELAWARE
Wilmington

FLORIDA
Daytona Beach
Deerfield Beach
Destin Beach (2 locations)
Fort Lauderdale Area
(3 locations)
Fort Myers
Jacksonville (2 locations)
Melbourne
Miami Area (3 locations)
Naples
Orlando Area (8 locations)
Palm Beach Area (3 locations)
Pensacola
Tampa Area (3 locations)

GEORGIA
Atlanta (8 locations)
Savannah

IDAHO
Boise

ILLINOIS
Chicago Area (8 locations)
Fairview Heights
Peoria

INDIANA
Ft. Wayne
Hobart
Indianapolis (3 locations)

KANSAS
Olathe
Overland Park

KENTUCKY
Bellevue
Lexington
Louisville

LOUISIANA
Baton Rouge
Lafayette
New Orleans (2 locations)

MARYLAND
Baltimore
Gaithersburg
Towson

MASSACHUSETTS
Boston Area (2 locations)

MICHIGAN
Ann Arbor (2 locations)
Detroit Area (10 locations)

MINNESOTA
Bloomington
Maple Grove
Roseville

MISSISSIPPI
Biloxi

MISSOURI
Branson
Independence
St. Louis
St. Peters

NEVADA
Lake Tahoe
Las Vegas (5 locations)

NEW JERSEY
Edison
Trenton (3 locations)
Weehawken

NEW MEXICO
Albuquerque

NEW YORK
Dobbs Ferry

NORTH CAROLINA
Asheville
Charlotte
Fayetteville

OHIO
Akron
Canton
Cleveland Area (3 locations)
Columbus (2 locations)
Dayton
Toledo

OKLAHOMA
Norman
Oklahoma City (2 locations)
Tulsa

OREGON
Portland

PENNSYLVANIA
Philadelphia
Pittsburgh (2 locations)

SOUTH CAROLINA
Charleston
Greenville
Hilton Head
Myrtle Beach (5 locations)

TENNESSEE
Memphis (3 locations)
Nashville (3 locations)

TEXAS
Amarillo
Austin Area (5 locations)
Beaumont
Corpus Christi (3 locations)
Dallas/ Ft. Worth (26 locations)
El Paso
Galveston
Houston (45 locations)
Kemah (7 locations)
Lubbock
McAllen
San Antonio (7 locations)

UTAH
Salt Lake City (2 locations)

VIRGINIA
Alexandria
Chesapeake
Fairfax
Fredericksburg
McLean
Norfolk
Sterling

WASHINGTON
Seattle
Vancouver

FINANCIALS

TABLE OF CONTENTS

SELECTED FINANCIAL DATA

The following table contains selected consolidated financial data for each of the past five fiscal years. All numbers are in thousands, except per share data:

Year Ended December 31,	2003	2002	2001	2000	1999
Income Statement Data					
Revenues	**$1,105,755**	$894,795	$746,642	$520,980	$438,986
Operating costs and expenses:					
Cost of revenues	**321,783**	257,945	219,684	156,787	136,321
Restaurant labor	**323,284**	259,198	215,662	147,192	125,566
Other restaurant operating expenses	**269,948**	222,711	185,186	122,099	101,563
General and administrative expenses	**51,704**	43,384	38,004	26,652	21,354
Depreciation and amortization [1]	**48,825**	40,480	34,753	27,100	22,230
Asset impairment expense [1]	**13,144**	2,200	2,394	6,292	—
Restaurant pre-opening expenses	**8,650**	4,591	2,598	3,402	3,764
Store closings and charges [3]	—	—	—	2,000	2,945
Total operating costs and expenses	**1,037,338**	830,509	698,281	491,524	413,743
Operating income	**68,417**	64,286	48,361	29,456	25,243
Other (income) expense:					
Interest (income) expense, net	**9,561**	4,997	9,402	6,617	1,965
Other, net	**1,463**	(887)	(56)	887	(178)
Total other (income) expense	**11,024**	4,110	9,346	7,504	1,787
Income before taxes	**57,393**	60,176	39,015	21,952	23,456
Provision for income taxes	**11,492** [2]	18,654	12,095	7,302	8,080
Net income	**$45,901**	$41,522	$26,920	$14,650	$15,376
Earnings per share information:					
Basic:					
Net income	**$1.66**	$1.60	$1.24	$0.63	$0.58
Average number of common shares outstanding	**27,600**	25,900	21,750	23,400	26,675
Diluted:					
Net income	**$1.62**	$1.54	$1.19	$0.62	$0.57
Weighted average number of common shares and equivalents outstanding	**28,325**	26,900	22,535	23,600	27,025
Other Data					
EBITDA (Earnings before interest, taxes, depreciation and amortization)					
Total Operating Income	**$68,417**	$64,286	$48,361	$29,456	$25,243
Depreciation and amortization	**48,825**	40,480	34,753	27,100	22,230
Asset impairment expense	**13,144**	2,200	2,394	6,292	—
EBITDA	**$130,386**	$106,966	$85,508	$62,848	$47,473
Balance Sheet Data (At End of Period)					
Working capital (deficit)	**$(38,977)**	$(55,685)	$(6,017)	$(39,657)	$17,430
Total assets	**1,102,786**	933,015	690,171	663,875	496,726
Short-term notes payable and current portion of notes and other obligations	**$1,963**	1,783	—	60	93
Long-term notes and other obligations, noncurrent	**$299,736**	189,404	175,000	155,000	68,060
Stockholders' equity	**$604,551**	$567,075	$393,671	$364,553	$377,348

(1) In 2003, 2002, 2001 and 2000, we recorded asset impairment charges of $13.1 million ($9.1 million after tax), $2.2 million ($1.5 million after tax), $2.4 million ($1.6 million after tax) and $6.3 million ($4.3 million after tax), respectively, related to the adjustment to estimated fair value of certain restaurant properties and assets. The Company considers the asset impairment charges as additional depreciation and amortization, although shown as a separate line item in the consolidated income statements.

(2) In 2003, we recognized a $6.3 million income tax benefit for a reduction of the valuation allowance and deferred tax liabilities attributable to tax benefits deemed realizable and reduced accruals.

(3) In the second quarter of 2000, we recorded a $2.0 million special charge to expense merger costs for our initial failed offer to acquire Rainforest Cafe. We incurred $2.9 million in store closings and special charges during 1999, which comprised the net result of $3.7 million in transaction costs as the result of a terminated merger agreement with another company during the first quarter of 1999, and the reversal of an accrual (income) of $0.7 million related to favorable lease settlement terminations during the second quarter of 1999.

EBITDA is not generally accepted accounting principles ("GAAP") measurements and is presented solely as a supplemental disclosure because the Company believes that they are widely used measures of operating performance in the restaurant industry. EBITDA is not intended to be viewed as a source of liquidity or as a cash flow measure as used in the statement of cash flows. EBITDA is simply shown above as it is a commonly used non-GAAP valuation statistic.

MANAGEMENT'S DISCUSSIONS

FORWARD LOOKING STATEMENTS

In this report, we have made forward-looking statements. Our forward-looking statements are subject to risks and uncertainty, including without limitation, our ability to continue our expansion strategy, our ability to make projected capital expenditures, as well as general market conditions, competition, and pricing. Forward-looking statements include statements regarding:

- future capital expenditures (including the amount and nature thereof);
- business strategy and measures to implement that strategy;
- competitive strengths;
- goals;
- expansion and growth of our business and operations;
- future commodity prices;
- availability of food products, materials and employees;
- consumer perceptions of food safety;
- changes in local, regional and national economic conditions;
- the effectiveness of our marketing efforts;
- changing demographics surrounding our restaurants;
- the effect of tax laws, and any changes therein;
- same store sales;
- earnings guidance;
- the seasonality of our business;

- weather acts of God;
- food, labor, fuel and utilities costs;
- plans;
- references to future success as well as other statements which include words such as "anticipate," "believe," "plan," "estimate," "expect," "intend" and
- other similar expressions.

Although we believe that the assumptions underlying our forward-looking statements are reasonable, any of the assumptions could be inaccurate and, therefore, we cannot assure you that the forward-looking statements included in this report will prove to be accurate. In light of the significant uncertainties inherent in the forward-looking statements, the inclusion of such information should not be regarded as a representation by us or any other person that our objectives and plans will be achieved.

FINANCIAL CONDITION AND RESULTS OF OPERATIONS

Introduction

We own and operate full-service, casual dining restaurants. As of December 31, 2003, we operated 286 restaurants. In addition to these units, there were several limited menu restaurants and other properties and two restaurants that were closed temporarily for renovation.

During 2003, we completed a series of relatively small acquistions, including: separate acquistions of several well-known individual upscale Houston restaurants; Ocean Journey (a 12 acre aquarium complex in Denver, Colorado); the Holiday Inn on the Beach in Galveston, Texas; and the Galveston Flagship Hotel (subject to an existing lease), for an aggregate cash purchase price of all such aquisitions of approximately $27.0 million, plus the assumption of $11.4 million of non-recourse long-term note payable. These aquisitions include certain future commitments as described in Note 7, in Notes to the Consolidated Financial Statements, Commitments and Contingencies in the paragraph titled "Building Commitments". The estimated cost of such future commitments are included in the Contractual Obligations table amounts under Other Long-Term Obligations, that is included within the discussion of Liquidity and Capital Resources.

In February 2002, we acquired 15 seafood restaurants located primarily in Michigan and Florida in connection with the acquisition of C.A. Muer, Inc., (the "Muer Acquisition"). In August 2002, we purchased 27 Chart House seafood restaurants, located primarily on the East and West Coasts of the United States. These acquisitions included plans for the redevelopment of ten additional lower profitability restaurants, which were also then acquired, into Joe's Crab Shack restaurants, and the sale or disposal of approximately six additional acquired, but non-strategic locations. In October 2002, we purchased 27 Texas-based Saltgrass Steak House restaurants.

The Specialty Growth Division is primarily engaged in operating complementary entertainment and hospitality activities, such as miscellaneous beverage carts and various kiosks, amusement rides and games and some associated limited room and service hotel and motel type properties, generally at locations in conjunction with our core restaurant operations. The total assets, revenues, and operating profits of these complementary "specialty" business activities are considered not material to the overall business (yet complementary nevertheless) and below the threshold of a separate reportable business segment under SFAS No. 131.

The Company is in the business of operating restaurants and the above-mentioned complementary activities. The Company does not engage in real estate operations other than those associated with the ownership and operation / management of its business. The Company owns a fee interest (own the land and building) in a number of properties underlying its businesses, but it does not engage in real estate sales or real estate management in any significant fashion or format. The Chief Executive Officer, who is responsible for the Company's operations, reviews and evaluates both core and non-core business activities and results, and determines financial and management resource allocations and investments for both business activities.

The restaurant industry is intensely competitive and is affected by changes in consumer tastes and by national, regional, and local economic conditions and demographic trends. The performance of individual restaurants may be affected by factors such as: traffic patterns, demographic considerations, marketing, weather conditions, and the type, number, and location of competing restaurants.

We have many well established competitors with greater financial resources, larger marketing and advertising budgets, and longer

MANAGEMENT'S DISCUSSIONS OF

FINANCIAL CONDITION AND RESULTS OF OPERATIONS

histories of operation than ours, including competitors already established in regions, where we are planning to expand, as well as competitors planning to expand in the same regions. We face significant competition from mid-priced, full-service, casual dining restaurants offering or promoting seafood and other types and varieties of cuisine. Our competitors include national, regional, and local chains as well as local owner-operated restaurants. We also compete with other restaurants and retail establishments for restaurant sites. We intend to pursue an acquisition strategy.

Results of Operations

Restaurant Profitability

The following table sets forth the percentage relationship to total restaurant revenues of certain restaurant operating data for the periods indicated:

Year Ended December 31,	**2003**	**2002**	**2001**
Revenues	100.0%	100.0%	100.0%
Cost of revenues	29.1	28.8	29.4
Restaurant labor	29.2	29.0	28.9
Other restaurant operating expenses	24.4	24.9	24.8
Restaurant level profit	17.3%	17.3%	16.9%

Year ended December 31, 2003 Compared to the Year ended December 31, 2002

Revenues increased $210,960,436, or 23.6%, from $894,794,621 to $1,105,755,057 for the year ended December 31, 2003, compared to the year ended December 31, 2002. The total increase/change in revenue is comprised of the following approximate amounts: 2003 restaurant openings – $81 million; 2002 acquistions incremental revenues for 2003 over 2002 partial year results – $139 million; restaurant closings decrease to 2003 revenues – $8 million; same store sales (locations open 2003 and 2002) – decrease $2 million. The total number of units open as of December 31, 2003 and 2002 were 286 and 267, respectively.

As a primary result of increased revenues, cost of revenues increased $63,838,636, or 24.7%, from $257,944,741 to $321,783,377 in the year ended December 31, 2003, compared to the same period in the prior year. Cost of revenues as a percentage of revenues for the year ended December 31, 2003, increased to 29.1%, from 28.8% in 2002. The increase in cost of revenues as a percentage of revenues primarily reflects the higher cost of sales from the Saltgrass and other 2002 acquisitions, and higher product costs at the Company's seafood restaurants.

Restaurant labor expenses increased $64,086,435, or 24.7%, from $259,197,964 to $323,284,399 in the year ended December 31, 2003, compared to the same period in the prior year, principally as a result of increased revenues. Restaurant labor expenses as a percentage of revenues for the year ended December 31, 2003, increased to 29.2% from 29.0% in 2002, principally due to inefficiencies attributable to a comparatively large number of new unit openings during the 2003 period.

Other restaurant operating expenses increased $47,236,875, or 21.2%, from $222,710,506 to $269,947,381 in the year ended December 31, 2003, compared to the same period in the prior year, principally as a result of increased revenues. Such expenses decreased as a percentage of revenues to 24.4% in 2003 from 24.9% in 2002, as a

primary result of lower rent expense from the acquired Saltgrass Steak House restaurants.

General and administrative expenses increased $8,320,301, or 19.2%, from $43,383,799 to $51,704,100 in the year ended December 31, 2003, compared to the same period in the prior year, and decreased as a percentage of revenues to 4.7% in 2003 from 4.8% in 2002. The dollar increase was a result of increased personnel and travel required to support our operations. Such expenses decreased as a percentage of revenues as a result of increased revenues from acquisitions and new restaurants thereby leveraging our corporate expenses.

Combined depreciation and amortization expense and asset impairment expense increased an aggregate of $19,288,838, or 45.2%, from an aggregate of $42,680,020 to $61,968,858 in the year ended December 31, 2003, compared to the same period in the prior year. The increase for 2003 was primarily due to the addition of new restaurants and equipment and restaurant acquisitions. Asset impairment expense of $13,100,000 relating to six underperforming and three closed restaurants was included in the 2003 amount, and $2,200,000 was included for 2002. Included in the 2003 amounts were four Landry's division, three Joe's Crab Shack, and two Crab House restaurants. The Company expects that asset impairment charges for 2004, if any, would be significantly less than amounts recorded in 2003.

The significant increase in impairment charges in fiscal 2003, resulted from 2003 sales declines in these restaurants, additional further deterioration in the specific restaurant's profitability, perceived 2003 deterioration of the market area and/or specific location, and management's 2003 downward revised outlook for further opportunity and/or improvement of forecasted sales and profitability trends for such specific property. Assets that were impaired are primarily leasehold improvements and to a lesser extent equipment. the following is a summary of related charges and expense:

Year Ended December 31,	**2003**	**2002**	**2001**
Asset Impairment	**$13,100,000**	$2,200,000	$2,394,000
Accrued Estimated Lease Termination Payments	**1,300,000**	—	—
Estimated Severance Costs	—	—	—
	$14,400,000	$2,200,000	$2,394,000

Restaurant pre-opening expenses were $8,650,178 for the year ended December 31, 2003, compared to $4,590,972 for the same period in the prior year. The increase for the 2003 period was attributable to an increase in units opened in 2003 as compared to 2002.

The increase in net interest expense in the year ended December 31, 2003, as compared to the prior year, is primarily due to our higher borrowings. Other expense for 2003 is primarily expenses related to abandoned development projects. Other expense (income) for 2002 includes additional income of $1,100,000 for a settlement from a vendor, and a gain of $875,000 on investment assets held for sale reduced by a loss of $1,500,000 on similar assets during the last six months of 2002.

Provision for income taxes decreased by $7,162,860 to $11,491,778 in the year ended December 31, 2003 from $18,654,638 in 2002 primarily due to changes in our pre-tax income offset by a $6,300,000 income

MANAGEMENT'S DISCUSSIONS OF
FINANCIAL CONDITION AND RESULTS
OF OPERATIONS

tax benefit gained from a reduction of the valuation allowance and deferred tax liabilities attributable to tax benefits deemed realizable and reduced accruals. The previously established valuation allowance was reduced at December 31, 2003, due to the strong 2003 and future forecasted profitability of the Rainforest Café restaurants, 2003 completion of a successful transition from a tax-loss incurring stand-alone public company to a highly profitable and taxable income producing wholly-owned subsidiary of Landry's, coupled with the approaching end of specific recognition limitations on allowable deductions and tax assets and the 2003 resolution of certain tax issues, which caused management to believe that a portion of the deffered tax assets previously reserved would more likely than not be realized and accruals reduced. Additional future evalutions may provide, in subsequent periods, the additional reduction of the remaining disclosed valuation allowance.

Year ended December 31, 2002 Compared to the Year ended December 31, 2001

Revenues increased $148,152,334, or 19.8%, from $746,642,287 to $894,794,621 for the year ended December 31, 2002, compared to the year ended December 31, 2001. The increase in revenues was primarily attributable to revenues from new restaurant openings, a small same store sales increase for the Company's seafood restaurants, offset by a slight decline in Rainforest Cafe restaurant revenues, and the inclusion of 2002 revenues from the Muer (since February 2002), Chart House (since August 2002) and Saltgrass Steak House restaurants (since October 2002) acquisitions.

As a primary result of increased revenues, cost of revenues increased $38,261,051, or 17.4%, from $219,683,690 to $257,944,741 in the year ended December 31, 2002, compared to the prior year. Cost of revenues as a percentage of revenues for the year ended December 31, 2002 decreased to 28.8% from 29.4% in 2001. The decrease in cost of revenues as a percentage of revenues primarily reflects menu changes and lower product costs in 2002 as compared to 2001, partially offset by the inclusion of Saltgrass Steak House restaurants (since October 2002) with higher than Company average cost of sales margins.

Restaurant labor expenses increased $43,535,944, or 20.2%, from $215,662,020 to $259,197,964 in the year ended December 31, 2002, compared to the prior year. Restaurant labor expenses as a percentage of revenues for the year ended December 31, 2002, increased to 29.0% from 28.9% in 2001, as a primary result of higher labor costs at the restaurants purchased in recent acquisitions, partially offset by increases in hourly labor productivity.

Other restaurant operating expenses increased $37,524,400, or 20.3%, from $185,186,106 to $222,710,506 in the year ended December 31, 2002, compared to the prior year, principally as a result of increased revenues. Such expenses increased as a percentage of revenues to 24.9% in 2002 from 24.8% in 2001, as a primary result of higher marketing and advertising expenses, partially offset by lower utility costs.

General and administrative expenses increased $5,380,311, or 14.2%, from $38,003,488 to $43,383,799 in the year ended December 31, 2002, compared to the prior year, and declined as a percentage of revenues to 4.8% in 2002 from 5.1% in 2001. The dollar increase resulted primarily from increased personnel to support our expanded operations. The decrease as a percentage of revenues is the primary result of increased

leverage from higher revenues increasing more than expenses.

Combined depreciation and amortization expense and asset impairment expense increased an aggregate of $5,532,695, or 14.9%, from an aggregate of $37,147,325 to $42,680,020 in the year ended December 31, 2002, compared to the prior year. The dollar increase was primarily due to the addition of new restaurants and equipment and the restaurant acquisitions in 2002, and asset impairment charges of $2,200,000 in 2002, compared to $2,394,000 in 2001.

Restaurant pre-opening expenses were $4,590,972 for the year ended December 31, 2002, compared to $2,598,293 for the same period in the prior year. The increase for the 2002 period was attributable to an increase in units opened in 2002 as compared to 2001.

The decrease in net interest expense for the year ended December 31, 2002, as compared to the prior year, is substantially due to reduced borrowings as a result from repayments using proceeds of a secondary stock offering we completed in April 2002. Also, the average borrowing rate declined by approximately 1.3 percentage points between December 31, 2001 to December 31, 2002. The change in other expense (income), includes additional income of $1,100,000 from a settlement from a vendor and a gain of $875,000 on investment assets held for sale reduced by a loss of $1,500,000 on similar assets during the last six months of 2002.

Provision for income taxes increased by $6,558,908 to $18,654,638 in 2002 from $12,095,730 in 2001 primarily due to changes in our pre-tax income.

Liquidity and Capital Resources

During the year, the Company increased its total borrowing capacity to $350 million through the closing of two separate financing agreements, which allow for increased financing permitted under the existing agreements. The terms of these agreements are outlined below. With the financing we intend to continue our planned growth. We plan to fund 2004 capital expenditures and any additional restaurant or business acquisitions out of proceeds from existing cash balances, 2003 tax refunds aggregating $9 million, cash flow from operations and availability under our existing credit facilities. We expect to spend approximately $100.0 million on capital expenditures in 2004, on opening approximately 20 restaurants, refurbishments of existing restaurants and other projects. As a result of our tax loss carryforwards and deferred tax assets, including amounts attributable to the acquisition of Rainforest Cafe, we expect our cash flow from operations to be subject to reduced federal income tax payments for the foreseeable future, which will therefore provide additional cash flow for funding our business activities and debt service. As of January 30, 2004, the Company had approximately $38 million available under the existing credit facilities for expansion and working capital purposes.

In October 2003, the Company refinanced its bank credit facility by issuing long-term notes totaling $150.0 million through a private placement of debt (the "Senior Notes") and amending and extending the existing bank credit facility to a four-year $200.0 million revolving credit facility (the "Bank Credit Facility"). The Senior Notes mature in October 2009 through October 2013, and the Bank Credit Facility matures in October 2007. Interest on the Senior Notes is paid quarterly at an average rate of 5.95%. Interest on the Bank Credit Facility is payable monthly or quarterly at LIBOR or the bank's base rate plus a

MANAGEMENT'S DISCUSSIONS OF

FINANCIAL CONDITION AND RESULTS OF OPERATIONS

Contractual Obligations (in thousands)	Less than 1 Year	2-3 Years	4-5 Years	After 5 Years
Operating Leases	$44,927	$85,468	$72,038	$279,319
Long-Term Debt	1,963	4,013	4,510	169,213
Unconditional Purchase Obligations	37,509	7,946	3,745	1,771
Other Long-Term Obligations	2,222	4,444	11,788	15,000
Total Cash Obligations	$86,621	$101,871	$92,081	$465,303

Other Commercial Commitments (in thousands)	Less than 1 Year	2-3 Years	4-5 Years	After 5 Years
Line of Credit	—	—	$122,000	—
Standby Letters of Credit	$10,084	—	—	—
Total Commercial Commitments	$10,084	—	$122,000	—

financing spread. The Company's financing spread under the Bank Credit Facility is presently 1.875% for LIBOR borrowings. The Senior Notes and Bank Credit Facility are secured by stock of subsidiaries, and governed by certain financial covenants, including maximum leverage ratio, maximum indebtedness, net worth, and fixed charge ratio tests. The Bank Credit Facility additionally provides for limitations on annual capital expenditures to prescribed amounts, maximum annual cash dividends and limitations on repurchases of common stock. The Bank Credit Facility also provides the ability to add an additional $25.0 million of capacity within the facility and other permitted indebtedness.

A wholly-owned subsidiary of ours assumed an $11.4 million 9.39% non-recourse, long-term note payable (due May 2010) in connection with an asset purchase in March 2003. Principal and interest payments under this note aggregate $102,000 monthly.

During the year ended December 31, 2003, the Company repurchased $8.4 million of common stock. In September 2003, the Company authorized an open market stock repurchase program for $60.0 million. The Company expects to make opportunistic repurchases of its common stock.

As of December 31, 2003, the Company had contractual obligations as described below. These obligations are expected to be funded primarily through cash flow from operations, working capital and additional financing sources in the normal course of business operations.

From time to time, we review opportunities for restaurant acquisitions and investments in the hospitality, entertainment, amusement, food service and facilities management and other industries. Our exercise of any such investment opportunity may impact our development plans and capital expenditures. We believe that adequate sources of capital are available to fund our business activities through December 31, 2004

As a primary result of establishing long-term borrowings, the Company will incur higher interest expense in the future. However, the Company has mitigated a portion of the higher immediate interest expense by entering into two fair value hedges aggregating notional amounts of $75.0 million, whereby the Company swapped higher fixed interest rates of the Senior Notes for floating interest rates equal to three (3)-month LIBOR plus 1.71%.

Since April 2000, we have paid an annual $0.10 per share dividend, declared and paid in quarterly amounts. The Company is currently reviewing its dividend policy to determine if the annual per share dividend will be increased in 2004.

Seasonality and Quarterly Results

Our business is seasonal in nature. Our reduced winter volumes cause revenues and, to a greater degree, operating profits to be lower in the first and fourth quarters than in other quarters. We have and continue to open restaurants in highly seasonal tourist markets. Joe's Crab Shack restaurants tend to experience even greater seasonality and sensitivity to weather than our other restaurant concepts. Periodically, our sales and profitability may be negatively affected by adverse weather. The timing of unit openings can and will affect quarterly results.

Critical Accounting Policies

Restaurant and other properties are reviewed on a property by property basis for impairment whenever events or changes in circumstances indicate that the carrying amount of an asset may not be recovered. The recoverability of properties that are to be held and used is measured by comparison of the estimated future undiscounted cash flows associated with the asset to the carrying amount of the asset. If such assets are considered to be impaired, an impairment charge is recorded in the amount by which the carrying amount of the assets exceeds their fair value. Properties to be disposed of are reported at the lower of their carrying amount or fair value, reduced for estimated disposal costs, and are included in other current assets.

We operate approximately 300 properties and periodically we expect to experience unanticipated individual unit deterioration in revenues and profitability, either on a short-term and occasionally longer-term situation. When such occurs and we evaluate that the associated assets are impaired, then we will record an asset impairment expense in the quarter such evaluation is made. Due to our average restaurant net investment cost, generally excluding the owned land component, of approximately $2 million, such amounts could be significant when and if they occur. However, such asset impairment expense is excluded from our credit covenant calculations, do not affect our financial liquidity, and are usually excluded from many valuation model calculations.

We follow the intrinsic value method of accounting for stock

MANAGEMENT'S DISCUSSIONS OF

FINANCIAL CONDITION AND RESULTS OF OPERATIONS

options, and as such do not record compensation expense related to amounts outstanding.

Recent Accounting Pronouncements

The Financial Accounting Standards Board ("FASB") issued FASB Interpretation No. ("FIN") 46, "Consolidation of Variable Interest Entities" in January 2003. This interpretation provides guidance on the identification of, and financial reporting for, variable interest entities. Variable interest entities are entities that lack the characteristics of a controlling financial interest or lack sufficient equity to finance its activities without additional subordinated financial support. FIN 46 requires a company to consolidate a variable interest entity if that company is obligated to absorb the majority of the entity's expected losses or entitled to receive the majority of the entity's residual returns, or both. The Company does not believe that FIN 46 will have a material impact on the Company's consolidated financial statements.

The FASB issued SFAS No. 148 "Accounting for Stock-Based Compensation—Transition and Disclosure" in December 2002. SFAS No. 148 provides alternative methods of transition for a voluntary change to the fair value based method of accounting for stock-based employee compensation. SFAS No. 148 also amends the disclosure requirements of SFAS No. 123 to require more prominent and frequent disclosures in financial statements about the effects of stock-based compensation. The transition guidance and annual disclosure provisions of SFAS No. 148 are effective for financial statements issued for fiscal years ending after December 15, 2002. The interim disclosure provisions were adopted for the three months ended March 31, 2003. Adoption of SFAS No. 148 did not materially impact our consolidated financial statements.

The FASB issued Interpretation No. 45, "Guarantor's Accounting and Disclosure Requirements for Guarantees, including Indirect Guarantees of Indebtedness of Others" in November 2002. Interpretation No. 45 provides guidance on the recognition and disclosures to be made by a guarantor in its interim and annual financial statements about its obligations under certain guarantees. The initial recognition and measurement provisions of Interpretation No. 45 are effective for guarantees issued or modified after December 31, 2002, and are to be applied prospectively. The disclosure requirements are effective for financial statements for interim or annual periods ended after December 15, 2002. The Company's adoption of Interpretation No. 45 in 2003 did not materially impact our consolidated financial statements.

The FASB issued Statement of Financial Accounting Standards (SFAS) No. 144, "Accounting for the Impairment or Disposal of Long-Lived Assets," in 2001. SFAS No. 144 supersedes SFAS No. 121, "Accounting for the Impairment of Long-Lived Assets to Be Disposed Of," and resolves significant implementation issues that had evolved since the issuance of SFAS No. 121. SFAS No. 144 also establishes a single accounting model for long-lived assets to be disposed of by sale. SFAS No. 144 is effective for financial statements issued for fiscal years beginning after December 15, 2001, and its provisions are generally to be applied prospectively. Adoption of SFAS No. 144, in 2002, did not materially impact our consolidated financial statements.

The FASB issued SFAS No. 146, "Accounting for Costs Associated with Exit or Disposal Activities," in June 2002. SFAS No. 146 provides guidance on the recognition and measurement of liabilities for costs associated with exit or disposal activities. SFAS No. 146 is effective for exit or disposal activities that are initiated after December 31, 2002. The Company's adoption of SFAS No. 146 in 2002 did not materially impact our consolidated financial statements.

The FASB issued statement of Financial Accounting Standards (SFAS) No. 150 in May 2003. SFAS No. 150 establishes standards for classification and measurement of certain financial instruments with characteristics of both liabilities and equity. SFAS No. 150 is effective for interim periods beginning after June 15, 2003. The Company's adoption of SFAS No. 150 did not materially impact our consolidated financial statements.

Impact of Inflation

We do not believe that inflation has had a significant effect on our operations during the past several years. We believe we have historically been able to pass on increased costs through menu price increases, but there can be no assurance that we will be able to do so in the future. Future increases in restaurant labor costs, including expected future increases in federal minimum wages, land and construction costs could adversely affect our profitability and ability to expand.

REPORT OF INDEPENDENT AUDITORS

To the Board of Directors and Shareholders of Landry's Restaurants, Inc.:

We have audited the consolidated balance sheets of Landry's Restaurants, Inc. and Subsidiaries as of December 31, 2003 and 2002, and the consolidated statements of income, stockholders' equity, and cash flows for the years then ended. These financial statements are the responsibility of the Company's management. Our responsibility is to express an opinion on these financial statements based on our audits. The financial statements of Landry's Restaurants, Inc. and Subsidiaries as of December 31, 2001, and for the year then ended were audited by other auditors who have ceased operations and whose report dated February 4, 2002, expressed an unqualified opinion on those statements.

We conducted our audits in accordance with auditing standards generally accepted in the United States. Those standards require that we plan and perform the audit to obtain reasonable assurance about whether the financial statements are free of material misstatement. An audit includes examining, on a test basis, evidence supporting the amounts and disclosures in the financial statements. An audit also includes assessing the accounting principles used and significant estimates made by management, as well as evaluating the overall financial statement presentation. We believe that our audits provide a reasonable basis for our opinion.

In our opinion, the 2003 and 2002 financial statements referred to above present fairly, in all material respects, the consolidated financial position of Landry's Restaurants, Inc. and Subsidiaries at December 31, 2003 and 2002 and the consolidated results of its operations and its cash flows for the years then ended, in conformity with accounting principles generally accepted in the United States.

ERNST & YOUNG LLP
Houston, Texas
February 11, 2004

REPORT OF INDEPENDENT PUBLIC ACCOUNTANTS

To Landry's Restaurants, Inc.:

We have audited the accompanying consolidated balance sheet of Landry's Restaurants, Inc. (a Delaware corporation) and subsidiaries as of December 31, 2001 and the related consolidated statements of income, stockholders' equity and cash flows for each of the three years in the period ended December 31, 2001. These financial statements are the responsibility of the Company's management. Our responsibility is to express an opinion on these financial statements based on our audits.

We conducted our audits in accordance with auditing standards generally accepted in the United States. Those standards require that we plan and perform the audit to obtain reasonable assurance about whether the financial statements are free of material misstatement. An audit includes examining, on a test basis, evidence supporting the amounts and disclosures in the financial statements. An audit also includes assessing the accounting principles used and significant estimates made by management, as well as evaluating the overall financial statement presentation. We believe that our audits provide a reasonable basis for our opinion.

In our opinion, the financial statements referred to above present fairly, in all material respects, the financial position of Landry's Restaurants, Inc., and subsidiaries as of December 31, 2001 and the results of their operations and their cash flows for each of three years in the period ended December 31, 2001, in conformity with accounting principles generally accepted in the United States.

ARTHUR ANDERSEN LLP
Houston, Texas
February 4, 2002

Note: The report of Arthur Andersen LLP presented below is a copy of a previously issued Arthur Andersen LLP report and said report has not been reissued by Arthur Andersen LLP nor has Arthur Andersen LLP provided a consent to the inclusion of its report.

7

CONSOLIDATED BALANCE SHEETS

Year Ended December 31,	2003	2002
Assets		
CURRENT ASSETS:		
Cash and cash equivalents	$35,211,319	$13,878,199
Accounts receivable—trade and other	23,271,831	19,910,006
Inventories	47,772,298	40,879,375
Deferred taxes	6,858,350	6,227,519
Other current assets	7,490,383	11,774,016
Total current assets	120,604,181	92,669,115
PROPERTY AND EQUIPMENT, net	965,574,991	830,930,131
GOODWILL	7,527,547	2,434,547
OTHER ASSETS, net	9,078,787	6,981,286
Total assets	$1,102,785,506	$933,015,079
Liabilities and Stockholders' Equity		
CURRENT LIABILITIES:		
Accounts payable	$82,894,048	$71,748,874
Accrued liabilities	74,512,641	74,237,570
Income taxes payable	211,131	584,531
Current portion of long-term notes and other obligations	1,963,189	1,783,427
Total current liabilities	159,581,009	148,354,402
LONG-TERM NOTES, NET OF CURRENT PORTION	299,735,906	189,403,599
DEFERRED TAXES	23,395,713	11,540,594
OTHER LIABILITIES	15,522,129	16,641,047
Total liabilities	498,234,757	365,939,642
Commitments and Contingencies		
STOCKHOLDERS' EQUITY:		
Common Stock, $0.01 par value, 60,000,000 shares authorized, 27,653,852 and 27,771,479 issued and outstanding, respectively	276,539	277,715
Additional paid-in capital	439,616,066	441,338,043
Deferred Compensation	(1,868,750)	—
Retained earnings	166,526,894	125,459,679
Total stockholders' equity	604,550,749	567,075,437
Total liabilities and stockholders' equity	$1,102,785,506	$933,015,079

The accompanying notes are an integral part of these consolidated financial statements.

8

CONSOLIDATED STATEMENTS OF

INCOME

Year Ended December 31,	2003	2002	2001
REVENUES	$1,105,755,057	$894,794,621	$746,642,287
Operating Costs and Expenses:			
Cost of revenues	321,783,377	257,944,741	219,683,690
Restaurant labor	323,284,399	259,197,964	215,662,020
Other restaurant operating expenses	269,947,381	222,710,506	185,186,106
General and administrative expenses	51,704,100	43,383,799	38,003,488
Depreciation and amortization	48,824,493	40,480,020	34,752,942
Asset Impairment expense	13,144,365	2,200,000	2,394,383
Restaurant pre-opening expenses	8,650,178	4,590,972	2,598,293
Total operating costs and expenses	1,037,338,293	830,508,002	698,280,922
OPERATING INCOME	68,416,764	64,286,619	48,361,365
Other Expense (Income):			
Interest expense, net	9,561,482	4,997,022	9,402,351
Other, net	1,462,450	(886,657)	(56,285)
	11,023,932	4,110,365	9,346,066
INCOME BEFORE INCOME TAXES	57,392,832	60,176,254	39,015,299
PROVISION FOR INCOME TAXES	11,491,778	18,654,638	12,095,730
NET INCOME	$45,901,054	$41,521,616	$26,919,569
Earnings per Share Information:			
BASIC			
Net income	$1.66	$1.60	$1.24
Average number of common shares outstanding	27,600,000	25,900,000	21,750,000
DILUTED			
Net income	$1.62	$1.54	$1.19
Average number of common and common share equivalents outstanding	28,325,000	26,900,000	22,535,000

The accompanying notes are an integral part of these consolidated financial statements.

CONSOLIDATED STATEMENTS OF

STOCKHOLDERS' EQUITY

	Common Stock Shares	Amount	Additional Paid-In Capital	Deferred Stock Compensation	Retained Earnings	Total
BALANCE, January 1, 2001	21,498,352	$214,984	$301,225,712	$ —	$63,111,962	$364,552,658
Net income	—	—	—	—	26,919,569	26,919,569
Dividends paid	—	—	—	—	(2,167,959)	(2,167,959)
Purchase of common stock held for treasury	(3,506)	(35)	(64,797)	—	(11,572)	(76,404)
Exercise of stock options and tax benefit	501,523	5,015	4,437,744	—	—	4,442,759
BALANCE, December 31, 2001	21,996,369	219,964	305,598,659	—	87,852,000	393,670,623
Net income	—	—	—	—	41,521,616	41,521,616
Dividends paid	—	—	—	—	(2,500,387)	(2,500,387)
Issuance of common stock, net	5,297,500	52,975	132,524,341	—	—	132,577,316
Purchase of common stock held for treasury	(304,904)	(3,049)	(5,317,638)	—	(1,413,550)	(6,734,237)
Exercise of stock options and tax benefit	782,514	7,825	8,532,681	—	—	8,540,506
BALANCE, December 31, 2002	27,771,479	277,715	441,338,043	—	125,459,679	567,075,437
Net income	—	—	—	—	45,901,054	45,901,054
Dividends paid	—	—	—	—	(2,768,997)	(2,768,997)
Purchase of common stock held for treasury	(468,823)	(4,688)	(6,347,881)	—	(2,064,842)	(8,417,411)
Exercise of stock options and tax benefit	251,196	2,512	2,676,904	—	—	2,679,416
Issuance of restricted stock	100,000	1,000	1,949,000	(1,950,000)	—	—
Amortization of deferred compensation	—	—	—	81,250	—	81,250
BALANCE, December 31, 2003	27,653,852	$276,539	$439,616,066	$(1,868,750)	$166,526,894	$604,550,749

The accompanying notes are an integral part of these consolidated financial statements.

CONSOLIDATED STATEMENTS OF

CASH FLOWS

Year Ended December 31,	**2003**	**2002**	**2001**
Cash Flows From Operating Activities:			
Net income	**$45,901,054**	$41,521,616	$26,919,569
Adjustments to reconcile net income to net cash provided by operating activities:			
Gain on sales of assets	—	(154,957)	(565,822)
Depreciation and amortization	**48,824,493**	40,480,020	34,752,942
Asset impairment expense	**13,144,365**	2,200,000	2,394,383
Deferred taxes, net	**11,224,288**	6,807,586	9,678,776
Deferred rent and other charges (income)	**(182,876)**	541,874	(241,155)
Changes in assets and liabilities:			
(Increase) decrease in trade and other receivables	**(3,342,672)**	(3,826,716)	(2,865,441)
(Increase) decrease in inventories	**(6,651,658)**	(4,044,169)	1,189,511
(Increase) decrease in other assets	**2,502,092**	(6,709,943)	3,425,250
Increase (decrease) in accounts payable and accrued liabilities	**10,110,805**	34,822,440	14,283,233
Total adjustments	**75,628,837**	70,116,135	62,051,677
Net cash provided by operating activities	**121,529,891**	111,637,751	88,971,246
Cash Flows From Investing Activities:			
Property and equipment additions	**(162,894,783)**	(115,903,544)	(73,462,974)
Proceeds from sale of property and equipment	—	2,097,870	750,000
Business acquisitions, net of cash acquired	**(27,035,893)**	(161,108,095)	(32,580,607)
Net cash used in investing activities	**(189,930,676)**	(274,913,769)	(105,293,581)
Cash Flows From Financing Activities:			
Proceeds from sale of common stock	—	132,577,316	—
Purchases of common stock for treasury	**(8,417,411)**	(6,734,237)	(76,404)
Proceeds from exercise of stock options	**1,826,816**	7,134,631	3,548,144
Borrowings (payments) under credit line, net	**(49,000,000)**	15,595,886	19,940,037
Borrowings (payments) on Senior Notes and other debt	**148,093,497**	—	—
Dividends paid	**(2,768,997)**	(2,500,387)	(2,167,959)
Net cash provided by financing activities	**89,733,905**	146,073,209	21,243,818
Net Increase (Decrease) in Cash and Equivalents	**21,333,120**	(17,202,809)	4,921,483
Cash and Cash Equivalents at Beginning of Year	**13,878,199**	31,081,008	26,159,525
Cash and Cash Equivalents at End of Year	**$35,211,319**	$13,878,199	$31,081,008

Supplemental Disclosures of Cash Flow Information:

Cash paid during the period for:			
Interest	**$8,675,327**	$5,567,196	$10,230,853
Income taxes	**$5,698,821**	$8,689,374	—

The accompanying notes are an integral part of these consolidated financial statements.

NOTES TO CONSOLIDATED
FINANCIAL STATEMENTS

1. NATURE OF BUSINESS AND SUMMARY OF SIGNIFICANT ACCOUNTING POLICIES
Nature of Business

Landry's Restaurants, Inc. (the "Company") owns and operates primarily restaurants under the trade names of Landry's Seafood House, Joe's Crab Shack, The Crab House, Charley's Crab, The Chart House and Saltgrass Steak House. In addition the Company owns and operates domestic and licenses international rainforest themed restaurants under the trade name Rainforest Cafe.

Principles of Consolidation

The accompanying financial statements include the consolidated accounts of Landry's Restaurants, Inc., a Delaware holding company and its wholly and majority owned subsidiaries and partnership.

Revenue Recognition

The Company records revenue from the sale of food, beverage, alcohol, and retail as products are sold. Proceeds from the sale of gift cards are recorded as deferred revenue and recognized as revenue when redeemed by the holder.

Accounts Receivable

Accounts receivable is comprised primarily of amounts due from the Company's credit card processor and receivables from national storage and distribution companies with which we contract to provide services. Transactions between the Company and the national storage and distribution companies do not have an impact on our consolidated statements of income. In connection with these services, certain of our inventory items are conveyed to the storage and distribution companies at cost (including freight and holding charges but without any general overhead costs). These transactions do not impact the consolidated statements of income as there is no profit recognition and no revenue or expenses are recognized in the financial statements since they are without economic substance other than drayage. We reacquire these items, although not obligated to, when subsequently delivered to the restaurants at cost plus the distribution company's contractual mark-up. Also included in accounts receivable is income tax receivables of $9.2 million and $3.1 million in 2003 and 2002, respectively.

Inventories

Inventories consist of food and beverages used in restaurant operations and complementary retail goods and are recorded at the lower of cost or market value as determined by the average cost for food and beverages and by the retail method on the first-in, first-out basis for retail goods. Inventories consisted of the following:

December 31,	2003	2002
Food and beverage	$32,458,803	$29,124,594
Retail goods	15,313,495	11,754,781
	$47,772,298	$40,879,375

Property and Equipment

Property and equipment are recorded at cost. Expenditures for major renewals and betterments are capitalized while maintenance and repairs are expensed as incurred.

The Company computes depreciation using the straight-line method. The estimated lives used in computing depreciation are generally as

follows: buildings and improvements—5 to 40 years; furniture, fixtures and equipment—5 to 15 years; and leasehold improvements—shorter of 30 years or lease term, including extensions where appropriate.

Interest is capitalized in connection with restaurant construction and development activities, and other real estate development projects. The capitalized interest is recorded as part of the asset to which it relates and is amortized over the asset's estimated useful life. During 2003, 2002 and 2001, the Company capitalized interest costs of approximately $2,050,000, $1,959,000 and $2,437,000, respectively.

Restaurant and other properties are reviewed for impairment on a property by property basis whenever events or changes in circumstances indicate that the carrying amount of an asset may not be recovered. The recoverability of properties that are to be held and used is measured by comparison of the estimated future undiscounted cash flows associated with the asset to the carrying amount of the asset. If such assets are considered to be impaired, an impairment charge is recorded in the amount by which the carrying amount of the assets exceeds their fair value. Properties to be disposed of are reported at the lower of their carrying amount or fair value, reduced for estimated disposal costs, and are included in other current assets.

Pre-Opening Costs

Pre-opening costs are expensed as incurred and include the direct and incremental costs incurred in connection with the commencement of each restaurant's operations, which are substantially comprised of training-related costs.

Development Costs

Certain direct costs are capitalized in conjunction with site selection for planned future restaurants, acquiring restaurant properties and other real estate development projects. Direct and certain related indirect costs of the construction department, including interest, are capitalized in conjunction with construction and development projects. These costs are included in property and equipment in the accompanying consolidated balance sheets and are amortized over the life of the related building and leasehold interest. Costs related to abandoned site selections, projects, and general site selection costs which cannot be identified with specific restaurants are charged to operations.

Advertising

Advertising costs are expensed as incurred during such year. Advertising expenses were $34 million, $32 million and $22 million in 2003, 2002 and 2001, respectively.

Goodwill

Goodwill is not amortized, but instead tested for impairment at least annually. Other intangible assets are amortized over the life of the related agreement. These amounts are included in goodwill and other assets in the accompanying consolidated balance sheets, respectively.

Financial Instruments

The Company utilizes interest rate swap agreements to manage its exposure to interest rate risk. The Company's interest rate swap agreements qualify as fair value hedges. As such, the gains or losses on the swaps are offset by corresponding gains or losses on the related debt.

NOTES TO CONSOLIDATED
FINANCIAL STATEMENTS

Earnings Per Share and Stock Option Accounting

Basic earnings per share is computed by dividing net income by the weighted average number of shares of common stock outstanding during the year. Diluted earnings per share reflects the potential dilution that could occur if contracts to issue common stock were exercised or converted into common stock. For purposes of this calculation, outstanding stock options are considered common stock equivalents using the treasury stock method, and are the only such equivalents outstanding.

The Company follows the intrinsic value method of accounting for stock options, and as such does not record compensation expense related to amounts outstanding.

Cash Flow Reporting

For purposes of the consolidated financial statements, the Company considers all highly liquid investments with original maturities of three months or less to be cash equivalents.

Segment Reporting

As of December 31, 2003, the Company operated 286 casual full-service dining restaurants which are a part of a single operating segment. The restaurants operate principally in the United States and provide similar products to similar customers. The restaurants generally possess similar pricing structures resulting in the potential for similar long-term expected financial performance characteristics. Revenues are from the sale of food, beverages and complementary retail items.

The Specialty Growth Division is primarily engaged in operating complementary entertainment and hospitality activities, such as miscellaneous beverage carts and various kiosks, amusement rides and games and some associated limited room and service hotel and motel type properties, generally at locations in conjunction with our core restaurant operations. The total assets, revenues, and operating profits of these complementary "specialty" business activities are considered not material to the overall business (yet complementary nevertheless) and below the threshold of a separate reportable business segment under SFAS No. 131.

The Company is in the business of operating restaurants and the above-mentioned complementary activities. The Company does not engage in real estate operations other than those associated with the ownership and operation / management of its business. The Company owns a fee interest (own the land and building) in a number of properties underlying its businesses, but it does not engage in real estate sales or real estate management in any significant fashion or format. The Chief Executive Officer, who is responsible for the Company's operations, reviews and evaluates both core and non-core business activities and results, and determines financial and management resource allocations and investments for both business activities.

Use of Estimates

The preparation of financial statements in conformity with accounting principles generally accepted in the United States requires management to make estimates and assumptions that affect the reported amounts of assets and liabilities and disclosures of contingent assets and liabilities at the date of the financial statements and the reported amounts of revenues and expenses during the reporting period. Actual results may differ from those estimates and services.

Recent Accounting Pronouncements

The Financial Accounting Standards Board ("FASB") issued FASB Interpretation No. ("FIN") 46, "Consolidation of Variable Interest Entities" in January 2003. This interpretation provides guidance on the identification of, and financial reporting for, variable interest entities. Variable interest entities are entities that lack the characteristics of a controlling financial interest or lack sufficient equity to finance its activities without additional subordinated financial support. FIN 46 requires a company to consolidate a variable interest entity if that company is obligated to absorb the majority of the entity's expected losses or entitled to receive the majority of the entity's residual returns, or both. The Company does not believe that FIN 46 will have a material impact on the Company's consolidated financial statements.

2. ACQUISITIONS

In February 2002, the Company acquired C.A. Muer, Inc., the owner and operator of 15 seafood restaurants ("Muer Acquisition"), in a stock purchase transaction for approximately $28.5 million. In August 2002, the Company acquired, in an asset purchase transaction, 27 Chart House seafood restaurants located primarily on the East and West Coasts of the United States from Angelo and Maxie's, Inc. for approximately $45.5 million, as well as assumption of selected trade payable related liabilities. Both of these acquisitions included plans for the redevelopment of 10 additional lower profitability restaurants, also then acquired, into Joe's Crab Shack restaurants, as well as the sale or disposal of six acquired but non-strategic locations. In October 2002, the Company acquired 27 Saltgrass Steak House restaurants in a stock purchase transaction for approximately $73.0 million which included a $20 million promissory note issued to the seller. The Saltgrass acquisition provides for future contingent payments based on the financial performance of the acquired restaurants and a limited number of future restaurants. As such contingency payments have not been earned, no amounts have been accrued. Any related incentive payment is expected to require financial performance of the acquired business to be well in excess of historical financial performance. The acquisitions noted above are accounted for under SFAS 141 and results of operations are included in the accompanying financial statements from the date of acquisition. The assets acquired and liabilities assumed of the acquired businesses were recorded at estimated fair values using relevant comparables, appraisals, and records.

A summary of the assets acquired and liabilities assumed in the acquisitions follows (in 000's):

	Muer	Chart House	Saltgrass
Estimated fair value of assets acquired	$45,431	$57,385	$83,524
Liabilities assumed	(16,883)	(5,945)	(10,063)
Allocated purchase price	28,548	51,440	73,461
Less cash acquired and seller note	(895)	(163)	(21,200)
Net cash paid	$27,653	$51,277	$52,261

As a result of the acquisitions, the Company has recorded acquisition integration costs for the estimated incremental costs to exit and

NOTES TO CONSOLIDATED

FINANCIAL STATEMENTS

consolidate activities at various locations, to involuntarily terminate employees, and for other costs to integrate operating locations and other activities of the acquired business with the Company. Accounting principles generally accepted in the United States provide that these acquisition integration expenses, which are not associated with the generation of future revenues and have no future economic benefit, be reflected as assumed liabilities in the allocation of the purchase price. Acquisition integration for the 2002 acquisitions aggregated $6.9 million of which most liabilities were paid in 2002.

During 2003, the Company made several individual property acquisitions that aggregated $27 million, plus $11.4 million of assumed debt, and included $5.1 million of Goodwill additions.

3. PROPERTY AND EQUIPMENT AND OTHER ASSETS

Property and equipment is comprised of the following:

December 31,	2003	2002
Land	**$170,163,593**	$138,379,047
Buildings and improvements	**222,903,558**	195,445,593
Furniture, fixtures & equipment	**234,372,485**	179,119,008
Leasehold improvements	**498,030,942**	398,384,738
Construction in progress	**64,349,939**	86,968,286
	1,189,820,517	998,296,672
Less—accumulated depreciation	**(224,245,526)**	(167,366,541)
Property and equipment, net	**$965,574,991**	$830,930,131

The Company continually evaluates unfavorable cash flows, if any, related to underperforming restaurants. Periodically it is concluded that certain properties have become impaired based on the existing and anticipated future economic outlook for such properties in their respective market areas. As a result, the Company recorded asset impairment depreciation charges of approximately $13,100,000, $2,200,000, and $2,394,000 in 2003, 2002 and 2001, respectively, representing the difference between the estimated fair value and carrying value for those restaurant properties. Asset impairment expense of $13,100,000 relating to six underperorming and three closed restaurants was included in the 2003 amount, and $2,200,000 was included for 2002. Included in the 2003 amounts were four Landry's division, three Joe's Crab Shack, and two Crab House restaurants. The Company expects that asset impairment charges for 2004, if any, would be significantly less than amounts recorded in 2003.

The significant increase in impairment charges in fiscal 2003, resulted from 2003 sales declines in these restaurants, additional further deterioration in the specific restaurant's profitability, perceived 2003 deterioration of the market area and/or specific location, and management's 2003 downward revised outlook for further opportunity and/or improvement of forecasted sales and profitability trends for such specific property. Assets that were impaired are primarily leasehold improvements and to a lesser extent equipment. The following is a summary of related charges and expenses:

Year Ended December 31,	2003	2002	2001
Asset Impairment	**$13,100,000**	$2,200,000	$2,394,000
Accrued Estimated Lease Termination Payments	**1,300,000**	—	—
Estimated Severance Costs	—	—	—
	$14,400,000	$2,200,000	$2,394,000

The Company considers the asset impairment expense as additional depreciation and amortization, although shown as a separate line item in the Consolidated Income Statements. Estimated fair values of impaired properties are based on comparable valuations, cash flows and management judgement.

Other current assets are comprised of the following:

December 31,	2003	2002
Prepaid expenses	**$3,490,137**	$4,439,300
Assets held for sale (expected to be sold within one year)	**3,384,925**	3,585,925
Marketable securities	—	2,752,979
Deposits	**615,321**	995,812
	$7,490,383	$11,774,016

Other expense (income) for 2003 is primarily expenses related to abandoned development projects. Other income during 2002 includes additional income of $1,100,000 from a settlement from a vendor and $875,000 in unrealized gains on marketable securities classified as trading offset by a loss of $1,500,000 on marketable securities and other assets held for sale.

4. ACCRUED LIABILITIES

Accrued liabilities are comprised of the following:

December 31,	2003	2002
Payroll and related costs	**$15,533,279**	$14,708,991
Rent, insurance and taxes, other than payroll and income taxes	**37,028,881**	36,628,732
Deferred revenue (gift certificates)	**10,455,869**	9,085,304
Other	**11,494,612**	13,814,543
	$74,512,641	$74,237,570

5. DEBT

On October 1, 2003, the Company issued notes totaling $150.0 million through a private placement of debt (the "Senior Notes"). Proceeds from the Senior Notes were used to pay down amounts outstanding under the bank promissory notes and the bank syndicate credit facility. The debt offering consisted of four equal series of notes in the amount of $37.5 million, quarterly interest of 5.47%, 5.84%, 6.05% and 6.44%, with an average rate of 5.95%, and maturities on October 1, 2009, 2010, 2011 and 2013.

NOTES TO CONSOLIDATED

FINANCIAL STATEMENTS

Long-term debt is comprised of the following:

Year Ended December 31,	2003	2002
$200.0 million Bank syndicate credit facility, LIBOR + 1.875%, interest only, due October 2007	**$122,000,000**	—
$150.0 million Senior Notes, average 5.95%, interest only, maturities ranging from October 2009 to October 2013	**150,000,000**	—
$20.0 million seller note, 5.5% interest, quarterly principal and interest payments of $653,386, due 2009	**18,055,321**	19,621,614
$220.0 million Bank syndicate credit facility, LIBOR + 2.5%, interest only, due July 2004	—	171,000,000
Non-recourse long-term note payable, 9.39% interest, principal and interest aggregate $101,762 monthly, due May 2010	**11,318,664**	—
Other long-term notes payable with various interest rates, principal and interest paid monthly	**325,110**	565,412
Total Debt	**301,699,095**	191,187,026
Less current portion	**(1,963,189)**	(1,783,427)
Long-term portion	**$299,735,906**	$189,403,599

In connection with the Senior Notes, the Company entered into two interest swap agreements with the objective of reducing its exposure to interest rate risk and lowering interest expense. The agreements were effective beginning October 7, 2003 with maturity dates of six years and seven years for an aggregate notional amount of $75 million and interest at LIBOR plus 1.71%. The Company's interest rate swap agreements qualify as fair value hedges and meet the criteria for the "short cut method" under SFAS No. 133, "Accounting for Derivative Instruments and Hedging Activities."

On October 14, 2003, the Company entered into the Second Amended and Restated Credit Agreement (the "Bank Credit Facility") whereby the existing bank credit facility was amended and extended to a four-year $200.0 million revolving credit facility. The Bank Credit Facility provides the ability to add an additional $25.0 million of capacity within the facility and other permitted indebtedness. Interest on the Bank Credit Facility is payable monthly or quarterly at LIBOR or the bank's base rate plus a financing spread. The Company's financing spread is presently 1.875% for LIBOR, and 0.375% for base rate borrowings, and may be decreased or increased by 25 basis points as the Company's leverage ratio decreases or increases over predetermined ratios. The Bank Credit Facility and Senior Notes are secured by stock of subsidiaries, governed by certain financial covenants, including maximum leverage ratio, maximum indebtedness, net worth, and fixed charge coverage ratio tests. The Bank Credit Facility additionally provides for limitations on annual capital expenditures to prescribed amounts, maximum annual cash dividends and limitations on repurchases of common stock. As of December 31, 2003, the Company had $10,000,000 in trade letters of credit. As of January 30, 2004, the Company had approximately $38 million available under the existing credit facilities for expansion and working capital purposes.

In connection with the Saltgrass Steak House acquisition in October 2002, the Company financed a portion of the acquisition with a $20 million, 7 year, 5.5% note to the former owner of Saltgrass Steak House. Principal payments under the promissory note aggregate $1,654,000 in 2004, $1,747,000 in 2005, $1,845,000 in 2006, $1,949,000 in 2007, $2,058,000 in 2008 and $8,802,000 thereafter (through 2009).

The Company assumed an $11.4 million, 9.39% non-recourse, long-term mortgage note payable, due May 2010, in connection with an asset purchase in March 2003. Principal and interest payments aggregate $102,000 monthly.

Interest expense (income), net includes the following:

Year Ended December 31,	2003	2002	2001
Interest expense	**$9,634,872**	$5,133,219	$9,685,201
Interest income	**(73,390)**	(136,197)	(282,850)
	$9,561,482	$4,997,022	$9,402,351

6. INCOME TAXES

An analysis of the provision for income taxes for the years ended December 31, 2003, 2002, and 2001 is as follows:

	2003	2002	2001
Tax Provision:			
Current income taxes	**$267,491**	$9,939,230	$3,266,954
Deferred income taxes	**11,224,287**	8,715,408	8,828,776
Total provision	**$11,491,778**	$18,654,638	$12,095,730

The Company's effective tax rate, for the years ended December 31, 2003, 2002, & 2001, differs from the federal statutory rate as follows:

	2003	2002	2001
Statutory rate	**35.0%**	35.0%	35.0%
FICA tax credit	**(9.1)**	(6.6)	(7.3)
State income tax, net of federal tax benefit	**4.1**	1.2	0.6
Recognition of tax carryforward assets and other tax attributes	**(9.7)**	—	—
Other	**(0.3)**	1.4	2.7
	20.0%	31.0%	31.0%

The Company's actual cash payments for annual income taxes due are currently lower than the financial accrual rate due to significant differences between book and tax accounting and tax credit and loss carryforwards.

15

NOTES TO CONSOLIDATED

FINANCIAL STATEMENTS

Deferred income tax assets and liabilities as of December 31 are comprised of the following:

Year Ended December 31,	2003	2002
Deferred Income Taxes:		
Current assets—accruals and other	**$6,858,000**	$6,228,000
Non-current assets:		
AMT credit, FICA credit carryforwards, and other	**$27,122,000**	$21,128,000
Net operating loss carryforwards	**28,951,000**	28,633,000
Valuation allowance for carryforwards	**(26,236,000)**	(28,239,000)
Non-current deferred tax asset	**29,837,000**	21,522,000
Non-current liabilities — property and other	**(53,232,000)**	(33,063,000)
Net non-current tax asset (liability)	**$(23,395,000)**	$(11,541,000)
Total net deferred tax asset (liability)	**$(16,537,000)**	$(5,313,000)

At December 31, 2003 and 2002, the Company had operating loss carryovers for Federal Income Tax purposes of $77.0 million and $73.3 million respectively, which expire in 2009 through 2023. These operating loss carryovers, and certain other deductible temporary differences, are related to the acquisitions of Rainforest Cafe and Saltgrass Steak House, and their utilization is subject to an annual limitation. Because of this limitation, the Company established a valuation allowance to the extent it is more likely than not that these tax benefits will not be realized. In 2003, a reduction of the valuation allowance and deferred tax liabilities aggregating $6.3 million was recorded attributable to tax benefits deemed realizable and reduced accruals. The valuation allowance was reduced due to the strong 2003 and future forecasted profitability of the Rainforest Café restaurants, 2003 completion of a successful transition from a tax-loss incurring stand-alone public company to a highly profitable and taxable income producing wholly-owned subsidiary of Landry's, coupled with the approaching end specific recognition limitations on allowable deductions and tax assets and the 2003 resolution of certain tax issues, which caused management to believe that a portion of the deferred tax assets previously reserved would more likely than not be realized and accruals reduced.

The Company has general business tax credit carryovers and minimum tax credit carryovers of $21.3 million and $7.4 million, respectively. The general business tax credit carryover includes $1.5 million from Saltgrass which is fully reserved, and the minimum tax credit carryover includes $2.4 million from Rainforest which is fully reserved. The general business credit carryovers expire in 2009 through 2023 while the minimum tax credit carryovers have no expiration date. The use of these credits is limited if the Company is subject to the alternative minimum tax. The Company believes it is more likely than not that it will generate sufficient income in future years to utilize the non-reserved credits.

The Internal Revenue Service (IRS) has examined the Company's Federal Income Tax Returns and certain pre-acquisition returns for Rainforest Cafe for years 1997 through 2000. The fieldwork for the examination was completed without adjustment.

7. COMMITMENTS AND CONTINGENCIES
Lease Commitments

The Company has entered into lease commitments for restaurant facilities as well as certain fixtures, equipment and leasehold improvements. Under most of the facility lease agreements, the Company pays taxes, insurance and maintenance costs in addition to the rent payments. Certain facility leases also provide for additional contingent rentals based on a percentage of sales in excess of a minimum amount. Rental expense under operating leases was approximately $54.1 million, $42.9 million and $40.6 million, during the years ended December 31, 2003, 2002, and 2001, respectively. Percentage rent included in rent expense was $12.1 million, $10.1 million, and $10.3 million, for 2003, 2002 and 2001, respectively.

In 2001, the Company entered into a $15.3 million equipment operating lease agreement. The lease expires in 2011. The Company guarantees a minimum residual value related to the equipment of approximately 66% of the total amount funded under the agreement. The Company may purchase the leased equipment throughout the lease term for an amount equal to the unamortized lease balance. The Company believes that the equipment's fair value is sufficient that no amounts will be due under the residual value guarantee.

In 2002, the Company entered into a $6.9 million equipment operating lease agreement. The lease expires in 2012. The Company guarantees a minimum residual value related to the equipment of approximately 66% of the total amount funded under the agreement. The Company may purchase the leased equipment throughout the lease term for an amount equal to the unamortized lease balance. The Company believes that the equipment's fair value is sufficient that no amounts will be due under the residual value guarantee.

In connection with substantially all of the Rainforest Cafe leases, amounts are provided for tenant inducements, rent abatements, and scheduled increases in rent. Such amounts are recorded as other long-term liabilities on the Company's consolidated balance sheet, and amortized or accrued as an adjustment to rent expense, included in other restaurant operating expenses, on a straight-line basis over the lease term.

The aggregate amounts of minimum operating lease commitments maturing in each of the five years and thereafter subsequent to December 31, 2003, are as follows:

2004	$44,927,000
2005	44,368,000
2006	41,100,000
2007	38,438,000
2008	33,600,000
Thereafter	279,319,000
Total minimum rentals	$481,752,000

Building Commitments

As of December 31, 2003, the Company had future development, land purchases and construction commitments expected to be expended within the next twelve months of approximately $17.2 million, including completion of construction on certain new restaurants. In 2001, the Company entered into an agreement to construct and operate a convention center in the City of Galveston,

NOTES TO CONSOLIDATED

FINANCIAL STATEMENTS

Texas. The Galveston convention center construction costs will be funded by governmental agency bonds issued by the City of Galveston and serviced by certain hotel occupancy taxes. In connection with the convention center development and related management contract, the Company is to guarantee certain construction cost overruns and operating losses, if any, subject to certain rights of reimbursement. Under the agreements, the Company will have the rights to one-half of any profits generated by the operation of the convention center.

In 2003, the Company purchased from the City of Galveston the Flagship Hotel and Pier, subject to an existing lease. Under this agreement, upon termination of the existing lease, the Company has committed to spend an additional $15 million to transform the hotel and pier into a 19th century style Inn and entertainment complex complete with rides and carnival type games. The property is currently occupied by a tenant.

During November 2003, the Company purchased two casual Italian restaurants. Under the purchase agreement, the Company is committed to building an additional five casual Italian restaurants over the next 5 years, or make certain payments in lieu of development. In conjunction with the agreement to develop additional restaurants, the seller agrees to provide consulting services to ensure the consistency and the quality of the food and service are maintained through this transition period. The Company also has a commitment to build an additional 12 new Saltgrass restaurants within five years. To date, five restaurants have either opened or are under construction.

Loan Guarantee

Rainforest Cafe, a wholly-owned subsidiary of the Company, has guaranteed the borrowings of one of its foreign affiliates in which the Company owns a 20% interest. As a result of a settlement with the foreign affiliate during 2003, we remain subject to a pre-existing obligation as guarantor of the affiliate's loan up to $1,400,000. However, Rainforest Cafe's proportional share of the remaining outstanding loan balance is approximately $300,000.

Litigation and Claims

In January 2002, Rainforest Cafe, Inc., our wholly-owned subsidiary, was sued by EklecCo, L.L.C., in the Supreme Court of the State of New York in Onondaga County. EklecCo is seeking damages and costs as a result of Rainforest Cafe's alleged breach of a restaurant lease entered into in 1996 for a Rainforest Cafe unit formerly located in the Palisades Mall. Rainforest Cafe believes that it has no liability for damages beyond the personal property located in the premises at the time it vacated the premises. Rainforest Cafe is defending this case vigorously. Because the case is in its early stages, the financial impact to the Company, if any, cannot be predicted.

On July 31, 2002, and subsequently amended, a purported collective action lawsuit against the Company entitled Meaghan Bollenberg, et. al. v. Landry's Restaurants, Inc. was filed in the United States District Court for the Northern District of Illinois and subsequently moved to a Court in the Southern District of Texas. The lawsuit was filed by six plaintiffs who were servers on behalf of themselves and others similarly situated. The lawsuit alleges that the Company violated certain minimum wage laws under the federal Fair Labor Standards Act and seeks damages and costs. The Company is vigorously defending this litigation. Because the case is in its early stages, the financial impact to the Company, if any, cannot be predicted.

Former shareholders of approximately 4.4 million shares of Rainforest Cafe, Inc. dissented to the merger between the Company and Rainforest Cafe, seeking an amount in excess of the $3.25 per share paid in the merger. An appraisal proceeding was held before a Minnesota District Court Judge in early January 2003. The appraisal trial ended with a ruling in the Company's favor. In July 2003, the ruling was appealed by the dissenters. The appeal hearing was held and a ruling is expected by April 2004.

General Litigation

The Company is subject to other legal proceedings and claims that arise in the ordinary course of business. Management does not believe that the outcome of any of these matters will have a material adverse effect on the Company's financial position, results of operations or cash flows.

8. STOCKHOLDERS' EQUITY

In April 2002, the Company completed a public offering of 5,297,500 shares of the Company's common stock. Net proceeds of the offering to the Company were approximately $132.6 million and were used to repay outstanding borrowings.

In October 2002, the Company's board of directors authorized a $50.0 million open market stock buy back program. In September 2003, the Company authorized an additional open market stock repurchase program for $60.0 million.

In connection with the Company's stock buy back programs, the Company repurchased into treasury approximately 469,000, 305,000 and 3,500 shares of common stock for approximately $8.4 million, $6.7 million and $0.1 million, in 2003, 2002, and 2001, respectively.

Commencing in 2000, the Company began to pay an annual $0.10 per share dividend, declared and paid in quarterly installments of $0.025 per share.

NOTES TO CONSOLIDATED

FINANCIAL STATEMENTS

A reconciliation of the amounts used to compute net income per common share—diluted is as follows:

Year Ended December 31,	2003	2002	2001
Net Income	$45,901,054	$41,521,616	$26,919,569
Weighted average common shares outstanding	27,600,000	25,900,000	21,750,000
Dilutive common stock equivalents–stock options	725,000	1,000,000	785,000
Weighted average common and common equivalent shares outstanding–diluted	28,325,000	26,900,000	22,535,000
Net income per share—diluted	$1.62	$1.54	$1.19

Options to purchase approximately 200,000 shares in 2001 have been excluded from the calculation of diluted earnings per share as they were anti-dilutive.

The Company maintains two stock option plans, which were originally adopted in 1993, (the Stock Option Plans), as amended, pursuant to which options may be granted to eligible employees and non-employee directors of the Company or its subsidiaries for the purchase of an aggregate of 2,750,000 shares of common stock of the Company. The Stock Option Plans are administered by the Stock Option Committee of the Board of Directors (the Committee), which determines at its discretion, the number of shares subject to each option granted and the related purchase price, vesting and option periods. The Committee may grant either non-qualified stock options or incentive stock options, as defined by the Internal Revenue Code of 1986, as amended.

The Company also maintains the 1995 Flexible Incentive Plan, which was adopted in 1995, (Flex Plan), as amended, for key employees of the Company. Under the Flex Plan eligible employees may receive stock options, stock appreciation rights, restricted stock, performance awards, performance stock and other awards, as defined by the Board of Directors or an appointed committee. The aggregate number of shares of common stock which may be issued under the Flex Plan (or with respect to which awards may be granted) may not exceed 2,000,000 shares.

In June 2003, the Company established an equity incentive plan pursuant to which stock options or restricted stock of the Company may be granted to eligible employees of the Company for an aggregate of 700,000 shares of common stock of the Company. The Compensation Committee of the Board of Directors determines the number of shares, prices, and vesting schedule of individual grants. In addition, the Company will issue pursuant to an employment agreement, over its five year term, 500,000 shares of restricted stock, with a 10 year vest from grant date, and a minimum of 800,000 stock options. In August 2003, 100,000 restricted common shares were issued subject to vesting on the tenth anniversary. The unamortized balance of non-vested restricted common stock grants is reflected as deferred compensation included in stockholders' equity and the related expense is amortized over the vesting periods.

In March 2003, the Company established the 2002 Employee/Rainforest Conversion Plan pursuant to which stock options of the Company may be granted to employees, non-employee directors and consultants of the Company for up to an aggregate of 2,162,500 shares of Common Stock of the Company. The Compensation Committee of the Board of Directors determines the number of shares, prices and vesting schedule of individual grants.

The table below illustrates the effect on net income and earnings per share if compensation costs for the Company had been determined using the alternative accounting method based on the fair value prescribed by SFAS No. 123.

Year Ended December 31,	2003	2002	2001
Net income, as reported	45,900,000	$41,500,000	$26,900,000
Less: stock based compensation expense using fair value method, net of tax	(2,100,000)	(1,800,000)	(1,500,000)
Pro forma net income	$43,800,000	$39,700,000	$25,400,000
Earnings per share			
Basic, as reported	$1.66	$1.60	$1.24
Basic, pro forma	$1.59	$1.53	$1.17
Diluted, as reported	$1.62	$1.54	$1.19
Diluted, pro forma	$1.55	$1.48	$1.13

The fair value of each option grant is estimated on the date of grant using the Black-Scholes option-pricing model; amortization over the respective vesting periods; expected lives of 6 years; expected stock price volatility of approximately 40% and an interest rate of approximately 6% in 2001, and 2.9% in 2002. The weighted average fair value per share of options granted during 2002 and 2001 was $7.83, and $5.82, respectively. Options for 16,000 shares were granted in 2003 and were not deemed material for the above calculations.

In connection with the acquisition of Rainforest Cafe, the Company issued approximately 500,000 vested stock options to employees of Rainforest Cafe as replacement for existing options outstanding at the date of the merger, as required by the merger agreement. The fair value of these options was included in the purchase price of Rainforest Cafe.

At December 31, 2003, options for 2,410,874 shares were outstanding at prices ranging from $6.00 to $20.60 per share. As of December 31, 2003 all options have been granted at the stock price on the grant date and are generally exercisable beginning one year from the date of grant with annual vesting periods over three to five years.

NOTES TO CONSOLIDATED

FINANCIAL STATEMENTS

Year Ended December 31,	2003		2002		2001	
	Shares	Average Exercise Price	Shares	Average Exercise Price	Shares	Average Exercise Price
Options outstanding, beginning of year	2,694,470	$11.57	3,040,926	$9.93	3,169,803	$9.92
Granted	16,000	$20.26	464,135	$17.71	623,500	$9.83
Exercised	(251,196)	$7.28	(782,514)	$9.12	(501,523)	$7.05
Terminated	(48,400)	$14.36	(28,077)	$13.55	(250,854)	$10.67
Options outstanding, end of year	2,410,874	$11.97	2,694,470	$11.57	3,040,926	$9.93
Options exercisable, end of year	1,902,274	$11.82	1,726,368	$10.33	1,831,694	$10.99

The following table provides certain information with respect to stock options outstanding as of December 31, 2003:

Range of Exercise Prices	Stock Options Outstanding	Weighted Average Exercise Price	Weighted Average Remaining Life Outstanding
< $9.00	994,360	$7.59	6.3
$9.00 - $13.50	783,627	$12.84	3.4
$13.50 - $20.25	622,887	$17.73	8.0
> $20.25	10,000	$20.60	9.8
	2,410,874	$11.97	5.8

The following table provides certain information with respect to stock options exercisable at December 31, 2003:

Range of Exercise Prices	Stock Options Exercisable	Weighted Average Exercise Price
< $9.00	737,260	$7.45
$9.00 - $13.50	778,627	$12.84
$13.50 - $20.25	386,387	$18.24
	1,902,274	$11.82

9. CERTAIN TRANSACTIONS

In 1996, the Company entered into a Consulting Service Agreement (the "Agreement") with Fertitta Hospitality, LLC ("Fertitta Hospitality"), which is jointly owned by the Chairman and Chief Executive Officer of the Company and his wife. Pursuant to the Agreement, the Company provided to Fertitta Hospitality management and administrative services. In 2003, a new agreement was signed ("Management Agreement"). Under the Agreement, the Company received a fee of $2,500 per month plus the reimbursement of all out-of-pocket expenses and such additional compensation as agreed upon. Pursuant to the Management Agreement, the Company receives a monthly fee of $7,500 plus reimbursement of expenses. The Management Agreement provides for a renewable three-year term.

In 1999, the Company entered into a ground lease with 610 Loop Venture, LLC, a company wholly owned by the Chairman and Chief Executive Officer of the Company, on land owned by the Company adjacent to the Company's corporate headquarters. Under the terms of the ground lease, 610 Loop Venture pays the Company base rent of $12,000 per month plus pro-rata real property taxes and insurance. 610 Loop Venture also has the option to purchase certain property based upon a contractual agreement.

In 2002, the Company entered into an $8,000 per month, 20 year, with option renewals, ground lease agreement with Fertitta Hospitality for a new Rainforest Cafe on prime waterfront land in Galveston, Texas. The annual rent is equal to the greater of the base rent or percentage rent up to six percent, plus taxes and insurance. In 2003, the Company paid base and percentage rent aggregating $602,000.

As permitted by the employment contract between the Company and the Chief Executive Officer, charitable contributions were made by the Company to a charitable Foundation that the Chief Executive Officer served as Trustee in the amount of $170,000 and $197,720 in 2003 and 2002, respectively. The contribution was made in addition to the normal salary and bonus permitted under the employment contract.

The Company, on a routine basis, holds or hosts promotional events, training seminars and conferences for its personnel. In connection therewith, the Company incurred in 2003 and 2002 expenses in the amount of $138,000 and $229,746, respectively, at resort hotel properties owned by the Company's Chief Executive Officer and managed by the Company.

The Company and Fertitta Hospitality jointly sponsored events and promotional activities in 2003 and 2002 which resulted in shared costs and use of Company personnel or Fertitta Hospitality employees and assets.

The foregoing agreements were entered into between related parties and were not the result of arm's-length negotiations. Accordingly, the terms of the transactions may have been more or less favorable to the Company than might have been obtained from unaffiliated third parties.

■

NOTES TO CONSOLIDATED

FINANCIAL STATEMENTS

10. QUARTERLY FINANCIAL DATA (UNAUDITED)

The following is a summary of unaudited quarterly consolidated results of operations (in thousands, except per share data).

Quarter Ended:	**2003**	March 31	June 30	September 30	December 31
Revenues		$249,582	$299,890	$302,162	$254,121
Cost of Revenues		$73,322	$87,447	$88,168	$72,846
Operating income		$13,979	$27,150	$29,546	$(2,258)
Net income		$8,121	$16,906	$18,382	$2,492
Net income per share (basic)		$0.29	$0.61	$0.67	$0.09
Net income per share (diluted)		$0.29	$0.60	$0.65	$0.09

Quarter Ended:	**2002**	March 31	June 30	September 30	December 31
Revenues		$192,170	$231,938	$241,072	$229,615
Cost of Revenues		$55,401	$66,443	$68,995	$67,106
Operating income		$10,888	$21,115	$23,354	$8,930
Net income		$6,183	$15,045	$15,717	$4,577
Net income per share (basic)		$0.28	$0.58	$0.57	$0.17
Net income per share (diluted)		$0.27	$0.56	$0.55	$0.16

CORPORATE INFORMATION

Stock Information

The Company's common stock is traded on the New York Stock Exchange under the symbol "LNY".

Corporate Offices

Landry's Restaurants, Inc.
1510 West Loop South
Houston, Texas 77027
Phone: (713) 850-1010
Fax: (713) 386-7707
www.landrysrestaurants.com

The Company

   Landry's Restaurants, Inc., headquartered in Houston, Texas, owns and operates full-service casual dining restaurants under the names of Joe's Crab Shack, Rainforest Cafe, Landry's Seafood House, Willie G's Seafood & Steak House, Saltgrass Steak House, Chart House, Charley's Crab, Kemah Boardwalk, The Crab House, Aquarium, Cadillac Mexican Restaurant and others in 36 states and five international countries. The Company operates a total of 286 full-service restaurants with approximately 25,000 employees.

Transfer Agent

American Stock Transfer
New York, New York

10K Availability

   The Company will furnish to any stockholder, without charge, a copy of the Company's annual report filed with the Securities and Exchange Commission on Form 10-K for 2002 upon written request from the stockholder addressed to:

   MR. PAUL S. WEST
   Executive Vice President and
   Chief Financial Officer
   Landry's Restaurants, Inc.
   1510 West Loop South
   Houston, Texas 77027

In Memorium

James E. Masucci
Served on the Board 1993 – 2003

B

Dave and Buster's, Inc.
2003 Annual Report

2003

ANNUAL REPORT

DAVE & BUSTER'S, INC.
CONSOLIDATED BALANCE SHEETS

	February 1, 2004	February 2, 2003
	(In thousands)	

ASSETS

Current assets:		
Cash and cash equivalents	$ 3,897	$ 2,530
Inventories	26,233	26,634
Prepaid expenses	2,709	2,049
Other current assets	2,518	2,136
Total current assets	35,357	33,349
Property and equipment, net (Note 2)	247,161	249,451
Other assets and deferred charges	13,371	8,412
Total assets	$295,889	$291,212

LIABILITIES AND STOCKHOLDERS' EQUITY

Current liabilities:		
Current installments of long-term debt (Note 4)	$ 3,333	$ 8,300
Accounts payable	13,346	14,952
Accrued liabilities (Note 3)	12,898	12,201
Income taxes payable (Note 5)	2,889	325
Deferred income taxes (Note 5)	3,111	1,802
Total current liabilities	35,577	37,580
Deferred income taxes (Note 5)	13,620	14,065
Other liabilities	13,602	10,471
Long-term debt, less current installments (Note 4)	50,201	59,494
Commitments and contingencies (Notes 4, 6 and 11)		
Stockholders' equity (Note 7):		
Preferred stock, 10,000,000 authorized; none issued	—	—
Common stock, $0.01 par value, 50,000,000 authorized; 13,181,284 and 13,080,117 shares issued and outstanding as of February 1, 2004 and February 2, 2003, respectively	132	132
Paid-in capital	118,669	116,678
Restricted stock awards	905	608
Retained earnings	65,029	54,030
	184,735	171,448
Less treasury stock, at cost (175,000 shares)	1,846	1,846
Total stockholders' equity	182,889	169,602
Total liabilities and stockholders' equity	$295,889	$291,212

See accompanying notes to consolidated financial statements.

F-1

DAVE & BUSTER'S, INC.
CONSOLIDATED STATEMENTS OF OPERATIONS

	Fiscal Year Ended		
	February 1, 2004	February 2, 2003	February 3, 2002
	(In thousands, except per share amounts)		
Food and beverage revenues	$191,881	$192,882	$181,358
Amusement and other revenues	170,941	180,870	176,651
Total revenues	362,822	373,752	358,009
Cost of revenues	68,142	68,752	66,939
Operating payroll and benefits	105,027	114,904	110,478
Other store operating expenses	111,310	117,666	106,971
General and administrative expenses	25,033	25,640	20,653
Depreciation and amortization expense	29,734	30,056	28,693
Preopening costs	—	1,488	4,578
Total costs and expenses	339,246	358,506	338,312
Operating income	23,576	15,246	19,697
Interest expense, net	6,926	7,143	7,820
Income before provision for income taxes	16,650	8,103	11,877
Provision for income taxes (Note 5)	5,661	2,755	4,299
Income before cumulative effect of a change in an accounting principle	10,989	5,348	7,578
Cumulative effect of a change in an accounting principle (Note 1)	—	(7,096)	—
Net income (loss)	$ 10,989	$ (1,748)	$ 7,578
Net income (loss) per share — basic:			
Before cumulative effect of a change in an accounting principle	$ .84	$ .41	$ .58
Cumulative effect of a change in an accounting principle	—	(.55)	—
	$ .84	$ (.14)	$ .58
Net income (loss) per share — diluted:			
Before cumulative effect of a change in an accounting principle	$ .80	$ .40	$ .58
Cumulative effect of a change in an accounting principle	—	(.53)	—
	$ .80	$ (.13)	$ .58
Weighted average shares outstanding:			
Basic	13,128	12,997	12,956
Diluted	14,646	13,404	13,016

See accompanying notes to consolidated financial statements.

F-2

DAVE & BUSTER'S, INC.

CONSOLIDATED STATEMENTS OF STOCKHOLDERS' EQUITY

	Common Stock		Paid-in Capital	Retained Earnings	Restricted Stock	Treasury Stock	Total
	Shares	Amount					
				(In thousands)			
Balance, February 4, 2001	12,953	$131	$115,659	$48,200	$243	$(1,846)	$162,387
Net earnings.	—	—	—	7,578	—	—	7,578
Stock option exercises.	6	—	40	—	—	—	40
Tax benefit related to stock option exercises	—	—	2	—	—	—	2
Amortization of restricted stock awards . .	—	—	—	—	139	—	139
Balance, February 3, 2002	12,959	131	115,701	55,778	382	(1,846)	170,146
Net earnings.	—	—	—	(1,748)	—	—	(1,748)
Stock option exercises.	121	1	870	—	—	—	871
Tax benefit related to stock option exercises	—	—	107	—	—	—	107
Amortization of restricted stock awards . .	—	—	—	—	226	—	226
Balance, February 2, 2003	13,080	132	116,678	54,030	608	(1,846)	169,602
Net earnings.	—	—	—	10,989	—	—	10,989
Stock option exercises.	101	—	704	—	—	—	704
Tax benefit related to stock option exercises	—	—	137	—	—	—	137
Amortization of restricted stock awards . .	—	—	—	—	297	—	297
Fair value of warrants issued in connection with convertible subordinated notes.	—	—	1,150	—	—	—	1,150
Other	—	—	—	10	—	—	10
Balance, February 1, 2004	13,181	$132	$118,669	$65,029	$905	$(1,846)	$182,889

See accompanying notes to consolidated financial statements.

F-3

DAVE & BUSTER'S, INC.

CONSOLIDATED STATEMENTS OF CASH FLOWS

	Fiscal Year Ended		
	February 1, 2004	February 2, 2003	February 3, 2002
	(In thousands)		
Cash flows from operating activities:			
Income before cumulative effect of a change in an accounting principle	$10,989	$ 5,348	$ 7,578
Adjustments to reconcile income before cumulative change in an accounting principle to net cash provided by operating activities:			
Depreciation and amortization	29,734	30,056	28,693
Deferred income tax expense	864	6,504	467
Restricted stock awards	297	226	139
Gain on sale of assets	(8)	(223)	(505)
Changes in operating assets and liabilities, net of effect of business acquisition			
Inventories	401	(670)	(4,206)
Prepaid expenses	(660)	(607)	2,221
Other current assets	(382)	309	693
Other assets and deferred charges	(502)	940	—
Accounts payable	(1,606)	(1,039)	6,700
Accrued liabilities	697	1,116	4,035
Income taxes payable	2,564	(4,729)	1,487
Other liabilities	3,129	3,373	2,399
Net cash provided by operating activities	45,517	40,604	49,701
Cash flows from investing activities:			
Capital expenditures	(24,292)	(21,720)	(49,761)
Business acquisition	(3,600)	—	—
Proceeds from sales of property and equipment	471	750	474
Proceeds from sales/leasebacks	—	—	18,474
Net cash used in investing activities	(27,421)	(20,970)	(30,813)
Cash flows from financing activities:			
Borrowings under long-term debt	44,825	12,000	24,060
Repayments of long-term debt	(57,789)	(34,602)	(41,648)
Debt fee costs	(4,469)	—	—
Proceeds from exercises of stock options	704	977	42
Net cash used in financing activities	(16,729)	(21,625)	(17,546)
Increase (decrease) in cash and cash equivalents	1,367	(1,991)	1,342
Beginning cash and cash equivalents	2,530	4,521	3,179
Ending cash and cash equivalents	$ 3,897	$ 2,530	$ 4,521
Supplemental disclosures of cash flow information:			
Cash paid for income taxes — net of refunds	$ 1,798	$ 679	$ 2,590
Cash paid for interest, net of amounts capitalized	$ 5,428	$ 7,353	$ 7,261

See accompanying notes to consolidated financial statements.

F-4

DAVE & BUSTER'S, INC.

NOTES TO CONSOLIDATED FINANCIAL STATEMENTS
In Thousands Except Per Share Amounts

Note 1:   Summary of Significant Accounting Policies

Basis of Presentation — The consolidated financial statements include the accounts of Dave & Buster's, Inc. and all wholly-owned subsidiaries (the "Company"). All material intercompany accounts and transactions have been eliminated in consolidation. The Company's one industry segment is the ownership and operation of restaurant/entertainment complexes (a "Complex" or "Store") under the name "Dave & Buster's," which are principally located in the United States and Canada.

Use of Estimates — The preparation of financial statements in conformity with generally accepted accounting principles requires management to make certain estimates and assumptions that affect the amounts reported in the financial statements and accompanying notes. Actual results could differ from those estimates.

Fiscal Year — Our fiscal year ends on the Sunday after the Saturday closest to January 31. References to 2003, 2002, 2001 and 2000 are to the 52 weeks ended February 1, 2004, February 2, 2003 and February 3, 2002 and to the 53 weeks ended February 4, 2001, respectively.

Inventories — Food and beverage and merchandise inventories are reported at the lower of cost or market determined on a first-in, first-out method. Smallware supplies inventories, consisting of china, glassware and kitchen utensils, are capitalized at the store opening date, or when the smallware inventory is increased due to changes in our menu, and are reviewed periodically for valuation. Smallware replacements are expensed as incurred. Inventories consist of the following (in thousands):

	February 1, 2004	February 2, 2003
Food and beverage	$ 1,809	$ 1,693
Merchandise	2,393	3,165
Smallware supplies	16,715	16,274
Other	5,316	5,502
	$26,233	$26,634

Preopening Costs — All start-up and preopening costs are expensed as incurred.

Property and Equipment — Property and equipment are recorded at cost. Expenditures that substantially increase the useful lives of the property and equipment are capitalized, whereas costs incurred to maintain the appearance and functionality of such assets are charged to repair and maintenance expense. Interest costs capitalized during the construction of facilities in 2003, 2002 and 2001 were $170, $361 and $892, respectively. Property and equipment, excluding most games are depreciated on the straight-line method over the estimated useful life of the assets. Games are generally depreciated on the 150 percent-double-declining-balance method over the estimated useful life of the assets. Reviews are performed regularly to determine whether facts or circumstances exist that indicate the carrying values of our property and equipment are impaired. We assess the recoverability of our property and equipment by comparing the projected future undiscounted net cash flows associated with these assets to their respective carrying amounts. Impairment, if any, is based on the excess of the carrying amount over the estimated fair market value of the assets.

Goodwill — We adopted Statement of Financial Accounting Standards (SFAS) No. 142, *Goodwill and Other Intangible Assets,* effective January 1, 2002. Under SFAS No. 142, goodwill is no longer amortized, but instead is reviewed for impairment at least annually. Impairment is deemed to exist when the carrying value of goodwill is greater that its implied fair value. As a result of applying the new standard, our initial assessment of fair value of the Company resulted in a write off of all of our goodwill during the first quarter of 2002 for

DAVE & BUSTER'S, INC.

NOTES TO CONSOLIDATED FINANCIAL STATEMENTS — (Continued)

$7,100. This was recorded as a cumulative effect of a change in accounting principle in 2002. As a result of this write off, we have no recorded amounts of goodwill as of February 1, 2004 and February 2, 2003.

The following table reflects income before cumulative effect of a change in an accounting principle and net income adjusted to exclude amortization expense related to goodwill (including related tax effects) recognized in the periods presented (in thousands):

	Fiscal Year Ended		
	February 1, 2004	February 2, 2003	February 3, 2002
Income (loss):			
Reported income before cumulative effect of a change in an accounting principle	$10,989	$ 5,348	$7,578
Goodwill amortization, net of income taxes	—	—	223
Adjusted income before cumulative effect of a change in an accounting principle	$10,989	$ 5,348	$7,801
Reported net income (loss)	$10,989	$(1,748)	$7,578
Goodwill amortization, net of income taxes	—	—	223
Adjusted net income (loss)	$10,989	$(1,748)	$7,801
Earnings per share:			
Basic:			
Reported income before cumulative effect of a change in an accounting principle	$ .84	$ .41	$ .58
Goodwill amortization, net of income taxes	—	—	.02
Adjusted income before cumulative effect of a change in an accounting principle	$ .84	$ .41	$ .60
Reported net income (loss)	$ .84	$ (.14)	$ .58
Goodwill amortization, net of income taxes	—	—	.02
Adjusted net income (loss)	$ .84	$ (.14)	$ .60
Diluted:			
Reported income before cumulative effect of a change in an accounting principle	$ .80	$ .40	$ .58
Goodwill amortization, net of income taxes	—	—	.02
Adjusted income before cumulative effect of a change in an accounting principle	$ .80	$ .40	$ .60
Reported net income (loss)	$ .80	$ (.13)	$ .58
Goodwill amortization, net of income taxes	—	—	.02
Adjusted net income (loss)	$ .80	$ (.13)	$ .60

Income Taxes — We use the liability method which recognizes the amount of current and deferred taxes payable or refundable at the date of the financial statements as a result of all events that are recognized in the financial statements and as measured by the provisions of enacted tax laws.

DAVE & BUSTER'S, INC.

NOTES TO CONSOLIDATED FINANCIAL STATEMENTS — (Continued)

Stock-Based Compensation — At February 1, 2004, we had two stock-based compensation plans covering employees and directors. These plans are described more fully in Note 7. We have elected to follow recognition and measurement principles of Accounting Principles Board Opinion No. 25, *Accounting for Stock Issued to Employees* (APB No. 25), in accounting for stock-based awards to our employees and directors. Under APB No. 25, if the exercise price of an employee's stock options equals or exceeds the market price of the underlying stock on the date of grant, no compensation expense is recognized.

Although SFAS No. 123, *Accounting for Stock-Based Compensation,* allows us to continue to follow APB No. 25 guidelines, we are required to disclose pro forma net income (loss) and net income (loss) per share as if we had adopted the fair based method prescribed by SFAS No. 123. The pro forma impact of applying SFAS No. 123 in fiscal 2003, 2002 and 2001 is not necessarily representative of the pro forma impact in future years. Our pro forma information is as follows (in thousands, except per share data):

	Fiscal Year Ended		
	February 1, 2004	February 2, 2003	February 3, 2002
Net income (loss), as reported	$10,989	$(1,748)	$ 7,578
Stock compensation expenses recorded under the intrinsic method, net of income taxes	196	149	92
Pro forma stock compensation expense recorded under the fair value method, net of income taxes	(801)	(1,288)	(1,541)
Pro forma net income (loss)	$10,384	$(2,887)	$ 6,129
Basic earnings (loss) per common share, as reported	$ 0.84	$ (0.14)	$ 0.58
Diluted earnings (loss) per common share, as reported	$ 0.80	$ (0.13)	$ 0.58
Pro forma basic earnings (loss) per common share	$ 0.79	$ (0.22)	$ 0.47
Pro forma diluted earnings (loss) per common share	$ 0.71	$ (0.22)	$ 0.47

Inputs used for the fair value method for our employee stock options are as follows:

	Fiscal Year Ended		
	February 1, 2004	February 2, 2003	February 3, 2002
Volatility	0.59	0.62	0.65
Weighted-average expected lives	4.40	5.00	3.20
Weighted-average risk-free interest rates	2.82%	3.89%	4.59%
Weighted-average fair value of options granted	9.97	8.63	6.91

Foreign Currency Translation — The financial statements related to our operations of our recently acquired Toronto complex are prepared in Canadian dollars. Income statement amounts are translated at average exchange rates for each period, while the assets and liabilities are translated at year-end exchange rates. Translation adjustments are included as a component of stockholders' equity. Total currency adjustments recorded as of February 1, 2004 were insignificant.

Revenue Recognition — Food, beverage and amusement revenues are recorded at point of service. Foreign license revenues are deferred until the Company fulfills its obligations under license agreements, which is upon the opening of the complex or upon resolution of any outstanding accounts receivable from the licensee. The license agreements provide for continuing royalty fees based on a percentage of gross revenues, which are recognized when realization is assured. Revenue from international licensees for 2003, 2002 and 2001 was $331, $564 and $537, respectively.

DAVE & BUSTER'S, INC.

NOTES TO CONSOLIDATED FINANCIAL STATEMENTS — (Continued)

Advertising Costs — Advertising costs are recorded as expense in the period in which the costs are incurred or the first time the advertising takes place. These expenses were $8,023, $13,782 and $13,130 for 2003, 2002 and 2001, respectively.

Note 2: Property and Equipment

Property and equipment consist of the following (in thousands):

	Estimated Depreciable Lives (in years)	February 1, 2004	February 2, 2003
Land	—	$ 6,706	$ 6,706
Buildings	40	44,663	44,824
Leasehold and building improvements	shorter of 20 or lease term	154,707	148,332
Furniture, fixtures and equipment	5-10	106,009	97,635
Games	5	86,382	80,207
Construction in progress		5,560	1,458
Total cost		404,027	379,162
Less accumulated depreciation		156,866	129,711
Property and equipment, net		$247,161	$249,451

Note 3: Accrued Liabilities

Accrued liabilities consist of the following (in thousands):

	February 1, 2004	February 2, 2003
Compensation and benefits	$ 5,297	$ 3,248
Sales and use taxes	1,330	1,374
Real estate taxes	1,143	2,551
Other	5,128	5,028
Total accrued liabilities	$12,898	$12,201

Note 4: Long-Term Debt

Long-term debt consisted of the following (in thousands):

	February 1, 2004	February 2, 2003
Revolving credit facility	$10,517	$ 9,250
Term loan A	14,167	23,301
Term loan B	—	35,243
Convertible subordinated notes	28,850	—
	53,534	67,794
Less current installments	3,333	8,300
Long-term debt, less current installments	$50,201	$59,494

On August 7, 2003 we closed a $30 million private placement of 5.0 percent convertible subordinated notes due 2008 and warrants to purchase 574,691 shares of our common stock at $13.46 per share. The

DAVE & BUSTER'S, INC.

NOTES TO CONSOLIDATED FINANCIAL STATEMENTS — (Continued)

investors may convert the notes into our common stock at any time prior to the scheduled maturity date of August 7, 2008. The conversion price is $12.92 per share, which represents a 20 percent premium over the closing price of our common stock on August 5, 2003. If fully converted, the notes will convert into 2,321,981 shares of our common stock. After August 7, 2006, we have the right to redeem the notes and we may also force the exercise of the warrants if our common stock trades above a specified price during a specific period of time. The convertible subordinated notes have a maximum leverage ratio which is significantly less restrictive than the senior bank credit facility covenant. And in the event we were to pay a cash dividend to common stockholders, the convertible subordinated notes would be included in the distribution as if converted. The fair value of the warrants of $1,276 was recorded as a discount on the notes and is being amortized over the term of the notes. As a result, the effective annual interest rate on the notes is 7.5 percent. We used the net proceeds of the offering to reduce the outstanding balances of our term and revolving loans under our senior bank credit facility. We agreed with the bank that up to $4 million of the repaid balance could be borrowed to fund the purchase of the Dave & Buster's complex in Toronto. See Note 12.

On October 29, 2003, we amended our senior bank credit facility. The current facility includes a $45 million revolving credit facility and a $15 million term debt facility. The revolving credit facility may be used for borrowings or letters of credit. At February 1, 2004, we had $5,780 letters of credit outstanding, leaving $28,703 available for additional borrowings or letters of credit. Borrowings under the revolving credit facility bear interest at a floating rate based on the bank's prime interest rate (4.00 percent at February 1, 2004) or the one-month EuroDollar (1.13 percent at February 1, 2004), plus in each case a margin based on financial performance. The interest rate on the revolving credit facility was 3.87 percent at February 1, 2004. Borrowings on the term debt facility bear interest at a floating rate based on the three month EuroDollar (1.13 percent at February 1, 2004), or at our option, the bank's prime interest rate (4.00 percent at February 1, 2004), plus in each case a margin based on financial performance. The interest rate on the term debt facility was 3.91 percent at February 1, 2004. The amended facility is secured by all assets of the Company. The amended facility has certain financial covenants including a consolidated tangible net worth, a maximum leverage ratio and a minimum fixed charge coverage ratio. Any outstanding borrowings under the revolving credit facility are due at maturity on April 29, 2008. Borrowings under the term debt facility are repayable in 17 consecutive quarterly payments of $833 with the final payment due on April 29, 2008. The fair market value of our long-term debt approximates its carrying value.

In 2001, we entered into an interest rate swap agreement that expires in 2007, to change a portion of our variable rate debt to fixed-rate debt. Pursuant to the swap agreement, the interest rate on notional amounts aggregating $40,633 at February 1, 2004 is fixed at 5.44 percent. The agreement has not been designated as a hedge and adjustments are recorded to mark the instrument to its fair market value through current operations. The fair market value adjustment at February 1, 2004 is $443, which is included in current liabilities. As a result of the swap agreement, we recorded additional interest expense of $1,863, $1,803 and $858 in 2003, 2002 and 2001, respectively.

The following table sets forth the Company's debt payment commitments (in thousands):

| | Total | Payments Due by Period | | | |
		1 Year or less	2-3 Years	4-5 Years	After 5 Years
Long-term debt	$53,534	$3,333	$6,666	$43,535	$ —

DAVE & BUSTER'S, INC.

NOTES TO CONSOLIDATED FINANCIAL STATEMENTS — (Continued)

Note 5: Income Taxes

The provision for income taxes is as follows (in thousands):

	Fiscal Year Ended		
	February 1, 2004	February 2, 2003	February 3, 2002
Current expense (benefit)			
Federal	$4,353	$(3,876)	$3,149
State and local	444	235	504
Deferred expense	864	6,396	646
Total provision for income taxes	$5,661	$ 2,755	$4,299

As a result of a change in the tax law in 2001, we amended our 2001 federal income tax return, which resulted in a refund of approximately $2,900. The refund was received in 2003.

Significant components of the deferred tax liabilities and assets in the consolidated balance sheets are as follows (in thousands):

	February 1, 2004	February 2, 2003
Deferred tax liabilities:		
Accelerated depreciation	$19,370	$15,482
Capitalized interest costs	1,883	1,750
Prepaid expenses	451	18
Smallware	355	3,313
Other	777	451
Total deferred tax liabilities	22,836	21,014
Deferred tax assets:		
Preopening costs	4,184	3,298
Leasing transactions	1,351	1,365
Worker's compensation	570	484
Total deferred tax assets	6,105	5,147
Net deferred tax liability	$16,731	$15,867

The reconciliation of the federal statutory rate to our effective income tax rate follows:

	Fiscal Year Ended		
	February 1, 2004	February 2, 2003	February 3, 2002
Federal corporate statutory rate	35.0%	35.0%	35.0%
State and local income taxes, net of federal income tax benefit	2.2%	6.7%	3.1%
Goodwill amortization and other nondeductible expenses	2.8%	6.0%	1.0%
FICA tip credits	(6.6)%	(15.7)%	(4.3)%
Other	0.6%	2.0%	1.4%
Effective tax rate	34.0%	34.0%	36.2%

DAVE & BUSTER'S, INC.

NOTES TO CONSOLIDATED FINANCIAL STATEMENTS — (Continued)

Note 6: Leases

We lease certain property and equipment under operating leases. Some of the leases include options for renewal or extension on various terms. Most leases require the Company to pay property taxes, insurance and maintenance of the leased assets. Certain leases also have provisions for additional percentage rentals based on revenues. For 2003, 2002 and 2001, rent expense for operating leases was $24,437, $23,828 and $19,469, respectively, including contingent rentals of $683, $624 and $1,448, respectively. At February 1, 2004, future minimum lease payments required under operating leases (including the sale/leaseback transactions described below) are (in thousands):

2004	2005	2006	2007	2008	Thereafter	Total
$26,196	$25,130	$24,706	$24,062	$23,896	$283,341	$407,331

During 2001, we completed the sale/leaseback of two complexes and our corporate headquarters. Cash proceeds of $18,474 were received along with twenty-year notes aggregating $5,150. The notes bear interest of 7 percent to 7.5 percent. These locations were sold to non-affiliated entities. In 2000, we entered into a sale/leaseback transaction with Cypress San Diego I, L.P. an affiliate of Cypress Equities, Inc. for our San Diego, California complex pursuant to which we received $6,300 in cash and a promissory note for $1,600. A director of the Company is the managing member of Cypress Equities, Inc. In October 2003, Cypress San Diego I, L.P. sold its interest in the San Diego property to a third party unrelated to the Company. Lease payments to Cypress Equities, Inc. in 2003, 2002 and 2001 were $667, $1,000 and $1,000, respectively. As of February 2, 2003, the balance due Cypress Equities, Inc. was $20,235 and no amounts were due at February 1, 2004. The sale/leaseback transactions resulted in a loss relating to one complex of $272, which was recognized in 2001, and a gain related to our corporate headquarters of $232,which is being amortized over the term of the operating lease.

Future aggregating lease obligations under the sale/leaseback agreements, which are classified as operating leases, are as follows (in thousands):

2004	2005	2006	2007	2008	Thereafter	Total
$4,002	$4,051	$4,183	$4,225	$4,267	$58,589	$79,317

At February 1, 2004 and February 2, 2003, the aggregate balance of the notes receivable due from the lessors under the sale/leaseback agreements was $6,407 and $6,551, respectively. Future minimum principal and interest payments due to us under these notes are as follows (in thousands):

2004	2005	2006	2007	2008	Thereafter	Total
$652	$652	$652	$652	$652	$8,281	$11,541

Note 7: Common Stock

Treasury Stock — During fiscal 1999, our Board of Directors approved a plan to repurchase up to 1,000 shares of the Company's common stock. Pursuant to the plan, as of February 1, 2004, we are authorized to purchase an additional 825 shares.

Stock-Based Compensation — In 1995, we adopted the Dave & Buster's, Inc. 1995 Stock Option Plan (the "Plan"), which as amended covers 2,950 shares of common stock. The Plan provides that incentive stock options may be granted at option prices not less than fair market value at date of grant (110 percent in the case of an incentive stock option granted to any person who owns more than 10 percent of the total combined voting power of all classes of stock of the Company). Non-qualified stock options may not be granted for less than 85 percent of the fair market value of the common stock at the time of grant and are primarily exercisable over a three to five year period from the date of the grant.

DAVE & BUSTER'S, INC.

NOTES TO CONSOLIDATED FINANCIAL STATEMENTS — (Continued)

In 1996, we adopted a stock option plan for outside directors (the "Directors' Plan"), for a total of 190 shares of common stock. The options granted under the Directors' Plan vest ratably over a three-year period.

In 2000, we amended and restated the Dave & Buster's, Inc. 1995 Stock Incentive Plan to allow the Company to grant restricted stock awards. Recipients are not required to provide consideration to the Company other than render service and have the right to vote the shares and to receive dividends. In 2003 and 2001, we issued, 23.5 and 63.5 shares of restricted stock with market values of $9.27-$10.70 and $6.45-$7.90, respectively. The restricted shares vest at the earlier of attaining certain performance targets or in 2007. The total market value of the restricted shares, as determined at the date of issuance, is treated as unearned compensation and is charged to expense over the vesting period. The charge to expense for the restricted stock compensation was $333, $226 and $139 in 2003, 2002 and 2001, respectively.

A summary of the Company's stock option activity and related information is as follows (in thousands except share data):

| | Fiscal Year Ended | | | | | |
| | February 1, 2004 | | February 2, 2003 | | February 3, 2002 | |
	Options	Exercise Price*	Options	Exercise Price*	Options	Exercise Price*
Outstanding — beginning of year.....	2,498	$11.79	2,785	$11.81	1,892	$14.69
Granted.........................	256	9.96	112	8.62	1,133	7.30
Exercised	(101)	6.95	(121)	7.20	(6)	6.80
Forfeited	(236)	14.30	(278)	12.76	(234)	13.16
Outstanding — end of year..........	2,417	11.55	2,498	11.79	2,785	11.81
Exercisable — end of year	1,592	13.13	1,411	14.25	1,134	15.55
Weighted-average fair value of options granted during the year...........		$ 5.05		$ 4.89		$ 3.40

* Weighted average exercise price

As of February 1, 2004, exercise prices for 2,417 options ranged from $5.59 to $8.38 for 1,115 options, $8.39 to $16.76 for 688 options and $16.77 to $27.94 for 614 options. The weighted-average remaining contractual life of the options is 6.1 years.

Under a Shareholder Protection Rights Plan adopted by the Company, each share of outstanding common stock includes a right which entitles the holder to purchase one one-hundredth of a share of Series A Junior Participating Preferred Stock for seventy five dollars. Rights attach to all new shares of commons stock whether newly issued or issued from treasury stock and become exercisable only under certain conditions involving actual or potential acquisitions of the Company's common stock. Depending on the circumstances, all holders except the acquiring person may be entitled to 1) acquire such number of shares of Company common stock as have a market value at the time of twice the exercise price of each right, or 2) exchange a right for one share of Company common stock or one one-hundredth of a share of the Series A Junior Participating Preferred Stock, or 3) receive shares of the acquiring company's common stock having a market value equal to twice the exercise price of each right. The rights remain in existence until ten years after the Distribution, unless they are redeemed (at one cent per right).

DAVE & BUSTER'S, INC.

NOTES TO CONSOLIDATED FINANCIAL STATEMENTS — (Continued)

Note 8:   Earnings Per Share

The following table sets forth the computation of basic and diluted earnings per share (in thousands except share data):

	Fiscal Year Ended		
	February 1, 2004	February 2, 2003	February 3, 2002
Numerator for basic earnings per common share — net income	$10,989	$(1,748)	$ 7,578
Impact of convertible debt interest and fees	662	—	—
Income applicable to common shareholders	$11,651	$(1,748)	$ 7,578
Denominator for basic earnings per common share — weighted average shares	13,128	12,997	12,956
Dilutive securities:			
Employee stock options	357	407	60
Convertible debt	1,161	—	—
Denominator for diluted earnings per common share — adjusted weighted average shares	14,646	13,404	13,016
Diluted earnings (loss) per common share before cumulative effect of accounting change	$ 0.80	$ 0.40	$ 0.58
Cumulative effect of a change in accounting principle	—	(0.53)	—
Diluted earnings (loss) per common share	$ 0.80	$ (0.13)	$ 0.58

In 2003, 2002 and 2001, options to purchase 870, 992 and 1,489 shares of common stock, respectively, were not included in the computation of diluted net income per share because the exercise price was greater than the market price and the effect would have been antidilutive.

Note 9:   Related Party Activity

In 2000, the Company entered into a sale/leaseback transaction with Cypress San Diego I, L.P. an affiliate of Cypress Equities, Inc. for its San Diego, California complex. A director of the Company is the managing member of Cypress Equities, Inc. See Note 6.

In addition, the Company from time to time has engaged Cypress Equities, Inc. or its affiliates to provide brokerage services in connection with the leasing of commercial property or with the sale and leaseback of properties formerly owned by the Company. The amount of broker's commissions paid to Cypress Equities for such services was $332 in 2001 (none in 2003 and 2002).

As of February 1, 2004, there were no loans to officers. At February 2, 2003 an officer owed the Company $100, under the terms of a personal loan, which was non-interest bearing and payable on demand. This loan was in existence prior to the prohibition on loans to executive officers enacted under Section 402 of the Sarbanes-Oxley Act of 2002 and was therefore exempt from such prohibition. The loan was paid in full in April 2003.

Note 10:   Employee Benefit Plan

The Company sponsors a plan to provide retirement benefits under the provision of Section 401(k) of the Internal Revenue Code (the "401(k) Plan") for all employees who have completed a specified term of service. Company contributions may range from 0 percent to 100 percent of employee contributions, up to a

DAVE & BUSTER'S, INC.

NOTES TO CONSOLIDATED FINANCIAL STATEMENTS — (Continued)

maximum of 6 percent of eligible employee compensation, as defined. Employees may elect to contribute up to 50 percent of their eligible compensation on a pretax basis. Benefits under the 401(k) Plan are limited to the assets of the 401(k) Plan.

Note 11:   Contingencies

The Company is subject to certain legal proceedings and claims that arise in the ordinary course of its business. In the opinion of management, the amount of ultimate liability with respect to all actions will not materially affect the consolidated results of operations or financial condition of the Company.

Note 12:   Acquisition of Toronto, Canada Complex

On October 6, 2003, we completed the purchase of the Dave & Buster's complex in Toronto, Canada from a party that operated the facility under a license agreement with us. The purchase price was $4,122, including $3,600 in cash plus the forgiveness of $523 in certain receivables due from the licensee. The purchase gave us the opportunity to expand our North American operations. The historical results of operations of the Toronto complex are not material to our consolidated results.

Assets acquired and liabilities assumed have been recorded at their estimated fair values as determined by management. The following table summarizes the allocation of the purchase price (in thousands):

Current assets	$ 517
Property and equipment	4,750
Current liabilities	(1,145)
Total acquisition price	$ 4,122

Note 13:   Quarterly Financial Information (unaudited)

	Fiscal Year 2003 — Ended February 1, 2004			
	First	Second	Third	Fourth
	(in thousands, except per share amounts)			
Total revenues	$91,587	$88,309	$82,882	$100,044
Income (loss) before provision for income taxes	4,619	2,218	(773)	10,586
Net income (loss)	3,049	1,464	(510)	6,986
Basic net income (loss) per share	$ .23	$ .11	$ (.04)	$ .54
Basic weighted average shares outstanding	13,090	13,116	13,144	13,161
Diluted net income per share	$ .23	$ .11	$ (.04)	$ .46
Diluted weighted average shares outstanding	13,283	13,458	13,144	15,944

DAVE & BUSTER'S, INC.

NOTES TO CONSOLIDATED FINANCIAL STATEMENTS — (Continued)

	Fiscal Year 2002 — Ended February 2, 2003			
	First	Second	Third	Fourth
	(in thousands, except per share amounts)			
Total revenues	$97,242	$92,150	$84,550	$ 99,810
Income (loss) before provision for income taxes and cumulative effect of a change in an accounting principle(2)	4,592	1,451	(2,759)	4,820
Income (loss) before cumulative effect of a change in an accounting principle	· 2,916	921	(1,670)	3,181
Cumulative effect of a change in an accounting principle	7,096	—	—	—
Net income (loss)(1)	(4,180)	921	(1,670)	3,181
Basic income (loss) per share before cumulative effect of a change in an accounting principle	$ .22	$ .07	$ (.13)	$ .25
Basic net (loss) from cumulative effect of a change in an accounting principle	$ (.55)	—	—	—
Basic net income (loss)	$ (.32)	$ .07	$ (.13)	$ .25
Basic weighted average shares outstanding	12,971	12,986	13,003	13,029
Diluted income (loss) per share before cumulative effect of a change in an accounting principle	$ .22	$ .07	$ (.13)	$ .24
Diluted net (loss) from cumulative effect of a change in an accounting principle	$ (.53)	—	—	—
Diluted net income (loss)	$ (.31)	$ .07	$ (.13)	$ .24
Diluted weighted average shares outstanding	13,307	13,435	13,460	13,219

(1) In the first quarter of 2002, the Company adopted SFAS No. 142, which resulted in a charge of $7,096, to write off all of our recorded goodwill. The charge is presented as the cumulative effect of a change in accounting principle.

(2) In the second quarter of 2002, as part of general and administrative expenses, the Company incurred $1,200 of transaction costs related to a proposed merger agreement with D&B Holdings and D&B Acquisition Sub.

REPORT OF INDEPENDENT AUDITORS

Stockholders and Board of Directors
Dave & Buster's, Inc.

We have audited the accompanying consolidated balance sheets of Dave & Buster's, Inc. as of February 1, 2004 and February 2, 2002, and the related consolidated statements of operations, stockholders' equity and cash flows for each of the three fiscal years in the period ended February 1, 2004. These financial statements are the responsibility of the company's management. Our responsibility is to express an opinion on these financial statements based on our audits.

We conducted our audits in accordance with auditing standards generally accepted in the United States. Those standards require that we plan and perform the audit to obtain reasonable assurance about whether the financial statements are free of material misstatement. An audit includes examining, on a test basis, evidence supporting the amounts and disclosures in the financial statements. An audit also includes assessing the accounting principles used and significant estimates made by management, as well as evaluating the overall financial statement presentation. We believe that our audits provide a reasonable basis for our opinion.

In our opinion, the financial statements referred to above present fairly, in all material respects, the consolidated financial position of Dave & Buster's, Inc. at February 1, 2004 and February 2, 2003 and the consolidated results of its operations and its cash flows for each of the three fiscal years in the period ended February 1, 2004, in conformity with accounting principles generally accepted in the United States.

As discussed in Note 1 to the consolidated financial statements, effective January 1, 2002, the Company adopted Statement of Financial Accounting Standards No. 142, *Goodwill and Other Intangible Assets.*

ERNST & YOUNG LLP

Dallas, Texas
March 31, 2004

Present and Future Value Concepts

The concepts of present value (PV) and future value (FV) are based on the time value of money. The **time value of money** is the idea that, quite simply, money received today is worth more than money to be received one year from today (or at any other future date), because it can be used to earn interest. If you invest $1,000 today at 10 percent, you will have $1,100 in one year. So $1,000 in one year is worth $100 less than $1,000 today because you lose the opportunity to earn the $100 in interest.

In some business situations, you will know the dollar amount of a cash flow that occurs in the future and will need to determine its value now. This type of situation is known as a **present value** problem. The opposite situation occurs when you know the dollar amount of a cash flow that occurs today and need to determine its value at some point in the future. These situations are called **future value** problems. The value of money changes over time because money can earn interest. The following table illustrates the basic difference between present value and future value problems:

	Now	*Future*
Present value	?	$1,000
Future value	$1,000	?

Present and future value problems may involve two types of cash flow: a single payment or an annuity (which is the fancy word for a series of equal cash payments). Thus, you need to learn how to deal with four different situations related to the time value of money:

1. Future value of a single payment
2. Present value of a single payment
3. Future value of an annuity
4. Present value of an annuity

Most inexpensive handheld calculators and any spreadsheet program can perform the detailed arithmetic computations required to solve future value and present value problems. In later courses and in all business situations, you will probably use a calculator or computer to solve these problems. At this stage, we encourage you to solve problems using Tables C.1 through C.4 at the end of this appendix. We believe that using the tables will give you a better understanding of how and why present and future value concepts apply to business problems. The tables give the value of a $1 cash flow (single payment or annuity) for different periods (n) and at different interest rates (i). If a problem involves payments other than $1, it is necessary to multiply the value from the table by the amount of the payment.[1]

---

[1]Present value and future value problems involve cash flows. The basic concepts are the same for cash inflows (receipts) and cash outflows (payments). No fundamental differences exist between present value and future value calculations for cash payments versus cash receipts.

COMPUTING

FUTURE AND PRESENT VALUES OF A SINGLE AMOUNT

Future Value of a Single Amount

In future value of a single amount problems, you will be asked to calculate how much money you will have in the future as the result of investing a certain amount in the present. If you were to receive a gift of $10,000, for instance, you might decide to put it in a savings account and use the money as a down payment on a house after you graduate. The future value computation would tell you how much money will be available when you graduate.

To solve a future value problem, you need to know three items:

1. Amount to be invested.
2. Interest rate (i) the amount will earn.
3. Number of periods (n) in which the amount will earn interest.

The future value concept is based on compound interest, which simply means that interest is calculated on top of interest. Thus, the amount of interest for each period is calculated using the principal plus any interest not paid out in prior periods. Graphically, the calculation of the future value of $1 for three periods at an interest rate of 10 percent may be represented as follows:

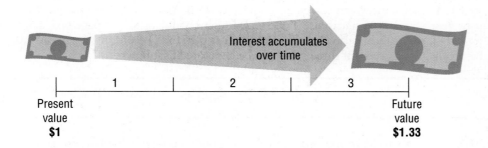

Interest accumulates over time

| | 1 | | 2 | | 3 | |

Present value **$1**

Future value **$1.33**

Assume that on January 1, 2006, you deposit $1,000 in a savings account at 10 percent annual interest, compounded annually. At the end of three years, the $1,000 will have increased to $1,331 as follows:

Year	Amount at Start of Year	+	Interest During the Year	=	Amount at End of Year
1	$1,000	+	$1,000 × 10% = $100	=	$1,100
2	1,100	+	1,100 × 10% = 110	=	1,210
3	1,210	+	1,210 × 10% = 121	=	1,331

We can avoid the detailed arithmetic by referring to Table C.1, Future Value of $1, on page 668. For $i = 10\%$, $n = 3$, we find the value 1.3310. We then compute the balance at the end of year 3 as follows:

> From Table C.1,
> Interest rate = 10%
> $n = 3$

$$\$1,000 \times 1.3310 = \$1,331$$

Note that the increase of $331 is due to the time value of money. It is interest revenue to the owner of the savings account and interest expense to the bank.

Present Value of a Single Amount

The present value of a single amount is the worth to you today of receiving that amount some time in the future. For instance, you might be offered an opportunity to invest in a financial instrument that would pay you $10,000 in 10 years. Before you decided whether to invest, you would want to determine the present value of the instrument.

To compute the present value of an amount to be received in the future, we must discount (a procedure that is the opposite of compounding) at i interest rate for n periods. In discounting, the interest is subtracted rather than added, as it is in compounding. Graphically, the present value of $1 due at the end of the third period with an interest rate of 10 percent can be represented as follows:

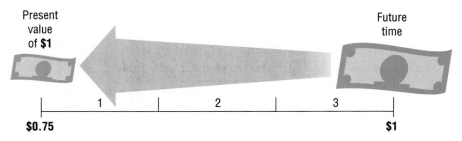

Assume that today is January 1, 2006, and you have the opportunity to receive $1,000 cash on December 31, 2008. At an interest rate of 10 percent per year, how much is the $1,000 payment worth to you on January 1, 2006? You could discount the amount year by year,[2] but it is easier to use Table C.2, Present Value of $1, on page 669. For $i = 10\%$, $n = 3$, we find that the present value of $1 is 0.7513. The present value of $1,000 to be received at the end of three years can be computed as follows:

> From Table C.2,
> Interest rate = 10%
> $n = 3$

$$\$1{,}000 \times 0.7513 = \$751.30$$

It's important to learn not only how to compute a present value but also to understand what it means. The $751.30 is the amount you would pay now to have the right to receive $1,000 at the end of three years, assuming an interest rate of 10 percent. Conceptually, you should be indifferent between having $751.30 today and receiving $1,000 in three years. If you had $751.30 today but preferred $1,000 in three years, you could simply deposit the money in a savings account that pays 10% interest and it would grow to $1,000 in three years. Alternatively, if you had a contract that promised you $1,000 in three years, you could sell it to an investor for $751.30 in cash today because it would permit the investor to earn the difference in interest.

What if you could only earn 6 percent during the three-year period from January 1, 2006, to December 31, 2008? What would be the present value on January 1, 2006, of receiving $1,000 on December 31, 2008? To answer this we would take the same approach, using Table C.2, except that the interest rate would change to $i = 6\%$. Referring to Table C.2, we see the present value factor for $i = 6\%$, $n = 3$, is 0.8396. Thus, the present value of $1,000 to be received at the end of three years, assuming a 6 percent interest rate, would be computed as $1,000 × 0.8396 = $839.60. Notice that when we assume a 6 percent interest rate the present value is greater than when we assumed a 10 percent interest rate

---

[2]The detailed discounting is as follows:

Periods	Interest for the Year	Present Value*
1	$1,000 − ($1,000 × 1/1.10) = $90.91	$1,000 − $90.91 = $909.09
2	$909.09 − ($909.09 × 1/1.10) = $82.65	$909.09 − $82.65 = $826.44
3	$826.44 − ($826.44 × 1/1.10) = $75.14[†]	$826.44 − $75.14 = $751.30

*Verifiable in Table C.2.

[†]Adjusted for rounding.

above. The reason for this difference is that, to reach $1,000 three years from now, you'd need to deposit more money in a savings account now if it earns 6 percent interest than if it earns 10 percent interest.

HOW'S IT GOING? A Self-Study Quiz

1. If the interest rate in a present value problem increases from 8 percent to 10 percent, will the present value increase or decrease?

2. What is the present value of $10,000 to be received 10 years from now if the interest rate is 5 percent, compounded annually?

3. If $10,000 is deposited in a savings account that earns 5 percent interest compounded annually, how much will it be worth 10 years from now?

After you're done, check your answers with the solution in the margin.

COMPUTING

FUTURE AND PRESENT VALUES OF AN ANNUITY

Instead of a single payment, many business problems involve multiple cash payments over a number of periods. An **annuity** is a series of consecutive payments characterized by

1. An equal dollar amount each interest period.
2. Interest periods of equal length (year, half a year, quarter, or month).
3. An equal interest rate each interest period.

Examples of annuities include monthly payments on a car or house, yearly contributions to a savings account, and monthly pension benefits.

Future Value of an Annuity

If you are saving money for some purpose, such as a new car or a trip to Europe, you might decide to deposit a fixed amount of money in a savings account each month. The future value of an annuity computation will tell you how much money will be in your savings account at some point in the future.

The future value of an annuity includes compound interest on each payment from the date of payment to the end of the term of the annuity. Each new payment accumulates less interest than prior payments, only because the number of periods remaining in which to accumulate interest decreases. The future value of an annuity of $1 for three periods at 10 percent may be represented graphically as

YOU SHOULD KNOW

An **annuity** is a series of periodic cash receipts or payments that are equal in amount each interest period.

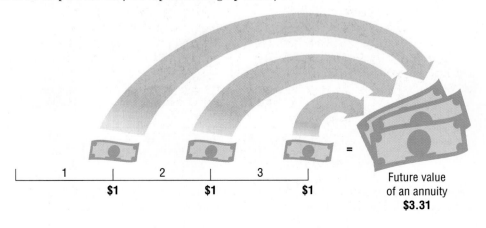

Future value
of an annuity
$3.31

Assume that each year for three years, you deposit $1,000 cash in a savings account at 10 percent interest per year. You make the first $1,000 deposit on December 31, 2006, the second one on December 31, 2007, and the third and last one on December 31, 2008. The first $1,000 deposit earns compound interest for two years (for a total principal and interest of $1,210); the second deposit earns interest for one year (for a total principal and interest of $1,100). The third deposit earns no interest because it was made on the day that the balance is computed. Thus, the total amount in the savings account at the end of three years is $3,310 ($1,210 + $1,100 + $1,000).

To calculate the future value of this annuity, we could compute the interest on each deposit, similar to what's described above. However, a faster way is to refer to Table C.3, Future Value of an Annuity of $1 for $i = 10\%$, $n = 3$ to find the value 3.3100. The future value of your three deposits of $1,000 each can be computed as follows:

From Table C.3,
Interest rate = 10%
$n = 3$

$$\$1,000 \times 3.3100 = \$3,310$$

The Power of Compounding

Compound interest is a remarkably powerful economic force. In fact, the ability to earn interest on interest is the key to building economic wealth. If you save $1,000 per year for the first 10 years of your career, you will have more money when you retire than you would if you had saved $15,000 per year for the last 10 years of your career. This surprising outcome occurs because the money you save early in your career will earn more interest than the money you save at the end of your career. If you start saving money now, the majority of your wealth will not be the money you saved but the interest your money was able to earn.

The chart in the margin illustrates the power of compounding over a brief 10-year period. If you deposit $1 each year in an account earning 10 percent interest, at the end of just 10 years, only 63 percent of your balance will be made up of money you have saved. The rest will be interest you have earned. After 20 years, only 35 percent of your balance will be from saved money. The lesson associated with compound interest is that even though saving money is hard, you should start now.

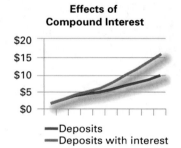

Effects of Compound Interest

— Deposits
— Deposits with interest

Present Value of an Annuity

The present value of an annuity is the value now of a series of equal amounts to be received (or paid out) for some specified number of periods in the future. It is computed by discounting each of the equal periodic amounts. A good example of this type of problem is a retirement program that offers employees a monthly income after retirement. The present value of an annuity of $1 for three periods at 10 percent may be represented graphically as

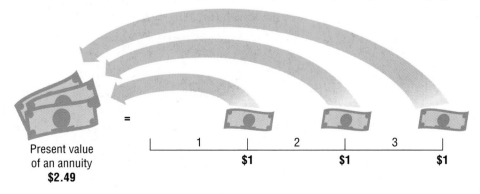

Present value
of an annuity
$2.49

Assume you are to receive $1,000 cash on each December 31, 2006, 2007, and 2008. How much would the sum of these three $1,000 future amounts be worth on January 1,

2006, assuming an interest rate of 10 percent per year? One way to determine this is to use Table C.2 to calculate the present value of each single amount as follows:

Year	Amount		Factor from Table C.2, $i = 10\%$		Present Value
1	$1,000	×	0.9091 ($n = 1$)	=	$ 909.10
2	1,000	×	0.8264 ($n = 2$)	=	826.40
3	1,000	×	0.7513 ($n = 3$)	=	751.30
			Total present value	=	$2,486.80

Alternatively, we can compute the present value of this annuity more easily by using Table C.4, as follows:

$$\$1,000 \times 2.4869 = \$2,487 \text{ (rounded)}$$

From Table C.4,
Interest rate = 10%
$n = 3$

Interest Rates and Interest Periods

The preceding illustrations assumed annual periods for compounding and discounting. Although interest rates are almost always quoted on an annual basis, many compounding periods encountered in business are less than one year. When interest periods are less than a year, the values of n and i must be restated to be consistent with the length of the interest period.

To illustrate, 12 percent interest compounded annually for five years requires the use of $n = 5$ and $i = 12\%$. If compounding is quarterly, however, the interest period is one quarter of a year (four periods per year), and the quarterly interest rate is one quarter of the annual rate (3 percent per quarter). Therefore, 12 percent interest compounded quarterly for five years requires use of $n = 20$ and $i = 3\%$.

COACH'S CORNER

The help function in Excel describes how to calculate the present value of an annuity using its PV worksheet function.

ACCOUNTING
APPLICATIONS OF PRESENT VALUES

Many business transactions require the use of future and present value concepts. In finance classes, you will see how to apply future value concepts. In this section, we apply present value concepts to three common accounting cases.

Case A—Present Value of a Single Amount

On January 1, 2006, General Mills bought some new delivery trucks. The company signed a note and agreed to pay $200,000 on December 31, 2007, an amount representing the cash equivalent price of the trucks plus interest for two years. The market interest rate for this note was 12 percent.

1. How should the accountant record the purchase?

Answer: This case requires the computation of the present value of a single amount. In conformity with the cost principle, the cost of the trucks is their current cash equivalent price, which is the present value of the future payment. The problem can be shown graphically as follows:

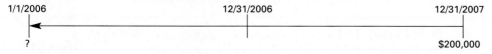

The present value of the $200,000 is computed as follows:

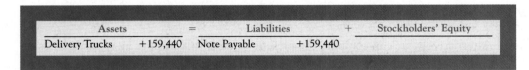

$$\$200,000 \times 0.7972 = \$159,440$$

From Table C.2,
Interest rate = 12%
$n = 2$

Therefore, the journal entry to record the purchase of the trucks is:

dr	**Delivery Trucks (+A)**.....................	**159,440**	
	cr **Note Payable (+L)**		**159,440**

Assets	=	Liabilities	+	Stockholders' Equity
Delivery Trucks	+159,440	Note Payable	+159,440	

2. What journal entry should be made at the end of 2006 and 2007 to record interest expense?

Answer: Each year's interest expense is recorded in an adjusting entry as follows:

FAST FLASHBACK

The interest formula is
$I = P \times R \times T$ where
I = interest
P = principal
R = rate of interest
T = time period

December 31, 2006

dr	**Interest Expense (+E, −SE)**	**19,132***	
	cr **Note Payable (+L)**		**19,132**

*$159,440 \times 12\% \times 12/12 = \$19,132$ (rounded).

Assets	=	Liabilities	+	Stockholders' Equity
		Note Payable	+19,132	Interest expense (+E) −19,132

December 31, 2007

dr	**Interest Expense (+E, −SE)**	**21,428***	
	cr **Note Payable (+L)**		**21,428**

*($159,440 + \$19,132) \times 12\% \times 12/12 = 21,428$ (rounded).

Assets	=	Liabilities	+	Stockholders' Equity
		Note Payable	+21,428	Interest Expense (+E) −21,428

3. What journal entry should be made on December 31, 2007, to record payment of the debt?

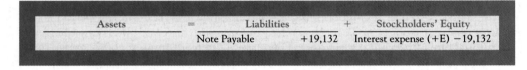

Note Payable (L)	
	159,440 Jan. 1, 2006
	19,132 Interest 2006
	21,428 Interest 2007
	200,000 Dec. 31, 2007

Answer: At this date the amount to be paid is the balance in *Note Payable*, after it has been updated for interest pertaining to 2007, as shown in the T-account in the margin. Notice that, just prior to its repayment, the balance for the note on December 31, 2007 is the same as the maturity amount on the due date.

The journal entry to record full payment of the debt follows:

dr	**Note Payable (−L)**	**200,000**	
	cr **Cash (−A)**		**200,000**

	Assets		=	Liabilities		+	Stockholders' Equity
Cash		−200,000		Note Payable	−200,000		

Case B—Present Value of an Annuity

On January 1, 2006, General Mills bought new milling equipment. The company elected to finance the purchase with a note payable to be paid off in three years in annual installments of $163,686. Each installment includes principal plus interest on the unpaid balance at 11 percent per year. The annual installments are due on December 31, 2006, 2007, and 2008. This problem can be shown graphically as follows:

1/1/2006	12/31/2006	12/31/2007	12/31/2008
?	$163,686	$163,686	$163,686

1. What is the amount of the note?

Answer: The note is the present value of each installment payment, $i = 11\%$ and $n = 3$. This is an annuity because the note repayment is made in three equal installments. The amount of the note is computed as follows:

> From Table C.4,
> Interest rate = 11%
> $n = 3$

$$\$163{,}686 \times 2.4437 = \$400{,}000$$

The acquisition on January 1, 2006, is recorded as follows:

dr	**Milling Equipment (+A)**	400,000	
	cr **Note Payable (+L)**		400,000

	Assets		=	Liabilities		+	Stockholders' Equity
Milling Equipment		+400,000		Note Payable	+400,000		

2. What journal entries should be made at the end of each year to record the payments on this note?

Answer:

December 31, 2006

dr	**Interest Expense (+E, −SE)**		
	($400,000 × 11% × 12/12)	44,000	
dr	**Note Payable (−L)** ($163,686 − $44,000)	119,686	
	cr **Cash (−A)**		163,686

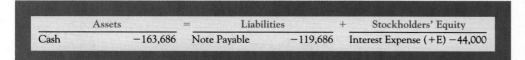

	Assets		=	Liabilities		+	Stockholders' Equity
Cash		−163,686		Note Payable	−119,686		Interest Expense (+E) −44,000

December 31, 2007

dr	Interest Expense (+E, −SE)	30,835*
dr	Note Payable (−L) ($163,686 − $30,835)....	132,851
	cr Cash (−A)		163,686

*Interest: [($400,000 − $119,686) × 11% × 12/12 = $30,835].

Assets	=	Liabilities	+	Stockholders' Equity
Cash −163,686		Note Payable −132,851		Interest Expense (+E) −30,835

Note Payable (L)

	400,000	Jan 1, 2006
Dec. 31, 2006 119,686		
Dec. 31, 2007 132,851		
Dec. 31, 2008 147,463		
	0	Dec. 31, 2008

December 31, 2008

dr	Interest Expense (+E, −SE)	16,223*
dr	Note Payable (−L) ($163,686 − $16,223)....	147,463
	cr Cash (−A)		163,686

*Interest: [($400,000 − $119,686 − $132,851) × 11% × 12/12 = $16,223 (adjusted to accommodate rounding errors)].

Assets	=	Liabilities	+	Stockholders' Equity
Cash −163,686		Note Payable −147,463		Interest Expense (+E) −16,223

Case C—Present Value of a Single Amount and an Annuity

On January 1, 2006, General Mills issued a four-year, $100,000 bond. The bond pays interest annually at a rate of 6 percent of face value. What would investors be willing to pay for the bond if they require an annual return of (a) 4 percent, (b) 6 percent, or (c) 8 percent?

Answer: This case requires the computation of the present value of a single amount (for the $100,000 face value paid at maturity) plus the present value of an annuity (for annual interest payments of $6,000). The problem can be shown graphically as follows:

COACH'S CORNER

Each interest payment of $6,000 is calculated as:

$100,000 × 6% × 12/12.

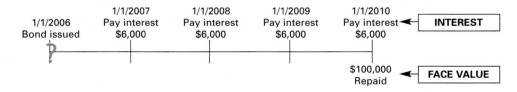

a. **4 Percent Market Interest Rate**

From Table C.2, Interest rate = 4% n = 4

The present value of the $100,000 face value is computed as follows:

$100,000 × 0.8548 = $85,480

From Table C.4, Interest rate = 4% n = 4

The present value of the $6,000 annuity is computed as follows:

$6,000 × 3.6299 = $21,780*

*Adjusted to accommodate rounding in the present value factor.

The present value of the total bond payments, computed using the discount rate of 4%, is

$107,260 (= $85,480 + $21,780)

b. 6 Percent Market Interest Rate

The present value of the $100,000 face value is computed as follows:

$100,000 × 0.7921 = $79,210

From Table C.2,
Interest rate = 6%
$n = 4$

The present value of the $6,000 annuity is computed as follows:

$6,000 × 3.4651 = $20,790*

From Table C.4,
Interest rate = 6%
$n = 4$

*Adjusted to accommodate rounding in the present value factor.

The present value of the total bond payments, computed using the discount rate of 6%, is

$100,000 (= $79,210 + $20,790)

c. 8 Percent Market Interest Rate

The present value of the $100,000 face value is computed as follows:

$100,000 × 0.7350 = $73,500

From Table C.2,
Interest rate = 8%
$n = 4$

The present value of the $6,000 annuity is computed as follows:

$6,000 × 3.3121 = $19,876*

From Table C.4,
Interest rate = 8%
$n = 4$

*Adjusted to accommodate rounding in the present value factor.

The present value of the total bond payments, computed using the discount rate of 8%, is

$93,376 (= $73,500 + $19,876)

COACH'S CORNER

The present values in *a*, *b*, and *c* demonstrate the calculation of the bond issue prices used in Chapter 10.

Of course, these calculations are just the starting point for understanding how bond liabilities are determined and reported. Chapter 10 describes the journal entries that would be used to enter this information into the accounting system.

TABLE C.1

Future Value of $1

Periods	2%	3%	3.75%	4%	4.25%	5%	6%	7%	8%
0	1.	1.	1.	1.	1.	1.	1.	1.	1.
1	1.02	1.03	1.0375	1.04	1.0425	1.05	1.06	1.07	1.08
2	1.0404	1.0609	1.0764	1.0816	1.0868	1.1025	1.1236	1.1449	1.1664
3	1.0612	1.0927	1.1168	1.1249	1.1330	1.1576	1.1910	1.2250	1.2597
4	1.0824	1.1255	1.1587	1.1699	1.1811	1.2155	1.2625	1.3108	1.3605
5	1.1041	1.1593	1.2021	1.2167	1.2313	1.2763	1.3382	1.4026	1.4693
6	1.1262	1.1941	1.2472	1.2653	1.2837	1.3401	1.4185	1.5007	1.5869
7	1.1487	1.2299	1.2939	1.3159	1.3382	1.4071	1.5036	1.6058	1.7138
8	1.1717	1.2668	1.3425	1.3686	1.3951	1.4775	1.5938	1.7182	1.8509
9	1.1951	1.3048	1.3928	1.4233	1.4544	1.5513	1.6895	1.8385	1.9990
10	1.2190	1.3439	1.4450	1.4802	1.5162	1.6289	1.7908	1.9672	2.1589
20	1.4859	1.8061	2.0882	2.1911	2.2989	2.6533	3.2071	3.8697	4.6610

Periods	9%	10%	11%	12%	13%	14%	15%	20%	25%
0	1.	1.	1.	1.	1.	1.	1.	1.	1.
1	1.09	1.10	1.11	1.12	1.13	1.14	1.15	1.20	1.25
2	1.1881	1.2100	1.2321	1.2544	1.2769	1.2996	1.3225	1.4400	1.5625
3	1.2950	1.3310	1.3676	1.4049	1.4429	1.4815	1.5209	1.7280	1.9531
4	1.4116	1.4641	1.5181	1.5735	1.6305	1.6890	1.7490	2.0736	2.4414
5	1.5386	1.6105	1.6851	1.7623	1.8424	1.9254	2.0114	2.4883	3.0518
6	1.6771	1.7716	1.8704	1.9738	2.0820	2.1950	2.3131	2.9860	3.8147
7	1.8280	1.9487	2.0762	2.2107	2.3526	2.5023	2.6600	3.5832	4.7684
8	1.9926	2.1436	2.3045	2.4760	2.6584	2.8526	3.0590	4.2998	5.9605
9	2.1719	2.3579	2.5580	2.7731	3.0040	3.2519	3.5179	5.1598	7.4506
10	2.3674	2.5937	2.8394	3.1058	3.3946	3.7072	4.0456	6.1917	9.3132
20	5.6044	6.7275	8.0623	9.6463	11.5231	13.7435	16.3665	38.3376	86.7362

TABLE C.2
Present Value of $1

Periods	2%	3%	3.75%	4%	4.25%	5%	6%	7%	8%
1	0.9804	0.9709	0.9639	0.9615	0.9592	0.9524	0.9434	0.9346	0.9259
2	0.9612	0.9426	0.9290	0.9246	0.9201	0.9070	0.8900	0.8734	0.8573
3	0.9423	0.9151	0.8954	0.8890	0.8826	0.8638	0.8396	0.8163	0.7938
4	0.9238	0.8885	0.8631	0.8548	0.8466	0.8227	0.7921	0.7629	0.7350
5	0.9057	0.8626	0.8319	0.8219	0.8121	0.7835	0.7473	0.7130	0.6806
6	0.8880	0.8375	0.8018	0.7903	0.7790	0.7462	0.7050	0.6663	0.6302
7	0.8706	0.8131	0.7728	0.7599	0.7473	0.7107	0.6651	0.6227	0.5835
8	0.8535	0.7894	0.7449	0.7307	0.7168	0.6768	0.6274	0.5820	0.5403
9	0.8368	0.7664	0.7180	0.7026	0.6876	0.6446	0.5919	0.5439	0.5002
10	0.8203	0.7441	0.6920	0.6756	0.6595	0.6139	0.5584	0.5083	0.4632
20	0.6730	0.5537	0.4789	0.4564	0.4350	0.3769	0.3118	0.2584	0.2145

Periods	9%	10%	11%	12%	13%	14%	15%	20%	25%
1	0.9174	0.9091	0.9009	0.8929	0.8850	0.8772	0.8696	0.8333	0.8000
2	0.8417	0.8264	0.8116	0.7972	0.7831	0.7695	0.7561	0.6944	0.6400
3	0.7722	0.7513	0.7312	0.7118	0.6931	0.6750	0.6575	0.5787	0.5120
4	0.7084	0.6830	0.6587	0.6355	0.6133	0.5921	0.5718	0.4823	0.4096
5	0.6499	0.6209	0.5935	0.5674	0.5428	0.5194	0.4972	0.4019	0.3277
6	0.5963	0.5645	0.5346	0.5066	0.4803	0.4556	0.4323	0.3349	0.2621
7	0.5470	0.5132	0.4817	0.4523	0.4251	0.3996	0.3759	0.2791	0.2097
8	0.5019	0.4665	0.4339	0.4039	0.3762	0.3506	0.3269	0.2326	0.1678
9	0.4604	0.4241	0.3909	0.3606	0.3329	0.3075	0.2843	0.1938	0.1342
10	0.4224	0.3855	0.3522	0.3220	0.2946	0.2697	0.2472	0.1615	0.1074
20	0.1784	0.1486	0.1240	0.1037	0.0868	0.0728	0.0611	0.0261	0.0115

TABLE C.3

Future Value of Annuity of $1

Periods*	2%	3%	3.75%	4%	4.25%	5%	6%	7%	8%
1	1.	1.	1.	1.	1.	1.	1.	1.	1.
2	2.02	2.03	2.0375	2.04	2.0425	2.05	2.06	2.07	2.08
3	3.0604	3.0909	3.1139	3.1216	3.1293	3.1525	3.1836	3.2149	3.2464
4	4.1216	4.1836	4.2307	4.2465	4.2623	4.3101	4.3746	4.4399	4.5061
5	5.2040	5.3091	5.3893	5.4163	5.4434	5.5256	5.6371	5.7507	5.8666
6	6.3081	6.4684	6.5914	6.6330	6.6748	6.8019	6.9753	7.1533	7.3359
7	7.4343	7.6625	7.8386	7.8983	7.9585	8.1420	8.3938	8.6540	8.9228
8	8.5830	8.8923	9.1326	9.2142	9.2967	9.5491	9.8975	10.2598	10.6366
9	9.7546	10.1591	10.4750	10.5828	10.6918	11.0266	11.4913	11.9780	12.4876
10	10.9497	11.4639	11.8678	12.0061	12.1462	12.5779	13.1808	13.8164	14.4866
20	24.2974	26.8704	29.0174	29.7781	30.5625	33.0660	36.7856	40.9955	45.7620

Periods*	9%	10%	11%	12%	13%	14%	15%	20%	25%
1	1.	1.	1.	1.	1.	1.	1.	1.	1.
2	2.09	2.10	2.11	2.12	2.13	2.14	2.15	2.20	2.25
3	3.2781	3.3100	3.3421	3.3744	3.4069	3.4396	3.4725	3.6400	3.8125
4	4.5731	4.6410	4.7097	4.7793	4.8498	4.9211	4.9934	5.3680	5.7656
5	5.9847	6.1051	6.2278	6.3528	6.4803	6.6101	6.7424	7.4416	8.2070
6	7.5233	7.7156	7.9129	8.1152	8.3227	8.5355	8.7537	9.9299	11.2588
7	9.2004	9.4872	9.7833	10.0890	10.4047	10.7305	11.0668	12.9159	15.0735
8	11.0285	11.4359	11.8594	12.2997	12.7573	13.2328	13.7268	16.4991	19.8419
9	13.0210	13.5975	14.1640	14.7757	15.4157	16.0853	16.7858	20.7989	25.8023
10	15.1929	15.9374	16.7220	17.5487	18.4197	19.3373	20.3037	25.9587	33.2529
20	51.1601	57.2750	64.2028	72.0524	80.9468	91.0249	102.4436	186.6880	342.9447

*There is one payment each period.

TABLE C.4

Present Value of Annuity of $1

Periods*	2%	3%	3.75%	4%	4.25%	5%	6%	7%	8%
1	0.9804	0.9709	0.9639	0.9615	0.9592	0.9524	0.9434	0.9346	0.9259
2	1.9416	1.9135	1.8929	1.8861	1.8794	1.8594	1.8334	1.8080	1.7833
3	2.8839	2.8286	2.7883	2.7751	2.7620	2.7232	2.6730	2.6243	2.5771
4	3.8077	3.7171	3.6514	3.6299	3.6086	3.5460	3.4651	3.3872	3.3121
5	4.7135	4.5797	4.4833	4.4518	4.4207	4.3295	4.2124	4.1002	3.9927
6	5.6014	5.4172	5.2851	5.2421	5.1997	5.0757	4.9173	4.7665	4.6229
7	6.4720	6.2303	6.0579	6.0021	5.9470	5.7864	5.5824	5.3893	5.2064
8	7.3255	7.0197	6.8028	6.7327	6.6638	6.4632	6.2098	5.9713	5.7466
9	8.1622	7.7861	7.5208	7.4353	7.3513	7.1078	6.8017	6.5152	6.2469
10	8.9826	8.5302	8.2128	8.1109	8.0109	7.7217	7.3601	7.0236	6.7101
20	16.3514	14.8775	13.8962	13.5903	13.2944	12.4622	11.4699	10.5940	9.8181

Periods*	9%	10%	11%	12%	13%	14%	15%	20%	25%
1	0.9174	0.9091	0.9009	0.8929	0.8550	0.8772	0.8696	0.8333	0.8000
2	1.7591	1.7355	1.7125	1.6901	1.6681	1.6467	1.6257	1.5278	1.4400
3	2.5313	2.4869	2.4437	2.4018	2.3612	2.3216	2.2832	2.1065	1.9520
4	3.2397	3.1699	3.1024	3.0373	2.9745	2.9137	2.8550	2.5887	2.3616
5	3.8897	3.7908	3.6959	3.6048	3.5172	3.4331	3.3522	2.9906	2.6893
6	4.4859	4.3553	4.2305	4.1114	3.9975	3.8887	3.7845	3.3255	2.9514
7	5.0330	4.8684	4.7122	4.5638	4.4226	4.2883	4.1604	3.6046	3.1611
8	5.5348	5.3349	5.1461	4.9676	4.7988	4.6389	4.4873	3.8372	3.3289
9	5.9952	5.7590	5.5370	5.3282	4.1317	4.9464	4.7716	4.0310	3.4631
10	6.4177	6.1446	5.8892	5.6502	5.4262	5.2161	5.0188	4.1925	3.5705
20	9.1285	8.5136	7.9633	7.4694	7.0248	6.6231	6.2593	4.8696	3.9539

*There is one payment each period.

FOR YOUR REVIEW

KEY TERMS TO KNOW

Annuity p. 661   **Present Value** p. 658   **Time Value of Money** p. 658
Future Value p. 658

FOR YOUR PRACTICE

QUESTIONS

1. Explain the concept of the time value of money.
2. Explain the basic difference between future value and present value.
3. If you deposited $10,000 in a savings account that earns 10 percent, how much would you have at the end of 10 years? Use a convenient format to display your computations.
4. If you hold a valid contract that will pay you $8,000 cash 10 years from now and the going rate of interest is 10 percent, what is its present value? Use a convenient format to display your computations.
5. What is an annuity?
6. Complete the following schedule:

	Table Values		
Concept	**i = 5%, n = 4**	**i = 10%, n = 7**	**i = 14%, n = 10**
FV of $1			
PV of $1			
FV of annuity of $1			
PV of annuity of $1			

7. If you deposit $1,000 at the end of each period for 10 interest periods and you earn 8 percent interest, how much would you have at the end of period 10? Use a convenient format to display your computations.

MULTIPLE CHOICE

1. You are saving up for a Porsche Carrera Cabriolet, which currently sells for nearly half a million dollars. Your plan is to deposit $15,000 at the end of each year for the next 10 years. You expect to earn 5 percent each year. How much will you have saved after 10 years, rounded to the nearest 10 dollars?
    a. $150,000.
    b. $188,670.
    c. $495,990.
    d. None of the above.
2. Which of the following is a characteristic of an annuity?
    a. An equal dollar amount each interest period.
    b. Interest periods of equal length.
    c. An equal interest rate each interest period.
    d. All of the above are characteristics of an annuity.
3. Which of the following is most likely to be an annuity?
    a. Monthly payments on a credit card bill.
    b. Monthly interest earned on a checking account.
    c. Monthly payments on a home mortgage.
    d. Monthly utility bill payments.

4. Assume you bought a plasma television, with no payments to be made until two years from now, when you must pay $6,000. If the going rate of interest on most loans is 5 percent, which table in this appendix would you use to calculate the television's equivalent cost if you were to pay for it today?
   - *a.* Table C.1 (Future Value of $1)
   - *b.* Table C.2 (Present Value of $1)
   - *c.* Table C.3 (Future Value of Annuity of $1)
   - *d.* Table C.4 (Present Value of Annuity of $1)

5. Assuming the facts in question 3, what is the television's equivalent cost if you were to pay for it today?
   - *a.* $5,442
   - *b.* $6,615
   - *c.* $11,100
   - *d.* $12,300

6. Assume you bought a car using a loan that requires payments of $3,000 to be made at the end of every year for the next three years. The loan agreement indicates the annual interest rate is 6 percent. Which table in this appendix would you use to calculate the car's equivalent cost if you were to pay for it in full today?
   - *a.* Table C.1 (Future Value of $1)
   - *b.* Table C.2 (Present Value of $1)
   - *c.* Table C.3 (Future Value of Annuity of $1)
   - *d.* Table C.4 (Present Value of Annuity of $1)

7. Assuming the facts in question 6, what is the car's equivalent cost if you were to pay for it today? Round to the nearest hundred dollars.
   - *a.* $2,600
   - *b.* $3,600
   - *c.* $8,000
   - *d.* $9,600

8. Which of the following statements are true?
   - *a.* When the interest rate increases, the present value of a single amount decreases.
   - *b.* When the number of interest periods increase, the present value of a single amount increases.
   - *c.* When the interest rate increases, the present value of an annuity increases.
   - *d.* None of the above are true.

9. Which of the following describes how to calculate a bond's issue price?

	Face Value	Interest Payments
a.	Present value of single amount.	Future value of annuity.
b.	Future value of single amount.	Present value of annuity.
c.	Present value of single amount.	Present value of annuity.
d.	Future value of single amount.	Future value of annuity.

10. If interest is compounded quarterly, rather than yearly, how do you adjust the number of years and annual interest rate when using the present value tables?

	Number of Years	Annual Interest Rate
a.	Divide by 4	Divide by 4
b.	Divide by 4	Multiply by 4
c.	Multiply by 4	Divide by 4
d.	Multiply by 4	Multiply by 4

MINI-EXERCISES

MC-1 Computing the Present Value of a Single Payment
What is the present value of $500,000 to be paid in 10 years, with an interest rate of 8 percent?

MC-2 Computing the Present Value of an Annuity
What is the present value of 10 equal payments of $15,000, with an interest rate of 10 percent?

MC-3 Computing the Present Value of a Complex Contract

As a result of a slowdown in operations, Mercantile Stores is offering to employees who have been terminated a severance package of $100,000 cash; another $100,000 to be paid in one year; and an annuity of $30,000 to be paid each year for 20 years. What is the present value of the package, assuming an interest rate of 8 percent?

MC-4 Computing the Future Value of an Annuity

You plan to retire in 20 years. Calculate whether it is better for you to save $25,000 a year for the last 10 years before retirement or $15,000 for each of the 20 years. Assume you are able to earn 10 percent interest on your investments.

EXERCISES

EC-1 Computing Growth in a Savings Account: A Single Amount

On January 1, 2004, you deposited $6,000 in a savings account. The account will earn 10 percent annual compound interest, which will be added to the fund balance at the end of each year.

Required (round to the nearest dollar):

1. What will be the balance in the savings account at the end of 10 years?
2. What is the interest for the 10 years?
3. How much interest revenue did the fund earn in 2004? 2005?

EC-2 Computing Deposit Required and Accounting for a Single-Sum Savings Account

On January 1, 2004, Alan King decided to transfer an amount from his checking account into a savings account that later will provide $80,000 to send his son to college (four years from now). The savings account will earn 8 percent, which will be added to the fund each year-end.

Required (show computations and round to the nearest dollar):

1. How much must Alan deposit on January 1, 2004?
2. Give the journal entry that Alan should make on January 1, 2004 to record the transfer.
3. What is the interest for the four years?
4. Give the journal entry that Alan should make on (a) December 31, 2004, and (b) December 31, 2005.

EC-3 Recording Growth in a Savings Account with Equal Periodic Payments

On each December 31, you plan to transfer $2,000 from your checking account into a savings account. The savings account will earn 9 percent annual interest, which will be added to the savings account balance at each year-end. The first deposit will be made December 31, 2004 (at the end of the period).

Required (show computations and round to the nearest dollar):

1. Give the required journal entry on December 31, 2004.
2. What will be the balance in the savings account at the end of the 10th year (i.e., 10 deposits)?
3. What is the total amount of interest earned on the 10 deposits?
4. How much interest revenue did the fund earn in 2005? 2006?
5. Give all required journal entries at the end of 2005 and 2006.

EC-4 Computing Growth for a Savings Fund with Periodic Deposits

On January 1, 2005, you plan to take a trip around the world upon graduation four years from now. Your grandmother wants to deposit sufficient funds for this trip in a savings account for you. On the basis of a budget, you estimate that the trip currently would cost $15,000. Being the generous and sweet lady she is, your grandmother decided to deposit $3,500 in the fund at the end of each of the next four years, starting on December 31, 2005. The savings account will earn 6 percent annual interest, which will be added to the savings account at each year-end.

Required (show computations and round to the nearest dollar):

1. How much money will you have for the trip at the end of year 4 (i.e., after four deposits)?
2. What is the total amount of interest earned over the four years?
3. How much interest revenue did the fund earn in 2005, 2006, 2007, and 2008?

EC-5 Computing Value of an Asset Based on Present Value

You have the chance to purchase an oil well. Your best estimate is that the oil well's net royalty income will average $25,000 per year for five years. There will be no residual value at that time. Assume that the cash inflow occurs at each year-end and that considering the uncertainty in your estimates, you expect to earn 15 percent per year on the investment. What should you be willing to pay for this investment right now?

COACHED PROBLEM

CPC-1 Comparing Options Using Present Value Concepts

After hearing a knock at your front door, you are surprised to see the Prize Patrol from a large, well-known magazine subscription company. It has arrived with the good news that you are the big winner, having won "$20 million." You discover that you have three options: (1) you can receive $1 million per year for the next 20 years, (2) you can have $8 million today, or (3) you can have $2 million today and receive $700,000 for each of the next 20 years. Your financial adviser tells you that it is reasonable to expect to earn 10 percent on investments. Which option do you prefer? What factors influence your decision?

GROUP A PROBLEM

PAC-1 Comparing Options Using Present Value Concepts

After completing a long and successful career as senior vice president for a large bank, you are preparing for retirement. After visiting the human resources office, you have found that you have several retirement options: (1) you can receive an immediate cash payment of $1 million, (2) you can receive $60,000 per year for life (your remaining life expectancy is 20 years), or (3) you can receive $50,000 per year for 10 years and then $70,000 per year for life (this option is intended to give you some protection against inflation). You have determined that you can earn 8 percent on your investments. Which option do you prefer and why?

GROUP B PROBLEM

PBC-1 Comparing Options Using Present Value Concepts

After incurring a serious injury caused by a manufacturing defect, your friend has sued the manufacturer for damages. Your friend received three offers from the manufacturer to settle the lawsuit: (1) receive an immediate cash payment of $100,000, (2) receive $6,000 per year for life (your friend's remaining life expectancy is 20 years), or (3) receive $5,000 per year for 10 years and then $7,000 per year for life (this option is intended to compensate your friend for increased aggravation of the injury over time). Your friend can earn 8 percent interest and has asked you for advice. Which option would you recommend and why?

COACH'S CORNER

All three scenarios require you to determine today's value of the various payment options. These are present value problems.

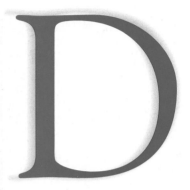

Reporting and Interpreting Investments in Other Corporations

You're probably already thinking about how you're going to celebrate the end of the term with your friends. Perhaps you'll dine out, go to a nightclub, or just simply relax in front of the TV at somebody's place. While you can't always control what your friends decide to do, by being involved in the decision making you can make sure they hear what you'd like before a decision is made.

The managers at Motorola feel the same way—not about end-of-term celebrations but instead about business decisions that are made by other companies that supply services to or buy products from Motorola. To ensure the impact on Motorola is considered in these decisions, Motorola might buy some of the stock issued by these other companies. As explained in Chapter 11, by becoming a common stockholder, Motorola gets one vote for each share it owns, to use when these other companies ask their stockholders to vote on important decisions. If Motorola buys enough common stock in other corporations, it could have a significant or possibly controlling influence over their decisions. In this appendix, you'll learn how Motorola accounts for the investments it makes in other corporations.

WHY
DOES A COMPANY INVEST IN OTHER CORPORATIONS?

A company can invest in either stock or bonds issued by another corporation. This appendix focuses on just stock investments. In principle, bond investments are accounted for in a manner similar to what we describe below for certain stock investments, but there are several technical differences that we leave for intermediate accounting courses.

A company might invest in stock issued by other corporations for one of four reasons:

1. **Take control.** A company might want to expand into other industries or markets, and the fastest way to do this is to take over control of another corporation (typically by buying more than 50 percent of its stock).

2. **Exert significant influence.** Instead of controlling the decisions of another corporation, the company might be satisfied with just having a significant influence on the decisions made by the other corporation. After buying 20–50 percent of the common stock of a supplier or customer, a company usually will be able to exert this significant influence.

3. **Passively invest in securities available for sale.** A company might have generated some extra cash from its operating activities, which it invests in another corporation's stock to earn dividends. The company doesn't become actively involved in the decisions made by the other companies. Rather, this is a passive form of investment where the company just plunks down some money and waits for the investment to pay off. Because these investments can be sold whenever the company is short of cash, they are called **securities available for sale**.

4. *Profit from buying and selling.* A company might actually be in the business of trading securities, which means trying to earn profits by buying securities at one price and selling them in the near future at a higher price. Investments made with this goal in mind are considered **trading securities**.

It's useful to understand these four reasons not only to be a wiser business person, but also because they relate to how investments in other corporations are accounted for. As Exhibit D.1 indicates, the methods used to account for these investments depend on the company's level of involvement in the other corporation and on the investing company's basic reason for investing in other corporations. As a guideline for determining the investor's level of involvement, the percent of stock ownership is considered, using percentages shown in the first column of Exhibit D.1. So, for example, an investor owning more than 50 percent of the stock of another corporation is presumed to control the other corporation. Other factors, like participation in setting operating and financing policies, also are considered. The following sections of this appendix discuss the different accounting methods listed in the third column of Exhibit D.1.

YOU SHOULD KNOW

Trading securities are purchased with the intent of selling them in the near future at a profit.

COACH'S CORNER

The fourth column in Exhibit D.1 will be most useful to you as a quick review of the different accounting methods. Don't spend time on it until after you read the following sections.

exhibit D.1 **Accounting for Investments in Other Corporations' Stock**

Level of Involvement in Decision Making (Percent of Ownership)	Reason for the Investment	Method of Accounting	How It Works
Control (more than 50%)	Take over the company →	Consolidation	Combine the financial statements of parent and subsidiaries
Significant Influence (20–50%)	Influence the company →	Equity	Record investment at cost, add % share of net income, deduct % share of dividends
Passive (less than 20%)	Invest excess cash to earn greater return	→ Market Value for Securities Available for Sale	Record investment at cost but adjust to market value at period-end; report dividends and realized gains/losses as investment income on the income statement; report unrealized gains/losses in stockholders' equity
Passive (less than 20%)	Securities trading	→ Market Value for Trading Securities	Record investment at cost but adjust to market value at period-end; report dividends and all gains/losses (either realized or unrealized) as investment income on the income statement

Consolidation Method for Investments Involving Control

When a company controls the decisions of other companies, it is called the **parent**. The **subsidiary** is the company that the parent controls. Although we haven't made a big deal out of it, in earlier chapters you've studied many companies that were the parent of several subsidiaries. For example, Mattel is the parent of Fisher-Price and American Girl, and Regis Corporation is the parent of Supercuts and Carlton Hair International. So how is it that you didn't know that these parent companies had invested in subsidiary companies until now? Why didn't they report an asset called investments? The answer is that the parent companies have accounted for their investments using the consolidation method.

Under the consolidation method, the parent company prepares a set of **consolidated financial statements** that combines the accounts of the parent company with the accounts of all its subsidiary companies. The parent doesn't report a separate investment account on its balance sheet because it includes all of the accounts of the subsidiaries in

YOU SHOULD KNOW

The **parent** company is the entity that controls another company. The **subsidiary** company is the entity that is controlled by the parent. **Consolidated financial statements** combine the financial statements of parent and subsidiary companies into a single set of financial statements.

exhibit D.2	Excerpt from Motorola's Consolidated Balance Sheet

MOTOROLA, INC. AND SUBSIDIARIES
Consolidated Balance Sheets (Partial)
(in millions)

	December 31	
	2003	**2002**
<u>Assets</u>		
Current Assets		
Cash	$ 7,877	$ 6,507
Accounts Receivable, Net	4,436	4,437
Inventories, Net	2,792	2,869
Other Current Assets	2,802	3,321
Total Current Assets	17,907	17,134
Property, Plant and Equipment, Net	5,164	6,104
Investments	3,335	2,053
Other Assets	5,692	5,861
Total Assets	$32,098	$31,152

its own consolidated financial statements. Basically, *the consolidation method can be thought of as adding together separate financial statements for two or more companies to make it appear as if a single company exists.* So, for example, the $7.8 billion of cash reported in the assets section of Motorola's balance sheet in Exhibit D.2 includes the cash in Motorola's bank accounts as well as the cash in its subsidiary companies' accounts. The same is true of the *Inventories* account, *Notes Payable* account, *Sales* account, and so on.

Motorola, Inc., is the parent of several subsidiaries, including Next Level Communications and General Instrument Corporation. Although these subsidiaries exist as separate legal entities, their financial successes and failures ultimately belong to Motorola, so it makes sense for Motorola to report them as if they were Motorola's own financial results. To inform you that the financial statements include the parent and subsidiary companies, the first financial statement note proudly announces that the financial statements are prepared on a consolidated basis. Also, the heading of each financial statement is marked as *consolidated*, as shown in Motorola's balance sheet in Exhibit D.2.

You probably will notice that, in Exhibit D.2, Motorola reports *Investments* totaling more than $3.3 billion at December 31, 2003. This particular line-item does *not* represent the amount Motorola has invested in subsidiaries because each account of each subsidiary already has been combined into the consolidated financial statements. Instead, the *Investments* account shown in Exhibit D.2 relates to investments where Motorola has either significant influence or passive interest in other corporations, as discussed in the following sections.

Equity Method for Investments Involving Significant Influence

The equity method is used when an investor can exert significant influence over an investee, which is presumed if the investor owns between 20 and 50 percent of the investee's outstanding voting stock. Because the investor does not actually control the investee's assets or its operating decisions, the accounts of the investee are not consolidated within each account of the investor. Instead, the investor records its investment in a single account called *Investments*. It's just like how you'd account for a building. Rather than record the stairs, doors, floors, and roofing in separate accounts, they're all included

COACH'S CORNER
The account name *Investments in Associated Companies* is also used for investments accounted for using the equity method.

in a single account. Under the equity method, the investor initially records its investment at cost and then, every year after that, records its share of the investee's net income and its share of dividends distributed by the investee for that year. These items affect the *Investments* account as follows:

- **Net income of investee.** When the investee reports net income for the year, the investor increases (debits) its *Investments* account for its percentage share of the investee's net income. The investee's earnings represent a future benefit to the investor because they imply the investor can expect to enjoy greater dividends or increased investment value in the future. The credit portion of the journal entry is recorded as *Investment Income*, which is reported on the income statement along with other non-operating items like interest expense and other gains and losses. (If the investee reports a net loss for the year, the investor records a debit to *Investment Loss* for its share of the net loss along with a credit that reduces its *Investments* account.)

- **Dividends received from investee.** If the investee pays dividends during the year, the investor increases *Cash* and reduces its *Investments* account when it receives its share of the dividends.

+ Investments (A) −	
Beginning balance	
Initial investment (also credit to Cash)	
Company's % share of investee's net income (also credit to Investment Income)	Company's % share of investee's dividends declared for the period (also debit to Cash)
Ending balance	

Purchase of Stock

To illustrate the equity method of accounting, let's assume that at the end of 2003, Motorola had no significant influence investments. On January 1, 2004, Motorola bought 40,000 common shares of Personal Communications Corporation (PCC) for $300,000 cash. PCC had 100,000 shares of common stock outstanding, so Motorola's purchase represented 40 percent and, therefore, Motorola was presumed to have significant influence over the investee (PCC). As a consequence, Motorola must use the equity method to account for this investment. The initial purchase of this investment is recorded at cost.

dr	**Investments (+A)**........................	300,000	
	cr **Cash (−A)**		300,000

Assets		=	Liabilities	+	Stockholders' Equity
Investments	+300,000				
Cash	−300,000				

Share of Net Income Earned

Because Motorola can influence PCC's processes for earning income, Motorola bases its investment income on PCC's earnings. During 2004, PCC reported net income of $250,000 for the year. Motorola's percentage share of PCC's income was $100,000 (40% × $250,000), which is recorded as follows:

dr	**Investments (+A)**........................	100,000	
	cr **Investment Income (+R, +SE)**..........		100,000

Assets		=	Liabilities	+	Stockholders' Equity	
Investments	+100,000				Investment Income (+R)	+100,000

If PCC were to report a net loss for the period, Motorola would have recorded its percentage share of the loss by decreasing the *Investments* account and recording an *Investment Loss*, which would be reported in the nonoperating section of the income statement, with interest revenue, interest expense, and gains and losses on sales of assets.

Dividends Received

Because Motorola can exert significant influence over PCC's dividend policies, any dividends it receives from PCC should *not* be recorded as investment income. Instead, any dividends it receives will reduce its *Investments* account because dividends reduce the underlying assets of PCC. Assume that, at the end of 2004, PCC declared and paid a cash dividend of $2 per share to stockholders. Motorola received $80,000 in cash ($2 × 40,000 shares) from PCC, which the equity method accounts for as follows:

dr	Cash (+A)	80,000	
	cr Investments (−A)....................		80,000

Assets		=	Liabilities	+	Stockholders' Equity
Cash	+80,000				
Investments	−80,000				

In summary, the effects for 2004 are reflected in the following T-accounts:

+ Investments (A) −			
Beg. bal.	0		
Purchase	300,000		
Share of PCC's net income	100,000	80,000	Share of PCC's dividends
End. bal.	320,000		

− Investment Income (R, SE) +			
		0	Beg. bal.
		100,000	Share of PCC's net income
		100,000	End. bal.

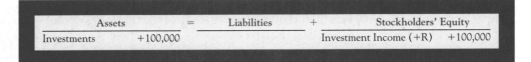

Assume that on January 1, 2005, Motorola bought 30 percent of the common stock of Intellicar Corporation (IC) for $120,000. IC reported net income of $100,000 for the year ended December 31, 2005. IC also declared and paid dividends totaling $50,000 for the year.

a. At what amount should Motorola report its investment in IC at December 31, 2005?

b. What amount should Motorola report as investment income?

When you're done, check your answers with the solutions in the margin.

Market Value Methods for Passive Investments

Before we discuss how the market value method is applied to securities available for sale and trading securities, let's consider the rationale for reporting these passive investments at market value. It's actually a rarity in accounting to report assets at market value because it means that, in some instances, they'll be reported at an amount higher than historical cost. Let's take a closer look at this approach, which is dubbed "mark-to-market accounting."

1. *Why are passive investments reported at fair market value on the balance sheet?* Two primary factors determine the answer to this question:

    - **Relevance.** Analysts who study financial statements often attempt to forecast a company's future cash flows. They want to know how a company can generate cash for purposes such as expansion of the business, payment of dividends, or survival during a prolonged economic downturn. One source of cash is the sale of passive investments. The best estimate of the cash that could be generated by the sale of these securities is their current market value.

    - **Measurability.** Accountants record only those items that can be measured in dollar terms with a high degree of reliability. Determining the fair market value of most assets is very difficult because they are not actively traded. For example, although the Empire State Building is the most important asset owned by the Empire State Company, its balance sheet reports the building in terms of its cost in part because of the difficulty in determining an objective value for it. Contrast the difficulty of determining the value of a building with the ease of determining the value of securities that Motorola owns. A quick look at stockcharts.com is all that is needed to determine the current price of IBM or Microsoft stock because these securities are traded each day on established stock exchanges.

2. *When the investment account is adjusted to reflect changes in fair market value, what other account is affected when the asset account is increased or decreased?* Under the double-entry method of accounting, every journal entry affects at least two accounts. An asset valuation account is added to or subtracted from the investment account (maintained at cost) to produce the market value that is reported on the balance sheet. The second account affected is **Unrealized Holding Gains or Losses** that are recorded whenever the fair market value of investments changes. These are called *unrealized* because no actual sale has taken place. Simply by holding the security, the value has changed. If the value of the investments increased by $100,000 during the year, an adjusting journal entry records the increase in the asset valuation account and an unrealized holding gain for $100,000. If the value of the investments decreased by $75,000 during the year, an adjusting journal entry records the decrease in the asset valuation account and an unrealized holding loss of $75,000. The financial statement treatment of the unrealized holding gains or losses depends on whether the investment is classified as securities available for sale or trading securities.

Securities Available for Sale

Exhibit D.3 on page 682 displays information from Note 2 of Motorola's financial statements, which indicates that most of the investments reported on Motorola's balance sheet are securities available for sale (in millions, securities available for sale account for $2,930 out of $3,335). The details reported in Exhibit D.3 indicate that Motorola's securities available for sale (or SAS for short) initially cost $500 million, but were worth $2.93 billion at December 31, 2003.

To simplify our look at the accounting procedures that ultimately led to the amounts in Exhibit D.3, let's assume that Motorola had no passive investments at the end of 2002. The way in which the market value method is applied to securities available for sale is shown below Exhibit D.3.

exhibit D.3	Motorola's Note Describing Securities Available for Sale (in millions)

	December 31, 2003
Securities available for sale (SAS)	
Investment in SAS (at cost)	$ 500
Allowance to value SAS at market	2,430
Market value of securities available for sale	2,930
Equity method and other investments	405
Total investments	$3,335

Purchase of Stock.   At the beginning of 2003, Motorola purchases 10 million shares of common stock of Wireless Networks Inc. (WNI) for $50 per share. There were 100 million outstanding shares, so Motorola owns 10 percent of WNI (10 ÷ 100), which is considered a passive investment in securities available for sale. Such investments are recorded initially at cost:

dr Investment in SAS (+A).................	500	
cr Cash (−A) (10 million shares × $50).....		500

Assets		=	Liabilities	+	Stockholders' Equity
Investment in SAS	+500				
Cash	−500				

After stock has been purchased, it can earn a return from two sources: (1) dividends, and (2) price increases. We will discuss price increases in a few moments, but for now let's focus on dividends.

Dividends Received.   Under the market value method, when dividends are received, the investor reports them as revenue on the income statement in an account called *Investment Income*. If Motorola receives a $1 per share cash dividend from WNI, which totals $10 million ($1 × 10 million shares), it would record the following journal entry:

dr Cash (+A)	10	
cr Investment Income (+R, +SE)..........		10

Assets		=	Liabilities	+	Stockholders' Equity	
Cash	+10				Investment Income (+R)	+10

Price Increases.   *At the end of the accounting period, passive investments are reported on the balance sheet at fair market value.* Let's assume that WNI had a $293 per share market value at the end of the year. That is, Motorola's investment had gained a whopping $243

per share ($293 − 50 = $243) for the year. Since the investment has not been sold, this is only a holding gain, not a realized gain. The market value method for SAS investments requires that, unlike dividends, all unrealized holding gains or losses should *not* be reported in the investor's net income. Because the investor expects to hold SAS investments into the future, it's likely that the value of the SAS investment will change again before any gain or loss is actually realized. Thus, unrealized gains or losses of this year might be recovered or become even larger next year. Either way, the unrealized gains and losses of this period are not likely to represent the true gains or losses that will be realized when the stock is ultimately sold, so they are not included in net income. Instead, they are recorded in a stockholders' equity account called *Unrealized Gains and Losses in Equity*. Only when the security is sold do the gains or losses become realized, at which time they are removed from stockholders' equity and included in net income.

In summary, reporting the SAS investment at market value requires adjusting it to market value at the end of each period using the account *Allowance to Value SAS at Market* along with a corresponding entry to *Unrealized Gains and Losses in Equity*. If the ending balance in the *Allowance to Value SAS at Market* account is a debit, it is added to the *Investment in SAS* account when it is reported on the balance sheet. If it is a credit balance, it is subtracted. The *Unrealized Gains and Losses in Equity* account is reported in the stockholders' equity section of the balance sheet, either increasing stockholders' equity (if it represents an unrealized holding gain) or decreasing it (if it represents an unrealized holding loss).

The following chart is used to compute any unrealized gain or loss in securities available for sale:

POINT OF INTEREST

Within the last two months of 1999, Yahoo!'s stock price jumped from $181 per share to $404. At the time of writing, it was trading at $32 per share.

COACH'S CORNER

Reporting the unrealized holding gain or loss in stockholders' equity has two purposes: (1) it reduces wild swings in net income, and (2) it informs users of the gains or losses that would occur if the securities were sold at market value.

Year	Market Value	−	Cost	=	Balance Needed in Valuation Allowance	−	Unadjusted Balance in Valuation Allowance	=	Amount for Adjusting Entry
2003	$2,930	−	$500	=	$2,430	−	$0	=	$2,430
	($293 × 10)		($50 × 10)				(We assumed there were no passive investments at the end of the prior year.)		An unrealized gain for the period

The adjusting entry at the end of 2003 is recorded as follows:

dr   **Allowance to Value SAS at Market (+A)**   2,430
     cr   **Unrealized Gains and Losses in Equity**
             (+SE)   2,430

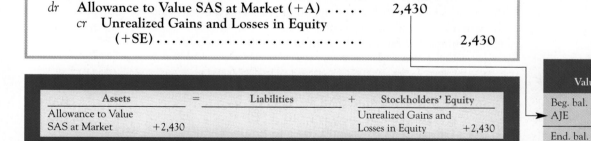

Assets	=	Liabilities	+	Stockholders' Equity
Allowance to Value SAS at Market +2,430				Unrealized Gains and Losses in Equity +2,430

Allowance to Value SAS at Market (A)	
Beg. bal. 0	
AJE 2,430	
End. bal. 2,430	

As Exhibit D.3 showed, the ending balance in *Allowance to Value SAS at Market* account is added to the *Investment in SAS* account balance when determining the amount to report as *Investments* on the balance sheet. If management intends to sell these investments within a year, they would be classified as current. Given that all of Motorola's investments appear below the current assets subtotal in Exhibit D.2 (on page 678), we can assume that Motorola's management expects to keep its SAS investments beyond the end of the upcoming year. The *Unrealized Gains and Losses in Equity* is reported in the stockholders' equity section just like retained earnings. If the balance is a net unrealized

exhibit **D.4**	**Balance Sheet Reporting of Unrealized Gains and Losses in Equity (in millions)**

	December 31, 2003
Stockholders' Equity	
Common Stock, $3 par value	
Authorized Shares: 2003 and 2002—4,200.0	
Issued and Outstanding: 2003—2,338.7; 2002—2,315.3	$ 7,017
Additional Paid-In Capital	2,362
Retained Earnings	3,103
Unrealized Gains and Losses in Equity	2,430
Total Stockholders' Equity	$14,912

loss, it would be reported as a negative amount, just like the treasury stock discussed in Chapter 11. Assuming that Motorola has a $2,430 credit balance in its *Unrealized Gains and Losses in Equity* account at the end of 2003, its stockholders' equity would be reported as shown in Exhibit D.4.

Sale of Stock.   When SAS investments are sold, three accounts on the balance sheet (in addition to *Cash*) can be affected:

- Investment in SAS.
- Allowance to Value SAS at Market.
- Unrealized Gains and Losses in Equity.

To illustrate, let's assume Motorola sold the WNI stock when the stock market reopened on January 2, 2004, after the New Year's holiday. If the stock price was still $293 per share that day, Motorola would receive (in millions) $2,930 cash ($293 × 10 million shares) for stock that cost $500, resulting in a realized gain of $2,430, which would be reported as investment income. Two journal entries are needed to record this sale. In entry 1, the cash received, stock given up, and gain realized by the sale are recorded. In entry 2, the valuation allowance and the related *Unrealized Gains and Losses in Equity* account would be eliminated because the gain has now been realized.

1.	dr	Cash (+A)...............................	2,930	
	cr	Investment in SAS (−A)		500
	cr	Investment Income (+R, +SE)		2,430
2.	dr	Unrealized Gains and Losses in Equity (−SE).	2,430	
	cr	Allowance to Value SAS at Market (+xA, −A)		2,430

Assets		=	Liabilities	+	Stockholders' Equity	
1. Cash	+2,930				Investment Income (+R)	+2,430
Investment in SAS	−500					
2. Allowance to Value					Unrealized Gains and	
SAS at Market (+xA)	−2,430				Losses in Equity	−2,430

Trading Securities

Trading securities are similar to securities available for sale in many ways. First, trading securities are considered passive investments because the investor does not acquire a sufficient quantity of stock to significantly influence the operating or financing decisions of the investee. Second, investments in trading securities are reported on the balance sheet at market value. Third, stock classified as trading securities also can earn a return from two sources: dividends and price increases.

Trading securities differ from securities available for sale in one small but very important way. Trading securities are purchased with the intent to profit *primarily* from price increases. *Buy low, sell high* is the motto of investors who invest in securities for trading purposes. This isn't the case with securities available for sale, where the investing company is likely to wait out periods of price changes because its goal is to safely "park" its excess cash in investments that generate a greater return than a bank's savings account.

Because trading securities are purchased with intent to profit from fluctuations in their stock prices, all gains and losses on trading securities are reported in the income statement regardless of whether they are realized or unrealized. In terms of accounting procedures, this means that rather than record unrealized gains and losses in a stockholders' equity account (as they were for securities available for sale), they are recorded in a temporary revenue or expense account, which is closed into retained earnings at the end of every year. If Motorola's investment in WNI stock had been considered an investment in trading securities (TS), the journal entry to adjust the *Investment in TS* to market value at the end of 2003 would have been:

dr	**Allowance to Value TS at Market (+A)**	2,430
cr	**Investment Income (+R, +SE)**	2,430

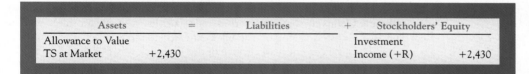

Assets	=	Liabilities	+	Stockholders' Equity
Allowance to Value TS at Market	+2,430			Investment Income (+R) +2,430

The journal entries to record the **purchase of stock** and **dividends received** for trading securities are identical to the journal entries used for securities available for sale (except that references to SAS in the account names are replaced with TS). And, similar to what you saw earlier for securities available for sale, the *Allowance to Value TS at Market* is combined with the *Investment in TS* account, with the total being reported on the balance sheet as *Investments*. Because investments in trading securities are intended to be sold in the near future, they are always classified as current assets.

Now that you've seen all four methods of accounting for investments in the stock of other corporations, return to Exhibit D.1 on page 677. Make sure you understand the final column that summarizes how the methods of accounting work for each type of investment.

FOR YOUR REVIEW

DEMONSTRATION CASE A—EQUITY METHOD FOR SIGNIFICANT INFLUENCE INVESTMENTS

On January 1, 2004, Connaught Company purchased 40 percent of the outstanding voting shares of London Company on the open market for $85,000 cash. London declared $10,000 in cash dividends and reported net income of $60,000 for the year.

Required:

1. Prepare the journal entries for 2004.
2. What accounts and amounts were reported on Connaught's balance sheet at the end of 2004? On Connaught's income statement for 2004?

Suggested Solution

1.

Jan. 1	dr	Investments (+A)	85,000	
	cr	Cash (−A)		85,000
Dividends	dr	Cash (+A) (40% × $10,000)...........	4,000	
	cr	Investments (+A)		4,000
Dec. 31	dr	Investments (+A) (40% × $60,000)	24,000	
	cr	Investment Income (+R, +SE)......		24,000

2. **On the Balance Sheet**

    Noncurrent Assets:

    Investments $105,000
         ($85,000 − $4,000 + $24,000)

    On the Income Statement

    Other Items:

    Investment income $24,000

DEMONSTRATION CASE B—MARKET VALUE METHOD FOR SECURITIES AVAILABLE FOR SALE

Howell Equipment Corporation sells and services a major line of farm equipment. Both sales and service operations have been profitable. The following transactions affected the company during 2004:

a. Jan. 1   Purchased 2,000 shares of common stock of Elk Company at $40 per share. This purchase represented 1 percent of the shares outstanding. Based on management's intent, the Elk Company shares are considered securities available for sale.
b. Dec. 28   Received $4,000 cash dividend on the Elk Company stock.
c. Dec. 31   Determined that the current market price of the Elk stock was $41.

Required:

1. Prepare the journal entry for each of these transactions.
2. What accounts and amounts will be reported on the balance sheet at the end of 2004? On the income statement for 2004?

Suggested Solution

1. *a.*

Jan. 1	dr	Investment in SAS (+A)	80,000	
	cr	Cash (−A)		
		(2,000 shares × $40 per share)		80,000

b.

Dec. 28	dr	Cash (+A)........................	4,000	
	cr	Investment Income (+R, +SE)		4,000

c.

Dec. 31	dr	Allowance to Value SAS at Market (+A)	2,000	
	cr	Unrealized Gains and Losses in Equity (+SE).................		2,000

Year	Market Value	−	Cost	=	Balance Needed in Valuation Allowance	−	Unadjusted Balance in Valuation Allowance	=	Adjustment to Valuation Allowance
2004	$82,000	−	$80,000	=	$2,000	−	$0	=	$2,000
	($41 × 2000 shares)								An unrealized gain for the period

2. On the Balance Sheet

Current or Noncurrent Assets:

Investment in SAS $82,000
    ($80,000 cost + $2,000 allowance)

Stockholders' Equity:

Unrealized gains and losses in equity   2,000

On the Income Statement

Other Items:

Investment income $4,000

DEMONSTRATION CASE C—MARKET VALUE METHOD FOR TRADING SECURITIES

Assume the same facts as in Case B, except that the securities were purchased for the purpose of active trading.

Required:

1. Prepare the journal entry for each of these transactions.
2. What accounts and amounts will be reported on the balance sheet at the end of 2004? On the income statement for 2004?

Suggested Solution

1. *a.*

Jan. 1	*dr*	Investment in TS (+A)	80,000	
	cr	Cash (−A) (2,000 shares × $40) . . .		80,000

b.

Dec. 28	*dr*	Cash (+A)	4,000	
	cr	Investment Income (+R, +SE)		4,000

c.

Dec. 31	*dr*	Allowance to Value TS at Market (+A) .	2,000	
	cr	Investment Income (+R, +SE)		2,000

Year	Market Value	−	Cost	=	Balance Needed in Valuation Allowance	−	Unadjusted Balance in Valuation Allowance	=	Adjustment to Valuation Allowance
2004	$82,000	−	$80,000	=	$2,000	−	$0	=	$2,000
	($41 × 2000 shares)								An unrealized gain for the period

2. **On the Balance Sheet**

Current Assets:

Investment in TS $82,000
    ($80,000 cost + $2,000 allowance)

On the Income Statement

Other Nonoperating Items:

Investment income $6,000
    ($4,000 dividend + $2,000
    unrealized gain)

KEY TERMS TO KNOW

Consolidated Financial Statements p. 677
Equity Method p. 678
Market Value Method p. 681

Parent Company p. 677
Securities Available for Sale p. 676
Subsidiary Company p. 677

Trading Securities p. 677
Unrealized Holding Gains and Losses p. 681

FOR YOUR PRACTICE

QUESTIONS

1. When is it appropriate to use consolidation, equity, or market value methods for an investment in another corporation?
2. How do the accounting methods used for securities available for sale and trading securities differ?
3. How do the accounting methods used for passive investments and investments involving a significant influence differ?
4. How do the accounting methods used for investments involving a significant influence and investments involving control differ?
5. What are consolidated financial statements and what do they attempt to accomplish?
6. Under the equity method, dividends received from the investee company are not recorded as revenue. To record dividends as revenue involves double counting. Explain.
7. What are the two sources of return for passive investments?
8. Where are unrealized gains and losses reported for securities available for sale? Where are unrealized gains and losses reported for trading securities? What's the reason for this reporting difference?

MULTIPLE CHOICE

1. Company A owns 40 percent of Company B and exercises significant influence over the management of Company B. Therefore, Company A uses what accounting method for reporting its ownership of stock in Company B?
   a. The consolidation method.
   b. The market value method for securities available for sale.
   c. The equity method.
   d. The market value method for trading securities.
2. Company A purchases 10 percent of Company X and intends to hold the stock for at least five years. At the end of the current year, how would Company A's investment in Company X be reported on Company A's December 31 (year-end) balance sheet?
   a. At original cost, in the Current Assets section.
   b. At the December 31 market value, in the Current Assets section.
   c. At original cost, in the Noncurrent Assets section.
   d. At the December 31 market value, in the Noncurrent Assets section.
3. Consolidated financial statements are required in which of the following situations?
   a. Only when a company can exert significant influence over another company.
   b. Only when a company has a passive investment in another company.
   c. Only when a parent company can exercise control over its subsidiary.
   d. None of the above.

4. When recording dividends received from a stock investment accounted for using the equity method, which of the following statements is true?
   a. Total assets are increased and net income is increased.
   b. Total assets are increased and total stockholders' equity is increased.
   c. Total assets are decreased and total stockholders' equity is decreased.
   d. Total assets and total stockholders' equity do not change.

5. When using the equity method of accounting, when is revenue recorded on the books of the investor company?
   a. When the market value of the investee stock increases.
   b. When a dividend is received from the investee.
   c. When the investee company reports net income.
   d. Both b and c above.

6. Dividends received from stock that is reported as *Securities available for sale* in the balance sheet are reported as which of the following?
   a. An increase to cash and a decrease to the investment account.
   b. An increase to cash and an unrealized gain on the balance sheet.
   c. An increase to cash and an increase to investment income.
   d. An increase to cash and an unrealized gain on the income statement.

7. Realized gains and losses are recorded on the income statement for which of the following transactions in *Trading securities* and *Securities available for sale*?
   a. When adjusting *Trading securities* to market value.
   b. When adjusting *Securities available for sale* to market value.
   c. Only when recording the sale of *Trading securities*.
   d. When recording the sale of either *Trading securities* or *Securities available for sale*.

8. Schlumber Corp. paid $200,000 to purchase 30 percent of the stock of Schleep, Inc., this year. At the end of the year, Schleep reported net income of $50,000 and declared and paid dividends of $20,000. If Schlumber uses the equity method to account for its investment in Schleep, at what amount would the investment be reported at the end of the year?
   a. $200,000
   b. $209,000
   c. $215,000
   d. $221,000

9. During the current year, Winterpeg Enterprises purchased common shares of Lakeview Development Corp. (LDC) for $200,000, received a $2,000 dividend from LDC, and saw the market value of its investment in LDC increase by $4,000 by year-end. If Winterpeg considers its investment in LDC to be securities available for sale, what amount will Winterpeg report as investment income on its income statement this year?
   a. $2,000
   b. $4,000
   c. $6,000
   d. None of the above.

10. Assume the same facts as described in 9, except that Winterpeg considers its investment in LDC to be trading securities. What amount will Winterpeg report as investment income on its income statement this year?
    a. $2,000
    b. $4,000
    c. $6,000
    d. None of the above.

MINI-EXERCISES

MD-1 Recording Equity Method Securities Transactions

On January 2, 2005, Ubuy.com paid $100,000 to acquire 25 percent (10,000 shares) of the common stock of E-Net Corporation. The accounting period for both companies ends December 31. Give the journal entries for the purchase on January 2, and for each of the following transactions that occurred during 2005:

July   2   E-Net declared and paid a cash dividend of $3 per share.

Dec. 31   E-Net reported net income of $200,000.

MD-2 Determining Financial Statement Effects of Equity Method Securities

Using the following categories, indicate the effects (direction and amount) of the transactions listed in MD-1. Use + for increase and − for decrease.

	Balance Sheet			Income Statement		
Transaction	Assets	Liabilities	Stockholders' Equity	Revenues	Expenses	Net Income

MD-3 Recording Trading Securities Transactions

During 2004, Princeton Company acquired some of the 50,000 outstanding shares of the common stock of Cox Corporation as trading securities. The accounting period for both companies ends December 31. Give the journal entries for each of the following transactions that occurred during 2004:

July	2	Purchased 8,000 shares of Cox common stock at $28 per share.
Dec.	15	Cox Corporation declared and paid a cash dividend of $2 per share.
	31	Determined the current market price of Cox stock to be $29 per share.

MD-4 Determining Financial Statement Effects of Trading Securities Transactions

Using the following categories, indicate the effects (direction and amount) of the transactions listed in MD-3. Use + for increase and − for decrease.

	Balance Sheet			Income Statement		
Transaction	Assets	Liabilities	Stockholders' Equity	Revenues	Expenses	Net Income

MD-5 Recording Available for Sale Securities Transactions

Using the data in MD-3, assume that Princeton Company purchased the voting stock of Cox Corporation for its portfolio of securities available for sale instead of its trading securities portfolio. Give the journal entries for each of the transactions listed.

MD-6 Determining Financial Statement Effects of Securities Available for Sale Transactions

Using the following categories, indicate the effects (direction and amount) of the transactions referenced in MD-5. Use + for increase and − for decrease.

	Balance Sheet			Income Statement		
Transaction	Assets	Liabilities	Stockholders' Equity	Revenues	Expenses	Net Income

MD-7 Recording the Purchase and Sale of a Passive Investment

Rocktown Corporation bought 600 shares of General Electric stock on March 20, 2004, for its trading securities portfolio at $29 per share. Rocktown sold the stock at $33 per share on June 23, 2004. Prepare the journal entries to record the transactions on each of these dates, assuming that the investment had not yet been adjusted to market value (that is, the investment was still recorded at cost at the time of sale).

EXERCISES

ED-1 Recording and Reporting an Equity Method Security

Felicia Company acquired 21,000 of the 60,000 shares of outstanding common stock of Nueces Corporation during 2004 as a long-term investment. The annual accounting period for both companies ends December 31. The following transactions occurred during 2004:

Jan. 10	Purchased 21,000 shares of Nueces common stock at $12 per share.
Dec. 31	Nueces Corporation reported net income of $90,000.
Dec. 31	Nueces Corporation declared and paid a cash dividend of $0.60 per share.
Dec. 31	Determined the market price of Nueces stock to be $11 per share.

Required:

1. What accounting method should the company use? Why?
2. Give the journal entries for each of these transactions. If no entry is required, explain why.
3. Show how the long-term investment and the related revenue should be reported on the 2004 financial statements of Felicia Company.

ED-2 Recording Holding Gains for Securities Available for Sale

On June 30, 2003, MetroMedia, Inc., purchased 10,000 shares of Mitek stock for $20 per share. The following information pertains to the price per share of Mitek stock:

	Price
12/31/2003	$24
12/31/2004	31

Required:

Assume that management considers the stock to be securities available for sale. Prepare the journal entries required on each date given.

ED-3 Recording Holding Gains for Trading Securities

Refer to the data in ED-2.

Required:

Assume that MetroMedia management purchased the Mitek stock as trading securities. Prepare the journal entries required on each date given.

ED-4 Reporting Holding Gains for Securities Available for Sale and Trading Securities

Refer to the data in ED-2.

Required:

1. Assume that management intends to hold the stock as securities available for sale for three years or more. Show how the stock investment and its holding gains would be reported at the end of 2004 and 2003 on the classified balance sheet and income statement.
2. Assume that management purchased the stock as trading securities. Show how the investment and holding gains would be reported at the end of 2004 and 2003 on the classified balance sheet and income statement.

ED-5 Recording Holding Losses for Securities Available for Sale

On March 10, 2004, Global Solutions, Inc., purchased 5,000 shares of Superior Technologies stock for $50 per share. The following information pertains to the price per share of Superior Technologies stock:

	Price
12/31/2004	$45
12/31/2005	42

Required:

Assume that management considers the stock to be securities available for sale. Prepare the journal entries required on each date given.

ED-6 Recording Holding Losses for Trading Securities
Refer to the data in ED-5.

Required:

Assume that Global Solutions purchased the Superior Technologies stock as trading securities. Prepare the journal entries required on each date given.

ED-7 Reporting Holding Gains for Securities Available for Sale and Trading Securities
Refer to the data in ED-5.

Required:

1. Assume that management intends to hold the stock as securities available for sale for three years or more. Show how the stock investment and its holding gains would be reported at each year-end on the classified balance sheet and income statement.
2. Assume that management purchased the stock as trading securities. Show how the investment and holding gains would be reported at each year-end on the classified balance sheet and income statement.

COACHED PROBLEMS

CPD-1 Recording Passive Investments and Investments for Significant Influence
On August 4, 2002, Cappio Corporation purchased 1,000 shares of Maxwell Company for $45,000. The following information applies to the stock price of Maxwell Company:

	Price
12/31/2002	$52
12/31/2003	47
12/31/2004	38

Maxwell Company declares and pays cash dividends of $2 per share on June 1 of each year.

Required:

1. Prepare journal entries to record the facts in the case, assuming that Cappio considers the shares to be securities available for sale.
2. Prepare journal entries to record the facts in the case, assuming that Cappio considers the shares to be trading securities.
3. Prepare journal entries to record the facts in the case, assuming that Cappio uses the equity method to account for the investment. Cappio owns 30 percent of Maxwell, and Maxwell reported $50,000 in income each year.

CPD-2 Comparing Methods to Account for Various Levels of Ownership of Voting Stock
Bart Company had outstanding 30,000 shares of common stock, par value $10 per share. On January 1, 2004, Homer Company purchased some of these shares at $25 per share, with the intent of holding them for a long time. At the end of 2004, Bart Company reported the following: net income, $50,000, and cash dividends declared and paid during the year, $25,500. The market value of Bart Company stock at the end of 2004 was $22 per share.

Required:

1. This problem involves two separate cases. For each case (shown in the table), identify the method of accounting that Homer Company should use. Explain why.
2. Give the journal entries for Homer Company at the dates indicated for each of the two independent cases. If no entry is required, explain why. Use the following format:

	Case A: 3,600 Shares Purchased	Case B: 10,500 Shares Purchased
1. Accounting method?		
2. Journal entries made by Homer Company:		
a. To record the acquisition of Bart Company at January 1, 2004.		
b. To recognize the income reported by Bart Company for 2004.		
c. To recognize the dividends declared and paid by Bart Company.		
d. Entry to recognize market value effect at end of 2004.		

3. Complete the following schedule to show the separate amounts that should be reported on the 2004 financial statements of Homer Company:

	Dollar Amounts	
	Case A	Case B
Balance sheet		
Investments		
Stockholders' equity		
Income statement		
Investment income		

4. Explain why assets, stockholders' equity, and revenues for the two cases are different.

GROUP A PROBLEMS

PAD-1 Recording Passive Investments and Investments for Significant Influence

On July 12, 2003, Rossow Corporation purchased 1,000 shares of Reimer Company for $30,000. The following information applies to the stock price of Reimer Company:

	Price
12/31/2003	$33
12/31/2004	28
12/31/2005	20

Reimer Company declares and pays cash dividends of $2 per share on May 1 of each year.

Required:

1. Prepare journal entries to record the facts in the case, assuming that Rossow considers the shares to be securities available for sale.

2. Prepare journal entries to record the facts in the case, assuming that Rossow considers the shares to be trading securities.

3. Prepare journal entries to record the facts in the case, assuming that Rossow uses the equity method to account for the investment. Rossow owns 30 percent of Reimer, and Reimer reported $50,000 in income each year.

PAD-2 Comparing the Market Value and Equity Methods

Lisa Corporation had outstanding 100,000 shares of common stock. On January 10, 2004, Marg Company purchased a block of these shares in the open market at $20 per share, with the intent of holding the shares for a long time. At the end of 2004, Lisa reported net income of $300,000 and cash dividends of $0.60 per share. At December 31, 2004, Lisa Corporation stock was selling at $18 per share.

Required:

1. This problem involves two separate cases. For each case (shown in the table), identify the method of accounting that Marg Company should use. Explain why.

2. Give the journal entries for Marg Company at the dates indicated for each of the two independent cases. If no entry is required, explain why. Use the following format:

	Case A: 10,000 Shares Purchased	Case B: 40,000 Shares Purchased
1. Accounting method?		
2. Journal entries made by Marg Company:		
a. To record the acquisition of Lisa Company on January 10, 2004.		
b. To recognize the income reported by Lisa Company for 2004.		
c. To recognize the dividends declared and paid by Lisa Company.		
d. Entry to recognize market value effect at end of 2004.		

3. Complete the following schedule to show the separate amounts that should be reported on the 2004 financial statements of Marg Company:

	Dollar Amounts	
	Case A	Case B
Balance sheet		
Investments		
Stockholders' equity		
Income statement		
Investment income		

4. Explain why assets, stockholders' equity, and revenues for the two cases are different.

A

Account A standardized format that organizations use to accumulate the dollar effects of transactions on each financial statement item. (8)

Accounting The process of capturing and reporting the results of a business's operating, investing, and financing activities. (6)

Accounting Period The time period covered by the financial statements. (7)

Accounting Process The process used by businesses to analyze and record transactions, adjust the records at the end of the period, prepare financial statements, and prepare the records for the next cycle. (147)

Accounts Payable Amounts owed by the business to suppliers for past transactions. (418)

Accounts Receivable (Trade Receivables, Receivables) Amounts owed to the business by customers for past transactions. (284)

Accrual Basis Accounting Records revenues when earned and expenses when incurred, regardless of the timing of cash receipts or payments. (94)

Accrued Expenses See *Accrued Liabilities*. (418)

Accrued Liabilities Previously unrecorded expenses that need to be adjusted at the end of the accounting period to reflect the amount incurred and its related payable account. (418)

Accrued Revenues Previously unrecorded revenues that need to be adjusted at the end of the accounting period to reflect the amount earned and its related receivable account. (137)

Acquisition Cost Cash equivalent amount paid or to be paid for an asset. (96)

Adjusted Trial Balance A list of all accounts and their adjusted balances to check on the equality of recorded debits and credits. (147)

Adjusting Journal Entries Entries necessary at the end of each accounting period to measure all revenues and expenses of that period. (138)

Aging of Accounts Receivable Method Using the age of each accounts receivable to estimate uncollectible amounts. (289)

Allowance for Doubtful Accounts (Allowance for Bad Debts, Allowance for Uncollectible Accounts, Reserve for Bad Debts) Contra-asset account containing the estimated dollar value of uncollectible accounts receivable. (286)

Allowance Method Bases bad debt expense on an estimate of uncollectible accounts. (286)

Amortization (1) For intangible assets, this is the systematic and rational allocation of the cost of an intangible asset over its useful life. (2) For bonds payable, this involves allocating any premium or discount over the life of the bond. (384)

Annuity A series of periodic cash receipts or payments that are equal in amount each interest period. (661)

Assets Probable future economic benefits owned by the business as a result of past transactions. (7)

Audit An examination of the financial statements to ensure that they represent what they claim and conform with generally accepted accounting principles. (19)

Audit Report Describes the auditors' opinion of the fairness of the financial statement presentations and the evidence gathered to support that opinion. (203)

Authorized Number of Shares Maximum number of shares of corporation's capital stock that can be issued. (475)

Average Cost Method See *Weighted Average Cost Method*. (332)

B

Bad Debt Expense (Doubtful Accounts Expenses, Uncollectible Accounts Expense, Provision for Uncollectible Accounts) Expense associated with estimated uncollectible accounts receivable. (286)

Balance When used as a noun, balance is the dollar amount recorded in an account; when used as a verb, balance is the act of ensuring total assets equals total liabilities plus stockholders' equity. (63, 104)

Balance Sheet (Statement of Financial Position) Reports the amount of assets, liabilities, and stockholders' equity of an accounting entity at a point in time. (7)

Bank Reconciliation Process of using both the bank statement and the cash accounts of a business to determine the appropriate amount of cash in a bank account, after taking into consideration delays or errors in processing cash transactions. (235)

Bank Statement Monthly report from a bank that shows deposits recorded, checks cleared, other debits and credits, and a running bank balance. (236)

Basic Accounting Equation (Balance Sheet Equation) Assets = Liabilities + Stockholders' Equity. (7)

Board of Directors A group of people elected by the stockholders of a company to oversee the decisions made by managers of the company. (191)

Bond Certificate The bond document that each bondholder receives. (425)

Bond Discount The difference between issue price and face value when a bond is sold for less than face value. (427)

Bond Premium The difference between issue price and face value when a bond is sold for more than face value. (427)

Bond Principal The amount (1) payable at the maturity of the bond and (2) on which the periodic cash interest payments are computed. (425)

Book Value See *Net Book Value*. (374)

C

Callable Bonds Bonds that may be called for early repayment at the option of the company that issued the bond. (435)

Capitalize To record a cost as an asset rather than an expense. (390)

Capitalized Interest Interest expenditures included in the cost of a self-constructed asset. (372)

Carrying Value See *Net Book Value*. (141)

Cash Money or any instrument that banks will accept for deposit and immediate credit to the company's account, such as a check, money order, or bank draft. (235)

Cash Basis Accounting Records revenues when cash is received and expenses when cash is paid. (93)

Cash Equivalents Short-term investments with original maturities of three months or less that are readily convertible to cash and whose value is unlikely to change. (521)

Cash Flows from Financing Activities Cash inflows and outflows related to external sources of financing (owners and creditors). (523)

Cash Flows from Investing Activities Cash inflows and outflows related to the purchase or sale of long-term assets. (523)

Cash Flows from Operating Activities (Cash Flows from Operations) Cash inflows and outflows directly related to earnings from normal operations. (522)

Certificate of Deposit A savings certificate, generally issued by commercial banks, entitling the holder to receive interest after a specified maturity date. (144)

Chart of Accounts A summary of all account names and corresponding account numbers used to record financial results in the accounting system. (49)

Classified Balance Sheet A balance sheet that classifies assets and liabilities into current and other (long-term) categories. (47)

Closing Entries Made at the end of the accounting period to transfer balances in temporary accounts to *Retained Earnings* and to establish a zero balance in each of the temporary accounts. (152)

Common Stock The basic voting stock issued by a corporation. (475)

Comparable Information Information that can be compared across businesses because similar accounting methods have been applied. (15)

Comprehensive Income Includes net income plus net unrealized gains or losses on securities available for sale and other adjustments (related to pensions and foreign currency

translation) which are directly credited or debited to the stockholders' equity accounts. (591)

Conservatism An accounting concept that suggests care should be taken not to overstate assets and revenues or understate liabilities and expenses. (66)

Consistent Information Information that can be compared over time because similar accounting methods have been applied. (192)

Consolidated Financial Statements The financial statements of two or more companies that have been combined into a single set of financial statements as if the companies were one. (677)

Contingent Liability Potential liability that has arisen as the result of a past event, not a liability until some future event occurs. (436)

Continuity Assumption See *Going Concern Assumption*. (587)

Contra-Account An account that is an offset to, or reduction of, another account. (141)

Contract Rate See *Stated Interest Rate*. (426)

Contributed Capital Results from owners providing to the business cash (and sometimes other assets). (48)

Convertible Bonds Bonds that may be converted to other securities of the issuer (usually common stock). (435)

Copyright A form of protection provided to the original authors of literary, musical, artistic, dramatic, and other works of authorship. (382)

Cost The amount of resources that a company sacrifices to obtain goods or services; often said to be incurred when the company pays cash or uses credit to acquire the item. (96)

Cost-Benefit Constraint Suggests that the benefits of accounting for and reporting information should outweigh the costs. (587)

Cost of Goods Sold (CGS) Equation BI + P − EI = CGS; beginning inventory plus purchases minus ending inventory. (328)

Cost Principle Requires assets to be recorded at the historical cash-equivalent cost, which is the amount paid or payable on the date of the transaction. (66)

Coupon Rate See *Stated Interest Rate*. (426)

Credit When used as a noun, credit is the right side of an account; when used as a verb, credit is the act of recording the credit portion of a journal entry to a particular account. (58)

Creditor Any business or individual to whom the company owes money. (8)

Credit Card Discount Fee charged by a credit card company for its services. (247)

Cross-Sectional Analysis Compares one company's financial results to that of other companies competing in the same industry. (196)

Cumulative Dividend Preference Preferred stock feature that requires specified current dividends not paid in full to accumulate for every year in which they are not paid. These cumulative preferred dividends must be paid before any common dividends can be paid. (485)

Cumulative Effects of Changes in Accounting Methods Amounts reflected on the income statement for adjustments made to balance sheet accounts when applying new accounting principles. (591)

Current Assets Assets that will be used up or turned into cash within 12 months or the next operating cycle, whichever is longer. (48)

Current Dividend Preference The feature of preferred stock that grants priority on preferred dividends over common dividends. (485)

Current Liabilities Short-term obligations that will be paid in cash (or fulfilled with other current assets) within 12 months or the next operating cycle, whichever is longer. (47)

D

Debit When used as a noun, debit is the left side of an account; when used as a verb, debit is the act of recording the debit portion of a journal entry to a particular account. (58)

Debt Covenants See *Loan Covenants*. (191)

Declaration Date The date on which the board of directors officially approves a dividend. (12)

Declining-Balance Depreciation The method that allocates the cost of an asset over its useful life based on a multiple of (often two times) the straight-line rate. (377)

Deferred Expenses Previously acquired assets that need to be adjusted at the end of the accounting period to reflect the amount of expense incurred in using the asset to generate revenue. (129)

Deferred Revenues Previously recorded liabilities that need to be adjusted at the end of the period to reflect the amount of revenue earned. (129)

Deferred Tax Items Caused by reporting revenues and expenses according to GAAP on a company's income statement at a time that differs from their reporting on the tax return. (379)

Depreciable Cost The portion of the asset's cost that will be used up during its life. It is calculated as asset cost minus residual value, and it is allocated to depreciation expense throughout the asset's life. (375)

Depreciation Process of allocating the cost of buildings and equipment over their productive lives using a systematic and rational method of allocation. (374)

Direct Method A method of presenting the operating activities section of the statement of cash flows, in which each line of the income statement is reported in terms of gross cash receipts and payments. (522)

Discontinued Operations Financial results from the disposal of a major component of the business. (590)

Discount Rate The interest rate used to compute present values. (427)

Dividends Payments a company periodically makes to its stockholders as a return on their investment. (9)

Dividends in Arrears Dividends on cumulative preferred stock that have not been declared in prior years. (479)

E

Earnings Forecasts Predictions of earnings for future accounting periods. (193)

Earned To have done what is necessary to obtain the right to receive payment. (93)

EBITDA Abbreviation for "earnings before interest, taxes, depreciation, and amortization," which is a measure of operating performance that some managers and analysts use in place of net income. (389)

Effective-Interest Method Amortizes a bond discount or premium on the basis of the market interest rate. (441)

Effective Interest Rate Another name for the market rate of interest on a bond. (427)

Equity Method Used when an investor can exert significant influence over an investee. It requires the investor to record its share of net income and dividends reported by the investee. (678)

Estimated Useful Life Expected service life of a long-lived asset to the present owner. (375)

Expenditures Outflows of cash for any purpose. (93)

Expenses Decreases in assets or increases in liabilities from ongoing operations, incurred to generate revenues during the current period. (10)

Extraordinary Items Gains and losses that are both unusual in nature and infrequent in occurrence. (590)

Extraordinary Repairs Infrequent expenditures that increase an asset's economic usefulness in the future, and that are capitalized. (373)

F

Face Value (Par Value) The amount of a bond payable at its maturity; used to compute interest payments. (426)

Factoring An arrangement where receivables are sold to another company (called a *factor*) for immediate cash (minus a factoring fee). (296)

Financial Accounting Standards Board (FASB) The private sector body given the primary responsibility to work out the concepts and detailed rules that become generally accepted accounting principles. (18)

Financial Statements Reports that summarize the financial results of business activities. (4)

Financial Statement Users People who base their decisions, in part, on information reported in a company's financial statements. (4)

Financing Activities Related to exchanging money with lenders or owners. (5)

Finished Goods Inventory Manufactured goods that are completed and ready for sale. (326)

First-In, First-Out (FIFO) Method Assumes that the first goods purchased (the first in) are the first goods sold. (330)

Fiscal Any matters relating to money; typically used to describe a specified period of time used for financial reporting. (7)

Fixed Assets Tangible assets that are fixed in place, such as land, buildings, and production equipment. (368)

Form 10-K The annual report that publicly traded companies must file with the SEC. (203)

Form 10-Q The quarterly report that publicly traded companies must file with the SEC. (203)

Franchise A contractual right to sell certain products or services, use certain trademarks, or perform activities in a certain geographical region. (383)

Free Cash Flow Computed as Cash Flows from Operating Activities − Dividends − Capital Expenditures. (538)

Full Disclosure Principle States that relevant information should be disclosed in either the main financial statements or the notes to the financial statements. (205)

Future Value The sum to which an amount will increase as the result of compound interest. (658)

G

Gains Increases in assets or decreases in liabilities from peripheral transactions. (91)

Generally Accepted Accounting Principles (GAAP) The rules used to calculate and report information in the financial statements. (18)

Going-Concern Assumption States that businesses are assumed to continue to operate into the foreseeable future. (587)

Goods Available for Sale The sum of beginning inventory and purchases for the period. (327)

Goodwill (Cost in Excess of Net Assets Acquired) For accounting purposes, the excess of the purchase price of a business over the market value of the business's assets and liabilities. (383)

Gross Profit (Gross Margin, Margin) Net sales less cost of goods sold. (249)

Gross Profit Percentage Indicates how much above cost a company sells its products; calculated as Gross Profit divided by Net Sales. (249)

H

Historical Cost Principle See *Cost Principle*. (66)

I

Impairment Occurs when the cash to be generated by an asset is estimated to be less than the carrying value of that asset, and requires that the carrying value of the asset be written down. (380)

Income from Operations (Operating Income) Equals net sales less cost of goods sold and other operating expenses. (91)

Income smoothing The dishonest practice of manipulating accounting estimates to keep net income levels stable or "smooth" over a series of periods. (297)

Income Statement (Statement of Income, Statement of Profit and Loss, Statement of Operations) Reports the revenues less the expenses of the accounting period. (10)

Incur To make oneself subject to; typically refers to expenses, which are incurred by using up the economic benefits of assets or becoming obligated for liabilities, resulting in a decrease in the company's resources in the current period. (93)

Indirect Method A method of presenting the operating activities section of the statement of cash flows, in which net income is adjusted to compute cash flows from operating activities. (523)

Industry Practices A constraint that recognizes that companies in certain industries must follow accounting rules peculiar to that industry. (587)

Intangible Assets Assets that have special rights but not physical substance. (369)

Interest Formula $I = P \times R \times T$, where I = interest calculated; P = principle; R = annual interest rate; and T = time period covered in the interest calculation (number of months out of 12). (292)

Internal Controls Processes by which a company provides reasonable assurance regarding the reliability of the company's financial reporting, the effectiveness and efficiency of its operations, and its compliance with applicable laws and regulations. (234)

Inventory Tangible property held for sale in the normal course of business or used in producing goods or services for sale. (325)

Inventory Turnover The process of buying and selling inventory. (337)

Investing Activities Involve buying or selling long-lived items such as land, buildings, and equipment. (5)

Investments in Associated (or Affiliated) Companies Investments in stock held for the purpose of influencing the operating and financing strategies for the long term. (678)

Issue Price The amount of money that a lender pays (and the company receives) when a bond is issued. (427)

Issued Shares Total number of shares of stock that have been sold; equals shares outstanding plus treasury shares held. (475)

J

Journal A record of each day's transactions. (57)

Journal Entry An accounting method for expressing the effects of a transaction on accounts in a debits-equal-credits format. (59)

Journalize The process of noting a transaction in the journal in the debits-equal-credits journal entry format. (61)

L

Last-In, First-Out (LIFO) Method Assumes that the most recently purchased units (the last in) are sold first. (330)

Ledger A collection of records that summarize the effects of transactions entered in the journal. (57)

Legal Capital The permanent amount of capital defined by state law that must remain invested in the business; serves as a cushion for creditors. (476)

Lenders A creditor that has loaned money to the company. (424)

Liabilities Probable debts or obligations of the entity that result from past transactions, which will be fulfilled by providing assets or services. (7)

Licensing Right The limited permission to use property according to specific terms and conditions set out in a contract. (382)

LIFO Reserve A contra-asset for the excess of FIFO over LIFO inventory. (339)

Line-Item An account name or title reported in the body of a financial statement; can represent a single account or the total of several accounts. (98)

Line of Credit A prearranged agreement that allows a company to borrow any amount of money at any time, up to a prearranged limit. (432)

Liquidity The ability to pay current obligations. (432, 576)

Loan Covenants Terms of a loan agreement that, if broken, entitle the lender to demand immediate repayment or renegotiation of the loan. (191)

Long-Lived Assets Tangible and intangible resources owned by a business and used in its operations over several years. (368)

Long-Term Assets Resources that will be used up or turned into cash more than 12 months after the balance sheet date. (48)

Long-Term Liabilities All of the entity's obligations that are not classified as current liabilities. (48)

Losses Decreases in assets or increases in liabilities from peripheral transactions. (91)

Lower of Cost or Market (LCM) Valuation method departing from the cost principle; recognizes a loss when asset value drops below cost. (336)

M

Manufacturing Company A company that sells goods that it has made itself. (232)

Market Interest Rate The current rate of interest that exists when a debt is incurred. Also called *yield, discount rate,* or *effective interest rate*. (427)

Market Value Method Reports securities at their current market value. (681)

Matching Principle Requires that expenses be recorded when incurred in earning revenue. (108)

Material Amounts Amounts that are large enough to influence a user's decision. (326)

Materiality A concept stating that relatively small amounts not likely to influence decisions are to be recorded and reported in the most cost-beneficial way. (326)

Merchandise Inventory Goods held for resale in the ordinary course of business. (325)

Merchandising Company A company that sells goods which have been obtained from a supplier. (232)

N

Net To combine by subtracting one or more amounts from another. (11)

Net Assets Shorthand term used to refer to assets minus liabilities. (383)

Net Book Value (Book Value, Carrying Value) The amount at which an asset or liability is reported after deducting any contra-accounts. (374)

Net Income Equal to revenues minus expenses. (10)

Net Income before Income Taxes Revenues and gains minus losses and all expenses except income tax expense. (92)

Net Sales Total sales revenue minus Sales Returns and Allowances, Sales Discounts, and Credit Card Discounts. (248)

Noncash Investing and Financing Activities Transactions that do not have direct cash flow effects; reported as a supplement to the statement of cash flows in narrative or schedule form. (538)

Noncumulative Preferred Stock Preferred stock that does not have cumulative dividend rights, such that dividend rights do not carry over from one year to the next. (485)

No-Par Value Stock Capital stock that has no specified par value. (476)

Notes (Footnotes) Provide supplemental information about the financial condition of a company, without which the financial statements cannot be fully understood. (16)

Notes Receivable Written promises that require another party to pay the business under specified conditions (amount, time, interest). (285)

NSF Checks (Not Sufficient Funds) Checks written for an amount greater than the funds available to cover them. (236)

O

Obsolescence The process of becoming out of date or falling into disuse. (324)

Operating Activities The day-to-day events involved in running a business. (5)

Operating Cycle (Cash-to-Cash Cycle) The time and activities needed for a company to sell goods and services to customers, collect cash from customers, and pay cash to suppliers. (233)

Operating Lease An arrangement where a fixed asset is rented from another company, but it is not recorded on the balance sheet. (386)

Ordinary Repairs and Maintenance Expenditures for the normal operating upkeep of long-lived assets, recorded as expenses. (373)

Outstanding Shares Total number of shares of stock that are owned by stockholders on any particular date. (475)

P

Paid-In Capital (Additional Paid-In Capital, Contributed Capital in Excess of Par) The amount of contributed capital less the par value of the stock. (473)

Par Value (1) For shares of stock, this is a legal amount per share established by the board of directors; it establishes the minimum amount a stockholder must contribute and has no relationship to the market price of the stock. (2) For bonds, see *Face Value*. (476)

Parent Company The entity that gains a controlling influence over another company (the subsidiary). (677)

Partnerships Business organizations owned by two or more people. Each partner often is personally liable for debts that the partnership cannot pay. (5)

Patent A right to exclude others from making, using, selling, or importing an invention. (382)

Payment Date The date on which a cash dividend is paid to the stockholders of record. (480)

Percentage of Credit Sales Method Bases bad debt expense on the historical percentage of credit sales that result in bad debts. (288)

Periodic Inventory System A system in which ending inventory and cost of goods sold are determined only at the end of the accounting period based on a physical inventory count. (240)

Permanent Accounts The balance sheet accounts that carry their ending balances into the next accounting period. (152)

Perpetual Inventory System A system in which a detailed inventory record is maintained recording each purchase and sale of inventory during the accounting period. (240)

Post-Closing Trial Balance Prepared as the last step in the accounting cycle to check that debits equal credits and that all temporary accounts have been closed. (152)

Preferred Stock Stock that has specified rights over common stock. (484)

Prepaid Expenses A general account name used to describe payments made in advance of receiving future services; typically includes prepaid rent, prepaid insurance, and other specific types of prepayments. (533)

Present Value The current value of an amount to be received in the future; a future amount discounted for compound interest. (427)

Press Release A written public news announcement normally distributed to major news services. (201)

Private Company A company that has its stock bought and sold privately. (5)

Profit An alternative term for net income. (10)

Pro Forma A method of reporting what a company's results would have been had certain events not occurred. (201)

Profitability Extent to which a company generates income. (576)

Public Company A company that has its stock bought and sold on public stock exchanges. (5)

Purchase Discount Cash discount received for prompt payment of an account. (243)

Purchase Returns and Allowances A reduction in the cost of purchases associated with unsatisfactory goods. (243)

R

Ratio (Percentage) Analysis An analytical tool that measures the proportional relationship between two financial statement amounts. (576)

Raw Materials Inventory Items acquired for the purpose of processing into finished goods. (325)

Receivables Turnover The process of selling and collecting on an account. The receivables turnover ratio determines how many times this process occurs during the period on average. (294)

Record Date The date on which the corporation prepares the list of current stockholders as shown on its records. Dividends are paid only to the stockholders who own stock on that date. (480)

Relevant Information Information that can influence a decision. It is timely and has predictive and/or feedback value. (192)

Reliable Information Information that is accurate, unbiased, and verifiable. (192)

Research and Development Costs Expenditures that may someday lead to patents, copyrights, or other intangible assets, but the uncertainty about their future benefits requires that they be expensed. (383)

Residual Value Estimated amount to be recovered, less disposal costs, at the end of the company's estimated useful life of an asset. (374)

Retained Earnings Cumulative earnings of a company that are not distributed to the owners; profits from the current year and all prior years that are reinvested ("retained") in the business. (48)

Revenue Principle Revenues are recorded when goods or services are delivered, there is evidence of an arrangement for customer payment, the price is fixed or determinable and collection is reasonably assured. (107)

Revenue Recognition Policy An accounting policy that describes when a company reports revenue from providing services or goods to customers. (108)

Revenues Increases in assets or settlements of liabilities from ongoing operations. (10)

S

Sales (or Cash) Discount Cash discount offered to customers to encourage prompt payment of an account receivable. (246)

Sales Returns and Allowances Reduction of sales revenues for return of or allowances for unsatisfactory goods. (245)

Securities and Exchange Commission (SEC) The U.S. government agency that determines the financial statements that public companies must provide to stockholders and the rules that they must use in producing those statements. (18)

Securities Available for Sale All passive investments other than trading securities (classified as either short term or long term). (676)

Segregation of Duties An internal control that involves separating employees' duties so that the work of one person can be used to check the work of another person. (234)

Separate-Entity Concept (Assumption) States that business transactions are separate from and should exclude the personal transactions of the owners. (7)

Service Company A company that sells services rather than physical goods. (232)

Solvency Ability to survive long enough to repay lenders when debt matures. (576)

Specific Identification Method A method of assigning costs to inventory, which identifies the cost of each specific item purchased and sold. (329)

Stated Interest Rate The rate of cash interest per period specified in a bond contract. Also called *coupon rate* or *contract rate*. (426)

Statement of Cash Flows Reports inflows and outflows of cash during the accounting period in the categories of operating, investing, and financing. (13)

Statement of Retained Earnings Reports the way that net income and the distribution of dividends affected the financial position of the company during the accounting period. (12)

Stock Dividend Declared by the board of directors to distribute to existing stockholders additional shares of a corporation's own stock. (481)

Stock Split An increase in the total number of authorized shares by a specified ratio; does not decrease retained earnings. (482)

Stockholders' Equity (Owners' Equity or Shareholders' Equity) The financing provided by the owners and the operations of the business. (7)

Straight-Line Amortization Simplified method of amortizing a bond discount or premium that allocates an equal dollar amount to each interest period. (440)

Straight-Line Depreciation Method that allocates the cost of an asset in equal periodic amounts over its useful life. (376)

Subsidiary Company A business that is controlled by another company (the parent). (677)

T

10-K See Form 10-K. (203)

10-Q See Form 10-Q. (203)

T-Account A simplified version of a ledger account used for summarizing transaction effects and determining balances for each account. (58)

Tangible Assets Assets that have physical substance. (368)

Technology Includes a company's Web site and computer programs written by its employees. (383)

Temporary Accounts Income statement accounts that are closed to *Retained Earnings* at the end of the accounting period. (151)

Tests of Liquidity Ratios that measure a company's ability to meet its currently maturing obligations. (581)

Tests of Profitability Ratios that compare income with one or more primary activities. (579)

Tests of Solvency Ratios that measure a company's ability to meet its long-term obligations. (582)

Ticker Symbol The two- to four-letter abbreviation used to identify a company on a public securities exchange. (197)

Time Period Assumption The assumption that allows the long life of a company to be reported in shorter time periods. (587)

Time-Series Analysis Compares a company's results for one period to its own results over a series of time periods. (195)

Time Value of Money The idea that money received today is worth more than the same amount received in the future because money received today can be invested to earn interest over time. (658)

Trademark An exclusive legal right to use a special name, image, or slogan. (382)

Trading Securities All investments in stocks or bonds that are held primarily for the purpose of active trading (buying and selling) in the near future (classified as short term). (677)

Transaction An exchange or an event that has a direct economic effect on the assets, liabilities, or stockholders' equity of a business. (50)

Transaction Analysis The process of studying a transaction to determine its economic effect on the business in terms of the accounting equation. (49)

Treasury Stock A corporation's own stock that has been issued but was subsequently reacquired by and is still being held by the corporation. (475)

Trial Balance A list of all accounts with their balances to provide a check on the equality of the debits and credits. (103)

U

Unearned Revenue A liability representing a company's obligation to provide goods or services to customers in the future. (94)

Unit-of-Measure Concept (Assumption) States that accounting information should be measured and reported in the national monetary unit. (8)

Units-of-Production Depreciation Method that allocates the cost of an asset over its useful life based on its periodic output in relation to its total estimated output. (376)

Unqualified Audit Opinion Auditors' statements that the financial statements are fair presentations in all material respects in conformity with GAAP. (193)

Unrealized Holding Gains and Losses Amounts associated with price changes of securities that are currently held. (681)

Useful Life The expected service life of an asset to the present owner. (374)

W

Weighted Average Cost Method Uses the weighted average unit cost of goods available for sale for calculations of both the cost of goods sold and ending inventory. (332)

Work in Process Inventory Goods in the process of being manufactured. (326)

Write-Off The removal from an uncollectable account and its corresponding allowance from the accounting records. (287)

Y

Yield See *Market Interest Rate*. (427)

Chapter 1

- BALANCESHEET
- GAAP
- DIVIDEND
- FLOW
- NETINCOME
- FASB
- ASSETS

Chapter 2

- ACCOUNT
- JOURNAL
- CONSERVATISM
- CREDIT
- LEFT
- TRANSACTION

Chapter 3

- MATCHING
- GAIN
- EXPENSES
- EXPENDITURE
- REVENUES

Chapter 4

- TRIALBALANCE
- PERMANENT
- TEMPORARY

Chapter 5

- CROSSSECTIONAL
- UNQUALIFIED
- RELIABLE
- PROFORMA
- DEBTTOASSETS
- COMPARABLE
- TIMESERIES

Chapter 6

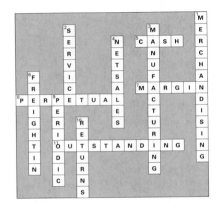

- CASH
- MARGIN
- PERPETUAL
- OUTSTANDING
- SERVICE
- MERCHANDISING
- RETURNS

Chapter 7

- AGING
- WRITEOFF
- FACTORING
- NOTES
- TRADE
- SMOOTHING

Chapter 8

- CONSERVATISM
- TURNOVER
- FINISHEDGOODS
- FIFO
- MATERIAL
- INCREASE
- LIFO

Chapter 9

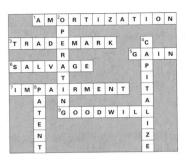

- AMORTIZATION
- TRADEMARK
- GAIN
- SALVAGE
- IMPAIRMENT
- GOODWILL
- PATENT
- CAPITALIZE

Chapter 10

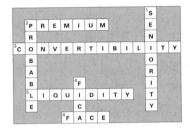

- PREMIUM
- CONVERTIBILITY
- LIQUIDITY
- FACE
- SENIORITY

Chapter 11

- SMALL
- ISSUED
- TREASURY
- RECORD
- DECLARATION
- PAYMENT
- PAR

Chapter 12

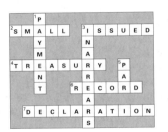

- FREE
- INVESTING
- FINANCING
- DIRECT
- INDIRECT
- OPERATING

Chapter 13

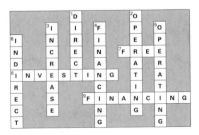

- EPS
- INVENTORY
- LIQUIDITY
- RECEIVABLES
- PROFITABILITY
- SOLVENCY
- CURRENT

Chapter 1

p. 3	Getty Images
p. 3	Corbis
p. 22	Foxtrot © 2002 Bill Amend. Reprinted with permission of Universal Press Syndicate. All rights reserved.
p. 23	Cartoon courtesy of Randy Glasbergen
p. 23	Courtesy of Krispy Kreme
p. 29	Courtesy of Procter & Gamble, Inc.
p. 30	Courtesy of Tootsie Roll Industries, Inc.
p. 32	Courtesy of Dave & Buster's, Inc.
p. 39	Courtesy of Landry's Restaurants, Inc.

Chapter 2

p. 45	Courtesy of Regis Corporation
p. 45	Courtesy of Regis Corporation
p. 45	Courtesy of Regis Corporation
p. 45	Courtesy of Regis Corporation
p. 45	Courtesy of Regis Corporation
p. 45	Courtesy of Regis Corporation
p. 50	CR100201 © Darren Jacklin
p. 73	Used with the permission of Hasbro, Inc.
p. 73	Courtesy of Half Price Books, Records, Magazines, Inc.

Chapter 3

p. 89	Courtesy of Regis Corporation
p. 89	Courtesy of Regis Corporation
p. 89	Courtesy of Regis Corporation
p. 89	Courtesy of Regis Corporation
p. 89	Courtesy of Regis Corporation
p. 89	Courtesy of Regis Corporation

Chapter 4

p. 135	Courtesy of Regis Corporation
p. 135	Courtesy of Regis Corporation
p. 135	Courtesy of Regis Corporation
p. 135	Courtesy of Regis Corporation
p. 135	Courtesy of Regis Corporation
p. 135	Courtesy of Regis Corporation
p. 167	Courtesy of Coach, Inc.
p. 181	Courtesy of Pacific Sunwear

Chapter 5

p. 189	Used with permission from Activision Publishing, Inc. © 2003
p. 202	Used with permission from Activision Publishing, Inc. © 2003
p. 204	Reproduced with permission of Yahoo! Inc. © 2003 by Yahoo! Inc. Yahoo! And the Yahoo! Logo are trademarks of Yahoo! Inc.
p. 228	Courtesy of Callaway Golf, Inc.

Chapter 6

p. 231	WAL-MART, the Wal-Mart logo, ALWAYS LOW PRICES, and ALWAYS are registered and/or unregistered trademarks of Wal-Mart Stores, Inc., Trademarks and photographs are used with permission of Wal-Mart Stores, Inc.
p. 231	WAL-MART, the Wal-Mart logo, ALWAYS LOW PRICES, and ALWAYS are registered and/or unregistered trademarks of Wal-Mart Stores, Inc., Trademarks and photographs are used with permission of Wal-Mart Stores, Inc.
p. 240	Getty Images
p. 240	Corbis
p. 240	Alien Technology Corporation

Chapter 7

p. 283	Courtesy of Skechers USA
p. 283	Photodisc Green/Getty
p. 283	Photodisc Green/Getty
p. 283	Kevin Jordan/Photodisc Red/Getty
p. 283	Andersen Ross/ Photodisc Red/Getty
p. 283	Jacobs Stock Photograph/ Photodisc Red/Getty
p. 310	Used with permission, Sears, Roebuck and Co.

Chapter 8

p. 323	Jeff Mitchell/Rueters/Corbis
p. 323	Oakley
p. 325	McGraw-Hill Higher Education
p. 325	McGraw-Hill Higher Education
p. 325	McGraw-Hill Higher Education
p. 325	McGraw-Hill Higher Education

Chapter 9

p. 367	Courtesy of Cedar Fair, C.P.
p. 367	Courtesy of Cedar Fair, C.P.
p. 367	Courtesy of Cedar Fair, C.P.
p. 367	Courtesy of Cedar Fair, C.P.
p. 369	PEANUTS © United Feature Syndicate, Inc.
p. 370	Courtesy of Cedar Fair, C.P.
p. 370	Courtesy of Cedar Fair, C.P.
p. 370	Courtesy of Cedar Fair, C.P.
p. 373	Courtesy of Cedar Fair, C.P.
p. 375	Corbis
p. 385	Courtesy of Cedar Fair, C.P.
p. 385	Courtesy of Cedar Fair, C.P.

Chapter 10

p. 415	Courtesy of General Mills
p. 415	Courtesy of General Mills
p. 415	Courtesy of General Mills
p. 415	Courtesy of General Mills
p. 415	Courtesy of General Mills
p. 423	Courtesy of Expedia, Inc.
p. 427	Courtesy of General Mills
p. 456	Used with the permission of The Reader's Digest Association, Inc.

Chapter 11

p. 471   Pablo Rivera/Superstock
p. 481   Courtesy of the Green Bay
         Packers

Chapter 12

p. 519   www.wonderfile.com
p. 519   Jim Cummins/Corbis
p. 519   Catherine Wessel/Corbis
p. 540   Pablo Rivera/Superstock

Chapter 13

p. 573   Courtesy of Landry's
         Restaurants, Inc.
p. 580   Courtesy of Landry's
         Restaurants, Inc.